THE OXFORD HANDBOOK OF

WOMEN, PEACE, AND SECURITY

THE OXFORD HANDBOOK OF

WOMEN, PEACE, AND SECURITY

Edited by

SARA E. DAVIES

and

JACQUI TRUE

OXFORD

UNIVERSITY PRESS

OXFORD
UNIVERSITY PRESS

Oxford University Press is a department of the University of Oxford. It furthers
the University's objective of excellence in research, scholarship, and education
by publishing worldwide. Oxford is a registered trade mark of Oxford University
Press in the UK and in certain other countries

Published in the United States of America by Oxford University Press
198 Madison Avenue, New York, NY 10016, United States of America.

Library of Congress Cataloging-in-Publication Data
Names: Davies, Sara E., editor. | True, Jacqui, editor.
Title: The Oxford handbook of women, peace and security / edited by Sara E. Davies and Jacqui True.
Other titles: Handbook of women, peace and security
Description: New York, NY, United States of America : Oxford University Press, 2019. |
Includes bibliographical references and index.
Identifiers: LCCN 2018008355 (print) | LCCN 2018025553 (ebook) | ISBN 9780190638283 (Updf) |
ISBN 9780190638290 (Epub) | ISBN 9780190638276 (hardcover : acid-free paper)
Subjects: LCSH: Women and peace. | Women and human security. |
Women—Violence against—Prevention—International cooperation. | United Nations.
Security Council. Resolution 1325. |
Classification: LCC JZ5578 (ebook) |
LCC JZ5578.O94 2019 (print) | DDC 303.6/6—dc23
LC record available at https://lccn.loc.gov/2018008355

1 3 5 7 9 8 6 4 2

Printed by Sheridan Books, Inc., United States of America

Contents

Acknowledgments   xi
List of Contributors   xiii

PART I. CONCEPTS OF WPS

1. WPS: A Transformative Agenda?   3
   SARA E. DAVIES AND JACQUI TRUE

2. Peace and Security from a Feminist Perspective   15
   J. ANN TICKNER

3. Adoption of 1325 Resolution   26
   CHRISTINE CHINKIN

4. Civil Society's Leadership in Adopting 1325 Resolution   38
   SANAM NARAGHI ANDERLINI

5. Scholarly Debates and Contested Meanings of WPS   53
   FIONNUALA D. NÍ AOLÁIN AND NAHLA VALJI

6. Advocacy and the WPS Agenda   67
   SARAH TAYLOR

7. WPS as a Political Movement   76
   SWANEE HUNT AND ALICE WAIRIMU NDERITU

8. Locating Masculinities in WPS   88
   HENRI MYRTTINEN

9. WPS and Adopted Security Council Resolutions   98
   LAURA J. SHEPHERD

10. WPS and Gender Mainstreaming   110
    KARIN LANDGREN

11. The Production of the 2015 Global Study   122
    LOUISE OLSSON AND THEODORA-ISMENE GIZELIS

PART II. PILLARS OF WPS

12. WPS and Conflict Prevention   135
    BELA KAPUR AND MADELEINE REES

13. What Works in Participation   148
    THANIA PAFFENHOLZ

14. What Works (and Fails) in Protection   161
    HANNAH DÖNGES AND JANOSCH KULLENBERG

15. What Works in Relief and Recovery   178
    JACQUI TRUE AND SARAH HEWITT

16. Where the WPS Pillars Intersect   193
    MARIE O'REILLY

17. WPS and Female Peacekeepers   206
    NATASJA RUPESINGHE, ELI STAMNES, AND JOHN KARLSRUD

18. WPS and SEA in Peacekeeping Operations   222
    JASMINE-KIM WESTENDORF

19. WPS and Peacekeeping Economies   237
    KATHLEEN M. JENNINGS

20. WPS in Military Training and Socialization   248
    HELENA CARREIRAS AND TERESA FRAGOSO

21. WPS and Policing: New Terrain   259
    BETHAN GREENER

22. WPS, States, and the National Action Plans   273
    MIRSAD MIKI JACEVIC

PART III. INSTITUTIONALIZING WPS

23. WPS inside the United Nations   293
    MEGAN DERSNAH

24. WPS and the Special Representative of the Secretary-General
    for Sexual Violence in Conflict   302
    ELEANOR O'GORMAN

25. WPS and the Human Rights Council   317
    RASHIDA MANJOO

26. WPS and International Financial Institutions   336
    JACQUI TRUE AND BARBRO SVEDBERG

27. WPS and the International Criminal Court   351
    JONNEKE KOOMEN

28. WPS and the North Atlantic Treaty Organization   364
    STÉFANIE VON HLATKY

29. WPS and the African Union   375
    TONI HAASTRUP

30. WPS and the Association of South East Asian Nations   388
    MA. LOURDES VENERACION-RALLONZA

31. WPS and the Pacific Islands Forum   402
    SHARON BHAGWAN-ROLLS AND SIAN ROLLS

32. WPS and the Organization of American States   413
    MARY K. MEYER MCALEESE

33. WPS and Civil Society   428
    ANNIKA BJÖRKDAHL AND JOHANNA MANNERGREN SELIMOVIC

34. WPS and Transnational Feminist Networks   439
    JOY ONYESOH

PART IV. IMPLEMENTING WPS

35. Delivering WPS Protection in All Female
    Peacekeeping Force: The Case of Liberia   451
    SABRINA KARIM

36. Securing Participation and Protection in
    Peace Agreements: The Case of Colombia   461
    ISABELA MARÍN CARVAJAL AND EDUARDO ÁLVAREZ-VANEGAS

37. WPS and Women's Roles in Conflict-Prevention: The Case of
    Bougainville   475
    NICOLE GEORGE

38. Women in Rebellion: The Case of Sierra Leone   489
    ZOE MARKS

39. Protecting Displaced Women and Girls: The Case of Syria   501
    ELIZABETH FERRIS

40. Donor States Delivering on WPS: The Case of Norway   516
    INGER SKJELSBÆK AND TORUNN L. TRYGGESTAD

41. WPS as Diplomatic Vocation: The Case of China   528
    LIU TIEWA

42. Women Controlling Arms, Building Peace:
    The Case of the Philippines   540
    JASMIN NARIO-GALACE

43. Testing the WPS Agenda: The Case of Afghanistan   553
    CLAIRE DUNCANSON AND VANESSA FARR

44. Mainstreaming WPS in the Armed Forces: The Case of Australia   569
    JENNIFER WITTWER

PART V. CROSS-CUTTING AGENDA?
CONNECTIONS AND MAINSTREAMING

45. WPS and Responsibility to Protect   585
    ALEX J. BELLAMY AND SARA E. DAVIES

46. WPS and Protection of Civilians   598
    LISA HULTMAN AND ANGELA MUVUMBA SELLSTRÖM

47. WPS, Children, and Armed Conflict   608
    KATRINA LEE-KOO

48. WPS, Gender, and Disabilities   618
    DEBORAH STIENSTRA

49. WPS and Humanitarian Action   628
    SARAH MARTIN AND DEVANNA DE LA PUENTE

50. WPS, Migration, and Displacement   643
    LUCY HALL

51. WPS and LGBTI Rights   657
    LISA DAVIS AND JESSICA STERN

52. WPS and CEDAW, Optional Protocol, and
    General Recommendations   669
    CATHERINE O'ROURKE WITH AISLING SWAINE

53. Women's Roles in CVE   680
    SRI WIYANTI EDDYONO WITH SARA E. DAVIES

54. WPS and Arms Trade Treaty   690
    RAY ACHESON AND MARIA BUTLER

55. WPS and Sustainable Development Goals   704
    RADHIKA BALAKRISHNAN AND KRISHANTI DHARMARAJ

56. WPS and the Convention against Torture   715
    ANDREA HUBER AND THERESE RYTTER

57. WPS and Climate Change   726
    ANNICA KRONSELL

PART VI. ONGOING AND FUTURE CHALLENGES

58. Global Study: Looking Forward   739
    RADHIKA COOMARASWAMY AND EMILY KENNEY

59. Measuring WPS: A New Global Index   751
    JENI KLUGMAN

60. Pursuing Gender Security   765
    AISLING SWAINE

61. The Challenge of Foreign Policy in the WPS Agenda   779
    VALERIE M. HUDSON AND LAUREN A. EASON

62. Networked Advocacy   792
    YIFAT SUSSKIND AND DIANA DUARTE

63. Women's Peacemaking in South Asia   803
    MEENAKSHI GOPINATH AND RITA MANCHANDA

64. WPS, Peace Negotiations, and Peace Agreements   815
    KARIN AGGESTAM

65. The WPS Agenda: A Postcolonial Critique   829
    SWATI PARASHAR

66. The WPS Agenda and Strategy for the Twenty-First Century   840
    CHANTAL DE JONGE OUDRAAT

67. The Challenges of Monitoring and Analyzing WPS for Scholars   850
    NATALIE FLOREA HUDSON

Index   863

Acknowledgments

We are immensely grateful to Angela Chnapko for her enthusiasm at our suggestion for an Oxford Handbook on Women, Peace, and Security. We are grateful to the reviewers for their helpful suggestions in the early stages of developing the Handbook.

It is important to state that the completion of this book would never have been realized without the tremendous support and assistance from three brilliant early career research scholars: Sarah Hewitt, Caitlin Mollica, and Maria Tanyag. Maria, in particular, was of tremendous assistance: her communication with contributors, assisting with organization of the contributors' workshop, and the tedious process of copy-editing for a handbook of this size. Thank you Maria. We also thank our partners for their support and care during the two years we have been working on editing this magnum opus volume!

We sincerely thank Aisling Swaine, then Director of the Center for Gender Equality in International Affairs at The Elliott School of International Affairs, George Washington University. In February 2017, Aisling kindly gave us her assistance and the assistance of her graduate students in organizing a venue for our contributors' workshop. Aisling is now at the London School of Economics and Political Science, and we look forward to future collaboration in the next workshop!

We are appreciative to those who have not contributed to the Handbook but have provided sage advice and guidance as it developed: Samanthi Gunawardana, Susan Harris Rimmer, Renee Jeffery, Sharon Pickering, and Lesley Pruitt.

Finally, we would like to thank the Australian Research Council College of Experts and the reviewers of our projects, DP 140101129 and LP 1048795, who have trusted us with a research grants to conduct this research on Women, Peace, and Security. This book reflects many of the discussions, fieldwork, workshops, conferences, and arguments we have had with scholars, practitioners, and advocates. We are so grateful to everyone who has taken the time to think about, engage, and write on topics for this Handbook. We have been honored to collaborate with such tremendous individuals who work every day to make tomorrow safer, more peaceful, just, and equal for all.

Sara E. Davies, Brisbane
Jacqui True, Melbourne

List of Contributors

Ray Acheson is Director of Reaching Critical Will, Women's International League for Peace and Freedom (WILPF), New York.

Karin Aggestam is Pufendorf Chair Professor of Political Science, Lund University, Sweden, and Honorary Professor at POLSIS, University of Queensland, Australia.

Eduardo Álvarez-Vanegas is former director of the conflict dynamics and peace negotiations area at the think-thank Fundación Ideas para la Paz (FIP), Bogotá, Colombia. Currently, he works at the United Nations Verification Mission in Colombia.

Sanam Naraghi Anderlini is Executive Director of International Civil Society Action Network, USA.

Radhika Balakrishnan is Faculty Director Center for Women's Global Leadership and Professor of Women's and Gender studies, Rutgers University New Jersey, USA.

Alex J. Bellamy is Professor of Peace and Conflict Studies at the School of Political Science and International Studies, University of Queensland. He is also Executive Director of the Asia Pacific Centre for Responsibility to Protect, Australia.

Sharon Bhagwan-Rolls is Coordinator at femLINKpacific, Fiji.

Annika Björkdahl is Professor of Political Science in the Department of Political Science at Lund University, Sweden.

Maria Butler is Global Programmes Director at the Women's International League for Peace and Freedom (WILPF), Geneva, Switzerland.

Helena Carreiras is Associate Professor of Sociology, ISCTE-University Institute of Lisbon, Portugal.

Isabela Marín Carvajal is a researcher at the think-tank Fundación Ideas para la Paz (FIP) and independent consultant in conflict and gender, Colombia.

Christine Chinkin is Emerita Professor of International Law and Director of the Centre on Women, Peace, and Security, London School of Economics and Political Science, UK.

Radhika Coomaraswamy is Lead Author of the Global Study on the Implementation of Security Council Resolution 1325 (2000) and Former Under-Secretary-General of the United Nations, Special Representative for Children and Armed Conflict, Colombo, Sri Lanka.

Sara E. Davies is Associate Professor and ARC Future Fellow at the School of Government and International Relations, Griffith University, Australia.

Lisa Davis is Associate Professor of Law and co-director of the Human Rights and Gender Justice (HRGJ) Clinic at the City University of New York (CUNY) School of Law and Senior Legal Advisor for MADRE.

Chantal de Jonge Oudraat is President of Women in International Security, Washington, DC, USA.

Devanna de la Puente is Inter-Agency Senior Gender Advisor (GenCap), Humanitarian Country Team, United Nations, Colombia.

Megan Dersnah is a Researcher at the Munk School of Global Affairs, University of Toronto, Canada.

Krishanti Dharmaraj is Executive Director of the Center for Women's Global Leadership, Rutgers University, New Jersey, USA.

Hannah Dönges is Doctoral Researcher at the Centre on Conflict, Development & Peacebuilding, Graduate Institute of International and Development Studies, Geneva, Switzerland.

Diana Duarte is Communications Director, MADRE, New York, USA.

Claire Duncanson is Senior Lecturer in International Relations in the School of Social and Political Science, University of Edinburgh, UK.

Lauren A. Eason is Senior Research Associate of The Woman Stats Project, and is based in Washington, DC.

Sri Wiyanti Eddyono is a lecturer in the Criminal Law Department and the director of Law, Gender and Society Centre at Faculty of Law, Universitas Gadjah Mada (UGM), Yogyakarta, Indonesia. She is also Adjunct Research Fellow at Monash Gender, Peace, and Security Centre.

Vanessa Farr specializes in conflict and gender, and is an independent consultant.

Elizabeth Ferris is Research Professor at Georgetown University, Washington, DC, USA.

Teresa Fragoso is PhD Candidate in Public Policy and President of the Commission for Citizenship and Gender Equality, Portuguese Public Administration, Portugal.

Nicole George is Senior Lecturer in Peace and Conflict Studies at the School of Political Science and International Studies, University of Queensland, Australia.

Theodora-Ismene Gizelis is Professor in the Department of Government, University of Essex, UK.

Meenakshi Gopinath is Founder-Director of Women in Security, Conflict Management, and Peace (WISCOMP), India.

Bethan Greener is Associate Professor at Massey University, New Zealand.

Toni Haastrup is Senior Lecturer in International Security and Deputy Director of Global Europe Centre, University of Kent, UK.

Lucy Hall is a lecturer in International Relations at the University of Amsterdam, Netherlands, Lecturer at the Faculty of Law, University of Amsterdam, Netherlands and a PhD candidate at the University of New South Wales, Sydney, Australia.

Sarah Hewitt is PhD Candidate at the Monash Gender, Peace, and Security Centre, Monash University, Australia.

Stéfanie von Hlatky is Associate Professor of Political Studies at Queen's University and Fellow at the Queen's Centre for International and Defence Policy, Canada.

Andrea Huber is Policy Director of Penal Reform International (PRI), Denmark.

Natalie Florea Hudson is Associate Professor of Political Science and Director of the Human Rights Studies Program, University of Dayton, Ohio, USA.

Valerie M. Hudson is Professor and George H. W. Bush Chair in the Department of International Relations of the Bush School of Government and Public Service at Texas A&M University, USA. She is also Director of the School's Program on Women, Peace, and Security.

Lisa Hultman is Associate Professor at the Department of Peace and Conflict Research, Uppsala University, Sweden.

Swanee Hunt is Founder of Inclusive Security, and Eleanor Roosevelt Lecturer in Public Policy, Harvard's Kennedy School of Government, USA.

Mirsad Miki Jacevic is Vice Chair of Inclusive Security, Washington, DC, USA.

Kathleen M. Jennings is head of research and development at the Faculty of Social Sciences, Oslo Metropolitan University.

Bela Kapur is Visiting Senior Fellow at the London School of Economics Centre for Women Peace and Security, UK.

Sabrina Karim is Assistant Professor of Government at Cornell University, USA.

John Karlsrud is Senior Research Fellow and Manager for the Training for Peace program, Norwegian Institute of International Affairs (NUPI), Norway.

Emily Kenney is Justice Specialist, Peace and Security, UN Women, New York, USA.

Jeni Klugman is Managing Director at the Georgetown Institute for Women, Peace and Security, and Fellow at the Women and Public Policy Program, Harvard Kennedy School, USA.

Jonneke Koomen is Associate Professor of Politics, Sociology, and Women's and Gender Studies at Willamette University, Oregon, USA.

Annica Kronsell is Professor of Political Science in the School of Global Studies at Gothenburg University, Sweden.

Janosch Kullenberg is PhD Fellow at the Bremen International Graduate School of Social Sciences (BIGSSS), Germany.

Karin Landgren is Executive Director of Security Council Report, New York, USA. She is a former SRSG and head of three UN peace operations.

Katrina Lee-Koo is Associate Professor in International Relations at the School of Social Sciences, Monash University, Australia.

Rita Manchanda is Consultant for Women in Security, Conflict Management, and Peace (WISCOMP), India.

Rashida Manjoo is Professor in the Department of Public Law, University of Cape Town, South Africa and the former United Nations Special Rapporteur on Violence Against Women, its Causes and Consequences.

Zoe Marks is Lecturer in Public Policy, Harvard Kennedy School, Harvard University, Cambridge, MA, USA.

Sarah Martin is Gender-Based Violence in Emergencies Consultant.

Mary K. Meyer McAleese is Professor of Political Science at Eckerd College, Florida, USA.

Henri Myrttinen is Head of Gender and Peacebuilding at International Alert, UK.

Jasmin Nario-Galace is Executive Director of the Center for Peace Education, Miriam College, Philippines.

Alice Wairimu Nderitu is armed conflict mediator, member of Women Waging Peace Network, and Commissioner of National Cohesion and Integration Commission, Kenya.

Fionnuala D. Ní Aoláin is Professor of Law at the University of Ulster Transitional Justice Institute, and Robina Chair in Law, Public Policy, and Society at University of Minnesota Law School, USA. She is United Nations Special Rapporteur for the Promotion and Protection of Human Rights while Countering Terrorism.

Eleanor O'Gorman is Senior Associate with the University of Cambridge Centre for Gender Studies, UK.

Marie O'Reilly is a peace and security consultant and Senior Adviser at Peace Is Loud, New York, USA.

Catherine O'Rourke is Senior Lecturer in Human Rights and International Law at the Transitional Justice Institute and School of Law, Ulster University Jordanstown, Northern Ireland.

Louise Olsson is Senior Researcher at the Peace Research Institute Oslo (PRIO), Norway.

Joy Onyesoh is WILPF International President, and formerly President of WILPF Nigeria.

Thania Paffenholz is Director of the Inclusive Peace & Transition Initiative, Graduate Institute of International and Development Studies, Geneva, Switzerland.

Swati Parashar is Senior Lecturer at the University of Gothenberg, Sweden.

Madeleine Rees is Secretary-General of the Women's International League for Peace and Freedom (WILPF), South Africa/Switzerland.

Sian Rolls is Communications Coordinator, Pacific Women Shaping Pacific Development Support Unit, Fiji.

Natasja Rupesinghe is Junior Research Fellow at the Norwegian Institute of International Affairs (NUPI), Norway.

Therese Rytter is Director of Legal and Advocacy Department, DIGNITY, Danish Institute Against Torture, Denmark.

Johanna Mannergren Selimovic is Associate Professor of Peace and Development and Senior Research Fellow at the Swedish Institute of International Affairs, Stockholm, Sweden.

Angela Muvumba Sellström is Researcher in the Department of Peace and Conflict Research at Uppsala University, Sweden.

Laura J. Shepherd is Professor of International Relations at the University of Sydney, Australia.

Inger Skjelsbæk is Research Professor at the Peace Research Institute Oslo (PRIO) and Associate Professor in the Department of Psychology, University of Oslo, Norway.

Eli Stamnes is Senior Research Fellow at the Norwegian Institute of International Affairs (NUPI), Norway.

Jessica Stern is Executive Director of Outright Action International, New York, USA.

Deborah Stienstra is Jarislowsky Chair in Families and Work, Professor in Political Science, and Director of the Centre for Families, Work, and Well-being, University of Guelph, Canada.

Yifat Susskind is Executive Director of MADRE, New York, USA.

Barbro Svedberg is Policy Specialist at the Swedish International Development Cooperation Agency (SIDA), Sweden.

Aisling Swaine is Assistant Professor in Gender and Security at the Gender Institute, London School of Economics and Political Science, UK.

Sarah Taylor is Research Fellow at the International Peace Institute, New York, USA.

J. Ann Tickner is Professor Emerita in the School of International Relations at the University of Southern California, USA, Distinguished Scholar in Residence at American University, Washington, USA, and Adjunct Professor, Centre for Gender, Peace, and Security, Monash University, Australia.

Liu Tiewa is Associate Professor at the School of International Relations and Diplomacy at Beijing Foreign Studies University. She is also Deputy Director of the Research Centre of the United Nations and International Organizations, Beijing Foreign Studies University, China.

Jacqui True is Professor of International Relations and Director of Monash Gender, Peace, and Security Centre, Monash University. She is also an Australian Research Council Future Fellow and Global Fellow at Peace Research Institute Oslo.

Torunn L. Tryggestad is Deputy Director of PRIO and Director of the PRIO Centre on Gender, Peace, and Security, Peace Research Institute Oslo (PRIO), Norway.

Nahla Valji is Senior Policy Advisor at the Peace and Security Division, UN Women, USA.

Ma. Lourdes Veneracion-Rallonza is Associate Professor, Department of Political Science, Ateneo de Manila University, Philippines.

Jasmine-Kim Westendorf is Senior Lecturer of International Relations, La Trobe University, Australia.

Jennifer Wittwer, CSM, RAN, is an international consultant on gender and Women, Peace and Security. She is a former Policy Specialist and Military Liaison Officer, Peacekeeping and Sexual Exploitation and Abuse, UN Women, New York, USA, and prior to that, was the Director of National Action Plan for Women, Peace and Security, Australian Defence Force, Australia.

THE OXFORD HANDBOOK OF

WOMEN, PEACE, AND SECURITY

PART I

CONCEPTS OF WPS

CHAPTER 1

....

WOMEN, PEACE, AND SECURITY
A Transformative Agenda?

....

SARA E. DAVIES AND JACQUI TRUE

WE live in a world where the scale and egregiousness of violent conflicts are increasing and where all evidence suggests that their effects on the human rights of women and girls are severe and intensifying. The Women, Peace, and Security agenda (WPS) stands at this juncture with significant potential to bring knowledge and social transformation to prevent conflicts, protect human rights, and promote recovery from conflict and insecurity. Yet there is a major disconnect between the great expectations of WPS advocates and the inadequate progress made by powerful institutions in meeting those expectations as enshrined in Resolution 1325. Indeed, the central argument in the United Nations Secretary-General commissioned Global Study on the Implementation of 1325 (2015), "Preventing Conflict, Transforming Justice, Securing Peace," was that "much of the progress toward the implementation of resolution 1325 continues to be measured in 'firsts', rather than as standard practice. Obstacles and challenges still persist and prevent the full implementation of the women, peace, and security (WPS) agenda" (UN Women 2015: 14).

The United Nations Security Council (UNSC) Resolution 1325 and seven subsequent resolutions make up the cross-cutting WPS agenda.[1] This agenda is a significant international normative and policy framework addressing the gender-specific impacts of conflict on women and girls. The Security Council itself has admitted deep concerns about the "persistent obstacles and challenges to women's participation and full involvement" (1820 [2008] preamble); the "underrepresentation of women at all stages of peace processes" (1888; 1889; 1960 preambles); and the negative impact of limited WPS implementation on "durable peace, security and reconciliation" (1889 [2009] preamble). It has urged the UN and member states to demonstrate "greater commitment to implement the women, peace, and security agenda, notably through more systematic and concrete reporting," and called for "women's full and meaningful participation and leadership in all efforts to maintain peace and security, including with regard to preventing conflict, sustaining peace, and responding to new threats" such as violent extremism, mass displacement, and climate change–induced disasters (UNSC 2017).

All WPS major policy forums and UNSC open debates on WPS have featured continual appeals to states and international institutions to scale up their commitments to implementing the WPS agenda. Repetition is necessary. Significant goals of the normative agenda, including to prevent conflict and promote peace through women's participation, are not easily achieved in short or medium time frames. There are, in essence, multiple time frames and scales of WPS, both institutional and localized, that need to be considered, as well as many intersections between WPS and other normative agendas that are contributing to an ever-evolving and dynamic realm of international affairs. The burden today is measuring progress in vastly different locations and situations from UN headquarters to peace operations on the ground; as well as being sure that the implementation gaps identified in the Global Study, for example, are receiving attention equal to the areas that are more readily accepted and implemented (Idris 2017).

In this volume, we draw on scholars, practitioners, and advocates' experiences from the Global North and South working on the WPS thematic agenda. We aim to draw on women's diverse practical experiences in promoting peace and inclusion and in developing a gender-sensitive and gender-inclusive theoretical perspective on peace and security. We also examine the broad cross-cutting projects of national and global security, and empowerment for all populations.

In this chapter, we build on feminist constructivist theories of normative change to put forward a pragmatist understanding of "women, peace, and security" as a "work in progress," wherein advocates and scholars work together with activist states to advance principles of equal and lasting peace. We argue that the theory and practice of WPS in conflict, post-conflict, and in peaceful situations—examined in this handbook—are best appreciated as a dynamic, normative agenda and iterative reform process committed to realizing a critical gender perspective on peace and security.

A FEMINIST PRAGMATIST APPROACH

WPS is characterized by tensions and ambivalences as state and non-state actors struggle, compete, and collaborate to define and implement the atypical security agenda. The agenda is expected to challenge the patriarchal normative framework and unequal political economies that underpin peace and security institutions, but, at the same time, to actively engage with these very institutions to transform gender power relations. It must straddle vital local networks where women are more likely to be present, but also ensure representation and engagement at the international and national levels of practice, in which elite men dominate.

WPS represents a pragmatic attempt on the part of women's rights activists to address the significant violence and inequality that characterizes conflict, particularly women's experience of it. It is not based on an *a priori* theory of gender and conflict but on a trial-and-error process committed to creating realizable pathways to gender equality, social justice, and peace. The normative agenda is the result of the practical capacities of diverse women's rights' actors around the world—scholars, activists, practitioners, political leaders, and policymakers—to build connections between their specific institutional and local contexts and the global norm, (Zwingel 2012).

WPS exemplifies the feminist pragmatist method as outlined by Tickner and True (2018). It aims to amplify voices of women from conflict zones, gender-based violence survivors, displaced and refugee women, *inter alia*, by bringing them to international fora to share their practical knowledge of how best to protect "vulnerable" populations and enable their participation. It seeks to bridge these voices with expert knowledge, which is often ignorant of peace and security solutions in local contexts and unaccountable to those most affected by international policies and interventions. In this process, the "truths" about conflict derive not from macro policy or data analysis but from on-the-ground experience. WPS advocates then make pragmatic choices about which issues are best pursued vis-a-vis states or the UN Security Council and which issues they must pursue outside institutions through social movement protest and activism.

In this volume, contributors evaluate the WPS normative agenda to ask "what works" and "what doesn't work" to deliver even more just and effective peace and security outcomes. Naturally, authors are concerned with what hasn't been achieved in the WPS agenda, but a number of contributors are also concerned with examining what aspects of the WPS agenda have been advanced, often in the face of great opposition and minimal resourcing. These contributions illustrate why we must study the WPS commitments and programs with an open, inquiring mind. WPS programs should be judged not only for their compromises and their use of discourse, but their usefulness and impact on end goals, such as "meaningful women's participation," "gender-responsive peace-building," and the like.

In addition to reflecting on what the WPS "community of practice" actually does, we observe the feminist pragmatist approach as a middle path for the ambitions of WPS against the harsh political realities. Politics among states has required compromise on some of the feminist revolutions required to transform global politics. For example, a major compromise is between a feminist, rights-based approach that advocates for women's equal participation in peace and security and opposes military solutions, and an instrumental approach that sees gender equality as a means to the ends of security, stability, and military effectiveness (see more on this discussion in part I). A pragmatic approach accepts that both rights-based and instrumental WPS approaches have the potential to recognize gender-specific experiences and impacts of conflict, as well as the need to prevent conflict in ways that enhance women's agency. Here we endorse the need for "pragmatism in the alternation between the use of soft and hard power," as Aggestam and Bergman-Rosamond (2016: 330) argue with respect to feminist foreign policy.

Concretely, the feminist pragmatist approach has enabled significant innovations in international peace and security processes—for example, the deployment of women protection advisors alongside gender advisors in peace operations, and the establishment of an Informal Experts Group on Women, Peace, and Security to routinely brief the Security Council on peace operations (see UNSCR 1960 [2009] and 2242 [2015], respectively). The inclusion of women's civil society in UNSC deliberations on political and peace missions is an important marker of progress. This is the first time the UNSC has agreed that, in principle, women's groups should participate in their meetings due to their particular risk of exclusion from political processes within a country under discussion. Would we have seen this or other innovations without first the "groundwork," without the pragmatic activism of the WPS community?

Feminist pragmatism has informed our approach in the handbook from the beginning and can be seen in the structure of the volume, the selection of sixty-seven chapters

authored and coauthored by nearly one hundred practitioners and scholars, and the selection of particular cases of WPS institutions and implementation. It has informed the
questions we ask ourselves and "our" institutions and those that the contributors in this
volume bring to the fore such as: Should we persist with a mainstream agenda that seeks
compromise rather than revolution, and how can we pursue the mainstreaming of WPS
without undermining essential reforms? These are possibly the most important questions
at this moment. The scholarship on international norm contestation discussing other cases
of normative diffusion and change may be helpful here. We learn from this literature that
ideas and interests that provide practical, feasible solutions often take over the agenda. In
the case of WPS, militaries and security sectors seek gender inclusion for operational effectiveness and are tending to leave other implementing actors behind in WPS national action
plans, and in so doing entrenching a militarized approach to WPS (e.g., see chapters 28 and
44 on the North Atlantic Treaty Organization [NATO] and Australia case in this volume).
But because these defense institutions are invested in WPS, this can lead to institutional
transformation as well as to greater uptake and investment by other state and non-state actors and new coalitions of these actors. Normative development and further acceptance of
WPS can be built upon by advocates who put forward alternative nonmilitary approaches,
harnessing women's agency and leadership in conflict prevention, peace mediation, and
peace-building. Similarly, local adaptation may not always reflect the full intent of WPS
resolutions, but it provides an opening that was not there before and would not be there
if we pushed for a "perfect" version of what the normative agenda should look like in that
local context. Thus, from a feminist pragmatist perspective, incremental progress may be
more generative of durable solutions to intractable problems than revolution.

WHAT IS ADDRESSED IN THIS BOOK AND WHY

The scholarship to date on WPS is immense and growing fast. Since the adoption of
Resolution 1325, there have been thousands of articles and hundreds of books devoted to
its discourse, its theoretical impact, and its practice. Despite the semblance of permanence
given by UNSC resolutions (UNSCR), the norm of WPS is a "work in progress"—its content is contested and dynamic rather than fixed. This is precisely as it should be and a central
theme throughout all chapters involves realizing that the WPS agenda is just beginning,
even after over a century of women's peace activism.

   We adopt a feminist constructivist approach to norms following Antje Wiener's (2009)
theory of contestation that judges norms in terms of their "meaning in use" rather than
their statement in treaties, laws, and policies. Focusing on fluid rather than fixed normative
meanings explains why norms such as WPS emerge and appear to diffuse rapidly, at the
same time as they rarely achieve their intended aims or have disappointing "concrete effects"
(Krook and True 2012: 105). As a broad and nonbinding UN normative framework, WPS
has changed as it has diffused across different sites.[2] The ambivalences in the normative
agenda explain both its success and its limitations with respect to actual implementation.

   As a "work in progress," it was intended that WPS would be holistically implemented
although *protection*, one of four pillars of WPS, has taken precedence in the norm's
meaning in use over the past decade. Conflict-related sexual violence was the substance of

five UN Security Council resolutions and fourteen presidential statements between 2008 and 2016 that were adopted with specific reference to action required, in stark contrast to no resolutions between 2000 and 2008 (Davies and True 2017: 703).[3] Non-state actors represented by the 1325 NGO Working Group have argued that the focus on protection against sexual violence highlights the victimization rather than the agency of women in peace and security. Domestic actors may also reject dominant "protection" frames using different frames as they adapt WPS for their own context. This can be seen in Asian states, where the "development" frame is predominantly used to localize WPS as a women's empowerment issue in the context of conflicts fueled and affected by poverty and underdevelopment (Association of Southeast Asian Nations [ASEAN] 2017). This normative contestation over the prioritizing of protection over participation in the WPS agenda has been a continual theme since 2008 (see Jansson and Eduards 2016; Kreft 2017).

However, as mentioned earlier, between 2000 and 2008 there were *no* WPS resolutions passed. The 2008 Resolution 1820 on sexual violence in conflict situations was narrow,[4] but it permitted the practices that have been, arguably, essential for achieving a broader engagement on the Security Council on matters pertaining to WPS in recent years (women's participation in peace-building, peace agreements, women protection advisors, women's expert testimony): the UN Secretary-General was authorized to convene a session of the UN Security Council to hear situations where widespread and systematic sexual violence against women was taking place, and to include evidence from other UN agencies and actors to inform the decisions of the Security Council. At the time this was seen as a dramatic expansion of the Security Council's purview, and diplomacy has been strong on both sides—with some member states advocating a broader mandate for WPS in the Security Council, and others consistently pushing back on these attempts.

There is justifiable concern about the location of the WPS agenda, its terminology, and a potential hierarchy among the four pillars pursued in local, national, and international forums. This concern was expressed in the 2015 UN Women's *Global Study on Women, Peace, and Security: Security the Peace*: "Frequently, women are portrayed alongside children, either in pictures or in the pages of reports, and they are almost universally shown as defenceless and vulnerable victims. This has had an effect in policy and in practice. Our most urgent interventions to assist women and girls in crisis situations are focused on their protection rather than their empowerment" (UN Women 2015: 86). Yet even crisis responses to protect women and girls should put in place some enabling mechanisms and be coherent with long-term peace-building efforts to empower women and girls. Women's groups are frequently the groups on the frontline of crisis response, and committed to remaining in-country for recovery and reconstruction despite resource-based constraints limiting the use of funds for long-term empowerment and prevention (Higelin and Yermo 2016; Davies 2017).

How has the WPS agenda been pursued to date? How should the WPS agenda be pursued in practice? These are the questions we asked of our contributors, and in answering these questions, they have had to engage with the normative and policy tensions involved in practically realizing the spirit and intent of UNSCR 1325.

Contention and concern does arise when the WPS thematic agenda refers to gender equality and gender mainstreaming in the defense forces, in peacekeeping operations, and more recently, in the promotion of women's roles and gender perspectives on preventing and countering violent extremism. Does gender mainstreaming in militaries and peacekeeping missions mean, by extension, that WPS legitimizes the use of violence? WPS's origins in the UN Security Council has meant that the agenda has had to follow its institutional conventions, but does this preclude multiple and intersecting WPS practices in other institutional contexts? To date, the UN General Assembly, the Human Rights Council, the Peacebuilding Commission, and Bretton Woods institutions left discussions on how to implement the WPS agenda to the UN Security Council, the UN Secretariat, and to a lesser extent, UN Women, and the Department of Peacekeeping Operations. The CEDAW (Convention on the Elimination of All Forms of Discrimination against Women) General Recommendation 30, however, makes it clear that the WPS agenda is not exclusively the purview of the UN Security Council. How then should WPS proceed and be coordinated, and where can political support be mobilized for its ongoing institutionalization and implementation?

We approached the structure of the handbook with a desire to be sensitive to these conceptual and structural disagreements but not to further binary, either/or positions. The introduction of the WPS agenda bridged a knowledge gap between acts of significant violence and the inequalities that characterize and enable such violence. The scholarship, policy engagement, and activism that have flowed since the introduction of Resolution 1325 seek to further bridge this gap. We contend, however, that greater advancement of the WPS agenda comes from attempts to pragmatically reconcile conceptual tensions. The feminist pragmatic method pays attention to how WPS is constituted by a community of practice and inquiry. As such, we have sought contributions in this handbook that pay particular attention to how WPS concepts, WPS pillars, and WPS practices are being contested, but also how they are being reconciled in practice.

The contestation of WPS meaning and practice is to be celebrated. Antje Wiener (2017: 173) argues, "[o]nce societal boundaries become blurred through border-crossing, it is international encounters that become the sites where contested norms of governance are most likely to become visible." In the case of WPS, the existence of contestation is vital to ensure that there are a variety of actors who can contribute their views. Legitimacy is achieved when representation is balanced and when access to contestation is continually expanded to new individuals and groups. We have structured this volume to deliberately include such an expansive cross section of voices, perspectives, and experiences.

The book is organized into six distinct areas of inquiry: part I—Concepts; part II—Pillars; part III—Institutions; part IV—Implementation; part V—Cross-Cutting agendas; and part VI—Future and Ongoing Challenges. Authors were deliberately selected to represent a cross section of scholars, policy practitioners, and activists. Particular attention was given to different local experiences of WPS in practice, scholarship, and activism. We live in a complex world where people have multiple loyalties, migrations, and locations. We have encouraged co-authorship to further promote learning across this diversity.

The first part of the book, *Concepts of WPS*, asks authors to engage with the criticisms but also the practical efforts. Starting from the history of feminist inquiry into peace and security by J. Ann Tickner, we then turn to examine the origins of the WPS agenda. Perspectives are deliberately drawn from those in civil society, academic, and diplomatic fields. Our authors come from alternative perspectives; they have different understandings of what choices prevailed and what compromises occurred when attempting to integrate gender perspectives and knowledge into a traditional peace and security institution. Resolution 1325 was intended to mainstream gender in peace and security policymaking—how this happened in practice is the concern of chapters by those who were involved in advocacy at the time, as well as those who have studied the passage of WPS resolutions subsequently. Finally, the section turns to the consequences of the male/female gender binary and what mainstreaming success the first eighteen years of Resolution 1325 can claim.

Having introduced the emergence and evolution of the WPS agenda in practice in the Security Council, the second part of the book turns to the *WPS Pillars*: specifically, the development and implementation of the four pillars—individually and holistically—since 2000. The first four chapters in this section examine the theory underlying each pillar, while the remaining four chapters examine the practice within each pillar to date. These chapters seek to provide a methodology to inform and document the community of practice that has developed for each pillar. Some of the chapters point to the conundrum raised already— that some pillars have received relatively more attention than others and that this has made the documentation of practice quite difficult. As such, these chapters demonstrate *why* it is important to study each respective pillar in its own right but also to recognize the interplay among the pillars to avoid silos.

Sensitive analysis that seeks to trace the conditions and opportunities for one pillar to promote or extend conversation and practice into another pillar is a point often made in this section. A clear example of this is how the original focus on the protection pillar, specifically protection of women in conflict and humanitarian situations, led to discussions about who is best placed to protect them. Practice soon led to awareness of the need for women to be mainstreamed into protection roles—primarily military roles. However, to achieve gender mainstreaming in the security sector, it has also been essential to integrate women personnel into political and justice institutions and in conflict prevention, civilian policing, and peace agreement negotiations. The chapters in this section demonstrate how ideas have shaped practical actions and the trial-and-error process that this has set in motion from the outset.

The *Institutionalization of WPS* in practice beyond one location (New York) and beyond one institution (the UN Security Council) is the purpose of the third section of the handbook. As previously noted, when WPS discourse is examined for meaning and import, the primary location that scholars turn to is the UN Security Council. However, as this section shows, not all *practitioners* turn to the Security Council to interpret the meaning and import of WPS in practice. There are many international and regional organizations working to realize WPS commitments, ever increasing in number, examined in this section. Some have a long-standing affiliation with the WPS agenda, such as the NATO, while others are yet to align their gender equality engagement with WPS obligations (i.e., the World Bank and International Monetary Fund). Regional organizations (ASEAN; the African Union; the Organization of American States; and the Pacific Islands Forum) are examined in this section as institutionally adapting the WPS agenda to guide and assist member states. The chapters in part III (as in the previous section), highlight how regional institutions may not always echo the precise language of the WPS resolutions, but there are, nonetheless, meaningful debates on gender inclusion and gender empowerment in local peace and security institutions that we should be aware of and monitor. How to advance such discussion so that transformation is not being held hostage to local "traditions" is the next puzzle for assisting local participation in the WPS agenda (George 2017).

In part III we also ask a selection of authors to take up CEDAW General Recommendation 30 by considering how agencies and organizations within the UN (aside from UN Women) can carry out their responsibility to the WPS agenda. The

Secretary-General annual report on WPS requires the UN system to report progress on mainstreaming the WPS agenda. Some organizations, like the Department of Peacekeeping are obvious locations to assess how the four pillars of WPS agenda are progressing; but we also have chapters that examine less-considered UN locations for WPS policymaking—such as the Human Rights Council, the International Criminal Court, and the World Bank. This section highlights the benefit of understanding WPS in different institutional environments and provides insight into the pragmatic pathways to mainstream WPS across a range of regional and international environments. These chapters find that advancement of respective WPS pillars is rarely neglected deliberately. Rather, in environments where there are competing resources, obligations, and local resistance, the task becomes focused on harnessing entry points and opportunities to build the WPS agenda while complementing existing remits.

Integrating WPS within existing remits demonstrates that the agenda is and should be core to conflict prevention, relief and recovery, peace processes, and the protection of civilians. Tragically for many populations at risk of violence and deprivation, the WPS agenda still lacks the perfect case of adoption, mainstreaming, and implementation, though there may be never be one given the dynamic situations of both conflicts and global politics. In part IV of the volume we take stock of the experience of *Implementing the WPS mandate*. Our authors examine a selection of conflicts, diplomatic actors, and conditions (such as displacement and disability) where a WPS mandate is intended to make a difference to the lives of conflict-affected women and girls. In this section we ask authors to explore the lessons learned in cases they examine, and what has had to be compromised, negotiated, and insisted on to bring WPS into the heart of peace and security situations where there are multiple agendas and needs. There are limited cases where WPS mandates have been pursued as a goal that is equally important to other goals in conflict, peace processes, and diplomacy. Making the case for WPS thus requires, as these chapters illustrate, a careful, often frustrating, compromise between the demand for evidence that a WPS focus works in a given setting when there may be little to be found, while avoiding simplistic gendered expectations that women are either the peacemakers or the victims, and so forth. These chapters illustrate the stark reality that practitioners face on the ground when needing to negotiate very different values and agendas between combatants, political leaders, and civilians. How to balance WPS values and competing local agendas lead us to ask when can WPS converge with other peace, security, humanitarian and development agendas without losing its focus and mandate?

Whether in a conflict or a diplomatic venue, there are always competing agendas. Is the success of some agendas also pivotal for the success and mainstreaming of the WPS agenda? In part V, we ask authors to consider what may be gained—and what may be lost—from pursuing *WPS as a Cross-Cutting agenda*. This section explores WPS advocacy that engages with other agendas advancing WPS perspectives on debates concerning arms control; migration; postcolonialism; conflict prevention; the responsibility to protect; torture; children's rights; the protection of civilians; as well as climate change; and countering violent extremism. Mainstreaming in these areas cannot stand alone without a specialized body of knowledge and practice on WPS and gender; likewise, WPS cannot advance gender mainstreaming without participation in areas that affect and determine the structures of gender relations. Given there remains so little understanding of the causes of women's marginalization in peace and security processes, as well as the consequences of this marginalization, the risk of issue-dilution from a broader focus needs to be weighed against the benefits of generating more evidence and awareness of the unequal gendered dynamics and effects of insecurity and conflict.

Division, doubt, and a lack of sustained interest persist despite almost two decades of scholarship, activism, and policymaking on the WPS agenda. These five sections of the handbook reveal the large ambition of the WPS project. This project was never going to be achieved without significant contestation as its full implementation is the promise of radical transformation of the structures and processes of the international system. It is important to pay attention therefore to what is possible and what is failing, what is not being delivered, and what is not being discussed, as well as who is present and who is absent from WPS debate and contestation. But it is equally important to build an evidence base of dialogue, compromise, policy, and practice. The success and failure of local adaptation, institutional engagement, and mainstreaming are all important lessons for progressing WPS. These may not be *best* practices, but they are good practices achieved in the face of diversity and opposition; and they are forging a dynamic normative agenda for WPS.

We invited contributors in the final section to think about the *Dynamic Normative Agenda of WPS* for the next twenty years of scholarship, advocacy, and practice. In part VI, authors put forward their most forceful recommendations for deepening engagement with gendered definitions of security, for networking advocacy with the use of technology, for attention to intersectionality, and for progressing peacemaking and foreign policy, because success depends upon gender equality and women's empowerment. They advocate for refinement in the methods of research and analysis, and for enhanced engagement between scholarship and practice in WPS.

Conclusion: A Dynamic Normative and Practical Agenda

As we have illustrated, conundrums and tensions continually surface at the heart of WPS: between the long-term quest for equal peace and the need for immediate gender-sensitive responses to conflict; between the importance of making visible women as agents and victims of war; between attentiveness to gender relations and the need to rethink gender as a binary concept; between the emphasis on nonviolent approaches to the resolution of conflict and support for gender equality across the security sectors that deploy violence; between the focus on conflict-affected, and often poor, countries and regions, and the practices of relatively stable, rich, and arms-trading nations that may foment war and conflict overseas. These tensions are both constitutive of the WPS normative agenda and productive in sustaining it. We think it is harmful to view the research in relation to WPS as progressive and its practice as regressive. Practice is often conducted in the face of immense policy and programmatic resistance. Different approaches will be taken and must be taken to fully realize the potential of WPS. Scholars must be sensitive to how the WPS agenda will be directly encountered by peace and security actors on the ground, including activists, practitioners, and politicians, many of whom may not have been introduced to gender analysis before.

As well as contestation of its meaning in use, WPS is having to accommodate cross-cutting issues such as terrorism, violent extremism, and climate change–induced displacement. Gender-specific protection and women's roles in preventing violence are being rethought and applied to a different set of issues (see UN Secretary-General 2016). The influence of gender-balance norms in economic governance following the global financial crisis has also influenced the broader normative environment for WPS. As a result, women's inclusion in peace processes has been promoted in a similar fashion to the advocacy for gender representation on corporate boards and the use of evidence on the investment returns from women's presence in decision-making. The discussion of women's representation in peace processes is in many respects an advance in the WPS agenda in progress. However, the fixation on the quantifiable nature of the number of women with a seat at the peace table must not become an end in itself, detracting from the substantive post-conflict gender-justice outcomes. To date, only the Colombian peace process "has addressed gender concerns (including sexual violence) in a systematic manner that exemplifies the aims of the Security Council Resolutions 1325 (2000) and 1820 (2008)" (United Nations Secretary-General [UNSG] 2017: 9–10; also see UNSG 2016: para 108). But that is not to prejudge the gender politics of peace implementation in Colombia discussed in several chapters in this handbook. The normative issues regarding *which women* and *what agendas* they bring remain largely sidelined by states. This is the *next* discussion that women's rights activists and scholars want to have. NGO advocates campaigning for "meaningful" women's participation (see Paffenholz et al. 2016; Women's International League for Peace and Freedom 2017) ask how can societies be rebuilt in ways that ensure the sustainability of peace and that recognize the agency of women? The language of meaningful participation is further echoed in the most recent UNSC resolutions and debates. It illustrates the evolving meaning-in-use of WPS.

We offer this volume consisting of sixty-seven chapters and nearly one hundred authors as a synthesis of the body of knowledge in the fast emerging field of WPS to this point, and as "toolkit" for practitioners to continue experimenting with as well. We hope that the Oxford handbook on WPS will spurn many debates and contestations, which are so crucial to further advancing the "Women, Peace, and Security" agenda and its vision for equal and lasting peace.

Notes

1. The subsequent seven resolutions are in order: UNSCR 1820 (2008); 1888 (2009); 1889 (2009); 1960 (2011); 2106 (2013); 2122 (2013); and 2242 (2015).
2. WPS UNSC resolutions have been adopted under chapter 6, rather than chapter 7 of the UN Charter, which makes them non-binding in international law on member states.
3. Resolutions 1888 (2008), 1889 (2009), 1920 (2013), 2122 (2014), 2242 (2015), and Security Council Resolution 2272 (2016). A seventh resolution was introduced in March 2016 on addressing and reporting sexual exploitation and abuse by UN peacekeepers.
4. It was a narrower focus in contrast to Resolution 1325, and it raised concern that the WPS thematic agenda was being reduced to one issue—protection—and, at that, a limited understanding of who experiences sexual violence.

REFERENCES

Aggestam, Karin, and Annika Bergman-Rosamond. "Swedish Feminist Foreign Policy in the Making: Ethics, Politics, and Gender." *Ethics and International Affairs* 30, no. 3 (2016): 323–334.

ASEAN. "Joint Statement on Promoting Women, Peace, and Security." November 16, 2017, http://asean.org/joint-statement-on-promoting-women-peace-and-security-in-asean/.

Davies, Sara E., and Jacqui True. "Norm Entrepreneurship in Foreign Policy: William Hague and the Prevention of Sexual Violence in Conflict." *Foreign Policy Analysis* 13, no. 3 (2017): 701–721.

Davies, Sara E. "Making These Beautiful Resolutions Real: Sara E. Davies in Conversation with Devanna de la Puente." *International Feminist Journal of Politics* 19, no. 1 (2017): 112–117.

George, Nicole. "Policing 'Conjugal Order': Gender, Hybridity, and Vernacular Security in Fiji." *International Feminist Journal of Politics* 19, no. 1 (2017): 55–70.

Higelin, Michelle, and Francisco Yermo. "Transforming Disaster into Opportunity: Shifting the Power." Action Aid Global, 2016.

Idris, Iffat. "Implementation of UN Security Council Resolution 1325 in Libya." *K4D Helpdesk Report*. Brighton, UK: Institute of Development Studies, 2017.

Jansson, Maria, and Maud Eduards. "The Politics of Gender in the UN Security Council Resolutions on Women, Peace, and Security." *International Feminist Journal of Politics* 18, no. 4 (2016): 590–604.

Kreft, Anne-Kathrin. "The Gender Mainstreaming Gap: Security Council Resolution 1325 and UN Peacekeeping Mandates." *International Peacekeeping* 24, no. 1 (2017): 132–158.

Krook, Mona L., and Jacqui True. "Rethinking the Life Cycles of International Norms: The United Nations and the Global Promotion of Gender Equality." *European Journal of International Relations* 18, no. 1 (2012): 100–124.

Paffenholz, Thania, Nick Ross, Steven Dixon, Anna-Lena Schluchter, and Jacqui True. "Making Women Count—Not Just Counting Women: Assessing Women's Inclusion and Influence on Peace Negotiations." Geneva: Inclusive Peace and Transition Initiative. The Graduate Institute of International and Development Studies and UN Women, 2016.

Tickner, J. Ann, and Jacqui True. A Century of International Relations Feminism: From World War One Women's Peace Pragmatism to the Women, Peace, and Security Agenda. *International Studies Quarterly* 62, no. 2. (2018): 221–233.

UN Secretary-General (UNSG). "Report of the UN Secretary-General on Women and Peace and Security." S/2016/822. New York: United Nations, September 29, 2016.

UN Secretary-General (UNSG). "Report of the Secretary-General on Conflict-Related Sexual Violence." S/2017/249. New York: United Nations, April 15, 2017.

UN Security Council (UNSC). "Resolution 1960, S/RES/1969 (2010)." New York: United Nations, December 16, 2010.

UN Security Council (UNSC). "Resolution 2242, S/RES/2242 (2015)." New York: United Nations, October 13, 2015.

UN Security Council. "Letter dated 20 October 2017 from the Chargé d'affaires a.i. of the Permanent Mission of France to the United Nations addressed to the Secretary-General, Transmits concept note for the Security Council open debate on the topic 'Women and peace and security', to be held on 27 Oct." S2017/2017/889. New York: United Nations, 23 October, 2017.

UN Women. "Transforming Justice, Securing the Peace. A Global Study on the Implementation of United Nations Security Council Resolution 1325 (2000)." Lead author: Radhika Coomaraswamy. UN Women, 2015, http://wps.unwomen.org/pdf/en/GlobalStudy_EN_Web.pdf.

Wiener, Antje. "Enacting Meaning-in-Use: Qualitative Research on Norms and International Relations." *Review of International Studies* 35 (2009): 175–193.

Wiener, Antje. "A Reply to My Critics." *Polity* 49, no. 1 (2017): 165–184.

Women's International League for Peace and Freedom. "Women's Meaningful Participation in Politics and Peace Processes: Where Do Member States Stand Now?," 2017. https://wilpf.org/wp-content/uploads/2017/10/FLYER_Member-States_Online.pdf.

Zwingel, Susanne. "How Do Norms Travel? Theorizing International Women's Rights in Transnational Perspective." *International Studies Quarterly* 56 (2012): 115–129.

CHAPTER 2

PEACE AND SECURITY FROM A FEMINIST PERSPECTIVE

J. ANN TICKNER

AT the 1985 Women's International Peace Conference held in Halifax, Canada, attended by women from all parts of the world, participants defined security in various ways depending on the most immediate threats to their survival. Some of the threats identified included freedom from fear of war or unemployment and the need for safe working conditions. Women from the Global South defined security broadly in terms of structural violence associated with imperialism, militarism, racism, and sexism (Tickner 1992: 54). In the same year, this definition of security was also affirmed in the report, *Equality, Development, and Peace*, which was released in Nairobi, Kenya, at the third United Nations Women's Conference. This conference met to review and appraise the achievements of the UN Decade for Women (1975–1985).[1]

The 1980s and the 1990s were also times when the international community more generally, responding to the new kinds of wars, began to define security in similarly broader terms, not just the national security of states.[2] But this insistence on defining peace and security comprehensively, to include the promotion of social justice and the elimination of violence in all its manifestations and at all levels of society, had been central to the international women's movements for much longer, stretching all the way back to the Women's Peace Congress held at The Hague, Netherlands, in 1915, which formulated a set of principles for a just settlement to World War I (Addams et al. 2003; Tickner and True (2018). The principles adopted at that meeting similarly noted the violence that women, and civilians more generally, suffered in times of war; the need for women to participate in peacemaking; and the desire to build what the women defined as "positive peace," a peace that includes social justice, not just the cessation of hostilities. All the statements coming out of the UN women's conferences from the beginning of the Decade for Women in Mexico City until Beijing in 1995 have adopted similarly broad definitions of peace and security, which culminated in UN Security Council Resolution 1325 (2000) and the adoption of the Women, Peace, and Security (WPS) agenda in the first decade of this century. Women's movements have always insisted that real security and just peace could never be achieved without similarly securing women's equal rights.

It has been the task of feminist scholarship in International Relations (IR) to analyze and explain the deep structural reasons why women's activism, participation, and knowledge about achieving peace and security have largely been ignored or not taken seriously by the international community. Using a broad multidimensional definition of security articulated by women peace activists over the past century, a definition that includes the security of individuals as well as states, and that extends to economic and environmental security as well as physical security, has been central to feminist IR scholarship. That scholarship, beginning in the late 1980s, started to address peace and security from a gendered perspective. Using a gender lens, feminists claim that true security cannot be achieved until unequal power structures of gender, race, and class are eliminated or at least diminished (Tickner 1992).

This chapter recognizes the importance of the intersection between women's activism and this emergent feminist scholarship. The interrelationship and tight links between the two have been crucial for the development of feminist theory. However, in this chapter I will focus on some of the ways in which IR feminist scholarship has defined, analyzed, and helped us understand the structural gendered insecurities that contribute not only to insecurities that women face *as women* but also to the multiple insecurities that we all face, as well as the obstacles to achieving genuine peace and social justice. Questioning the essentialist association of women and peace, feminists offer us a multilevel, multidimensional definition of security; they advocate seeing women as agents in all aspects of peace-building and peacemaking, positions that the international community is finally beginning to recognize. Drawing on feminist theory, feminists are also suggesting some new ways to think about building peace and security. Involving women as security providers and peace builders is vital to achieving security for us all.

ENGENDERING SECURITY

As feminists have noted both *security* and *peace* are profoundly gendered concepts. Security has been associated with a strong form of militarized masculinity and peace with a type of femininity where women are seen only as victims needing protection. In the discipline of International Relations, security is generally defined as *national* security, and when we think of a national security specialist, typically we think of a masculine protector. Despite women's entry into many militaries, war making is still seen primarily as men's business. The prioritizing of national security is manifested in many states in high levels of defense spending and the privileging of needs of warfare over welfare. Realism, the IR approach associated with security studies, assumes that states exist in a hostile international environment where conflict could break out at any time. Prescriptions for state survival are based on power maximization, strength, and autonomy, characteristics we associate with masculinity.

International Relations has focused its attention on the causes and consequences of war rather than on the insecurities that people suffer as a consequence of war, both during and after conflict. IR has typically used a certain threshold of battle deaths to define war[3]; yet in today's wars, civilians account for a large proportion of casualties, the majority of them women and children (True 2015). While acknowledging the toll that war takes on all civilians, feminists have investigated the degree to which women are made insecure during and after war by virtue of *being women*. As noted in 1915 by the women peace activists at The Hague and by all subsequent women's peace movements, tasks associated with caring for children, the wounded, the sick, and the elderly go up during war, and it is generally left to women to fulfill these responsibilities with shrinking resources. Women struggle to find resources to care for their families long after the fighting stops.

Beginning with the Bosnian wars of the 1990s when it was estimated that at least twenty thousand women were raped,[4] it was women's groups that first got the issue of rape in war and sexual and gender-based violence (SGBV) more generally onto the international agenda. As feminists have pointed out, rape is not just an accident of war but frequently part of military strategy. In ethnic wars, rape is used as a way of undermining the identity of entire communities (Tickner 2001: 50; Davies and True 2015). Thanks to the work of women peace activists, the UN has now recognized SGBV as being a serious problem and one that has been addressed in many of the UN Security Council resolutions that comprise the WPS agenda.

In the co-authored introduction to their edited volume, Kathleen Kuehnast and her co-editors claim that while conflict mortality that disaggregates by sex is virtually nonexistent, the female to male ratio of people dying from the effects of conflict seems to have gone up in the post–Cold War era (Kuehnast et al. 2011: 6). Feminists have drawn our attention to the fact that wars do not end when the fighting stops. And recent studies have shown the death rate of women is higher than that of men after the conflict is over (Kuehnast et al. 2011: 7; True 2012: 136). Every war generates large numbers of refugees and women and children make up almost 70 percent of the refugee population. Yet refugee camps, frequently run by male refugees or male humanitarian workers, are often violent places, sexual violence being a particular problem.[5] And women rarely have control over distribution of resources such as food and health services in refugee camps (Kuenhast et al. 2011: 8). Women's physical security is threatened more generally, particularly in militarized societies where the incidence of SGBV is often high.

Laura Sjoberg (2006: 160–161), writing on the wars in Iraq, noted the devastation caused by the sanctions imposed on Iraq in the 1990s, a period defined as the "interlude" between the First and Second Gulf Wars. Sanctions inevitably impose the greatest hardship on people rather than the governments at which they are aimed. Economic sanctions have disproportionately negative effects on women since they are already more socioeconomically and politically vulnerable.[6] In Iraq it was the poor, the sick, the elderly, and children—and the women who cared for them—who suffered. Women were also first to lose their jobs, something that frequently happens when women's wages are seen as supplementary to a family wage. In today's wars, men often disappear or are killed leaving women as sole family providers (Tickner 2001: 50).

Feminists have also pointed to the insecurity of women due to the presence of militaries not engaged in actual warfare. Katherine Moon's (1997) research on prostitution around US military bases in South Korea in the 1970s demonstrated that clean up of prostitution camps by the Korean government, aimed at inducing the US military to stay in Korea, became a matter of high security politics. The health monitoring and policing of female sex workers became a national security concern, thus sacrificing these women's security for the security of the state. Moon's study successfully demonstrates how often individuals' security is compromised in the name of national security.

Despite the high level of violence and insecurities that women, and civilians more generally, suffer during and after conflict, the rationale for war has been centered on the myth that wars are fought for the protection of women, children, and other vulnerable people. The idea that (young) males fight wars to protect vulnerable groups particularly "women and children"[7] has been an important motivator for military recruitment. As Judith Stiehm (1983) claimed, the concept of the *protected* is essential to the legitimation of military violence. Exploding the protector/protected myth helps us to understand who the real victims of violence are. Stiehm also reminds us that if we think of men as protectors, we must remember that they are usually protecting women from other men. Exposing this myth also helps us to see that women are not just helpless victims in conflict but persons who are actively engaged in the provision of security in multiple ways.

It is important to note that feminists do not define security in terms of physical security alone but also as economic security, and not only the economic insecurities associated with war. The concept *structural violence* was introduced into the peace research literature in 1971 by Norwegian peace researcher Johan Galtung (1971). Yet peace researchers rarely talked about the gendered effects of structural violence or the particular insecurities that women face as women.[8] While there are huge differences in the socioeconomic status of women depending on class, race, nationality, and geographic region, women are disproportionately located at the bottom of the socioeconomic scale in just about all societies. Globally, only one in two women participate in paid work compared to three in four men. At the same time, women undertake about three times more unpaid work than men. When women do engage in paid labor, they are often in part-time jobs or in work stereotypically associated with "feminine" skills that are low-paying; frequently women are paid less than men when they do the same work (United Nations Secretary-General's High Level Panel 2016: 21). Many of the hours spent in caring and reproductive tasks are imposing an ever heavier burden on women, not just because of conflict, as I have discussed, but because the effects of neoliberalism's scaling back of welfare benefits and social services (Tickner 2001: 77).

Feminists have suggested that these disturbing data are due to an international division of labor that had its origins in seventeenth-century Europe when definitions of male and female were becoming polarized in ways that were suited to the growing division between paid work done in factories and caring and reproductive unremunerated labor done in the home (Tickner 2001: 81). Even though a vast majority of women work outside the home, the association of women with the roles of caregiver, housewife, and mother has become institutionalized and affects the kind of paid work that is available to them, thus decreasing their economic security and autonomy. Women may choose occupations based on gendered expectations and socialization rather than on market rationality and profit maximization.

Closely tied with economic security is the issue of environmental security, a threat which grows ever more pressing and which also calls for a gendered analysis. Amid threats of global warming, natural disasters, and shrinking natural resources, everyone's security is threated by multiple environmental insecurities, yet it is the poor who suffer the most immediate dangers. While environmentalists have acknowledged these problems, there has been less focus on the gendered effects of environmental degradation that have strong negative effects on women's environmental insecurities. As gatherers of firewood and fuel, rural women in the Global South carry the responsibility for providing clean drinking water and energy for the household. With increased scarcity of firewood caused by over use and resulting desertification, women are foraging further for firewood that, besides being a source of airborne pollution, is being depleted faster than fossil fuel. Environmental damage has severe impacts on women's reproductive systems and toxicity from dangerous chemicals and waste dumps frequently are situated in poor communities (Tickner 2001: 116–121). Since women are the majority of the world's poor and are more dependent on natural resources for their livelihood, women are more vulnerable to the natural hazards associated with climate change, such as floods, landslides, and hurricanes.[9] But it is also the case that women can be agents for change: women have a strong body of knowledge that can be used in climate change mitigation and disaster relief. Household responsibilities place them in a strong position to be stewards of the natural environment. At the 2015 climate conference in Paris, Helen Clark, head of the United Nations Development Programme (UNDP), stressed that women's leadership at the local level is key to any successful strategy to combat climate change.[10]

IR feminists have been somewhat reluctant to investigate and analyze environmental insecurities, perhaps because the association of women with nature has been detrimental to seeing women as autonomous agents. However, indigenous scholarship is giving us some new tools with which to conceptualize environmental dangers. Indigenous peoples celebrate the connection of women with nature. Maori scholar Makere Stewart-Harawira claims that her research was driven by an accelerating sense of crisis in political, social, and economic structures and the fragility of the biosphere. She claims that what is needed to shape a world order that she sees on the brink of destruction is a return to what she calls the Maori "feminine principle," a reconciliation of the political and spiritual with a view to developing "new and sustainable ways of compassionate coexistence on this planet" (Stewart-Harawira 2007: 124–126). This holistic belief in the interconnectedness of all beings and in a symbiotic reciprocity between male and female is central to indigenous cosmologies. As Julius Kunnie (2006: 258) tells us, there is an implicit assumption in all indigenous cosmologies that all life is interconnected. There is no distinct word for "nature" among indigenous people because all of life is seen as coterminous with nature. As Stewart-Harawira (2005: 43–45) reminds us, this holistic way of thinking was common in ancient philosophies and survived in Western philosophy up until the Renaissance, but gradually gave way in the seventeenth century West to the Cartesian view of nature that elevated the mind over the body, men over women, and humans over nature. The critique of Cartesian dualisms has been central to Western feminist thinking and the similarity between feminist and indigenous knowledge is something that could give us fresh insights into ways to think about environmental issues

In this section I have shown how gendered structures of inequality have had particular effects on women's physical, economic, and environmental insecurities, insecurities that have been documented by women peace scholars and activists for over one hundred years. Since the 1980s, feminist scholars in IR have been analyzing and explaining these structures using a gendered lens. Drawing on the multiple insecurities of women, variously situated by race, class, and geographic location, IR feminists have preferred to use a multidimensional definition of security and one that is not tied to conventional notions of national security. But just as the association of women with nature has been problematic for Western feminists so too has the relationship with peace, an issue I take up in the next section.

WOMEN AND PEACE: A PROBLEMATIC ASSOCIATION

If men have been seen as agents in the provision of national security, women have been as-sociated with an essentialized notion of peace that lacks agency. It has often been claimed that women are more peaceful than men and less prone to conflict. While there is evidence to suggest that women have shown less support for men's wars (Tickner 2001: 60), the re-lationship between women and peace has been a contentious one for feminists. Feminist scholars have suggested that in male dominated societies the association of women with peace reinforces gender hierarchies and false dichotomies that contribute to the devaluation of both women and peace. However, even though many of the leaders of peace movements have been men, it has been the case that women have constituted the majority of peace activists, often forming separate movements that draw on maternal imagery to make their case. The women who constituted the Women's Strike for Peace in the United States in the early 1960s defended their right as mothers to de-escalate the nuclear arms race, which, they claimed, threatened the family rather than protected it. And the Women's Peace Camp at Greenham Common in the UK in the 1980s, protesting the staging of US cruise missiles, focused on the radical feminist principles of celebrating women's roles as nurturers and caregivers; this maternal imagery was also used in Argentina by the Mothers of the Plaza de Mayo protesting the disappearance of their husbands and sons (Tickner 2001: 58–59). While not relying specifically on maternal imagery, the International Coalition to Ban Landmines, a coalition of NGOs that included many women, led by Canadian activist Jody Williams, was successful in its efforts to bring about the 1997 Mine Ban Treaty, often referred to as the Ottawa Convention.[11] Moreover, women continue to play a central role in disarmament campaigns. Projects such as Reach Critical Will, the disarmament program of the Women's International League for Peace and Freedom (WILPF), works for disarmament and arms control of many different weapons systems and the reduction of military spending. It aims to include women in disarmament discussions and investigates the gendered aspects of the impact of weapons and disarmament processes.[12]

Protests that use maternalism to make their case have been criticized for celebrating women's maternal and peaceful roles, a move that feminists believe denies women's agency. And of course, not all women are mothers and not all women are peaceful. It has often been the case, however, that rather than essentializing women, feminists have used ma-ternalism strategically. Jane Addams provides us with an early example of this. Addams was both a theorist and an activist. As chair of the Women's Peace Congress in 1915 and the first president of WILPF, Addams came to pacifism though her work at Hull House, a settlement community in Chicago for immigrant women. Hers was a dynamic notion of peace—women of many nationalities living together and negotiating their differences, what she called "a sturdy and virile" internationalism (Fischer 2005: 3).

Like many thinkers at the end of the nineteenth century, Addams was also an evolu-tionist, believing that the world was progressing beyond what she termed "a juvenile pro-pensity for war" to a more cosmopolitan form of patriotism that extended beyond narrow tribal allegiances (Fischer 2005: 4). Addams applied this evolutionary paradigm to govern-ment, which she claimed was moving from a focus on militarism to one centered on social welfare. In *Newer Ideals of Peace*, Addams claimed that immigrant women, many of whom worked in city government, which she described as "enlarged housekeeping," were developing the kind of skills necessary to build a just peace (Fischer 2005: 6–7). For Addams, democracy, social justice, and peace were mutually defining concepts. Like other peace activists and suffragettes at the beginning of the twentieth century, maternalist rhetoric was an important tool, but it was used instrumentally to pursue a dynamic notion of peace strongly linked to social justice. And real peace could not be achieved without women's equality.

Contemporary feminists have continued to draw on this instrumental use of maternal thinking to construct a theory of peace that also includes gender equality. Sara Ruddick (1989) developed a sophisticated theory of maternalism that is careful to avoid essentialism. Ruddick claims that the idea of maternal peace rests on a myth that mothers are peacemakers and victims without power, a myth that is easily shattered by history. Women have supported men's wars in overwhelming numbers and some are fighters as well as mothers (Ruddick 1989: 219). Nevertheless, she claims, war is women's enemy, because it disrupts caregiving, a role that has traditionally been assigned to women, although both men and women bring maternal skills to peace work. Like Addams, Ruddick claims that thinking about peace arises from distinctive ways of doing care work, work that men are capable of performing also (Ruddick 1989: 13). Paraphrasing feminist philosopher Sandra Bartky, Ruddick states "[C]oming to have a maternal feminist and antimilitarist consciousness is the experience of coming to know what violence does to one's children and to oneself, as victim or perpetrator, and then casting one's lot in solidarity with women who resist violence" (Ruddick 1989: 244). Like other feminists, Ruddick is careful not to associate peace with passivity and victimhood. Peace-building and nonviolence require courage, struggle, and resistance, and a refusal to accept victimization, traits we see in women activists in conflict zones today. Ruddick concludes that it is easy to be skeptical about the idea of feminist maternal peace politics in a world filled with war. However, she argues, the work of peace-building is always specific, a particular resistance to particular violences, many of which are successful (Ruddick 1989: 245).

Building on Addams and Ruddick's claim that maternal thinking is relevant not only to the private sphere but has political significance also, Fiona Robinson extends an ethics of care to global issues, particularly those related to structural violence. Robinson claims that care as a practice must relate to particular contexts, just as Ruddick claims that peace-building must be specific and contextualized (Robinson 1999: 30). An "ethics of care" on a global scale breaks down the dichotomy between public and private, a move that is central to feminist thinking, and conceptualizes how to build social relations on a global scale. Responding to issues of poverty and structural violence, an important aspect of feminist thinking on security, Robinson claims that the eradication of poverty must start from the premise that responding morally to others is a learned capacity that emerges out of connections (Robinson 1999: 46). Feminist theory is particularly useful because its focus is on individuals located in particular structures of domination and oppression. What she calls a relational morality should encourage, not economic dependence, but interdependence through the creation of a sense of mutual respect and an atmosphere of trust among moral agents who respond to each other as concrete persons (Robinson 1999: 48).

Care ethics is one of the tools that Elisabeth Porter (2007) uses to build her feminist approach to peace-building. Like Robinson, Porter finds care ethics useful because it is contextualized, particular, and informal. She contrasts it with a justice approach to ethics that is based on individualized rights and the generalized "other." She claims that a feminist ethics is particularly useful for peace-building since feminist theory has always been concerned with breaking down dichotomies and the dualist way of thinking that characterizes so much of International Relations. A dualistic position, one that sees only right or wrong, friend or enemy, is at the root of violent insecurity. On the contrary, dialogue, openness to others, typical of feminist knowledge-building, is crucial for peace-building (Porter 2007: 43–46). Porter claims that feminist ethics rests on three pillars that are useful for peace-building: First, the starting point is women's lives in all their different manifestations—women living in war zones, women peace-builders, women campaigning against violence, women in NGOs, and in international governmental organizations. The focus is always on women's subordination and inequality, however it manifests itself. Second, a feminist ethic asks how male privilege has come to define what is security and insecurity. It investigates what are the necessary conditions for a sustainable peace that include reducing structural inequalities between women and men. It asks why have women been systematically excluded from peace tables and treated as second-class citizens in matters of security and peace-building. Third, the alternative ways of building peace that a feminist ethic proposes are contextual and emphasize personal experience and nurture, characteristics that echo Ruddick's maternal thinking and Robinson's ethics of care (Porter 2007: 56). Like Jane Addams also, all these feminists emphasize the importance of breaking down dualisms, being open to dialogue and listening to others, as well as allowing room for compromise positions.[13]

CONCLUSION

This chapter has attempted to show how feminists have contributed to redefining security away from a narrow understanding of national security toward a more comprehensive vision focused on human security. Human security places people rather than states at the center of international security. Even though women activists have been advocating this form of security for well over one hundred years, human security was not placed on the international agenda until the UNDP's 1994 Human Development Report, a report that equated security with people, rather than with states, and with development rather than with arms.[14] However, the report did not mention gender or women's particular insecurities, and it was not until the passage of Resolution 1325 and the ensuing WPS agenda that women's security became a concern for the international community. Contributions from feminist activists and scholars have emphasized that conceptualizing human security in a way that is truly inclusive must account for gendered insecurities that stem from exclusionary practices that perceive women as victims rather than security providers, and from the structural inequalities that contribute to women's economic, political, and social insecurities. Human security must also address issues of gender-based violence, and the structural insecurities that women suffer by virtue of being women. Feminists believe that real security or positive peace cannot be achieved without gender justice and the empowerment of women. Empowerment means the empowerment of all individuals, both women and men, in all their various roles as security providers. It involves exposing the myth of masculine protectors and feminized victims.

I have attempted to show how feminist scholars have constructed knowledge that contributes to our understanding of the deeper reasons why women suffer particular insecurities both physical and structural. I have suggested that strategic maternalism and a feminist ethic of care that is closely linked to maternalism are useful tools in this endeavor. Going at least as far back as The Hague peace conference of 1915, feminists, such as Jane Addams, who was both a scholar and a practitioner, have introduced maternalism as a practical strategy into peace politics. Strategic maternalism claims that bringing maternal qualities such as care to the peaceful resolution of disputes, qualities available to both women and men, are essential for achieving human security. Focusing on individuals rather than states and the concrete rather than the abstract, a feminist ethic of care promotes the breaking down of boundaries between "us" and "them" through a dialogic pragmatic approach that is consistent with feminist knowledge-building more generally. Introducing a multidimensional feminist perspective on peace and security that exposes the gendered inequalities that make us all less secure builds on a long tradition of feminist peace politics and the practical knowledge that has emerged from these feminist movements, knowledge that is essential if we are to work toward a world that is more secure for us all.

NOTES

1. UN Women Watch. http://www.un.org/womenwatch/daw/beijing/otherconferences/Nairobi/Nairobi%20Chapter%205-6.pdf.
2. The Nordic countries took the lead on this. Olaf Palme, then Prime Minister of Sweden, defined security in terms of joint survival rather than mutual destruction. See Independent Commission on Disarmament and Security Issues, (1982).
3. Uppsala Conflict Database Program is the most complete account of battle deaths by country; see http://www.ucdp.uu.se/.
4. According to an estimate by the Parliamentary Survey of Europe entitled, "Sexual Violence against Women in Armed Conflict," May 2009, http://assembly.coe.int/nw/xml/XRef/Xref-XML2HTML-en.asp?fileid=17743&lang=en.
5. After wars end, women and children make up more that 80 percent of the population of refugee camps (True 2012: 135).
6. See A. Cooper Drury and Durson Peksen, "Women and Economic Statecraft: The Negative Impact International Sanctions Visit on Women, September 6, 2012, http://journals.sagepub.com/doi/abs/10.1177/1354066112448200.
7. This term was used by Cynthia Enloe in an article in the *Village Voice* to remind us how often this phrase is used—in this case the media talking about the war between the United States and Iraq—to unproblematically lump these essentialized terms together when we talk about protection.
8. For a feminist critique of Galtung's concept, see Confortini, 2006.
9. For a comprehensive list of resources on women and climate change, see UN Women Watch, http://www.un.org/womenwatch/feature/climate_change/downloads/Women_and_Climate_Change_Factsheet.pdf.
10. Clark described a UNDP partnership with the Global Environmental Facility and Barefoot College of India that resulted in an initiative to train low-income women to install and maintain solar panels. See "Women Are Key to a Successful Climate Strategy," *Time* (website), December 1, 2015, http://time.com/4131575/women-leadership-climate-strategy/.

11. For a comprehensive discussion of the Mine Treaty, see United Nations Office for Disarmament Affairs, "Landmines," https://www.un.org/disarmament/convarms/Landmines/.

12. For resources on women's activism concerning disarmament and arms control today, see Reaching Critical Will, http://www.reachingcriticalwill.org/. See also chapter 54, this volume.

13. One example of women's negotiating skills is the nuclear accord between Iran and the P5+1 reached in 2015. Three women, two European and one American, were central to the success of this agreement. The lead negotiator Federica Mogherini, the European Union's chief diplomat, who faced criticism at first for being too young and inexperienced, is quoted as having said "the fact of having many women at the table helped us be concrete and pragmatic." Iran did not raise objections to this mostly women team, but they were unable to shake hands due to Iran's strict rules about interactions between men and women. See Suzanne Kianpour, "Iran Negotiations: The Women Who Made the Iran Nuclear Deal Happen," August 6, 2015, BBC News (website), http://www.bbc.com/news/world-us-canada-33728879.

14. See United Nations Development Programme, "Human Development Report 1994," http://hdr.undp.org/en/content/human-development-report-1994.

REFERENCES

Addams, J., E. G. Balch, and A. Hamilton. *Women at The Hague*. Amherst, MA: Humanity Books, 2003.

Davies, S. E. and J. True. Reframing Conflict-Related Sexual and Gender-Based Violence: Bringing Gender Analysis Back In. *Security Dialogue* 46 (2015): 1–18.

Confortini, C. "Galtung, Violence, and Gender: The Case for a Peace Studies/Feminist Alliance." *Peace and Change: A Journal of Peace Research* 39 (2006): 3.

Galtung, J. "A structural theory of imperialism." *Journal of Peace Research* 8 (1971): 81–117.

Fischer, M. "Addams's Internationalist Pacifism and the Rhetoric of Maternalism." *NWSA Journal*, 18, no. 3 (2005): 1–19.

Independent Commision on Disarmament and Security Issues. *Common Security: A Blueprint for Survival*. Oxford: Oxford University Press, 1982.

Kuehnast, K., C. de Jonge Oudraat, and H. Hernes, eds. *Women and War: Power and Protection in the Twenty-First Century*. Washington, DC: US Institute of Peace, 2011.

Kunnnie, J. "Indigenous African Knowledge: Human Rights and Globalization." In *Indigenous People's Wisdom and Power: Affirming Our Knowledge Through Narratives*, edited by J. Kunnie and N. Goduka, 257–270. Burlington, VT: Ashgate, 2006.

Moon, K. H. S. *Sex Among Allies: Military Prostitution in U.S. Korea Relations*. New York: Columbia University Press, 1997.

Porter, E. *Peacebuilding: Women in International Perspective*. New York: Routledge, 2007.

Robinson, F. *Globalizing Care: Ethics, Feminist Theory and International Relations*. New York: Westview Press, 1999.

Ruddick, S. *Maternal Thinking: Toward a Politics of Peace*. New York: Ballantine Books, 1989.

Sjoberg, L. *Gender, Justice, and the Wars in Iraq: A Feminist Reformulation of Just War Theory*. Lanham, MD: Lexington Books, 2006.

Stewart-Harawira, M. *The New Imperial Order: Indigenous Responses to Globalization*. London: Zed Books, 2005.

Stewart-Harawira, M. "Practising Indigenous Feminism." In *Making Space for Indigenous Feminism,* edited by J. Green, 124–139. London: Zed Books, 2007.

Stiehm, J. H. *Women and Men's Wars.* Oxford: Pergamon Press, 1983.

Tickner, J. A. *Gender in International Relations: Feminist Perspectives on Achieving Global Security.* New York: Columbia University Press, 1992.

Tickner, J. A. *Gendering World Politics: Issues and Approaches in the Post-Cold War Era.* New York: Columbia University Press, 2001.

Tickner, J. A., and J. True. "A Century of International Relations Feminism: From World War I Women's Peace Pragmatism to the Women, Peace, and Security Agenda." *International Studies Quarterly* 62, 2018.

True, J. *The Political Economy of Violence against Women.* New York: Oxford University Press, 2012.

True, J. "Winning the Battle but Losing the War: A Feminist Perspective on the Declining Global Violence Thesis." *International Feminist Journal of Politics* 17: 554–572, 2015.

United Nations Secretary-General's High Level Panel. "*Leave No One Behind: A Call to Action for Gender Equality and Women's Economic Empowerment,*" 2016, http://hlp-wee.unwomen.org/-/media/hlp%20wee/attachments/reports-toolkits/hlp-wee-report-2016-09-call-to-action-en.pdf?la=en.

CHAPTER 3

....

ADOPTION OF 1325 RESOLUTION

....

CHRISTINE CHINKIN

UN Security Council Resolution 1325 on Women and Peace and Security[1] was widely celebrated by women's NGOs who had advocated for its adoption. It was the first time that the Security Council had devoted a full session to debating women's experiences during and after conflict, and the resolution drew attention to the fact that "peace is inextricably linked with gender equality and women's leadership" (UN Women 2015: 5). However, although it was a "first", Resolution 1325 was not adopted in a vacuum; it can be seen alongside and in conjunction with a number of other thematic resolutions and broader policy initiatives around the same time within the Security Council, and, more generally, the UN. This chapter briefly outlines contemporaneous developments that are founded upon some of the same principles as Resolution 1325 in order to sketch the peace and security landscape in 2000 and to place the resolution in its legal and policy context. It argues that some of the goals of 1325 were already finding support in international law and relations but with variable application, especially with respect to women in conflict-affected situations.

The end of the Cold War had generated optimism for a "new world order" in which democracy, rule of law, and human rights would be the prevailing values,[2] but a different reality soon became clear. The violent conflicts that erupted in the former Yugoslavia, Somalia, Haiti, Burundi, the Caucuses, and elsewhere; the 1994 genocide in Rwanda; and the ensuing conflict in the Democratic Republic of Congo were all incidents of what were termed "new wars." Mary Kaldor identified a number of characteristics of these "new wars": they were fought by loose networks of state and non-state actors—armed militia, criminal gangs, and warlords—that operated across state borders; they were fought in the name of identity—ethnic, religious, or tribal—rather than for political ideas or geopolitical goals; they generated a distinctive and predatory war economy; and extreme violence was directed toward civilians, including highly visible atrocities—executions, torture, rape and other forms of sexual violence, suicide bombings, planting landmines, looting, arson—as a way to generate fear and cause people to flee (Kaldor 2012). Indeed, forced displacement is perhaps the defining characteristic of new wars.

The conflict in Bosnia was the archetypal example of "new wars." And it was in Bosnia that allegations of "massive, organized and systematic detention and rape of women" were brought to the attention of the Security Council and the public (UN Security Council 1993). Against this backdrop, and also that of revelations about the fate of so-called "comfort women" at the hands of the Japanese military in World War II (Dolgopol and Paranjape 1994), with their chilling resemblance to the crimes going on in Bosnia, women activists pursued a two-pronged campaign to have gender-based violence explicitly recognized as a violation of human rights law, and, as the decade progressed, of international criminal law. The first success was the groundbreaking formulation in 1992 by the Committee on the Elimination of Discrimination against Women (CEDAW) describing gender-based violence against women "as violence that is directed against a woman because she is a woman or that affects women disproportionately." The Committee asserted it to be "a form of discrimination that seriously inhibits women's ability to enjoy rights and freedoms on a basis of equality with men," and, as such, it comes within the definition of discrimination in article 1 of the 1979 Convention on All Forms of Discrimination against Women, despite the lack of any explicit reference to violence therein. Although the applicability of the Convention during armed conflict had not then been stipulated, the Committee also noted under paragraph 16 that "[w]ars, armed conflicts and the occupation of territories often lead to increased prostitution, trafficking in women and sexual assault of women, which require specific protective and punitive measures" (CEDAW 1992).

Campaigning and network building by the global women's movement led to the concept of gender-based violence being taken up by the World Conference on Human Rights in Vienna in 1993. The Declaration and Programme of Action adopted at Vienna affirmed that "violations of the human rights of women in situations of armed conflict are violations of the fundamental principles of international human rights and humanitarian law. All violations of this kind, including in particular murder, systematic rape, sexual slavery, and forced pregnancy, require a particularly effective response" (UN General Assembly 1993a). This assertion challenged the classic division between international humanitarian law and human rights law and thus also between violence against women committed in wartime and in so-called peacetime. Indeed, in its recognition of women's rights as "an inalienable, integral and indivisible part of universal human rights" (UN General Assembly 1993a), it was widely asserted that "the biggest winners" at the Vienna Conference were women (Whelan 2010: 186). The UN General Assembly (1993b) followed suit adopting the Declaration on the Elimination of Violence against Women (DEVAW) in December of the same year. In 2000, just a month before the adoption of Resolution 1325, at the Millennium Summit, the UN General Assembly (2000a) reiterated the need "to combat all forms of violence against women and to implement the Convention on the Elimination of All Forms of Discrimination against Women."

Individual criminal responsibility for the commission of sexual violence in conflict as an international crime was sought alongside the provision under human rights law for state responsibility for the wrongful acts of state agents (including military personnel) and for state failure "to exercise due diligence to prevent, investigate and, in accordance with national legislation, punish acts of violence against women, whether those acts are perpetrated by the State or by private persons" under article 4(c) of DEVAW. The first international criminal courts to be established since those following World War II at Nuremburg and Tokyo, the International Criminal Tribunal for former Yugoslavia (ICTY) in 1993 and the International Criminal Tribunal for Rwanda (ICTR) in 1994, provided for the criminal prosecution of

those violating international humanitarian law. The tribunals have subject matter jurisdiction with respect to war crimes, crimes against humanity, and genocide, and criminal
prosecution is either aimed at individual perpetrators or at force commanders through
command responsibility. In 1997 the Women's Caucus for Gender Justice was formed to
promote and defend women's concerns at the negotiations, first in the "prepcoms," and
then at Rome for the statute for a permanent International Criminal Court. By 1998, such
feminist advocates had the statutes, prosecution policies, and the early jurisprudence of the
ICTY and ICTR to draw upon. They succeeded in securing state-of-the-art provisions with
respect to sexual violence: "rape, sexual slavery, enforced prostitution, forced pregnancy,
enforced sterilization, or any other form of sexual violence of comparable gravity" were
spelled out as crimes against humanity (now decoupled from armed conflict), as "serious
violations of the laws and customs applicable in international armed conflict," and as serious violations of laws applicable in armed conflict of a non-international character.[3] In
addition, "[c]ommitting outrages upon personal dignity, in particular humiliating and degrading treatment," constituted a violation of the laws and customs of war in international
and non-international armed conflict.[4] Gender-based persecution was included as a crime
against humanity,[5] and provision was made for "[a] fair representation of female and male
judges."[6]

Resolution 1325 was not adopted under UN Charter Chapter VII and is therefore not
subject to the requirement in article 25 that UN member states "agree to accept and carry
out" decisions of the Security Council. However, these significant legal advances clarified
that rape and sexual violence constitute violations of human rights law and international humanitarian law and, through the evolving international criminal law, constitute
legal and practical tools for combating wartime violence against women. Without these
developments there would have been less reason for the explicit call in Resolution 1325 for
all parties to a conflict to respect international humanitarian law, human rights law, and the
Rome Statute.[7] They also imbued the resolution with the strong normative content it might
otherwise have lacked.

Civil society activism, especially that of NGOs lobbying and networking within international institutions, was crucial in achieving the reform necessary to take account of women's
human rights and to recognize the harms committed against women as violations of international law. So too was seeking new fora and international law-making processes for
achieving these objectives. Such activism and pursuit of legal change were also evident in
other initiatives that sought to mitigate the harms caused by conflict and its aftermath.
For example, the Landmines Convention stemmed from civil society outrage about the indiscriminate and ongoing harm the use of landmines caused to civilians (United Nations
1997). The preamble makes this clear: "[D]etermined to put an end to the suffering and
casualties caused by anti-personnel mines, that kill or maim hundreds of people every week,
mostly innocent and defenseless civilians and especially children, obstruct economic development and reconstruction, inhibit the repatriation of refugees and internally displaced
persons, and have other severe consequences for years after emplacement" (United Nations
1997). The movement for adoption of the Convention was initiated and progressed by a
global NGO coalition, the International Campaign to Ban Landmines (ICBL), supported
by like-minded states, notably Canada, Austria, and Norway (Cameron, Lawson, and
Tomlin 1998). It sought a new forum for treaty negotiation, deliberately working outside
the Geneva Disarmament Conference, the traditional location for disarmament issues,

preferring the more flexible diplomatic Ottawa process. The successful negotiation of the Landmines Convention, like that of the Rome Statute of the ICC a year later, demonstrated that strong coalitions—a partnership between like-minded states and NGOs—can be effective in securing change in international law, even against the interests of powerful states. There was a pattern throughout the 1990s of strategic coalition building, lobbying, and advocacy by civil society that took place within the UN human rights treaty bodies, at global summit meetings and at diplomatic negotiations, that led to normative developments with humanitarian objectives at their core. The adoption of Resolution 1325 fits this pattern: it was motivated by civil society for the advancement of women's interests, assisted by an international agency, the United Nations Development Fund for Women (UNIFEM) and involved engagement with like-minded states that instigated and supported the initiative through the relevant institutional processes. Strategic use of the Aria formula for information sharing with members of the Security Council, as described in chapter 6 in this volume, was also key.

The need to combat the violence experienced by civilians and their deliberate targeting in the context of new wars that was central to many of the campaigns previously described also galvanized the Security Council into several initiatives around protection of civilians in armed conflict in the 1990s. These took a number of different directions. First was the use of military operations for humanitarian purposes. Without referring to women or sexual violence but in response to "continuing reports of widespread violations of international humanitarian law occurring in Somalia, including reports of violence and threats of violence . . . deliberate attacks on non-combatants" in 1992, the Security Council adopted unanimously Resolution 794 (UN Security Council 1992). The resolution was widely considered to break new ground by authorizing "all necessary means" (that is military force) to relieve human suffering through the establishment of a "secure environment for humanitarian relief." This paved the way for recognition of violence against civilians as constituting a threat to international peace and security within the competence of the Security Council. It was, of course, a country-specific mandate and was followed by a slew of resolutions, notably with respect to Bosnia and Herzegovina and to Haiti, which mandated various measures in response to atrocities committed against civilians, including, in the context of Bosnia, the creation of the ICTY, and subsequently for Rwanda, the ICTR.

Later in the decade a second initiative gained momentum. Thematic resolutions for the protection of civilians were adopted (see chapter 46 in this volume), which were general rather than specific to a threat to international peace caused by the situation within a named country and accompanied by measures decided upon under UN Charter Chapter VII. The first such resolutions were directed at categories of people deemed especially vulnerable in armed conflict. One such category, children, was addressed first by the UN General Assembly. Following Graça Machel's (UN General Assembly 1996) pioneering report on children in armed conflict, the Assembly recommended that the Secretary-General appoint a Special Representative on the impact of armed conflict on children to report annually to it (UN General Assembly 1997a). Three years later, the Council took up this issue in its Resolution 1261 (UN Security Council 1999a). While primarily drafted in gender-neutral terms, including with respect to condemning the targeting of children in armed conflict and sexual violence, it also urged "all parties to armed conflicts to take special measures to protect children, in particular girls, from rape and other forms of sexual abuse and gender-based violence in situations of armed conflict and to take into account the special needs of the girl child throughout armed conflicts and their aftermath, including in the delivery of humanitarian assistance" (see chapter 47 in this volume). A year later, the UN Security Council (2000a) underlined "the importance of giving consideration to the special needs and particular vulnerabilities of girls affected by armed conflict, including, *inter alia*, those heading households, orphaned, sexually exploited and used as combatants." In 1998, following two reports of the Secretary-General on insecurity in Africa,[8] the Council adopted a thematic resolution on the protection of refugees and the humanitarian character of refugee camps that stressed the "security needs of women, children and the elderly, who are the most vulnerable groups in refugee camps and settlements" (UN Security Council 1998b).

The Council's thematic agenda for the protection more generally of all civilians in armed conflict commenced in 1999 following the report of the Secretary-General on conflict and insecurity in Africa (UN General Assembly 1998) and a further report on the protection of civilians in armed conflict (UN Security Council 1999b). Making the "human rights of women . . . an integral part of the United Nations human rights activities" (or "gender mainstreaming") and had become stated UN policy since the Vienna and Beijing Global Summits on Human Rights and Women respectively.[9] In line with this policy, both reports address the position of women in armed conflict, albeit not in great detail. In similar language to that of "new wars" the first report noted that in armed conflict, civilians had become "often the main targets, with women suffering in disproportionate numbers while often also being subjected to atrocities that include organized rape and sexual exploitation" (UN General Assembly 1998: para. 49). It also recognized the importance of eliminating discrimination against women, and, from an instrumental perspective, that "investing in women's capabilities and empowering them to exercise their choices is a vital and certain way to advance economic and social development" (UN General Assembly 1998: para. 89). The second report noted the differential impact of war on women and men: the dramatic increases in the number of children and women heads of households, the vulnerability of women and girls to gender-based violence and sexual exploitation, including rape and forced prostitution, and the disproportionate burden of displacement borne by them (UN Security Council 1999b: para. 18). Under the heading "Special measures for children and women," the Secretary-General also called for "parties to conflicts to make special arrangements to meet the protection and assistance requirements of children and women" (UN Security Council 1999b: Recommendation 21).

In Resolution 1265, on the protection of civilians in armed conflicts, the UN Security Council (1999c) noted that civilians "are increasingly targeted by combatants" and grouped women with children and "other vulnerable groups," while also recognizing the "direct and particular impact of armed conflict on women." The Council urged states to comply with human rights law, international humanitarian law, and refugee law, and expressed its "willingness to respond to situations of armed conflict where civilians are being targeted or humanitarian assistance to civilians is being deliberately obstructed." However, that resolution made no reference to the wider consequences of conflict for women as referred to in the report on *Protection of Civilians in Armed Conflict* (UN Security Council 1999b). The next resolution on the protection of civilians, Resolution 1296, continued in a similar vein, depicting women as a vulnerable group in need of protection (UN Security Council 2000b). The Council reaffirmed "its grave concern at the . . . particular impact that armed conflict has on women, children and other vulnerable groups" that "their special protection and assistance needs" be taken into account in peace operations, as well as the possibility of undertaking "special arrangements" when appropriate to ensure protection and delivery of humanitarian assistance (UN Security Council 2000b).

Some of the themes of Resolution 1325 had thus already entered into the Security Council's work through these generic resolutions. However, there is one obvious omission. Despite the limited reference to women's empowerment in the report on conflict and insecurity in Africa (UN General Assembly 1998), for instance, the representation of women is as in need of protection; there is no reference to women's active participation and representation in policy- and decision-making. Women's active agency was not recognized, as it had been in the requirement for equality in political participation in the 1979 Convention on the Elimination of All Forms of Discrimination against Women,[10] and specifically in the context of conflict in strategic objective E.1 in the Beijing Platform for Action: "Increase the participation of women in conflict resolution at decision-making levels." The stark omission of local women from the negotiations at Dayton (which brought an end to the war in Bosnia) and which took place in 1995 only months after the Beijing Conference, was a motivating factor in the push for adoption of Resolution 1325.

Thematic resolutions are the exception in the practice of the Security Council. The majority of its resolutions are directed at country-specific threats to international peace and security. In these resolutions the absence of—or minimal reference to—the concerns expressed in the thematic resolutions is striking. For example, two situations in 1999 led to an especially high level of intervention by the Security Council through the authorization of a civil presence with legislative and executive authority, including the administration of justice. In 1998 and 1999 the Security Council was faced with determining its response to the "grave humanitarian situation throughout Kosovo and the impending humanitarian catastrophe" (UN Security Council 1998c). Following the unauthorized NATO military intervention, acting under UN Charter Chapter VII the Council mandated the establishment of an international security presence (KFOR) and an international civil presence (UNMIK) (UN Security Council 1999d). UNMIK's mandate included the promotion of human rights but without any reference to harms committed against women or, indeed, protection of children and civilians. Later the same year, when violence erupted following the popular consultation in East Timor through which the Timorese people voted for independence, the Council did express that it was "[a]ppalled by the worsening humanitarian situation in East Timor, particularly as it affects women, children and other vulnerable groups" and emphasized the need "to ensure the protection of civilians at risk" (UN Security Council 1999e). It also referred to its deep concern at the "large-scale displacement and relocation of East Timorese civilians, including large numbers of women and children" (UN Security Council 1999f). However, neither the multinational force, the United Nations Mission in East Timor (UNAMET), nor the territorial administration, the United Nations Transitional Administration in East Timor (UNTAET), was mandated to take steps to address gendered crimes. Security Council awareness of the gendered dimensions of the violence did not result in explicitly mandated measures for their redress by UN authorized bodies. It seems that the Council did not relate its emerging thematic agenda to its direct in-country responses to threats to international peace and security, suggesting that in mandating specific powers it did not prioritize the former.

Other resolutions demonstrate an apparently haphazard concern about the position of women in conflict, sometimes referred to, more often not. For instance, in 1999 and 2000, in resolutions concerning the Democratic Republic of Congo and Haiti, there were no such mentions; in the case of Sierra Leone, the Council recalled its Resolution 1265 on protection of civilians and underlined the importance in the training of United Nations Mission in Sierra Leone (UNAMSIL) personnel of the "child and gender-related provisions" of relevant international law (UN Security Council 1999g). In imposing targeted sanctions on Taliban-controlled Afghanistan, preambular mention is made to "discrimination against women and girls," a somewhat minimalist reference in view of that regime's record of violence against women.[11] That the gender mainstreaming policy had not been fully internalized or insisted upon within the UN system (Gallagher 1997) is further demonstrated by its absence from the Brahimi Report on UN Peace Operations. The panel, which had been commissioned to "assess the shortcomings of the existing system [of conflict prevention, peace-making and peace-building]" and "to make frank, specific and realistic recommendations for change," made no recommendations with respect to the protection, inclusion, or participation of women. Indeed, in assessing the difficulties in securing implementation of peace, Brahimi noted the level of wartime casualties, population displacement, and human rights violations as adding to the complexities of peacemaking, but without any consideration of the gender dimensions or of the importance of participation by women (UN General Assembly 2000b). Yet the 1999 Secretary-General's Report on *Protection of Civilians in Armed Conflict* had recommended that the Council ensure "that the special protection and assistance requirements of children and women are fully addressed in all peacekeeping and peace-building operations" (UN Security Council 1999b: Recommendation 20) and Resolution 1325, adopted just two months later, expressed a "willingness to incorporate a gender perspective into peacekeeping operations."

What is evident from this brief survey of reports and resolutions is that by the end of the 1990s, there was Security Council acknowledgment of the deliberate targeting of civilians in armed conflict and of the "vulnerability" of women and girls to rape and sexual violence. The Security Council was becoming receptive to the importance of adopting provisions for the protection of civilians and "vulnerable" groups in conflict and for addressing the "special needs" of women and girls and making "special arrangements" for them, yet it only occasionally made any reference to the experiences of women in armed conflict in its country-specific UN Charter Chapter VII resolutions. There was no sense of a holistic or routine recognition of the need to take account of the gendered violations of international humanitarian or human rights law, although there were sufficient indicators that such acceptance would not be impossible to secure. In this sense the adoption of Resolution 1325 is perhaps unsurprising, but the warning signs that it would be seen more as rhetoric than as a blueprint for action and implementation were already present.

As the Security Council grew more ready during the 1990s to accept that harms to individuals could constitute threats to international peace and security, a number of policy-oriented reports and other initiatives within the UN focused on the need to safeguard the security of individuals rather than just that of the territorial state. There was a recognized urgency "to redefine our concept of security, as security for people, not security for land" (United Nations Development Programme [UNDP] 1993: iii). One illustration of this was the prominence accorded to the concept of human security in the 1990s, although there was no agreement about either its scope or formulation. A broad form of human security, encompassing development and disarmament, was pioneered by UNDP, notably in its 1994 *Human Development Report* (UNDP 1994), which emphasized material security—freedom from want—although the link with freedom from fear was also acknowledged. The report lists seven types of security: economic, food, health, environmental, personal, community, and political, of which only "personal security," referred to physical safety from violence (UNDP 1994). Gender security was not identified as a distinct category necessitating targeted measures for its achievement. The narrow form of human security was more directly concerned with freedom from physical harm and drew on the growing influence in international affairs of the link between security and human rights. In the words of the then Minister for Foreign Affairs of Australia, Gareth Evans (1995),

> the first [approach] is to develop the notion that "security," as it appears in the Charter, is as much about the protection of individuals as it is about the defence of the territorial integrity of states. "Human security," thus understood, is at least as much prejudiced by major intra-state conflict as it is by inter-state conflict. The second approach, which could either stand alone or be seen as reinforcing the "human security" approach, would pursue to its logical limits the international community's basic human rights, bearing in mind that the most basic human right of all, that of life, is violated on a very large scale in intra-state conflicts.

The high point of the human rights strand of human security thinking as directing policy may be the work of the International Commission on Intervention and State Sovereignty (ICISS), established by the Canadian government just one month before the adoption of Resolution 1325 in September 2000. The Commission was established in reaction to the legal and moral debates around the unauthorized NATO military intervention in Kosovo in March 1999, which had been in response to the oppression and human rights violations committed by the Serbian authorities against the Albanian population in Kosovo. This use of force was considered by many commentators to be in violation of the UN Charter, article 2 (4), which prohibits the use of force in international relations. Others considered military intervention when carried out for humanitarian purposes to be legitimate, even if technically illegal. After wide consultation to gauge broad global opinion, the Commission argued for a "Responsibility to Protect" as a principled response to such violence: "that sovereign states have a responsibility to protect their own citizens from avoidable catastrophe—from mass murder and rape to starvation—but that when they are unwilling or unable to do so, that responsibility must be borne by the broader community of states" (ICISS 2001; see also chapter 45 in this volume). The debate around intervention in Kosovo, the formation of the Commission and its enunciation of the Responsibility to Protect were thus contemporaneous with the adoption of Resolution 1325 and the more general focus on protection of civilians expressed in the thematic resolutions of the Council. These parallel developments highlighted the distinction between the *jus ad bellum* (the legal use of force) and the *jus in bello* (protective constraints on behavior in conflict), the former remaining seemingly impervious to the latter.

The decade that followed the end of the Cold War was in some ways one of optimism, in which ideas relating *inter alia* to human security, civilian protection, legal accountability, and gender equality were all given voice within the mainstream international institutions. But it was also a decade of extreme violence, new wars, and growing awareness of the threats of terrorism. The global women's movement that had gained traction since the UN Decade for Women (1975–1985) was especially focused on combating violence against women both in "peacetime" and in armed conflict. Taken together these diverse strands to some extent shifted the understanding of the Security Council's role in the maintenance of international peace and security, away from a classic state-oriented approach to one that takes account of the violence directed at people and bringing human rights and international humanitarian law into its decision-making and operations. They created an environment that was conducive to the acceptance of a Security Council resolution addressing women's experiences in armed conflict. But what especially differentiates Resolution 1325 from these other initiatives such as human security, the Responsibility to Protect, or disarmament, is the inclusion of a requirement of gender balance and a gender perspective in all policy and decision-making relating to conflict prevention, management, and resolution, as well as post-conflict reconstruction. This entailed making the rule of law, human rights, and democracy, a mantra that characterized the decade, equally applicable to women, ensuring women's inclusion and agency and not merely grouping them with other "vulnerable" groups needing protection and with "special" needs. Security Council Resolution 1325 gave institutional legitimacy to the goals of the women's movement, set a new standard for the Security Council, UN member states, and the UN system as a whole. It launched detailed studies into the impact of armed conflict on women and girls, the role of women in peace-building and the gender dimensions of peace processes and conflict resolution (United Nations 2002; Rehn and Sirleaf 2002).While conceived of as a human rights agenda, there was also an unexplained instrumentalization in the preambular assertion of Resolution 1325 that women's "full participation in the peace process can significantly contribute to the maintenance and promotion of international peace and security."

The adoption of 1325 has implications for the making of international law (the role of civil society within the international legal and institutional framework), for rethinking participation and empowerment, and the meaning of security and protection. However, in retrospect, the year 2000 was a pivotal moment when a more human-oriented international law seemed a real possibility (Teitel 2011), and before the turn back towards militarism and national security in the wake of the terrorist attacks of September 11, 2001. The price of bringing the pillars of women, peace, and security into the security agenda of the UN Security Council may have been the high one of losing the transformative potential sought by civil society (Otto 2015).

NOTES

1. UN Security Council, Resolution 1325. S/RES/1325. October 31, 2000, https://undocs.org/S/RES/1325(2000).
2. For example. George Bush, Address before a Joint Session of the Congress on the State of the Union, *January 29, 1991*.
3. Rome Statute of the International Criminal Court, Articles 7 (1) (g); 8 (2) (b) (xxii). United Nations Human Rights, Office of the High Commissioner, 1998, http://www.ohchr.org/EN/ProfessionalInterest/Pages/InternationalCriminalCourt.aspx.
4. Rome Statute, Articles 8 (2) (b) (xxi) and (2) (c) (ii).
5. Rome Statute, Article 7 (1) (h).
6. Rome Statute, Article 36 (8) (a) (iii).
7. For examples, paras. 9–11 of UN Security Council Resolution 1325.

8. UN General Assembly (1998) and UN Security Council (1998a).
9. See Part I, para 18 of the Vienna Declaration and Programme of Action and paras. 221 –231(b). The definition of gender mainstreaming and the strategy to promote it are outlined under the "Agreed Conclusions" of the Economic and Social Council (ECOSOC) (UN General Assembly 1997b).
10. See Articles 7 and 8, for example, in UN General Assembly (1979).
11. Noted in UN Security Council (1999h, 2000c).

REFERENCES

Cameron, M., R. Lawson, and B. Tomlin. (eds). *To Walk Without Fear: The Global Movement to Ban Landmines*. Toronto: Oxford University Press, 1998.

Committee on Elimination of Discrimination against Women (CEDAW). *"CEDAW General Recommendation No. 19: Violence against Women,"* 11th Session. UN Women, 1992, http://www.un.org/womenwatch/daw/cedaw/recommendations/recomm.htm.

Dolgopol, U., and S. Paranjape. *Comfort Women: The Unfinished Ordeal*. Geneva: International Commission of Jurists, 1994.

Evans, G. *Cooperating for Peace*. Award Lecture. University of Louisville. October 24, 1995, http://foreignminister.gov.au/speeches/1995/gecopce.html.

Gallagher, A. "Ending the Marginalisation: Strategies for Incorporating Women into the United Nations Human Rights System." *Human Rights Quarterly* 19 (1997): 283–333.

International Commission on Intervention and State Sovereignty (ICISS). *The Responsibility to Protect*. Ottawa: International Development Research Centre, 2001.

Kaldor, M. *New and Old Wars: Organised Violence in a Global Era*, 3rd ed. Cambridge: Polity Press, 2012.

Otto, D. "Women, Peace and Security: A Critical Analysis of the Security Council's Vision." University of Melbourne, Legal Studies Research Paper No. 705, 2015.

Rehn, E., and E. Johnson Sirleaf. "Women, War, Peace: The Independent Experts' Assessment on the Impact of Armed Conflict on Women and Women's Role in Peace-Building." Report. New York: United Nations Development Fund for Women, 2002.

Teitel, R. *Humanity's Law*. Oxford: Oxford University Press, 2011.

UN Development Programme (UNDP). *Human Development Report 1993*. New York: UNDP, 1993.

UN Development Programme (UNDP). *Human Development Report 1994*. New York: UNDP, 1994.

UN General Assembly. "Comprehensive review of the whole question of peacekeeping operations in all their aspects." A/55/305–S/2000/809, 55th session, August 21, 2000b.

UN General Assembly. Convention on the Elimination of All Forms of Discrimination against Women. UN Women, 1979, http://www.un.org/womenwatch/daw/cedaw/text/econvention.htm.

UN General Assembly. *Declaration on the Elimination of Violence against Women (DEVAW)*. A/RES/48/104, 85th Plenary meeting, December 20, 1993b, http://www.un.org/documents/ga/res/48/a48r104.htm.

UN General Assembly. "Report of the Expert of the Secretary-General, Ms. Graça Machel, Submitted Pursuant to General Assembly Resolution 48/157." Impact of Armed Conflict on Children. A/51/306, 51st Session, August 26, 1996.

UN General Assembly. "Report of the Economic and Social Council for 1997." A/52/3, 52nd session, September 18, 1997b.

UN General Assembly. "Report of the Secretary-General. The Causes of Conflict and the Promotion of Durable Peace and Sustainable Development in Africa." A/52/871—S/1998/318, 52nd Session, April 13, 1998.

UN General Assembly. "Resolution 51/77." A/RES/51/77, 51st Session, February 20, 1997a.

UN General Assembly. "United Nations Millennium Declaration." Resolution adopted by the General Assembly 55/2. A/RES/55/2, 55th Session, September 18, 2000a.

UN General Assembly. *Vienna Declaration and Programme of Action.* July 12, 1993a. A/CONF.157/23.

United Nations. "Convention on the Prohibition of the Use, Stockpiling, Production and Transfer of Anti-Personnel Mines and on Their Destruction." Oslo, September 18, 1997, UNTS, vol 2056, p. 211.

United Nations. "Women, Peace, and Security: Study Submitted by the Secretary-General Pursuant to Security Council Resolution 1325 (2000)." New York: United Nations, 2002.

UN Security Council. "Report of the Secretary-General, Protection for Humanitarian Assistance to Refugees and Others in Conflict Situations." S/1998/883, September 22, 1998a.

UN Security Council. "Report of the Secretary-General to the Security Council on the Protection of Civilians in Armed Conflict." S/1999/957, September 7, 1999b.

UN Security Council. "Resolution 794 [Somalia]." S/RES/794, 3145th meeting, December 3, 1992.

UN Security Council. "Resolution 820." S/RES/820, 3200th meeting, April 17, 1993.

UN Security Council. "Resolution 1203 [Kosovo]." S/RES/1203, October 24, 1998c.

UN Security Council. "Resolution 1208 [on the maintenance of the security and civilian and humanitarian character of refugee camps and settlements in Africa]." S/RES/1208, November 19, 1998b.

UN Security Council. "Resolution 1244 [on the situation relating Kosovo]." S/RES/1244, 4011th meeting, June 10, 1999d.

UN Security Council. "Resolution 1261 [on children in armed conflicts]." S/RES/1261, 4037th meeting, August 25, 1999a.

UN Security Council. "Resolution 1264 [on the situation in East Timor]." S/RES/1264, 4045th meeting, September 15, 1999e.

UN Security Council. "Resolution 1265 [on protection of civilians in armed conflicts]." S/RES/1265, 4046th meeting, September 17, 1999c.

UN Security Council. "Resolution 1267 [on the situation in Afghanistan]." S/RES/126, 4051st meeting, October 15, 1999h.

UN Security Council. "Resolution 1270 [on the situation in Sierra Leone]." S/RES/1270, 4054th meeting, October 22, 1999g.

UN Security Council. "Resolution 1272 [on the situation in East Timor]." S/RES/1272, 4057th meeting, October 25, 1999f.

UN Security Council. "Resolution 1296 [on protection of civilians in armed conflicts]." S/RES/1296, 4130th meeting, April 19, 2000b.

UN Security Council. "Resolution 1314 [on the protection of children in situations of armed conflicts]." S/RES/1314, 4185th meeting, August 11, 2000a.

UN Security Council. "Resolution 1333 [on the situation in Afghanistan]." S/RES/1333, 4251st meeting, 19 December 19, 2000c.

UN Women. "Preventing Conflict, Transforming Justice, Securing the Peace. A Global Study on the Implementation of United Nations Security Council Resolution 1325." New York: United Nations, 2015.

Whelan, D. *Indivisible Human Rights: A History.* Philadelphia: University of Pennsylvania Press, 2010.

CHAPTER 4

....

CIVIL SOCIETY'S LEADERSHIP IN ADOPTING 1325 RESOLUTION

....

SANAM NARAGHI ANDERLINI

Prologue

....

LONDON: OCTOBER 31, 2000, I sat with my bellyful of babies (two of them) glued to my computer, awaiting news of the events in the UN Security Council. Without Twitter or Facebook or smartphone, I was relying on old fashioned phone calls and emails from my colleagues in New York, with whom we had formed the ad-hoc NGO working group on Women, Peace, and Security. I had pangs of regret for missing the events. The group had nominated me to deliver our collective statement at the first ever open debate on women, peace, and security in the Security Council on October 23rd, 2000, but I could not travel. My pregnancy had been through too many cliffhangers, and, at five months, I was already huge, so as much as I had wanted to travel and speak, the thought of prompting premature birth or harming my babies trumped my ego or professional excitement. So I held the fort in London and waited for the news.

It finally came in the afternoon London time. The UN Security Council had unanimously adopted resolution 1325 on "Women and Peace and Security." Through emails and phone calls, we whooped for joy, talked to the media, and thought we were on the cusp of changing the business of global war and peacemaking forever. Still, I did not quite believe that we—a group of women peace and rights activists—had done it, given how far-fetched the idea of a Security Council resolution had been when we first started out.

The Personal

....

In the seventeen years since UNSCR 1325 was adopted, the resolution has been both depersonalized by bureaucracies and academia, and claimed by countless people who take credit for its passage. Some are UN technocrats, others are erstwhile US presidential candidates. After all, as Noeleen Heyzer, the former head of the United Nations Development Fund for Women (UNIFEM) said, "There are many hands beating the drums of success."[1] Indeed there were. But it started as a personal, human, participatory, and radical (for its time) process, with just a handful of people imagining a change and deciding to act. I had the privilege of being among them. Each of us has her own memories of where it started and why.

My story starts in a walk-up office under the Vauxhall Bridge in London. I was 26 years old when I took my job as assistant speechwriter for the Secretary-General of International Alert (IA). I was drawn to the organization by the audacity of its mission—to prevent and transform violent conflicts and to end wars. I wanted to make a difference in the world and IA seemed to be the right place to start. On my first day I discovered my office-mate was a Hutu woman from Rwanda. She'd fled the 1994 genocide. I felt privileged and awed to be among a cohort of men and women as deeply committed to ending wars and horrific conflicts around the world as I was. Innovation and pushing new boundaries was the air we breathed because it was the 1990s, the Cold War had ended, and the world was changing.

Across the hall, the elegant Ndeye Sow was a key figure in IA's Burundi team, running conflict resolution programming as part of a global effort to mitigate a brewing genocide. Ndeye was pioneering work with Hutu and Tutsi women in Burundi. Her approach was to provide safe spaces for women from across the warring communities to meet and experience the conflict from each other's perspectives. By doing so, enable them to recognize that they had more in common based on their gender identity—i.e. as Burundian women—than they had differences based on their ethnicity. They fostered the first Burundian women's peace coalitions, which in later years informed and influenced many other women's peace coalitions. Ndeye's experience was one of the factors that inspired me to mobilize women for peacemaking in other countries and across contexts.

By 1997, Eugenia Piza Lopez had arrived in our midst to head up IA's advocacy program. She was a genius at strategic policy planning. Under her leadership, IA launched a thousand ships from the International Action Network on Small Arms (IANSA) to the Women Building Peace Campaign that culminated in the Security Council in October 2000. But I'm jumping ahead. The first stop is May 1998 and a packed steaming conference room in London. After years of mulling and months of planning at IA, we were co-hosting the first global conference on women's experiences of conflict and peacebuilding with some fifty women from conflict zones worldwide. The aim of the conference was to better understand the role women play in peacebuilding and reconstruction efforts. Presentations were organized under the themes of human rights and human security; the impact of armed conflict on women's lives; from armed conflict to peace: women's testimonies; collective strategies for peace and security; democracy and peacebuilding; and women, peacebuilding and foreign policy. It was the nascent start of what would become the "Women Building Peace from the Village Council to the Negotiating Table" campaign that we would later develop at IA and launch with a myriad partners globally.

On the first day, I sat mesmerized as courageous, audacious women from Guatemala, South Africa, Afghanistan, and Israel stepped up to the podium to tell their tale. They were superheroes in their own right, ending violence, military occupation, and fighting for equality and justice in their societies. But invisibility was their curse. Then on stage a Rwandese woman stood to speak. Her eyes were deep brown wells of sorrow but when she spoke, her voice was strong and the message rang clear. She spoke of the need for reconciliation and looking to the future for the children who had survived. Later I discovered she had lost countless relatives in the genocide. I don't know how she had the courage to wake up in the morning, let alone to look forward, to see the need to focus on those who survived, and to have a superhuman heart to still have compassion. I often think back to that day, recognizing that she changed the course of my own life and path. That was my moment of clarity. Concepts of conflict prevention and transformation, early warning indicators, which were powerful in theory but not tangible in practice, came together as it became clear that ultimately it is people who hold the power to make the decisions about wars, acts of violence, and acts of peace. Women in particular were leading much of this work but with no recognition. I wanted to shed the cloak of invisibility and silence and instead elevate and amplify the work and experiences of women as peace-builders globally.

In the subsequent days, it was extraordinary to hear how despite the unique country settings and cultures, there was a universality in the women's experiences—of trauma, of survival, of engagement, activism, and a passion for peace in their own communities and nations. We understood that these women did not represent all women. We knew then that women who dare to become peace-builders are the exception and the exceptional. But we also knew that they exist in every society, and they rise up in every conflict. Our collective discussions led us to a shared conclusion and the impetus to say: *We need to elevate women's experiences in the global policy arena. We need to create the language and the policy parameters to talk about these experiences within international peace and security policy institutions and frameworks.*

In the months that followed, we developed the concept of the campaign, the pillars of the work, and core partners. We launched the campaign at the May 1999 Hague Appeal for Peace (HAP) Conference, in partnership with UNIFEM (the United Nations Development Fund for Women, predecessor to UN Women) and welcomed others. The campaign comprised four "Ps," the pillars of our work:

- Partnerships and consultations with women's organizations and peace organizations around the world;
- Public outreach through a postcard campaign to send the message from women to Kofi Annan, UN Secretary-General;
- Peace prize for women annually; and
- Policy making and influence targeting the UN Security Council, the European Commission, and the Organization for Security and Cooperation in Europe (OSCE).

Years later, Betty Reardon, the doyenne of peace education and one of our key partners in New York, recalled how as we washed our hands together in the bathroom I had said "If Al Gore can go to the Security Council, why can't we?" I laughed the first time she retold this story. I had forgotten it, but it was a familiar sentiment. I've always been allergic to "no" and "you can't," and had a preference for "why not?" over "why?"

The Policy Framing: Empirical, Analytical, and Conceptual

Box 4.1. Message on a Postcard:

Dear Secretary-General Kofi Annan,

Women everywhere applaud the efforts made for peace by the United Nations. Women recognise the progress made in including women in peace making and peace building efforts within the UN itself and the pledges made to women during the UN Fourth World Conference on Women in 1995. However, we believe that five years later not enough has been done to make these pledges a reality. They must be implemented, as sustainable peace can only be achieved with the full participation of women from all levels of society. We ask the governments of the international community and the United Nations to stand by the commitments they have made to women. These are to:

1. Include women in peace negotiations as decision-makers
2. Put women at the heart of reconstruction and reconciliation
3. Strengthen the protection and representation of refugee and displaced women
4. End impunity for crimes committed against women and ensure redress
5. Give women and women's organisations the support and resources they need to build peace

---

At IA, Eugenia Piza Lopez led our team; Ancil Adrian Paul was program manager focused on the partnerships and, later, the OSCE and European Union work; and I as senior policy adviser was charged with analysis and conceptual framing to make the case for the agenda and partnerships to reach the UN Security Council. We were well aware of the need for a solid conceptual and empirical foundation for our advocacy work. So we set about developing the materials.

Our starting point was chapter E on Women and Armed Conflict of the 1995 Beijing Platform for Action (BPFA). We knew that during the Beijing conference women from Northern Ireland, Israel, Palestine, Guatemala, Rwanda, and Bosnia had lobbied for this new theme. The BPFA text addresses two key elements. First, because they were in the midst of their peace talks back home, which the Northern Irish, Israelis, and Palestinians and Guatemalans had fought for, women's participation in peace processes was included. Second, the Rwandese and the Bosnians, still fresh from the horrors of the genocide and the war, introduced the theme of protection, and with it, matters of sexual violence and women's experiences of displacement. The issue of women's rights was of course integral to the entire document.

For the empirical or "evidence" base, between the summer of 1998 and March 2000, in conjunction with partners around the world and UNIFEM, we did research, focus group interviews, and synthesized the findings into various documents. We aimed for March 2000 as it was in time for the Beijing +5 review that was scheduled to take place at the UN Commission on the Status of Women (CSW) in New York. The publications that became part of our "calling card" to the policymakers we met with included the following:

- The 1998 conference proceedings published as *Women, violent conflict, and peacebuilding: global perspectives* (International Alert 1999)

- The in-country consultations distilled into five key demands and put on the back of thousands of postcards addressed to then UN Secretary-General, Kofi Annan (see Box 4.1).
- A policy brief, *Mainstreaming Gender in Peacebuilding: A Framework for Action* first published in 1998, which provided short and clear explanations of the issues, the rationale for the relevance of gender to peace-building and practical recommendations for action (Women Action 2000).
- *Women at the Peace Table: Making a Difference*, which offered an analysis of in-depth interviews with some fifteen women who had been involved in key peace negotiations, which I wrote and UNIFEM published. It was released just prior to the first UN Security Council debate on women, peace, and security in March 2000 during the Commission on the Status of Women (CSW) meetings at the UN (UN Women, 2000).

We were conscious that our vision and the goal of the campaign was highly ambitious. We assumed and embraced the principles of equal rights as a baseline for our efforts, and we were taking a step further to assert our rights to have a voice and influence in the last bastion of male-dominated political and military spaces—where global matters of war, peace, and security were determined. In seeking to enter that space, our goal was not just to acquire equal access or a space at the table to maintain the status quo. Our agenda was to fight for women's equal rights and the opportunity to transform the terms of the discussions, to change business as usual, to shift the paradigm from war to peace. Put another way, our cause was not about ensuring that women, or our daughters have equal rights to join the military, to have equal rights to fight, die, kill, and maim; our cause was and continues to be to ensure that neither our daughters nor our sons have to be drafted into militaries or armed groups to bear witness or engage in the horrors of war.

We were also acutely aware of the need for empirical underpinnings and a strong conceptual framework to situate the agenda and our advocacy so that we could make a compelling case that was both practical and inspirational. The publications listed earlier provided both the evidence base that we could access at the time. With Professor Donna Pankhurst at Bradford University, I also co-authored *Mainstreaming Gender in Peacebuilding: A Framework for Action*, published in 1998 (Naraghi-Anderlini and Pankhurst 1999). It was a succinct piece that distilled some of the existing scholarly and academic work in gender studies as well as peace and conflict studies. In addition, it created a cohesive narrative for the policy community. Many of the issues we highlighted would later gain traction and continue to be explored today in the field of women, peace, and security. For example, we addressed the heterogeneity of women's experiences—as victims and survivors, as fighters and political actors, and as peace-builders. We pointed out the tensions that exist between individual women who are elevated to participate in peace processes (as political agents) compared to women's organizations and civil society presence. We touched on the importance of fostering political will and cultural change within existing institutions. Lastly, we also tackled the question of gender versus women, and we raised the need for more attention to men and masculinities in the context of peace and war. While many of these issues were being addressed by academics, they had not yet entered the world of policy and practice. As activist-advocates our goal was to not only shed light on this important area of study and work, but also to establish a new vocabulary and set of concepts in the policy realm to enable implementation of the ideas and expansion of existing practices globally. This was the rationale for aiming our advocacy at the UN Security Council, the EU and the OSCE.

The Partners, the Politics, and the Nitty Gritty

From the outset, forming partnerships had been a key pillar of the Women Building Peace campaign, and critical to the strategy. The partnerships forged at the Hague Appeal for Peace were expanded as the months went on. The Ford Foundation, with Mahnaz Isfahani as a key force, funded our advocacy work with a $180,000 grant. It enabled our team to participate in regional meetings globally, as women's organizations met with states to prepare for the review of the 1995 Beijing Platform for Action. Throughout the latter half of 1999 and early 2000, members of our team attended the regional meetings, reconnecting with local partners, and distributing the Women Building Peace campaign materials. We had determined that if our campaign priorities could be seeded into the outcomes' documents of the regional meetings, then our chances of ensuring strong member-state support for the agenda at the March 2000 CSW meetings would be greater. Moreover, given that the CSW in 2000 was focused on "Beijing+5," with a view to updating the core commitments in the original BPFA, we recognized the opportunity could not be missed to gain traction and support among more UN member states.

We were deliberate in our messaging. We understood that the multilateral system was struggling with the rise of internal conflicts. The principles of noninterference in domestic affairs and recognizing the sovereignty of states tied the hands of the UN. We were offering an alternative or a new opening as a pathway to adapt the institutions better to the changing nature of warfare: *Women in civil society build peace. They can make a difference. Work with them.* It was not just adding to the litany of problems or reinforcing stereotypes of women as victims. It was a positive message at a time of change and it inspired people to contemplate the possibility of new approaches.

In the European regional meeting where the United States and Canada also participated, our colleagues from Bosnia, Croatia, and Macedonia provided the ultimate boost. Their stories of war and resilience, and their demand for respectful treatment and equal say, were heard loud and clear in the Palais de Nations in Geneva. As usual, the absurdity of well-meaning but gender- blind international efforts in the midst of their tragedy came to light. I remember a Bosnian chemist turned peace-builder who told me adamantly that the internationals came and offered her a "cow." "Imagine that!" she exclaimed, "What was I meant to do with a cow?! I'm a Chemist."

As we mobilized more civil society support for the idea of a Security Council resolution, we also took every opportunity to advocate the message of "women build peace" to the governments that participated. The US team, led by Linda Tarr-Whelan and staffed with exquisite professionalism by Sharon Kottok and others, became good allies. They welcomed our input into their drafting of the regional government reports that would ultimately be negotiated with other countries at the March 2000 CSW meetings. We also broke new ground at the regional meetings, by advocating for greater civil society representation in the formal state gatherings. Our days and nights were dedicated to a mix of advocacy among our NGO cohorts, drafting texts and assisting those who would represent the NGO community in conveying the key messages.

For me personally, and coming from IA, it was imperative that every opportunity for formal representation was given to the women who were at the literal frontlines of the wars and peacemaking efforts. Authenticity mattered then as it does now, and the principle of "show not tell" was very apt. So on the topic of women as peace-builders, we all voted for our Macedonian colleague to represent us. We helped draft her two-minute speech together to capture the critical messages we hoped to convey. She practiced with us, and delivered it beautifully. Months later at the UN, she approached me with a giant hug saying, "I was the first ever Macedonian woman to represent my country at an international event." She continued to be a powerful voice at the UN.

As the regional meetings concluded, we focused our attention to the UN in New York, and specifically on members of the Security Council at the time. Our first port of call was Slovenia who had appointed Danilo Turk as their first ambassador to the UN. We approached the mission to determine whether they could lead on the issues during their presidency of the Council. While they expressed some interest, the timing was not right, so we had to scout out other missions in the run up to the March 2000 CSW. We reached out to the New York NGOs to build our coalition, and in the initial stages, we were met with much suspicion. For me, as a relative newcomer to the world of NGOs and the UN, the tensions and competition were at times confounding. I was focused on the higher goal and assumed that our collective efforts were for the greater good, so the pettiness of institutional turf warfare was at times difficult. The New York organizations were suspicious of IA and assumed we were a heavyweight organization—not a women's organization—that came to overshadow their work. It took some time to foster the personal and professional relationships to demonstrate that we were not in the business of takeovers, but rather that we needed the partnerships to achieve the goal we had in mind.

Ultimately we founded the ad hoc NGO working group on women, peace, and security (which is now an established coalition in the UN New York scene; see chapter 6 in this volume). The original members were the Women's International League for Peace and Freedom (WILPF) represented by Felicity Hill and Isha Dyfan, The Hague Appeal for Peace led by Cora Weiss, Amnesty International represented by Florence Martin (who also gave us access to the French mission), the Women's Commission for Refugee Women and Children represented by Maha Muna and Ramina Johal, and Betty Reardon who brought us the weight of Columbia University.

As March 2000 beckoned, thousands of women activists descended onto New York. In those days, the NGO community was more organized. For example, for each of the topics of the Beijing Platform for Action there were NGO caucuses, so that we could meet and strategize collectively. We also had passes that enabled us to enter the UN buildings, often sit in on the debates, and have better direct access to our government representatives in the cavernous UN conference rooms in which they were negotiating the Beijing +5 agreement.[2] So we could reach them and find out what issues were on the table, the sticking points and obstacles, and offer up fresh language on a daily basis. Our Women and Armed Conflict caucus, chaired by the formidable Felicity Hill of WILPF with me representing IA and the Women Building Peace campaign, became the hub of our advocacy activities. We met every day to track the progress in the negotiations and determine which of our priorities were included and which needed more work. We also consulted the caucus that numbered some sixty organizations from conflict-affected countries worldwide about the demand for a Security Council resolution. The support was resounding. In the meantime our collaboration with UNIFEM was ongoing. They had reached out to other Security Council members to gauge the level of interest in the agenda.

In the first week of March 2000, Noeleen Heyzer hosted a gathering to launch the *Women at the Peace Table: Making a Difference* publication, which I had researched and authored (UN Women 2000). Palestinian negotiator Hanan Ashrawi, and former governmental minister Mu Sochua of Cambodia, who had both been at the peace tables in their respective countries, gave compelling speeches about the necessity of women's presence in peace processes. On the eve of March 8, 2000, Heyzer hosted a cocktail reception as an informal launch of the publication, with Ambassador Anwarul Chowdhury of Bangladesh as the keynote speaker. Amidst the glad-handing and upbeat speeches, Heyzer publicly presented fifteen copies of *Women at the Peace Table* to Ambassador Chowdhury, "as gifts to him and his Security Council colleagues." Then she thanked him for championing the cause, and for working with us to attain a Security Council resolution on the topic of women, peace, and security. Ambassador Chowdhury, ever the seasoned diplomat with a big heart, accepted the challenge with grace and promised to keep us informed.

Of course these public acts and declarations were the result of much "behind the scenes" negotiations and advocacy. Ambassador Chowdhury was already at work with the Council members on the issues at hand with a draft statement in play. So by the afternoon of the same day, we heard the news. The Security Council under Bangladesh's presidency for that month was issuing a formal statement, for the first time in its history, recognizing that "peace is inextricably linked with equality between women and men" and highlighting women's experiences of conflict and their contributions to peacemaking and conflict resolution (United Nations Security Council 2000). The devil as usual was in the details. The statement could have been issued by the presidency of the Council alone. Instead it was a formal press statement with the words negotiated by all members and its unique reference number, SC/6816, indicated that the topic was now on the formal agenda of the Council.

We cheered Ambassador Chowdhury for cracking open the doors to the impenetrable Security Council and then went back to work. As the CSW negotiations lumbered on more slowly than anyone had anticipated, our campaign advocacy was gathering steam. At the caucus meeting, I proposed inviting government representatives to join us and hear directly from women from the war-affected countries about their needs and their request: a resolution from the Council. We fanned out across the UN to reach any of the missions we could access. Within a few days, we held our gathering in a packed room with government representatives mixed in with NGOs. It was an emotional and politically powerful event. Most of the state officials had never encountered women from the front lines of wars. Yet in that ninety-minute meeting, they heard powerful testimony from Jessica Nkuuhe talk about the rise of the Lord's Resistance Army (LRA) in Uganda, the devastating impact of sanctions from an Iraqi woman, the war widows' village in Colombia, and a representative from almost every other conflict ongoing at the time. As each speaker tackled different issues—from humanitarian aid to women at the peace table—they ended with a shared message: join us in calling for a Security Council resolution.

"In the six years I've come to the CSW, I'd never been invited to the NGO caucuses," Linda Tarr-Whelan told me later on. It was a generational shift, I believe. As a young activist, I could not understand why we would not engage and work with our states. Adversarial relationships had their limits. But we were also cautious. When I was asked to meet with the more senior US representatives, I demurred because they would not let my colleagues from the Ad Hoc NGO working group join in. We did not want to be co-opted by any state, particularly the powerful ones. As a follow-up to that gathering and with the Security Council presidential statement issued, it seemed obvious that we should invite the members of the Security Council to a similar meeting. We drafted the invitations and issued them through Ambassador Chowdhury. A few days later the Security Council delegation—fourteen men and one woman—led by Ambassador Chowdhury, sat shoulder to shoulder with us women in a cramped basement room. We presented our case, provided them with the background documentation, and made our demand. Consummate diplomats that they were, they gave no formal commitments, but the ground was being set and the momentum was positive.

While these larger group events were taking place, the working group members were plotting out likely allies in the Council that we could approach to pass the baton forward from the Bangladeshi presidency onwards. We also agreed to initiate our own draft of a Security Council resolution. Florence Martin of Amnesty International had some experience in legal drafting and had been actively seeking to secure a resolution to protect women's rights in times of conflict. She took the pen and provided us with the first skeleton draft. It made the task much easier for the rest of us, as we were able to focus on the substantive issues we each wanted to include.

As with all efforts to write by committee, the draft ballooned, and we had fraught negotiations among ourselves. It was tough because we were a diverse group consisting of human rights organizations, alongside one that was committed to nuclear disarmament and disarmament issues, and another focused on refugee issues, and one on conflict transformation, together with inputs from multiple countries. Everyone was lobbying for their own priorities. But we had to be savvy and realistic about how far we could aim for the ideal without risking losing the real. It was a life lesson. From the outside it is very easy to be critical of systems, but when you want to engage you have to be constructive, strategic, and practical as well. Less is often more.

With the new draft in hand, we consulted even more widely with our partners to ensure that it encapsulated the most critical issues. Then once again, we fanned out to talk to government upon government. Our pack of documents now included this draft resolution. Following consultations with Ambassador Chowdhury, we approached the Jamaican ambassador who was the only woman at the Council in 2000. She was enthusiastic about the agenda but had committed to the children and armed conflict (CAC) debate during her presidency in July. We all agreed that women's leadership should not be tied to a children's agenda as it would detract from the essence of our purpose to amplify women's agency rather than package them together as "womenandchildren", and relegate women to the status of passive victims or being infantilized, and thus in need of only men's protection. Canada was also a strong supporter, but they too had committed to CAC. Among the P5, the United Kingdom was equivocating. We did not know why, except to assume that they did not want to lead alone. The United States was suddenly silent and unresponsive. This was perhaps indicative of the extent of the gap between the Security Council work and the gender equality team that, although they had led their CSW delegation, had no permanent home either in the State department or the US mission at the UN.[3] The French who had been strong supporters were quiet again, as a new Ambassador was sworn in. Finally, Russia and China were reluctant at best, despite our efforts to invite them to lunch events and other meetings.

Meanwhile the Beijing+5 negotiations reached a deadlock because of the sudden influx of conservative and evangelical lobbyists. They arrived at the UN in the hundreds, young men in identical navy suits and ties, and young women who were pristine, poised, and aggressive. Their agenda was to dismantle many of the BPFA commitments, particularly in the realm of reproductive health and rights. They created a deadlock in the negotiations. The state representatives went home in late March, with a promise to return to New York in April to complete the process. During that time our working group kept on. We took the time to connect our advocacy with country missions in New York with their national ministries. So I found myself in Paris and London sharing our information and keeping the momentum alive. Back in New York, our colleagues kept abreast with the Security Council members. In May we reconvened in New York.

One morning an opportunity presented itself and I grabbed it. The Namibian Foreign Minister attended a vast NGO meeting in the UN building. He spoke movingly of his commitment to NGOs, because when he had been a liberation fighter and banned from the UN building, the NGOs had supported him. He ended his speech and with cheers from the crowd left the hall. I jumped out of my seat and ran after him. He had just settled into a cozy corner in the smoke-filled Vienna Café in the basement of the UN nursing an espresso. I approached him, introduced myself, made the case for inclusive peace processes, and women's peace-building, and pitched the "ask": would Namibia, which at the time held a nonpermanent seat at the Security Council, consider sponsoring the Security Council resolution on this topic. Whether I was convincing or he just wanted to have his coffee in peace, I'll never know. But his answer was not negative. He smiled and nodded, then suggested I contact his mission and his ambassador to follow up. A gentle passing of the buck but it was a mini-coup.

We wrote to the mission and a few days later our delegation met with the Namibian Ambassador in the UN Delegates' Lounge. The mission was already considering the topic of gender and peacekeepers and had held a summit in their capital, Windhoek. They were contemplating a resolution during their October presidency. We welcomed the idea, recognizing from our discussions with the P5, especially the Russians and the Chinese, that they were concerned about the expansion of the Security Council's agenda into the realm of human rights, refugee protection, and other sectors. In their view such matters were dealt with by other arms of the UN system, namely the United Nations Economic and Social Council (ECOSOC), the Human Rights Commission, and the United Nations High Commissioner for Refugees (UNHCR). Moreover, while the UN's charter mandated the organization to engage in peacemaking, there were still no systems in place. At best the UN Secretary-General could appoint an envoy and conduct quiet diplomacy. With our message of inclusive peace-making and civil society engagement, we were literally in uncharted territory.

Peacekeeping was one of the traditionally mandated areas of the Council and it was the perfect anchor or "foot in the door." With all the diplomatic skills we could muster, we suggested they consider a more comprehensive agenda; one that combined peacekeeping with conflict prevention, peacemaking, and post-conflict recovery—all with a focus on women of course. In the midst of the discussions, we shared our panoply of reports and background evidence. We then proffered the text of the resolution we had crafted. The proverbial "here is one we prepared earlier." The Ambassador agreed to consider our proposal and, introduced us to the "young lady," Aina Liyambo, in his team, who would be our point of contact. She was tall and elegant with a smile on her face but giving nothing away. Little did we know then that without Aina as an ally within, the impetus for carrying the agenda forward and ultimately getting Resolution 1325 passed would have been much less.

Then the waiting game began. Throughout the summer of 2000, we heard little from the Security Council or Namibia. No decisions were made. Despite our best efforts we were feeling rudderless. Then toward late August, the news came through, Namibia was taking up the theme for October. The pace of activity and the levels of formality changed immediately. Once Namibia agreed, UNIFEM stepped in and became the channel between civil society and the member states. Of course, the Security Council members negotiated the final version of the resolution. Throughout that process, Aina Liyambo kept a firm hand in ensuring the voice and spirit of civil society were alive. In reading Resolution 1325, many of the elements that came from our campaign and civil society community are evident, compared to subsequent resolutions that have been typically state led and drafted. For example, Resolution 1325 does not limit its applicability to countries that are on the Security Council's agenda. Any country—any women in any country that is affected by conflict or not— can say, "There's a Security Council resolution, we want to work on this." Whereas in Security Council resolution 1820, adopted in 2008, which was proposed and first drafted by the United States, it immediately limits the application of the resolution to countries that are on the Council's agenda. So if a country is not on their agenda, in principle, the government can say, "This isn't relevant to us."

In Resolution 1325 we reference the prevention of conflict. This is critical. We wanted an end to war-making. It is not about making war safer for women, as my friend, colleague, and president of The Hague Appeal for Peace, Cora Weiss, says (2011). There are also details about the gender aspects of disarmament, demobilization, reintegration, on refugee repatriation, elections and constitutional processes. All of these issues are relevant to current contexts including in relation to Daesh/Islamic state. There is reference to Article 41 of the UN Charter about sanctions. Iraqi women included this, saying that sanctions were devastating to them. These details came to us from women in war zones and stayed in. We also asked for benchmarks and timelines, to track implementation. The Security Council members, however, removed all the accountability measures. Some years later, I met a UN bureaucrat who very proudly said that the night before the debate he had edited the resolution down to 1.5 pages. No one knows what he deleted in his pursuit of a short document.

The Final Sprint

As the governments negotiated their text in private, we in civil society prepared for the Security Council's designated meeting on the resolution. The date was set: October 31, 2000. The Namibians were calling for an Aria Formula meeting on October 23, allowing non–Security Council members to be invited to speak on the topic at hand. I produced the first draft statement and like all our other materials, over countless email exchanges among the core group and the wider listserv of the Women and Armed Conflict Caucus, we reached consensus on the final speech that would be delivered on our behalf. The working group agreed that International Alert should represent the group at the Arria Formula, and that I would be the speaker. But as September rolled into October, my twin pregnancy, initially fraught with misdiagnosis, was growing rapidly. I had trouble navigating the passages in the London Underground, let alone airports and airplanes. So the day came, with Eugenia Piza Lopez representing us at the Security Council. One week later, my colleagues from the working group gathered in the public gallery while I was at my laptop in London, as we all waited to see if the resolution would be adopted.

Epilogue

A week after Resolution 1325 was adopted, our team was basking in its success at a meeting with IA's board of directors. We reported on the resolution and our work leading up to it, expecting congratulations. Instead one of the directors, a Baroness in the House of Lords, looked at us with disdain and said, "Fine, so now they've passed this resolution, what's next? What are you doing now?" I was taken aback by her cynicism. "They passed it last week," I replied, "Let's give it some time," naively assuming that once a body as prestigious as the Security Council adopted a resolution, it would take on the responsibility of bringing its provisions to life: a false assumption if ever there was one.

The question prompted us to ask "what next?" and we realized that we still had work to do: to transform the words on paper into reality in people's lives. Here too, women peacemakers around the world who are connected together through this nascent global women's peace movement would have to take the lead. In December 2000, I drafted and published a short brief called the *ABCs of 1325*. This brief explained the resolution in simple language and identified both its significance and shortcomings. It also outlined what we achieved and where we fell short, as well as offered recommendations for how to take it forward (Naraghi-Anderlini 2000).[4] In New York Felicity Hill produced a detailed annotated version of the resolution, and WILPF took on the task of translating Resolution 1325 into as many languages as possible with volunteers offering their services.

Retrospectively, it is clear that Resolution 1325 was a product of a particular moment in our recent history. It came in that brief window between the end of the Cold War that gave rise to civil wars, and 9/11, which set us on a path toward the interminable war on terror. Those few years between 1991 and 2000 revealed the constraints and limitations of the principles of sovereignty. However, they also gave space for an expanding discourse on nontraditional security issues—from HIV/AIDS to Child Solders, to the notion of "Responsibility to Protect," and, of course, the concept of "Human Security." The women, peace, and security agenda is firmly situated in that space. It was innovative for other reasons too.

First, Resolution 1325 was driven by civil society. We had the vision, the strategy, the tools, and tactics, not to mention the relentless hard work and singular pursuit that drove our efforts. It was and is an achievement in terms of advocacy because we succeeded in getting governments to embrace and own our vision and agenda. As civil society alone, we could not have secured a resolution in the Security Council. That remains an arena for state action, so we needed those states to join in. At the time, the protocol for formal interaction with the Council was through a UN entity, hence UNIFEM played a pivotal role in facilitating access and sharing documents and information. Each sector had its role and its comparative advantages. It was a collaborative process. I would like to see that collaboration develop, because as problems on the ground become increasingly complicated, each of us has a different strength to bring to the table. It is even more important to work together as equal partners.

Civil society organizations have a degree of independence to raise uncomfortable truths and to delve into issues that have yet to become a concern for states. They have a long-term commitment to advocacy issues, which enables the development of expertise and a willingness to innovate. But civil society alone cannot end wars or enable the reform of a nation's security sector. We can encourage, provide ideas and solutions, lead and support, but ultimately it is the job of governments to commit to long-term good governance. The UN system could play a critical role by upholding the highest standards of practice and ideals of the UN charter and other policies that have evolved over the decades. It can be a guide for member states and diplomats. Indeed, it should represent the "gold standard" in peacemaking efforts, adapting and applying policy tools, such as the women, peace, and security agenda, to improve its own practices. Where we have witnessed this form of teamwork between states, multilaterals, and civil society—even in limited ways as in Colombia where the peace process became more inclusive over time—the results are groundbreaking. The willingness to collaborate and respect must exist in the first place. It is akin to an orchestra: each instrument has its own unique sound and role. If played in harmony the effect is transformative, but if not coordinated, it is cacophonic, and, ultimately, detrimental to all.

The second impact of Resolution 1325 is that women brought the human face of war into the Security Council and other spaces where the fate of humanity was decided, but where human beings, most affected, rarely had any presence. This is a profound achievement. Until then, security was framed as a state issue with a focus on state and armed actors. This agenda is forcing us to say, "there are other people involved," and, particularly, they have a stake and a role in sustaining and promoting peace. We are transforming twenty-five hundred years of history. For twenty-five hundred years, military and apolitical elite have determined the course of the future in war and peace. In the last sixteen years, we have prompted a change globally. Peace is not the absence of war. Peace is not just power-sharing between predatory states and militias or groups that are willing to use violence. Peace is also the people who, in the midst of war, work for peace and maintain normalcy and provide education and health and so forth for their communities. The *positive side of peace is the transformative element.* Peace processes cannot be seen as just political or security blueprints. They are and must be societal processes. Resolution 1325 agenda helped set the course for us.

Finally, in New York and in other Western capitals, the agenda has become overbureaucratized, theorized, analyzed, and erased of its humanity. Yet, on the ground and in countries affected by war—past and present (and no doubt the future)—the word and spirit of the document resonates in ways that we could never have imagined. I was in Sri Lanka in 2015, fourteen years after 1325 was adopted, and a police officer from Jaffna said Resolution 1325 matters to the people there. It frames the issues they face. A female politician, though skeptical of the UN, said that when she found out about Resolution 1325 and the subsequent resolutions, particularly Security Council Resolution 1889, her views changed. She said "This is about and for us, as people, women." In Somalia in 2012, Resolution 1325 was the impetus for enabling me to work with women's organizations to ensure a quota for them in their transition process. In the Syrian and Yemeni talks now, it is hard to imagine how women would be recognized if Resolution 1325 had not been adopted so long ago.

CONCLUSION

We all agree implementation remains shaky and problematic in most instances. Governments and the UN, have failed in their responsibilities. While there are growing forces to push the ball forward, there are plenty still married to the status quo. Sexism, racism, cronyism, inertia, and apathy are all alive and well. Our agenda started with women in war zones demanding to be heard and have a seat at the table. Their call to action has already inspired youth to mobilize with similar demands. Despite all the difficulties, the idea of inclusivity in war and peace, of recognizing the differential needs and capacities of women and men, of valuing civil society, cannot be rescinded or erased. At its best, Resolution 1325 still has transformative capacities, but only if those who adopt and utilize it value that quality.

On a personal note, my contribution to furthering this implementation comes in the form of practice, policy advocacy, and ongoing analysis and documentation. In 2015 through the International Civil Society Action Network (ICAN), which I lead, we published the *Better Peace Tool* that provides practical guidance and a simple framework on "why women peacebuilders matter" and "how to include them in peace processes" (ICAN 2015).[5] A key goal now is to "deepen the bench" with regard to international and national level expertise among practitioners and the diplomatic corps so that they can be the implementers and innovators in each setting. As the first senior advisor on gender and inclusion in the UN Standby Team of Mediation Experts, I implemented much of what we have long advocated for and succeeded in enabling Somali women's participation in the Garowe 2 talks in 2012, as well as garnering commitments in the peace accords to their inclusion in the transitional governmental structures. However, I also saw firsthand how commitments on paper can be erased in practice, when the states or the UN, which are signatories and responsible for implementation, renege on their commitments. Thus it brings us full circle to the importance of enabling and sustaining strong independent civil society movements—women's movements—that understand the issues and have the resources and capacities to be active on the ground and, at the same time, are guaranteed seats at key decision-making tables, maintaining their independent voices so as to hold the powerful actors accountable. At ICAN we are committed to providing the resources, technical know-how, and access that such groups need.

Ultimately, the women, peace, and security agenda is one that was ahead of its time. As we look at the complexity of contemporary wars and rising extremism today, with gender being more relevant than ever as a frame of analysis, and women still present and active in all spheres, the agenda remains relevant. The creativity and commitment of the few who imagined it and mobilized the many who now support this agenda is itself a lesson. Each of us matters. In our communities, NGOs, government, or multilateral bureaucracies, media outlets, parliaments, or universities, each of us has agency, and when we link arms and unite, we represent the greater majority of people who strive for peace, rather than the minority who use arms and violence to further their goals. We, who are active in this agenda are the spirit of Resolution 1325. In turn, this resolution is about and for all of us, regardless of sex, gender, race, or religion—because it is about inclusivity and ending wars. It is about the achievability of peace, if we choose to participate and be counted. It is about recognizing and never again erasing any women's rights or their leadership to define and determine how peace and security are realized. It is an agenda that remains on the right side of the future.

NOTES

1. In conversation with author, October 2001, New York.
2. In subsequent years a number of factors contributed to the deterioration of the NGO caucuses and access to state representatives. For example, the sudden arrival and

aggressive lobbying by evangelical movements made governments more reticent to engage with NGOs. The renovation of the UN building for years and tightened security created a physical separation between the NGOs and the states. Some of the thematic caucuses remained strong (e.g., reproductive health) but others lacked the resources to sustain organized advocacy. For the women, peace, and security community with the adoption of Resolution 1325 by the UNSC, much of our attention and focus was turned to developments at Council and not at the CSW.

3. It took eight years before the Office for Global Women's Affairs was launched at the State Department providing a much-needed point of contact and connectivity within the system.

4. Naraghi-Anderlini, Sanam, "The A-B-C to UN Security Council Resolution 1325 on Women, Peace and Security," 2000, https://www.researchgate.net/publication/265451303_THE_A-B-C_TO_UN_SECURITY_COUNCIL_RESOLUTION_1325_ON_WOMEN_AND_PEACE_AND_SECURITY.

5. "The Better Peace Tool," ICAN, 2015, http://www.icanpeacework.org/wp-content/uploads/2017/03/Better-Peace-Tool-English.pdf.

REFERENCES

ICAN (International Civil Society Action Network). "Better Peace Initiative: The Better Peace Tool." ICAN 2015, http://www.icanpeacework.org/our-work/better-peace-initiative/.

International Alert. "Women, Violent Conflict, and Peacebuilding: Global Perspectives. International Conference, London, May 1999, http://repository.forcedmigration.org/show_metadata.jsp?pid=fmo:2676.

Naraghi-Anderlini, Sanam. "The A-B-C To UN Security Council Resolution 1325 on Women, Peace, and Security." 2000, https://www.researchgate.net/publication/265451303_THE_A-B-C_TO_UN_SECURITY_COUNCIL_RESOLUTION_1325_ON_WOMEN_AND_PEACE_AND_SECURITY.

Narghi-Anderlini, Sanam. *Women at the Peace Table: Making a Difference*. UN Women, 2000, http://www.unwomen.org/en/digital-library/publications/2000/1/women-at-the-peace-table-making-a-difference.

Naraghi-Anderlini, Sanam, and Donna Pankhurst. *Mainstreaming Gender in Peacebuilding: A Framework for Action; From the Village Council to the Negotiating Table; The International Campaign to Promote the Role of Women in Peacebuilding*. 1998: https://www.worldcat.org/title/mainstreaming-gender-in-peacebuilding-a-framework-for-action-from-the-village-council-to-the-negotiating-table-the-international-campaign-to-promote-the-role-of-women-in-peacebuilding/oclc/56009340.

United Nations Security Council. "Peace Inextricably Linked with Equality between Men and Women, Says Security Council." Press Release SC/6816, 2000, http://www.un.org/press/en/2000/20000308.sc6816.doc.html.

Weiss, Cora. "We Must Not Make War Safe for Women." Open Democracy, 2011, https://www.opendemocracy.net/5050/cora-weiss/we-must-not-make-war-safe-for-women.

Women Action. "Women Building Peace: From the Village Council to the Negotiating Table." Women Action 2000, http://www.womenaction.org/global/peacebuilding.html.

CHAPTER 5

....

SCHOLARLY DEBATES
AND CONTESTED
MEANINGS OF WPS

....

FIONNUALA D. NÍ AOLÁIN AND NAHLA VALJI

THE Women, Peace, and Security (WPS) agenda was launched in 2000 with the passage of
United Nations Security Council Resolution 1325 and had the laudable aim of mainstreaming
gender in all aspects of conflict prevention, management, and resolution. In particular, the
UN resolutions and their implementation, including the National Action Plans on WPS,
stress the value of women's contributions to conflict transformation and peacemaking.
Generally, gender mainstreaming has been understood as encouraging female representation in peace negotiations (ideally equal with male participation); gendering the terms of
political agreements by including references to specific issues deemed of concern to women
(e.g., quotas in political participation and non-discrimination); gendering peace-building
work, including peacekeeping; and preventing sexual violence in conflict through accountability and political condemnation (Cohn 2008: 185–206).

This chapter sets out some of the critiques in theory and practice that have emerged over
the past decade for the WPS agenda. First, we traverse theoretical critiques that focus on
the conceptual and institutional limitations of the agenda, its reliance on particular kinds
of political and gender tropes to enable its adoption, and the continuing kinds of political
support that the agenda attracts. Second, we then address the historically based critiques of
WPS to situate the agenda within a longitudinal assessment of women's activism in the politics of war and peace. Third, we explore the policy and practical engagements of this agenda
to hone in on what WPS has actually achieved in practice. Our analysis shows that the limits
of its practical success (or the complexity of the success that has been realized) underscore
some of the broader conceptual and historical analysis just outlined.

Critically analyzing the contested meanings of WPS demands attention to both macro
and micro practices. It requires paying attention to the text of the various Security Council
resolutions that have forged the identity and content of WPS,[1] as well as the pragmatic and
sometimes cynical adaption and application of those resolutions at United Nations, regional,
state, and local levels, as featured across the chapters in this handbook. It also demands recognition of a broader history of gendered exclusions in international law generally defined

(Charlesworth et al. 1991: 613), and the law and practice of war and peace in particular. Feminist interventions have been largely marginalized in international law scholarship, women's needs and rights therefore remain excluded from mainstream legal regulation regarding the use of force, development, and international financial regulation. The laws of war broadly ignore the specificity of women's contribution to combat. As civilians, their needs and rights are assumed identical to men (Gardam and Jarvis 2001). WPS is still a relatively young body of norms and practices as compared to such fixed rules as the law of armed conflict or human rights norms (Chinkin 2017). The institutions applying WPS have only done so for a very short period of time. In this sense, we acknowledge that a trenchant critique speaks to a "work-in-progress" and not to a completed project, so there is a danger in prematurely categorizing the strengths and weaknesses of WPS. Nonetheless, our critique offers an important way to identify the strengths and weaknesses of WPS, as well as alternative political and legal spaces to advance the interests of women in situations of conflict, insecurity, and emergency.

The chapter proceeds in two main sections. The first addresses a range of scholarly critiques that have coalesced around the WPS agenda. These include essentialism, specifically the centrality of victimhood and protection discourses to enhancing the power of WPS's normative content; the geographies where WPS has purchase and those wherein it does not; and the increased scholarly and community resistance to WPS inciting a search for other political and legal avenues to place women squarely into the fulcrum of peace and security regulation. The second section addresses the theory and practice of feminist institutionalism as a way to better understand the success and failure of WPS, and points to the importance of a layered understanding of how various institutional actors advance this agenda or pose sizeable barriers to its success.

SCHOLARLY CRITIQUES OF WOMEN, PEACE, AND SECURITY

Criticisms of the WPS agenda abound, including its selectivity (applying WPS to some conflicts and not others), its essentialism (treating women primarily as victims not as autonomous actors with the capacity to shape peace and security processes), and its failure to challenge the war system from a feminist perspective (accepting the bona fides of war in contrast to a long feminist tradition of peace activism internationally) (Otto 2010). In this section, we chart the contours of these debates.

Essentialism: Victimhood and Protection Discourses

Influential legal scholars have critiqued the creation process for the Security Council norm including the trade-offs and costs to women of being placed in the "war and peace" paradigm of legal regulation. Scholars have paid close attention to the compromises and inconsistencies that follow from endorsing the use of force under Chapter VII of the UN Charter, the inequality reflected in the composition of the UN Security Council, and the lack of enforcement capacity engaged by Resolution 1325 (Otto 2009). The story of women's entry into the state arena of war and peace, epitomized by the role and importance of the United Nations Security Council, is told elsewhere in this handbook.[2] That entry point, and in particular, the value placed by states on "protecting" women in situations of armed conflict, as well as the high-profile recognition given to sexual violence of women during armed conflict by combatants and armed actors, has given rise to one of the most sustained critiques of WPS. There is no question that the lack of attention paid by states to women's experiences of war, female vulnerability in armed conflict, and the use of sexual violence as a method and means of warfare constituted a lacuna in international law and security policy (Ní Aoláin 2000a: 46). However, four successive resolutions of the Security Council and a dedicated institutional architecture of the UN focused only on this issue has raised concerns, including by those advocates who were originally part of this effort (Engle 2017; Goetz and Jenkins 2017). Invoking sexual violence as the primary basis upon which women gain legitimacy, visibility, and standing in the war-and-peace arena has manifold implications. First, invoking women primarily as victims creates and reinforces sexist stereotypes about women's agency, thereby marginalizing the possibility of other roles. Painting this victimhood as tied mainly to sexual violence further denudes women's agency and presumes it characterizes their dominant experience of conflict. It also presumes that, in general, victimhood is coded female, excluding the experiences of men in general, and specifically with respect to sexual violence (Carpenter 2006). Second, victimhood implies that the primary role of the international community is to provide paternalistic protection for women. There is, as Sjoberg and Peet (2011: 163–164) have argued a "dark side of the protection racket," whereby protection is traded for silence and acquiescence in legal and political systems that produce and enable conflict in the first place. There is equally the risk that discourses of protectionism reflected in such doctrines as R2P and humanitarian intervention are used to justify military interventions (Heathcote 2012).

Continuums and Categories of Violence

There is a growing awareness on the limits of the violence that is seen and called into view by the WPS agenda. Substantial legal consideration has been given to sexual violence occurring during armed conflict through WPS, specifically to rape. This effort builds on the work done previously by ad hoc tribunals and was signaled by the war crimes provisions of the Statute of the International Criminal Court. However, a concentration on high-profile extraordinary violence has obscured attention from the regular violence that women routinely experience in conflict and post-conflict societies. It eclipses the links between daily experiences of intimate partner violence and larger scale issues of conflict and violence. For example, growing research is pointing to a link between laws which prevent violence against women and greater resilience to state-level conflict. Similarly, there is growing acknowledgment that one of the greatest commonalities held by extremists and terrorists is a past history of violent misogyny.

WPS has not sought to engage with this parallel and coexistent violence that shapes and frames the pre-, during, and post-conflict experiences of many women. Thus, there is an ongoing lack of engagement in addressing the consequences of distinguishing between "exceptional" and "ordinary" violence against women, and an institutional distancing from exploring relationships of the continuity between the two. To give just one example, in the field of transitional justice, early efforts to render mechanisms gender-sensitive focused largely on including sexual violence by political actors in mandates of justice mechanisms. Little was done to interrogate the time frames covered by these mechanisms. For women, conflict violence continues beyond the signing of a peace agreement. With direct roots in the conflict itself, the use of patriarchal definitions of "war" and "peace" render their experiences invisible and beyond redress.

The categorization of certain kinds of acts as "private" and not "public" is a fundamentally gendered process. It has been exposed by feminist scholars as illustrating the challenges to enabling female-centered harms to be legally "counted."[3] The arbitrary nature of such distinctions in conflict settings ignores the linkages between the violence generated by generally male combatants in the public sphere,[4] and the violence perpetrated by combatants and other men in the private sphere. Moreover, the distinction ignores the continuities of violence for women (Swaine 2012; Sigsworth and Valji 2012), and underappreciates the extent to which women are the ongoing targets of multiple forms of violence before, during, and after violent political conflicts.[5] In some sense, while the enormity of this task is not the sole domain of WPS, the dominance of a narrowed definition of violence has influenced the shape and understanding of women's experience of conflict in general and sexual violence in particular within WPS. Thus in practice, WPS has not addressed the relationship between private and public violence in conflict and post-conflict settings; the gendered nature of the conditions conducive to the production of violence that create specific vulnerabilities for women; and the relationship of structural violence including gendered poverty and socioeconomic exclusion that shape conflict-related harms for women.

The challenge for feminist scholars and advocates in the WPS arena is compounded by the fact that an uncritical and narrowly liberal conception of gender accountability and equality directs our gaze away from the cultural, material, and geopolitical sites in which war, peace, and transition practices have emerged. The export or expansion of highly constrained, masculine, international legal tools and rules can reflexively deploy an uncritical, liberal, feminist positioning with little capacity to recognize its own hegemony and privilege. In doing so, the entry of feminists into the war and peace arena, given a narrative dominated by sexual harms, may reframe the language of intervention, militarism, and transition to include certain kinds of harms to certain women. However, this does little transformative work to address the construction of the terrain itself, nor the manipulation of the female body within it. Specifically, the Security Council resolution may invoke the specter of harm to women as a rationale for intervention in places as disparate as Afghanistan and Libya, but women are never the real reason for military action. Moreover, the rhetoric of protection is understood as a chimera to protect the military, economic, and geopolitical interests that dominate the use of force in international law and state practice.

Feminist scholars critiquing the evolution of WPS are mindful that tackling a highly selected menu of "women's issues," such as a primary and excessive focus on sexual violence, allows states to maintain a comfortable and familiar role—as patriarchal protectors of women.[6] Bearing in mind the multiple dimensions of justice at play in such contexts, it remains striking that distributive justice remains well off the menu of issues and solutions to the causes that produce extreme violence against women in conflict situations, even as international institutions profess greater engagement with the harms experienced by women in war. We acknowledge the harm spectrum is not necessarily "set-up" in trade-off form.

However, the fixated concentration on cataloging sexual harms, particularly in political cultures that dismiss the legal status of economic and equality rights, result in de-facto hierarchies perpetuating and reinforcing the validation of certain harms and the omission of others.

The lack of attention to continuums of violence reinforces the very inequalities feminists seek to address. For example, in the context of violent extremism, some have engaged religious leaders recently to issue *fatwas* condemning the use of sexual violence by extremists. The fatwas do not, however, talk to the broader rights of women or equality, focusing on a particular at the expense of the general (Werft 2017). Paradoxically, the very process by which sexual harms are elevated in legal norms such as WPS reflects how popular narratives and cultural discourses can act as a means to further subjugate women. These narratives and discourses entrench rather than undo presumptions about honor (both individual and communal), the purity of the female body, and status loss when sexual harm is experienced. In the context of conflict-related sexual violence, the passive, dependent, innocent, shamed, and vulnerable woman trope is seen to be essential to mobilizing law and protection (read also *intervention*) for the geopolitical sites in which harms occur.

The Geographies of Gender and Conflict

Resolution 1325 made no distinction in the context to which the norms being produced would apply. Given the focus on prevention as one of the key pillars of the resolution, its application should in theory be open-ended to any country or region in the world. It may apply beyond the scope of armed conflict and countries specifically slated on the Security Council agenda. In practice, WPS has been applied highly selectively by the Security Council and by member states. Two distinct patterns arise. The first is state willingness to apply Resolution 1325 and the seven subsequent resolutions to conflicts "elsewhere" but not to conflicts at home. Perhaps the most striking example of this disjunction has been the trenchant unwillingness of the United Kingdom to recognize the application of Resolution 1325 and its progeny to the conflict in Northern Ireland (Ní Aoláin 2016). Thus, one of the most prominent conflicts that took place in a Western European democracy throughout the course of the late twentieth century has been omitted through definition by the state, notwithstanding consistent local feminist agitation to force recognition.[7] A similar example is seen in the case of India wherein, despite Kashmir and a history of tensions with Pakistan, it insists that the WPS agenda has no domestic relevance.

Another dimension to the externalized application of WPS has been the persistent practice of states in producing National Action Plans to implement the agenda but whose sole focus is externalized. More aptly described as "international" action plans, they are exclusively focused on the role of the state in conflicts in other states rather than recognizing internal conflict and/or the contribution of the producing states to conflict. Given the roots of WPS in a mobilization of a world free of conflict and military spending, states recognizing their own responsibilities for propagating conflict continues to represent the ideal. Sweden briefly came close to this ideal in questioning their own arms sales to Saudi Arabia under a feminist foreign policy. A good example of the external but narrow focus of national action plans is the US plan (United States National Action Plan on Women, Peace, and Security 2016). The plan makes little mention of US engagement in a series of conflicts, namely Iraq, Afghanistan, Yemen, and Syria, with direct consequences on women affected by and participating in US military action (including bombing, military administration, detention, and other practices). Rather, it has a focus on supporting WPS in a more generic globalized way.

The second dimension of critical perspectives on conflict geographies involved in WPS relates to the close inspection of certain conflicts at the expense of others. Despite its broad descriptive reach, in practice some conflicts and not others have had far more WPS exposure. Until relatively recently, the conflicts coming within the scope of the WPS agenda have been narrowly defined along conventional armed conflict classification. The narrow lens has left untouched a number of conflict afflicted geographies and contexts where women have been excluded from conflict resolution, and where the harms they experience are rendered almost entirely invisible to the WPS agenda (Ní Aoláin 2016). There is also a pattern of invocation whereby WPS will be engaged in some (though not all) classic inter-state conflicts when there is a clear and recognized application of the Geneva Conventions of 1949 and all their attendant obligations. Yet, the invocation is not consistently used for internal armed conflicts, which are regulated by Protocol II Additional to the Geneva Conventions of 1949; conflicts involving Common Article 3 of the Geneva Convention; conflicts involving occupation specifically those to which the 4th Geneva Convention applies;[8] and mixed-conflicts involving both elements of internal/international armed conflict and the regulation of terrorism or counter-extremism.

While there are some highly visible examples of inter-state conflict in the contemporary moment, in reality the vast majority of conflicts fall outside of that specific legal framework. Internal armed conflict such as civil war dominates as the war context of our times. Moreover, as UN Security Council Resolution 2243 partly recognizes, the terrain of war and peace that occupies states is far from orthodox. The terrain includes terrorism (Arimatsu and Choudhury 2014), "hot-spots" (Tams 2009), and designated sites of hostilities within a state that do not require the entire inter-state conflict apparatus being activated. The patchwork application of WPS in practice undermines its claims to universal and consistent application. It underscores how the political underpinnings of the WPS doctrine is vulnerable to the political winds of state interest. Lastly, it demonstrates the extent to which WPS is avoided as a vehicle that might directly or indirectly impinge on state latitude with respect to the legal obligations that apply in internal conflicts and situations of terrorism.

Resisting a Bad Deal

Another recent critique advanced by one of the authors of this chapter is the failure by states, advocates, and scholars to treat women's resistance to ill-conceived and inequitable conflict resolution as a valid exercise of political power (Ní Aoláin 2017). Without including a framework of resistance in its worldview, WPS may become increasingly irrelevant to women on the ground in conflict zones. For women in war zones, their homegrown understanding of local peace and security needs differs substantially from the internationally mediated peace processes driven by bilateral and regional interests. In some conflicts, it is apparent that local women perceive international interventions, including but not limited to Resolution 1325, as part of the problem and not the solution (Autesserre 2014). As the abject failures of many humanitarian and other interventions cogently illustrate, local sentiments are often right about what works—building and supporting women's organizing; local level conflict resolutions; platforms for dialogue; and more inclusive governance processes. They also know what does not work in conflict resolution in the long-term.

Articulating their viewpoint is not easy for women's organizations given that funds to support women's movements and political participation in conflict zones are frequently premised implicitly and explicitly on their willingness to be partners in implementing Resolution 1325.[9] Examples of resistance to an essentializing assumption of women in relation to peace and security abound. These include the participation of women in both state and non-state armed forces in conflicts around the globe (Allison 2009; MacKenzie 2012). Women's roles as combatants is gaining increased recognition, but still requires practical implementation on the ground in conflict sites. This is vital to ensure their ability to serve on equal terms as their male counterparts, for their ability to exercise command and control functions within militaries, and for their right to equal treatment in processes of disarmament, demobilization, and reintegration (DDR) (O'Rourke 2013; Berdak 2015).

Women's resistance to simplified conflict resolution, and activism for comprehensive peace-building are less visible in the spaces where international donors support. This is in part because women are quintessentially viewed as agents of peace-making such that it is generally assumed they will be on the side of reconciliation and conflict resolution no matter what the context or the "deal" on the table. Yet, women's civil society organizations are increasingly articulating their unhappiness with elitist and superficial conflict resolution that does not address the political root causes of conflict and people's everyday needs (Gibbings 2011; Political Settlements Research Program [PSRP] n.d.). For example, in Cyprus where the long-running peace negotiations have created a marginalized Women's Technical Committee and relegated all gender issues related to the conflict to this committee, women's civil society groups are debating the value of "staying in or coming out" of peace talks. For these women, being included within the framework of the formal talks provides a fig leaf of gender validation for the male political leaders negotiating the conflict's end. However, it offers no meaningful engagement with issues of peace and security from a gender perspective. Such an engagement would include women at the table to structure the form and timetable for DDR; broadening the scope and application of reconstruction; negotiating the content of political representation; and addressing the specific and gender aspects of individuals at the community and family level. The same might well be said of efforts to include Syrian women in the failed Geneva negotiation process (Enloe 2014). Here, and in other conflict zones, external resistance to the official peace agenda may be a more effective course of action for women's organizations. This resistance may deliver much needed dissent as well as occasional concrete gains as a result of putting external pressure on negotiations.

In the Israeli-Palestinian context, for instance, Palestinian women's organizations have stepped away from participating in joint "woman-to-woman" peace projects with Israeli groups. They argue that such engagement only creates cosmetic individual changes while leaving intact issues of structural discrimination and power inequality. These inequalities fundamentally affect Palestinian women's capacity to engage on an equal and fair basis in intra-communal dialogue. Yet, these dialogues provide cover for international organizations and interested third parties who can claim that positive women's work is being done in conflict. In reality, such work may politically disable women's organizations from confronting the Israeli occupation in tangible and direct ways. It leads to a feminization of relatively powerless peace-building that is entirely divorced from the political realpolitik (Sharoni 2012).

In conclusion, a highly salient question today is: To what extent is women's resistance, including nonviolent protest, considered a relevant part of the WPS agenda (see Chapter 12 in this volume)? This question seems all the more relevant as we have witnessed an upsurge in women's national protest activities such as in Poland, the United States, and Ireland. While these visible aspects of protest are not conflict-related, they underscore that protest and resistance are an integral part of the conflict resolution landscape. Moreover, to what extent does the WPS agenda affirm the right to actively work against any conflict resolution that is unrepresentative, insufficiently grounded in conflict transformation, and which fails to address the root causes of conflict? For many women in conflict sites, resistance activism reflects an emphasis on action and not words, on struggle rather than coexistence, and on the everyday as the place in which this work is done. Instead, as we witness the weakness of many post–Cold War peace deals to deliver anything beyond negative peace on the ground or to simply limit public violence between male combatants without corresponding political and economic capacity building (see, e.g., Northern Ireland and Bosnia), there is a growing need to reconsider the value of resistance within and beyond peace processes. This is perhaps an essential ingredient to reimagining inclusive and transformative peace premised on female political agency and empowerment and not merely about adding women, and stirring them into to an already well-cooked political compromise between male elites. Affirming resistance says that dissent is a vital part of securing peace, and that women have an equal entitlement to oppose any peace process.

The Gendered Histories of War and Peace

While WPS is the first formal engagement by the United Nations Security Council in the gendered terrain of war and peace, women are not new actors in this domain. As the meticulous work of Dianne Otto has revealed, as well as the work of Tickner and others in this volume, women have had a sustained historical engagement with the regulation of war and the challenges of peace (Otto 2016). The core point here, of course, is that the dominant preoccupation of women has been to advance peace by influencing foreign policy, regulating the arms trade and limiting the influence of its beneficiaries, educating for peace, and ensuring the processes that enable the peaceful resolution of disputes between states through economic and commercial incentives are supported. While paying some rhetorical homage to peace, WPS has not welded its ideological or rhetorical capacity to these long-standing values and aims. Hence, the deep critique by Otto (2016: 4–5) and others, that in fact WPS has a largely "ritualistic" modus operandi. This involves the acceptance of certain highly stratified gender norms which do little to undo the global security apparatus. Instead, such an approach enables and sustains war economics, supports the global arms trade, and necessarily weakens the kind of international institutional infrastructure that might meaningfully broker peace through economic, commercial, and ethical incentives.

INSTITUTIONALISM AND WPS

Where does WPS "fit" within the institutional architecture of the United Nations, and what organs of the United Nations have a formal or informal role in advancing the mandate contained within the United Nations Security Council Resolutions? Understanding the institutional positioning of WPS enables us to gauge the relative power or powerlessness of the WPS agenda, as well as the kinds of institutional pressures and funding capacities that support or disable it. It allows us to better understand how women fare in masculine institutional settings and how policies and practices specifically addressed toward women can be tamed or diverted from having meaningful institutional effects (Chappell 2014; Mackay et al. 2010; Chappell and Waylen 2013). There is a tendency in the study of international institutions, as Barnett and Finnemore (1999: 719) have pointed out, to foreground the "input" and "output" of these bodies, and to pay little attention to the institutional cultures that sustain and enable their particular modalities of operation. In paying close attention to the dynamics of political and legal institutions, we have a cogent means of determining what role gender plays in shaping institutional dynamics and how gender "influences institutional outcomes and opportunities" (Chappell 2010: 183).

Attention to gender also reveals what Goetz terms as "gender capture," which follows from men's historical and modern dominance of power positions within organizational structures including the United Nations (Goetz 2007). Here, we take seriously the insights from Chappell and Waylen's feminist analysis of political institutions which engages the very challenging task of looking *within* institutions for "formal and informal practices." Codified rules and unwritten expectations are an important aspect of thinking about when, how, why, and with what outcomes women engage in institutional processes.

WPS sits with in overlapping architectures within the UN system. Normatively, it belongs to the United Nations Security Council, the apex of deliberations and power within the UN system. Its operationalization, however, falls to highly specific agencies and departments within the UN system. States have also independently adopted WPS into their foreign policy structures. There is thus a "push-pull" dimension to policymaking and enforcement for WPS. To a large extent these institutional dynamics, both within and between states, and within and between UN entities, have shaped the evolution of the agenda to date. For example, the push for a dedicated resolution on sexual violence in conflict emanated from within the feminist and international gender justice community as an effort to right a centuries-long injustice in the application of international law. Consequently, the protection stream established an institutional architecture at the United Nations including a Special Representative of the Secretary-General on Sexual Violence who is appointed to serve as the UN spokesperson and political advocate on conflict related sexual violence; an inter-agency committee and network called UN Action Against Sexual Violence in Conflict; and a dedicated team of experts on rule of law and sexual violence. This institutional architecture together with the strength of two permanent members of the Security Council in championing this issue led to a situation where for some years, protection considerations were far more visible.

Beyond the institutional bifurcation of the WPS agenda, there is also the consideration that WPS elements are far-reaching. They include aspects that span the mandates of different lead entities: the Department of Political Affairs (DPA) on elections, prevention, and mediation; Department for Peacekeeping Operations (DPKO) on protection and peacekeeping, DDR, security sector reform, and more; Department of Field Support (DFS) on issues of sexual exploitation and abuse; Peacebuilding Support Office (PBSO) on gender in post-conflict recovery and peace-building; and the Office of the United Nations High Commissioner for Human Rights (OHCHR) on transitional justice in addition to other agencies. As well as their own policy and programming work, UN Women is tasked with coordinating and leading the UN system vis-à-vis WPS. It is also responsible for holding all actors to account through reporting to the Security Council.

In actual fact, however, UN Women has never been provided the concrete tools for effective accountability in the system, or the formal clarification of its "lead" role. With respect to the contestations of WPS that this chapter has discussed, this lends itself to wide-ranging interpretations of WPS within the UN itself: from a view that it is sufficient to add a few women to mediation processes and in senior positions to achieve the goals of the agenda, to more transformative interpretations. One does not need to look further than the annual Secretary-General's report to the Security Council on WPS to realize the negotiated space that the WPS agenda occupies. The annual report is written largely by committee and negotiated line by line. The report constitutes technical reporting on the number of gender advisers deployed to peace talks and the percentage of consultations by mediators with civil society, but no analysis of the quality of consultations, the advice of advisers, or the overarching goals and impact. To effect greater change will require a shift not just within the UN, but also within the countries that support the WPS agenda. There must be a move from the narrow technical exercise of checking boxes on the number of women in peace processes and truth commissions, to a wholesale rethinking of what the WPS agenda is intended to achieve, taking into account the rich, scholarly debates, as well as in supporting multiple pathways to real transformation.

NOTES

1. *See generally* United Nations Security Council (UNSC), 2000; 2008; 2009; 2010; 2013; 2015.
2. See chapter 3 in this volume; and chapter 4 in this volume.
3. Notably, some standard scholarly work simply ignores the gendered complexity of civilian casualties (Seybolt et al. 2013).
4. Sjoberg and Peet (2011: 175) in discussing civilian targeting argue that the civilian/combatant distinction, fundamental to the operational premise of the law of armed conflict, contains a fundamental skew that exposes civilians (who are de facto primarily women and children in most conflicted societies) to greater harm.
5. O'Rourke (2013: 95 cited Corporación Humanas and UNIFEM 2005: 73), in a close analysis of the disarmament, demobilization, and reintegration (DDR) in Colombia, references local organizations identifying an alarming increase in levels of domestic violence as relationships were "forged or reignited between former combatants and members of the civilian population."

6. Otto (2009: 15–16) discussed additional factors for the adoption of UN Security Council Resolution 1325 at that particular time. Sjoberg and Peet (2011: 176) discussed how "belligerents justify wars as necessary to protect 'their women and children' both as innocent people themselves and as a symbol of the purity of the nation and the state."

7. The state position has maintained that the formal requirements of the Geneva Conventions and Additional Protocols were not met by the threshold of conflict in Northern Ireland and on that basis it is excluded. Notably the application of the Geneva Convention was and remains controversial for the United Kingdom in Northern Ireland (Ní Aoláin 2000b).

8. The most notable example in this context is the failure to consistently invoke the WPS Agenda in the context of the Israeli Occupation of the Occupied Palestinian Territories, and specifically to the military campaign conducted on Gaza—Operation Cast Lead (PCHR 2009).

9. Little funds do exist for women's organizations in fragile contexts. As the Global Study on Resolution 1325 (UN Women 2015: 380) found, less than 2 percent of peace and security funds to fragile contexts go to supporting gender equality. A fraction of this goes to women's organizations.

REFERENCES

Allison, M. *Women and Political Violence: Female Combatants in Ethno-National Conflicts.* Oxford: Routledge, 2009.

Arimatsu, L., and M. Choudhury. The Legal Classification of the Armed Conflicts in Syria, Yemen, and Libya. Chatham House, 2014, https://www.chathamhouse.org/sites/files/chathamhouse/home/chatham/public_html/sites/default/files/20140300ClassificationConflictsArimatsuChoudhury1.pdf.

Autesserre, S. *Peaceland: Conflict Resolution and Everyday Politics of International Intervention.* New York: Cambridge University Press, 2014.

Barnett, M., and M. Finnemore. "The Politics, Power, and Pathologies of International Organizations." *International Organization* 53, no. 4(1999): 699–732.

Berdak, O. "Reintegrating Veterans in Bosnia and Herzegovina and Croatia: Citizenship and Integration Effects." *Women's Studies International Forum* 49 (2015): 48–56.

Carpenter, R. C. *Innocent Women and Children: Gender Norms and the Protection of Civilians.* London: Ashgate, 2006.

Chappell, L. "Comparative Genders and Institutions: Directions for Research." *Perspectives on Politics* 8, no. 1 (2010): 183–189.

Chappell, L. "New, Old, and Nested Institutions and Gender Justice Outcomes: A View from the International Criminal Court." *Politics & Gender* 10, no. 4 (2014): 572–594.

Chappell, L., and G. Waylen. "Gender and the Hidden Life of Institutions." *Public Administration* 91, no. 3 (2013): 599–615.

Charlesworth, C., C. Chinkin, and S. Wright. "Feminist Approaches to International Law." *American Journal of International Law* 85, no. 4 (1991): 613–645.

Chinkin, C. "Adoption of 1325 Resolution." In *Oxford University Press Handbook on Women, Peace, and Security*, edited by Sara E. Davies and Jacqui True. Oxford: Oxford University Press, 2017.

Cohn, C. "Mainstreaming Gender in UN Security Policy: A Path to Political Transformation." In *Global Governance: Feminist Perspectives*, edited by S. M. Rai and G. Waylen, 185–206. New York: Palgrave MacMillan, 2008.

Coomaraswamy, R. "Preventing Conflict, Transforming Justice, Securing the Peace: A Global Study on the Implementation of United Nations Security Council Resolution 1325." UN Women, 2015, http://wps.unwomen.org/index.html.

Corporación Humanas and UNIFEM. "Riesgos para la seguridad de las mujeres en procesos de reinserción de excombatientes." Corporación Humanas, 2005, http://www.humanas.org.co/archivos/riesgosparalaseguridaddelasmujeres.pdf.

Engle, K. "A Critical Genealogy of the Centrality of Sexual Violence to Gender and Conflict." In *The Oxford Handbook on Gender and Conflict*, edited by F. Ní Aoláin, N. Cahn, D. Hayes, and N. Valji, 132–144. Oxford: Oxford University Press, 2017.

Enloe, C. "Cynthia Enloe's Report from the Syrian Peace Talks." Women's International League for Peace & Freedom [blog], January 30, 2014, http://wilpf.org/cynthia-enloes-report-from-the-syrian-peace-talks/.

Gardam, J. and M. Jarvis. *Women, Armed Conflict, and International Law*. The Hague: Kluwer Law International, 2001.

Gibbings, S. L. "No Angry Women at The United Nations: Political Dreams and the Cultural Politics of the United Nations Security Council Resolution 1325." *International Feminist Journal of Politics* 13, no. 4 (2011): 522–538.

Goetz, A. M. "Gender Justice, Citizenship, and Entitlements: Core Concepts, Central Debates, and New Directions for Research." In *Gender Justice, Citizenship and Development*, edited by M. Mukhopadhyay and N. Singh, 15–57 . Ottawa: International Development Research Centre, 2007.

Goetz, A. M., and R. Jenkins. "Participation and Protection: Security Council Dynamics, Bureaucratic Politics, and the Evolution of the Women, Peace, and Security Agenda." In *The Oxford Handbook on Gender and Conflict*, edited by F. Ní Aoláin, N. Cahn, D. Hayes, and N. Valji, 119–132 . Oxford: Oxford University Press, 2017.

Heathcote, G. *The Law on the Use of Force: A Feminist Analysis*. Oxford: Routledge, 2012.

Mackay, F., M. Kenny, and L. Chappell. "New Institutionalism through a Gender Lens: towards a Feminist Institutionalism?" *International Political Science Review* 31, no. 5 (2010): 573–588.

MacKenzie, M. *Female Soldiers in Sierra Leone; Sex, Security and Post-Conflict Development*. New York: NYU Press, 2012.

Ní Aoláin, F. *The Politics of Force: Conflict Management and State Violence in Northern Ireland*. Belfast: Blackstaff Press, 2000b.

Ní Aoláin, F. "Rethinking the WPS Agenda through the Lens of Resistance." Just Security [blog], April 17, 2017, https://www.justsecurity.org/39982/rethinking-women-peace-security-agenda-lens-resistance/.

Ní Aoláin, F. "Sex-Based Violence and the Holocaust—A Re-Evaluation of Harms and Rights in International Law. *Yale Journal of Law and Feminism* 12, no. 1 (2000a): 43–84.

Ní Aoláin, F. "The 'War on Terror' and extremism: Assessing the Relevance of the WPS Agenda. *International Affairs* 92, no. 2 (2016): 275–291.

O'Rourke, C. *Gender Politics and Transitional Justice*. Oxford: Routledge, 2013.

Otto, D. "The Exile of Inclusion: Reflecting on Gender Issues in International Law over the Last Decade." *Melbourne Journal of International Law* 10 (2009): 11–26.

Otto, D. "The Security Council's Alliance of 'Gender Legitimacy': The Symbolic Capital of Resolution 1325." In *Fault Lines of International Legitimacy*, edited by H. Charlesworth and J. M. Coicaud, 239–276. New York: Cambridge University Press, 2010.

Otto, D. "WPS: A Critical Analysis of the Security Council's Vision." London School for Economics and Political Science: Centre for Women, Peace, & Security, November 5, 2016, http://www.lse.ac.uk/women-peace-security/assets/documents/2016/wps1Otto.pdf.

Palestinian Center for Human Rights (PCHR). "Through Women's Eyes: A PCHR Report on the Gender-Specific Impact and Consequences of Operation Cast Lead." September 28, 2009, http://pchrgaza.org/en/?p=6500.

Political Settlements Research Program (PSRP). "Gender: Women's Inclusion Studies." n.d., http://www.politicalsettlements.org/about/how/themes/gender/.

Seybolt, T. B., J. D. Aronson, and B. Fischoff, B., eds. *Counting Civilian Casualties: An Introduction to Recording and Estimating Nonmilitary Deaths in Conflict*. Oxford: Oxford University Press, 2013.

Sharoni, S. "Gender and Conflict Transformation in Israel/Palestine." *Journal of International Women's Studies* 13, no. 4 (2012): 113–128.

Sigsworth, R., and N. Valji. "Continuities of Violence against Women and the Limitations of Transitional Justice: The Case of South Africa." In *Gender in Transitional Justice*, edited by S. Buckley-Zistel and R. Standley, 115–135. London: Palgrave Macmillan, 2012.

Sjoberg, L. and J. Peet. "A(nother) Dark Side of the Protection Racket: Targeting Women in Wars." *International Feminist Journal of Politics* 13, no. 2 (2011): 163–182.

Swaine, A. "Transition or Transformation: An Analysis of Before, During, and Post-Conflict Violence against Women in Northern Ireland, Liberia, and Timor-Leste." Unpublished PhD thesis, University of Ulster, 2012 (on file with authors).

Tams, C. J. "The Use of Force against Terrorists." *European Journal of International Law* 20, no. 2 (2009): 359–397.

United Nations Security Council (UNSC). "Resolution 1325 (2000) [Women and Peace and Security]." October 31, 2000, S/RES/1325 (2000), http://www.un.org/en/ga/search/view_doc.asp?symbol=S/RES/1325(2000).

United Nations Security Council (UNSC). "Resolution 1820 (2008) [Women and Peace and Security]." S/RES/1820 (2008), June 19, 2008, http://www.un.org/en/ga/search/view_doc.asp?symbol=S/RES/1820(2008).

United Nations Security Council (UNSC). "Resolution 1888 (2009) [Women and Peace and Security]." S/RES/1888 (2009), September 30, 2009, http://www.un.org/en/ga/search/view_doc.asp?symbol=S/RES/1888(2009).

United Nations Security Council (UNSC). "Resolution 1889 (2009) [Women and Peace and Security]." S/RES/1889 (2009), October 5, 2009, http://www.un.org/en/ga/search/view_doc.asp?symbol=S/RES/1889(2009).

United Nations Security Council (UNSC). "Resolution 1960 (2010) [Women and Peace and Security]." S/RES/1960 (2010), December 16, 2010, http://www.un.org/en/ga/search/view_doc.asp?symbol=S/RES/1960(2010).

United Nations Security Council (UNSC). "Resolution 2106 (2013) [Women and Peace and Security]." S/RES/2106 (2013), June 24, 2013, http://www.un.org/en/ga/search/view_doc.asp?symbol=S/RES/2106(2013).

United Nations Security Council (UNSC). "Resolution 2122 (2013) [Women and Peace and Security]." S/RES/2122 (2013), October 18, 2013, http://www.un.org/en/ga/search/view_doc.asp?symbol=S/RES/2122(2013).

United Nations Security Council (UNSC). "Resolution 2242 (2015) [Women and Peace and Security]." S/RES/2242 (2015), October 13, 2015, http://www.un.org/en/ga/search/view_doc.asp?symbol=S/RES/2242(2015).

"United States National Action Plan on Women, Peace, and Security." The White House, June 2016, https://www.usaid.gov/sites/default/files/documents/1868/National%20Action%20Plan%20on%20Women%2C%20Peace%2C%20and%20Security.pdf.

Werft, M. "Female Muslim Clerics Issue Fatwa on Child Marriage & Marital Rape." Global Citizen, April 28, 2017, https://www.globalcitizen.org/en/content/female-muslim-clerics-issue-fatwa-on-child-marriag/.

CHAPTER 6

....

ADVOCACY AND THE WOMEN, PEACE AND SECURITY AGENDA

....

SARAH TAYLOR

"WOMEN and peace and security" (WPS), resolution 1325, became an official item on the UN Security Council's (UNSC) agenda in 2000. The resolution brought to the fore a number of concerns for women and girls in armed conflict as was increasingly recognized at the international level, including in the Beijing Platform for Action (section E), and the Windhoek Declaration. Encompassing the rights of women and girls in all stages of conflict, the breadth of the WPS agenda allows for tremendous scope in its inflection points. The agenda covers human rights violations, gender-specific humanitarian concerns, prevention of conflict, protection and assistance during conflict, accountability for crimes committed during war, conflict prevention, conflict resolution, and post-conflict reconstruction. Indeed, the argument is often made that full implementation of the WPS has the potential to address the roots of substantive matters of international peace and security. Particularly spurred by the adoption of UN Security Council Resolution 1325, normative policy frameworks have been developed globally. Women's rights advocates have had some success at leveraging these resolutions. However, implementation in specific conflicts remains uneven at best, "[i]ncluding the continued exclusion of women from peace negotiations and the persistence of sexual violence with little access to assistance"(Human Rights Watch [HRW] 2015).

This chapter first outlines different approaches to women, peace, and security advocacy, specifically tensions between incrementalist approaches and those that demand structural change at the outset. Here the chapter addresses some of the political calculations that are made to achieve broad, if contested, goals. The second section examines implementation of the WPS agenda in the UNSC as a case study, arguing that there has been slow, though sporadic, implementation and expansion of the agenda in the work of the Council. In conclusion, the chapter then suggests a number of ways to assess advocacy on women, peace, and security.

What are some of the achievements in the WPS agenda from an advocacy perspective? The adoption of the first resolution, Resolution 1325, is often pointed to as a success, so much so that it is difficult to find text that does not refer to the "landmark resolution 1325."

To be sure, this resolution was the result of hard and strategic work by international and NGO representatives in New York. (Cohn 2004) These activists leveraged the work that had been done for many years by grassroots civil society, United Nations champions, and member states in the years just prior to the adoption of the resolution. It built on work that had been done at the Fourth UN World Conference on Women in Beijing and 1995 (see also chapter 4 in this volume).

Subsequent years have seen a rapidly intensifying set of policies and institutions in international organizations. After a relatively quiet period between 2000 and 2008, since 2008 there has been a proliferation of UNSC resolutions, senior appointments, and commitments regarding this agenda. WPS national action plans from governments have been increasingly adopted, there are now eight WPS resolutions, and special representatives on various aspects of the agenda have been appointed in the United Nations, the African Union, NATO, and other multilateral institutions (see part III).[1]

However, even an assessment of founding Resolution 1325 should be tempered by recognition of what the resolution does and does not include. The embedding of the WPS agenda in the UNSC is not without its problems. Indeed, just as the argument can be made that the WPS agenda will influence the Security Council, the case can be made that the Council will weaken core components of the agenda in return. The assertion is that inculcation of WPS in the Council conscribes the issue, weakening if not removing the transformational elements like prevention of conflict, and the anti-militarism of many WPS advocates. Some have argued that the cooption of the WPS agenda by the UNSC has effectively gutted attempts to implement WPS obligations globally (Otto 2010). And a huge gap remains in the exclusion of populations that are traditionally ignored and simultaneously targeted in conflict, including indigenous populations and LGBTI (see chapter 51 in this volume).

As advocates who worked on its adoption relate, Resolution 1325 is absent substantive points on the prevention of conflict itself and on reference to small arms and light weapons. The resolution is primarily about the management of conflict, rather than the creation of peace (Cohn 2008). For example, Resolution 1325 does not actually include mention of the impact of small arms and light weapons on women and girls in conflict. This reference did not occur until resolution 2117 (2013), which referenced women, peace, and security concerns, and resolution 2122 (2013), which referenced small arms and light weapons. I would argue here that this is where we see the glimmer of possibility for WPS to bring about change in the Council: that in fact there has not been a regression of the WPS agenda in the Council, but that there has been incremental, though sporadic, implementation and expansion of it in the work of the Council. Some of this is a fundamental challenge for the UNSC itself, in its inability to move past genuine political disagreements, and some of it is a lack of willingness to expend political capital within the UNSC on WPS matters, which is still seen as secondary to the immediate work of peace and security.

Whose goals count in advocacy on women, peace, and security? What counts as success when these goals are deeply contested? To a certain degree, context counts regarding whose goals and advocacy objectives are recognized in policy and programming. National and regional organizations will have different goals than international organizations who are pushing for multilateral policies. That being said, the targets of this advocacy—including member states and multilateral institutions such as the United Nations—are more amenable to advocacy that speaks to their own institutional priorities. This is where discourse and framing matters. This is not, obviously, something that is unique to the WPS field.

The question then becomes whether there is utility in seeing a historically unified vision for women, peace, and security, or if that would impose a false unity on the positions of previous advocates. Sometimes these arenas are inherently difficult to quantitatively or qualitatively assess. Do new UN Security Council resolutions count as success in multilateral policy advocacy? This would be a simplistic and reductionist means of measuring success, failing to take into account the most basic assessments of content. But who then assesses the worth and utility of these resolutions? Continuing with the example of the UN Security Council, where negotiations are notoriously held in secret and NGOs carefully guard their access to private information regarding their knowledge of these negotiations, it is unusual to see public discourse on the value of WPS resolutions. And yet in 2008, there was a public split in the NGOs who have traditionally worked on the WPS agenda at UN headquarters in New York. The subject—sexual violence in conflict—and it was the first time the UNSC was taking a specific aspect of the WPS agenda and pursuing a separate resolution on it.

The split, which can be seen in practice and policy literature and analyses in the intervening years, pitted those who saw sexual violence in conflict as one of the main violations women and girls face in that situation against those who saw the broad implications of focusing on the victimization of women and girls as inherently damaging to the feminism at the root of WPS.

For better or worse, the split regarding sexual violence in conflict is more or less settled at this point, at least in the eyes of policymakers. Sexual violence in conflict has a specific stream of work, focused primarily on protection, and—within the UN±a set of policies and institutions that deal specifically with this issue (see chapter 24 in this volume). Advocates working on the issue continue to emphasize the connections between addressing these protection concerns and ensuring the agency of women and girls.

As one of the most "advocacy heavy" locations for WPS policy development, the next section addresses advocacy success at the UN Security Council. This is not a comprehensive accounting for and assessment of WPS implementation at the Council, but rather an evaluation of what success has looked like in an emblematic case, and an accounting of some of the political dynamics that have helped and hindered this advocacy work. This assessment is based in large part on the strategies and impact of the primary civil society WPS advocacy actor at UN Headquarters, the NGO Working Group on Women, Peace, and Security (NGOWG).[2] The NGOWG has a consensus-driven approach to advocacy, meaning the public positions of the group are agreed upon by all members of the group, and meaning that there are certain positions the group cannot take given the constraints of certain individual member organizations.

CASE STUDY: ASSESSING WPS ADVOCACY IN THE UN SECURITY COUNCIL

Implementation, particularly in the UNSC, has progressed in fits and starts. As the NGOWG noted in 2013, WPS matters are not a "red line" for Council members (NGOWG 2013). Rather, the Council has historically tended to support the agenda in principle and to maintain WPS components in its country-specific work only when this does not present political problems. In addition to this lack of political investment, and indeed in part because of this, major challenges to implementation of the WPS agenda have included inconsistency in reporting, lack of information on urgent country situations, lack of gender analysis in peacekeeping and special political mission leadership briefings to the UNSC, and inconsistency in the Council's products. In addition, the Council's work on WPS has been notoriously conscribed on controversial efforts that edge into the most deeply rooted conflicts within the Council's membership—that is, conflict prevention and sovereignty.

In reality, success can only be measured by what kind of impact proposed policies have in communities that have been—or continue to be—impacted by conflict. There are far too many examples of cases where the Security Council has shirked its self-imposed responsibilities on women, peace, and security. As an example, in October 2014 in Tabit, Darfur, credible evidence surfaced of yet another attack by Sudan military forces and state sanctioned actors. According to Human Rights Watch, "Sudanese army troops carried out a series of attacks against the civilian population of the town of Tabit in North Darfur, Sudan. The attacks included the mass rape of women and girls and the arbitrary detention, beating and ill-treatment of scores of people"(HRW 2015). In this case, despite the presence of a UN peacekeeping mission in Darfur (UNAMID), the Council was only able to agree upon a brief press statement, with the anodyne request to allow UN access to "verify whether these incidents have occurred." The statement was lacking any reference to services for survivors, and to any strong call on the Sudan government to address the charges.

But the Council has been able to address some situations consistently and with a certain degree of political commitment. As an example, in September 2009, in the Guinea capital of Conakry, political protest in the context of elections erupted into violence. State security actors opened fire on peaceful demonstrators in the Conakry stadium, and many of the women detained by these security forces were raped. Human Rights Watch research indicated that "the killings, rapes, and other abuses committed by the security forces on and after September 28 [rose] to the level of crimes against humanity" (HRW 2009). The Council took rhetorical action, and supported the UN system in its efforts to promote accountability for the crimes. In October, the Council produced a presidential statement (PRST) condemning the violence. By December of 2009, the Commission of Inquiry, with the then-rare inclusion of a gender expert, had relayed their findings to the Secretary-General, who then submitted it to the Council. The Council subsequently adopted another PRST in February of 2010.

As in other areas of the Council's work, there are clearly remaining challenges for the UNSC's implementation of the WPS agenda. Despite more than seventeen years of effort—and, indeed, certain successes—in ensuring that the core components of this agenda are incorporated into the Council's daily work, robust and consistent implementation remains elusive. Department of Peacekeeping Operations (DPKO) and Department of Political Affairs (DPA) reports and the UNSC mandates are still sporadic in addressing these issues. The years since the fifteenth anniversary of 1325 have seen significant fluctuations in addressing WPS concerns, with removal of key language in, for example, the 2017 mandate for the UN mission in Afghanistan. While the negotiations on these texts are not public, the general understanding is that WPS elements were seen as less of a priority than streamlining and shortening the mandate. When the UN and the Council do address WPS, they tend to focus on one or two elements of the agenda, such as protection and CRSV (conflict-related sexual violence), rather than the full scope that includes women's rights, participation, and significant roles in conflict prevention. This challenge is fed and compounded by two key obstacles: the continuing ad hoc nature of "official" and substantive information flowing into the UNSC, and accountability: both for the Council's directives/instructions and for the Council's own work.

In discussions and debates in the UNSC, which include closed briefings, open debates, and closed negotiations, barriers exist because of a lack of transparency, lack of meaningful debate, and a lack of leadership, among other things. As a result, outcomes of the UNSC, which include PRSTs, resolutions, sanctions, and letters to relevant parties, are often bereft of consistent messaging and content, particularly regarding WPS.[3] This stems from a lack of clarity on options, and results in inconsistency, and lack of follow-up on previous WPS requests from the UNSC. This is compounded by the challenges of information flowing into the Council, including briefings by Special Representative(s) of the Secretary-General (SRSG), Arria Formula meetings (one of the few opportunities for civil society to address Council Members), and UN reports. Here, barriers include inconsistent inclusion of WPS-specific information, the lack of gender-disaggregated data and gender-specific analysis, and a correlating lack of targeted recommendations.

Since 2013 there has been growth in the policy/normative framework attempting to address these very barriers. Resolution 2122 (2013), for example, has a wealth of operative paragraphs focusing on the work of the Council itself, in addition to directives to key actors (DPKO/ DPA; heads of missions, etc.) to remain appraised of women's human rights in conflict situations, ensure appropriate support/programming for women's engagement in prevention/peacebuilding work, and the like. (UNSCR2122–OP 5). The Council has tasked itself with incorporating the WPS agenda into all of its work (UNSCR2122–OP 3), and has solidified its recognition of the key role of civil society in WPS implementation (UNSCR2122–OP 6). UNSCR 2242, adopted on the occasion of the fifteenth anniversary of SCR 1325, focuses in part on the establishment of clear lines of information into the UNSC (this is discussed in detail next). In addition, key resolutions on other matters, such as Resolution 2117 (2013), with its focus on small arms and light weapons, have included specific language on WPS in operative paragraphs, including women's protection and participation concerns.

The Council itself consists of five permanent members (United States, United Kingdom, France, China, Russia), and ten elected members who rotate in for two-year terms on the Council. Given the nature of issues the Council addresses, it is small wonder that there is disagreement among these member states as to what belongs on the Council's agenda, and what action the Council should take. As seen recently in Syria, but also in many prior cases, national and regional considerations of the member states often trump what the outside world sees clearly as cases in which the Council has obligations regarding international peace and security. The permanent members are constantly navigating a long-term ideological split between the "P3" (USA, UK, France) and a loose China/Russia alliance. Elected members struggle with large workloads and a lack of insight into the opaque workings of the Council (Security Council Report 2017). Long-staked out positions by the P3, which tend to favor the thematic issues and more interventionist approaches are anathema to the sovereignty-focused positions of China and Russia. Human rights and international humanitarian law obligations have been held at bay by the realities of the politics within the Council: from the Cold War through to today, there seems little scope to move member states beyond their national political priorities. What leverage, then, is there to hold over

Council Members, to demand accountability for the requests and demands it itself makes? International human rights and humanitarian law certainly play a role here, but the limits of both, and of naming and shaming efforts, have been well demonstrated.

WPS advocacy actors have taken different approaches to push for implementation given these political realities. One clear objective of the NGOs with WPS advocacy goals at the UNSC for a number of years has been a mechanism specific to the inconsistent information, analysis, and recommendations that flow into and are produced by the UNSC. Broadly put, the key areas of concern revolve around three issues: First, information flow into the Council, including peacekeeping and political mission country reports, briefings from heads of missions, and briefings on urgent crisis situations; second, the barriers to information from civil society experts, and analysis and discussion of this information leading to appropriate policy/programming responses; and third, accountability for all actors concerned, including the Council, other member states, UN actors, and non-state actors.[4]

In 2010 NGOWG launched an advocacy ask for the Council to establish a formal means to address this gap via a proposal for a "Comprehensive and Transparent System of Implementation" (unfortunately shortened to the CaTSI). The policy brief recommended four actions:

- Oversight and leadership within the Security Council;
- Consistent, meaningful information on the key areas of the women, peace, and security agenda;
- Expertise and analysis to contextualize information/data from the field; and
- A clear set of options—particularly those that draw on current operational capabilities—for the Security Council and UN enities.[5]

Up until this point, the most concrete action the Council had taken to embed the WPS agenda in its own work was in its resolutions on sexual violence in conflict. In the year prior to the CaTSI, and in response to a number of WPS resolutions, notably 1888 and 1889, UN actors developed a set of information-gathering processes and targets intended to both measure and prompt implementation of the Women, Peace, and Security agenda. This includes the MARA on sexual violence in conflict, which is primarily reliant on Women Protection Advisors (WPAs) working in peacekeeping missions, whose reporting is increasingly forming the basis for the SRSG's annual report to the Security Council on conflict related sexual violence. The broader WPS indicators, established by Resolution 1889 (2009), are intended to gauge longitudinal progress on the entire scope of the agenda. They are broadly grouped in the pillars of prevention, protection, participation, and, the more recently added, relief and recovery, with responsibility for data collection assigned to UN entities and member states. These indicators allow for tracking and comparison of the data, thereby providing a means to assess general progress over time. However, the Council does not receive this information on a country by country basis. Despite encouragement from civil society, to date these indicators are not reflected in regular country reports received by the UN Security Council. The information collected on some of the indicators is reflected in the annual WPS report of the Secretary-General, providing longitudinal tracking that would be useful in country-specific reports.

Momentum built between the tenth anniversary in 2010 and the fifteenth anniversary for the Council to be more accountable to its WPS obligations, particularly given that the two other thematic agendas—those focusing on children in conflict and on protection of civilians (see chapters 46 and 47 in this volume) already had reporting mechanisms of a kind. The NGOWG, in its monthly policy briefs, used analysis of the Council's work to highlight the impact of the ad hoc approach, and to subsequently call for the establishment of a mechanism.

By the time of the fifteenth anniversary, there was luck that added to the combined weight of five years of advocacy: perhaps most importantly, the president of the UNSC happened (via the alphabet) to be Spain for the anniversary, and this was someone who became an early and strong champion of the mechanism and was willing to commit political capital to the cause. UN Women, as the secretariat for the report assessing the implementation of Resolution 1325, commissioned a chapter specifically on the need for such a mechanism and detailing what such a group could do. Much also hinged on the pressure on potential dissenters—expected to be Russia and China—to not be the first UNSC member to veto a WPS resolution.

In October 2015, these ingredients came together in Resolution 2242, OP 5, subsections a and b, which expressed in part "its intention to convene meetings of relevant Security Council experts as part of an Informal Experts Group on Women, Peace and Security to facilitate a more systematic approach to Women, Peace and Security within its own work and enable greater oversight and coordination of implementation efforts;" and "decides to integrate women, peace and security concerns across all country-specific situations on the Security Council's agenda . . ." While the group is still relatively young (by the timeline of UNHQ), it has met numerous times on six countries—Iraq, Mali, Central African Republic, Afghanistan, Yemen, and the Lake Chad Region. The group, chaired in 2017 by permanent UNSC member United Kingdom and by elected members Sweden and Uruguay, has gradually developed its working methods, including increased transparency regarding its work.[6]

The core question is whether member states and others will be able to overcome what at times appear to be fundamental challenges to real accountability on these matters. Ultimately, there is certainly opportunity—realistic opportunity—for the UNSC to be far more engaged in a practical manner on WPS from a quotidian approach. Opportunities to address the substantive, overarching challenges are of course far less certain. The assessment of possibility for fundamental change to a degree depends on how much capacity there is for this daily work to shift the institution over the long-term, and whether that is a worthwhile goal. The value of that goal shows its worth when the triumvirate of actors—the United Nations, governments, and, crucially, feminist civil society—are able to work together to ensure progress, not to lose ground. This can be, to a certain degree, institutionalized, but will always be dependent on both political positions of governments (which can change dramatically with national elections), and on the commitment of individual policymakers. I would argue, therefore, that this change is both a worthwhile and possible goal, but that it will always be a precarious one.

The relevance of the UNSC in and of itself—adopting mission mandates with strong WPS elements one day and allowing the continuing flows of small arms in same country the next—points to both the challenge of the UNSC to engage on international peace and security, and to work on WPS. The expectation of changing the UNSC as an institution, including bringing about fundamental change in its approach not only on WPS but human rights, is dependent on the constant monitoring of the work of the Council, and the tireless chipping away at the Council's daily work. While changing the UNSC itself is not the primary goal of WPS work, it is nonetheless a necessary precondition for the Council to be a productive locus for WPS policy. The daily grind of this work matters, but only when it is part of broader, global efforts to create change, and only when it is reflective of what communities affected by conflict actually need.

CONCLUSION

What does the experience of the NGOWG pushing the UNSC on consistency tell us? I would argue that in some ways success is in the eye of the beholder. Ultimately the effectiveness of any of these tools hinges not just upon creative and strategic design of policy frameworks and institutions, but upon the political will in the UNSC to utilize them.

This approach to addressing WPS in the Council is important both symbolically, and in its substantive impact f . It is perhaps in the tenacity of civil society advocates working at UNHQ that we see the most concrete examples of the scope for WPS matters to move the UNSC's needle. For more than eleven years, these advocates have successfully managed to convince the UNSC to ensure a civil society representative speaks in the Council at every WPS open debate, traditionally held in October. It is difficult to overemphasize how unusual this is, as Council members are traditionally only briefed by UN representatives. And yet, as the October anniversary of the adoption of Resolution 1325 evolved to include the spring debate on sexual violence in armed conflict, this debate also developed the tradition of a civil society speaker. In 2015, the regular "Protection of Civilians" debate also included a woman civil society speaker. And so, despite themselves, the Council is now regularly briefed on women's participation in peace talks, on the impact of conflict related sexual violence, of the need for accountability—from women from Mali, Afghanistan, Central African Republic, Somalia, and more.

Any advocacy approach that seeks to move accountability forward in the Council needs to be resilient to the political ebbs and flows within the Council. This includes changing dynamics in UNSC due to elections, and the lack of transparency of information that flows into and out of the Council. Seventeen-plus years of WPS implementation has been responsive to some of these dynamics, though this can never in itself be sufficient for the women and girls whose lives have been upended by conflict.

NOTES

1. Add to this list the Special Representative of the UN Secretary-General on Sexual Violence in Conflict and the Special Representative of the NATO Secretary-General on Women, Peace and Security.
2. The NGOWG is a coalition of international NGOs who focus on WPS implementation at the UNSC. The membership is made up of service providers, grassroots networks, human rights organizations, and academic centers. The NGOWG currently consists of Amnesty International; CARE International; Consortium on Gender, Security, and Human Rights; Global Justice Center; Human Rights Watch; Inclusive Security; International Alert; MADRE; Nobel Women's Initiative; Oxfam; Refugees International; Saferworld; Women's

International League for Peace and Freedom; and Women's Refugee Commission. More at http://www.womenpeacesecurity.org.

3. In the hierarchy of Council products, resolutions—which include mandates for UN peacekeeping and political missions—are the strongest, and can call for the most significant consequences and actions under international law. These are voted on by Council members. Presidential Statements, or PRSTs, are consensus documents that are negotiated by all Council members, and are seen as being less powerful that resolutions.
4. UNSC Resolution 2122 (2013) OP 1., OP 2.
5. A summary of the CaTSI can be found here: http://www.peacewomen.org/e-news/article/ngo-working-group-women-peace-and-security.
6. Summaries of the IEG meetings can be found on Security Council Report's section on women, peace, and security.

REFERENCES

Cohn, Carol. Helen Kinsella and Sheri Gibbing, "Women, Peace, and Security: Resolution 1325," (with Helen Kinsella and Sheri Gibbings). *International Feminist Journal of Politics* 6, no. 1: 130-140 (2004),

Cohn, Carol. "Mainstreaming Gender in UN Security Policy: A Path to Political Transformation?" In *Global Governance: Feminst Perspectives* edited by Shirin M. Rai and Georgina Waylen, London: Palgrave, 2008 https://www.amherst.edu/media/view/92331/original/mainstreaming+gender+in+UN+security+policy.pdf.

Human Rights Watch. "Mass Rape in North Darfur: Sudanese Army Attacks against Civilians in Tabit." February 11, 2015, https://www.hrw.org/report/2015/02/11/mass-rape-north-darfur/sudanese-army-attacks-against-civilians-tabit.

Human Rights Watch. "'Bloody Monday': The September 28 Massacre and Rapes by Security Forces in Guinea." December 17, 2009, https://www.hrw.org/report/2009/12/17/bloody-monday/september-28-massacre-and-rapes-security-forces-guinea.

NGO Working Group on Women, Peace, and Security (NGOWG) . "Mapping Women, Peace, and Security in the UN SC." Annual tracking reports on WPS in the UN Security Council.

Security Council Report. Annual crosscutting report on women, peace, and security. NGOWG. Annual Report, Executive Summary, 2013.

Otto, Diane. "Power And Danger: Feminist Engagement with International Law through the UN Security Council." *The Australian Feminist Law Journal* 32, no. 1 (2010).

Security Council Report. "Security Council Elections 2017: Research Report." April 2017.

CHAPTER 7

....

WPS AS A POLITICAL
MOVEMENT

....

SWANEE HUNT AND ALICE WAIRIMU NDERITU

HISTORY IN A NUTSHELL

THIS is a movement spanning the globe, which has gathered strength for decades, with antecedents stretching back centuries. The narrative has many possible idioms—democratization, military efficiency, human solidarity, and sustainable peace among others. We have chosen a chronology laced with stories. History is, after all, chunks of real life. As part of the movement, we bear persuasive and personal witness to the WPS policies and principles. We ourselves have experienced the hurdles and opportunities:

(Swanee) It was 2003, just after the US "shock and awe" bombing of Baghdad. I wangled an hour at the Pentagon, where I described to a General why he would require an inclusive group of local decision-makers as he stepped into the void left by Saddam Hussein.

"Women know which angry teenagers have guns under their mattresses. They go places men can't. They build bridges more easily across religious divides. They have maternal standing that helps them counter violent extremism. General, you need this 51 percent of the population on your side to achieve your mandate."

After three cups of coffee, it was time to go. "Madam Ambassador, when we get the place secure, we'll turn to women's issues." But we weren't talking about cervical cancer. We were talking about security.

(Alice) In 2008, after Kenya's bitter presidential election left more than 1,000 dead, I co-founded Uwiano Platform for Peace, a partnership between the government and more than a thousand NGOs under a network called PeaceNet Kenya. The 2013 elections were coming up, and deep ethnic divisions hadn't healed. I knew people wanted to avoid bloodshed, but they didn't know how to help. So why not use something practical, like cell phones? With UNDP's help, we distributed them far and wide. I mean 700,000 of them.

It's hard to explain to civilians "conflict indicators for an early warning system." So we said, "Look through your window and tell us what you see. Are children not going to school? Are markets closed? Are young men standing in small groups? Text us a tip; we'll get the police there." These are the details of life that women notice, and they sent us several hundred thousand tips. Two servers crashed! One woman said, "Don't tell him I contacted you, but my son is out blocking the road. I want him home, safe."

We saw the gap, and we filled it. When people relayed sensitive information, we were on the other end of the phone, ensuring that police would act. Cell phones are tangible; trust isn't, but trust is crucial for real security. We understood.

The description that follows lays out key milestones and motivators of the movement—as well as illustrative obstacles and opportunities that lie ahead.

PRECURSORS AND EARLY MEETINGS

The modern WPS undertaking grew from other broad social campaigns, particularly the push for women's rights that swelled in the 1960s and the wider struggle for human rights. This was not, of course, the first international attempt to assert women's rights and influence in security matters. Notably, twelve hundred activists from opposing sides in Europe and North America had braved wartime travel in 1915 to gather in The Hague, aiming to develop their "unique vision in which peace, gender equality and human rights were intimately intertwined" (McCarthy 2015). Although they were unsuccessful in stopping World War I or preventing a second global cataclysm two decades later, their work—built partly on that of late nineteenth century suffragettes—was foundational.

Still, it isn't easy to pinpoint precisely when a separate WPS movement emerged, or to disentangle security from other issues that loomed large on the so-called women's agenda of the late twentieth century. Certainly "feminism" or "women's liberation" was fundamental. Across the globe from roughly the 1960s to the 1990s, this trend encompassed evolving and varying political, economic, and social aspects, depending on region and context. The amalgam of issues worldwide ranged from voting rights, to reproductive rights, to property rights; from domestic violence, to female genital mutilation, to rape; from child custody, to inheritance rights, and on and on. Widespread media focus on the concurrent US struggle for civil rights also contributed to "consciousness raising" about exclusion and inequality, along with nonviolent tactics (such as those introduced by Mahatma Gandhi) used to combat those problems. Civil disobedience opened doors for civil society.

A wider concern for people out of power produced the 1993 Vienna Declaration of the United Nations World Conference on Human Rights. That work also set the stage for women's participation in peace and security matters, as well as better protection for females—two themes that would soon compete for policymakers' attention. The "human security" doctrine, a term first used in a 1994 UN development report, recast governments' basic goals for their citizens. It's important to recall the ferment of those early years after the 1989 fall of the Berlin Wall. Activists, policymakers, and scholars revisited security questions in a post–Cold War context no longer dominated by competing communist and capitalist dogmas. A window opened, allowing in fresh thinking about insecurity and inequality.

In much of Latin America, ideological battles hinged on different issues because of the local political environment. From 1964 to 1985, the struggle for women's rights in Brazil was being waged against the backdrop of one of the region's multiple military dictatorships, so "security" was a loaded term. Democracy proponents included those protesting male-female inequality. But they joined others: university professors, trade unionists, and Catholic priests schooled in "liberation theology" who defended the poor. Jacqueline

Pitanguy, co-founder of Brazil's first feminist organization, made common cause with other human rights groundbreakers.

> By 1964, the feminist movement got going, and we began organizing in collectives. Civil society had a monopoly on human rights work, given violations by military governments. . . . In the '70s, we were gaining space on human rights among labor unions. And the UN Decade of the Woman (1975–1985) was very significant. We were under a dictatorship but we had UN protection when they organized an important meeting in Rio in '75. There was a synergy between what was happening locally and internationally. Because we women are more vulnerable, we are more capable—we have insider knowledge, legitimacy (Pitanguy 2016).

The UN: Catalytic Converter

The UN imprimatur was complicated.[1] Any organization whose member nations included so many ethnicities had to deal with concern for cultural appropriateness. Despite these problems, no other group had the mandate and wherewithal to go forward globally. Organizers of the first UN World Conference on Women in Mexico City, which took place in 1975, selected three themes: equality, development, and peace (UN 1996). Out of that meeting came two similar gatherings at five-year intervals. After the second conference, in Copenhagen, Nairobi was chosen to host.

> (Alice) I remember that as a mixed blessing, with hopes for change and opportunities yet so much negative media coverage. Men said that women from abroad were coming to tell us how to behave. Helping prepare for the conference was Wangari Maathai, our human rights and environmental icon who later won the Nobel Peace Prize. She was divorced, and government and church leaders condemned her for "wanting to wear the trousers." They were referring to 1922 when Mary Muthoni Nyanjiru, protesting colonial injustice, shamed the timid men at her side by throwing her skirt over her shoulder to reveal her nakedness. She shouted just before being shot and killed that they were cowards and could trade their trousers for her dress. More than 60 years later, we had officials saying Wangari had no right to be involved. That got us riled up!

Years later, reflecting on that conference and others, former US ambassador to the Commission on the Status of Women, Arvonne Fraser, described how governments were forced to respond to what was essentially a revolution. "Kenya, at first eager to have the 1985 conference, tried to slow down and hinder preparations as it saw the enthusiasm among women . . ." (Fraser 2014).

Rape Weaponized

In the 1990s, women were experiencing violent conflict in places as disparate as Colombia, Sri Lanka, and Uganda. Still the world was shocked by the organized rape camps of the murderous three-and-a-half-year Bosnian war. Those horrors were taking place within "civilized" Europe where the post-Holocaust mantra *never again* had long seemed so solid. The fact that UN forces with limited mandates at times stood by as impotent witnesses was nearly inconceivable and displayed the international community at its worst.

The women's stories spoke truth no statistic could.

> Rada: We were like calves grazing by an active volcano. . . .
> Danica: Then the nationalists came in, and people just went crazy. . . .
> Kristina: You learn to feel in your gut when to go hide. . . .
> Alma: Men feared being killed. We women were afraid of being caught alive.
> Emsuda: A mother and father had to watch their daughter being raped. Sons had to watch their mothers being raped. . . .
> Kada: If nothing else, we can at least try to be sure that all we experienced in Srebrenica isn't forgotten. . . . (Hunt 2004: 15, 9, 16, 201, 51, 193).

At the same time, outsiders failed to deter the inconceivably brutal war crimes being committed in the small African country of Rwanda. In one hundred days, 800,000 men, women, and children were hacked to death by Hutu extremists (Hunt 2017). As in Bosnia, rape was also a favorite weapon in the Rwandan case. Mama Diane points toward the village square, where the mob of men assailed her:

> I was 16 years old, still a child. I looked like a madwoman—in the street, naked. Everyone saw me. After, I had to tell my story. . . . My testimony about my attack was even on the radio. So everyone knew. Everyone knows a mad person (Hunt 2017: 206–207).

Beijing: Critical Mass

This systematic rape was galvanizing. In the wake of the 1993 Vienna Human Rights conference, with its Program for Action still fresh on activists' minds, full-bore planning began for the fourth UN meeting on women. It was to be held in China, of all places, despite perennial concerns about huge numbers of political prisoners. The stories of sex-selective abortions and infanticide (under the one-child policy) added to the tension, as did the presence of Bosnian and Rwandan survivors. Small wonder that US First Lady Hillary Clinton's (1995) striking message that "human rights are women's rights and women's rights are human rights, once and for all" was a clarion call for a new movement in which security is a human right, and that right belongs to women as well as men.

More than seventeen thousand participants had gathered in Beijing, along with some thirty thousand at the parallel NGO forum. It was big news. One author of this chapter (Alice) vividly recalls two things: first, widespread media reports that Kenyan President Moi had told his conference representative to leave in China whatever was learned there.[2] Second, in the same vein, African men were often overheard saying to activists, "Oh, you're some of the women who have been 'Beijinged.'" Moi was right to be worried. On top of the expected emphasis on development, the delegates were paving the way to a bold paradigm of women's protection and full participation in decision-making.

Filipina ceasefire expert Irene Santiago, executive director of the NGO forum, reminisces: "Those women, in the mud, in the rain, they were there for a purpose. The words I heard applied over and over about the meeting were 'life changing'" (Santiago 2015b).

On that point also, Turkish participant Zeliha Ünaldi, later a UN gender officer, reflected on eight days of a trans-Siberian train ride from Warsaw to Beijing with more than two hundred new friends from twenty-nine different countries:

> We were dedicated to transforming the world. . . . When I recall the tents with thousands of women, two words come to mind: sisterhood and peace. I still believe in sisterhood, even though it may sound ancient to the younger generation. The Beijing Declaration and Platform for Action and the subsequent five years helped me understand the power in us and of us as the global women's movement (Ünaldi 2015).

That individual and collective power was unleashed as the returnees combatted crises and conflicts—not only in Bosnia and Rwanda, but also in Israel and Palestine, Northern Ireland, South Africa, and beyond. Activist and chronicler par excellence Sanam Naraghi-Anderlini explains:

> The focus on women's experiences in war, articulated in Chapter E (Women and Armed Conflict) of the final platform, doesn't just dwell on women's victimization; it calls for the increased involvement of women in resolving conflicts. The conference delegates, governmental and nongovernmental, couldn't have known their words were launching a global revolution—inspiring women to challenge the last bastion of male-dominated decision-making (Anderlini 2007: 5-6).[3]

One of those inspired was Luz Méndez, a member of Guatemalan National Revolutionary Unity. Beijing was a source of courage for her; the blunt message that "women's rights are human rights" had a sharp point (Hunt 2005: 260).[4] Méndez was initially the only woman in the peace talks that ended more than three decades of bloody war. Supporting proposals from women's organizations, she developed strategies to advance women's rights, tailored to the three groups around the negotiating table—her rebel colleagues, the government, and the UN. As a result, equal rights provisions were inserted into the peace accords (see Nobel Women's Initiative, n.d.).

THE MAKING OF SECURITY COUNCIL RESOLUTION 1325

The energy of women like Luz Méndez—fueled by the Beijing conference—was unstoppable. Over the next several years the UN had a tiger by the tail, and that tiger was civil society on the hunt for a Security Council resolution to further the goals of WPS advocates. In the run-up to the June 2000 five-year implementation review of the Beijing Declaration and Platform for Action, activists criss-crossed cultures. They tapped their networks to generate consensus and to pressure key diplomats. Their own ethnic and other diversity was a major strength. Veteran Cora Weiss, president of The Hague Appeal for Peace, was famous for constantly bringing in the next generation. Ironically, some critics (forgetting the cacophony of warlords) called the women disorganized because they didn't speak with one voice on issues such as pacifism versus military intervention to end genocide.

Civil society groups negotiated among themselves to produce a draft resolution and worked with helpful governments—Bangladesh, Canada, Jamaica, and Namibia all had temporary Security Council seats—to enlist others. After Bangladesh and Namibia took preliminary steps during their respective Council presidencies in March and May of 2000, the resolution was adopted unanimously in October. In less than a year, the Organization for Security and Cooperation in Europe and the European Union took similar actions. It's a fact of diplomatic practice that countries, for expediency's sake, may sign pacts with a metaphorical wink and a shrug because "everyone knows" that implementation may not be politically feasible. Still, even getting these words on paper was an enormous accomplishment. In the broadest sense, the actions of certain high-level diplomats were all the more remarkable as they cajoled other governments to sign on given the huge gap in everyday experience between policymakers negotiating agreements and women making peace in communities while dealing with material realities of life amid conflict. Long story short, far from a powerful cabal of states *imposing* action, the great UN was *responding* to activists determined to secure what would become "basic law" for their cause. Within the international system, it might be termed a "soft law," but it was still an essential turning point. There was no playbook; this was movement "improv."

SWINGING DOORS

Judging by their treatment of women at home, for many countries Resolution 1325 was a mere fig leaf to cover continuing institutional pathologies and misogyny. It's amazing that WPS advocates have made such headway despite facing powerful and entrenched machismo. After 2000, advocacy around the world accelerated. But too often resistance to change outside was mirrored by tired inertia from UN Member States and officials who responded only grudgingly to demands from women and a few good men. Typical of that resistance was the much anticipated "Brahimi report" of the Panel on UN Peace Operations. Published in 2000, the seventy-three-page document contained nary a word about 51 percent of the world's population.

> (Swanee) During a small UN meeting with the storied Algerian official, I asked, in my most sanitized, diplomatic tone, about the dangerous omission. But compared to those with formal heft, my words had no traction.
>
> Still, a movement was coalescing. A year earlier, building on my experience with Bosnian women during and after the war, we had brought to Harvard's Kennedy School of Government 110 women from ten conflict zones. To my surprise, an additional 100 policymakers and more than 70 researchers came from distant, and close, parts. They were eager to be in an unprecedented mix with women from war zones who were learning that they were not alone and, moreover, that their experiences were valued by those wanting to understand what causes violent confrontation and how to prevent it. Our guests from conflict zones formed the nucleus of a new NGO, dubbed Women Waging Peace (now Inclusive Security).
>
> Throughout the next two decades, as our staff worked with several thousand women leaders, policy officials, and academics, we were often up against worthy men who, despite best intentions, found it inordinately tough to move from aspirational agreement to action. One memorable day, as I pursued the brilliant US Director of Policy Planning, Richard Haass, down a State Department corridor, he paused. "You're pushing on an open door," he assured me graciously. "Perhaps," I thought to myself, "but it's a swinging door, as likely to keep you out as let you in."

Holding the door wide open was Haass's deputy, Ambassador Donald Steinberg. He was enthusiastic about the hypothesis that women are integral to stopping war partly because of his experience during the recurring conflict in Angola. But year after year, Steinberg was a voice calling in the wilderness. The bias that security is a man's sphere was chasm-deep, perhaps due to ignorance of what women bring, or an unconscious dread of appearing "womanish"—that is, weak. But even if others in the military or elsewhere considered his notion soft around the edges, Steinberg never folded. As he said more than once, "There's nothing soft about it" (Steinberg 2012). Carrying forward the metaphor, even when the security door has let in "protection," it has kept out "participation." The separation, however, is artificial.

In 2013, Oksana Romaniuk, an opponent of the pro-Russian Ukrainian government's efforts to control the media, was the victim of a defamatory pseudo-documentary. She recalls, "The police interrogated my parents and colleagues; they took my laptop and tried to keep me from working" (Romaniuk 2016). Still, she redoubled her efforts to promote better journalism which included securing bulletproof vests when reporters covering revolutionary demonstrations were targeted by government troops. In a sense, her best protection was her enhanced participation.

But when Iraqi female members of parliament say their greatest impediment is the expense of bodyguards, or when a Mexican politician describes death threats to her family as she advocates for a law to combat cartels, we can see why policymakers—mostly male—may not promote women's participation in security matters in a bid to protect them. Even so, advocates for WPS have pushed back against shielding professional women from dangerous jobs.

Canadian Lt. General Roméo Dallaire (who commanded UN troops sent to pacify Rwandan extremists), for example, looks beyond the distinction between women as victims and actors:

> I was involved with the 2005 comprehensive peace agreement for Darfur. Women were nowhere. And so we had a senator that was with us from Canada, Mobina Jaffer, who brought together women and [they] forced themselves into the meetings. I mean they sometimes demonstrate so much more courage in breaking, literally breaking open doors. And men, no matter how . . . well, I could even say pompous . . . how pretentious they will be in their positions of authority, tend to be caught off-guard and are not sure how to handle a strong, female presence (Dallaire 2016).

Senator Jaffer recalls her determination to ensure women's participation in those negotiations, and the pragmatic results when their voices were added:

> Every time I asked where the women were, people would say, "What are you doing? It's fragile enough. If you introduce the women, it will not work." The mediator brought 17, 18 women from the camps, and the peace process changed, because when people were talking about water rights, the women would say, "What are you talking about? This river dried up a long time ago . . ." (Jaffer 2010).

Lt. General Dallaire agrees. According to him:

> There is an enormous amount of potential power in women to bring reasonableness around the table. They can be a lot more demanding, a lot pushier, a lot more even aggressive in their

positions and not fear being shunned or aggressively responded to. But on the contrary, once they crack that door open, it's pretty damned hard to throw them out, because they tend to bring out some pretty solid arguments that often catch men off-guard (Dallaire 2016).

However, doors often opened straight into another wall whether they cracked open figuratively or literally. In fact, most governments had little at stake when it came to making a place for women in security matters. As a former senior US envoy to the UN put it, "my recollection, alas, is there was not much high-level attention devoted to 1325 after it was adopted, with the bulk of follow-up left to the UN Secretariat" (Wolff 2016). Thus, for more than two decades, the movement has been shaped by tension as diplomats and other officials are torn between a focus on altruistic response to atrocities and an upstream bet that women will themselves address issues such as sexual violence if they're in positions of leadership. Here, Ambassador Anwarul Chowdhury weighs in: "The main question is not to make war safe for women, but to structure peace in a way that there is no recurrence of war and conflict." Importantly, women must be the architects of that structure (Chowdhury 2010).

EMBEDDED

For those of us who have devoted most of our professional lives to this field, it's heartening to see how "women, peace, and security" has picked up speed since the international meetings focused on global women's rights and human rights began some four decades ago. The mobilization from Beijing to Security Council Resolution 1325 provided a platform for an ever-growing contingent of implementers. Looking ahead, it's reassuring how WPS is being implanted in academic, philanthropic, policy-planning, military, and electoral spheres. Thinkers have begun to recognize—and analyze why—peace and security are more obtainable and less fragile if women are fully participating in decision-making. Research centers have sprung up on most continents, and related courses are offered across the world. The topic has been adopted by philanthropic heavyweights in the United States, Europe, and Asia. Recently, even foreign policymaking powerhouses such as the US Council on Foreign Relations have opened their thinking to what before was considered a marginal idea. Special envoys for WPS are being appointed by countries and multilateral organizations. Slowly, the critical need for women in peace processes is being recognized at a global scale.

Gradual progress in implementing WPS is also evident in different national contexts. In Afghanistan, donor support has included funding to train women in mediation (and some of those leaders have negotiated with Taliban forces to release hostages, as we authors heard during workshops; see Gibson 2014). The UN Special Envoy for Syria created an advisory group of women to seek their perspectives on the main obstacles to negotiations. The 2012–2016 Colombian government talks with the rebel FARC included creation of a gender subcommission comprising representatives of both parties. In the Philippines, when the government signed a major peace agreement with the Moro Islamic Liberation Front in 2014, women were 50 percent of the government's negotiating team and 25 percent of the signatories—and a female headed the Office of the Presidential Adviser on the Peace Process, which presides over five distinct peace tables. Women leaders supported the inclusion of other females in the process, which led to provisions in the accord on women's rights to "meaningful political participation" and "lawful employment," as well as special development programs and protections (Santiago 2015a: 12).

Meanwhile, the UN is also slowly moving forward on women's participation in global security. The Department for Peacekeeping Operations has a mandate under UNSCR 2242 to double the number of female peacekeepers by 2020. That's a stretch, given the small pool of women among member states' militaries. Still, one encouraging indicator comes from NATO countries where, based on a robust percentage of female applicants to military colleges, the needle should begin to shift soon.[5] The WPS movement has likely benefited from the increased acceptance of gender-based electoral quotas, now used in half the countries of the world (Quota Database ,n.d.). For example, in Rwanda women now hold 64 percent of the seats in parliament, and Rwanda is far ahead of any other country in the percentage of women legislators. When the killings stopped, Rwandans discovered that chaos had cracked open the patriarchal culture. With a pull from top leaders,[6] women became three of twelve drafters of a constitution that established a 30 percent quota throughout government. A five-tiered system of women's councils funneled civil society leaders into those government positions. Then women from the 30 percent in parliament gave up their seats for their less experienced sisters and ran against the men.

The broader impact on peace and security was also evident. Rwandan women headed a truth and reconciliation process in which two million alleged perpetrators faced the families of victims, a process key to achieving stability in the collapsed social structure. Despite concerns about its uneven transition to democracy, Rwanda's progress two decades after genocide is astounding. The society is remarkably corruption-free; women (although they may struggle financially) can now own property; life expectancy has risen from 48 to 58 years; boys and girls attend secondary schools in equal numbers; violence against women, while still prevalent, is dramatically reduced; and much more.[7]

Finally, no indicator is more reassuring than the fresh proliferation of National Action Plans, or NAPs, to implement Resolution 1325. With that development, the WPS cause, originally powered by individual activists and civil society groups, is acquiring a broad cadre of newly educated allies—both career civil servants charged with negotiating and implementing such plans (many of whom have become advocates after learning new ways of operating and cooperating) and political leaders using the documents for various ends. Increasingly, the plans are tools to help a government focus on emerging threats beyond traditional security. For example, Kenya's 2015 plan and Jordan's draft strategy advance women's participation in countering violent extremism. NAPs in Sierra Leone and Liberia elevate women's roles in combating pandemics, and the Finnish plan supports women's organizations dealing with climate change (Inclusive Security 2017).

Still, there are plenty of obstacles ahead for WPS. A particularly significant obstacle is the disconnect between NAPs and women on the ground.

> (Alice) In Africa, at a meeting looking at NAP implementation, a Maasai friend named Mary Simat asked me: "So what exactly happened in the year 1325 that we are celebrating today?" And this is a woman who's involved, a very powerful grassroots organizer. When I explained, Mary added, "Why don't we know about these things? Who do they write them for?"

A paper resolution or plan is a crucial asset for advocates. However, the future of WPS must be measured by whether the Mary's of the world are not only aware of, but also living out, those words. That's a tall order because if the mid-level drafters of NAPs are forthright in their plans for change, their political leaders (and bosses) must face a humbling roster of faults. Pointing them out is hardly a prescription for the career advancement of those authors. Given these and a litany of other challenges, it's astonishing that more than sixty countries and regions have created plans. Clearly, the value outweighs the cost.

And So. . . .

Since the 2016 US presidential election, many of us have been re-examining our assumptions about the WPS movement. The Hillary Doctrine, as scholars have dubbed it, holds that *the subjugation of women is a direct threat to the common security of our world . . .* (Hudson and Leidl 2015: 3). With a different election result, the might of the international system's powerhouse nation could have been oriented toward the human rights heralded by the US First Lady in Beijing. But as we have seen, a movement does not follow a straight path. There are detours, switchbacks, and reverses. So now, more than most of us imagined, nations huge to miniscule, Global South to Global North, must play vital roles ensuring that the rights of women are inextricably linked to peace and to security. *Once and for all.*

NOTES

1. For many in the United States, the major funder, it was tainted with international socialism/communism.
2. The Kenyan leader also described the conference as a "meeting of women aimed at pushing for immoral traits and un-African culture" (Obonyo 2017).
3. Minor edits for brevity's sake were approved by Ms. Anderlini.
4. Additional information was gleaned from author Hunt's personal email exchanges with Ms. Méndez.
5. A recent study compared percentages of women on active military duty in NATO member and partner nations to the—usually significantly higher—percentages of women among all applicants to their respective military colleges. For example, while only 4 percent of the Polish military on active duty is female, 35 percent of applicants to military colleges were female. Corresponding figures for four other countries were as follows—Czech Republic 13:32; Greece 16:29; France 15:27; and Japan 6:27. (North Atlantic Treaty Organization 2015: 11, 13).
6. War changed gender roles in Rwanda. One of the authors (Alice Nderitu) was part of a 2003 consultative process in Rwanda, working with the premise that women were key to preventing another genocide and advising the government on roles they could play. She notes, "The women's inclusion in decision-making was deliberate, and Rwanda's leadership deserves praise for it."
7. See Hunt, *Rwandan Women Rising*, for details.

REFERENCES

Anderlini, S. N. "*Women Building Peace: What They Do, Why It Matters.*" Boulder, CO: Lynne Rienner, 2007.

Chowdhury, Anwarul K. "10 Years On, The Promises to Women Need to Be Kept." In *Women and Conflict: A Frontline Issue?* NATO Review, October 13, 2010, http://www.nato.int/docu/review/2010/Women-Security/Women-resolution-1325/EN/index.htm.

Clinton, H. Video of speech in Beijing. PBS, "Washington Week," 1995, http://www.pbs.org/weta/washingtonweek/web-video/hillary-clinton-declares-womens-rights-are-human-rights.

Dallaire, R. Personal interview by Swanee Hunt, March 14, 2016.

Fraser, Arvonne. "UN Decade for Women: The Power of Words and Organizations." In *Women and Social Movements, International: 1840 to Present*, edited by Kathryn Kish Sklar, Thomas Dublin. Alexander Street Database, 2014, http://alexanderstreet.com/products/women-and-social-movements-international (http://wasi.alexanderstreet.com/help/view/un_decade_for_women_the_power_of_words_and_organizations#_edn12).

Gibson, C. "Photos: Equipping Women to Push for Inclusion in the Afghan Peace Process." Inclusive Security [Blog], July 30, 2014, https://www.inclusivesecurity.org/2014/07/30/photos-equipping-women-push-inclusion-afghan-peace-process/.

Hudson, V. M., and P. Leidl. *The Hillary Doctrine: Sex & American Foreign Policy.* New York: Columbia University Press, 2015.

Hunt, S. *This Was Not Our War: Bosnian Women Reclaiming the Peace.* Durham, NC: Duke University Press, 2004.

Hunt, S. "Moving Beyond Silence: Women Waging Peace." In *Listening to the Silences: Women and War,* edited by Helen Durham and Tracey Gurd, 251–271. The Netherlands: Martinus Nijhoff, 2005.

Hunt, S. *Rwandan Women Rising.* Durham, NC: Duke University Press, 2017.

Inclusive Security. "National Action Plan Resource Center." Countries, 2017, https://actionplans.inclusivesecurity.org/.

Jaffer, M. "Women and Peace Negotiations in Darfur." Institute for Inclusive Security Policy Forum, November 17, 2010, https://www.youtube.com/watch?v=755YwYpzEmU.

McCarthy, H. Introduction. "Women, Peace, and Transnational Activism, A century on." *History & Policy,* March 30, 2015, http://www.historyandpolicy.org/dialogues/discussions/women-peace-and-transnational-activism-a-century-on.

Nobel Women's Initiative. "Meet Luz Méndez, Guatemala." Activist Spotlight, n.d., https://nobelwomensinitiative.org/activist-spotlight-luz-mendez-guatemala/.

North Atlantic Treaty Organization. "Summary of the National Reports of NATO Member and Partner Nations to the NATO Committee on Gender Perspectives." Report Summary, 2015, http://www.nato.int/nato_static_fl2014/assets/pdf/pdf_2017_01/20170113_2015_NCGP_National_Reports_Summary.pdf.

Obonyo, O. "Foreign Influence' Agenda is Gaining Ground." Daily Nation, January 1, 2017, http://mobile.nation.co.ke/news/politics/3126390-3503510-item-1-e3b5p3z/index.html.

Pitanguy, Jacqueline. Personal interview by editorial assistant Deborah Cavin, December 12, 2016.

Quota Database. Gender Quotas Database. International IDEA, Inter-Parliamentary Union, and Stockholm University, n.d., http://www.quotaproject.org/aboutQuotas.cfm.

Romaniuk, O. Personal interview by Deborah Cavin, January 13, 2016. Additional information available at Inclusive Security, https://www.inclusivesecurity.org/experts/oksana-
romaniuk/.

Santiago, I. Research Paper. "The Participation of Women in the Mindanao Peace Process."
Prepared for the United Nations Global Study on 15 Years of Implementation of UN Security
Council Resolution 1325 (2000). New York, UN Women, October 2015.

Santiago, I. International Peace Institute Global Observatory. UN Conference on Women in
Beijing, October 21, 2015, https://www.youtube.com/watch?v=d-xspyMdpd4.

Steinberg, D. "Beyond Victimhood: The Crucial Role of Marginalized Groups in Building
Peace." USAID, February 6, 2012,

Ünaldi, Z. "The Power in Us and of Us." In *The Beijing Platform for Action Turns 20*. UN
Women, July 30, 2015, http://beijing20.unwomen.org/en/news-and-events/stories/2015/7/
beijing-what-the-power-in-us-and-of-us.

United Nations (UN). "Report of the Fourth World Conference on Women, Beijing, 4–5
September 1995." Annex II, Statement by Boutros Boutros-Ghali, Secretary-General of
the United Nations. New York, 1996, http://www.un.org/esa/gopher-data/conf/fwcw/off/
a-20a1.en.

Wolff, A. Personal e-mail to Ambassador Hunt's editorial assistant Deborah Cavin,
December 6, 2016.

CHAPTER 8

LOCATING MASCULINITIES IN WPS

HENRI MYRTTINEN

FROM the very outset, the United Nations Women, Peace, and Security (WPS) policy architecture has had an unclear relationship with men, boys, and masculinities. With "masculinities," I refer to the ways in which men and boys are socially expected, and expect themselves, to enact their gendered selves in any given situation, and how this is reflected in societal power dynamics. Masculinities are multiple, constructed, dynamic, and contested, and not tied to bodies generically considered as being biologically male, but this conceptualization already goes far beyond the ways in which masculinities are present in or engaged with in the WPS policy realm.[1]

I argue that this unclear relationship is due to three somewhat interlinked reasons: First, ever since UN Security Council Resolution 1325 (2000), the term "gender" has been used rather imprecisely in the UN Security Council's WPS resolutions.[2] Most often, it is used interchangeably with or seen as pertaining only to "women" or "women and girls." On occasion, it is used more comprehensively to include men, women, boys, and girls, though this tends to be usually more implicit than explicit. When the term gender is used more comprehensively in these documents, however, the position of those who do not identify according to gender binaries remains vague. While a broader understanding of the term gender also covers intersex, trans, third gender, and other gender identities, to date no UNSC WPS resolution has explicitly used language that goes beyond the gender binary (Hagen 2016).

Second, gender tends to be seen in WPS policy and peace-building practice as something that is extraneous to issues of peace and security, as a kind of technical add-on, rather than as something which lies at the heart of all human behavior and thus is also inextricably interwoven into all matters of conflict and peace (Myrttinen et al. 2014). The conflation of gender with women leads to an "invisibilization of masculinities and hyper-visibilization of femininities," rendering women, girls, and femininities as exceptional, as compared to men and masculinities who are de facto seen as the norm (Puechguirbal 2010: 175). In a similar vein, Hilary Charlesworth (1994: 445) stresses that "[t]he imbalance in men's representation in national and international government structures allows male life experiences to be regarded as a general, rather than a gendered, category. By contrast, 'women's concerns' are regarded as a distinct and limited category, relegated to a specialized and marginalized sphere and regulated, if at all, in a weaker way." Furthermore, the casting of women and girls as being *essentially* only victims of conflict and/or peace-builders often has very real, and retrograde impacts on their practical possibilities of participating in post-conflict political decision-making processes (Cano Vinas 2015; Debusscher and Martin De Almagro 2016).

Third, and in part due to the view of gender as an "add-on" to the peace and security agenda, men and boys are for the most part rendered invisible as gendered actors in peace and conflict (El-Bushra 2012; Myrttinen et al. 2014; Wright 2014). Thus, while men and boys are ubiquitous in these contexts as fighters, as peace negotiators, as refugees, as victims and survivors, as aid givers, as media, and as bystanders, they are seldom seen *as men*, that is, as gendered beings performing their masculinities in relation to societal expectations about the appropriate behavior for ("manly") men. Equally, collective institutions involved in conflict and peace, such as state and non-state security forces, the United Nations, national governments, or NGOs are seldom analyzed as gendered—and often masculine-coded—constructions.

In this chapter, I examine how and when men and boys appear in key texts that constitute the WPS policy architecture especially the respective UNSCRs. Using the example of conflict-related sexual and gender-based violence (SGBV), which has been one of the main focus areas of the WPS-related SCRs, I then analyze the gendered consequences of the contested and uneven expansion of the agenda to also include men and boys. I then discuss some of the potential reasons for the lack of a comprehensive gender analysis as the basis of the UNSCR-based WPS policy architecture. Lastly, I consider possibilities for using the spaces within the policy architecture to create more radical, transformative change.

MEN AND BOYS IN THE WOMEN, PEACE, AND SECURITY UNSC RESOLUTIONS

While men and boys, and the various formal and informal institutions they inhabit, de facto play a variety of very central roles in processes of conflict and peace, they remain spectral in the language of the WPS policy architecture. The absence of men and boys in WPS policy texts is despite the fact that they tend to be the main perpetrators of conflict-related violence (sexual and otherwise), form the majority of direct casualties, and are often a key demographic militating against increased women's participation.

Although many of the WPS SCRs focus on conflict-related sexual violence, the gender of the perpetrators of the violence is not explicitly stated. Given that the majority of armed actors are men and boys, one might assume that this may in part be taken for granted as being male, and militarized and violent masculinities are specifically mentioned in the Global Study (UN Women 2015). Victimhood, in particular with respect to SGBV, is mostly assumed to be female, as for example UNSCR 2106 remains ambivalent about the possibility of male or non-gender binary victims[3] (cf. Dolan 2014a; Kirby and Shepard 2016: 252; Puechguirbal 2010; Sjoberg 2016).

The few times men and boys they are mentioned explicitly in the resolutions, they are cast in a more positive (or potentially positive) light than as perpetrators of violence or obstacles to gender equality: UNSCR 2106 (2013) mentions men and boys both as potential partners in preventing violence against women and girls, and, somewhat obliquely, as being "also affected" by sexual and gender-based violence. More explicitly, the preamble of UNSCR 2242 (2015) "re-iterat[es] the important engagement by men and boys as partners in promoting women's participation in the prevention and resolution of armed conflict, peacebuilding and post-conflict situations." This inclusion of "men and boys as partners" reflects a broader shift toward engaging with men in gender issues, be it through the growth of the international MenEngage network, campaigns such as UN Women's He4She, or, more controversially, Iceland's "barbershop" initiative to create men-only spaces at the UN to discuss gender issues. While this engagement with men and boys has been lauded by some as a necessary step to increasing gender equality (e.g., Vess et al. 2013), others fear a dilution of the gender equality agenda (e.g., Ward 2016), and yet others are critical and in between, giving qualified support (Duriesmith 2017; Flood 2015; Myrttinen 2018; Myrttinen et al. 2014). For the most part, however, the actors with agency, be they the perpetrators of violence, the mostly male intervening peacekeepers, or the male-dominated UN Security Council itself, which "re-iterates," "expresses concern," for or "remains seized of" WPS issues, continue to be ungendered or invisible in WPS resolutions and documents.

MEN AND BOYS IN THE GLOBAL STUDY

In 2014–2015, UN Women co-ordinated a global review process of fifteen years of implementing UNSCR 1325 as part of an UN-mandated High Level Review process, resulting in what is commonly referred to as the "Global Study" (UN Women 2015; see also chapter 11 and chapter 58 in this volume). The lengthy process of compiling this study involved a number of opportunities for civil society organizations to give their input through written submissions and a series of workshops. Several NGOs, including my organization, International Alert, used the opportunity to jointly push through co-authored submissions for a broader approach to gender, peace, and security (Conciliation Resources et al. 2015; DCAF and International Alert 2015). Echoing wider concerns, we called explicitly for critically examining masculinities and including diverse sexual orientations and gender identities, while not dropping women's rights and gender equality from the agenda. In at least some of the workshops organized to give input to the Global Study, the need for addressing masculinities in the review process were also raised, although at least at the workshop which I attended as a participant, this was very literally a last-minute add-on.[4]

The end result of the Global Study, however, was rather disappointing from a standpoint of broadening the scope of the agenda from Women, Peace, and Security to Gender, Peace, and Security (GPS). In the 418 pages of the Global Study:

- "Boys" are mentioned five times in relation to their educational performance compared to girls;
- "Men and boys" are mentioned once as potential combatants and once as receiving preferential treatment to "women and girls" when it comes to nutrition;
- Possibilities of changing of male behavior are mentioned five times;
- Masculinities are mentioned twice in the context of "violent masculinities" and twice as "militarized masculinities";

- Men and boys come up thirteen times as part of the phrase "men, women, boys and girls";
- LGBT (lesbians, gays, bisexuals, trans—with intersex persons, queer and other sexual orientations and gender identities left unmentioned) are mentioned twice.

These figures, as low as they are, are however somewhat inflated by the fact that a number of these mentions are made twice, when the phrase in question is used in the main text and repeated in the summarizing bullet points at the end of a section. Thus, the tentative policy space which had been opening up to broaden the WPS agenda and make it more comprehensive, intimated in UNSCRs 2106 and 2242 (not to mention decades of work in academia and by civil society actors), were largely ignored by the Global Study.

THE CONSEQUENCES OF INVISIBILIZING MASCULINITIES—THE EXAMPLE OF SGBV AGAINST MEN AND BOYS

The consequences of this invisibilization of men and boys in the WPS policy architecture are both harmful and beneficial at the same time to men and boys, as well as differently for women and girls. Overall, however, they tend to stabilize patriarchal binary views of gender roles (Dolan 2014a; Puechguirbal 2010) and gender hierarchies of inequality (Ward 2016). Women and girls are relegated to positions of victimhood (and sometimes assumed to have "innate" peacefulness) with little agency, reaffirming views of male strength and power, casting some men as violent without questioning how these masculinities are co-constructed by men and women. Thus, the gendered underpinnings of power, the gendered dynamics of violence, and the gendered nature of institutions remain unquestioned.

I will explore here some of these impacts by looking at the push to include a recognition of men and boys as potential victims of SGBV. Conflict-related SGBV has been one of the main focus areas of WPS resolutions, in particular after UNSCR 1820, and at least since 2010, there has been a push by victims/survivors' organizations, local and international NGOs, vocal activists and academics, to include language on men and boys as victims/survivors of SGBV as well. As, for example, a comparison between Dolan (2014b) and its rejoinder (Ward 2016) shows, the debates between the proponents and opponents of a broadening of the scope have at times been quite acrimonious.

Although the issue has not been fully taken into account in all SGBV frameworks and remains in part contested, there is an increasing recognition of men and boys' vulnerabilities in this respect. Agencies such as the Inter-Agency Standing Committee (2015), the International Committee of the Red Cross (2014), the International Criminal Court's Office of the Prosecutor (ICC/OTP 2014), and the United Nations High Commissioner for Refugees (2012) are addressing men and boy's SGBV victimization, and global policy documents such as the UK Foreign and Commonwealth Office (FCO)'s Principles for Global Action (UK FCO 2017) expressly include men and boys as victims and survivors. In the WPS architecture, the issue is reflected, to a degree, in UNSCR 2106, part of the

UK government's Preventing Sexual Violence Initiative (PSVI), including the declaration of the G8 Summit in April 2013 and at the PSVI Summit in London in 2014 (G8 2013; cf. Kirby 2015; Ward 2016).

One of the most obvious results of the lack of addressing men, boys, and masculinities in the WPS policy architecture is to implicitly or explicitly deny the possibility that men and boys may be victims, especially those considered to be "able-bodied" and of "fighting age," especially if they are clearly civilian and thus fall under international legal protective norms—and form a large part of direct civilian casualties (cf. Carpenter 2006). The inclusion of boys and men as potential victims of conflict-related SGBV is an important step in creating both the policy practical space for working on the issue, at least as far as male victims/survivors of this particular type of violence are concerned. However, merely adding men and boys to the list of potential victims of one type of violence is not enough to understand the gendered dynamics and implications of this, nor does it automatically mean adequate services will be provided—in particular when these services are already often woefully lacking for women and girl victims, despite having been on the WPS agenda as a supposed priority for much longer (cf. Kirby 2015: 470).

Progress thus has been slow on first recognizing SGBV against women and girls as a serious problem that needs to be addressed, and this was followed by the difficult process of recognizing men and boys as victims. The struggle to recognize other gender identities in this regard is on-going, and there is a continued lack of adequate funding for victims/survivors across the board, regardless of gender identity. This progress, however, has been far greater than on the side of addressing perpetration, where the patriarchal structures and norms that underpin SGBV and the problematic masculinities of the majority of perpetrators have only begun to be addressed by local-level actors (cf. Flood 2015; Myrttinen et al. 2014; Wright 2014).[5]

This points to a risk in shifting the focus of the Women, Peace, and Security agenda to one based on gender, peace, and security. We can see signs of this in the Global Study: Men and boys are added to the mantra-like litany of "women and girls," without reflecting on what that addition means in terms of actually engaging with the construction of masculinities and femininities, and their relationship to each other. The risk is that neither "adding women and stir" nor "adding men and stir" addresses the gendered inequalities and identities which reproduce violent conflict and vulnerabilities.

WHY ARE MEN INVISIBILIZED IN WOMEN, PEACE, AND SECURITY?

I tentatively propose five potential reasons to explain why men and boys remain invisiblized in the WPS architecture. The first is the history of WPS, which is closely linked to the second, which is the historical and continuing lack of serious attention paid to women and girls' very real needs and vulnerabilities in conflict affected situations. The historical trajectory of WPS can be traced at least back to the 1915 founding Women's Peace conference held at the Hague (see Tickner and True 2018), giving it an immensely rich and varied basis of experience, research, and theory to draw upon. The studies of men, boys, and masculinities in conflict and peace are of a much later provenance and are heavily indebted to the groundwork laid by feminist research and theory—indeed would not exist in their current state without it (see, for example, Connell 1995; and Hearn 1998). The WPS agenda continues to be driven, to a wholly different degree than is the case for men and boys, by the continued woeful disregard of women and girls' needs and vulnerabilities, their agency, and the lack of their possibilities of meaningful political, social, and economic participation in conflict-affected contexts.[6]

While the first two reasons are partly positive and ameliorative, the other three reasons I put forward are less so. The third reason, I argue, is a widespread lack of political will or even intellectual laziness among many peace-building actors to engage seriously with gender as a critical analytical tool with a radical, transformative potential (cf Wright 2018). Most actors seem unwilling to use gender analysis of power differentials, of identities, and of social, economic, and political convictions, let alone as a basis to critically question and transform these. This is especially the case when this might mean applying gender analysis to oneself and one's actions. It is always far easier to "do gender" onto others and demand that others, especially in the Global South or "the poor," need to go through radical transformations. Fourth, echoing Cynthia Enloe (2017) and Nadine Puechguirbal (2010), an approach to broadening the WPS agenda by uncritically "adding men and boys" without critically examining masculinities runs the risk of stabilizing and "updating" a patriarchal status quo rather than questioning it. This does not mean that there is a deliberate patriarchal plan to co-opt the WPS agenda, but rather that as a dynamic, deeply ingrained system of power and of making sense of the world, it requires a lot of conscious determination and energy to escape the pull of patriarchal systems—and most individuals and institutions are too enmeshed in it, both consciously and subconsciously, to do so.

Lastly, and fifth, the debate is also about setting the policy agenda and, more mundanely, providing access to resources. Rather than seeing a broadening of WPS to include masculinities and other gender identities as an enrichment, it has often come to be seen as a zero-sum game, where the focus on gender—and specifically men and boys—would mean a move away from the already paltry support given to women and girls' needs and a dilution of the WPS message, in particular if already meager funds for promoting women and girls' rights, supporting gender equality, or, for that matter, to provide support for women SGBV survivors are further cut to accommodate work with men and boys (Kirby 2015: 471; Ward 2016). Ideally, of course, this would not be the case, and the addressing of masculinities, and including men, boys, and other gender identities in a GPS, would bring with it an increase in the amount of resources available. However, given the already inadequate financial and political support available for this kind of work, this threat of diminishing support is a very real one.[7]

Conclusion

The UNSC resolutions that form the lattice of the WPS agenda do not, for the most part, explicitly mention men, boys, and masculinities, or the gender of perpetrators and peace-building actors, let alone the power they wield that has numerous negative consequences. Male perpetrators of various forms of violence and the often complex, gendered dynamics which underpin that violence remain unexamined and unchallenged—and therefore un-changed. Similarly, men's practices and attitudes which prevent increased women's social, political, and economic participation, and the gendered ideologies that underpin them, continue to be largely unchallenged at the global policy level, despite decades of feminist activism and feminist-inspired research. Furthermore, the patriarchal institutional cultures and structures of the UN, nation-states, and other international and national institutions remain similarly unquestioned. Also, the very real needs and vulnerabilities of men and boys, not to mention those with other gender identities, which go beyond the current im-portant but narrow focus of sexual violence in conflict, remain unaddressed. Lastly, women and girls remain conceptually relegated to "outlier" status and essentialized as either polit-ically powerless victims or innate peacemakers, while men, male-dominated institutions, and masculine-coded ways of "doing" peace and security remain unchallenged as the seem-ingly ungendered norm.

What is needed, in my mind, is a broadening of the WPS agenda to a GPS one that makes use of the small policy spaces that have opened up in terms of including men and boys, and thus masculinities, to not only address very real needs of men and boys (including but going beyond sexual violence in conflict). The politics of peace and security need to be critically re-examined by recognizing the gendered ways in which men and boys are al-ready present as agents for positive and negative change in situations of peace and conflict. Only by recognizing the impacts of dominant patriarchal and heteronormative norms,—expectations as well as ways of being and acting as men and women and as persons with other gender identities, can we together challenge social norms and behaviors that per-petuate violence and discrimination. This includes critically examining, challenging, and transforming the very institutions themselves who are directly tasked with building peace and providing security and the ways with which they try to achieve this.

Echoing comments made by Cynthia Enloe (2015), there are two ways of integrating masculinities into WPS work. One is easier, more comfortable, and more palatable, and stabilizes patriarchal power and gendered inequalities—this would be the approach of merely adding tokenistic language of men and giving disproportionate recognition to those men who embrace equality and peace. The other way is more radical and more transform-ative, and requires keeping the agenda uncomfortable for the powers that be and the gen-dered structures we inhabit and reproduce. It requires taking gender seriously as a starting point of critical analysis, of masculinities and femininities, including of ourselves.

NOTES

1. I use the term "WPS policy architecture" here to refer to the family of UNSCRs following on from UNSCR 1325 (2000)—1820 (2008), 1888 (2009), 1889 (2009), 1960 (2010), 2106 (2013), 2122 (2013), and 2242 (2015)—and related documents such as National Action Plans (NAPs) for implementing 1325 and 1820, regional protocols, declarations, and the like.
2. For the purpose of this chapter, I will focus mainly on the various UNSCR resolutions and directly related documents such as the UNSCR 1325 Global Study as the main framework of the WPS Agenda at the United Nations. Mapping the understandings of, as well as the usage of, the term "gender" by the multitude of actors who implement and use the WPS

agenda at local, national, and international levels is beyond the scope of this chapter, but there is a range of uses and understandings from what Cynthia Enloe refers to as "women and children" to more complex, intersectional, and relational understandings of gender (cf. El-Bushra 2012).

3. UNSCR 2016 states "[. . .] sexual violence in armed conflict and post-conflict situations disproportionately affects women and girls, as well as groups that are particularly vulnerable or may be specifically targeted, while also affecting men and boys and those secondarily traumatized as forced witnesses of sexual violence against family members [. . .]"

4. At the Global Study input workshop held in The Hague coinciding with the 100th anniversary of the Women's International League for Peace and Freedom (WILPF) in April 2015 which I attended as a participant, the word "masculinities" was added on at the behest of the participants, in ballpoint pen, to the printed agenda of items to be discussed just as the input session was about to start.

5. As Sjoberg (2016) reminds us, recognizing women as potential perpetrators of conflict-related SGBV has been its own complicated, slow-moving process.

6. While I highlight conflict-affected contexts here due to the WPS context, it should be noted that not a single country at peace currently is gender equal either.

7. Given very different (and often inaccurate) ways in which funding for WPS/GPS work or supporting gender equality is tracked by different donors, it is difficult to say whether or not this has materialized. Anecdotal evidence has been contradictory and different from one country context to the next as to whether there is indeed a shift of funds away from working on women and girls to working with men and boys instead, but on the whole, as also evidenced by the Global Study, gender work in general struggles with funding issues.

References

Cano Vinas, M. *Gender Audit of the Peace, Security and Cooperation Framework for the Democratic Republic of Congo and the Region.* London: International Alert, 2015.

Carpenter, R. C. "Recognizing Gender-Based Violence against Civilian Men and Boys in Conflict Situations." *Security Dialogue* 37, no. 1 (2006): 83–103. doi:10.1177/0967010606064139.

Charlesworth, H. "Transforming the United Men's Club: Feminist Futures for the United Nations." *Transnational Law and Contemporary Problems* 4 (1994): 421–454.

Conciliation Resources, International Alert, and Saferworld. *Peacebuilders' Reflections on Gender, Peace, and Security—Joint Submission to the Global Study on Women, Peace, and Security.* London: Conciliation Resources, International Alert, and Saferworld, 2015.

Connell, R. W. *Masculinities.* Cambridge, UK: Polity Press, 1995.

DCAF and International Alert. *Promoting Gender Equality through Security Sector Reform—DCAF and International Alert Contribution to the Global Study on Women, Peace, and Security.* Geneva/London: Geneva Center for the Democratic Control of Armed Forces and International Alert, 2015.

Debusscher, P., and M. Martin De Almagro. "Post-Conflict Women's Movements in Turmoil: The Challenges of Success in Liberia in the 2005-Aftermath." *Journal of Modern African Studies* 54, no. 2 (2016): 293–316.

Dolan, C. "Has Patriarchy Been Stealing the Feminists' Clothes? Conflict-Related Sexual Violence and UN Security Council Resolutions." *IDS Bulletin* 45, no. 1 (2014a): 80–84.

Dolan, C. "Letting Go of the Gender Binary: Charting New Pathways for Humanitarian Interventions on Gender-Based Violence." *International Review of the Red Cross* 96, no. 894 (2014b): 486–501.

Duriesmith, D. "Engaging Men and Boys in the Women, Peace and Security Agenda: Beyond the "Good Men" Industry". *LSE Women, Peace and Security Working Paper 11/2017*. London: LSE WPS Centre, 2017.

El-Bushra, J. *Gender in Peacebuilding: Taking Stock*. London: International Alert, 2012.

Enloe, C. 2015. Untitled presentation at the "Women: powerful agents for peace and security" conference, February 16–17, 2015, Amsterdam, Netherlands.

Enloe, C. 2017. "The Persistence of Patriarchy." *New Internationalist*, October 1, 2017.

Flood, M. "Work with Men to End Violence against Women: A Critical Stocktake." *Culture, Health & Sexuality* 17, no. 2 (2015): 159–176.

G8. "*G8 Declaration on Preventing Sexual Violence in Conflict*." Foreign & Commonwealth Office, April 11, 2013, https://www.gov.uk/government/uploads/system/uploads/attachment_data/file/185008/G8_PSVI_Declaration_-_FINAL.pdf.

Hagen, J. "Queering Women, Peace, and Security." *International Affairs* 92, no. 2 (2016): 313–332.

Hearn, Jeff. *The Violences of Men*. London: Sage, 1998.

ICC/OTP. "Policy Paper on Sexual and Gender-Based Crimes." The Hague: International Criminal Court/Office of the Prosecutor, 2014.

Inter-Agency Standing Committee. "Guidelines for Integrating Gender-Based Violence Interventions in Humanitarian Action." Geneva: Inter-Agency Standing Committee, 2015.

International Committee of the Red Cross. "Sexual Violence in Armed Conflict." *International Review of the Red Cross* 894 (2014).

Kirby, P. "Ending Sexual Violence in Conflict: The Preventing Sexual Violence Initiative and Its Critics." *International Affairs* 91, no. 3 (2015): 457–472.

Kirby, P., and L. Shepherd. "Reintroducing Women, Peace, and Security." *International Affairs* 92, no. 2 (2016): 249–254.

Myrttinen, H. "Stabilizing or Challenging Patriarchy? Sketches of Selected "New" Political Masculinities," *Men and Masculinities*, 1–19 (2018). doi:10.1177/1097184X18769137

Myrttinen, H., J. Naujoks, and J. El-Bushra. *Rethinking Gender in Peacebuilding*. London: International Alert, 2014.

Puechguirbal, N. "Discourses on Gender, Patriarchy, and Resolution 1325: A Textual Analysis of UN Documents." *International Peacekeeping* 17, no. 2 (2010): 172–187.

Sjoberg, Laura. *Women As Wartime Rapists—Beyond Sensation and Stereotyping*. New York: New York University Press, 2016.

Tickner, J. A., and J. True. "A Century of International Relations Feminism: From World War One Women's Peace Pragmatism to the Women, Peace, and Security Agenda." *International Studies Quarterly* 62 (2018).

UK FCO. *Principles For Global Action—Preventing and Addressing Stigma Associated with Conflict-Related Sexual Violence*. London: UK Foreign and Commonwealth Office Preventing Sexual Violence in Conflict Initiative, 2017.

United Nations High Commissioner for Refugees. *Working with Men and Boy Survivors of Sexual and Gender-Based Violence in Forced Displacement*. Geneva: United Nations High Commissioner for Refugees, 2012.

UN Women. "Preventing Conflict, Transforming Justice, Securing the Peace—A Global Study on the Implementation of United Nations Security Council Resolution 1325." UN Women, 2015, http://wps.unwomen.org/.

Vess, J., G. Barker, S. Naraghi-Anderlini, and A. Hassink. *The Other Side of Gender: Men as Critical Agents of Change*. Washington DC: United States Institute of Peace, 2013.

Ward, J. "It's Not about the Gender Binary, It's about the Gender Hierarchy: A Reply to 'Letting Go of the Gender Binary,'" *International Review of the Red Cross* 98, no. 1 (2016): 275–298. doi:10.1017/S1816383117000121.

Wright, H. *Masculinities, Conflict, and Peacebuilding: Perspectives on Men through a Gender Lens*. London: Saferworld, 2014.

Wright, H. "The Masculinities Turn: Reviving a Radical Women, Peace and Security Agenda?", Paper presented at the 7th Annual International Feminist Journal of Politics Conference, April 2–3, 2018, San Francisco, USA.

CHAPTER 9

....

WPS AND ADOPTED
SECURITY COUNCIL
RESOLUTIONS

....

LAURA J. SHEPHERD

A decade ago, the "Women, Peace, and Security agenda" did not exist. There was, of course, concerted effort from women's movements and civil society organizations to push to center stage the issues with which the Women, Peace, and Security (WPS) agenda is now concerned: the importance of listening to and valuing women's experience in conflict and post-conflict situations, for example, and the need to ensure that women are equally represented in the institutions of peace and security governance, including peace negotiation, peace-building activities, and peacekeeping. But these issues and concomitant demands for action did not cohere to form a specific and recognized "agenda" until relatively recently. Following the adoption in 2000 of the foundational resolution in the Women, Peace, and Security architecture, UN Security Council Resolution 1325, there were no further resolutions adopted under the title of "Women and peace and security" until 2008. So it certainly was not common to speak of a Women, Peace, and Security agenda until at least 2008, when the second resolution was adopted, Resolution 1820. After 2008, as more resolutions under the thematic title of Women and peace and security were adopted at the UN Security Council, feminist scholars and activists began to debate not only the content of the resolutions but what that content meant for the contours and priorities of the emergent WPS agenda.

In this chapter, I draw out some of the key themes of the adopted resolutions, and develop two core arguments. The first argument I seek to make is that the WPS resolutions have been inconsistent in their presentation of key thematic priorities and issue areas, with emphasis being afforded to different priorities at different times. Broadly what we see at this stage (at the time of writing) is the division of the agenda into primarily protection-related activities and advocacy on the one hand, and primarily participation-related activities and advocacy on the other. Second, and relatedly, I argue that, with the most recent adoption of Resolution 2242, it is possible to identify a critical political juncture in the development of the WPS agenda, which has potentially profound implications for future activities and advocacy in this space.

Mapping the Women, Peace, and Security agenda

In this section, I analyze the formation of the WPS agenda and explore its provisions and principles through a discussion of the adopted resolutions. The key priorities of each resolution are summarized in Table 9.1.

The foundational WPS resolution is comprehensive in its coverage of both the issues that women face in conflict and post-conflict situations and the gendered dynamics of peace and security.[1] The articulation of priorities and principles in Resolution 1325 is widely described as creating three (sometimes four) "pillars" of WPS activity: the *protection* of women's rights and bodies particularly in conflict situations; the *prevention* of violence, specifically, but importantly not limited to, conflict-related sexualized violence (a point to which I return later); and the *participation* of women in all forms of peace and security governance and

Table 9.1 Summary of Key Priorities of Each WPS Resolution

Resolution (Year)	Key issues and core provisions
UNSCR 1325 (2000)	Representation and participation of women in peace and security governance; protection of women's rights and bodies in conflict & post-conflict situations.
UNSCR 1820 (2008)	Protection of women from sexualized violence in conflict; zero tolerance of sexualized abuse and exploitation perpetrated by UN Department of Peacekeeping Operations personnel.
UNSCR 1888 (2009)	Creation of office of Special Representative of the Secretary-General on Conflict-Related Sexual Violence (CRSV); creation of UN Action as an umbrella organization addressing issues related to CRSV; identification of "team of experts"; appointment of Women's Protection Advisors (WPAs) to field missions.
UNSCR 1889 (2009)	Need to increase participation of women in peace and security governance at all levels; creation of global indicators to map implementation of UNSCR 1325.
UNSCR 1960 (2010)	Development of CRSV monitoring, analysis, and reporting arrangements; integration of WPAs to field missions alongside Gender Advisors.
UNSCR 2106 (2013)	Challenging impunity and lack of accountability for CRSV.
UNSCR 2122 (2013)	Identifies UN Women as key UN entity providing information and advice on participation of women in peace and security governance; whole-of-UN accountability; civil society inclusion; 2015 high-level review of implementation of UNSCR 1325.
UNSCR 2242 (2015)	Integrates WPS in all UNSC country situations; establishes Informal Experts Group on WPS; adds WPS considerations to sanctions committee deliberations; links WPS to countering terrorism and violent extremism (CT/CVE).

Source: Kirby and Shepherd (2016a: 251).

decision-making. The fourth pillar relates to *relief and recovery* in post-conflict and conflict-affected environments, but I do not engage with that pillar here as it is much less prevalent in discussions about the adopted resolutions (see chapter 15 in this volume).

The division of the WPS agenda into these pillars is an heuristic device, one that bears close resemblance not only to the ways in which priority is afforded to certain issues in practice but also the organization of the WPS policy architecture. In my view, there have been two "agenda-setting" resolutions (UNSCR 1325 and UNSCR 2242), two "participation" resolutions (UNSCR 1889 and UNSCR 2122), and four "protection" resolutions (UNSCR 1820, UNSCR 1888, UNSCR 1960, and UNSCR 2106). "Prevention" is articulated inconsistently across the suite of WPS resolutions, hence Soumita Basu and Catia Confortini's (2017) claim that it is the "weakest 'p' in the pod," is an argument I find wholly plausible.

The "agenda-setting" text of Resolution 1325 performs a number of significant functions in the germination of the WPS agenda that was to develop from this hard-fought resolution (see chapter 4 in this volume). First, it locates the WPS agenda squarely under the auspices of the UN Security Council, through its preambular statement that reaffirms "the primary responsibility of the Security Council under the Charter for the maintenance of international peace and security" (UN Security Council 2000, Preamble).[2]

Second, the resolution attempts to balance protection and participation. While the protection of women is given priority in the text, this prioritization is alongside the infantilization of women through their association with children such that it states "civilians, particularly women and children, account for the vast majority of those adversely affected by armed conflict" (see UN Security Council 2000, Preamble). The first operative paragraph of the resolution also prioritizes participation in the Council as it "*[U]rges* Member States to ensure increased representation of women at all decision-making levels in national, regional and international institutions and mechanisms for the prevention, management, and resolution of conflict" (see UN Security Council 2000, para. 1, emphasis in original). This illustrates the tension in the WPS from the very beginning, regarding the desired focal point of activities and advocacy.

Third, and relatedly, the foundational resolution commits member states to the recognition of women's roles in violence prevention with the Council "*[R]eaffirming* the important role of women in the prevention and resolution of conflicts and in peace-building" (UN Security Council 2000, Preamble). This is potentially deeply subversive, given the feminist and anti-militarist politics of the organizations involved in lobbying around the WPS agenda from the outset. Relatedly, prevention has received less attention than protection and participation in subsequent years (discussed in the following). In the remainder of this section, I explore the constitution of participation, protection, and violence prevention in the architecture of the WPS agenda.

Participation

In Resolution 1325, participation is emphasized in the Preamble, which references "the importance" of women's "equal participation and full involvement in all efforts for the maintenance and promotion of peace and security" (UN Security Council 2000, Preamble). Participation is "important" because of the "role" women play "in the prevention and resolution of conflicts and in peace-building" (UN Security Council 2000, Preamble). As I have written elsewhere, there is certain essentialism at work here, which ascribes to women, by virtue of their femininity, superpowers when it comes to the "maintenance and promotion of peace and security" (UN Security Council 2000, Preamble; see Shepherd 2011).

In Resolution 1325 (and the same is true in Resolution 1820), participation is not afforded the same textual priority as protection in the Preamble, which means that protection still appears first (see UN Security Council 2000, Preamble; UN Security Council 2008, Preamble). However, the first two operative paragraphs relate explicitly to representation and the "participation of women at decision-making levels in conflict resolution and peace processes" (UN Security Council 2000, para. 2). Women's participation is articulated as an element of the Secretary-General's "strategic plan," lending the normative argument a certain technical and procedural credibility. This is reinforced in Resolution 1820, which includes a strong statement (although again only in the Preamble) about

> the persistent obstacles and challenges to women's participation and full involvement in the prevention and resolution of conflicts as a result of violence, intimidation and discrimination, which erode women's capacity and legitimacy to participate in post-conflict public life, and . . . the negative impact this has on durable peace, security and reconciliation, including post-conflict peacebuilding (UN Security Council 2008, Preamble).

Here, "durable peace, security and reconciliation," priorities whose significance would be hard to dispute, are put at risk by the "obstacles and challenges to women's participation." The articulation of "obstacles and challenges" positions inhibitors outside of the women themselves—it is not a capacity or capability deficit but a structural impediment (or series of structural impediments, actually) that is having a negative effect on "durable peace, security and reconciliation." Similar to the articulation in Resolution 1325 of the "strategic priority" of women's participation, this configuration locates both the solution and the problem as external to women themselves, who can then retain their status as peaceful superheroines *extraordinaire*.

Participation is represented as "equal and full" in the first three adopted resolutions (see also UN Security Council 2009a, Preamble; participation is only mentioned once in Resolution 1888). The duality of this construction intrigues me. The motif of equality has been deconstructed by many feminist scholars, who argue that gender equality is too often conceived in narrow and binary terms, such as manifesting in the "balance" between women and men. Further, to modify "full" with "equal" creates an interesting tension given that "equal" has textual priority, and it limits the fullness of "full participation." This construction changes in Resolution 1889 which introduces a requirement for participation to be "full, equal and *effective*" (UN Security Council 2009b, Preamble, emphasis added). Resolution 1889 has been classified as a "participation" resolution and it certainly has a strong participation theme. The resolution opens with extensive Preambular material positioning participation. The first operation paragraph "*[U]rges* Member States, international and regional organisations to take further measures to improve women's participation during all stages of peace processes, particularly in conflict resolution, post-conflict planning and peacebuilding" (UN Security Council 2009b, para. 1, emphasis in original). Articulating participation as a comprehensive requirement across peace and security governance activities (expressed as "all stages of peace processes") constructs participation not as a gift or chimera but as an integral component of effective governance.

Resolution 2106, in line with Resolution 1889, also represents a requirement for participation to be "effective" which is interesting (UN Security Council 2013a, para. 16). In the next adopted resolution, Resolution 2122, "equal" has fallen out of the configuration completely, leaving instead a series of statements about "women's empowerment, participation, and human rights" from the Preamble through to the operative paragraphs (UN Security Council 2013b, Preamble, para. 1, 4, 7, 7b, 7c, 8, and 14). The only modifier to "full" is "meaningful," which is enabling rather than limiting.

By way of a brief aside, the story and language of Resolution 2122 are both particularly interesting. The adoption of Resolution 2106 brought the total number of protection resolutions to four, with just one "participation" resolution (Resolution 1889). During the period between June (when Resolution 2106 was adopted) and October (marking the adoption of Resolution 2122), anecdotal accounts report frantic mobilization of civil society organizations in a concerted advocacy campaign aimed at generating support for a second WPS resolution in 2013. These mobilizations were taking place in an environment marked by a distinct lack of appetite for the proliferation of resolutions and one in which the United States—a powerful member of the UN Security Council and one which happens to be penholder on resolutions related to sexual violence in conflict—might perceive a second resolution as a challenge or slight to the earlier adoption of Resolution 2106. I have also heard tales of texts negotiated at unusual speed, and efforts made by states supportive of the WPS agenda to influence diplomats and missions represented on the Council in the hope that the wisdom of a second resolution would be received.[3] "Participation" is certainly a prominent focus of Resolution 2122 with the first operation paragraph committing the Council itself "to focus more attention on women's leadership and participation in conflict resolution and peacebuilding" (UN Security Council 2013b, para. 1). In Resolution 2242, the most recent of the WPS resolutions, "leadership" is prominently related to participation (UN Security Council 2015, para. 13), and participation is again articulated with "effective" and "meaningful" (UN Security Council 2015, para. 1).

Protection

Turning now to the constitution of protection, beyond its representation in the Preambular material, "protection" is afforded textual priority over rights in Resolution 1325, which is interesting. For example, paragraph 6 refers to the "protection, rights and the particular needs of women" (UN Security Council 2000, para. 6). This configuration is subverted a few paragraphs later, however, as the resolution calls for "[M]easures that ensure the protection of and respect for human rights of women and girls" (UN Security Council 2000, para. 8c). Here it is the rights rather than the bodies of women *per se* that are deserving or in need of protection. The final mention of protection in the foundational resolution again reverses the logic, calling on "all parties to armed conflict to respect fully international law applicable to the rights and protection of women and girls" (UN Security Council 2000, para. 9).

Resolution 1820, the second adopted resolution, explicitly links protection to sexual violence, in a discursive move that has been highly influential in determining the parameters of the WPS agenda. Broader issues of women's rights are simply not represented in this resolution. The articulations of rights in the text relate to international human rights law (UN Security Council 2008, Preamble), the UN Convention on the Rights of the Child

(UN Security Council 2008, Preamble), and the primary obligation of states to respect and protect the human rights of their citizens (UN Security Council 2008, Preamble). It is also noteworthy not only that there is no association forged between women and rights in this second, long-awaited, eagerly anticipated resolution, but also that every reference to rights appears in the Preambular material. The substance of the resolution makes no mention of rights at all. "Violence," by contrast, appears forty times, and thirty-three of these representations modify "violence" with the prefix "sexual." The kind of violence from which women require protection, therefore, is sexual violence. Even in those textual articulations of violence that are not prefixed with sexual, the modification is still manifest, as in the Preamble which condemns "violence against women and children in situations of armed conflict, including sexual violence in situations of armed conflict" (UN Security Council 2008, Preamble; see also para. 10, which articulates a need for "protection from violence, including in particular sexual violence"), and similarly where "other forms of violence against civilians" are appended to the primary object of sexual violence (UN Security Council 2008, para. 6).

Resolution 1820 set the nascent WPS agenda on a particular trajectory in its powerful articulation of protection in—and only in—relation to women's bodies and specifically those bodies violated in sexual and gender-based attacks. Resolution 1888 continues the development of the protection pillar along similar lines, calling for: "[s]pecific provisions, as appropriate, for the protection of women and children from rape and other sexual violence in the mandates of United Nations peacekeeping operations including, on a case-by-case basis, the identification of women's protection advisers" (UN Security Council 2009a, para. 12). The discursive association between protection and sexual violence is reinforced in Resolution 1888. Again a close reading of the resolution demonstrates that general rights protection is relegated to the Preamble of the resolution while the operative paragraphs include protection language specific to women only in relation to the violated bodies of women. The resolution does mention "witness protection" in para. 9, but in response to the deployment of "a team of experts to situations of particular concern with respect to sexual violence in armed conflict," thus determining the context of protection again as a product of its association with sexual violence (UN Security Council 2009a, para. 9).

The heavy emphasis put on the protection of women's bodies rather than their rights in conflict and post-conflict environments in the two resolutions subsequent to Resolution 1325 had a significant impact on the formation of the WPS agenda. The effect of these next two resolutions' focus on protection rather than participation or prevention should not be underestimated either. Resolution 1889 can be read as an attempt to redress the emergent imbalance between the pillars given its prevalent participation focus as discussed earlier. While the resolution offers a particular construction of protection, it is a construction at odds with the association of protection with sexual violence offered in Resolutions 1820 and 1888. The construction of protection in these resolutions relies on a female subject who is both violated and passive. Resolution 1889 opens with a Preambular statement that challenges this construction immediately, "*stressing* the need to focus not only on protection of women but also on their empowerment in peacebuilding" (UN Security Council 2009b, Preamble). The Preamble further associates protection explicitly with participation. Moreover, it associates the participation of women with the creation and durability of peace: "*Recognizing* that . . . adequate and rapid response to their particular needs, and effective institutional arrangements to guarantee [women and girls'] protection and full participation in the peace process, particularly at early stages of post-conflict peacebuilding, can significantly contribute to the maintenance and promotion of international peace and security" (UN Security Council 2009b, Preamble, emphasis in original).

As noted, however, the Preambular material is not necessarily significant in the context of a UN Security Council resolution. Resolution 1889, though, continues to reorient protection away from women's bodies and toward their rights in the operative paragraphs. The second paragraph—affording this construction significant textual priority—calls for parties to conflict to respect "international law applicable to the rights and protection of women and girls" (UN Security Council 2009b, para. 2; the first paragraph of the resolution focuses on participation as outlined previously). Even "women protection advisors" are textually subordinate to "gender advisors" (UN Security Council 2009b, para. 7). There is only one articulation of protection with sexual violence and the way that this is configured in the text diminishes much of the power of the articulation in the previous resolution. Resolution 1889 asks all parties to conflict to "ensure the protection of all civilians inhabiting such camps, in particular women and girls, from all forms of violence, including rape and other sexual violence" (UN Security Council 2009b, para. 12). Here, "all forms of violence" is the dominant representation of violence with "rape and other sexual violence" appended as subordinate.

Although it is widely held to be a "protection" resolution (it is certainly not, as noted earlier, a "participation" resolution), Resolution 1960 is actually a sexual violence resolution. This is evident in simple numerical terms: the word "protection" appears six times in the text of the resolution (notably only once in the body of the resolution itself and only then in the context of the phrase "women protection advisors"; see UN Security Council 2010, para. 10). In comparison, the phrase "sexual violence" appears forty-five times. The construction of protection in this resolution relates primarily to the protection of civilians, with "women and girls" constituted as a subcategory of civilians deserving of "special protection due to the fact that they can be placed particularly at risk" (UN Security Council 2010, Preamble). The particular form of violence from which civilians (and, by association, "women and girls") require protection is articulated in the Preamble, which stresses the importance of "protection of civilians, including the prevention of and response to instances of sexual violence in armed conflict" (UN Security Council 2010, Preamble). This is reinforced in the early operative paragraphs that describe at length the Council's recognition of the problem of sexual violence and its desire to see better data collected and reported in order to inform better responses.

Resolution 2106 (re)produces very similar logics to those that organize Resolution 1960, down to oddly similar numerical representations. Resolution 2106 also has six mentions of protection, but has forty-seven rather than forty-five mentions of sexual violence. Again, the first textual articulation of protection is in the Preamble and relates to "protection of civilians" (UN Security Council 2013a, Preamble). By contrast to Resolution 1960, however, Resolution 2106 "stresses women's participation as essential to any prevention and protection response" in the first operative paragraph (UN Security Council 2013a). This association between protection and participation relates to but is distinct from the representation of protection in Resolution 1889 discussed earlier. Although protection is still articulated in terms of bodies rather than rights, women's agency—and the ways in which it might be violently curtailed—remains in view in this particular representation of protection. The discursive construction of protection achievements as a result of women's participation in peace and security governance is shown both in the inclusion of women in the formation of "prevention and protection" responses, and in the recognition of the "important roles that civil society organizations, including women's organizations, and networks can play in enhancing community-level protection against sexual violence in armed conflict and post-conflict situations" (UN Security Council 2013a, para. 21).

In Resolution 2122, the Council:

> [E]xpresses its intention to include provisions to facilitate women's full participation and protection in: election preparation and political processes, disarmament, demobilization and reintegration programs, security sector and judicial reforms, and wider post-conflict reconstruction processes where these are mandated tasks within the mission (UN Security Council 2013b, para. 4, emphasis in original).

Protection is firmly affixed to participation here and elsewhere in this resolution. The Preamble, in fact, produces a governing statement related to the whole of the WPS agenda where it comments on "the implementation of resolution 1325 (2000) and subsequent resolutions to advance women's participation and protection" (UN Security Council 2013b, Preamble). In doing so, Resolution 2122 solidifies the association between participation and protection, as well as the centrality of this association to the WPS agenda. Interestingly, there is only a single reference to protection in the most recent resolution, Resolution 2242 (2015). The meaning of this articulation is profoundly ambivalent: the resolution comments on "the importance of integrating gender considerations across humanitarian programming by seeking to ensure the provision of access to protection and the full range of medical, legal, and psychosocial and livelihood services, without discrimination" (UN Security Council 2015, para. 16). It specifies neither protection from what, nor protection for whom.

Prevention

Finally, I want to examine prevention, the "weakest 'p' in the pod" (Basu and Confortini 2017). In Resolution 1325, "prevention" is firmly articulated with conflict. It appears three times and in each representation is associated with conflict either directly (as in the phrase "conflict prevention"; see UN Security Council 2000, Preamble) or indirectly (as in the phrase "prevention, management, and resolution of conflict"; see UN Security Council 2000, para. 1). This articulation is reproduced in a number of resolutions. For example, Resolution 1820 mentions "prevention and resolution" of conflict four times (UN Security Council 2008, Preamble, para. 12), while the Preambular material of Resolution 1889 reproduces the articulation of conflict prevention and conflict resolution three times (UN Security Council 2009b, Preamble). In Resolution 1888, however, the type of violence with which the agenda is concerned is narrowed down and specified as sexual violence (UN Security Council 2009a, para. 12).This articulation is reinforced in both Resolutions 1960 (UN Security Council 2010, Preamble) and 2106 (UN Security Council 2013a, Preamble). A tension emerges, therefore, between the broad remit of violence prevention in one set of adopted resolutions, and a narrow focus on preventing sexual violence in conflict in another sequence of resolutions.

As we might expect, given the unique circumstances surrounding the adoption of Resolution 2122, adopted as it was on the back of the adoption of Resolution 2106 and—as legend has it, at least—in something of a hurry, the prevention language in Resolution 2122 confounds this tension, representing prevention both in relation to conflict/conflict resolution and sexual violence. Resolution 2122 actually features the most frequent and comprehensive representations of prevention, more so even than the most recent adopted resolution (which takes an interesting turn vis-à-vis prevention, as I discuss in what follows). Although the Preambular material links prevention to sexual violence (in comments on the "monitoring, prevention and prosecution of violence against women in armed conflict and post-conflict situations"; see UN Security Council 2013b, Preamble), this is one of only two such representations in the resolution. The resolution constructs an association between prevention and conflict through repeated articulation (UN Security Council 2013b, Preamble, paras 2, 7, 15).

The final point I would make in relation to Resolution 2122 is the way in which prevention is linked not only to conflict but also to women's agency. The resolution requests of the Secretary-General that they report to the Council "on progress in inviting women to participate, including through consultations with civil society, including women's organizations, in discussions pertinent to the prevention and resolution of conflict, the maintenance of peace and security and post-conflict peacebuilding" (UN Security Council 2013b, para. 2). The value afforded to women's participation in these activities is significant not only through textual placement (in the second operative paragraph of the resolution) but also through the positioning of the request to the Secretary-General himself (thus far, sadly, the Secretary-General has always been a "he"). This valuing is reinforced later in the resolution when the Council "*recognizes* with concern that without a significant implementation shift, women and women's perspectives will continue to be underrepresented in conflict prevention, resolution, protection and peacebuilding for the foreseeable future" (UN Security Council 2013b, para. 15, emphasis in original). This articulation presupposes that the representation of women in conflict prevention is valuable (given that the Council notes "with concern" the possibility of underrepresentation). It constructs women as important political actors with responsibilities in all spheres of peace and security governance—including the prevention of violence.

Interestingly, in Resolution 2242 there is a shift from the articulation of women as agents of violence prevention to the articulation of gender equality and women's empowerment as a precondition for effective violence prevention: "women's and girls' empowerment and gender equality are critical to conflict prevention and broader efforts to maintain international peace and security" (UN Security Council 2015, Preamble). In the context of the discursive formation of the adopted resolutions as a whole, this equates or at least associates women's empowerment with gender equality and further links empowerment/equality to effective conflict prevention. This seems in line with Cora Weiss's oft-quoted idea that the purpose of the WPS agenda should not be to "make war safe for women" but rather to "abolish war" (Weiss 2011). Resolution 2224 seems to suggest that "international peace and security"—perhaps extending to the abolition of war—can be achieved through the participation of women, founded on principles of gender equality. The resolution reinforces, for example, the importance of women's representation "at all decision-making levels in national, regional and international institutions and mechanisms for the prevention, and resolution of conflict" (UN Security Council 2015, para. 1) in the first (very substantial) operative paragraph.

There is, however, a new articulation of prevention in this most recent resolution that is of some significance: the prevention of terrorism and violent extremism. Resolution 2242 "[C]alls for the greater integration by Member States and the United Nations of their agendas on women, peace and security, counter-terrorism and countering-violent extremism which can be conducive to terrorism" (UN Security Council 2015, para. 11, emphasis in original). Just as women's participation is articulated as critical to effective conflict prevention, in this most recent resolution the participation of women is positioned as "core" to UN efforts in this space. The resolution recommends that the forthcoming Secretary-General's *Plan of Action to Prevent Violent Extremism* should "integrate women's participation, leadership and empowerment as core to the United Nation's strategy and responses" in the field of terrorism and violent extremism (UN Security Council 2015, para. 13). This articulation changes the nature of prevention as it has been constituted thus far in the adopted resolutions.

Where to from here? Fractured Futures of Women, Peace, and Security

Staying faithful to the textual composition of the WPS agenda (though always attuned to the multiple ways in which these texts are interpreted and translated into practice in local, national, regional, and international contexts), in this final section I turn briefly to the futures of WPS, as constituted in the most recent resolution, Resolution 2242.[4] As just noted, both participation and prevention take on new inflections in the most recent WPS resolution. In addition to the alignment of the WPS agenda with efforts to counter terrorism and violent extremism across the UN system and within member states, there are other dimensions of Resolution 2242 that represent new possible futures for the WPS agenda. These dimensions include "the engagement by men and boys as partners in promoting women's participation in the prevention and resolution of armed conflict, peacebuilding and post-conflict situations" (UN Security Council 2015, Preamble), and the integration of WPS priorities and principles across all areas of the Council's work (although this should be read in the light of Christine Chinkin's analysis in chapter 3 where she argues that the WPS thematic agenda is rarely taken up in the resolutions with specific conflict mandates). The Council suggests that this can be facilitated through the formation of an Informal Experts Group on Women, Peace, and Security (UN Security Council 2015, para. 5a), the integration of WPS considerations in work on country settings (UN Security Council 2015, para. 5b), and through the granting of an audience to civil society organizations or representatives so that they might brief the Council "in country-specific considerations and relevant thematic areas" (UN Security Council 2015, para. 5c).

I choose to end here, as it brings my analysis full circle, back to the women and allies who agitated for the Security Council to listen to and acknowledge their expertise on matters of peace and security in the late 1990s. They are the civil society organizers who were the progenitors of the WPS agenda. The agenda is, as discussed here, manifested in but not wholly captured by the adopted resolutions. The activism, advocacy, and associated practices of state and non-state actors alike are integral to the consideration of the WPS agenda (see chapters 33 and 34 in this volume). But the resolutions—the most recent of which marginally brings the importance of civil society knowledge and authority back into focus—are the architecture through which the WPS agenda is embedded across the UN system. They inform the implementation of the agenda at the national level. As such, they are deserving of our analytical consideration.

Notes

1. As I have argued elsewhere, however, the overall perception of women in peace and security that is created and perpetuated in Resolution 1325 is the idea of *women-in-need-of-protection*, an issue to which I return in the text; see Shepherd (2008; 2011).
2. The distinction between Preambular statements and operative paragraphs is significant. The introductory remarks in the Preamble to a resolution often include the language that state negotiators have not been able or willing to include in the operative paragraphs, which are the actionable content of the resolution and which therefore has much greater political significance.
3. These anecdotes were relayed to me during a field trip to New York for an unrelated project, in informal conversations with various research participants.
4. For a more comprehensive overview, please see Kirby and Shepherd (2016b).

References

Basu, S., and Confortini, C. "Weakest 'P' in the 1325 Pod? Realizing Conflict Prevention through Security Council Resolution 1325." *International Studies Perspectives* 18, no. 1 (2017): 43–63.

Kirby, P., and Shepherd, L. J. "Reintroducing Women, Peace, and Security." *International Affairs* 92, no. 2 (2016a): 249–254.

Kirby, P., and Shepherd, L. J. "The Futures Past of the Women, Peace, and Security Agenda." *International Affairs* 92, no. 2 (2016b): 373–392.

Shepherd, L. J. *Gender, Violence, and Security: Discourse as Practice.* London, Zed Books, 2008.

Shepherd, L. J. "Sex, Security, and Superhero(in)es: From 1325 to 1820 and Beyond." *International Feminist Journal of Politics* 13, no. 2 (2011): 504–521.

UN Security Council. Resolution 1325 (2000). S/RES/1325, 2000, http://www.un.org/en/sc/documents/resolutions/2000.shtml.

UN Security Council. Resolution 1820 (2008). S/RES/1820, 2008, http://www.un.org/en/sc/documents/resolutions/2008.shtml.

UN Security Council. Resolution 1888 (2009a). S/RES/1888, 2009a, http://www.un.org/en/ga/search/view_doc.asp?symbol=S/RES/1888(2009).

UN Security Council. Resolution 1889 (2009b). S/RES/1889, 2009b, http://www.un.org/en/ga/search/view_doc.asp?symbol=S/RES/1889(2009).

UN Security Council. Resolution 1960 (2010). S/RES/1960, 2010, http://www.un.org/en/sc/documents/resolutions/2010.shtml.

UN Security Council. Resolution 2106 (2013). S/RES/2106, 2013a, http://www.un.org/en/ga/search/view_doc.asp?symbol=S/RES/2106(2013).

UN Security Council. Resolution 2122 (2013). S/RES/2122, 2013b, http://www.un.org/en/ga/search/view_doc.asp?symbol=S/RES/2122(2013).

UN Security Council. Resolution 2242 (2015). S/RES/2242, 2015, http://www.un.org/en/sc/documents/resolutions/2015.shtml.

Weiss, C. "We Must Not Make War Safe for Women." *50:50 Inclusive Democracy*, 2011, https://www.opendemocracy.net/5050/cora-weiss/we-must-not-make-war-safe-for-women.

CHAPTER 10

WPS AND GENDER MAINSTREAMING

KARIN LANDGREN

RESOLUTION 1325 AND UNITED NATIONS PEACE OPERATIONS

CONSIDERATION of gender perspectives at all stages of peace processes is a hallmark of UN Security Council Resolution 1325, the landmark resolution that changed the way the United Nations Secretariat and the Security Council think about peace operations. In a 2005 statement, the Security Council "stressed the importance of bringing gender perspectives to the centre of all United Nations efforts related to peace and security."[1] Since the adoption of Resolution 1325 in 2000, the UN Security Council has shown considerable dedication to discussing Women, Peace, and Security (WPS). Related references in the mandates given to UN peace operations have also grown. The Council has applied its attention unevenly, however, both to the different facets of Resolution 1325 and to the practice of UN peace operations in implementation and reporting.

The work UN peace operations are assigned is complex to begin with. The UN Security Council normally mandates every operation with dozens of major tasks. Resolution 1325 and subsequent WPS resolutions have added to this complexity in three ways: first, in terms of addressing sexual violence against women in conflict settings; second, in insisting on women's representation in peace processes and in the UN; and third, in understanding the differentiated needs and perspectives of men and women in the work of UN peacekeeping and peace-building. This chapter focuses on institutional gender perspectives and their mainstreaming in UN peace missions, and sets out four principal recommendations at the end. These areas of work require targeted investment if the full aims of Resolution 1325 and subsequent resolutions are to be fulfilled.

MANDATE COMPLEXITY

Using the gender mainstreaming logic of Resolution 1325, a peace operation should develop its strategy and tasking by taking gendered aspects into account.[2] UN peace mission mandates are problematic in their ambitious complexity (United Nations 2015a: 182), featuring tasks or components that can number upwards of two dozen. Weighty mandates are rarely superfluous: all the assigned tasks are usually central to peace and participatory democracy. Their development has, on the whole, been too perfunctory, however. Mandating should follow a discerning case-by-case, mission-by-mission examination of what an operation can reasonably expect to deliver in a challenging political, security, and reform context. Building on a coherent political strategy, the UN can seek to prioritize and stagger the work as well as bring on board locally represented UN agencies, funds, and programs to a greater extent than at present. It goes without saying that the implementation of mandates may be compromised by difficult political contexts and insecure operating environments.

RESOLUTION 1325's COMPLEXITY

Adding to the problem of mandate complexity, the distinct elements within Resolution 1325 are insufficiently teased apart by the UN Security Council (SCR Cross-Cutting Report 2010). Christine Bell has proposed a "layered" set of components for gender in peace agreements. I find them applicable *mutatis mutandis* to assessing gender in the work of peace operations, namely:

(a) the inclusion of women in peace process negotiations, and support to women to participate effectively;
(b) the inclusion of provisions designed to address the particular needs of women;
(c) an assessment of the implications for women and men of any provision in the peace agreement, including provision for legislation, policies, or programs in any area and at all levels, with a view to ensuring that men and women benefit equally, and inequality is not perpetuated (Bell 2015).

Women's participation in peace agreements has grown steadily since 2000 (see chapters 12 and 13 in this volume). The mere presence of women is no guarantee that the UN has integrated a gender perspective, however.

Mandate provisions addressing the particular needs of women have most often pertained to protection, especially from sexual and gender-based violence (SGBV) (see, for example, SCR 1888 (2008), and 1960 (2010)), extending the United Nations Mission in Liberia). The Security Council has devoted commendable attention to SGBV, and until October 2013, all its resolutions pertaining to Resolution 1325 were protection-focused. This should not become the sole proxy for the "four Ps" of Resolution 1325 (prevention, participation, protection, and peace-building or relief and recovery; see part II of this handbook). The issues are too easily conflated, especially as the case for women's participation is frequently still argued on the basis of women as victims of conflict, rather than as a matter of their right to inclusion (United Nations 2015b: 86). What remains weakest in practice, speaking from my experience of leading UN peace missions in the aftermath of conflict, is assessment of the differentiated implications for women and for men of the legal, policy, structural, and programmatic actions supported by UN field operations.

The United Nations Mission in Liberia (UNMIL) has had a solid record in mainstreaming Resolution 1325 since its establishment in 2003 (see UN Security Council Resolution 1509). This is fitting: Liberian women had publicly pressured President Charles Taylor and the Accra Peace Agreement negotiators to end the country's long-running war, and the 2003 Accra Peace Agreement stipulated that all elective and non-elective positions were to reflect gender balance. In 2011, the Women's Situation Room was founded in Liberia with the primary aim of keeping elections peaceful (United Nations 2015b: 202). Female leadership was also visible through Ellen Johnson Sirleaf, a two-term president who took office in 2006, and two successive Special Representatives of the Secretary-General from 2008 to 2015.

UNMIL demonstrated good examples of engagement with women in order to understand and incorporate their perspectives in its work. In its intensive support to the Liberian constitutional review process, UNMIL assisted a dedicated consultation process with women in different parts of the country. Subsequently, women were strongly represented at the first constitutional review conference in April 2015. In responding to Liberia's Ebola crisis in 2014, UNMIL drew on its uniquely strong local presence compared to other international partners. UNMIL also supported information, practical engagement, and defused conflict through engagement with local communities, including with women. The Ebola epidemic in Liberia had gendered aspects, such as in the preponderance of female caregivers among the afflicted, and the high-risk environment of obstetrics for both mothers and midwives (see also Davies and Bennett 2016). A few months into the crisis UNMIL and its integrated Human Rights component began an internal Ebola Rights Watch initiative drawing attention to these and other gendered aspects of Ebola, including livelihood implications for market women of Ebola-related border closures. In 2014, the Secretary-General's reporting on gender in the work of UNMIL was independently assessed as "robust" (Security Council Report 2014).

ENGAGED LISTENING TO WOMEN AND CONNECTING WITH COMMUNITIES

"Sit on the ground and talk to people. That's the most important thing." — Dag Hammarskjöld [3]

Among the reasons UNMIL has been comparatively successful in integrating gendered considerations are the community links fostered through the fifteen UNMIL field offices that were maintained for most of its tenure. Many were in remote county capitals. Overall, the UN has become better at listening to communities. By the mid-1990s, the Office of the United Nations High Commissioner for Refugees (UNHCR) had understood that technically impeccable designs—for refugee camp layout, lighting, latrines, and distribution of ID cards—nonetheless created serious protection problems for women and children. Good technical solutions had ignored disastrous social consequences. For instance, even the size of water jugs was revisited. A large container appeared efficient, but if most women and girls were unable to carry it without male support, sexual exploitation was all but inevitable.

These issues, which now seem self-evident, were a breakthrough in the delivery of humanitarian assistance along with the legendary *Do No Harm* used by UNHCR as a staff training tool (see Anderson et al. 2012). While many United Nations peace operations already work closely with local populations and communities, a contextualized understanding of how societies think and act is yet to become the norm in the UN's peacekeeping and political arenas (United Nations 2015a: 165). Security concerns and local politics represent the most formidable barriers to stronger channels of direct community engagement, and in this respect UNMIL has been unusually privileged. Liberia remained largely peaceful during UNMIL's tenure (2003 to 2018). UNMIL was widely appreciated and trusted by the Liberian public, including through its broadcasting arm, UNMIL Radio. Very few observers considered the mission to be partisan, and UNMIL had a good relationship with the government and civil society alike. UNMIL was able to cultivate extensive local relationships through a civilian presence in every one of Liberia's fifteen counties, and uniformed personnel stationed in many more locations. While costly to maintain given Liberia's rugged and rainy terrain, UNMIL's dispersed presence provided a remarkable window on national developments beyond the insular information environment of the capital, Monrovia. Further payoffs from the widespread UNMIL presence included a strong sense of UN solidarity with local populations, daily support to local authorities, a trusted convening role among mistrustful people, and engagement in small projects, including for local mediation skills. The option of quotidian interaction with local communities is vanishingly rare in UN political and peacekeeping operations, however. As a colleague from Baghdad reminded me, he was not even permitted to walk around inside the Green Zone, and local engagement in a number of other mission locations had similar restrictions for security reasons.

To build better listening into the insecure environments of peace operations, the High-Level Panel recommended "forums in which senior mission leadership can participate in structured, regular engagement with local communities, including women, youth, religious and other leaders who can provide feedback to the mission on its work" (United Nations 2015a: 255). These require careful design and should include, but not be limited to, the annual "Open Days on Women, Peace, and Security that have been led by the heads of UN peace operations since 2010. Other approaches could include the use of oral histories compiled by and with accessible populations, perception surveys, UN-supported immersion studies for mission leaders, and active use of local docents" (USIP 2009: 92).

This is important because nuanced views and a deep understanding of local conflict dynamics should be the basis for mandates and protection strategies in UN peace operations, according to the 2015 High-Level Panel which called for those operations to adopt a more "people-centred approach" (United Nations 2015a: 250–251). The UN must look at local sources of resilience and self-protection, it said, with the best information often coming from communities themselves (United Nations 2015a: 98). It stands to reason, as the Panel says, that the UN should listen to all possible sources and levels of expertise before settling on strategies to support preventing recurrence of conflict, encouraging reconciliation, securing transitional justice, and strengthening governance (United Nations 2015a: 153).

Active listening can yield surprises. In 2013, I sat down with a group of forty women in Gbarnga, Central Liberia, to listen to their views on peacetime life and issues that needed resolution. Their expectation that UNMIL would step in to solve all manner of problems was striking. Among the unexpected concerns they raised was dissatisfaction with legislation giving inheritance rights to widowed spouses. Many Liberian communities have long had a relaxed approach to out-of-wedlock heterosexual relationships, and although marriage is regarded as highly desirable, it can occur after the birth of one or several children, or not at all. The legislation, which was intended to protect their rights, had made their lot worse. They protested: "Now it's even harder to get men to marry us!" A lively discussion of human rights followed. The point here is the risk involved in policymakers substituting their own assumptions about the perspectives of those they serve.

In short, strengthening engagement with affected populations is indispensable to understanding gender perspectives on peace process issues. This element has received comparatively limited emphasis in interactions between the UN Secretary-General and the Security Council, and between the Secretary-General and the leadership of peace operations. An exception is through UN Security Council Resolution 1960, which encourages the Secretary-General to improve missions' capacity to communicate effectively with local communities. The Secretary-General therefore should expect peacemakers to acquire a deep understanding of local context, and should himself be attentive to listening skills, curiosity, and compassion when making senior appointments. The shift to a more people-centered approach would require a cultural change at senior levels, however, and such transformations can be the hardest.

RAISING THE PROFILE OF RESEARCH IN PEACE OPERATIONS

Social and cultural barriers to women's engagement are often complex, and there is limited evidence that the UN's current gender mainstreaming in the realm of peace and security has had discernible impact on promoting gender equality (Gizelis and Olsson 2015: 10). Strengthening research feedback loops to UN peace operations can support operations struggling to internalize gender perspectives and establish genuine accountability in this sphere. At root, local research and improved monitoring are essential but can be challenging for peace operations working in insecure settings. The UN's own lessons learned in peace operations, already collected on a voluntary basis, are an important resource. More can be done in collating and sharpening major lessons learned, including on mainstreaming gender perspectives.[4]

There appears to be relatively good awareness among UN policymakers of the broad-brush findings of research into women, peace, and security, in particular those that have been quantified, such as the superior durability of inclusive peace agreements and the persistent low levels of women in mediation processes. Data-based findings appear persuasive. This may be especially true when outcomes are framed as globally beneficial outcomes, such as improved peace and security for all. Framing inclusivity within mainstream narratives of success can also help avoid ghettoization as a "women's issue." In addition to "headline data," "mantra-based" practices have also proven useful, including the annual "16 Days of Activism against Gender-Based Violence."

Not all policymakers actively seek out research and evaluation, however. Parts of the UN have a weak learning culture, and dialogue between practitioners and academics can be erratic. Research brings fresh ideas to organizations, strengthens the credibility that comes with evidence-based policy, opens pathways for cooperation with other organizations, and promotes staff development. For the leadership of UN peace operations, the presentation of findings matters. Absorbing the sprawling 2015 report, "Preventing Conflict, Transforming Justice, Securing the Peace: A Global Study on the Implementation of UN Security Council Resolution 1325" (United Nations 2015b) is a challenge for peace operations leadership at 420 pages and with some two hundred recommendations (see chapter 11 in this volume on the production of the study).

The practice of benchmarking and the use of indicators are helpful in peace operations, in my experience. The WPS Implementation Matrix is a useful illustration of the status of, and responsibility for, relevant recommendations. Likewise, the "Secretary-General's Report on Mainstreaming a Gender Perspective into All Policies and Programmes in the UN System" (United Nations 2015c) is a positive contribution to communicating and visualizing progress. Practical guidance for overcoming common barriers to women's inclusion and incorporating perspectives on the differential impact of conflict on men and women can also be found in the Better Peace Tool (2015), and in the "Enhancing Gender-Responsive Mediation: A Guidance Note" (2013).

Gender rarely features in the non-UN mainstream publications consulted by UN mission leadership, including the colloquial periodicals focused on international peace and security. Such publications, which are widely read, combine factual reporting with strategic advocacy and set out political pathways and practical actions that resonate with policymakers. The UN and partners should pursue a strategy for enhancing their attention to gender perspectives.

SUPPORTIVE ORGANIZATIONAL STRUCTURES FOR GENDER MAINSTREAMING

Structural support for gender perspectives within UN peace operations has long come primarily from a senior gender adviser in mission (see UN Security Council Resolution 2106). This role has been elevated and strengthened in recent years. For instance, UN Security Council Resolution 2242 has called for such advisers to be located in the office of the head of mission (the Special Representative of the Secretary-General), and the Secretary-General decided that such advisers would be supported by gender expertise embedded in functional mission components as well.[5] Less quantifiably, but just as critical, is the personal interaction between the gender advisor and related components with the head of mission and other sections. Similarly, gender mainstreaming must be adopted in the interaction within the UN Country Team as a whole, and with local women and women's organizations.

The UN Secretariat and peace operations themselves can continue to strengthen the sense of shared ownership of such operations among UN agencies, funds, and programs, including UN Women, which has briefed the Security Council repeatedly in recent years (United Nations 2015b: 53, 54). Despite documented good practices, however (United Nations 2015b: 277–278), informal consensus suggests that gender advisors in UN peacekeeping missions struggle to have the desired impact. They may be viewed as responsible for "taking care of" Resolution 1325 on behalf of the entire mission, which fundamentally misunderstands the concept of mainstreaming. In practice, both human rights and gender perspectives can still feel like bolted-on extras in the work of peace operations. Unlike human rights components in field operations, however, which represent and retain a close link to the Office of the High Commissioner for Human Rights (OHCHR), gender advisers are untethered to another weighty operational agency, which can make them easier to ignore (United Nations 2015b: 278–280). The Global Study (United Nations 2015b: 277) notes that staff teams with gender-related responsibilities are prone to being under-ranked, understaffed, and under-resourced. It is perhaps unsurprising that "[d]espite the presence of gender advisers and gender units, UN peace missions have seemed to have only a 'marginal impact' in terms of transmitting the values of UNSCR 1325 to the national contexts" in which they operate (Olonisakin et al. 2010: 229).

CONTINUE TO SHARPEN FOCUS BY THE UN SECURITY COUNCIL

The UN Security Council's devotion to gender mainstreaming has improved steadily, but remains sporadic, peaking seasonally during the annual UN Security Council discussion on Women, Peace, and Security (United Nations 2015a: 79). This discussion, too, often skews toward sexual and gender-based violence. Indeed, Ambassador Anwarul Chowdhury, who as Bangladesh's Permanent Representative to the UN in New York had been instrumental in the adoption of Resolution 1325, remarked a decade later that the Security Council had not internalized gender concerns into operational behavior, and commitment to the resolution remained weak (United States Institute of Peace 2010).

Since 2012, there have been signs of more creative uptake of the gender agenda by the Security Council. In May 2012 the Portuguese Security Council presidency organized a so-called Arria-formula—meeting with gender advisors in UN peacekeeping missions. The meeting was a first and has been repeated in subsequent years.[6] In 2013, the Security Council adopted Resolution 2122, with a deepened focus on the participation aspects of the WPS agenda. Among other things, the Security Council sought more, and more regular, information on these aspects, including through briefings by the Executive Director of UN Women, and in the briefings and reports by senior UN officials, including Special Representatives.[7]

The Global Study noted a positive trend of coverage of WPS issues in the Secretary-General's country-specific reports. It added, however, that the Security Council could significantly underscore the importance of this agenda "simply by asking mission leadership follow-up questions when they come to New York to brief, in line with resolution 2122. If Council members exhibit greater commitment then it will likely result in the Secretariat and mission leadership approaching the task with more attention" (United Nations

2015b: 335). The Study further suggested that the Council seek more analytical, less descriptive reporting on gender issues in peace operations, including a "separate, more analytical section dedicated to capturing the country's and the mission's progress, challenges and recommendations towards better implementation of women, peace and security" (United Nations 2015b: 336).

Security Council members must demonstrate an expectation that Special Representatives heading peace operations be able to speak fluently to the issue.[8] Similar recommendations are made by the 2015 High Level Independent Panel on Peace Operations (HIPPO; United Nations 2015a) and 1325 Reports (United Nations 2015b: 239–243). A significant advance was made when, following the 2015 peace and security reviews, the Security Council adopted Resolution 2242. As a result, an Informal Experts Group on Women, Peace, and Security was established. UN Women has coordinated the convening of relevant UN actors, as well as civil society, to brief the Security Council on gender aspects of country situations on its agenda. These briefings were reported to have improved the quality of information presented to the Security Council.[9]

For its own credibility on the WPS agenda, the UN will need to address the poor representation of women within its own senior ranks (Landgren 2015). On taking his oath of office, incoming Secretary-General António Guterres committed the UN to respect for gender parity in a range of senior appointments, with a view to reaching gender parity among Under-Secretaries General and Assistant Secretaries-General by the end of his tenure.[10] Members of the Security Council should also make greater effort toward parity in their selection of ambassadors to the United Nations.

CONCLUSION

The WPS agenda is ambitious. While its contours and application have at times bred contentious discussion in the UN Security Council, a consensus has broadly held. Engagement with WPS has advanced steadily, if slowly. In addition to increased references to gender dimensions in the country-specific reports of the Secretary-General, these are now also noted in other thematic reports, including on access to justice, security sector reform, and small arms.[11] For several years, "Arria-formula" meetings of the Security Council with UN gender advisors have been used. It has also been suggested that the Convention on the Elimination of Discrimination Against Women (CEDAW) be referenced more actively given its near-universal ratification among 189 States.[12] The Council's own approach remains "uneven," however, and the Council and UN Secretariat alike share a "detrimental culture" regarding the women's agenda as an add-on (Security Council Report Cross-Cutting Report 2014: 41).

Creative, coordinated strategies that bring partners together will continue to be needed. Other politically contested fields where the UN is engaged, including with HIV/AIDS and narcotic drugs policy, have been targets of strategies to address unproductive and harmful practices. The strategies involve coordinated global research, advocacy, member state pressure, high-profile individual champions, and media attention.[13] The road from policy to practice, however, may remain rough. In 2015, the High-Level Panel found that there was

[a]n uneven commitment to this agenda at the most senior levels and within the ranks of all mission personnel—civilian and uniformed—and at Headquarters; there is a failure to understand the integration of gender and the advancement of the Women, Peace, and Security agenda as a responsibility of all staff (United Nations 2015a: 239, vi).

If gendered understandings are to enter the bloodstream of UN peace operations, four positive measures discussed in this chapter should be given higher priority:

1. Peace operations need to incorporate engaged listening and consultations with local populations, especially women, which go beyond *pro forma* encounters;
2. Mission and headquarters' leadership must refine and communicate more extensively on relevant research and lessons learned with respect to gender outcomes;
3. Gender advisors within UN peace operations should have a stronger institutional base; and
4. The UN Secretary-General and the Security Council ought consistently to demonstrate their expectation that mission leaders understand and have endeavored to integrate gender perspectives, including through performance accountability measures.

The expectations placed on a UN peace operation in respect of local gender relations can be startlingly high, not least when set against limited capacity and resources on the ground. A constant in peace operations, moreover, is the broad mix of nationalities and cultures among personnel contributing to wide differences in attitudes and perceptions. It is not unusual to encounter gender bias, both overt and unconscious. The day-to-day of peace operations is a constant reminder that there is no such thing as gender neutrality, in our own lives or in the lives of those served by the UN. It is only by closer engagement with each other and with communities that our understanding of gender can become less abstract, and with that, our actions more effective.

Notes

1. S/2005/636 of 10 October 2005, para. 5, referring to the adoption of SCR1325 in 2000.
2. For a definition of gender mainstreaming see International Forum for the Challenges of Peace Operations 2016. http://www.challengesforum.org
3. "Dag Hammarskjöld: A Secretary-General for All." United Nations Association—UK, Autumn 2011, https://www.una.org.uk/magazine/autumn-2011/dag-hammarskj%C3%B6ld-secretary-general-all.
4. For interesting reflections from J-M Guéhenno, then USG for Peacekeeping, see "Shifting Attitudes? DPKO Comments During Debates." Security Council Report, 2010, http://www.securitycouncilreport.org/atf/cf/%7B65BFCF9B-6D27-4E9C-8CD3-CF6E4FF96FF9%7D/WPS%202010%20Sidebar4.pdf.
5. A/70/357–S/2015/682, "The Future of United Nations Peace Operations:Implementation of the Recommendations of the High-Level Independent Panel on Peace Operations: Report of the Secretary-General." United Nations Digital Library, para. 67, September 15, 2015, https://digitallibrary.un.org/record/802167?ln=en.

6. What's in Blue. "Arria Meeting with Gender Advisors." Security Council Report, May 17, 2012, http://www.whatsinblue.org/2012/05/arria-meeting-with-gender-advisers.php.

7. "Women, Peace, and Security." Cross-Cutting Report. Security Council Report, April 16, 2014, http://www.securitycouncilreport.org/atf/cf/%7B65BFCF9B-6D27-4E9C-8CD3-CF6E4FF96FF9%7D/cross_cutting_report_2_women_peace_security_2014.pdf.

8. As well as inviting women to participate, Resolution 2122 "requests the Secretary-General and his Special Envoys and Special Representatives to United Nations missions, as part of their regular briefings, to update the Council on progress in inviting women to participate, including through consultations with civil society, including women's organizations, in discussions pertinent to the prevention and resolution of conflict, the maintenance of peace and security and post-conflict peacebuilding."

9. "Over the course of 2016, the 2242 Group met on four situations: Mali, Iraq, Central African Republic, and Afghanistan. At each meeting, Council experts received briefings from senior leadership of field missions, in each instance at the level of either Special Representative or Deputy Special Representative. It seems that the meetings of the 2242 Group have enabled the Council to make some headway with another recommendation emanating from the 2015 peace and security reviews, namely better information leading to better outcomes. Council members have observed improvement in the quality of gender information presented to the Council during briefings, an increase in the number of questions posed by Council members to Special Representatives regarding their mission's implementation of women, peace and security obligations, and a greater willingness to include gender specific language when renewing mandates of peace operations. However, such improvement has largely been limited to the countries considered by the 2242 Group, rather than extending to broader improvement across all country-specific situations considered by the Council. Additionally, some Council members report only incremental improvement in gender analysis in written reports by the Secretary-General on country-specific situations, remarking that most women, peace and security reporting continues to be descriptive rather than analytical." From "Women, Peace, and Security." SCR, October 2016 Monthly Forecast, http://www.securitycouncilreport.org/monthly-forecast/2016-10/women_peace_and_security_8.php.

10. United Nations Secretary-General. "Secretary-General-Designate António Guterres' Remarks to the General Assembly on Taking the Oath of Office." December 12, 2016, https://www.un.org/sg/en/content/sg/speeches/2016-12-12/secretary-general-designate-ant%C3%B3nio-guterres-oath-office-speech.

11. Commenting in late 2013, the NGO Security Council Report noted increased references: "Meanwhile, recent Secretary-General's reports on other thematic issues demonstrate an improvement in the Secretariat's own cross-cutting approach to the women, peace and security agenda. The report on the rule of law included many such references, including an assessment completed by UN Women regarding the extent to which women's empowerment and gender equality is considered in the work of the UN on access to justice (S/2013/341). The report on security sector reform recommended that such programmes include a consistent gender dimension (S/2013/480). The small arms report highlighted emerging concerns about the issue of illicit small arms in armed conflict and the linkages to sexual violence in conflict (S/2013/503)." From "Women, Peace, and Security." SCR, October 2013 Monthly Forecast, http://www.securitycouncilreport.org/monthly-forecast/2013-10/women_peace_and_security_3.php.

12. Including its General Recommendation No. 30 on women in conflict prevention, conflict, and post-conflict situations.
13. For example, work ahead of the 2016 UNGASS on drugs included a Lancet Commission, contributions by the International Center for Science in Drug Policy, important NGO coalitions around the International Drug Policy Consortium and Harm Reduction International, and Transform Drug Policy Foundation; LSE IDEAS with expert group reports endorsed by five Nobel Prize-winning economists; significant media coverage—and a follow-up UNGASS in 2019.

References

Anderson, Mary B., Dayna Brown, and Isabella Jean. "The Listening Project." In *Time to Listen: Hearing People on the Receiving End of International Aid.* Cambridge, MA: CDA Collaborative Learning Projects, November 2012.

Bell, Christine. "Text and Context: Evaluating Peace Agreements for Their 'Gender Perspective.'" Political Settlements Research Programme, University of Edinburgh, 2015, http://www.politicalsettlements.org/files/2016/05/20151011_R_Bell_GJA_Text-and-Context.pdf.

"The Better Peace Tool." International Civil Society Action Network, 2015, http://www.betterpeacetool.org/.

Davies, Sara E., and Belinda Bennett. "A Gendered Human Rights Analysis of Ebola and Zika: Locating Gender in Global Health Emergencies." Chatham House, September 1, 2016, https://www.chathamhouse.org/publication/ia/gendered-human-rights-analysis-ebola-and-zika-locating-gender-global-health.

"Enhancing Gender-Responsive Mediation: A Guidance Note." Organization for Security and Co-operation in Europe, October 28, 2013, http://www.osce.org/gender/107533.

Gizelis, T-I., and L. Olsson, eds. *Gender, Peace, and Security: Implementing UN Security Council Resolution 1325.* New York: Routledge, 2015.

Landgren, Karin. "The Lost Agenda: Gender Parity in Senior UN Appointments." Global Peace Operations Review, December 2015, http://peaceoperationsreview.org/commentary/the-lost-agenda-gender-parity-in-senior-un-appointments/.

Olonisakin, F., K. Barnes, and E. Ikpe. *Women, Peace, and Security: Translating Policy into Practice.* New York: Routledge, 2010.

Security Council Report Cross-Cutting Report No. 2: "Women Peace, and Security." October 2010, http://www.securitycouncilreport.org/cross-cutting-report/lookup-c-glKWLeMTIsG-b-6239031.php.

Security Council Report Cross-Cutting Report No. 2: "Women, Peace, and Security." October 2014, http://www.securitycouncilreport.org/atf/cf/%7B65BFCF9B-6D27-4E9C-8CD3-CF6E4FF96FF9%7D/cross_cutting_report_2_women_peace_security_2014.pdf.

United Nations. "Uniting our Strengths for Peace—Politics, Partnership, and People. Report of the High-Level Independent Panel on Peace Operations." A/70/95 S/2015/446, 2015a, http://www.un.org/ga/search/view_doc.asp?symbol=A/70/95.

United Nations. "Preventing Conflict, Securing Justice, Transforming the Peace—A Global Study on the Implementation of Security Council Resolution 1325." UN Women, 2015b, http://wps.unwomen.org/.

United Nations. "Secretary-General's Report on Mainstreaming a Gender Perspective into All Policies and Programmes in the UN System." E/2015/58, 2015c.

United Nations Security Council. "Resolution 1509 (2003) S/RES/1509." http://www.securitycouncilreport.org/atf/cf/%7B65BFCF9B-6D27-4E9C-8CD3-CF6E4FF96FF9%7D/Liberia%20SRes1509.pdf

United Nations Security Council. "Resolution 2008 (2011) extending the United Nations Mission in Liberia (UNMIL)." New York: United Nations, September 16, 2011, https://www.un.org/press/en/2011/sc10388.doc.htm

United Nationsl Security Council. "Resolution 2106" S/RES/2106, June 24, 2013, New York: United Nations

United States Institute of Peace. "Looking for Justice: Liberian Experiences with and Perceptions of Local Justice Options." 2009.

United States Institute of Peace. "Women, Peace, and Security: Fulfilling the Vision of 1325." Discussion. 10-year anniversary of SCR 1325, July 27, 2010, http://www.usip.org/events/women-peace-and-security-fulfilling-the-vision-1325.

CHAPTER 11

....

THE PRODUCTION OF THE 2015 GLOBAL STUDY

....

LOUISE OLSSON AND THEODORA-ISMENE GIZELIS

"This is not rhetoric, [Phumzile Mlambo-Ngcuka] said, adding that the findings were backed by "extensive" evaluations, statistics and academic research."[1]

PENDING the fifteen-year anniversary of UN Security Council Resolution 1325, the first resolution on Women, Peace, and Security (WPS), the Security Council identified the need for a High-level Review to take stock of progress. To inform the review, the Secretary-General was instructed to commission a "Global Study on the implementation of resolution 1325, highlighting good practice examples, implementation gaps and challenges, as well as emerging trends and priorities for action" (UN Women 2015d). The result was the report "Global Study on UNSC Resolution 1325: Preventing Conflict, Transforming Justice, Securing the Peace," launched on October 14, 2015. In the introduction of the document, Secretary-General Ban Ki Moon states that the Global Study "offers new evidence, ideas and good practices that can help generate new commitments and implement old ones" (UN Women 2015d: 4). The results from the Global Study were presented at the anniversary Open Debate where the Executive Director of UN Women, as can be seen in the initial quote, opted to emphasize the scholarly foundations of the study by claiming that the recommendations rest on research and are evidence-based.

Academics and policymakers can probably all agree on the need for a more solid research base for WPS implementation. Basing our discussions on the production and content of the Global Study, this chapter argues that this requires improving the dialogue across scholars and practitioners. The chapter also outlines examples of what such a dialogue can contribute for further implementation. In particular, the chapter highlights the importance of careful selection and critical evaluation of academic research based on clear criteria. In fact, drawing on academic research for such a broad evaluation of existing WPS implementation as was attempted in the Global Study requires careful consideration on concepts, design, and comparability of the selected evidence.

Moreover, this chapter argues that we need to recognize that different research fields contribute different pieces of the puzzle on how to move forward on implementation. We focus specifically on two key fields. First, *conceptually focused feminist research* (henceforth called feminist research)[2] has repeatedly pointed out that Resolution 1325 consists of many contested, and sometimes contradictory, postulates and ideas. As a document produced after a politicized process, the Global Study consequently only presents some of the potential interpretations and assessments of Resolution 1325 and its content. Thus, feminist research points out that it is essential to consider the political context during the production of the report and its impact on the content and use of selected academic research to support most of the Global Study's recommendations. Second, the assertion by the UN that the study relies on evidence based in statistics and other forms of *systematic empirical research* (hereafter empirical research)[3] raises further concerns by this research field about the validity of such claims. As we discuss in this chapter, the report does not systematically compile or collect existing empirical research, a necessary condition to substantiate the conclusions of a document with the purpose of evaluating existing policies and programs, highlighting emerging patterns and providing evidence to set priorities of action. In fact, the Global Study refers to a small number of peer-reviewed and published academic research in a field which has grown considerably over the last decade.

We begin by discussing the politics of measuring the implementation of Resolution 1325 and producing the Global Study. This paints a picture of the context and brings out some of the main contentions. We then look closer at the content of the Global Study with the purpose of displaying what a strengthened research-policy dialogue could contribute to further improving implementation. Here we raise key points from the two complementary research traditions; empirical research, which tests assumptions on data to find evidence-based paths forward often using quantitative methodology; and the more conceptual feminist research which critically discusses the foundations for WPS work and its key arguments. We focus our discussion primarily on two chapters from the Global Study: chapter three on women's participation; and chapter six on militarization and on the conduct of the CSO survey. These chapters are illustrative examples that provide insights into how the content and recommendations of the Global Study can be further developed through increased research-policy collaboration.

THE POLITICS OF MEASUREMENT
AND PRODUCTION

The importance of the Global Study should be understood in two contexts. First, monitoring and reporting on Resolution 1325 (i.e., measuring progress) has been one of a few tools available for pushing implementation of what is a rather toothless document. Second, the text of Resolution 1325 is rather vague and contains contested elements while seeking to create groundbreaking change in an increasingly hostile environment. The starting point for the Global Study is, hence, quite demanding, attempting to reconcile diverge goals and viewpoints. The following section outlines the highly politicized process that led to the production of the study.

The Politics of Measuring Resolution 1325

Resolution 1325 builds on a substantive international legal framework on human rights and gender equality, not least the Convention on the Elimination of all forms of Discrimination Against Women, as well as a long list of policy documents and political decisions, such as the Beijing Platform for Action.[4] Yet, it is a thematic resolution using only vague wordings and without institutionalized follow-up mechanisms. Thus, Resolution 1325's normative imperative has been stronger than the degree of embodiment and legal worth of the text. This imperative has been used to try to influence the behavior of the Security Council, the Secretariat, and member states (Tryggestad 2009: 544). To that end, many actors promoting WPS have requested increasingly more targeted and detailed monitoring and reporting to ensure accountability (Labonte and Curry 2016: 311). Resistance to such efforts has been steadily growing. For example, an attempt to reach a decision on WPS indicators for oblig-atory reporting by all member states was thwarted in the Open Debate in 2010. This speaks to the disparity of preferences between more conservative state actors—unsympathetic either to radical changes in gender equality or to expansive applications of international norms at the expense of national sovereignty—and more liberal states who seek to forward the WPS framework (see Basu 2016).

In addition to existing political conflicts, the actual text of Resolution 1325, and, subsequently, the WPS agenda and the Global Study, reflect fundamental contentions in their theoretical underpinnings. This stems, as Arat notes, from the fact that the UN has been central to advancing women's rights in two ways. First, by forwarding a liberal discourse on women's rights, and, second, by providing a platform for trans-national women's activism where the latter often has been used for "introducing dif-ferent feminist theoretical frameworks" (2015: 674). As Tryggestad (2009) has argued, the Resolution 1325 had primarily been adopted as a concession to women's organiza-tions' hard work and recognized them as actors for peace. But in addition, the resolution included efforts by member states forwarding gender equality as part of their foreign policy; the Department of Peacekeeping Operations' aim to mainstream gender in peace operations; professional women in the UN system who were fighting for increased par-ticipation in peace operations; and actors addressing sexual exploitation and abuse by peacekeepers (Tryggestad 2009; see also Olsson 2000). Hence, the resolution came to embrace a range of theoretical standpoints that were not easily reconcilable—from the more radical, postcolonial, and critical feminisms to the dominant liberal feminism (Olsson and Gizelis 2014; Arat 2015).

The Politics of the Production Process

After Resolution 2122 outlined the mandate of the Global Study in October 2013, competi-tion over the interpretation of Resolution 1325 inevitably became part of the process and an equally politicized process of designing the actual production started. An *Independent lead author*, Radhika Coomaraswamy (Sri Lanka) was appointed. Coomaraswamy had previ-ously served as a Special Representative for Children and Armed Conflict (2006–2012) and as Special Rapporteur on Violence against Women (1994–2003). A "High-level Advisory Group for the Global Study on SCR 1325" (henceforth, the Advisory Group) was formed. It consisted of seventeen members (of which three were men), and its role is described as providing "engaged advice on the Global Study process on a regular basis" (UN Women 2015d). Members included Ms. Leymah Gbowee (Liberia), Anwarul Chowdhury (Bangladesh), Elisabeth Rehn (Finland), and Luz Mendez (Guatemala).[5] In addition, trying to ensure that WPS was not kept on a side track from other ongoing UN reviews, most notably the High-level Independent Panel on Peace Operations (HIPPO), one member from the Advisor Group, Youssef Mahmoud (Tunisia) was a member of the HIPPO.[6] The assignment to practically coordinate and support the production of the Global Study and the review in the Security Council was handled by creating "a small Secretariat hosted by UN Women and supported by the Standing Committee on Women, Peace and Security of the Inter-Agency Network on Women and Gender Equality in close coordination with the Executive Office of the Secretary-General" (UN Women 2014). In a manner, this was designed to decrease institutional competition.

A consultative and inclusive production approach was designed thereby underlining the political, rather than scientific, character of the process. Given the demanding context of the Global Study, seeking to create a broad support base was rational. Many specialists on WPS were engaged to contribute with analyses. In addition, sixty member states and international and regional organizations made submissions. Much material was collected during twelve consultations conducted in different settings. For example, joint consultations were conducted in the EU, AU, and NATO, and in a regional consultation with civil society of, for example, the MENA region, South-Pacific, Latin America (UN Women 2015a). In this work, consulting women affected by armed conflict was a stated priority. Women's NGOs were also invited to provide information through a survey. This survey, conducted under the auspices of the Global Network of Women Peacebuilders, Cordaid, the International Civil Society Action Network, and the NGO Working Group on Women, Peace, and Security, generated responses from 317 organizations in seventy-one countries. In addition, forty-seven civil society organizations, academics, and research institutes provided inputs via a public website (UN Women 2015b).

The result of the entire production process was a four-hundred-plus-pages-long document launched by the Secretary-General on October 14, 2015. As noted by Jenkins (2015), it is a sweeping document balancing a broad and ambitious agenda with the need to protect the reputation of the UN. The Global Study's recommendations converge into a set of guiding principles with conflict prevention as the leading theme. Local women peacebuilders are depicted as being at the forefront of sustainable peace and confronting current security challenges. The report is divided into ten topics including a chapter that outlines the normative framework for WPS and a chapter on general recommendations and guidelines. The thematic entities cover topics such as women's participation in peace processes and in peace operations, and new challenges such as addressing violent extremism—portrayed as the most urgent current security concern. The last three thematic chapters focus on the intersection of WPS and the preventive toolkit of the Security Council—mostly perceived as underutilized. For instance, in chapter 11, the Global Study outlines a framework of allowing the flow of information across the whole system while engaging with the Human Rights Council with years of experience in creating commissions and establishing fact-finding missions (p. 328). Finally, the last chapter highlights the challenges of financing, a key topic for civil society organizations given the financial challenges they are constantly facing when seeking to contribute to the implementation of WPS.

Due to the Open Debate being moved up a week for the Spanish Prime Minister to chair the meeting, it was held the day before the release of the Global Study. By the time it was launched, a select number of recommendations had already been included in the Secretary General's own yearly report on WPS published in September 2015. The Secretary General's report also included recommendations from the two parallel UN reviews, the HIPPO, and the *Advisory Group of Experts on the 2015 Review of the United Nations Peacebuilding Architecture* (see United Nations 2015c). Even further weeding of the recommendations was then done into Resolution 2242, the eighth resolution on WPS.

STRENGTHENING THE RESEARCH-POLICY DIALOGUE ON WPS

Although one cannot dispute the importance and the high-level of ambition behind the Global Study, the report itself is neither designed in accordance with accepted practices of research methodology (which is used to ensure that conclusions are empirically supported), nor does it engage with ongoing research debates. While we agree with Jenkins (2015) that the Global Study is a political document, we still argue that there is a need to seriously engage with it from the viewpoint of two leading research perspectives, the empirical and the feminist. Interestingly, they converge on key concerns on "theoretical standpoints and concepts," and "data collection, measurement and voice"—though the two reflect different epistemological and ontological perspectives.

Differences in Understandings? Theoretical Standpoints and Concepts

As noted by Arat (2015), the UN's work on gender equality encompasses an interesting amalgamation of processes related to varying theoretical standpoints. These contestations are also found in Resolution 1325 and, hence, brought into the Global Study. As an illustration, the first recommendation focusing on prevention uses terminology on structural inequality and violent masculinities most often found in feminist theory, whereas the second recommendation instead uses liberal terminology by underlining that Resolution 1325 is in its essence a human rights' mandate (p. 13). A more in-depth engagement with previous research could have enriched the Global Study by providing clarification and nuance.

A chapter where this engagement with research could have been particularly fruitful is chapter six, "Keeping the Peace in an Increasingly Militarized World." In much feminist literature, "gender" is considered fundamental as it perceives current assumptions about security in the world to lean toward hyper-masculinist, which, in turn, are seen as reinforcing militarism. Therefore, articles in feminist research have argued that peacekeeping, considered as a tool in this militarized world, cannot be used to increase women security (for example, see Whitworth 2004; Willet 2010; Khalid 2015; Shepherd 2016). In policy, Women's International League for Peace and Freedom represents this strand of thinking and has considered the resolution as a platform for counteracting war as such, and not an instrument to handle the consequences of war for women (Tryggestad 2009). When the Global Study uses a quote stating that "Women, peace and security is about preventing war, not about making war safer for women," one can almost hear the echo from the Congress of Women hundred years earlier (p. 191).[7]

This theoretical standpoint contrasts quite clearly with a feature that has become a dominant theme in Resolution 1325, women's rights to be included in military peacekeeping—often used as a key indicator for measuring progress. Hence, the Global Study displays an uneasy balancing, but it lands in an emphasis on demilitarization: "[U]ltimately, for advocates of sustainable peace and security interlinked with development and human rights, the value of the WPS agenda is its potential for transformation, rather than greater representation of women in existing paradigms of militarized response" (p. 135). Unsurprisingly, this standpoint does not appear to have been supported in the Security Council Open Debate in 2015 where the dominant liberal and functional standpoints in this political context were displayed through the emphasis on the need to increase the number of women peacekeepers instead (Security Council 2015). Engaging with feminist research could have assisted in bringing out the tensions, the disagreement, and the potentially very different pathways for WPS in the future.

Another fundamental concern for both empirical and feminist research relates to key concepts. Concepts are central for researchers as they assist in the development of an understanding on how a phenomenon should be understood and to ensure accuracy and consistency across studies. The Global Study contains a vast number of concepts, such as "conflict prevention," "protracted conflict," and "insecurity." Feminist research has been quite successful in providing in-depth insights into what different definitions can mean for what is labeled as important—for example, that limitations in how we understand a phenomenon affect whether or not women's key concerns are incorporated. For instance, if we see "peace" merely as the absence of violent conflict, this disregards the fact that there might not even be peace for women since their security, and economic and political access, have not been an integral part of the peace process (see chapter 2 in this volume; also Meintjes, Turshen, and Pillay 2001). An understanding of this is hinted in the Global Study, which states that "the content of what we mean by 'peace' and 'security' is evolving . . ." (p. 13). However, it misses the opportunity on providing clearer direction of the goals of WPS in relation to the achievement of positive peace or more gender aware security.

In fact, one could argue that the Global Study's lack of discussion of how key concepts are defined and measured across the different studies referred to in the document constitute one of its major flaws for formulating recommendations. A prerequisite of empirical research, and hence evidence-based policy, is the ability to define fuzzy concepts. When concepts are well-defined, one can then develop relevant measurements which can assess, evaluate, observe, and appraise a phenomenon in a fruitful way. While measurements are often associated with the process of quantifying characteristics of phenomena (e.g., peace processes and outcomes), the role of measurement is broader by defining the spectrum of possible outcomes or states of a phenomenon that can be observed. The scaling of possible states of a phenomenon permits researchers, practitioners, and academics alike to compare and evaluate the alternative states of a phenomenon (see Landman 2000; Podsakoff et al. 2012).

These problems can be exemplified by chapter 3, "Women's Participation and a Better Understanding of the Political" in the Global Study. More specifically, how is women's participation in peace processes defined and measured in order to arrive at conclusions on how to move forward? Seen from this perspective, chapter 3 spans all aspects of a peace process which is not defined or clarified—for example, without outlining differences between process phases, tasks, or actor compositions (for their importance, see Walter 2002). Even more importantly, in the Global Study, women are consistently mentioned as one group, whether it concerns women in leading state positions or women in grassroot organizations taking part in a peace process. Women are treated as having similar characteristics—for example, bringing a "particular quality of consensus building to public debate" which, in turn, is argued to increase the chance for peace (p. 42). This is underlined in the chapter's introductory quote by O'Reilly, Ó Súilleabháin, and Paffenholz (2015: 37), stating that women are rarely belligerents, but that their input is necessary for peace. The assumptions about women in the Global Study risks essentializing their role both in conflict and peace although research studies, empirical as well as feminist, warn against such oversimplifications (see, for example, Willett 2010; Pratt and Richter-Devroe 2011; Karim and Beardsley 2017). For instance, Alison (2009) and Cohen (2013) problematize the role of former female combatants for peace and prevention of conflict. Hence, treating women as one coherent group results in unsubstantiated assumptions that all women have the same political perspectives and work toward the same goals. That is not to say that women's activism is not important. There is some research showing the importance of strong autonomous women's movements in driving different forms of social change, yet more systematic studies are required to support existing evidence.

Another discussion in the Global Study concerns the ways in which women's participation can be assisted. Research findings underline the need to place these considerations within the context of the broader findings of research on durable peace. For example, the Global Study highlights the need to minimize obstacles to women's meaningful participation especially in peace processes (pp. 48–53), often stressing the activism of women's organizations in multitrack peace processes (pp. 54–55). However, empirical research has found multitrack processes to be very few in number, rendering them unique cases. This means that we cannot learn much on how to move forward from them. Moreover, in general, most multitrack interventions to end violent armed conflicts are rather ineffective and only bring results in very specific conditions (Böhmelt 2010). Research even highlights situations where "quick fix" increases in women's participation by simply raising the number without considering the political context may become counter-productive because doing so can lead to either very short-term changes or even backlash (Bjarnegård and Melander 2013; Karim and Beardsley 2013, 2015, 2017; Olsson and Gizelis 2015). So, while we must pay much more attention to women's participation, research points to serious gaps in our knowledge before we can make evidence-based recommendations.

What Is Measured and Who Matters? Measurement, Data, and Voice

The "local" must clearly be the most important factor in our analysis. Nevertheless, women spoke with one voice from every continent to convey a key message to the Security Council: the United Nations must take the lead in stopping the process of militarization and militarism that began in 2001 in an ever-increasing cycle of conflict (p. 17).

A key concern in feminist research is the political consequences of what is measured and who provides information. It even argues that uncritical measurements and reporting constitute a problem when seeking to accomplish what it sees as the resolution's main aims—decreasing militarization and preventing war. The reason is that measurements and reporting risk turning WPS into a depoliticized, technocratic process (Davies and True 2017; True 2015). Susan Willett (2010) even argues that the power inequalities of the UN as an institution has tended to overshadow the gender discourse. Whitworth (2004) claims that the current focus on women's roles in peace-building have become idealized and gender mainstreaming policies are thus rendered as empty "spaces" for alternative voices to be heard without challenging the dominant and militaristic discourse.[8] Overall, the Global Study actually fails to address that there is very little research on what women bring to the table when they have a voice or the effectiveness of gender mainstreaming programs (Gizelis and Krause 2015).

In a manner of speaking, this is related to a concern in empirical research. Empirical research is often critical of the low methodological quality of approaches used in policy reports to measure implementation such as unclear selection criteria of interviewees and non-random surveys among others. According to empirical research, there is more to drawing conclusions than compilation and using numbers. Importantly, transparent criteria are required to guide the collection of data for analysis. The criteria's role is twofold: first, transparency allows other researchers or policymakers to use the criteria in different contexts and therefore ensure comparability of key findings and recommendations. Second, clear criteria allow different viewpoints to be included in the selection process or at least have an equal chance to be selected. Let us here focus on the Civil Society Organization (CSO) Survey for the Global Study on Women, Peace, and Security, which was used in order to harvest the voices of "local women" in combination with the consultations. The Global Study highlights that the CSOs that participated in the survey were self-selected (p. 6). To some extent the large number of CSOs included is reassuring. The sample, even though not random or systematic, is at least comprehensive. However, it raises the question of selection. For example, did specific types of organizations not engage with the Global Study—either by choice or because they could not access the website (p. 106)? And, if this was the case, what are the implications for interpreting the policy recommendations?

This consideration is relevant for both empirical and feminist researchers who converge in noting differences between the Global North and the Global South on what is considered to be the most central aspects of WPS. Member states from the Global North have tended to advocate for civil and political rights, participation, and protection from violence whereas non-Western states have instead focused on socioeconomic rights and empowerment (Labonte and Curry 2016: 313). It is, therefore, relevant to consider if similar differences might be reflected in the survey had it been designed systematically to reveal such patterns? Here, the lack of contextualization and any recognition of regional concerns are striking given that 40 percent of CSO respondents were in Africa and 30 percent in Asia, two regions that have disproportionally experienced conflict and intervention. If anything the Global Study promotes the assumption that CSOs represent one body and speak with one voice. And yet, studies on women's organizations show that policies advocated by the UN and external donors might often lead to decoupling and failures if not contextualized (Gizelis and Joseph 2016). Regional variations in terms of the priorities given in survey responses can speak to the relevance of engaging with literatures that outline different WPS pathways and plausible outcomes (p. 111).

CONCLUSIONS AND THE WAY FORWARD

The Global Study is an outcome of a political process. Hence, the final report's lack of engagement with academic research is not surprising. However, we argue that such an engagement is critical if we are to chart a successful way forward. Notably, empirical research underlines the importance of clarity in key concepts when developing recommendations based on lessons drawn over space and time. Similarly, feminist research brings out key considerations when using measurements and reporting to advance implementation in order for WPS to be a platform for transformative change. They both underline the importance of including alternative and dissenting voices. This is an issue which to an extent has been echoed in both feminist and empirical research concerns in relation to the need for transparency in the collection of data and analysis of data to reveal trends in differences between regions, countries, and socioeconomic groups. Collectively, these research perspectives strongly argue that not all women speak with one voice, but that all women matter. As the 2020 anniversary year draws nearer, an in-depth engagement with research can contribute to a strengthened process forward on WPS.

NOTES

1. Original quote reads "she" (name inserted by authors) and is from Security Council (2015).
2. In the UN context, Arat (2015) identifies Liberal feminism, Marxist feminism, Radical feminism, Socialist feminism, Third World feminism, and Critical feminism in relation to the use of intersectionality. In this paper, we refer primarily to critical feminist research.
3. Here we mean primarily positivist research that uses rigorous empirical methods to explore and test ideas and suggestions. In a sense, we mean a form of "empirical feminism" in research (see Reiter 2015).
4. See chapter 3 in this volume where Christine Chinkin analyses the international legal framework within which made UNSCR 1325 possible; also Tryggestad 2009; Labonte and Curry 2016: 312.
5. For a full list, see UN Women (2015d).
6. This did not happen automatically. The first appointment of the HIPPO panel included very few women and no coordination with the WPS. This led to massive protests resulting in revisions.
7. Similar to when the congress in the Hague in 1915 found that "[t]his International Congress of Women opposes the assumption that women can be protected under the conditions of modern warfare" (International Congress of Women 1915).
8. See also Cohn 2008.

REFERENCES

Alison, M. *Women and Political Violence: Female Combatants in Ethno-National Conflict.* New York: Routledge, 2009.

Arat, Z. "Feminisms, Women's Rights, and the UN: Would Achieving Gender Equality Empower Women?" *American Political Science Review* 109, no. 4 (2015): 674–689.

Basu, S. "Gender as a National Interest in the UN Security Council." *International Affairs* 2 (2016): 255–273.

Bjarnegård, E., and E. Melander. "Revisiting Representation: Communism, Women in Politics, and the Decline of Armed Conflict in East Asia." *International Interactions* 4 (2013): 558–574.

Böhmelt, T. "The Effectiveness of Tracks of Diplomacy Strategies in Third-Party Interventions." *Journal of Peace Research* 2 (2010): 167–178.

Cohen, D. K. "Female Combatants and the Perpetration of Violence: Wartime Rape in the Sierra Leone Civil War." *World Politics* 3 (2013): 383–415.

Cohn, C. "Mainstreaming Gender in UN Security Policy: A Path to Political Transformation?" In *Global Governance: Feminist Perspectives*, edited by S. Rai and M. G. Waylen, 185–206. New York Palgrave Macmillan, 2008.

Davies, S. E., and J. True. "Connecting the Dots: Pre-existing Patterns of Gender Inequality and the Likelihood of Widespread and Systematic Sexual Violence." *Global Responsibility to Protect* 1 (2017): 65–85.

Gizelis, T.-I., and J. Joseph. "Decoupling Local Ownership? The Lost Opportunities for Grassroots Women's Involvement in Liberian Peacebuilding." *Cooperation and Conflict* 4 (2016): 539–556.

Gizelis, T.-I., and J. Krause. "Exploring Gender Mainstreaming in Security and Development." In *Gender, Peace, and Security: Implementing UN Security Council Resolution 1325*, edited by L. Olsson and T-I. Gizelis, 165–184. London: Routledge, 2015.

International Congress of Women. The Hague, 1915, http://www.ub.gu.se/kvinndata/portaler/fred/samarbete/pdf/resolutions_1915.pdf.

Jenkins, R. The Practical Is the Political: The UN's Global Study on Women, Peace, and Security. Global Peace Operations Review, 2015, http://peaceoperationsreview.org/thematic-essays/practical-political-un-global-study-women-peace-security/.

Karim, S., and K. Beardsley. "Female Peacekeepers and Gender Balancing: Token Gestures or Informed Policymaking?" *International Interactions* 4 (2013): 461–488.

Karim, S., and K. Beardsley. "Ladies Last: Peacekeeping and Gendered Protection." In *Gender, Peace and Security: Implementing UN Security Council Resolution 1325*, edited by L. Olsson and T-I. Gizelis, 62–96. London: Routledge, 2015.

Karim, S., and K. Beardsley. *Equal Opportunity Peacekeeping: Women, Peace, and Security in Post-Conflict States*. Oxford: Oxford University Press, 2017.

Khalid, M. "Feminist Perspectives on Militarism and War." In *The Oxford Handbook of Transnational Feminist Movements*, edited by R. Baksh and W. Harcourt, 632–650. Oxford: Oxford University Press, 2015s.

Labonte, M., and G. Curry. "Women, Peace and Security: Are We There Yet?" *Global Governance* 22 (2016): 311–319.

Landman, T. *Issues and Methods in Comparative Politics*. London: Routledge, 2000.

Meintjes, S., M. Turshen, and A. Pillay. *The Aftermath: Women in Post-Conflict Transformation*. London: Zed Books, 2001.

O'Reilly, M., Ó Súilleabháin, A., and Paffenholz, T. *Reimagining Peacemaking: Women's Roles in Peace Processes*. New York: International Peace Institute, June 2015.

Olsson, L. "Mainstreaming Gender in Multidimensional Peacekeeping: A Field Perspective." *International Peacekeeping* 7, no. 3 (2000): 1–16.

Olsson, L., and T.-I. Gizelis. Commentary: "Advancing Gender and Peacekeeping Research." *International Peacekeeping* 21, no. 4 (2014): 520–528.

Olsson, L., and T.-I. Gizelis, eds. *Gender, Peace, and Security: Implementing UN Security Council Resolution 1325*. London: Routledge, 2015.

Podsakoff, P. M., S. B. MacKenzie, and N. P. Podsakoff. "Sources of Method Bias in Social Science Research and Recommendations on How to Control It. *Annual Review of Psychology* 63 (2012): 539–569.

Pratt, N., and S. Richter-Devroe, S. "Critically Examining UNSCR 1325 on Women, Peace, and Security." *International Feminist Journal of Politics* 4 (2011): 489–503.

Reiter, D. "The Positivist Study of Gender and International Relations." *Journal of Conflict Resolution* 7 (2015): 1301–1326.

Security Council. "Security Council Unanimously Adopts Resolution 2242 (2015) to Improve Implementation of Landmark Text on Women, Peace, Security Agenda." Meetings Coverage, October 13, 2015, http://www.un.org/press/en/2015/sc12076.doc.htm.

Shepherd, L. J. "Making War Safe for Women? National Action Plans and the Militarisation of the Women, Peace, and Security agenda." *International Political Science Review* 3 (2016): 324–335.

True, J. "Winning the Battle but Losing the War on Violence: A Feminist Perspective on the Declining Global Violence Thesis." *International Feminist Journal of Politics* 4 (2015): 554–572.

Tryggestad, T. L. "Trick or Treat? The UN Implementation of Security Council Resolution 1325 on Women, Peace and Security." *Global Governance* 15 (2009): 539–557.

United Nations. "Report of the Secretary-General on Women and Peace and Security." S/2015/716, 2015.

UN Women. "Global Study on the Implementation of Security Council Resolution 1325 (2000)." Peace Women, 2014, http://peacewomen.org/sites/default/files/GS1325-2pager-10dec2014.pdf.

UN Women. "Consultations." 2015a, http://wps.unwomen.org/en/global-study/consultations.

UN Women. "Global Study Consultation—Global Civil Society." 2015b, http://wps.unwomen.org/en/highlights/global-civil-society-consultation.

UN Women. "High-level Advisory Group for Global Study on SCR 1325(2000)." 2015c, http://wps.unwomen.org/en/global-study/high-level-advisory-group

UN Women. "High-Level Review." 2015d, http://www.unwomen.org/en/news/in-focus/women-peace-security/2015.

Walter, B. F. *Committing to Peace: The Successful Settlement of Civil Wars*. Princeton and Oxford: Princeton University Press, 2002.

Whitworth, S. *Men, Militarism, and UN Peacekeeping: A Gendered Analysis*. Boulder, CO: Lynne Rienner, 2004.

Willett, S. "Introduction: Security Council Resolution 1325: Assessing the Impact on Women, Peace and Security." *International Peacekeeping* 17, no. 2 (2010): 142–158.

PART II

PILLARS OF WPS

CHAPTER 12

WPS AND CONFLICT PREVENTION

BELA KAPUR AND MADELEINE REES

ONE of the most incomprehensible characteristics of the human species is our absolute refusal to eschew extremities of violence in order to win an argument! That argument is almost always linked to power—*who* has it, *who* wants it, and *what* they want to do with it. And power is highly gendered. As a result, in a modern era when we can achieve the most unimaginable feats of brilliance in seeking to understand ourselves and our place in the universe, we have signally failed to prevent our destructive impulses. An ever more voracious arms industry and economic models that have led to monstrous and unsustainable inequalities further fuel these impulses. The consequences are livid. If we are to be serious about preventing violent conflict, then we have to rethink "security" and what it means and address the causes of our perceived need for militarized security; a mind shift which we, so far, have been unable to realize. Stuck in this intransigent narrative of a never-ending dialectic of violence, what will it take to make that shift possible?

After declining for much of the 1990s, (notwithstanding the conflicts in Rwanda and Bosnia-Herzegovina), the incidence of violent conflict in the twenty-first century has been steadily increasing. This refers to both civil war and internationalized conflict (internal conflicts in which other states intervene militarily on one or both sides), with major civil wars having almost tripled from four in 2007 to eleven in 2014 (Von Einsiedel 2014: 2). As well as new outbreaks of armed conflict, relapse into civil war is high, with 90 percent of civil wars in the 2000s occurring in countries that had experienced civil war in the previous thirty years (World Bank 2011: 1).

This chapter sets out a practical, integrated roadmap for academics, policymakers, and field-based practitioners alike to connect local, national, regional, and global efforts for peace and security, sustainable development and human rights. We describe this roadmap as "integrated" because it consciously takes into account and synthetizes a number of academic disciplines and practical approaches, including economic, legal, political, and security (usually construed as militarized security), in order to more effectively and comprehensively respond to the inherently multifaceted causes and drivers of conflict. We take as a starting point the broader approach set out in 2015 by the UN Advisory Group of Experts on Peacebuilding;

that "sustaining peace should be understood as encompassing not only efforts to prevent re-lapse into conflict, but *also to prevent lapse into conflict in the first place*" (emphasis added) (UN Advisory Group 2015: 12). The goal must be to build and sustain peace.

THE CURRENT STATE OF CONFLICT PREVENTION POLICY

Recent peace and security reviews initiated by the United Nations have drawn attention to the structural causes and underlying drivers of conflict. These reviews have also documented and exposed the international community's resounding failure to prevent conflict in recent years. The Advisory Group of Experts' review of the UN's Peacebuilding Architecture (UN Advisory Group) analysis of factors driving conflict and rendering it more intractable to resolution range from extremism and organized crime to the proliferation of small and light weapons, weak governance, and corruption (UN Advisory Group 2015: 14–15). Significantly, the UN Advisory Group asserted that "economic and social grievances are often amongst the root causes leading to conflict" (UN Advisory Group 2015: 19).

The 2015 High Level Independent Panel review of UN Peace Operations (UN HIPPO) defined the way in which the prevention of armed conflicts is approached as "ad hoc . . . with many disparate and disconnected perspectives—diplomatic, political, developmental, and economic among others," which do not constitute "a sustained international effort to prevent conflict" (UN HIPPO 2015: 31).

Conflict prevention has also become the poor little sister of the international norma-tive Women, Peace, and Security framework, encompassed in the eight related resolutions of the UN Security Council, adopted from 2000 to 2015 (Otto 2016: 8). Overall, scant at-tention has been paid to the role of women in preventing conflict, notwithstanding the finding of the 2015 Global Study on Implementation of UN Security Council resolution 1325 (Global Study) that "the objective of UN Security Council resolution 1325 [on Women, Peace and Security] . . . at its core, [was] the prevention of armed conflict and a roll back of the escalating levels of militarization making homes, communities and nations less rather than more secure" (Global Study 2015: 194).

Specifically, the Security Council has maintained a largely ambivalent approach toward getting behind women and promoting their role in preventing conflict. At best, the Security Council has urged "the Secretary-General and his/her special envoys to invite women to participate in discussions pertinent to the prevention and resolution of conflict."[1] Yet not-withstanding this "urging," the Security Council has consistently veered away from following up and actually holding the Secretary-General and his special envoys and representatives to account for these internationally legally mandated responsibilities. Further, the Security Council itself has shown little consistent interest to meet and hear directly from women activists from countries under the Council's purview at UN Headquarters in New York and during Security Council visits to UN peace operations. Likewise, there has been little discus-sion in academic and policymaking circles on women's potential to prevent conflict.

Instead, this "prevention space" has been largely subsumed by high profile attention, policy development, monitoring, reporting, and funding on the specific issue of the prevention of sexual violence against women and girls in conflict.[2] Important as this is, it is only one element of women's experience of conflict and, as the Liberian peace activist and Nobel Laureate Leymah Gbowee powerfully reminded states at the Global Summit to End Sexual Violence in Conflict in 2014, we should not think for one minute that we can stop sexual violence in armed conflict. The only way stop sexual violence in armed conflict is to prevent the conflict in the first place.

The 2015 Global Study noted two categories around which approaches to conflict prevention have generally been grouped. First, short- and medium-term operational measures, which encompass the adoption and execution of practical strategies that monitor and prepare for the potential for violence, such as early warning and response, preventative diplomacy, peacekeeping, and the use of information and communications technology (Global Study 2015: 194-195). Second, longer-term measures of structural prevention that address the foundational roots of war and militarism. These measures aim to bring about a reduction in the potential for armed or political violence over time and promote nonviolent means to address acute needs and rights entitlements. They include efforts to address structural inequality and violence, promote human rights and human security, and engage in demilitarization, disarmament, and reduction in spending on armaments (Global Study 2015: 204).

Building upon the findings of the three peace and security related reviews of 2015, the new Secretary-General of the United Nations, Antonio Guterres, in his first address to the Security Council in early January 2017, called for a "whole new approach" to prevent conflict which connects "efforts for peace and security, sustainable development and human rights, not just in words, but in practice" (Guterres 2017).

In this chapter, we build upon increasing research relating to the structural causes that lead to conflict and violent conflict or relapse into conflict. These causes include "gender, the constructs of masculinities shaped and perpetuated by conflict, patriarchy, militarism and violence, the political economy of war, and the impact of neo-liberalism" (Rees and Chinkin 2016: 1213). Evidence increasingly suggests that addressing these underlying gendered structural causes that lead to conflict and violent conflict, with emphasis on gender inequalities and their manifestations, will have a transformative effect on building and sustaining peace. We propose four transformational shifts connecting peace and security, human rights, and sustainable development to help contribute to a more methodological approach to preventing conflict and sustaining peace.

The four transformational shifts are:

- Transforming gender relations;
- Challenging, transforming, and eliminating violent militarized power relations and militarization;
- Ensuring sustainable equitable social and economic development; and
- Promoting restorative agency.

Patriarchy and Militarization: The Impact on Women and Preventing Conflict

"An attitudinal shift is needed away from a primary focus on military responses, towards investment in peaceful conflict prevention strategies" (Global Study 2015: 195).

Recent statistical research has confirmed the experience of decades of women's peace movements: the cultural role assigned to women and the overall impact of gender in society has a relationship to intrastate (Caprioli 2005) and interstate violence (Caprioli and Boyer 2001). Specifically, the research postulates that the higher the level of gender inequalities within a state, the greater the likelihood such a state will experience internal and interstate conflict. This is, in short, because states characterized by gender discrimination and structural hierarchy are permeated with, and supported by, norms of violence that make conflict more likely. These states are, as such, "primed for violence" (Caprioli 2005: 172). Further research has indicated that the physical security of women is strongly associated with the peacefulness of the state, the degree to which the state is of concern to the international community, and the quality of relations between the state and its neighbor. These findings, together with the breadth and depth of experience of women's peace movements, suggest that the level of physical security of women is one of the most likely indicators for predicting conflict and that the security of women influences the security of the state (Hudson 2008/2009).

It is the gendered social and economic inequalities between women and men, grounded in gendered hierarchies, which make women most vulnerable to violence and abuse in any context. More specifically, it is not just poverty that heightens women's vulnerability to violence; it is women's impoverished situation relative to men—with respect to income, property, employment, and the consequent access to power—that is at the root of violence against women (True 2012: 5). Violence against women inhibits the accessing of rights and participation in public life. Hence it feeds an intractable cycle of exclusion, disempowerment, and discrimination.

This cycle is predicated upon the dominance and survival of "patriarchy." Patriarchy is a system requiring the maintenance of gender inequalities to ensure the attainment, exercise, and retention of power, in the main by a relatively small number of men, who wield influence and control over the majority of men and women. Patriarchy is dependent upon and reinforces a particular type of masculinity as the norm, a norm prepared to use violence to win the "argument." Maintenance of the patriarchic system requires the building and entrenching of particular structures; specifically hierarchies in which women adopt, or are forced into adopting, a subordinate gender role. This sustains the social and economic and power structures of patriarchy. A straightforward example of patriarchy at work is the exclusion of care work from formal economic analysis; it simply disappears from the books, is generally ignored or undervalued by the political and economic elite, and yet conversely is worth billions to the economy of all countries. The work of—in the main—women in raising children, caring for the elderly, and having responsibility for the overall welfare of families, both immediate and extended, is deemed to be irrelevant in assessing how well an economy is performing. In a patriarchal system, care work is just what women are supposed to do.

Under patriarchy, some women are more privileged by virtue of their class, race, ethnicity, color, sexual orientation . . ., a long list of intersecting identities which are used to create and sustain inequalities and othering. But within each category, men will still be privileged over women. When there is tension among men, especially during the run up to violent conflict and the conflict itself, gender roles tend to be intensified; the men to become first protectors, and then warriors; the women to be protected and to support their men. The manipulation of identities; nationalism, religious affiliation, ethnicity, and so on, all can be dragged in to create or drive conflict and ensure the maintenance of power or indeed provoke attempts to seize power. And it never ends well.

The intensification of traditional gender roles and the increasing marginalization of women in public life is, therefore, an early warning sign of the potential for conflict to descend into violent conflict. In the former Yugoslavia just prior to the conflict, the number of women in Parliament fell from above 25 percent to below 6 percent. Men increasingly interacted with men of the same ethnic group in a variety of social locations. In a retrospective hosted by the Women's International League for Peace and Freedom (WILPF) in 2014, Bosnian women remarked that if only they had known then what they know now, (i.e., how the changes in the social conduct of their men folk were identifiers of polarizations and developing violent identities), they would not have had the same sense of denial of impending violence; they could have seen war coming. Similarly, following the annexation of the Crimea by the Russian Federation and the eruption of fighting in eastern Ukraine in 2014, the creation and dissemination of the "heroic warrior" narrative became ubiquitous in Ukraine, to the extent that it even included the women in uniform. However, women's participation in the military is highly gendered in terms of practice and perception; beauty contests for those women in uniform being just one manifestation of the questionable "liberating" impact of serving in the military in Ukraine, one which is not exclusive to that State.

It is opportune to mention that the increasing number of women in the military results directly from the deliberate militarization of Security Council resolution 1325. Instead of women changing the militarized system, the system has co-opted women into it! This is evidenced by, inter alia, the emphasis on women in the military in Security Council Resolution 1325 national action plans, the decision to introduce conscription for women in Norway and Sweden, the international praise heaped on South Africa for reaching over 30 percent women in its military, and the considerable efforts of UN peacekeeping to increase the number of women in blue . . . yet where is the equivalent push and encouragement from international actors to increase the numbers of women in governance and decision-making structures and in formal economic activity? And where is the thinking on how to actually achieve women's greater participation in these spheres through properly funded child care, healthcare, education, and reproductive rights? The shift toward, effectively, the militarization of the international women, peace, and security agenda was surreptitiously made; the language of participation quietly converted into military speak, the rationale for Security Council resolution 1325 silently subverted. Yet, as a system, patriarchy is not changed by the addition of a few women into positions of power. The structure of power and the gendered assumptions that sustain it are flawed and must be changed.

The increasing understanding of gender dynamics as a predictor of violent conflict is contrasted with the increasing focus and resources of international actors on militarized approaches to security and resolution of disputes. In 2016, global military expenditure was an estimated US$1686 billion, representing an increase of about 0.4 percent in real terms from 2015, and equivalent to 2.2 percent of global gross domestic product (SIPRI 2017). By early 2017, the global transfer of major weapons systems had risen over the past five years to the highest volume since the end of the Cold War, with many countries of the Middle East nearly doubling imports (Dehghan 2017). Similarly, the budget for UN peacekeeping has increased annually in recent years (though 2016–2017 saw a 0.4 percent decrease from 2015–2016) (UN Peacekeeping 2017) at the expense of UN development funding, reflecting the quasi knee-jerk reaction of the international community for militarized responses to threats and breaches to international peace and security, which—in the main—serve to freeze peace processes and manage conflicts as opposed to resolving them.

Indeed, as the Global Study pointed out, this militarized approach to security "is not the 'prevention' envisaged 15 years ago [in Security Council resolution 1325]. A militarized view of conflict prevention sells resolution 1325 short of its transformative vision for a more equal, just and peaceful world, and neglects a proven tool, [women], to achieve this" (Global Study 2015: 24). We find ourselves in this situation, in part, as a result of the exclusion from Security Council resolution 1325 of all references to disarmament and militarism championed by WILPF in the negotiations. This absence has left the door wide open for the co-option of women into the security part of the resolution in its traditional, militarized interpretation and at the expense of how to secure peace. As a result, and somewhat ironically, the international Women, Peace, and Security agenda has actually cemented the idea that securing international peace relies on military peace and securitized states (Otto 2016: 10)!

Conversely, while international actors—both states and international and regional organizations and alliances, including the United Nations—continue to rely on the use of force as a central means to prevent and resolve conflict, the meaning of "security" as experienced by the people living in insecure, fragile, and conflict-affected contexts is undergoing transformation. No longer is "security" understood as referring solely to physical security, and especially relating to the security of the state, provided through militarized approaches and specifically, armaments.

Instead, those on the receiving end of "insecurity" are redefining security more broadly to incorporate the human dimensions of what "feeling secure and insecure" means to them as individuals, families, and communities. They describe security as requiring not just physical security, but other measures too, including economic, health, food, shelter, and environmental aspects (see chapter 60 in this volume). This approach to security necessitates that security is built from the ground up as opposed to having security "done" to them exogenously. To state the obvious, only through participation in the approach to security can there be prospects for ensuring success. This broader human-centered approach recognizes the roles of women in sustaining security within their families, communities, and wider society.

In short the evidence now shows that there are two realities that must inform strategies and approaches to security and the prevention of conflict:

1. the realization that gender-based violence arising from gendered structural violence is a predictor of armed conflict; and
2. the reality that, on the ground, women are central actors in sustaining security.

It is clear, however, that actions taken so far are the antithesis of what needs to be done to make and sustain peace.

The Four Transformational Shifts to Prevent Conflict

Shift 1: Transforming Gender Relations

The nexus between political economy and gender relations is causal in the buildup to conflict or its avoidance. We have asserted that gender relations are a product of patriarchy and of the consequent political economy. Logically, therefore, ending patriarchy and fundamentally changing the structures which underpin the design of political economy will transform gender relations. Which is where we come to the "if only"; if only we could ensure that from early childhood, all children were enabled to understand themselves as having a biological sex and a gender, but instead of co-opting the biological sex to ascribe characteristics, gender is used to be inclusive of multiple, and not binary, identities—all of equal value and import. Naturally, such an approach requires legal frameworks and social and cultural contexts to re-enforce it. Indeed, in Sweden, there are progressive schools that are developing such approaches but clearly the results will take time to permeate into society more broadly.

Suggested ways forward might include:

- Engaging with men to challenge and broaden current concepts of masculinity;
- Investing in education with curricula that supports the approaches just mentioned (also noting evidence that suggests that boys with higher levels of education are less likely to use violence[3]);
- Effective application of human rights, especially social, cultural, and economic rights, and an insistence on non-discrimination; this must be applied so as to break gendered discrimination—from education, to employment, to social welfare, land rights, inheritance, rights to nationality, and rights of property ownership;
- Ensuring economic value is ascribed to unpaid work, predominantly undertaken by women;
- Supporting women to see agency in the work they do in—for example, in caring roles—and "degendering" particular types of employment, such as nursing or policing;
- Ensuring committed political, policy, and funding support for implementation of the Sustainable Development Goals.

These are the headlines. There are multiple issues to be considered under each of them, which fall beyond the scope of this article.

Shift 2: Challenging, Transforming, and Eliminating Violent Militarized Power Relations and Militarization

Militarism as a way of thought and the militarization of societies, such that perceived threats are likely to be met with weaponry rather than words, is a root cause of conflict and violent conflict (WILPF 2015: 1). This is because militarism and cultures of militarized masculinities create and sustain political decision-making whereby resorting to the use of force becomes a normalized mode for dispute resolution (Global Study 2015: 207). As the UN Advisory Group of Experts explained, while militarized responses can be effective in the immediate context of halting violence, they tend to address symptoms rather than root causes. "The very nature of such responses, with their emphasis on short term security, can sometimes reduce support and detract attention from achieving sustainable peace" (UN Advisory Group 2015: 46).

Challenging militarism is therefore a key strategy to prevent conflict and sustain peace. None of the eight Security Council resolutions on Women, Peace, and Security call for disarmament. This is notwithstanding the reality that conflict prevention cannot take place without disarmament and the references to disarmament in the Charter of the United Nations (including the obligation of the Security Council to promote the establishment and maintenance of international peace and security "with the least diversion for armaments of the world's human and economic resources").[4]

The 2013 Arms Trade Treaty (ATT) makes it mandatory for arms exporting states to assess the risk that their weapons will be used to commit or facilitate serious acts of gender-based violence or serious acts of violence against women and children and to deny authorization of any sales that present such a risk.[5] It was only due to the interventions of WILPF, which galvanized other local and international NGOs to advocate for the gendered impact of weaponry, that such language was included.

The Committee on the Elimination of Discrimination Against Women (the CEDAW Committee) has followed up on this ATT provision in General Recommendation 30 on women in conflict prevention, conflict, and post-conflict. After referring to the direct and indirect impact of the proliferation of conventional weapons on women as victims of conflict-related gender-based violence, as victims of domestic violence, and also as protestors or actors in resistance movements,[6] the Committee recommends state parties address the gendered impact of international transfers of arms, especially small and illicit arms including through the ratification and implementation of the ATT.[7] However, while the references to gender-based violence and violence against women and children represent an important step forward in the recognition of the gendered impact of the proliferation and use of arms, we are still confronted by the overall objective of the ATT, which is to prevent and eradicate the *illicit* trade in conventional arms and not to prevent and eradicate the transfer of arms per se (on this point see chapter 54 in this volume).

Given its founding principle as a peace organization—to save "succeeding generations from the scourge of war"—the United Nations, led by the new Secretary-General, should more robustly and visibly promote disarmament as a central strategy to prevent conflict. In his first public pronouncement on the need to prioritize prevention, the Secretary-General called for a "surge in diplomacy for peace" as a means of preventive action. Though recognizing that "war is never inevitable. It is always a matter of choice: the choice to exclude, to discriminate, to marginalize, to resort to violence," the Secretary-General has, to date, been disappointingly silent on the need for disarmament (Guterres 2017). It is critical that the Secretary-General take firm unequivocal steps to reframe the ongoing "prevention" debate; beyond elaboration of early warning measures and increased public and private mediation, the Secretary-General must—and must be seen to—advocate robustly for a world without weapons. Disarmament must be a key element of his platform to prevent conflict if the universal calls for conflict prevention are to make real headway in the world today.

Suggested ways forward might include:

- Civil Society Organizations (CSOs) documenting and reporting on prevalence of arms and their use;
- CSOs advocating against the sale and use of arms;
- UN Human Rights Treaty Bodies to highlight the legal obligations on arms producing states for their impact on human rights and in particular the impact on women;
- Increased multidisciplinary research on nonviolent conflict resolution alternatives;
- Constant exposure of the economic costs to countries which prioritize the purchase of weaponry over the protection of human rights and how "moving the money" from the arms trade and military defense to sustainable development would lead to enhanced and real security.

Shift 3: Ensuring Sustainable Equitable Social and Economic Development

Our economic systems are now globalized. The hegemony of neoliberalism has been accepted even as the world economic crisis of 2008 exposed it as a shibboleth. The dominant theory perpetuated by neo-liberalism has led to enormous inequality with the oft-quoted figure of 1 percent owning the vast majority of the world's wealth. It has led to the politics of austerity across much of the world—developing and so-called developed countries alike—and the attendant assault on social and economic rights. Indeed, instead of progressive realization of such rights, most children will be less able to access healthcare, education and employment than their parents.

And there is a gender dimension to neo-liberalism (Hozic and True 2016). The politics of austerity have hit women harder and in more aspects of their lives. In so doing, austerity measures have shown that they are the antithesis of what needs to be done to redress the power structures within households and society more broadly. Economic structural adjustment or neoliberal reform inhibits the participation of women in public life and, as per the preceding analysis, exacerbates still further the potential for violence. It is recognized that inequalities in access to and enjoyment of economic and social rights constitute a root cause of conflict (UN OHCHR 2014). Ergo: given the increasing inequalities arising directly from impact of austerity measures, we are right on course for major and violent conflict, or, indeed, conflicts.

There is an urgent need, therefore, to rethink how the relationship with economics and human rights impacts gender and peace. One way of doing so is to examine the role and impact of the international financial institutions (IFIs), the development banks, and, in particular, the World Bank (see chapter 26 in this volume). These institutions are hugely influential in how states structure their budgets, and, therefore, influence the organization and how priorities made. Hence, IFI conditionalities can fundamentally transform the political and social contract of a country. For example, post-conflict Bosnia-Herzegovina not only had to transition from war to a (so-called) peace, but also to move from a centralized socialist system into the brick wall of free market capitalism.

To summarize, instead of investing in programs to address the consequences of conflict, such as reparations, particular types of healthcare, education, infrastructure repair, job creation, and the like, the conditionalities imposed by the IFIs on loans, insisted, inter alia, on reductions in welfare (despite the inevitable needs after conflict), the privatization of virtually anything owned by the Bosnian state, and an increase in indirect taxes, such as VAT which hit the poorest most. Bosnia-Herzegovina is subject to some 187 conditionalities. The impact these have had on social and economic rights has been highlighted to the UN human rights treaty bodies and addressed through the concluding observations by the Committees on Economic, Social, and Cultural Rights, and the Elimination of All Forms of Discrimination Against Women. Significantly, the treaty bodies' recommendations relate to the State of Bosnia-Herzegovina and not to those institutions imposing the conditionalities (True et al. 2017).

The IFIs and the World Bank in particular have long argued that their remit is economic only and that human rights are political, hence the responsibility of the borrowing State. This precept is gradually being challenged on several grounds. It is simply illogical to pretend that economics lives in isolation from politics; political choices and policies obviously have an impact on human rights, and law, therefore, has a role in regulation of those policies so as to protect rights. Soft law is pointing us in a direction that will compel hard law regulation. The "pointing" needs to be accelerated through intelligent submissions to CEDAW and other treaty bodies. If such an approach is adopted it would do the following:

Bring the World Bank and their associated development banks into the discussions on prevention, (see chapter 26, this volume), which if done from an evidence-, experiential-, human rights–based perspective would show the extent of inequalities and the developing fault lines. Bring their existing work, for example, on laws that prevent women entering the work force, into the diagnosis of the gendered political economy in any given country. As previously outlined, that diagnosis would indicate how and in what way the social and economic structures predispose that society to violence. The state, with the support of the international community and with targeted financial support, could then seek to redress inequalities through specific policies. Self-evidently, this analysis and solution is predicated upon the participation of civil society. The role of the IFIs in preventing conflict should be integrated into the observations and recommendations of the UN human rights system, including treaty bodies, special procedures, and the UPR process, as a way of "normalizing" their responsibilities.

Addressing inequalities in the distribution of economic and social rights and the structures that underpin such discrimination is critical to eliminate this root cause of conflict and violent conflict (True et al. 2017). A great deal of work has been undertaken on the justiciability of economic, social, and cultural rights. Without the empowerment provided by equal access to and delivery of economic, social, and cultural rights through national legal frameworks, in accordance with international standards, there can be no real addressing of the underlying grievances and creation of positive peace. Indeed, without the realization of economic, social, and cultural rights, civil and political rights cannot be sustained. Human rights—in particular, economic, social, and cultural rights— can be used to support a theory of change to realize social or transformative justice (Rees and Chinkin 2016: 1220).

Shift 4: Promoting Restorative Agency: Facilitating Circumstances Whereby People Feel Renewed in Their Exercise of Power, Agency, and Participation; Giving Power Back to People; Building Reciprocity and Solidarity across Communities and Borders

In essence, building peace and preventing violence means simply this: understanding that we cannot all do everything, and looking up to see where our allies are and how to link our "causes." How a passion for saving the environment means an automatic connection with those who oppose militarism, how opposing militarism links you to those addressing the creation of violent masculinities, how working on masculinities leads you to those working on discrimination against women and violence . . . and so the process grows. The movement exists, we just have not quite worked out how to transition through the dividing membranes . . .but as we know, membrane is permeable!

CONCLUSION

How to do that, we conclude? It's an oxymoron to say we can conclude on prevention. It is ongoing, arduous, and it shifts—what must be done changes over time. But it doesn't have to be like that. In this chapter, we have tried to pull some of the pieces together to show that prevention is, in fact possible. It's a "simple" question of actually believing what empirical evidence presents, and changing the policies, practices, and ideologies that move us to conflict—even if violent conflict is not what is actually wanted. Arguments can be won through rational debate, the application of law and the common sense to realize that violence will not, ultimately, win the argument.

It is not naïve to believe we can stop war, or to want to stop war. We have argued that war flows from a particular social, cultural, and political model which then drives economic practice: patriarchy, unspoken except by feminists, but exposed by activists and now by academic research. It is a chameleon, which means we need to shine Cynthia Enloe's feminist spotlight to seek it out—in our households, our places of work, our schools, institutions, and in all our laws and policies, to name just a few. If we fail in one, it will undermine what we can achieve in another—all are integrated and intrinsic to the changes needed for peace to be realized.

NOTES

1. Security Council resolution 1325 (2000) "reaffirms the important role of women in the prevention and resolution of conflicts and in peacebuilding, and stressing the importance of their equal participation and full involvement in all efforts for the maintenance and promotion of peace and security, and the need to increase their role in decision making

with regard to conflict prevention and resolution," http://www.un.org/en/peacekeeping/issues/women/wps.shtml.

Security Council resolution 1820 (2008) "urges the Secretary-General and his Special Envoys to invite women to participate in discussions pertinent to the prevention and resolution of conflict . . . ," http://www.un.org/en/peacekeeping/issues/women/wps.shtml.

Security Council resolution 2122 (2013) "requests the Secretary-General and his Special Envoys and Special Representatives to UN missions, as part of their regular briefings, to update the Council on progress in inviting women to participate, including through consultations with civil society, including women's organizations, in discussions pertinent to the prevention and resolution of conflict, the maintenance of peace and security and post-conflict peacebuilding," http://www.un.org/en/peacekeeping/issues/women/wps.shtml.

2. See Security Council resolutions 1888 (2009), 2106 (2013), and 2242 (2015), http://www.un.org/en/peacekeeping/issues/women/wps.shtml.

See International protocol on documentation and investigation of sexual violence in conflict, accessible at https://www.gov.uk/government/publications/international-protocol-on-the-documentation-and-investigation-of-sexual-violence-in-conflict-training-materials-introduction.

3. See Sonke Gender Justice [website]. http://www.genderjustice.org.za.
4. Charter of the United Nations. Article 26, June 26, 1945, http://www.un.org/en/charter-united-nations/index.html.
5. The Arms Trade Treaty. Article 7(4), 2013, https://unoda-web.s3.amazonaws.com/wp-content/uploads/2013/06/English7.pdf.
6. CEDAW General Recommendation 30. UN Document CEDAW/C/GC/30, October 18, 2013, http://www.ohchr.org/documents/hrbodies/cedaw/gcomments/cedaw.c.cg.30.pdf, para. 32.
7. CEDAW General Recommendation 30, para. 33(e).

REFERENCES

Caprioli, M. "Primed for Violence: The Role of Gender Inequality in Predicting Internal Conflict." *International Studies Quarterly* 49, no. 2 (2005): 161–178.

Caprioli, M., and M. A. Boyer. "Gender, Violence, and International Crisis." *Journal of Conflict Resolution* 45, no. 4 (August 2001): 503–518.

Dehghan, S. K. "Global Arms Trade Reaches Highest Point since Cold War Era." *The Guardian*, February 19, 2017, https://www.theguardian.com/world/2017/feb/20/global-arms-weapons-trade-highest-point-since-cold-war-era.

Guterres, A. "Secretary-General's Remarks to the Security Council Open Debate on Maintenance of International Peace and Security: Conflict Prevention and Sustaining Peace." United Nations Secretary-General, January 10, 2017, https://www.un.org/sg/en/content/sg/statement/2017-01-10/secretary-generals-remarks-security-council-open-debate-maintenance.

Hozic, A. and J. True. *Scandalous Economics: Gender and the Politics of Financial Crises.* New York: Oxford University Press, 2016.

Hudson, V.M., B. Balliff.-Spanvill, M. Caprioli, R. McDermott, and C. F. Emmett. "The Heart of the Matter: The Security of Women and the Security of States." *International Security* 33, no. 3 (2008/2009): 7–45.

Otto, D. "Women, Peace, and Security: A Critical Analysis of the Security Council's Vision." LSE Centre for Women, Peace, and Security Working Paper Series January 2016, http://eprints.lse.ac.uk/69472/?from_serp=1 .

Rees, M., and C. Chinkin. "Exposing the Gendered Myth of Post Conflict Transition: The Transformative Power of Economic and Social Rights." *New York University Journal of International Law and Politics* 48, no. 4 (2016): 1211–1226.

SIPRI. Trends in World Military Expenditure, 2016. SIPRI Factsheet, April 2017, https://www.sipri.org/sites/default/files/Trends-world-military-expenditure-2016.pdf.

True, J. *The Political Economy of Violence Against Women.* New York: Oxford University Press, 2012.

True, J., C. Chinkin, M. Rees, N. Porobić Isaković, G. Mlinarević, and B. Svedberg. "A Feminist Perspective on Post Conflict Restructuring and Recovery—The Case of Bosnia and Herzegovina." WIPLF, August 30, 2017.

UN Advisory Group "The Challenge of Sustaining Peace." The Report of the Review of the United Nations Peacebuilding Architecture, 2015, http://www.un.org/pga/wp-content/uploads/sites/3/2015/07/300615_The-Challenge-of-Sustaining-Peace.pdf.

UN HIPPO. "Uniting our Strengths for Peace—Politics, Partnerships, and People." The Report of the High Level Independent Panel on Peace Operations. UN Document A/70/95-S/2015/446, 2015, http://www.un.org/en/peacekeeping/resources/reports.shtml.

UN OHCHR. UN Office of the High Commissioner for Human Rights (OHCHR), Transitional Justice and Economic, Social, and Cultural Rights. UN Document HR/PUB/13/5, UN Sales No. E.14.XIV.3, 2014.

UN Peacekeeping Approved Resources for Peacekeeping Operations for the Period from July 1, 2016 to June 30, 2017. Note by the Secretary-General. "UN Document A/C.5/70/24, 2017.

UN Women. "Transforming Justice, Securing the Peace. A Global Study on the Implementation of United Nations Security Council Resolution 1325 (2000)." Lead author: Radhika Coomaraswamy. UN Women, 2015, http://wps.unwomen.org/pdf/en/GlobalStudy_EN_Web.pdf.

Von Einsiedel, S., L. Bosetti, R. Chandram, J. Cockayne, J. de Boer, and W. Wan. Major "Major Recent Trends in Violent Conflict." *Occasional Paper 1.* Tokyo. United Nations University Centre for Policy Research, November 2014, http://collections.unu.edu/eserv/UNU:3212/unu_cpr_conflict_trends.pdf.

WILPF 2015. "WILPF Manifesto." April 17, 2015, https://wilpf.org/wp-content/uploads/2015/07/Manifesto-2e-print-bleed.pdf.

World Bank. Facts and Figures. World Development Report, 2011, http://web.worldbank.org/archive/website01306/web/pdf/english_wdr2011_facts_figures%20no%20embargo.pdf.

CHAPTER 13

....

WHAT WORKS IN PARTICIPATION

....

THANIA PAFFENHOLZ

RESOLUTION 1325 was widely hailed as a milestone and an unprecedented achievement, as it marked the first time the UN Security Council (UNSC) recognized the importance of including women in all aspects of conflict prevention, peace negotiations, and peace-building. Since its adoption in 2000, the international community has developed an extensive normative framework on Women, Peace, and Security (WPS), including seven subsequent resolutions.[1] Indeed, as the "Global Study on the Implementation of United Nations Security Council Resolution 1325" (hereafter referred to as the "Global Study") notes, "it is hard to think of one resolution that is better known for its name, number, and content than resolution 1325" (UN Women 2015: 28). Women's participation in peace talks has been a recurrent theme within the WPS agenda. A range of specific commitments has been made to increase women's representation in peace processes and to render peace negotiations more gender sensitive. In 2012, UN Women (2012: 3) reported an increase in consultations with women's groups in peace negotiations, as well as a higher number of women within mediation teams, yet the overall numbers of women in high level peace negotiations remain low. Despite some progress, participation of women in peace negotiations remains the exception rather than the norm, and it is constantly challenged by those in power of the process. Women's participation remains a contested affair (Paffenholz et al. 2016: 18).

While for a long time most of the debates focused on a rights-based understanding of women's participation and gender-sensitivity, the focus has only recently shifted toward a different framing of the debate around the effectiveness of women's participation for peace processes. The reasons for this shift can be found in the fact that fifteen years of rights-based advocacy has not led to substantial changes in the practice of women's participation in peace talks. Nevertheless, until recently, research about the possible effects of women's participation on peace negotiations and under which conditions these are achieved (or not) has been rather limited. Within this newer research there are two main strands. First, there is research that makes statistical correlations and causations regarding women's participation and the reduction in violence after peace agreements (Stone 2014). Second, there is qualitative research showing how and under which conditions women's participation in peace negotiations can have positive effects (Paffenholz et al. 2016). The later research shows that it is not women's participation as such, but rather the degree of women's actual influence on peace negotiations that increases the likelihood of the signing and implementation of peace agreements (Paffenholz et al. 2016).

This chapter provides an overview of the development of the discourses within the WPS agenda and its relation to peace negotiations.[2] It aims at demonstrating how the discourse has shifted from "counting women" to "making women count" (Paffenholz et al. 2016). The chapter then seeks to also explain the substance behind this recent shift to come to a better understanding of what "making women count" entails in peace negotiations—for example, what is meant by "meaningful" women participation. It also illustrates implications of this changed policy discourse for the continued participation of women in ongoing peace talks.

COUNTING WOMEN AND GENDER PROVISIONS

Women's participation has always been one of the four pillars of the WPS agenda, besides prevention, protection, peace-building, and recovery. Resolution 1325 itself mentions women's "full participation in the peace process" and encourages "the Secretary-General to implement his strategic plan of action (A/49/587) calling for an increase in the participation of women at decision making levels in conflict resolution and peace processes" (UN Security Council Resolution 2000: 2). Over the years, the WPS discourse in both policy and academia has focused on different arguments for women's participation. This section aims to provide an overview of these main discussions on women's participation in peace processes.

From its outset, the 1325 agenda took a primarily normative and rights-based approach. One of the major arguments of this approach is that, as women make up half the population, they deserve equal rights in all forms of political participation (Barnes 2011: 19; O'Reilly and O Suilleabhain 2013: 4; Gibbings 2011: 528). Accordingly, women's participation in peace talks is also perceived as strategically important. Their inclusion is vital in order to push for human rights and women's issues within new legal and institutional frameworks in political transition processes, and thus ensure the long-term participation of women in political institutions (Chinkin 2003: 7; Bell and O'Rourke 2010: 948; UN Women 2012: 12). Interestingly, Resolution 1325 does not even call for "equal" participation of women in peace talks, which can—according to Aroussi (2015: 155)—be seen as a major drawback for the WPS agenda from its start.

This paradigm drew upon two other main fields of research that emerged in the post–Cold War era: firstly, on the notion of human security (Kaldor 1999), and secondly, on the work of feminist scholars who examined the gendered impact of both war and peace. These scholars found that since conflicts affect women and men differently, it is important to include both women and men in peace negotiations (Willett 2010: 144). A perspective emerged that gives agency to women as the largest excluded group from political decision-making.

After the adoption of Resolution 1325, researchers wanted to better understand the evidence around women's participation and its relationship to the adoption of the resolution. Hence, numerous studies focused on references to women and gender-sensitive language in peace agreements flourished. Ellerby (2016) found that out of fifty-four negotiated peace processes between 1991 and 2014, only 65 percent include any reference to women and/or gender. Other scholars have argued that Resolution 1325 has had a positive impact with regard to increasing the number of references to women and gender issues in peace agreements. Bell and O'Rourke's (2010: 954) research shows that only 11 percent of peace agreements made specific reference to women before the year 2000. In only ten years after 2000, such references increased by 27 percent.

The policy world has primarily aimed to increase the numbers of women included in peace talks. These arguments have been reflected in several policy documents subsequent to Resolution 1325. For example, UNSC Resolution 1889 (2009) calls for the greater use of gender advisors, and for taking into consideration women's empowerment in post-conflict planning. In addition, UNSC Resolution 2122 (2013) requests that the UN Secretary-General supports the appointment of more women mediators. It also calls on peace process parties to "facilitate the equal and full participation of women at decision-making levels." Furthermore, a report of the Secretary General published in 2010 contained seven commitments that aimed at increasing women's representation and including a gender aspect in peace negotiations (UNSG 2010). Specific measures outlined in these commitments notably demanded increasing the number of women in peace talks, both as participants and as mediators. In 2012, UN Women released a report that focused on how the number of women participants in peace processes could be increased. It found that in thirty-one major peace processes between 1992 and 2011, only 4 percent of signatories, 2 percent of chief mediators, and 9 percent of negotiators were women (UN Women 2012: 3).

FACTORS CONSTRAINING WOMEN'S PARTICIPATION

When it comes to barriers to women's participation, True's research (2013: 5) found that the context of the political economy can often reinforce gender inequalities. This occurs especially where military security strategies are implemented at the expense of, and without paying attention to, political and economic stabilization. Moreover, as Moosa et al. (2013: 459) argue, there are several factors that restrict women's participation in formal peace processes, including restrictive patriarchal norms and attitudes; a culture of violence against women; the "multiple work burdens" that women often face (including house-hold, children, and employment); lower levels of education; lack of long-term sustainable funding for women's organizations; and a lack of access to decision-makers, mainly by rural women. Domingo et al. (2015: 24) found that other major obstacles to women's participation include peace processes that are often militarized; gender agendas that are often seen as less important than other transformative agendas; and the commitment-implementation gap. Another interesting study by Goetz and Jenkins (2016: 213) shows that women's groups often face stricter conditions than others regarding participation in peace negotiations. For example, during talks in Northern Uganda in 2008 and in Syria in 2012, the UN's chief mediator demanded that "any women's groups invited to participate must represent the full diversity of women's groups, country-wide"—a condition that was not imposed upon other civil society organizations (Goetz and Jenkins 2016: 219). The research of Paffenholz et al. (2016: 5) confirms this finding and also highlights the fact that women's groups were the sole sector in peace negotiations that could participate only after they or their external supporters applied massive pressure. This was far less the case for other groups wanting to participate (2016: 18).

MAKING WOMEN COUNT

Even before Resolution 1325, research studies were set up to try to establish a link between women's participation and the outcomes of peace negotiations. Research based on experimental studies collected by the GlobalEd project showed that introducing women into "a decision-making environment can substantially alter the behaviour of the group" (Boyer et al. 2009: 37). This study found that female negotiators are more likely to interact with their counterparts, and work in a collaborative and creative manner, than male negotiators. Furthermore, another experimental study conducted in the context of the Israel-Palestine conflict found that respondents rated female negotiators' trustworthiness higher than that of male negotiators, even when the same compromise was offered (Maoz 2009: 532). It also showed that gendered stereotypes portraying women as more peace-oriented than men could lead to a self-fulfilling prophecy. In other words, the stereotypes grant them increased capability to wage or promote peace through garnering support, as proposals by female mediators were considered more credible and less self-interested (Maoz 2009: 531).

Other studies looked more into the longer-term effects of women's participation and of gender-sensitive language in peace talks. Domingo et al. (2015: 22) asserted that gender-sensitive agreements help improve women's access to representation in post-agreement political transition phases. Moreover, Anderson and Swiss (2014: 35) found that countries with peace agreements that include specific references to women's rights are more likely to adopt quotas than in cases where there is no reference to women's issues. Stone's research (2014) found that women's participation increases the prospects of short-term durability of peace (defined as the non-recurrence of armed conflict within one year), although there appears to be no significant effect in the long-term (five years). This study also argued that the use of gender quotas has a positive impact on the durability of peace. Aroussi (2015: 153), on the other hand, argued that quantitative data can only provide limited understanding of the actual implementation of women's rights and issues in peace agreements. High levels of representation do not necessarily lead to improvement in women's rights (Aroussi 2015: 181).

A substantial shift in the literature emerged with research showing that the short- and long-term effects of women's participation in peace talks only occur if women have an influence on the process. As Ellerby (2016: 6) argued with respect to research on women's participation in peace processes, "having an empirical framework of substantive representation and participation rather than just counting the number of times women and/or gender is mentioned in agreements is important." The study "Making Women Count—not Just Counting Women," which informed the Global Study's participation chapter,[3] argued that voices of women who are included in peace negotiations are nonetheless often excluded from decision-making. Thus, approaches that focus on how many women are represented are insufficient. Based on twenty-eight cases of women's formal and substantive participation in peace processes derived from a data set of forty peace negotiations,[4] the study found that only when women had an influence inside or outside of the official talks was there an increase in peace agreements signed and implemented. The study had wide-ranging influence on policy processes. For example, UN Security Council Resolution 2242 on women's roles in countering violent extremism and terrorism "*encourages* those supporting peace processes to facilitate women's meaningful participation in negotiating parties' delegations to peace talks." In addition, the General Assembly's (GA) discussion in October 2016 and various events during the GA saw both UN agencies and member states talking about "meaningful" women's participation or "making women count."

This demonstrates a successful paradigm shift in the WPS discourse that has been directly influenced by research, although what exactly entails "meaningful" participation seems not to be fully clear. The research findings of Paffenholz et al. (2016) centering on women's influence and meaningful participation are analyzed in what follows. This will involve consideration of what women's influence entails and what factors support or hinder meaningful women's participation in peace processes.

What Works and What Does Not for Women's Participation

References to "meaningful" or "influential" or "effective" women's participation entered the WPS agenda unreservedly since UNSC Resolution 2242 (2015), even if they had been mentioned in various earlier policy documents. But what is behind the meaning of "meaningful" participation? It obviously refers to more than mere formal representation at the negotiation table. The following part of the chapter aims to deconstruct what meaningful participation means by discussing key research findings from Paffenholz et al. (2016). It is not women's participation in peace negotiations per se that contributes to reaching and sustaining peace agreements, but rather that women's influence is needed in the process. Women's influence is best understood in relation to an intertwined set of key process and context factors in circumstances where they have been in place in negotiation cases where women's presence lead to more sustainable outcomes. It also applies in circumstances where these factors had not been in place and there was no correlation between women's presence—even in high numbers—and increased outcomes.

The first factor is related to the structure and design of the process of participation. Most research and policy studies on women's participation in peace and transition processes have focused on the official negotiation table as the sole space for participation (Bell and O'Rourke 2010; Ellerby 2016; Ellerby 2013; Nakaya 2003; and Taylor 2015). However, the research of Paffenholz et al. (2016) has found that there are many other ways to effectively include women in peace processes, including and beyond the official negotiation table. Seven modalities through which women can potentially gain meaningful influence on the process were identified: direct representation at the negotiation table; observer status; consultations; inclusive commissions; high-level problem-solving workshops; public decision-making; and mass action. These modalities and the conditions under which women have exerted influence in each of the modalities are discussed in the following paragraphs. The modalities were first identified by Paffenholz (2014) for the purposes of civil society inclusion in peace negotiations, and have since been adapted for use in relation to women's inclusion (Paffenholz et al. 2016).

Direct representation at the negotiation table

Apart from participating as members of official negotiation delegations, there have also been some instances in which separate women's delegations have been created alongside other involved actors. Moreover, participation of different groups at the negotiation table can also be facilitated through the creation of special working groups, sub-committees or technical committees. Our research has found that women's quotas can be effective in ensuring a higher representation of women at the negotiation table. This is evident in the case of the Yemeni National Dialogue, which had a 30 percent women's quota (Paffenholz and Ross 2016). However, representation does not necessarily lead to influence. Oftentimes, women as members of negotiation delegations are more likely to push for their party's interests than for women's issues per se. For example, in Nepal during the Constituent Assembly negotiations from 2008 to 2012, women who were represented in high numbers with 197 out of 601 seats across delegations primarily took the position of their political parties. Women did not manage to unite to pass certain citizenship laws for the benefit of women and children as their parties decided to vote against them (Inclusive Peace & Transition Initiative 2016). In cases where women in different delegations coordinated strategically to advance common interests, they gained more influence. For example, in the Democratic Republic of Congo (DRC) Inter-Congolese Dialogue (1999–2003), women across delegations united to push for the signing of a peace agreement during a fragile moment. Women-only delegations were also very effective even if seen in only a few cases. For example, in Northern Ireland the women's coalition—comprised mostly of women activists—successfully pushed for inclusion of women in the agenda. The coalition was also instrumental in the successful negotiation of the wider peace deal.

Observer Status

Depending on the case, women observers being in the room have been able to informally lobby or advise the mediation team or the negotiating parties. Observer status provides direct presence during talks, though often at the expense of limited influence. In the case of Liberia in 2003, women observers were influential because they collaborated successfully with strong women activists outside of the talks. They were able to do so by keeping these activists informed of the negotiation agenda.

Consultations

Consultations can take place in different formats. They can be formally mandated or exist informally. They can also be elite-based, broad-based, or even public. The results of consultation processes can vary quite considerably. Much depends on the transfer strategies to the official negotiation table or the ways in which concerns raised during consultations are channeled to mediation teams and negotiating parties. In the cases studied, consultations constituted the most frequently used participation modality. While most broad-based consultations have included women, women-only consultations are rare However, they do seem to become increasingly popular among mediators as observed in

Yemen (2013–2014), Syria (2015–onwards), and Libya (2015). The research showed that women were most likely to have an impact on peace processes through consultations when they succeeded in jointly promoting positions on women's issues with clear explanations of their demands. In South Africa in 1990, nationwide public consultations conducted by the Women's National Coalition influenced the drafting of the Women's Charter for Effective Equality, which, in turn, helped shape equality provisions in the 1997 constitution (Paffenholz et al. 2016: 33).

Inclusive Commissions

Women participate in commissions which tend to be established in the implementation phase of a peace agreement. However, in some cases these commissions are tasked with preparing or conducting peace negotiations. In other cases, commissions can also take on the role of permanent constitutional bodies as in Kyrgyzstan in 2013 and in Kenya in 2008. Gender equality provisions and particularly quotas have helped increase the number of women in commissions. Such provisions are especially useful when they are explicitly defined in the peace agreement. They can also influence the language in peace agreements or constitutional documents. In the cases examined, women participated in commissions across all negotiation phases. The research found that women were more likely to exercise influence over peace processes through their participation in commissions if they were involved as early as possible.

High-Level Problem-Solving Workshops

Sometimes referred to as "Track 1.5," high-level problem-solving workshops can provide informal and unofficial participation spaces involving representatives close to negotiation party leaders. Such meetings can serve as an alternative to official negotiations at which leaders might refuse to meet in public (Paffenholz 2014). In the cases studied, women tended to be underrepresented in high-level problem-solving workshops. Yet, there were occasions in which women managed to influence peace processes through joint positions in workshops specifically designed for addressing tensions and grievances of women. For example, this was the case in the DRC during the Inter-Congolese Political Negotiations in 2002. As with consultations, effective transfer and communication strategies are essential in order for participants in high-level workshops to influence formal negotiations in a meaningful way.

Public decision-making processes such as elections and referenda can serve to ratify peace agreements, new constitutions, or other relevant decisions pertaining to peace and transition processes. Strong public endorsement, which was the case in Northern Ireland's referendum on the Good Friday Agreement, can increase the legitimacy of an agreement. This can also raise the chances of its long-term sustainability. On the other hand, a public rejection of such a major document can also put the entire process on hold, as in the rejection of the Annan Peace Plan in Cyprus in 2004. While this is another modality through which women have participated in peace and transition processes, there are few reliable gender-disaggregated data on women's voting patterns in public decision-making processes. In Northern Ireland, available survey data showed that women were not much more supportive of the peace agreement than men.

Mass action is often based on bottom-up initiatives with a common objective—for example, to create strong public pressure on established political and economic elites or against an ongoing crisis or conflict (Paffenholz 2014). Women's groups have been more active than any other groups in collectively organizing in favor of peace agreements. In Somaliland in 1991, women's groups organized demonstrations at key venues of the peace talks, which led to their participation as observers at the Boroma peace conference. Their demands were also acknowledged in the following national Guurtii conference, resulting in the formalization of a national charter. The Northern Ireland Women's Coalition also successfully used mass mobilizations to push for the ratification of the Good Friday Agreement in 1998. In Liberia in 2003, the Women in Peacebuilding Network (WIPNET) arranged demonstrations at important venues and during key moments of the negotiations that were instrumental for reaching a final agreement.

Enabling and Constraining Process Factors

Next to modalities of women's inclusion, the design of a peace process reveals that there are a set of process factors that can either enable or constrain women's influence (Paffenholz et al. 2016: 38–49). **Gender-sensitive selection criteria and procedures** supporting women's presence are a precondition for influence. Similarly, **decision-making procedures** can also enable or constrain participants' contributions in negotiation processes and affect whether representation is purely nominal or not. When no procedures are in place to explicitly enable women's influence on decision-making processes, this can limit their influence considerably.

Women's coalitions or caucuses can enable women to find common ground on specific issues. In the cases examined, propositions from women's groups that formed coalitions were much more likely to be considered and taken into account by the negotiating parties. When women sit in consultations or other modalities further away from the official negotiation table, effective **transfer strategies** can determine whether and to what extent different positions actually influence the official peace process. Transfer mechanisms may involve the sharing of documents such as reports and non-papers with representatives of formal Track 1 processes or through public reports and press statements. The research found that women's groups who used a variety of different transfer strategies were more likely to increase their influence.

Conflict parties and mediators can also influence women's participation in peace and transition processes. Thus, mediators with a positive attitude toward women's participation were able to significantly increase both the representation and influence of women. The **early involvement of women in the process** can also positively influence women's overall impact, not least by setting a precedent for the entire peace and transition process.

Support structures, particularly including technical support centers with access to computers and internet, and gender- and other issue-specific advice can help render women's contributions to peace and transition processes more effective. Adequate **funding** is another important factor in order to enable women's effective participation throughout all different modalities of negotiation. In particular, it can help strengthen the preparedness of women's groups and cover travel costs where necessary.

Monitoring mechanisms are crucial to keep track of the implementation of peace agreements. Yet, the research found that in most cases, monitoring mechanisms were weak. Moreover, women's involvement in such mechanisms has been particularly weak, even when women achieved a relatively high degree of influence over the negotiation process. Thus, there is little knowledge about whether gender and other provisions that had been pushed by women during the talks and subsequently made it into the agreement have ever been implemented and led to change.

The second set of factors that can affect women's influence relate to the general context in which the peace and transition process takes place (Paffenholz et al. 2016: 50–54). The research found that **elite resistance** is often an obstacle with regard to broadening participation and, for women's participation specifically. Negotiating parties and other elites often try to establish selection criteria and decision-making procedures in a way that will strengthen their own positions at the expense of their opponents. In this context of contested participation, women's participation is most often not a priority and is generally not considered politically important. When quotas were in place, male elites managed successfully to include women from their constituencies.

Public buy-in can also be a crucial factor in determining the outcome of a peace process. In the cases examined, some women's groups used public campaigns to generate momentum for peace. For example, the Northern Ireland Women's Coalition played a significant role in supporting the broad-based civil society campaign in favor of the Good Friday Agreement. By generating broad public buy-in for a process, women have been able to significantly influence the outcome. **Regional and international actors** can also push for the participation of women and women's issues in peace negotiations. The **presence of strong women's groups**, networks, or movements with experience and resources to lobby for meaningful women's participation has facilitated women's involvement in peace processes as seen in Kenya, Northern Ireland, and Liberia. **Regional and international women's networks** can support local women's groups. For example in Liberia (2003–2011), women's networks arranged mass protests outside the main venue of the peace talks in neighboring Sierra Leone with the support of a regional women's network that was also active in Sierra Leone.

Similarly, another significant factor is the **preparedness of women** based on experience and substantive expertise in previous campaigns and mobilization efforts. Throughout the 1980s, women's organizations in South Africa, which were first established in 1911, were able to draw on long-standing experience in order to unite against the apartheid regime. The **heterogeneity of women's identities** can both enable and constrain women's influence. Women do not only identify themselves with their gender, but also with other groups such as faith, nationality, or political party. Thus, women often represent a plethora of different views and agendas during peace and transition processes. Such differences in some cases have been overcome by creating common ground and forming coalitions. In other cases, these different identifies have been used by women in a proactive and positive way. For example, in Kenya, women used their party affiliations to proactively influence the negotiation agenda, while women in Liberia used their identities as wives to influence the men in the talks.

At the same time, **attitudes and expectations surrounding societal gender roles** can either facilitate or challenge women's influence in peace and transition processes. In DRC in 1999, Afghanistan in 2001, and Yemen in 2013, women's rights were contentious issues, and female participants to negotiations were oftentimes threatened or even sexually harassed and assaulted. Women in Papua New Guinea / Bougainville in 1997, however, had traditionally recognized roles as mediators. The tradition in turn enabled them to be significantly involved in the process. **Prior commitments to women's rights or gender provisions** can also support the meaningful participation of women. Notably, they provide a legal basis for women to claim their legitimacy to participate in peace and transition processes. For example, in Yemen, the transitional governance agreement of the Gulf Cooperation Council (GCC) in 2011 included provisions foreseeing the participation of women in the National Dialogue Conference (2013–2014).

Conclusions and Next Steps

This chapter has presented an overview of the shifting discourse in the policy world starting from advocacy for women's representation at the peace table since the landmark Resolution 1325, toward the acknowledgement in the Global Study that the mere presence of women by numbers is not a sufficient condition for their "meaningful" participation (UN Women 2015). The chapter has then discussed what the term "meaningful" women's participation entails and provided the reader with a better understanding of the enabling and constraining conditions that have been in place in those cases where women were included in the negotiation or through other modalities of inclusion. However, the shift in discourse has yet to be seen in practice. This would require the UN, regional organizations, member states, and NGOs to collaborate in a joint effort to make the evidence available to decision-makers, experts, and women's organizations. It also entails pushing for the design of peace negotiations and the presence of necessary political and financial conditions which together would allow women to take up influential roles.

On the research side, to further advance this agenda more research is needed to understand women's preferences in negotiations. For example: ascertaining the degree to which they really have joint interests; deconstructing women identities and their impact on the processes; making stronger differentiation between women's presence and gender issues; understanding the kinds of pushback that women have experienced, and what the best responses are; identifying the roles of different outside actors in supporting women in peace processes; and discerning what types of women's participation, which types of provisions, and what other conditions need to be in place prior to and during official talks that allow for women's participation, which will all set the preconditions for social change.

Notes

1. These are resolutions 1820 (2008), 1888 (2009), 1889 (2009), 1960 (2010), 2106 (2013), 2122 (2013), and 2242 (2015).
2. I would like to express my gratitude to Nicola Ann Hardwick for her substantial contribution in writing this chapter, as well as to Dominique Marion Fraser for her support with background research.
3. The study results were integrated into the participation chapter of the Global Study in 2015; the full study was published as a stand-alone report in 2016: see Paffenholz et al 2016.

4. For more detailed information on the case studies and methodology, see "Broadening Participation," Inclusive Peace and Transition Initiative, http://www.inclusivepeace. org/content/broadening-participation. The full list of cases is as follows: Aceh (Peace Negotiation 1999–2003); Afghanistan (Negotiations and Political Transition 2001–2005); Benin (Political Transition 1990–2011); Burundi (Peace Negotiations and Implementation 1996–2013); Colombia (Peace Negotiations 1998–2002); Cyprus (Negotiations 1999–2004); Darfur (Peace Negotiations 2009–2013); DR Congo (Inter-Congolese Dialogue 1999–2003); Egypt (Political Transition 2011–2013); El Salvador (Peace Negotiation and Implementation 1990–1994); Eritrea (Constitution-Making 1993–1997); Fiji (Political Transition / Constitution–Making 2006–2013); Georgia-Abkhazia (UN Negotiations 1997–2007); Guatemala (Peace Process 1989–1999); Israel-Palestine (Geneva Initiative 2003–2013); Israel-Palestine (Oslo I 1991–1995); Kenya (Post-Election Violence 2008–2013); Kyrgyzstan (Political Reforms 2013 to present); Liberia (Peace Agreement and Implementation 2003–2011); Macedonia (Ohrid FA Peace Process 2001–2013); Mali (Political Transition 1990–1992); Northern Mali (Peace Negotiation 1990–1996); Mexico (Chiapas Uprising and Peace Process 1994–1997); Moldova-Transnistria (Negotiations 1992–2005); Nepal (Peace Agreement and Constitution-Making 2005–2012); Northern Ireland (Good Friday 2001–2013); Papua New Guinea (Bougainville Peace Negotiations 1997–2005); Rwanda (Arusha Peace Accords 1992–1993); Solomon Islands (Townsville Peace Agreement and Constitution-Making 2000–2014); Somalia (National Peace Conference 1992–1994); Somalia (National Peace Conference 2001–2005); Somalia (Djibouti Process 1999–2001); Somaliland (Post-Independence Violence Negotiations 1991–1994); South Africa (Political Transition 1990–1997); Sri Lanka (Ceasefire, Peace Negotiation, and Elections 2000–2004); Tajikistan (Peace Negotiations and Implementation 1993–2000); Togo (Political Transition 1990–2006); Turkey Armenia Protocols 2008–2011); Turkish-Kurdish (Peace Process 2009–2014); and Yemen (National Dialogue 2011–2014).

REFERENCES

Anderson, M., and L. Swiss. "Peace Accords and the Adoption of Electoral Quotas for Women in the Developing World, 1990–2006." *Politics and Gender* 10 (2014): 33–61.

Aroussi, S. *Women, Peace, and Security: Repositioning Gender in Peace Agreements.* Cambridge, UK: Intersentia: Law and Cosmopolitan Values, 2015.

Barnes, K. "The Evolution and Implementation of UNSCR 1325: An Overview." In *Women, Peace and Security: Translating Policy into Practice*, edited by Funmi Olonisakin, Karen Barnes, and Eka Ikpe, 15–34. New York: Routledge, 2011.

Bell, C., and C. O'Rourke. "Peace Agreements or Pieces of Paper? Impact of UNSC Resolution 1325 on Peace Processes and Their Agreements. *International and Comparative Law Quarterly* 59, no. 4 (2010): 941–980.

Boyer, M. A., B. Urlacher, N. F. Hudson, A. Niv-Solomon, L. L. Janik, M. J. Butler, S. W. Brown, and A. Ioannou. "Gender and Negotiation: Some Experimental Findings from an International Negotiation Simulation." *International Studies Quarterly* 53, no. 1 (2009): 23–47.

Chinkin, C. "Peace Agreements as a Means for Promoting Gender Equality and Securing the Participation of Women." Background paper for the UN Division for the Advancement of Women Meeting of Experts. Ottawa, Canada, 2003.

Domingo, P., R. Holmes, T. O'Neil, N. Jones, K. Bird, A. Larson, E. Presler-Marshall, and C. Valters. "Women's Voice and Leadership in Decision-Making: Assessing the Evidence." London: Overseas Development Institute, 2015, https://www.odi.org/publications/9514-womens-voice-leadership-assessment-review-evidence.

Ellerby, K. "(En)gendered Security? The Complexities of Women's Inclusion in Peace Processes." *International Interactions* 39, no. 4 (2013): 435–460.

Ellerby, K. "A Seat at the Table Is Not Enough: Understanding Women's Substantive Representation in Peace Processes." *Peacebuilding* 4, no. 2 (February 18, 2016): 136–150.

Gibbings, S. L. "No Angry Women at the United Nations: Political Dreams and the Cultural Politics of United Nations Security Council Resolution 1325." *International Feminist Journal of Politics* 13, no. 4 (2011): 522–38.

Goetz, A. M., and R. Jenkins. "Agency and Accountability: Promoting Women's Participation in Peacebuilding." *Feminist Economics* 22, no. 1 (2016): 211–236.

Inclusive Peace and Transition Initiative. "Women in Peace & Transition Processes. Nepal (2008–2012)." Geneva: Inclusive Peace and Transition Initiative (Graduate Institute of International and Development Studies), 2016.

Kaldor, M. *New and Old Wars: Organized Violence in a Global Era.* Stanford, CA: Stanford University Press, 1999.

Maoz, I. "The Women and Peace Hypothesis? The Effect of Opponent Negotiators' Gender on the Evaluation of Compromise Solutions in the Israeli-Palestinian Conflict." *International Negotiation* 14, no. 3 (2009): 519–536.

Moosa, Z., M. Rahmani, and L. Webster. "From the Private to the Public Sphere: New Research on Women's Participation in Peace-Building." *Gender and Development* 21, no. 3 (2013): 453–472.

Nakaya, S. "Women and Gender Equality in Peace Processes: From Women at the Negotiating Table to Postwar Structural Reforms in Guatemala and Somalia." *Global Governance* 9, no. 4 (2003): 459–476.

O'Reilly, M., and A. Ó Súilleabháin. "Women in Conflict Mediation: Why It Matters." Issue Brief. International Peace Institute, 2013.

Paffenholz, T. "Civil Society and Peace Negotiations: Beyond the Inclusion-Exclusion Dichotomy." *Negotiation Journal* 30, no. 1 (2014): 69–91.

Paffenholz, T., and N. Ross. "Inclusive Political Settlements: New Insights from Yemen's National Dialogue." *PRISM* 6, no. 1 (2016): 199–210.

Paffenholz, T., N. Ross, S. Dixon, A. L. Schluchter, and J. True. "Making Women Count—Not Just Counting Women: Assessing Women's Inclusion and Influence on Peace Negotiations." Inclusive Peace and Transition Initiative (Graduate Institute of International and Development Studies). UN Women, 2016.

Paffenholz, T., M. O'Reilly, and A. O'Suilleabhain. "Women's Participation and a Better Understanding of the Political." In *A Global Study on the Implementation of United Nations Security Council Resolution 1325.* UN Women, 2015.

Stone, L. "Women Transforming Conflict: A Quantitative Analysis of Female Peacemaking." Working Paper. South Orange, NJ: Seton Hall, 2014.

Taylor, S. *A Better Peace? Including Women in Conflict Negotiations.* New York: The New School, 2015.

True, J. "Women, Peace, and Security in Post-Conflict and Peacebuilding Contexts." Policy Brief. Norwegian Peacebuilding Resource Centre, March 2013.

United Nations Security Council Resolution 1325. 2000. S/RES/1325.

United Nations Security Council Resolution 1889. 2009. S/RES/1889.

United Nations Security Council Resolution 2122. 2013. S/RES/2122.

United Nations Security Council Resolution 2242. 2015. S/RES/2242.

United Nations Secretary General (UNSG). "Women's Participation in Peacebuilding." Report of the Secretary-General. A/65/354—S/2010/466, 2010.

UN Women. "Women's Participation in Peace Negotiations: Connections between Presence and Influence." October 2012, http://www.unwomen.org/~/media/ headquarters/attachments/sections/library/publications/2012/10/ wpssourcebook-03a-womenpeacenegotiations-en.pdf.

UN Women. *Preventing Conflict, Transforming Justice, Securing the Peace: A Global Study on the Implementation of United Nations Security Council Resolution 1325.* New York: UN Women, 2015.

Willett, S. "Introduction: Security Council Resolution 1325: Assessing the Impact on Women, Peace, and Security." *International Peacekeeping* 17, no. 2 (2010): 142–158.

CHAPTER 14

··

WHAT WORKS (AND FAILS) IN PROTECTION

··

HANNAH DÖNGES AND JANOSCH KULLENBERG

PROTECTION AT THE FOREFRONT

THE idea that UN peacekeeping missions should protect civilians in armed conflict has steadily gained momentum since Kofi Annan first formulated it in 1998.[1] This is reflected in the development of two separate but interconnected Security Council thematic agendas: Protection of Civilians (POC) and Women, Peace, and Security (WPS). This chapter critically explores the evolution of both of these agendas from the late 1990s to the present and considers their operationalization in two peacekeeping missions, namely, the UN Stabilization Mission in the Congo (MONUSCO) and the United Nations Mission in South Sudan (UNMISS).

Though the POC concept in UN peacekeeping has developed considerably since its first use in the mandate of the UN peacekeeping mission in Sierra Leone in 1999, its practical implementation seems to lag behind. The ambiguous wording of protection in guidance and peacekeeping mandates has long left open how protection is to be achieved on the ground. This ambiguity has required individual peacekeeping missions to translate ambitious mandates into practice through developing protection tools and activities on ad hoc basis and in consideration of the country context, the available budget, and human resources capacity.[2] The specific protection of women and girls, one of the three pillars of the WPS agenda, experiences similar operationalization and implementation dilemmas.

Recurring failures to protect civilians have partially sparked conceptual and practical developments. They also underscore the limited understanding of protection practices in general, and in protection of women and girls in particular. So far, a comprehensive picture of what peacekeeping missions actually do on the ground to protect civilians and implement WPS is missing across practice and academia. Therefore, this chapter explores the implementation of WPS and POC under the guiding question of what works and fails in protection, and to what extent do the separate but interconnected agendas reinforce each other.

We argue that despite their practical overlap and implications for the physical security of populations in armed conflict, the two agendas have evolved in rather disconnected ways. However, we also observe that attention to gendered vulnerabilities in protection has increased through reference to WPS. Specific references in peacekeeping mandates were mostly in relation to sexual violence but also in the context of pushing for more female peacekeepers.[3] On the operational side, we find that the development of gender-specific methods to protect women and girls is moving forward. Yet, particularly during times of decreasing peacekeeping budgets, much work is required to avoid the potential "siloing" effect of compartmentalizing protection into ever more specific mandates. There also remains the risk that despite the increased attention to gender-based vulnerabilities, UN peacekeeping still implements protection with the same tools—predominantly male soldiers. This entails the risk of lacking gender sensitivity and subsuming women under the general group of civilians in their daily protection tasks. Ironically, there exists the parallel tendency that civilians are only perceived as victims and those are, in return, essentialized into women and children, so that the agency of local communities is neglected and the protection concerns of boys and men overlooked of women and local communities more generally (on the latter point, see Carpenter 2006 and Chapter 8).

This chapter combines specific field-based expertise in the Democratic Republic of Congo (DRC) and in the Republic of South Sudan with secondary literature on POC implementation in other contexts. In this approach, we aim to provide an assessment neither of the UN peacekeeping's efficacy, nor its achievements concerning protection and gender mainstreaming (see chapters 10 and 46 in this volume). Instead, we highlight and discuss implementation issues that we identified during field research. We proceed in three steps. Firstly, we touch upon different ways the POC concept and the WPS agenda have evolved, where they intersect, and where they diverge (for a more detailed description of the evolvement of the two agendas, see chapter 46 in this volume). We then chronologically trace this development in the mandates of MONUSCO, and UNMISS. In both DRC and South Sudan, armed actors have used sexual violence widely and systematically. Subsequently, the missions have responded with the development of specific instruments. Based on our field research, we focus on three examples at the intersection of POC and WPS practices: Women Protection Advisors (WPAs); community-based protection; and inter-organizational cooperation on monitoring and reporting.

AN AMBIGUOUS AGENDA: PROTECTION IN PEACEKEEPING AND PROTECTION OF WOMEN

Although overlapping in many aspects, the peacekeeping and gender literature are relatively disconnected, mirroring a separate evolvement of the WPS and the POC agendas through different agents and constituencies. To be sure, the two agendas share a number of commonalities. Both emerged in the same period and are centered on the idea of human security and share the historical roots of protection failures in Rwanda and Srebrenica. However, while POC was developed mainly in the halls of international organizations themselves, WPS was originally driven by NGOs and the activism of women's rights advocates from outside the UN system.[4]

Another commonality is that both agendas are difficult to pin down. They seem to reinforce each other conceptually and politically in the sense that they push for a rights-based protection of individuals. The two agendas, however, have kept the definition of protection broad and relatively ambiguous. There still is no common definition of the protection of civilians across the UN. DPKO developed an operational concept of POC only in 2010, stating that it consists of three pillars, namely: protection of political processes, protection against physical violence, and building a protective environment (DPKO 2010; Francis and Popovski 2012: 84–85). This conceptualization was, however, so broad that it was of limited use for its implementation on the ground. In the most recent guidance, DPKO and the Department of Field Support's (DFS) *Policy on the Protection of Civilians in UN Peacekeeping* (UN DPKO/DFS 2015), a definition for POC is finally provided as "all necessary means, up to and including the use of deadly force, aimed at preventing or responding to threats of physical violence against civilians, within capabilities and areas of operations, and without prejudice to the responsibility of the host government to protect its civilians" (p. 5). Although this definition gives some clarity sixteen years after POC was first conceived, it has not problems of implementation.

Similarly to POC, the WPS agenda could also be formulated more precisely despite its intersectional nature. "Resolution 1325" is widely referred to within the floors of DPKO as a term or concept that symbolically stands for WPS, but most staff would probably have difficulties to state whether it is about gender, women, or sexual violence.[5] Despite protection being one of the four WPS pillars, it is rarely explained what kind of *protection* is actually meant and how peacekeepers could achieve this. Resolution 1325 (UN Security Council 2000b) and the subsequent seven resolutions building on it do not sufficiently specify the content of reforms, the nature of services to be provided, the procedures needed to protect women, or their right to participate. "UN Action, the Office of the Special Representative of the Secretary General on Sexual Violence in Conflict (OSRSG-SVC) and other actors have subsequently issued guidance, but the dissemination, comprehension, and use of these documents leave much to be desired."[6] We conclude that both agendas have neglected building on each other to specify how protection can be conceptualized and how it might be achieved.

THE IMPLICATIONS OF MONUSCO AND UNMISS PEACEKEEPING MANDATES FOR POC AND WPS

Systematic and widespread sexual violence against women and girls makes the cases of DRC and South Sudan central to the study of POC efforts and their alignment with WPS. This section shows the development of the mandates as well as the impact that practices on the ground also had on the development of the two agendas.

Both MONUSCO and UNMISS operate under a Chapter VII mandate through which the Security Council authorizes the use of force in the effort to maintain international peace and security. UNMISS' mandate has been under Chapter VII since the existence of the mission in South Sudan with the country's independence in 2011. MONUSCO's mandate is often described as the "most robust" one currently held by a peacekeeping operation (Rhoads 2016). However, the UN organization mission in the DRC started out as a small scale observation mission with a Chapter VI mandate in 1999 (Reynaert 2011: 14). MONUSCO, then named MONUC until June 30, 2010,[7] was only the second peacekeeping mission that received a POC mandate by 2000 (see UN Security Council 2000a, Resolution

1291). For this purpose, MONUC received a Chapter VII mandate and an increase of troop strength to 5,537 military personnel within two years.

In reality, the mission continued to be severely under-equipped and practically functioned like an observer mission (Reynaert 2011: 15). This gap between the mission's protection mandate and its actual capacity became particularly obvious in 2002, when RCD-Goma rebels killed 160 civilians in Kisangani (Rhoads 2016). In response, the Security Council called on the member states to contribute personnel to enable MONUC to reach its earlier authorized strength of 5,537. The Council also called for the protection of civilians with Resolution 1417 (UN Security Council 2002), and has reaffirmed this call in every subsequent resolution.[8] When MONUC peacekeepers were again unable to adequately respond to a particularly severe protection crisis in 2003 that left four hundred people dead in Bunia, the Security Council supported a more robust interpretation of the mandate.

As MONUC's robustness in the use of force to prevent atrocities and abuses against civilians is strengthened, the language of resolutions for gender sensitivity and against sexual violence also continuously develops. Resolution 1493 (UN Security Council 2003) is the first of MONUC's resolutions that explicitly refers to Resolution 1325 and specifically mentions "sexual violence against women and children." After 2003, subsequent Security Council resolutions on MONUSCO regularly recall preceding WPS and POC resolutions to condemn systematic violence against civilians, and in particular sexual violence. In 2007, the Security Council condemned sexual violence, and called on the Congolese government to end such violence by "[bringing] the perpetrators, as well as the senior commanders under whom they serve, to justice" (UN Security Council 2007, Resolution 1794). The Council also appealed to member states to provide medical, humanitarian, and other assistance to victims of sexual violence. Resolution 1794 made explicit reference to the protection of the rights of women and took into account gender considerations set out in Resolution 1325. Further, it requested the mission to "undertake a thorough review of its efforts to prevent and respond to sexual violence, and to pursue a comprehensive mission-wide strategy." Tellingly, the resolution links the prevention of and protection from sexual violence to the mandate of the mission even before the adoption of Resolution 1820 (UN Security Council 2008). The latter declared sexual violence in conflict as a threat to international peace and security, and gave peacekeeping operations the mandate to intervene.

In the same period, Resolution 1590 (UN Security Council 2005) provided the mandate for the predecessor mission of UNMISS, also known as the United Nations Mission in Sudan (UNMIS) which, had only mentioned "women" in relation to female and child combatants within Disarmament, Demobilization, and Reintegration (DDR) programs, and among vulnerable internally displaced groups and returning refugees. Similar to Resolution 1565 of MONUSCO, women were mentioned solely as a sub-category of vulnerable populations[9] and not in their own right under Resolution 1590. The first UNMISS mandate (UN Security Council 2011, Resolution 1996) required the peacekeeping mission "to use all necessary means, within the limits of its capacity and in the areas where its units are deployed to carry out its protection mandate." Moreover, the resolution made explicit reference to Resolutions 1325 and 1820; as well as 1889 (UN Security Council 2009b) and 1960 (UN Security Council 2010b)—two further resolutions adopted on conflict related-sexual violence. Curiously, however, Resolution 1996 mentions these resolutions only in relation to the pillar of participation in peace-building without connecting WPS to the protection mandate. The UNMISS' Resolution 2109 (UN Security Council 2013b) holds the protection mandate of 2011 constant but is the most crucial resolution for advancing WPS focus within UNMISS. This resolution refers to the importance of gender expertise and a training for the mission. It welcomes the appointments of WPAs and, therefore, marks the first mission to deploy them.

Both peacekeeping missions have had difficulties in cooperating with host country security forces who have themselves proven to be major threats to the security and well-being of local civilians. In 2009, during joint military operations of MONUC and the Congolese Armed Forces (FARDC) entitled "Kimia II," it became obvious that government security forces, including the police, were some of the worst human rights violators. MONUC reacted by developing a policy paper that set out the conditions under which the mission would provide support to FARDC units. The so called "conditionality policy" specifies that "MONUC will not participate in or support operations with FARDC units if there are substantial grounds for believing that there is a real risk that such units will violate international humanitarian, human rights or refugees law in the course of the operation" (S/2009/ 623: 4; UN Security Council 2009c, Resolution 1906: 6). Like other protection innovations, MONUCO'S conditionality policy was subsequently mainstreamed by the Secretary General in the Human Rights Due Diligence Policy in late 2013 (Aust 2014). However, the implementation of the policy is frequently challenging, as UN peacekeepers are often operationally dependent on the host country's security forces. Drawing clear red lines can lead to disengagement and loss of oversight. Therefore, this approach may increase the risk of human rights violations. The recent rupture of collaboration between UN and Congolese forces because of two red-listed Congolese generals serves as an example of this dilemma.[10]

Because of the human rights abuses and atrocities committed by government security forces during the Juba crisis, collaboration with government security forces was suspended though Resolution 2132 (United Nations Security Council 2013c) on December 24, 2013. This resolution stressed POC and increased the force level of UNMISS in South Sudan. Subsequently, the UN Security Council (2014, Resolution 2155) formally eliminated the mandate components of capacity building for South Sudanese armed forces after they were found to be responsible for the lion share of mass atrocities committed in 2013 (AUCISS 2014; UN Security Council 2015a, 2015b). The protection mandate is elaborated in detail in six sections of Resolution 2155. Yet, according to several interviews we conducted in Juba in 2015, while the POC mandate in Resolution 2155 (UN Security Council 2014b) was indeed more detailed, it did not allow for any new actions that could not have been done under the previous mandate.[11]

Even as Resolution 2155 authorizes "all necessary measures" to protect civilians, this did not represent additional mandate language that will make civilians safer. Rather, this depends on what troops are able and willing to do to protect civilians. It is the first resolution that referred to "UNMISS protection of civilians sites" and the responsibility of the UN peacekeepers to "maintain public safety of and within" them. Accounts of sexual violence also triggered increased attention to civilian protection within the mandate.[12] Finally, the POC and WPS agendas converge in the mandate. For example, the first section on protection of civilians asks for "specific protection for women and children, including through the continued use of the Mission's Child Protection and Women Protection Advisers" (Resolution 2155). Emphasizing compliance with the Human Rights Due Diligence Policy (HRDDP), two subsequent resolutions reinstall coordination with police services on POC-related activities (UN Security Council 2015b, Resolution 2252; and UN Security Council 2016, Resolution 2327); and a further resolution on training for the Joint Integrated Police (UN Security Council 2016, Resolution 2327).

Critical for progress regarding the protection of women and girls is political pressure on the host country. In DRC, the "listing" process of the FARDC for the two issues of sexual violence and child recruitment—done through the yearly reports of the respective OSRSGs—has proven very effective (see chapter 24 in this volume). From the Congolese perspective, the army's listing for sexual violence and child recruitment is not only a hindrance for the deployment of Congolese troops as peacekeepers in other countries, but more generally very embarrassing. Doing something about this was often described in interviews as relatively easy as compared to some of the other challenges. In 2014, President Joseph Kabila gave these issues priority by appointing a "Presidential Adviser on Sexual Violence and Child Recruitment" and providing her with sufficient authority to quickly obtain results. At the same time, from 2014 onward, MONUSCO mandates regularly refer to the ongoing efforts of the Congolese Government in combating sexual violence in an effort to maintain the pressure. For example, UN Security Council (2015a) Resolution 2211 welcomes the appointment of Kabila's "Presidential Adviser on Sexual Violence and Child Recruitment," but urges the government to implement the two national action plans against sexual violence and child recruitment by the FARDC.

The analysis of Security Council mandates for MONUC/MONUSCO and UNMISS shows that mandates mainly evolve as a response to stark protection failures, which in turn act as shocks to the existing system. Ambitious mandates are adopted but not necessarily matched with the capacities needed to fulfill them both in terms of POC and WPS. Grave protection failures continuously urged the Security Council to take a more decisive stance. In response, the Council urged the missions to become more active and innovative in protection. As the first peacekeeping mission where POC was prioritized (in 2008), MONUSCO has been at the forefront of protection through developing and testing protection measures that were later mainstreamed to other peacekeeping contexts. However, other missions have not only taken from MONUSCO but also contributed through their own experiences. In the case of South Sudan, the POC sites have proven a milestone for the question of whether and how to protect civilians on UN premises. The first WPAs were also deployed in South Sudan.

As a consequence of the shock-led development and the connected challenges in regards to specifying practical meaning of mandates and securing necessary funding, we can observe an accompanying time lag both in troop numbers and female personnel to fulfill, for instance, WPA roles. The result is that although MONUSCO and UNMISS protection mandates have been formulated more and more explicitly to address POC and WPS, particularly for conflict-related sexual violence (CRSV), they remain far from being concrete operationalization and practices.

PROTECTION PRACTICES IN THE DRC AND IN SOUTH SUDAN

These abstract protection mandates highlight the need to scrutinize the ways that peacekeeping missions develop instruments and practices to operationalize it on the ground. The following section examines how the protection mandate has been implemented by

UNMISS and MONUSCO in three examples. As previously highlighted, MONUSCO has had a predominant role in this process of implementing POC. Other missions have heavily built on MONUSCO's experience, adopted many of its instruments, and adapted them as appropriate for the context. In return, we find, MONUSCO has recently learned from the protection practices of other missions, for instance from UNMISS in regards to sheltering vulnerable populations on its premises. We thus argue that the protection practices of these two missions are indicative of the wider organizational field that has had to learn by practice how to implement POC and WPS. Often implementation is weak and fragmented, but efforts within missions to implement the two agendas in tandem are taking place despite their continued separation in Security Council processes.

At the time of writing the DRC is embroiled in a deepening political crisis, which is exacerbating ethnic and militia violence. South Sudan is in a downward spiral of an escalating conflict too. In both cases, POC still seems to be an "impossible mandate." In DRC, cooperation with the state in security matters has been hampered by the fact that Congolese Security forces remain the main perpetrator of human rights abuses in the country.[13] In many interviews across both missions, protection experts did not seem very optimistic: "Something positive? Here in South Sudan? (. . .) Uniformed personnel is [sic] committing rapes with impunity. Weak institutions make it very difficult to protect. Protection is primarily the role of the Government of South Sudan, but the Government of South Sudan is talking like it's UNMISS responsibility."[14]

We, however, argue that particularly because of these imminent challenges it is important to understand the actual POC practices taking place. The following section identifies the relative strengths and weaknesses of protection efforts. In this section, therefore, we aim to shed light on some of the most important ways protection has been implemented and how they relate to the WPS agenda by presenting three examples on WPAs, community-based protection, and monitoring and reporting arrangements.

Introducing Women Protection Advisors—An Attempt to Align POC and WPS?

The progress of hiring more female staff is slow both for international and national personnel. Their embeddedness make hiring more female staff challenging in particular sociocultural contexts (see MONUSCO 2014). In 2009, the Security Council decided "to include specific provisions, as appropriate, for the protection of women and children from rape and other sexual violence" including, on a case-by-case basis, the identification of Women Protection Advisers (WPAs) (UN Security Council 2009a, Resolution 1888). WPAs were intended to serve as a "further bridge between operational protection and gender-sensitivity skill sets" (UN Women 2010: 16).

UNMISS deployed its first set of WPAs in April 2012, and therefore was the first peacekeeping operation to do so. From July 2012 to April 2013, six WPAs were appointed within the Human Rights Division, including four at the state level in Jonglei, Lakes, Unity, and Upper Nile. In April 2014, a Senior WPA (SWPA) was appointed to advise the Special Representative of the Secretary-General (SRSG) on the implementation of Resolutions

1920 (UN Security Council 2010a), 1888, 1960, and 2106 (UN Security Council 2013a). The advisor was also tasked to expedite the establishment of the Monitoring, Analysis, and Reporting Arrangements on Conflict-Related Sexual Violence (MARA). However, the SWPA as well as the WPAs seem poorly integrated in the operationalization and practices of protection.[15] In South Sudan, the priorities of the SWPA were monitoring and evaluation of conflict-related sexual violence (e.g., rape, abduction, sexual slavery, enforced prostitution, trafficking). Despite available funding, some positions remained unfilled throughout 2015 because of a perceived lack of senior applicants with gender expertise willing to work in remote locations of South Sudan.[16] However, given the rest and recuperation (R&R) patterns of South Sudan as a duty station, in two out of six weeks there were no WPAs present, because there is only one WPA covering all field locations. The absence was noticeable during field visits.

This lack of continuous staff presence, for example, is different from the bigger operational offices working on child protection, which are also prominently engaging on monitoring, reporting, and direct engagement with armed parties on the ground. Closer or more constant interaction with women on the POC sites and beyond them may at times exist through engaged personnel from the Relief, Reintegration and Protection Section after Civil Affairs Division. These have proved essential for finding ways to ameliorate the security situations within the sites.[17]

Although MONUSCO received the mandate to identify WPAs among MONUC's gender advisers and human rights protection units as early as 2009 through Resolution 1906, the deployment of WPAs was stalled due to negotiations between implementing partners and funding issues. In 2014, the Security Council insisted on the quick "implementation, analysis and reporting arrangements on CRSV and the swift deployment of WPAs" (UN Security Council 2014a, Resolution 2147). Consequently MONUSCO's Sexual Violence in Conflict Unit was dismantled and redeployed in 2014 as WPAs.[18]

In the DRC, the implementation of the WPS agenda and more specifically the "Monitoring, Analysis, and Reporting Arrangements on Conflict-Related Sexual Violence" through the WPAs was initially envisioned as a triangular structure between gender advisers, human rights protection units such as the WPAs, and the third part being fulfilled by the Senior Protection Advisor.[19] On one hand, WPAs belonging to the Gender Unit would conduct gender mainstreaming, awareness raising, and training. On the other, WPAs from the Joint Human Rights Office (JHRO) would be involved in verification of incidents, monitoring, and reporting. Although both were mandated to work on CRSV, the human rights WPAs would focus on CRSV, whereas the gender WPAs would, at least initially, work on Sexual Gender-Based Violence (SGBV) thus pertaining also to violence perpetrated in non-armed conflict areas. The SWPA was not the supervisor of the WPAs and in fact did not have a section or much staff. Rather, the three independent parts of the triangle (gender unit, JHRO and SWPA) were intended to work collaboratively.

This triangular structure of SWPA, Gender WPAs, and Human Rights WPAs was implemented comparatively well in DRC. However, the implementation still led to tensions on the division of roles and responsibilities among the different elements. For partners outside the mission, the triangular structure and particularly the two kinds of WPAs and their diverging tasks were often confusing.[20] As one MONUSCO official described, "[A]ll actors orient themselves towards the WPAs to report and exchange on conflict-related sexual violence. But the Gender WPAs are not really trained for that. So they write reports, which quickly get to New York, getting attention for something which is not theirs. However, since they are not trained for this work, they have made mistakes in their investigation and reporting, which ironically, the JHRO gets then blamed for."[21] To make matters even more confusing for external partners, the implementing entity for sexual violence responses in DRC is UN Women and not the WPA team. In addition, the Senior WPA, who was working in the office of the Deputy-SRSG (Rule of Law) in Goma, had a very small team with no direct authority over the WPAs.

The Senior WPA, taken aback by this impractical arrangement, tried to quickly establish a "Women Protection Team" after her arrival but this strategy did very little to alter this situation. More recently, the *Consolidation* process within peacekeeping has provided a bit more clarity by integrating all WPAs and the SWPA into JHRO. However, barriers to acquiring funding and subsequently integrating the WPAs into the mission's activities remained. The SWPA and the WPAs are dependent on extra-budgetary funding and thus more volatile. As a result to shifting staff, there are currently only five WPAs deployed in Goma, Kalemie, Bunia, and Beni, in addition to on at the operational headquarters. They represent "only" national staff and UN volunteers as opposed to the more authoritative international professional staff. This highlights the imbalance with MONUSCO's other specialized protection mandates, such as Child Protection with thirty-five posts, or other missions such as UNMISS which has fifteen WPAs and MINUSCA with ten WPAs.

Community-Based Protection

UN peacekeeping has increasingly recognized that community-based protection is a more legitimate and effective approach. Peacekeeping is linked to international discourses about local ownership that require a minimum of participation for the intervention to appear legitimate and sustainable. Community-based protection relates to a tough learning curve of international protection actors, realizing they were simply not able to protect civilians by themselves. Given the unwillingness and inability of host governments to protect their own population, peacekeeping has increasingly worked with local populations directly.

In the DRC, the development of community-based protection mechanisms was specifically spurred by the failure to intervene against the 2008 Kiwanja massacre. This shortcoming highlighted that the local peacekeeping contingent had simply not understood the escalating local conflict dynamics. The mission was quite detached from the realities on the ground. For example, the locally deployed peacekeepers did not speak French or Swahili, let alone local languages. They were rotated too quickly to familiarize themselves with the environment. To close the gap with the local population and gain a better understanding of the threats, MONUSCO institutionalized joint protection missions (JPTs). Yet, they quickly realized that a more permanent civilian presence was needed on the ground (UNDPKO/DFS-OHCHR 2013; MONUSCO 2014).

Firstly, the mission developed a new staff category that would stay on the peacekeeping bases and liaise with local communities. So-called Community Liaison Assistants (CLAs) briefed the peacekeeping contingents, and developed measures to intensify MONUSCO's interaction with local communities. Based on their local focal points, the CLAs, for instance, managed an early warning system called "Community Alert Networks" through which the population can call for assistance in case of security threats. CLAs also worked with communities not only to identify threats and opportunities in an effort to strengthen their resilience, but also to inform MONUSCO's protection strategies.[22]

In South Sudan, women participating in a "women's security" meeting on the POC site in Bentiu suggested that the times of patrolling would be announced in the different tribal languages on the site. This is done so that local women could coordinate to meet in groups and go out in time to join the peacekeepers who were on their way or returning from a point approximately five kilometers away from the site (which the women used as a main route). This consultation as part of a weekly scheduled women's security meeting has been a way to tailor peacekeeping protection for a group of women most vulnerable to physical threats of sexual violence and abuse such as those leaving the sites. It also came without substantive additional costs for the mission.

Secondly, firewood patrols were established around the main base in Unity on Bentiu POC where about half or approximately one hundred thousand of the people living on UNMISS bases live. These patrols were perceived as significantly increasing the security of females living on the site.[23] During field research in South Sudan in May 2016, it was discussed at a women's security meeting on Bentiu POC site how these firewood patrols could be conducted so that women could use the peacekeepers' presence better by coordinating more closely on the times the patrols would take place; and in starting official announcements in the different tribal languages on site. Solely through consultations with the women on the site, protection efforts could strengthen local female agency with no additional resources required.

MARA and Inter-Organizational Cooperation

In conflict environments, data assessments often remain vague and are constrained by access for experts and/or the media. A systematic account, even just for those killed in conflict, is missing, and a lack of attention to the harms to the civilian population has been criticized in the case of South Sudan (Kristof 2016). In addition, the plethora of organizational entities collecting and analyzing data apply different methodologies, standards, and foci. As a result, a great variety of reports is produced that are at times diverging in their content. Conflicting numbers and narratives are problematic in so far as they also lead to diverging understanding of the problem and recommended responses.[24]

One response to this situation is the development of the Monitoring, Analysis, and Reporting Arrangements (MARA) on Conflict-Related Sexual Violence. According to its Provisional Guidance Note, the "purpose of MARA is to ensure the systematic gathering of timely, accurate, reliable and objective information on conflict-related sexual violence against women, men and children in all situations of concern" (OSRSG-SVC 2011: 4). It would then also directly feed into the protection efforts of peacekeeping operations by contributing to the development of Comprehensive Strategies to combat sexual violence at country-level. Further, the information from MARA would also feed into the establishment of protection mandates through the Security Council. Monitoring and protection should therefore reinforce each other in the sense that monitors "should be aware of and be able to refer survivors to such services where possible. Increased availability of services will, in turn, result in more accurate information related to sexual violence" (OSRSG-SVC 2011: 4).

Aimed at technical level and within the UN, WPAs (if they are in place) are responsible for convening a Working Group on Conflict-Related Sexual Violence under Resolution 1960. This group is supposed to be "a technical level, UN-led and UN-comprised body expected to review information, monitor and verify incidents of sexual violence, analyze data, trends, and patterns, prepare reports, and build capacity to strengthen MARA" (OSRSG-SVC 2011: 7). However, for this to work and for different members of the Working Group to feel comfortable with sharing information without harming their informants and/or aid/protection recipients, confidentiality mechanisms may have to be increased to further the willingness and diligence for sharing relevant data.

Following its provisions, all of this information could and should feed into the MARA under WPA coordination and lead. This itself also would be a primary exercise in coordination as it "is foreseen that MARA will draw on information gathered from a variety of sources in a given country context, including local government authorities and institutions, health and psychosocial service providers, UN Civilian, Police and Military Peacekeeping presence, UNCT actors, local and international NGOs, civil society organizations, religious institutions and faith-based networks" (OSRSG-SVC 2011: 5).

A systematic monitoring for protection purposes remains rather limited. For instance at UNMISS, a database had been started and it had been the responsibility of one staff member whose termination of post also temporarily put a stop on the database. As for troop presence and its implications for human rights reporting and documentation, the current reach is limited and even more difficult to organize. For most areas where human rights violations take place, for example in Upper Nile and Unity, force protection through coordinating on a joint patrol and fact-finding mission may take time. One can imagine that if not even killings can be assessed, how much harder it is to conduct a representative survey on the issues of SGBV. Lastly, different databases particularly on sexual violence experienced by women living on POC sites are maintained by NGOs working on protection efforts (for example by the International Refugee Council and Nonviolent Peace Force in South Sudan who survey women on the POC sites). A systematic monitoring of atrocities committed outside of the POC sites goes well beyond UNMISS's capacities, as most of its resources are bound to the sites and its patrol range is limited (despite notable efforts of establishing a Forward Operating base in Southern Unity, which has seen some of the worst and widespread sexual and gender-based violence).

In the DRC, the implementation of MARA is also limited and has to deal with many of the same problems. Like the WPA, MARA is a required headquarters' concept but lacking the necessary funding and operational integration in the mission. In addition to an HQ driven process that appears detached from the ground, MONUSCO also seems to have not made MARA implementation a priority. MARA had been coordinated by a UN Volunteer and when that person left in March 2017, there remains no dedicated focal point.[25] One interviewee summarized the issue strikingly: "[W]ithout manpower these things don't get done. I have the impression there are more people busy with this in

NY [New York] and universities worldwide than in the missions."[26] Another UN official expressed the concern that WPAs and MARA resemble "lip service" from headquarters instead of a more practical and sustainable approach for protection against sexual violence.[27]

The MARA guidelines foresee that the SRSG or Resident Humanitarian Coordinator not only provide information on various violations for the annual Secretary-General report, but also "initiate a strategy for engagement with parties aimed at securing specific commitments to prevent and address conflict-related sexual violence. SRSG on Sexual Violence in Conflict (SViC) will also provide support to UN field teams in the implementation of resolution 1960" (OSRSG-SVC 2011: 2). In South Sudan, the government and the opposition had signed such agreements before the latest upsurge in violence. Yet the agreements and the ceasefire that the conflict parties had agreed upon have been ignored. Moreover, CRSV has become even worse. It is hard to know in which ways MARA may lead to deterrence in the long run though we agree that deterrence seems to be a necessary starting point.[28]

CONCLUSION: GENDERED PROTECTION MOVING FORWARD

"Gender has always been the stepchild of peacekeeping," a UN peacekeeping official noted,[29] implying that gender-sensitive approaches have not come naturally within DPKO. However, rapid developments have been made since the cascade year of 2008 when the POC and WPS agendas started to reinforce each other through a shared focus on CRSV. MONUSCO and UNMISS mandates reflect the rising attention to the WPS agenda, and CRSV in particular, within the UN system. These important peacekeeping operations have also sparked practical protection developments, although often only in the aftermath of atrocities or as a response to high-profile protection failures. The window of opportunity still exists to align the policy and the practical developments through headquarters conceptualization and operationalization in pragmatic support of the field offices. Currently, success often overly depends on the engagement and leadership of field personnel.

In this chapter, we have highlighted important developments in protection practices and the intersection of both the protection and the WPS agenda. We identified three examples that point to the central role of protective presence, deterrence, and coordination within the UN system and local interlocutors. These examples highlight that progress has been made but that headquarters-driven processes need to be supported more effectively. More research is needed on how to more efficiently mainstream protection issues especially the protection of women and girls within peacekeeping. So far, it has been difficult to recruit protection and gender specific experts in peacekeeping operations and to integrate them sufficiently in the mission structures. Complementing the increase of female and gender specific staff, specific expertise is also built through targeted training in gender and protection issues. All peacekeepers receive relevant training upon and during their deployment, but UN mission personnel questioned whether the limited hours and content of training translate into actual practices. Increasingly the national security forces are also trained on protection matters by the missions' substantive sections (i.e.. Human Rights, Civil Affairs WPAs, Child Protection, and the like). From our experience, we have a critical perception on these trainings that often seems appreciated by organizations, because they are relatively easy to do. Still, these trainings have to prove their impact on the ground.

Additionally, further scrutiny is needed on how strengthening female mission components affect protection outcomes and where they may have the strongest impact. Our research suggests that this may be at the field office level and that troop contingents should be trained there. Arguably, coordination structures within the UN system have improved but key barriers remain. These include the persistence of turf wars and silo implementation and the continued lack of information sharing in protection practices. During times of decreasing peacekeeping budgets, the risk of "compartmentalization" is particularly salient and might require a more effective consolidation of protection functions. Coordination problems in protection should be addressed both within the academic, policy, and operationalization and practical spheres.

Possible ways forward are in the continued sensitization needed on the "protective" mindset vis-à-vis women and girls. This may start by asking questions of which vulnerabilities are faced by groups and listening to the populations themselves. This can also be done through developing and maintaining close ties with the communities, for example under the Civil Affairs section. Empowerment and inclusion of the civilian population is happening within both agendas but may not be pushed for by the same set of actors. While we both have stories to tell about protection failures and successes around accounting for local women's knowledge, the examples are still too few and "innovations remain piecemeal and limited" (UN Women 2015: 144). In addition to protection of civilians not being a typical task of the militaries of troop-contributing countries (TCCs), the non-response to violations of human rights and International Humanitarian Law (IHL) weighs heavily not only on the peacekeeping mission and the civilian population of a country, but also on the UN as a whole. Substantive results ultimately still remain driven by individuals, even though we have elucidated on protection tools and structures. If UN peacekeeping wants to continue engaging in proactive protection, it is important to find ways for changing the incentive structure in peacekeeping in a way that rewards tailored and brave protection efforts across battalions and individuals.

Notes

1. See United Nations Secretary-General (1998). "Report of the Secretary-General on the work of the Organization: The Causes of Conflict and the Promotion of Durable Peace and Sustainable Development in Africa." S/1998/318, April 1998, http://documents.wfp. org/stellent/groups/public/documents/eb/wfp000065.pdf.
2. The focus is on the protection efforts of United Nations peacekeeping missions but we acknowledge that other UN and non-UN entities have their role to play, sometimes in collaboration with the given peacekeeping mission.
3. For more detailed analysis of The Security Council's engagement with WPS, see the annual and monthly analysis of the NGO Working Group on WPS on http://www. womenpeacesecurity.org/publications/. For instance, in their analysis of last year, they

have found 75 percent of Security Council resolutions mentioning WPS. See also "NGO Working Group on WPS (2016)."

4. Cohn, Kinsella, and Gibbings 2004.

5. This statement is based on our individual fieldwork at DPKO.

6. Author exchange with former WPA, October 2017.

7. The UN peacekeeping mission in the Congo was named MONUC from 1999–2010 and renamed MONUSCO July 1, 2010. Throughout the text we refer to the same mission (as MONUSCO) and only use MONUC when chronologically appropriate.

8. S/RES/1355 (2001) reminded all parties of their obligations with respect to the security of civilian populations under the Fourth Geneva Convention relative to the Protection of Civilian Persons in Time of War, but does not restate MONUC's POC mandate.

9. Most often, they seem to appear as the conglomerate "women and children."

10. Here the solution could be to refocus on the original intent of the HRDDP to provide robust mitigation measures to troops at risk of committing violations. Other than categorical decisions, the point is to use conditionality to guide behaviour.

11. Author interviews with UNMISS personnel in Juba, May 2015.

12. They were reported as shocking in the terms of their scale, but also in the victimization of groups that had been seen as "taboos" in traditional society fabrics (i.e., pregnant and married women). Author interview with international sexual violence analyst/expert in Juba, June 2016.

13. While they regularly commit approximately 55–60 percent of all human rights violations, their track record on sexual violence is slightly better. The 2016 Secretary-General report on CRSV indicates that Congolese security forces were responsible for 32 percent out of 514 verified cases (even if the 2,593 reported cases include many that could not be verified due to time and resource constraints).

14. Author interview with UNMISS personnel in Juba, June 2015.

15. Interviews with UNMISS personnel in Juba, June 2015 and May 2016.

16. Interview with UNMISS personnel in Juba, June 2015.

17. Interviews with UNMISS personnel in Juba, June 2015 and May 2016; and in Malakal and Bentiu, May 2016.

18. Email correspondence with former MONUSCO official, June 2017.

19. Author interview with MONUSCO personnel in Goma, March 2016.

20. This issue becomes even more salient because other actors (e.g., the International Rescue Committee, among others) frequently have similarly complicated structures, which hinders the necessary coordination between entities.

21. Author interview with MONUSCO personnel in Goma, April 2016.

22. For more information on the CLAs, see MONUSCO's 2014 Best Practice Review.

23. Author interviews with female IDPs on Bentiu POC, and with UN bureaucrats in Juba and in Bentiu, May 2016. For a more detailed elaboration on diverging protection dynamics on the POC sites, compare Dönges, 2016.

24. This is indeed the reason why the 2015 HIPPO report recommended the streamlining of monitoring and reporting arrangements, which was later picked up by the SG's decision for consolidation.

25. Author interview with MONUSCO staff, June 2017.

26. Email correspondence with UN official, June 2017.

27. Author interview with MONUSCO official, June 2017.

28. According to UN Women (2015: 13), the MARA has led to very few prosecution, but possibly deterrence.
29. Telephone interview with UN peacekeeping official, New York, January 2017.

REFERENCES

African Union Commission of Inquiry on South Sudan, Final report. 2014. Addis Ababa: AU.

Aust, Helmut Philipp. "The UN Human Rights Due Diligence Policy: An Effective Mechanism against Complicity of Peacekeeping Forces?" *Journal of Conflict and Security Law* 20, no. 1 (2014): 61–73.

Carpenter, Charli. *Innocent Women and Children. Gender, Norms and the Protection of Civilians.* Aldershot, UK: Ashgate, 2006.

Cohn, Carol, Hellen Kinsella, and Sheri Gibbings. "Women, Peace, and Security Resolution 1325." *International Feminist Journal of Politics* 6, no. 1 (2004) 130–40.

Dönges, Hannah. "Protection of Civilians Needs to Be Understood as a Collaborative Strategy and Not a Campsite." *Global Peace Operations Review* (June 2016), 12–21. New York University Center on International Cooperation, 2016.

DPKO/DFS-OHCHR. "Report on the Joint Protection Team (JPT) Mechanism in MONUSCO." United Nations, 2013.

Francis, A., V. Popovski, and C. Sampford. "The Responsibility to Protect and the Protection of Civilians: A View from the United Nations." In *Norms of Protection: Responsibility to Protect, Protection of Civilians and Their Interaction*, edited by A Francis, V. Popovski and C. Sampford. United Nations University Press, 2012.

Kristof, Nicholas. "Are as Many Civilians Dying in South Sudan as in Syria?" *The New York Times Opinion.* 2016. https://kristof.blogs.nytimes.com/2016/03/11/are-as-many-civilians-dying-in-south-sudan-as-in-syria/

MONUSCO. Civil Affairs Section. *CLA Best Practice Review.* August 2014, https://janoschkullenberg.files.wordpress.com/2014/09/cla-review-final_270814.pdf.

NGO Working Group on Women, Peace, and Security. "Mapping Women, Peace and Security in the UN Security Council: 2016." Policy Brief, 2016, http://www.womenpeacesecurity.org/files/NGOWG-Mapping-WPS-in-UNSC-2016.pdf.

Reynaert, Julie. "MONUC/ MONUSCO and Civilian Protection in the Kivus." IPIS, 2011, https://monusco.unmissions.org/sites/default/files/monuc-monusco_and_civilian_protection_in_the_kivus_0.pdf.

Rhoads, Emily Paddon. *Taking Sides in Peacekeeping: Impartiality and the Future of the United Nations.* New York: Oxford University Press, 2016.

UN DPKO/DFS. Operational Concept on the Protection of Civilians in United Nations Peacekeeping Operations, 2010, http://www.peacekeeping.org.uk/wp-content/uploads/2013/02/100129-DPKO-DFS-POC-Operational-Concept.pdf

UN DPKO/DFS-OHCHR. "Report on the Joint Protection Team (JPT) Mechanism in MONUSCO." United Nations, 2013.

UN DPKO/DFS. "The Protection of Civilians in United Nations Peacekeeping." April 1, 2015, http://providingforpeacekeeping.org/wp-content/uploads/2017/08/2015-07-Policy-on-PoC-in-Peacekeeping-Operations.pdf.

UN Office of the Special Representative of the Secretary-General on Sexual Violence in Conflict. Provisional Guidance Note—Implementation of Security Council Resolution 1960 (2010) On Women, Peace and Security (conflict-related sexual violence)", July 2011. http://www.refworld.org/pdfid/4e23ed5d2.pdf.provisional

United Nations Secretary-General. "Report of the Secretary-General on the Work of the Organization: The Causes of Conflict and the Promotion of Durable Peace and Sustainable Development in Africa." S/1998/318, 1998.

United Nations Security Council. *Resolution 1291.* "The Situation Concerning the Democratic Republic of the Congo." S/RES/1291, 2000a.

United Nations Security Council. *Resolution 1325.* "Women and Peace and Security." S/RES/1325, 2000b.

United Nations Security Council. *Resolution 1417.* "The Situation in the Democratic Republic of the Congo." S/RES/1417, 2002.

United Nations Security Council. *Resolution 1493.* "The Situation Concerning the Democratic Republic of the Congo." S/RES/1493, 2003.

United Nations Secretary-General. *Resolution 1590.* "Report of the Secretary-General on the Sudan." S/RES/1590, 2005.

United Nations Security Council. *Resolution 1794.* "The Situation Concerning the Democratic Republic of the Congo." S/RES/1794, 2007.

United Nations Security Council. *Resolution 1820.* "Women and Peace and Security. S/RES/1820, 2008.

United Nations Security Council. *Resolution 1888.* "Women and Peace and Security." S/RES/1888, 2009a.

United Nations Security Council. *Resolution 1889.* "Women and Peace and Security." S/RES/1889, 2009b.

United Nations Security Council. *Resolution 1906.* "The Situation Concerning the Democratic Republic of the Congo." S/RES/1906, 2009c.

United Nations Security Council. *Resolution 1920.* "The Situation Concerning Western Sahara." S/RES/1920, 2010a.

United Nations Security Council. *Resolution 1960.* "Women and Peace and Security." S/RES/1960, 2010b.

United Nations Security Council. *Resolution 1996.* "Reports of the Secretary-General on the Sudan." S/RES/1996, 2011.

United Nations Security Council. *Resolution 2106.* "Women, Peace, and Security." S/RES/2106, 2013a.

United Nations Security Council. *Resolution 2109.* "Reports of the Secretary-General on the Sudan and South Sudan." S/RES/2109, 2013b.

United Nations Security Council. *Resolution 2132.* "Sudan and South Sudan." S/RES/2132, 2013c.

United Nations Security Council. 2014a. *Resolution 2147.* "Democratic Republic of the Congo." S/RES/2147 (2014).

United Nations Security Council. 2014b. *Resolution 2155.* "Reports of the Secretary-General on the Sudan and South Sudan." S/RES/2155 (2014).

United Nations Security Council. *Resolution 2211.* "Democratic Republic of the Congo." S/RES/2211, 2015a.

United Nations Security Council. *Resolution 2252.* "Reports of the Secretary-General on the Sudan and South Sudan." S/RES/2252, 2015b.

United Nations Secretary-General. *Resolution 2327.* "Reports of the Secretary-General on the Sudan and South Sudan." S/RES/2327, 2016.

UN Women. *Addressing Conflict-Related Sexual Violence. An Analytical Inventory of Peacekeeping Practice.* New York: United Nations, 2010.

UN Women. "Preventing Conflict, Transforming Justice, Securing the Peace—A Global Study on the Implementation of the United Nations Security Council Resolution 1325." UN Women, 2015, http://wps.unwomen.org/.

CHAPTER 15

WHAT WORKS IN RELIEF AND RECOVERY

JACQUI TRUE AND SARAH HEWITT

MUCH of the analysis and discussion of Women, Peace, and Security (WPS) has centered on enhancing protection from sexual and gender-based violence (SGBV) and increasing women's participation in peace and security especially in the security sector and during peace processes. We argue that the transformative potential of WPS as promoted in resolution 1325 has yet to be fully realized because of the failure to address the structural causes of violent conflict and to build the long-term structural foundations of peace. This structural dimension is relevant across the whole WPS agenda, but it is especially core to the "relief and recovery" pillar of WPS, which involves, *inter alia*, "building back better." The relief and recovery (R&R) pillar is the most underdeveloped, under-researched and misinterpreted of the four WPS pillars. Advocates and scholars often refer to prevention, protection, and participation, leaving off R&R, with scant literature explicitly addressing what it includes and what it does not. R&R has even been consigned to the recovery of sexual violence survivors alone (Schaper 2017), indicating a problematic interpretation of its potential coverage and intent. In this chapter, we redress that situation. We define the R&R pillar and demonstrate its potential to connect WPS to the achievement of women's social and economic rights, to economic recovery that promotes gender equality, and to transformative reparations that redress gender injustices after conflict, disaster, or humanitarian crisis. Within "relief and recovery," there are opportunities to bridge the divide between "relief" or short-term humanitarian assistance that responds to women's needs, and "recovery" or the long-term development frameworks and initiatives that address the strategic interests of Resolution 1325 in gender equality, conflict-prevention, and sustainable peace.

Having considered the "meaning-in-use" (Wiener 2014) of R&R in UN Security Council resolutions, we discuss R&R in the WPS agenda with respect to four interrelated themes: (1) securing women's social and economic rights; (2) developing a gender perspective and promoting women's participation in economic recovery; (3) providing post-conflict financing and conducting gender budgeting; and (4) ensuring gender-transformative reparations and transitional justice, including responsiveness to SGBV survivors for women's political and economic empowerment. More than the economic recovery or empowerment of women, and the provision of physical security, we see R&R as the complex work of reweaving the social and economic fabric of societies after traumatic and/or violent events.

Herein lies the chance to transform violent gender relations and hierarchies that subordinate, discriminate, and marginalize women and minority groups by creating opportunities for greater levels of participation and agency in renegotiating peaceful societies.

WHAT IS RELIEF AND RECOVERY?

WPS "relief and recovery" is defined interchangeably with multiple sets of concepts using *relief, recovery, peace-building, empowerment, rehabilitation*, and *reconstruction*, leading to considerable ambiguity in its interpretation and confusion in its implementation. Indeed, the Global Study on the implementation of 1325 after fifteen years coins the fourth WPS pillar "peacebuilding and recovery" without any particular rationale or justification (UN Women 2015).[1] We retain the phrase "relief and recovery" to indicate a broad definition inclusive of disaster and humanitarian crises, though this chapter primarily deals with recovery from conflict. As shown in Table 15.1, within WPS resolutions "relief and recovery" is referred to variously via mention of peace-building, post-conflict recovery, disarmament, demobilization and reintegration (DDR) efforts, security sector reform (SSR), transitional justice, and wider UN peace-building and development agendas that relate to the Peacebuilding Commission and Fund and the UN Sustainable Development Goals (SDGs) (UNSG 2016).

Resolution 1325 is rather narrow in its articulation of R&R focusing on short-term post-conflict efforts. The diffusion of National Action Plans (NAPs), one of the key WPS implementing mechanisms, progressed slowly after the Secretary-General called for them in 2004 and only gained momentum around 2010 (True 2016). Moreover, apart from the 2008–2009 UN System-wide Action Plan on 1325 (UNSG 2005) that interprets R&R in terms of equal access to services and aid distribution, there was little expansion of the fourth pillar's definition and broadening intent until Resolutions 1888 and 1889 in 2009.[2]

Beyond the UN Security Council resolutions and NAPs, two major UN frameworks exist for implementing the WPS R&R pillar incorporating Resolution 1888 and 1889. The UN Strategic Results Framework (UN 2011) for WPS implementation 2011–2020, and the UN Secretary-General's Seven-Point Action Plan on gender-responsive peace-building (UNSG 2010b). These frameworks are the most definitive in implementing R&R yet they do not address the issue comprehensively or in terms of women's socioeconomic rights and gender/economic reparative justice. The Strategic Results Framework explicitly names "relief and recovery" and requires women's and girls' specific relief needs to be met, and women's capacities as agents in relief and recovery to be reinforced, in conflict and post-conflict situations as one of the four WPS pillars. Specific implementation outputs, targets, and indicators within this pillar include the financing and funding of gender equality programming and planning in R&R, addressing and responding to the needs of vulnerable groups, especially internally displaced persons, SGBV and war crime victims, disabled, female heads of households, female ex-combatants, refugees, returnees and women living with and affected by HIV. Transitional justice mechanisms, reparations, and DDR programs are required to be gender-responsive and inclusive with equitable access to economic recovery, employment, and livelihood services for women and girls.

Concurrently, the Seven-Point Action Plan on gender-responsive peace-building aims to institutionalize women's participation and gender analysis in all post-conflict planning in

Table 15.1 UN Security Council Resolutions on WPS

	Description
1325 (2000)	Adopt a gender perspective during repatriation, resettlement, and for rehabilitation, reintegration, and post-conflict reconstruction, and support women in the implementation of peace agreements.
1820 (2008)	Support development and strengthen judicial, heath, and civil society capacities to provide sustainable assistance for victims of sexual violence.
1888 (2009)	Increase access to healthcare, psychosocial support, legal assistance, and socioeconomic reintegration services for victims of sexual violence and implement measures through post-conflict strategies to reduce sexual violence.
1889 (2009)	Support women's mental health and sexual and reproductive health. Ensure women and girls' livelihoods, land, and property rights, enhance socioeconomic conditions through education, income generating activities, employment, and women's participation in decision-making and post-conflict planning throughout the recovery process, including in DDR programs and aid management. Ensure women's engagement in public decision-making and economic recovery in order to be effective. Improve financing of women's empowerment and gender initiatives and implement funding tracking mechanisms. Appoint gender advisors and/or women protection advisors to assist in addressing women and girls' recovery needs in post-conflict situations and implement gender mainstreaming throughout peace-building and recovery processes.
1960 (2010)	Increase access to healthcare, psychosocial support, legal assistance, and socioeconomic reintegration for victims of sexual violence, explicitly those in rural areas and people living with disabilities.
2106 (2013)	Ensure women's participation in all aspects of mediation, post-conflict recovery, and peace-building. Support strengthening multisectoral services and capacities of health and civil society structures to support women and girls, particularly those living with and affected by HIV and AIDS and survivors of sexual violence.
2122 (2013)	Include women's participation and protection in DDR, electoral processes, security sector and judicial reforms, and wider post-conflict reconstruction processes. Develop funding mechanisms to support capacities of civil society and women in implementation of 1325. Commend the Peacebuilding Commission's declaration on women's economic empowerment for peace-building (PBC/7/OC/L.1 2013).
2242 (2015)	Integrate gender considerations and women's participation across humanitarian programming and response including in medical, legal, and psychosocial and livelihood services. Increase international development cooperation related to women's empowerment and gender equality, and track funding through initiatives such as the Global Acceleration Instrument.

Descriptions of resolutions[15] were compiled by the author from statistics located at: http://www.peacewomen.org/member-states.

order to enhance the capacity to address gender inequalities in post-conflict state building (UNSG 2010b).[3] The Seven-Point Plan calls for increased financing of gender equality and women and girls' empowerment initiatives in post-conflict situations. It establishes a benchmark to dedicate at least 15 percent of all UN-managed peace-building funds to support projects where gender equality and women's empowerment are the principal objective. It commits to achieving gender parity in post-conflict employment programs where neither sex receives more than 60 percent of employment person-days and payment is received daily by women themselves. As well, the Seven-Point Plan promotes women's access to security and justice, including legal support services and minimum standards of gender responsiveness in Truth and Reconciliation Commissions (TRCs), reparation programs, and related bodies. It mandates women's and civil society's participation in the setting of economic recovery priorities, the planning and implementing of development, social, environmental, and physical infrastructure programs.

Only the Strategic Results Framework specifically refers to "relief and recovery" thus, whereas the Seven-Point Action Plan employs the R&R synonyms of "peacebuilding and economic recovery." This indicates inconsistencies and perhaps a lack of dedicated thought into the definition of R&R as a WPS pillar. Nonetheless, both UN frameworks set impressive goals toward gender-sensitive and inclusive "relief and recovery." However, we need to judge this WPS pillar by the practical usefulness of the stated commitments and implementation frameworks. From a feminist pragmatist perspective, it is what they "do" or enable, not what they "say," that matters most.

In the following sections we consider challenges to these implementation frameworks with respect to their core precepts: (1) securing women's social and economic rights; (2) bringing a gender perspective and women's participation into economic recovery; (3) integrating gender budgeting within post-conflict financing; and (4) transforming reparations and transitional justice (including responsiveness to SGBV survivors) to empower women economically.

Securing Women's Economic and Social Rights

Women's capacity to participate in relief and recovery is closely linked to their enjoyment of socioeconomic security and rights. Taken together, poverty, unequal gender norms, and impunity for—and fear of—violence, prevent women from participating in and benefiting from post-conflict processes (True 2012: 145-7). This is a major setback for peace, reconciliation, and the long-term recovery of societies. Governments and the international community must attend to the protection of women's economic and social rights in post-conflict settings, and integrate them with efforts to create stability and security.

Women's economic and social rights tend to be seen as optional, but they are crucial foundations for sustainable development and growth that peace-agreements and post-conflict governance should secure. Women's rights to security and justice and the prevention of SGBV depend upon the prioritization of women's economic and social rights (cf. UNSG 2010a: para. 46). For example, if key economic and social rights are not secured early enough after conflict, such as those to land and housing, to transact in one's own legal name, to equality in marriage, and to freedom of mobility, then many women who are already poor and marginalized will be denied opportunities for both economic and political participation in peace and reconstruction.[4] Moreover, access to sexual and reproductive health is fundamental, including pregnancy care, abortion services, post-SGBV psychosocial care, and HIV-related care. They are often stigmatized and denied with considerable negative impact on women's ability to participate in post-conflict recovery processes (see Pierson and Thomson 2018). Ensuring safe and quality sexual and reproductive healthcare is thus imperative in both emergency responses and long-term development interventions as often, post-conflict countries have poor healthcare infrastructure.

Transitions from conflict or disaster are windows of opportunity for fundamentally challenging and targeting structural disadvantage through the realization of these rights (Rees and Chinkin 2016: 1225). This includes investing in both physical infrastructure, such as bridges, roads, water, and sanitation, electricity and telecommunication systems, as well as social infrastructure that improves living standards and quality of life and develops people's capabilities in areas like education, health, and community engagement (Seguino 2016: 7). Spending on social infrastructure has been shown to have a positive effect on addressing inequalities between groups, including between women and men, with economy-wide benefits (Seguino 2016: 8). At present, however, socioeconomic rights are not at all operationalized in peace-building processes to create economic opportunities for women (True et al. 2017). In many post-conflict countries there is a lack of information to assess the status of women's economic and social rights, and loss of access to resources during conflict. Legislation to ensure economic protection, compensation, social protection and labor rights is also often not in place after conflict. Yet the marginalization experienced by women in post-conflict societies is the result of gendered economic discrimination, exploitation, and violence.

Gendered socioeconomic inequalities tend to exclude women from participating in security decision-making and reinforce a culture of impunity for violence against women. For example, in post-genocide Rwanda the 70 percent of households headed by females fell into poverty at greater rates than male-headed households because they lost their access to or ownership of land (Rombouts 2006: 205). Land was either transferred to a son or other male relative or sold for economic survival reasons.[5] Moreover, for women survivors of SGBV, recovery, protection, and prevention of future violence, "is often tied to their ability to move on and generate incomes for themselves and children" (Anderlini 2010: xiv; True 2012: 151).[6] Despite this, most resources are directed toward legal justice remedies for violence in post-conflict contexts, which do not create economic security and may inadvertently marginalize women's basic needs. Resolution 1889 (2009: para. 10) stresses the need to support women's socioeconomic rights in post-conflict settings, but it does not provide specific mechanisms or a plan of action for realizing these rights through state or other institutions.

GENDER PERSPECTIVE AND WOMEN'S PARTICIPATION IN ECONOMIC RECOVERY

The UN Secretary-General's Seven-Point Plan for gender-responsive economic recovery seeks to promote women's economic participation but does not recognize this structural oppression of women prior to and during conflict. Post-conflict conditions tend to exacerbate women's already unequal economic and social status relative to men, and add-on measures do little to change this situation. In often dire economic situations after conflict that foster corruption and criminality, marginalized groups of women experience extreme income inequality, working in the informal economy and in the most precarious employment positions in the labor market. As well, they suffer from pre-conflict legacies of poor investment in gender-equal economic and social development with respect to education, health, housing, food security, water, property, and land rights. The 2011 World Bank Development Report concurs that while the impact of armed conflict falls directly on young males, who are the majority of fighting forces, women and children suffer disproportionately from war's indirect effects (World Bank 2011).[7] Increases in female heads of households, gender discrimination in employment, exploitation in incipient sex industries and trafficking networks, female displacement and resettlement in urban slums, and gender bias in DDR processes make up a pattern of gendered marginalization after conflict that constrains economic recovery in post-conflict settings and women's participation in that recovery. The preference for employing men is widespread in post-conflict countries (Jennings 2014). Suggesting employment programs that specifically target women as a beneficiary group and that neither sex receives more than 60 percent of the positions created by economic reconstruction programs is an important corrective. However, the UN, donors, and the international community need to lead the way by supporting programs that are culturally sensitive (for instance, in Afghanistan, women would be ostracized if they engage in road-building, but in Kenya it is acceptable) (Anderlini 2010; True 2013).

Post-conflict conditions often exacerbate gender inequality with gender discrimination in employment, female displacement and resettlement in urban slums, gender bias in DDR programs, sexual exploitation and trafficking, all contributing to the gendered marginalization that constrains economic and social recovery (True 2013: 3). Women are often forced into precarious employment conditions in the informal economy and low-earning positions, which is reinforced by neoliberal assumptions underpinning post-conflict recovery, privileging productive economies and devaluing reproductive economies. This vulnerability can be heightened by loan and austerity measures imposed by international financial institutions and development banks, such as the World Bank and International Monetary Fund (True et al. 2017). In conflict and post-conflict periods, changes in household and community gender relations and roles are directly linked to adaption of productive and reproductive economies for economic survival. With losses of men due to conflict, female seclusion in domestic and household spheres is unsustainable. This is reflected in increases of female heads of households and women's labor participation rates in conflict and post-conflict settings (Justino 2012). However, greater participation in productive economies is generally concomitant with increased caring and reproductive responsibilities, doubling if not tripling women's work burdens. Additionally, within the productive sectors, women are still largely segregated in unskilled, low-wage, and informal jobs, and potentially risky and unprotected work, such as survival sex in peacekeeping economies and militarized states (UN Women 2015: 42).

The effects of conflict and peacekeeping missions are also enduring. For example, more than ten years after the Bosnian conflict, government trafficking data show that women continue to be both imported and exported, albeit with the number of foreign women decreasing and the number of Bosnian victims increasing significantly (Jennings and

Nikolić-Ristanović 2009).These numbers reflect the economic desperation and lack of alternative economic opportunities that many women face. The UN response has been to enforce a zero-tolerance policy on sexual relationships with locals and a code of conduct for peacekeepers that treats sexual misconduct as an exceptional occurrence rather than a political economy based on unequal gendered social relations.[8] This policy approach deals with the issue of sexual exploitation and abuse on "an individual level, with application and sanctions restricted to UN personnel" (Jennings and Nikolić-Ristanović 2009: 20).

Administrative rules and regulations, however, cannot eliminate the economic incentives for sex work and for the culture of violence against women. In conflict and post-conflict countries where there are usually few income-generating alternatives, unless plans for women's economic empowerment are prioritized, peace-building processes tend to create new forms of gendered exploitation (such as early marriage, trafficking, and prostitution). In Syria's war economy, women have been used as a form of currency to further political, military, and economic goals by being sold into marriage, kidnapped for ransom, traded for weapons and safe travel, and for basic necessities such as rent (Carrié et al. 2017). In Jordan, Iraq, and Lebanon, incidences of child marriage have increased alarmingly among Syrian refugees, often reasoned to protect young girls from the threat of SGBV and ease pressures on dwindling family economic resources and opportunities (Save the Children 2014).[9] Likewise, widespread early marriage in Sri Lanka during and after the conflict has resulted in severe vulnerability, especially for widows, to coercive transactional sex to secure basic economic necessities (Davies and True 2017: 7–8).

In addition to employment barriers and vulnerabilities, women may experience violent backlash from returning male family members who often insist that they revert to traditional gender roles.[10] This is reinforced by R&R initiatives that prioritize (male) ex-combatant and male employment and income generation programs, curtailing women's potential newfound freedoms and participation in the political, economic, and social spheres. This is illustrated by the exclusion of women in post-conflict decision-making that determines the "power-distribution, wealth-sharing patterns, social development priorities, and approaches to justice" (UN Women 2015: 168). Women's inclusion in the planning, designing, and implementing of post-conflict and humanitarian relief and recovery cannot be overemphasized.

Post-Conflict Financing and Gender Budgeting

The UN has committed to increasing the financing for gender equality and for women and girl's empowerment in post-conflict situations (UNSG 2010a: para. 35, 36). This is crucial since gender analysis of post-conflict budgets shows that up until 2010 only meager resources were committed to these goals. In a 2010 report, the UNDP conducted a gender-specific budget analysis to reveal the gendered priorities of peace-building (UNDP 2010). While the attention to gender equality and women's needs were low priorities in the overall peace-building budgets of twelve post-conflict countries, the least attention to gender issues was evident in spending on economic recovery and infrastructure, demonstrating the lack of integration and bias toward political/military security even in gender mainstreamed programs. At the same time, this UNDP report reviewed economic reconstruction aid addressing the economic security pillar of peace operations to four post-conflict countries (East Timor, Sierra Leone, Kosovo, and South Sudan). It found very limited resources were allocated to promote gender equality or women's specific needs (UNDP 2010).

In the Post-Conflict Needs Assessments, less than 5 percent of activities and only 3 percent of budget lines mentioned either gender equality or women's needs (UNDP 2010: 6). Yet in all four post-conflict countries, critical gender gaps between women and men exist, including, for example, with respect to access to education and health, water for domestic consumption, agricultural inputs, and economic opportunities (UNDP 2010: 35). Women were also excluded from the planning of economic reconstruction in Sierra Leone, Timor-Leste, Kosovo, and Southern Sudan. This UNDP evaluation found that none of the countries had an economic policy adviser with gender budget analysis training and skills. Thus, to implement Resolution 1325 in post-conflict contexts the UN and donor governments must focus on actually implementing gender-responsive financing, planning, and budgeting as well as strengthening in-country and donor accountabilities.

The lack of financing and funding for the implementation of the WPS agenda and targeted action for women and girls in post-conflict and humanitarian settings was highlighted in the Global Study. OECD-DAC (2017) data show that aid is generally directed toward supporting gender-equality in health, education, and government and civil society where significant gaps remain in the economic and productive sectors and in peace and security. Moreover, despite increasing recognition of the impact of SGBV, due to its invisibility, violence against women is not considered a priority in many emergency responses and is subsequently under-resourced (Barclay et al. 2016: 11). Even within this asymmetrical deployment of aid, only 1.7 percent of projects in 2016 using the IASC Gender Marker[11] included targeted action for women and girls (GAI 2017: 7).

The target of 15 percent of funds directed toward gender equality programming and policy across the UN system is a positive step. Although many UN agencies have failed to achieve this, the Peacebuilding Fund surpassed this target and has directed 20 percent of funding to gender responsive programming in 2016. The Peacebuilding Fund has also rolled out gender promotion initiatives to encourage proposals with a gender-focus.[12]

Resolution 2242 (2015) established the Global Acceleration Instrument (GAI) for WPS and Humanitarian Action, which is a multilateral fund intended to promote women's engagement in peace, security, and humanitarian affairs in order "to attract resources, coordinate responses and accelerate [WPS] implementation" (UN Women 2017: opening para. 17). Launched in 2016, the GAI addresses financing gaps and under-resourcing of women's humanitarian and peace-building efforts across the peace and security and development continuum (UN Women 2017). It aims to bridge the gap between the recognition of the benefits of women's participation in conflict prevention, humanitarian action, and peace-building, and the lack of investment in local women's civil society organizations (UN Women 2016: 7). Moreover, the GAI is a tool to localize and implement global development, and humanitarian and gender commitments, such as SDGs goals 4, 5, and 16, to conflict-affected countries (UN Women 2017: 13), providing a more holistic approach to funding local humanitarian, development, and peace-building actors.

GENDER-TRANSFORMATIVE JUSTICE

Transitional justice processes are often not considered under the R&R ambit; generally they are included and discussed under the protection and participation pillars. However, transitional justice is a critical and core aspect of R&R, especially in linking redress for past crimes with wider economic redistribution and development initiatives aimed at enhancing women's socioeconomic rights (Davies and True 2017: 12). Funding for implementing individual or collective reparations for women survivors of war/conflict and gross violations of human rights, disproportionately affects the economic livelihoods of widows, female heads of households, young women, and former female combatants. Reparations help to either reinforce or subvert some of the preexisting structural gender inequalities that result in systematic discrimination against women (Rubio-Marin 2006: 25; Durbach et al 2017). Attending to reparations shifts our attention away from the overwhelming attention given to criminal justice and what to do with the perpetrators, toward the victims of violence and how to assist them to reclaim their lives and potentialities (Rubio-Marin 2006: 23–24). Shifting the focus from individual to collective reparations helps us to think further about violent social structures and the prevention of future violence (True 2012: 157-8). As Rees and Chinkin (2016: 1223) state, reparations are "key to breaking the cycle of violence." And finally, designing reparation programs that address community development in a future-oriented way is a crucial strategy to counter the unequal gender dimensions of recovery and peace-building. Thus, reparations targeted at women survivors—widows and family members of deceased combatants as well as combatants themselves and victims of conflict-related SGBV—should be designed for the long-term economic development and empowerment of women and their families. Individual compensation or delivery of basic needs through social welfare institutions will not address existing gender inequalities and deficits in women's post-conflict participation (Rees 2012).[13]

In Timor-Leste, where 40 percent of the population lives in poverty, the Truth and Reconciliation Commission (known by its Portuguese acronym CAVR) framed reparations and its recommendations in broad recovery terms with key measures for women (CAVR 2006). Social services, material support, and economic empowerment through livelihood activities, group counseling, and community education were all conceived as reparations programs. Women-friendly recommendations that emerged from the CAVR process included support to single mothers and victims of sexual violence and scholarships for their children; support for the disabled, widows, and torture victims; and support to the most affected communities. Specific measures were suggested to encourage women's participation and were largely successful (True 2012: 157–158). Transitional justice mechanisms must create gender-sensitive spaces (cf. UNSG 2010a: para. 48) but so must they actually provide the financing so that reparations can be fully implemented.

Many transitional justice mechanisms are brokered during peace negotiations in which women are largely excluded. Consequently, little attention is paid to women's experiences of conflict where transitional processes are likely to reflect men's experiences, concerns, needs, and priorities, and could reinforce preexisting structural gender inequalities

(UN Women 2015: 110; Rees and Chinkin 2016: 1224). Women's participation and consultation in designing and implementing transitional processes cannot be overemphasized, where one size does not fit all. Where transitional justice mechanisms may be absent, an "economic reparative" approach focusing on economic relief and recovery can serve as one way of providing justice that addresses women's needs in the post-conflict phase (Davies and True 2017: 1331–1332). Broadening conceptions of transitional justice beyond a human rights approach by addressing the political economy of post-conflict contexts may provide women with the justice they require, while recognizing that women's justice needs will not be homogenous. For instance, regarding reparations, in Côte d'Ivoire, women were more likely to mention individual reparations compared to women in Central African Republic, who emphasized the need for psychosocial counseling (UN Women 2015: 115–116).

However, psychosocial support must not reinforce female-victimhood stereotypes. In conflict-affected Afghanistan, the United Nations Population Fund (UNFPA) has launched four mobile women-friendly health spaces and psychosocial experts to assist survivors of gender-based violence, especially Yazidi women and girls (cf. UNSG 2016: para. 33). In Burundi, Rwanda, and the Democratic Republic of the Congo (DRC), Switzerland has developed a program to provide a holistic set of services for victims of violence targeted at medical care, legal services, and socioeconomic integration (UNSG 2016: para. 33). A key aspect of transitional processes is psychosocial recovery that works concurrently with gender-transformative reparations and justice mechanisms (UN Women 2015: 69). Mental healthcare must be tailored toward specific contexts where one-on-one counseling may not be appropriate compared to traditional healing rituals, community dialogue, or engagement in livelihood projects.

CONCLUSION: ONGOING CHALLENGES AND OPPORTUNITIES

Mainstreaming gender equality and women's empowerment goals in relief and recovery requires an integrated framework for action. Post-conflict financing and needs assessments must involve gender-sensitive economic analysis and gender-responsive budgeting so that resources on the ground equally benefit women as well as men as well as addressing inequalities among diverse groups of women. Regular audits of post-conflict financing should be put in place to hold donor and recipient governments accountable. This includes ensuring reparations that can contribute to women's economic empowerment. Collective reparations programs for gendered harms through transitional justice mechanisms should be designed in order to develop the economic and political capacities and livelihoods of women and girls in post-conflict societies.

Actual resource commitments and specific targets within WPS NAPs could be one vehicle for implementing more fully and connecting humanitarian assistance and R&R to long-term structural issues that are beyond immediate assistance.[14] As this chapter has illustrated, however, post-conflict, humanitarian, and disaster approaches have inadequately addressed gender inequalities and women's experiences typically resulting in ineffective interventions. Without women's meaningful input and consultation across diverse groups into the design of relief and recovery programs, vital resources and assistance won't reflect their needs and concerns. A "one-size-fits-all" mentality results in funds and resources going toward initiatives that aren't even helpful or that don't assist women in their relief and recovery (UN Women 2015: 168). Social accountability could prove a useful alternative in approaching gender-sensitive R&R. It involves community members coming together with service users (mainly women), service providers, and local authorities to assess interventions, identify issues, and jointly design solutions to improve outcomes. This participatory method is facilitated via Community Score Cards and is complimentary with peace and security and development agendas (Care International 2015). Incorporating such participatory approaches into R&R efforts would facilitate women's participation in decision-making processes in key recovery aspects such as employment, health, and education.

The current siloing of humanitarian relief responses, sustainable development approaches focused on resilience building, and security approaches addressing women's participation, protection, and prevention roles represents a major challenge to realizing the WPS R&R pillar. To more effectively promote its implementation, WPS provisions need to be embedded into all UN Security Council resolutions on post-conflict countries' donor and country fragile state and/or post-conflict strategy and planning; conflict-affected and post-conflict countries should be priority countries in the implementation and monitoring of donor/developed country WPS NAPs; and gender equality must be practically realized in development aid strategies, support and financing for post-conflict countries.

NOTES

1. In this chapter we retain "relief and recovery" as a WPS pillar rather than adopt "peacebuilding," which is a more general term that lacks the specificity of the relief and recovery phase.

2. Consultations around developing a UN-wide framework on the implementation of Resolution 1325 only started in earnest in 2004. The System-Wide Action Plan was adopted for 2005–2007 and renewed for 2008–2009, and it served as a coordination, reporting, and accountability tool; see Office of the Special Adviser on Gender Issues and Advancement of Women, "Independent Evaluation of the System-wide Action Plan for 2008–2009 for Security Council Resolution 1325 (2000), Women, Peace and Security." July 26, 2010, http://www.peacewomen.org/assets/file/PWandUN/UNImplementation/evaluation_of_the_1325_swap_26th_july_10.doc.

3. See also UNDP, "The Eight Point Agenda: Practical Positive Outcomes for Girls and Women in Crisis." Crisis Prevention and Recovery, 2010, http://www.undp.org/content/dam/undp/library/crisis%20prevention/undp-cpr-8-point-agenda-practical-positive-outcomes-girls-women-crisis.pdf.

4. See A. M. Ibanez and A. Moya, "The Impact of Intra-State Conflict on Economic Welfare and Consumption Smoothing: Empirical Evidence for the Displaced

Population in Colombia," HiCN Working Paper 23, University of Sussex, Falmer-Brighton, 2006.

5. See P. Justino and P. Verwimp, *Poverty Dynamics, Violent Conflict, and Convergence in Rwanda* (Brighton, UK: Households in Conflict Network, 2006)—based on panel data on Rwanda following the same households before and after conflict. T. Brück and K. Schindler, "Small Landholder Access in Post-War Northern Mozambique," *World Development* 37 (2009): 1379–1389; and T. Bundervoet, "Estimating Poverty in Burundi," HiCN Working Paper 20, University of Sussex, Falmer-Brighton, 2006—find similar results for Mozambique.

6. See also "DRC: Sexual Violence Prevention and Re-Integration Funding 'Falls through Cracks,'" *IRIN News*, November 4, 2009.

7. Analyzing adult mortality as a result of armed conflict, political scientists Q. Li and M. Wen find that over time women's mortality that is attributable to war is as high as men's, due to war's lingering social and economic effects: "The Immediate and Lingering Effects of Armed Conflict on Adult Mortality: A Time-Series Cross-National Analysis," *Journal of Peace Research* 42 (2005): 471–492; also H. Ghobarah et al., "Civil Wars Kill and Maim People—Long After the Shooting Stops," *American Political Science Review* 97, no. 2 (2003): 189–202, show that the risk of death and disability from infectious diseases rises sharply in conflict-affected countries, and that women and children are the majority of the long-term victims.

8. See O. Simic, "Does the Presence of Women Really Matter? Towards Combating Male Sexual Violence in Peacekeeping Operations," *International Peacekeeping* 17, no. 2 (2012), 188–199; D. Otto, "Making Sense of Zero-Tolerance Policies in Peacekeeping Sexual Economies," in *Sexuality and the Law: Feminist Engagements*, eds. V. E. Munro and C. F. Stychin, 259–280 (New York: Routledge-Cavendish, 2007).

9. Save the Children (2014) estimates that rates of child marriage in the Syrian refugee community in Jordan increased from roughly 12 percent in 2011 to as high as 25 percent in 2013. [AU: Add this source link here or full ref. in ref. list DONE.]

10. See True's discussion in chapter 3 of *Political Economy of Violence against Women*, (New York: Oxford University Press, 2012, 35–52).

11. The IASC Gender Marker is a tool that codes, on a 0–2 scale, whether or not a humanitarian project is designed to effectively respond to the different needs of men, women, girls, and boys within the affected population.

12. See Hansen and Lorentzen (2017).

13. See Rees (2012).

14. Some NAPs, especially from African countries, specifically address a relief and recovery pillar. For instance, Kenya's NAP has specific R&R objectives to promote a gender perspective and ensure women's inclusion in humanitarian, early recovery, relief, and peace-building programs, including disaster-risk management, with a specific focus on refugee and internally displaced women and girls (2016–2018 Kenya National Action Plan, 54); see also C. Reiling, "Dueling Models: Tackling Women's Empowerment through Both Security and Development," European Conference on Politics and Gender, Lausanne, Switzerland, June 8–10, 2017.

15. See S/RES/1325 (2000); S/RES/1820 (2008); S/RES/1960 (2010); S/RES/1888 (2009); S/RES/1889 (2009); S/RES/2106 (2013); S/Res/2122 (2013); S/RES/2242 (2015).

References

Anderlini, S. N. "WDR Gender Background Paper." Background Paper for the 2011 World Development Report. February 19, 2010, https://openknowledge.worldbank.org/bitstream/handle/10986/9250/WDR2011_0033.pdf?sequence=1&isAllowed=y.

Barclay, A., M. Higelin, and M. Bungcaras. *On the Frontline: Catalysing Women's Leadership in Humanitarian Action*. World Humanitary Aid Summit, ActionAid International, 2016.

Care International. "Beyond 2015 for Women, Peace, and Security: Care Austria Position on the 15th Anniversary of UNSCR 1325." Women-Peace Security Agenda, 2015, https://www.care.at/wp-content/uploads/2015/10/09_20141103_Beyond-2015-for-Women-Peace-and-Security.compressed.pdf.

Carrié, S., R. Zayat, and A. Masi. "In Syria's War Economy, Women Have Become a Form of Currency." *Syria Deeply*, September 15, 2017, https://www.newsdeeply.com/syria/community/2017/09/15/in-syrias-war-economy-women-have-become-a-form-of-currency.

Comissao de Acolhimento, Verdade e Reconciliacao (CAVR) (Commission for Reception, Truth, and Reconciliation). "Chega!" The Report of the Commission for Reception, Truth, and Reconciliation Timor-Leste." Final Report, 2006, http://www.etan.org/news/2006/cavr.htm.

Davies, S., and J. True. "When There Is No Justice: Gendered Violence and Harm in Post-Conflict Sri Lanka." *International Journal of Human Rights* 21, no. 9 (2017). 1320-1336.

Durbach, A., L. Chappell and S. Williams. "Foreword: Special Issue on 'Transformative Reparations and Sexual Violence Post-Conflict: Prospects and Problems." International Journal of Human Rights 21, 9 (2017): 1185–1192

Hansen, J. M., and J. Lorentzen. "Gender Financing at the UN Peacebuilding Fund." *PRIO Gender, Peace, and Security Update*, PRIO, 2017.

Jennings, K. M. "Service, Sex, and Security: Gendered Peacekeeping Economies in Liberia and the Democratic Republic of the Congo." *Security Dialogue* 45, no. 4 (2014), 1–18.

Jennings, K. M., and V. Nikolić-Ristanović. "UN Peacekeeping Economies and Local Sex Industries: Connections and Implications." MICROCON (Micro Level Analysis of Violent Conflict) Research Working Paper 176. Institute of Development Studies at the University of Sussex, UK, 2009.

Justino, P. *Women Working for Recovery: The Impact of Female Employment on Family and Community Welfare after Conflict*. New York: UN Women, 2012.

Organisation for Economic Cooperation and Development (OECD). "Aid in Support of Gender Equality and Women's Empowerment: Donor Charts." OECD, 2017, http://www.oecd.org/development/gender-development/Aid-to-Gender-Equality-Donor-Charts-2017.pdf.

Pierson, C., and J. Thomson. "Can Abortion Rights be Integrated into the Women, Peace and Security Agenda." *International Feminist Journal of Politics*, https://doi.org/10.1080/14616742.2017.1413583, 2018.

Rees, M. "The Gendered Dimensions of Human Trafficking." CDDRL Working Papers, no. 7, Program on Human Rights, Center on Democracy, Development, and the Rule of Law. Freeman Spogli Institute for International Studies, Stanford University, June 2012.

Rees, M., and C. Chinkin. "Exposing the Gendered Myth of Post Conflict Transition: The Transformative Power of Economic and Social Rights." *New York University Journal of International Law and Politics* 48, no. 4 (2016): 1211–1226.

Rombouts, H. "Women and Reparations in Rwanda: A Long Path to Travel." In *What Happened to the Women? Gender and Reparations for Human Rights Violations*, edited by Ruth Rubio-Marin. New York: Social Science Research Council, 2006.

Rubio-Marin, R., ed. *What Happened to the Women? Gender and Reparations for Human Rights Violations*. New York: Social Science Research Council, 2006.

Save the Children. *Too Young to Wed: The Growing Problem of Child Marriage among Syrian Girls in Jordan*. United Kingdom, 2014.

Schaper, H. "The UN's Women, Peace, and Security framework in the Context of the 2012–2016 Colombian Peace Process. A Window of Opportunity for Enhancing Women's Rights?" PhD dissertation, Tartu Ülikool, 2017.

Seguino, S. *Financing for Gender Equality in the Context of the Sustainable Development Goals*. New York: UN Women, 2016.

True, J. *The Political Economy of Violence against Women*. New York: Oxford University Press, 2012.

True, J. "Women, Peace, and Security in Asia Pacific: Emerging Issues in National Action Plans for Women, Peace and Security." Asia-Pacific Regional Symposium on National Action Plans on Women, Peace, and Security, UN Women and the Embassy of Japan, Bangkok, Thailand, July 11–13, 2016.

True, J. "Women, Peace, and Security in Post-Conflict and Peacebuilding Contexts." *Norwegian Peacebuilding Resource Centre Expert Analysis*, March 14, 2013.

True, J., C. Chinkin, M. Rees, N. P. Isaković, G. Mlinarević, and B. Svedberg. "A Feminist Perspective on Post-Conflict Restructuring and Recovery: The Case of Bosnia and Herzegovina." Geneva, Sarajevo: Women Organizing for Change in Bosnia and Herzegovina and Women's International League for Peace and Freedom, 2017.

United Nations (UN). "UN Strategic Results Framework on Women, Peace, and Security: 2011–2020." July 11, 2011, http://www.un.org/womenwatch/ianwge/taskforces/wps/Strategic_Framework_2011-2020.pdf.

UN Development Programme (UNDP). *"The Price of Peace: Financing for Gender Equality in Post-Conflict Reconstruction*. New York: United Nations Development Programme, 2010.

UN Secretary-General (UNSG). "Report of the Secretary-General on Women and Peace and Security (S/2016/822)." New York: United Nations, September 29, 2016.

UN Secretary-General (UNSG). "Report of the Secretary-General on Women and Peace and Security (S/2015/716)." New York: United Nations, September 16, 2015.

UN Secretary-General (UNSG). "Report of the Secretary-General on Women's Participation in Peacebuilding (A/65/354–S/2010/466)." New York: United Nations, September 7, 2010a.

UN Secretary-General (UNSG). "Report of the Secretary-General on Women's Participation in Peacebuilding (A/65/354–S/2010/466)." Tracking Progress: 7-Point Action Plan, 2010b, http://www.un.org/en/peacebuilding/pbso/pdf/seven_point_action_plan.pdf.

UN Secretary-General (UNSG). "Report of the Secretary-General on Women and Peace and Security (A/65/354–S/2005/636)." New York: United Nations, October 10, 2005.

UN Security Council. Resolution 1889, S/RES/1889 Adopted by the Security Council, 13 October, 2009.

UN Security Council. Resolution 2242, S/RES/2242 Adopted by the Security Council, 13 October, 2015.

UN Women. *Preventing Conflict, Transforming Justice, Securing the Peace: A Global Study on the Implementation of United Nations Security Council Resolution 1325*. New York: UN Women, 2015.

UN Women. "The Global Acceleration Instrument (GAI) for Women, Peace, and Security and Humanitarian Action Terms of Reference. February, 2016.

UN Women. "The Global Acceleration Instrument (GAI) for Women, Peace, and Security and Humanitarian Action: Annual Report January–December 2016." 2017.

Wiener, A. *A Theory of Contestation*. Berlin Heidelberg: Springer-Verlag, 2014.

World Bank. *World Development Report: Conflict and Development*, Washington DC: International Bank for Reconstruction and Development / World Bank, 2011.

CHAPTER 16

WHERE THE WPS PILLARS INTERSECT

MARIE O'REILLY

POPULISTS and autocrats are threatening the post–Cold War international order based on human rights and the rule of law (Aghekyan et al. 2017). As repressive dictatorships bomb civilians in Syria and Yemen, "strongman" rule is devastating civil and political institutions in Egypt, Ethiopia, and Venezuela. Patriarchal nationalism is rebounding in the West: from the rise of Donald Trump in the United States to Vladimir Putin's consolidation of power in Russia and beyond, and the growth of far-right nationalist parties across the European continent. Over a century ago, a similar kind of belligerent nationalism produced the "war to end all wars" with an estimated thirty-eight million casualties. In response to the devastation of World War I, more than 1,100 women from twelve countries gathered in The Hague, Netherlands, in 1915. They called on governments to begin negotiations to end the war and commit to a new strategy to ensure that a "permanent peace" would follow (Addams et al. 1915).

The Hague Congress envisioned a system of international cooperation that could produce a positive peace beyond the absence of war. To prevent conflict, it suggested states resolve their disputes through mediation or arbitration, and exert social, moral, and economic pressure on any state that resorts to arms. To sustain peace, it argued foreign policy and issues of self-government should be subject to democratic control in which women's representation and political rights are equal to men's. Significantly, the congress' resolutions also protested vehemently against the "odious wrongs" done to women during war (Addams et al. 1915).

Looking back, we see the early origins of the four core pillars of UN Security Council Resolution 1325, namely prevention of armed conflict; women's participation; protection of women during war; and inclusive relief and recovery (Otto 2016). Following The Hague Congress, the Women's International League for Peace and Freedom (WILPF) carried forth these pillars of women's peace activism to succeeding generations (see Tickner and True 2018). A variety of multilateral fora throughout the twentieth century re-emphasized the need for conflict prevention, women's participation in peace and security processes, women's protection during war, and women's involvement in recovery thereafter—though typically not all four together. As chapters 3 and 4 discussed, the Fourth World Conference on Women in Beijing in 1995 brought them to the fore again as interrelated means for achieving peace and security and advancing women's rights (United Nations 1996: 56–65).

Yet, despite the formal interlinking of these pillars in Resolution 1325 in 2000, which laid the foundation for a new global policy framework on Women, Peace, and Security (WPS) for the twenty-first century, these priority areas have suffered a very uneven and siloed implementation. How has this influenced their impact? To what extent does progress for one pillar depend on the others? In the context of a backlash against women's rights and increasing belligerence in many places, is there a point of intersection that advocates, policymakers, and researchers could double down on to transform implementation of the agenda as a whole? This chapter examines progress and pitfalls in prevention, participation, protection, and relief and recovery since 2000. It explores the interdependence of these four pillars and argues that greater emphasis on a new kind of participation, through transformative feminist leadership, would lead to gains in all four areas and beyond.

UNEVEN IMPLEMENTATION OF RESOLUTION 1325

Emphasis on Protection

Protection has been the dominant pillar in the WPS policy framework since the year 2000. After the Security Council articulated the links between the four pillars in Resolution 1325, it went on to issue four resolutions devoted to combatting sexual violence in conflict between 2008 and 2013 (also see chapter 9 in this volume).[1] Collectively, these were valuable steps in establishing the multilateral protection framework, leading to

- Security Council recognition of conflict-related sexual violence as a tactic of war and threat to international peace and security;
- creation of a special representative of the UN Secretary-General dedicated to the issue of sexual violence in conflict;
- a mechanism for monitoring and reporting on this kind of violence and its perpetrators;
- "women protection advisors" deployed to UN missions to support strategies for combatting sexual violence as well as monitoring and reporting; and
- application of targeted sanctions to some perpetrators of conflict-related sexual violence (Goetz and Jenkins 2015).

This normative progress since Resolution 1325 built on significant advances in jurisprudence since the 1990s. International courts and tribunals handling wars in Sierra Leone, Rwanda, and Yugoslavia, as well as the International Criminal Court, had already recognized widespread and systematic conflict-related sexual violence as war crimes, crimes against humanity, and acts of genocide. Since 2000, academic researchers have also conducted extensive, multi-country explorations of patterns of sexual violence in conflict situations; motivations related to ideology, social hierarchy, and instrumental gains; as well as enabling structures of gender inequality (Davies and True 2015).

Despite these advances in research and international policy frameworks, women continue to be targeted during war. The global focus on protection has led to gains in the number of security sector personnel trained to respond to gender-based violence in conflict (UN Secretary-General 2016: 2). But given the lack of robust data, it's difficult to measure whether the rate of conflict-related sexual violence has been increasing or declining in the last two decades (Mack et al. 2012). What is clear is that even in settings notorious for such violence that have received significant international attention, such as the Democratic Republic of the Congo, sexual and gender-based violence against women and men continues to be carried out by state actors and rebel groups alike (O'Reilly 2016).

Participation Lags Behind

The predominant focus on women as victims in the WPS agenda has to some extent reinforced stereotypes that women are inherently vulnerable rather than agents of change. As such, it is perhaps unsurprising that participation has received less attention compared to protection, in both normative frameworks and scholarly research. Following Resolution 1325, Security Council Resolutions 1889 and 2122 primarily addressed women's participation in peacebuilding, a topic the Security Council was slower to act on (UNSC 2009b; 2013b). A third resolution, 2242, covered all four pillars, including participation (UNSC 2015). The Security Council has acknowledged its own imbalanced approach to the WPS agenda. Articulating its intention "to focus more attention on women's leadership and participation in conflict resolution and peacebuilding," the Council recognized in 2013 that without "a significant implementation shift" women will continue to be underrepresented (UNSC 2013b: 3, 5–6).

Impact has been mixed in the area of participation. Women's participation in peace and mediation processes remained static between 2000 and 2010, but limited data suggests some increases thereafter (Council on Foreign Relations, 2018). Nevertheless, skeptics suggest that meaningful participation as opposed to tokenistic representation remains rare in practice. Indeed, it has been easier to insert language relating to women's rights and protection in peace agreements than for women themselves to participate in creating these agreements (Bell and O'Rourke 2010; Castillo-Diaz and Tordjman 2012). In UN peace operations, amid zigzag progress, the proportion of women serving in senior leadership roles reached a high of 25 percent in 2016 compared to a low of 2 percent in 2006 (United Nations 2017). But women's representation among peacekeeping troops remains stuck at 4 percent (UN Secretary-General 2017). Secretary-General Antonio Guterres' milestone achievement of gender parity in his senior management group in 2018 suggests greater improvement in the realm of peace and security may now be within reach.

Part of the challenge in measuring change is the dearth of documentation, analysis, and scholarly literature focused specifically on women's participation in peace and security processes, despite significant academic research on the impact of women's empowerment on socioeconomic development outcomes, for example. Nonetheless, Thania Paffenholz has shown that in the cases where women exerted influence on a peace process, a peace agreement was more likely to be reached and the agreement more likely to last (O'Reilly et al. 2015). Statistical analysis supports this finding: women's inclusion in peace talks increases the quality and durability of peace (Krause et al. 2018).

Relief and Recovery: A Siloed Latecomer

Compared to protection and participation, the pillar of relief and recovery has arguably received less attention in the Security Council's "soft law" on WPS. Relief and recovery, also
referred to as post-conflict peace-building, was added as a fourth pillar in the WPS agenda
by the UN Secretary-General in 2007.[2] Its essence, however, had already been featured in
Resolution 1325 with references to gender perspectives in post-conflict resettlement, rehabilitation, and reintegration processes, as well as in post-conflict governance and security mechanisms. As previously noted, a focus on women's participation in post-conflict
peace-building re-emerged in Resolution 1889 (UNSC 2009b). Resolution 2122 (2013b) later
emphasized the need to support local women's peace-building initiatives after conflict.

Despite these mentions, post-conflict peace-building is not typically considered the domain of the UN Security Council (notwithstanding security-sector issues such as disarmament, demobilization, and reintegration). As such, other bodies and frameworks including
the Sustainable Development Goals, UN Peacebuilding Architecture, and UN Development
Programme have arguably made greater strides in articulating the links between women's
inclusion and post-conflict recovery, and advancing targets and indicators for women's
political and economic participation in post-conflict settings. In 2010, the UN Secretary-
General created a seven-point action plan to improve gender-responsive peacebuilding by
UN entities. However, five years later, the UN's high-level review of the implementation
of Resolution 1325, known as the *Global Study*, concluded that "while some progress has
been made in the area of processes, not enough impact has yet been felt in the daily lives of
women in post-conflict contexts" (Coomaraswamy 2015: 170).

Nonetheless, there are signs of progress in other areas relevant to relief and recovery.
For example, the proportion of women represented in constitution-making in countries
affected by conflict and unrest has grown steadily over the past two decades (Tamaru and
O'Reilly, 2018). Women have also successfully seized opportunities to increase their representation in politics in many post-conflict countries (Tripp 2015). In part thanks to the
Security Council's inclusion of gender-sensitive approaches to disarmament, demobilization, and reintegration (DDR) in country-specific resolutions, gender mainstreaming has
been incorporated into more DDR programs. However, as these programs frequently consider women as victims rather than agents of change, they continue to fall short beyond
initial disarmament and demobilization phases (Coomaraswamy 2015).

Prevention Falls by the Wayside

If relief and recovery has seen some progress in a variety of domains, prevention of armed
conflict has largely fallen by the wayside in the WPS agenda. No WPS resolution passed
by the Security Council has been dedicated to this issue. On the contrary, skeptics suggest
that WPS has become more concerned with making war safe for women than preventing
the outbreak of conflict in the first place. Despite the Security Council's assertion in 2000
that "peace is inextricably linked with equality between women and men," the term "prevention" is now frequently associated with the narrow lens of preventing conflict-related
sexual violence in gender-related policies or with generic calls for women's participation in

conflict prevention (Basu and Confortini 2016). Broader conflict prevention issues such as disarmament—a widely held feminist goal (see chapter 54 in this volume)—barely feature in the eight resolutions. "Disarmament," when it appears, relates to disarming individuals after conflict as part of context-specific disarmament, demobilization, and reintegration processes. Though links between gender and arms control are now reflected in the Small Arms and Light Weapons agenda, prevention remains largely unrelated to minimizing the buildup of arms, which is the Security Council's responsibility under Article 26 of the UN Charter (Otto 2016).

Following the *Global* Study, the Security Council responded to calls for a greater focus on conflict prevention, noting in Resolution 2242 the need to "invest more in conflict prevention and women's empowerment," including in efforts to combat violent extremism (UNSC 2015). But compared to normative advances in the protection and participation pillars, emphasis on conflict prevention beyond a box-ticking exercise has fallen short. Like most policymakers, scholars have yet to fully explore the gendered causes of conflict and their implications for preventing it (Basu and Confortini 2016). There is also a lack of documentation and analysis of women's experiences in conflict prevention. Moreover, feminists calling for a change in the dominant, militarized approach to conflict resolution have failed to significantly influence the WPS agenda as it has unfolded in the UN Security Council—home to the largest arms exporters in the world. As such, the transformative change that Resolution 1325 made possible has not yet been realized.

WHY PARTICIPATION MATTERS FOR PROTECTION, PREVENTION, AND RECOVERY

There are many reasons why implementation of Resolution 1325 and its successors have faltered. Among them is this unbalanced approach to developing the WPS framework and the frequent treatment of protection and recovery issues as distinct from participation and prevention. Even in protection, which has benefitted from the most concerted efforts, the relevant chapters in this handbook reveal that improvements in women's safety and security during war have been uneven. Why do these pillars need to be approached in a more integrated way?

The Benefits of Women's Participation for Protection and Recovery

Perhaps the most straightforward argument for overcoming the "chronic protection-representation dilemma" that has plagued the field of WPS is that without protection it is extremely difficult for women to participate in public life (Kirby and Shepherd 2016: 381). This is true and significant. It's also an argument that has frequently been abused. When framed in sequential terms, the same argument has been used to hold women back for years. Women's safety and security has to come first, and then later they might be in a position to participate in politics, which is to say "just be patient and let us men deal with the conflict." Furthermore, the women's protection-for-empowerment narrative has been used, among other reasons, to justify launching wars in Iraq and Afghanistan (Hudson 2012). As previously noted, in an area where protection approaches have been dominant, this safety-first approach has not succeeded in stemming the tide of conflict-related sexual violence. And even in wars that have not seen widespread sexual and gender-based violence, as in Guatemala in the 1990s (Cohen and Nordås 2016), women have still largely been excluded from decision-making in formal peace processes. Besides, men are victimized during war and in some conflicts deliberately targeted for sexual violence, but this does not preclude men from participating in peace and security decision-making.

Women's representation in decision-making processes that will affect their lives is a basic right and fundamental to any democratic process. It also connects to protection in the reverse direction to that already described because participation matters for protection. Policies for preventing sexual and gender-based violence are likely to be stronger if victims' experiences inform them (Charles and Mackay 2013). Broader frameworks addressing peace and conflict issues are more likely to address women's particular concerns if women can meaningfully participate in creating them. For example, even as women draw from multiple, intersecting identities in peace processes, in cases where women have been able to offer meaningful inputs, as in Northern Ireland, Guatemala, and Burundi, peace agreements have addressed their gender-specific concerns (Bell and O'Rourke 2010). Such provisions don't guarantee changes on the ground, but they do offer a tool for women to advocate for their rights and their security after war ends. They also set a precedent for future engagement if conflict breaks out again.

Although there is some debate over the impact of women's representation in security forces, in part due to a lack of robust data and low participation rates, this kind of participation may also contribute to protection. For example, analysis of the integration of women into policing in the United States between the 1970s and 1990s shows that as female representation increases, violent crimes against women are reported at higher rates (Miller and Segal 2013). Particularly in conservative cultures, female police officers have greater access to female civilians and their concerns. When it comes to relief and recovery, women's participation in the security sector can increase citizens' trust in these institutions while also improving intelligence gathering, reporting rates of gender-based violence, and treatment of female victims, witnesses, and suspects (Coomaraswamy 2015: 180).

Participation, Gender Equality, and Conflict Prevention

Recent scholarly research has significantly advanced our understanding of the connections between women's participation, gender equality, and peace writ large. Cumulatively, it suggests that conflict is less likely to break out or recur where women are treated as equals in society and when they participate in policymaking. This takes us beyond the argument of participation for the sake of protecting other women to participation's benefits for societies at large. Even as women play myriad roles in peace and conflict at the individual level, from belligerents to peacemakers to indifferent observers, on average women show less interest in going to war than men. This does not mean that women are inherently more peaceful: gender differences in attitudes toward particular aspects of war vary across time, issues, and cultures (Reiter 2015). But gender differences on the acceptability of war are large, statistically significant, and consistent in cross-national surveys: women are much less likely to approve of war (Eichenberg and Read 2016). Moreover, countries where women are more politically engaged display higher gendered differences in relation to many security issues (Eichenberg and Read 2016).

It's perhaps unsurprising then that research also shows how women's participation in politics—the domain where decisions about war and peace are made—correlates with less aggressive state action. Cross-national quantitative studies have shown that higher levels of female representation in parliament reduces the risk of interstate war (Caprioli and Boyer 2001), civil war (Melander 2005a), and domestic human rights abuses (Melander 2005b). In fact, as the percentage of women in the legislature increases by 5 percent, a country is five times less likely to use violence when confronted with an international crisis (Caprioli and Boyer 2001).[3]

Women's political and social participation has also been associated with decreases in the likelihood that countries recently at war will slip back into conflict again. Globally, the rate of conflict relapse has increased every decade since the 1960s; in the 2000s, 90 percent of conflicts occurred in countries that had already experienced war (World Bank 2011). In other words, conflict prevention today often means avoiding the recurrence of war. Analysis of fifty-eight conflict-affected states between 1980 and 2003 found that when women are absent from parliament, the risk of conflict recurrence increases over time. But "when 35% of the legislature is female, this relationship virtually disappears, and the risk of relapse is near zero" (Demeritt and Nichols 2014: 362). Other scholars have found that where women enjoy a higher pre-war social status—independent of levels of economic development—local cooperation with UN peace-building efforts is greater, thus "decreasing the probability of conflict responses toward activities in peacebuilding missions" (Gizelis 2011: 537). Indeed, scholars have established that gender equality more broadly is a better predictor of a state's peacefulness than a country's levels of democracy, religion, or wealth (Hudson et al. 2012). Where women are more empowered in various walks of life, countries are less likely to go to war or experience internal crime and violence (Hudson et al. 2012). Feminists have been calling for greater attention to conflict prevention for over a century. What we now know is that in situations where gender equality is higher and women can participate in public life, prevention is more likely.

BEYOND PARTICIPATION: TRANSFORMATIVE FEMINIST LEADERSHIP

Despite the advances in policy and research, and increased advocacy showing the linkages between Resolution 1325's four pillars, women's participation continues to be regarded as a contentious issue for many states, not least many of those on the UN Security Council (Taylor 2013). The protection agenda has been more acceptable than participation or prevention as it does not challenge patriarchal dynamics of war. On the contrary, it sometimes reinforces stereotypes of women as victims and men as protectors as well as perpetrators. Meanwhile, without meaningful participation (see chapter 13 in this volume), many peace negotiations fail to address the root causes of conflict or gain sufficient traction to prevent war from breaking out again. Why have arguments for a more integrated approach to the WPS pillars failed to deliver sufficient change on their own? Is there a kind of participation that could contribute to a transformation that will be harder to reverse?

Right and Reason Are Not Enough

Women have an equal democratic right to be included in peace and security decision-making. Though not unproblematic, instrumental arguments in favor of women's participation or rationalizing participation as a contributor to other accepted priorities such as protection or peace and security, can also help women realize this right. As scholars Anne Marie Goetz and Rob Jenkins (2016: 16) explain in a wide-ranging review of states' responses to demands for gender-equality policies:

> Instrumental appeals on issues that ought to be considered a matter of equal rights . . . are often condemned for their tendency, over time, to distort feminist agendas—toward comfortable accommodation and away from radical change. Despite these criticisms, there is ample evidence from a range of policy arenas that such tactics can be of crucial importance in the "long game" of outmaneuvering anti-reform coalitions.

Instrumental arguments have complemented the rights-based approach in convincing (predominantly male) policymakers to establish significant international frameworks on more inclusive approaches to peace and security. National frameworks are now following suit as more than seventy countries have adopted national action plans for implementing Resolution 1325 (see chapter 22).

Nonetheless, most of these frameworks have not meaningfully questioned the deep gendered structures and oppressive expressions of power that need to be understood and replaced in order to transform the traditional approaches to peace and security that are falling short in the face of twenty-first century conflicts. Neither has women's mere "taking part" in peace and security processes always been sufficient. Conflict prevention and resolution are deeply gendered tasks that go beyond involving women. A culture of prevention cannot be created until men and women understand and change those constructions of masculinity that contribute to war, and harm men too, as warriors and victims (see chapter 8 in this volume). Similarly, in the realm of protection, even if conflict-related sexual violence can be partly explained by opportunistic gains or the creation of bonds of loyalty among soldiers (Cohen 2016), systemic gender inequality is undoubtedly a structural enabler of this violence that needs to be addressed (Davies and True 2015).

Transformative Feminist Leadership

Since policy frameworks and attempts to merely increase the *numbers* of women in peace and security processes have not sufficed, there is growing recognition that women's leadership—not just participation—is badly needed to advance change. The UN Secretary-General's first recommendation in his 2016 report on WPS is to bring "women's participation *and leadership* to the core of peace and security efforts" (UN Secretary-General 2016: 30, emphasis added). Gender-equality experts in other fields such as development and human rights have proposed a particular form of leadership called "transformative feminist leadership." This type of leadership focuses on how women's movements can succeed in the deeper change of social structures as well as the advancement of women and other marginalized genders. According to Srilatha Batliwala (2011: 51), the starting point for this kind of leadership is analysis of gender and social discrimination in a particular setting, followed by attempts to transform structures, institutions, and practices toward a more equitable state of affairs. Given the fundamental changes required in the current structures and conceptualizations of peace and security as well as the shift in social norms surrounding women's roles, the transformative feminist leadership framework could usefully be applied to the field of WPS. Let's unpack the meaning of this term and its relevance for this domain.

Leadership for WPS needs to be transformative in its *goals*, since a deeper shift in attitudes and power structures is needed to address how female leaders in politics, policymaking, and social movements are constrained by the patriarchal systems around them. Fortunately, there are new openings for transforming gendered structures in peace and security beyond the UN Security Council. Frameworks such as CEDAW General Recommendation 30, the Arms Trade Treaty, the Sustainable Development Goals, and national feminist foreign policies are integrating gender perspectives and gender analysis in a way that moves toward the transformational (Swaine and O'Rourke 2015; True 2016).

Leadership in this domain also needs to be transformative in its *style*. Distinct from "great man" theories of leadership focused on heroic individuals' characteristics and behaviors, transformational leadership theory presents leadership as a collaborative process in which leaders understand and engage their followers in a way that changes individuals as well as social systems (Burns 1978; Bass 1985). This approach marries well with feminist principles of collaboration, inclusiveness, and egalitarianism, in which individual and social transformations are closely linked (Wakefield 2017). It also ties to the idea of more inclusive approaches to security that prioritize the protection, well-being, and participation of individuals and groups (human security) rather than the narrower, state-centric conceptualization of national security (see chapter 2 in this volume).

The *feminist* dimension is also significant for helping ensure success. Analysis of a cross-national dataset from seventy-one countries over thirty years shows that the most decisive factor in combating violence against women was the strength of feminist mobilization rather than, for example, the number of female legislators or levels of national wealth (Htun and Weldon 2012). Strong local feminist movements leverage international policy frameworks to realize rights in practice, "magnify[ing] the effects of these treaties by highlighting the gap between ratification and compliance" (Htun and Weldon 2012: 558). Indeed, many civil society organizations working on women's rights in other domains are already adopting transformative feminist leadership practices to great effect (Wakefield 2017).

In the field of WPS, this kind of leadership is needed in formal, elite settings as well as mass social movements. Feminist bureaucrats at the UN contributed significantly to creating the policy window for change in this field. Feminist politicians at national levels can help create a global environment that is more receptive to women's leadership in peace and security through feminist foreign policies, such as the one currently being pioneered by Sweden. Given the disconnect between formal peace and security processes at national and international levels and informal peacemaking initiatives at subnational levels where women are more likely to be in leadership positions, there is a need for greater mobilization of feminist leaders in both realms. Formal and informal leadership among women can be connected through issue networks (Sikkink 1993) and by alliances that leverage the diverse resources and skills of each.

Transformative leadership is needed among men as well as women. Feminist bureaucrats and civil society activists who have advanced WPS have been male as well as female. Particularly in light of the resurgence of patriarchal nationalism, there is a need for male champions of gender equality to be heard; for manipulated "masculine" traits of honor and bravery to be called into question; and for a more critical and nuanced understanding of men's diverse roles in war and peace. If applied more comprehensively to WPS through collaboration with men and more long-term funding, training, and support for movement-building among women's organizations and others working in this field, this kind of leadership could help (1) better define the problem with the status quo, (2) generate new solutions, and (3) influence the political climate for change. These are the three streams necessary to shift social norms now that a policy window has opened (Kingdon 1995).

CONCLUSION

Decades of advocacy for more inclusive approaches to peace and security have led to significant policy advances in the realm of women, peace, and security. In terms of impact, however, the gains in preventing conflict, protecting women, and advancing more inclusive participation in peacemaking and recovery have been very uneven. Most men who dominate the field of peace and security continue to think that women do not have a significant role to play (e.g., Busby and Hurlburt 2017). As a result, greater attention is now needed to women's participation: this is where the four core pillars of Resolution 1325 intersect, as participation significantly influences prevention, protection, and recovery. But our understanding of participation needs to go beyond merely "taking part." To more effectively challenge the gendered power structures that continue to hinder progress, women seeking peace and equality need to take a transformative, feminist approach in their leadership alongside like-minded men.

NOTES

1. UN Security Council Resolutions 1820 (2008), 1888 (2009), 1960 (2010), and 2106 (2013).
2. In 2007, the UN Secretary-General also included a "normative" pillar.
3. This paragraph and the next draw from O'Reilly, *Why Women?*

REFERENCES

Addams, Jane, Emily Greene Balch, and Alice Hamilton, eds. *Women at The Hague: The International Congress of Women and Its Results* (New York: MacMillan, 1915), 150–159.
Aghekyan, E., J. Dunham, S. O'Toole, S. Repucci, and V. Tucker. *Freedom in the World 2017*. Washington, DC: Freedom House, 2017.

Bass, B. M. *Leadership and Performance*. New York: Free Press, 1985.

Basu, S., and C. C. Confortinia. "Weakest 'P' in the 1325 Pod? Realizing Conflict Prevention through Security Council Resolution 1325." *International Studies Perspectives* (2016): 1–21.

Batliwala, S. *Feminist Leadership for Social Transformation: Clearing the Conceptual Cloud.* New Delhi: CREA, 2011, https://www.uc.edu/content/dam/uc/ucwc/docs/CREA.pdf.

Bell, C., and C. O'Rourke. "Peace Agreements or Pieces of Paper? The Impact of UNSC Resolution 1325 on Peace Processes and Their Agreements." *International and Comparative Law Quarterly* 59, no. 4 (2010): 941–980.

Burns, J. M. *Leadership*. New York: Harper & Row, 1978.

Busby, J., and H. Hurlburt. "Do Women Matter to National Security? The Men Who Lead U.S. Foreign Policy Don't Think So." *Washington Post*, February 2, 2017, https://www.washingtonpost.com/news/monkey-cage/wp/2017/02/02/do-women-matter-to-national-security-the-men-who-lead-u-s-foreign-policy-dont-think-so/.

Caprioli, M., and M. Boyer. "Gender, Violence, and International Crisis." *Journal of Conflict Resolution* 45 (2001): 503–518.

Castillo-Diaz, P., and S. Tordjman. *Women's Participation in Peace Negotiations: Connections between Presence and Influence.* New York: UN Women, 2012.

Charles, N., and F. Mackay. "Feminist Politics and Framing Contests: Domestic Violence Policy in Scotland and Wales." *Critical Social Policy* 33, no. 4 (2013): 593–615.

Cohen, D. K. *Rape During Civil War*. Ithaca, NY: Cornell University Press, 2016.

Cohen, D. K., and R. Nordås. "Sexual Violence in Armed Conflict (SVAC) Dataset." Updated November 2016—Version 1.1, http://www.sexualviolencedata.org/dataset/.

Coomaraswamy, R. *Preventing Conflict, Transforming Justice, Securing the Peace.* New York: UN Women, 2015.

Council on Foreign Relations. "Women's Roles in Peace Processes" database, updated January 2018, https://www.cfr.org/interactive/interactive/womens-participation-in-peace-processes/explore-the-data.

Davies, S. E., and J. True. "Reframing Conflict-Related Sexual and Gender-Based Violence: Bringing Gender Analysis Back In." *Security Dialogue* 46 (2015): 495–512.

Demeritt, J. H. R., and A. D. Nichols. "Female Participation and Civil War Relapse." *Civil Wars* 16, no. 3 (2014).

Eichenberg, R. C., and B. M. Read. "Gender Difference in Attitudes towards Global Issues." In *Handbook on Gender in World Politics*, edited by J. Steans and D. Tepe-Belfrage, 234–244. Northampton, MA: Elgar, 2016.

Gizelis, T. I. "A Country of Their Own: Women and Peacebuilding." *Conflict Management and Peace Science* 28, no. 5 (2011): 522–542.

Goetz, A., and R. Jenkins. "Feminist Activism and the Politics of Reform: When and Why Do States Respond to Demands for Gender-Equality Policies?" United Nations Research Institute for Social Development, Working Paper 2016-13, 2016.

Goetz, A., and R. Jenkins. "Taking Stock: Protection without Empowerment? Evolution of the Women, Peace, and Security Agenda since the Beijing Platform for Action." In *Women and Girls Rising: Progress and Resistance around the World*, edited by E. Chesler and T. McGovern, 69–81. New York: Routledge, 2015.

Htun, M., and S. L. Weldon. "The Civic Origins of Progressive Policy Change: Combating Violence against Women in Global Perspective." *American Political Science Review* 106, no. 3 (2012): 548–569.

Hudson, H. "A Double-Edged Sword of Peace? Reflections on the Tension between Representation and Protection in Gendering Liberal Peacebuilding." *International Peacekeeping* 19 (2012): 443–460.

Hudson, V., B. Ballif-Spanvill, M.. Caprioli, and C. F. Emmett. *Sex and World Peace.* New York: Columbia University Press, 2012.

Kingdon, J. *Agendas, Alternatives, and Public Policies.* New York: Harper Collins, 1995.

Kirby, P., and L. J. Shepherd, L. J. "The Futures Past of the Women, Peace and Security Agenda." *International Affairs* 92 (2016): 373–392.

Krause, J., W. Krause, and P. Braenfors. "Women's Participation in Peace Negotiations and the Durability of Peace." *International Interactions* (2018).

Mack, A., S. Merz, M. Bui, T. Cooper, G. Echlin, J. L. Gray, K. Harris, and L. Ridway. *Human Security Report 2012: Sexual Violence, Education, and War—Beyond the Mainstream Narrative.* Vancouver: Human Security Press, 2012.

Melander, E. "Gender Equality and Intrastate Armed Conflict." *International Studies Quarterly* 49, no. 4 (2005a): 695–714.

Melander, E. "Political Gender Equality and State Human Rights Abuse." *Journal of Peace Research* 42, no. 2 (2005b): 149–166.

Miller, A., and C. Segal. "Do Female Officers Improve Law Enforcement Quality? Effects on Crime Reporting and Domestic Violence Escalation." University of Zurich, UBS International Center of Economics in Society, Working Paper No. 9, 2013.

O'Reilly, M. "The Democratic Republic of Congo." In *From Global Promise to National Action,* edited by A. Amling and M. O'Reilly, 9–24. Broomfield, CO: One Earth Future Foundation; Washington, DC: Inclusive Security, 2016.

O'Reilly, M. *Why Women? Inclusive Security and Peaceful Societies.* Inclusive Security, 2015, https://www.inclusivesecurity.org/publication/why-women-inclusive-security-and-peaceful-societies/.

O'Reilly, M., A., Ó Súilleabháin, and T. Paffenholz. *Reimagining Peacemaking: Women's Roles in Peace Processes.* New York: International Peace Institute, 2015, https://www.ipinst.org/wp-content/uploads/2015/06/IPI-E-pub-Reimagining-Peacemaking.pdf.

Otto, D. Women, Peace, and Security: A Critical Analysis of the Security Council's Vision. London: LSE Women, Peace, and Security Working Paper Series, 2016.

Reiter, D. "The Positivist Study of Gender and International Relations." *Journal of Conflict Resolution* 59, no. 7 (2015): 1301–1326.

Sikkink, K. "Human Rights, Principled Issue-Networks, and Sovereignty in Latin America." *International Organization* 47, no. 3 (1993): 805–831.

Swaine, A., and C. O'Rourke. *Guidebook on CEDAW General Recommendation No. 30 and the UN Security Council Resolutions on Women, Peace, and Security.* New York: UN Women, 2015.

Tamaru, N., and M. O'Reilly. *How Women Influence Constitution Making after Conflict and Unrest.* Washington, DC: Inclusive Security, 2018.

Taylor, S. "Women, Peace, and Politics at the UN Security Council." *The Global Observatory,* July 17, 2013, https://theglobalobservatory.org/2013/07/women-peace-and-politics-at-the-un-security-council/.

Tickner, J. Ann, and Jacqui True. A Century of International Relations Feminism: From World War One Women's Peace Pragmatism to the Women, Peace, and Security Agenda. *International Studies Quarterly* 62, 2. 2018, https://doi.org/10.1093/isq/sqx091

Tripp, Aili Mari. *Women and Power in Postconflict Africa*. Cambridge: Cambridge University Press, 2015.

True, J. "How Effective Is Gender Mainstreaming in International Peace and Security Policy?" In *Handbook on Gender in World Politics*, edited by J. Steans and D. Tepe-Belfrage, 457–466. Northampton, MA: Elgar, 2016.

United Nations. "Report of the Fourth World Conference on Women, Beijing, September 4–5, 1995." New York, 1996.

United Nations. "System-Wide Strategy on Gender Parity." New York, 2017.

United Nations Secretary-General. "Report of the Secretary-General on Women and Peace and Security." New York, S/2016/822, 2016.

United Nations Secretary-General. "Report of the Secretary-General on Women and Peace and Security." New York, S/2017/861, 2017.

United Nations Security Council (UNSC). 2000. Resolution 1325.

United Nations Security Council (UNSC). 2008. Resolution 1820.

United Nations Security Council (UNSC). 2009a. Resolution 1888.

United Nations Security Council (UNSC). 2009b. Resolution 1889.

United Nations Security Council (UNSC). 2010. Resolution 1960.

United Nations Security Council (UNSC). 2013a. Resolution 2106.

United Nations Security Council (UNSC). 2013b. Resolution 2122.

United Nations Security Council (UNSC). 2015. Resolution 2242.

Wakefield, S. "Transformative and Feminist Leadership for Women's Rights." Oxfam America Research Backgrounder Series, 2017, https://www.oxfamamerica.org/static/media/files/Transformative_and_Feminist_Leadership_for_Womens_Rights.pdf.

World Bank. "World Development Report 2011." Washington, DC, 2011.

CHAPTER 17

WPS AND FEMALE PEACEKEEPERS

NATASJA RUPESINGHE, ELI STAMNES, AND JOHN KARLSRUD

WOMEN'S participation in peacekeeping operations has always been a clear and concrete goal to rally around for the Women, Peace, and Security (WPS) agenda. Of the four principle pillars of UN Security Council Resolution 1325,[1] "participation" is arguably the most relevant and most contested when discussing WPS and female peacekeeping personnel. This aim is often referred to as "gender balancing," which the UN Department of Peacekeeping Operations (DPKO) defines as "the degree to which men and women hold the full range of positions in a society or organisation" (United Nations 2014: 21). In other words, gender balancing seeks to attain parity between male and female personnel in peacekeeping operations. In the fifteen years since the passing of Resolution 1325, we have seen modest improvements in women's participation in peacekeeping. Today, all peacekeeping missions have female personnel but progress on increasing female police and female military troops in particular has been slow. The *Preventing Conflict Transforming Justice Securing the Peace—A Global Study on the Implementation of United Nations Security Council resolution 1325* (Global Study) assessed the progress and challenges related to the implementation of the resolution. It was commissioned by UN Secretary-General Ban Ki Moon who pointed out that peacekeeping remains one of the most challenging areas for ensuring women's equal and meaningful participation (Coomaraswamy 2015).

This chapter will provide an overview of the participation of female peacekeeping personnel in UN missions, tracing key target and agenda-setting policy events, as well as examining causes for the slow progress in female participation. The chapter will consider female participation in the military, police, and civilian components of UN peacekeeping operations. It then critically discusses the drawbacks of the "gender-balancing" agenda advanced by the UN, which critics argue has often amounted to "tokenism." This necessary, but insufficient goal of increasing numbers alone, has been prioritized over the more comprehensive and potentially transformative goal of gender mainstreaming. Gender mainstreaming in peacekeeping is defined as "a way of guaranteeing that the concerns, requirements and opinions of women and men are included equally into every aspect of peacekeeping." Moreover, each component of the mission should include a "gender perspective in all its functions and tasks from start-up to draw-down" (United Nations 2014: 21–22).

Failing to address the complexity of gender relations and the militarized, masculine, institutional structures within peacekeeping missions themselves will ultimately constrain gender equality. Seeking to situate the WPS agenda within the broader context of UN peace operations, the chapter concludes by reflecting on some of the possible implications of the trend toward militarization and securitization within peacekeeping which will have consequences for women's active and quality participation in peacekeeping.

Background: WPS and Peacekeeping

Increasing the participation of women in peacekeeping missions, sometimes known as "gender balancing" has been a clear and concrete goal of the WPS agenda. Prior to the adoption of Resolution 1325, women's organizations, civil society, feminist scholars, as well as the UN had been advocating for increased representation of women in UN peacekeeping missions. However, specific requests for increasing the number of female peacekeepers only came in the 1990s, some fifty years after the deployment of the UN's first mission (Väyrynen 2004: 1). During this time, the wars in Rwanda and Bosnia and the use of rape as a weapon of war had elevated the issue of sexual and gender-based violence (SGBV) to the attention of the international community. These and other civil wars such as in Liberia and Sierra Leone also demonstrated clearly how armed conflict adversely impacts women.

While gender equality was moving to the forefront of the UN's agenda, the 1990s also saw the expansion of UN peacekeeping mandates which became more multidimensional in scope. The mandates were increasingly incorporating humanitarian, development, and peace-building initiatives to respond to complex intra-state conflicts. Evolving from more traditional, lightly armed military missions—usually tasked with keeping warring interstate belligerents apart, overseeing ceasefires, or monitoring peace processes—multidimensional peacekeeping missions developed to perform a variety of tasks. Examples of these tasks include restructuring state institutions; training host country police and armed forces; supporting the disarmament, demobilization, and reintegration of former combatants; organizing elections; facilitating local conflict resolution and early warning; and protecting civilians. This led to a demand for new personnel with skill sets that go beyond military capacity (Bertolazzi 2010: 6). DPKO in particular came under increasing pressure to reflect gender equality in its peacekeeping missions (Simić 2014). In 1995, the Secretary-General announced his commitment toward increasing women's participation in field missions, following ten years of concerted pressure brought on by women's mobilizations during the UN Decade for Women (1975–1985) (Olsson et al. 2015: 37).

Following the 1995 Beijing Women's Platform for Action, attention to both gender and women's issues within the UN intensified. One of the key recommendations sought to ensure 30 percent female representation in UN decision-making to ensure women's active participation in public and private life (United Nations 1995). It was not until the Lessons Learned Unit of the DPKO launched the "Windhoek Declaration and Namibia Plan of Action" that calls for mainstreaming a gender perspective in peace operations were advanced.[2] The key finding of this report was that missions in Namibia and South Africa had been more successful *because* these had a higher percentage of female personnel (Carey 2001: 53-54, emphasis added). This view is still central in ongoing discussions within and outside the UN on increasing women's participation in peacekeeping.

The adoption of Resolution 1325 on October 31, 2000 (see chapters 3 and 4 in this volume) formalized the commitment to deploy female peacekeepers (Tryggestad 2009). In its eighteen provisions, the resolution requested action on a number of peacekeeping-related issues and urged the Secretary-General "to seek to expand the role and contribution of women in United Nations field-based operations, and especially among military observers, civilian police, human rights and humanitarian personnel" (UN Security Council 2000). It recognized "the urgent need to mainstream a gender perspective into peacekeeping operations" and that field operations should where appropriate include a gender unit (UN Security Council, 2000). The resolution also recognized that armed conflict impacts women differently. Consequently, it encouraged the use of gender-sensitive training guidelines and materials on protection, rights, and the particular needs of women. However, the resolution omitted the ambitious US recommendation to establish a mandated, expert panel or working group to report on mechanisms ensuring equal participation of women in peace operations (Carey 2001: 53). This absence of accountability provisions, we argue, is part of the reason why the implementation of Resolution 1325 in general has been uneven and slow.

Participation of Female Peacekeepers

Since 2000, a substantial body of literature has also emerged focusing on gender-based participation in peace operations (Olsson et al. 2015: 38). Gender statistics provided by the UN contain information about Uniformed Personnel: the military which is subcategorized into "Military Experts" and "Troops"; and the police which is subcategorized into "Individual Police" and "Formed Police Units." Few countries produce assessments of female participation in national forces or their contributions to UN peacekeeping. There is no data on the number of women in the civilian component disaggregated per mission.[3] Existing figures, however, confirm that there is a positive trend of increasing female participation in peacekeeping.

Women are now represented in all fifteen UN peace operations worldwide. During the Cold War period from 1957 to 1989, only twenty women served in peacekeeping missions, mainly as support staff, particularly as nurses or in medical units (Bertolazzi 2010: 8). By 1993, eleven out of nineteen UN peacekeeping missions had significant civilian components, and almost one-third of this staff were women (Bertolazzi 2010: 12). Female uniformed personnel participation remained low for almost a decade between 1999 and 2009, at approximately 1 percent globally (Dharmapuri 2013:2). In 2005, DPKO affirmed its commitment to gender equality and stated that it sought to achieve a 50–50 gender balance in civilian professional posts in the "near future" (Simić 2014: 186). In 2006, the DPKO Policy Directive on "Gender Equality" was launched to define "requirements for ensuring the equal participation of women, men, girls and boys in all peacekeeping activities" (United Nations 2006: 2).[4] For example, Principle III of the policy required DPKO and peacekeeping missions to set standards for attaining gender balance and the equal participation of women in decision-making (United Nations 2006: 3). At the tenth anniversary of Resolution 1325, the stagnating rates of female participation in peacekeeping was raised again thus putting pressure on the UN to put in place specific targets. In 2009, Ban Ki-Moon launched a campaign to increase the number of women peacekeepers to 10 percent in military contingents, and 20 percent in police components by 2014. In 2009, Ban Ki-Moon launched a campaign to increase the number of women in the police component of peacekeeping operations to 20 percent. (End note: United Nations, "United Nations in Global Effort to Increase Number of Female Police in Peacekeeping Operations," PKO/218-WOM/1751, New York: United Nations, 7 August 2009.)

As of 2016, women constitute 3 percent of the 125,000 military personnel, 10 percent of the 13,000 police personnel, and just under 30 percent of the 6,800 international civilian staff in peacekeeping and special political missions (UNPOL 2017; United Nations 2017c). For military peacekeeping personnel, that figure has remained largely stagnant since 2011. Over the past two decades, the number of women peacekeepers has only risen incrementally from 1 percent in 1993 (Coomaraswamy 2015). As Figure 17.1 illustrates, the ambitious targets set in 2005 and 2009 have not been met but modest improvements have been made in participation in the police contingent which rose from 7 to 10 percent (Karim and Beardsley 2013; UN POL 2017; also see chapter 21 in this volume). Resolution 2242 (UN Security Council 2015) recently set another target encouraging "efforts to incentivise a greater number of women in militaries and police deployed to United Nations peacekeeping operations, and call[ing] upon the Secretary General to initiate, in collaboration with Member States, a revised strategy, within existing resources, to double the numbers of women in military and police contingents of UN peacekeeping operations" by 2020 (para. 8).

As Figure 17.2 shows, MONUSCO (510) in the Democratic Republic of the Congo (DRC), and UNAMID (459), the UN-African Union hybrid mission in Darfur, have the largest number of female military peacekeeping personnel, followed by UNIFL (404) in Lebanon, UNMISS (380) in South Sudan, and UNISFA (326) in Abyei, Sudan. Looking at the percentage of female uniformed personnel per mission (Figures 17.3, 17.4, and 17.5), however, is revealing. In MONUSCO, women comprised only 3 percent of military personnel and 12 percent of police personnel. In UNAMID, 4 percent of military personnel are female, while 8 percent are police.

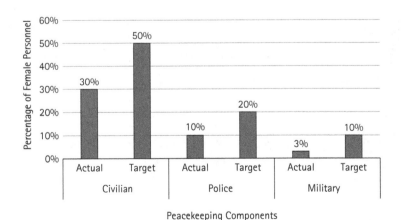

FIGURE 17.1 Targets and actual percentages of female peacekeeping personnel.
Source: Authors compiled data from United Nations (2017c), Women in Peacekeeping, http://www.un.org/en/peacekeeping/issues/women/womeninpk.shtml

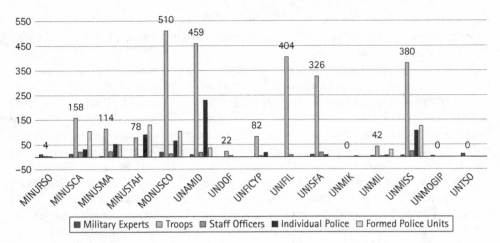

FIGURE 17.2 Number of females in uniformed personnel positions per mission.

Source: Authors compiled data from United Nations (2017a), Gender Statistics,
http://www.un.org/en/peacekeeping/contributors/gender/2017gender/may17.pdf.

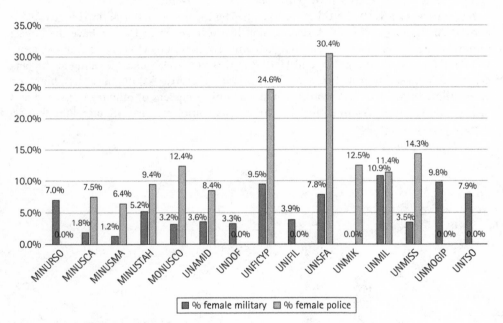

FIGURE 17.3 Percentage of female military and police personnel per mission.

Source: Authors compiled data from United Nations (2017a), Gender Statistics.

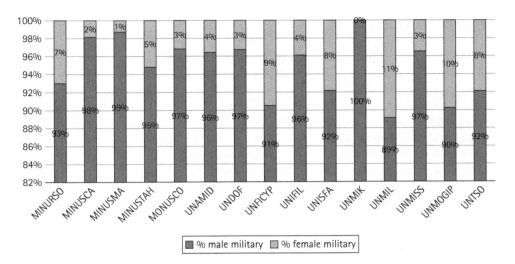

FIGURE 17.4 Percentage of male and female military personnel per mission.

Source: Authors compiled data from United Nations (2017a), Gender Statistics.

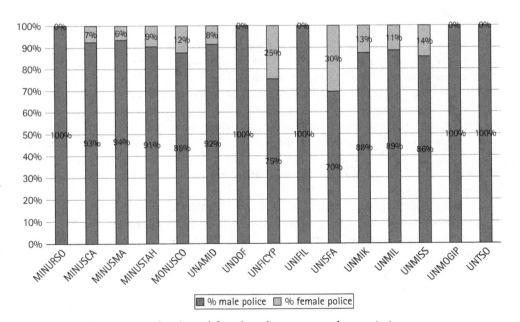

FIGURE 17.5 Percentage of male and female police personnel per mission.

Source: Authors compiled data from United Nations (2017a), Gender Statistics

Women in Leadership Roles

An increase in the appointments of women as special representatives of the Secretary-General (SRSG) and deputy SRSG (DSRSG) started in 2002. However, women's participation in peace operations particularly at the director level has been limited (Dharmapuri 2013: 3). In May 2014, the UN appointed its first female commander of a peacekeeping force to its mission in Cyprus (UNFICYP). Major General Kristin Lund joined Lisa Buttenheim, the mission's SRSG. This made UNFICYP the first ever mission to have dual female leadership. In May 2015, almost 40 percent of peacekeeping missions were led by women (Coomaraswamy 2015: 35). Of the fifteen peacekeeping operations worldwide, MINUSTAH's SRSG and DSRSG are both female, MINURSO is led by a female SRSG, and three missions (MINUSTAH, MINUSCA, and UNAMID) have female DSRSGs.

Slow Progress and Barriers to Implementation

What accounts for the low participation of women in peacekeeping despite the relatively strong commitments expressed in DPKO and WPS-related resolutions from UNSC? To answer this question, it is necessary to turn to domestic dynamics in Troop Contributing Countries (TCCs). While the former UN Secretary-General Ban Ki-moon and DPKO through the Office of the Military Affairs have encouraged TCCs to deploy more women, and the UN Security Council regularly calls on member states to deploy more peacekeepers, their appeals cannot actually be enforced. Female deployment remains the preserve of TCCs. Therefore, achieving a gender balance in UN peace operations is largely dependent on the national recruitment policies of TCCs. The top TCCs contributing female military personnel are Ethiopia, Ghana, Nigeria, South Africa, and Uruguay. For police, these are Bangladesh, Ghana, India, Nigeria, and Rwanda (UN Women 2017). Developed countries do not readily supply their own troops, opting instead to provide logistical and financial support. Meanwhile, countries from the Global South and lesser developed countries supply the troops.

Beardsley and Karim (2015) find that TCCs' decision to deploy female peacekeepers is conditioned by the prevalence of the "gendered protection" norm. This norm prevents TCCs from sending women to the most dangerous countries and therefore accounts for variation in deployment patterns of female peacekeepers (Karim and Beardsley 2013; Beardsley and Karim 2015). In the United Nations Multidimensional Integrated Stabilization Mission (MINUSMA) in Mali, which is considered to be one of the most deadly peacekeeping operations in history, only 1.8 percent of the military personnel of the 10,791 troops deployed by December 30, 2016 were women. This figure was well below the 3.8 percent average (Cold-Ravnkilde and Albrecht 2016; United Nations 2016: 12). The presence of female personnel is pertinent because in certain communities women are not allowed to speak in the presence of men. Yet, many of the African troop-contributing countries have not deployed women, citing harsh conditions and the asymmetrical threat environment, including armed and terrorist groups. Where women are deployed, they often perform support staff functions (Cold-Ravnkilde and Albrecht 2016). Similarly, in MONUSCO in the DRC, which conducts "peace enforcement" operations, the rate of female participation in the military component has hovered at around 2 percent compared to the 10 percent rate among the police (Olsson et al. 2015).

Most peacekeeping operations are today deployed with a Chapter VII mandate by the UN Security Council, enabling them to use force in self-defense or in defense of the mandate. Chapter VII missions, which require larger troop presence and combat skills, appear to constrain TCCs from sending female troops because they have low numbers of women available to serve in combat roles, and domestic policies deter women from engaging in combat (Coomaraswamy 2015: 139; Crawford et al. 2015). This is problematic because female peacekeepers are not sent to where they are most often needed such as in situations where there are high rates of sexual and gender-based violence as well as low female political participation in peace processes.

In 2015, two review processes were designed to take stock of peace operations, the UN peace-building architecture, and the implementation of Resolution 1325. Both the High-Level Independent Panel on Peace Operations (HIPPO) report and the 1325 Global Study recognized the key role played by female peacekeepers for mission success. While the HIPPO report has been criticized for not taking advantage of the critical window of opportunity in the reform process for moving the issue of female peacekeepers forward, it does include a section on implementation of the WPS agenda (Ramos-Horta et al. 2015: 70–80). It also makes other substantive references to gender and women. This is an improvement from the 2001 Brahimi Report which only made a reference to gender once in its concluding chapter (Olsson and Tryggestad 2001). The HIPPO report recognized the importance of increasing the number of female peacekeepers and urged that "[t]roop-and police-contributing countries should implement their national action plans on Security Council resolution 1325 (2000) or develop such plans, and redouble efforts to increase the number of women serving in the national security sector" (Ramos-Horta et al. 2015: 67). Furthermore, it called on the UN Secretariat to develop a gender-sensitive force and police generation strategy (Ramos-Horta et al. 2015). The HIPPO also urged the Secretariat and field missions to conduct gender-sensitive analysis throughout planning, implementation, review, evaluation, and mission drawdown processes (Ramos-Horta et al. 2015: 79).

The issue of women's participation in peacekeeping was a prominent theme in the Global Study which assessed the progress and challenges in the implementation of Resolution 1325. Specific recommendations included advocating for gender-responsive budgeting and financial tracking of investments on gender equality in missions as an example of technical accountability mechanism. The Global Study echoing the HIPPO report, advocated for a "gender-balance premium" to incentivise member states to contribute more female uniformed personnel (Coomaraswamy 2015; Ramos-Horta et al. 2015).[5] To make mission life more "gender-sensitive," the report advocates for adopting as standard practice a gender-budgetary analysis to address gender-specific aspects of deployment such as family leave accommodation, recreational space, medical care, and internal compound safety (Coomaraswamy 2015: 142).

Rationales for Increasing Participation of Female Peacekeepers

From our analysis of these developments in the fifteen-year history of female participation in peacekeeping, we identify at least four rationales attached to increasing women's participation in peacekeeping. First, women are considered indispensable to performing certain activities that demand gender sensitivity, such as addressing the needs of female ex-combatants, interviewing and assisting survivors of sexual and gender-based violence, and conducting house and body searches (United Nations 2017c). In some contexts, it is culturally unacceptable for women to speak with men publicly such that mixed-patrols are necessary for interacting with local communities (Heinecken 2015).

Second and relatedly, it is argued that women have an advantage in fostering commu-nity relations (e.g. DeGroot 2001). The assumed conciliatory attributes of women, in-cluding communication skills, empathy, sensitivity, and approachability, are believed to make female peacekeepers more responsive and sensitive to local needs. It is therefore not surprising that the highest representation of women is in the civilian component of peace-keeping missions where they often undertake activities requiring community engagement, such as confidence-building, local conflict resolution, and reconciliation. While granular data on the specific roles and responsibilities within mission components is not available, a cursory overview suggests that women are confined to performing "soft" roles. They tend to be in humanitarian, development, and peace-building activities, as well as support staff roles if deployed to military contingents.

Third, it is hoped that women personnel, particularly police and troops, function as role models for local women. Here, it is the presence of female uniformed personnel that contributes to challenging gender inequality norms in the host society as well as inspiring local women to seek employment in traditionally male dominated occupations (Carey 2001). The United Nations Mission in Liberia (UNMIL), which deployed the first all-female Indian Formed Police Unit (FPU), has often been commended for inspiring Liberian women to join the security sector (UN News 2016, see also chapter 35 in this volume).

Fourth, the presence of women can temper levels of sexual exploitation and abuse (SEA) perpetrated by peacekeeping personnel (Bridges and Horsfall 2009; see also chapter 18 in this volume). In UN Security Council Resolution 1820 in 2008, troop contributing coun-tries and police contributing countries were called upon to provide more female troops to combat sexual violence (Simić 2014: 188). This rationale gained renewed thrust in recent years after the UN has come under increasing scrutiny over the conduct of its peacekeepers in countries such as the Democratic Republic of Congo and the Central African Republic. The UN claims that the pacifying presence of women reduces aggressiveness and hyper-masculinity that are entrenched in peacekeeping. Indeed, some evidence does show that women temper the behavior of their male colleagues and bolster accountability (Karim and Beardsley, 2013: 473).

As we see from these four rationales, functionalist arguments have often taken prece-dence. Together, these rationales highlight that increasing the number of women in UN peacekeeping missions will lead to greater operational effectiveness. DPKO has published a number of guidelines to enhance the operational effectiveness of the military in UN op-erations through gender balancing that reflects these four rationales.[6] However, we identify a number of flaws in the functionalist approach to gender balancing in peacekeeping that may explain the continued low prevalence of female participation.

First, these arguments subvert the rights-based approach to female participation for achieving gender equality. A rights-based approach argues that women's participation should be an end in itself and not a means to achieving mission success. The gender-balancing rationales previously outlined also suffer from deeper flaws. Gender balancing has been criticized for advancing an "add women and stir" approach, where women's perspectives are simply added to existing frameworks. This amounts to simply adding women to areas where they have been traditionally excluded, such as peacekeeping missions. Simić (2014) argues that DPKO has focused on implementing policies that strive to achieve a gender balance at the expense of more comprehensive reforms required for fostering actual gender equality.

Second, as stated earlier, gender disaggregated data are often not available from missions. These functionalist rationales thus lack empirical backing and risk perpetuating "essentialist" understandings of men and women (e.g. Simić 2014). Recent empirical research by Heinecken (2015) has shown that women peacekeepers' relations with local communities are context-specific. In her qualitative comparative study, Heinecken finds that determinants such as race, ability to speak the local language, and respect for local culture have been more important in fostering community relations than gender.

Third, it is not certain that female military peacekeepers are so different from their male counterparts. Sion (2009) has found that some female military peacekeepers are actually conservative in their ideology and do not necessarily join missions with the aim of liberating local women in conflict. Many female peacekeepers aspire to join international forces not to improve gender equality, but due to career prospects, attractive income, and other professional benefits (Sion 2009).

Gender-balancing policies are often based on essentialized assumptions of men and women. These gender stereotypes rest on assumptions that women are inherently more peaceful than men, a view that has been interrogated by a range of feminist and other scholars. Elshtain's famous binary of the male "just warrior" and the female "beautiful soul" is therefore deeply imbued in rationales for increasing participation of women in peacekeeping (see Elshtain 1995). Female peacekeepers are pushed into specific tasks simply because they are women, rather than being taken seriously in their capacity as soldiers or peacekeepers. This might increase the operational effectiveness of the mission, but does little to improve gender equality. Scholars who take this view argue that working toward more equitable gender relations involves much more than merely adding the perspective and participation of women. As we discuss in the final section, social structures, institutions, and the hierarchy of masculinity and femininity must be the subject of investigation and change (Stamnes 2012: 182). Unless these are dealt with, the women who are added may simply be co-opted into the prevailing structures with female leaders expected to, for instance, "act like men." The UN strategy of gender mainstreaming, which will be discussed next, takes (at least a proportion of) these insights on board.

Gender Mainstreaming. As previously pointed out, gender balancing has limited transformational potential in itself. It needs to be accompanied by a change in the structures in which women are included for actual gender equality to occur. Gender mainstreaming aims to contribute to this by seeking to institutionalize gender perspectives and gender equality (Jennings 2011). It is "a global strategy for promoting gender equality" established through the Platform for Action at the United Nations Fourth World Conference on Women in Beijing in 1995 (OSAGI 2001), and reinforced through several UN documents and resolutions (see UN Women 2017). Its starting point is that gender is socially constructed and that the attributes and opportunities associated with being male and female are context-/time-specific and changeable (Office of the Special Advisor on Gender Issues and Advancement of Women [OSAGI] 2001). "It is a strategy for making women's as well as men's concerns and experiences an integral dimension of the design, implementation, monitoring and evaluation of policies and programmes in all political, economic and societal spheres so that women and men benefit equally and inequality is not perpetrated" (United Nations 1997/2). In the context of peacekeeping, it is defined as "a way of guaranteeing that the concerns, requirements and opinions of women and men are included equally into every aspect of peacekeeping"; and that each component of the mission should include a "gender perspective in all its functions and tasks from start-up to draw-down" (United Nations 2014: 21–22).

The UN DPKO has made some progress in mainstreaming a gender perspective in peace operations. Almost every directive for the military and police components of missions now include specific instructions to address women's particular security concerns, and to engage with local female leaders and women's groups. One common means of operationalizing "gender mainstreaming" is through the deployment of "gender advisors." In 2000, only two peacekeeping missions had gender advisors. Now, all multidimensional peacekeeping operations have "gender units" and women's protection advisors.

Almost all mission mandates also reflect specific provisions of WPS. However, Kreft (2017) finds that mission mandates are usually gender-mainstreamed when the conflict in question is marked for having high levels of sexual violence. She argues that this in effect renders Resolution 1325 to be "selectively activated, accrediting women's empowerment within the framework of CRSV [conflict-related sexual violence], rather than recognizing their right to fully and equally participate in society" (Kreft 2017: 154). Moreover, a gender perspective is still to a large extent understood and operationalized as a focus on "women only" concerns.

The Global Study recognizes concrete progress in efforts to integrate a gender perspective into UN peacekeeping operations. However, it concedes that these efforts are often ad hoc, unsystematic, and do not reflect the "core business" of the UN (Coomaraswamy 2015: 144). Creating new positions for gender focal points, advisors, and units risk segregating gender issues to one part of the mission, instead of integrating them comprehensively in the overall design, implementation, and monitoring of the mission. One could say that it simply ends up as a box-ticking exercise which risks undermining the intended purpose of the gender mainstreaming strategy. (Chapter 16 in this volume identifies the "box-ticking exercise" and "siloed implementation" phenomena in the South Sudan and Democratic Republic of Congo missions.)

GENDER PERSPECTIVES ON FEMALE PEACEKEEPERS' WORKING CONDITIONS

There is also a need to examine the challenges in the daily realities of female peacekeepers from a more comprehensive gender perspective. Such a task requires taking into account social structures, institutions, and gender hierarchies. While there is a steady increase in female participation in peacekeeping missions, they may still face barriers when they are deployed that limit their full potential (Heinecken 2015; Karim 2016). Empirical evidence has demonstrated that female peacekeepers, including military personnel, may be prevented from leaving the base, forced to be accompanied by men, and not allowed to drive. This creates an "access gap" inhibiting female peacekeepers from doing community outreach (Karim 2016). Female military peacekeepers have, for example, been bullied by their male counterparts in Liberia, and denigrated by host state national forces and rebel groups in the DRC and Sudan. It is also common that female peacekeepers face sexual harassment and are not taken seriously as peacekeepers (Heinecken 2015: 245). In Sudan, bringing women on patrols has even been considered a liability because rebel groups have considered the presence of uniformed women to be disrespectful to their culture (Heinecken 2015: 246).

UN peacekeeping operations are increasingly being called upon to intervene in volatile conflicts where there is no peace to keep. This is evident, for example, in Mali where the mission is faced with terrorist and armed groups. Battle fatigue from Afghanistan and Iraq, and the enduring effects of economic austerity, have elevated UN peacekeeping as a possible low-cost tool to be deployed to deal with threats at the lower end of the conflict spectrum (Karlsrud 2017). There has been a surge in demand for "blue helmets" to intervene in so-called "asymmetric" contexts under Chapter VII mandates, or in situations where non-state armed groups increasingly use anti-civilian violence and target peacekeepers as a deliberate strategy (see e.g., Boutellis and Fink 2016).

Both the Global Study and HIPPO cautioned against the increasing trend toward militarization of peacekeeping (Coomaraswamy 2015; Ramos-Horta et al. 2015). Mission mandates have evolved to become more robust. They now enable missions to respond to asymmetric threats, resembling stabilization, peace-enforcement and even counterterrorism operations (Karlsrud 2015; 2017). This is characterized by an increased authorization and willingness to employ the use of force by peacekeepers (Hunt 2017). In this context, UN peacekeeping operations may be compelled to employ a "Fortress" approach, which is a model of protection characterized by an "over-reliance on physical security tools like 'T' walls and heavily armed military escorts" (United Nations 2008, para. 286). Evidence of this can be seen in MINUSMA, where peacekeepers in the north are confined behind high protective walls and barriers (Andersson and Weigand 2015: 11). In general, peacekeeping operations themselves are becoming militarized, relying on surveillance drones, intelligence units, and armed private security companies in exceptional cases (Willmot et al. 2015). We are thus arguably seeing a reification of hyper-militarized peacekeeping masculinities (Enloe 2000). In a context like Mali, where peacekeepers (both male and female) hesitate to leave their vehicles and engage with locals due to the threat of attacks (Cold-Ravnkilde and Albrecht 2016), it is likely that women in the mission will be shielded even further. More granular research that looks at the experience of female peacekeepers in the mission setting is needed to understand the gendered impact of these changing institutional security procedures.

CONCLUSION

While there has been slow progress to female participation in peacekeeping—in police and military components particularly—there is also evidence of an upwards trend. Attention to TCC national policies is critical to determining female participation. A significant bulk of norm entrepreneurship on women's participation in military and particularly infantry units should be directed here. Enhancing accountability at the level of mission leadership in the field, as well as leadership at headquarter level, will be critical to ensuring female participation. Accountability in mission leadership also augments the sense of individual responsibility to achieve gender equality in the mission context. It is necessary, however, to critically re-examine the rationales for women's participation in peacekeeping. This re-examination should be informed by more evidence-based research on women's impact on peacekeeping dynamics and outcomes. Developing an evidence-base is crucial to nuance the "essentialist" perspectives in the functionalist arguments we have seen so far. This also needs to be balanced with a pragmatic understanding that policymakers in the UN need to provide convincing arguments to encourage TCCs to deploy more women. While gender-balancing might amount to a tokenistic numbers game like gender quotas, it is a neces- sary but insufficient strategy to ensure quality participation, which can be challenging in militarized contexts like peacekeeping.

Gender mainstreaming arguably possesses greater transformative potential in that it can provide a more comprehensive understanding of what constitutes gender perspectives, policies, and practices in the peacekeeping context. This means moving beyond "add women and stir" approaches and tick-box exercises to satisfy external pressure. Involving women from a diverse spectrum of society, including women's groups, NGOs, religious and marginalized groups, to the design, implementation, and monitoring of programs is one means through which gender mainstreaming can become more system-wide (True 2011). However, without challenging the institutions that perpetuate gender inequality and the gendered impact of the trend toward militarization and securitization of peace operations, women's meaningful and quality participation is at risk.

Notes

1. See UN Security Council (2000). S/RES/1325 is founded on four principle pillars which call for the increased participation of women in all levels of decision-making including national, regional, and international institutions; in mechanisms of conflict prevention, management, and resolution; in peace processes, mediation, and negotiation; as well as in peace operations as civilians, police, and troops, and in leadership roles at the UN; the protection of women and girls from sexual and gender-based violence; the prevention of violence against women and the importance of gender mainstreaming, defined as "the process of assessing implications for men and women of any planned action, including legislation, policies, or programmes in all areas and at all levels" (cite).
2. See United Nations, "Windhoek Declaration."
3. Contemporary peacekeeping operations are usually multidimensional, consisting of mil- itary, police, and civilian personnel.
4. This Policy Directive (United Nations 2006) was updated to a Policy on "Gender Equality in UN Peacekeeping Operations" (United Nations 2010).
5. Premiums are extra funds paid to member states in exchange for specialized capacities.
6. See "DPKO/DFS Guidelines: Integrating a Gender Perspective into the Work of the United Nations Military in Peacekeeping Operations," UN Department of Peacekeeping Operations and Department of Field Support, March 1, 2010, http://www.peacewomen. org/node/89767.

References

Andersson, R., and F. Weigand. "Intervention at Risk: The Vicious Cycle of Distance and Danger in Mali and Afghanistan." *Journal of Intervention and Statebuilding* 9, no. 4 (2015): 519–541.

Beardsley, K., and S. Karim. "Ladies Last: Peacekeeping and Gendered Protection." In *Gender, Peace, and Security: Implementing UN Security Council Resolution 1325*, edited by L. Olsson and T-I. Gizelis. London: Routledge, 2015.

Bertolazzi, F. "Women with a Blue Helmet: The Integration of Women and Gender Issues in UN Peacekeeping Missions." Working Paper Series, Santo Domingo: UN-INSTRAW, 2010, http://www.operationspaix.net/DATA/DOCUMENT/1656~v~Women_with_a_Blue_Helmet__The_Integration_of_Women_and_Gender_Issues_in_UN_Peacekeeping_Missions.pdf.

Boutellis, A., and N. C. Fink. *Waging Peace: UN Peace Operations Confronting Terrorism and Violent Extremism*. New York: International Peace Institute, 2016.

Bridges, D., and D. Horsfall. "Increasing Operational Effectiveness in UN Peacekeeping: Toward a Gender-Balanced Force." *Armed Forces & Society* 36, no. 1 (2009): 120–130.

Carey, H. F. "'Women and Peace and Security': The Politics of Implementing Gender Sensitivity Norms in Peacekeeping." *International Peacekeeping* 8, no. 2 (2001): 49–68.

Cold-Ravnkilde S. M., and P. Albrecht. *Female Peacekeepers Are Vital for the UN Mission in Mali*. DIIS Policy Brief, 2016, http://pure.diis.dk/ws/files/712641/Gender_in_Minusma_WEB.pdf.

Coomaraswamy, R. *Preventing Conflict, Transforming Justice, Securing the Peace—A Global Study on the Implementation of United Nations Security Council Resolution 1325*. New York: UN Women, 2015, http://www.refworld.org/docid/561e036b40c.html.

Crawford K. F., J. H. Lebovic, and J. M. Macdonald. "Explaining the Variation in Gender Composition of Personnel Contributions to UN Peacekeeping Operations." *Armed Forces & Society* 41, no. 2 (2015): 257–281.

De Groot, J. "A Few Good Women: Gender Stereotypes, the Military, and Peacekeeping." In *Women and International Peacekeeping*, edited by L. Olsson and T-I. Tryggestad. London: Frank Cass, 2001.

Dharmapuri, S. *Not Just a Numbers Game: Increasing Women's Participation in UN Peacekeeping*. Providing for Peacekeeping. New York: International Peace Institute, 2013, http://www.operationspaix.net/DATA/DOCUMENT/8074~v~Not_Just_A_Numbers_Game__Increasing_Womens_Participation_in_UN_Peacekeeping.pdf.

Elshtain J. B. *Women and War*. Chicago: University of Chicago Press, 1995.

Enloe, C. *Maneuvers: The International Politics of Militarizing Women's Lives*. Los Angeles: University of California Press, 2000.

Heinecken, L. "Are Women 'Really' Making a Unique Contribution to Peacekeeping?" *Journal of International Peacekeeping* 19 (2015): 227–248.

Hunt, C. T. "All Necessary Means to What Ends? The Unintended Consequences of the 'Robust Turn' in UN Peace Operations." *International Peacekeeping* 24, no. 1 (2017): 108–131.

Jennings, K. M. "Women's Participation in UN Peacekeeping Operations." NOREF Report, Oslo, September 2011, https://www.files.ethz.ch/isn/137505/Women%E2%80%99s%20participation%20in%20UN%20peacekeeping.pdf.

Karim, S., and K. Beardsley. "Female Peacekeepers and Gender Balancing: Token Gestures or Informed Policymaking?" *International Interactions* 39, no. 4 (2013): 461–488.

Karim, S. "Reevaluating Peacekeeping Effectiveness: Does Gender Neutrality Inhibit Progress?" *International Interactions* (2016), 1–26.

Karlsrud, J. "The UN at War: Examining the Consequences of Peace-Enforcement Mandates for the UN Peacekeeping Operations in the CAR, the DRC, and Mali." *Third World Quarterly* 36, no. 1 (January 2015): 40–54.

Karlsrud, J. "Towards UN Counter-Terrorism Operations?" *Third World Quarterly* (January 2017): 1–17.

Kreft, A. K. "The Gender Mainstreaming Gap: Security Council Resolution 1325 and UN Peacekeeping Mandates. *International Peacekeeping* 24, no. 1 (2017): 132–158.

Office of the Special Advisor on Gender Issues and Advancement of Women (OSAGI). "Gender Mainstreaming: Strategy for Promoting Gender Equality." August 2001, http://www.un.org/womenwatch/osagi/pdf/factsheet1.pdf.

Olsson, L., and T. L. Tryggestad. "Introduction." In *Women and International Peacekeeping*, edited by L. Olsson and T. L. Tryggestad, 1–8. London: Frank Cass, 2001.

Olsson, L., A. Schjølset, and F. Möller. "Women's Participation in International Operations and Missions." In *Gender, Peace, and Security: Implementing UN Security Council Resolution 1325*, edited by L. Olsson and T-I. Gizelis, 37–61. London: Routledge, 2015.

Ramos-Horta, J. et al. "Report of the High-level Independent Panel on Peace Operations on Uniting Our Strengths for Peace: Politics, Partnership, and People." June 17, 2015, http://www.unic.or.jp/files/peace_operations.pdf.

Sion, L. "Can Women Make a Difference? Female Peacekeepers in Bosnia and Kosovo." *Commonwealth & Comparative Politics* 47, no. 4 (2009): 476–493.

Simić, O. "Increasing Women's Presence in Peacekeeping Operations: The Rationales and Realities of 'Gender Balance.'" In *Rethinking Peacekeeping, Gender Equality, and Collective Security. Thinking Gender in Transnational Times*, edited by G. Heathcote and D. Otto. London: Palgrave Macmillan, 2014.

Stamnes, E. "The Responsibility to Protect: Integrating Gender Perspectives into Policies and Practices." *Global Responsibility to Protect* 4 (2012): 172–197.

True, J. "Feminist Problems with International Norms: Gender Mainstreaming and Global Governance." In *Conversations in Feminist International Relations: Past, Present and Future* edited by J. Ann Tickner and Laura Sjoberg. New York: Routledge, 2011.

Tryggestad, T.L. "Trick or Treat? The UN and Implementation of Security Council Resolution 1325 on Women, Peace, and Security." *Global Governance: A Review of Multilateralism and International Organizations* 15, no. 4 (2009): 539–557.

United Nations. "Beijing Declaration and Platform of Action, Adopted at the Fourth World Conference on Women." *RefWorld*, October 27, 1995, http://www.refworld.org/docid/3ddeo4324.html.

United Nations. "ECOSOC Agreed Conclusions," 1997/2, A/52/3. July 18, 1997, https://www.un.org/womenwatch/osagi/pdf/ECOSOCAC1997.2.PDF.

United Nations. "Windhoek Declaration." Namibia, May 31, 2000, http://www.un.org/womenwatch/osagi/wps/windhoek_declaration.pdf.

United Nations. "Gender Equality in UN Peacekeeping Operations." Department of Peacekeeping Operations. DPKO Policy Directive. November 2006, http://www.un.org/en/peacekeeping/documents/gender_directive2006.pdf.

United Nations. "Gender Forward Looking Strategy 2014–2018." Department of Peacekeeping Operations and Department of Field Support. 2014, http://www.un.org/en/peacekeeping/documents/DPKO-DFS-Gender-Strategy.pdf.

United Nations. "Policy on Gender Equality in UN Peacekeeping Operations." Department of Peacekeeping Operations and Department of Field Support. July 26, 2010, http://www.un.org/en/peacekeeping/documents/gender_directive_2010.pdf.

United Nations. "Report of the Independent Panel on Safety and Security of UN Personnel and Premises Worldwide." Brahimi Safety and Security Report, June 9, 2008.

United Nations. "Report of the Secretary-General on the Situation in Mali." S/2016/1137, December 30, 2016.

United Nations. "Summary of Troop Contributions to UN Peacekeeping Operations by Mission, Post and Gender." Gender Statistics, 2017a, http://www.un.org/en/peacekeeping/contributors/gender/2017gender/may17.pdf.

United Nations. "Use of Force by Military Components in United Nations Peacekeeping Operations." Department of Peacekeeping Operations and Department of Field Support, 2017b.

United Nations. "Women in Peacekeeping." 2017c, https://peacekeeping.un.org/en/women-peacekeeping.

UN News. "Hailed as 'Role Models,' All-Female Indian Police Unit Departs UN Mission in Liberia." *UN News*, February 12, 2016, http://www.un.org/apps/news/story.asp?NewsID=53218#.WVkSpOk8xPY.

UNPOL. "UN Police GenderInitiatives." 2017, https://police.un.org/en/un-police-gender-initiatives.

UN Security Council. Security Council Resolution 1325 [on women and peace and security]. S/RES/1325 (2000), October 31, 2000, http://www.refworld.org/docid/3b00f4672e.html.

UN Security Council. Security Council Resolution 2242 [on women and peace and security]. S/RES/2242 (2015), October 13, 2015, http://www.refworld.org/docid/562097f44.html.

UN Women. "Gender Mainstreaming." 2017, http://www.unwomen.org/en/how-we-work/un-system-coordination/gender-mainstreaming#sthash.Rd2RNncV.dpuf.

Väyrynen, T. "Gender and UN Peace Operations: The Confines of Modernity." *International Peacekeeping* 11, no. 1 (2004): 125–142.

Willmot H., S. Sheeran, and L. Sharland. "Safety and Security Challenges in UN Peace Operations." *International Peace Institute* (2015), 1–48.

CHAPTER 18

WPS AND SEA IN PEACEKEEPING OPERATIONS

JASMINE-KIM WESTENDORF

IN 2015, revelations emerged that peacekeepers from France, Chad, and Equatorial Guinea had regularly raped homeless and starving boys aged 8 to 15 in refugee camps in the Central African Republic, and that a French military commander had tied up and undressed four girls and forced them to have sex with a dog, after which one of the girls died (Aids Free World 2015; Deschamps et al. 2015). Although alarming, these revelations were not surprising: interveners in peace operations (including military and civilian peacekeepers, aid workers, diplomats, private contractors, and others associated with missions) have been implicated in the sexual exploitation and abuse (SEA) of local women and children in nearly every UN peacekeeping operation (PKO) since the end of the Cold War.

According to the UN, *sexual exploitation* is "any actual or attempted abuse of a position of vulnerability, differential power, or trust, for sexual purposes, including, but not limited to, profiting monetarily, socially or politically from the sexual exploitation of another," while *sexual abuse* is "the actual or threatened physical intrusion of a sexual nature, whether by force or under unequal or coercive conditions" (United Nations Secretary General [UNSG] 2003: 1). The impact of such behaviors is significant: In 2013, a UN investigation declared SEA "the most significant risk to UN peacekeeping missions, above and beyond other key risks including protection of civilians" (Awori et al. 2013: 1). Moreover, UN officials and state delegates to the UN have often claimed it undermines the organization's credibility and capacity (e.g., United Nations 2006). Scholarly research has also demonstrated its long-term impacts, including embedding sex work and trafficking in postwar economies (Jennings and Nikolić-Ristanović 2009: 9; Jennings 2010; True 2012: 141). Further, SEA undermines the international community's capacity to achieve the goals set out in the Women, Peace, and Security (WPS) framework, in particular, the mandates that the protection needs of women be given particular attention in PKOs, that special measures be taken to protect women and girls from gender-based violence, and that women be included at all levels of decision-making in peace processes.

This chapter[1] addresses two questions. First, what is the relationship between SEA and WPS, and what impact does the former have on the international community's efforts regarding the latter? Second, why have SEA policies and frameworks been pursued largely in isolation from broader WPS frameworks, and what practical and conceptual gains are to be had from a closer integration of the two? The chapter proceeds in three sections. The first maps the extent and characteristics of SEA in PKOs and their links to WPS outcomes. The second investigates how the international community has attempted to prevent and hold individuals accountable for SEA through the development of policy frameworks, training programs, and institutional mechanisms, and the extent to which these have interacted or aligned with WPS policies, programs and mechanisms. The final section addresses the practical and conceptual implications of the current approach to SEA policy. In particular, it considers UN policies on transactional sex and relationships between peacekeepers and beneficiaries in order to understand the assumptions underpinning UN SEA policy, and how these assumptions operate against fundamental WPS values.

SEA in UN Peace Operations

Awareness of SEA in PKOs first emerged during the UN Transitional Authority in Cambodia (UNTAC) in 1993, when the number of prostitutes in Cambodia grew from 6000 to more than 25,000 within a year of the peacekeepers' arrival (Whitworth 2004: 68). The widespread use of prostitutes by peacekeepers involved violence and the sexual abuse of girls, and Cambodian sex-workers complained to the UN at the time that "UNTAC customers could be more cruel" than Cambodians (Whitworth 2004: 67–68). The UN response was threefold: the head of mission declared that "boys will be boys" (Ledgerwood 1994), mission leadership advised peacekeepers not to wear uniforms when visiting brothels nor park UN vehicles directly outside, and an additional eight hundred thousand condoms were shipped to Cambodia to prevent the spread of HIV (Simić 2012: 41).

In 1995, the issue of peacekeeper SEA arose in Bosnia-Herzegovina, with reports that women and girls were being trafficked to work as sex slaves in brothels frequented by UN personnel, and later, of the complicity of peacekeepers in sex trafficking. It was not until 1999, however, that negative media and rising public attention prompted the UN Mission in Bosnia and Herzegovina and Office of the High Commissioner for Human Rights to develop policy responses to address peacekeepers' involvement in the sex trade (Simić 2012: 42). Once underway, the UN response failed to provide adequate protection to victims, and peacekeepers found to have been involved in trafficking and forced prostitution returned home before charges could be laid, thereby avoiding prosecution (Human Rights Watch 2002: 55).

Shortly thereafter, consultants hired by United Nations High Commissioner for Refugees (UNHCR) and Save the Children UK raised the alarm that UN and NGO staff were abusing and exploiting local women and children in refugee camps in Guinea, Liberia and Sierra Leone (UNHCR and Save the Children UK 2002). A subsequent Office of Internal Oversight Services (OIOS) investigation verified that SEA was prevalent. The cases it documented included a sexual relationship between a UN civilian staff member and a 17-year-old refugee in exchange for school fees, the violent rape of girls by NGO staff, the rape of boys by UN peacekeepers, the exchange of sex for food provided by NGO staff, and the refusal of international staff to take responsibility for children they fathered (UNSG 2002: 9–11). The Secretary-General subsequently declared that

> [SEA] by humanitarian staff cannot be tolerated. It violates everything the UN stands for. Men, women and children displaced by conflict or other disasters are among the most vulnerable people on earth. They look to the UN and its humanitarian partners for shelter and protection. Anyone employed by or affiliated with the UN who breaks that sacred trust must be held accountable and, when the circumstances so warrant, prosecuted (UNSG 2002: 1).

In response, the United Nations General Assembly (UNGA) adopted Resolution 57/306 "[e]xpressing its grave concern at incidents of [SEA] against vulnerable populations," and directing the Secretary-General to extend remedial and preventive measures to all peace and humanitarian operations, ensure that reporting and investigative procedures are in place, and maintain data on SEA. It "encouraged" all UN bodies and NGOs to do the same (UNGA 2003: 1–2). The Secretary-General consequently issued a bulletin establishing a zero-tolerance policy on SEA for all UN staff, and outlining the duties of mission leadership to ensure accountability, including through referring cases to national authorities for criminal prosecution. It obliges all UN staff to report SEA, and it is binding on all UN civilian staff and any agencies and individuals who have cooperation agreements with the UN. Military and police contingents in PKOs are bound through a Memorandum of Understanding between the UN and troop contributing countries (TCCs), and mission experts are bound through signed individual undertakings. The zero-tolerance bulletin is the cornerstone of SEA policy, and reinforced the mandate laid out in Resolution 1325 for peacekeepers to protect women from post-conflict sexual and gender-based violence (SGBV). However, as this chapter demonstrates, SEA policy has been developed in isolation from the WPS agenda, with severe consequences for effectiveness.

Since the introduction of the zero-tolerance policy, military, civilian, and police peacekeepers have continued to perpetrate SEA. The 2017 annual Secretary-General's report *Special Measures for Protection from Sexual Exploitation and Abuse* included the most comprehensive breakdown of allegations to date (UNSG 2017). It reported that in 2016, 103 allegations were recorded involving personnel in peacekeeping and special political missions, an increase from 69 in 2015. Sexual abuse accounted for 57 percent of allegations, with nearly two-thirds involving children. Sexual exploitation accounted for the remaining 43 percent of allegations. Any allegations involving children are recorded as sexual abuse, regardless of the nature of the acts.

Of the allegations, seventy-three related to military personnel, twenty-three to civilian personnel, and seven to police. Personnel in all three groups are considered *peacekeepers* as they are deployed as part of a PKO; there is often an assumption that the term applies only to military personnel. It is unlikely, however, that these statistics accurately reflect the scale of SEA in peace operations: research suggests that UN data is unreliable due to poor data-management, potential false allegations, and likely under-reporting of SEA (Grady 2016: 942). Rates are probably much higher: in Liberia, an estimated fifty-eight thousand women aged 18 to 30 years-old engaged in transactional sex in the first nine years of UNMIL—more than 75 percent with UN personnel, and more than half reported their first encounter happened before they were 18 (Beber et al. 2017).

These examples highlight key themes in peacekeeper SEA: the widespread abuse of children; the perpetration of SEA by the range of military, police, and civilian peacekeepers and humanitarian staff deployed into peacekeeping contexts; repeated rounds of policy development that have not effectively prevented SEA; and the diversity of behaviors that SEA encompasses, which poses challenges for policy responses. In fact, the differences between the behaviors are perhaps greater than the overarching descriptor "sexual exploitation and abuse" suggests. Although united by the sexual nature of the behaviors involved, the behaviors are only loosely related in practice—for example, rape or child abuse is significantly different to negotiated, consensual, transactional sex between adults, even in a context of unequal power dynamics. It follows that policies need to be sensitive to the various forms of SEA, and the various factors that contribute to them (Westendorf and Searle 2017).

So, why do peacekeepers perpetrate SEA? One explanation revolves around gendered power dynamics and masculinity. While this applies to both military and civilian peacekeepers, scholarship has focused on the former. For instance, military peacekeepers have told researchers that they need to prove they are not homosexual by "going out and getting a woman," that disciplining soldiers for sexual harassment "[limits] the military's capacity to produce effective soldiers" (Razack 2000: 138), and that "satisfying" their sex drives is fundamental to their masculinity (Higate 2007: 106). Henry's analysis of peacekeeper SEA highlights other explanations that have been marshalled to explain conflict-related sexual violence (CRSV) and military prostitution, and are equally relevant to SEA by military peacekeepers. These include military cultures, the politics of race in civilian-military relations, the role international relations have played in military prostitution, economies shaped by military presence, and the intersection of interests between international and local actors in the control of women's sexuality and bodies (Henry 2013: 127). As Enloe argues "[t]here is nothing inherent in [PKOs] that makes soldiers immune to the sort of sexism that has fuelled military prostitution in wartime and peacetime" (Enloe 2000: 101). It is also relevant to recognize the latent coloniality in the peacekeeping project (Razack 2004), the importance of which, in relation to SEA, is underscored by the explanation given by a French MONUC civilian peacekeeper who admitted having sex with twenty-four underage girls. He said, "over there, the colonial spirit persists. The white man gets what he wants" (*UN News Service* 2004).

The implications of peacekeeper SEA are significant for the implementation of the WPS agenda. Peacekeepers are mandated by Resolution 1325 to attend to the specific protection needs of women in conflict and post-conflict contexts, and all parties to a conflict are instructed to respect international law and "take special measures to protect women and girls from gender-based violence" (Article 10). The perpetration of SEA directly contravenes this resolution. SEA also throws into question the extent to which member states have complied with Resolution 1325's mandate that gender perspectives and training be embedded in PKOs, which would help prevent SEA. Furthermore, a mandate for women's inclusion at all levels of decision-making and peace processes, and for measures that support local women's peace initiatives, lie at the heart of Resolution 1325 (Articles 1 and 8). SEA actively undermines these goals: by perpetrating SEA against women and children, peacekeepers undermine their capacity to participate actively in the political space. When PKOs fail to prevent or hold perpetrators accountable for such acts, they send the message that women are neither respected nor seen as valuable participants in the peace process.

The disconnect between WPS and SEA policy is problematic for the implementation of both frameworks. To understand how the decoupling occurred and its implications, it is necessary to unpack how the international community has attempted to prevent and hold individuals accountable for SEA and why policies have been unable to effectively limit SEA.

A Brief History of UN SEA Policy

Since the adoption of the zero-tolerance bulletin, successive revelations about SEA have prompted renewed cycles of policy development, which have revolved around prevention, enforcement, and more recently, victims' needs. In 2004, international media documented the SEA of young girls in internally displaced person (IDP) camps by UN peacekeepers in Bunia, Democratic Republic of the Congo (DRC; Holt and Hughes 2004), which jolted the UN into a new wave of investigations and policy development that shifted focus from prevention to enforcement. The Special Committee on PKOs requested the Secretary-General provide a comprehensive report and strategy on SEA by UN peacekeeping personnel (UNGA 2007). Investigated by Jordanian prince Zeid Ra'ad Zeid Al-Hussein, the report entitled *A comprehensive strategy to eliminate future sexual exploitation and abuse in UN peacekeeping operations*, (or "the Zeid Report") was introduced to the General Assembly in 2005 by the Secretary-General, who described existing measures to address SEA as "manifestly inadequate" and called for a fundamental shift in approach (UNSG 2005). The report argued that the problem of SEA in PKOs encompassed four areas: rules on standards of conduct; the investigative process; organizational, managerial, and command responsibility; and individual disciplinary, financial, and criminal accountability (Al-Hussein 2005). The report's recommendations in each area were comprehensive, with a recurring emphasis on agency systems and processes to strengthen accountability. These recommendations were broadly accepted by the Special Committee on Peacekeeping Operations, whose report (A/59/19.Add1) was endorsed by the UNGA in Resolution 59/300, which formally adopted the Zeid Report's comprehensive strategy.

However, while the UN Secretariat, General Assembly, and Security Council were concerned with enforcement and accountability, the field-level of PKOs was still struggling with basic questions of how to implement SEA policies. For example, in reviewing MONUC's response to SEA in the aftermath of the Zeid Report, the former MONUC Director of the Office for Addressing SEA described the policy vacuum the Office encountered when it began operating in 2005. Despite overarching frameworks prohibiting SEA, there were no rules or procedures for conducting investigations, the UN's responsibility to victims was unclear, and there was no guidance on how to address paternity claims (Dahrendorf 2006: 4). In documenting lessons learned, Dahrendorf argued that specific training is needed for field managers and commanders in how to create and maintain an environment that prevents SEA and mitigates their tendency to "down-play the issue, or even cover up," and that mission-specific training describing the impact and context of SEA is necessary (Dahrendorf 2006: 11–14).

This call for a policy approach that goes beyond implementing and upholding rules to understand the environments in which SEA occurs and its impacts, has gone largely unheeded. Although new operational directives such as curfews, non-fraternization policies, requirements to wear uniforms outside compounds, and off-limits locations has resulted in a decrease in reported incidents, evidence suggests that SEA has simply been pushed underground (Dahrendorf 2006: 13–14; Grady 2016: 942; Deschamps et al. 2015: 16). Further, the focus on procedures for investigations conflicts with the reality that SEA, like most forms of SGBV, is probably underreported and difficult to "prove" to UN investigative standards, even in the UN's own assessment (Deschamps et al. 2015: 16). Many factors contribute to this: victims may refuse to give evidence against soldiers because of fear of retribution; it is difficult to generate witness evidence because of people movements in emergency settings; there is confusion over who is responsible for investigating; the departure or repatriation of alleged perpetrators and the UN's lack of authority over TCCs regarding investigative processes; and the fact that officials—both in UN missions and in the militaries of TCCs— have been reticent to hold perpetrators accountable for SEA (Stern 2015: 13–17; Holt and Hughes 2004; Deschamps et al. 2015: i, iv, 77–78; Burke 2012; Bolkovac and Lynn 2011). A gendered analysis of SEA also reveals that stigma and structural gender inequalities in the conflict environment are important obstacles to reporting all forms of sexual and gender-based violence (Davies and True 2015).

In 2008, the UNGA introduced the first Comprehensive Strategy on Assistance and Support to Victims of SEA by UN Staff and Related Personnel, which aimed to ensure that complainants, survivors, and children receive appropriate medical, legal, psychosocial, and other assistance (except compensation) in a timely and effective manner (UNGA 2008: 2). This was the first time SEA policy shifted from administrative procedures for investigations toward the needs of affected individuals and their families. The fact that earlier SEA policy did not draw on the 1985 General Assembly Declaration on the Basic Principles of Justice for Victims of Crime and Abuse of Power demonstrates how it has been siloed from other relevant policy frameworks.

In 2010, the Inter-Agency Standing Committee (IASC) commissioned a global review to investigate the extent of SEA policy implementation since the Zeid Report. The review was damning. It found that understanding and acceptance of new policies by staff and managers remained low, leadership by senior managers was critically absent, policies and guidance had generally not been communicated to the field, and implementation was "patchy, poor or non-existent "(IASC 2010). However, little happened until the 2015 CAR crisis.

Following the 2015 revelations of SEA by French Sangaris soldiers in the Central African Republic (CAR), an independent panel was appointed to investigate SEA by international peacekeeping forces in CAR, and produced the report *Taking Action on Sexual Exploitation and Abuse by Peacekeepers*. It documented "gross institutional failure" within the UN's response, including that survivors received inadequate care and protection, additional victims were identified but not followed up to take testimony, and the head of Mission failed to take "any action" to end abuse or report allegations appropriately (Deschamps et al. 2015: i). The report acknowledged that the Sangaris forces were not under UN command and therefore not bound by UN SEA frameworks. The report nonetheless called for a fundamental shift in how the UN, including TCCs, understand and frame SEA. The Panel argued that SEA can no longer be perceived as simply a personnel conduct and discipline issue, but should be understood as a violation of basic human rights and a form of CRSV that triggers the Security Council's mandated protection responsibilities, regardless of whether alleged perpetrators are under UN command. Reporting on SEA allegations against non-UN forces under Security Council mandates has subsequently been included in the annual Secretary-General's report on SEA.

The CAR scandal led to a shift in the UN leadership's action on SEA. First, the Secretary-General demanded the resignation of General Babacar Gaye, the head of mission, who ignored reports of SEA occurring on his watch. Then, the Secretary-General declared in his statement to the Security Council that the Secretariat could not alone address the "global scourge" of SEA by troops in peace operations, and placed responsibility for ensuring justice for victims "squarely" on TCCs. He went on to say that

> It is time to ask individually as Member States—and collectively as an institution—are we doing enough to report misconduct and punish those responsible? I must speak candidly. The answer is no. Too many incidents go unreported. Too few cases are prosecuted. Too often, justice is denied. . . . Even one case of sexual exploitation and abuse erodes the trust of the most vulnerable population we are sent to safeguard. Let us pledge to do more—much more — together to protect civilians and uphold the values of the United Nations (UNSG 2015).

This call for states to take greater responsibility for preventing and ensuring accountability for SEA suggests that the UN recognizes that its policies are not working. The zero-tolerance policy has not effectively prevented SEA, and many states have been unwilling to properly implement it among their personnel deployed to PKOs. The Secretary-General also expanded the OIOS' powers to include detailed reporting on the countries of personnel involved for greater TCC accountability, the number of victims, and whether a paternity claim has been lodged. The premise for this change appears to be that "naming and shaming" countries whose personnel perpetrate SEA will prompt states to take prevention and accountability measures more seriously. Lastly, the Secretary-General appointed Jane Holl Lute as the first Special Coordinator on Improving UN Response to SEA, to streamline SEA policy.

In response to these developments, the UN Security Council adopted Resolution 2272 in March 2016, endorsing the Secretary-General's decision to repatriate military or police units of a contingent where "credible evidence of widespread or systematic" SEA by that unit exists. The Council requested that the Secretary-General replace all units of a troop-contributing or police-contributing country in a particular PKO where that country fails to appropriately investigate allegations against their personnel, hold perpetrators accountable, or inform the Secretary-General of progress. Enhanced measures to strengthen prevention include a Secretariat-wide communications and information strategy, an e-learning program, and a request that TCCs certify that personnel have not engaged in prior misconduct during peacekeeping deployments (UNSG 2016). There are also new reporting requirements for TCCs regarding the progress and outcomes of SEA investigations. These details will be publicly reported, and influence the Secretary-General's decisions on whether a TCC should contribute to PKOs.

Resolution 2272 was met with resistance from Egypt and Russia in the UNSC who argued the policy amounted to "collective punishment" (Charbonneau 2016), but Russia eventually voted in favor while Egypt abstained. A key objection was the unfair burden of responsibility Resolution 2272 places on less developed states, which contribute the bulk of military personnel to PKOs, for responding to a complex issue that even developed state armies continued to struggle with. However, the resistance to Resolution 2272 also illuminates the problem with assuming that SEA is antithetical to the goals of TCCs in peace operations, when in fact TCCs contribute troops for a range of reasons that may not align with protecting civilians, promoting human rights, and embodying UN principles (Paris 2002; Neack 1995; Victor 2010).

In 2017, newly appointed Secretary-General Antonio Guterres made SEA policy reform a priority, appointing a High Level Task Force, led by the Special Coordinator on SEA, to develop a strategy that delivers "visible and measurable improvements" in the UN's prevention and response to SEA (UNSG 2017). Key innovations of the new policy include acknowledging that the system-wide nature of the SEA problem requires a multi-stakeholder response, a victim-centred approach, and greater transparency of reporting and investigations. In a major departure from previous policy, and explicitly connecting SEA to WPS for the first time, the Report identified gender inequality as the root of SEA and advocated that increasing the number of women in UN peacekeeping would help address SEA. Further, the Secretary-General committed to developing a special protocol on preventing SEA that would include strict rules regarding non-fraternization, certification of mandatory pre-deployment training, restrictions on the consumption of alcohol, and a written acknowledgement from every individual deployed that they understand UN values and principles, and commit to following SEA rules.

Two themes emerge from this account of SEA policy development. First, these policies—including the adoption of Resolution 2272—reflect an individualized understanding of SEA, and target individual compliance primarily through standards of conduct, recruitment standards and training, and threats of punishment, rather than addressing the complex mix of factors that operate in distinct ways to produce SEA. Additionally, this train-and-punish approach obscures the practical challenges that mid- to high-ranking officials pose when they refuse to deal with allegations or are simply too occupied with "hard security" issues to take "gender issues" seriously (Westendorf 2013, Westendorf 2017). The capacity of both civilian and military personnel in a mission tasked with investigating these crimes is shaped by whether the mission's institutional culture supports their role and prioritizes accountability mechanisms. Further, a compliance-based approach assumes that robust accountability mechanisms deter rules breaches—a logic for which there is little evidence in relation to CRSV more broadly (Kirby 2015: 464), and which is undermined by low rates of criminal charges or material punishments for perpetrators of SEA.

Secondly, the individualized approach to SEA has isolated it from the WPS framework, by focusing on conduct and discipline rather than broader issues of gender, protection, and human rights. It is worth noting that Resolution 2272 was not listed as a WPS resolution, despite clear connections and the mandate for WPS mechanisms to include SEA allegations in reporting to the Secretary-General (UNSC 2016: para. 13). In-fact, SEA remains listed on the UN's Peacekeeping website as a conduct and discipline issue only. Engagement with WPS frameworks has been absent from policy development processes, and SEA operational policy has been delinked from Protection of Civilians (POC) and Children in Armed Conflict thematic agendas despite synergies (Westendorf and Searle 2017). Indeed, SEA is siloed from POC and WPS references in mission mandates (as chapter 35 in this volume discusses). What is particularly troubling is that the delinking seems to be one-sided: those working on WPS see SEA as within their purview, as evidenced by the significant attention given to SEA in the 2015 Global Study on 1325, which argued that increasing women's presence in peace operations was crucial to reducing SEA (Coomaraswamy 2015).

IMPLICATIONS OF DELINKING SEA AND WPS

What are the impacts of delinking SEA policy from the WPS framework more broadly? Firstly, by dealing with SEA as an individualized conduct and discipline issue only, policies and their implementers are constrained in addressing the structural gender inequalities that shape the choices made by perpetrators (and sometimes, victims.) One example that highlights the lack of sensitivity to gender experiences and constructs in missions has been the UN policy on transactional sex.

The zero-tolerance bulletin prohibits any "exchange of money, employment, goods, or services for sex." However, PKOs are normally deployed into contexts where the intersection of CRSV, gender inequality, stigma, and material deprivation, creates the conditions for "survival" sex economies to flourish. For example, in 2003, when displaced civilians from Bunia in eastern DRC took refuge in and around UN headquarters, an extensive survival sex economy was established. *The Independent* reported the story of 13-year-old Faela, who became pregnant after being raped by militias and whose father refused to support her because of the shame of being an unmarried mother. In the IDP camp, she and her baby faced starvation; so, along with other girls in similar situations, every night she climbed through the fence into the compound where Uruguayan and Moroccan peacekeepers were based.

> "If I go and see the [MONUC] soldiers at night and sleep with them, then they sometimes give me food, maybe a banana or a cake," she says, looking down at her son. "I have to do it with them because there is nobody to care, nobody else to protect Joseph except me. He is all I have and I must look after him. . . . Going over to the camp is OK because the soldiers are kind to me and don't point their guns like the other soldiers did," Faela says (Holt and Hughes 2004).

A *Washington Post* investigation in Bunia documented similar stories, with one 14 year-old known locally as "the one-dollar UN girl" telling reporters "I'm sad about it. But I needed the dollars. I can't go farm because of the militias. Who will feed me? . . . But at least they paid us. I was worthless anyhow. My honour was lost [due to wartime rape]" (Wax 2005). A characteristic of transactional sex is that it "involves a level of agency and negotiation" even though it is negotiated in the context of often-extreme deprivation, desperation, and insecurity (Otto 2007: 260–261).

Research on transactional sex reveals the need to incorporate a gender analysis into SEA policy. The presence of agency and negotiation in transactional sex means that such transactions are sometimes interpreted by the men involved as being driven by the women, who, they argue, "enthusiastically" compete to attract peacekeepers' attention (Higate 2007: 106). Others interpret their actions as benevolent: peacekeepers told Higate that their sexual "transactions" were acceptable because the "donated" food, resources, or money made women more secure (Higate 2007: 100). That some parents see their child's participation in transactional sex as key to their family's economic survival may bolster this impression (Save the Children UK 2006: 13). These justifications operate despite peacekeepers receiving mandatory pre-deployment training that identifies transactional sex as breaching UN codes of conduct. The phenomenon of transactional sex economies in PKOs highlights a limited understanding of gender and the local context, and the disconnect between the list of rules that peacekeepers are expected to follow and their understanding of why those rules are important. The zero-tolerance policy on transactional sex reinforces the "women as victims" mentality often noted as a challenge to WPS implementation, while also missing the opportunity to address the underlying causes of SGBV. Incorporating an interrogation of gendered post-conflict dynamics, sexual violence, and the implications of sex between peacekeepers and locals into training would improve the capacity of peacekeepers to understand to the particular vulnerabilities of women in post-conflict contexts, as Resolution 1325 mandates. It would also provide a foundation from which peacekeepers can navigate their interactions with local communities, including sexual interactions. Furthermore, situating SEA policy and training within the WPS frameworks that push peacekeepers to respond to the particular needs, capacities, and vulnerabilities of civilians, would give it a broader conceptual framework from which to address the motivating and permissive factors that give rise to SEA. Operationally, connecting WPS and SEA might limit competition for time, resources, and influence that gender-related work in PKOs often suffers from.

A second illustrative example is the way SEA policy addresses the issue of peacekeepers engaging in consensual, non-transactional relationships with locals, and how this undermines core WPS goals of empowering women to participate in all levels of peace and decision-making processes. In addition to banning sex with children under 18 years-old and transactional sex, the zero-tolerance bulletin states that "sexual relationships between UN staff and beneficiaries of assistance, since they are based on inherently unequal power dynamics, undermine the credibility and integrity of the work of the UN and are strongly discouraged" (UNSG 2003). Staff involved in such relationships are required to report them to their Head of Mission or Office. This has been a source of significant confusion in practice—for instance, during interviews in East Timor, two heads of UN agencies reported that they did not feel comfortable discussing or passing judgment on such relationships if they are between consenting adults, suggesting that the training they receive does not equip them for complex conversations about power and gender in such contexts (Author interview 2016c; Author interview 2016b). Crucially, the lack of clarity over such relationships and whether they constitute SEA undermines the integrity of SEA policy more broadly. As one international humanitarian agency in Geneva noted, "because the behaviours are lumped together as SEA, it risks people not taking the whole policy seriously. Instead of raising the bar, it results in misunderstandings and misperceptions"(Author interview 2016a). More importantly, by suggesting that *all* relationships between peacekeepers and beneficiaries—understood to mean the whole local population in peacekeeping contexts—are inherently unequal and therefore probably exploitative, the policy suggests that adults in conflict-affected communities do not have the capacity to exert agency and freely consent in their sexual relationships. The policy thereby inadvertently infantilizes and disempowers local women rather than ensure that peacekeepers see them as individuals with valuable contributions to make to local and national peace-building and decision-making. This risks reinforcing the power dynamics in relationships with local populations that "permit" UN peacekeepers to engage in exploitative and abusive relationships, and fails to equip peacekeepers with the concepts required to distinguish between exploitative and non-exploitative relationships.

Re-linking SEA policy to WPS would help address these tensions, by situating it within the WPS agenda's concern for gender, power, and protection issues. If SEA policies and training drew on the language of gender and the conceptual framework around women's roles and vulnerabilities in conflict and peace processes—which are the foundation of WPS and currently absent from SEA policy discourse—they would provide peacekeepers with a better understanding of *why* the SEA rules are important rather than simply *what* the rules are. Furthermore, couching SEA policy within the WPS framework and language would give peacekeepers and those involved in SEA accountability processes a conceptual framework for *how* to navigate the sometimes complicated negotiation of relationships with locals, particularly sexual relationships that are consensual, but where consent does not rest on equal, non-hierarchical power relations. Importantly, this conceptual framework would help prevent the infantilization and disempowerment of women by foregrounding their agency, while providing peacekeepers with an understanding of the gendered, racialized, and economic context in which it is exercised. Equipping peacekeepers with a language of power dynamics—that can encompass gender, race, and economics—and a lens through which to make sense of their own positionality and its implications, is crucial to preventing and ensuring accountability for SEA. It would provide all personnel involved—including peacekeepers, the UN Secretariat, TCCs, UN Funds and Agencies—with a better grounding from which to understand why certain behaviors are unacceptable in the context of PKOs, identify SEA, and hold perpetrators accountable.

This leads to the question of why SEA policies have been pursued in isolation from the WPS agenda. The individualization of SEA and focus on conduct and disciplinary responses reflects a broader trend related to gender issues: technocratic "fixes" have been prioritized over efforts that address the underlying causes of gendered inequality and violence. Increasing women's participation has been prioritized over gender mainstreaming in part because it makes less prominent the need to address the persistent inequalities between women and men that give rise to women's disenfranchisement (Krook and True 2012: 115–117; chapter 14 in this volume illustrates this in relation to the DPKO). Similarly, by focusing on the technocratic responses to SEA—training, administrative procedures, and the associated bureaucratic structures—it appears as if the international community is taking concrete steps to address SEA, while inadvertently reinforcing the image of local women as victims lacking agency, and torpedoing more nuanced understandings and responses. This narrowing of focus inevitably isolates responses from broader frameworks—in this case, from WPS, as well as POC and Children in Armed Conflict agendas, all of which are more explicitly intersectional and human rights–based than SEA policy.

CONCLUSIONS

This chapter has demonstrated the challenges peacekeeper SEA poses to the international community's capacity to realize Resolution 1325's vision for women's participation and protection. Further, when peacekeepers abuse and exploit local women and children, they not only abrogate their responsibilities to WPS principles, but undermine the overarching goals of PKOs in terms of building peace and promoting human rights. The individualized understanding of SEA has narrowed the focus of policy to conduct and discipline interventions, at the expense of addressing the intersecting contextual, normative, and structural factors that shape the choices perpetrators, and sometimes victims, make. It has isolated SEA policy from frameworks that offer conceptual and operational benefits, including WPS. Stronger linkages between WPS and SEA may help address the failings of

SEA policies to date, by situating them within a broader analysis of the intersecting set of gendered and other dynamics that lead to women's disenfranchisement and their particular vulnerabilities in conflict and post-conflict environments. Moreover, couching SEA within the WPS framework would provide peacekeepers and those involved in training and accountability processes with a language of power and gender, and the concomitant conceptual frames—which extend to race, economics, and other sources of power imbalances. This is crucial to ensuring that individuals understand why SEA policies exist and how they provide a guide to navigating sexual interactions with locals, and to ensuring accountability for perpetrators who breach those policies.

NOTE

1. This research was funded by a grant from the Transforming Human Societies Research Focus Area at La Trobe University. Earlier parts of this project were undertaken collaboratively with Louise Searle.

REFERENCES

AIDS Free World. "The UN's Dirty Secret: The Untold Story of Child Sexual Abuse in the Central African Republic and Anders Kompass." 2015, http://www.codebluecampaign.com/carstatement/.

Al-Hussein, Zeid Ra'ad. "A Comprehensive Strategy to Eliminate Future Sexual Exploitation and Abuse in United Nations Peacekeeping Operations (A/59/710)." New York: United Nations, 2005.

Author interview, international humanitarian agency, Geneva, 2016a.

Author interview, senior UN agency official, East Timor, 2016b.

Author interview, senior UN official, East Timor, 2016c.

Awori, Thelma, Catherine Lutz, and Paban Thapa. "Final Report: Expert Mission to Evaluate Risks to SEA Prevention Efforts in MINUSTAH, UNMIL, MONUSCO, and UNMISS." Never officially released by the UN, but leaked in 2013, https://static1.squarespace.com/static/514a0127e4b04d7440e8045d/t/55afcfa1e4b07b89d11d35ae/1437585313823/2013+Expert+Team+Report+FINAL.pdf.

Beber, Bernd, Michael Gilligan, Jenny Guardado, and Sabrina Karim. "Peacekeeping, International Norms, and Transactional Sex in Monrovia, Liberia." *International Organization* 71, no. 1 (2017): 1–30.

Bolkovac, Kathryn, and Cari Lynn. *The Whistleblower: Sex Trafficking, Military Contractors, and One Woman's Fight for Justice.* New York: Palgrave Macmillan, 2011.

Burke, Roisin. "Attribution of Responsibility: Sexual Abuse and Exploitation, and Effective Control of Blue Helmets." *Journal of International Peacekeeping* 16 (2012): 1–46.

Charbonneau, Louis. "U.N. Adopts Resolution on Combating Sex Crimes by Peacekeepers." *Reuters,* 2016, http://in.reuters.com/article/un-peacekeepers-sexcrimes-idINKCN0WD2IM.

Coomaraswamy, Radhika. "Preventing Conflict, Transforming Justice, Securing the Peace: A Global Study on the Implementation of United Nations Security Council Resolution 1325." NY: UN Women, 2015, http://www2.unwomen.org/-/media/files/un%20women/wps/highlights/unw-global-study-1325-2015.pdf?vs=2435.

Dahrendorf, Nicola. "Sexual Exploitation and Abuse: Lessons Learned Study, Addressing Sexual Exploitation and Abuse in MONUC." New York: UNDPKO, 2006.

Davies, S. E., and Jacqui True. "Reframing the Prevention of Conflict-Related Sexual and Gender-Based Violence." *Security Dialogue* 46, no. 6 (2015): 495–512.

Deschamps, Marie, Hassan B. Jallow, and Yasmin Sooka. "Taking Action on Sexual Exploitation and Abuse by Peacekeepers: Report of an Independent Review on Sexual Exploitation and Abuse by International Peacekeeping Forces in the Central African Republic." UN External Independent Panel, 2015.

Enloe, Cynthia. *Maneuvers: The International Politics of Militarizing Women's Lives.* Berkeley: University of California Press, 2000.

Grady, Kate. "Sex, Statistics, Peacekeepers, and Power: UN Data on Sexual Exploitation and Abuse and the Quest for Legal Reform." *Modern Law Review* 79, no. 6 (2016): 931–960.

Henry, Marsha. "Sexual Exploitation and Abuse in UN Peacekeeping Missions: Problematising Current Responses." In *Gender, Agency, and Coercion*, edited by Sumi Madhok, Anne Phillips, and Kalpana Wilson, 122–142. Houndmills, UK: Palgrave Macmillan, 2013.

Higate, Paul. "Peacekeepers, Masculinities, and Sexual Exploitation." *Men and Masculinities* 10, no. 1 (2007): 99–119.

Holt, Kate, and Sarah Hughes. "Sex and Death in the Heart of Africa." *Independent*, May 25, 2004, http://www.independent.co.uk/news/world/africa/sex-and-death-in-the-heart-of-africa-564563.html.

Human Rights Watch. "Hopes Betrayed: Trafficking of Women and Girls to Post-Conflict Bosnia and Herzegovina for Forced Prostitution." Vol. 19, no. 9 (D). New York: Human Rights Watch, 2002. https://www.hrw.org/reports/2002/bosnia/Bosnia1102.pdf.

Inter-Agency Standing Committee. "Global Review of Protection from Sexual Exploitation and Abuse by UN, NGO, IOM, and IFRC Personnel." United Nations Office for the Coordination of Humanitarian Affairs, 2010.

Jennings, Kathleen. "Unintended Consequences of Intimacy: Political Economies of Peacekeeping and Sex Tourism." *International Peacekeeping* 17, no. 2 (2010): 229–243.

Jennings, Kathleen, and Vesna Nikolić-Ristanović. "UN Peacekeeping Economies and Local Sex Industries: Connections and Implications." MICROCON Research Working Paper No. 17, 2009, http://papers.ssrn.com/sol3/papers.cfm?abstract_id=1488842.

Kirby, Paul. "Ending Sexual Violence in Conflict: The Preventing Sexual Violence Initiative and Its Critics." *International Affairs* 91, no. 3 (2015): 457–472.

Krook, Mona Lena, and Jacqui True. "Rethinking the Life Cycles of International Norms: The United Nations and the Global Promotion of Gender Equality." *European Journal of International Relations* 18, no. 1 (2012): 103–127.

Ledgerwood, Judy L. "UN Peacekeeping Missions." Analysis from the East-West Center 11. Asia Pacific Issues. Honolulu: East-West Center, 1994, http://www.seasite.niu.edu/khmer/ledgerwood/PDFAsiaPacific.htm.

Neack, Laura. "UN Peace-Keeping: In the Interest of Community or Self?" *Journal of Peace Research* 32, no. 2 (1995): 181–196.

Otto, Dianne. "Making Sense of Zero Tolerance Policies in Peacekeeping Sexual Economies." In *Sexuality and the Law*, edited by Vanessa Munro and Carl Stychin, 259–282. Abingdon: Routledge-Cavendish, 2007.

Paris, Roland. "International Peacebuilding and the 'Mission Civilisatrice.'" *Review of International Studies* 28, no. 4 (2002): 637–656.

Razack, Sherene. "From The 'Clean Snows of Petawawa': The Violence of Canadian Peacekeepers in Somalia." *Cultural Anthropology* 15, no. 1 (2000): 127–163.

Razack, Sherene. *Dark Threats and White Knights*. Toronto: University of Toronto Press, 2004.

Save the Children UK. "From Camp to Community. Liberia Study on Exploitation of Children." Save the Children (UK), 2006.

Simić, Olivera. *Regulation of Sexual Conduct in UN Peacekeeping Operations*. New York: Springer, 2012.

Stern, Jenna. "Reducing Sexual Exploitation and Abuse in UN Peacekeeping: Ten Years after the Zeid Report." Policy Brief No. 1. Civilians in Conflict. Stimson Centre, 2015, http://www.stimson.org/sites/default/files/file-attachments/Policy-Brief-Sexual-Abuse-Feb-2015-WEB.pdf.

True, Jacqui. *The Political Economy of Violence against Women*. New York: Oxford University Press, 2012.

United Nations General Assembly (UNGA). " UN Comprehensive Strategy on Assistance and Support to Victims of Sexual Exploitation and Abuse by UN Staff and Related Personnel." A/RES/62/214, 2008, http://repository.un.org/bitstream/handle/11176/268157/A_RES_62_214-EN.pdf?sequence=1&isAllowed=y.

United Nations General Assembly (UNGA). "Declaration of Basic Principles of Justice for Victims of Crime and Abuse of Power." A/RES/40/34, 2016, http://www.un.org/documents/ga/res/40/a40r034.htm.

United Nations General Assembly (UNGA). "Report of the Special Committee on Peacekeeping Operations and Its Working Group on the 2005 Resumed Session." UN Doc A/61/19 (Part III), June 12, 2007.

United Nations General Assembly (UNGA). "Investigation into Sexual Exploitation of Refugees by Aid Workers in West Africa." A/RES/57/306, 2003, http://www.un.org/en/ga/search/view_doc.asp?symbol=A/RES/57/306.

United Nations High Commissioner for Refugees (UNHCR) and Save the Children UK. "Sexual Violence & Eploitation: The Experience of Refugee Children in Guinea, Liberia, and Sierra Leone." London, 2002, https://www.streetchildrenresources.org/resources/sexual-violence-exploitation-the-experience-of-refugee-children-in-guinea-liberia-and-sierra-leone

United Nations. Press Release. "Problem of Sexual Abuse by Peacekeepers Now Openly Recognized, Broad Strategy in Place to Address It, Security Council Told." UN Security Council, SC/8649, 2006, http://www.un.org/press/en/2006/sc8649.doc.htm.

United Nations Secretary-General (UNSG). "Comprehensive Review of the Whole Question of Peacekeeping Operations in All Their Aspects (A/59/710)." A/59/710, 2005, https://documents-dds-ny.un.org/doc/UNDOC/GEN/N05/247/90/PDF/N0524790.pdf?OpenElement.

United Nations Secretary-General (UNSG). "Investigation into Sexual Exploitation of Refugees by Aid Workers in West Africa." A/57/465, 2002, https://reliefweb.int/report/guinea/investigation-sexual-exploitation-refugees-aid-workers-west-africa-a57465.

United Nations Secretary-General (UNSG). "Secretary-General's Bulletin: Special Measures for Protection from Sexual Exploitation and Sexual Abuse." ST/SGB/2003/13, 2003, https://oios.un.org/resources/2015/01/ST-SGB-2003-13.pdf.

United Nations Secretary-General (UNSG). "Secretary-General's Bulletin: Status, Basic Rights and Duties of United Nations Staff Members (ST/SGB/2002/13)." United Nations, 2002.

United Nations Secretary-General (UNSG). "Special Measures for Protection from Sexual Exploitation and Sexual Abuse." A/70/729, UN General Assembly: Secretary-General, 2016.

United Nations Secretary-General (UNSG). "Special Measures for Protection from Sexual Exploitation and Abuse: A New Approach A/71/818." New York: UN, 2017, http://undocs.org/A/71/818.

United Nations Secretary-General (UNSG). United Nations Web Services. "Secretary-General's Remarks to Security Council Consultations on the Situation in the Central African Republic." United Nations, 2015, http://www.un.org/sg/statements/index.asp?nid=8903.

United Nations Security Council (UNSC). "Security Council Resolution 2272 (2016) [on Sexual Exploitation and Abuse by United Nations Peacekeepers." S/RES/2272 (2016). United Nations Security Council, 2016, http://www.refworld.org/docid/56e915484.html.

UN News Service. "UN Civilian Worker in DR of Congo Accused of Child Molestation.," November 1, 2004.

Victor, Jonah. "African Peacekeeping in Africa: Warlord Politics, Defense Economics, and State Legitimacy." *Journal of Peace Research* 47, no. 2 (2010): 217–229.

Wax, Emily. "Congo's Desperate 'One-Dollar U.N. Girls.'" *Washington Post*, March 21, 2005, http://www.washingtonpost.com/wp-dyn/articles/A52333-2005Mar20.html.

Westendorf, Jasmine-Kim. "'Add Women and Stir': The Regional Assistance Mission to Solomon Islands and Australia's Implementation of United Nations Security Council Resolution 1325." *Australian Journal of International Affairs* 67, no. 4 (2013): 456–474.

Westendorf, Jasmine-Kim, and Louise Searle. "Sexual Exploitation and Abuse in Peace Operations: Trends, Policy Responses, and Future Directions." *International Affairs* 93, no. 2 (2017): TBC.

Whitworth, Sandra. *Men, Militarism, and UN Peacekeeping: A Gendered Analysis.* Boulder, CO: Lynne Rienner, 2004.

....

CHAPTER 19

WPS AND PEACEKEEPING ECONOMIES

....

KATHLEEN M. JENNINGS

IN recent years, increasing analytical attention has been paid to the question of how international interveners—be they peacekeepers, peace-builders, humanitarians, or aid workers—relate to the community in which they find themselves.[1] The idea underpinning much of this work is that attempts to determine the impacts of peacekeeping (and other forms of international intervention) should also take into account factors falling outside of the formal activities and mandate of the mission. These informal factors include the ways in which interveners live, move, and spend in their off-duty, as well as on-duty, time. The impacts unfolding from peacekeepers' daily lives may in fact be more immediate, visible, and beneficial (or harmful) to local people living alongside peace operations than most of the mission's prescribed tasks and activities. This analytical focus on the "everyday" has become increasingly influential in peacekeeping, peace-building, and political economy scholarship.[2] It owes an obvious, though often unacknowledged (McLeod 2015), debt to feminist scholarship's focus on the "private."

One way to conceptualize the everyday encounters between international interveners and local residents of peacekeeping sites is through the notion of the "peacekeeping economy." In its most basic formulation, the peacekeeping economy refers to economic activity that either would not occur, or would occur at a much lower scale and pay-rate, without the international peacekeeping (or peace-building) presence. While the term may be used narrowly to refer only to the attributable economic flows of peacekeeping, I use the concept more broadly. Peacekeeping economy serves as shorthand for the ecosystem of formal, informal, and sometimes illicit transactions and interactions that allow peacekeeping missions and peacekeepers to function, and the services and establishments in and through which this activity occurs. This expansive political economic approach has the advantage of focusing attention on the "everyday" peacekeeping experienced by those living in, and alongside, peacekeeping missions, while still retaining a concern for the structuring authority of markets, governance, and domestic and international institutions (Jennings 2016b). Indeed, the peacekeeping economy can be understood as a concentration of the larger post-conflict political economy, rather than a temporary distortion of it. It describes not only specific economic flows or the establishment of certain enterprises and infrastructure, but also raises the larger question of gendered roles and relations in conflict-affected societies.

As such, the peacekeeping economy, and its constitutive transactions and interactions, is as important to the Women, Peace, and Security (WPS) agenda as it is to peacekeeping. This is because the pillars of the WPS agenda, especially participation, protection, and prevention (see chapters 12 and 16 in this volume), are forwarded through, and impacted or undermined by, the entirety of peacekeepers' actions and presence. This implies that analyses of WPS focusing on systemic, organizational, political, or cultural factors should be supplemented by studies that also take into account the broader political-economic ramifications of peace operations—including the "extracurricular" activities of peacekeepers—in order to give a holistic account of the real gains and challenges to WPS objectives.

This chapter is an attempt to provide such analysis. I use the concept of the "peacekeeping economy" to illuminate the interaction and tension between the objectives of WPS and everyday life in peacekeeping sites. I focus especially on two sources of friction between peacekeeping economies and the WPS agenda. First is the direct contradiction between the protection and prevention imperatives of WPS, and the explosive growth of the local sex industry that is characteristic to peacekeeping economies. The second source of friction stems from peacekeeping economies' strongly hierarchical and gendered distribution of labor and resources, and the arguably lasting implications this has for gender relations and gender equality in conflict-affected societies. This latter argument hinges on a broad conceptualization of the WPS agenda, one that connects particular problems of violence, exploitation, and lack of female participation to the wider political economy of peace and security, and not least the "gendered social and economic inequalities between women and men" (True 2012: 5). I contend that the everyday political-economic context in which peacekeeping missions unfold thus challenges the WPS aims of gender equality. It puts into question the very issues of protection, participation, and prevention that peacekeeping missions are meant to assist.

PEACEKEEPING ECONOMIES

One of the earliest appearances of the term "peacekeeping economies" comes in Elisabeth Rehn and Ellen Johnson Sirleaf's report entitled *Women, War, and Peace* (2002: 62). They use peacekeeping economies descriptively to refer to "industries and services such as bars and hotels that spring up with the arrival of large, foreign, comparatively well-paid peacekeeping personnel." Subsequently, Higate and Henry (2004) added analytical heft to the notion of the peacekeeping economy. They use the term to identify the diverse opportunities for income generation provided by the arrival of a UN mission, and are concerned with how militarized (peacekeeping) masculinities are constructed through and across the spaces of the peacekeeping economy, as well as the effects this has on local women's security.[3] In a series of publications dating from 2009–2016, my colleagues and I build further on the idea of the peacekeeping economy as both describing a phenomenon common to peacekeeping and peace-building environments, and as an analytical tool that enables rich analysis of the everyday interactions between peacekeepers and locals.[4] In this section, I will briefly describe what is meant by the peacekeeping economy, and how using this concept facilitates a more inclusive understanding of the operation of WPS objectives in peacekeeping sites.

As previously noted, peacekeeping economy refers to economic activity that either would not occur, or would occur at a much lower scale and pay-rate, without the international peacekeeping presence.[5] Specifically, it encompasses jobs available to local staff in UN offices or NGOs that accompany the UN presence (occasionally professional but usually administrative or unskilled, as well as subcontracted work such as maintenance and security); unskilled and mainly informal work that locals do for individual internationals (such as cleaning, cooking, gardening, or other housework); jobs in the establishments and enterprises that cater primarily to internationals; and participation in the sex industry. Within the host society, peacekeeping economies include skilled and unskilled workers; local and foreign (expatriate) businesspeople; political, economic, and military elites; landlords; professionals; tradespeople; service workers (sex workers, domestic workers, security guards, drivers, others); and people working in both the formal and informal economies. International civilian, military, and police peacekeeping and peace-building personnel are also necessarily involved in the peacekeeping economy. Peacekeeping economies as described here are also found in peace-building sites. The key distinction is that peace-building refers also to actors and activities that may represent increased revenues (via aid flows or budget support) to the host country, while this is not the case for peacekeeping missions. That peacekeeping missions' budgets largely circumvent the host nation is, in fact, significant to the peacekeeping economy concept because it facilitates a focus on the peace-keeping "everyday" and on the enterprises, services, and sectors that develop or expand to accommodate peacekeepers' wants and needs. That said, it makes little sense to distinguish between peacekeepers and peace-builders in terms of individual users or beneficiaries of peacekeeping economies.

Peacekeeping economies are most evident in urban areas where international personnel are most concentrated, as well as those places in rural areas where a military and/or civilian UN presence is located. In these places, the peacekeeping economy affects labor markets; the building or rehabilitation of infrastructure, including housing and office stock, airports and ports, and accommodation and leisure facilities; the cost-of-living, primarily in terms of housing, leisure activities, and certain goods and services; the built environment; and the way space is configured or controlled. In many cases, the peacekeeping economy also affects the banking system and availability of financial services (see chapter 26 in this volume). Finally, the peacekeeping economy is the context in which most of the contact between local residents and international personnel takes place. It may also be the source of the only *concrete* benefits that many locals receive out of the peacekeeping mission, such as income or increased trade or job possibilities.

Yet even where the peacekeeping economy creates employment opportunities for local women and men, the infrastructure, services, and skills it generates are not of a type necessarily beneficial to the society at large (Beber et al 2016; Ammitzboell 2007). Instead, the enterprises of the peacekeeping economy comprise a high-end, niche market that caters primarily to needs, tastes, and consumption habits typical to the global North. This does not, however, imply that peacekeeping economies are simply temporary bubble economies unconnected to the "real" economy of host countries. While it is true that the dollarized peacekeeping economy often functions as a parallel economy to that operating in the local currency (Edu-Afful and Aning 2015), there is significant imbrication between the two. More so, the peacekeeping economy captures and channels investment and infrastructure development in specific ways. In most cases, it is *instead of* rather than *in addition to* other forms of investment and development (Jennings 2015). This is why the peacekeeping economy can be understood as a concentration of the larger post-conflict political economy, rather than a distortion of it.

Peacekeeping economies are also inescapably gendered. Close attention to peacekeeping economies through a feminist political economy lens "reveals the workings of power not only through visible coercion that is direct in its effects but also in the material basis of relationships that govern the distribution and use of resources, benefits, privileges, and authority within the home and society at large" (True 2012: 7). Their chief beneficiaries are predominantly men: local or national politico-economic and military elites, diaspora returnees, local and expatriate businesspeople, those active in wartime (often illicit) networks, and peacekeepers themselves. As Edu-Afful and Aning (2015: 392) argue, "the peacekeeping economy 'system' is set up to continue to reward those who already have the most," thus reinforcing "hierarchies of inclusion and exclusion" in host countries. That the consuming side of the peacekeeping economy is lopsidedly male is also important. While globally international civilian peacekeepers are estimated to comprise approximately 30 percent women,[6] peacekeeping missions overall are largely staffed by men.[7] This drives the kinds of services and entertainment venues that flourish in peacekeeping economies, which target a clientele that is presumed to be single (or at least alone), transient, and male. These services and enterprises do not, however, automatically disappear once missions are drawndown. Moreover, because peacekeeping missions are non-family accompanied—that is, peacekeepers do not bring spouses, partners, and children to the mission area—there is not the counterweight of "family-friendly" entertainment, of nannies and child-minders, international schools, health, and other services found in expatriate-heavy, non-peacekeeping locales.

The "maleness" of the peacekeeping economy does not, however, imply a lack of "women's work." Quite the opposite: even without the demand for child-minding and other forms of care work, the informal or illicit sectors encompassed by the peacekeeping economy comprise jobs that are women-dominated, such as domestic work, hostessing and waitressing, and sex work. There is also evidence that formal sector jobs encompassed by the peacekeeping economy, such as clerical and administrative support in UN offices, are more likely to employ women, while men are more likely to be employed as mechanical or maintenance staff. This division of labor reflects the prevailing understanding of what are "appropriate" jobs for women and men (Aning and Edu-Afful 2013). The overall picture is that positions of power, ownership and influence in both the formal and informal or illicit sectors of peacekeeping economies tend to be occupied by men; while women are concentrated in low-level service work, usually with a great deal of direct contact with (and potential vulnerability to) their customers and employers.

In short, peacekeeping economies, and women's and men's participation in them, are structured along highly gendered lines, in a way that aligns closely with stereotypical or "traditional" gender roles. This does not mean that peacekeeping economies are necessarily harmful to either local individuals or the community as a whole. Indeed, many individuals' livelihoods are directly sustained by peacekeeping economies. However, it cannot be maintained that peacekeeping economies affect everyone equally, benignly, or advantageously. The knock-on effects of the peacekeeping economy also have gendered ramifications. For example, the presence of peacekeepers and other international interveners drives up housing costs, displacing many residents out of city centers to outlying suburbs. Longer commutes into the city center for work put yet more pressure on women's time, which is already burdened by the care responsibilities disproportionately carried by women. The presence of missions can also drive up prices on certain staples, even in the shops and markets not normally patronized by peacekeepers. Finally, the relative paucity of remunerated care work—aside from housecleaning—in the peacekeeping economy, alongside the growth in the sex industry, makes for an economy that is not just gendered but also heavily sexualized in terms of access, opportunities, and ramifications for gender roles and relations.

PEACEKEEPING ECONOMIES AND THE WPS AGENDA

This is the backdrop against which to problematize how peacekeeping economies interact with and affect the WPS agenda, particularly the key objectives on protection against gender-specific human rights violations, the prevention of conflict, and recognition of women's participation across these objectives. Briefly, Resolution 1325 calls upon "all parties to armed conflict to respect fully international law applicable to the rights and protection of women and girls, especially as civilians (para. 9)" and to "take special measures to protect women and girls from gender-based violence, particularly rape and other forms of sexual abuse, and all other forms of violence in situations of armed conflict (para. 10)." Meanwhile, "prevention" in Resolution 1325 refers both to the inclusion of women in conflict prevention mechanisms (para. 1), as well as the prevention of violence against women and children in conflict situations. Protection and prevention are thus centered on violence (protection from violence, prevention of violence), and on the preservation and defense of women's rights. There is a strong emphasis in subsequent resolutions on conflict-related sexual violence (CRSV), which straddles the protection and prevention imperatives. Relatedly, there is also the acknowledgment that peacekeepers themselves engage in harmful, exploitative, and abusive sexual behavior against women, men, and children living in peacekeeping sites (see chapter 18 in this volume).

The most direct, and negative, link between peacekeeping economies and WPS objectives is connected to the explosive growth of the sex industry in peacekeeping host countries—and not uncommonly, in neighboring countries. Examples from Cambodia, Bosnia, Kosovo, Liberia, Haiti, and the Democratic Republic of the Congo[8] demonstrate that the strong association between militarism and the sex industry is not limited to state militaries or active conflicts. It is also a dominant feature in peacekeeping environments, in which civilian as well as uniformed peacekeepers partake. Significantly, the entertainment infrastructure in peacekeeping economies plays an enabling role. Its venues—high-end restaurants, bars, clubs, hotels, and brothels—are key facilitators of sexual transactions, providing a relatively safe, vetted meeting point where services can be procured. Moreover, the surge in demand created by a large cohort of interveners incentivizes both voluntary migration and human trafficking, involving peacekeepers in organized criminal activity that undercuts the governance, security, and human rights goals of the peace operation (Mendelson 2005). In short, while peacekeepers' patronage of peacekeeping sex industries is not generally considered equivalent to CRSV,[9] it is untenable to argue that the peacekeeping sex industry is somehow incidental or unrelated to the protection and prevention imperatives of WPS. Conversely, the expansion and entrenchment of sex industries during peacekeeping missions, as evidence from the Balkans shows, does not necessarily abate after missions are drawn down (Jennings and Nikolic-Ristanovic 2009). The related entertainment infrastructure may be profitably re-oriented instead toward sex tourism (Jennings 2010). Once again, this is intrinsically in opposition to the WPS principles of protection from, and prevention of, violence against women, and the defense of women's rights.

Significant though the connection is between peacekeeping, sex industries, and protection and prevention, it does not entirely capture the ways in which peacekeeping economies are relevant to WPS. It is only with a broader perspective on the WPS agenda that the issue of peacekeeping economies becomes most salient. This approach recognizes that participation is not limited to peace processes; and that protection and prevention go beyond physical violence or CRSV, to also encompass protection of women's social and economic rights and prevention of further backsliding on gender equality in conflict-affected countries (True 2012). For while peacekeeping economies can have beneficial impacts on local livelihoods, this should not obscure the more complicated, and potentially troubling, ramifications for WPS aims of gender equality.

One aspect of this is the aforementioned sexualization of the peacekeeping economy, which affects even those jobs, services, and people not directly or indirectly involved in transacting sex. As Oldenburg (2015: 324) argues with relation to what she terms the "market of intervention" in Goma, "access . . . privileges young women, particularly in the realm of intimate relations, and has consequences for gendered identities and images of gender roles" both for women and men. Oldenburg shows how (young) women's bodies and sexuality become their primary means to achieve resources, connections, and mobility in these environments. In turn, this bodily reliance has generational and gendered ramifications in terms of interpersonal relationships, the limited opportunities (and increased resentment) of young men, and the wider patterns of gendered participation and belonging in these political economies. While Oldenburg stresses that young women's actions in the "market of intervention" can be economically and socially empowering, the flip side is that they are still heavily dependent on men. They are vulnerable to the whims both of their patrons and of the men in their familial and social circle, whose resentment can be expressed through violence or exclusion. The larger point is that in these economies, social status and economic participation is achieved at least in part through one's willingness and ability—mediated by sex, age, and physical appearance—to strategically use one's own body and femininity in ways that, while they may be beneficial for some, actually buttress regressive understanding of gender roles, masculinity, and femininity.[10]

That many of the characteristic features of peacekeeping economies reinforce rather than disrupt gendered roles and hierarchies also affects how money, power, and time is concentrated and valued in conflict-affected societies. For example, the feminized labor of domestic service is largely ignored by missions, despite the prevalence of peacekeepers living in private accommodation who employ maids. This form of labor is taken for granted despite the potential for exploitation in terms of wages and working conditions, as well as in terms of unwanted sexual contact between domestic workers and their employers (Jennings 2014). Conversely, the masculinized, corporatized realm of private security is vetted and regulated by the mission's internal security department even while the purveyor of that security—the (mostly) men guarding compounds around the clock—are subject to similarly precarious conditions as female service workers. Both are characterized by low or inconsistent pay, long hours, lack of legal protections, lack of contract, and physical insecurity.

In other words, service work—even when performed by male bodies—is feminized, "private," and outside the purview of the mission as a political economic actor. Simultaneously, missions reward (such as through the leasing of property and granting of contracts) those with resources, connections, and corporate form—however obtained, structured, and shady. A paradigmatic example is the leasing of Pan African Plaza, the site of UNMIL's headquarters, from a Libyan-Liberian consortium connected to the late Libyan leader Muammar Gaddafi. Although these deals are justified by the speed with which peacekeeping missions must establish themselves, combined with the often-limited selection of properties to lease and services to contract, the UN's unwillingness to confront the political economy in which it is implicated outlasts the chaotic start-up period.

Finally, the peacekeeping economy reinforces dynamics operating in the wider political economy, even if it does not alone create these dynamics. These include "a gap between symbolic (and sometimes substantive) advancements in women's rights in certain spheres, and the structural and socioeconomic constraints that impede their implementation or equitable distribution . . . [and] the political cooptation of women's empowerment and emancipation" (Lake and Berry 2017). In this way, the gendered peacekeeping economy fits the typical pattern of "backlash" against women in conflict-affected societies and economies (Pankhurst 2008; Meintjes et al. 2001; Cockburn and Zarkov 2002). Pillay (2001) argues that these economies are characterized by the reassertion of male dominance over women's productive and reproductive labor. It serves as a means of controlling the economic threat posed to men's interests and identities by women who may have gained a greater degree of power during the conflict period. As Turshen (2001: 85) asserts, the post-conflict period is one in which "men reassert control through economic violence against women." This process also occurs in situations where women are, by necessity or choice, the sole or primary breadwinners, thus indicating a contradiction between economic realities and the imperative felt by some to return to, or re-impose, conservative and regressive understandings of masculinity and femininity.

Yet there are specific interventions that peacekeeping missions could take to counter some of the inequities of the peacekeeping economy. These actions would have positive implications for the wider post-conflict political economy. They include guidance to peacekeepers on how to fairly treat their employees, especially domestic staff, in terms of hiring, firing, and compensation levels; working toward gender-equal distribution of mission jobs and contracts; more mission oversight of the subcontractors they employ with respect to labor standards, protections, and employee pay; vetting of landlords the mission rents from so as to ensure that warlords and/or those that gained property through illicit or criminal means are not rewarded; and greater efforts to procure goods and supplies locally by means of prioritizing women-owned businesses or co-operatives, and working with local suppliers to improve livelihoods and forestall potential negative side-effects on local markets. Better enforcement of the zero-tolerance policy against transactional sex would help mitigate against the typical explosion of the sex industry in peacekeeping sites. These are relatively straightforward interventions. While they may not dramatically affect the balance of power or structure of the peacekeeping economy, they could at least improve conditions for many of the local women and men involved in it. They could also have important signaling effects regarding missions' commitment to protect the economic rights and well-being of local residents.

CONCLUSION

The peacekeeping economy can be understood as a concentration of the larger post-conflict political economy, rather than a temporary distortion of it. Accordingly, the peacekeeping economy raises the larger question of gendered roles and relations in conflict-affected societies. It is overstated to claim that a peacekeeping operation, and the political economy it helps create and perpetuate, is the decisive factor in determining the evolution or regression of gendered relations in post-conflict societies. However, this does not imply that the multifarious gendered impacts of that operation or economy can be ignored, even (or especially) where these are unintended and unconstructive. Nor should it be assumed that these effects will disappear with the mission.

It is possible to imagine a political economy of peacekeeping that is more preventive of harms, and protective of women's rights, including their economic and social rights as well as their civil and political rights. Such change would require more decisive, and necessarily political, engagement on the part of missions, from the national to the grassroots levels. It requires an emphasis on economic and political justice for communities and individual women and men. It would also involve a re-orientation of peacekeeping away from aloof patrols and fortified bases toward dialogue with locals about their everyday needs and challenges, and greater openness to building mutual trust and accountability. Lastly, it would necessitate the acceptance by the peacekeeping apparatus of some responsibility for the gendered political economy it creates and partakes in.

NOTES

1. For example, Smirl (2008, 2015); Duffield (2010); Higate and Henry (2009); Autesserre (2014); Pouligny (2006); Elias and Rethel (2016).
2. See, for example, Richmond and Mitchell (2012); Mac Ginty (2013); Björkdahl and Mannergren Selimovic (2016).
3. For a more traditional approach to the economic impact of peacekeeping operations/peacekeeping economies, see Carnahan, Durch, and Gilmore (2006); Beber et al. (2016).
4. See: Jennings and Nicolic-Ristanovic (2009); Jennings (2010, 2014, 2015, 2016a, 2016b); Jennings and Bøås (2015); Aning and Edu-Afful (2013); Edu-Afful and Aning (2015); Henry (2015); Oldenburg (2015).
5. The rest of this section draws particularly on Jennings (2010; 2014; 2016b).
6. See United Nations Peacekeeping, https://peacekeeping.un.org/en/women-peacekeeping
7. The UN provides monthly statistics on the sex-breakdown of uniformed personnel (military and police) in peacekeeping missions, but not of civilian personnel. See https://peacekeeping.un.org/en/gender.
8. See, among many, on sex industries in peacekeeping sites: Rehn and Johnson Sirleaf (2002); Simic (2010); Whitworth (2004); Higate (2003); Harrington 2005); True (2012); Enloe (1989).
9. Although, see Gowrinathan and Cronin-Furman (2017), who position the connected issue of peacekeeper involvement in sexual exploitation and abuse as CRSV.
10. See also Jennings and Nikolic-Ristanovic (2009) for a similar analysis from Bosnia and Kosovo.

REFERENCES

Ammitzboell, Katarina. "Unintended Consequences of Peace Operations on the Host Economy from a People's Perspective." In *Unintended Consequences of Peacekeeping Operations*, edited by Chiyuki Aoi, Cedric de Coning, and Ramesh Thakur, 69–89. Tokyo: United Nations University Press, 2007.

Aning, Emmanuel Kwesi, and Fiifi Edu-Afful. "Unintended Impacts and the Gendered Consequences of Peacekeeping Economies in Liberia." *International Peacekeeping* 20, no. 1 (2013): 17–32.

Autesserre, Séverine. *Peaceland: Conflict Resolution and the Everyday Politics of International Intervention*. Cambridge: Cambridge University Press, 2014.

Beber, Bernd, Michael Gilligan, Jenny Guardado, and Sabrina Karim. "Challenges and Pitfalls of Peacekeeping Economies." Working Paper, July 2016, https://www.nyu.edu/projects/beber/files/Beber_Gilligan_Guardado_Karim_PK_Economy.pdf.

Björkdahl, Annika, and Johanna Mannergren Selimovic. "A Tale of Three Bridges: Agency and Agonism in Peace Building." *Third World Quarterly* 37, no. 2 (2016): 321–335.

Carnahan, Michael, William Durch, and Scott Gilmore. "Economic Impact of Peacekeeping: Final Report." New York: UN Department of Peacekeeping Operations, 2006.

Cockburn, Cynthia, and Dubravka Zarkov, eds. *The Postwar Moment: Militaries, Masculinities, and International Peacekeeping*. London: Lawrence & Wishart, 2002.

Duffield, Mark. "Risk-Management and the Fortified Aid Compound: Everyday Life in Post-Interventionary Society." *Journal of Intervention and Statebuilding* 4, no. 4 (2010): 453–474.

Edu-Afful, Fiifi, and Kwesi Aning. "Peacekeeping Economies in a Sub-Regional Context: The Paradigmatic Cases of Liberia, Sierra Leone, and Côte d'Ivoire." *Journal of Intervention and Statebuilding* 9, no. 3 (2015): 391–407.

Elias, Juanita, and Lena Rethel, eds. *The Everyday Political Economy of Southeast Asia*. Cambridge: Cambridge University Press, 2016.

Enloe, Cynthia. *Bananas, Beaches, and Bases: Making Feminist Sense of International Politics*. Berkeley: University of California Press, 1989.

Gowrinathan, Nimmi, and Kate Cronin-Furman. "UN Peacekeepers: Keeping the Peace or Preventing It?" Al-Jazeera, May 2, 2017, http://www.aljazeera.com/indepth/opinion/2017/04/peacekeepers-keeping-peace-preventing-170430102118379.html.

Harrington, Carol. "The Politics of Rescue: Peacekeeping and Anti-Trafficking Programmes in Bosnia-Herzegovina and Kosovo." *International Feminist Journal of Politics* 7, no. 2 (2005): 175–206.

Henry, Marsha G. "Parades, Parties and Pests: Contradictions of Everyday Life in Peacekeeping Economies." *Journal of Intervention and Statebuilding* 9, no. 3 (2015): 372–390.

Higate, Paul, ed. *Military Masculinities: Identity and the State*. Westport, CN: Praeger, 2003.

Higate, Paul, and Marsha Henry. "Engendering (In)security in Peace Support Operations." *Security Dialogue* 34, no. 4 (2004): 481–498.

Higate, Paul, and Marsha Henry. *Insecure Spaces: Peacekeeping, Power, and Performance in Haiti, Kosovo and Liberia*. London: Zed Books, 2009.

Jennings, Kathleen M. "Unintended Consequences of Intimacy: Political Economies of Peacekeeping and Sex Tourism." *International Peacekeeping* 17, no. 2 (2010): 229–243.

Jennings, Kathleen M. "Service, Sex, and Security: Gendered Peacekeeping Economies in Liberia and the Democratic Republic of the Congo." *Security Dialogue* 45, no. 4 (2014): 1–18.

Jennings, Kathleen M. "Life in a 'Peace-Kept' City: Encounters with the Peacekeeping Economy." *Journal of Intervention and Statebuilding* 9, no. 3 (2015): 296–315.

Jennings, Kathleen M. "Blue Helmet Havens: Peacekeeping as Bypassing in Liberia and the Democratic Republic of the Congo." *International Peacekeeping* 23, no. 2 (2016a): 302–325.

Jennings, Kathleen M. "Blue Helmet Havens: Gendered Peacekeeping Economies in Liberia and the Democratic Republic of the Congo." PhD diss., University of Oslo, 2016b.

Jennings, Kathleen M., and Morten Bøås. "Transactions and Interactions: Everyday Life in the Peacekeeping Economy." *Journal of Intervention and Statebuilding* 9, no. 3 (2015): 281–295.

Jennings, Kathleen M., and Vesna Nikolić-Ristanović. "UN Peacekeeping Economies and Local Sex Industries: Connections and Implications." MICROCON Working Paper 17. Bristol: MICROCON, 2009.

Lake, Milli, and Marie Berry. "Women and Power After War." Denver Dialogues [Blog], June 6, 2017, http://politicalviolenceataglance.org/2017/06/06/women-and-power-after-war/.

Mac Ginty, Roger. "Introduction: The Transcripts of Peace: Public, Hidden, or Non-Obvious?" *Journal of Intervention and Statebuilding* 7, no. 4 (2013): 423–430.

McLeod, Laura. "A Feminist Approach to Hybridity: Understanding Local and International Interactions in Producing Post-Conflict Gender Security." *Journal of Interventional and Statebuilding* 9, no. 1 (2015): 48–69.

Meintjes, Sheila, Anu Pillay, and Meredeth Turshen, eds. *The Aftermath: Women in Post-Conflict Transformation.* London: Zed Books, 2001.

Mendelson, Sarah E. *Barracks and Brothels: Peacekeepers and Human Trafficking in the Balkans.* Washington, DC: CSIS, 2005.

Oldenburg, Silke. "The Politics of Love and Intimacy in Goma, Eastern DR Congo: Perspectives on the Market of Intervention as Contact Zone." *Journal of Intervention and Statebuilding* 9, no. 3 (2015): 316–333.

Pankhurst, Donna. "Gendered Peace." In *Whose Peace?: Critical Perspectives on the Political Economy of Peacebuilding*, edited by Michael Pugh, Neil Cooper, and Mandy Turner, 30–46. Basingstoke, UK: Palgrave, 2008.

Pillay, Anu. "Violence against Women in the Aftermath." In *The Aftermath: Women in Post-Conflict Transformation*, edited by Sheila Meintjes, Anu Pillay, and Meredeth Turshen, 35–45. London: Zed Books, 2001.

Pouligny, Béatrice. *Peace Operations Seen from Below: UN Missions and Local People.* Bloomfield, CT: Kumarian Press, 2006.

Rehn, Elisabeth, and Ellen Johnson Sirleaf. *Women, War and Peace: The Independent Experts' Assessment on the Impact of Armed Conflict on Women and Women's Role in Peace-Building.* New York: UNIFEM, 2002.

Richmond, Oliver P., and Audra Mitchell, eds. *Hybrid Forms of Peace: From Everyday Agency to Post-Liberalism.* Basingstoke, UK: Palgrave Macmillan, 2012.

Simic, Olivera. *Regulation of Sexual Conduct in UN Peacekeeping Operations.* Heidelberg: Springer, 2010.

Smirl, Lisa. "Building the Other, Constructing Ourselves: Spatial Dimensions of International Humanitarian Response." *International Political Sociology* 2 (2008): 236–253.

Smirl, Lisa. *Spaces of Aid: How Cars, Compounds, and Hotels Shape Humanitarianism.* London: Zed Books, 2015.

True, Jacqui. *The Political Economy of Violence Against Women.* Oxford: Oxford University Press, 2012.

Turshen, Meredeth. "Engendering Relations of State to Society in the Aftermath." In *The Aftermath: Women in Post-Conflict Transformation*, edited by Sheila Meintjes, Anu Pillay, and Meredeth Turshen, 78–96. London: Zed Books, 2001.

Whitworth, Sandra. *Men, Militarism, and UN Peacekeeping: A Gendered Analysis.* Boulder, CO: Lynne Rienner, 2004.

CHAPTER 20

....

WPS IN MILITARY TRAINING AND SOCIALIZATION

....

HELENA CARREIRAS AND TERESA FRAGOSO

THE WPS agenda has put a special emphasis on the need to increase the presence of women in military forces and strengthen a gender perspective in the planning and conduct of military operations. The under representation of women in national militaries and peace operations, as well as the lack of gender awareness in military training and missions, led to repeated appeals aimed at the development of concrete policies targeting these problems. Both individual countries and international and regional security organizations have been developing tools to implement the WPS agenda in this respect. A robust set of policy instruments and rules began to emerge in the past decade (Barnes 2011). However, evaluation reports point to persistent implementation problems in the inclusion of a gender perspective in international military missions.

While acknowledging notable progress in some areas, reports from the United Nations, European Union (EU), and NATO highlight systematic obstacles and challenges preventing much of that progress to become standard practice. These include, among others, limited human and financial resources attached to implementation, uneven awareness of the resolutions and related organizational guidelines, broad range of potential interventions and lack of criteria for prioritizing, ambiguity of policy documents, lack of accountability mechanisms, flaws in the gender adviser system, and the absence of pre-deployment training (Olsson and Tejpar 2009; Lackenbauer and Langlais 2013; UN Women 2015).

At the national level, the situation of gender integration in military forces varies significantly across countries but important changes have been taking place. On the one hand, in countries where integration patterns between the armed forces and societies intensified, the representation of women grew, many restrictions were lifted, including those preventing women's access to combat or close to combat areas and training.[1] In addition, today more positions than ever are formally open to women. Some of these changes have been, at least partially, a result of the global WPS agenda and the pressure put on national states by international alliances and organizations. On the other hand, empirical studies still report, in most cases, persistent glass ceiling effects, occupational segregation, and more dramatically, increasingly reported situations of sexual harassment and assault (Bastick et al. 2007; Carreiras 2010; Obradovic 2014).

The overall situation of gender integration in national militaries is thus diverse and to a certain extent paradoxical. Although it is expected to find spillover or dissemination effects from the international to the national level, it is also fundamental to acknowledge that the extent to which international organizations such as the UN, NATO, or the EU are able to implement Resolution 1325 is very dependent on the willingness of member states to do so. Even if international military missions have specific planning, engagement rules, and organizational outlook, their forces are composed of contributing countries' personnel with concrete institutional, cultural, and identity backgrounds, as well as diverse levels of experience and training in terms of gender.

The attention given to the specific conditions and contexts for the implementation of the WPS agenda at the national level has been comparably lower than the one directed at the international arena. At the national level, policy and research efforts have centered on assessing the implementation of national action plans. This approach has frequently been done from a strictly administrative point of view or based on formal quantitative indicators and not on in-depth qualitative studies. Furthermore, there are very few truly comparative studies addressing the variety of factors that affect policies and practices in terms of the implementation of the WPS agenda.

This chapter aims at contributing, even if modestly, to a much needed and overdue discussion on the articulation of both international and national policy levels. It specifically examines the way policies on gender integration affect military training and socialization. It explores the hypothesis that a lack of congruence between national policies on gender integration in the military and the requirements of Resolution 1325 account for many of the implementation problems identified at the level of international military missions.

Since comparative data on gender representation and policies in the armed forces around the world are scarce, we concentrate on Western states' militaries or those belonging to NATO countries. Data and studies allowing comparative and longitudinal analyses are available for this group. While the quality of the data still raises several concerns, the existence of an institutional core and a progressively standardized data collection procedure[2] allow for an easier assessment of both policies and practices at domestic and alliance level (Carreiras 2006; Schjølset 2010; Obradovic 2014).

FACTORS THAT AFFECT NATIONAL POLICIES ON GENDER IN THE ARMED FORCES

The extent to which Western democracies have integrated women in their armed forces varies significantly across time and space. While some countries grant military women similar rights and opportunities to men, others keep them in symbolic positions and restrict their access from certain—mostly combat related—roles and positions. In most of the Western world the dominant trend has been that of a steady increase in number and representation. Cycles of expansion and contraction, however, have been recorded. There is also a significant diversity concerning recruitment, training, retention, or integration policies. Such variation ranges from an almost total absence, rank limitations, segregated training, and severe functional restrictions, to relatively open career patterns, fully integrated training and access to combat roles.

Research has shown that national policies vary according to political, organizational, and socioeconomic variables. In a study on the participation of women in NATO forces, Carreiras found that such differences were not a direct consequence of the amount of time women had served. Rather, they were related to organizational factors, namely all-volunteer versus conscript recruitment systems, and above all, to the political and economic situation of women in society at large (Carreiras 2006). The study showed that gender integration clearly reached higher levels in countries more exposed to the democratization of gender relations in society, and to external political pressures to achieve gender equality in the military. Likewise, gender inclusiveness was higher where the military opened up to society due to organizational shifts towards professionalization and where gender equality policies were implemented in the armed forces.

Contrarily, and regardless of the moment when women joined the military, in countries where those external influences had not been felt with the same intensity, where the military remained closer to a mass-army format, and where women had not reached a qualified position in the social structure; there were lower levels of gender inclusiveness in the military. The author concluded that "change towards greater gender equality in the armed forces will not occur automatically as a consequence of time or the increase in relative numbers. . . . it will probably depend more on the extent to which external variables, such as women's position in society at large, might influence policy orientations and decision-making processes within the armed forces" (Carreiras 2006: 127).

In the same vein, researching the armed forces in Europe, Forster showed that existing differences in gender integration were related to the type of military institution (Forster 2005; also see Eulriet 2009; Hazelzet 2013). Variation depended on the military's overall degree of convergence with society, and that convergence patterns might develop for different reasons (Forster 2005). Three groups of states were identified. In the first group, mainly composed of West European and North American states, more women were likely to serve in the future, to hold senior and command positions, and experience greater workplace equality. These were states where civil-military convergence had taken place and the armed forces lost organizational autonomy in determining what internal changes are acceptable. Pressures to change in this respect have mainly, although not exclusively, derived from external legal factors.

In the second group of countries, mainly composed of Central and Eastern European countries, convergence on gender matters took place whereas in other areas the military remained strikingly different from society. In these cases there was a functional rather than normative rationale to promote an equality agenda. Yet the expectation was still that these states would face challenges that would progressively undermine the gate-keeping power of their armed forces. Finally, for the third group of cases where the military's position as arbiter of internal change remained fundamentally unchallenged, poorly developed civil societies and weak economies meant that neither the legal structure and human rights advocacy groups, nor military personnel themselves had enough power to impact significantly on the armed forces, or even on society more widely. The fact that the equality agenda had not been advanced in society at large was thus seen as explaining the absence of military-society convergence. Rather than resisting change, the armed forces simply reflected prevailing social trends.

In addition, another assessment of the role of women in NATO showed the persistence of diversity across countries, particularly in recruitment and retention strategies, among

member states (Schjølset 2010). While in some West European and North American countries, a strong emphasis on strategies for reducing the gender gap in the armed forces
coincided with higher levels of female personnel, favorable numbers were not always
preceded by distinct recruitment and retention strategies. The UK and France, for instance,
seem to have been able to increase women's participation without many policy initiatives.
Conversely, countries that have implemented strong policies toward recruiting and retaining women did not always reach their quantitative goals. Scandinavian countries, such
as Norway, have not been able to reach the desired recruitment objectives. This is so despite
a variety of enabling conditions in place, including active recruitment policies, a high level
of female participation in public and political life, and a strong public discourse on gender
equality (see chapter 40, this volume). What this shows is that political efforts do not always
lead to practical success. Providing women with equal opportunities might not be enough
to motivate them for military service.

A more recent study highlighted the increased pressures exerted by public international
organizations such as the UN's move to promote gender integration under Resolution 1325,
or NATO's quest for standardization and consistency among member countries. Moreover,
domestic women's movements were also identified as another major factor contributing to
greater gender integration in the military (Obradovic 2014). A strong correlation seems to
exist between greater gender integration and growing civil-military convergence. Despite
each having a different focus, all these studies underline that gender integration in the military is shaped by various societal processes and not by a single major factor. Hence, both
domestic and international factors play a role in explaining the gender gap in the armed
forces. Against this background, it is now important to look at how, in these countries, military policies on the one hand, and actual results and practices on the other, reflect WPS
concerns and goals.

GENDER-RELATED POLICIES IN NATO

Two recent reports mapping the situation of women and gender policies in NATO between 1999 and 2015 identify remarkable progress in the reporting by member states
of specific gender policies or regulations in the armed forces (NATO 2015a; NATO
2015b). Despite the fact that only seventeen of the twenty-eight member states have developed national action plans for implementing Resolution1325 and related resolutions,
awareness seems to have grown significantly. While in 1999, only 21 percent of NATO
members indicated they had specific legislation targeting gender issues, in 2013 the
overwhelming majority (93 percent) did so. Progress has also been made in terms of
training, a key area under Resolution 1325. In 2000, no NATO member reported specific training on gender awareness, whereas in 2013, 63 percent informed of the existence of such training. Likewise, the establishment of workgroups monitoring national
action plans or supporting military women has shown an exponential growth from
only 4 percent in 2005 to 75 percent in 2013. The reports indicate that by 2015, over
two-thirds of NATO members had dedicated positions or departments supporting
gender integration in the armed forces as well as women's professional networks (see
chapter 28, this volume).

Another interesting development has been an increased focus on recruitment and retention policies for women. There is now a trend towards reducing gender disparities in enlistment processes and uniformity in physical and intellectual standards for men and women. In 1999, 26 percent of NATO members were reporting equal enlistment processes (identical competency and physical tests), and by 2015 this number had increased to 65.4 percent. Formal restrictions to women's access to different positions have also been reduced, and most intensely in the last couple of years. The percentage of countries that opened up all positions to women rose from 70.3 percent in 2014 to 85 percent in 2015. In what concerns gender specific training for operations, policies appear to be very positive. In 2015, more than 90 percent of NATO member nations reported the inclusion of gender in pre-deployment training and exercises, and more than 73 percent reported the inclusion of gender in operational planning (NATO 2015b: 30).

In a less positive vein, one of the reports (NATO 2015a) notes that although all NATO countries accept women in the armed forces, there are still countries that formally limit their full access to some positions, especially related to combat roles and submarines.

Another very important policy area regards sexual harassment and assault prevention. Here, the quality of data from the two reports raises considerable doubts. While in 2013 only 29 percent of the countries reported training concerning sexual assault prevention or sexual assault prevention advisors (NATO 2015a), in 2015 (only two years later) references are made to a much higher percentage of countries reporting such policies. Almost 80 percent of NATO member nations reported to have training and programs related to the prevention of sexual harassment. More than 60 percent reported strategies, appointed personnel, and developed formal procedures to prevent and report cases of sexual harassment against men and women (NATO 2015b).

Still, it is relevant to note that in 2015 the NATO Committee on Gender Perspectives highlighted the issues of sexual harassment and sexual and gender based violence (SGBV) as major challenges. The committee also stressed the way these problems degrade operational effectiveness and readiness as well as recruitment and retention. It made concrete recommendations to the Military Committee: "a. that leaders at all levels should uphold core values and standards of behavior to demonstrate their commitment to an environment free from harassment and SGBV and perpetrators (. . .); b. that Nations should create and implement a credible reporting process that collects data and drives appropriate support to victims of harassment and SGBV (. . .); and c. that Nations should seek to develop a gender advisor framework for their armed forces to build capacity in gender perspectives in order to enhance operational effectiveness" (NATO 2015b: 33).

One problematic aspect of the data used in these reports is that they do not allow for an in-depth description of the nature and contents of the policy measures referred to by each country. For instance, in the case of gender training, it is not possible to know whether such measures refer to a minimal approach, as in the inclusion of a single and fragmentary reference to gender in a syllabus, or to a consolidated and systematic approach in training schemes. This makes it impossible to fully evaluate the training focus, relevance, or impact. In some areas, however, it is possible, even if with some limitations, to compare policy goals and actual results.

THE CURRENT SITUATION OF WOMEN IN
THE ARMED FORCES

In the face of an obvious underrepresentation or absence of women from peace processes and conflict resolution instances, the WPS agenda has put great emphasis on the need to raise the number of women in military forces and missions. Various policy instruments, from the level of the resolutions to that of national action plans, urge decision-makers to redress the numerical imbalance between men and women in national forces and international military missions alike. As noted by Schjølset (2010), "[A]t both national and international levels, recruitment of women is believed to be strategically important both with respect to increasing military capacity to manage commitments relevant to defense and security, and with respect to exporting national identity abroad." The greater presence of women has been considered a necessary condition for narrowing the gender gap in military and security forces.

Skepticism has grown toward the so-called "nominal approach" to equality, whereby the focus is laid on raising representation levels without consideration of the structural asymmetries in the distribution of power and resources. This approach has been criticized for its supposedly excessive focus on numbers (Barnes 2011). "To add women and stir" is not enough to challenge structural inequality and foster real change (Darmaphuri, 2011). However, it has also been argued, with as much intensity, that a politics of presence is necessary even if not sufficient for transforming dominant structures of privilege and subordination. Theories of gender in organizational settings have put forward the idea that numbers affect the social experience of groups. Research on minorities in organizations and tokenism has shown the importance of relative numbers in determining the resources and possibilities for groups to influence power structures inside organizations (see for examples Kanter 1977). Other variables such as the level of intrusiveness, sex-typing of occupations or, most importantly, the social status of the minority group, must be considered too (Blalock 1970; Yoder 1991). Relative numbers cannot be excluded from the set of determinants of a group's power and performance in work settings.

Policies concerning representation and relative numbers are thus meaningful to understand the kind of environment where military training and socialization take place. In the NATO case, the overall pattern that emerges from a longitudinal analysis of representation indicates that the representation of women in the armed forces has been growing (see Figure 20.1). Moreover, spillover effects have been observed when new members joined the alliance (Obradovic 2014). In 2015, women represented 10.8 percent of the armed forces of NATO members, compared to 7.14 percent in 1999. While the data show a growth, women's representation increased at a rather slow pace, rising by 3.7 percent in sixteen years.

In what concerns women's presence in the occupational structure, data for 2015 confirm a preexisting trend. The majority of women are still concentrated in support areas, such as logistics and medical services, administration, finances, and personnel (79.3 percent), while a lower number is serving in operational areas such as infantry (12.5 percent) or technical

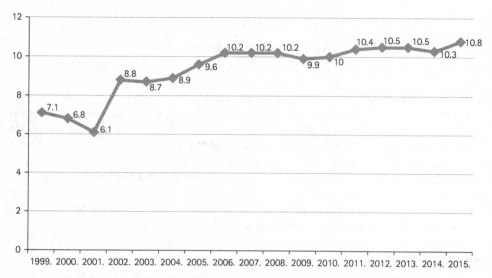

FIGURE 20.1 Percentage of women in the Armed Forces of NATO countries, 1999–2015.

Source: NATO (2015b: 9).

areas such as communications (8 percent) (NATO 2015b: 23). Strikingly, a study conducted in 2000 pointed to a very similar pattern showing that even if the relative weight of each of these different types of functions in the overall military organizational structure is taken into account, women were clearly over represented in the so-called traditional female areas (Carreiras 2006). The one remarkable exception in 2015 seems to be a rise in the percentage of women in combat areas such as infantry where only 7 percent of the women served in 2000.

The gender balance in terms of the rank structure is much less asymmetric. Data for 2015 show that if we compare the relative weight of men and women in each rank category within the overall military structure, the representation of men and women by rank is similar (see Figure 20.2).

Despite a notable increase in representation levels, and even considering that the proportion of women varies by occupation, unit, rank, or service in each country, global percentages with the exception of Hungary, the United States, and Latvia, point to a *token* situation where women represent less than 15 percent of the whole group. Being a minority of a less valued social status and often considered potentially intrusive, women have thus to face the usual consequences of tokenism. Women end up facing performance pressures due to excessive visibility, social isolation resulting from the exaggeration of differences, and boundary heightening, also referred to as encapsulation deriving from stereotyping.

The very slow pace of growth in women's representation levels and the still dominant pattern of occupational segregation are not consistent with the aims of WPS. They constitute major challenges that still hinder an effective implementation of the agenda. Hence, it comes as no surprise that one of the areas where greater incongruence exists between policies and actual practices is the involvement of women in international operations. While formal policies have been drawn concerning gender in operational training or a

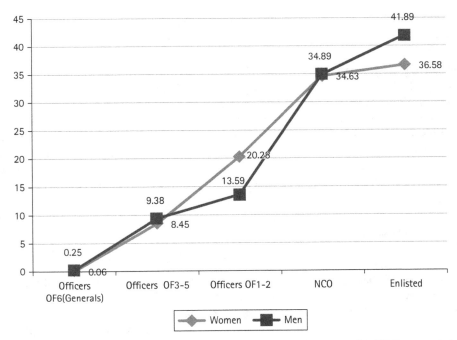

FIGURE 20.2 Percentage of men and women in the Armed Forces of NATO countries, by rank (2015).

Source: NATO (2015b: 25).

system of gender advisors, the actual proportions of women deployed in operations is in sharp contrast with policy orientations. For example, in 2015 women made up for only 6 percent of the personnel deployed in all types of operations by NATO member states, and 6.4 percent of the personnel deployed in NATO operations (NATO 2015b: 30). Even if this is a higher percentage than the one reported in UN operations where women make up for no more than 0–4 percent, it is far from mirroring the robust policy frame that NATO has been developing in terms of gender mainstreaming. Likewise, while the number of trained gender advisors has been increasing (from 381 in 2014 to 440 in 2015), only 33 (7.5 percent) have been deployed.[3]

Some reasons for these disparities have already been identified. Countries tend to select participants in international missions from more operational units that already have a lower representation of women in the first place. A deliberate lack of political will to involve women, however, as well as cultural resistances, cannot be ruled out as causes for the observed imbalance. One of the few studies that build on comparative empirical evidence on women's participation in peacekeeping, Karim and Beardsley's (2017) research concluded that there is a gender protection norm operating in decision-making about women's deployments that tend to keep women away from dangerous mission scenarios. They also show that in international military missions women face rampant discrimination; they are confined to particular gendered roles; and their participation is thwarted by "old boys networks" that prevent them from having influence within missions (Karim and Beardsley 2017).

CONCLUSION

One starting assumption of this chapter was that policies and practices of gender integration at the national level have a greater impact on what happens at the level of international operations than is usually assumed. Factors such as the ability to recruit and retain women; the existence of restrictions on positions that women can hold, especially in combat roles; awareness of the gender dimensions of security; and consequent attention given to gender mainstreaming in military training and socialization are particularly constraining in this respect. Research has shown that the number of women in national armed forces provides a pool from which international deployments depend. Meanwhile, missions consisting of personnel from member states with better records on gender equality, sexual exploitation, and abuse allegations are fewer (Karim and Beardsley 2017). However, the relation between national and international policies is not direct.

The data we analyzed show that the steady, even if slow, growth in representation of women in national militaries has not translated into an identical increase in women's presence in international military forces. That the relative success in recruiting and retaining women in national forces does not automatically reduce the gender gap in international missions should not detract from an equally pressing observation. Uneven gender representation, segregation, and lack of awareness within national contingents will strongly contribute to the gender gap at the international level. Data on gender occupational segregation in national forces or the disjuncture between apparently widespread gender operational training policies and the modest deployment of women to missions or even the cultural resistance therein, seem to confirm this argument.

There is also a second disjuncture to acknowledge. At both domestic and international levels, the fact that policies have been designed and implemented does not necessarily translate into effective results. While recognizing states that have made more formal commitments are more likely to carry out integration, "de jure policies do not automatically translate into de facto opportunities, and domestic interest groups know they must use both legal and political instruments to ensure that they do" (Williams 2000: 270). It is thus crucial to analyze the conditions under which the efficacy of policies vary by considering both external variables (e.g., institutional anchorage, articulation, or conflict with policies of other gender regimes), and internal features (flexibility versus rigidity, stability versus volatility, coherence, coordination, forms of implementation, and control).

The relation between domestic and international level policies is complex and multidirectional. This chapter has put emphasis on the need to examine national policies and its implementation, in the face of a lack of attention being directed to this policy level when it comes to evaluating accomplishments and gaps in the WPS agenda more globally. It is, of course, equally important to understand how international processes, actors, and institutions contribute to domestic policy change and cross-national policy convergence. This requires the development of comparative research that digs into the way different factors combine to explain policy decisions and processes.

While the endorsement of policy instruments at the international level often facilitates their diffusion, there are many factors that seem to complicate policy implementation at the national level. Policymakers' motivation for voluntarily adopting policy instruments cannot be exclusively explained by rational attempts to improve policy effectiveness. Policy adoption is often motivated by concerns of legitimacy and perceived pressure to conform with international norms (Busch et al. 2004). Even in cases where different instruments and policy measures related to WPS have been adopted, their adoption has probably been driven more by legitimacy concerns than by a rooted belief that such mechanisms and tools will positively affect military effectiveness. This hypothesis deserves and requires the development of further research.

One conclusion, however, can already be drawn. Both normative and structural shifts are necessary not only at the level of international missions and peacekeeping but also at the national level. Without aiming at a specific list of substantive recommendations, it would be crucial to strengthen the articulation and coherence of WPS related policies at different levels. This would probably require the reinforcement of mechanisms that favor policy diffusion not only through cooperative harmonization of domestic practices by means of international legal agreements or supranational law but also by means of more interdependent diffusion of practices through cross-national imitation, emulation, or learning.

NOTES

1. Major transformations in women's military roles happened in recent years, the most visible being the lifting of combat restrictions in the United States in 2013 and the announcement of a move in that direction in the UK. These changes were precipitated by the wars in Iraq and Afghanistan, which included both shifts in the deployment of women to combat areas and the frameworks behind those deployments.
2. In 2015, the Office of the Gender Advisor of the International Military Staff at NATO HQ (IMS GENAD), as the secretariat to the NATO Committee on Gender Perspectives (NCGP), began to forward a standardized online questionnaire to all NATO member and partner nations.
3. The interpretation of these findings requires great caution since the way different countries conceive or interpret the position of gender advisor might vary significantly. The disparity in numbers between the countries, varying for instance between 1 in the United States and 195 in Spain, does not allow for great trust in the validity of comparisons.

REFERENCES

Barnes, K., and E. Ikpe, eds. *Women, Peace, and Security: Translating Policy into Practice.* New York: Routledge, 2011.

Bastick, M., K. Grimm, and R. Kunz. *Sexual Violence in Armed Conflict: Global Overview and Implications for the Security Sector.* Geneva: DCAF, 2007.

Blalock, H. *Towards a Theory of Minority Group Relations.* New York: Capricorn, 1970.

Busch, P. O., H. Jorgens, and K. Tews. "The Global Diffusion of Regulatory Instruments: The Making of a New International Environmental Regime." *European Integration Online Papers* (EIoP) 8, no. 21 (2004).

Carreiras, H. *Gender and the Military, Women in the Armed Forces of Western Democracies.* London and New York: Routledge, 2006.

Carreiras, H. "Gendered Culture in Peacekeeping Operations." *International Peacekeeping* 17, no. 4 (2010): 471–485.

Dharmapuri, S. "Just Add Women and Stir?" *Parameters* 41, no. 1 (2011): 56–70.

Eulriet, I. "Towards More Coherence? Policy and Legal Aspects of Gender Equality in the Armed Forces of Europe." *Journal of European Integration* 31, no. 6 (2009): 741–756.

Forster, A. *Armed Forces and Society in Europe.* Basingstoke, UK: Palgrave Macmillan, 2005.

Hazelzet, H. "Gender and European Union's Common Security and Defense Policy." *Gender Violence in Armed Conflicts. IDN Cadernos* 11. Lisbon: IDN, 2013.

Kanter, R. M. *Men and Women of the Corporation.* New York: Basic Books, [1977]1993.

Karim, S., and K. Beardsley. *Equal Opportunity Peacekeeping.* Oxford: Oxford University Press, 2017.

Lackenbauer, H., and R. Langlais. *Review of the Practical Implications of UNSCR 1325 for the Conduct of NATO-Led Operations and Missions.* Swedish Defence Research Agency (FOI), 2013.

NATO. "UNSCR1325 Reload Report. An Analysis of Annual National Reports to the NATO Committee on Gender Perspectives from 1999–2013: Policies, Recruitment, Retention & Operations. Findings & Recommendations." NATO, 2015a, http://www.nato.int/issues/nogp/meeting-records/2015/UNSCR1325-Reload_Report.pdf.

NATO. "Summary of the National Reports of NATO Member and Partner Nations to the NATO Committee on Gender Perspectives." NATO, 2015b, http://www.nato.int/nato_static_fl2014/assets/pdf/pdf_2017_01/20170113_2015_NCGP_National_Reports_Summary.pdf.

Obradovic, L. *Gender Integration in NATO Military Forces: Cross-National Analysis.* Farnham, UK: Ashgate, 2014.

Olsson, L., and J. Tejpar, eds. *Operational Effectiveness and UN Resolution 1325—Practices and Lessons Learned from Afghanistan.* Stockholm: Swedish Defence Research Agency, 2009.

Schjølset, A. "Closing the Gender Gap in the Armed Forces: The Varying Success of Recruitment and Retention Strategies in NATO." *PRIO Policy Brief* 4, 2010.

Seifert, R. War and Rape: Analytical Approaches. Geneva, Switzerland: Women's International League for Peace and Freedom (WILPF) 1993.

UN Women. "Preventing Conflict, Transforming Justice, Securing the Peace. A Global Study on the Implementation of United Nations Security Council Resolution 1325." New York: UN Women, 2015.

Williams, John Allen. "The Postmodern Military Revisited." In *The Postmodern Military: Armed Forces after the Cold War*, edited by C.C. Moskos, J. A. Williams, and D. R. Segal. New York: Oxford Unviersity Press, 2000.

Yoder, J. "Rethinking Tokenism: Looking beyond Numbers." *Gender and Society* 5, no. 2 (1991):178–192.

CHAPTER 21

WPS AND POLICING
New Terrain

BETHAN GREENER

IN theory, the Women, Peace, and Security (WPS) and international policing agendas have the potential to work together to significantly advance peace, security, and gender justice objectives. As detailed in the part I of this handbook, the four main pillars of WPS are prevention, participation, protection, relief and recovery. Policing speaks to all of these. Although an immediate assumption may be that policing is primarily about protection, international policing arguably better serves prevention and participation objectives. Good police work, after all, aims to preempt and deter crimes before they can occur. In carrying out the role of protection, the police open public space. Moreover, gender mainstreaming efforts within policing institutions have increased the participation of women in public roles with high levels of authority. Finally, police can also play a role in relief and recovery, particularly through their contributions to the justice system.

Central to this chapter is the question: what impact has WPS had on international policing and vice versa? In attempting to answer this question, this chapter adopts a problem-solving approach. It seeks to identify how policing contributes, or could contribute, to the normative feminist aim of promoting gender justice (Ackerly and True 2010: 2)[1] by focusing on the relationship between international policing and the WPS agenda. It investigates the current status of women's participation in policing; the question of gender sensitive protection provided through policing; and the police's responsibility in supporting the WPS agenda on relief and recovery. It finds that a range of ideological and practical barriers have combined to stymie the promise of international policing in advancing the WPS agenda and vice versa. Yet it also notes recent achievements and advocates for an even closer working relationship between policing and WPS.

INTERNATIONAL POLICING

For the purposes of this chapter, "international policing" refers to both the policing of peace and stability operations, as well as to capacity building and police reform projects. The use of police in international settings has increased substantially since the 1990s. This is in part a response to the increasing number of peace and stability operations, and the broadening of roles undertaken within and after these operations (Greener 2011). This chapter speaks predominantly to UN engagement in international policing efforts given the significant policing numbers deployed, the range of missions undertaken, and the UN's centrality to international norm development around international policing.[2]

International policing roles have included stability-type tasks and capacity building–type tasks. Police personnel can potentially undertake more "active" roles in the earlier phases of a peace operation when an executive policing mandate can allow external police the power of arrest in circumstances where local law and order has broken down. Such roles tend to be sited within a robust peacekeeping or peace enforcement frame; and are rare occurrences, with Kosovo and Timor Leste being the main cases in point. With regard to the second category of capacity building, less obviously interventionist roles can occur either in later or more permissive stages in a mission, or they can occur within more generic security sector reform (SSR) efforts. These may involve external police in roles such as monitoring, training, mentoring, capacity building, or programs to "reform, rebuild, and restructure" existing police capabilities (Greener 2009). Significantly, gender training and gender mainstreaming is increasingly supposed to constitute an important part of such security sector reform efforts in UN and other missions (see Kleppe 2008; Bastick and Valasek 2008; Ibrahim et al. 2015).

In terms of concerns raised about the international policing agenda, there are doubts about the capacity of police personnel from outside a jurisdiction to successfully "police" or "reform" a local police service in an area that they are not connected to, nor necessarily very familiar with, or where they are reliant on local attitudes toward policing and reform efforts (Baker 2009: 329). The success of policing is also dependent on whether or not there is any local or international appetite or ability to press on with broader political, social, or security sector reforms (see O'Neill 2005). For example, in the Solomon Islands, efforts to reform the police were initially impeded by a failure to indict certain political "big fish" and a reluctance to address the root causes of conflict (see Braithwaite et al. 2010). Additional problems can also arise when the crucial working relationship between policing, justice, and corrections is not prioritized. The limited quantity and variable quality of the police personnel deployed in such missions pose barriers too.

There are never enough civilian police available to deploy on international operations in a timely fashion. In Africa, in 2009, for example, the UN Security Council had authorized the use of sixty-four hundred police for the UN Assistance Mission in Darfur (UNAMID), but were only able to deploy three thousand, while only six hundred of the fourteen hundred police requested were deployed for the UN Mission in the Congo (MONUC) (Williams 2009). The issue of getting enough police on the ground, particularly within short time frames, continues to be problematic with few missions ever reaching full deployment (Rappa 2016). Getting women to deploy has been even more challenging, as discussed in more detail in what follows. Concerns over quantity, however, have been overshadowed by concerns over the quality of police deployed in missions to date.

A lack of cultural sensitivity and language barriers have in the past been significant issues, and have exacerbated other problems, such as personnel lacking basic policing skill sets. Moreover, police operating outside of their own domestic jurisdictions tend to receive better pay while, at the same time, they may feel less ethical constraints and be less accountable to oversight mechanisms. This has led to claims that these personnel are not "securely grounded in 'local' and/or 'national' accountability structures" (Sheptycki 2007: 41). As such Hills suggested in 2009 that there was no evidence for any form of a global or transnational police ethic ensuring ethical behavior. Wiatrowski and Goldstone (2010: 82) similarly bemoaned the lack of international police that are able to "follow and teach the principles of democracy-friendly policing," which the UN seeks to instill.

Abuse of office, unwillingness to carry out policing tasks, or corrupt, immoral, or illegal behavior have been reported in a number of missions. These problems of quality have had gendered dimensions. Harris and Goldsmith (2010: 302) have noted how male-dominated international missions can allow the "old culture" of sexist policing to reemerge, potentially further enabling unacceptable behavior and compounding difficulties met in addressing that behavior. For example, in 2015, of the sixty-nine claimed instances of sexual exploitation and abuse (SEA) by UN peacekeepers, only twelve cases had resulted in charges being laid by May 2016. Eight of these charges were against military personnel, three against police, and one against civilian personnel. In early 2016, forty-four allegations of SEA had been recorded by the UN, four of which involved police (UN 2016). Even those countries which pride themselves on high standards of democratic and human rights–oriented policing at home have had to grapple with instances of those same police personnel engaging in crimes when deployed abroad in UN missions (see Code Blue 2016; Boutlilier 2017).

Given these problems, then, what are the possible benefits of the rise of international policing for the WPS agenda? Here we consider the WPS agenda and its four pillars, beginning with recognition that international police can play an important role in providing for the physical protection of individuals as well as in creating a more general protective and secure environment.

INTERNATIONAL POLICING AND WOMEN PEACE AND SECURITY

Prevention and Protection

Starting with the notion of "protection," the UN Police Vision to 2020 emphasizes that:

> UN Police play an important role in the protection of civilians, primarily in the second (physical protection) and third tiers (protective environment), as described in the 2010 DPKO/DFS operational concept (UN Police Division 2014: 9).

Protection is clearly stated here as a central objective of international policing. Prevention is also alluded to by the mention of a contribution to a "protective environment." Moreover, in carrying out these protection and prevention roles, the overall nature of the human rights–oriented model of policing being promulgated in international policing effort helps to create space for the WPS agenda.

The "United Nations Criminal Justice Standards for Peacekeeping Police" (UN Crime Prevention and Criminal Justice Branch 1994) constituted the first significant set of international policing guidelines. Drawing from lessons learned in Cambodia and Bosnia, it was created specifically for UN policing missions. This small blue book covers procedures for activities such as lawful arrest, the minimization of the use of force, and the humane handling of victims and prisoners. This emphasis on human rights–centered policing has become even more insistent in the UN in recent years (Bayley 2006: 8; author attendance at UN Police Division meetings in 2007 and 2009). Recent UN pre-deployment training materials seek to promote accountable, transparent, and humane approaches to policing among UNPOL and in sector reform efforts undertaken in country (UN DPKO 2009). Moreover, the minimization of the use of force, particularly lethal force, has continued to be a central theme in international policing mandates, doctrine and policy (Rotmann 2009). International policing provides a less militarized form of security in post-conflict and other sites; potentially aligning with feminist calls to demilitarize domestic and international society (Enloe 2000).

Having argued that policing is less militaristic and that the overall goal of policing is to build a web of trust and cooperation between police and the local community (Wiatrowski and Goldstone 2010: 80), however, it must be noted that the UN has also increased its use of more militaristic Formed Police Units (FPUs)[3] (UN Police Division 2014: 9). In 2016, FPU personnel accounted for almost three-quarters of deployed UN Police (Caparini 2017: 12). FPUs have come under fire for a variety of reasons including overzealous use of force and lack of discipline. There has been talk of revisiting the role of FPUs in UN missions (Durch and Ker 2013), and, notably, it could be useful to revise the use of FPUs to help further the WPS agenda as alternative models of civilian policing are more receptive to the WPS agenda.

Being "available," "helpful," and "fair and respectful," as per the ideal characteristics of civilian police officers (Bayley and Perito 2010: 84-6), combined with the shift toward a community policing focus (Fielding 1995; Fridell 2004), can help to challenge the hyper-masculine nature of policing and to increase space for WPS objectives. Indeed, it is significant that community policing has "implicitly embraced 'feminine' qualities" (Miller 1999: 68) although recent work underscores the ongoing gendered nature of policing writ large (Loftus 2009; Atkinson 2016). A civilian model of community policing also emphasizes the proactive prevention of crime as well as the creation of a "protective environment" that helps to care for the more vulnerable in society and to promote participation in public life—issues which are often gendered.

More specifically, there is an increasingly active interest in, and express promotion of, gender issues within the international policing arena. For example, the UN Police Division recently developed an overarching Strategic Guidance Framework for International Police Peacekeeping (SGF). This SGF is comprised of five policy documents. The first is fundamentally important, as it is the main strategic document which maps the overall roles and objectives of UN policing. The remaining four are subsidiary documents on administration, capacity building, command, and operations. The main strategic document, called the "DPKO/DFS Policy on UN Police in Peacekeeping Operations and Special Political Missions," directly emphasizes the need for UN police to "provide support that is gender-responsive" (UN DPKO and DFS 2014: 8).

Such policy developments have been explicitly connected to the WPS agenda, with express recognition that the eight UN Security Council Resolutions from 1325 onwards have helped motivate change (UN Police Division, n.d.). There is also a direct and prompt mention of the centrality of gender-mainstreaming and these WPS resolutions in a mid-2016 "External Review of the Functions, Structure, and Capacity of the UN Police Division."

The UN Police Division has therefore expressly recognized the centrality of a gender perspective, a phenomenon not necessarily matched by other UN agencies. Speculation might suggest that this is because of the nature of the job which requires interacting closely with an often traumatized population. Perhaps it is also a result of a growing recognition that the WPS agenda aids operational success.

In terms of how this translates into the practice of international policing, the UN Police Division runs standardized training for United Nations Police, including pre-deployment and in-service training which incorporates gender modules. In November 2015, a comprehensive UNPOL Gender Toolkit was then widely disseminated amongst UN police to help bring gender considerations further to the fore. This toolkit is a "repository of standardized processes, procedures, and templates on gender mainstreaming of policing in peacekeeping based on best practices" (UN Police Division 2016a: 19). Modules on gender mainstreaming in the mission, promoting gender equality in the host state, and capacity building of the host state in preventing and responding to SGBV are available free online. These packages are freely available for all UNPOL personnel, but they have also been promoted more widely through social media and other avenues—for example, being disseminated through a public Facebook campaign in early 2017. However, although UNPOL receive induction training that has a gender component in field missions which is compulsory, this induction training can vary depending upon the mission—particularly upon whether or not there are Gender Advisors or Gender Focal Points in those missions.

In addition, specific issues such as sexual abuse and exploitation (SEA) perpetrated by UN personnel are also now being more systematically addressed. In 2015, the UN Office of Internal Oversight Services (OIOS) released a formal evaluation of SEA issues (UN OIOS 2015a). Although some of its claims were challenged by the UN Department of Peacekeeping Operations (DPKO) and the Department of Field Services (DFS; see responses included at the end of the document), the report clearly outlined a number of salient difficulties met in halting SEA practices in missions. By the end of 2016, the UN had consequently added new recruitment protocols, implemented a member state investigation office and created Immediate Response Teams (IRTs) to respond to allegations of sexual abuse (UN 2016).[4]

Moreover, not only is it the case that the UN is looking to tackle problems among UNPOL themselves, but there is also a strong emphasis on improving gender-sensitive policing when deployed in mission. A case in point is South Sudan. Criticism about a lack of protection for civilians, particularly a lack of willingness to respond to instances of SGBV, had plagued the mission. Police officers were given additional SGBV training (Report of the Secretary General 2015) and new police escort initiatives put into place (Quinn 2017). Thus, although at times international policing personnel may fail in their duty to protect and serve, or may even perpetrate crimes themselves, these recent initiatives signal a willingness to bring gender more to the fore in policing missions. This argument is supported by independent evaluations (Donadio and Rial 2015: 30) and evaluations by the UN's Office of Internal Oversight Services, though the latter also notes that only a limited number of SEA perpetrators were arrested and that crimes still persisted (UN OIOS 2016: 24–26).

The implementation of efforts to inculcate gender-sensitive policing within UNPOL and across police reform efforts made by UNPOL is therefore still a little patchy. It is also still focused on narrower issues such as sexual violence—a concern raised by the 2015 *Global Study on 1325*, which noted that, of thirty-three benchmarks adopted by five peacekeeping missions, none specifically referred to gender-specific issues or gender equality. Of 105 indicators attached to these benchmarks, only 5 were on gender issues with most relating to sexual violence (UN Women 2015). However, these developments suggest that the *policy* frameworks around UN policing which take gender seriously may be starting to impact policing *practice*, and, perhaps, other initiatives might follow.

Finally in 2015, the UN Security Council adopted an unprecedented resolution focused solely on the role that UN police play in international affairs. Though not specifically geared toward advancing WPS, fundamental to UN Security Council Resolution 2185 are a number of assertions as to what role international police should be playing with regards to gender. For example, this policing resolution brings the WPS agenda to attention:

> *Taking note* of and *encouraging* the increased participation of female police in United Nations peacekeeping operations and special political missions, thereby contributing to the effectiveness of relevant mandate implementation, including by providing diverse perspectives which can assist in building trust with local communities; improving the protection of women and children from violence and abuse; and facilitating gender-sensitive police approaches and mentoring (UNSCR 2185 [2014]).

Indeed, encouraging female participation in UN policing has, in particular, been a major focus at the UN Police Division since at least 2009.

International Policing and Participation

We can begin a consideration of participation by asking "where are the policewomen"—both within contributing missions, and within countries that either host those international policing efforts. The "Global Effort" was initiated in 2009 to further gender-sensitive policing aims by recruiting more women to UNPOL positions. Concerted efforts have been made to increase the number of women deployed with the stated aim of deploying at least 20 percent women across UNPOL missions (UN Police Division, n.d.), an important effort, albeit short of the 35 percent recommended to initiate cultural change (Childs and Krook 2008). Since 2010, the UN's own Standing Police Capacity is also supposed to be populated by a minimum of 65 percent of members which have "gender" as an occupational specialization (UN OIOS 2015b: 15). This particular initiative potentially moves the UN away from an approach which merely focuses on "adding women" to solve gender issues and toward a more holistic understanding of some of the broader questions at play in the WPS agenda.

Yet the goal of "adding women" continues to be a major focus for UN policing and has been explicitly reaffirmed through Security Council Resolution 2242 in 2015, which calls for the UN to double its female police representation in five years. For example, an International Female Police Peacekeeper Network has been created. Interaction has been formalized with the International Association of Women Police in efforts to stimulate recruitment, retention and advancement (UN Police Division, n.d.; UN Police Division 2016d: 35). Recently strengthened UNPOL partnerships with groups such as UN Women (UN Police 2014: 17) and all-female training modules (since 2014) are also intended to support this objective (UN Police Division 2016c: 27).

Recent figures suggest that these initiatives will indeed help to increase numbers. In 2009, the number of female police officers stood at about nine hundred, or a total of seven percent of twelve thousand police deployed on UN missions. This had increased to thirteen hundred officers, or ten percent of thirteen thousand by 2016 (UN Police Division, n.d.). A specific national example of this dynamic at work is found in Rwanda in 2009. According to a UN Women report, there were only fifty serving female police officers in the whole national police force in 2009. Yet by 2015, Rwanda had become the top contributor of female police officers to UN missions with 114 women deployed overseas (UN Women 2016).[5] This case also highlights the fact that there have been significant increases in the proportion of serving female police in countries that have hosted international policing missions. Following concerted recruitment drives, and in a similar pattern to the Rwandan case noted earlier, there was a shift from females making up 6 percent of the Liberian police force in 2007, to them constituting 17 percent by 2016 (UN Women 2016; Bacon 2015). Note too that this phenomenon has also been repeated in non-UN police reform efforts. In Afghanistan in 2007, for example, there were only 475 serving police women, but after concerted recruitment efforts by external donors this had increased to 1,690 by early 2014 (Moetsabi 2014).

Some initiatives that have occurred along the way to "get more women in" have had a wide range of consequences. The UN deployment to Liberia included an all-female Formed Police Unit from India which aimed to increase local female participation in the police force. "Acting as visible role models while on guard duty, managing public order situations and during night patrols these officers helped inspire girls to join the police," thus tripling the number of women in the Liberian Police in a few years as previously noted (UN Police Division 2016a: 19; also see chapter 35 in this volume). The broader impact of role modeling is clear here. Yet, in addition to concerns about instrumentalization and overburdening these women police officers (see Pruitt's 2016 discussion about these women working a "double shift" as they carried out police and volunteer work in the community), FPUs have also been criticized for their more militarized approaches to policing, as noted earlier. This is based on their primary role as mobile units used to respond to public disorder and to disperse crowds (Durch and Ker 2013). Indeed the UN has an entirely separate doctrine for the specific use of FPUs in missions (UN DPKO 2009).

One issue here, then, is that trends show that the greatest increase in women as UNPOL has come from their engagement in FPUs (Donadio and Rial 2015: 18). Such a trend may in part be because many women police may not yet have the seniority needed to be deployed as Individual Police Officers (IPOs). Deployment of more women through FPU's does therefore provide another avenue for participation, and could potentially provide an entry point for women into other international policing roles. Such deployment may also have positive benefits for women who have traditionally been sidelined out of more active police roles (Pruitt 2016). However, research also needs to be done to ensure that 'getting more women in' via FPUs helps rather than hinders 'getting women in' via other IPO or Special Police Team (SPT) roles; civilian policing better aids the broader WPS agenda and mitigates militarization concerns.

The agenda to "get more women in" to international policing efforts is therefore gaining some ground but numbers remain limited. In 2016 women still only made up just over six and a half percent of FPU personnel and nineteen and a half percent of IPOs within UNPOL's ranks (Caparini 2017: 22). Moreover, even less examined is whether the increasing rates of women's participation in police services or in public spaces also lends itself to the "relief and recovery" aspect of the WPS agenda.

Relief and Recovery

The main aims of the WPS pillar on relief and recovery are undermined when the ability of women and girls to have their needs met, and their capacities to act as agents, are limited by broader political and social issues manifested in the police and justice sectors (see chapter 15, this volume). For instance, immediately after major UN operations in Timor Leste, women engaged in police and public roles to a greater degree than ever before (Myrttinen 2009: 13, 16). Opportunities for the advancement of gender justice were created. Yet despite initial promise, Timor Leste has demonstrated how difficult it can be for women to be fully accepted in policing roles; and for changes in the numbers of police women to aid gender justice overall. Thus, despite various UN missions having emphasized gender mainstreaming, despite SGBV constituting the bulk of crimes in Timor Leste, and despite increases in the number of local female police officers, the highest national police law did not make any mention of gender issues. Moreover, Vulnerable Person Units have been severely under resourced, and local police have been accused of a range of abuses including trafficking in women (Myrttinen 2009: 23–27). Notably, in this case these shortcomings were at least in part due to this being a case of "do as we say not as we do," with UNPOL practice not always living up to its rhetoric (Myrttinen 2014: 182).

Even in cases where female police are accepted to a certain degree it can be difficult to create sustainable change. In MINUSTAH, following a UN resolution which specifically focused on SGBV issues in Haiti (Donadio and Rial 2015: 15), international police purposefully trained female Haitian police officers on issues specific to SGBV. As one Canadian UNPOL member noted though, following their training, these women were instead given administrative tasks rather than investigating crimes of sexual violence or putting in practice the skills they had learned (Menard 2009: 4). As Harris and Goldsmith (2010: 296) suggest, "gender-sensitising a police force is not as simple as establishing rules [and recruiting more women], but may hinge on deeper change in the broader community."

If we exclude the notion of women being able to be active agents through their participation in political and social life in roles as policewomen, the pillar of "relief and recovery" is perhaps the least obvious when it comes to the contributions made by international policing. However, although not expressly considered here, such policing clearly contributes to a related site of action—that of the justice system—which in turn contributes significantly to relief and recovery. Moreover, at its best, an early "engendering" of a fledgling or reformed police service within a country (Harris and Goldsmith 2010) should help to further support shifts in societal attitudes away from gender discrimination, thereby enabling recovery processes. Also potentially key would be police engagement in post-conflict efforts, such as in responding appropriately to domestic violence, which can peak when men are demobilized after conflict, or in Truth and Reconciliation processes, which can address previous wrongs and enable restorative as well as retributive justice. This latter point is vital as recent research has suggested that a focus on formal retributive justice in international policing missions has at times resulted in an "entrenchment of patriarchal systems and attitudes, which has limited the ability of women to appeal to the state to defend their human rights" (Hawksley and Georgeou 2015: 135).

Despite all the difficulties previously noted, attempting both to support and encourage women into policing roles at international and domestic levels, and to recognize the need for gender-sensitive policing at home and abroad, is therefore fundamentally important to furthering the WPS agenda.

Conclusions: WPS and Policing

The relationship between international policing and the WPS agenda is fraught but also charged with potential. The deployment of international police officers has at times seen those officers fail to prevent or protect populations from SGBV, or has seen those officers themselves be charged with SEA crimes. Some of these issues have in part been enabled by a hyper-masculine environment in international policing missions. Such an environment has presented challenges not only for populations in countries hosting those missions, but also for women seeking to deploy in those missions alongside their male counterparts. It has contributed to the fact that the number of women deploying for international missions is *even lower* than those within domestic settings. Lastly, it contributes to difficulties in pushing through gender-sensitive policies and particularly practices. Yet there are some signs that the international policing and WPS agendas may be starting to achieve a degree of synchronicity.

Police offer a less militarized model for providing security in conflict and post-conflict zones. The human-rights based policing models being promulgated in civilian community policing efforts have moved international policing efforts toward a less hyper-masculine ethos. This shift not only opens up space within policing organizations for recruiting and retaining women but also lends itself to support for a more gender sensitive society as a whole. This model of policing contributes to the WPS goals of prevention, protection, and participation, as well as to relief and recovery. As society changes and sexism is challenged, the police as an organization which *reflects society* (Bayley 2001 and 2006) will also necessarily change in response to this. The police as an organization which both *constitutes and challenges society* may also help continue to present challenges to gender norms, particularly if international policing is able to act as a transmission belt for WPS values globally (Greener 2012).

International policing as a specific phenomenon can clearly contribute to WPS objectives and has increasingly referred in policy and practice to this gender agenda. UN training and policy now emphasize that female participation, the need for gender-sensitive policing, and gender equality are all fundamental to the success of international policing efforts. These aims are interrelated. Having more police women in police organizations begins to alter the nature of that organization. It then allows a different approach to the provision of security, which better supports female victims, enables women to be seen as sites of public authority and not just as victims, as well as encourages other women to challenge existing gender stereotypes.

The WPS agenda can similarly contribute to the betterment of international policing. Women are more likely to be successful in certain types of policing (Rabe-Hemp 2009). For instance, they use less lethal force (Paquette 2016) and far less complaints are laid against female police (Mazurana 2002). Therefore, efforts to generate more women in police uniforms in international and domestic settings could also have far reaching consequences for how populations are policed and for how policy priorities are developed. These factors, and recent developments that provide evidence for the assertion that gender is being taken seriously in the realm of international policing, mean that the international policing and WPS agenda still have the capacity to achieve greater things together.

Notes

1. The overarching system which promotes international policing action, particularly UN policing, is thus not directly challenged here. There are other works which have convincingly suggested that the UN peacekeeping system is a form of "riot control" (Pugh 2004) or "imperial policing" (Rubenstein 2010) and, more specifically, that UNSCR1325 and subsequent WPS resolutions are merely mechanisms for recognizing the validity of concerns about sexual violence in peacekeeping while at the same time "embedding opposition to violence against women within the militarized projects of political and economic transformation which characterize the new wars" (Harrington 2011: 566). Some aspects of these narratives about the nature of the international system are mentioned, but they do not constitute the main focus of this piece.
2. Currently the UN typically requires approximately fourteen thousand police annually for operational deployments; see the UN Police Division website for up-to-date data. Additional international policing efforts can be bilateral reform programs or regional programs, such as the police-led Pacific Islands Forum mandated Regional Assistance Mission to Solomon Islands (RAMSI), EULEX in Kosovo, or the EU Police Program in Afghanistan.
3. The UN Police Division (http://www.un.org/en/peacekeeping/sites/police/units.shtml) suggests that an FPU "consists of approximately 140 Police Officers, trained and equipped to act as a cohesive unit capable of accomplishing policing tasks that individual police officers could not address. Well-trained FPUs can operate even in "high-risk" environments. FPUs have three core duties: public order management, protection of United Nations personnel and facilities and support to such police operations that require a concerted response but do not respond to military threats."
4. However, some of the issues raised in the 2015 report appear to remain outstanding. These include the possibility for confusion around the legal status of police on deployment. Although typically dubbed a civilian for the purposes of law, thereby opening the possibility of being tried by the host state, at times police contributing countries have instead utilized the national repatriation and closed court-martial route, particularly in the case of Formed Police Units which sometimes operate under military chains of command, resulting in a lack of transparency and charges of impunity (UN OIOS 2015a: 17–18). Another note of ongoing interest was the disparate rate of convictions for police as opposed to military personnel charged with SEA crimes over the period 2010–2012—5.3 percent as opposed to 45.7 percent (UN OIOS 2015a: 20). There may well be more work to do here in teasing out these particular issues, but, overall, there are indications that the UN is attempting to enforce, and to clarify, a zero tolerance policy toward SEA (UN Secretariat 2003).
5. Fundamentally, too, this effort to increase the number of women working in international police missions has gone hand in hand with more localized efforts to increase the number of police women within national contingents. In terms of one of the UN's top police contributing countries (PCCs), for example, India has suggested it will seek to

reserve a minimum of one-third of its police positions at home for women (Young 2015). Other countries, such as New Zealand, have recently called for no less than an equal participation of men and women in their national police forces (Shipman 2017).

REFERENCES

Ackerly, B., and J. True. *Doing Feminist Research in Political and Social Science*. Houndsmills, UK: Palgrave, 2010.

Atkinson, C. "Patriarchy, Gender, Infantilisation: A Cultural Account of Police Intelligence Work in Scotland." *Australian and New Zealand Journal of Criminology* (2016): 1–18.

Bacon, L. "Liberia's Gender Sensitive Police Reform: Improving Representation and Responsiveness in a Post-Conflict Setting." *International Peacekeeping* 22, no. 4 (2015): 372–397.

Baker, B. "Policing Post Conflict Societies: Helping Out the State." *Policing and Society* 19 (2009): 329–332.

Bastick, M., and K. Valasek. *Gender and Security Sector Reform Toolkit*. Geneva: DCAF/OSCE / UN-INSTRAW, 2008.

Bayley, D. *Democratizing the Police Abroad: What to Do and How to Do It*. Washington DC: US Department of Justice, 2001.

Bayley, D. *Changing the Guard: Developing Democratic Police Abroad*. Oxford: Oxford University Press, 2006.

Bayley, D. H., and R. M. Perito. *The Police in War: Fighting Insurgency, Terrorism, and Violent Crime*. Boulder CO: Lynne Rienner, 2010.

Braithwaite, J., S. Dinnen, M. Allen, V. Braithwaite, and H. Charlesworth. *Pillars and Shadows; Statebuilding as Peacebuilding in Solomon Islands*. Canberra, Australia: ANU, 2010.

Boutlilier, A. "Alleged Sex Abuse by Peacekeepers 'Tip of the Iceberg.'" *Toronto Star*, January 14, 2017, https://www.pressreader.com/canada/toronto-star/20170114/281479276109704.

Caparini, M. *Challenges in Deploying Effective Police to International Peace Operations*. Oslo: NUPI, 2012, https://brage.bibsys.no/xmlui/bitstream/handle/11250/2451656/NUPI_Working_Paper_877_Caparini.pdf?sequence=2.

Carpenter, A. and C. Sharwood-Smith. "Developments in United Nations Police Peacekeeping Training." In *Police Organization and Training: Innovations in Research and Practice*, edited by M. R. Harberfield et al., 179–190. New York: Springer, 2012.

Childs, S., and M. L. Krook. "Critical Mass Theory and Women's Political Representation." *Political Studies* 56 (2008): 725–736.

Code Blue. "Media Highlights: Reports of Sexual Abuse by Canadian Peacekeepers in Haiti." Code Blue, August 2, 2016, http://www.codebluecampaign.com/archived-news/2016/8/1-1.

Donadio, M., and J. Rial. "The Women, Peace, and Security Agenda in the Year of Its Review: Integrating Resolution 1325 into the Military and Police; An Analysis Based on Three UN Missions: MINUSTAH (Haiti), MONUSCO (Democratic Republic of the Congo), and UNFIL (Lebanon)." Resdal, March 2015, http://www.resdal.org/The_Women_peace_and_security.pdf.

Durch, W., and M. Ker. *Police in UN Peacekeeping: Improving Selection, Recruitment, and Deployment*. Providing for Peacekeeping No. 6. New York: International Peace Institute, 2013.

Enloe, C. *Maneuvers: The International Politics of Militarizing Women's Lives*. Berkeley: University of California Press, 2000.

"External Review of the Functions, Structure, and Capacity of the United Nations Police Division." May 31, 2016, http://www.un.org/en/peacekeeping/documents/policereview2016. pdf.

Fielding, N. *Community Policing*. Oxford: Oxford University Press, 1995.

Fridell, L. "The Defining Characteristics of Community Policing." In *Community Policing: The Past, Present, and Future*, edited by L. Fridell and M. Wycoff, 3–12. Washington DC: Police Executive Research Forum, 2004.

Greener, B. K. "UNPOL: Police as Peacekeepers." *Policing and Society* 19 (2009): 106–118.

Greener, B. K. "The Rise of Policing in Peace Operations." *International Peacekeeping* 18 (2011): 183–195.

Greener, B. K. "International Policing and International Relations." *International Relations* 26, no. 2 (2012): 181–198.

Harrington, C. "Resolution 1325 and Post-Cold War Feminist Politics." *International Feminist Journal of Politics* 13, no. 4 (2011): 557–575.

Harris, V., and A. Goldsmith. "Gendering Transnational Policing: Experiences of Australian Women in International Policing Operations." *International Peacekeeping* 17, no. 2 (2010): 292–306.

Hawksley, C., and N. Georgeou. "Transitional Justice as Police-Building in Solomon Islands: Tensions of Statebuilding and Implications for Gender." In *Current Issues in Transitional Justice* (Springer Series in Transitional Justice 4), edited by N. Szablewska and S. D. Bachmann, 133–160. Switzerland: Springer, 2015.

Hills, A. "The Possibility of Transnational Policing." *Policing and Society* 19 (2009): 300–317.

Ibrahim, A. F., A. S. Mbayo, R. Mcarthy. *Integrating Gender in Security Sector Reform and Governance Tool 8*. Toolkit for Security Sector Reform and Governance in West Africa. Geneva: DCAF, 2015. http://www.dcaf.ch/Publications/Tool-8-Integrating-Gender-in-Security-Sector-Reform-and-Governance.

Kleppe, T. T. *Gender Training for Security Sector Personnel – good practices and lessons learned*. Geneva: DCAF, 2008. https://www.files.ethz.ch/isn/142762/Tool_12_Gender%20Training%20for%20Security%20Sector%20Personnel.pdf.

Loftus, B. *Police Culture in a Changing World*. Oxford: Oxford University Press, 2009.

Mazurana, D. "Do Women Matter in Peacekeeping? Women in Police, Military, and Civilian Peacekeeping." *Canadian Women Studies* 22, no. 2 (2002): 64–71.

Menard, A. Presentation 2. *UNSCR 1820: A Roundtable Discussion with Female UN Police Officers Deployed in Peacekeeping Operations*. Pearson Peacekeeping Centre, August 6, 2009, http://www.iansa-women.org/sites/default/files/newsviews/Roundtable%20Report_Women%20in%20POs_NYC%20Aug%20%2009.pdf.

Miller, S. L. *Gender and Community Policing: Walking the Talk*. Boston: Northeastern University Press, 1999.

Moetsabi, T. "Afghan Police Force Recruits Women to Fight Crime and Stigma." UNDP, Our Stories, 2014, http://www.undp.org/content/undp/en/home/ourwork/ourstories/afghan-women-join-police-force.html.

Myrttinen, H. "Poster Boys No More: Gender and Security Sector Reform in Timor-Leste. *Geneva Centre for the Democratic Control of Armed Forces Policy Paper No. 31*. Geneva: DCAF, 2009.

Myrttinen, H. "Do as We Say, Not as We Do? Gender and Police Reform in Timor-Leste". In *Security Sector Reform in Southeast Asia*, edited by F. Heiduk, 181–200. Houndsmills: Palgrave Macmillan, 2014.

O'Neill, W. G. "Police Reform in Post-Conflict Societies: What We Know and What We Still Need to Know." *International Peace Academy Policy Paper*, 2005, https://www.ipinst.org/wp-content/uploads/publications/polreferpt.pdf.

Paquette, D. "One Way to Curb Police Brutality That No One is Talking About." *Washington Post Online*, Wonkblog, July 14, 2016, https://www.washingtonpost.com/news/wonk/wp/2016/07/14/the-kind-of-police-officer-whos-less-likely-to-shoot-and-kill/?utm_term=.d7c09bdc3b95.

Pruitt, L. *The Women in Blue Helmets: Gender, Policing, and the UN's First All-Female Peacekeeping Unit*. Los Angeles: University of California Press, 2016.

Pugh, M. "Peacekeeping and Critical Theory." *International Peacekeeping* 11 (2004): 39–58.

Quinn, B. "Makeshift Justice the Only Recourse for Ill-Protected Women at South Sudan Camp." *The Guardian*, January 16, 2017, https://www.theguardian.com/global-development/2017/jan/16/makeshift-justice-ill-protected-women-south-sudan-un-camp-malakal-protection-of-civilians-sexual-violence.

Rabe-Hemp, C. E. "POLICEwomen or policeWOMEN?: Doing Gender and Police Work." *Feminist Criminology* 4, no. 2 (2009): 114–129.

Rappa, R. "The Challenges of Full Deployment on UN Peace Operations." *Global Peace Operations Review*. September 7, 2016, https://peaceoperationsreview.org/wp-content/uploads/2016/09/gpor_monthly_newsletter_sep_2016.pdf.

Report of the UN Secretary-General. "Sudan (Darfur)." Sexual Violence in Conflict, March 23, 2015, http://www.un.org/sexualviolenceinconflict/countries/sudan-darfur/.

Rotmann, P. *First Steps towards a UN Police Doctrine for Peace Operations 2001–2006*. Geneva: Geneva Centre for the Democratic Control of the Armed Forces, 2009.

Rubenstein, R. A. "Peacekeeping and the Return of Imperial Policing." *International Peacekeeping* 17 (2010): 457–470.

Rubin, A. "Afghan Policewomen Struggle against Culture." *New York Times*, March 1, 2015, https://www.nytimes.com/2015/03/02/world/asia/afghan-policewomen-struggle-against-culture.html?_r=0.

Sheptycki, J. "The Constabulary Ethic and the Transnational Condition." In *Crafting Transnational Policing: Police Capacity-Building and Global Policing Reform*, edited by A. Goldsmith and J. Sheptycki, 31–71. Oxford and Portland OR: Hart, 2007.

Shipman, J. "Police Want More Women on Beat." *Newshub*, January 14, 2017, http://www.newshub.co.nz/home/new-zealand/2017/01/police-want-more-women-on-beat.html.

UN. "Update on Allegations of Sexual Exploitation and Abuse in United Nations Peacekeeping Operations and Special Political Missions." May 17, 2016, http://www.un.org/en/peacekeeping/documents/updatesea.pdf.

UN Crime Prevention and Criminal Justice Branch. *United Nations Criminal Justice Standards for Peace-Keeping Police*. Vienna: United Nations Office at Vienna, 1994.

UN DPKO *UN Peacekeeping PDT Standards, Core Pre-Deployment Training Materials*, 1st ed., Unit 2—Part 2: "How UN Peacekeeping Operations Function." New York: UNDPKO, 2009.

UN DPKO and DFS. *UN Police in Peacekeeping Operations and Special Political Missions*. Policy, February 1, 2014, http://www.un.org/en/peacekeeping/sites/police/documents/Policy.pdf.

UN OIOS. "Evaluation of the Enforcement and Remedial Assistance Efforts for Sexual Exploitation and Abuse by the United Nations and Related Personnel in Peacekeeping Operations." Assignment No. IED 15-001, May 15, 2015a.

UN OIOS. "Programme Evaluation of the Standing Police Capacity." Assignment No. IED-14-012, June 12, 2015b.

UN OIOS. "Evaluation of the Results of National Police Capacity-Building in Haiti, Côte d'Ivoire, and the Democratic Republic of the Congo by United Nations Police in MINUSTAH, UNOCI, and MONUSCO." Assignment No. 16-014, September 29, 2016.

UN Police Division. *Global Effort and Gender Initiatives*. United Nations Police [website], n.d., http://www.un.org/en/peacekeeping/sites/police/initiatives/globaleffort.shtml.

UN Police Division. "UN Police Towards 2020: Serve and Protect to Build Peace and Security—A Vision and Multi-year Strategy." UNPOL, March 2014, http://www.un.org/en/peacekeeping/sites/police/documents/2020.pdf.

UN Police Division. "Developing a Professional Police Service in Liberia." *UN Police Magazine* 13 (2016a): 18–19.

UN Police Division. "Launching the United Nations Police Gender Toolkit." *UN Police Magazine* 13 (2016b): 28–29.

UN Police Division. "Taking Stock of Gender Mainstreaming and Increasing Female United Nations Police." *UN Police Magazine* 13 (2016c): 26–27.

UN Police Division. "Police Women in Peace Operations." *UN Police Magazine* 13 (2016d): 35.

UN Secretariat. "Secretary-General's Bulletin: Special Measures for Protection from Sexual Exploitation and Abuse." ST/SGB/2003/13, October 9, 2003, https://oios.un.org/resources/2015/01/ST-SGB-2003-13.pdf.

UN Security Council Resolution 2185. (2014). http://www.securitycouncilreport.org/atf/cf/%7B65BFCF9B-6D27-4E9C-8CD3-CF6E4FF96FF9%7D/s_res_2185.pdf.

UN Women. "Keeping the Peace in an Increasingly Militarized World." In *Transforming Justice, Securing the Peace. A Global Study on the Implementation of United Nations Security Council Resolution 1325 (2000)*. Lead author: Radhika Coomaraswamy. UN Women, 2015, http://wps.unwomen.org/pdf/en/GlobalStudy_EN_Web.pdf.

UN Women. "Women Police Climb the Ranks across Africa." UN Women, April 12, 2016, http://www.unwomen.org/en/news/stories/2016/4/women-police-climb-the-ranks-across-africa.

Wiatrowski, M. D., and J. A. Goldstone. "The Ballot and the Badge: Democratic Policing." *Journal of Democracy* 21 (2010): 79–92.

Williams, P. "Peace Operations in Africa: Seven Challenges, Any Solutions?" *Conflict Trends*, October 2009, https://journals.co.za/content/accordc/2009/3/EJC16058.

Young, G. "Women on the Beat: How to Get More Female Police Officers around the World." *The Guardian*, July 28, 2015, https://www.theguardian.com/global-development-professionals-network/2015/jul/28/women-police-afghanistan-pakistan-india.

....

CHAPTER 22

WPS, STATES, AND THE NATIONAL ACTION PLANS

....

MIRSAD MIKI JACEVIC

OVER the last decade, the international community, national governments, and local civil society organizations have dedicated attention and resources to realizing the objectives of the United Nations Security Council Resolution 1325 through national action plans (NAPs). Since 2005, NAPs have become tools for institutionalizing the Women, Peace, and Security (WPS) agenda. These plans aim to "translate" international legal framework around WPS, Resolution 1325, and seven subsequent resolutions, plus many operational documents and guidelines, into a domestic strategy with specific national and local objectives. Currently, sixty-five countries have adopted such strategies and twelve more are underway. NAPs are a fairly recent approach, with more than 70 percent adopted since 2010.[1] As some time-bound plans have expired, governments have revised and renewed them: seventeen countries have issued a second NAP, and six of those countries are on their third or fourth. Governments now recognize that NAPs enable them to collaborate with grass-roots organizations on projects that enhance security at the local level, while at the same time fulfilling their international obligations.

Yet, significant gaps remain between the promise of NAPs and the goal of safer, more stable countries and local communities. Inclusive Security's "high-impact NAP" methodology posits that these plans *can* achieve this goal when inclusively designed, effectively monitored and evaluated, adequately resourced, and fully supported politically. Using this framework and illustrative country examples, this chapter reviews NAP progress and challenges to date, critically examines the current "state of the field" and emerging trends, and offers lessons learned to translate WPS commitments into action.

HISTORY OF NATIONAL ACTION PLANS

....

In October 2000, the UN Security Council unanimously passed Resolution 1325, calling for equal participation of women in preventing violence, stopping war, and helping rebuild communities and countries after the conflict. The resolution recognized that women, who

typically suffer disproportionally in war, are also critical agents in building peace and security. Two years later, UN Women (then UNIFEM) commissioned Elisabeth Rehn and
Ellen Johnson Sirleaf (2002) to independently assess and document women's critical peace-
building roles in conflict-affected countries. This report highlighted an immediate, apparent need to effectively translate this international framework into actionable changes at
the national and local levels. As early as 2002, the Security Council began recommending
"national action plans." Despite repeated calls to operationalize Resolution 1325,[2] it took
several more years until the first NAP was launched by Denmark in 2005.

There are various forms in which governments have attempted to institutionalize this agenda
in their policymaking. Some governments, like Thailand and Colombia for example, include
provisions on peace and security in their overall gender equality plans. Others, like Albania,
mention gender in the commitments of different departments, like the Ministry of Interior
"Action Plan on Diversity" and Ministry of Defense "Human Resource Policy." There are also
plans and strategies with broader implications for multilateral organizations, including the
European Union, Organization for Security and Cooperation in Europe, the African Union,
and the Pacific Islands Forum, among others. Finally, some countries have bound together to
create regional plans. For example, the Bujumbura Plan of Action brought together thirty-two
representatives of the governments of Rwanda, Burundi, and the Democratic Republic of the
Congo (DRC), together with the Conference of the Great Lakes region for the period from
2009 to 2012 to focus on increasing women's mediation efforts in that region.

For the purpose of this chapter, I focus on a "typical" strategy, developed at a country
level. A national action plan on Resolution 1325 is an official government policy that

- explains the national and international legal and policy framework on WPS;
- articulates a government's commitments and priorities regarding WPS;
- outlines specific actions that various ministries, agencies, and institutions will undertake to fulfill commitments and achieve change;
- promotes coordination across these governmental bodies and (in some instances)
  clarifies the specific role and contributions of civil society;
- offers additional tools for successful implementation, such as monitoring and evaluation (M&E) systems or coordination structures;
- specifies human, technical, and financial resources needed for implementation; and
- explains the reporting and accountability measures.

WHY DEVELOP A NAP?

In recent decades, the world has grown more violent: 2015 saw 121 recorded armed conflicts,[3]
and in 2014, more people died in war-related battles than since the end of the Cold War
(Pettersson and Wallensteen 2015). One in every 113 people on the planet is currently displaced by violence, the highest number ever recorded.[4] Plainly, traditional approaches to
peace and security are failing. We need to employ all available assets to prevent wars and
end conflicts including an often overlooked but critical resource: women.

Though causal links are difficult to establish with existing data, NAPs can help reduce a country's gender gap and this, in turn, increases stability and fosters peace. Over 60 percent of countries with NAPs have grown more peaceful since adopting them,[5] and nearly 90 percent of countries with NAPs have seen their gender gap shrink.[6] Furthermore, more than 40 percent have seen an increase in GDP growth.[7] Increasingly, research demonstrates that women's contributions to peace and security matter. Overall trends are indicative of women's critical contributions to stabilizing their countries and communities: A peace agreement is more likely to last at least fifteen years if women participate in its creation;[8] higher levels of female participation in parliament reduce the risk of civil war (Melander 2005); and, gender equality is a better predicator of a state's peacefulness than other factors, such as democracy or national wealth (Hudson et al. 2012). These are just a few examples of evidence showing that women's empowerment and gender equality are associated with stability (Hudson et al 2015). Simply put, investing in these plans and facilitating direct investments in women's contributions to conflict prevention and resolution is just smart governance. If properly designed, and implemented with serious commitment, including political will and adequate funding, these plans have shown a potential of being a tool for making this agenda institutional.

True (2016) analyzes the global patterns of the spread of WPS policies through the vehicle of NAPs, which mark a key phase in the diffusion process from international to national jurisdictions. According to a dataset, which includes fifty-five NAPs up to December 2015, the following factors increase the chances that a country will develop a NAP:

- Unreserved adoption of CEDAW (the Convention to End All Forms of Discrimination against Women) Treaty;
- The degree of democracy;
- The presence of women in power (in both parliament and the executive);
  - Countries adopting NAPs have 24 percent women ministers whereas non-adopting states have just 16 percent women ministers (global average is 18.5 percent);
  - Countries adopting NAPs have 24 percent women in parliament versus non-adopting states have 18 percent (global average in 2015 was 22 percent);
  - Based on descriptive evidence, additional elements also matter for WPS norm diffusion:
- Period effects—many of NAPs were adopted around the tenth anniversary of 1325;
- A country's engagement in transnational advocacy networks;
- A country's membership in an intergovernmental organization that has committed to implementing the WPS agenda (for example, 57 percent of NATO members, 61 percent of EU members, and 57 percent of the Organization for Security and Cooperation in Europe (OSCE) members have NAPs. But just 20 percent (i.e., two) countries have NAPs in ASEAN, a regional organization that has not committed to implementing WPS).
- The majority of states with a NAP are Northern and/or developed nations (thirty out of fifty-five) but many different types of states adopt NAPs, including countries affected by conflict and those not affected by conflicts. This shows that NAPs are not just taken up by fragile, conflict-affected countries under the tutelage of international organizations or powerful states.

- Even though the adoption and implementation of NAPs is slow, True (2016) concludes that "the relationship between prior commitments to women's rights, democratic governance, the presence of women in positions of political power, and the adoption of NAPs regardless of a country's conflict or non-conflict status, together suggest strong potential for future WPS policy diffusion and norm alignment across states."

However, several words of caution are due. As the rest of this chapter will show, making rhetorical proclamations and using NAPs as a "check the box" exercise does not represent actual "institutionalization" of WPS. Major gaps remain. First, most governments still need to create a plan in the first place; more than two-thirds of UN member states do not have a NAP. Of those that have, none have really reached "high impact." Most inaugural NAPs focus heavily, sometimes exclusively, on intra-governmental processes and require or show little actual progress; many of those include vague objectives like "awareness raising" without any clarity of intended results. The weakest link, both in the technicial and conceptual application of NAPs, is their capacity to monitor implementation and explain actual change in the lives of ordinary people in conflict areas. In some cases, both civil society and governments view Resolution NAPs as a "panacea" for addressing all gender issues and gaps, some of which might be better addressed in other specialized programs and policies. As I will show, there are some attempts at good practice, which focus more on actual change, not just the process and path to creating "High Impact NAPs." Still, much criticism remains, and it is premature to proclaim any real successes. These plans, however, are a tool that have the potential of ensuring that women, peace, and security commitments become more systemic and permanent. In short, to enable this agenda and ensure its effectivness, many other tools (policies, programs, projects, Networks) need to be strengthened, and, hopefully, complement and supplement the efforts of the NAPs.

Inclusive Security is an international advocacy organization focused on realizing the promise and potential of Resolution 1325. Its National Action Plan Initiative has provided technical assistance to over thirty governments to create, implement, monitor, and evaluate national action plans (NAPs) and similar inter-agency policies. This experience points to many other critical reasons to develop these strategies. First, NAPs focus on concrete actions that lead to changes in attitudes, behaviors, and policy, with an emphasis on mainstreaming issues of gender into the national peace and security agenda. For example, after Bosnia and Herzegovina implemented two NAPs (NAP I 2010–2013; NAP II 2014–2017), the number of women participating in international peace missions tripled. Significantly, women now lead their deployment units.[9] Additionally, the inclusive design processes needed to create an effective NAP often result in increased cooperation across government ministries and agencies. In Afghanistan, the 2015–2019 NAP was the product of several years' collaboration between representatives from more than twenty institutions that worked to create strategies to enhance inclusive security at the local level. As a result, the Ministry of Hajj and Religious Affairs instituted a regular monthly sermon calling for tolerance, and emphasizing respect for women's rights (Jacevic 2014).

Next, in several cases NAPs have presented a coordinated platform to channel international aid to specific projects that the national government prioritized with local civil society. During the International Colloquium from Women's Leadership in Peace and Security in Monrovia, Liberia, in March 2009, the organizers facilitated direct linkages to fund projects in security sector reform and transitional justice, which were clearly outlined in the Liberian NAP (Braun 2009).

NAPs also allow unique opportunities for government representatives to constructively engage with nongovernmental actors. This is a relatively new phenomenon and extremely complex for policymakers, as peace and security matters are often a sensitive topic for any government. The potential for engagement was highlighted in a 2016 report that analyzed the design and implementation of national polices in Serbia, the Philippines, Sierra Leone, and the DRC, four countries that all adopted their NAPs in 2010. Their political, social, and economic contexts vary widely, and importantly, recent conflicts in each country played out very differently during the course of the NAP's implementation, from ongoing violence in Eastern Congo to the negotiations in Mindanao to the Ebola crisis in Sierra Leone. Interviews with scores of government officials at all levels, representatives of international community, civil society actors, and women leaders all pointed to the opening channels of communication and improvement in their collaboration. The inquiry's main finding states,

> Indeed, this otherwise uncommon participatory policymaking has become standard practice for creating NAPs around the world. It brings to life the spirit of inclusion set forth in Resolution 1325 and is particularly significant in the aftermath of conflict, when there is a need to build trust between citizens and the state and to increase communication around peace and security issues. In particular, the involvement of civil society organizations as intermediaries between citizens and political elites allows for increased participation by women, who often faces greater barriers to entry in other intermediary structures such as political parties (Amling and O'Reilly 2016: 5).

HIGH IMPACT NAP METHODOLOGY

Based on extensive field work and contacts with women leaders in scores of conflict affected countries, along with direct engagement with more than thirty governments, Inclusive Security identified four key challenges in the design and implementation of NAPs: (1) lack of political will; (2) failure to include relevant design and monitoring and reporting methods; (3) no defined budget or timeline; and, (4) lack of "buy-in" due to limited or no consultation with a wider set of government agencies, as well as groups like civil society, minorities, and men. In an effort to address identified gaps and begin bridging this divide, Inclusive Security developed the "high-impact national action plans" methodology to guide the work with national governments and multilateral institutions. The term and concept first appeared in the monitoring and evaluation guide, *What Matters Most: Measuring Plans for Inclusive Security*, and was also cited in the National Action Plan chapter of UN Women's 2015 Global Study on the implementation of Resolution 1325.[10]

A NAP on the path to being high-impact has the following four elements:

1. Inclusive design process and established coordination system for implementation;
2. Results-based monitoring and evaluation plan;
3. Identified and allocated implementation resources; and
4. Strong and sustained political will.

Instead of providing a "wish list" of unrealistic goals or unclear targets, a high-impact NAP (see Figure 22.1) signals a government's commitment to the principles of Resolution 1325

4. STRONG AND SUSTAINED POLITICAL WILL

A NAP's success depends on the commitment of key policymakers, at leadership and technical levels.

1. INCLUSIVE PROCESS AND COORDINATION STRUCTURE

2. RESULTS-BASED MONITORING & EVALUATION SYSTEM

An inclusive process for designing and implementing the NAP helps to ensure that the priorities and needs of diverse constituencies are addressed, and contributes to a greater sense of legitimacy, buy-in, and ownership of the plan across communities.

An established body of knowledge suggests that national plans are more likely to be realized if (1) they are designed with results in mind, (2) they are measurable, and (3) there is a plan for monitoring and evaluation to track implementation.

3. RESOURCES IDENTIFIED AND ALLOCATED

The activities in the NAP need to be realistically analyzed for cost, and the plan itself requires a corresponding and sufficient budget for realizing its objectives and activities.

FIGURE 22.1 Qualities of a high-impact NAP.

Source: Amling and O'Reilly (2016: 5).

through designating responsibilities, establishing reporting measures to ensure accountability, and encouraging coordination and dialogue among governments, civil society organizations, and other groups tasked with realizing a country's NAP.

Component 1: Inclusive Design Process and Coordination System for Implementation

An inclusive design ensures the various government ministries and agencies responsible for the NAP are represented in both the creation and implementation of the plan. This also requires a coordination system that allows for increased communication and efficiency. In the case of Bosnia and Herzegovina (2014–2017), the Gender Agency leads the Coordination Board, comprised of twenty government institutions and one civil society representative. Following on a request for membership from the Agency, each of the ministries and agencies appoints its own representative, typically a mid-level technical civil servant (though often not with background in gender). Civil society, which is organized in a separate network supported by the UN Women country office, nominates its representative, like in almost all other countries, with the notable exception of the Netherlands, civil society representation is much smaller, compared to the government officials. Importantly, many of its twenty-five members were deeply involved in developing the first and second Bosnian NAPs and were also responsible for implementation of the plan. To increase effectiveness of their operations, the Agency adopted Terms of Reference for each member with explicit roles and responsibilities, which enhanced individual contributions, continuity, and collective coordination. Similarly, for Liberia's NAP (2009–2013), the Liberian government created a National Steering Committee (NSC) that brought together gender focal points in fourteen ministries and each relevant government institution, including the National Parliament and security sector services. This national body coordinates with County Steering Committees (CSCs) in place to further strengthen Liberian NAP localization, which includes representatives of local police forces as well as boarder police and immigration officials, and a Civil Society Monitoring Observatory group tasked with implementing activities and producing a shadow report.

Ideally, civil society groups should be involved from the very start of the process and formally included in the coordination mechanism, as equal partner to its governmental counterparts in all stages of design, implementation, and monitoring of the plan. This structure should include representatives from the main implementing ministries and institutions, as well as those whose contributions are important, such as statistical agencies and members of Parliament. Ideally, the coordination board will clearly define roles and responsibilities for its members to facilitate transparent decision-making. Inclusive processes also mean that civil society and other stakeholders have been consulted not only throughout the design process, but also within validation workshops and meetings *prior* to the plan's adoption, as this is often where critical recommendations are made about what activities to take and how to measure their effectiveness. In many cases, it is then the Coordination Board that decides and implements those recommendations; in other instances, the decisions are made by the higher political authority like the Cabinet or the Prime Minister's office; yet in other, the main implementing ministry creates the actual final framework for implementation—still, the main point is that along this path, input is sought and included from civil society organizations. For instance, Afghan Women's Network (AWN), the leading umbrella organization of over one hundred women's NGOs, greatly shaped the development of the Afghan NAP. Its representatives, Samira Hamidi and Hasina Safi, were members of the NAP Steering Committee from the very first meeting. In addition to coordinating this national network, they had been working on WPS issues both regionally and internationally, so their experience and pragmatic approach helped inform the process and build the capacity of the government representatives, most of whom had little exposure to Resolution 1325. Based on their positive contributions to the Steering Committee, the Ministry of Foreign Affairs, which coordinated the NAP creation, partnered with AWN to lead six provincial consultations across the country to ensure input from local government and civil society representatives.

Effective civil society integration was also a hallmark of the Netherlands NAP creation process, where Dutch civil society groups played key roles throughout all three iterations of the Netherlands NAP (2008–2011, 2012–2015, and 2016–2019). The second NAP (2012–2015) was the first ever to be co-signed by civil society, with more than fifty civil society and academic institutions partnering with the Dutch government on joint implementation. While coordination challenges remain, having the Dutch NGOs as official co-signers of the policy ensured both their ownership of its implementation, and also more effective advocacy from "inside" the structures. Additionally, it provided a concrete example of the "revolutionary potential of the UN Security Council WPS mandates" (True 2016) to concretely and jointly work from all sectors to realize the promise of 1325 and related resolutions.

There are three core challenges to an inclusive design and coordination process:

1. Confusion regarding civil society's role and a lack of transparent civil society engagement mechanisms

Japan in 2015 provides a good example of this challenge. Despite a transparent NAP drafting process involving twelve meetings and six local consultations, Japanese civil society reported that the Ministry of Foreign Affairs made significant last minute changes to the plan without further consultation or consensus. Specifically, the "term 'gender' was deleted almost completely in the Japanese language version and replaced by other terms with different implications and connotations."[11]

2. Lack of local stakeholder involvement

The Global Network of Women Peacebuilders (GNWP) has championed localization of 1325 across dozens of countries; they also supported the localization of Sierra Leone's NAP (2010–2014) at the community level across all fourteen districts. As the Ministry of Social Welfare seemed to have a better presence in some local districts over others, these localization activities had varied results. In Moyamba district, for example, the local government officials reported little awareness of the NAP and, despite having an office in the district, the Ministry could not report on any implementation activities (Amling and O'Reilly 2016:5).

3. Lack of coordination focal points or explicit "terms of reference" for implementing and coordinating institutions

In Indonesia, all twenty-four ministries that signed on to the NAP (2014–2019) make up the coordinating committee and must be consulted at decision-points. However, there are no formal ministerial focal points, and this has led to cumbersome coordination and a lack of sustained institutional knowledge.[12] Even when appointed, focal persons change often, are not empowered to make decisions on behalf of their ministries, and usually assume this responsibility as an "add-on" to their already busy work portfolios.

Component 2: Results-Based Monitoring and Evaluation plan

A results-based monitoring and evaluation (RBM&E) process takes implementation-focused M&E a step further, addressing the "so what?" question regarding data collection. A results-based plan is just that: A plan designed with results in mind (see Figure 22.2). It includes a framework or matrix linking one step to the next, assigning lead and supporting agencies responsible for implementing actions, and reporting on measurable qualitative

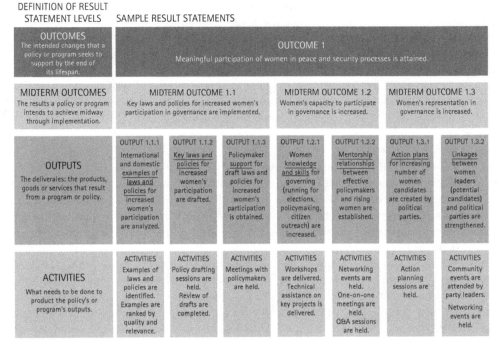

FIGURE 22.2 Sample logical framework.

Source: Lippai and Young (2014).

and quantitative indicators. These benchmarks of success are critical for several reasons; one, they can verify if the intended change has been achieved or how much progress has been made toward reaching the goal. Second, developing indicators can be a useful exercise in the design phase that can make the actual implementation process much easier. In several countries I have worked in, government officials and civil society representatives often report that using the activities to make SMART (specific, measurable, achievable, relevant, and time-bound indicators) allows them to "translate" intended results into a set of concrete actions with specified results. Third, if used in the NAP or its accompanying M and E plan, indicators allow us to track and make often-needed course corrections in real time, rather than to wait for the end of the implementation cycle. Finally, and most relevantly, indicators are the key part of "NAPs' story board" allowing for clear and specific answers to the question, "what difference have we made?" A "High Impact NAP" should tell a story of change, in terms of policy, process, and impact, with both data and narratives that will encourage further investments and improvements in making the WPS agenda more institutional. The NAP design framework specifies clear reporting mechanisms, time frames, and budget for all activities. Lead implementing agencies should report annually (or otherwise regularly) on results and produce both midterm and final reviews. Results-based planning enables implementers and policymakers to determine midterm outcomes and activities that build to the final objectives. Transparent roles and responsibilities and clear links from one step to the next provide the foundation necessary for relevant actors to monitor progress and evaluate results of the NAP.

Angelic Young, director of the NAP program at Inclusive Security, worked in partnership with UN Women to support the Jordanian National Commission for Women (JNCW) to draft Jordan's first National Action Plan (JONAP, expected 2017). The JONAP is supported by a logical framework that includes SMART (specific, measurable, achievable, relevant and time-bound) outcomes, mid-term outcomes, outputs, and indicators. It will be accompanied by a monitoring and evaluation strategy. The process has been inclusive; JNCW convened a group of key government and civil society leaders to form a JONAP Coalition. The Coalition is the body responsible for designing the JONAP; a steering committee comprised of senior government representatives will approve the final document.

While a few national action plans have included such frameworks with specified outcomes, outputs, and indicators, the vast majority of NAPs are missing RBM&E elements throughout their design and implementation. Finland's NAP (2012–2016) lacked specific activities with assigned responsibilities, leaving too much room for interpreting which ministry or department should implement each section of the NAP. The Finnish government dedicated significant resources and political will to this agenda; for example, they pioneered the twinning concept to assist governments and civil society in Afghanistan, Nepal, and Kenya to create their NAPs. Despite these initiatives and overall Finnish leadership on this agenda globally, the lack of a clear logical framework and system to track actual achievements led to a situation where results were neither captured nor attributed. In another case, the second Dutch NAP (2012–2015) purposefully left out set indicators and detailed action plans to maximize flexibility to rapidly changing contexts.[13] Indistinct roles and responsibilities, coupled with a lack of defined indicators and reporting guidance, resulted instead in inconsistent data collection and under reporting. Additional core challenges to implementing an RBM&E plan include a lack of technical capacity and skills, and a dearth of dedicated resources. Finally, committing to monitor progress is inherently a political decision; sometimes, measurement of performance may be embarrassing or resisted by some ministries.

Component 3: Resources Identified and Allocated for Implementation

Inadequate human, technical, and financial resources are most often the biggest reported barriers to implementing the NAPs and realizing WPS objectives. An effectively financed NAP should include appropriate amounts costed out prior to implementation, and a budget allocating sufficient funds to NAP implementation activities. Ideally, a transparent financing mechanism is put in place and dedicated funds are then disbursed to implementing agencies with clear guidance on how to track and report on received funding. While all governments operate under resource constraints, funding for WPS activities should be made available and dedicated. The UN Secretary-General's Seven-Point Action Plan (2010) on Gender-Responsive Peacebuilding stated that 15 percent of post-conflict project funding should be dedicated to addressing gender-equality (Jenkins 2015). The Global Study calls for the same (still unmet) 15 percent gender target to be applied to *all* peace and security spending, including in UN missions.[14]

Unfortunately, there are not that many concrete example of resourcing that can be found. Only a handful of countries have attempted to directly reference it in their NAPs, such as Ireland, Norway, Rwanda, Sweden, and the UK, undertaking institutional audits to identify resource and capacity constraints prior to developing their respective NAPs. The second Dutch NAP (2012–2015) includes a table outlining annual contributions (in Euros or in person hours) of various NAP activities.

The United Kingdom's first National Action Plan on Women, Peace, and Security was adopted in 2014 for implementation through 2017. A delegation of government and civil society representatives responsible for the plan attended the September 2016 National Action Plan Academy, co-hosted by the Organization for Security and Cooperation in Europe and Inclusive Security.

The purpose of the convening was to build participants' knowledge and skills to design future action plans using results-based management principles. After the Academy, the UK government did a mapping of existing commitments to implement national and local policies related to women, peace, and security. The unit at the Foreign and Commonwealth Office in charge of drafting the next NAP then provided government funding for UK civil society organizations to conduct consultations with beneficiaries in target countries. The core team responsible for revising the Resolution 1325 NAP reviewed the mapping and results of consultations to identify key gaps and potential objectives to prioritize in the new plan.[15]

In some instances, NAP activities are either not specifically budgeted, or the budget includes unrealistically low funding for the scope of work. Rwanda's NAP (2009–2012) was launched without allocated funding, but instead stated the need "to hold roundtables with donors to secure required funding" (Miller et al. 2014). While the budget for Sierra Leone's plan (2010–2014) identifies potential *sources* of funds, including from domestic (private sector, government, nongovernment) and international entities, members of civil society reported that the budget numbers were not a genuine reflection of implementing agencies' costs (Amling and O'Reilly 2016: 63). Shifting national priorities or donor-driven outcomes present another obstacle, and can lead to a NAP's "pillars" being disproportionally funded. For example, outside funding tends to favor protection efforts, often with desired quick results, like setting a target number of shelters. This sometimes comes at the expense (literally) of investing in less tangible and more long-term outcomes such as an increase in women leading local mediation efforts. Finally, a lack of clarity around how or when allocated money will be disbursed can negatively affect NAP resourcing. Germany's NAP (2012–2016) simply mentions that ministries will take NAP activities into consideration "when employing the funds at their disposal," without further elaboration (Amling and O'Reilly 2016: 63).

Component 4: Strong and Sustained Political Will

The starting point for attempting to define "political will" is identifying *whose* will is needed to accomplish a stated objective, policy, or agenda. From a high-impact NAP perspective, political will means that critical government ministries and agencies recognize the value of their NAP, are committed to its progress, and take action to implement it. The commitment of high-level government officials is important, but it is often the mid-level civil servants (not political appointees who change often) that determine the success of NAP's implementation. They can drive buy-in and broad ownership among ministries and agencies across the government. In Nigeria (2013–2017), Esther Eghobamien-Mshelia, Director of Women and Gender Affairs for the Ministry of Social Development, has been the government's key NAP champion. Her influence and experience led to implementation efforts gaining momentum at the end of 2015, even though the plan launched in 2013. In countries affected by conflict, buy-in and ownership is not limited to the capital; provincial and local governments must also be committed to NAP implementation.

Another key demonstration of political will is that the government includes the NAP in peace and security dialogues, strategies, and processes, *not* only those related to gender equality and women's rights. Often, the personal perceptions of key national and local policymakers' around women's inclusion present the biggest barriers to securing the necessary political will. As was the case in Germany, an early barrier to adoption is the resistance to creating a separate national policy focused on women's inclusion in peace and security. Despite being the country's first female chancellor, Angela Merkel reportedly stated her opposition to a NAP in 2006, saying the following:

> Many of the concerns of Resolution 1325 have already been integrated in various federal government action plans . . . In my opinion, this provides better chances of reaching these objectives than a further separate action plan, as a mainstreaming approach in all relevant policy areas allows us to react much more flexibly to current problems in crisis-ridden regions (Bucurescu 2011: 40–41).

Germany eventually reconsidered and launched their NAP in 2012, years later than many of their Western European counterparts.

Other core challenges related to political will include, bureaucratic infighting, frequent political transitions, and constantly shifting priorities. For example, Iraq (2014–2018) became the first Middle Eastern country with a NAP, and Iraqi Prime Minister Haider al-Abadi signed on to an "Emergency NAP" in May 2015 focused on the participation, protection, and prevention efforts in the conflict with ISIS/ISIL. However, two months later he dissolved the Iraqi Ministry of Women's Affairs, who oversaw and coordinated both NAPs, effectively ceasing all support for their implementation (Rayman et al. 2016).

ADDITIONAL TOOLS AND FRAMEWORKS
TO LINK TO THE NAPs

The effective design, implementation, and monitoring of national action plans is enshrined in recent global tools such as the UN's Sustainable Development Goals (SDGs), Resolution 2242, and CEDAW General Recommendation 30 (Gordon 2015). Resolution 2242 calls for more NAPs and their enhanced alignment with other national strategies, inclusive design, regular reporting to the Security Council during Open Debate, and for development of Regional Action Plans.[16] The Resolution specifically calls for a systemic inclusion of civil society and requires adequate resources dedicated to implementation. However, systemic integration of this agenda still varies. In 2015, the UN released the SDGs, seventeen objectives to guide international development. Unfortunately, despite advocacy of some member states and civil society, there is no explicit mention of WPS. Still, there is some space to influence this agenda via Goal 5 ("Achieve gender equality and empower all women and girls") and Goal 16 ("Promote peaceful and inclusive societies for sustainable development, provide access to justice for all, and build effective, accountable, and inclusive institutions at all levels."). An Inter-Agency Expert Group on SDG Indicators created a set of benchmarks for governments to track progress. As many NAPs already include women, peace and security indicators, it is critical to align specific targets with those proposed for Sustainable Development Goals 6 and 15.

Since 1979, 187 out of 194 UN member states have ratified CEDAW. Unlike a "soft law" like Resolution 1325, CEDAW provides a legally binding accountability framework on which governments are obliged to regularly report. The Review Committee tracks compliance with clear parameters to ensure women's participation in the political, economic, and social life of their nations. In October 2013, the Committee expanded the reporting requirements by adding General Recommendation 30. This amendment expands CEDAW's mandate to address women's situation in all stages of the conflict cycle, from conflict prevention, internal and international wars, all forms of political violence, and post-conflict reconstruction. It mandates member states to collect data on the Women, Peace, and Security agenda and report on the national government's compliance with UN benchmarks on implementing Resolution 1325. Point 28 requires that governments ensure NAPs are aligned with CEDAW and budgets are allocated for their implementation. Most relevantly, the monitoring and reporting section mandates:

> The States parties are to provide information on the implementation of the Security Council agenda on women, peace and security, in particular resolutions 1325 (2000), 1820 (2008), 1888 (2009), 1889 (2009), 1960 (2010) and 2106 (2013), including by specifically reporting on compliance with any agreed United Nations benchmarks or indicators developed as part of that agenda.

KEY EMERGING TRENDS

In addition to these tools and guidance, several trends are increasingly becoming significant in how we institutionalize the WPS agenda and feature prominently in the latest NAPs.

Preventing/Countering Violent Extremism (P/CVE)

Resolution 2242 calls for "the greater integration by member states and the United Nations of their agendas on women, peace and security, counter-terrorism and countering-violent extremism which can be conducive to terrorism."[17] Point 13 of Resolution 2242 urges member States and the United Nations system to "ensure the participation and leadership of women and women's organizations in developing strategies to counter terrorism and violent extremism which can be conducive to terrorism."[18] The Kenyan NAP (2016–2020) calls for women's participation throughout the design and execution of relief and recovery programs, including efforts related to the security situation in areas affected by Al Shabab and other terrorist groups. It also includes an output dedicated to ensuring women's inclusion (particularly refugees and internally displaced persons) in humanitarian, early recovery, relief, and peace-building efforts. Supporting the inclusion of women, men, boys, and girls in conflict prevention work is also a key priority in Sweden's revised NAP (2016–2020). Among other prevention efforts, the plan includes an output for including women and their experiences in designing conflict early warning and analysis mechanisms and the "inclusion of gender perspectives in measures intended to counteract and prevent conflict, radicalization and violent extremism."[19]

In addition to being grounded in results-based design methodology, the Jordan NAP is also unique in that it incorporates an emphasis on women's role in preventing and countering violent extremism. Though still in draft as of this writing, it is expected that the JONAP will include activities to enhancing women's leadership (particularly young women) on the prevention of violent extremism and building community cohesion and resilience. The JONAP will also address the need for sensitization materials that emphasize women's participation in conflict prevention and the role of religious leaders in supporting women's participation. JONAP drafters envision holding awareness-raising sessions in collaboration with religious and intellectual leaders, creating and promoting education resources related to women's roles (especially young women) in combating radical ideologies and violent extremism, and enhancing extracurricular activities that enrich boys' and girls' lives and promote their participation in active citizenship and good governance.

Environment/Climate Change

While debates surrounding women's access to and management of natural resources in peace-building have been ongoing for decades, their specific roles in combating climate change are garnering increased global attention. Certain national action plans have integrated environment and climate change–related indicators and goals. Japan's NAP emphasizes the need for a human security focus, and highlights Japan's prioritization of women's protection during and participation following natural disasters.[20] The second Finnish NAP has an objective charging the Ministries of Foreign Affairs, Environment, and Interior with promoting women's active participation in environment and security and mitigating climate change.[21] The plan also has specific indicators on funding for "green economy projects" with a gender objective and funding for women's participation as delegates in international climate and other environment cooperation.[22]

Localization

Local action plans (LAPs) and other localization mechanisms are increasingly used to operationalize Resolution 1325 at the local and community level. As part of a GNWP-supported project in Serbia, the Association Women of the South and the Association Dea Dia produced guidelines for implementing Resolution 1325 in the Pirot municipality in February 2015.[23] Additionally, with technical support from Inclusive Security, the Agency for Gender Equality in Bosnia and Herzegovina worked with local government and civil society actors to develop LAPs in five pilot municipalities in 2015, addressing women's daily security concerns, including protection from gender-based violence, human trafficking, access to legal protection, and environmental and infrastructure concerns.[24] The OSCE's mission in Bosnia and Herzegovina is utilizing local field offices and their influence on mayors to develop six more municipal strategies, including in areas affected by the recent migrant crisis and 2014 catastrophic floods.

Increased Roles of Regional/International Organizations in Promoting NAP Development.

Adopting a national plan for implementing Resolution 1325 is increasingly viewed as a way for non-NAP countries to demonstrate their commitment to and meet criteria for joining regional/international alliances such as the European Union, OSCE, and NATO. While Moldova does not yet have a NAP, Moldova and NATO have agreed on two-year Individual Partnership Action Plans (IPAPs) since 2006 that outline the country's commitments to further its partnership with NATO. The 2014–2016 IPAP emphasizes implementation of Resolution 1325, and it focused on improved education and training for security and armed forces.

Following a year-long relationship building process, NATO's Science for Peace and Security Programme (NATO SPS) approached Inclusive Security in 2015 and suggested they partner with Moldova on their proposal to improve Resolution 1325 implementation within their Defense Ministry. Similarly, Montenegro folded their NAP development into the NATO integration process. As part of the accession road map, the Ministry of Defense was provided a list of twenty-seven commitments, one of which specifically called for actions related to 1325, suggesting the development of a national action plan.

CONCLUSION

More than a decade has passed since then UN Secretary General Kofi Annan issued a call to start the process of institutionalizing the WPS agenda by developing national action plans as a means to translate the international normative advances into national strategies that realize the promise of 1325. Subsequent UN resolutions, including the last one 2242 passed in 2015, further emphasized this need, asking for increased commitments from member states to develop and implement NAPs. Other parts of the international norm-making have followed, including importantly, CEDAW's Committee Recommendation Number 30 from 2013. Multilateral organizations from OSCE to AU and ASEAN have issued various proclamations of their own, as did regional organizations such as the Economic Community of West African States (ECOWAS) and the Union for the Mediterranean. As of early 2017, more than one-third of UN member states have adopted NAPs, with a handful approaching their fourth version.

NAPs face a number of limitations, particularly in the implementation phase. Most plans are heavily internally focused, emphasizing intra-government coordination and many bureaucratic barriers to an inclusive decision-making. Yet, NAPs also represent an important instrument, both of policy and practice and advocacy, to continue to strengthen institutional efforts for change. Using the High Impact Framework, we have highlighted concrete examples of best practice and lessons learned that can ensure NAPs can achieve the desired change: inclusive design process, and an established coordination system for implementation; results-based monitoring and evaluation plan; allocated implementation resources; and sustained political will are the core components of a framework that can help governments and their partners in civil society reach the ultimate goal, making communities around the world safe and secure for all.

NOTES

1. See Inclusive Security: National Action Plan Resource Center, "The Power of a Plan," n.d., https://actionplans.inclusivesecurity.org/.
2. See UN Security Council, "Statement by the President of the Security Council" (October 31, 2002), UN Doc. S/PRST/2002/32; UN Security Council, "Women and Peace and Security: Report of the Secretary-General" (October 13, 2004), UN Doc. S/2004/814; UN Security Council, "Statement by the President of the Security Council" (March 7, 2007), UN Doc. S/PRST/2007/5; UN Security Council, "Women and Peace and Security: Report of the Secretary-General" (September 25, 2008), UN Doc. S/2008/622.
3. Uppsala Conflict Database (2015): http://ucdp.uu.se/#/year/2015.
4. See UNHCR "With 1 human in every 113 affected, forced displacement hits record high." 20 June, 2016, http://www.unhcr.org/en-au/news/press/2016/6/5763ace54/1-human-113-affected-forced-displacement-hits-record-high.html
5. Figure derived using data extracted from the World Economic Forum, annual Gender Gap Report, years 2006–2016.
6. Figure derived using data extracted from the World Economic Forum, annual Gender Gap Report, years 2006–2016.
7. Figure derived using data extracted from the World Bank, annual GDP reports, years 2006–2015.http://www.worldbank.org.
8. Statistical analysis by Laurel Stone, as featured in O'Reilly, M., A. O'Suilleabhain, and T. Paffenholz, "Reimagining Peacemaking: Women's Roles in Peace Processes," International Peace Institute (June 2015), 12–14.
9. See "Assessment of the Action Plan for the Implementation of UNSCR 1325 in Bosnia and Herzegovina 2010–2013," conducted for Inclusive Security at the request of the Gender Equality Agency of Bosnia and Herzegovina (January 2010), http://www.peacewomen.org/assets/file/bosniaherzegovina_nationalactionplan_2010.pdf
10. "The Institute for Inclusive Security coined and developed the term 'high-impact NAP' and has developed numerous resources on the topic. For more information on NAPs, including a training course on the development of high-impact NAPs, see https://actionplans.inclusivesecurity.org/"; UN Women, "Preventing Conflict, Transforming Justice, Securing the Peace: A Global Study on the Implementation of United Nations Security Council resolution 1325," Key Actors for Women, Peace and Security: Monitoring and Accountability (chap. 10), 241, http://www.peacewomen.org/sites/default/files/UNW-GLOBAL-STUDY-1325-2015%20(1).pdf.
11. Asia-Japan Women's Resource Center, "Statement of the Civil Society Working Group on the official announcement of Japan's National Action Plan on 'Women, Peace, and

Security'" (December 17, 2015), http://www.ajwrc.org/eng/modules/bulletin/index.php?page=article&storyid=145.

12. Based on Inclusive Security's assessments conducted in Jakarta in March 2015 and August 2015.

13. Ministry of Foreign Affairs of the Netherlands, *Women: Powerful Agents for Peace and Security: Dutch National Action Plan (2012–2015): For the Implementation of UN Security Council Resolution 1325 on Women, Peace, and Security* (November 2011), 8, http://www.peacewomen.org/assets/file/NationalActionPlans/dutch_nap_2012-2015.pdf.

14. UN Women, "Preventing Conflict, Transforming Justice . . ." (chap. 10), 16, http://www.peacewomen.org/sites/default/files/UNW-GLOBAL-STUDY-1325-2015%20(1).pdf.

15. Author's email correspondence with representatives of the UK Foreign and Commonwealth Office's Conflict Department, which manages the coordination of the UK NAP.

16. Operative (para. 2), 3.

17. United Nations Security Council, Resolution 2242, S/RES/2242 (2015), http://www.securitycouncilreport.org/atf/cf/%7B65BFCF9B-6D27-4E9C-8CD3-CF6E4FF96FF9%7D/s_res_2242.pdf.

18. Ibid., point 13.

19. Government Offices of Sweden, *Women, Peace & Security: Sweden's National Action Plan for the implementation of the UN Security Council's Resolutions on Women, Peace and Security 2016–2020* (2016), 12, http://www.government.se/contentassets/8ae23198463f49269e25a14d4d14b9bc/women-peace-and-security-eng.pdf.

20. Ministry of Foreign Affairs of Japan, *National Action Plan on Women, Peace, and Security* (September 29, 2015), 4, http://www.mofa.go.jp/files/000101798.pdf.

21. Ministry of Foreign Affairs of Finland, *Finland's National Action Plan 2012–2016* (2012), 22, http://www.peacewomen.org/assets/file/finland_nap_2012.pdf.

22. Ibid., 45.

23. Kingdom of the Netherlands, *Guidelines for the Implementation of the United Nations Security Council Resolution 1325—Women, Peace, and Security, in the Municipality of Pirot* (February 2015), https://actionplans.inclusivesecurity.org/wp-content/uploads/2015/02/Guidelines-for-the-Localization-of-the-UNSCR-in-Pirot-Municipality.pdf.

24. UN Women, "Preventing Conflict, Transforming Justice . . ." (chap. 10), 243.

REFERENCES

Amling, A., and M. O'Reilly. *From Global Promise to National Action*. Inclusive Security and One Earth Future Foundation, 2016, 5, 63.

Braun, M. D. *Colloquium Marks a New Era for Women in Liberia*. Washington, DC: National Geographic Society, 2009.

Bucurescu, A. M. "Security Council Resolution 1325 on Women, Peace and Security: Effective Ways to Implement It at a National Level: National Action Plans or Gender Mainstreaming Approach? A Comparative Case Study on Swedish and German Implementation Designs." PhD Dissertation, Uppsala University, Sweden, 2011, 40–41.

Gordon, A. *Applying Global Tools to Improve National Action Plans on UN Security Council Resolution 1325*. Inclusive Security, 2015, https://www.inclusivesecurity.org/publication/applying-global-tools-to-improve-national-action-plans-on-un-security-council-resolution-1325/.

Hudson, V., B. Ballif-Spanvill, M. Caprioli, and C. F. Emmett. *Sex and World Peace.* New York: Columbia University Press, 2012.

Hudson, V. M. and P Leidl. The Hillary Doctrine: Sex & American Foreign Policy (New York: Columbia University Press, 2015).

Jacevic, M. "The Latest Country to Adopt a Women, Peace, and Security Policy May Surprise You." Inclusive Security, 2014, https://www.inclusivesecurity.org/2014/11/19/latest-country-to-adopt-women-peace-and-security-policy/.

Jenkins, R. "The Practical Is the Political: The UN's Global Study on Women, Peace, and Security." *Global Peace Operations Review,* 2015, http://peaceoperationsreview.org/thematic-essays/practical-political-un-global-study-women-peace-security/.

Melander, E. 2005. "Gender Equality and Intrastate Armed Conflict." *Institutional Studies Quarterly* 49, no. 4 (November 14, 2005): 695–714.

Miller, B., M. Pournik, and A. Swaine. *Women in Peace and Security through United Nations Security Resolution 1325: Literature Review, Content Analysis of National Action Plans, and Implementation.* The George Washington University Institute for Global and International Studies, 2014, http://www.peacewomen.org/assets/file/NationalActionPlans/miladpournikanalysisdocs/igis_womeninpeaceandsecuritythroughunsr1325_millerpournikswaine_2014.pdf.

Pettersson, T., and P. Wallensteen. "Armed Conflicts, 1946–2014," *Journal of Peace Research* 52 (2015): 4.

Rayman, P. M., S. Izen, and E. Parker. *UNSCR 1325 in the Middle East and North Africa: Women and Security.* United States Institute of Peace Special Report 388, 2016, https://www.usip.org/sites/default/files/SR388-UNSCR-1325-in-the-Middle-East-and-North-Africa-Women-and-Security.pdf.

Rehn, E., and E. J. Sirleaf. "Women, War, and Peace: The Independent Experts' Assessment on the Impact of Armed Conflict on Women and Women's Role in Peace-Building," United Nations Development Fund for Women, 2002, https://www.unfpa.org/sites/default/files/pub-pdf/3F71081FF391653DC1256C69003170E9-unicef-WomenWarPeace.pdf.

True, J. "Explaining the Global Diffusion of the Women, Peace and Security Agenda." *International Political Science Review* 37, no. 3 (2016): 307–323.

UN Secretary-General (UNSG). "Report of the Secretary-General on Women's Participation in Peacebuilding (A/65/354–S/2010/466)." Tracking Progress: 7-Point Action Plan, 2010. http://www.un.org/en/peacebuilding/pbso/pdf/seven_point_action_plan.pdf.

PART III

INSTITUTIONALIZING WPS

CHAPTER 23

....

WPS INSIDE
THE UNITED NATIONS

....

MEGAN DERSNAH

THE adoption of UN Security Council Resolution 1325 marked a turning point in terms of incorporating women and gender considerations for the first time into the work of the Security Council. Fifteen years on, the Women, Peace, and Security (WPS) agenda is well established within the UN system. UN agencies and programs are increasingly incorporating gender and women's rights considerations into their peace and security work. They are also increasingly coordinating their efforts to ensure coherent, efficient, and ultimately more beneficial program outcomes for the populations they serve (UNSC 2015, 2016).

This chapter seeks to explain and analyze the factors that have contributed to this progress to date, while also addressing the challenges that remain for advancing the WPS agenda within the UN system. First, it looks at the creation of UN Women as a focal point for coordination around gender equality within the UN system, and particularly taking the lead on driving the WPS agenda forward. Second, it then explores the role that UN Women has played in the successes of this agenda, before highlighting some of the challenges that remain to be overcome for its continued progress. The chapter argues that UN Women is struggling to find its institutional location in advocating for the WPS agenda. This is reflected in the fact that UN Women remains weakly represented in the field and lacks a voice in the Inter-Agency Standing Committee, a key humanitarian decision-making body of the UN. UN Women's struggle to situate itself within the UN system is also reflected in the significant challenges that remain for advancing gender mainstreaming within the UN more broadly. The success of the WPS agenda depends on the existence of a coherent and unified approach to gender equality amongst all UN humanitarian, peace, and security stakeholders.

The structure of this chapter is as follows. It will first provide an overview of the creation of UN Women and its mandate to lead on the WPS agenda. It will then outline some successes thus far, before explaining how the organization has been struggling to find its institutional location and voice. Finally, it will conclude by explaining the impact this confusion can have on the possibility of strengthening the WPS agenda within the UN system moving forward.

UN Women: Driving Gender Equality and the WPS Agenda within the UN

In 2009, as part of its broader efforts to ensure system-wide coherence within the UN system, the General Assembly passed a resolution that strongly supported the strengthening of the institutional arrangements for support of gender equality and the empowerment of women, through the consolidation of existing UN entities doing gender-related work.[1] The following year, UN Women—the United Nations Entity for Gender Equality and the Empowerment of Women—was created. It merged four previously distinct entities within the UN system, each one focused on gender equality and women's empowerment. The four entities were the Division for the Advancement of Women (DAW); the International Research and Training Institute for the Advancement of Women (INSTRAW); the Office of the Special Adviser on Gender Issues and Advancement of Women (OSAGI); and the United Nations Development Fund for Women (UNIFEM).

UN Women was envisioned to be the center of the gender equality architecture of the UN system by combining the mandates and assets of the four existing gender equality entities, and performing new and additional functions to close the gaps in the gender equality work of the UN system (UNGA 2010). The vision was that UN Women would address significant gaps in the ability of the UN system to respond to country demand for support in advancing gender equality. These gaps were a result of inadequate coordination and coherence across the UN; weak linkages between intergovernmental agreements and implementation on the ground; lack of accountability in relation to leadership and voice on gender equality in the UN system; inadequate authority for the organizations and individuals in the UN system tasked with supporting gender equality; and, importantly, inadequate resources (UN Women 2011). The creation of UN Women was therefore a historic step by UN member states to accelerate the focus on gender equality and women's empowerment across the UN system and also to improve the accountability, efficiency, and effectiveness of its gender initiatives through better coherence and coordination (UN Women 2013a).

Since its creation, UN Women has spearheaded and amplified gender mainstreaming efforts within the UN system. None of UN Women's predecessors had an equivalent mandate, and UN Women in its early years has begun to take promising steps toward defining its role in coordinating this issue within the UN system (UN Women 2016). Moreover, UN Women has taken steps to advance the focus on gender equality more broadly in policy and programming. Among UN Women's key contributions are the following. It has been proactive in establishing as well as revitalizing several mechanisms that support the advancement of gender mainstreaming and collaboration in the domain of gender equality work such as regional and country level Gender Theme Groups, which strengthen the "gender agenda" at all levels of UN functioning (UN Women 2016). It has also been driving the UN system-wide action plan (SWAP) for gender equality, a framework that addresses key areas of importance to improve gender mainstreaming within the institutions of the UN including those related to peace and security as well as humanitarian affairs (UN ECOSOC 2014). UN-SWAP assigns performance standards for the gender-related work of all UN entities thereby ensuring greater coherence and accountability. All UN organizations are required, based on a set of fifteen indicators, to adopt policies and practices to institutionalize gender equality considerations in their operations and architecture.

This broader focus on driving gender mainstreaming across the UN system, and in particular coherence and cooperation in the way that gender equality is being addressed, is the context for understanding the advancement of the WPS agenda in recent years. UN Women has been designated and is now unequivocally seen as a lead agency for the WPS agenda within the UN system. This is a major step toward addressing the fragmented approach to WPS that previously existed within the UN system (Dersnah 2016). Disconnection between the previous gender entities within the UN, such as UNIFEM, OSAGI, and DAW, created at best a piecemeal approach to addressing the WPS agenda. At worst, this disconnect was reflected in bureaucratic infighting that led to considerable inefficiencies and duplicated resources (Dersnah 2016). With a dedicated Peace and Security section that is actively involved in both normative development and inter-agency coordination, and support from the Intergovernmental Support Division and the UN System Coordination Division, UN Women is much more strongly positioned to provide a coherent and consolidated approach to advance the WPS agenda. It is better able to provide stronger leadership and visibility for the agenda (UN Women 2013b). Indeed, the creation of UN Women and its leadership on this agenda is a marker of the increasing strength of gender equality norms within the UN system, and particularly the growing strength of the WPS agenda.

This enhanced role extends to providing leadership on the coordination of gender mainstreaming into peace and security work across the UN system by working with influential actors, namely the Department of Political Affairs (DPA); the Peacebuilding Support Office (PBSO); the Office of the High Commissioner for Human Rights (OHCHR); and the Department for Peacekeeping Operations (DPKO). UN Women is active in providing technical leadership in conflict and post-conflict contexts to ensure that gender considerations are incorporated across peace and security work such as in the design of gender-responsive humanitarian interventions. For example in 2015, UN Women's technical support ensured the prioritization of women's leadership and gender-responsive allocations of resources for infrastructure and livelihoods in humanitarian action plans in Myanmar, Nepal, and Vanuatu (UN ECOSOC 2016). In the State of Palestine, the deployment of a Gender Adviser to the Office for the Coordination of Humanitarian Affairs ensured that gender was mainstreamed into the terms of reference for hiring in each humanitarian cluster. These examples, among others, illustrate that UN Women is not only defining its role at the policy and normative level at UN headquarters, but also beginning to carve out its space at the country and regional levels. It is mainstreaming gender into the work that takes place in fragile, conflict and post-conflict countries to ensure that the WPS agenda is advanced in practice.

UN Women's leadership has particularly strengthened the WPS agenda within the UN system at the global level too. For example, the 2015 publication of the global study on the implementation of Resolution 1325 (see Chapter 11 and Chapter 58), and the adoption of Security Council Resolution 2242 (2015) are two of the most recent milestones driven by UN Women for advancing the WPS agenda within the UN. Beyond this, three separate institutional reviews in 2015 each put forward gender-specific recommendations for the UN to improve its coherence, coordination, and gender expertise in the domain of peace and security (UNSC 2016). These were the high-level review on the implementation of Resolution 1325; the high-level Independent Panel on Peace Operations; and the review of the United Nations peace-building architecture.

Moreover, a set of twenty-six globally relevant indicators to measure the implementation of Resolution 1325 were developed with strong contributions from UN Women's Peace and Security team. The indicators were adopted in 2010 to monitor the implementation of the WPS resolutions and for voluntary reporting by member states. The Seven-Point Action Plan on Gender-Responsive Peacebuilding and the Strategic Framework for United Nations Action against Sexual Violence in Conflict, together add weight to the mechanisms that aim to strengthen the UN system's accountability to the WPS agenda.

Beyond these specific examples of UN Women's institutional leadership for the WPS agenda at the global level, there is broader, albeit more limited, evidence that the WPS agenda is also slowly progressing within the policies and practices of other entities across the UN system. At the policy level, all UN agencies that work in peace, security and humanitarian contexts have now developed their own gender policies that guide gender mainstreaming into their development or humanitarian mandates, either as stand-alone or in conjunction with other organizations (UN Women 2015). For example, the United Nations Development Programme (UNDP) has their *Eight Point Agenda for Women's Empowerment and Gender Equality in Crisis Prevention and Recovery*. This policy emphasizes practical, positive outcomes for women and girls in crisis. It focuses not only on the immediate aftermath of conflict but also on providing a response that works toward building stronger, sustainable, and equitable societies in the aftermath of conflict for women and girls (UNDP, n.d.). Moreover, the Department of Political Affairs (DPA) and DPKO revised directives, guidance and training to emphasize gender mainstreaming, including in peacekeeping and political participation in 2016 (UNSC 2016). Many UN entities are now also screening financial allocations using gender marker systems. Gender marking is a crucial tool for gender-sensitive planning and monitoring. For example, the Office for the Coordination of Humanitarian Affairs (OCHA) made it mandatory to list gender allocations in projects using the Inter-Agency Standing Committee gender marker (UNSC 2016). The existence of these policies within individual UN agencies, particularly when they are accompanied with reporting mechanisms, serves as an accountability structure to the obligations within the WPS agenda.

Tangible outcomes in incorporating gender equality into humanitarian programming also demonstrate the growing, although still limited, strength of the WPS agenda across UN agencies tasked with peace and security programming. For example, all UN mediation support teams since 2012 have included a woman, and more peace agreements have provisions in support of women's human rights (UNSC 2016). Gender-focused budget allocations have increased over time across UN entities. In 2015, UNDP allocated almost $82 million compared with $72 million in 2014.[2] UN Women allocated $41.6 million in 2015, a figure more than double the $17.7 million they allocated for peace, security and humanitarian action in the previous year (UNSC 2016). The proportion of allocations targeting gender equality as a program's principal objective has increased too, for example, with UNICEF's proportion over three years increasing from 11 to 19 percent in 2014 (UNSC 2015). The UN Peacebuilding Fund has also exceeded a 15 percent UN-wide target, allocating 15.7 percent of funds to projects with the principal objective of gender equality and women's empowerment in 2015 (UNSC 2016).

These achievements indicate that progress has been made on advancing the WPS agenda within the UN system, and that UN Women has played a role in driving this— either through direct involvement or because of its broader mandate to advance the gender mainstreaming agenda across all UN entities. Yet, despite the progress that has been made, challenges remain in advancing the WPS agenda. These challenges are the result of both UN Women's continued weak positioning and voice in the UN. More broadly, they reflect systemic challenges that persist for advancing gender issues within the UN system. The following section will address these challenges in turn.

The Challenges of Advancing WPS within the UN System

While UN Women has made great strides to advance the gender mainstreaming agenda within the UN system, and the WPS agenda in particular, challenges remain. UN Women is struggling to find its institutional location and voice within the UN, limited by confusion concerning its role and place. This is especially the case because it is not the only institution responsible for implementing the WPS agenda, even though it is the designated coordinator within the UN system. Moreover, it is considerably smaller than some entities who have long been working in the area of peace and security. This confusion is exacerbated by the fact that UN Women is not yet a loud voice in institutional mechanisms that govern humanitarian action, such as the Inter-Agency Standing Committee, because it lacks operational capacity in-country. Finally, the advancement of the WPS agenda is limited by a continued systematic rejection of gender mainstreaming across the UN system.

UN Women is experiencing the growing pains of defining itself as an actor within the UN system, and there remains confusion around its role and place, especially in advancing the WPS agenda. UN Women is only now beginning to carve out and define its role at the normative and policy level, as well as in the coordination and field-level programming and practical support for the WPS agenda. Broadly speaking, UN Women has primarily focused on establishing itself at the global level in its initial years (Dersnah 2016). This is reflected in the fact that UN Women's positioning as UN system coordinator is much more consistently acknowledged at the global level than in the field, including in the area of WPS (UN Women 2016). UN Women continues to have a relatively small presence in-country, especially compared to other major players. Consequently, it has not yet been able to consistently define its "value-added" in comparison to these existing actors in these contexts.

UN Women is still defining and clarifying the role that it should play in coordination and technical support in field operations, despite the fact that it officially holds the coordinating mandate for gender across the UN system. There remains a lack of clarity in terms of how this role should be conceived. As a recent UN Women report highlighted, "UN Women has not yet clearly articulated, demonstrated or operationalized the notion that UN coordination is part of a synergistic approach that is inherent in its mandate and/or that better UN system coordination leads to changes for women's rights and gender equality" (UN Women 2016: 12). UN Women has implemented its UN coordination role in a highly complex environment, characterized by the challenge of vertical accountability mechanisms. This means that entities are accountable to their own headquarters and compete over resources, which in turn limit their ability and willingness to focus on jointly identified priorities (UN Women 2016). Given the vertical structure of the UN, coordination relies on the voluntary cooperation of UN entities. How other UN actors perceive and make use of UN Women's expertise is therefore strongly influenced by their own needs and interests. The impact UN actors are able to make is greatly affected by competing interests, and by their capacity to demonstrate their individual authority and expertise in practice.

Coordination for advancing gender equality and the empowerment of women in fragile, conflict and post-conflict contexts presents an added challenge. UN Women's ability to advance the WPS agenda in these contexts can be ad hoc or dependent on various entities' willingness to engage with them and with specific gender issues. Despite the push at headquarters level to ensure coordination and the advancement of gender equality goals, it remains common for UN agencies and entities to implement the WPS agenda in ways that are inconsistent with each other. For example, a recent study of the Inter-Agency Standing Committee's 2008 Gender Policy showed that the way gender, age, and diversity are addressed and incorporated into the directives and operational guidelines of the committee were highly inconsistent. This is in part because of the variation between entities within the committee as well as the lack of strong leadership on gender from within that would ensure gender is consistently incorporated (IASC 2015). This inconsistency can include anything from differing definitions of gender to the total omission of any reference to gender equality in their documentation. While there has been an increase in attention to gender issues, UN entities are not yet functioning in a coordinated and consistent way to advance this agenda in practice.

The inconsistent approach to how gender is incorporated into Inter-Agency Standing Committee's gender policies is complicated by the fact that the committee does not have a strong lead on gender mainstreaming. While UN Women is active in the committee's Gender Reference Group, which gives it some voice to influence decision-making, UN Women's application to join the committee was recently rejected (IASC 2015). This has been linked to the argument that UN Women is not sufficiently operational to be a relevant player in the context of humanitarian action, even though it has played a coordination role in these contexts (UN Women 2016). Actual or perceived gaps in UN Women's operational capacity have limited its ability to contribute to or lead inter-agency discussions at both the field and global level (UN Women 2016). Whereas UN Women has a strong mandate to lead on the WPS agenda that is accountable to the Security Council, there is slippage when it comes to humanitarian coordination—a dimension integral to the WPS agenda implementation. As such, UN Women is not in a strong position to influence the Inter-Agency Standing Committee's work and improve coordination across the institution (IASC 2015). This fragmentation has a significant impact on UN Women's ability to play an effective coordinating role on the WPS agenda.

Beyond the challenges of coordination and the complexities of showing leadership in an area where there are numerous actors operating in different ways, UN Women has faced challenges more broadly in its mandate to promote gender mainstreaming. While progress has been made in recent years in putting gender equality at the forefront of discussions within the UN, there remains serious resistance to this agenda. For evidence of this resistance we can look no further than at the results of the UN-SWAP. While the SWAP has so far been unprecedented in its effects, the current state of gender mainstreaming within the UN—which has been revealed in the initial data gathering for the SWAP—is indicative of how far gender mainstreaming efforts have been lagging over the past fifteen years.

Gender mainstreaming has formally been a goal within the UN system since 1997. The 2014 review of findings established that even when accountable to the SWAP indicators, most UN entities have very limited performance around improving their gender architecture and ensuring gender parity (UN ECOSOC 2014).[3] For example, while 96 percent of UN entities have gender focal points or equivalent in place to support the incorporation of gender concerns into their work, the strength of the gender focal point system is undermined by the lack of seniority of the focal point and the failure to formalize their functions (UN ECOSOC 2014).[4] As of 2015, all eight multidimensional peacekeeping missions had gender units led by senior advisers, and the eight traditional peacekeeping missions had gender focal points (UNSC 2016). Yet, gender focal points and advisers must also be present in all UN agencies working on WPS to ensure these issues are advocated in all policies and practices of every relevant entity.

This lack of gender focal points, as well as their low levels of authority, can have an impact on the strength of gender mainstreaming broadly, and on the WPS agenda specifically. Gender focal points across the UN system are often those responsible for implementing the WPS agenda in practice. An absence of a gender focal point, or a focal point without sufficient seniority to make an impact in decision-making, could mean that WPS considerations take a back seat to competing priorities. This is especially the case in contexts where UN Women may not be present in decision-making due to its low country-level representation. By default, gender focal points located in these other UN agencies become key advocates for WPS priorities.

Moreover, one need look no further than the representation of women in professional posts within the UN system to see that the UN is not delivering on its gender mainstreaming commitments. The hiring and representation of women in the UN system remains characterized by considerable gender inequality. A 2014 report of the Secretary-General on the status of women in the UN system noted that there is an inverse relationship between the level and representation of women. At the lowest professional levels, women make up over 50 percent of the staff, whereas at the highest level, women only make up 26.7 percent (UNGA 2014).[5] While women are well represented in entry-level positions, this does not equate to the representation of women in decision-making positions (UNGA 2014). In fact, between 2014 and 2015, the proportion of women in senior positions in peace operations declined (UNSC 2016). A 2013 General Assembly resolution expressed serious concerns that the goal to have 50/50 representation of men and women had not been met, especially at senior levels, and that the representation of women in the UN system remains almost static (UNGA 2013). The consistently poor representation of women within the UN system is one indicator that suggests a broader challenge in advancing the WPS agenda within the UN itself. Without the representation of women in senior decision-making positions, and given a lack of institutional focal points and gender policies that support the incorporation of gender considerations into all UN work, systematic progress will remain a challenge. While progress has certainly been made to institutionalize this agenda, these efforts are made within an institutional environment that remains at best indifferent to gender mainstreaming priorities, and actively resistant at worst.

Conclusion

This chapter has analyzed and explained the factors that have contributed to progress to date in advancing the WPS agenda within the UN system. It also addressed the challenges that continue to limit its institutionalization in practice. Ultimately, it is a mixed picture. The critical role played by the creation of UN Women and its mandate for gender mainstreaming within the UN have helped give the WPS agenda a higher profile across the UN system. We can see that, in recent years, attention to the WPS agenda has increased based on the growth of resolutions and references in the Security Council (see chapter 6 in this volume), and commitments to its institutionalization in policy and practice. However, this chapter has also identified institutional challenges to the implementation of the WPS agenda. UN Women continues to experience confusion and/or pushback in its role in advancing the WPS agenda. This results from having neither a strong presence at the country level nor an influential voice in institutional decision-making bodies such as in the Inter-Agency Standing Committee. This is exacerbated by a UN system that lacks coordination in its approach to WPS, and which has shown only limited progress in systematic gender mainstreaming. Some of these challenges may be offset as UN Women continues to establish itself within the UN system. It may gradually find a louder voice and increase its involvement in key decision-making forums. However, for the WPS agenda to succeed, there must be representation of gender advocates across the UN system. For that reason, the success of the WPS agenda is crucially linked to the success of the gender mainstreaming project more broadly and across the UN system. These responsibilities must be consistent and coordinated, and must emerge from all UN stakeholders involved in peace and security work.

Notes

1. At the 2005 World Summit, the Outcome Document called for a study on a fundamental restructuring of the UN system. A High-Level Panel was created in 2006 to explore how the UN system could work more coherently and effectively across the world in the areas of development, humanitarian assistance, and the environment. In the report of the High-Level Panel, one recommendation was for the establishment of one gender entity within the UN system. See the report at http://www.un.org/events/panel/resources/pdfs/HLP-SWC-FinalReport.pdf.
2. Of these, $28 million targeted the strengthening of institutions in order to deliver universal access to basic services, including rule of law and support for victims of sexual and gender-based violence; $16.5 million targeted emergency jobs, livelihoods, and early recovery; and $15 million promoted gender-responsive national budgets and development strategies.
3. Only 19 percent of UN entities rated as meeting or exceeding requirements in 2013, which is up from 13 percent in 2012.
4. Only 53 percent of focal points are at a P-4 level and above (P-4 is mid-level career and requires a minimum of seven years of work experience), and only 42 percent of entities with focal points have written terms of reference and only 31 percent have at least 20 percent of their time allocated to focal point duties.
5. The report shows the following statistics: The inverse relationship between the level and the representation of women continues: P1 (54.3 percent), P2 (57.9 percent), P3 (45.3 percent), P4 (40.5 percent), P5 (34.2 percent), D1 (32.4 percent), D2 (30.1 percent), and ungraded (26.7 percent).

REFERENCES

Dersnah, Megan. "Feminist Practice in an International Bureaucracy: Contestation over the Field of Peace and Security at the United Nations." PhD dissertation, University of Toronto, 2016.

IASC. "Executive Summary: Review of the IASC 2008 Gender Equality in Humanitarian Action Policy Statement." May 2015.

UN ECOSOC (UN Economic and Social Council). "Mainstreaming a Gender Perspective into All Politics and Programmes in the United Nations System: Report of the Secretary General." E/2014/63, 2014.

UN ECOSOC (UN Economic and Social Council). "Mainstreaming a Gender Perspective into All Policies and Programmes in the United Nations System: Report of the Secretary-General." E/2016/57, April 8, 2016.

UNGA (UN General Assembly). "Comprehensive Proposal for the Composite Entity for Gender Equality and the Empowerment of Women: Report of the Secretary-Genera." A/64/588, 2010.

UNGA (UN General Assembly). "Follow-up to the Fourth World Conference on Women and Full Implementation of the Beijing Declaration and Platform for Action and the Outcome of the Twenty-Third Special Session of the General Assembly." A/68/140, 2013.

UNGA (UN General Assembly). "Improvement in the Status of Women in the United Nations System: Report of the Secretary-General." A/69/346, 2014.

UNSC (UN Security Council). "Report of the Secretary-General on Women and Peace and Security." S/2015/716, September 16, 2015.

UNSC (UN Security Council). "Report of the Secretary-General on Women and Peace and Security" S/2016/822, September 29, 2016.

UN Women. "Strategic Plan 2011–2013." UNW/2011/9, 2011.

UN Women. "Joint Evaluation of Joint Programmes on Gender Equality in the United Nations System." Final Synthesis Report, 2013a.

UN Women. "The Contribution of UN Women to Increasing Women's Leadership and Participation in Peace and Security and in Humanitarian Response." Thematic Evaluation Final Synthesis Report, September 2013b.

UN Women. "The Effect of Gender Equality Programming on Humanitarian Outcomes." With Institute of Development Studies, April 2015.

UN Women. "Coordinating for Gender Equality Results: Corporate Evaluation of UN Women's Contribution to UN System Coordination on Gender Equality and the Empowerment of Women." May 2016.

CHAPTER 24

....

WPS AND THE SPECIAL REPRESENTATIVE OF THE SECRETARY-GENERAL FOR SEXUAL VIOLENCE IN CONFLICT

....

ELEANOR O'GORMAN

My focus in this chapter is the institutionalization of the Women, Peace, and Security (WPS) agenda, looking at the case study of the *role* and *office* of the Special Representative of the Secretary-General on Sexual Violence in Conflict (SRSG–SVC), first appointed in 2010. I will examine the implications of having a dedicated leadership role and office on SVC in terms of embedding change in UN operations. In addition, I question the extent to which the existence of this new structure generates tensions or synergies between the protection and participation (empowerment) commitments of UN Security Council Resolution 1325 (2000) on WPS.

The analysis set out here is based on primary document review and observation of UN and civil society organizations and operations on gender, conflict and peace-building issues over the past two decades. During 2012, I led a major five-year review of the network of UN agencies, funds, and programs called UN Action Against Sexual Violence in Conflict that had driven the SVC agenda within the UN. UN Action paved the way, along with other advocacy efforts, for WPS with UN Security Council Resolutions 1820 (UN Security Council [UNSC] 2008), 1888 (UNSC 2009a), 1889 (UNSC 2009b), and 1960 (UNSC 2010), which underpin the appointment of a dedicated SRSG on the issue of Sexual Violence in Conflict. I revisit that 2012 review (O'Gorman 2013) as well as subsequent UN reports and related sources. The objective is to draw out learning and insights on the challenges and opportunities for institutionalizing the combatting of SVC within the UN system as part of the WPS agenda.

The chapter centers around (1) the *policy and institutional developments* leading up to and following the creation of the post of UN SRSG-SVC called for in Resolution 1889 (2009b); (2) the *challenges and opportunities* during 2010–2016 in embedding and realizing the new

UN architecture on combatting SVC; and (3) the *lessons and insights on the institutionalization of WPS* that arise from the case study of the Office of the SRSG-SVC and UN Action structures and approach. Finally, the chapter concludes with (4) suggested next steps to renew and refocus the UN mandate, institutional arrangements, and actions on SVC toward the *practical implementation* of WPS commitments contained in Resolution 1325 and successor UN Security Council Resolutions (UNSCRs).

POLICY AND INSTITUTIONAL DEVELOPMENTS OF SVC AT THE UN

Operating paragraph 9 of Resolution 1888 in 2009 called on the Secretary-General to appoint a dedicated SRSG-SVC:

> . . . to provide coherent and strategic leadership, to work effectively to strengthen existing United Nations coordination mechanisms, and to engage in advocacy efforts, *inter alia*, with governments, including military and judicial representatives, as well as with all parties to armed conflict and civil society, in order to address, at both headquarters and country level, sexual violence in armed conflict, while promoting cooperation and coordination of efforts among all relevant stakeholders, primarily through the inter-agency initiative "United Nations Action against Sexual Violence in Conflict."

The Swedish politician and former EU commissioner Margot Wallström was appointed the first SRSG-SVC. Insider femocrats, member state diplomats, and civil society leaders credit her with maintaining relations with the Security Council and UN member states, as well as building strong visibility and communications for the agenda and its implementation. She also oversaw the setting up of the Office and the establishment of the Rule of Law Team of Experts from April 2010–2012. These initiatives are part of Resolution 1888 and its call to accelerate and resource a dedicated focus on investigation and prosecution of SVC violations at the country level.

In June 2012, Zainab Hawa Bangura of Sierra Leone, a former government minister inherited the ongoing transition of strengthening the Office of SRSG-SVC as part of the existing peace and security, and gender architecture of the UN. She is credited with driving forward a strong sense of national ownership and working with governments on the ground to champion actions and advocacy. On her watch, accountability and action at the national level advanced with visits, evidence gathering, and the operationalization of key provisions in the WPS resolutions. By the time the first SRSG was appointed in 2010, she stepped onto an unusually high-functioning, empowered, and resourced structure of UN coordination on SVC in New York. UN Action was established in 2007 and grew to be a network of thirteen United Nations entities[1] that provided system-wide coordination on prevention and response to sexual violence in conflict. It essentially grew from the personal and professional initiative and commitment of senior UN officials (mainly female but with some key male supporters) to work across mandates, structures, and internal competitiveness. They intended to help the UN get its act together on improving the system-wide response to sexual violence in conflict, and to campaign for recognition of this issue at the UN Security Council as well as calling for a dedicated SRSG.

These reforms were spurred in a context of growing international concern and campaigning for more action in response to the reports of sexual violence and rape emanating from the war in the Democratic Republic of the Congo (DRC) that found expression in events such as the "Brussels Call to Action to Address Sexual Violence in Conflict and Beyond, International Symposium on Sexual Violence in Conflict and Beyond, Brussels, June 21--23 2006." Kathleen Cravero, former Deputy Head of UNAIDS, and Assistant Secretary-General and head of the Bureau for Crisis Prevention and Recovery at the United Nations Development Programme (UNDP) is credited with having spearheaded this drive with her inclusive and strategic leadership. In essence, it had the elements of a "start-up" company when it first emerged. As it settled down, it established structures of a Steering Committee led by Principals from the member entities, a Focal Point Committee that carried much of the working level implementation forward, and a small Secretariat to backstop the mechanism. Three pillars of work emerged from this process that guided and structured the work of the network. These are advocating for action, knowledge generation, and country-level action.

The main conclusion of the 2013 review was the unique achievement of the network to overcome assumed and historic competitiveness, infighting, and bureaucracy that typifies UN inter-agency relations among the myriad of programs, funds, and offices that make up the UN system (O'Gorman 2013). Indeed, it was UN Action that helped build the case and momentum for the appointment of a dedicated SRSG on SVC that was called for in Resolution 1888. Some of the resources and successes of UN Action included inter-agency cooperation on SVC where most members could look beyond their own mandates and pool efforts to find new ways of working in New York and in field operations to address SVC. Alongside this ran UN Action's Multi-Partner Trust Fund (MPTF) that was set up in early 2009 and within a year mobilized over $5.4 million to fund UN Action initiatives such as the Stop Rape Now website, technical missions to the DRC to support the UN mission, and the establishment of the new Office of the SRSG-SVC and the Team of Experts.

The new SRSG-SVC was to become the permanent chair of UN Action and build on the coordination and inter-agency work that evolved to that point. The institutional adaptation and integration of the Office of the SRSG into the UN system and in relation to UN Action and its small secretariat took time to embed as both successive SRSGs brought their own backgrounds, strengths, and vision to interpreting the mandate and engaging and leading the existing platform. This proved more challenging than it should have been given the evolution of UN Action.

EMBEDDING THE NEW UN ARCHITECTURE ON COMBATTING SVC

The main challenge was one of "leadership following functions" in terms of inheriting and building upon the existing inter-agency forum of UN Action to accelerate implementation of the Security Council resolutions across peacekeeping, humanitarian, human rights, diplomatic/peacemaking, and development/peace-building operations. The mandate requires the support of and the ability to influence the work of other key UN offices, agencies, and programs. These include the UN Department of Peacekeeping Operations (DPKO), the Department of Political Affairs (DPA) for peacemaking and peace-building, as well as protection practices and programs ranging across the United Nations Population Fund (UNFPA), UNICEF, and the World Health Organization (WHO), to shape the delivery of integrated services to survivors. It has been challenging to know where the remits of the UN Action network and the SRSG begin and end, or overlap.

It was also not clear how the SRSG could cohere the assets, resources, and political capital at her disposal. These include (i) being chair of the UN Action network, giving access and opportunity to coordinate with the myriad of UN agencies, funds, and programs relevant for her in the SVC mandate; (ii) having a private office and staff to support the SRSG mandate; (iii) hosting the UN Action Secretariat in the SRSG office; (iii) having access through UN Action to an established trust fund for financing the private office, Team of Experts, and country-level initiatives that go beyond the SRSG office and entail joint UN projects at New York and field levels; and (iv) navigating expectations to work within wider UN structures such as the Security Council as well as UN member states at country level to advocate implementation of the WPS resolutions. In addition to this, the SRSG is expected to be "the voice" and "spokesperson" in the UN on SVC and to champion the agenda by raising the profile of particular situations.

While UN Action had established strengths, and a credible portfolio of inter-agency projects and initiatives, the Office of the SRSG also launched new initiatives and moved with an understandable impetus and desire to create a track record for itself that was distinct from UN Action. For example, staff in the SRSG office assumed direct contact with specific UN leadership teams at country level. They were undertaking missions and often agreeing to actions with little or no reference to previous or ongoing work by UN Action that was funding UN initiatives at country level and had on its Steering Committee the representatives of all entities working in country. At a minimum this created confusion, and diluted energies and resources. In some cases, it undermined the work and remit of UN Action by neither acknowledging what existed nor inviting UN Action for shared planning and advice. It also beset the first steps of engaging with the data problem when the SRSG launched its own work on the Monitoring and Reporting Arrangements called for in UN Security Council Resolution 1960 (2010). The office also unilaterally prepared guidance and ways forward with little reference or consultation with preexisting efforts on wider data and SVC capacities that were supported via UN Action. Such efforts involved core data collection by UN agencies such as UNICEF and UNFPA. This trend of independent and parallel tracks became more obvious as the office became fully staffed with various specialists, and targeted certain country situations and themes.

Lack of coordination or failure to capture institutional synergies could be seen in fundraising approaches, in access and use of the MPTF by the Office of the SRSG, and in communications and policy engagement functions to the UN system and with member states. This can be witnessed most visibly in the creation of separate websites with the SRSG setting up its own portal separate from the very successful, campaign-driven, UN Action website.[2] The websites have some coordination by this point but the purpose and audiences for both remain puzzling and only an insider with background knowledge could figure out the evolution of these different UN windows for showcasing the UN role and response to combatting SVC. On reflection, some consideration and pre-planning based on the existing strengths and resources of the UN Action network and the mandate of the SRSG would have made this integration of the new role and function into the still young architecture on SVC in the UN a lot easier. One cannot identify a particular political logic of why the evolution occurred in this way, except a working assumption by newly recruited staff that the SRSG office was starting from scratch, when it was not.

An unintended and unplanned consequence of the appointment of an SRSG-SVC was the positioning of this new role in the wider context of the UN architecture on WPS that now included the new gender entity of UN Women. Margot Wallström took up her appointment as SRSG-SVC in June 2010. A General Assembly resolution (A/RES/64/289) in July 2010 established the UN Entity for Gender Equality and the Empowerment of Women (UN Women) that became operational in January 2011. There was always likely to be potential for institutional tensions between the role of UN Women and any SRSG position related to gender or WPS that would be established. This lack again of pre-planning and failure to rethink or rework relevant structures and offices to ensure the agenda of SVC could be effectively pursued is not new. It reflects a logic of "adding on," like one who builds rooms onto a house as the number of residents increases but never considers redesigning the house to make it fit for new reality of more residents.

Another working logic voiced by many UN officials and 1325 activists interviewed for the 2013 review is that Security Council members were very resistant to having a dedicated SRSG on WPS owing to the wide agenda of 1325 that covered many UN mandates and areas of engagement in global peace and security. The Council was more prepared to countenance Resolution 1820 and the case for a dedicated SRSG on SVC as they could focus it on "protection" and a specific aspect of the impact of violent conflict. More feminist voices highlighted that this Security Council discourse was very gendered as protection was more appealing and appeasing to male decision makers and big powers than were any notions of agency, participation or empowerment that a wider mandate than SVC might involve (see chapters 6 and 12 in this volume).

The importance of the UN Action trust fund to the success of the SRSG office cannot be underestimated. By June 2017, it had mobilized some $42 million since its launch in January 2009.[3] The MPTF has supported global and national projects to test and advance implementation of new resources and approaches on the ground and contributed directly *to institutionalizing the focus on sexual violence in conflict within the UN system itself.* It incentivized cooperation with financial resources by requiring joint projects that ranged across, health, data, mediation, peacekeeping, and deployment of additional experts to UN Missions. The MPTF has been a vital source of independence and traction for the SVC architecture and agenda, and can be considered a critical part of the institutionalization of SVC at the UN. For example, in DRC, the MPTF funded the deployment of a Senior Coordinator within the UN mission and bridging to the wider range of agencies and programs that led to the first Comprehensive Strategy to combat SVC. This paved the way for the establishment of the first ever Sexual Violence Unit in a UN Mission (MONUSCO) to coordinate and take forward the Comprehensive Strategy and related Action Plan with the UN, government, NGO partners, and donors. Another example was funding the critical post of Program Manager for the Joint Government/UN Gender-Based Violence Program in Liberia that included SVC, notably in services for survivors and in addressing impunity. The funding for training and deployment of Women Peace Advisers to UN Missions as dedicated senior advisers to UN operations on monitoring, reporting, and accountability continues this stream of surge capacity at field level.

The SRSG office and UN Action enabled joint efforts to create and clarify operational guidance on core peace and security activities and approaches at the UN to better respond to and prevent sexual violence in conflict. This included "UN DPA Guidance for Mediators: Addressing Conflict-Related Sexual Violence in Ceasefire and Peace Agreements" and "Guidance Note of the Secretary-General on Reparations for Conflict-Related Sexual Violence," (UN DPA 2012; UN OHCHR and UN Women 2014). Two important initiatives to institutionalize the accountability part of the mandate of the SRSG-SVC center on (1), the Team of Experts on the Rule of Law and Sexual Violence in Conflict (ToE) that were also called for UNSCR 1888 and were established at the same time as the Office of the Secretary-General (OSRSG) in 2010; and (2), the Monitoring and Reporting Arrangements (MARA) called for in Resolution 1960.

The Team of Experts on the Rule of Law and Sexual Violence in Conflict brings together the Office of the Special Representative, the Department of Peacekeeping Operations, the Office of the United Nations High Commissioner for Human Rights (OHCHR), and the United Nations Development Programme (UNDP). It works directly on support to governments and national authorities to investigate and bring cases to address the impunity that is long-standing around SVC. Countries where the team has been deployed to give assistance include the Central African Republic, Colombia, Côte d'Ivoire, the Democratic Republic of the Congo, Guinea, Iraq, Liberia, Mali, Somalia, South Sudan, and countries neighboring the Syrian Arab Republic (Lebanon, Jordan and Turkey). Technical areas of support have included protection of victims, support to criminal investigations, military justice, as well as outcomes such as reparations for survivors. Much of the support, backed up by an international roster of experts centers on capacity building and working with governments. The annual reports of the Team provide case studies of particular support at country level that leverages national and other UN capacities and interventions. The link to increased or successful prosecutions is made, but as with all capacity building efforts seeking to reshape dynamic political or legal processes, the issue of contribution can be difficult to unpack among the many actors and actions working on the ground. For example, in its 2016 report, the Team of Experts state that the results in Cote d'Ivoire led to a scenario where

> reported cases of sexual violence have progressively decreased from a high of 180 cases noted in the 12 December 2014 Secretary-General's report on conflict-related sexual violence, to only 34 cases documented by ONUCI in the 2016 report. At least 23 perpetrators of these crimes were arrested, nine of whom were tried and sentenced. This has ultimately resulted in the de-listing of the FACI [armed forces of Cote d'Ivoire] from the annex of the Secretary-General's annual report on conflict-related sexual violence (UN Team of Experts 2016: 19, 22). [text added by author]

The establishment of the MARA accountability and reporting mechanism on SVC by the Security Council includes the listing of alleged perpetrators; the report by the SRSG-SVC of January 2012 (UNSC 2012) included for the first time an Annex of List of Parties Credibly Suspected of Committing or Being Responsible for Patterns of Rape and Other Forms of Violence in Situations of Armed Conflict on the Security Council Agenda. In this way, MARA has linked effectively to sanctions regimes with the list serving "as a basis for more focused United Nations engagement with those parties, including, as appropriate, measures in accordance with the procedures of the relevant sanctions committees" (UN Security Council 2010: Resolution 1960, operating para. 3). Accountability and armed groups were given an extra dimension in Resolution 2242 (UNSC 2015e) to mark the fifteenth anniversary of Resolution 1325. It addressed among other themes women's roles in countering violent extremism and terrorism and the use of sexual violence by listed terrorist groups. It dedicated three whole operating paragraphs (11–13) to the role of women in preventing violent extremism (PVE) and counter terrorism (CT).

The SRSG uptake on these new provisions can be seen in a Special Report submitted to the Security Council in December 2016 on the SVC perpetrated by ISIL in Syria and Iraq (OSRSG-SVC 2016). The focus of the report is "the use of sexual violence by violent extremist groups as a tactic of terrorism." It came on the back of the visit to the Middle East by SRSG Bangura during 2015. For this report, an expert was deployed to border areas to gather witness statements and evidence on patterns and trends. Consequently, the report documents supporting evidence for widespread and strategic use of sexual violence and sexual slavery by ISIL in recruitment of fighters, the funding of ISIL activities with links to trafficking of women and girls, and the targeting communities and clearing of territory through use of SVC.

While the use of rape as a weapon of war by extremist groups is a reality and needs to be recognized, witnessed, evidenced, and prosecuted as part of the SVC mandate, the linkage of WPS to PVE and CT objectives remains contested and controversial among women's organizations and peace-building organizations of all types.[4] There are concerns that this focus further instrumentalizes women and creates potential new risks. Over the past decade, international aid strategy and allocations in conflict-affected countries have been influenced by an increasing trend to securitization, where peace-building, peace support, conflict prevention, and women, peace, and security objectives are pitted against development assistance, being actively and specifically designed and targeted for, and framed more in terms of stabilization and security rather than peace or development.

The policy gains and contributions for UN Action and the SRSG-SVC began with Resolution 1820, owing to the success of a coalition of women's organizations, civil society leaders and activists, UN member state government leaders, officials and diplomats, and UN officials and bureaucrats. Four UNSCRs defined and expanded the mandate of the SRSG: 1820 (2008), 1888 (2009), 1960 (2010), and 2106 (2013). Most recently, paragraph 22 of Resolution 2106 (2013) requested that the SRSG-SVC report annually on the implementation of resolutions 1820 (2008), 1888 (2009), and 1960 (2010), and to recommend strategic actions. This amounts to a rolling mandate for the Office and the Role.

One of the indicators developed to track the implementation of Resolution 1325 (2000) is the "extent to which United Nations peacekeeping and special political missions include information on violations of women's and girls' human rights in their periodic reporting to the Security Council." The 2011 Women Peace and Security Report of the Secretary-General (UNSC 2011, operating para. 7) reported that "of the 58 country reports submitted by peacekeeping and political missions to the Security Council during 2010, 52 (90%) addressed women and peace and security issues—mainly sexual and gender-based violence, human rights violations and political participation." There are also annual reports by the Secretary-General to the Security Council on Conflict Related Sexual Violence (CRSV). UN Mission reports to the Security Council include sections on CRSV, and this is a consideration in recent Security Council mandates for peace operations. This accountability and reporting at the level of the Security Council is a notable shift and carries forward the spirit of UNSCR 1325 in ensuring gender is a matter of international peace and security. (UNSC 2015a, 2015b, 2017)

Challenges for Implementation

However, as the Global Study (UN Women 2015) clearly underlined, the increasing deepening of the normative framework for WPS is not leading to sufficiently greater action or impact on the ground in conflict situations or in the corridors of decision-making and power in New York, Geneva, or member state capitals, confirming the sense of many operational actors and staff (civil society organizations [CSOs], international NGOs, diplomats, officials, activists, field offices). The institutional energies and resources need to be redirected. This consensus emerged from both states and civil society debates around the fifteenth Anniversary and UN High-Level Review in October 2015. Specific tensions emerged as the SVC agenda was bedding into the UN system and the wider field of peace and security. The need to include men who are survivors of SVC in analysis, services, and accountability emerged as a strong theme (for example, Cain 2015; Sivakumaran 2007). This focus has sometimes risked creating a false parity that suggests reducing the focus on women and girls by calling for a "gender-inclusive" approach and sublimating yet again the case, the specific risks, attitudes, power dynamics, and ideas that took years to bring recognition of rape in war as a weapon and as a crime against humanity. Data consistently confirm that it is overwhelmingly girls and women who are targeted, and practitioners and professionals would not dispute that approaches should be inclusive of all survivors, and that accessing, understanding, and identifying the nature and impact of SVC on men and boys is part of that effort. In a context of underfunded and precarious responses, this remains challenging and sometimes a red herring in operational debates about responding to SVC.

A related ongoing tension for insitutionalizing SVC has been the constant call for a "threshold of credibility" regarding data on prevalence and impact of SVC in general to prove that is meets the threshold of a security concern (Steinberg 2008). As stated in WHO meeting report (2008: 10), "Demands for more and better data will not go away. Data is needed to justify why rape was put on the political agenda and why it should remain there." Some of these demands are logical in gathering information for advocacy, shaping responses, and accessing and reporting on funding for interventions related to SVC. However, there is also a lingering sense that SVC is held to a higher threshold that consciously or unconsciously reinforces the history of silence, shame, marginalization, as well as the difficulties for women and girls in conflict zones in being believed and being counted.

On a more positive note, there has been progress by specialist agencies in the UN on building improved, more sensitive, and better data collection systems for meeting demands of (i) providing medical and psychosocial services; (ii) documenting risk and therefore protection needs; and (iii) enabling accountability. Systems such as Gender-Based Violence Information Management System (GBVIMS) were supported and helped in terms of interagency cooperation through UN Action forum and funding.[5] So too was the UN Action

Summary of WHO's "Ethical and Safety Recommendations for Researching, Documenting, and Monitoring Sexual Violence in Emergencies"; this preceded and predated the UK-led 2014 initiative for an International Protocol on the Documentation and Investigation of Sexual Violence in Conflict.

The battle of terminology and concepts causes internal tensions among activists, professionals, and decision makers on the nature of sexual violence in conflict; this pits SVC against CRSV, gender-based violence (GBV), and violence against women (VAW). The move from SVC to CRSV in describing the focus of the mandate of the SRSG and UN Action has drawn some criticism and yet can also be seen as an attempt to focus the efforts of a dedicated office. An "Analytical Framing of Conflict-Related Sexual Violence" was set out in the Report of the Secretary-General to the Security Council on Conflict-Related Sexual Violence of January 13, 2012 (UNSC 2012). It highlighted parameters such "incidents or patterns . . . of sexual violence, that is rape, sexual slavery, forced prostitution, forced pregnancy, enforced sterilization or any other form of sexual violence of comparable gravity against women, men or children. [. . .] patterns occur in conflict or post conflict settings [. . .] may be evident in the profile and motivations of the perpetrator(s), the profile of the victim(s), the climate of impunity/State collapse, cross border dimensions and/or the fact that they violate the terms of a ceasefire agreement."

There are concerns that the "continuum of violence" which sees SVC and GBV as part of underlying norms and behaviors that are structural and require long-term transformation will be undermined by singling out SVC for targeted actions of protection, prevention, and accountability. The concern is that in its place there will be a hierarchy of gender and violence whereby a narrower definition of sexual violence in conflict, perpetrated by parties to conflict, and attested as patterns of conflict-related violence would be considered and addressed as a priority and major security concern. GBV and VAW that includes *all* situations that pertain to issues of forced and /or early marriage, inter-personal violence, domestic abuse, trafficking, sexual exploitation and abuse, and so forth, would lose out. There is some anecdotal evidence of that, in that simply by virtue of being elevated to the level of Security Council, as the lead body of the UN of global peace and security, and with annual thematic and country-level (UN peace operations) reporting, SVC is already singled out for more political attention and support by influential decision makers who may not readily engage or be interested in broader GBV/VAW campaigns. Many activists would argue it needed to be elevated, as rape in war was not being taken seriously as a weapon of war and a potential war crime. GBV has long-standing history with its own networks that has to some extent drawn more heavily on the humanitarian norms and practices.

VAW is a strong rallying point for global action and campaigns with engaged civil society activism and dedicated trust funds competing to raise funds for country level actions.

In a related sense, the overlap and tension between SVC and WPS remits spillover in agenda- and priority-setting across the UN on what to bring to the Security Council's attention or reflect on in work of the UN teams and missions at the country level. There is the concern of the decoupling of "protection" from prevention and participation in the WPS agenda by singling out SVC for attention and action as the only or reduced interpretation for action by the Security Council and UN Member States in implementing Resolution 1325. One of main findings of Global Study was that the emphasis on protection took over participation on the agenda of the Security Council. The findings were certainly not news to feminist activists, women's organizations, or civil society leaders and UN senior officials who had waged long campaigns to bring about 1325 and 1820. Yet these arguments of parsing the definitions of SVC come face to face with operational realities where scarce resources and often marginalized (female) staff working in very complex and pressured setting of UN Missions at the country level seek to keep Resolutions 1325 and 1820 on the agenda and to work together on the realities of the situation on the ground.

Lessons and Insights from SRSG-SVC and UN Action

What can we learn about the institutionalization of WPS from the experience of the SRSG-SVC? New York is a long way from Aleppo, Goma, Juba, and Mosul, and SRSGs leading UN missions on the ground straddle an expectation to be part of the machine in New York and keep political engagement active while driving forward operational and advocacy impact and change on the ground—this is the front line of the work in terms of supporting survivors, investigating violations, and exercising accountability. The UN Gender Architecture remains a work in progress. New mechanisms need to bring along and build upon ongoing achievements in other agencies and offices. The SRSG-SVC requires support and space to set an agenda while harnessing the existing resources and achievements of the UN—each individual incumbent of the SRSG post will bring their own strengths and focus to the position.

It may be more than coincidence that the first incumbent in the post of SRSG-SVC extended her influence and impact by going on to pioneer "feminist foreign policy" as the Minister for Foreign Affairs in Sweden; this experiment is similarly testing and driving the institutionalization of WPS agenda. The Office of the SRSG and UN Action together as an ecosystem for combating SVC have influenced and in all likelihood accelerated the example-setting that required leadership and proactive take-up of key UN actors, including DPKO and DPA in the fields of peacekeeping and peace processes. It also strengthened the cross-UN platform for health-related and humanitarian response programming to advance their integrated support to survivors (e.g., medical care, psychosocial support, rehabilitation, support for return to family and community). Relations with civil society and women's organizations need to change fundamentally in terms of the attitudes and nature of participation in multilateral system at the UN. This is not unique to SVC or the gender architecture but is a question of power, position, and assumptions about who is "in the room" for decision making and debate. The current model is based, at best, on consultation and select participation. Money remains as a key factor. This is attested by the vital importance of the MPTF to drive change in terms of (i) providing incentives for inter-agency cooperation; (ii) being an incubator of learning and new practices; (iii) ensuring rapid set up of SRSG office and Team of Experts to implement critical commitments of Resolution 1888; (iv) and be a focus for donor activism. Male champions in the system are an important resource, notably the UN Secretary-General and the still predominantly male SRSGs who are in charge of the leading UN Missions and Operations on the ground and can set the tone for how SVC and wider GBV considerations will be treated and addressed. Greater management accountability is also helping to increase engagement.

CONCLUSION

Future institutionalization of the SVC and WPS mandates needs to take account of the ongoing reforms of the UN in terms of global peace and security. During 2015 there were three major reviews on peace and security at the UN. The Global Study on the Implementation of Resolution 1325 was one (UN Women 2015). The other two were the High-Level Independent Panel on United Nations Peace Operations (UNSC 2015c) and the Advisory Group of Experts for the 2015 Review of the United Nations Peacebuilding Architecture (UNSC 2015d). All three reviews were planned separately with intense timelines. There was a glaring missed opportunity to carry out a comprehensive review of the UN system on peace and security and a sense that silos were reinforced. Nonetheless worthy efforts were made by the different panels to link up and coordinate, and to all make recommendations on WPS. Getting women, peace, and security into the DNA of analysis and decisions to rebuild and reform the UN remains a critical task for the SRSG-SVC in coming years.

The institutionalization of WPS faces the challenge of developing effective means and ways of translating the resolutions into actions. There is the challenge of working in new ways within the preexisting and enduring peace and security structures of the UN, as well as the recently reformed gender structures that created UN Women. Part of the learning from the evolution of the office of the SRSG-SVC is the difficult and ongoing work of reforming and coordinating the existing offices and mandates that all directly deal with WPS issues of protection, participation, and peace-building. The tendency of all new offices and entities to clarify and embed their offices can lead to an incentive to develop a body of work or actions that can be directly attributed to them. The reality is that WPS and SVC actions require collaboration, coordination, and acknowledgment of comparative advantages and expertise to work on different fronts (health, rule of law, peacekeeping, and so on). These high-level and challenging skills and the authority to facilitate and coordinate such actions in the implementation of WPS agenda are the real challenge. One dedicated office—whether it is narrowly focused on SVC or expanded to WPS—would still remain bound in this systemic way of working to be effective and improve the situation on the ground for women and girls caught up in conflict.

We cannot speak yet of a coherent, established, and accepted WPS architecture at the UN. Indeed, there is a fundamental question of whether a separate or distinctive WPS architecture is the most strategic or effective way to proceed in terms of reforming and transforming long-standing UN peace and security, humanitarian, and peace-building operations to implement WPS commitments in war-torn areas. What we can speak of is a normative framework of UN Security Council Resolutions, UN Reports, National Actions Plans on 1325 as well as some new, dedicated capacities including the UN Action platform and the SRSG-SVC, as well as Trust Funds, rule of law expert teams, and so forth. There is a need for gender-mandated agencies and roles across the UN to move beyond the rhetoric of a split between 1325 and 1820 that has pitted participation against protection. This means reuniting Resolutions 1820 with 1325 and ending the split of these agendas at the Security Council. Given the track record and evidence of some successes on SVC in a relatively short time frame, there is a need to return to the winning formula of activism inside and outside of the UN that brought together coalitions of CSOs, NGOs, key member states, leading diplomats, professionals, and academics who championed, agitated, and painstakingly built the platform for action.

A more ambitious and political systemic approach by decision-makers, officials, and civil society partners to UN institutionalization of WPS would allow more fundamental questioning of gendered assumptions and implications of the *status quo* analysis and responses to violent conflict that permeate UN peace operations. This kind of systemic approach is well supported by academic and grassroots work being carried out on feminist political economy and conflict, for example (Cohn 2013; Duncanson 2016; True 2012; WILPF 2014, 2016a, 2016b). Its elevation and application to the leadership of operationalizing WPS resolutions could transform, reinvigorate, and increase effectiveness and the likelihood of success of a host of UN actions, resources, and capabilities in crisis situation with real results for women, girls, and their communities. This ambition can contribute to the desperately needed reform and transformation of core business and operating models of the UN to respond to contemporary crises and global political dynamics.

Lastly, there is a need to recapture the global feminist political engagement and debate that led to 1325 and 1820. This is about making meaningful civil society engagement happen and not simply talk about it, through: (i) direct briefings to the Security Council by women representatives and leaders from conflict-affected countries; (ii) direct funding to international and national NGOs and local civil society organizations from UN Trust Funds as a matter of course and not experiment in aiming for the very low bar of 15 percent quota for gender-related allocations from peace-building and post-conflict reconstruction funds that are in place at the UN; (iii) requiring and releasing agreed outcomes and action points from consultations and meetings of civil society women representatives with UN leaders whether at UN missions and team in country or with SRSGs and the Secretary-General in New York; and (iv), participation of civil society representatives in follow-up and implementation of UN reforms.

Notes

1. The 13 entities include UN Department of Political Affairs (UN DPA) UN Department for Peacekeeping Operations (UNDPKO), United Nations Development Programme (UNDP), UN Children's Program (UNICEF), UN Population Fund, (UNFPA), World Health Organization (WHO), UN Entity for Gender Equality and the Empowerment of Women [UN Women, since 2010], UN High Commissioner for Refugees (UNHCR), UN Office for the Coordination of Humanitarian Affairs (UN OCHA), UN Office of the High Commissioner for Human Rights (OHCHR), UN Office for Drugs and Crime (UNODC), UN Peace Building Support Office (UN PBSO), Joint United Nations Programme on HIV/AIDS (UNAIDS)

2. See Stop Rape Now, UN Action against Sexual Violence in Conflict, http://www.stoprapenow.org.

3. See Multi-Partner Trust Fund Office, "United Nations Fund for Action against Sexual Violence," UNDP, 2017, http://mptf.undp.org/factsheet/fund/UNA00?fund_status_month_to=6&fund_status_year_to=2017.

4. For example, see piece by Syrian activist Maria Al Abdeh, "Conflict in Syria: Stop Instrumental sing Women's Rights," Open Democracy (April 19, 2017), where she highlights the impact of counter terrorism approaches on financing of community projects as well as lack of balance by international community in addressing sources of sexual violence, https://www.opendemocracy.net/5050/maria-al-abdeh/syria-instumentalising-women-s-rights.

   Anna Möller-Loswick, a policy officer at the peace-building NGO Saferworld, makes a similar point and highlights the impact on women's organizations and peace work where new funding incentives force them to adapt to PVE and CT frameworks of donors to secure funding for their work; this also places women at risk of being seen as intelligence gatherers. SaferWorld (April 26, 2017), https://www.saferworld.org.uk/resources/news-and-analysis/post/221-the-countering-violent-extremism-agenda-risks-undermining-women-who-need-greater-support.

5. The Gender-Based Violence Information Management System (GBVIMS) initiative was launched in 2006 by UNOCHA, UNHCR, and the IRC (International Refugee Council). Over the past ten years it has been implemented in more than twenty countries. Today, the GBVIMS Steering Committee now consists of UNFPA, UNICEF, UNHCR, IRC, and IMC (International Medical Corps). For more, see http://www.gbvims.com/what-is-gbvims/gbvims-background/.

References

Cain, M. "Hope in the Shadows: Male Victims of Sexual Assault in the Democratic Republic of the Congo." *Knowledge & Action*, Humanity in Action, 2015, http://www.humanityinaction.org/knowledgebase/657-hope-in-the-shadows-male-victims-of-sexual-assault-in-the-democratic-republic-of-the-congo.

Cohn, C., ed. *Women and Wars*. Cambridge: Polity Press, 2013.

Duncanson, C. *Gender and Peacebuilding*. Cambridge: Polity Press, 2016.

Office of the SRSG-SVC. "Special Report of the Special Representative of the Secretary-General on Sexual Violence in Conflict." Submission to the Security Council Committee pursuant to resolutions 1267 (1999), 1989 (2011), and 2253 (2015), concerning ISIL (Da'esh), Al Qaeda, and associated individuals, groups, undertakings, and entities. S/2016/1090, December 2016, http://www.un.org/ga/search/view_doc.asp?symbol=S/2016/1090.

O'Gorman, E. "Review of UN Action against Sexual Violence in Conflict (2007–2012)." Stop Rape Now, 2013, http://www.stoprapenow.org/uploads/advocacyresources/1401281502.pdf.

Sivakumaran, S. "Sexual Violence against Men in Armed Conflict." *European Journal of International Law* 18, no. 2 (2007): 253–276, https://doi.org/10.1093/ejil/chm013.

Steinberg, D. "Combating Sexual Violence in Conflict: Using Facts on the Ground." Speech by Donald Steinberg, Deputy President, International Crisis Group, to United Nations Action against Sexual Violence in Conflict in Geneva. December 17, 2008, https://www.crisisgroup.org/global/combating-sexual-violence-conflict-using-facts-ground.

True, J. *The Political Economy of Violence against Women*. Oxford: Oxford University Press, 2012.

UN Action. *Summary of Ethical and Safety Recommendations for Researching, Documenting, and Monitoring Sexual Violence in Emergencies*. Geneva: World Health Organization, 2007.

UNDPA. *UN DPA Guidance for Mediators: Addressing Conflict-Related Sexual Violence in Ceasefire and Peace Agreements*. New York: United Nations, 2012.

UN OHCHR and UN Women. *Guidance Note of the Secretary-General on Reparations for Conflict-Related Sexual Violence*. New York: United Nations, 2014.

United Nations Security Council (UNSC). Resolution 1325: Women, Peace, and Security. October 31, 2000.

United Nations Security Council (UNSC). Resolution 1820: Women, Peace, and Security. June 19, 2008.

United Nations Security Council (UNSC). Resolution 1888: Women, Peace, and Security. September 30, 2009a.

United Nations Security Council (UNSC). Resolution 1889: Women, Peace, and Security. October 5, 2009b.

United Nations Security Council (UNSC). Resolution 1960: Women, Peace, and Security. December 16, 2010.

United Nations Security Council (UNSC). "Report of the Secretary-General on Conflict-Related Sexual Violence." S/2011/598, September 29, 2011, http://www.un.org/en/ga/search/view_doc.asp?symbol=S/2011/598.

United Nations Security Council (UNSC). "Report of the Secretary-General on Conflict-Related Sexual Violence." S/2012/33, September 13, 2012, http://www.un.org/en/ga/search/view_doc.asp?symbol=S/2012/33.

United Nations Security Council (UNSC). Resolution 2242: Women, Peace, and Security. October 13, 2015e.

United Nations Security Council (UNSC). "Report of the Secretary-General on Conflict-Related Sexual Violence." S/2015/203, March 23, 2015a, http://www.un.org/en/ga/search/view_doc.asp?symbol=S/2015/203.

United Nations Security Council (UNSC). "Report of the Secretary-General on Women, Peace, and Security." S/2015/716, September 16, 2015b, http://www.un.org/en/ga/search/view_doc.asp?symbol=S/2015/716.

United Nations Security Council (UNSC). "Report of the Secretary-General on The Future of United Nation Peace Operations: Implementation of the Recommendations of the High-Level Independent Panel on Peace Operations." S/2015/682, September 2, 2015c, http://www.un.org/en/ga/search/view_doc.asp?symbol=S/2015/682.

United Nations Security Council (UNSC). "Challenge of Sustaining Peace: Report of the Advisory Group of Experts on the Review of Peacebuilding Architecture." S/2015/490, June 30, 2015d, http://www.un.org/ga/search/view_doc.asp?symbol=A/69/968.

United Nations Security Council. "Report of the Secretary-General on Conflict-Related Sexual Violence." S/2016/361/Rev.1, June 2016a, http://www.un.org/ga/search/view_doc.asp?symbol=S/2016/361/Rev.1.

United Nations Security Council (UNSC). "Report of the Secretary-General on Women, Peace, and Security." S/2016/822. September 29, 2016b, http://www.un.org/en/ga/search/view_doc.asp?symbol=S/2016/822.

United Nations Security Council (UNSC). "Report of the Secretary-General on Conflict-Related Sexual Violence." S/2017/249, April 15, 2017, http://www.un.org/ga/search/view_doc.asp?symbol=S/2017/249.

UN Team of Experts. "Annual Report 2016." Team of Experts/Rule of Law/Sexual Violence in Conflict, 2016, http://stoprapenow.org/uploads/advocacyresources/1493911578.pdf.

UN Women. "Transforming Justice, Securing the Peace. A Global Study on the Implementation of United Nations Security Council Resolution 1325 (2000)." Lead author: Radhika Coomaraswamy. UN Women, 2015, http://wps.unwomen.org/pdf/en/GlobalStudy_EN_Web.pdf.

WHO. "Data Report on Behalf of UN Action and with Support of UNFPA and UNICEF." Geneva: WHO, 2008.

WILPF. "Women Organising for Change in Syria and Bosnia and Herzegovina: Conference Report." Geneva: WILPF, 2014, http://wilpf.org/wp-content/uploads/2014/07/Women-Organising-for-Change-in-Bosnia-and-Syria.pdf.

WILPF. "Feminist (Re)interpretation of the Dayton Peace Accords: An Intimate Dialogue on How Societies Transit from War to Peace and How Feminist Approach to Peacebuilding Can Help Create Strong and Long-Lasting Peace." Working Document, Women Organising for Change in Syria and Bosnia and Herzegovina project. Geneva: WILPF, 2016a, http://womenorganizingforchange.org/Development/wp-content/uploads/2016/02/DPA-report-FINAL.pdf.

WILPF. "Concept and Framework for the Development of a Gender-Sensitive Reparations Programme for Civilian Victims of War in Bosnia and Herzegovina." Women Organising for Change in Syria and Bosnia and Herzegovina project. Geneva: WILPF, 2016b, http://womenorganizingforchange.org/Development/wp-content/uploads/2016/02/Reparations-BiH.pdf.

Websites ConsultedPeace Women: http://www.peacewomen.org

Security Council Report: http://www.securitycouncilreport.org

Stop Rape Now: http://stoprapenow.org/advocacy-resources/

Office of the Special Representative of the Secretary-General for Sexual Violence in Conflict: http://www.un.org/sexualviolenceinconflict/

United Nations Security Council: http://www.un.org/en/sc/documents/

UN Women: http://www.unwomen.org

CHAPTER 25

··

WPS AND THE HUMAN
RIGHTS COUNCIL

··

RASHIDA MANJOO

WHETHER in times of conflict, post-conflict, transitions, displacements, or peace, violence against women impairs and nullifies women's realization of their human rights; prevents women from participating in their community as full and equal citizens; reinforces male dominance and control; supports discriminatory gender norms; and also maintains systemic inter-gender and intra-gender inequalities. These consequences, among others, are exacerbated during times of conflict and post-conflict. It has been recognized that "violence against women is an obstacle to the achievement of the objectives of equality, development and peace in all societies, to a greater or lesser degree, women and girls are subjected to physical, sexual and psychological abuse that cuts across lines of income, class and culture" (UN General Assembly 1995).[1] Under international law, states have an obligation to respect, protect, and fulfill all human rights including the obligation to respond to and prevent gendered human rights violations that disproportionately impact women and girls.

This chapter provides an overview of the work, whether explicit or implicit, of the United Nations Human Rights Council (the Council)[2] and its mechanisms, which illustrates its concerns about Women, Peace, and Security (WPS) and the need to address how this impacts the exercise and realization of all human rights by women.[3] The significance of interrogating the work of the Council lies in the imperative to address the human rights of women in a holistic manner. This requires all UN oversight mechanisms and also agencies to reinforce and strengthen both the normative and the implementation aspects of issues that adversely impact the promotion, protection, and realization of human rights.

The temporal period covered is 2006 to 2016. The chapter includes a general overview of the Council and its mechanisms, as well as the relevant research focus areas of its Advisory Committee. It provides an analysis of applicable resolutions adopted by the Council; an analysis of the investigations of country situations mandated by the Council, whether through Commissions of Inquiry, Fact Finding Missions, Commissions on Human Rights, or Investigations. It then offers some reflections on the work of the Council in the Universal Periodic Review process, and, finally, addresses the engagement of the Special Procedures system with WPS. The chapter concludes by highlighting some of the gaps and challenges that are reflected in the functioning of the Council as regards WPS.

The Council in its work program underscores the need to focus on the promotion and protection of all human rights: civil, political, economic, social, and cultural rights, including the right to development. This framing also includes looking at violence against women, whether perpetrated by state or non-state actors, as a human rights violation in and of itself. For a long time, traditional human rights advocacy viewed gender-based violence through a public/private binary where states are responsible only for violence against women committed in the public sphere while ignoring the reality that violence crosses the public and private domains, ranging from intimate and interpersonal violence to structural, systematic, and institutional forms of violence. Currently, a greater focus on the mainstreaming and specificity on the human rights of women in general, and violence against women in particular, is also reflected in the policies, processes, and practices in the different mechanisms of the Council.

General Overview of the Human Rights Council

The Human Rights Council, which was established by the General Assembly in March 2006, is an intergovernmental body within the United Nations system and it is responsible for strengthening the promotion and protection of human rights globally (UN General Assembly 2006). It consists of forty-seven member states of the United Nations, elected by the General Assembly, and it reports annually on its activities to the General Assembly. The Council replaced the United Nations Commission on Human Rights, which was created in 1946, a year after the adoption of the UN Charter. The predecessor had the mandate to draft the Universal Declaration on Human Rights and other relevant human rights instruments. The creation of a new body to fulfill the human rights promise of the United Nations Charter, arose out of concerns and criticisms, including in respect of issues such as the politicization, effectiveness, credibility, and objectivity of the Commission on Human Rights.

The work of the Council is undertaken through three regular sessions per year, and when necessary, special sessions are also held. It is administratively supported by the Office of the High Commissioner of Human Rights in Geneva. Its work includes both a thematic and a country situation focus, whether through directly addressing situations of human rights violations; monitoring human rights thematic issues; conducting reviews of human rights developments in all 193 member states of the United Nations; adopting resolutions; and producing reports and making recommendations.

In 2007 the Council adopted, after an institution-building process, procedures and mechanisms to guide its work. This process acknowledged the Council's status as a cooperative mechanism based on interactive dialogues, interactions that privilege dialogue over confrontation, and consensus as opposed to polarization (UN General Assembly 2006; UN Human Rights Council 2007a). The Council has established some new mechanisms and processes. These include the Universal Periodic Review process; the setting up of an Advisory Committee; and establishing a complaints procedure to allow for individuals and organizations to file complaints about human rights violations, with the Council having the power to address such complaints. The Commission on Human Rights, the predecessor of the Council, was prevented through a 1947 Economic and Social Council resolution from having the power to take action in respect of any complaints concerning human rights (UN Economic and Social Council 1947). Thus a complaints procedure, that grants powers to the Council to act on allegations received, is a positive development and a welcome addition to the human rights architecture. The addressing of complaints and the findings of the Council are generally deemed confidential, and can result in a decision to keep the country situation under review or to discontinue the review.

The hosting of a full-day panel discussion followed by an interactive dialogue with states on different thematic issues is also a current process. Women's human rights has been one of the thematic focus areas in the Council's annual interactive session. In terms of a Council resolution (UN Human Rights Council 2007b), the focus of the 2016 annual discussion on the human rights of women included two themes—"Violence against Indigenous Women and Girls and Its Root Causes" and "Women's Rights and the 2030 Agenda for Sustainable Development" (UN Human Rights Council 2016a). The theme of violence against women is a common one during the annual day of discussion, and WPS has been touched upon in previous years. The Council inherited the system of Special Procedures which was established by its predecessor, and which consists of independent experts, working groups, and special rapporteurs.

The Advisory Committee can be an important driving force of the Council's thematic focus areas, including in highlighting current areas of concern and normative developments and gaps. This committee was created through the Council's institution-building resolution to function as a "think tank" to provide it with expertise and advice on thematic human rights issues (UN Human Rights Council 2007a: paras. 65 to 84). It is not an independent autonomous body that can decide on what thematic issues it considers as relevant or a priority for research, but this committee works under the direction of the Council. Areas of focus for research have included, among others, albinism, corruption, international solidarity, missing persons, the right to peace, and post-disaster and post-conflict situations. The 2017 agenda includes a request for research on the integration of a gender perspective. Interestingly, the Council in 2011 requested this Committee to develop a Draft Declaration on the Right of Peoples to Peace (UN General Assembly 2010c). This was preceded by a request in 2009 to the High Commissioner for Human Rights to host a workshop on the right to peace and to produce a report (UN Human Rights Council 2008a; UN General Assembly 2010a). The final draft declaration developed by the Advisory Committee was presented to the Council in 2012, and it is unclear as to further developments regarding this draft declaration (UN General Assembly 2012a). The Draft Declaration focuses on standards relating to international peace and security that are core to the right to peace. It also includes relevant standards in the areas of peace education, development, the environment, and victims and vulnerable groups as elements of positive peace. Women experiencing from violence are included in Article 11(3) of the Draft Declaration under the category of victims and vulnerable groups, who have a right to truth, restoration of rights, and effective and full redress among others. However, there is no reference in the Draft Declaration to Security Council resolutions linked to WPS.

In 2012, the Advisory Committee made a proposal to the Council on the need for research on the protection of human rights in post-conflict and post-disaster situations. Subsequently, the Council adopted a resolution in 2013 (UN General Assembly 2013a), and the Advisory Committee presented its final research-based report to the Council in 2015 (UN General Assembly 2015a). The report adopted a holistic approach to the normative analysis by highlighting state obligations emanating from international law including human rights, humanitarian, refugee, and criminal law, as applicable to international and non-international armed conflict, post-conflict, and peace-building contexts. These obligations also extend to post-conflict reconstruction and recovery as well as transitional contexts. The focus on affected persons includes women and girls, children, older persons, indigenous peoples and minorities, LGBTI persons, and persons with disabilities.

Paragraph 31 of the report explicitly references Security Council Resolution 1325 as regards representation of women in all decision-making processes and mechanisms. This paragraph also highlights the need for effective remedies for violence against women and the need for the human rights–based approach in this regard. Paragraph 85 calls for the implementation of the four pillars of the women, peace, and security agenda—participation, protection, prevention, and relief and recovery—as reflected in Security Council Resolutions 1325 and 1820. Of concern is the fact that despite the Advisory Committee sending out a questionnaire to Member States, civil society, and UN agencies, the response rate was just thirty-nine responses. Surprisingly, no UN agency responded to the questionnaire that was sent out specifically to all agencies in 2014. It can be assumed that the low response rate as well as the lack of information from relevant UN agencies negatively impacted the information that was available to highlight practices on the ground, in respect of the WPS.

Resolutions Adopted by the Human Rights Council between 2006 and 2016

Over ten years, the Council has adopted numerous resolutions that either explicitly mention, or implicitly refer to, aspects linked to the Security Council resolutions dealing with WPS. Relevant resolutions broadly deal with the issues of human rights and transitional justice[4]; sexual violence (UN General Assembly 2010b); elimination of discrimination against women (UN General Assembly 2013b); violence against women (UN General Assembly 2014a); and accelerating efforts to eliminate all forms of violence against women, among others (UN General Assembly 2013c; 2016a). There is no specific resolution dedicated to WPS, but references are made in different resolutions including as follows: women in situations of armed conflict (UN Human Rights Council 2009); or conflict related sexual violence (UN General Assembly 2011a); and sexual violence particularly in conflict and post-conflict situations (UN General Assembly 2012b). Resolutions dealing with violence against women often refer to the "prevalence of violence against women and girls, including domestic violence, [which is] exacerbated in armed conflict and humanitarian crisis situations" (UN General Assembly 2015b).

In addition, resolutions that deal with trafficking also recognize the heightened vulnerability to trafficking of women and children in humanitarian crisis situations, including conflict and post-conflict environments (UN General Assembly 2016b). Resolutions that deal with the elimination of discrimination against women also recognize the negative impact of armed conflict and natural disasters on women and girls' health and well-being (UN General Assembly 2016c). The resolution on the impact of arms transfers and human rights acknowledges that arms transfers can have a seriously negative impact on the human rights of women and girls due to the widespread availability of arms, as it may increase the risk of sexual and gender-based violence (UN General Assembly 2016d). A resolution on human rights and transitional justice reaffirms the important role of women in the prevention and resolution of conflicts and in peace-building (UN General Assembly 2016e).

Despite a commitment to gender integration, as well as specificity in terms of women's human rights, the Council has passed resolutions that do not include, either explicitly or implicitly, the nexus between health, education, development, the right to food, water, and sanitation, among others, and the specific needs of women in contexts of conflict and post-conflict. A resolution adopted on the thirtieth anniversary of the Declaration on the Right to Development acknowledges the human rights of all, including the goal of achieving gender equality and the empowerment of women and girls (UN General Assembly 2016f: para. 12). However, most resolutions that deal with the right to development fail to acknowledge the link between the right to development and WPS.[5] Various resolutions on education make no explicit mention of the right of women and girls to education, let alone make reference to this right in conflict and post-conflict settings.[6] A resolution on realizing the equal enjoyment of the right to education by every girl highlights concern that humanitarian crises and armed conflicts are depriving children, especially girls, of access to education (UN General Assembly 2016g: preamble and 2(m)).

As is acknowledged in policy developments on WPS, women's health issues are of serious concern in such contexts. One Council resolution explicitly draws the link by recognizing that the risk of maternal mortality and morbidity is exacerbated in armed conflict and humanitarian emergencies (UN General Assembly 2016h). Often there is no explicit mention in resolutions of how women are denied protection from and prevention of violence in conflict, post-conflict, and peace-building environments, and how these must be addressed.[7] Resolutions that deal with the standard of physical and mental health do not make explicit mention of the need for specific attention to women's needs in such contexts (UN General Assembly 2010d, 2013d). One resolution highlights the importance of capacity building and strengthening the participation of women in decision-making processes and developing gender-sensitive multisectoral health policies (UN General Assembly 2016i). It is clear that the Council resolutions on health do not consistently reflect the nexus and the need to pay specific attention to the issue of women and girls' health needs in general, and in situations of conflict and post-conflict specifically.

The preceding brief analysis of some of the resolutions adopted by the Council raise questions about whether principles of gender integration, mainstreaming, and intersectionality are sufficiently understood, and whether they are taken into account in the negotiation process when resolutions are being developed. Also, it is unclear whether there is a sufficient knowledge base in such processes that understands the synergies and linkages between a holistic understanding of human rights promotion and protection, and WPS.

COMMISSIONS OF INQUIRY, FACT-FINDING MISSIONS, AND COMMISSIONS ON HUMAN RIGHTS

The widespread and systematic human rights violations faced by women in conflict and post-conflict situations, including sexual and gender-based violence, can amount to crimes against humanity, war crimes, and genocide, in some contexts. The killing of women as strategic targets for the purpose of terrorizing civilian populations, and also the targeting of women human rights defenders as the symbolic targets of politically motivated killings during conflicts and transitions can also amount to violations of international laws (UN Human Rights Council 2012).

As part of the protection and promotion of all human rights, the mandate of the Council includes the responsibility to address situations of human rights violations, including gross and systematic violations, as experienced by women in different country contexts. This requires proactive action by the Council through receiving reports and communications, and also considering information about triggers and early warning signs that are brought to the attention of the Council, including through findings and recommendations that are reflected in the reports of Special Procedures mandate-holders. Consideration of such information can lead to the adoption of resolutions that set up Commissions of Inquiry (COI), Fact-Finding Missions, Investigations, and Commissions on Human Rights. The appointment of a country-specific mandate-holder is also an option in such circumstances.

The Council's Agenda Item 4 focuses on human rights situations that require its attention to address gross and systematic violation of human rights. Unfortunately, not all states are supportive of resolutions relating to the scrutiny of country-specific situations without the consent of the implicated state. This is a challenge to the Council's credibility and legitimacy, as political considerations lead to politicization of the issue and to compromising of the Council's work on promoting and protecting all human rights. The lack of universal support for a resolution under Agenda Item 4 can lead to the Council considering a resolution under Agenda Item 10, which relates to the provision of technical assistance and capacity building to address the human rights situation, even when there is evidence of gross and systematic human rights violation. In addition, in such circumstances, the Council can opt to adopt a resolution under Agenda Item 2 mandating the High Commissioner of Human Rights to investigate and report on country situations where there are reports of gross violations of human rights. These various options have disadvantages, including allowing for the continuation of gross human rights violations and impunity for such violations; accepting the politicization of human rights issues due to the intransigent and unethical support of some states as regards the scrutiny of states that are implicated in gross human rights violations; and also by imposing a human and financial burden on the Office of the High Commissioner of Human Rights, without factoring in increased budgets for carrying out investigations.

The Council's resolutions have established mechanisms to investigate situations of serious violations of international human rights law and international humanitarian law. The countries that are reviewed in what follows include the Democratic Republic of Korea, Eritrea, Sri Lanka, Occupied Palestinian Territory, Libya, Syria, Burundi, and South Sudan. This analysis briefly highlights findings linked to WPS emanating from the inquiry and investigation reports, as well as references to this issue in relevant resolutions. In 2013 the Council established a COI on Human Rights in the Democratic Republic of Korea with the mandate to investigate systematic, widespread, and grave violations of human rights, with a view to ensuring full accountability, in particular for violations that may amount to crimes against humanity (UN General Assembly 2013e). The report includes findings of gender-based discrimination and violence against women, especially linked to the *songun* system, which further increases the vulnerability of women.[8] The COI report also highlights other violations such as freedom of movement, and sexual and reproductive rights. However, the resolutions adopted in respect of this COI do not make explicit mention of WPS.[9]

The 2014 resolution establishing a COI on Eritrea (UN General Assembly 2014b) was mandated to investigate all alleged violations of human rights as outlined in the reports of the Special Rapporteur on the situation of human rights in Eritrea (UN General Assembly 2013f; 2014c). The reports presented in 2015 and 2016 pay special attention to allegations of sexual and gender-based violence.[10] The reports highlight that sexual violence, which occurs in the military, detention centers, and at the country's borders, largely goes unpunished. Again, the Council resolutions do not mention WPS explicitly, but the issues of child marriages, forced marriages, female genital mutilation, and violence against women are addressed in the report.[11]

The 2014 resolution on promoting reconciliation, accountability, and human rights in Sri Lanka (UN General Assembly 2014d) requires the High Commissioner to undertake a comprehensive investigation into alleged serious violations and abuses of human rights and related crimes by all sides to the conflict during the period 2002 to 2011. The High Commissioner appointed three experts to play a supportive and advisory role to its internal staff team. There was a common understanding that the report would be a human rights investigation report, and not a criminal investigation report. The COI report has a dedicated section on sexual and gender-based violence with findings that indicate that sexual violence is used as part of torture; that government security forces are largely responsible for such human rights violations; and that there are grounds to conclude that there have been human rights violations that can amount to war crimes and crimes against humanity.[12] The Council resolutions are not explicit about WPS,[13] but there is one resolution explicitly mentioning sexual and gender-based violence (UN General Assembly 2014d).

There have been numerous resolutions and a few COIs on the situation in the Occupied Palestinian Territory (OPT). The 2014 resolution mandated the High Commissioner to dispatch an independent, international COI, who would be appointed by the President of the Council, to investigate all violations of international humanitarian law and human rights law in the OPT, and East Jerusalem, particularly in the occupied Gaza Strip due to the most recent military operations (UN General Assembly 2014e). The report of the COI reveals violations of principles of distinction, proportionality, and precaution, which adversely impact civilians in general, and women in particular. This has rendered women and children vulnerable to death and injury, with an increase in death rates of women from 14 percent in 2009 to 20.2 percent in 2014.[14] There is no specific mention of sexual and gender-based violence in the report or in the Council resolutions.[15]

The resolution on technical assistance and capacity building to improve human rights in Libya was adopted in 2015 and it mandated the High Commissioner to send a mission to investigate violations and abuses of international human rights, in coordination with the UN Support Mission in Libya, and to provide the Council with a comprehensive report (UN General Assembly 2015c). The report "Investigation by the Office of the United Nations High Commissioner for Human Rights on Libya"[16] makes explicit mention of Security Council Resolutions 1325 and 1820. It has a dedicated section on sexual and gender-based violence and discrimination against women. It also highlights that there have been a series of attacks by armed groups on women who are promoting equality, social justice, and accountability; that women migrants and women in detention centers are particularly vulnerable and subject to sexual violence and exploitation; that other rights of women are routinely violated, such as freedom of movement, forced modesty dress codes, and issues relating to access to justice. The recommendations in the report emphasize the need for protection measures.[17] Generally the relevant Council resolutions do not explicitly mention the Security Council resolutions on WPS,[18] but some resolutions mention sexual violence against women and the empowerment of women and girls (UN General Assembly 2011b; 2014f), and the equal and effective participation of women in all activities relating to the prevention and resolution of armed conflict (UN General Assembly 2015c; 2016j).

In 2011 a Council resolution mandated the investigation of all alleged violations of international human rights law, through an Independent International COI for the Syrian Arab Republic (UN Human Rights Council 2011). Numerous resolutions have been adopted and eight reports have been produced by the COI. The 2015 and 2016 reports highlight that civilians continue to be the main victims of the conflict (UN Human Rights Council 2015; 2016b). The "Report on the Independent International Commission of Inquiry on the Syrian Arab Republic: They came to Destroy: ISIS Crimes against Yazidi"[19] includes a separate section on the treatment of Yazidi women and girls aged nine and above, including pervasive sexual violence and sexual slavery. It exposes how unmarried women are most vulnerable to forced marriages; the virginity testing that takes place to confirm if women have lied about their marital status; and it notes that over 3200 Yazidi women and children are still being held hostage by ISIS. Yazidi women and girls are controlled in a manner consistent with ISIS ideology and women are deemed to be property that can be bought and sold as slaves. In terms of rape, although there are no allegations of mass rapes taking place, women are often considered to be sex slaves, are forced to take birth control, and any resistance to rape results in gang rape. Numerous Council resolutions on Syria mention Security Council Resolution 1325 and emphasize the importance of women's participation in peace-building; violations of women's rights are condemned; the need to protect women against gender-based violence is stressed; and the state is encouraged to take measures linked to the empowerment of women[20] and to comply with international law.[21]

With regard to Burundi, the 2015 resolution requested the High Commissioner to urgently organize and dispatch a team of independent experts to investigate violations and abuses of human rights with a view to preventing further deterioration of the human rights situation. The members of the UN Independent Investigation on Burundi include existing independent experts within the UN system, with one Special Rapporteur from the African Union and two from the UN Special Procedures system. The report on Burundi has a specific section on sexual and gender-based violence and highlights that women and girls who are attempting to flee Burundi are subject to sexual violence as a form of punishment, that incidents of sexual mutilation were noted, and that security force staff are allegedly perpetrators of sexual violence.[22] A 2016 resolution authorizes the formation of a COI with a mandate to include the provision of support and expertise for the immediate improvement of the human rights situation and to identify alleged perpetrators of human rights violations and persons involved, with a view to ensure full accountability (UN General Assembly 2016k). Council resolutions on Burundi do not mention WPS or Security Council Resolution 1325, but some resolutions do mention CEDAW and the need for meaningful participation of women in all processes (UN General Assembly 2015d; 2016k).

The current conflict-related crisis situation in South Sudan that started in 2013, has led to numerous developments, including the Secretary General's 2014 report advising the Security Council that there existed reasonable grounds to believe that crimes against humanity had been committed. The African Union established a COI and the same conclusion about crimes against humanity was reached. A Peace Agreement was signed in 2015 to stop the fighting and also to establish a Transitional Government of Unity. The Council adopted a resolution in 2015 requesting the High Commissioner to urgently undertake a mission to engage with the government, to monitor and report on the situation of human rights, and to conduct a comprehensive assessment of allegations of violations and abuses with a view to ensuring accountability and complementarity with the African Union COI (UN General Assembly 2015e). The High Commissioner dispatched a team in October 2015 and an assessment report was presented to the Council in March 2016.[23] The assessment reveals that sexual and gender-based violence is continuous and that government forces and affiliated militia are apparently primarily responsible. The assessment report led to the adoption of a resolution for the establishment of a Commission on Human Rights for South Sudan for a period of one year (UN General Assembly 2016l). Paragraph 14 of this resolution makes explicit reference to WPS resolutions. The three members of the Commission on Human Rights will conduct the investigation and present a report in 2017 to the Council. The Council convened a special session on the situation of human rights in South Sudan in December 2016, despite objections by the government that viewed this as an unjustified intervention. The various Council resolutions often make explicit mention of Security Council Resolution 1325, women's empowerment, women's engagement, and participation in decision-making and peace-building processes and forums (UN General Assembly 2015e; 2016l), and the protection of women's rights broadly, including addressing women's vulnerability as refugees (UN General Assembly 2012d; 2013g).

A common finding in the reports just discussed is a recommendation to the Security Council to refer the country situation to the International Criminal Court, and also to adopt targeted sanctions against those responsible for gross violations of human rights. In conclusion, the report on "Investigation by the Office of the High Commissioner for Human Rights on Libya" is the most explicit as regards mentioning Security Council resolutions and WPS.[24] Other resolutions and reports include information that implicitly acknowledge principles and areas of focus linked to WPS. It is unclear as to the precise reasons for the inclusion or non-inclusion of the WPS focus in different resolutions emanating from the Council. The assumptions can include speculations about the political and diplomatic dimensions of the debates; the reluctance of other oversight mechanisms in the UN system to apply the WPS normative understandings to all conflicts; or the silo mentality that is visible when the issue of violence against women is under discussion, which articulates sexual violence in conflict as "different."

THE UNIVERSAL PERIODIC REVIEW PROCESS

The Universal Periodic Review (UPR)[25] is a new mechanism created to periodically review the human rights record of all 193 UN member states (UN General Assembly 2006). It does this by reviewing information that is submitted by the state under review,

UN agencies, mechanisms, and civil society. The process also includes a three-hour discussion with the Working Group (troika), as well as an interactive dialogue when the outcome report is presented to the Council at one of its regular sessions. The objective of the review is to provide an opportunity for states to report on the human rights situations in their countries, for the review process to assess a state's human rights record, to identify gaps and challenges, to discuss positive state practices, and to make recommendation to the state under review. This is the first time that the UN has a system that treats all states equally as regards the review of their human rights record. In 2007 the Council adopted an institution-building package (UN Human Rights Council 2007a) to guide their work broadly, including the methodology for conducting the UPR (UN General Assembly 2011c; 2011d). Importantly, the process of the entire review is non-adversarial in nature, to ensure a constructive interactive dialogue that can result in an outcome document and agreement. This also ensures that the review contributes to the Council's goal of "changing the reality on the ground." Recommendations that are made in the outcome report can either be noted or supported by the state under review. The Council has no powers of enforcement, and hence it is unclear as to what remedies exist regarding noncooperation of states, either with the UPR process or with the implementation of recommendations.

As regards the implementation of the recommendations that are supported and/or noted in the UPR, it is the reviewed state that bears ultimate responsibility for this. The third cycle of the UPR will commence in 2017 and the reports emanating from the second cycle of the review indicate that states had been questioned about their implementation of, and compliance with, the recommendations that emanated in the first review cycle. There are concerns that there is no specific UPR monitoring mechanism that can review the implementation and compliance with the recommendations to ensure a coherent, sustained, and substantive follow-up process. There has been advocacy on this issue, including a recent civil society call to the High Commissioner for such a mechanism to be created.

A brief analysis of some of the UPR outcome reports reveals that it is mostly in conflict and post-conflict contexts that references are made to the principles articulated in the WPS documents. For example, the outcome report on Colombia recommends that sexual and gender-based violence must be addressed more broadly in the spirit of Security Council Resolution 1820. The recommendation was supported by the State (UN General Assembly 2009b). On the other hand, the report on Algeria recommends the need for accountability for crimes committed during the armed conflict, and thus the need for a review of the National Peace and Reconciliation Commission, but the relevant recommendation does not link this to WPS. The recommendation was noted by the state (UN General Assembly 2008).

In some reports, there is a broad but generic reference to the principles articulated in Security Council resolutions on WPS; while in other instances Security Council Resolution 1325 is explicitly mentioned. This is reflected in the outcome reports of, among others, Cyprus, Guinea-Bissau, Somalia, Uganda, France, Mali, Democratic Republic of the Congo, Nigeria, Central African Republic, Afghanistan, Cyprus, Kazakhstan, El Salvador, Iraq, Angola, Madagascar, Lao People's Democratic Republic, Armenia, Guyana, Kenya, Kuwait, Gambia, and Mongolia.[26] A majority of these states supported the recommendations related to WPS. Algeria, Kazakhstan, and Armenia noted the relevant recommendations.

Recommendations, to a large extent, focus on the need for women's participation broadly in decision-making forums, including in peace processes and associated mechanisms; the need for development of, or implementation of, national action plans (where they have been developed) in line with the relevant Security Council resolutions; highlighting the reality of impunity and the lack of justice for crimes committed against women; the need to address accountability gaps as regards the criminal prosecution for sexual and gender-based violence; the need to ensure training and guidance on the protection, human rights, and needs of women and girls, especially regarding sexual violence; the need to combat gender-based discrimination in all processes; and to promote leadership and equal participation of women. The analysis seems to indicate a focus in the UPR on women's human rights broadly and also some specificity where relevant on issues linked to WPS. The wording of the recommendations seems to indicate a formulaic and narrow approach that does not acknowledge that violence against women functions on a continuum, whether it occurs in times of peace, conflict, or post-conflict. Also, the recommendations do not draw linkages between individual, communal, institutional, and structural factors that are implicated in human rights violations that women and girls experience, including in conflict and post-conflict contexts.

SPECIAL PROCEDURES MECHANISM

The system of Special Procedures consists of independent human rights experts with mandates to investigate, report on, and advise on thematic and country-specific human rights issues and situations. The experts are not remunerated for the work that they carry out, and they are not UN employees. As mentioned previously, the Special Procedures system is one that the Council inherited from its predecessor, the Commission on Human Rights, which had no powers to address complaints in respect to human rights (UN Economic and Social Council 1947). It was only in 1967, after receiving numerous individual petitions, that the Commission established an ad-hoc working group to investigate the situation in Southern Africa in general and South Africa under apartheid in particular.[27] The 1973 coup in Chile led to the establishment of an ad-hoc Working Group in 1975 which was tasked to look into the human rights situation in the country. In 1979 a Special Rapporteur and two experts replaced the working group, with a focus on the issue of disappearances in Chile. This then led in 1980 to the creation of the first thematic Special Procedures mechanism with a global mandate—the Working Group on Enforced Disappearances.[28]

By 1990, there were six thematic mandates created including enforced disappearances; extrajudicial, summary, or arbitrary executions; religious intolerance; mercenaries; torture and the sale of children. Currently there are forty-three thematic and fourteen country mandates covering all regions of the world. The thematic mandates in broad terms cover all civil, political, economic, social, and cultural rights. There are thematic mandates that also include specificity on certain issues and groups—for example, Special Rapporteurs on violence against women, migrants, indigenous peoples, internally displaced persons, food, water and sanitation, development, and culture; an independent expert on the enjoyment of all rights of older persons; a Working Group of experts on people of African descent; and also a Working Group on the issue of discrimination against women in law and in practice among others. The country mandates include countries experiencing internal armed conflict, such as Eritrea, Somalia, Sudan, and the Syrian Arab Republic. There are also country mandates where there are concerns about human rights promotion and protection, such as in Iran, Belarus, Myanmar, and the Democratic Republic of Korea.[29]

The selection and appointment procedures of mandate-holders are reflected in different Council resolutions (UN Human Rights Council 2007a; UN General Assembly. 2011c). The criteria applicable include expertise, experience in the field of the mandate, independence, impartiality, objectivity, personal integrity, gender balance, equitable geographic representation, and representation of different legal systems. A Code of Conduct binds mandate-holders, and since 2005 there is also a coordinating committee to facilitate coordination among mandate-holders. In practice, mandate holders produce thematic reports that contribute to furthering the conceptual and normative understanding of their mandates. They conduct investigative visits to countries at the invitation of governments, and produce reports and recommendations. They address complaints on specific allegations of human rights violations and send communications to states. They provide technical assistance on request to states. Lastly, they participate in relevant conferences, panels, and workshops. The majority of mandate-holders report annually to both the Council and the General Assembly where they provide information that highlights whether states' are meeting their obligations regarding the promotion and protection of human rights.

A brief overview of the reports produced by different mandates reveals that all mandate-holders attempt to integrate a gender perspective into their work, including making references and recommendations pertaining to WPS, albeit to differing degrees. The reports of the Special Rapporteurs on the Situation of Human Rights Defenders, Torture, and Violence against Women have consistently highlighted the manifestations and prevalence of violence against women, its numerous causes and consequences, and also the culture of impunity that has led to the normalization of this human rights violation, including in conflict and post-conflict situations.[30] The Special Rapporteur on the rights of Freedom of Peaceful Assembly has in recent reports highlighted legal and non-legal challenges faced by women who are involved in protests and political life, and also how the rise of fundamentalism and extremism is impacting women's rights to freedom of peaceful assembly and of association (UN General Assembly 2014g; UN Human Rights Council 2016c). This has an impact on women's participation in both public and private life, as engaged citizens who are exercising agency, including in electoral processes. The reports of the Special Rapporteur on the promotion of truth, justice, reparations, and guarantees of non-recurrence highlight the need for women's participation in transitional processes and mechanisms, including truth commissions; and the need to obtain justice, accountability, and effective redress for sexual and gender-based violations. The 2012 report presented to the General Assembly explicitly mentions the need to factor in the Security Council resolutions on WPS in transitional justice processes (UN General Assembly 2012e). The Special Rapporteur on Terrorism has highlighted the gendered effects of counterterrorism measures on women, including by extremists groups and also state authorities. Direct violations include sexual violence, torture, intimidation, the direct targeting of pregnant women who are seen as potential terrorists, and maternal mortality due to restrictions on freedom of movement. Indirect violations include the diversion of funding to counterterrorism measures at the expense of addressing the needs of civilians, including health, education, food, water and sanitation needs, and building an effective and responsive justice system, among others (UN General Assembly 2007; 2009c).

CONCLUSION

The intrinsic link between human rights and WPS is, in practice, acknowledged in the work of the Council, sometimes explicitly, but more often not in a substantive, holistic, and comprehensive manner. As previously mentioned, resolutions, reports emanating from Commissions of Inquiry, Special Procedures mechanisms, and UPR outcome reports do reflect the Councils concern about the human rights of women broadly, and the protection, participation, and redress rights of women in conflict and post-conflict situations. The wording of the recommendations in reports seem to indicate a formulaic and narrow approach that does not acknowledge that violence against women functions on a continuum, whether it occurs in times of peace, conflict, or post-conflict. Also, the recommendations do not draw linkages between individual, communal, institutional, and structural factors that are implicated in human rights violations that women and girls experience in conflict and post-conflict contexts. The limited and sometimes gender-neutral framing of human rights is reinforced by the failure to acknowledge the specificities of women's lives and realities, thereby ignoring the need for a more situated articulation of the human rights of women. It is necessary to go beyond the public space when reference is made to women's right to a life free of all forms of violence in order to address the interconnected and interlocking character of women's public and private lives, and the ways in which violence impacts the realization of all human rights and the ability to exercise effective citizenship.[31] In conclusion, the lack of consistency in developing a coherent, integrated, and sustained approach in the policymaking, reporting, and accountability work of the Human Rights Council has resulted in gaps with regard to its commitment to WPS.

NOTES

1. Beijing Declaration and Platform for Action—General Assembly A/52/231 (1995).
2. For information pertaining to the processes and mechanisms regarding the UN Human Rights Council, see https://www.ohchr.org/EN/HRBodies/HRC/Pages/AboutCouncil.aspx
3. I would like to thank Rebecca Gore, Pretty Mubaiwa, Nondu Phenyane, and Jayshall Vassen—students at the University of Cape Town—for research assistance.
4. These include UN Human Rights Council (2008b); UN General Assembly (2009a); UN General Assembly (2012c).

5. A/HRC/RES/4/4 (2007), A/HRC/RES/6/9 (2007), A/HRC/RES/15/25 (2010), A/HRC/
   RES/18/26 (2011), A/HRC/RES/19/34 (2012), A/HRC/RES/21/32 (2012), A/HRC/RES/24/
   14 (2013), A/HRC/RES/27/2 (2014), A/HRC/RES/30/28 (2015), A/HRC/RES/33/14 (2016).
6. A/HRC/RES/15/11 (2010), A/HRC/RES/17/3 (2011), and A/HRC/RES/27/6 (2014).
7. A/HRC/RES/11/8 (2009), A/HRC/RES/15/17 (2010), A/HRC/RES/18/2 (2011), A/HRC/
   RES/21/6 (2012), and A/HRC/RES/27/11 (2014).
8. Report of the Commission of Inquiry on human rights in the Democratic People's
   Republic of Korea, A/HRC/25/63 (2014: paras. 35, 42), https://www.ohchr.org/EN/
   HRBodies/HRC/RegularSessions/Session25/Pages/ListReports.aspx
9. A/HRC/RES/28/22 (2015), A/HRC/RES/31/18 (2016), A/HRC/RES/13/14 (2010), A/HRC/
   RES/16/18 (2011), A/HRC/RES/19/13 (2012), A/HRC/RES/22/13 (2013), A/HRC/RES/25/25
   (2014).
10. Reports of the Commission of Inquiry on Human Rights in Eritrea: A/HRC/29/42
    (2015), http://www.ohchr.org/EN/HRBodies/HRC/CoIEritrea/Pages/ReportCoIEritrea.
    aspx; A/HRC/32/47 (2016: paras. 45,47, 48), http://www.ohchr.org/EN/HRBodies/HRC/
    CoIEritrea/Pages/2016ReportCoIEritrea.aspx. OK
11. A/HRC/RES/20/20 (2012), A/HRC/RES/21/1 (2012), A/HRC/RES/23/21 (2013), A/HRC/
    RES/26/24 (2014), A/HRC/RES/29/18 (2015), and A/HRC/RES/32/24 (2016).
12. Comprehensive Report of the Office of the United Nations High Commissioner for
    Human Rights on Sri Lanka, A/HRC/30/61 (2015: paras. 36–37), http://www.ohchr.org/
    EN/HRBodies/HRC/Pages/OISL.aspx.
13. A/HRC/RES/30/1 ((2015), A/HRC/RES/19/2 (2012), and A/HRC/RES/22/1 (2013).
14. Report of the Independent Commission of Inquiry established pursuant to Human
    Rights Council—Gaza Conflict, A/HRC/ 29/52 (2015: paras. 19, 36, 39, 40), http://www.
    ohchr.org/EN/HRBodies/HRC/CoIGazaConflict/Pages/ReportCoIGaza.aspx#report.
15. A/HRC/RES/19/18 (2012), A/HRC/RES/22/25 (2013), A/HRC/RES/25/30 (2014), and A/
    HRC/RES/16/32 (2011).
16. Investigation by the Office of the United Nations High Commissioner for Human Rights
    on Libya: Report of the Office of the United Nations High Commissioner for Human
    Rights, A/HRC/31/47 (2016: paras. 34–38, 51), http://www.ohchr.org/EN/HRBodies/
    HRC/Pages/OIOL.aspx.
17. Investigation by the Office of the United Nations High Commissioner for Human Rights
    on Libya: Detailed Findings, A/HRC/31/CRP.3 (2016: para. 176), http://www.ohchr.org/
    EN/HRBodies/HRC/Pages/OIOL.aspx.
18. A/HRC/RES/19/39 (2012), A/HRC/RES/22/19 (2013), A/HRC/RES/18/9 (2011).
19. Report of the Independent International Commission of Inquiry on the Syrian Arab
    Republic: "They Came to Destroy": ISIS Crimes against the Yazidis, A/HRC/32/CPR.2
    (2016: para 45, 51, 54, 55, 65, 69, 76, 82), http://www.ohchr.org/EN/HRBodies/HRC/
    IICISyria/Pages/Documentation.aspx.
20. A/HRC/RES/21/26 (2012), A/HRC/RES/23/26 (2013), A/HRC/RES/30/10 (2015), A/HRC/
    RES/31/17 (2016), and A/HRC/RES/33/23 (2016).
21. A/HRC/RES/26/23 (2014), A/HRC/RES/28/20 (2015), A/HRC/RES/29/16 (2015), A/HRC/
    RES 31/25 (2016).
22. Report on the United Nations Independent Investigation on Burundi (UNIB) A/HRC/
    33/37 (2016: para. 57–60), http://www.ohchr.org/EN/HRBodies/HRC/CoIBurundi/
    Pages/CoIBurundi.aspx.

23. Assessment mission by the Office of the High Commissioner for Human Rights to Improve Human Rights, Accountability, Reconciliation, and Capacity in South Sudan A/HRC/31/49 (2016), http://www.ohchr.org/EN/HRBodies/HRC/RegularSessions/ Session31/_layouts/15/WopiFrame.aspx?sourcedoc=/EN/HRBodies/HRC/ RegularSessions/Session31/Documents/A-HRC-31-49_en.doc&action=default&Defau ltItemOpen=1.

24. Report on the United Nations Independent Investigation on Burundi (UNIB) A/HRC/ 33/37 (2016: para. 176), http://www.ohchr.org/EN/HRBodies/HRC/CoIBurundi/Pages/ CoIBurundi.aspx.

25. For all information pertaining to the processes and mechanisms regarding the Universal Periodic Review, see http://www.ohchr.org/EN/HRBodies/UPR/Pages/UPRMain.aspx.

26. A/HRC/13/7 (UPR 2010); A/HRC/15/10 (UPR 2010); A/HRC/18/6 (UPR 2011); A/HRC/ 19/16 (UPR 2011); A/HRC/23/3 (UPR 2013); A/HRC/23/6 (UPR 2014); A/HRC/25/16 (UPR 2014); A/HRC/25/6 (UPR 2013); A/HRC/25/11 (UPR 2014); A/HRC/26/4 (UPR 2014); A/ HRC/26/14 (UPR 2014); A/HRC/27/5 (UPR 2014); A/HRC/28/10 (UPR 2014); A/HRC/ 28/5 (UPR 2014); A/HRC/28/14 (UPR 2014); A/HRC/28/11 (UPR 2014); A/HRC/28/13 (UPR 2014); A/HRC/29/7 (UPR 2015); A/HRC/29/11 (UPR 2015); A/HRC/29/16 (UPR 2015); A/HRC/29/10 (UPR 2015); A/HRC/29/17 (UPR 2015); A/HRC/28/6 (UPR 2014); A/ HRC/30/6 (UPR 2015).

27. CHR RES 2 (XXIII).

28. CHR RES 20 (XXXVI).

29. For all information pertaining to the Special Procedures mechanisms, see https://www. ohchr.org/EN/HRBodies/SP/Pages/Welcomepage.aspx

30. See reports of mandate-holders at http://www.ohchr.org/EN/HRBodies/SP/Pages.aspx.

31. See, generally, the reports of Rashida Manjoo, former UN Special Rapporteur on Violence against Women, including A/69/368 (2014), A/HRC/17/26 (2011), A/HRC/17/16 (2012), and A/HRC/20/16 (2012).

References

UN General Assembly. *Beijing Declaration and Platform for Action*. Fourth World Conference on Women, Beijing. New York: United Nations, 1995.

UN Economic and Social Council. Resolution 75. ECOSOC/RES/75 (V) (1947), 1947.

UN General Assembly. Resolution 60/251. Human Rights Council, 60th Session, A/RES 60/ 251, April 3, 2006.

UN General Assembly. "Report of the Special Rapporteur on the Promotion and Protection of Human Rights and Fundamental Freedoms while Countering Terrorism." Martin Scheinin. Human Rights Council, 4th Session, A/HRC/4/26, January 29, 2007.

UN General Assembly. "Report of the Working Group on the Universal Periodic Review: Algeria." Human Rights Council, 8th Session, A/HRC/8/29, May 23, 2008.

UN General Assembly. Resolution 12/11. "Human Rights and Transitional Justice." 12th Session, A/HRC/RES/12/11, October 12, 2009a.

UN General Assembly. "Report of the Working Group on the Universal Periodic Review: Colombia." Human Rights Council, 10th Session, A/HRC/10/82, January 9, 2009b.

UN General Assembly. "Protection of Human Rights and Fundamental Freedoms while Countering Terrorism." 64th Session, A/64/211, August 3, 2009c.

UN General Assembly. "Report of the Office of the High Commissioner on the Outcome of the Expert Workshop on the Right of Peoples to Peace." Human Rights Council, 14th Session, March 17, 2010a.

UN General Assembly. "Resolution 13/20: Rights of the Child: The Fight against Sexual Violence against Children." Human Rights Council, 13th Session, A/HRC/RES/13/20, April 15, 2010b.

UN General Assembly. "Resolution 14/3: Human Rights Council, 14th Session, A/HRC/RES/14/3, June 23, 2010c.

UN General Assembly. "Resolution 15/22: Right of Everyone to the Enjoyment of the Highest Attainable Standard of Physical and Mental Health." Human Rights Council, 15th Session, A/HRC/RES/15/22, October 6, 2010d.

UN General Assembly. "Resolution 17/11: Accelerating Efforts to Eliminate All Forms of Violence against Women: Ensuring Due Diligence in Protection." Human Rights Council, 17th Session, A/HRC/RES/17/11, July 14, 2011a.

UN General Assembly. "Resolution 17/17: Situation of Human Rights in the Libyan Arab Jamahiriya." Human Rights Council, 17th Session, A/HRC/RES/17/17, July 14, 2011b.

UN General Assembly. "Resolution 16/21: Review of the Work and Functioning of the Human Rights Council." Human Rights Council, 16th Session, A/HRC/RES/16/21, April 12, 2011c.

UN General Assembly. "Decision 17/119: Follow-up to the Human Rights Council Resolution 16/21 with Regard to the Universal Periodic Review." Human Rights Council, 17th Session, A/HRC/DEC/17/119, July 19, 2011d.

UN General Assembly. "Report of the Human Rights Council Advisory Committee on the Right of Peoples to Peace." Human Rights Council, 20th Session, A/HRC/20/31, April 16, 2012a.

UN General Assembly. "Resolution 20/12: Accelerating Efforts to Eliminate All Forms of Violence against Women: Remedies for Women Who Have Been Subjected to Violence." Human Rights Council, 20th Session, A/HRC/RES/20/12, July 16, 2012b.

UN General Assembly. "Resolution 21/15: Human Rights and Transitional Justice." 21st Session, A/HRC/RES/21/15, October 11, 2012c.

UN General Assembly. "Resolution 21/28: Technical Assistance and Capacity-Building for South Sudan in the Field of Human Rights." Human Rights Council, 21st Session, A/HRC/RES/21/28, October 11, 2012d.

UN General Assembly. "Promotion of Truth, Justice, Reparation, and Guarantees of Non-Recurrence." 67th Session, A/67/368, September 13, 2012e.

UN General Assembly. "Resolution 22/16: Promotion and Protection of Human Rights in Post-Disaster and Postconflict Situations." Human Rights Council, 22nd Session, A/HRC/RES/22/16, April 10, 2013a.

UN General Assembly. "Resolution 23/7: Elimination of Discrimination against Women. Human Rights Council." 23rd Session, A/HRC/RES/23/7, June 20, 2013b.

UN General Assembly. "Resolution 23/25: Accelerating Efforts to Eliminate All Forms of Violence against Women: Preventing and Responding to Rape and Other Forms of Sexual Violence." Human Rights Council, 23rd Session, A/HRC/RES/23/25, June 25, 2013c.

UN General Assembly. "Resolution 23/14: Access to Medicines in the Context of the Right of Everyone to the Enjoyment of the Highest Attainable Standard of Physical and Mental Health." Human Rights Council, 23rd Session, A/HRC/RES/23/14, June 24, 2013d.

UN General Assembly. "Resolution 22/13: Situation of Human Rights in the Democratic People's Republic of Korea." Human Rights Council, 22nd Session, A/HRC/RES/22/13, April 9, 2013e.

UN General Assembly. "Report of the Special Rapporteur on the Situation of Human Rights in Eritrea." Sheila B. Keetharuth. Human Rights Council, 23rd Session, A/HRC/23/53, May 28, 2013f.

UN General Assembly. "Resolution 23/24: Technical Assistance and Capacity-Building for South Sudan in the Field of Human Rights." Human Rights Council, 23rd Session, A/HRC/RES/23/24, June 27, 2013g.

UN General Assembly. "Resolution 26/15: Accelerating Efforts to Eliminate All Forms of Violence against Women: Violence against Women as a Barrier to Women's Political and Economic Empowerment." Human Rights Council, 26th Session, A/HRC/RES/26/15, July 11, 2014a.

UN General Assembly. "Resolution 26/24: Situation of Human Rights in Eritrea." Human Rights Council, 26th Session, A/HRC/RES/26/24, July 14, 2014b.

UN General Assembly. "Report of the Special Rapporteur on the Situation of Human Rights in Eritrea." Sheila B. Keetharuth. Human Rights Council, 26th Session, A/HRC/26/45, May 13, 2014c.

UN General Assembly. "Resolution 25/1: Promoting Reconciliation, Accountability, and Human Rights in Sri Lanka." Human Rights Council, 25th Session, A/HRC/RES/25/1, April 9, 2014d.

UN General Assembly. "Resolution S-21/1: Ensuring Respect for International Law in the Occupied Palestinian Territory, including East Jerusalem." Human Rights Council, 21st Session, A/HRC/RES/S-21/1, July 24, 2014e.

UN General Assembly. "Resolution 25/37: Technical Assistance for Libya in the Field of Human Rights." Human Rights Council, 25th Session, A/HRC/RES/25/37, April 15, 2014f.

UN General Assembly. "Report of the Special Rapporteur on the Rights to Freedom of Peaceful Assembly and of Association." Maina Kiai. Human Rights Council, 26th Session, A/HRC/26/29, April 14, 2014g.

UN General Assembly. "Final Research-Based Report of the Human Rights Council Advisory Committee on Best Practices and Main Challenges in the Promotion and Protection of Human Rights in Post-Disaster and Post-Conflict Situations." Human Rights Council, 28th Session, A/HRC/28/76, February 10, 2015a.

UN General Assembly. "Resolution 29/14: Accelerating Efforts to Eliminate All Forms of Violence against Women: Eliminating Domestic Violence." Human Rights Council, 29th Session, A/HRC/RES/29/14, July 22, 2015b.

UN General Assembly. "Resolution 28/30: Technical Assistance and Capacity-Building to Improve Human Rights in Libya." Human Rights Council, 28th Session, A/HRC/RES/28/30, April 7, 2015c.

UN General Assembly. "Resolution 30/27: Technical Cooperation and Capacity-Building for Burundi in the Field of Human Rights." Human Rights Council, 30th Session, A/HRC/RES/30/27, October 12, 2015d.

UN General Assembly. "Resolution 29/13: Mission by the Office of the United Nations High Commissioner for Human Rights to Improve Human Rights, Accountability, Reconciliation, and Capacity in South Sudan." Human Rights Council, 29th Session, A/HRC/RES/29/13, July 23, 2015e.

UN General Assembly. "Resolution 32/19." Human Rights Council, 32nd Session, A/HRC/RES/32/19, July 19, 2016a.

UN General Assembly. "Resolution 32/3: Trafficking in Persons, Especially Women and Children: Protecting Victims of Trafficking and Persons at Risk of Trafficking, Especially Women and Children in Conflict and Post-Conflict Situations." Human Rights Council, 32nd Session, A/HRC/RES/32/3, July 20, 2016b.

UN General Assembly. "Resolution 32/4: Elimination of Discrimination against Women." Human Rights Council, 32nd Session, A/HRC/RES/32/4, July 15, 2016c.

UN General Assembly. "Resolution 32/12: Impact of Arms Transfers on Human Rights." Human Rights Council, 32nd Session, A/HRC/RES/32/12, July 15, 2016d.

UN General Assembly. "Resolution 33/19: Human Rights and Transitional Justice." Human Rights Council, 33rd Session, A/HRC/RES/33/19, October 5, 2016e.

UN General Assembly. "Resolution 31/4: Commemoration of the Thirtieth Anniversary of the Declaration on the Right to Development." Human Rights Council, 31st Session, A/HRC/RES/31/4, April 8, 2016f.

UN General Assembly. "Resolution 32/20: Realizing the Equal Enjoyment of the Right to Education by Every Girl." Human Rights Council, 32nd Session, A/HRC/RES/32/20, July 18, 2016g.

UN General Assembly. "Resolution 33/18: Preventable Maternal Mortality and Morbidity and Human Rights." Human Rights Council, 33rd Session, A/HRC/RES/33/18, October 10, 2016h.

UN General Assembly. "Resolution 32/16: Promoting the Right of Everyone to the Enjoyment of the Highest Attainable Standard of Physical and Mental Health through Enhancing Capacity-Building in Public Health." Human Rights Council, 32nd Session, A/HRC/RES/32/16, July 19, 2016i.

UN General Assembly. "Resolution 31/27: Technical Assistance and Capacity-Building to Improve Human Rights in Libya." Human Rights Council, 32nd Session, A/HRC/RES/31/27, April 20, 2016j.

UN General Assembly. "Resolution 33/24: Situation of Human Rights in Burundi." Human Rights Council, 33rd Session, A/HRC/RES/33/24, October 5, 2016k.

UN General Assembly. "Resolution 31/20: Situation of Human Rights in South Sudan." Human Rights Council, 31st Session, A/HRC/RES/31/20, April 27, 2016l.

UN Human Rights Council. "Resolution 5/1: Institution-Building of the United Nations." Human Rights Council, A/HRC/RES/5/1, June 18, 2007a.

UN Human Rights Council. "Resolution 6/30: Integrating the Human Rights of Women throughout the United Nations System." A/HRC/RES/6/30, December 14, 2007b.

UN Human Rights Council. "Resolution 8/9: Promotion on the Right of Peoples to Peace." 28th meeting, A/HRC RES/8/9, June 18, 2008a.

UN Human Rights Council. "Resolution 9/10: Human Rights and Transitional Justice." 9th Session, September 18, 2008b.

UN Human Rights Council. "Resolution 11/2: Accelerating Efforts to Eliminate All Forms of Violence against Women." 11th Session, A/HRC/RES/11/2, June 17, 2009.

UN Human Rights Council. "Resolution S-17/1: Situation of Human Rights in the Syrian Arab Republic." A/HRC/RES/S-17/1, 2011.

UN Human Rights Council. "Report of the Special Rapporteur on violence against women, its causes and consequences" A/HRC/20/16 Rashida Manjoo 23 May, 2012.

UN Human Rights Council. "Report of the Independent International Commission of Inquiry on the Syrian Arab Republic" 2015 A/HRC/30/48, 15 August, 2015.

UN Human Rights Council. "Summary Report of the Annual Full-Day of Discussion on Women's Human Rights." 33rd Session, A/HRC/33/68, September 14, 2016a.

UN Human Rights Council. "Report of the Independent International Commission of Inquiry on the Syrian Arab Republic." 31st Session, A/HRC/31/68, February 11, 2016b.

UN Human Rights Council. "Report of the Special Rapporteur on the Rights to Freedom of Peaceful Assembly and of Association." 32nd Session, May 31, 2016c.

CHAPTER 26

....

WPS AND INTERNATIONAL FINANCIAL INSTITUTIONS

....

JACQUI TRUE AND BARBRO SVEDBERG

WHAT is the relationship between the policy development and lending programs of the International Finance Institutions (IFIs) and the Women, Peace, and Security (WPS) agenda? Why is there an apparent disconnect between the priorities of IFIs and their focus on women's economic empowerment and gender-based violence on the one hand, and the principles of the WPS agenda on the other, including sexual and gender-based violence (SGBV) in fragile and conflict-affected states? The mandates and contemporary practices of IFIs are informed by a neo-liberal economic growth agenda rather than international human rights norms or security mandates, as is the case with the WPS agenda. Can IFIs, therefore, be agents for promoting and enforcing the WPS agenda? If so, how can we bridge the gap and ensure greater synergies between the policy and implementation strategies of IFIs and WPS?

This chapter consists of two main parts. In the first section, we explore how and why IFIs, specifically the International Monetary Fund (IMF) and the World Bank, are important institutions for advancing the WPS agenda. We make the case for the relevance of the WPS agenda to IFIs, given their institutional mandates and commitment to gender and global development agendas, as well as their more recent emphasis and commitment with respect to "fragility, conflict and violence" (FCV) contexts. In the second part, we examine practical ways to integrate these agendas—bringing IFIs into WPS and vice versa. We evaluate existing initiatives—development and financial commitments to FCV states, donor, and conflict-affected country WPS National Action Plans, and World Bank country strategies—to identify entry points and opportunities for bolstering the political economy tools of the to-date largely security and human rights–focused WPS agenda.

THE MUTUAL RELEVANCE OF IFIs AND WPS

....

IFIs are important institutions for advancing and implementing the WPS agenda because they are often the primary funders of post-conflict recovery and economic reconstruction, which ensures the non-recurrence of conflict and violence. Yet IFIs are largely neglected as implementers of WPS. An economic analysis that highlights gender-based structural inequalities and discrimination in access to resources is frequently under-explored in the WPS agenda. This has resulted in women's political and civil rights, in the realm of peace and security, being more fully developed than the equally necessary economic and social rights. Structural inequalities between women and men compound the inequalities visible in security and political institutions and peace negotiations; as a consequence, political and decision-making power is typically concentrated in the hands of a few men, sustaining systems of gender inequality and exclusion even after conflict.

IFIs are relevant WPS actors in a range of ways. As major stakeholders in post-conflict recovery processes and economic reform programs they directly influence the power dynamics of decision-making and negotiations with conflict-affected governments, including their gender dynamics. IFIs consist of member states with WPS obligations sometimes clearly manifested in WPS national action plans (NAPs) (for example, Norway includes key responsibilities for IFIs in its NAP). Some member states see IFIs as key actors in implementing the WPS agenda. They may direct state priorities to support women's security and participation through the mechanisms of funding and loans, and through their coordination role vis à vis other financial institutions or donors. A macroeconomic analysis framework shapes all technical advice, policies, and programs for fragile or conflict-affected states with the potential to influence the prevention of, or recovery from, conflict.

IFIs are increasingly engaged in post-conflict relief and recovery processes (see chapter 15 in this volume). For example, the World Bank provides development grants through the International Development Association (IDA) for humanitarian support and relief and recovery, as well as negotiating with governments that require substantial lending for institutional restructuring, infrastructure, and physical reconstruction (see for instance, the recent multibillion dollar programs in Iraq and Afghanistan). The combination of support to governance and infrastructure-building has a major bearing on the distribution and redistribution of power in post-conflict societies, affecting the achievement of gender-equal participation and protection. Post-conflict transitions are an opportunity to establish new institutional rules and to create conditions for stability, security, justice, equality, and economic recovery. These processes are also an opportunity to redress inequalities, including gender inequalities, which may have contributed to the causes of conflict, and, if addressed within a broader political and economic transition, may contribute to sustainable peace. IFIs have disproportionate negotiation power in these transitions, relative to typically weak governments with limited state capacity.

The IMF and World Bank respectively, both finance and coordinate economic development and recovery programs in fragile and conflict-affected states. Both historically and today, they are significant actors in postwar recovery (see Gailbraith 1975). The IMF is a monetary institution, rather than a development institution, and its primary purposes are to promote monetary cooperation, assist in the establishment of a multilateral system of payments for transactions, promote orderly and stable exchange rates, and help correct balance-of-payment problems. To do so, the IMF engages in three primary activities: surveillance, which includes regular consultations with member states to monitor exchange rate and balance-of-payments policies and provide macroeconomic and monetary advice; the provision of financing to member states to counteract balance-of-payments problems; and technical training and support assistance. The IMF engages in post-conflict states by setting out an Article V Agreement with the post-conflict government, which includes directives regarding financial, legal, and regulatory reform. All IMF member states are subject to surveillance of their economic and financial policies and settings to ensure the stability of international finance and trade. These are called "Article IV consultations" evaluating each borrowing country's economic health. In recent years, the IMF has begun to service only developing nations rather than all of its member states, becoming less a monetary institution and more a development financing institution. As a result, its focus, once solely macroeconomic, now includes governance; labor market issues; law reform; budgetary allocations and monitoring compliance with standards and codes for banking, accounting, auditing, corporate governance, and related issues (see Boon 2007).

The World Bank Group, includes four financial institutions and one center for dispute resolution: The International Bank for Reconstruction and Development (IBRD), the IDA, the International Finance Corporation (IFC), the Multilateral Investment Guarantee Agency (MIGA), and the International Center for Settlement of Investment Disputes (ICSID). The World Bank engages in complex and diverse initiatives, including financial operations, such as lending programs; investments, research, and dialogues about policies that may affect economic development and specific projects; technical assistance, including training and capacity building; and the provision of theoretical and practical information about development activities. The Bank's Articles of Agreement set forth its basic purposes, which are to assist in the economic reconstruction and development of member states, promote balanced growth in international trade and the maintenance of equilibrium in balance of payments, increase productivity, and raise the standards of living in less-developed areas of the world.

Despite the relevance of IFIs in achieving WPS goals, such as, supporting women's agency to prevent violent conflict, and respecting women's rights and gender equality in "relief and recovery," their implementing role has been neglected by the United Nations (UN), member states and civil actors as well as the institutions themselves. Seen as "non-political," their mandate is focused on economic interests and operations. Over the past decade, however, the IMF and the World Bank have come to realize that "fragility, conflict and violence" (FCV) are major breaks on stability, poverty alleviation, and the shared economic prosperity at the core of their mission (World Bank 2012). The UN's joint General Assembly and Security Council "sustaining peace" Resolution 2282 (2016) recognizes that "the scale and nature of the challenge of sustaining peace can be met through close strategic and operational partnerships between the UN and its key stakeholders," which includes IFIs (para. 18; see also, para. 30[d]). It calls on the UN Secretary-General to explore options for strengthening collaboration between the United Nations and the World Bank in conflict-affected countries.[1] As a result, in April 2017, the UN and the World Bank signed a partnership framework focused on conflict prevention and sustaining peace in conflict-affected contexts.[2] This collaboration also responds to "the need for integrated and coherent development and security strategies in post-conflict countries as a means of addressing fragmented and siloed approaches to peacebuilding funding," as highlighted in the most recent report of the UN Peacebuilding Commission (2016: para. 11). Members of the Commission stressed the importance of conflict prevention and addressing root causes at the earliest possible stage, as well as the need to integrate a gender perspective into all aspects of institution-building (UN Peacebuilding Commission 2016: para. 54).

Within the new expanded commitment and collaboration with UN agencies, the World Bank in particular, has responsibilities to address the prevention of conflict and coordination of post-conflict financing (see Buvinic et al. 2013). This updated and substantially expanded mandate effectively requires the Bank to implement the WPS agenda, recognizing the gender-specific causes and consequences of conflict and violence, as well as of economic growth and development. The Bank now has a unique opportunity to lessen the impact of the legacy of conflict on (global) economic development by aligning its strategies and objectives promoting women's economic participation with the rights-based peace and security principles of the WPS agenda.

Given that 2 billion people are affected by FCV and 46 percent of the world's population are expected to be affected by 2030,[3] the World Bank now employs a "broad approach to fragility by focusing on prevention, and engaging during active conflict, transition and recovery."[4] The IDA mechanism within the Bank provides loans and grants to the world's poorest countries to boost economic growth, reduce inequalities, and improve people's living conditions. It is the single largest source of donor funds for basic social services in these countries. IDA grants aim to provide the financing needed to rebuild states recovering from conflict; to make states resilient to threats including conflict, disease, and humanitarian emergencies; and to develop infrastructure, enabling people to resume peaceful and constructive lives.[5] Currently programming in four areas is being evaluated to generate evidence on what works with respect to basic service delivery in weak states, including (1) job opportunities for at-risk youth; (2) breaking poverty traps and (3) vulnerability (focusing in particular, on child labor and gender-based violence); and (4) the political economy of post-conflict reconstruction—which refers to projects in African countries that are providing access to unbiased information to support women's political participation and peace-building. A WPS perspective is implied if not explicit in these programs. These evaluations provide an opportunity to take WPS principles into consideration, but there should also be a human rights obligation under the Convention on the Elimination of all forms of Discrimination Against Women (CEDAW) General Recommendation 30 on conflict and post-conflict situations.

During an Article IV consultation, an IMF team visits a country to assess economic and financial developments and discuss the country's economic and financial policies with government and central bank officials. It provides technical assistance in post-conflict transitions to rebuild fiscal institutions with respect to revenue (taxation) and expenditure (public spending). Among the IFIs, the IMF has a particularly important role to play in coordinating gender-sensitive post-conflict financing through multiple mechanisms[6] and leveraging investment from multilateral and private sources to ensure coherence in the goals of this financing. IMF bilateral surveillance and loans frequently require conditions on loans, especially those providing budgetary support to governments. These conditionalities generally demand structural reform to open markets and address inefficiencies in the public and private sectors (see Kentikelenis et al. 2016). Impact assessment of macroeconomic and structural reform policies is carried out to identify any negative effects and implement mitigating policies. However, this assessment does not address the gender bias toward private investment in the "productive" economy over public investment in the "reproductive" economy. This imbalance in investment may stifle domestic demand and fuel inequalities including disenfranchised militarized masculinities (see True et al. 2017). Overall, the IMF approach to financial stability in conflict-affected states makes it increasingly difficult to introduce transformative reform programs that prioritize economic, social, and cultural (ESC) rights obligations through spending on health, education, and other basic human needs. As such, it has been subject to strong criticism over the past two decades for imposing "austerity" and rapid macroeconomic adjustment on poor countries seeking to rebuild their societies.[7]

From a WPS perspective the gendered impacts of austerity are crucial to take into account. Women were disproportionately the losers of austerity policies in non-conflict countries after the Global Financial Crisis (Hozic and True 2016; UNICRI 2014) and of structural adjustment policies implemented in developing countries in the 1980s (Elson 1991). In post-conflict states, women tend to be more vulnerable than men in terms of livelihoods and income-earning opportunities, as well as in terms of physical insecurity through displacement, disability and poor health due to conflict (Ghobarah et al. 2004; see chapters 48 and 50 in this volume). They are more likely to be widowed and thus responsible for a household with the loss of the main earner, to be without property or rights to property, and to face difficulties in finding employment and accessing credit or capital in order to start businesses (True 2012; Ni Aoláin et al. 2011). Women also frequently lack proper social protection and have limited access to, and control over, economic and financial resources due to pre-conflict institutions and the breakdown of existing social support and networks as the result of conflict. Thus, further retrenchment in state services and redistribution during post-conflict transitions has detrimental consequences, undermining women's opportunities for economic and political participation. In addition, redistribution and retrenchment increase the vulnerability of some groups of women and girls to gender-based violence, such as trafficking, early and forced marriage, abuse, and sexual harassment.

In short, IFIs through their lending and development programs have significant, gender-specific impacts on post-conflict societies (see True et al. 2017). To make good on their increased commitment to allocate more resources and programming to fragile, conflict-affected states while ensuring progress toward gender equality, a more coherent WPS strategy and role for IFIs is needed. With the integration of a WPS lens, respective IMF and World Bank approaches to (financial) stability and conflict-prevention in fragile and conflict-affected states could be transformative. For example, women's participation in peace-building could be explicitly targeted as a marker of stability and peace, and women's realization of economic and social rights could become an end in itself, enabling broader prosperity and lasting peace. At present though, the IMF and World Bank are driven by an instrumental approach; prioritizing gender equality interventions as "smart economics," because they deliver on the core goals of eradicating poverty and promoting sources of productivity and growth (World Bank 2012).[8] A WPS rights-based approach would enable a more holistic and sustainable path, addressing both conflict and development, and their gendered drivers.

OPPORTUNITIES AND ENTRY POINTS
FOR WPS IN IFIS

In theory, WPS and IFI mandates, as explored in the first part of this chapter, are mutually reinforcing. IFIs provide sustainable financing for gender-inclusive peace and post-conflict recovery promoted by WPS, as well as for stability and development to prevent the recurrence of conflict. But what are the practical opportunities for institutionalizing WPS awareness and commitments within IFIs? In this section, we examine possible entry points for WPS in decision-making processes, from the leadership and board levels of the IMF and World Bank, to the institutional operational and country levels with WPS academic and civil society input.

We accept that the practices and operations of the IFIs are difficult to change as a result of their neo-liberal commitments and approach to economic growth-driven development that privilege productive over reproductive economies (Prugl 2016). However, there are opportunities for a transformative approach involving IFIs and other development partners where they can bring the experience of conflict into financing and development plans and better understand the care economy and its contribution to the macroeconomy, especially in the recovery of conflict-affected societies. Member states also have the potential to ensure greater synergy between the broader development and WPS agendas, and the financial and political support provided to the IFIs. The commitment to the Sustainable Development Goals by both governments and the IFIs, especially the World Bank, can provide a strong entry point for WPS integration and gender sensitive analysis and programming.

Political Leadership and State Commitment

There is an opportunity to bring WPS concerns to the highest level of IFIs, that is, at the CEO and board level of political decision-making. In the IMF, the Managing Director (MD) has considerable influence on the overall direction of the institution. That gender analysis of macroeconomic and fiscal policies has made inroads into the IMF is accredited to the political leadership of Christine La Garde, now in her second term as IMF MD. We were told that, "if gender is seen as important—it will be heard."[9] However, the approach still largely sees women as inputs to growth and productivity, drawing correlations between women's labor market participation and GDP increases and the fiscal policies needed to support that participation with no particular focus on fragile or conflict-affected states.[10] As La Garde said at the 2017 W20 conference in Berlin, "Give us the numbers—then we can measure and move forward."[11]

In the World Bank, leadership also matters as an entry point for WPS. The Executive Board, made up of twenty-six Directors representing member states and their regions, approves all negotiated country partnership frameworks and lending programs as well as the strategic policies governing its operations.[12] Board members can ask direct and strategic questions to any unit in the Bank about the gender-inclusive governance or gender-analysis of their strategy and loan programs. Some of these executive directors and their advisors are mandated through their country National Action Plans to advance the WPS agenda with respect to IFIs as implementing partners.[13] With more understanding of WPS and its direct connection to the mandate of the organization, these state representatives could leverage greater accountability to the WPS agenda at the World Bank through, a "friends of WPS" group, a model developed in several UN fora, at the Bank and through the Bank's informal gender network.

The spring and annual meetings of the World Bank and IMF, which showcase research and feature side panels on relevant development themes, are an opportunity for WPS civil society to raise awareness and demonstrate the connection between WPS and the achievement of sustainable development (for example, as we show next with respect to the integration of WPS within the Bank's gender strategy). This is also an opportunity for direct dialogue with the management of the Bank, and state representatives.

States are already influential in promoting their political agendas through the World Bank Trust fund mechanism. Norway, Sweden, and other like-minded states, for example, integrate human rights in Bank programming through the Nordic Trust Fund, promoting knowledge and learning on human rights for Bank staff. Other trust funds, such as the Fragility and Conflict Partnership Trust Fund managed by Switzerland, supports partnership and strengthening the relationships between the UN and the World Bank to promote more effective and sustainable responses in conflict-affected contexts. One of the Bank's largest trust funds, the State and Peacebuilding Trust Fund, was established to finance innovative approaches to state and peace-building in regions affected by FCV. This mechanism could be used to advance and integrate a WPS approach across Bank programming in a comprehensive way. No one has yet to take up this particular opportunity; it could be an avenue for advocacy in the future.

Institutional Operations

IMF Article IV consultations and staff missions often meet with parliamentarians and representatives of business, labor unions, and civil society.[14] At present, gender analysis and gender equality issues in macroeconomic monetary and fiscal policies are not mandatory and are only discussed in these negotiations, including where there is an IMF loan package, when governments raise them.[15] However, given that IMF officials meet with social partners to governments, there is an opportunity for civil society organizations focused on women's rights in conflict-affected countries, where loans are conditional on structural reform packages, to meet with IMF economists. Currently, these processes are not inclusive and would require more openness and transparency to allow women's organizations to effectively participate as part of the Article IV assessments. IMF understanding of the WPS participation pillar in connection with the post-conflict recovery pillar would increase the likelihood of more accurate and gender-aware macroeconomic analysis.

IMF gender assessment of the macroeconomic impact of loans is presently being piloted in Egypt, Rwanda, and Uganda, but it is not yet rolled out to all loan recipient countries. Gender budgeting and impact assessment of loans, which could be useful for analyzing the impact on women's socioeconomic rights in post-conflict settings are still very marginal to IMF analysis. Moreover, in its current piloting stage, such analysis is largely carried out by research staff with an interest in gender issues, as essentially "voluntary work," that is, it is in addition to their core work program.[16]

Within the World Bank there are two country strategic processes influencing and determining the framework for programs: The Systematic Country Diagnostics (SCD), which is prepared by Bank staff in consultation with national authorities and other stakeholders, and the Country Partnership Framework (CPF). The former aims to identify the key challenges and opportunities in a specific country context to accelerate progress toward the development objectives consistent with the Bank's goals. Despite being a reference point for broad consultations and analysis, the process is selective and not mandatory or systematically inclusive for women civil society's groups, resulting in limited and/or the absence of a comprehensive gender and conflict-sensitive analysis. This is despite the fact that there is both a Gender unit and a unit dedicated to Fragility, Conflict, and Violence (FCV) within the "Cross-Cutting Solutions" branch of the Bank.

The updated World Bank Gender Strategy 2016–2022 seeks to address gender in FCV. The Bank strategy recognizes that addressing gender gaps is critical to the consolidation of peace and security in FCV affected contexts. It states that gender disparities

> reflect norms and dynamics that entrench inequalities and factors of exclusion that perpetuate conflict and instability. Addressing persistent gender challenges, therefore, is as much a security imperative as it is a longer-term recovery and development priority (World Bank 2016: 18).

Closing gender gaps, however, is a limited approach in that it focuses our attention on the male-as-norm standard of economic and political participation. It is also possible that gender gaps could be reduced—since they are calculated based on averages across all women and all men—irrespective of regional location, ethnic or religious group, and other risk factors for vulnerability, without actually changing the material conditions for the realization of women's human rights (see Arat 2015).

Within the Bank's gender strategy there is nonetheless an opening for WPS analysis to further expand the FCV focus. Indeed, as we next demonstrate, the five areas of the strategy's focus closely linked to the WPS agenda are (1) gender-based violence (GBV), (2) masculinities, (3) political and civic engagement of women and girls,(4) women's access to the labor market, and (5) finance and services.

INTEGRATING WPS IN THE WORLD BANK'S 2016–2020 GENDER STRATEGY

With respect to GBV, a WPS lens offers both a more specific context for addressing the root causes of GBV and a broader analysis of its connections to masculinities and the everyday use of violence to win power over resources and decision-making. The World Bank's turn to GBV, which some argue is a classic case of mission creep,[17] is driven by a concern for the non-market barriers to individual women's engagement in the formal economy and overall to economic growth and productivity. In the World Development Report (World Bank 2012), GBV is seen as an outcome of "sticky" gendered social norms that exist apart from, rather than embedded within, economic structures and practices. This conceptualization of norms, however, was challenged in the UN Secretary-General's High-Level Panel final report on Women's Economic Empowerment (United Nations 2017). The panel stated that

> renewed focus should be not just on gendered social norms but also on economic norms affecting women's economic empowerment . . . it is essential to change economic norms to address the devaluation of care work and the stigmatization of the informal economy, which leads to ignoring agricultural workers . . . (2017: 7).

The WPS agenda, set within a human rights framework, links women's socioeconomic rights not only to the prevention of GBV, but to the prevention of armed conflict, where various forms of GBV often become endemic and integral to warfare (see Rees and Chinkin 2015).

The Bank's approach to GBV is also driven by risk management concerns.[18] After allegations of negative social and environmental impact, including sexual harassment of female staff and sexual exploitation of girls in the community by contractors, the Bank canceled funding for the Uganda Transport Sector Development Project in December 2015. Following the report of an Inspection Panel into the project,[19] which recommended that the Bank take a number of immediate actions in October 2016, President Jim Yong Kim launched a Global Gender-Based Violence (GGBV) Task Force to strengthen the institution's response through its development projects to issues involving sexual exploitation and abuse (SEA). President Kim acknowledged that

> large infrastructure projects—including those supported by the World Bank—which involve a substantial influx of workers into a community, can expose women and girls to risks of sexual exploitation and abuse, unless adequate measures are taken to prevent and address such risks.[20]

The taskforce consists of external GBV experts and Bank staff and builds on existing Bank initiatives to address GBV. Bringing cases to the inspection panel has now been demonstrated to be a potentially effective approach for raising WPS protection issues. It is interesting to see how in the World Bank GBV and SEA are institutionally connected, whereas in the UN Security Council they are considered distinct issues and frameworks (see chapter 18). As a result of the connection between GBV and SEA, the Bank's new gender strategy seeks to connect GBV to women's economic livelihoods through specific projects. However, while these projects might be underpinned by the idea that empowering women economically could serve as a protective mechanism against GBV, they are disconnected from the broader macroeconomic reforms affecting gender equality and women's economic opportunities (see True 2012). They are also disconnected from the gender strategy objective focused on masculinities and engaging men and boys. Moreover, there is no compulsory ex-ante gender assessment of the likely impact of World Bank projects on women's access to jobs, to finance and services, or GBV in development or FCV situations. The Bank Gender Unit reviewed 25 SCDs between November 2014 and December 2016 looking closely at gender gaps in endowments, jobs, and actions as the basis for policy dialogue (World Bank 2016). While the Bank guidelines have strong references to "do no harm," this is not reflected in the analytical or process practice, especially related to women or gender equality.

In terms of the Bank, gender strategy objectives focused on women's access to labor markets, finance, and services. SCD processes should include gender and conflict expertise in the core country analysis team, and make use of that expertise, drawing on non-Bank country-specific feminist political economy analysis to ensure the gender strategy is implemented in the core documents. The gender strategy recognizes that men and women are differently affected by conflict and reconstruction after conflict and allows for the creation of gender and social inclusion platforms on request from countries. Bank projects under this platform include technical support to Sri Lanka on a women's economic empowerment strategy and a project on girls' schooling in Afghanistan. There is also a Middle East and North Africa Regional Gender Action Plan in Syria, Jordan, and Lebanon funded by the Bank's State and Peacebuilding Fund aimed at promoting women's economic empowerment initiatives. Overall, however, these projects lack a holistic approach to the gendered nature and impact of conflict. With a WPS lens, we would expect that analysis of the care and remittance economies and the functions they perform in societies recovering from conflict and violence should form part of the gender analysis of the opportunities and constraints for women's participation in format markets.

With respect to the Bank's gender strategy objective of promoting women's voices and participation, a WPS perspective could provide significant insights on their peace and stability dividends. At present the Bank's approach is minimalist—it is essentially a mandate to consult with women's organizations in country, in SCDs, around key "gender gaps" with respect to the health and education endowments, jobs, and assets. Women's participation has been generally low in processes contributing to the development of Bank policy and country frameworks. However, there were consultative processes with extensive input from academics and women's civil society groups during the development of the 2015 Gender Strategy and the 2016 World Bank Safeguards, as well as consultations with women's civil society groups in a few but not all conflict-affected country processes, such as Colombia and Afghanistan (but not in Bosnia or Sri Lanka), for example.

During the IDA 18 process consultations were also held with a number of civil society organizations, but the gender analysis was weak and disconnected from the complex experience and needs of women and girls for both social and economic development. It provided only selective areas of importance to enhance gender equality, socioeconomic rights, and the inclusion of women (World Bank 2015). One avenue for promoting women's participation and voice could be through the inclusion of country-level women's organizations in the design, reporting, and supervision of IDA 18 and all SCDs, investments, and opportunities. This approach could redress the problem of "inconsistent demand from clients" for gender analysis and programs addressing gender equality outcomes cited by Bank and IMF officials as a barrier.[21] For instance, the Trust Fund financing mechanism could be reformed to enable co-design with people who will be affected by the dispersal of funds, especially where they are for job creation and GBV prevention. Consultations with citizens should also occur prior to Bank programming in all countries. By arranging inclusive consultations with women's civil society groups early in the diagnostic analysis they could assist with identifying the key gender-specific areas of concern, and provide input to each of the thematic areas, especially infrastructure, macroeconomic reform, and governance, not merely "women's issues." In FCV contexts, it is crucial to consider the connection between broader security concerns for women (including but going beyond GBV) and opportunities for their economic and social development.

Civil society has the potential to increase the awareness of WPS concerns in World Bank policy and country operations through direct contact with Bank officials. Country teams are highly influential in the diagnostics and the negotiations of country strategic frameworks and programs. We were told that Bank country directors "depend often on the willingness, understanding and capability" of the national team.[22] Creating spaces for joint dialogues and public events with Bank officials and country teams, therefore, would be a start to addressing the lack of "gender skills" across the Bank, which prevents them from raising gender issues with client governments. The "Women's Eyes on the World Bank" campaign that began in the late 1990s had a significant impact on the Banks awareness of gender (O'Brien et al. 2000). WPS advocates could take up this model and create a "WPS

Eyes on the World Bank" campaign to monitor Bank policies and operations and (as an alternative to the fixation with "gender gap") the gap between *what the Bank says and what it does* on gender equality in FCV settings. In addition, WPS advocates should demand a consultative approach to all Bank research and flagship report processes that includes local women's organizations in FCV and post-conflict countries to bring a practice-based WPS perspective.

Conclusion

The current roles and functions of IFIs enable them to make substantial contributions to the implementation and development of the participation, prevention, protection, and relief and recovery pillars of the WPS agenda. For institutions such as IFIs external to the UN Security Council, it is critical that their mandates, policies, and programs connect explicitly with these pillars. Participation of women in FCD economies and economic governance is crucial if they are to fully recover from conflict and for women to contribute to the prevention of violent conflict in the future. Gender-sensitive protection of human rights, including through appropriately gender-inclusive economic reforms and recovery is a necessary foundation for that participation. Factoring in these WPS principles within IFI internal decision-making processes is essential to the effective implementation of IFI's own stability, growth, and development mandates.

At present, World Bank and IMF officials do not see their work as informed by or relevant to the Women, Peace, and Security agenda. A WPS lens could provide a helpful framework for them to address the connections between gender and security, economic recovery, and sustainable development with a transformative rather than an instrumentalist approach to women's participation. As a case in point, the World Bank's gender strategy refers to the transformative potential of conflict to alter traditional gender norms, including women's political and civic participation and engagement in economic and labor market opportunities. But it falls short of comprehensibly addressing the structural gender inequalities that may be root causes of violence and responding to economic and social injustices that frequently result from conflict and militarization (see United Nations Women 2015). Bank engagement and programming in fragile and conflict-affected contexts must be recognized as a security as well as a development imperative, critical for building peaceful and inclusive societies. Financing priorities should be based on the joint assessments among government, civil society, and the Bank. They should be coordinated and sequenced on the basis of what is realistic for any given country to implement given the often devastating impact of conflict on institutions and state and societal capacities.

To be fully realized as a normative agenda and effectively implemented, WPS must extend well beyond the UN Security Council. We recommend expanding the institutional responsibilities for WPS to explicitly include IFIs. IFIs have crucial roles to play in WPS financing and strategies for the prevention of conflict, the human rights protection of civilians, the gender-equal participation of women and men in economic recovery, and the reconstruction of societies toward sustainable peace.

Notes

1. UN Security Council Resolution 2282 para. 20. "*Requests* the Secretary-General to explore options for strengthening the United Nations–World Bank collaboration in conflict-affected countries in order to (a) assist such countries, upon their request, in creating an enabling environment for economic growth, foreign investment and job creation, and in the mobilization and effective use of domestic resources, in line with national priorities and underscored by the principle of national ownership; (b) marshal resources, and align their regional and country strategies, to promote sustainable peace; (c) support the creation of enlarged funding platforms bringing together the World Bank Group, multilateral and bilateral donors and regional actors to pool resources, share and mitigate risk, and maximize impact for sustaining peace; (d) enable and encourage regular exchanges on priority peacebuilding areas."

2. "UN-World Bank Joint Statement on Signing of New Framework to Build Resilience and Sustain Peace in Conflict Areas," April 22, 2017, http://www.worldbank.org/en/news/press-release/2017/04/22/un-world-bank-joint-statement-on-signing-of-new-framework-to-build-resilience-and-sustain-peace-in-conflict-areas.

3. See "Fragility, Conflict, and Violence," updated February 9, 2017, http://www.worldbank.org/en/research/dime/brief/fragility-conflict-and-violence.

4. FCV mandate: http://www.worldbank.org/en/topic/fragilityconflictviolence.

5. The International Development Association is overseen by 173 shareholder nations, and complements the World Bank's original lending arm—the International Bank for Reconstruction and Development, which functions as a self-sustaining business and provides loans and advice to middle-income and credit-worthy poor countries. IBRD and IDA share the same staff and headquarters and evaluate projects with the same rigorous standards.

6. In 2008, the UN and World Bank signed the "Partnership Framework for Crisis and Post-Conflict Situations," where they acknowledged shared objectives and the need to cooperate in post-conflict situations. However, the framework was not actioned due to the lack of clear division of roles and capacities coordinating their partnership.

7. For a summary of critical research on the negative impacts of IFIs in post-conflict settings, see "World Bank, IMF, and Armed Conflicts," February 2, 2004, http://www.brettonwoodsproject.org/2004/02/art-35157/. Research evidence fails to strongly support the theory of austerity. In May 2016, the IMF's own economists published a study, which issues a strong warning that austerity policies can do more harm than good. They argued that there is no evidence across three decades of IMF technical assistance and lending that fiscal consolidation leads to economic growth. See "Austerity Policies Do More Harm Than Good, IMF Study Concludes," May 27, 2016, https://www.theguardian.com/business/2016/may/27/austerity-policies-do-more-harm-than-good-imf-study-concludes.

8. With respect to regional banks, the Asian Development Bank (ADB) has funded some WPS projects on women's participation in peace-building in Nepal and analysis of women's situation in the conflict and peace process in Myanmar. The ADB is committed to increasing the loans that directly address gender disparity and, given the number of poor, conflict-affected countries in the region, these are relevant to WPS. The Global Study (UN Women 2015) reports that 54 percent ($2.49 million) of project loans and grants approved by the ADB in 2014 for fragile states in Asia and the Pacific were tagged as interventions with effective gender mainstreaming. Only 14 percent of rated funds

(E638,000) were allocated to projects focused specifically on promoting gender equality, while almost 30 percent ($1.32 million) had no gender elements (UN Women 2015: 378). The gender mainstreaming approach of the ADB enables the use of a gender marker across all its loans and investments, which is not yet the case for the African Development Bank (AfDB).

9. Personal interview with IMF analyst, February 28, 2017, Washington, DC.

10. La Garde at W20 also stated, "Funding is needed but women also need the right policies." She gave an example of enabling bank credit policies in Kenya.

11. For a full transcript of the W20 panel, see "Full W20 Summit 2017 Berlin," YouTube, April 25, 2017, https://www.youtube.com/watch?v=h64QaR7LYeI.

12. See the structure of the Executive Board of the World Bank at "Board of Directors," The World Bank, January 16, 2018, http://www.worldbank.org/en/about/leadership/directors.

13. Germany's WPS strategy principles for implementation support "joint initiatives and joint programmes at global, regional and national levels with . . . the World Bank and other international financial institutions (IFI)" (24); and Canada's NAP states that they will "[c]ontinue to engage in policy dialogue with multilateral partners—including through . . . the World Bank and other international financial institutions . . . to encourage the strengthening of their capacities to plan for, implement and report on issues of WPS in peace operations, fragile states and conflict-affected situations." Further, one of the goals in Norway's WPS NAP is to "promote the integration of a gender perspective into work carried out by the World Bank and the regional banks in fragile states and into various funding mechanisms for reconstruction efforts."

14. International Monetary Fund, "Surveillance," https://www.imf.org/external/about/econsurv.htm.

15. Personal interview, the World Bank, March 1, 2017 Washington, DC.

16. Personal interview with IMF analyst, February 28, 2017, Washington, DC.

17. Personal interview, international development consultant, March 1, 2017, Washington, DC.

18. See "Uganda Transport Sector Development Project Fact Sheet (Updated)," June 7, 2017, http://www.worldbank.org/en/country/uganda/brief/uganda-transport-sector-development-project-fact-sheet for Inspection of the TSDP had been registered by the Inspection Panel in September 2015. It concerned complaints received from the Bigodi and Nyabubale-Nkingo communities located along the Kamwenge to Fort Portal Road. The Request contained numerous allegations of adverse environmental and social impacts stemming from the project's construction works, including impacts related to road safety and compensation for land acquisition, as well as serious allegations of road workers' sexual relations with minor girls in the community, and sexual harassment of female employees. [AU: URL was not working; slight edit seemed to fix it; As meant?]

19. "Republic of Uganda: Transport Sector Development Project—Additional Financing (P121097)," August 4, 2006, http://ewebapps.worldbank.org/apps/ip/PanelCases/98-Inspection%20Panel%20Investigation%20Report.pdf.

20. "World Bank Launches Global Task Force to Tackle Gender-Based Violence," October 13, 2016, http://www.worldbank.org/en/news/press-release/2016/10/13/world-bank-launches-global-task-force-to-tackle-gender-based-violence.

21. Personal Interview, World Bank, March 1, 2017, Washington, DC.

22. Ibid.

References

Arat, Zehra F. Kabasakal. "Feminisms, Women's Rights, and the United Nations: Would Achieving Gender Equality Empower Women?" *American Political Science Review* 109, no. 4 (2015): 674–689.

Boon, Kristin. "Open for Business: International Financial Institutions, Post-Conflict Economic Reform, and the Rule of Law." *New York University International Law and Politics* 513, 9, 2007: 513–581.

Buvinic M., M. Das Gupta, U. Casabonne, and P. Verwimp. "Violent Conflict and Gender Inequality: An Overview." *World Bank Research Observatory* 28, no. 1 (2013): 110–138.

Elson, D. *Male Bias in the Development Process.* Manchester: University of Manchester Press, 1991.

Galbraith, J. K. *Money, Whence it Came, Where it Went?* Princeton, NJ: Princeton University Press, 1975.

Ghobarah, H. A., P. Huth, and B. Russett. "Comparative Public Health: The Political Economy of Human Misery and Well-Being." *International Studies Quarterly* 48, no. 1 (2004): 73–94.

Hozic, A., and J. True, ed. *Scandalous Economics: The Politics of Gender and Financial Crises.* New York: Oxford University Press, 2016.

Kentikelenis, A. E., Thomas H. Stubbs, and L. P. King. "IMF Conditionality and Development Policy Space, 1985–2014." *Review of International Political Economy* 23, no. 4 (2016): 543–582.

Ni Aolain, F., D. F. Haynes, and N. Cahn. *On the Frontlines: Gender, War, and the Post-Conflict Process.* Oxford: Oxford University Press, 2011.

O'Brien, R., A. M. Goetz, J. A. Scholte, and M. Williams. *Contesting Global Governance: Multilateral Economic Institutions and Global Social Movements.* Cambridge: Cambridge University Press, 2000.

Prügl, E. "Neoliberalism with a Feminist Face: Crafting a New Hegemony at the World Bank." *Feminist Economics* 23, no. 1 (2016): 30–53.

Rees, M., and C. Chinkin. "Exposing the Gendered Myth of Post Conflict Transition: The Transformative Power of Economic and Social Rights." *New York University Journal of International Law and Politics* 48, no. 4 (2015): 1211–1226.

True, J. *The Political Economy of Violence against Women.* New York: Oxford University Press, 2012.

True, J., C. Chinkin, M. Rees, N. P. Isaković, G. Mlinarević, and B. Svedberg. *A Feminist Perspective on Post-Conflict Restructuring and Recover: The Case of Bosnia and Herzegovina.* Geneva, Sarajevo: Women Organizing for Change in Bosnia and Herzegovina, Women's International League for Peace and Freedom, 2017.

UNICRI (United Nations Interregional Crime and Justice Research Institute) "The Impacts of the Crisis on Gender Equality and Women's Wellbeing in European Union (EU" Mediterranean Countries." Geneva, UNICRI, 2014.

United Nations. "Report of the UN Secretary-General's High Level Panel on Women's Economic Empowerment. Leaving No One Behind, Taking Action for Transformative Change on Women's Economic Empowerment." New York: UN, 2017.

United Nations Security Council. "Resolution 2282", S/RES/2282, 27 April, 2016.

UN Women. "Preventing Conflict, Transforming Justice, Securing the Peace: A Global Study on the Implementation of United Nations Security Council Resolution 1325." New York: UN Women, 2015.

UN Peacebuilding Commission. "Report of the Peacebuilding Commission on Its Ninth Session." UN General Assembly 70th Session, Agenda Item 31, September 2016.

World Bank. "World Development Report: Gender Equality and Development." Washington, DC, 2012.

World Bank. "ID17 Mid Term Review: Gender Equality Progress Report." Washington, DC: IDA DFiRM and DFi, September 28, 2015.

World Bank. "World Bank Gender Strategy 2016–2022." Washington, DC, 2016.

CHAPTER 27

....

WPS AND THE INTERNATIONAL CRIMINAL COURT

....

JONNEKE KOOMEN

THE Women, Peace, and Security (WPS) resolutions highlight the key role of the International Criminal Court (ICC) in the development of a "comprehensive normative framework with regard to sexual violence in conflict" (UN Women 2015: 13). This chapter examines the ICC from a WPS perspective and points to the key role of advocates and GOs in monitoring the Court's gender justice commitments. In this first section, I lay out how the Court's founding treaty, the Rome Statute, contributes to the WPS agenda. I focus on the Statute's definitions of crimes, gender-sensitive rules, and provisions for victims' participation and reparations. I also highlight the Statute's commitment to women's decision-making and gender expertise, as well as its framework for national and local implementation and dissemination. In the next two sections, I examine difficulties and "implementation gaps" in the institutionalization of the WPS agenda at the ICC and recent efforts by its second chief prosecutor, Fatou Bensouda, to strengthen the Court's gender justice framework (Chappell 2016: 2, 197). The final section reflects on ongoing challenges facing the ICC and considers ways that WPS advocates can productively support the Court's work in very challenging international political circumstances.

ICC Contributions to the WPS Agenda

....

The WPS resolutions repeatedly point to the ICC's key role in promoting accountability for sexual and gender-based violence in armed conflict. As a result of sustained advocacy by feminist and human rights activists, the ICC's founding treaty, the Rome Statute of 1998 (entered into force in 2002), offers an unprecedented legal framework dedicated to ending impunity for sexual gender-based violence in armed conflict (Glasius 2006). Supported by 120 state parties at the 1998 Rome Conference, the Statute features "the most advanced articulation of sexual and gender-based crimes of any international tribunal and sets a new standard for the conception of these crimes" (Chappell 2016: 32). Feminist advocates and women's rights groups ensured that the Statute's definitions of war crimes and crimes against humanity include rape, sexual slavery, enforced prostitution, forced pregnancy, enforced sterilization, and other forms of sexual violence (Article 7[1][g]; Article 8[2][b][xxii]; and 8[2][e][vi]). The Rome Statute recognizes persecution based on gender as a crime against humanity (Article 7[1][h]) and prohibits gender discrimination in its interpretation (Article 21[3]). States' widespread support for the Statute reflects a growing international consensus about the criminalization of sexual violence in conflict, albeit with key exceptions (as discussed in Chappell 2016: 100; Bedont and Hall-Martinez 1999).

As a result of sustained civil society advocacy, the ICC became the first international criminal court to establish reparations provisions and formally recognize victims in judicial proceedings. Article 79 of the Statute laid the foundations for the establishment of an independent Trust Fund for Victims (TFV), which offers general assistance programs and implements the Court's reparations decisions after convictions. Activists also successfully pushed for procedures and rules to allow for victim participation in Court proceedings (Article 68[3]), provisions that did not exist in international criminal tribunals. The Statute allows the Court to "take appropriate measures to protect the safety, physical and psychological well-being, dignity and privacy of victims and witnesses," with particular attention to age, gender, sexual and gender-based violence, and violence against children (Article 68[1]). Relatedly, the prosecutor must consider the "interests and personal circumstances of victims and witnesses," especially when investigating sexual violence, gender-based violence, and violence against children (Article [54][1][b]). The Rules and Procedures of Evidence state that survivor testimony on sexual violence does not need corroboration and victim-witnesses may not be questioned about their previous sexual history (Rule 63[4] and 71). Chappell (2014: 186) argues that these "formal rules . . . [remove] the long-held view that a woman's testimony is worth less than a man's in a situation of sexual violence." Together, these important developments in international criminal justice are described as the Court's "victims' mandate" (Pena and Carayon 2013: 519).

Feminist advocates made compromises during the Rome Statute negotiations. The Statute offers the first definition of gender in international law: ". . . it is understood that the term 'gender' refers to the two sexes, male and female, within the context of society. The term 'gender' does not indicate any meaning different from the above" (Article 7[3]). This definition—described by prominent scholars as narrow, "oddly worded" and "circular"— is the product of contentious debates about gender during the negotiations (Oosterveld 2005: 56; see also Copelon 2000). While the Women's Caucus at Rome advocated for a feminist understanding of gender as a social construct, right-wing groups insisted on a binary definition of gender and wording that precludes alternative interpretations (Glasius 2006; Chappell 2016: 44–47). Despite these controversies, the director of the Women's Caucus explained that it is highly significant that, for the first time, an international criminal law treaty included a definition of gender (Alda Facio in 1999, cited in Chappell 2016: 47).

Women's rights advocates successfully lobbied for the representation and participation of women in all organs of the Court. The Statute requires the prosecutor and the registrar to consider gender balance in staff appointments (Article 44[2]), and gender and geographical representation in the election of ICC judges (Article 36[8][a]). UN Women's 2015 Global Study on the implementation of UN Security Council Resolution 1325 (hereinafter referred to as the *Global Study*) notes that the ICC's current staffing composition, its senior leadership, and elected judges successfully reflect the Court's commitment to gender parity (UN Women 2015: 105). Relatedly, the Statute provides for professional appointments with expertise on "violence against women or children" and "sexual and gender violence" in all organs of the Court, including Chambers (Article 36[8][*b*]) and the Office of the Prosecutor (OTP) (Article 42[9]). The Women's Caucus at Rome proposed that judges should have "gender expertise," language which would include sexual violence experienced by men. However, the Statute employs the narrower formulation of "violence against women" due to pressure from conservative groups during Rome negotiations (Chappell 2016: 63; Bedont and Hall Martinez 1999: 77). In 2008, Luis Moreno Ocampo named Catharine MacKinnon as special gender adviser to the prosecutor. In a move welcomed by feminist advocates and civil society groups, the second prosecutor appointed Brigid Inder as MacKinnon's successor. Inder, who was the executive director of Women's Initiatives for Gender Justice and a key participant in feminist international law and WPS advocacy networks, served in this capacity from 2012 to 2016.

Building Global Accountability

ICC supporters proclaim the Court is at the "forefront of gender justice." The president of the Assembly of State Parties, for example, argues that the ICC will help end "the culture of impunity for gender-based crimes" through its investigations and prosecutions, and by encouraging national authorities to conduct their own domestic proceedings (Intelmann 2013). The architects of the Court envisioned that state parties would adopt gender-sensitive legal standards and procedures articulated in the Rome Statute in their domestic legal systems through the guiding principle of complementarity. Under this principle, the Office of the Prosecutor can only indict and prosecute a case when national authorities are "unable" or "unwilling" to "genuinely" do so (Article 17). As such, the architects of complementarity viewed the principle as an accountability catalyst. As the principle of complementarity requires states to routinely investigate and prosecute gross violations of human rights, states would have to change their domestic laws and procedures in line with ICC standards.

The first ICC prosecutor articulated a vision he termed *positive complementarity*. Drawing on Article 93(10) of the Rome Statute, Moreno Ocampo argued that "the effectiveness of the International Criminal Court should not be measured by the number of cases that reach it. On the contrary, complementarity implies that the absence of trials before this Court, as a consequence of the regular functioning of national institutions, would be a major success." This understanding of complementarity allows the OTP to actively assist and encourage domestic proceedings, promote national capacity judicial building, and cooperate with national and international networks including as "a proactive use of OTP information to help states fulfill their obligations" (Moreno Ocampo 2003: 2). Moreno Ocampo's approach was reiterated in the Office of the Prosecutor's 2014 gender policy. As I discuss in what follows, these complementarity mechanisms have the potential to meaningfully reinforce and extend the WPS agenda through the adoption in national legislation and local practice of the Rome Statute's definitions of crimes, standards, and procedures, including on victim and witness support and reparations.

The Challenge of Implementation

Women's rights advocates and many other observers celebrated the innovations of the Rome Statute. As the Court began its work in 2003, however, practitioners, activists, and scholars monitored the institutionalization of the Statute's gender justice commitments with considerable concern. This section lays out key problems characterizing the ICC's gender justice project in the Court's first decade. I focus on the work of the first prosecutor and briefly lay out challenges related to reparations and victim representation.

The Prosecutor

The first three ICC judgments did not result in any convictions for sexual and gender-based violence. The Lubanga trial (2009–2012), the ICC's first, raised serious doubts about the Court's capacity to pursue criminal accountability for sexual and gender-based violence. Moreno Ocampo indicted Thomas Lubanga for crimes related to the recruitment of child soldiers in Ituri, eastern Democratic Republic of the Congo (DRC), focusing on the period between 2002 and 2003. Women's rights advocates and survivors' groups raised concerns about the prosecutor's handling of the case. Women's Initiatives for Gender Justice (WIGJ), the successor of the Women's Caucus at Rome, played an important role in monitoring the OTP's work. WIGJ argued that the prosecutor's charges did not reflect the scope of Lubanga's alleged crimes and maintained that the Rome Statute required the prosecutor to investigate evidence of sexual and gender-based violence. In turn, the prosecutor defended his "limited charging strategy" by claiming that sexual violence investigations were difficult to conduct and that survivors were reluctant to talk to investigators. Legal scholar Niamh Hayes disputes this, noting that ICC investigators in the DRC found evidence of crimes of rape, torture, and enslavement during their initial investigations, yet OTP leadership "instructed them to pursue evidence relating only to the conscription and use of child soldiers" (Hayes 2013: 11; Glassborow 2008). In addition, WIGJ researchers independently identified over thirty survivors in Ituri who could identify militia perpetrators and were willing to provide statements to the OTP, information WIGJ provided to the OTP (Chappell and Inder 2014; Chappell 2014).

After a trial described by commentators as "shambolic," Lubanga was found guilty of recruiting child soldiers in 2012 (Hayes 2013: 16). The prosecutor refused to amend Lubanga's charges despite protests and legal interventions from prominent NGOs (Avocats Sans Frontières et al. 2006; WIGJ 2010). While the prosecutor highlighted the sexual and gender-based dimensions of the crime of recruiting child soldiers in opening and closing statements, observers argued that prosecutors did not adequately address this during the trial itself (Chappell 2014: 189–190). Hayes argues that Moreno Ocampo sought to "camouflage the gaping omissions in his own indictment." The OTP effectively "name-check[ed]" sexual violence "for rhetorical and emotive effect," while refusing to investigate and charge these crimes (Hayes 2013: 14). The Lubanga judgment and sentencing decision strongly criticized the prosecutor's approach (ICC 2012c; ICC 2012d; see also discussion in Hayes 2013: 10–25)

The ICC's second trial, the trial of Germain Katanga and Mathieu Ngudjolo Chui, also focused on violence in Ituri in 2003. This was the ICC's first trial featuring sexual violence charges (Katanga and Ngudjolo Chui's joint case was eventually severed). In 2012, Ngudjolo Chui was acquitted of all charges including sexual violence (ICC 2012a). Katanga was convicted for crimes against humanity (murder) and war crimes (murder, attacking a civilian population, destruction of property, and pillaging) in 2014. However, he was acquitted of all charges related to sexual violence including rape and sexual slavery, and the recruitment of child soldiers. While the trial chamber ruled that sexual violence had taken place in attacks on Borogoro village, it determined that the prosecution had not established the accused's responsibility (ICC 2014c).

The ICC's first trials exposed serious flaws in the OTPs investigations of sexual and gender-based crimes. Hayes (2013: 25) writes that the Lubanga case "set a particularly ignominious precedent for the coherence, efficiency, and professionalism of international criminal prosecutions." Both trial chambers concluded that the prosecutors did not have a trusted presence in the DRC. The OTP relied heavily on secondary materials obtained from the UN through confidentiality agreements and, the defense argued, it violated its obligations to disclose potentially exculpatory evidence. Judges found that prosecutors employed so-called intermediaries to connect them to former child soldiers and other witnesses. These decisions had far-reaching implications for the quality of evidence from former child soldiers presented during trials (Buisman 2013: 31). The flawed investigations cast serious doubts on the prosecutor's capacity to pursue justice for sexual and gender-based crimes and the Court's ability to ensure witnesses and survivors' meaningful participation in the proceedings.

The OTP also faced serious difficulties confirming charges for sexual and gender-based crimes during the tenure of the first prosecutor. Notably, in 2011, the ICC pre-trial chamber declined to confirm the prosecutor's charges against Callixte Mbarushimana, including a broad range of charges related to sexual and gender-based violence. The *Mbarushimana* decision illustrated a broader problem. Although the OTP pursued charges for sexual and gender-based violence in a majority of its cases during the first decade of the Court's existence, half of these did not make it through the confirmation of charges stage (WIGJ 2012: 106–107; Hayes 2013: 27–28). In other words, the prosecutor's charges relating to sexual or gender-based crimes were much less successful in the confirmation stage than charges for murder, pillage, and attacks on civilian populations. Hayes attributes this to poor quality evidence offered by prosecutors, including their reliance on open source and indirect information in place of witness testimony (Hayes 2013: 28).

Reparations and Victims' Provisions

While "[c]omprehensive, sustainable and transformative reparations for victims are both a right and an integral aspect of peacebuilding," the Global Study argues that reparations are rarely implemented, funded, or oriented to address survivors' needs (UN Women 2015: 115). The ICC's reparations regime illustrates this challenge. The Court's independent Trust Fund is hampered by limited funds and indigent defendants. The development of the ICC's reparation provisions has also been slow. Judges are responsible for the implementation of the Rome Statute's victims' mandate and reparations are the subject of ongoing legal deliberation. In 2012, the Lubanga trial chamber laid out the principles and procedures that should govern reparations provisions (ICC 2012b). The first of its kind, this ruling provided for many types of reparations including symbolic and collective reparations. It also emphasized "principles of gender-inclusiveness, non-discrimination, flexibility, responsiveness to the needs of vulnerable victims and the importance of victims' agency in the design and priorities for reparations programmes" (WIGJ 2012: 206). After long delays, appeals and procedural questions about how victims should be idenitified, judges approved a TFV proposal to provide symbolic collective reparations to Ituri communities in 2016 and, in December 2017, held Lubanga responsible for $10,000,000 in victim reparations, the largest reparations order to date (ICC 2016a; Brodney and Regué 2018).

Legal representatives for victims have long raised concerns about how reparations will be implemented. Luc Walleyn, for example, questioned the viability of collective reparations for his clients. He argued that "[C]hild soldiers are not a community . . . It is not like a village that has been victimized. They are very often in conflict with their own families. I cannot see my clients as a group. They are really individuals" (cited in IRIN 2012). In March 2017, the Katanga trial chamber made the Court's first award for individual and collective damages. Victims were awarded $250 in symbolic reparations, as well as collective reparations in the form of support for housing, income-generating activities, education, and psychological support (ICC 2017). Reparations are currently being deliberated in the Al Mahdi case.

In addition to the challenges related to reparation provisions, scholars and practitioners have expressed concern that the Court's celebrated victims' provisions do not provide meaningful representation. Victims' participation in ICC proceedings is mediated through common legal representatives, some of whom are tasked with representing thousands of victims. Critics argue that Court practices effectively serve to bureaucratize victimhood and do not necessarily allow for substantive participation by survivors (Kendall and Nouwen 2013). In response, the registry, the ICC's administrative organ, has reviewed its victims' participation procedures. Pretrial chambers have now simplified the victim application process (Pena and Carayon 2013).

GENDER JUSTICE DEVELOPMENTS

While the first prosecutor faced serious criticism from women's rights advocacy groups, many welcomed the election of Fatou Bensouda as the ICC's second chief prosecutor. Bensouda, who began her tenure in June 2012, has been widely praised for strengthening the work of the OTP. She is credited for developing its prosecutorial strategy, appointing highly respected advisors, and pursuing meaningful collaborations with civil society groups, among other initiatives. These initiatives have strengthened the Office's work in pursuing accountability for sexual and gender-based crimes.

Notably, Bensouda's OTP produced a Policy Paper on Sexual and Gender-Based Crimes, the first of its kind offered by an international criminal court. Released in 2014, the policy paper articulates principles and lays out specific strategies to strengthen the OTP's investigation practices, charging strategy, and measures related to witness safety and well-being, among other aspects of its work. The Global Study describes the policy paper as "an important shift in the OTP's methods, signaling the operationalization of a gender-conscious approach to prosecution which should allow it to better account for the full range of SGBV crimes committed" (UN Women 2015: 104). Overseen by Brigid Inder, Bensouda's gender advisor until 2016, the policy explicitly references states' 1325 obligations. States have the primary responsibility for investigating and prosecuting crimes, including sexual and gender-based violence. The OTP also suggests it can offer support and assistance to states as part of its vision of "positive complementarity" (ICC 2014a: para. 110). Inder emphasized that "continuous leadership on these issues is critical for the Policy to be fully implemented" (WIGJ 2016).

Bemba

The Bemba case illustrates important and paradoxical developments in the Court's gender justice work. The Court's third trial and fourth judgment centered on sexual violence. In 2016, Jean-Pierre Bemba, a former DRC vice-president and senator, was found responsible for rape, murder, and pillage committed by soldiers under his command in the Central African Republic (CAR) from 2002 to 2003 (ICC 2016d). The 2016 judgment marked the ICC's first conviction for rape as a war crime and as a crime against humanity, as well as its first conviction for command responsibility. The International Federation for Human Rights (FIDH) and its CAR member association concluded that "[T]he trial has . . . undeniably contributed to raising awareness of a destructive effect that the usage of sexual violence as a systematic weapon of war has on women and men and has helped to break the silence and the stigmatization of victims of rape" (FIDH 2016). However, the ICC's appeals chamber reversed Bemba's conviction by a 3:2 majority in June 2018. Following this far-reaching decision, Melinda Reed of WIGJ points out that, "as of today, there has not been a single successful conviction for sexual and gender-based crimes" at the ICC (WIGJ 2018).

The Bemba case is instructive for WPS advocates in several respects. First, the case shows that activists, including survivors, must continually pressure the Court to live up to its gender justice commitments. Survivors and human rights activists in CAR coordinated with FIDH to focus international attention on the case. Advocates collected evidence of atrocities themselves, strategically engineered a state referral, and pushed an apparently reluctant ICC prosecutor to investigate the case. Survivors formed organizations and mobilized themselves as witnesses and victims; over 5,000 victims participated in the Bemba procedings (Glasius 2009: 53; FIDH 2016).

Second, *Bemba* illuminates the complexities of sexual and gender-based violence experienced by women, men, and children in armed conflict. The OTP reportedly initially viewed the CAR situation as its flagship sexual violence case and pursued only rape, torture, and pillaging charges against Bemba in 2008. Again, women's rights groups criticized Moreno Ocampo's "limited charging strategy," arguing that charges focused on rape detracted from survivors' experiences. Bernadette Sayo, a survivor of the 2002–2003 violence in CAR and subsequently a prominent women's rights advocate, explained in 2007 that ". . . it would be unnatural to prosecute someone for her rape but not for the killing of her husband: 'it is the same suffering'" (cited in Glasius 2009: 58). While murder charges were later added to Bemba's indictment during confirmation of charges in 2009, judges declined to confirm torture charges and other charges related to sexual violence against Bemba. In a ruling strongly criticized by women's rights advocates and feminist scholars, the pretrial chamber opposed the cumulative charging of rape and torture, arguing that "the act of torture identified by the Prosecution was 'fully subsumed by the count of rape'" (in Hayes 2013: 40; Chappell 2016: 117–118). Hayes argues that judges displayed "extreme reticence to progressively interpret the law on sexual and gender-based crimes" in this decision (Hayes 2013: 39)

WPS resolutions focus on women and girls as the primary victims of sexual violence (see also Mibenge 2013; Koomen 2013). Resolution 2106 in 2013 was the first WPS resolution to note sexual violence faced by men and boys, though Dolan suggests that this "rather tentative" acknowledgment appears to be a "reluctant compromise" (Dolan 2014a: 80; Dolan 2014b: 488, fn 9). The Statute of Rome arguably offers a broader framework for understanding the gendered dimensions of sexual violence and the Bemba trial, in particular, sheds light on the dynamics surrounding sexual violence against men. While other international tribunals have charged sexual violence against men as torture, cruel treatment, and sexual violence, Bemba had been the first person held accountable for the rape of men, women, and children by an international criminal court, as well as the first person convicted for rape based in part on the testimony of male survivors, prior to his 2018 acquital (Hayes 2016). Evidence related to the rape of men and boys also features in the ongoing Ntaganda and Ongwen cases.

Ongoing Cases

NGOs and scholars have welcomed the success of Bensouda's OTP in gaining confirmation for sexual and gender-based violence charges by pretrial chambers. Relatedly, the Office appears to have moved away from the first prosecutor's limited charging strategy. Pena and Carayon (2013: 526) attribute this development in part to advocacy by victims' groups during the Lubanga trial.

The prosecutor was successful in gaining confirmation for all sexual and gender-based violence charges in the case against Bosco Ntaganda in 2014. For the first time, an ICC pretrial chamber unanimously confirmed all the prosecutor's sexual and gender-based violence charges. This is particularly noteworthy because Ntaganda's original 2006 arrest warrant did not include these charges (ICC 2014b; WIGJ 2014: 110–111). The OTP is also prosecuting Ntaganda for sexual violence committed against child soldiers within his own militia. These charges, a first of their kind at an international criminal tribunal, could develop legal understandings of the gendered dynamics of child recruitment. Ntaganda was the first case to reach the confirmation stage under Bensouda's leadership. This milestone suggests that the OTP has strengthened its understanding of the relationship between sexual and gender-based violence and other types of crimes. It has also improved its institutional commitment to gender mainstreaming, and its capacity to conduct investigations. Last, the OTP was successful in gaining confirmation of sexual and gender-based charges in the Gbagbo and Blé Goudé case in 2014 (WIGJ 2014).

Dominic Ongwen's trial, which began late 2016, also points to potentially promising developments in the pursuit of gender justice at the ICC and for the WPS agenda more broadly. An alleged senior commander in the Lord's Resistance Army, Ongwen faces numerous charges including rape, sexual slavery, enslavement, torture, and outrages upon personal dignity. Ongwen is the first ICC defendant to face charges for forced pregnancy and forced marriage. While forced marriage is not explicitly enumerated in the Rome Statute, the Chamber ruled it may constitute a crime against humanity ("other inhumane acts"). Like Ntaganda, Ongwen's 2005 arrest warrant did not include any charges related to sexual and gender-based violence. The prosecutor added these after his 2015 arrest. Notably, the prosecutor's pretrial brief includes a specific section on sexual and gender-based violence crimes thereby indicating a more developed theory of the ways these crimes are integrated into the case (ICC 2016b). Moreover, as Dieneke De Vos (2016) notes, the case "marks another breaking point—the Prosecution has classified acts of sexual violence against women and girls not just as sexual violence (rape and sexual slavery), but as torture and outrages upon personal dignity." The Ongwen case also features procedural innovations relevant to sexual and gender-based violence. Acknowledging survivors' difficult circumstances and trauma, judges allowed prosecutors to present witness testimony from victims of forced marriage via video link before the start of trial (ICC 2016c).

In short, the work of the second prosecutor suggests promising new directions in the pursuit of accountability for sexual and gender-based violence, despite the potentially enormous implications of Bemba's acquittal. Bensouda has emphasized institutional capacity building, the development of a robust gender policy, and enhanced investigations. Under her leadership, the OTP has succeeded in confirming charges for sexual and gender-based violence. Despite profound challenges facing the court, ongoing trials may be able to expand the WPS framework's understanding of the scope, nature and dynamics of sexual and gender-based violence and further the pursuit of individual criminal accountability for these atrocities.

Ongoing Challenges and Advocacy

The adoption of the Rome Statute marked "momentous progress" toward the WPS goal of promoting international accountability for sexual and gender-based violence in armed conflict (UN Women 2015: 103). Yet the ICC's achievements, like the WPS agenda more broadly, are still "measured in 'firsts,' rather than as standard practice" (UN Women 2015: 15). The unfolding international·political climate does not bode well for the nascent Court for it must rely on state parties, the UN Security Council, and the broader international community to assist its efforts in investigating atrocities and arresting suspects. Moreover, the ICC faces opposition from key state parties and the African Union. Notably, leaders from South Africa, Kenya, Burundi, and Gambia have on various occasions threatened to withdraw their countries from the Treaty of Rome. However, most of these withdrawal efforts have since been successfully stalled or overturned. The Court also faces the prospect of rejuvenated opposition to its existence from the United States. While the Obama and Bush administrations took limited and tentative steps to cooperate with the ICC on occasions where US geopolitical interests aligned with the Court's work, the Trump administration appears unlikely to continue these overtures. Court officials warn that budget pressure from the Assembly of State Parties as well as the Security Council's refusal to fund its own referrals severely undermine the Court's ability to carry out its mandate. In particular, cost-saving measures hamper OTP investigations and stunt the institutionalization of the Court's victims' provisions and reparations regime including the Trust Fund for Victims

(UN Women 2015: 118–119). Opposition, lack of cooperation, and funding gaps therefore combine to pose serious impediments to the promising work of the second prosecutor on gender justice.

In these very challenging circumstances, civil society organizations, human rights groups and women's rights activists remain central to the success of the ICC and the institutionalization of its gender justice mandate. In these indispensable advocacy efforts, the WPS agenda serves as a key strategic and substantive focus. Notably, the Global Study calls on WPS advocates to continue to support state ratification of the Rome Statute and promote domestic legislation in line with the Statute's women's rights standards (UN Women 2015: 124). As the Global Study emphasizes, it is not enough for states to adopt the Statute's definitions of crimes into national legislation. The Court's potential to contribute to the WPS agenda requires "the domestication of the full Rome Statute architecture," including its "comprehensive framework for investigating and prosecuting SGBV as international crimes, dedicated procedures for victim and witness support that are matched with adequate resources for their implementation, and provision for necessary reparations" (UN Women 2015: 107).

Advocates can productively emphasize the WPS commitments made by states and international organizations to promote enhanced cooperation with the Court. WPS National Action Plans (NAPs) provide important opportunities for states to reaffirm their commitment to the ICC (see chapter 22 in this volume). Several governments, including France and the United Kingdom, already explicitly reiterate their support for the ICC in their Plans, whereas the US NAP is notably silent about the role of the ICC in the WPS agenda. NAP deliberations, reviews, and renewals allow activists to highlight state parties' legal obligations under the Rome Treaty. The NAPs help reiterate their funding and budget commitments, as well as mobilize support for the Trust Fund for Victims. In turn, the institutional overlap between the ICC and the WPS agenda at the Security Council provides advocates with critical opportunities to press for improved Council cooperation with the Court. As the prosecutor repeatedly emphasizes in her regular reports to Resolution 1593 (Darfur referral), the Security Council has not provided adequate public and diplomatic support for the ICC's work. It has not funded investigations triggered by its own referrals, and neither has it taken meaningful actions to enforce ICC arrest warrants or address state non-compliance (see, for example, Bensouda 2017; 2016). In these difficult circumstances, advocates' strategic appeals to the Council's WPS commitments serve to publicize ongoing Security Council obstruction. Most ambitiously, perhaps, the WPS agenda may help advocates make inroads into future debates surrounding Security Council referrals to the ICC including the very challenging task of encouraging the Council to develop and apply consistent standards to guide its referrals.

REFERENCES

Avocats Sans Frontières. Center for Justice and Reconciliation. Coalition Nationale pour la Cour Pénale Internationale—RCD. Fédération Internationale des Ligues des Droits de l'Homme. Human Rights Watch. International Center for Transitional Justice. Redress. Women's Initiatives for Gender Justice. Joint letter to the Chief Prosecutor of the International Criminal Court. July 31, 2006, http://www.hrw.org/news/2006/07/31/dr-congo-icc-charges-raise-concern.

Bedont, B., and K. Hall-Martinez. "Ending Impunity for Gender Crimes under the International Criminal Court." *The Brown Journal of World Affairs* 6, no. 1 (1999): 65–85.

Bensouda, F. "Statement of ICC Prosecutor, Fatou Bensouda, before the United Nations Security Council on the Situation in Darfur, pursuant to UNSCR 1593 (2005)." June 8, 2017, https://www.icc-cpi.int/Pages/item.aspx?name=170608-otp-stat-UNSC.

Bensouda, F. "Statement of ICC Prosecutor, Fatou Bensouda, before the United Nations Security Council on the Situation in Darfur, pursuant to UNSCR 1593 (2005)." New York, December 13, 2016, https://www.icc-cpi.int/Pages/item.aspx?name=161213-otp-stat-unsc-darfur.

Brodney, M., and M. Regué. "Formal, Functional, and Intermediate Approaches to Reparations Liability: Situating the ICC's 15 December 2017 Lubanga Reparations Decision." EJIL Talk [blog], January 4, 2018. https://www.ejiltalk.org/formal-functional-and-intermediate-approaches-to-reparations-liability-situating-the-iccs-15-december-2017-lubanga-reparations-decision/

Buisman, C. "Delegating Investigations: Lessons to be Learned from the Lubanga Judgment." *Northwestern Journal of International Human Rights* 11, no. 30 (2013): 30–82. http://www.scholarlycommons.law.northwestern.edu/njihr/vol11/iss3/3.

Chappell, L. "Conflicting Institutions and the Search for Gender Justice at the International Criminal Court." *Political Research Quarterly* 67 (2014): 183–196.

Chappell, L. *The Politics of Gender Justice at the International Criminal Court: Legacies and Legitimacy.* New York: Oxford University Press, 2016.

Chappell, L., and B. Inder. "Advocating for International Gender Justice: A Conversation with Brigid Inder." *International Feminist Journal of Politics* 16, no. 4 (2014): 655–664.

Copelon, R. "Gender Crimes as War Crimes: Integrating Crimes against Women into International Criminal Law." *McGill Law Journal* 46 (2000), 217–240.

De Vos, D. "ICC Trial against Dominic Ongwen Commences: Some Thoughts on Narratives." IntLawGrrls [blog], December 8, 2016, http://www.ilg2.org/2016/12/05/a-day-to-remember-ongwens-trial-starts-on-6-december/.

Dolan, C. "Has Patriarchy Been Stealing the Feminists' Clothes? Conflict-Related Sexual Violence and UN Security Council Resolutions." *IDS Bulletin* 45, no. 1 (2014a): 80–84.

Dolan, C. "Letting Go of the Gender Binary: Charting New Pathways for Humanitarian Interventions on Gender-Based Violence." *International Review of the Red Cross* 96, no. 894 (2014b): 485–501.

Fédération Internationale des Ligues des Droits de l'Homme (FIDH). Press release. "21 March: ICC to Issue Long-Awaited Verdict in Trial Against Jean-Pierre Bemba." Worldwide Movement for Human Rights, March 17, 2016, http://www.fidh.org/en/region/Africa/central-african-republic/21-march-icc-to-issue-long-awaited-verdict-in-trial-against-jean.

Glasius, M. "'We Ourselves, We Are Part of the Functioning': The ICC, Victims, and Civil Society in the Central African Republic." *African Affairs* 108, no. 430 (2009): 49–67.

Glasius, M. *The International Criminal Court: A Global Civil Society Achievement.* London: Routledge, 2006.

Glassborow, K. ICC Investigative Strategy Under Fire. *Institute for War and Peace Reporting.* October 27, 2008, https://iwpr.net/global-voices/icc-investigative-strategy-under-fire.

Hayes. N. "The Bemba Trial Judgement: A Memorable Day for the Prosecution of Sexual Violence by the ICC." *PhD Studies in Human Rights* [blog], March 21, 2016, http://www.humanrightsdoctorate.blogspot.com/2016/03/hayes-bemba-trial-judgement-memorable.html.

Hayes, N. "Sisyphus Wept: Prosecuting Sexual Violence at the International Criminal Court." In *Ashgate Research Companion to International Criminal Law: Critical Perspectives*, edited by W. Schabas, Y. McDermott, and N. Hayes, 7–43. Farnham, Surrey: Ashgate Publishing, 2013.

Intelmann, T. "Gender Justice and International Criminal Court." *Huffington Post*, June 13, 2013, http://www.huffingtonpost.com/tiina-intelmann/gender-justice-and-the-in_b_3431280.html.

International Criminal Court (ICC). Press Release. "Katanga Case: ICC Trial Chamber II Awards Victims Individual and Collective Reparations." ICC Doc. No. ICC-CPI-20170324-PR1288, March 24, 2017, http://www.icc-cpi.int/Pages/item.aspx?name=pr1288.

International Criminal Court (ICC). "Situation in the Democratic Republic of the Congo in the case of the Prosecutor v. Thomas Lubanga Dyilo. Order Approving the Proposed Plan of the Trust Fund for Victims in Relation to Symbolic Collective Reparations." Trial Chamber II. ICC Doc. No. ICC-01/04-01/06-3251, October 21, 2016a, http://www.icc-cpi.int/CourtRecords/CR2016_22094.PDF.

International Criminal Court (ICC). "Situation in Uganda in the Case of the Prosecutor v. Dominic Ongwen. Prosecution's Pre-Trial Brief." Office of the Prosecutor. ICC Doc. No. ICC-02/04-01/15-533, September 6, 2016b, http://www.icc-cpi.int/CourtRecords/CR2016_06511.PDF.

International Criminal Court (ICC). "Situation in Uganda in the Case of the Prosecutor v. Dominic Ongwen. Prosecution's Request to Admit Evidence Preserved under Article 56 of the Statute." Office of the Prosecutor. ICC Doc. No. ICC-02/04-01/15-464, June 13, 2016c, http://www.icc-cpi.int/CourtRecords/CR2016_04258.PDF.

International Criminal Court (ICC). "Situation in the Central African Republic in the Case of the Prosecutor v. Jean-Pierre Bemba Gombo. Judgment Pursuant to Article 74 of the Statute." Trial Chamber III., ICC Doc. No. ICC-01/05-01/08-3343, March 21, 2016d, http://www.icc-cpi.int/CourtRecords/CR2016_02238.PDF.

International Criminal Court (ICC). "Policy Paper on Sexual and Gender-Based Crimes." Office of the Prosecutor. June 2014a, http://www.icc-cpi.int/iccdocs/otp/OTP-Policy-Paper-on-Sexual-and-Gender-Based-Crimes--June-2014.pdf.

International Criminal Court (ICC). "Situation in the Democratic Republic of the Congo in the Case of the Prosecutor v. Bosco Ntaganda. Decision Pursuant to Article 61(7)(a) and (b) of the Rome Statute on the Charges of the Prosecutor Against Bosco Ntaganda." Pre-Trial Chamber II. ICC Doc. No. ICC-01/04-02/06-309, June 14, 2014b, http://www.icc-cpi.int/CourtRecords/CR2014_04750.PDF.

International Criminal Court (ICC). "Situation in the Democratic Republic of the Congo in the Case of the Prosecutor v. Germain Katanga. Judgment Pursuant to Article 74 of the Statute." Trial Chamber II. ICC Doc. No. ICC-01/04-01/07-3436-tENG, March 7, 2014c, http://www.icc-cpi.int/CourtRecords/CR2015_04025.PDF.

International Criminal Court (ICC). "Situation in the Democratic Republic of the Congo in the Case of the Prosecutor v. Mathieu Ngudjolo Chui. Judgment Pursuant to Article 74 of the Statute." Trial Chamber II. ICC Doc. No. ICC-01/04-02/12-3-tENG, December 26, 2012a, http://www.icc-cpi.int/CourtRecords/CR2013_02993.PDF.

International Criminal Court (ICC). "Situation in the Democratic Republic of the Congo in the Case of the Prosecutor v. Thomas Lubanga Dyilo. Decision Establishing Principles to be Applied to Reparations." Trial Chamber I. ICC Doc. No. ICC-01/04-01/06-2904, August 7, 2012b, https://www.icc-cpi.int/pages/record.aspx?uri=1447971.

International Criminal Court (ICC). "Situation in the Democratic Republic of the Congo in the Case of the Prosecutor v. Thomas Lubanga Dyilo. Decision on Sentence Pursuant to Article 76 of the Statute." Trial Chamber I. ICC Doc. No. ICC-01/04-01/06-2901, July 14, 2012c, http://www.icc-cpi.int/CourtRecords/CR2012_07409.PDF.

International Criminal Court (ICC). "Situation in the Democratic Republic of the Congo in the Case of the Prosecutor v. Thomas Lubanga Dyilo. Judgment Pursuant to Article 74 of the Statute." Trial Chamber I, ICC Doc. No. ICC-01/04-01/06-2842, April 4, 2012d, http://www.icc-cpi.int/CourtRecords/CR2012_03942.PDF.

IRIN. "Thorny Issue of Reparations for Lubanga's Victims." IRIN News, April 10, 2012, http://www.irinnews.org/news/2012/04/10/thorny-issue-reparations-lubanga%E2%80%99s-victims.

Kendall, S., and S. Nouwen. "Representational Practices at the International Criminal Court: The Gap between Juridified and Abstract Victimhood." *Law & Contemporary Problems* 76 (2013), 235–262.

Koomen, J. "'Without These Women, the Tribunal Cannot Do Anything': The Politics of Witness Testimony on Sexual Violence at the International Criminal Tribunal for Rwanda." *Signs: Journal of Women in Culture and Society* 38, no. 2 (2013): 253–277.

Mibenge, C. S. *Sex and International Tribunals: The Erasure of Gender from the War Narrative.* Philadelphia: University of Pennsylvania Press, 2013.

Moreno Ocampo, L. "Ceremony for the Solemn Undertaking of the Chief Prosecutor of the International Criminal Court. Statement Made by Mr. Luis Moreno-Ocampo." The Hague, June 16, 2003, http://www.iccnow.org/documents/MorenoOcampo16June03.pdf.

Oosterveld, V. "The Definition of Gender in the Rome Statute of the International Criminal Court: A Step Forward or Back for International Criminal Justice?" *Harvard Human Rights Journal* 18 (2005): 55–84.

Pena, M., and G. Carayon. "Is the ICC Making the Most of Victim Participation?" *International Journal of Transitional Justice* 7, no 3 (2013): 518–535.

Rome Statute of the International Criminal Court, opened for signature July 17, 1998, 2187 UNTS 3 (entered into force July 1, 2002), http://legal.un.org/icc/statute/99_corr/cstatute.htm

UN Women. "Preventing Conflict, Transforming Justice, Securing the Peace: A Global Study on the Implementation of United Nations Security Council Resolution 1325." New York: UN Women, 2015, http://wps.unwomen.org/en.

Women's Initiatives for Gender Justice (WIGJ). Press Release. "Bemba Conviction Overturned by the ICC Appeals Chamber." June 12, 2018, http://4genderjustice.org/pub/Statement-Bemba-Appeal-Judgment-June-2018.pdf.

Women's Initiatives for Gender Justice (WIGJ). Press Release. "Special Adviser on Gender Completes Her Mandate." August 26, 2016, http://www.4genderjustice.org/pub/Special-Adviser-on-Gender-completes-her-mandate.pdf.

Women's Initiatives for Gender Justice (WIGJ). *Gender Report Card on the International Criminal Court 2014.* The Hague, December 2014, http://www.iccwomen.org/documents/Gender-Report-Card-on-the-ICC-2014.pdf.

Women's Initiatives for Gender Justice (WIGJ). *Gender Report Card on The International Criminal Court 2012.* The Hague, November 2012, http://www.iccwomen.org/documents/Gender-Report-Card-on-the-ICC-2012.pdf.

Women's Initiatives for Gender Justice (WIGJ). *Legal Filings: The Prosecutor v. Jean-Pierre Bemba Gombo and The Prosecutor v. Thomas Lubanga Dyilo.* The Hague, February 2010, http://www.iccwomen.org/publications/articles/docs/LegalFilings-web-2-10.pdf.

CHAPTER 28

WPS AND THE NORTH ATLANTIC TREATY ORGANIZATION

STÉFANIE VON HLATKY

As the world's most powerful political-military organization, the North Atlantic Treaty Organization (NATO) might seem like an unlikely candidate when it comes to championing gender-based reforms. Yet, the Alliance has been quite active in promoting the Women, Peace, and Security (WPS) agenda over the last decade, adapting the objectives of UN Security Council Resolution 1325 and follow-on resolutions (1820, 1888, 1889, 1960, 2106, 2122, and 2422) to the performance of its core tasks: collective defense, crisis management, and cooperative security. Taken together, the appropriation of these resolutions by governments and international organizations has been dubbed the WPS agenda.

To demonstrate its commitment to the WPS agenda, NATO has integrated the Resolution 1325 vocabulary into successive Summit declarations, the Secretary-General's annual reports, and key official documents. During the 2016 NATO Summit in Warsaw, the Communiqué stated that: "Our ongoing efforts and commitment to integrate gender perspectives into Alliance activities throughout NATO's three core tasks will contribute to a more modern, ready, and responsive Alliance" (Warsaw Communiqué 2016). During the 2018 NATO Summit in Brussels, a new WPS policy and action plan were adopted. In addition, NATO created a permanent position to advise the Secretary General, the North Atlantic Council (NAC) and the International Staff, on how to best integrate the gender-based concepts at the heart of Resolution 1325. NATO's commitment to the WPS agenda, thus, appears quite far-reaching.

Like most international security organizations that have taken on the task of implementing Resolution 1325, one of the main challenges involves incorporating the varying interpretations of what gender means into NATO policy, operational planning, and missions. After all, gender roles vary across cultural contexts and NATO is an organization counting twenty-nine member states and an additional twenty-one partners under the auspices of the Euro-Atlantic Partnership Council (EAPC). Still, the Alliance, with the help of both internal and external gender experts, has developed an important number of gender guidelines to harmonize gender awareness across the organization. Recent research which analyses NATO's publicly available guidelines demonstrates that there is nevertheless a significant divide between how civilians and the military have approached the WPS agenda, perhaps mirroring existing intra-Alliance professional divides (Hardt and von Hlatky 2017).

While the civilian and military administrative bodies of NATO, the International Staff (IS) and the International Military Staff (IMS), are supported by a Women, Peace, and Security Office and Gender Advisors (GENAD) respectively, the permanent representatives, who are the Ambassadors heading the national delegations, tend to rely on their own capitals, rather than NATO, for foreign and defense policy leadership and guidance. Ultimately, NATO is an Alliance of sovereign states, and the normative shift undertaken with the WPS agenda can only progress as quickly as consensus decision-making will allow. The Alliance's complex organizational structure, which has civil-military cooperation at its core, has both benefited and hampered the implementation of Resolution 1325 at NATO. On the one hand, there are multiple entry points within the organization for knowledge on gender to be introduced and shared. For example, NATO's Secretary-General Jens Stoltenberg has been an ardent defender of Resolution 1325, proudly proclaiming himself to be a feminist.

On the other hand, there is no baseline understanding when it comes to identifying WPS priorities, with significant variation across countries and between civilian and military professional cultures. This chapter provides an overview of the progress that has been made to date, drawing from existing academic scholarship and policy reports that have been funded or produced by NATO. The focus of this chapter is on how NATO has attempted to guide state behavior when it comes to the WPS agenda. I argue that there are two main mechanisms through which NATO presses allies to advance WPS priorities. The first mechanism is reporting, especially the annual questionnaire compiled by nations at the request of the IMS Office of the Gender Advisor. The second mechanism is operational. NATO allies and partners, through their joint participation in operations and missions, have developed certain common practices when it comes to integrating a gender perspective as part of their operational plans.

The chapter is divided into three main sections: the first provides an overview of the literature on gender as it relates to international security; the second section discusses NATO's reporting requirements on the representation of women and examines other organizational practices in support of the WPS agenda; and, finally, the third section investigates how gender guidelines have been integrated into missions and operations. In the conclusion, I address the way ahead for the Alliance, arguing that the return of deterrence and collective defense as core NATO focus areas, will reduce the salience of gender issues in the near future. To secure the progress made thus far, NATO will have to protect its institutional memory through the work of the Women, Peace, and Security Office and military gender advisors. This can be achieved through the continued collection of data, and the creation of reports and guidance notes, as well as through the provision of expert advice to NATO officials and practitioners.

Debates in the Literature

The literature that discusses the WPS agenda as it applies to NATO is a combination of feminist scholarship and reports compiled by practitioners to assess the progress made by governments and international security organizations on Resolution 1325. In addition, NATO has encouraged more cooperation between academic researchers and practitioners through its Science for Peace and Security (SPS) Programme. Established in 1958, the SPS program has funded several research and training projects related to WPS. Specifically, funding for WPS initiatives has been a core objective since 2007, when NATO adopted its first official policy on Resolution 1325. This kind of research was greatly facilitated when NATO made available its annual country reports on women in the military, compiled by the IMS Office of the GENAD, though gender in the armed forces is admittedly only a small portion of what is covered under Resolution 1325 (Carreiras 2006; Figueroa and Palomo 2015).

In the scholarly literature, feminist researchers and gender theorists have long studied the impact of gender on conflict, often offering a critical analysis of initiatives such as Resolution 1325. Indeed, gender theorists offer both critical and sociological accounts of female and male participation in military organizations, conflict, and war, and they are often skeptical when analyzing attempts by the international community to "mainstream" gender issues (Peterson 1992; Tickner 1992). Speaking to the adoption of Resolution 1325 more specifically, Charli Carpenter decries the neglect of men and boys as important actors that should be included in the cornerstone UN resolution but that are obscured by the label of *Women,* Peace, and Security (Carpenter 2006). She points out that men and boys who are subjected to military violence have been omitted from the debate, given the resolution's explicit focus on women and girls. Similarly, Laura Sjoberg (2007) challenges gender stereotypes that color the debate on gender and armed conflict by pointing out the role of female perpetrators of sexual violence, thereby problematizing some of the essentializing assumptions that underlie the WPS agenda, namely that women, by their simple inclusion, can bring about peaceful change. Indeed, the feminist literature highlights that the goal of making the practice of security and defense more gender sensitive is often more complex than presented in the succinct text of UN resolutions and National Action Plans (NAP).

By contrast, a review of the literature also reveals an important body of work that is more policy oriented and certainly more optimistic in tone. These contributions often come in the form of best practices or progress reports, but do find echoes in the standpoint feminist literature, which argues that more women in the military improves outcomes because they bring unique skills to the table (Bridges and Horsfall 2009). This line of argument is very much at the center of NATO's WPS agenda, which has enshrined the message that the inclusion of more women in leadership positions and in the military improves policy and operational outcomes. Reports commissioned by NATO, demonstrated that gender awareness remained low across the organization (Lackenbauer and Langlais 2013). NATO practitioners then realized that pointing to Resolution 1325 and NAPs was not enough to change policy and operational planning processes, and thus they started examining more practical tools, such as training.

Adding to the challenge of low awareness, the WPS agenda was faced with a gap in understanding between competing visions of what gender means in the NATO context. Recent research shows that while some NATO practitioners view the WPS agenda through the prism of representation goals—for example, how many women are represented within NATO structures—others view the integration of gender analysis into day-to-day tasks as the overarching priority (Hardt and von Hlatky 2017). In reality, both issues are equally important, though not always evenly represented in NATO's gender policies. The most authoritative documents to date are the NATO/EAPC Implementation Plan on Resolution 1325 and the Bi-Strategic Command Directive 40-1, which has also led to an Action Plan to ensure compliance. These guiding policies and supporting documentation ultimately cover a pretty broad scope and provide objectives and action items related to gender equality, the integration of a gender perspective in NATO's core tasks, and sexual violence prevention.

Another segment of the literature focuses on women's integration into NATO countries' national armed forces. For example, Lana Obradovic uses NATO data to address recruitment challenges, the role of the women's movement, and the overarching community of practice which emerged with the creation of Resolution 1325 (Obradovic 2015). The most important finding in her work is the identification of a gap between North American and European approaches to gender mainstreaming, an observation that is important in the NATO context. For example, there is variation when it comes to the adoption of national action plans, linked to the implementation of Resolution 1325, or the participation of women in national armed forces. Indeed, NATO observers tend to assume that the biggest cultural or professional gap will manifest itself between the traditional NATO allies and the newer members from the Baltics and Central Europe, so Obradovic's finding is counterintuitive in this respect.

There are other experts who have been very influential in NATO debates on gender, even though they are examining non-NATO case studies. Indeed, research focusing on NATO's partner nations has been particularly useful in defining the vocabulary and conceptual reference points for the Alliance's WPS agenda. Sweden, for example, was given the position of GENAD for Allied Command Operations for several years. This position has meant that a lot of the lessons learned from the Swedish context were transferred to NATO. Robert Egnell's work is important in this respect (Egnell 2014). He argues that, for successful implementation, the narrative surrounding WPS matters, noting that presenting gender-based reforms as necessary for operational effectiveness yields more acceptance than a rights-based approach, when you implore on members of the armed forces to embrace Resolution 1325 because it is the right thing to do. The Swedish armed forces were also among the first to appoint senior GENADs to work within defense headquarters to advise key military leaders, under the Chief of Joint Operations.

Australian experts have also been quite present in WPS debates. Jennifer Wittwer (2013; also see chapter 44 in this volume) for instance, who has worked on the gender file in the Australian, NATO, and UN contexts, focuses on operational planning and capability building as the mechanisms through which the gender perspective should be integrated into organizational practices. She also highlights the importance of the interplay between official actors, namely governments and member-based organizations like NATO, and nongovernmental organizations and civil society. What comes across in Wittwer's analysis is that this knowledge exchange has been key to advancing best practices in support of the WPS agenda, especially when it comes to monitoring Resolution 1325 and integrating a gender perspective in military operations.

REPORTING

To monitor the implementation of 1325 across NATO member states and partners, we should look to both national and alliance-level mechanisms. At the national level, most NATO member states have a national action plan to monitor the implementation of

Resolution 1325 across different security, defense and development organizations (Figueroa and Palomo 2015). Through this mechanism, countries can track progress annually when it comes to the representation of women in government and the armed forces, the development of new gender awareness training packages, as well as how programs are designed and delivered to account for the gender perspective.

At the Alliance level, NATO tracks data on the representation of women across NATO institutions through its annual Diversity Report (Nordick 2015). At the NATO Headquarters, for example, the 2015 Diversity Report (Figure 28.1) show that women make up 39 percent of civilian staff. However, when one looks at the two most senior levels, the proportion of women drops down to 16 percent (Nordick 2015) Updated reports show very slow progress on this front.

NATO is facing important recruitment and retention problems, which help explain why these numbers are stagnating. Family-friendly policies and NATO events to boost staff awareness on representation issues are some of the measures that have been introduced to encourage more women to pursue careers at NATO and to reach the highest levels of leadership. In 2016, a major milestone was the appointment of Rose Gottemoeller as the first female Deputy Secretary-General. Still, when one looks at NATO's senior leadership, from the military representatives to the Assistant Secretary-Generals, there are no women represented. The picture looks better for the Permanent Representatives, as there are currently nine female Ambassadors out of twenty-nine representing allied states at the NATO headquarters.

As a parallel effort, the International Military Staff's Office of the Gender Advisor (IMS GENAD) compiles annual reports submitted by member nations, tracking the number of women in their armed forces, accounting for rank and service. These reports also include information about women-friendly policies and various research and policy initiatives aimed to improve the representation of women in the military. Collecting this data serves as a kind of benchmarking exercise, where NATO states can compare each other's performance regarding women in the armed forces. But more importantly, the tracking and

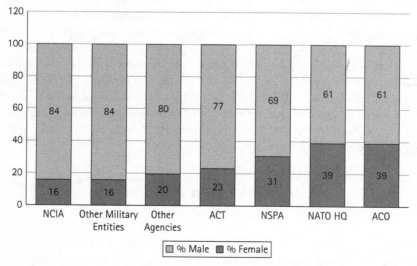

FIGURE 28.1 NATO-wide civilian staff—by NATO, body, and gender.

analysis of these data help the IMS GENAD formulate guidelines for member states and the consolidation of best practices to share across the Alliance and with partner nations. The other two NATO GENADs, which sit at Allied Command Operations and Allied Command Transformation, are focused on operational planning and gender training respectively. Their roles are, therefore, more focused on gender mainstreaming within the Alliance, as opposed to gender balancing, which is about improving the representation of women at all levels. Gender mainstreaming, for its part, "has to do with operational effectiveness" and "recognizes the role of gender integration in international peace and security, as well as the understanding that policies and programs may have different impacts on men and women" (de Jonge Oudraat 2013: 613).

Finally, the role of the WPS Office is also very important to draw lessons from the various reporting procedures, at both the national and alliance levels. The WPS office is headed by a Special Representative (SR) for Women, Peace, and Security—currently Ambassador Clare Hutchinson, who is an important contact within NATO for targeted advice on gender issues at the strategic level. To this end, she is sometimes asked to brief the North Atlantic Council, the Alliance's highest decision-making body. The Special Representative also has an important outreach and public diplomacy role, representing NATO internationally at conferences and forums where the WPS agenda is advanced. In addition to the GENADs and the SR for WPS, each NATO division has a gender focal point, who is meant to track the gender file as it relates to their respective unit. Though focal points have no specific reporting requirements, they are tasked with overseeing key documents to make sure that attention is paid to Resolution 1325. These focal points can suggest that the language be tweaked to account for Resolution 1325 or raise this as a point of discussion in meetings. In addition, the focal points coordinate with the WPS Office to develop internal good practices when it comes to integrating a gender perspective in NATO's day-to-day tasks.

These institutional arrangements demonstrate clear political will to make Resolution 1325 and the WPS agenda a priority, but implementation continues to be a challenge, as NATO experiences high turnover of staff and, therefore, both progress and the retention of institutional memory depend a lot on the personal commitment of individuals who are tasked with the gender file (Hardt 2016). Civilian staff also seem less certain about how to implement the gender perspective as part of their day-to-day tasks (Hardt and von Hlatky 2017). On the military side, however, dynamics are a bit different because there has been a greater opportunity to institutionalize gender awareness in the context of missions and operations and to share these lessons widely within and outside of the military community (Hardt and von Hlatky 2017).

OPERATIONS

To situate the implementation of Resolution 1325 within the context of NATO missions and operations, an overview of certain guidelines is in order. The NATO/EAPC Women, Peace, and Security Agenda 2016–2018 lays out NATO's commitments as they relate to incorporating a gender perspective for crisis management and NATO-led missions. This document notes that to enhance the operational effectiveness and to ensure implementation of Resolution 1325 and related Resolutions, NATO and its operational partners will ensure that a gender perspective is included in conflict analysis, planning, execution, assessment and evaluation of any NATO-led operation or mission (NATO/EAPC 2016: 16).

The stated intention, therefore, is to perform a gender analysis long before operations begin, suggesting that gender should be mainstreamed throughout the process of operational planning, from conflict analysis to the execution of missions on the ground.

The primary means through which this is achieved is with the appointment of GENADs who can be attached to the Command Group and by making sure that senior commanders have received appropriate gender training. In addition, NATO recommends that female soldiers participate in operations, which is an important distinction as GENADs are not necessarily women. Despite having these overarching guidelines, it is up to the individual NATO allies and partners to take action: "The provision of trained troops and experts on gender issues, as well as a better gender balance in NATO-led forces, depend entirely on national decisions" (NATO/EAPC 2016: 17).

When it comes to the deployment of gender advisors and overall training related to gender in operations, there have been remarkable changes at NATO between 2002 and 2013 (Figure 28.2). This evolving picture is certainly due to the fact that more and more NATO member states have adopted national action plans on Resolution 1325, but also that there might be a powerful socialization process at play. Indeed, by encouraging the deployment of GENADs as part of its missions, NATO is creating a demand for this type of expertise, which then encourages states to meet this demand. Moreover, by requiring and providing gender-based training in preparation for NATO-led operations and missions, the Alliance is further reinforcing the norm of gender mainstreaming across the organization.

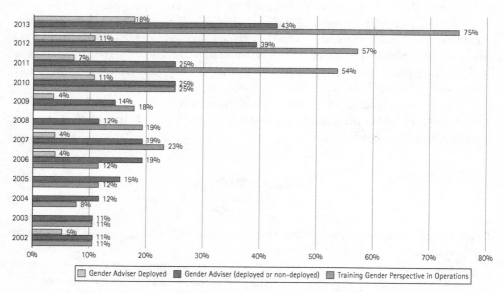

FIGURE 28.2 Percentage of NATO member states reporting on the use of deployed gender advisors, non-deployed gender advisors, and training for gender in operations, 2002–2013.

While these trends are encouraging, it is noteworthy that the deployment of gender expertise on the civilian side is not monitored to the same extent. Moreover, gender training packages that are offered by Allied Command Transformation or the NATO school in Oberammergau, which is more focused on operational training, cater to the military and do not directly address the policy planning tasks of NATO practitioners in the headquarters. Referring back to the earlier statement from the NATO/EAPC WPS Agenda, it would appear that there are fewer resources to support the integration of a gender perspective in conflict analysis and planning, as opposed to missions and operations (Hardt and von Hlatky 2017).

Additionally, many of the military's lessons were not necessarily learned through training, but were picked up from the field. In Afghanistan, for example, NATO forces realized that paying attention to gender and social dynamics was necessary for successful engagement with the community. Indeed, the nexus of gender and security is often tackled through the prism of cultural awareness and understanding, which are especially salient during international missions. The impact of gender on military practice has been examined in the scholarly literature, as mentioned earlier, but has seldom been addressed in a multinational, operational settings. Resolution 1325 on WPS (and follow-on resolutions) gave attention to this important aspect of international missions.

To support the narrative that diversity breeds success, the NATO Committee on Gender Perspectives started to compile case studies from NATO missions in Kosovo and Afghanistan, to show how the inclusion of a gender perspective could support commanders' intent. In a report titled "How Can Gender Make a Difference to Security Operations," one of those case studies is focused on how a Dutch GENAD, who was also a Lieutenant Commander, introduced women's markets for the International Security Assistance Force (ISAF). Not only was the initiative a positive opportunity for local Afghan women, who made money and learned English, but it allowed the Dutch contingent to foster meaningful contacts within the community (NATO Committee on Gender Perspectives [NCGP] 2011). Such contacts with local women proved useful for the ISAF mission as soldiers needed to assess local needs in the delivery of security and when overseeing development programs. As the report notes, "engaging local women provided NATO with a better understanding of the local context in which it operated" (NCGP 2011: 27).

Some studies go a bit further, claiming that women may have comparative advantages on the battlefield, linked to a natural inclination toward cooperative strategies, communication, and community building (Disler 2010). NATO has also embraced the idea that women can bring unique skills to the table, though it is not a widely accepted concept as some states' national defense preferences tend to favour gender neutrality over gender specificity. This gender-as-difference approach has been criticized by certain scholars who take issue with gender analyses that treat women as a homogeneous group (True 2016).

Beyond creating ties with local communities and intelligence gathering, however, these reports fall short of offering a compelling assessment of how gender perspectives can improve "hard security" tasks, such as targeting decisions and combat. This challenge replicates itself as NATO turns to Forward Presence as an operational priority, the deployment of battlegroups in Poland and in the Baltics to bolster the Alliance's deterrence capabilities. NATO's gender practitioners are addressing this challenge by including gender-based scenarios in military exercises and by stressing the importance of local community engagement for deterrence missions as well. Though GENADs continue to be active in Operation

Resolute Support, ISAF's follow-on mission in Afghanistan, there is still much work ahead to deliver a compelling gender analysis for traditional defense and deterrence tasks.

In terms of best practices, NATO frequently turns to the UN for guidance on how to implement Resolution 1325 in operational contexts. Indeed, the UN has developed a gender strategy for peacekeeping operations to address the unique needs of women and girls in the communities where peacekeepers are deployed. Here too, the UN relies on GENADs and gender focal points to make sure the gender perspective is considered in all aspects of the missions, for the uniformed and un-uniformed personnel deployed on UN peace support operations. To this end, the Gender Forward Looking Strategy promotes gender mainstreaming during all phases of mission planning, encourages mission designs that address gender inequality and discrimination, and encourages a more streamlined training approach for all UN personnel (United Nations 2014). The UN, much like NATO, has also pushed for more women to be deployed on operations, though this has not always been a priority for troop contributing countries (Crawford et al. 2015).

CONCLUSION

This chapter has provided an overview of NATO policies and operational considerations linked to the implementation of Resolution 1325 and follow-on resolution. It focused primarily on reporting mechanisms and the operational context to show how gender mainstreaming guidelines are translated into practice, for both civilian and military personnel. In so doing, this chapter also notes that there are important and visible differences in terms of how the WPS Agenda is carried out. Some of those differences can be attributed to differences in national culture, since NATO is an alliance with twenty-nine member states and a broad network of partners. Other differences are more salient across the civilian-military divide. Civilian and military institutions very often have different professional cultures and practices, which makes the translation of best practices more complex. To bridge that gap, the challenge will be to provide gender training that is tailored to civilian tasks, such as committee work and the development of NATO policies, as well as military ones, with variants for the strategic, operational, and tactical levels. A step in this direction is the development of training, supported by the NATO Science for Peace and Security Program that is meant to provide baseline knowledge on gender for both civilians and military personnel across NATO institutions.

Even beyond fostering a common understanding on gender, the Alliance faces a more immediate challenge as member states shift their attention away from Afghanistan and turn back to a more traditional defense posture, in response to the security threats posed by Russia, which are especially acute for NATO's Baltic and central European allies. While the gender perspective was fairly intuitive to work with during ISAF, it has so far proven more challenging for gender experts to perform gender analysis in support of enhanced Forward Presence—the deployment of allied battlegroups to bolster NATO deterrence on the Eastern flank. While it is possible to offer such an analysis, as community-based engagement and defense cooperation will still be part of those efforts, there has been much less research and policy analysis dedicated to the intersection of gender and deterrence, as these concepts relate to NATO. Indeed, some issues are seen as "outside the scope" of gender. However, investigating gender perspectives on the harder edge of the security spectrum is nonetheless possible if subject matter experts from each respective field collaborate. For NATO, that would mean a collaboration between gender and deterrence experts in the context of enhanced Forward Presence, the NATO battlegroups in Lithuania, Estonia, Latvia, and Poland. As attention ebbs and flows on gender issues, NATO should still resource and fund gender expertise and capabilities to support the Alliance's work, to both preserve institutional memory and to refine gender mainstreaming tools and training for civilian and military personnel. This is indeed essential moving forward as gender-based analytical skills are becoming part of the core competencies of security and defense professionals, at NATO and beyond.

REFERENCES

Bridges, Donna, and Debbie Horsfal. "Increasing Operational Effectiveness in UN Peacekeeping toward a Gender-Balanced Force." *Armed Forces & Society* 36, no. 1 (2009): 120–130.

Carreiras, Helena. *Gender and the Military: Women in the Armed Forces of Western Democracies.* London and New York: Routledge, 2006.

Carpenter, R. Charli. "Recognizing Gender-Based Violence against Civilian Men and Boys in Conflict Situations." *Security Dialogue* 37, no. 1 (2006): 83–103.

Crawford, Kerry F., James H. Lebovic, and Julia M. Macdonald. "Explaining the Variation in Gender Composition of Personnel Contributions to UN Peacekeeping Operations." *Armed Forces & Society* 41, no. 2 (2015): 257–281.

de Jonge Oudraat, Chantal. "UNSCR 1325—Conundrums and Opportunities." *International Interactions* 39, no. 4 (2013): 612–619.

Disler, Edith A. "The Feminine as a Force Multiplier." In *Attitudes Aren't Free: Thinking Deeply about Diversity in the US Armed Forces*, edited by James E. Parco and David A. Levi, 363–379. Maxwell, AL: Air University Press, 2010.

Egnell, R., P. Hojem, and H. Berts. *Gender, Military Effectiveness, and Organizational Change: The Swedish Model.* London: Palgrave Macmillan, 2014.

Figueroa, Cristina, and Jesus Palomo. *UNSCR 1325 Reload: Analysis of Annual National Reports to the NATO Committee on Gender Perspectives from 1999–2013—Policies, Recruitment, Retentions, and Operations. Findings and Recommendations.* Brussels: NATO Emerging Security Division, 2015.

Hardt, Heidi. "How NATO Remembers: Explaining Institutional Memory in NATO Crisis Management," *European Security* (December 2016): 1–29.

Hardt, Heidi, and Stéfanie von Hlatky. "NATO's Gender Turn: Adaptation in International Security Organizations." Paper presented at International Studies Association Annual Convention, Baltimore, MD, February 23 2017.

Lackenbauer, Helene, and Richard Langlais, eds. *Review of the Practical Implications of UNSCR 1325 for the Conduct of NATO-Led Operations and Missions.* Brussels: NATO, 2013.

NATO Committee on Gender Perspectives. *How Can Gender Make a Difference to Security Operations.* Brussels: NATO, 2011.

NATO/EAPC. *Women, Peace and Security Agenda 2016–2018: Policy, Action Plan, and Strategic Report.* Brussels: NATO, 2016.

Nordick, Tara. *2015 Annual Diversity Report.* NATO Headquarters. Brussels: Diversity and Inclusion, 2015.

Obradovic, Lana. *Gender Integration in NATO Military Forces: Cross-National Analysis.* Farnham, UK: Ashgate, 2015.

Peterson, V. Spike. *Gendered States: Feminist (Re)Visions of International Relations Theory.* Boulder, CO: Lynne Rienner, 1992.

Sjoberg, Laura. "Agency, Militarized Femininity, and Enemy Others: Observations from the War in Iraq." *International Feminist Journal of Politics* 9, no.1 (2007): 82–101.

Tickner, J. Ann. *Gender in International Relations: Feminist Perspectives on Achieving Global Security.* New York: Columbia University Press, 1992.

True, Jacqui. "How Effective Is Gender Mainstreaming in International Peace and Security Policymaking?" In *Handbook on Gender in World Politics*, edited by Jill Steans and Daniela Tepe-Belfrage, 457–467. Cheltenham, UK: Edward Elgar, 2016.

United Nations. "Gender Forward Looking Strategy 2014–2018." New York: Department of Peacekeeping Operations and Department of Field Support (DPKO/DFS), 2014.

Warsaw Summit Communiqué. Issued by the Heads of State and Government Participating in the Meeting of the North Atlantic Council. Warsaw, July 8–9, 2016.

Wittwer, Jennifer A. "The Gender Agenda: Women, Peace, and Security in the Conduct of NATO-led Operations and Missions." *Australian Defence Force Journal* 191 (2013): 57–67.

CHAPTER 29

WPS AND THE AFRICAN UNION

TONI HAASTRUP

INTRODUCTION

IN 2016, the African Union (AU) issued its first ever implementation report of the Women, Peace, and Security (WPS) agenda. This report was compiled by the Office of the Special Envoy on Women, Peace, and Security, which was created in 2014 as a dedicated regional hub for ensuring AU compliance with the WPS agenda. As a hub of practice, the context of this office and the work it does is essential to understanding the contributions of the African region to the WPS landscape. While previous research on WPS has focused mainly on the language of the Security Council resolutions, the role of certain states, and the performance of the United Nations at the institutional and field levels, the increased roles of regional security institutions like the AU also demands attention. In recent times, analysis from the European regional perspective has begun to address the institutional adaptations of the WPS and the use of WPS in the European Union's missions (Guerrina and Wright, 2016; Deiana and McDonagh, 2017; Muehlenhoff 2017; Haastrup, 2018), there remains, however, limited understanding of the African regional cases (see Olonisakin et al. 2011; Haastrup, 2013). Where these exist, they are descriptive in the main and increasingly dated (see Hendricks 2015; Hudson 2016, for exceptions).

Yet, Much of what we see articulated in the first WPS resolution, UN Security Council Resolution 1325, has origins in the concerns of African women's groups and regional security institutions (Diop 2011: 173). In this chapter, I reflect on how the AU has engaged the global WPS agenda, locating the AU as a "site of practice" (see Gelot 2017; Bueger 2015; Neumann 2013; Schatzki 2005). The idea of the AU as a "site of practice" for Africa's take on the WPS agenda is useful because it emphasizes the implications of the actions of individuals or a specific set of actors, the processes they engage in, or sets of actions they perform, within a given time and space (Bicchi and Bremberg 2016). The practice approach allows not only for a focus on what the African Union and its agents do when they "implement" or "take WPS seriously," but also on how they understand WPS in the African context (Gelot 2017; also Bicchi and Bremberg 2016: 394). By applying a practice approach to understanding the

WPS agenda in the African context I focus specifically on the work of AU practitioners, particularly the Office of the AU Special Envoy for WPS, and the institutional environment and the localized framework that practitioners draw upon (knowledge and processes). This focus enables me to observe "socially meaningful patterns of action, which, in being performed more or less competently, simultaneously embody, act out, and possibly reify background knowledge and discourse in and on the material world" (Adler and Pouliot 2011: 4). Although the AU does not have a formally named regional action plan (RAP), the 2009 AU Gender Policy is widely considered the default RAP because it sets out the continental agenda. The AU Gender Policy is comprehensive in the way it gives attention to both regional frameworks and references the founding resolutions of the WPS agenda, Resolution 1325, and the subsequent Resolution 1820. However, this policy was not created in a vacuum; rather it is dependent on the interaction of other regional legal frameworks, regional instruments and the practices of certain actors in what practice approaches delineate as a community of practice (Adler and Pouliot 2011). It is this community of practice that is the focus of this chapter. The community of practice

> [e]ncompasses not only the conscious and discursive dimensions, and the actual doing for social change, but also the social space where structure and agency . . . . [It] constitutes the normative and epistemic ground for action [including] agents, made up of real people, who—working via network channels, across national borders, across organizational divides, and in the halls of government—affect political, economic, and social events (Adler and Pouliot 2011: 18–19).

Thus, by examining this regional community of practice through the AU case, a new story is added to the WPS narrative that emphasizes the localized context and gives Africa and Africans agency within the global context. This chapter will proceed as follows: Drawing on legal documents, official papers, and secondary sources, the first section analyzes the evolution of the AU's African Peace and Security Architecture in parallel to the development of a gender-aware peace and security agenda. In the second section, the chapter examines the evolution of the local/regional gender regime and its intersection with the global WPS agenda. Next, the chapter uses illustrative examples to explore the areas of priority thus far in the WPS work of the AU. These two sections underscore the mutually constituted process of interaction where learning, knowing, and doing is happening within a WPS community of practice. By focusing on the work that dominates the implementation of the WPS agenda via the Office of the AU Special Envoy for Women, Peace, and Security, this chapter concludes that practitioners' priorities have contributed to the making of an Africanized WPS agenda.

Locating the WPS Agenda in The African Peace and Security Architecture

The AU, which succeeded the Organization for African Unity (OAU), was formally launched in 2001. Between its creation in 1963 and the post–Cold War period, the OAU had failed in its ambition to integrate the social, economic, and political apparatuses of African states and people so that people felt security and peace thrived. By 1999, when negotiations were finalized to create a new continental organization, it was clear that peace and security issues, linked to resolving violent conflict and protecting the most vulnerable, would be the main focus of the AU. The Constitutive Act of the African Union committed to accelerating integration, and addressing the many challenges on the continent linked to poverty, health, universal education, state fragility, and insecurity. The AU is thus tasked with ensuring the peace and security of the entire continent. Moreover, this new security agenda finds form in conceptual understandings of security as human security. Despite its critical take on who should be the subject of security, human security is still gendered in that it reifies a gender-neutral human without attention to the experiences of gender hierarchies. It is this that makes the AU an appropriate venue through which to engage with the meanings and practices of the WPS agenda in Africa, since its remit goes beyond traditional military defense toward addressing new forms of insecurities, and especially is we are to see changes in the lived experiences of Africans. Further, as the majority of the AU's budget is directed toward peace and security issues, the gendering of the AU is dependent on an assessment of its peace and security apparatuses. As part of integrating new institutional norms, the structures of the AU are intended to bring about institutional innovation.

The primary route for this peace and security innovation has been the African Peace and Security Architecture (APSA). The APSA is an innovation in that it broadens the remit of the AU in the area of peace and security at the same time as broadening what constitutes peace and security. The APSA includes the Peace and Security Council, the Regional Economic Communities (RECs), and Regional Mechanisms (RMs),[1] as well as the Peace and Security department, the latter of which takes its mandate from the Constitutive Act and Protocol Relating to the Establishment of the Peace and Security Council (PSC Protocol) (see also Ndiaye 2016). In 2000, the AU established the Women and Gender Directorate[2] within the chairperson's office. The role of this Directorate was to "integrate, support, implement and develop mechanisms to mainstream gender awareness" across all AU structures including the RECs and RMs (Haastrup 2013: 105).

In 2002, the AU adopted the PSC Protocol, which sets out the functions of the Peace and Security Council (PSC; African Union 2001). In justifying the creation of the PSC (and the APSA), the signatories acknowledged the negative impact of militarized conflict, especially on *women and children*. In doing so, it committed the AU Commission to human rights training that prioritizes the needs of women and children. The AU's PSC is the tangible representation of an evolved and comprehensive peace and security regime, and an example of a collective security arrangement. It is the main decision-making organ of the APSA with the responsibility for preventing, managing, and resolving conflicts on the continent. The APSA relies on the integration of the peace and security mechanisms of RECs and RMs to be successful. Because the PSC reflects the leadership of the member states, it already fails in the area of participation, since the majority of heads of states in Africa are men. Nevertheless, the authority of the PSC in promulgating the WPS agenda is important to its institutionalization. The PSC has, therefore, instituted the practice of an annual open session on the WPS agenda. These formal sessions allow for the discussion of progress and shortcomings in the implementation of the WPS agenda in Africa. Moreover, it provides an opportunity for participants to interrogate the role of the AU in the WPS implementation process. The Open Sessions further encourage engagement between civil society, media, government officials, and others. As part of the 407th meeting of the PSC, which was launched in December 2013, the Open Session focused on "Women and

Children in Situations of Conflict in Africa." This meeting adopted the *AU Gender Training Manual for AU Peace Support Operations*. The Manual is a course that reinforces the tenets of the Maputo Protocol and the WPS agenda on how AU personnel should act in conflict situations. The October 2016 Open Session focused on the Role of the Media in Enhancing Accountability on Women, Peace, and Security Commitments in Africa. The Open Session was also a recommitment to expedite National Action Plans (NAPs) on the WPS agenda. These Open Sessions simultaneously create the space for learning, knowing, and acting toward the progressive implementation of the WPS in Africa to enact positive change. It thus underscores the AU as a site of practice for the WPS agenda in Africa. The peace and security department (PSD) is the operational epicenter of the APSA. Situated within the AU Commission, the PSD plans the work of the APSA with respect to conflict prevention, management and in some instances post-conflict reconstruction. The PSD, therefore, is responsible for designing and implementing the peace support operations that dominate the AU's peace and security work. Additionally, the PSD is responsible for gender mainstreaming and consequently implementing the provisions of the WPS under the aegis of the Office of the Special Envoy for WPS.

Of these regional institutional innovations, the most significant is the creation of the Office of the AU special envoy for WPS (OSE), which was created in 2014 by former AU chairperson Nkosasana Dlamini-Zuma. Due to its location within the AU, the chairperson and the OSE are considered to be essential within the APSA. The adoption of the WPS agenda, for now, is considered important to the full realization of the continental security architecture. But, what this really means requires a consideration of the practices and priorities of those tasked with implementation.

BUILDING A GENDER SENSITIVE PEACE AND SECURITY ARCHITECTURE

The inception of the WPS agenda in 2000, which began with the adoption of Resolution 1325, coincided with the launch of the AU itself. As a new institution, the AU had a unique opportunity to include this new global perspective within its nascent processes. Moreover, given that the WPS agenda prioritizes a gender-equal perspective with respect to how security is enacted, its aims were very much aligned with the commitment of the AU to gender equality as a fundamental part of its new regional integration project (Haastrup 2013: 104; Haastrup 2015; Hendricks 2015). Indeed, the journey toward the first WPS resolution, Resolution 1325, was determined, in part, by African regional perspectives. African feminists were actively involved in getting the issues that became part of the WPS onto the Security Council agenda. It is worth noting the work of Femmes Africa Solidarite (FAS), founded by Bineta Diop, now the current AU Special Envoy on WPS, and the African Women's Committee on Peace and Development (AWCPD). FAS, an umbrella organization for women-focused civil society organizations, and AWCPD campaigned for gender mainstreaming in regional institutions and have been instrumental to all the major gender equality milestones of the AU. One of their early successes was the adoption of the principle of gender parity within the AU and the Durban Declaration on Mainstreaming Gender and Women's Effective Participation in the African Union (AWCPD and FAS 2002). In observing recent trends regarding the inclusion of gender perspectives at the African regional level, it is clear that third-world feminism (which is concerned with gender power relations in the context of the global political economy of the postcolonial state) has played a role (see also Haastrup 2013). Indeed, third-world feminism has informed the development of these African perspectives and facilitated the Africanization of global frameworks (see also Lorber 1998; Saunders 2002; United Nations Economic Commission for Africa [UNECA] 2008). At the same time, the new agenda with respect to gender equality interacts with contemporary notions of pan-Africanism, defined as "as an insurrectionary discourse that emerged in direct opposition to European capitalism, manifest in the worst forms of human exploitation, and occupation" (Abbas and Mama 2015: 3–4).

In 1994, the Dakar Fifth Regional Conference on Women adopted an African Platform for Action, which informed the Beijing Declaration and Platform for Action and the subsequent 2000 Windhoek Declaration, which directly influenced the provision of Resolution 1325. From the outset, Africans have been involved in the mission of the WPS agenda. It is thus unsurprising that the AU has also taken up the discourse that aims to prioritize gender perspectives in the institutionalization and practice of peace and security on the continent. As Article 4 (I) of the AU's Constitutive Act indicates, members of the Union are tasked with the promotion of gender equality. The WPS agenda was thus being introduced to a new institution with a renewed commitment to taking gender seriously for the whole continent. The Constitutive Act provision, however, was not the only African commitment to taking gender seriously and improving the lives of women in Africa. Indeed, for the AU and civil society groups on the continent, the adoption of the WPS would only be one way of reinforcing Africa's long-standing commitments to global gender norms. Among its other commitments was the development of its own gender regime, and, by extension, a gender-sensitive peace and security architecture. While this story is often missing from dominant narratives of the WPS, the agency of African women is especially important to understanding the AUs approach to the agenda.[3]

In Africa, concerns around the role of women in the politics of peace and security are certainly not recent. In 1981, the African Charter on Human and People's Rights (ACHPR) emphasized the necessity of equality in law and advocated against gender discrimination (Art. 18). Specifically, states are asked to ensure that discrimination against women and the protection of their (and children's) rights within domestic legislation is in accordance with international legal frameworks. This framework is limited, however, in its consideration of what a gender perspective may entail, as it focuses on understanding women's right in the context of their role in the family. In other words, notions of gender as a category distinct from women is a conflation that dominates policy framing in Africa and limits women's agency as it reduces their participation to the private sphere of the family and thus fails to consider *how* political and social issues impact women. In the ACHPR, for example, Article 23 deals specifically with security issues, but no link is made to considerations of gender or women.

The 2003 adoption of the Protocol to the African Charter on Human and Peoples Rights on the Rights of Women in Africa (the Maputo Protocol) was thus seen as major progress beyond the ACHPR. The Maputo Protocol is innovative for pushing beyond the legal allowances of the initial Charter. It explicitly commits the AU, and it member states (which now includes all African countries) to thirty-two articles aimed at social, economic, and political rights and empowerment. Articles 9–11, specifically, echo the concerns raised by Resolution 1325. In particular, Article 10, on the "Right to Peace," argues that women have a right to peaceful existence and participation in the promotion of peace. Similarly, Article 11 deals with the protection of "Women in Armed Conflicts," and requires that, the practices of member states in conflict aim to protect women, and other vulnerable peoples from "rape and other forms of sexual exploitation" (Art. 11).

The following year, the Solemn Declaration on Gender Equality in Africa (SDGEA) was adopted to bring forward the aspirations of the Maputo Protocol (African Union 2004). This was the first concrete policy instrument for attaining gender equality on the continent. "It provides a regulatory framework for implementing gender equality policies through mainstreaming" (Haastrup 2013: 103). For example, Article 2 of the SDGEA specifically deals with Peace and Security. Making specific reference to Resolution 1325, the SDGEA commits AU member states to

> ensur[ing] the full and effective participation and representation of women in peace processes including the prevention, resolution, management of conflicts and post-conflict reconstruction in Africa . . . and to also appoint women as Special Envoys and Special Representatives of the African Union (Art. 2, sec. 18).

The SDGEA is monumental because it spearheaded the "Gender Is My Agenda Campaign" (GIMAC) launched in 2006 to continue the work of activists in a more targeted way. In 2008, the Sixth African Development Forum was dedicated to Gender Equality, Women's Empowerment, and Ending Violence against Women in Africa. A joint venture of the AU, UNECA, and the African Development Bank, the forum emphasized that despite the acceptance of the WPS agenda as an additional frame for safeguarding women in conflict and post-conflict settings, implementation had been slow. Some of the blame, it was argued lay in the context. This context went beyond the usual trope of African conflict although this too was a focus. In the outcome report, other sources of insecurity were acknowledged including, financial volatility, food and fuel crises, and climate change—thus the focus was on the impact of everyday insecurities (UNECA, 2008: 2).

On conflict and post-conflict–based insecurity, often the starting point of much WPS discussion, the outcome report noted that the still limited number of NAPs, the lack of knowledge on the part of women's grassroots organizations, and the tendency of political elites to sideline women in negotiations compounded the failures of the WPS to take hold (UNECA 2008: 3). Subsequent to this report, a few more countries launched NAPs.[4]

These culminated in the 2009 Gender Policy. The Gender Policy was driven by the need to develop and outline a strategy for the implementation of the SDGEA, including the WPS agenda. Concerning peace and security issues specifically, the Gender Policy cites the "domesticating" of Resolution 1325 and 1820 (the WPS agenda) as fundamental to the gender work of the AU (African Union 2009). Indeed, Resolution 1325 is mentioned six times as a framework reference alongside other African frameworks as a path to realizing gender equality and paying attention to the gendered nature of insecurity in Africa.

Close readings of all these formal frameworks reinforce two discursive nodes of gender and security in Africa. In the context of the AU's priorities, in particular through its adoption of WPS, the first discursive node conflates women with gender. The gender policy is primarily a policy about the greater inclusion and visibility for women on the African continent. The second discursive node is that of the protection of women. To an extent, this appears to be a consequence of the first. The trope of that has been fundamental to the WPS agenda as well (see Willet 2010) and appears to have found fertile ground in the African context. By engaging with the local frameworks, however, it is evident that the WPS agenda does not necessarily impose this particular trope, but rather that it is conducive to the meanings enacted by the AU. In other words, the Gender Policy is a confluence of processes, practitioner experiences, and the evolution of gender-knowledge. Taken together, these factors have produced a roadmap for the implementation of the WPS agenda in Africa.

PRACTICING WOMEN, PEACE, AND SECURITY AGENDA IN AFRICA

In the aftermath of producing the Gender Policy, the AU has lived up to its role of being a site of practice from which Africa's WPS community can begin to enact change. The AU declared 2010–2020 the "African Women's Decade," thus committing the institution to the promotion of women's rights and gender equality. On the fifteenth anniversary of the first WPS resolution, African Heads of States declared 2015 to be the "Year of Women's Empowerment and Development Towards Africa's Agenda 2063" (African Union 2015). Following this, 2016 was then declared the "Year of Human Rights with a Particular Focus on the Rights of Women."

Beyond simply committing to the WPS agenda, AU actors have, to an extent, leveraged the framework, in addition to other localized ones, to bolster the impact of the AU in interpreting and effecting gender-sensitive security on the continent. This has been primarily through the office of the Special Envoy, but also beyond it. In this section, I consider some illustrative examples of where the WPS agenda has been particularly useful for the work of the AU via the Special Envoy. In this way, I reflect on an African interpretation of the WPS, one that uses the local frameworks described earlier. Furthermore, I explore the implications of this interpretation for the advancement of a gender-sensitive peace and security agenda on the continent.

The Special Envoy provides guidance and leadership on the institutionalization of the WPS agenda within the AU and on the continent as a whole. This role is undertaken on behalf of the Commission Chairperson, and it sends a strong message regarding the importance of the WPS agenda to the main work of the AU. While the core aim of the WPS envoy is to support the implementation of the agenda at the regional level, there is an additional broader commitment to amplifying the "voices and concerns" of women so that they are a part of the peace and security processes on the continent (Diop 2014). In addition, the OSE was given a special mandate to monitor progress on the implementation of the WPS agenda across the continent focusing on the AU organizations, the member states, and the RECs and RMs. Specifically, the OSE supports the development of NAPs and RAPs. Moreover, through the OSE, the Africa Gender Scorecard[5] will expand to consider WPS concerns. Thus, through the activities of the envoy, this institution is well placed to *Africanize* the WPS agenda so that it works for and in Africa.

The AU's WPS envoy has sought to directly engage with women affected by conflict in a variety of ways, including supporting participation efforts. Following her appointment, Bineta Diop traveled to meet women's groups and governmental representatives for women's ministries. By going to member states directly, the OSE is able to mediate national and local concerns with continental ones. Moreover, she provides a physical connection between the regional agenda and national ones. For instance, by supporting the creation of the Regional Platform of Women in the Sahel, the Special Envoy seeks to bring together key stakeholders to create an advocacy platform, capable of directly responding to persistent insecurity in the Sahel, particularly in Niger and Mali. Whereas Mali has a NAP, Niger does not. By encouraging this type of grouping then, the OSE is able to direct the learning between the two countries, while also creating the pathway to increasing Africa's NAP by one. In the case of the Central African Republic (CAR), the Special Envoy launched a project to support the participation of women in peacemaking, peace-building, and the reconstruction of the country. The participation of women in CAR's peace settlement was especially salient given the impact of the conflict on women, most notably their experiences of sexual violence within IDP camps (Musau 2015). The project coincided with a joint visit with UN Women executive director and the launch of the NAP to implement the WPS agenda. This one example is a tangible expression of the Special Envoy's ambition to actively link the national and continental contexts of the WPS agenda in Africa. In Nigeria, the OSE also took an active role in raising and maintaining awareness about the abduction of school-aged girls by the terrorist group Boko Haram in Chibok, Northern Nigeria.

In examining the priority areas of the OSE in Mali, CAR, and Nigeria, it is unsurprising that the AU's WPS practice has been most visibly focused on tackling sexual violence in conflict and post-conflict situations. Despite the existence of NAPs in these countries, conflict-related sexual violence remains a persistent problem, which suggests that NAPs themselves are not enough. The parallel persistence of limited resources has made it difficult to implement their aspirations. As Aisling Swaine (2009; 2015) argues, NAPs provide the incentive to act for states, but at best constitute only one dimension of implementing the WPS agenda, and are certainly not the antidote to fixing what's wrong.

Despite the persistence of conflict-related sexual and gender-based violence within AU member states, the OSE continue to focus on this aspect of the WPS agenda in terms of tangible outcomes. The protection of women (and girls) from sexualized violence is a key tenet of the WPS agenda, featuring consistently across all eight resolutions, sometimes to the detriment of other priorities, as argued by other authors in this handbook. In the African case, it is also supported by Article 11 of the *Maputo Protocol*, which obligates states' parties to protect "asylum seeking women, refugees, returnees and internally displaced persons" from sexual violence and exploitations (African Union 2003). The scandals surrounding the sexual violation of women and girls by peacekeepers has galvanized the WPS special envoy's mission regarding a zero tolerance code of conduct for AU troops, also known as the Policy on Sexual Exploitation and Abuse (SEA). The main motivation for this policy was the case of Somalia, following accusations that the troops of the African Union Mission to Somalia (AMISOM) sexually exploited and raped vulnerable women and girls. Somalia has been embroiled in conflict for over two decades. The United National Development Programme's Gender Inequality Index has consistently ranked Somalia very low (UNDP 2012)[6] in the areas of maternal mortality; child marriages of young girls; violence against women; and a hostile atmosphere to equality through the persistence of discriminatory traditional jurisprudence. In 2007, mandated by the United Nations, the AU launched AMISOM as a response to the conflict related insecurity in the country. It is a peace support mission with a military, civilian, maritime, and humanitarian component. "Gender" features as one of the six units of AMISOM's civilian component. The Gender Unit is considered an innovation of AMISOM and AU peace support missions more broadly. The Gender Unit is tasked with conducting training on gender sensitivity for the military, police, and civilian dimension of AU engagement in Somalia and with implementing Resolution 1325.

The majority of the training on gender focuses on the prevention of sexual violence or exploitation, and public awareness-raising about the criminality of sexual violence against women. Indeed, one of the achievements of AMISOM in this regard was the Policy on Prevention and Response to Sexual Exploitation and Abuse in 2013. Because the contributing member states are responsible for disciplining troops, the extent of the AU's contribution was the Policy. By 2014, members of the Ugandan contingent were suspended from the AMISOM mission allegedly because they sexually violated Somali women and girls. Soon, Human Rights Watch (HRW) released their report "The Power These Men Have Over Us— Sexual Exploitation and Abuse by African Union Forces in Somalia," accusing AMISOM soldiers of sexual abuse (Human Rights Watch 2014). A blow to the progress being made, the initial AU response was defensive (African Union 2014). Nevertheless, an investigation was promised.

The existence of the zero tolerance policy in the context of Africa's WPS supported the ensuing full-scale investigation into the precise allegations contained in the HRW report. This shows, further, evidence of the community of practice at work in the context of the AU. The result was a robust investigation between November 2014 and February 2015. While the AU's response has been deemed to be swift, it has not been able to prevent similar abuses in the Central African Republic where the Ugandan contingent of the African Union Regional Task Force have been accused of sexual exploitation (Human Rights Watch 2017). As this HRW Report notes, the problem is that "[t]he AU does not have a comprehensive conduct and discipline policy for AU peacekeepers or soldiers who commit sexual exploitation and abuse."

Moreover, the AU does not have an independent investigative mechanism and, consequently, the best efforts of the WPS community of practice are perhaps not enough to result in the immediate cessation of these violations. In analyzing the various practices of the OSE, the dominant linkages made between gender and security focus on sexual violence against women, despite some of the more recent work on participation and supporting women's agency which has included a commitment to training women mediators and the establishment of the African Women's Leadership Network in 2017 (AWLN). Overall, there is a reinforcement that equates gender to women. Moreover, in this particular narrative of gender, the possibility of vulnerable men is excluded as persons also needing security. Given that the majority of allegations investigated have involved women and girls, this is perhaps unsurprising.

As a further move to institutionalizing the zero tolerance practice, the majority of AU troops receiving training are men, as the recruitment of women into military ranks does not feature as a significant priority. Whereas, the UN has pioneered all women police units, drawing them from India and China, the AU has yet to take this step. Perhaps inadvertently then, men are situated as perpetrators vis-à-vis women as victims. This is, of course, contrary to the Special Envoy's promise to look "beyond seeing women only as victims and men as only as [*sic*] victimizers" (Diop 2014: 4). A further consequence of existing practice is that AU peacekeepers are positioned as protectors of women's virtue against Somali men. This is because the new commitment of the AU and AMISOM does not address dismantling systems that initially allowed their male Somali intermediaries to procure women and girls for exploitation. In other words, in context of this example, the patriarchal system of Somalia and the Ugandan command is not addressed by current interventions. Thus, despite the gains made in establishing the Policy, it is inward looking to the AU institution rather than the society itself and the root causes of violence and conflict. As such, it is evident that the specific context within which WPS operates, as well as the material constraints of the AU and its relationship to its member states, can constrain practitioners' intent.

Conclusion

Despite the wealth of information and research on Africa, the continent remains marginalized as a *source of knowledge* on international relations practices. Addressing the WPS agenda in the context of the AU is thus an important opportunity to "flip the script." Whereas the discourse around global governance has rightly emphasized Africa's marginalization; inadvertently, this narrative has also reproduced this narrow perception of Africa's capacity to act as a site of knowledge about global governance. Given this, the analysis conducted in this chapter takes African perspectives from the periphery to the center, where understandings of the global governance with respect to WPS are created.

There is now a well-established network of frameworks that embed WPS on the continent. This has been informed by a certain understanding of feminism and a new pan-Africanist push via the AU and women's movements there. They count as part of their success the adoption of NAPs in seventeen member states. As one of the global obligations for implementing the WPS, it is unsurprising that progress on NAPs has been a feature of the limited studies on Africa and the WPS (for example, Olonisakin et al. 2011; Hendricks 2015).

But, many fail to examine its institutionalization within the regional context, which is the main arbiter for peace and security on the continent (for exception, see Diop 2011). Moreover, when they do, they focus on the UN framed agenda itself, trying to establish linear causal links that explain successes or failures. In these framings, there is often not much room for the ways in which localized practices provide the space to remake or reproduce what the WPS actually means in an African context. By focusing on *practice*, as the interaction of learning, knowing, and doing in the context African and global policy frameworks, one can observe how the discursive frame for WPS in Africa and the practices of the OSE create new meanings and simultaneously reinforce old ones. In engaging Africa as a community of practice vis-à-vis the AU, this chapter realizes Africa's contribution to the WPS agenda.

Looking within and beyond the UN resolutions that we are told constitute the WPS agenda, it becomes clear that African activists and institutions have been engaging with the WPS agenda for a long time. Moreover, their focus unsurprisingly is on a notion of gender equality that prioritizes women. Frameworks like the Maputo Protocol, while elucidating on the gendered power relations that contribute to discriminatory practices, have failed to be realized, in practice, and to address the gendered assumptions around women's roles and participation in public life. It is thus unsurprising then that even when the AU's WPS aims seem to be working, it still ends up reinforcing problematic narratives or becomes constrained by the security context. By engaging with the WPS as a community of practice, a series of multifaceted interactions between frameworks, people, and the social environment, this analysis challenges the persistent critique of institutions' abilities to implement the WPS. In effect, it becomes difficult to claim a set of causal links from which one might declare the AU a success or failure when it comes to WPS progress and regress. Rather, this chapter has sought showcase the AU as a site of practice, wherein knowledge and learning about the WPS take place simultaneous with efforts to implement Resolution 1325 within a very specific context. It is within this complexity that the relationship between the Women, Peace, and Security in the African Union is knowable, and can be understood.

NOTES

1. RECs and RMs include the Arab Maghreb Union (AMU), Common Market for East and Southern Africa (COMESA), Community of Sahel-Saharan States (CEN-SAD), Economic Community of West African States (ECOWAS), Inter-Governmental Authority for Development (IGAS), and the Southern Africa Development Community (SADC).
2. This is now the Women, Gender, and Development Directorate.
3. Natalie Hudson (see chapter 67 in the volume) argues that in its first two decades, non-Western contributions to WPS tended to be underappreciated.
4. In 2017, only seventeen African countries had NAPs making up about 31 percent of the continent. These countries include Burkina Faso; Burundi; Central African Republic; Cote D'Ivoire; the Democratic Republic of Congo; Gambia; Ghana; Guinea; Guinea-Bissau; Liberia; Mali; Nigeria; Rwanda; Sierra Leone; Togo; and Uganda.
5. The Africa Gender Scorecard was launched in 2015. It is used to track Africa's achievements in gender equality and women's empowerment as part of the African Union's 2063 Agenda.
6. Somalia has not been recorded on the Gender Inequality Index since 2012 due to lack of reliable data as a result of the ongoing conflict.

REFERENCES

Mama, A., and H. Abbas. "Editorial: Feminism and Pan-Africanism." *Feminist Africa* 20 (2015): 1–6.
Adler, E., and V. Pouliot. "International Practices." *International Theory* 3 (2011): 1–36.
African Union. "African Union Gender Policy."Addis Ababa: African Union, 2009.
African Union. "AU Declaration on 2015 Year of Women's Empowerment and Development towards Africa's Agenda 2063." Addis Ababa: African Union, 2015.
African Union. Press Release. "The African Union Strongly Rejects the Conclusions Contained in the Report of the Human Rights Watch on Allegations on Sexual Exploitation and Abuse by AMISOM." Addis Ababa: African Union, September 8, 2014, http://amisom-au.org/2014/09/the-african-union-strongly-rejects-the-conclusions-contained-in-the-report-of-the-human-rights-watch-on-allegations-on-sexual-exploitation-and-abuse-by-amisom/.

African Union. "Protocol Relating to the Establishment of the Peace and Security Council." Addis Ababa: African Union, 2001.

African Union. "The Protocol to the African Charter on Human and Peoples' Rights on the Rights of Women in Africa." Addis Ababa: African Union, 2003.

African Union. "Solemn Declaration on Gender Equality." Addis Ababa: African Union, 2004.

African Women's Committee for Peace and Development (AWCPD) and Femmes Africa Solidarité (FAS). "Durban Declaration on Mainstreaming Gender and Women's Effective Participation in the African Union." June 30, 2002, https://oldsite.issafrica.org/uploads/DURBANGENDER.PDF.

Bicchi, F., and N. Bremberg. European Diplomatic Practices: Contemporary Challenges and Innovative Approaches. *European Security* 25 (2016): 391–406.

Bueger, C. "Making Things Known: Epistemic Practices, the United Nations, and the Translation of Piracy." *International Political Sociology* 9 (2015): 1–18.

Deiana, M., and K. McDonagh. "'It is important, but . . .': Translating the Women, Peace, and Security (WPS) Agenda into the Planning of EU Peacekeeping Missions." *Peacebuilding* 6, no. 1 (2017): 34–48.

Diop, B. "The African Union and the Implementation of UNSCR 1325." In *Women, Peace, and Security: Translating Policy into Practice*, edited by F. Olonisakin, K. Barnes, and E. Ikpe, 173–183. London: Routledge, 2011.

Diop, B. "Statement of the Special Envoy of the Chairperson of the African Union on Women, Peace, and Security to the United Nations Security Council during the Open Debate on Women, Peace, and Security." April 28, 2014, http://www.peaceau.org/en/article/statement-of-the-special-envoy-of-the-chairperson-of-the-african-union-commission-on-women-peace-and-security-to-the-united-nations-security-council-during-the-open-debate-on-women-peace-and-security-25-april-2014-new-york#sthash.fhybKnib.dpuf.

Gelot, L. "Civilian Protection in Africa: How the Protection of Civilians Is Being Militarized by African Policymakers and Diplomats." *Contemporary Security Policy* 38, no. 1 (2017): 161–173.

Guerrina, R., and K. Wright. "Gendering Normative Power Europe: Lessons of the Women, Peace, and Security Agenda." *International Affairs* 92, no. 2 (2016): 293–312.

Haastrup, T. "Where Global Meets Local: The Politics of Africa's Emergent Gender Equality Regime." In *Handbook of Africa's International Relations*, edited by T. Murithi, 103–111. Abingdon, UK, and New York: Routledge, 2013.

Haastrup, T. "Are Women Agents? Reading 'Gender' in Africa's Rights Frameworks." *E-International Relations*, October 26, 2015, http://www.e-ir.info/2015/10/26/are-women-agents-reading-gender-in-africas-rights-frameworks/.

Haastrup, T. "Creating Cinderella? The Unintended Consequences of the Women Peace and Security Agenda for the EU's Mediation Architecture." International Negotiation 23, no. 2 (2018): 218-237.

Hendricks, C. "Women, Peace, and Security in Africa: Conceptual and Implementation Challenges and Shifts." *African Security Review* 24, no. 4 (2015): 364–375.

Hudson, H. "Decolonizing the Mainstreaming of Gender in Peacebuilding: Toward an Agenda for Africa." *African Peacebuilding Networking Papers* 8 (2016): 1–33.

Human Rights Watch. "The Power These Men Have Over Us—Sexual Exploitation and Abuse by African Union Forces in Somalia." September 8, 2014, https://www.hrw.org/report/2014/09/08/power-these-men-have-over-us/sexual-exploitation-and-abuse-african-union-forces.

Human Rights Watch. "Central African Republic: Ugandan Troops Harm Women, Girls. Repeated Sexual Exploitation and Abuse." May 15, 2017, https://www.hrw.org/news/2017/05/15/central-african-republic-ugandan-troops-harm-women-girls.

Lorber, J. *Gender Inequalities: Feminist Theories and Politics*. Los Angeles: Roxbury, 1998.

Musau, Z. "Women Seek Greater Role in Rebuilding Central African Republic." *Africa Renewal Online*, 2015, http://www.un.org/africarenewal/web-features/women-seek-greater-role-rebuilding-central-african-republic.

Muehlenhoff, H. L. "Victims, Soldiers, Peacemakers, and Caretakers: The Neoliberal Constitution of Women in the EU's Security Policy." *International Feminist Journal of Politics* 19, no. 2 (2017) 153–157.

Ndiaye, M. "The Relationship between the AU and the RECs/RMs in Relation to Peace and Security in Africa: Subsidiarity and Inevitable Common Destiny." In *The Future of African Peace Operations: From Janjaweed to Boko Haram*, edited by C. De Coning, L. Gelot, and J. Karlslund. Chicago, IL: University of Chicago Press, 2016.

Neumann, I. B. *Diplomatic Sites: A Critical Inquiry*. London: Hurst, 2013.

Olonisakin, F., K. Barnes, and E. Ikpe, eds. *Women, Peace, and Security: Translating Policy into Practice*. London: Routledge, 2011.

Saunders, K. *Feminist Post-Development Thought: Rethinking Modernity, Post-Colonialism, and Representation*. London: Zed Books, 2002.

Schatzki, T. R. "Peripheral Vision: The Sites of Organizations." *Organization Studies* 26 (2005): 465–484.

Swaine, A. "Assessing the Potential of National Action Plans to Advance the Implementation of United Nations Security Council Resolution 1325." *Yearbook of International Humanitarian Law* 12 (2009): 403–433.

Swaine. A. "Implementing UNSCR 1325: The Role of National Action Plans." *OpenDemocracy*, October 13, 2015, https://www.opendemocracy.net/5050/aisling-swaine/implementing-resolution-1325-role-of-national-action-plans.

United Nations Development Programme (UNDP). Somalia Human Development Report 2012: Empowering Youth for Peace and Development (2012). http://hdr.undp.org/sites/default/files/reports/242/somalia_report_2012.pdf

United Nations Economic Commission for Africa (UNECA). "The Sixth African Development Forum." Addis Ababa, UNECA, November 19–21, 2008, http://repository.uneca.org/bitstream/handle/10855/2993/bib-24641_I.pdf?sequence=1.

Willett, S. "Introduction. Security Council Resolution 1325: Assessing the Impact on Women, Peace, and Security." *International Peacekeeping* 17, no. 2 (2010):142–158.

CHAPTER 30

....

WPS AND THE ASSOCIATION OF SOUTH EAST ASIAN NATIONS

....

MA. LOURDES VENERACION-RALLONZA

SOUTH East Asia (SEA) has experienced many conflicts, as each historical period has brought new challenges to the region. For example, Cold War *realpolitik* saw the United States of America and the former Union of the Soviet Socialist Republic wage proxy wars in Cambodia, Laos, and Vietnam until 1975; the Khmer Rouge rule of Cambodia from 1975 was punctuated by the commission of genocide and other mass atrocity crimes against its people; and Vietnam's invasion of Cambodia in 1979 ended the Khmer Rouge regime four years later. In the Philippines, at the tail-end of the 1960s, the communist front took up arms in the name of social justice and the national democratic struggle, while the Moros in the south fought for the right to self-determination. In Indonesia, ethno-nationalist struggles unfolded in Aceh (1976–2005), East Timor (1975–1999 [vote on self-determination]), and West Papua (1969-ongoing sporadic conflict); while in 1998 following the end of former President Soeharto's regime, ethnic and religious conflicts emerged in Poso, Ambon, West Kalimantan, North Maluku, and Central Kalimantan. In Myanmar (Burma), ethnic-based, political armed struggles connected with autonomy erupted beginning in 1948, throughout the Kachin, Karenni, Kayin, Rakhine, and Shan regions, making this the longest recorded civil war.

Efforts to resolve the conflict within the region has seen several permutations. In the case of Cambodia, the strategy was to pursue justice through the Extraordinary Chambers of the Courts of Cambodia (ECCC), mandated to prosecute those allegedly involved in the perpetration of atrocity crimes during the Khmer Rouge regime. In the Philippines, Indonesia, and Myanmar, the key approach was to conduct peace negotiations.[1] For example, in the Philippines, the formal peace process comprised of forging agreements between the Moro National Liberation Front (MNLF),[2] the Moro Islamic Liberation Front (MILF),[3] and the Communist Party-National Democratic Front-Alex Boncayao Brigade (CPP-NDF-ABB).[4] In Indonesia, a peace settlement was entered into with the Free Aceh Movement or *Gerakin Aceh Merdeka* (GAM) in 2005; while in Myanmar, ceasefire agreements have been intermittently brokered with ethnic rebels since the 1990s, leading to the current attempt to bring eighteen armed groups together under the National Ceasefire Agreement (as of early 2018 ten rebel groups have signed the agreement).

These have been positive steps to resolve conflicts, however, new combatants, new justifications for the use of violence, and renewed tensions sporadically reemerge throughout the region. Over the last decade, there has been a spate of ethno-religious separatism leading to terrorist attacks in southern Thailand. In the case of Myanmar, ethnic conflict has continued and intensified with violence between Buddhist and Muslim communities in the Rakhine State, leading to mass displacement of the Rohingya population. In the Philippines, the government continues to reconfigure its response to the Mindanao conflict, as combatants now resort to criminal gang activity, sporadic acts of terrorism, and emerging fronts of violent extremism.

Brunei Darussalam, Cambodia, Indonesia, Lao PDR, Malaysia, Myanmar, the Philippines, Singapore, Thailand, and Vietnam are members of the Association of South East Asian Nations (ASEAN). As a regional institution, "ASEAN is frequently said to be the most successful regional organization in terms of the promotion of regional peace and stability" (Prasetyono 2007: 2). Furthermore, the organization "is proud of the fact that compared with neighboring regions, relations among member states are relatively harmonious and security is for the most part assured" (Vatikiotis 2009: 28). The principle of nonintervention, or the normative belief that member countries should not interfere in the domestic affairs of other members, has informed the public response to conflict and peace situations in the territories of ASEAN Member States (AMS). However, despite the articulation of noninterference, individual AMS have been involved in trying to resolve internal armed conflicts through informal diplomacy, third party mediation, and Track One conflict resolution. For example, in the 1980s and 1990s, AMS aimed to resolve the Cambodian conflict; Thailand and Malaysia conducted bilateral cooperation on the resolution of the communist insurgency in the latter part of the 1980s; and Indonesia assisted the Philippines in brokering peace with the MNLF (Vatikiotis 2009: 28). More recently, Malaysia has also served as the third party facilitator in the peace negotiations between the Philippine Government and the MILF. To bring the GAM armed insurgency under control in Aceh, five AMS, namely, Brunei Darussalam, Malaysia, the Philippines, Singapore, and Thailand, along with Norway, Switzerland, and the European Union, undertook the Aceh Monitoring Mission (AMM) from September 15, 2005 to December 15, 2006. According to Schulze, the Memorandum of Understanding between Indonesia and GAM, the AMM required the participation of AMS because "the Indonesian government objected to a purely European monitoring force"(**************Schulze 2007: 8).

But as previously stated, the involvement of AMS has been largely individualized; the institutional response[5] has not been the norm. However, such precedents, along with existing institutional instruments and mechanisms, may be further maximized, particularly in the context of the ASEAN's commitment to promote and protect human rights,[6] including women's human rights in conflict situations. In other words, although peace, security, and human rights are sensitive subjects for the AMS, it is still possible (albeit painstakingly gradual) to find common ground and commit to collective action. For example, in the case of women's human rights in situations of armed conflict, the 2013 Declaration on the Elimination of Violence against Women and Violence against Children in the ASEAN explicitly "acknowledges the importance of intensifying the efforts of ASEAN Member States to promote the rights of women and children, as well as to prevent and protect them from and respond to all forms of violence, abuse and exploitation of women and children particularly for those who are in vulnerable situations" including "women and children in armed conflict . . ."[7]

Given this contextual institutional milieu, this chapter will explore the potential of invoking both United Nations Security Council Resolution 1325 on Women, Peace, and Security (WPS), and the Convention on the Elimination of All Forms of Discrimination Against Women (CEDAW), specifically general recommendation (GR) 30, to strengthen the ASEAN institutional discourse on advancing the human rights of women in conflict situations in the region. Drawing from the collectively held advocacy addressing conflict-related sexual and gender-based violence (CRSGBV), the nexus of Resolution 1325 and CEDAW GR 30 may actually be the much needed discursive common ground.

Nexus of Resolution 1325 and CEDAW GR 30: An Overview

According to the United Nations Development Fund for Women (UNIFEM), CEDAW and the Resolution 1325 complement and strengthen each other:

> While both CEDAW and Resolution 1325 are important in their own right, there is also a synergy between the two sets of standards that canbe used greatly to enhance their implementation and impact. Resolution 1325 helps to broaden the scope of CEDAW's application by clarifying its relevance to all parties in conflict and in peace. CEDAW, in turn, provides concrete strategic guidance for actions to be taken on the broad commitments outlined in Resolution 1325. Drawing on these instruments together will enable advocates to maximize the impact of norms and standards for gender equality in all conflict and post-conflict interventions.

The concept of gender equality anchors these two frameworks. Gender equality seeks to dismantle the unequal power relations between women and men that render the former more vulnerable, particularly in situations of conflicts. Furthermore, it seeks to provide women special protection as part of the vulnerable groups; and to ensure their active and meaningful participation in all stages of conflict transformation.

Both Resolution 1325 and CEDAW GR 30 apply to various types and stages of conflict and post-conflict reconstruction. Specifically, they have the propensity to support the applicability of standards toward each other, and the monitoring and reporting processes of both can mutually reinforce each other. CEDAW is a human rights treaty that must be acceded or ratified by state parties—needless to say, it is binding only to them. In contrast, Resolution 1325 is a United Nations Security Council resolution and, thus, automatically binding to all members of the UN.

CEDAW offers the substantive framing to Resolution 1325 regarding women's status in society, including the backdrop for conflict-related SGBV and exclusion of women in the peace process. On the practical and implementation side, CEDAW has a reporting mechanism that is likewise legally binding, while Resolution 1325 on WPS does not. At most, member states are urged to draft and finance their respective national action plans (NAPs) on WPS. Nonetheless, both CEDAW and Resolution 1325 complement each other.

> The nexus of these two important instruments can be illustrated in the way Resolution 1325 can be strengthened through CEDAW as the latter has already set in place a standard and mechanism i.e. Committee on the Elimination of Discrimination Against Women established since 1982 that produces periodic reporting on UN Member States' compliance or implementation of the Convention—governments are compelled to report and civil society organizations (CSOs) provide validation through its own submission. On the other hand, CEDAW's theme on women and armed conflict should be maximized to integrate reporting on the implementation of UN resolutions 1325 and 1820 on sexual violence against women in armed conflict situation; in the same way that the global indicators for the implementation of Resolution 1325 can serve as very good benchmarks for CEDAW (GPPAC-SEA, n.d.: 6).

And in the context of the ASEAN—through the ASEAN Human Rights Declaration (AHRD) that announced its commitment to "international human rights instruments to which ASEAN members states are parties"—both Resolution 1325 and CEDAW are taken as international standards that need to be adhered to. Specific to CEDAW GR 30, the mandate is for state parties to

> (1) report on the legal framework, policies and programmes that they have implemented to ensure the human rights of women in conflict prevention, conflict and post-conflict; (2) collect, analyze and make available sex-disaggregated statistics, in addition to trends over time, concerning women, peace and security; and (3) provide information on the implementation of the Security Council agenda on Women, Peace and Security, in particular resolutions 1325 (2000), 1820 (2008), 1888 (2009), 1889 (2009), 1960 (2010) and 2106 (2013), including by specifically reporting on compliance with any agreed United Nations benchmarks or indicators developed as part of that agenda (Gordon 2015: 5).

WOMEN, PEACE, AND SECURITY: THE INSTITUTIONAL DISCURSIVE TERRAIN IN ASEAN MEMBER STATES

By the end of 2016, sixty-three countries have adopted their NAPs on WPS. The Philippines was the only AMS on the list; Cambodia, Myanmar, and Indonesia also have their NAPs, but they were not as detailed in their consideration of WPS as the Philippines.

To date, the Philippines has adopted three National Action Plans on Women, Peace, and Security. The first generation NAP was adopted in 2010; the second generation was launched in 2014, which amended the first to streamline the action points and indicators; and the third was adopted in March 2017. Building on the first two Philippine NAPs, the third generation "NAP WPS 2017–2022," serves as a roadmap for the current Philippine government and has the following new features: (1) framing in the new NAP integrates the language provided by CEDAW, including the precepts of human security as stipulated in CEDAW GR 30, and the key recommendations of the 2015 Global Study on the Implementation of Resolution 1325; it also seeks to incorporate a gender perspective in the government's Six Point Peace and

Development Agenda and in the Philippine Development Plan; (2) privileging of women's agency as it intends to highlight their contribution, both as leaders and participants, in conflict transformation, the security sector, and in post-conflict economic reconstruction; (3) strengthening of coordinative mechanisms on the protection of women, as it broadens the scope of situations that affect women to include vertical (armed) and horizontal conflicts, as well as various emergency situations (conflict affected/vulnerable communities in natural disaster situations), and specifically calls for a gender approach to transitional justice; and (4) institutionalizing multilevel implementation, monitoring, and evaluation that will involve strategic action planning for implementation by national government agencies, drafting of regional-level action plans, and involvement in national and subnational bodies involved in disaster risk reduction, peace and order, and development. Most recently, the Autonomous Region in Muslim Mindanao (ARMM), the region where most of the armed conflict in the name of the right of self-determination of the Moros has taken place, adopted the first ever ARMM regional action plan on Women, Peace, and Security (RAP WPS).

In Cambodia, the Council of Ministers approved the National Action Plan to Prevent Violence against Women (NAP VAW II) 2014–2018 in December 2014. WPS language appears in Strategic Area 3 on policy formulation and implementation specific to addressing violence against women (VAW), and in Strategic Area 4 on capacity building for the Cambodian police to implement the village safety policy, both within the framework of Resolution 1325. In the *Gender Assessment* that was conducted on VAW in 2014, one of the policy recommendations listed in connection with "strengthening the policy environment toward preventing violence against women and girls" was a "review of Operational Standards and Codes of Conduct" for policy harmonization with national and international legal frameworks, including Resolution 1325. Furthermore, in light of policy recommendations for legal protection and multisectoral services on improving "access to redress and services for women and girls at increased risk or who face specific challenges to access to justice," the provision for "effective redress to victims of gender-based violence, in particular sexual violence against women committed during the Khmer Rouge regime" was explicitly mentioned (Canbodian Ministry of Women's Affairs 2014a: 21, 24). A similar *Gender Assessment* was conducted on the rights of vulnerable groups of women and girls in the same year and included in this category were "women who experienced sexual violence and/or forced marriage during the Khmer Rouge regime." The policy recommendation for this group of vulnerable women was specific to health and social benefits (Camnbodian Ministry of Women's Affairs 2014b: 22). Taken together, despite the fact that the NAP VAW II is not a specific national action plan on WPS, it nonetheless included relevant items related to women's protection in the context of post-armed conflict. To a large extent, its framing reflects the language of CEDAW.

On the other hand, Indonesia's Presidential Regulation Number 18 in 2014 acknowledged the need to protect women and girls during armed conflict, and to provide mechanisms that would address the rights of women and girl's during social conflict and violence. The presidential regulation also recognizes the need to improve the lives of women and girls who have been affected by conflict, and increase their participation in peace-building initiatives (Kholifa 2014). Accordingly, by virtue of a Presidential Decree, Indonesia launched its NAP on the Empowerment and Protection of Women and Children in Social Conflicts 2014–2019 (known as RAN P3A-KS).[8]

There are several features of the Indonesian NAP. First, it defines conflict as those related "to social or communal (or ethnic and religious)" tensions and does not recognize "separatist/independence struggles such as those in Aceh, Papua, and Maluka" as legitimate conflicts, in the context of WPS (Veneracion-Rallonza 2016: 168). Relatedly, the NAP was anchored on Law No. 7 on the management of social conflict, and on Presidential Decree No. 8 on the protection of women in social conflict. Second, the Indonesian NAP draws from the Universal Declaration on Human Rights (UDHR); Law No. 11 (2005) on the Ratification of the International Covenant on Economic, Social, and Cultural Rights (ICESCR); and Law No. 12 (2005) on the Ratification of the International Covenant on Civil and Political Rights (ICCPR), as well as the country's various Development Plans. Finally, the NAP serves as a guideline for Indonesian national and local government institutions to protect and empower women and children during social conflict situations.[9] Although the language of the Indonesian NAP is more expansive in the way that it frames human rights, it nonetheless limits the context of "conflict" to horizontal (and not vertical) ones which, in turn, marginalizes women in the context of non-social armed conflicts.

In Myanmar, the government initially embarked on an explicit initiative related to WPS. Indeed, in 2014, a multi-stakeholder gathering was convened to discuss the impact of armed conflict on women and their contribution to peace processes. It was organized by the Ministry of Social Welfare, Relief, and Resettlement, the Myanmar Women's Affairs Federation, and the UN System in the country. Today, despite concerns of widespread VAW in the context of armed conflict in the country, similar spaces to discuss the issue are no longer available. Even the Myanmar National Action Plan on the Advancement of Women 2011–2015 that followed the language of the Beijing Platform for Action (BPFA) included all the critical areas of concern except "women in armed conflict." This was a telling sign that there was no acknowledgment of the conflict context as well as the conflict-related women's human rights violations. Instead, "women in armed conflict" was changed to "women and emergencies" and efforts to address this concern were meant to "strengthen mechanisms to ensure women's protection and participation in emergency preparedness and response in conjunction with the Myanmar Action Plan on Disaster Risk Reduction."[10] In other words, there was no mention of women in the situations of armed conflict.

NAPs are largely time-bound implementation roadmaps for governments. Accordingly, they reflect the institutional framing of governments themselves. In referring to the NAPs of the Philippines, Cambodia, Indonesia, and Myanmar, it is interesting to note the diversity in terms of referencing and understanding WPS. As such, whether explicit or implicit, based on international and/or domestic mandate, as well as CEDAW and/or Resolution 1325, WPS is discursively present in these AMS.

Strengthening the Discourse through the WPS and CEDAW GR 30 Nexus

WPS and Conflict-Related Sexual and Gender Based Violence

Women's human rights are no longer alien concepts in the ASEAN. Structurally, institutional bodies such as the ASEAN Intergovernmental Commission on Human Rights (AICHR) and the ASEAN Commission on the Protection and Promotion of the Rights of Women and Children (ACWC) have been established. The former touches on women's human rights as part of its broader mandate on human rights and the latter was explicitly created to address the rights of women and children. The AICHR was born out of the ASEAN Political and Security Community (APSC) while the ACWC was conceived within the ambit of the ASEAN Social and Cultural Community (ASCC). Both have the mandate to codify international and regional standards, and both can complement and mutually reinforce each other with regard to the promotion and protection of women's human rights.

Discursively, women's human rights are present in key regional consensus documents, namely the Declaration on the Advancement of Women in the ASEAN (1988),[11] the ASEAN Summit Declaration on HIV/AIDS (2001),[12] ASEAN Declaration against Trafficking in Persons Particularly Women and Children (2004),[13] ASEAN Declaration on the Protection and Promotion of the Rights of Migrant Workers (2007),[14] Ha Noi Declaration on the Enhancement of Welfare and Development of ASEAN Women and Children (Ha Noi Declaration) (2010),[15] and the Declaration on the Elimination of Violence against Women and the Elimination of Violence against Children in ASEAN (DEVAWC).[16] However, the Ha Noi Declaration and the DEVAWC are the only two, which reference WPS. For example, the Ha Noi Declaration identified in one of its operational clauses the need "to encourage closer regional cooperation in promoting and protecting the rights of women and children, especially those living under disadvantaged and vulnerable conditions, including those in disaster and conflict affected areas." Similarly, DEVAWC referenced Resolution 1325 (2000), and follow up resolutions 1820 (2008), 1888 (2009), and 1889 (2009), and acknowledged in its preamble the importance of promoting the rights of women and preventing VAW in situations of vulnerability, including armed conflict. According to Veneracion-Rallonza (2016), "each of these declarations had their respective focus and discursive construction as regards women's human rights," some highlighted women's "vulnerability and protection," while others privileged the "agency-empowerment" discourse.

The ASEAN Regional Action Plan on the Elimination of Violence against Women (RAP EVAW) 2016–2025 acknowledged women's vulnerability to violence in diverse situations, including those living in conflict-affected areas.[17] Aside from CEDAW, it referred to Resolutions 1325, 1820, 1888, and 1889 on WPS. Under its Action Plan 2 on the "protection and support services for victims/survivors," item 18 seeks to "incorporate the prevention of and response to all forms of VAW into the planning and delivery of disaster risk reduction programs and protocols as well as in all humanitarian responses following natural disasters, conflict situations, or other emergencies." Furthermore, Action Point 5, item 45, on "research and data collection," calls for a national data collection system on "VAW in disaster and conflict situations." Apart from these items, however, there was no other clear articulation of WPS in the RAP EVAW. In fact, none of the submitted initiatives of AMS listed in Part II of the document mentioned anything on VAW in conflict situations.

Earlier on, in April 2014, AICHR held their second consultation meeting with ACWC on the AHRD and the DEVAWC. During this meeting, both agreed on four priority areas, namely, trafficking in persons (especially, women and children), disability, education, and gender, peace, and security. During the fourteenth meeting of the ACWC held in Jakarta from February 28 to March 2, 2017, one of the approved new projects was on "Advancing Gender, Peace and Security in the ASEAN." As part of this project, an ACWC Fellowship Program on "Advancing Gender, Peace and Security in ASEAN" was hosted by the Asia Pacific Centre on "The Responsibility to Protect" at the University of Queensland from

March 27–30, 2017. The week-long activity provided lectures and exchanges with the ACWC on mass atrocity crimes, conflict-related sexual and gender-based violence (CRSGBV), WPS, CEDAW GR 30, transitional justice, and displacement. The goal of the fellowship was to strengthen key commitments among attendees with respect to the APSC, AEC, and ASCC; collaboration with other ASEAN sectoral bodies; addressing the needs of women and children as vulnerable groups; and contributing to a gender-sensitive culture of prevention and a culture of peace. Additionally, they reiterated the project on "Gender, Peace, and Security: Advancing Women's Roles in Peace Mediation in Southeast Asia—Progress, Opportunities, and Challenges." Interestingly, a significant outcome at the end of this fellowship was an agreement among the ACWC members "to propose an ASEAN statement on Women, Peace, and Security for adoption at the 31st ASEAN Summit in November 2017 in the Philippines."

Having these discursive and structural elements in the ASEAN can be seen as building blocks to advance WPS in the region more emphatically, particularly in light of CRSGBV. The preponderant focus on the women's "vulnerability and protection" discourse lays the foundation for a discursive frame, which requires states to address mass atrocity crimes against women, including rape and sexual violence. In fact, during the 2013 UN Security Council Open Debate on WPS, H. E. Ambassador Le Hoai Trung, Permanent Representative of the Socialist Republic of Vietnam, spoke on behalf of the ASEAN and declared their "readiness and commitment to join efforts with the international community to ensure the elimination of sexual violence in armed conflict, and implement effective measures of accountability and redress in the field of women and peace and security."[18] The following year, at the same forum, H. E. Ambassador Nguyen Phuong Nga, Permanent Representative of the Socialist Republic of Vietnam, on behalf of the ASEAN acknowledged "sexual violence and organized crime targeting women and girls are still a source of serious concern in many regions,"[19] and she called for the integration of WPS in regional mechanisms such as the AICHR and ACWC (Veneracion-Rallonza 2016: 175). Furthermore, during the same year, eight AMS, namely Cambodia, Indonesia, Malaysia, Myanmar, the Philippines, Thailand, and Vietnam, signed the 2013 UN Declaration of Commitment to End Sexual Violence in Conflict. Relatedly, Ambassador Nguyen Phuong Nga reaffirmed the framework commitment of the ASEAN:

> Perpetrators of sexual violence must not go unpunished. But more importantly, victims of conflict-related sexual violence must be provided with assistance and services tailored to their specific needs. They must be protected against stigmatisation and exclusion, and given the opportunity and capability to re-engage and re-integrate with their communities . . . the ASEAN is strongly committed to ending sexual violence wherever it occurs, and ASEAN member states have been fulfilling their respective obligations and commitments under the Convention on the Elimination of All Forms of Discrimination of Women (CEDAW) and the Beijing Platform for Action.[20]

In 2015, H. E. Ambassador Nguyen Phuong Nga shared that the "ASEAN is gravely troubled by the violation of the rights of women and girls, in conflicts and by extremist non-state actors" and that they "particularly deplore sexual violence against women and girls, especially when it is deployed as a tactic of war." Further, they declared that "regional organizations play an essential role in implementing global obligations and commitments to better protect women and girls from sexual violence, discrimination and social exclusion and promote the role of women in conflict resolution and peace processes, including through supporting their Member States in doing so."[21] The message on the role of regional organizations in contributing to women's participation and empowerment—including in the context of peace and security—was likewise articulated by the ASEAN in the 2016 WPS Open Debate in the UN.

CEDAW GR 30: Interfacing Conflict-Related Sexual and Gender-Based Violence and Transitional Justice

In the case of CEDAW, its GRs guide state members and highlight specific issues and concerns that require states attention. The recommendations are intended to "provide authoritative guidance to state parties on legislative, policy and other appropriate measures to ensure full compliance with their obligations under the Convention to protect, respect and fulfil women's human rights."[22] In the past few years, the CEDAW Committee issued Concluding Observations and Recommendations to Cambodia, the Philippines, Indonesia, and Myanmar, in connection with the human rights of women in conflict situations. For example, for Myanmar, the CEDAW Committee in 2008 raised the issue of sexual violence in armed conflict in its review of the Combined Second and Third Periodic Reports.[23] Specifically, it articulated its deep concern for the prevalence of crimes, including rape, against Shan, Mon, Karen, Palaung, and Chin women by the state security forces. Accordingly, it recommended that efforts should be strengthened in combatting impunity, improving the victims' access to justice, engendering capacity development for the security forces, monitoring the situation of women in conflict-affected areas, and formulating and implementing a policy that would integrate Resolutions 1325 and 1820.

In the case of Indonesia, the CEDAW Committee, in its 2012 review of the Combined Sixth and Seventh Periodic Reports, noted the issue of VAW in armed conflict. In particular, it highlighted instances of systemic rape and sexual violence, which occurred during the 1965 political unrest in the conflict in East Timor Province and Aceh, as well as those in East Java and Papua Provinces in the May 1998 riots, and in the militarization in Maluku Province and Poso (Central Sulawesi Province) that have not been fully addressed.[24] The Committee expressed its concerns regarding, the issue of impunity, the lack of support for victims, and the increasing incidence of social conflicts that increases internal displacement. Given these concerns, the committee's recommendation was for was meant for policy formulation and the strengthening of women's participation in post-conflict reconstruction and peace-building.

In 2013, the Fourth and Fifth Periodic Reports for Cambodia, raised concerns that the ECCC has "not adequately addressed cases of gender-based violence, in particular, sexual violence against women committed under the Khmer Rouge Regime." The Committee thus recommended, that the Cambodian Government "incorporate effectively the provisions of the Convention and of Resolution 1325 into its post-conflict programmes."[25] In the Policy Brief that the Ministry of Women's Affairs (MoWA) released in connection with their Gender Assessment on the Rights of Vulnerable Groups of Women and Girls, Cambodia recognized the CEDAW Committee's observations that "women who suffered from sexual violence during the Khmer Rouge regime" must be considered in the formulation of government policy.

Finally, the Philippines Combined Seventh and Eighth Periodic Reports were discussed by the Committee in 2016.[26] In their review, the Committee lauded the Philippines for the adoption and implementation of the NAP on Resolution 1325 and 1820 from 2010 to 2016. However, it was still concerned with the issue of SGBV and trafficking in the context of armed conflict in the country. Likewise, the Committee noted the inadequacy of the justice system to provide redress for women who fell victims to such crimes. Accordingly, the Committee recommended that the Philippines "further accelerate its achievement of substantive gender equality and the full realization of women's human rights, in particular by strengthening a gender-sensitive approach to . . . peace and security, transitional justice" to "ensure the active and meaningful participation of women and women's rights organizations in such processes." Given, advancements in transitional justice in the Philippines, the Committee recommended that the system must provide and enforce remedies for women that are "effective, gender-sensitive, and proportionate to the gravity of the harm suffered."

As related to SGBV, CEDAW GR 30, under the provision on access to justice, Articles 1–3, 5(a), and 15, called for measures to advance transitional justice that incorporates mechanisms reflective of the right to truth, right to justice, right to reparation, and with a guarantee of non-repetition. It also called for women's participation in these mechanisms and the creation of appropriate support systems. Relatedly, the 2015 Global Study on the Implementation of UN Security Council Resolution 1325 acknowledged that one of the gains of implementing 1325 in the last fifteen years was the recognition of transitional justice as integral to building sustainable peace.

> Support for transitional justice mechanisms and processes has become not only a critical component of efforts to strengthen the rule of law post-conflict, but a regular feature of post-conflict recovery, and integral to the peacebuilding agenda. Rooted in the premise that in the wake of mass human rights violations, the social fabric of society needs to be rebuilt, transitional justice comprises the full range of processes and mechanisms associated with a society's attempt to come to terms with a legacy of large-scale human rights abuses. These may include both judicial and non-judicial mechanisms and processes including institutional reforms, prosecutions, truth telling, reparations programmes, traditional justice and the vetting of public officials.

CEDAW, and more specifically, GR 30, provide the institutional discourse on seeking redress for CRSGBV by implementing transitional justice mechanisms that have been recommended by the Global Study. At the level of the ASEAN, since AICHR and ACWC were both mandated to ensure the adherence of AMS to international standards, CEDAW GR 30 offers specific and concrete guidance for the redress of past women's human rights violations, including CRSGBV, through transitional justice. In this regard, both institutional bodies can use these instruments to guide Cambodia, the Philippines, Indonesia, and Myanmar in appropriately and fully responding to violence committed against women within their own conflict contexts. It is thus worth exploring, how the WPS agenda in the ASEAN may converge on the issues of CRSGBV and transitional justice when informed by Resolution 1325 and CEDAW.

At the recently held 2017 ASEAN Summit chaired and hosted by the Philippines, the Joint Statement on Promoting Women, Peace, and Security in ASEAN was adopted by the heads of state/governments of the AMS. Procedurally, the Joint Statement came from the ACWC and the initiative was said to have been led by the Philippine representative as part of the highlights of the Philippine ASEAN chair. Substantively, it referred to both CEDAW (but not GR 30) and Resolution 1325 (and all subsequent WPS resolutions) to frame the ASEAN message on WPS. Specific to SGBV, the Joint Statement seeks to

> encourage the inclusion of the women, peace and security agenda in policies and programmes for the protection of women and girls from sexual and gender-based violence before, during, and after armed conflict, and the creation of greater and wider spaces for participation in peacebuilding and post-reconstruction processes.

Although not explicit to transitional justice, at the very least the Joint Statement offers a clear entry point.

CONCLUSION

This chapter has explored the potential of invoking Resolution 1325, as well as subsequent resolutions, and CEDAW, particularly GR 30, to advance women's human rights in conflicts occurring throughout the ASEAN region. These global instruments are part of the institutional discourse and mechanisms that the ASEAN, as a collective, adheres to. They also anchor NAPs in several AMS that have experienced—in and are still experiencing—conflict situations. But more importantly, the interface of these global instruments complement and mutually reinforce each other in addressing the issue of past and current conflict-related sexual and gender-based violence and in advancing transitional justice.

NOTES

1. This study covers only the ASEAN Member States (AMS). Timor Leste, although a country in the Southeast Asian region with a history of armed conflict and having gone through the process of negotiated peace settlement and establishing transitional justice mechanisms, is not included in the discussion since it is not a member of the ASEAN.
2. The Final Peace Agreement (FPA) was signed between the Philippine Government and the Moro National Liberation Front in 1996.
3. The Framework Agreement on the Bangsamoro (FAB) was signed in 2012, followed by the signing of the various Annexes on Transitional Arrangement and Modalities, on Revenue Generation and Wealth-Sharing, and on Power-Sharing in 2013, and the Annex on Normalization in 2014. These were collectively brought together in the Comprehensive Agreement on the Bangsamoro (CAB) signed in 2014.
4. The first signed agreement was the Comprehensive Agreement on the Respect for Human Rights and International Humanitarian Law (CARHRIHL) in 1998.
5. The exception would be in dealing with the Cambodian conflict when ASEAN issued a statement deploring the escalation of the conflict in Indochina and "called for conformity to the principles of the UN Charter as well as the Bandung Declaration" and "further urged the UN Security Council to discuss the issue and take appropriate measures."

For full discussion, refer to Sundararaman, Shankari, "ASEAN Diplomacy in Conflict Resolution: The Cambodian Case" (1997), http://www.idsa-india.org/an-oct-7.html.

6. The ASEAN Human Rights Declaration was adopted in November 2012, and within which it declared its commitment to "international human rights instruments to which ASEAN Member States are parties."

7. Preamble Paragraph 8. Declaration on the Elimination of Violence against Women and Elimination of Violence against Children in ASEAN. http://asean.org/?static_post=declaration-on-the-elimination-of-violence-against-women-in-the-asean-region-4

8. The Indonesian National Action Plan on the Empowerment of Women and Children during Social Conflicts (June 3, 2014), http://peacewomen.org/sites/default/files/NAP-indonesia.pdf.

9. In the context of social conflicts, protection means efforts "to prevent and deal with all types of violence and breaches of women and children's human rights, as well as to provide for the basic and specific needs for women and children through conflict resolution as an integrated part of conflict resolution activities," while empowerment pertains to initiatives "to strengthen human rights, improvement of the quality of life, and intensify the participation of women and children in peace building."

10. The Myanmar National Action Plan on the Advancement of Women 2011–2015 (updated May 13, 2010), http://www.burmalibrary.org/docs09/UNCT_UNCountryTeam_Annex2-Plan%20of%20Action_eng.pdf.

11. Declaration on the Advancement of Women in the ASEAN (July 5, 1988), http://www.asean.org/communities/asean-socio-cultural-   community/item/declaration-of-the-advancement-of-women-in-the-asean-region-bangkok-thailand-5-july-1988.

12. The ASEAN Summit Declaration on HIV/AIDS, Brunei Darussalam (November 5, 2001), http://asean.org/?static_post=7th-asean-summit-declaration-on-hivaids-brunei-darussalam-5-november-2001.

13. ASEAN Declaration against Trafficking in Persons, Particularly Women and Children (November 29, 2004), http://asean.org/storage/2012/05/ASEAN-Declaration-against-Trafficking-in-Persons-Particularly-Women-and-Children-TPPWC.pdf.

14. ASEAN Declaration on the Protection and Promotion of the Rights of Migrant Workers (January 13, 2007), http://www.ilo.org/dyn/migpractice/docs/117/Declaration.pdf.

15. Ha Noi Declaration on the Enhancement of Welfare and Development of ASEAN Women and Children (October 28, 2010), http://asean.org/?static_post=ha-noi-declaration-on-the-enhancement-of-welfare-and-development-of-asean-women-and-children.

16. The Declaration on the Elimination of Violence against Women and the Elimination of Violence against Children in ASEAN (October 9, 2013), see note 7.

17. The ACWC Regional Plan of Action on the Elimination of Violence against Women (2016)   https://acwc.asean.org/wp-content/uploads/2016/10/Final-ASEAN-RPA-on-EVAW-IJP-11.02.2016-as-input-ASEC.pdf.

18. Statement of H. E. Ambassador Le Hoai Trung, Permanent Representative of the Socialist Republic of Viet Nam (October 14, 2013), https://unoda-web.s3-accelerate.amazonaws.com/wp-content/uploads/assets/special/meetings/firstcommittee/68/pdfs/GD_14-Oct_Viet%20Nam.pdf.

19. Statement of H.E. Ambassador Nguyen Phuong Nga, Permanent Representative of the Socialist Republic of Viet Nam on behalf of the Association of Southeast Asian Nations (October 2014) http://www.peacewomen.org/sites/default/files/scwps2014_statement_vietnam_0.pdf.

20. ASEAN Commits to Eliminating Sexual Violence, Asian Trade Union Council (April 17, 2015), http://aseantuc.org/2015/04/1742015-asean-commits-to-eliminating-sexual-violence/.

21. Statement of H. E. Ambassador Nguyen Phuong Nga, Permanent Representative of the Socialist Republic of Viet Nam on behalf of the Association of Southeast Asian Nations (October 12, 2015) https://papersmart.unmeetings.org/media2/7652372/viet-nam-asean.pdf.

22. See Operative Clause 1 of CEDAW General Recommendation No. 30 (October 18, 2013), http://www.ohchr.org/Documents/HRBodies/CEDAW/GComments/CEDAW.C.CG.30.pdf.

23. CEDAW, Concluding Observations on the Combined Second and Third Period Reports of Myanmar, Adopted by the Committee in its 42nd Session (November 7, 2008), http://hrlibrary.umn.edu/research/myanmar/Annex%20N%20-%202008%20Concluding%20Observations%20CEDAW.pdf.

24. CEDAW, Concluding Observations on the Sixth and Seventh Periodic Report of Indonesia, Adopted by the Committee in its 52nd Session (July 27, 2012), http://www2.ohchr.org/english/bodies/cedaw/docs/co/CEDAW-C-IDN-CO-6-7.pdf.

25. CEDAW, Concluding Observations on the Fourth and Fifth Periodic Report of Cambodia, Adopted by the Committee at its 56th Session (December 5, 2013), http://docstore.ohchr.org/SelfServices/FilesHandler.ashx?enc=6QkG1d%2fPP RiCAqhKb7yhsglff%2fiazrVw%2bcyfdY9GxZ62YXIcKp9qTzonRzgoWWfPCW uduIoAQDgIdC71U7lPYiIffLoiBHKqR9Sh2Vo3nWax969tKGbDUkflPsXeZyF 8sAhoDtowkyo5T8krCgqvhQ%3d%3d.

26. CEDAW, Concluding Observations on the Combined Seventh and Eighth Periodic Reports of the Philippines, Discussed by the Committee in its 1405th and 1406th Meetings (July 25, 2016), http://tbinternet.ohchr.org/_layouts/treatybodyexternal/Download.aspx?symbolno=CEDAW%2fC%2fPHL%2fCO%2f7-8&Lang=en.

References

Cambodian Ministry of Women's Affairs (MoWA). Policy Brief 7 in *The Cambodia Gender Audit 2014.* 2014a.

Cambodian Ministry of Women's Affairs (MoWA). Policy Brief 9 in *The Cambodia Gender Audit 2014.* 2014b.

Gordon, Ariel. "Applying Global Tools to Improve Implementation of National Action Plans on United Nations Security Council Resolution 1325." Inclusive Security, December 2, 2015, .

GPPAC–SEA (Global Partnership for the Prevention of Armed Conflict–Southeast Asian). "On the Nexus of CEDAW and UNSCR 1325: Towards the Promotion and Protection of Women's Human Rights in Southeast Asia." GPPAC-SEA and Asian Circle 1325, n.d., https://www.peaceportal.org/documents/10156/0/Policy+Brief+on+the+Nexus+of+CEDA W+%26+UNSCR+1325.

Kholifa, Dwi Rubiyanti. "Indonesian Implementation of UNSCR 1325: Adapting to the National Context," April 8, 2014, https://www.womenpeacemakersprogram.org/news/indonesian-implementation-of-unscr-1325-adapting-to-the-national-context/.

Prasetyono, Edy. "Traditional Challenges to States: Intra-ASEAN Conflicts and ASEAN Relations with External Powers." 2007, .

Schulze, Kirsten. "Mission Not So Impossible: The AMM and the Transition from Conflict to Peace in Aceh, 2005-2006," Working Paper # 131 S. Rajaratnam School of International Studies. 2007, https://www.rsis.edu.sg/wp-content/uploads/rsis-pubs/WP131.pdf.

Vatikiotis, Michael. "Managing Armed Conflict in Southeast Asia: The Role of Mediation." *Southeast Asian Affairs* (2009): 28–35.

Veneracion-Rallonza, Ma. Lourdes. "Building the Women, Peace, and Security Agenda through Multi-Focal Norm Entrepreneurship." *Global Responsibility to Protect* 8, nos. 2–3 (2016): 158–179.

CHAPTER 31

WPS AND THE PACIFIC ISLANDS FORUM

SHARON BHAGWAN-ROLLS AND SIAN ROLLS

DESPITE the efforts of women and young women to engage in peace and security in Pacific Island countries and territories, their participation in formal conflict prevention, management, and post-conflict recovery efforts remains a challenge. In addition, their efforts to engage with formal oversight and accountability mechanisms for the security sector are still not fully realized. Women still struggle to be heard at the negotiating table in leadership roles and are not given sufficient recognition and resources to do their work. This is symptomatic of a broader problem in the region—related to women's absence from political decision-making at all levels of society, coupled with their lack of safety in public and private spaces, and with continued high levels of sexual and gender-based violence (SGBV). The lack of institutional and governance structural support means that the invisibility of women and the lack of women's formal participation in the peace and security structures continues to occur despite the commitments in the Pacific region to gender equality, including in the peace and security arena.

Even though Pacific Island Forum (PIF) leaders endorsed and committed to the 2012 Gender Equality Declaration, which included temporary special measures, such as legislation to establish reserved seats for women and political party reforms, to accelerate women's full and equal participation in governance reform at all levels, and women's leadership in all decision-making, Pacific Island legislatures have some of the world's lowest numbers of women among their elected representatives. As of July 2015, women legislators across the Pacific accounted for less than 6 percent of all parliamentarians (Inter-Parliamentary Union 2017).

Women entering politics face local cultural obstacles and gender bias, including opposition from men in parliament. The Fiji Parliamentary elections in 2014 saw 44 female candidates (17.7 percent) out of the total number of 248 candidates in the first general elections, following the military coup of December 2016. In the lead up to the elections and since, there has also been an incremental representation of women in political parties including leadership positions. In the Solomon Islands, while women played a leading role in brokering peace during the height of the ethnic tensions in 2000, only two women have ever been elected to the Solomon Islands parliament. In Tonga, where the government is yet to ratify the UN Convention on the Elimination of All forms of Discrimination against

Women (CEDAW), the 2018 snap elections saw the election of two women, including Akosita Lavulavu who is now the first Tongan woman to be elected for a second term in parliament in 2016. Additionally, although women are increasingly accepted in general decision-making roles across the Pacific, they remain poorly represented in media content where national development priorities, in particular national budget allocations, are determined.

The year 2015 marked the fifteenth anniversary of UN Security Council Resolution 1325 on Women, Peace, and Security (WPS). It was one of three distinct, yet interconnected reviews taking place at the United Nations that include the Peacebuilding Architecture Review and the Peace Operations Review Panel. According to Radhika Coomaraswamy (UN Women 2015), the difference between the Global Study on the implementation of Resolution 1325 and other reports and reviews was its focus on amplifying the voices of women from the field to the Security Council, even if some of the truths they speak may at times be unpalatable.

The fifteenth anniversary of Resolution 1325 came at a time when there was growing recognition to the changing nature of conflict. Specifically, across the Pacific region, women have consistently communicated the need to address the root causes of our region's political fragility and insecurity and the interconnections between disasters, humanitarian crises and conflicts (Bhagwan-Rolls 2016b). The fifteenth anniversary of Resolution 1325 was an opportune moment to review the impact of the resolutions' recommendations and activities as a basis for deciding future directions in the Pacific. This involved an examination of the mechanisms for advancement and continuity of practice to sustain the peace-building activities and policies initiated in the region and the articulation of action-oriented strategies with existing regional mechanisms.

Women, of course, have proven for longer than fifteen years that they are not simply vulnerable to crises and have repeatedly demonstrated leadership that must be integrated into political processes. As Dr. Abigail Ruane (Bhagwan Rolls 2015) of the Women's International League for Peace and Freedom (WILPF) notes, women display "powerful leadership" as " . . . peace and . . . human rights activists" yet they "continue to be excluded, marginalised, their rights ignored and their voices side-lined." The recommendations of the Global Study identified and refined by Pacific women through femLINKpacific and the Global Partnership for the Prevention of Armed Conflict (GPPAC), are those which prioritize the "development" of "processes and priorities" at "the community level up" as it is acknowledged that Resolution 1325 allows for the "transformation" of "spaces and processes for women's equal participation—in all our diversities" (Bhagwan Rolls 2016a).

This chapter will argue that despite women's demonstrated ability to participate in the peace and security field, regional mechanisms in the Pacific have not adapted to incorporate their leadership and skills. We suggest that the focus now must be to motivate a shift from writing national action plans (NAPs), originally attached to the Resolution 1325 framework, to generating concrete action and the allocation of funding and resources to achieve them. This chapter proceeds in five sections. First, we introduce the WPS agenda as it is understood across the Pacific. Second, we provide an analysis of the networks and groups in the Pacific advocating for the Women, Peace, and Security. Next, we provide an outline of Resolution 1325 and the UN process responsible for its development. Then we reveal the regional activities associated with Resolution 1325, and finally, we examine the role of the media in providing meaningful support for the implementation of the WPS agenda.

Introduction to WPS in Pacific

The adoption of the Pacific Regional Action Plan on Women, Peace, and Security (RAP-WPS) (2012–2015) has been recognized as a key regional mechanism to support the advancement of gender equality and women's rights in the Pacific region. Specifically, this regional action plan envisioned women's equal participation within member states, UN agencies, and Regional Inter-Governmental Organizations (RIGOs), whether it is to prevent the resurgence of violent and armed conflict, to engage in the reform of national and local governance systems, or in advocating for compliance with human rights standards such as CEDAW. The RAP-WPS is part of a legacy of women's peace activism and, according to the Pacific Islands Forum Secretariat (PIFS) (2015), the [RAP-WPS] provided a framework to enhance women and young women's leadership in conflict prevention and peace-building, mainstream gender in security policymaking, and ensure women and girls' human rights are protected in humanitarian crises, transitional contexts, and post-conflict situations. It also sets out a regional mechanism to support regional and national efforts.

The decision to employ a regional approach to WPS was endorsed by a series of regional intergovernmental meetings in 2010 and 2011, including the Pacific Women's Triennial and Ministerial Conference. Pacific Forum Leaders upon the recommendation of the Forum Regional Security Committee (FRSC), acknowledged that participation in the integration of WPS recommendations and strategies would benefit the broader national peace, security platform, and humanitarian processes, and was not simply limited to the responsibility of small and under-resourced national women's machineries. Since the adoption of the Pacific RAP-WPS, the Autonomous Bougainville government adopted an action plan in 2013 and the Solomon Islands government finally launched its NAP on WPS in 2017. However, providing resources for these NAPs, particularly for women's civil society engagement and monitoring, remains challenging. According to Agnes Titus of the Nazareth Centre in Bougainville (2017),

> we came up with the Gender Equality, Women Empowerment, Peace and Security Policy. That document actually has helped our government and civil society to work hand in hand (. . .) and now we need to come back together and review.[1]

In the Solomon Islands, the NAP is closely linked to the advocacy of WPS activism. The 2014 session of the CEDAW reporting process for the Solomon Islands highlighted the link between the Convention and WPS, and resulted in the concluding remarks of the CEDAW committee, which stressed the need for the adoption of a NAP. Now adopted, the Plan comes at a timely juncture with the exit of the Regional Assistance Mission to the Solomon Islands. As Josephine Teakeni, a network leader from the Solomon Islands, observes, "there are still a lot to be done in terms of addressing women's peace initiative activities through policies and through making things happen".[2]

ANALYSIS OF THE NETWORK AND
GROUPS WITHIN IT

Since 2007, femLINKpacific has convened a regional media and policy network on Resolution 1325 to inform and transform notions of security and to ensure proposed strategies are inclusive of women's human security priorities. Through the network, the engagement and participation of local women leaders provides a mirror we can hold up to governance systems and processes to remind them of the commitments to women's human rights, peace, and security. In 2009, the organization assumed the role of the GPPAC Pacific secretariat. In 2015, the network provided input for the Global Study report lead authored by Radhika Coomaraswamy.

Building on the legacy of the Pacific feminist movement, our early work on awareness raising and advocacy with respect to Resolution 1325 is now widely acknowledged throughout the region:

> The gender, peace, and security network which leads feminist peace advocates in Bougainville, Fiji, Tonga and Solomon Islands set up by femLINK[pacific] is another important network that has been long standing.[3] (Claire Slatter)

The GPPAC Pacific Regional Secretariat, builds on a feminist media and policy network model (2007–2010), the "1325 network," and extends to link with a core set of partners from Fiji, Papua New Guinea including Bougainville, the Solomon Islands, Tonga, and Vanuatu, as well as developing partnership in Tahiti and New Caledonia. These women and civil society led groups are committed to enhancing collaboration and adapting our regional network model and practice at the local and national level. Sharon Bhagwan-Rolls, femLINKpacific's executive producer-director (and co-author of this chapter) is also the chair of the GPPAC Board and was a member of the UN high level advisory group for the Global Study on the implementation of UNSCR 1325.

GPPAC Pacific convenes an annual Regional Civil Society Organisation (CSO) Forum on Peace and Human Security, bringing together regional network partners as well as developing partnerships, with similar networks also working in the Pacific including the Pacific Conference of Churches (PCC), World Association for Christian Communication (WACC) Pacific, World Association of Community Radio Broadcasts (AMARC) Pacific, Pacific Centre for Peacebuilding and Transcend Oceania. Our collective goal is to progress gender inclusive conflict prevention and human security, and to work together to strengthen the regional intergovernmental architecture. The GPPAC Pacific network activities are also designed to hold accountable political commitment to the implementation of the goals of WPS, in terms of integrating participation, protection, and prevention into policies and action to strengthen the capacities of CSOs and women's organizations to contribute to the advancement of the conflict, prevention, and human security agenda, and to strengthen collaboration across regional network. In this respect, media and communications is utilized as a way to make the regional network visible and to review gender inequality indicators.

This cooperation across the regional network demonstrates the importance of investing in the sustainability of the network, which is not just limited to the resourcing of activities that enable network strengthening, but also the localization activities and the amplification of key themes and messages via intergovernmental processes, national and regional media networks, as well as via other civil society processes and networks.

Since 2000, members of our GPPAC Pacific network have experienced a range of natural disasters, from severe droughts in Papua New Guinea, to intense tropical cyclones in countries including Tonga, Vanuatu, and Fiji, to earthquakes and flooding affecting the Solomon Islands. The estimated average annual direct loss caused by natural disasters in the region amounts to $284 million.[4]

At the global level, Pacific member states have been consistent in stressing the connection with environment security including the impact of climate change at the annual UN Security Council open debate on Resolution 1325. The Global Study on Resolution 1325 (UN Women 2015) highlighted that "as natural disasters increase in frequency and severity due to climate change and environmental degradation, the international community must respond through inclusive strategies that recognize women's agency and respect their rights and needs." The report further noted the need to transform the way women are portrayed, to ensure that strategies do not perpetuate the universal image of women being defenseless and vulnerable victims, and thus produce policies and practices that focus attention on protection rather than empowerment.

Evidence from recent natural disasters in the Pacific highlights the need to support women's leadership and amplify their voices at every level so that National Disaster Management Committees, as well as development partners, ensure women's leadership in preparedness and in decision-making for the planning and implementation of recovery strategies, including the development of appropriate security in evacuation centers and affected communities.

Subsequently, the adoption of Resolution 2242 in 2015 puts women, peace, and human security at the center of addressing the current global challenges of rising violent extremism, climate change, and displacement. This is critical, particularly as eighteen years since the adoption of Resolution 1325, we continue to need to strengthen the integration of development, conflict prevention, and human security agendas with a gender perspective.

Progressing "Women, Peace, and Security, and the Humanitarian Agenda: Participation, Preparedness, and Protection" is now a priority for femLINKpacific. The goal of the network through the innovative Women's Weather Watch program is to develop and communicate clear strategies and recommendations linked to 1325, drawing evidence from recent natural disasters in the Pacific in order to support women's leadership and amplify their voice at every level so that National Disaster Management Committees, as well as development partners, ensure women's leadership in preparedness, decision-making in planning, and implementation of recovery strategies, including ensuring security in evacuation centers and affected communities.

RESOLUTION 1325 AND THE BROADER UN PROCESS

The world has also changed dramatically since the adoption of Resolution 1325, and new obstacles to gender equality, peace, and security have arisen, while old issues remain unresolved. Climate change has become an increasingly urgent problem, exacerbating conflicts and raising tensions. Violence and conflict, therefore, undermine collective efforts and hopes for development, equality, and stability. As such, we must ensure that our peace-building efforts bring sustainable results. This is only possible if the process is inclusive and builds on the potential and strengths of all actors.

There is quality data, both comprehensive and comparable, of the high prevalence and severity of violence committed against women in the Pacific by both intimate partners and strangers. Research like the Family Health and Safety Studies of 2015, conducted by UN Women, in Samoa, the Solomon Islands, Kiribati, Vanuatu, and Fiji, indicates the Pacific has some of highest rates of violence against women in the world, "with . . . incident [rates]" of intimate partner violence at "more than 60 percent for women aged 14–49 in Fiji, Solomon Islands and Kiribati," while "60 percent of women in Samoa and Tonga experienced non-partner violence."

The recent debates within and outside the Security Council demonstrate a strong recognition of the role of women in peace-building and recovery. While the global normative frameworks for empowering women in peace-building efforts are in place, implementation remains slow. There are even more impediments when it comes to country-level implementation. Given this, it is essential that the voices of local women are amplified to ensure that states are compelled to re-examine efforts, successes, and challenges in securing sustainable peace. This is a unique opportunity to integrate women's participation and the WPS agenda more generally, into the DNA of the UN's peace and security architecture.

At the regional level, the GPPAC Pacific network's regional strategy will continue to contribute to enhancing the visibility and participation of women and young women in political leadership at the local and national levels. The network will also undertake strategic and systematic collaboration with government officials from the subnational to regional level to integrate international gender equality standards and conventions and regional policy commitments into local and national development and political processes.

This is even more essential now and while the UN system was consulting women for the 2015 Global Study report, the Pacific Islands Forum decided that a review of the Pacific RAP-WPS would proceed without substantive consultation with women's civil society, nor the input and advice of the Reference Group appointed to guide the implementation of the action plan.

The focus of the GPPAC Pacific network is now to ensure that there is greater accountability by RIGOs to support and enhance gender-inclusive conflict prevention and human security, based on the findings and recommendations from peace-building networks in line with the recommendations of The Global Partnership for the Prevention of Armed Conflict (GPPAC) recommendations to the Global Study, which stressed the need to

1. Provide long-term support to local civil society, and to women as agents within civil society movements;
2. Adopt a gender, peace, and human security strategy to implement the WPS agenda;
3. Support access to and capacity building on communication and technology, enabling women to enhance their voices and document their perspectives in policymaking.

Ultimately, the first fifteen years of progressing Resolution 1325 in the Pacific highlighted the value of and the need to continue to invest in networks of civil society experts who have monitored the implementation of Resolution 1325 and are using 1325 as an instrument to prevent conflict and the resurgence of violence, and to strengthen women's agency in both.

REGIONAL ACTIVITIES

In many violent situations in the Pacific region, women and women's organizations have demonstrated their capacity to contribute to solutions, whether as mediators or as part of groups working to improve conditions in local communities. Furthermore, women's organizations have provided safe havens for women and children affected by violence, as well as demanded accountability and respect for human rights. They are also part of the legacy of activism, which gave voice and attention to the issue of a nuclear free and independent Pacific Island region. femLINKpacific has contributed to informing and transforming notions of security, and to ensuring that the strategies implemented by states are inclusive of women's human security priorities. Moreover, through its community media network and the engagement of local women leaders, a process has been established that reminds governments of their commitments to the human rights of women, and their peace and security. Furthermore, this network has provided quantitative and qualitative evidence, which informed the development of the RAP-WPS.

Efforts to engage with the regional security architecture in the Pacific, such as the PIF Regional Security Committee have waxed and waned, particularly since asking the question: If the UN member states have the Security Council, do we have anything in our Pacific region? Drawing on the legacy of women's activism to hold the UN system accountable, it makes sense that the regional WPS networks would not only hold our national governments accountable but also the RIGOs, such as PIFS, which is tasked with the responsibility of supporting Pacific leaders.

In 2007, the Gender, Conflict, Peace, and Security workshop for Pacific Forum Regional Security officials—co-convened by PIFS, the United Nations Development Programme (UNDP) Pacific Centre, and femLINKpacific—set the scene for women's engagement in what was already an evolving regional architecture

This workshop signified a new style of collaboration between PIFS, development partners, the United Nations (including the UNDP Pacific Centre), and civil society to raise awareness and understanding of gender issues in conflict, peace-building, and security in the region. The goal of the workshop was to facilitate a shift toward a more gender responsive security framework at national and regional levels, and it called for the need to support women's participation in all aspects of conflict prevention, peace negotiations, and post-conflict recovery in the region. It was the first time that women were able to formally engage with Forum officials on security issues.

Subsequent collaborations, including the UNDP, PIFS, University of South Pacific (USP), and the femLINKpacific human security consultations with government, women's groups, and civil society (2008), and the UNDP and PIFS Regional Ministerial Conference on Security Sector Governance held in Tonga in 2009, built on regional commitments to gender equality.

The formulation of the RAP was the result of a commitment by PIFS to a biannual dialogue between Forum officials and CSOs on regional security issues. This dialogue also resulted in the placement of two civil society representatives on the RAP working group.

The June 2015 decision by the FRSC reflected the importance of supporting the expanding scope of the WPS agenda in the region to reflect key gender inequality and security priorities in the context of sustainable development, in line with the Leaders Gender

Equality Declaration, as well as supporting the continued mainstreaming of Women, Peace, and Security commitments into National Security Policies, in line with the Security Sector Governance Principles endorsed by Leaders in 2014. However, the institutional reform within the Pacific Islands Forum has resulted in dwindling spaces for engagement despite the need for greater accountability to progressing the WPS agenda in the region and demonstrated success of earlier collaborations.

So, while the adoption of a RAP-WPS is recognized as a key regional mechanism for supporting the advancement of gender equality and women's rights in the Pacific region, including enabling their equal participation within member states, UN agencies, and RIGOs, civil society no longer has a clear channel to engage with Forum Regional Security Officials. This further marginalizes women.

The Role and Importance of the Media

The WPS agenda must continue to evolve as well as amplify the commitments by political leaders to gender inclusive conflict prevention and human security. Additionally if the Sustainable Development Goals (SDGs) are to truly transform the lives of women in their homes and families, and demonstrate the nexus between peace, development, and humanitarian situations, we need to ensure women and communities are connected to information and communication systems and that local and national decision-making is accountable, participatory, and transformative.

Since 2001, femLINKpacific's community media network has demonstrated the role of new and traditional media in building and sustaining peaceful communities

The development and production of media content by the network continues to ensure the availability of information. The network provides quantitative and qualitative evidence, which assists in the development of local and national action plans on WPS, and also informs the development of the RAP-WPS. An example of localizing network priorities is femLINKpacific's Women's Human Security First campaign, which has highlighted that development processes and priorities must be defined from the community level up, particularly to prevent conflict over resources.

Our regional media and policy network on Resolution 1325 has consistently been communicating the need to transform notions of security, particularly to ensure strategies are inclusive of women's human security priorities. Through community radio and television broadcasts and a range of media initiatives we have localized the resolutions to make the connection with human rights, peace, human security, and development. In this way, we have acted as a regional network of communicators and peace-builders. The development and production of community media content provided evidence which informed the development of the RAP-WPS in October 2012.

Human security for the network is about transforming spaces and processes for women's equal participation, in all their diversities; it is about environment security, including protection from the negative impact of extractive industries, intensifying natural disasters, and the impact of climate change on food and nutrition security. Moreover, it is about ensuring that the women of the Pacific Islands have a police force that is resourced and responsive.

Since introducing Fiji and the Pacific's first women-led community radio station in 2004, femLINKpacific has also developed and sustained a regional media network, which has expanded across the twenty-two Pacific Island countries and territories. This network links peace-builders and community media activists through their various media and information platforms, including publications, radio programs, television, and online media platforms.

Since 2016, femLINKpacific's role as a media network has been recognized as a partner of the UN Women Media Compact, obtained UN media accreditation at the World Humanitarian Summit in Istanbul. Furthermore since 2003 it has been the Pacific coordinator of the Global Media Monitoring Project (GMMP), and an active member of AMARC in the Asia-Pacific region. FemLINKpacific also collaborates with a range of civil society partners demonstrating the application of solutions-based journalism and proving to be an important platform and voice for a diverse range of women responding to the consistent underrepresentation of women in news media content.

CONCLUSION

The adoption of a RAP-WPS has been recognized as a key regional mechanism to support the advancement of gender equality and women's rights in the Pacific region, enabling women to be equal participants with member states, UN agencies, and RIGOs in the prevention of the resurgence of violent and armed conflict, as well as the reform of national and local governance systems, and in advocating for compliance with human rights standards such as CEDAW. It is part of a legacy of women's peace activism which brought voice and attention to the issue of a nuclear free and independent Pacific Island region. But, as we have found, a plan is not enough. If women are not resourced and supported, we cannot make our plans work. The best way forward for the future requires a shift from action plans to concrete action and the allocation of funding and resources to achieve this. It involves implementing accountability measures to monitor the human rights of women, as well as the provision of resources to conflict prevention and human security within the regional intergovernmental peace-building architecture, and the support for accessible fora so that we can continue to engage and collaborate with civil society partners and allies working on peace and security.

Thus, the collective and individual voices of women continue to be fundamental to advancing women's rights at national and international levels. While there is no one-size-fits-all RIGOs or civil-society approach to collaboration, there is a critical need to enhance collaborative practices given that both sectors often have the means and understanding to help prevent the root causes of conflict in their regions and to build strong and inclusive democratic institutions. Processes can include direct channels of communication. Spaces for interaction and joint analysis between officials from regional organizations and civil society representatives can contribute to strengthening peace and security cooperation, by enabling the participation of women in decision-making processes on peace-building, conflict prevention, and democratic governance, according to the principles enshrined in Resolution 1325 and CEDAW. Therefore, the evolving regional intergovernmental architecture in the Pacific Island region urgently requires an important anchor that will ensure that representatives of member states tasked with advancing commitments to peace and security do so, through a range of processes, including information sharing, conflict analysis, early warning, coordinating early response, enhancing credibility of peace processes, convening conflicting parties, strengthening dialogue, and conducting mediation.

The next phase of implementation of Resolution 1325 should be about operationalizing women's inclusion as a critical component to institutional effectiveness, rather than about making the linkages between the participation of women in peace processes and sustainable peace. It is about taking bold steps at the regional and national levels to invest in peace, which in our experience includes an end to increased militarism and militarization. It requires that national and regional security structures respond to human security issues, as this is where the resources are needed, including early warnings systems, prevention of conflict mechanisms, and imaginative, nonviolent methods for the protection of civilians. There is a need to reprioritize to ensure that the local comes first, and that the mechanisms implemented are informed by women at the local and national levels, as this will ensure that women are free, more equal, and supported in their attempts to mobilize to become peacebuilders on their own terms and in their own way.

NOTES

1. Tawake, F., "Here Are the Women—Pacific (2017): Agnes Titus," femLINKpacific, 2015, http://www.femlinkpacific.org.fj/index.php/en/actions/here-are-the-women/538-here-are-the-women-pacific-2017-agnes-titus.
2. Rolls, S., "FemTalk: Women Continue to Lead for Peace as RAMSI Leads," femLINKpacific, June 27, 2017, https://www.facebook.com/notes/femlinkpacific/femtalk-women-continue-to-lead-for-peace-as-ramsi-leaves/10155531893084295/.
3. Pacific Feminist Forum, "Pacific Feminist Forum Opening," FemTalk 89 FM, November 28, 2016, https://www.mixcloud.com/femlinkpacific/femtalk89fm-day-one-pacific-feminist- forum-opening/.
4. "Pacific Islands: Disaster Risk Reduction and Financing in the Pacific," World Bank, April 1, 2012, http://www.worldbank.org/en/results/2012/04/01/pacific-islands-disaster-risk-reduction-and-financing-in-the-pacific.

REFERENCES

Bhagwan Rolls, S. "Act to Ensure Participation for Prevention." *Islands Business* (November 2015).

Bhagwan Rolls, S. "FemTALK1325+16: Not Just Another Anniversary." Pasifika Peace Talanoa, ed. 2., femLINKpacifica, 2016a, http://www.femlinkpacific.org.fj/images/PDF/Policy/PPT_2_2016.pdf.

Bhagwan Rolls, S. "Policy for Peace: Communicating Women, Peace, and Security in Humanitarian Crises." A FemLINKpacific Policy Initiative, 2016b, http://www.femlinkpacific.org.fj/images/PDF/Policy/PolicyForPeace_2016.pdf.

Inter-Parliamentary Union. "Women in National Parliaments." May 1, 2017, http://www.ipu.org/wmn-e/world.htm.

Pacific Islands Forum Secretariat. "Review of the Regional Action Plan on Women, Peace, and Security." June 2015.

UN Women. "Transforming Justice, Securing the Peace. A Global Study on the Implementation of United Nations Security Council Resolution 1325 (2000)." Lead author: Radhika Coomaraswamy. UN Women, 2015, http://wps.unwomen.org/pdf/en/GlobalStudy_EN_Web.pdf.

···

CHAPTER 32

WPS AND THE
ORGANIZATION OF
AMERICAN STATES

···

MARY K. MEYER MCALEESE

AT first glance, the Organization of American States (OAS) appears to be resistant to recognizing and implementing the United Nations Security Council Resolution 1325 and the eight additional resolutions that have defined the Women, Peace, and Security (WPS) agenda since 2000.[1] The OAS has not developed a Regional Action Plan (RAP) for implementing Resolution 1325, and until recently only a handful OAS documents expressly refer to the resolution or use the trope, "Women, Peace, and Security." Moreover, the OAS is not specifically named in the section on regional organizations in the comprehensive 2015 Global Study on the Implementation of United Nations Security Council Resolution 1325 (UN Women 2015). Through April 2018, only eight states in the Americas have developed a National Action Plan (NAP) for implementing Resolution 1325: Argentina, Brazil, Canada, Chile, El Salvador, Guatemala, Paraguay, and the United States (PeaceWomen 2018). However, a closer look into the OAS and the inter-American system demonstrates that important work is well underway relating to each of the four "pillars" that define the UN's WPS agenda.

Resolution 1325 calls for women's *participation* at all levels of decision-making, the *protection* of women and girls from sexual and gender-based violence (SGBV), and the *prevention* of violence against women through the promotion of women's rights, accountability, and law enforcement (Miller et al. 2014: 2). The fourth pillar, *relief and recovery*, focuses on meeting the specific needs of women and girls displaced by violence, survivors of gender based violence, and those with disabilities, and calls for women to be at the center of relief and recovery work (PeaceWomen 2013). These four interrelated pillars are important instrumental steps in the mainstreaming of gender perspectives in contemporary peacemaking and peacekeeping efforts and are essential to advancing the WPS agenda. Feminist scholars and activists add a fifth, more transformative pillar focused on long-term peace-building that eliminates all forms of structural violence underlying conflict and human insecurity.

Although the particular forms of conflict envisioned by Resolution 1325 are currently less prevalent in the Americas than elsewhere, the four pillars of the WPS agenda are relevant to the nations of the Western Hemisphere. Many countries in the Americas face enormous levels of physical insecurity and violence related to the prevalence of drug cartels, traffickers of all sorts, and criminal gangs. Many countries record high rates of homicide, femicide, and SGBV, and displacement caused by such widespread insecurity. Nearly all countries experience persistent structural violence linked to income inequality, gender discrimi-nation, and economic underdevelopment. Despite its curious silence on Resolution 1325 and the WPS agenda, the OAS, and more specifically its Inter-American Commission of Women, has long been working in each of the policy areas or pillars of the WPS agenda. This work takes a distinctly regional approach that is framed by the political, social, and economic conditions, and issues confronting the countries of the Americas. Despite clear obstacles, the translation of the UN's WPS agenda is underway at the OAS, but its articula-tion is inflected by the specific concerns, political agendas, and policy frames of the actors, mechanisms, and institutions in the region.

This chapter explores the ways and extent to which the OAS and the inter-American system have been engaged in work relating to the pillars of the UN's WPS agenda. It takes a largely institutionalist approach and policy perspective, but is informed by other approaches such as discourse analysis to address the following questions: First, what are the key actors, mechanisms, and legal and policy frameworks in the OAS system that are relevant to the WPS agenda? Second, how and to what extent are these actors, mechanisms, and frameworks incorporating WPS pillars into all facets of policy action in the Americas? Finally, what will be needed to articulate and implement further the UN's WPS agenda into the regional, national, and local discourses in ways that measurably improve the lives of women and girls across the hemisphere?

The chapter proceeds in four sections, beginning with a brief discussion of the unique history of the OAS system and the historic work of the Inter-American Commission of Women, which has been dedicated to advancing women's human rights, equality, devel-opment, and security in the Western Hemisphere since 1928. The second section analyzes the specific legal and policy initiatives framing women's human rights and gender equality in the inter-American system since the 1990s and the strengthening and modernization of that work since the year 2000. The third section addresses the extent to which the inter-American women's human rights and gender equality framework matches the pillars of the UN's WPS agenda, and the final section briefly considers the question of "localization" of the WPS agenda in the Western Hemisphere. Ultimately the chapter aims at indicating fur-ther avenues for academic research, policy development, and political action to make the WPS agenda come meaningfully alive for all women in the Americas.

THE OAS SYSTEM AND THE INTER-AMERICAN INSTITUTIONAL ARCHITECTURE

The OAS is a regional intergovernmental organization with a complicated history and place in the inter-American system of nation-states. It is often ignored or marginalized in the con-temporary study of the international relations of the Western Hemisphere, a field dominated by realist, structural realist, and dependency theory approaches, and one that almost completely ignores questions of women and gender politics (Domínguez and Covarrubias 2015; Escudé 2015; Tickner 2008; Arceneaux and Pion-Berlin 2007). The few contemporary liberal institutionalist studies of the region's international relations tend to downplay the effectiveness or even the relevance of the OAS, particularly in light of newer experiments in regional economic integration and political cooperation (for example, Mercosur, UNASUR, ALBA, or CELAC[2]) that challenge the OAS as a tool of US regional hegemony and assert the autonomy of Latin American states (see for example, Legler 2015; Fontana and Pereyra 2009; Herz 2011; Tickner 2015; Meyer McAleese 2016; Mace and Loiseau 2009).

With its roots stretching back to the nineteenth Century, the OAS was created at the Ninth International Conference of American States held in Bogotá, Colombia, in 1948. Among the preexisting inter-American bodies and commissions incorporated into the new OAS architecture was the Inter-American Commission of Women, most commonly known by its Spanish acronym, CIM (*Comisión Inter-Americana de Mujeres*). The CIM has been an important norm entrepreneur and protagonist for advancing women's human rights in the Americas since 1928. Its first major accomplishment was its pathbreaking Convention on the Nationality of Women, adopted by the Seventh International Conference of American States at Montevideo, Uruguay, in 1933. Its second major accomplishment was its successful drafting of two new fundamental human rights instruments for women in the hemisphere, both of which were adopted at the Bogotá meeting on May 2, 1948: The Inter-American Convention on the Granting of Civil Rights to Women, and the Inter-American Convention on the Granting of Political Rights of Women (Inter-American Commission of Women 2016a; Meyer 1999).

Since 1948, the CIM has expanded its work on the advancement of women's rights and equality into such issues or policy areas as education, health, economic development, and more recently violence against women (more on this to follow). The CIM's Assembly of Delegates meets every three years to chart the strategic program of work for the Commission, and its Executive Committee meets at least once a year to navigate timely issues within the OAS. Its Washington-based Secretariat provides full-time gender policy expertise within and across the inter-American system. The Secretariat's technocratic—or "femocratic"— work tends to lack the political limelight, but it produces model legal and public policy frameworks adopted by the CIM Assembly of Delegates, the OAS General Assembly, and more recently the triennial meetings of the Summit of the Americas.[3] These legal and policy frameworks are then implemented through other mechanisms, commissions, and agencies across the OAS/inter-American system and by its member states.

The CIM and its legal and policy initiatives have encountered obstacles and resistance within the OAS system and from member states. Through the years the CIM's Secretariat has worked tirelessly with minimal staff, tiny budgets, and tight space (Meyer McAleese 2009). According to the Executive Secretary's 2016 Report to the Thirty-Seventh Assembly of Delegates, "of the more than 1,700 mandates handed down to the OAS by the General Assembly and other authorities, the CIM has more than 250 (15.4%), including specific and permanent mandates from its Assembly of Delegates and Executive Committee, the OAS General Assembly and the Summits of the Americas" (Inter-American Commission of Women 2016b: 2). Yet in 2016, the CIM Secretariat counted only 2 percent of OAS staff (six full-time staff and two consultants), received only 1.7 percent of the OAS budget, and competed for scarce resources with other commissions, agencies, and programs working on women and gender issues across the hemisphere (Inter-American Commission of Women 2016b: 3; Anderson 2016).

STRENGTHENING THE OAS's WOMEN's HUMAN RIGHTS AND GENDER EQUALITY REGIME

Despite limited resources (and patriarchal resistance), the 1990s and 2000s were decades of significant policy development and institutional modernization for the CIM. Particularly since 1999, the CIM strategically positioned itself as "the Hemisphere's political forum and reference point for the full citizenship of women, from a human-rights perspective," and aims at the "institutionalization of a rights-based and gender equality approach in the [OAS's] main forums, programs, and institutional planning" (Inter-American Commission of Women 2016b: 2). The CIM claimed this position through careful work and the formal adoption by the OAS General Assembly of two key human rights and public policy instruments: The 1994 Inter-American Convention on the Prevention, Punishment, and Eradication of Violence against Women (commonly known as the Belém do Pará Convention), and the 1999 Inter-American Program on the Promotion of Women's Human Rights and Gender Equity and Equality (commonly known as the Inter-American Program, or IAP). Both instruments deserve discussion to demonstrate how the CIM has continued its pathbreaking women's rights work, how it modernized and strengthened its role as a "high level policy forum" in the inter-American system, and how its work relates to the four pillars of the WPS agenda (Anderson 2016; OAS 2018).

The Belém do Pará Convention on Violence against Women

In the early 1990s the CIM played a key role in drafting and shepherding to adoption in the OAS General Assembly the Convention of Belém do Pará, which entered into force in 1995 (Organization of American States 1995; Meyer 1999). This Convention was the first of its kind in the world but, perhaps due to its regional focus, is often overlooked in broader discussions of women's human rights or efforts to eradicate SGBV at the global and grassroots levels. One of the Convention's key advances is its comprehensive definition of violence against women in Article 2 which goes beyond domestic or family violence in the private sphere to include violence occurring in the community (for example, in schools, in the workplace, and so on) and all public spaces, as well as violence perpetrated or condoned by agents of the state.[4] Another key advance is Article 7, which establishes the state's responsibility and enumerates the state's duties in stemming all forms of violence against women via national legislation, law enforcement, and policy development, aimed at preventing, punishing, and eradicating all social practices that tolerate or condone such violence (Organization of American States 1995).

The Convention was careful to engage two other inter-American entities to help establish its juridical force. The Inter-American Commission of Human Rights, another autonomous commission within the OAS system, was empowered to investigate complaints lodged by individuals or groups against a state thought to be in violation of the Convention, while the Inter-American Court of Human Rights was empowered to hear cases referred to it by that Commission and interpret and apply the Convention's law. Progress in establishing the authority of the Convention since 1995 has been slow but measurable. A few cases asking the

Inter-American Commission of Human Rights and the Court of Human Rights to apply the Convention have been successful. Perhaps the best known is the 2006 "Cotton Fields" case in which the Inter-American Court of Human Rights found the state of Mexico responsible for failing to exercise its due diligence in preventing and punishing the violent deaths of three young women near Cuidad Juárez, a city at the US-Mexican border with one of the highest rates of femicide and gender-based violence in the hemisphere (Arango et al. 2011; Celorio 2011; Osuna 2008; Boero 2011; Staudt 2008).

Getting states to develop and implement policies in keeping with their responsibilities under the Belém do Pará Convention has been slow and uneven. In its 2004 ten-year review of the Convention's implementation, the CIM recognized a gaping lack of progress. It worked with other governmental and nongovernmental stakeholders to create an independent implementing body known as the MESECVI (Follow Up Mechanism to the Belém do Pará Convention). The MESECVI, comprised of a Committee of Experts (CEVI), works with states to collect and publish data on violence against women in the region, develop indicators for measuring implementation of the Convention, issue reports, make recommendations to states, and encourage civil society organizations to participate in the process by submitting parallel reports. Since 2004, this detailed work has paid off as the CIM and the MESECVI have produced highly detailed, clear, and user-friendly guides and reports to hold states accountable in implementing the Convention. Specifically, the detailed *Practical Guide to the System of Progress Indicators for Measuring the Implementation of the Belém do Pará Convention* (Inter-American Commission of Women and MESECVI 2015) and the *Overview of the Implementation of the Belém do Pará Convention* (MESECVI et al. 2015), both published twenty years after the Convention's entry into force, are impressive in their clarity and comprehensiveness.

Nevertheless, the findings in the *Overview* document are disheartening, showing very uneven and anemic levels of states' compliance with their duties to implement the Convention by developing a national plan (49 percent), passing appropriate legislation (39.19 percent), providing specialized services (41.67 percent) and access to justice (22.92 percent) for women victims of violence, gathering information and statistics (18.75 percent), and allocating budget resources to combat violence against women (17.71 percent) (MESECVI et al. 2015). In any case, the CIM's legal and policy work concerning the Belém do Pará Convention is highly relevant to the second pillar of the UN's WPS agenda concerning prevention of all forms of gender based violence, particularly SGBV in places of violent conflict. It also speaks to the WPS agenda's participation and protection pillars. CIM's work demonstrates that clear albeit limited steps have been taken to prevent and punish such violence in both public and private spaces in the Americas, and it provides gender policy expertise and accessible models for other governmental and nongovernmental actors at all levels to consider adapting to other parts of the world.

The Inter-American Program

In the wake of the successful adoption of the Belém do Pará Convention in 1994 and the impact of the 1995 UN Women's Conference in Beijing, the CIM implemented its Strategic Plan of Action for 1995–2000, which launched a renewed effort to strengthen and modernize its central role in gender policy work in the Americas. The outcome was the CIM's

"Inter-American Program," approved by the OAS General Assembly in 1999 (CIM 2000). The IAP's first Objective was "to systematically integrate a gender perspective in all organs, organizations, and entities of the inter-American system;" its subsequent objectives and lines of action provide clear statements of how that should be accomplished (CIM 2000). Through the IAP, the CIM placed itself at the hub of advancing the full range of women's rights and gender equality policies in the inter-American system. It acts inside the OAS Secretariat and with other OAS components to infuse gender mainstreaming into every policy area by providing policy expertise, advisory services, capacity building, and gender training via workshops and virtual short courses. In its 2016 report, the CIM Executive Secretary highlighted such work in support and coordination with the OAS Secretariats for Multidimensional Security, for Political Affairs, for Access to Rights and Equity, and for Legal Affairs. In addition, the report outlined the CIM's cooperation and advisory services provided to other autonomous specialized organizations such as the Pan-American Health Organization (Inter-American Commission of Women 2016b: 19–21).

Moreover, the IAP situates the CIM to work "horizontally" with member states on capacity building and providing legal and policy models, seminars, trainings and workshops, and related support for governmental ministries to infuse the inter-American women's rights and gender equality regime into the state and local levels. The IAP also empowers the CIM to cooperate and coordinate with other inter-governmental organizations outside of the OAS system, such as UN Women and the Economic Commission for Latin America and the Caribbean (ECLAC), as well as with nongovernmental and civil society organizations working in the region at all levels to advance the women's rights and gender equality agenda (CIM 2000; Inter-American Commission of Women 2016a and 2016b). For example, with the support of the governments of Chile and Trinidad and Tobago, the CIM undertook a project focused on capacity building with the Organization of Eastern Caribbean States (OECS) and its six member states (Antigua and Barbuda, Dominica, Grenada, Saint Lucia, Saint Kitts and Nevis, and Saint Vincent and the Grenadines) to compile data, hold focus groups, workshops, and roundtables with local stakeholders, and ultimately produce a sub-regional report on the implementation of their Belém do Pará commitments. Importantly, these countries had some of the weakest participation and/or lowest compliance rates in the MESECVI evaluation previously discussed, even though gender-based violence is "a topic of great interest to the Caribbean region" (Inter-American Commission of Women 2016b: 10–11).

The IAP and CIM's impact on furthering gender mainstreaming within the inter-American system is also seen in the increased articulation of mandates relating to "gender issues" in the high-level Summit of the Americas process. Seventeen gender mandates were included in the 2001 Plan of Action at the Quebec Summit alone, constituting over 60 percent of all gender mandates produced by the Summit process between 1994 and 2012 (Gender Issues, n.d.; Summits of the Americas Secretariat, n.d.). Interestingly, most of the gender mandates adopted by the Summits of the Americas prior to 2009 tended to address general principles of women's human rights and gender equality in the political, economic development, and social policy areas. At the 2012 Summit of the Americas in Cartagena, Colombia, which focused on Citizen Security and Transnational Organized Crime, one finds the first set of mandates that infuse a gender perspective into discussions of public security (see OAS Secretariat for Multidimensional Security 2012).

In short, since the adoption of the IAP in 1999, the CIM has clearly strengthened and modernized itself and its work to infuse women's rights and gender equality in and across the inter-American system. The creation of the MESECVI in 2004 and the subsequent development of its evaluation process for the implementation of the Belém do Pará Convention along with the CIM's regular strategic planning documents and periodic reports are examples of the CIM's increasingly thorough and professional gender policy work. While other international, regional, and organizational factors were surely at play in the gender politics under review, it must be noted that the strengthening and modernization of the CIM is largely due to its professional and expert staff. In 2009, the CIM Secretariat got even stronger, when Carmen Moreno, formerly the director of the United Nations International Research and Training Institute for Women (UN-INSTRAW), was appointed Executive Secretary of the CIM. Moreno brought with her Hilary Anderson (also from UN-INSTRAW) to serve as Gender Senior Specialist at the CIM. With the rest of the CIM staff, these women have further modernized the approach, discourse, and visibility of the CIM's women's rights and gender equality work inside the OAS system in ways that are directly relevant to the UN's WPS agenda (discussed later). Moreover, they pushed the region's gender regime even further by working to reframe the regional discussion of "citizen security" in terms of "*gender*, peace, and security."

LOCATING THE WOMEN, PEACE, AND SECURITY AGENDA IN INTER-AMERICAN FRAMEWORKS

According to the Executive Secretary's 2016 report, today the CIM defines its work in terms of the "OAS's four thematic pillars and its programs, forums, and strategies: Substantive political citizenship of women for democracy and governance; Women's human rights and gender violence; Women's economic security and citizenship; and Citizen security from a gender approach." The report adds a "fifth pillar and one of CIM's main mandates: the institutionalization of an approach based on rights and gender equality within the work of the OAS" (Inter-American Commission of Women 2016b: 2). These pillars are strikingly similar to the four pillars of the UN's WPS agenda discussed earlier: women's participation, women's protection, prevention of violence against women and gender-based violence, and women-centered relief and recovery. Both sets advance instrumental gender perspectives in policymaking aimed at ending all forms of violence and redefining human security.

As we have seen, the CIM has led the way in advancing hard law regarding women's political and civil rights to participate in the political process and decision-making as well as in the prevention and punishment of violence against women in the Western Hemisphere. Since 2009, the CIM has worked to mainstream gender issues into the region-wide debates about multidimensional and citizen security aimed at protecting women, girls, and other vulnerable groups. It has long worked on advancing gender equity policies in education, health, economic development, social policy, and more. Yet, it remains curious that specific references to Resolution 1325 and the trope "women, peace, and security" are so few, and arise so late in the documentary records of the inter-American system even though CIM is clearly working in these issues areas. Indeed, it is UN-related entities working in the region such as UN Women and ECLAC, or regional civil society networks like RESDAL (Network for Security and Defense in Latin America) that speak directly of Resolution 1325 and the WPS agenda in regional fora (ECLAC 2016a, 2016b, and 2015; ECLAC and UN Women 2016; RESDAL 2015). Only a handful of such direct references are articulated inside the OAS system.

The first reference appears in the CIM's 2011 "Briefing Note: A Rights-Based and Gender Equality Approach to Citizen Security in the Americas," which mentions Resolution 1325 only once, on the last page of the six-page technical note (discussed later) (CIM 2011). The second reference dates from October 13, 2015 on the occasion of the fifteenth anniversary of Resolution 1325 at the United Nations in New York, when the Chief of Staff of the Assistant Secretary General of the OAS delivered a short speech (seven paragraphs) prepared by the CIM to commemorate the anniversary at the UN Security Council (Laínez 2015). A third reference relates to a Policy Roundtable event titled, "Gender, Peace, and Security," held on March 17, 2016 at the OAS's Hall of the Americas and co-sponsored by the OAS, the CIM, the Embassy of the Principality of Liechtenstein, and UN Women. The event included welcoming remarks by the Assistant Secretary General of the OAS and a keynote address by the Foreign Minister of Liechtenstein who saluted Resolution 1325 and the WPS agenda in their speeches (Méndez 2016; Frick 2016).

When asked why there was so little direct naming of Resolution 1325 or the WPS Agenda inside the OAS system, the CIM's Gender Senior Specialist Hilary Anderson—who edited UN-INSTRAW's 2006 policy and planning guide on Women, Peace, and Security—explained that there are three arguments blocking a specific incorporation of Resolution 1325 and WPS into the regional policy discourse. The first is that 1325 is considered "a UN thing." Some believe that it should stay within the UN, seeing this as a question of "different organization, different agenda" (Anderson 2016). A second and related argument is that some states prefer to keep the UN Security Council out of regional affairs, reflecting the deeply embedded defense of national sovereignty and autonomy in the region as well as a nod to the region's own security and defense arrangements. The third argument is that Resolution 1325 is considered simply "not relevant" to some states because there is "no formal conflict" in the region, at least not of the type envisioned in Resolution 1325 (Anderson 2016).

The contemporary cases of Colombia and Haiti notwithstanding, the regional challenges and discourse regarding "security" have changed since the 1990s and the three-pronged ending of the Cold War, of the civil wars in Central America, and of military rule in several important South American states. Today's high levels of violence associated with criminal cartels, traffickers, and gangs fueled by the underlying structural violence of neoliberal globalization, social inequality, and economic underdevelopment have shifted regional debates about "security" (see Mattar Nasser 2010; Placencia et al. 2009). A bifurcated or double-discourse about security has emerged, with one line addressing the more traditional national security and defense concerns of states in a discourse about "multidimensional security," and another line addressing the more local concerns about personal safety and policing in the discourse of "public security" and "citizen security." Until recently, the endemic violence against women, particularly femicide and SGBV, has tended to be missing from either of these discourses. A preliminary reading suggests that the multidimensional security policy arena within the OAS is lagging or is more resistant to gender mainstreaming, as fewer references to women's rights, security, and gender equality appear in the available documents (see for example, Organization of American States Permanent Council 2016). However, the "citizen security" policy arena appears to be more open to gender framing and mainstreaming (see OAS Secretariat for Multidimensional Security 2012).

According to Ms. Anderson, the CIM's 2011 "Briefing Note: A Rights-based and Gender Equality Approach to Citizen Security in the Americas," was written "to contextualize security" and "to frame WPS for the Americas" in politically and policy relevant terms (Anderson 2016). The "Briefing Note" specifies the different ways women experience violence compared to men (for example, sexual assault or harassment, rape and sexual torture, femicide, "honor" crimes, forced sexual exploitation, child marriage, and the like) and underscores the ways "gender differences intersect with differences in economic status, ethnicity, age, physical capacity, sexual orientation, gender identity and other factors that affect certain people's vulnerability" (CIM 2011). It frames violence against women as a question of public security and points out the limits of traditional approaches. Citing Charlotte Bunch, as well as the World Bank, the "Briefing Note" asserts:

> The global change in the nature of conflict—from interstate and civil wars to local conflicts, political repression and organized crime—demand a change of focus in security policy that recognizes the threats inherent in poverty, HIV, racism, domestic violence, ethnic conflict, and population displacement, among other factors. However, the same institutional weakness that allows the existence and growth of organized crime and the violence it implies also hinders the formulation of an adequate response to these new, or emerging, threats (CIM 2011).

The "Briefing Note" goes on to offer a set of policy recommendations based on UN as well as OAS agreements and resolutions, including Resolution 1325 and subsequent resolutions, along with the Belém do Pará Convention.

Since 2011, the CIM has shifted its language to using the trope "*gender*, peace, and security," and has advanced this agenda into several new areas in the OAS's citizen security policy arena. Most notably, it launched work on violence against women in politics, including attention to political violence more generally which limits women's political participation in the electoral process and access to positions of political leadership. It has prepared a fact sheet on the issue, secured the adoption of a Declaration on the issue by the Conference of States Party to the Belém do Pará Convention in 2015, and developed a Model Law on the topic (CIM 2017; Inter-American Commission of Women 2016a: 7). The CIM also frames child and forced marriage, as well as teenage pregnancy as citizen security issues, and is even raising interesting discussions about gender and cybersecurity. Moreover, the CIM is working with others to inject women's rights and gender equity into debates on regional drug policies and incarceration rates, which have been especially onerous for women (OAS 2018; Washington Office on Latin America et al. 2016). While the CIM's "gender, peace, and security"—or GPS—efforts seem to be making some headway in the citizen security policy arena, its gender mainstreaming work in the multidimensional security arena appears to be just getting under way. Further progress will largely depend on overcoming resistance in government ministries and in the military and policing institutions inside member states.

THE CHALLENGES AHEAD

Translating the pillars of the UN's WPS agenda through the OAS's GPS framework and on to the national and local levels remains a major challenge. As noted earlier, as of April 2018 only eight states in the region had developed a NAP for implementing Resolution 1325: Argentina, Brazil, Canada, Chile, El Salvador, Guatemala, Paraguay, and the United States (see PeaceWomen 2018). Chile was the first state in the Americas to do so in 2009, thanks in part to the leadership of its President, Michele Bachelet, who went on to serve as UN Women's first director between 2010 and 2013 before returning to Chile for a second term as president. Guatemala is the most recent, though its NAP has yet to be published (PeaceWomen 2018). Curiously, many Latin American states, including Brazil, Chile and Guatemala, participate in UN Peacekeeping missions around the world, particularly in Haiti, Democratic Republic of the Congo, and the Middle East (Matijascic 2014; Rebelo 2014; RESDAL 2015; Valdes 2008; Benítez 2007; Malcorra 2010; United Nations Peacekeeping 2016). Despite a certain desire to keep the UNSC at arm's length in the Americas and a real uneasiness in the region about sending military missions to other countries in the Global South, one would expect more states to have embraced 1325 and adopted NAPs, at the very least to comply with Resolution 1325 in such peacekeeping missions.

Yet, as Miller et al. (2014: 4) found in their literature review on the implementation of Resolution 1325, "a 1325 NAP or RAP is neither necessary for promoting gender mainstreaming nor is it sufficient." The experience of the partial implementation of the Belém do Pará Convention is instructive regarding prospects for the advancement of the UN's WPS or the CIM's GPS agendas. With half-hearted compliance levels in developing the Convention's NAPs and widespread neglect in providing adequate budget and financial resources to implement them after twenty years, it is difficult not to be pessimistic. Moreover, reporting fatigue seems to be an emerging obstacle, as some states complain about having to submit so many reports to different international governmental human rights bodies that seem to ask for the same information (Anderson 2016). In an environment of limited resources, weak state capacity, multiple policy demands, and persistent patriarchal attitudes about women, such reporting fatigue is not a promising sign for advancing the WPS or GPS agendas in the Western Hemisphere.

Ultimately, there will be thirty-five different stories about whether and how the UN's WPS or the OAS's GPS agendas can be fully infused and implemented in all corners of the Americas. This study of CIM's work suggests that regionalization is not a one-way process: it may also mean responding to UN-level agendas through legal, political, and policy frameworks articulated in the region's own terms. The CIM's work also indicates the importance of long-term strategies and strategic coalitions along the way. Implementing the WPS and GPS agendas in the Americas will depend on the strength, strategies, and insistence of the region's gender heroes, femocrats, and gender rights activists working in inter-governmental organizations, government ministries, civil society organizations, and academia. Increasing the visibility of the WPS and GPS agendas and explaining their relevance to the challenges of "security" in the Western Hemisphere will be particularly important along with strengthening local and regional networks, building political pressure, and increasing women's representation in political leadership roles at the national, municipal, and community levels. A key challenge is to get the region's military establishments and policing services on board without militarizing "security" any further in the region and without militarizing the WPS or GPS agendas. In the end, a great deal of work lies ahead for political leaders, policy experts, political activists, and academics to translate high-level principles, promises, and policy initiatives from mere lip service into meaningful social and political change. Realizing this goal is relevant to everyone's peace and security in the Americas.

NOTES

1. The other eight resolutions are UN Security Council Resolutions 1820, 1888, 1889, 1960, 2106, 2122, 2242, and 2331. For simplification, the shorter "Resolution 1325" will refer to the entire set of subsequent resolutions that define the WPS agenda.
2. Mercosur is an economic customs union in South America which includes Argentina, Brazil, Paraguay, Uruguay, and Venezuela (suspended in December 2016), and several associate members. UNASUR is the Union of South American Nations founded by Brazil. ALBA is the Bolivian Alliance for the Peoples of Our America founded by Venezuela. CELAC is the Community of Latin American and Caribbean States which grew out of the earlier Rio Group states.
3. The Summits of the Americas Process emerged to reorganize inter-American relations and discuss regional issues after the end of the Cold War. The first Summit of the Americas was held in Miami in 1994. The early Summits of the Americas were technically outside of the OAS but subsequent summits were eventually institutionalized and brought under the umbrella of the OAS system (Summits of the Americas Secretariat n.d.: 2–3).
4. The Belém do Pará Convention's Article 2 specifies violence "that occurs in the community and is perpetrated by any person, including, among others, rape, sexual abuse, torture, trafficking in persons, forced prostitution, kidnapping and sexual harassment in the workplace, as well as in educational institutions health facilities or any other place; and that is perpetrated or condoned by the state or its agents regardless of where it occurs" (Organization of American States 1995).

REFERENCES

Anderson, Hilary. Gender Senior Specialist, CIM. Personal interview at the Inter-American Commission of Women, Organization of American States, Washington, DC, October 17, 2016.

Arango, Bustamante, Diana Marcela, and Paola Andrea Vásquez Henao. "La Convención Belém do Pará: Un Balance de su Aplicación en la Jurisprudencia de La Corte Interamericana, a 16 Años de su Entrada En Vigor." *Civilizar: Ciencias Sociales Y Humanas (Colombia)* 11, no. 20 (2011): 15–35.

Arceneaux, Craig L., and David Pion-Berlin. "Issues, Threats, and Institutions: Explaining OAS Responses to Democratic Dilemmas in Latin America." *Latin American Politics and Society* 49, no. 2 (2007) (Summer): 1–31.

Benítez, Raúl. "America Latina: Operaciones de Paz y Acciones Militares Internacionales de las Fuerzas Armadas." *Foro Internacional* 47, no. 1 (187) (2007): 99–116.

Boero, Susana Chiarotti. "Women's Citizen Security." *University of Miami Law Review* 65, no. 3 (2011): 797–817.

Celorio, Rosa M. "The Rights of Women in the Inter-American System of Human Rights: Current Opportunities and Challenges in Standard Setting." *University of Miami Law Review* 65, no. 3 (2011): 819–866.

CIM. "Inter-American Program on the Promotion of Women's Human Rights and Gender Equity and Equality." OAS, 2000, http://www.oas.org/en/CIM/docs/PIA[EN].pdf.

CIM. "Briefing Note: A Rights-Based and Gender Equality Approach to Citizen Security in the Americas." Washington, DC: Organization of American States, 2011, http://www.oas.org/en/cim/security.asp.

CIM. "Latest News." OAS, 2017, http://oas.org/en/cim/.

Domínguez, Jorge I., and Ana Covarrubias, eds. *Routledge Handbook of Latin America in the World*. New York: Routledge, 2015.

ECLAC (Economic Commission for Latin America and the Caribbean). "Report of the Twenty-Second Meeting of Specialized Agencies and Other Bodies of the United Nations System on the Advancement of Women in Latin America and the Caribbean (Santo Domingo, July 29, 2015)." Doc.LC/L.4076. Santiago, Chile, 2015, http://www.cepal.org/sites/default/files/events/files/c1501118.pdf.

ECLAC. "40 Years of the Regional Gender Agenda." ECLAC, 2016a, http://www.cepal.org/en/print/37909.

ECLAC. "XIII Regional Conference on Women in Latin America and the Caribbean: Programme." Text. *XIII Regional Conference on Women in Latin America and the Caribbean*. October 25, 2016b, http://conferenciamujer.cepal.org/13/en/programme.

ECLAC and UN Women. "Declaration of the Machineries for the Advancement of Women in Latin America and the Caribbean to the Sixtieth Session of the Commission on the Status of Women." In *Fifty-Third Meeting of the Presiding Officers*. Santiago, Chile, 2016, http://www.cepal.org/sites/default/files/events/files/c16001131.pdf

Escudé, Carlos. "Realism in the Periphery." In *Routledge Handbook of Latin America in the World*, edited by Jorge I. Domínguez and Ana Covarrubias, 45–57. New York: Routledge, 2015.

Fontana, Andrés, and Darío M. Pereyra, eds. *La OEA Y La Agenda Interamericana*. Buenos Aires: Universidad Nacional de la Matanza y Prometeo Libros, 2009.

Frick, H. E. Aurelia. "Gender, Peace, and Security. Keynote Speech by H. E. Aurelia Frick, Minister of Foreign Affairs, Education & Culture, Principality of Liechtenstein." Inter-American Commission of Women and OAS, March 17, 2016, http://www.oas.org/es/CIM/docs/Speech_Canciller_Liechtenstein.pdf

"Gender Issues." *Follow-up and Implementation: Mandates—Gender Issues*. Summits of the Americas and Organization of American States, n.d., http://summit-americas.org/sisca/ge.html

Herz, Mônica. *The Organization of American States (OAS): Global Governance Away from the Media*. New York: Routledge, 2011.

Inter-American Commission of Women. "Strategic Plan 2016–2021 of the Inter-American Commission of Women (Draft)." OAS and Inter-American Commission of Women, 2016a, http://oas.org/en/CIM/assembly.asp

Inter-American Commission of Women. "Report of the Executive Secretary of the CIM to the Thirty-Seventh Assembly of Delegates of the Inter-American Commission of Women." Organization of American States and Inter-American Commission of Women, 2016b, http://oas.org/en/CIM/assembly.asp

Inter-American Commission of Women, and MESECVI. *Practical Guide to the System of Progress Indicators for Measuring the Implementation of the Belem Do Para Convention.* OAS. Official Records, OEA/Ser.L/II.6.15. OAS, 2015.

Laínez, Francisco. "Address of Francisco Laínez, Chief of Staff of the Assistant Secretary General [of the OAS], on the 15th Anniversary of the UN Security Council Resolution 1325 on Women, Peace, and Security." Organization of American States, 2015, http://www.oas.org/en/media_center/speech.asp?sCodigo=15-0079

Legler, Thomas. "Beyond Reach? The Organization of American States and Effective Multilateralism." In *Routledge Handbook of Latin America in the World*, edited by Jorge I. Dominguez and Ana Covarrubias, 311–328. New York: Routledge International Handbooks, 2015.

Mace, Gordon, and Hugo Loiseau. "Cooperative Hegemony and Summitry in the Americas." *Latin American Politics and Society* 47, no. 4 (2009): 107–134.

Malcorra, Susana. "What Is the Role of the United Nations, Particularly for Peacekeeping Forces and Missions in Post-Disaster Situations? An Overview from a Gender Perspective." In *Sesión Especial Sobre Haiti Y Chile: (Re)construir La Igualdad*. ECLAC. July 13–16, 2010, http://www.cepal.org/mujer/noticias/paginas/2/38882/ponencia_susanamalcorra.pdf.

Matijascic, Vanessa Braga, ed. *Operações de Manutenção de Paz Das Nações Unidas: Reflexões e Debates*. Coleção Paz, Defesa e Segurança Internacional. São Paolo, Brazil: Editora Unesp., 2014.

Mattar Nasser, Reginaldo, ed. *Novas Perspectivas sobre os Conflitos Internacionais*. São Paolo, Brazil: Editora Unesp., 2010.

Méndez, Nestor H. E. "Remarks for the Assistant Secretary General of the OAS, H. E. Nestor Méndez." Hall of the Americas, OAS, Washington, DC: OAS and Inter-American Commission of Women, 2016, http://www.oas.org/es/cim/docs/Speech_ASG_GenderPeaceSecurity.pdf.

MESECVI, Organization of American States, and Canadian International Development Agency. *Overview of the Implementation of the Belem Do Para Convention*. Washington, DC: OAS, 2015.

Meyer, Mary K. "Negotiating International Norms: The Inter-American Commission of Women and the Convention on Violence against Women." In *Gender Politics in Global Governance*, edited by Mary K. Meyer and Elisabeth Prügl, 58–71. Boulder, CO: Rowman and Littlefield, 1999.

Meyer McAleese, Mary K. "The CIM and the Inter-American Convention on Violence against Women: Still Marginalized after All These Years." From *International Studies Association Annual Convention*. New York, 2009.

Meyer McAleese, Mary K. "International Relations—General." In *Handbook of Latin American Studies—Social Sciences*, Vol. 71, 331–350. Hispanic Division of the Library of Congress. Austin: University of Texas Press, 2016.

Miller, Barbara, Milad Pournik, and Aisling Swaine. *Women in Peace and Security through United Nations Security Resolution 1325: Literature Review, Content Analysis of National Action Plans, and Implementation*. Institute for Global and International Studies, GIS WP13/GGP WP 09. Washington, DC: The George Washington University, 2014, . http://www.peacewomen.org/node/90901

OAS. "OAS: Inter-American Commission of Women."2018, http://www.oas.org/en/cim/

OAS Secretariat for Multidimensional Security. *Report on Citizen Security in the Americas 2012: Official Statistical Information on Citizen Security Provided by the OAS Member States.* OES/ Ser.D/ XXV.2. Washington, DC: OAS Hemispheric Security Observatory, 2012, http:// www.oas.org/dsp/alertamerica/Report/Alertamerica2012.pdf

Organization of American States. *Inter-American Convention on the Prevention, Punishment, and Eradication of Violence against Women.* Organization of American States, 1995, http:// www.oas.org/en/CIM/docs/Belem-do-Para[EN].pdf.

Organization of American States, Permanent Council, Committee on Hemispheric Security. "Advancing Hemispheric Security: A Multidimensional Approach (Draft Resolution)." OEA/Ser.G CP/CSH-1725/16 rev. 4. May 3, 2016. Washington, DC: OAS, 2016, http://www. oas.org/en/council/CSH/

Osuna, Karla I. Quintana. "Recognition of Women's Rights before the Inter-American Court of Human Rights." *Harvard Human Rights Journal* 21 (2008): 301–312.

PeaceWomen. "Women, Peace, and Security Panel Series: Relief and Recovery Pillar." Women's International League for Peace and Freedom, May 23, 2013, http://www.peacewomen.org/ assets/file/wps_panel_series_relief_and_recovery_summary.pdf.

PeaceWomen. "Who Implements: Member States." Women's International League for Peace and Freedom, 2017, http://www.peacewomen.org/member-states.

Placencia, Luis Gonzáles, Metztli Álvarez, and José Luis Arce, eds. *Inseguridad: Perspectivas Desde América Latina.* Guanajuato, México: Secretaria de Seguridad Pública del Estado de Guanajuato, Instituto Estatal de Ciencias Peñales del Estado de Guanajuato, y Editorial Miguel Angel Porrúa, 2009.

Rebelo, Tamya Rocha. "O Equilibrio de Género Nas Operações de Paz: Avanços e Desáfios." In *Operações de Manutenção de Paz Das Nações Unidas: Relfexões E Debates,* edited by Vanessa Braga Matijascic, 71–104. Coleção Paz, Defesa e Seguranca Internacional. São Paolo, Brazil: Editora Unesp., 2014.

RESDAL. "RESDAL Presentó en Montevideo Diéz Recomendaciones Para Incorporar El Enfoque de Género en las Operaciones de Paz." *RESDAL-Red de Seguridad Y Defensa de America Latina,* 2015, http://www.resdal.org/new_12.html.

Staudt, Kathleen. "Gender, Governance, and Globalization at Borders: Femicide at the US-Mexico Border." In *Global Governance: Feminist Perspectives,* edited by Shirin M. Rai and Georgina Waylen, 234–253. New York: Palgrave MacMillan, 2008.

Summits of the Americas Secretariat. "About the Summits of the Americas." Summits of the Americas and Organization of American States, n.d., http://summit-americas.org/pre-vious_summits.html.

Tickner, Arlene B. "Latin American IR and the Primacy of *lo práctico.*" *International Studies Review* 10, no. 4 (December 2008): 735–748.

Tickner, Arlene B. "Autonomy and Latin American International Relations Thinking." In *Routledge Handbook of Latin America in the World,* edited by Jorge I. Domínguez and Ana Covarrubias, 74–84. New York: Routledge, 2015.

UN Women. "Transforming Justice, Securing the Peace. A Global Study on the Implementation of United Nations Security Council Resolution 1325 (2000)." Lead author: Radhika Coomaraswamy. UN Women, 2015, http://wps.unwomen.org/pdf/en/GlobalStudy_EN_Web.pdf.

United Nations Peacekeeping. "Troop and Police Contributors." United Nations Peacekeeping, 2016, https://peacekeeping.un.org/en/troop-and-police-contributors.

Valdés, Juan Gabriel. "La MINUSTAH Y La Reconstrucción del Estado Haitiano." *Estudios Internacionales (Santiago)* 40, no. 159 (2008): 129–142.

Washington Office on Latin America, International Drug Policy Consortium, Dejusticia, Inter-American Commission of Women, and Organization of American States. *Women, Drug Policies, and Incarceration: A Guide for Policy Reform in Latin America and the Caribbean.* Washington, DC: WOLA, IDPC, Dejusticia, CIM, 2016.

CHAPTER 33

....

WPS AND CIVIL SOCIETY

....

ANNIKA BJÖRKDAHL AND JOHANNA MANNERGREN SELIMOVIC

CIVIL society stands at the core of the development of the Women, Peace, and Security (WPS) agenda. Locally and nationally, women's civil society organizations (CSOs) are key spaces for women's social and political engagement with the power to end wars and build peace. CSOs demonstrate that women's agency, voice, and capacities are critical to local dialogues, better policies, and more equitable peace deals, which establish a solid foundation for the new postwar order. Globally, civil society has united to encourage the United Nations (UN) and the international community to recognize the gendered impacts of armed conflict and the active roles played by women, as well as men, toward build lasting and sustainable peace. UN Security Council Resolution 1325 adopted in 2000, was the culmination of decades of activism and advocacy work by CSOs. The resolution recognized the importance of non-state actors by calling on the adoption of mechanisms to support local women's peace initiatives. This was the first time that international law acknowledged the right to inclusion of non-state actors in peace processes (Falch 2010).

The contributions of civil society can be understood by investigating three key phases in the evolution of the WPS agenda: norm-making through advocacy and agenda-setting; the institutionalization of the norms; and implementation and practice. The history of women's activism reveals how normative assumptions concerning suffrage, welfare, peace, and development were constantly negotiated in a complicated web of parallel and independent institutions operating in global, national, and local spaces. In this chapter, we trace the role and activities of women's CSOs in advocating and setting the WPS agenda, advancing its institutionalization, and implementing the agenda in practice. In doing so, we aim to explore the implementation of WPS in practice and shed light on how women activists emplaced in local, national, transnational, or global spaces conceptualize and contribute to the institutionalization of the WPS agenda. In turn, this chapter sheds light on CSOs' ability or inability to affect states and other actors with meeting their WPS responsibilities. Some central moments and events related to the WPS agenda at local, national, and global levels are used to illustrate our argument. We see that CSOs often are successful in framing, promoting, and implementing the ideas, norms, and values that underpin the WPS agenda. They connect grass-roots movements with elite structures and open up space for marginalized voices and agency. They provide care and support to victims when state institutions fail and contribute to peace-building through interethnic dialogue, thereby providing a critical space for a radical reformulation of the meaning of peace. However, the role of civil society is not clear-cut. Its space is constantly in danger of shrinking as a result of political or economic changes. CSOs can be co-opted or marginalized in their relationship to state actors. There is tension between the inherent heterogeneity of civil society and the need to unite around common issues, and there may not always be agreement between the priorities of grass-roots movements and global civil society.

What is civil society?

Civil society is a broad term that includes a heterogeneous society and interlinked networks of organizations at the international, transnational, national, local, and grass-roots level. In classical political theory, according to Neera Chandhoke, civil society is conceptualized as "the space where ordinary men and women through the practices of their daily life acquire political agency and selfhood" (quoted in Shepherd 2015: 895). Civil society "includes those political, cultural and social organizations of modern societies that are autonomous of the state, but *part of the mutually-constitutive relationship between state and society*" (Lipschutz 1999: 101). Thus, the "identity" of civil society is produced through its relationship with the state (Mohan 2002). Civil society as a concept "carries connotations of civility and virtue" (Scholte 2002: 19).

Yet, it is a concept loaded with tensions. Often civil society actors and movements strive for independence, but find their relevance in their interdependence with all aspects of society. Civil society is seen to produce the social glue that holds societies together and as constructive spaces for collaboration, but CSOs may also strive for radical upheaval of oppressive structures (Pfaffenholz 2014).

These understandings of civil society connect with the notion of global civil society, which has a transnational character in the sense that it is not necessarily constrained by international borders or situated in any particular state (Kaldor 2003). In some research, civil society is seen as a unitary actor, while others emphasize the importance of "local level" participation through CSOs. Here, we understand CSOs to be both "global civil society" as well as the multitude of local grass-roots–based associations that may or may not be linked up to transnational networks. Their different positionalities come with different roles that, depending on contexts and times, may converge. This chapter zeros in on the endeavor of women's CSOs to construct, diffuse, institutionalize and implement the WPS agenda.

WOMEN'S CIVIL SOCIETY ORGANIZATIONS AND THE IMPLEMENTATION OF WPS

The WPS agenda interlinks three key concerns: women's participation, the gendered nature of conflict, and women's postwar priorities. This normative agenda sees the exclusion of women from formal decision-making processes as part of a vicious circle that renders their voices, conflict-related experiences, and concrete needs invisible (Aharoni 2014).

The forging of a global consensus around norms pertaining to women's rights and gender equality underpinning the WPS agenda comprises a unique example of the dynamic picture of norm construction, diffusion, and institutionalization. Due to the declarative nature of Resolution 1325, Sarai Aharoni argues that it is "partially a regulative norm" (i.e., a norm that establishes recognized standards and constrains behavior) and partially a "constitutive norm that defines the identity of actors," especially states, but also international organizations and CSOs (Aharoni 2014: 2). Thus, the production of Resolution 1325 was constitutive of transnational women's networks and the women's CSOs that comprise them.

Agenda-Setting and Advocacy

Civil society plays an important role in the agenda-setting and advocacy that paved the way for the WPS agenda. Agenda-setting is about gaining influence and shaping the agenda through efforts to bring a particular issue to the forefront, push for a particular problem definition, or introduce new ideas (Keck and Sikkink 1998). An advocate may contribute to shaping the agenda by introducing a new idea, by bringing a particular issue to the forefront, and by keeping the idea on the agenda. The bulk of what advocates do can be termed as persuasion, to convince others to take on board the ideas they propagate and mobilize support for the new agenda. It is also about overcoming skepticism, contestation, and structural constraints (Björkdahl 2008). In the aftermath of the Cold War an ideational space opened up due to the changed perceptions of peace and security. Old and new ideas surfaced. Yet, only a limited number of ideas can be noticed and reacted to, regardless of their acuity. Ideas linked to gender equality and women's rights that underpin the WPS agenda were among those ideas whose time had come. Women's CSOs were key actors ready to invest energy in promoting these ideas in order to shape the global peace and security context.

The WPS agenda was not a new idea at the end of the Cold War but built upon ideas and actions of protest movements that had evolved throughout the twentieth and twenty-first centuries. The feminist and the pacifist movements shared an anti-militaristic transformative agenda in response to the violent patriotism of the two horrific World Wars, which translated into the post–Cold War engagement for the WPS agenda. A case in point is the Women's International League for Peace and Freedom (WILPF), a CSO that came into being in 1915 and has been a central transnational actor in the development of Resolution 1325 (Björkdahl and Mannergren Selimovic 2016). By engaging with the UN, new spaces for women's transnational activism were established and ideas about WPS were diffused globally. The UN's International Women's Decade (1975–1985) contributed to bringing about a new era in women's activism (Tinker and Jaquette 1987). The four UN women's conferences in Mexico City (1975), Copenhagen (1980), Nairobi (1985), and Beijing (1995) mobilized thousands of women (Friedman 2007). The conference in Beijing became the "turning point" for the involvement of civil society in the global peace and security structure and the conference proceedings were precedent in their focus on women's participation as a transformative force (Naraghi-Anderlini 2007: 7).

Since the conference, the number and importance of women's CSOs have grown around the globe. Innovative networks that connected local grass-roots organizations with global institutions empowered women and created space for women's agency (True and Mintrom 2001). These organizations were part of a larger global movement that broadened the understanding of security to include human security. The Agenda for Peace launched in 1992, by then UN Secretary-General Boutros-Boutros Ghali, brought into focus peacebuilding and opened up space for bottom-up approaches, and the thinking on Women, Peace, and Security as a coherent agenda took off (Pratt and Richter-Devroe 2011: 491). In 2000, at the fifth review conference of the 1995 Beijing Declaration, a number of key nongovernmental organizations (NGOs) came together in the NGO Working Group on Women and Armed Conflict (NGOWG) with the explicit aim to lobby for a UN Security Council resolution on the protection of women in conflict and their right to participation in peace processes (Pratt and Richter-Devroe 2011: 492; Hill et al. 2003). Women's CSOs worked together with UN bodies and a number of governments to draft the key pillars of Resolution 1325 (see chapter 4 in the volume).

Women activists as well as feminist scholars point out that Resolution 1325 has evolved into an important site for civil society activism. This work has to a large degree shaped the present directions for CSOs concerned with women and peace in their strategic choices as well as the topics they have conceived of as central to the WPS agenda. Thus, the establishment of the resolution meant the making of a new international norm, and it is pertinent to notice the increasing influence of women's CSOs as norm entrepreneurs spearheading the norm development underpinning Resolution 1325 (Tryggestad 2009).

Institutionalization

For a set of norms, such as those inherent in the WPS agenda, to be maintained over time and to eventually affect practice, they need to be institutionalized. The process of institutionalization is characterized by how an idea, norm, or set of norms becomes mainstreamed into discourse and procedures, and thereby is able to create changes in policies and programs that affect future practices. Changes in rhetoric and discourse are often the first indications of institutionalization, and they may be followed by procedural and policy changes as well as the setup of new institutional mechanisms and allocations of financial resources to advance the new agenda. Once institutionalized, collectively held norms will become powerful and introduce practices not previously considered relevant or efficient, and thus induce new patterns of behavior (Björkdahl 2008: 138).

Transnational networks of women's CSOs spearheaded the institutionalization of the WPS norms, and they were able to provide the political momentum and societal pressure for the establishment of gender mainstreaming institutions (True and Mintrom 2001). A study of 157 country cases conducted by Mintrom and True found that transnational networks, such as those with a presence at United Nations global women's conferences, were strongly associated with the discursive changes and the adoption of international and national institutional mechanisms designed to promote greater gender equity (True and Mintrom 2001). Through these transnational civil society networks, information, resources, and strategies were shared and this contributed to consolidating the WPS agenda (True 2003). Powerful slogans such as "democracy without women is no democracy," and "women's rights are human rights and human rights are women's rights" helped change the global discourse about women in international relations. Discursive changes were important since they tend to incrementally translate into changes in policy and practice.

CSOs also worked with and empowered key gender entrepreneurs and "femocrats," and feminist policymakers built bridges to women's CSOs, feminist activists, and feminist research while working within institutions to change them from the inside. Thus, jointly they were able to ensure gender mainstreaming and to promote key mechanisms through which gender can be taken into account, such as compiling gender-disaggregated data, gender budgeting, integration of gender analysis into conflict programming and early warning, as well as establishing gender focal points (True 2003; Aharoni 2014).

The development of the International Criminal Court (ICC) exemplifies how global civil society can play a key role in the establishment and institutionalization of the WPS agenda in an international body beyond the Security Council (Chappell 2015). In the 1990s, following the landmark achievements of the ad hoc tribunals for the wars in Bosnia-Herzegovina and Rwanda concerning the criminalization of conflict-related sexual violence, advocacy began for a permanent international criminal court. A core body of about twenty-five CSOs formed the Coalition for the International Criminal Court (CICC) to advocate for a legal framework that institutionalizes jurisdiction on conflict-related sexual violence (Glasius 2007). Their efforts bore fruit. The 1998 Rome Statue of the ICC establishes that rape, sexual slavery, enforced prostitution, forced pregnancy, and enforced sterilization are crimes against humanity (Article 7 [1]). Further, it establishes the protection of victims and witnesses with special regards for victims of sexual or gender-based violence, as well as the fair representation of male and female judges. The CICC has grown to 2,500 organizations from 150 countries that closely monitor the politics around the court (International Criminal Court 2014).

An important achievement for the long-term institutionalization of the WPS agenda at the ICC was the Gender Policy Paper, launched by the Office of the Prosecutor in 2014. The policy document was developed through close consultations with civil society and draws up guidelines for the integration of a gender perspective and analysis throughout all stages of the court's work including prosecutions. The policy paper states that a gender analysis should be undertaken of all crimes under its jurisdiction, and that a gender perspective must be integrated in all its interactions with witnesses. The policy also stresses the need for continued consultations with victim organizations, thus institutionalizing the active presence of civil society at the court (International Criminal Court 2014: 5).

Likewise, women's CSOs are a driving force behind institutionalization processes at the national level. Potentially powerful, national platforms for CSOs are the National Action Plans (NAPs). They were established in a concomitant resolution in 2009, Resolution 1889, as a means to realize the Resolution 1325 agenda at national level. The NAPs can be read as blueprints for how states prioritize, outlining key areas that states will monitor and work on in order to implement Resolution 1325 (George and Shepherd 2016). In Resolution 1889, civil society actors were identified as key to the process of localizing the global WPS agenda, and the development of NAPs typically involve consultation with local civil society (Björkdahl and Mannergren Selimovic 2015). However, a number of case studies reveal that the extent of the influence of CSOs on the process of developing NAPs is highly dependent on local dynamics. In Nepal, for example, the NAP was developed in an inclusive, ongoing process with strong local grounding in CSOs (Miller et al. 2014: 115), whereas in Bosnia-Herzegovina the role of CSOs was more marginal (Björkdahl and Mannergren Selimovic 2015).

Implementation and Practice

Implementation is the process of moving an idea from concept to reality. In this case, it is about enacting the actual set of norms pertaining to women's rights in peace and conflict (Finnemore and Sikkink 1998; Aharoni 2014). The task is to implement and put into operation Resolution 1325 recommendations and to ensure that women's groups receive concrete, practical, financial and technical support. Case studies demonstrate that Resolution 1325 is being implemented in different ways at the global, national, and local level, indicating that multiple interpretations are possible of the WPS agenda, and possibly the emerging norm is vague and ambiguous (Joachim and Schneiker 2012). Thus, to realize the WPS agenda's transformative potential, it needs to move from commitments to accomplishments.

CSOs are often delegated to implement the agenda in cooperation with international and national organizations, states, and various other actors concerned with translating the rhetoric of WPS into practice. Grass-roots organizations play an important bridging function as their work is grounded in practice. A visible practice with high impact is how in the midst of war and conflict, CSOs have often engaged in efforts to end violence. Women's organizations have in several instances managed to persuade opposite sides to the negotiation table, thus participating as a driving force through direct action. The Liberian grass-roots movement, "women mass action for peace," was able to force an end to the civil war in 2003 by approaching rebel groups and persuading many of them to hand in their guns (Mannergren Selimovic et al. 2012: 71). In Libya women were involved in the negotiations of local truces (Kammars Larsson and Mannergren Selimovic 2014). In the ongoing conflict in Syria, the Syrian Women's Advisory Board, composed of twelve independent civil society representatives, give recommendations to the UN Special Envoy for Syria in order to assist the peace talks and end war (UN Women 2016).

Evidence points to the crucial role of such involvement as it is through peace negotiations that the new social contract and the new postwar order are established. Two strategies have emerged as crucial for the involvement of civil society and women. First, to invite representatives from women's CSOs to the formal negotiation process to allow for actors beyond the (often male) political and military elite (UN Women 2015). Second, to give more weight to informal processes (so called track II negotiations). Both these strategies recognize the need to take on the perspectives of civil society representatives. The implementation of Colombia's gender-sensitive peace accord will potentially have a deep impact when it comes to women's participation in transitions from war to peace (see chapter 36 in this volume). The Colombian case is unprecedented and a blueprint of the gains made in the implementation of the 1325 agenda. This is made clear when comparing it to the Bosnian peace negotiations in 1995, in which no women participated. Civil society was completely sidelined, despite being very active in interethnic cooperation and other peace efforts immediately after the ceasefire (Lithander 2000). In the time span between these two processes, from 1995 to 2016, the WPS agenda brought recognition and legitimacy to civil society actors' right to participate.

A common and crucial role for CSOs in fragile societies transitioning from war to peace is to provide service to citizens when the state fails to do so. They may provide psychosocial care to victims; launch microcredit schemes that help women support their families; escort vulnerable victims to court proceedings; or run mobile gynecologist clinics. One such example, is the widow's organization AVEGA (Association de Veuves du Genocide Agahozo) in Rwanda. With thousands of members organized in local self-help groups, AVEGA is a support system and a powerful advocacy platform that helps women who have suffered multiple harms. They are widows, but may also be rape victims and HIV positive as a consequence, and have taken on the caring for orphans (Avega-Agahozo, n.d.).

Many women's organizations are involved in addressing conflict-related sexual violence and strive for acknowledgment of these crimes in ways that aim to construct victimhood as a site for powerful agency. In the countries of former Yugoslavia, the Women's Court is a transformative initiative that was launched by a number of CSOs. Not a legal court, it functions as a platform for personal narratives that are made public in order to make the crimes against women public, prevent further silence, impunity, and retroactive revision of history. It is also a case of rare cooperation across ethnic divides, which builds upon decades of women's cooperation since the end of the war in 1995. In the court's hearing in Sarajevo in May 2015, thirty-eight women survivors of war violence testified in public, in person, without interruptions (Clark 2016). The deeply personal stories were amplified through this collective action of defiance and resistance against the dominant, gendered nationalist narratives (cf. Mibenge 2013: 4).

The engagements of CSOs, however, to address crucial gaps in states' commitments to the WPS agenda come with a risk. States may outsource service provision to (often internationally funded) civil society and thus may avoid a long-term integrated strategy for addressing gender justice gaps. Paradoxically, it may mean that a service-providing civil society may in effect uphold the status quo and hinder state level transformations toward a gender-just peace. A way to detect this discrepancy is to closely monitor the implementation of the NAPs. A case in point is the Bosnian action plan, adopted in 2010. One of its goals is to develop cooperation with civil society actors in the national implementation of Resolution 1325. Yet, the future role envisioned for CSOs in the NAP text is only as service providers, expected to step in where state institutions are unable or unwilling. The same tendency can be noted in the NAP for Rwanda. Thus, civil society is engaged primarily as a space for service provision, filling in implementation gaps that states do not address (Björkdahl and Mannergren Seimovic 2015).

CONCLUSION AND CHALLENGES AHEAD

This chapter has discussed the role civil society plays with regards to the WPS agenda. From agenda-setting to institutionalization and implementation at the local, national, and global level, women's CSOs emerge as key actors. Their crucial role is reflected in Resolution 2122 (2013), which encourages women's full participation in all levels of decision-making and pays special attention to the role of civil society (UN 2013).

Nevertheless, several gaps and contentions have emerged in our overview. We can see that, concerning *agenda-setting*, there are some topics that have been pushed to the margins. The topic of anti-militarization, at the center of the women's movement for more than a century, is not so salient in the agenda of global civil society. Some critics claim that prominent CSOs for strategic reasons have toned down anti-militarism in favor of the key themes of Resolution 1325 agenda (Gibbings 2011). Yet, as evidenced in the UN Women's Global Study, it remains a top priority among many local CSOs. The study, based on wide consultations of women's groups, concludes as follows: "Women spoke with one voice from every continent to convey a key message to the Security Council. The United Nations must take the lead in stopping the process of militarization and militarism" (UN Women 2015: 25; see also McLeod 2011). How to bridge this apparent gap in priorities between different sections of civil society will be an important task ahead.

When it comes to conflict-related sexual violence, CSOs have been, as we previously noted, very successful in their advocacy. The challenge ahead is to make sure it remains a top priority as the gaps are still daunting when it comes to institutionalizing and implementing efforts to address these crimes. CSOs will also need to engage with the ongoing debate on how not to let "hyper-attention" to rape and a discourse of victimhood privilege a passivizing objectification of women. Initiatives such as the Women's Court presented earlier are promising in this regard.

Concerning *institutionalization,* we can see that NAPs are potentially powerful instruments that CSOs can use to encourage states to institutionalize the WPS agenda at the national level. Yet, civil society actors are sometimes sidelined in the NAP processes and the space for CSOs varies widely from context to context. A great challenge for civil society is to find ways to engage with the institutionalization processes in meaningful and inclusive ways, both in countries that have not yet commenced the NAP process, and others who will revise existing NAPs.

With regards to *implementation*, women's CSOs at the local level engage in a great variety of activities that directly implement the ideas and ideals of the WPS agenda. We have already pointed out that a negative consequence is that states can refrain from long-term strategies for implementation. Another aspect of this relationship is that it may undermine the watchdog function of civil society. As CSOs, in effect, become subsidiary implementers of state politics, they may find it hard and too costly to criticize the state.

With the latest addition of the UN Security Council resolutions on Women, Peace, and Security, Resolution 2242 (2015), a new avenue has opened up for CSOs to exert influence, which ultimately may strengthen their role in agenda-setting at the highest level. The resolution commits the council to regularly engage with civil society actors through briefings, and calls for the creation of an Informal Experts Group whose recommendations will feed into all missions of the Security Council. Such structures can strengthen a more systematic and coordinated approach that opens up opportunity for the sustained involvement of CSOs at the highest level (UN 2015).

CSOs are heterogeneous and active in a multitude of local, national, and global spaces. In this they are unique in the connections made between global elites and grass-roots activists. This connection is crucial for the advancement of the WPS agenda. From the cases of Colombia and Syria we note that there is a need for CSOs to mobilize donors and advocates to support the implementation of WPS in regions and in local sites where resistance against these norms is firm. Thus, the grounding of the WPS agenda is imperative for its potential to have a truly transformative effect on societies, which allows them to escape cycles of conflict and turn from gender inequality to gender justice.

REFERENCES

Aharoni, S. "Internal Variation in Norm Localization: Implementing Security Council Resolution 1325 in Israel." *Social Politics* 21, no. 1 (2014): 1–25.

Avega-Agahozo. Home Page, n.d., http://avega.org.rw

Björkdahl, A. "Norm Advocacy: A Small State Strategy to Influence the EU." *Journal of European Public Policy* 15, no. 1 (2008): 135–154.

Björkdahl, A., and J. Mannergren Selimovic. "Gender—The Missing Piece in the Peace Puzzle." In *Dimensions of Peace: Disciplinary and Regional Approaches*, edited by Oliver P. Richmond, S. Pogodda, J. Ramovic, 181–192. London: Palgrave McMillan, 2016.

Björkdahl, A., and J. Mannergren Selimovic. "Translating UNSCR 1325 from the Global to the Local: Protection, Representation, and Participation in the National Action Plans of Bosnia-Herzegovina and Rwanda. *Conflict, Security and Development* 15, no. 4 (2015): 311–335.

Chappell, L. *The Politics of Gender Justice at the International Criminal Court.* Oxford: Oxford University Press, 2015.

Clark, J. N. "Transitional Justice as Recognition: An Analysis of the Women's Court in Sarajevo." *International Journal of Transitional Justice* 10 (2016): 67–87.

Falch, Å. "Women's Organizations: A Driving Force Behind Women's Participation and Rights." *PRIO Policy Briefs* 3. Oslo: Prio, 2010, https://gps.prio.org/utility/DownloadFile.ashx?id=68&type=publicationfile.

Finnemore, M. and K. Sikkink. "International Norm Dynamics and Political Change." *International Organization* 52, no. 4 (1998): 887–917.

Friedman, E. "Gender the Agenda: The Impact of the Transnational Women's Rights Movement at the UN Conferences in the 1990s." *Women's Studies International Forum* 26, no. 4 (2007): 313–331.

George, N., and Shepherd, L. "Women, Peace and Security: Exploring the Implementation and Integration of UNSCR 1325." *International Political Science Review* 37, no. 3 (2016): 297–306.

Gibbings, S. L. "No Angry Women at the United Nations: Political Dreams and the Cultural Politics of United Nations Security Council Resolution 1325." *International Feminist Journal of Politics* 13, no. 4 (2011): 522–538.

Glasius, M. *The International Criminal Court: A Global Civil Society Achievement.* Abingdon, UK: Routledge, 2007.

Hill, F., M. Aboitiz, and S. Poehlman-Doumbouya. "Nongovernmental Organizations' Role in the Build up and Implementation of Security Council Resolution 1325." *Journal of Women in Culture and Society* 28, no. 4 (2003): 1255–1269.

International Criminal Court. "Policy Paper on Sexual and Gender-Based Crimes." June 2014, https://www.icc-cpi.int/iccdocs/otp/otp-policy-paper-on-sexual-and-gender-based-crimes--june-2014.pdf

Joachim, J. and A. Schneiker. "Changing Discourses, Changing Practices? Gender Mainstreaming and Security." *Comparative European Politics* 10, no. 5 (2012): 528–563.

Kaldor, M. *Global Civil Society. An Answer to War.* Cambridge: Polity Press, 2003.

Kammars Larsson, D., and J. Mannergren Selimovic. "Gender and Transition in Libya." UI Paper no 8. Stockholm: The Swedish Institute of International Affairs, 2014.

Keck, M., and K. Sikkink. *Activist Beyond Borders. Advocacy Networks in International Politics.* Ithaca, NY: Cornell University Press, 1998.

Lipschutz, R. D. "Bio Regionalism, Civil Society, and Global Environmental Governance." In *Bioregionalism*, edited by M. V. McGinns, 101–120. London and New York: Routledge, 1999.

Lithander A., ed. *Engendering the Peace Process: A Gendered Approach to Dayton and Beyond.* Stockholm: Kvinna till Kvinna, 2000.

Miller, B., M. Pournik, and M. A. Swaine. *Women in Peace and Security through United Nations Security Resolution 1325: Literature Review, Content Analysis of National Action Plans, and Implementation.* Institute of Global and International Studies, The George Washington University, 2014.

Mannergren Selimovic, J., A. Söderberg Jacobson, and Å. Brandt Nyquist. *Equal Power— Lasting Peace. Obstacles for Women's Participation in Peace Processes.* Stockholm: Kvinna till Kvinna, 2012.

McLeod, L. "Configurations of Post-Conflict: Impacts of Representations of Conflict and Post-Conflict upon the (Political) Translations of Gender Security within UNSCR 1325." *International Feminist Journal of Politics* 13, no. 4 (2011): 594–611.

Mibenge, C. S. *Sex and International Tribunals. The Erasure of Gender from the War Narrative.* Philadelphia: University of Pennsylvania Press, 2013.

Mohan, G. "The Disappointments of Civil Society: The Politics of NGO Intervention in Northern Ghana." *Political Geography* 21, no. 1 (2002):125–154.

Naraghi-Anderlini, S. *Women Waging Peace: What They Do and Why It Matters.* Boulder, CO: Lynne Rienner, 2007.

Pfaffenholz, T. "Civil Society and Peace Negotiations: Beyond the Inclusion–Exclusion Dichotomy." *Negotiation Journal*, 30, no. 1 (2014): 69–91.

Pratt, N., and S. Richter-Devroe. "Critically Examining UNSCR 1325 on Women, Peace, and Security." *International Feminist Journal of Politics* 13, no. 4 (2011): 498–503.

Rome Statute of the International Criminal Court, 1998, https://www.icc-cpi.int/nr/rdonlyres/ea9aeff7-5752-4f84be940a655eb30e16/0/rome_statute_english.pdf.

Scholte J. A. "Civil Society and Democracy in Global Governance." *Global Governance* 8, no. 3 (2002): 281–304.

Shepherd, L. "Constructing Civil Society: Gender, Power, and Legitimacy in United Nations Peacebuilding Discourse. *European Journal of International Relations* 21, no. 4 (2015): 887–910.

Tinker I., and J. Jaquette. "UN Decade for Women: Its Impact and Legacy." *World Development* 15, no. 3 (1987): 419–427.

True J., and M. Mintrom. "Transnational Networks and Policy Diffusion: The Case of Gender Mainstreaming." *International Studies Quarterly* 45, no. 1 (2001): 29–59.

True, J. "Mainstreaming Gender in Global Public Policy." *International Feminist Journal of Politics* 5, no. 3 (2003): 368–396.

Tryggestad, T. "Trick or Treat? The UN and the Implementation of Security Council Resolution 1325 on Women Peace and Security." *Global Governance* 15, no. 4 (2009): 539–557.

United Nations (UN). "Security Council Resolution 2242." UN Doc. S/RES/UN 2242, October 13, 2015.

United Nations (UN). "Security Council Resolution 2122." UN Doc. S/RES/UN 2122, October 18, 2013.

UN Women. "Women of Syria: A Strong Constituency for Peace." September 1, 2016, http://www.unwomen.org/en/news/stories/2016/9/women-of-syria-a-strong-constituency-for-peace.

UN Women. "Preventing Conflict, Transforming Justice, Securing the Peace. A Global Study on the Implementation of United Nations Security Council Resolution 1325." New York: UN Women, 2015, http://www.peacewomen.org/sites/default/files/UNW-GLOBAL-STUDY-1325-2015%20(1).pdf.

CHAPTER 34

WPS AND TRANSNATIONAL FEMINIST NETWORKS

JOY ONYESOH

WOMEN, Peace, and Security (WPS) discourses and practices provide opportunities and an enabling environment for women to participate meaningfully in navigating conflict resolution and peace processes. UN Security Council Resolution 1325 and its subsequent resolutions are broad blueprints for the substantive engagement of women in the international (and national) peace and security discourse. Resolution 1325 signaled a shift from the militaristic security discourse to a more comprehensive focus on human security. This takes into cognizance the different factors that affect the security of humans and especially women in times of conflict and peace. In conflict areas around the world, women are mobilizing and networking toward ensuring the resolution of conflict and the protection of women from all kinds of discrimination and violence. Women and girls continue to experience war and armed conflicts in a disproportionate way including being targets of gender-based and sexual violence (GSBV) (Cohn 2013). The perceived and experienced vulnerabilities of women and children, and the expansive contribution women bring to the table have been a propelling force behind the WPS agenda. Resolution 1325 on WPS provides the framework for women to express their agency in reknitting the social, economic, political, and cultural fabrics of their societies during and after conflict (Delargy 2013). This process has motivated women to build alliances across borders, sharing experiences and building a network of support systems, especially within similar contexts. The WPS agenda has become a unifying process for women sharing the vision of substantively participating in the process of building peace and stability in their societies.

This chapter aims to address the following questions: What is a transnational feminist network and how does it serve in the implementation of the WPS agenda? How does the Women's Situation Room (WSR), as an example of a transnational feminist network, perform a decolonizing function for the WPS agenda?

The Women's Situation Room is a women led, civil society initiative, that seeks to increase women's substantive participation in political processes and conflict prevention in accordance with UNSCR 1325. I use the example of the WSR throughout this chapter to illustrate the promises and pitfalls of feminist transnational networks in implementing the

WPS agenda. My purpose is to build a bridge between theoretical and contextual debates around WPS and states' responsibility toward its successful implementation. I first discuss the transnational origins of WSR as spaces for the substantive implementation of WPS. Second, I examine the WSR process in the Nigerian context. Finally, I discuss the challenges of WSR in implementing the WPS agenda from a postcolonial feminist perspective, and explore avenues for the institutionalization of WPS through the Women's Situation Room.

The conceptual underpinnings of the WPS agenda revolve around gender being linked to conflict and women's agency as peacemakers. Advocates of WPS understand gender as a system of power that impacts on processes of conflict, conflict prevention and resolution, and peace-building. Pratt and Richter-Devroe (2011) emphasize the importance of studying and understanding the way gender intersects with other root causes of conflict and war in the translation and implementation of the WPS agenda. They discuss the importance of context in the translation of the WPS agenda and the careful navigation of the discourse on gender being central to the causes of war and conflict so as to avoid stereotyping women from the Global South as victims without agency. There is, however, an understanding that gender inequality, among other factors, is intrinsically linked in a nonlinear relationship to the causes and consequences of conflict (Cohn 2013). Access to the negotiation table and peace talks, as well as the ability to participate actively in times of conflict in the defense of the community is linked to gender constructions and identity (De Alwis et al. 2013). The WPS agenda in the Global South has nuances of the valorization of conflict that is associated with patriarchy, colonialization, representation, and identity politics. Mills (2009) a postcolonial feminist posits that women's marginalization, oppression, and inequality are historically located and thus cannot be framed by gender alone. She argues that a material feminist analysis is critical for social movements and feminist struggle if an understanding of structures and representations are to be understood. Her argument makes a case for the contextualization of the WPS agenda. The National Actions Plans (NAP) on WPS, while not the only way of implementing UNSCR 1325 and related resolutions, provide a pathway for a contextual analysis of the WPS agenda.

WOMEN'S SITUATION ROOM AND TRANSNATIONAL FEMINIST NETWORKS

Moghadam (2005: 4), describes transnational feminist networks (TFN) as "structures organized above the national level that unite women from three or more countries around a common agenda . . ." Comfortini (2012) understands transnational feminist practices as a shift in analysis from local, regional, and national cultures to processes and relations across cultures that take cognizance of the local in relation to the larger cross-national processes. Deepening her insights, this chapter invokes an understanding of TFNs as tools and practices shaped by diverse understanding and subjectivities of individual and collective agency around a common agenda across national borders (Nagar and Swarr 2010). From this perspective, the Women's Situation Room (WSR) project can be analyzed as a TFN engrained into local context but within a larger cross-national structure.

In tracing the evolution of transnational feminist mobilization, Tripp (2006) notes that the mid-1800s marked the beginning of the "first wave of transnational feminist movement," which focused on issues of peace and suffrage. The second wave started in 1945, when women became active in efforts to secure independence for their countries and resist colonization. It was during this period that many women's movements emerged in the Global South independent of the women's movements in the West. The third wave of transnational feminist movement spans from 1985 to today, and this period marks the challenge of the ideological dominance of the North by the Global South. Yet, transnational feminist movements nevertheless push toward the consolidation of a common agenda. The transnational feminist paradigm draws from postcolonial feminist theories, which promote contextual analysis, diverse subjectivity, and recognize the impact of colonial legacies, which continuously shape the social, economic, and political oppression of women and men (Nagar and Swarr, 2010). Transnational feminist practices involve social movements across borders and cultures that work together to understand the role of gender, the state, and civil society forces in resisting patriarchal and capitalist structures.

WSR was established in 2011 by the Angie Brooks International Centre in Liberia as a process to support women's active participation in peacebuilding in accordance with UNSCR 1325. Concerns surrounding the 2011 elections in Liberia and the understanding that women need to participate substantively in the prevention of electoral violence motivated the International Centre to establish the WSR. The objective of the WSR is to provide a platform for women's groups to strategize, plan, and respond rapidly to election related issues in a coordinated manner. Furthermore, the WSR works to establish a network of women peace activists in African countries that are conducting elections, activists equipped with the requisite skills and knowledge to prevent and respond to political and electoral violence and emergencies before, during, and after the election. In addition, they aim to successfully replicate the African Union Best Practice as part of the Gender Is My Agenda Campaign (GIMAC) in African countries having elections, and to strengthen women's solidarity beyond borders by showcasing their ability to constructively launch preventive measures ensuring elections take place in a manner that fosters an enabling environment and an all-inclusive process.

The WPS agenda provides a framework for the implementation of the WSR in countries of replication. UNSCR 1325 and related resolutions recognize that peace is inextricably linked with equality between women and men. Furthermore, it affirms the importance of equal access and the full participation of women in power structures and in all efforts geared toward peace and security. The resolution is rooted in the premise that women's inclusion, their presence and participation in the process, their perspectives, and their contributions to the crucial dialogues will improve the chances of attaining viable and sustainable peace. The resolution is cognizant of gender as a resource for sustainable peace which is in consonance with the WSR mottos, "Peace is in our Hands" and "Investing in Peace" reaffirming the importance of an inclusive peace process that engages all stakeholders irrespective of gender and affiliations. The WSR process, implements the WPS agenda by translating UNSCR 1325 and related resolutions into context specific actions, such as capacity building, advocating for an inclusive peace process, intervention and mediation by national and transnational women representatives, coordination of activities of women and youth groups on peace campaigns, political, legal, gender, and conflict analysis, media engagement and training, observation of the election polling process, and recording and documenting the WSR replication process. The WSR sets up a physical situation room that receives calls of incidents and situations happening around the country, especially in targeted regions which have been identified as "hot spots" for violence. WSR works toward the quick resolution of the conflicts by engaging a team of African women mediators, police, the electoral monitoring body, and other stakeholders. The physical room has incident report collation officers, analysts, a team of women mediators from across the region, as well as a national and international coordinator. The manner of setting up the physical room depends on the context and dynamics within the country. One remarkable feature of the room is the mass number of women that participate in conflict resolution, early warning, and response structures at different levels.

WSR has gained currency in Africa as a process that mobilizes women in collaboration with youth to ensure their active participation in peaceful and democratic electoral processes. Key stakeholders in countries of replication are engaged and lobbied to commit to peace before, during, and after elections, and a robust mass media campaign is one of the distinguishing bedrocks of the WSR process. The WSR aims at achieving long-lasting effects, therefore, it does not end with the announcement of election results but includes relevant follow-up activities as deemed necessary by women in the country of replication, thereby making the connection between women's essential role in conflict prevention and peace processes, and women's active participation in the electoral process, specifically related to observing, monitoring, and reporting on electoral and gender-based violence during and after the elections.

Since its adoption as a best practice by the African Union in 2012, the WSR has been replicated in Senegal in February 2012, Sierra Leone in November 2012, Kenya in March 2013, Nigeria in March 2015, Uganda in 2015 and Ghana in December 2016. The common agenda of the WSR in all countries of replication is the substantive participation of women in peace-building, using UNSCR 1325 as a tool for promoting the participation of women and eliciting state and international support of the process. The implementation of WSR in the country of replication is designed to culturally translate UNSCR 1325 to respond to local realities shaped by the countries' political contexts, with lessons learned and best practices recorded for use in future replications. By integrating perspectives from other countries of replication, networking with women from other African countries, and inviting them to participate in the countries of replication's implementation process, a cross-national TFN emerges that builds on the expertise of the women involved and their experiences of past replication.

WOMEN'S SITUATION ROOM IN NIGERIA

Before the Nigerian parliamentary election in 2015, tensions were building as a result of divisive campaigns and violence during political rallies, which were occurring during the primaries of the general elections of 2015. This was of particular concern to women's organizations, as violence is one of the major factors that deters women from participating in mainstream politics, either as voters or candidates. This warranted the need for the WSR in Nigeria, a process to promote nonviolence and women's roles as peacemakers as conceptualized in UNSCR 1325. In August 2013, Nigeria launched the first NAP on

UNSCR 1325 and related resolutions. The NAP is anchored on three priorities: increased political empowerment for women and engagement at all levels of decision-making; a more effective and credible justice and security environment for women during and after conflict; and an allocation of greater and more sustainable financial resources to support women in recovery processes.

The process was replicated in Nigeria in ten states: Anambra, Benue, Enugu, Gombe, Imo, Kaduna, Lagos, Plateau, Rivers, and the Federal Capital Territory (Abuja). The ten states were selected based on early warning reports of violence, and these states were tagged as hot spots. The Nigerian women established the Women's Situation Room/Nigeria Platform for Peaceful Elections (NWPPE), which comprised sixteen women's national networks in Nigeria. This platform was inaugurated in December 2014, and chaired by the Women's International League for Peace and Freedom, Nigeria (WILPF) with support from UN Women and the United Nations Development Fund. The WSR-Nigeria's national secretariat was in Abuja with state secretariats in the ten states. A national coordinator oversaw the national secretariat of WSR, while state coordinators were responsible for the state secretariats.

The WSR in Nigeria engaged with two of the priorities of the Nigeria NAP on UNSCR 1325 and related resolutions—namely, increased political empowerment and a more effective and credible justice system. This was translated to actionable activities at different levels and involving multiple stakeholders, such as mapping of stakeholders in the implementation of the WPS agenda, training state coordinators of the WSR on UNSCR 1325 and related resolutions, training of media representatives on gender-sensitive reporting, youth groups trained on being peace ambassadors and leading peer-to-peer peace advocacy, hosting of town hall meetings to understand the local realities and to advocate for community engagement with elements of the Nigerian NAP on WPS and also strategically engaging political parties and the diplomatic community.

During the 2015 general election in Nigeria, the Women's Situation Room aimed at creating an early warning and early response mechanism by training state coordinators, networking with media, partnering with traditional gatekeepers, the Independent Electoral Commission and the Nigeria Police Force, as well as conducting training and deploying an all-female team of three hundred election observers in the ten states considered hotspots for the March 28, 2015, general elections. During the election, WSR provided a mediation mechanism through a team of eminent women from Nigeria and Africa who made timely interventions to incidents reported to the room with the support of the Independent National Electoral Commission and the Nigeria Police Force—Gender Force Unit Intervention Desks. Incidents reported from the field by the WSR election observers and the general public (by calling into the physical room on the toll-free hotlines) were collated; the data then disaggregated by type of incident and gender and further analyzed by the team of experts; and then passed to the team of women mediators, Nigeria's Police Force and the Independent National Electoral Commission (INEC), who resolved the incidents in a timely manner. The nature of the incident determined which group responded. For example, incidents of electoral violence were handled by the police desk in the situation room, while electoral process issues were dealt with by the INEC. Due to the high level of awareness that was created using the mass media, the physical situation room received a total of 4,973 calls, from the thirty-six states of Nigeria during the elections, even though the WSR was implemented in only ten states.

The WSR, Nigeria, provided further opportunities for women to mobilize around issues of collective interest, and more specifically the peace and stability of the country. These mobilizations in turn enhanced women's participation as voters, mediators, observers, and analysts in the evolving political process. WSR mobilization and advocacy activities are a tangible way of expressing the concepts and rationale of the WPS agenda, in particular the *participation, promotion, and prevention* pillars. The process provided clarity and a pathway for ongoing implementation of the NAP in Nigeria. Despite the fact that UNSCR 1325 had been in existence for over fifteen years and the Nigerian NAP for close to three years, the awareness and engagement with both tool and framework within the country was significantly low. During the Women, Peace, and Security training sessions of the state coordinators, media representatives, and other stakeholders (which were conducted by the WSR National Coordinator), a pre-evaluation assessment was done to ascertain the level of awareness on UNSCR 1325. The assessment showed that 85 percent of the participants had no knowledge of 1325, while the 15 percent who were familiar with the terms did not have an understanding of what the resolution or the NAP was all about. The low awareness and engagement of key stakeholders typifies some of the challenges in implementing WPS agenda within countries.

The targeted actions of WSR in Nigeria on improving local understandings of the WPS agenda, by creating awareness, building capacity, and creating a process of engagement with the framework of the WPS agenda, creates a responsive mechanism that holds the state accountable for its commitment toward the implementation of the WPS agenda. The Women's Situation Room acts as a transnational feminist network for implementing the WPS agenda. It provides local, national, and transnational feminists a resource for strategizing and collaborating while resisting the simple dichotomy of geographical proximity in order to create a fully transnational agenda (Dube, 2002).

INSTITUTIONALIZATION OF WOMEN, PEACE, AND SECURITY AGENDA THROUGH THE WOMEN'S SITUATION ROOM

The WSR is conceptualized as a process to increase women's substantive participation in implementing the WPS agenda within country and transnationally. It builds on the normative framework of gender equality and the multiple roles of women in conflict and peace-building. The WSR, with its expansive and diverse women's groups membership, becomes a veritable tool for the institutionalization of the WPS agenda within and across countries. This is through the fostering of women's participation in the electoral process as coordinators, voters, observers, mediators, incident reporters and analysts.

The early warning and early response mechanism that is a hallmark of the WSR process is one that can be operationalized alongside the electoral process, thereby enlarging the space for women's participation in the peace process in formal spaces and institutionalizing the implementation of the WPS agenda within states. In recognition of the need to enlarge the formal space for women's participation aside the electoral phase, WSR Nigeria, after the replication during the 2015 general elections, expanded the scope of the implementation process, by establishing a network and process in 2016, ahead of the 2019 general election. The network architecture includes 744 community organizers, 36 state coordinators, 6 geo-political zone coordinators, a national coordinator, and a loose affiliation to the transnational body. The objectives of the expanded network are to empower political constituencies by strengthening and empowering women at the local and national level to organize, mean-ingfully participate, and provide gender perspectives on policy issues. Second, it aims to en-gender political space through robust strategic political party and assembly engagement and enhanced understanding and dialogue on gender with key stakeholders. Third, the network seeks to create enabling conditions by preventing violence through establishing women-led early warning and conflict-prevention mechanisms at the community and state level as a human rights protection tool, and to promote women's solidarity across borders and show-case their ability to constructively launch preventive measures to ensure elections take place in a manner that fosters an enabling environment and an all-inclusive process. Fourth, they endeavor to promote empowered women's participation by increasing women's substan-tive participation in political processes, and by supporting and encouraging candidates to run in the election. Finally, the network aims to sustain gender change through an ongoing mentorship for aspiring women candidates and newly elected female parliamentarians by conducting leadership training for women leaders.

This expanded translation of the WSR, as seen in the current model of Nigeria, engages diverse stakeholders in creating an enabling environment for women's substantive participa-tion in the peace process beyond the electoral phase of the country. The state, as the principal stakeholder, has the responsibility of creating effective and inclusive policies and programs that ensure women's access to quality healthcare, quality education, means of economic pro-duction, decision-making and inclusive democratic governance. Their commitment to de-liver on their responsibilities is constantly under focus. As women's capacities are enhanced at community and national levels, they become more capable of holding the state account-able at different levels of representation. They achieve this by demanding that the state im-plement their duty to prevent all forms of violence and discrimination against women, by enacting and implementing gender-sensitive laws and policies, and by promoting women's substantive participation in decision-making and leadership positions. States with the polit-ical will to implement the WPS agenda can thus partner with women networks at different levels to push for a transformative agenda that is committed to comprehensive human se-curity. This partnership institutionalizes the WPS agenda and makes it more sustainable to translate the agenda into actionable activities at different levels within the state.

CHALLENGES OF THE WOMEN'S SITUATION ROOM IN IMPLEMENTING THE WPS AGENDA

The WSR has some success in the implementation of the WPS agenda, but this has not been without some challenges. These issues include the translation of the WPS within local contexts; local tensions and competition between WSR leading actors over leadership; the narrow focus of the WSR on electoral periods, which prevents long-term sustainability; its replicability to other contexts; and finally the lack of adequate funding of the process, which limits the focus and time frame of implementation.

The translation of the WPS agenda by the Women's Situation Room process highlights some of the challenges faced by women's movements within and across states in forging a common agenda. The issues of voice, participation, and empowerment are closely linked to the issues of translation of the WPS agenda. Even though there is an understanding that women are not a homogenous group, within the women's movement pushing the WPS agenda, there is always the challenge of inclusiveness throughout the process. The probing question is how do we engage with the different subgroups of women to ensure that their issues and concerns are on the table and that they are given the space to express their lived experiences? The silencing of certain narratives from the agenda is one that activists constantly have to deal with when working in different contexts. For instance, there are women living with different forms of disabilities that rarely have a platform to express their concern; they are unconsciously excluded from the very agenda that seeks to include their perspectives. Most times women with "ability" assume that they can speak (and indeed go on to speak) for this subgroup without critical reflection on the silencing this enacts. There is, therefore, an urgent need for a reframing of the engagement process to ensure that it takes into consideration the diversity within the women's groups.

The tensions between the women's national groups and the transnational body are an interesting configuration that highlight the utility of political boundaries in transnational-feminist networks. The domestic agenda of the women's groups comes into play, each seeking ownership of the process, bringing to the fore vexed questions on authenticity, representations, identity, and situated knowledge. All these affect the process of implementation, creating limitations on moving a common agenda forward. These previously listed challenges may not be unconnected to the global dilemma of donors negotiating the meaning and legitimacy of the activities of women's organizations or the shrinking space of women's formal participation in leadership. This creates situations whereby women are subtly driven by the need to be relevant and visible so as to access funds and negotiate space for participation. Thus, the process if not carefully navigated degenerates into turf control, silencing certain narratives and distorting of the WPS agenda.

In all the countries of replication except Nigeria, the Women's Situation Room has been conducted through the founding transnational body, the Angie Brooks International Centre (ABIC). This has affected the continuity of the process because of several factors, one of which is the replication of the process close to the elections, thereby limiting the scope of intervention to the active electoral phase. Furthermore, the process is constrained by women within the country of replication not committing to the broader agenda because of inadequate understanding of the process as being integral to the WPS agenda. Finally, the question becomes how to move the agenda forward after the elections, as the structure put in place is usually ad hoc and primarily for the purposes of the elections. However, the latter is connected to the ease of mobilization of financial resources, as it is easier to mobilize resources for women's political participation much closer to the elections. Most development agencies and donors have dedicated funding for women's political participation, but these are not readily available until close to the elections. This reality has negatively affected women's substantive participation in politics.

CONCLUSION

How does WSR as a transnational feminist network serve in the implementation of the WPS agenda? The previous exploration of the process of the WSR as a TFN shows that it connects experts and increases communication, political expertise, and bargaining for women's inclusion and substantive participation in mediation. Furthermore, the WSR advances the WPS agenda by employing the knowledge of the African eminent women, experts in analyzing conflict and gender within and across state boundaries, to implement conflict prevention through the early warning and response mechanism. It also expands the space for women's participation in formal leadership by training and deploying an all-female observers team, thereby dismantling patriarchal stereotypes of women's participation in the electoral process. The WSR builds solidarity among peace activists by forging a common agenda across national boundaries.

Second, as demonstrated by the case of the Women's Situation Room in Nigeria, the scope of the implementation of the WSR can be expanded beyond the electoral phase to include a holistic mechanism for conflict prevention and the promotion of women's participation in politics and decision-making at different levels. Institutionalizing the WPS agenda by keying into the mobilized constituency of the network and supporting the implementation process at different levels especially for states that have NAPs on WPS or other strategic gender polices or framework.

Third, currently the WSR has been replicated in only African countries; this model presents opportunities for further transnational feminist solidarity across other regions. The model could be adapted to suit different contexts.

Finally, the WSR functions as a postcolonial feminist strategy that takes account of the local and historical realities of women in multiple spaces in forging a common agenda for the implementation of the WPS Agenda. It recognizes, as such, that there is a need to enhance women's agency in demanding their rights, no matter what their perceived positioning.

REFERENCES

Cohn, C., ed. *Women and Wars: Contested Histories, Uncertain Futures.* Hoboken, NJ: John Wiley & Sons, 2013.

Confortini, Catia C. *Intelligent Compassion: Feminist Critical Methodology in the Women's International League for Peace and Freedom.* New York: Oxford University Press, 2012.

De Alwis, M., J. Mertus, and T. Sajjad. "Women and Peace Processes." In *Women and Wars: Contested Histories, Uncertain Futures*, edited by C. Cohn, 169–191. Hoboken, NJ: John Wiley & Sons, 2013.

DeLargy, P. "Sexual Violence and Women's Health in War." In *Women and Wars: Contested Histories, Uncertain Futures*, edited by C. Cohn, 54–79. Hoboken, NJ: John Wiley & Sons, 2013.

Dube, M. W. "Postcoloniality, Feminist Spaces, and Religion." In *Postcolonialism, Feminism, and Religious Discourse*, edited by Laura E. Donaldson and Kwok Pui-Lan, 100–120. New York: Routledge, 2002.

Mills, S. *Gender and Colonial Space.* Manchester, UK: Manchester University Press, 2009.

Moghadam, V. M. *Globalizing Women: Transnational Feminist Networks*. Baltimore: Johns Hopkins University Press, 2005.

Nagar, R., and A. Swarr. "Theorizing Transnational Feminist Praxis. In *Critical Transnational Feminist Praxis*, 1–20. Albany, NY: SUNY, 2010.

Pratt, N., and S. Richter-Devroe. "Critically Examining UNSCR 1325 on Women, Peace, and Security." *International Feminist Journal of Politics* 13, no. 4 (2011): 489–503.

Tripp, A. M. "The Evolution of Transnational Women's Feminisms." In *Global Feminism: Transnational Women's Activism, Organizing, and Human Rights*, edited by M. M. Ferree and A. M. Tripp, 51–75. (2006).

PART IV

IMPLEMENTING WPS

CHAPTER 35

....

DELIVERING WPS PROTECTION IN ALL FEMALE PEACEKEEPING FORCE
The Case of Liberia

....

SABRINA KARIM

ACCORDING to Rachel Mayanja, Special Gender Advisor to the UN Secretary–General, "without women's participation in peace efforts there can be no peace and security" (Cordell 2011: 3). Consequently, the deployment of female peacekeepers has recently become recognized as not simply "desirable, but an operational imperative" (Cordell 2011: 2). This is based on the presupposition that increasing the participation of female peacekeepers within a mission will improve the protection of local women by helping to empower women in the host community, to reduce conflict and confrontation, to improve access and support for local women, to provide role models for women in the community, to provide a greater sense of security to local populations, and broaden the skill set available within a peacekeeping mission (United Nations 2017). Consequently, female peacekeeper's potential to aid with *protection* and conflict *prevention* have served as justification for increased female peacekeeping *participation*. The peacekeeping mission in Liberia (the UN Mission in Liberia, UNMIL) has been touted as one of the most successful UN peacekeeping missions when it comes to implementing the key pillars of the Women, Peace, and Security (WPS) agenda: participation, protection, and prevention.[1] The mission was one of the first to incorporate components of the WPS agenda in its peacekeeping mandates (Karim and Beardsley 2017), and was home to the first all-female formed police units (Pruitt 2016).

Despite its many successes, however, upon closer inspection the mission has suffered from challenges associated with implementing the participation, protection, and prevention pillars. This chapter explores female peacekeeper participation, as well as their protection and prevention role in UNMIL. In addition, it examines some of the barriers that exist which inhibit them from more fully participating, protecting local women, and preventing violence. Participation in this chapter refers to the full and equal participation and representation of women at all levels of decision-making within the mission; protection refers to addressing the rights and needs of local women and girls in conflict and post-conflict settings, including reporting and prosecution of sexual and gender-based violence; and prevention refers to preventing the emergence, spread, and re-emergence of violence (Peacewomen 2013). The innovation of the all-female formed police unit (FFPU) increased the number of women in the UNMIL mission (participation), helped provide protection to women, and played a major role in the country's overall security (prevention). Yet, even with this innovation, their successes were sometimes overshadowed by other women conducting activities that are considered traditionally feminine, such as the provision of health services to locals and teaching cooking and dance classes to young Liberian children.

Moving forward, this chapter first gives a short background on the conflict in Liberia, it then provides a description of participation by female peacekeepers as well as their role in providing protection. The chapter concludes by demonstrating that even with the innovation of the FFPU, female peacekeepers still face a multitude of barriers that prevent them from fully advancing the WPS agenda.

Background on Liberia and the UN Mission in Liberia

Civil unrest in Liberia began in 1980, when a small group of indigenous officers from the Armed Forces of Liberia (AFL), led by Master Sergeant Samuel Doe, stormed the presidential palace and killed then-president William R. Tolbert, Jr. Doe was the first "indigenous" Liberian to govern the country, which since its inception as a country in 1847, was led by "Americo-Liberians" or "Congo"——freed slaves from the United States (Ciment 2013). In the late 1980s, widespread discontent with the Doe regime led to the onset of an insurgency commanded by Charles Taylor. In December 1989, Charles Taylor led the National Patriotic Front for Liberia (NPFL) into Liberia, and in 1990, two different factions defeated Samuel Doe. However, Charles Taylor and rival groups engaged in a violent power struggle until 1997 when he was elected president by 75 percent of the vote in the first round. Within several months in office, Charles Taylor began to suppress the activities of political opponents and the regime slid back into authoritarianism. By July 2000, a new armed opposition group, Liberians United for Reconciliation and Democracy (LURD) launched attacks on the government forces and advanced near the capital. Taylor declared a state of National Emergency in 2002. The situation deteriorated over the prevailing year and Taylor, who faced military defeat, resigned and fled Liberia in August 2003. One month later, the United Nations Mission in Liberia (UNMIL), with thousands of international troops, entered the country.

The mandate of UNMIL was a multidimensional one from the beginning. Among other stipulations, it stated, that the mission objectives included providing support for the implementation of the ceasefire agreement, observing and monitoring the implementation of a ceasefire agreement, providing security at key sites, implementing a disarmament, demobilization and reintegration program for ex-combatants, ensuring human rights protections, and restructuring the police force.[2] The original mandate in 2003 also stated that the United Nations Security Council (UNSC) reaffirms the "importance of a gender perspective in peacekeeping operations and post-conflict peace-building in accordance with resolution 1325" (adopted in 2000). It also "recalls the need to address violence against women and girls as a tool of warfare, and encourages UNMIL as well as the Liberian parties to actively address these issues."[3] At the time, such language relating to the WPS agenda was relatively new for the UN.

PARTICIPATION OF FEMALE PEACEKEEPERS in UNMIL

The first pillar of the WPS agenda requires women's representation in peacekeeping missions. In the early years of the mission, women constituted, on average, 2 percent of military personnel, 18 percent of police, 30 percent of international civilian staff, and 25 percent of national civilian staff (UNMIL 2010). In 2012, the numbers were, on average, 3 percent for the military and about 15 percent for the police (Karim and Beardsley 2017). At the drawdown phase of the peacekeeping mission,[4] in 2016, the percentage of females in the military was 9 percent, and in the police 11 percent.[5] These numbers can be compared to the global average for female peacekeepers of 3 percent in the military and 10 percent in the police.[6] While, as a mission, Liberia is not ranked among the top missions for the highest number of women (such as the United Nations Peacekeeping Force in Cyprus [UNFICYP] among others), the Liberian government and United Nations did make a conscious effort to recruit women into the mission (Kuehnast et al. 2011).

To gain a better understanding of factors that might influence women's participation in UNMIL, it is important to understand the recruitment processes for peacekeepers. After the UNSC passes a resolution for the creation or the continuation of a peacekeeping mission, each UN member country has to decide whether it will send contributions to the mission (and to which missions globally), how many contributions it will send, and the composition of the contribution. Military contributions may come in the form of contingents or groups of soldiers under the guidance of a commander, or they may come in the form of military observers, who deploy as individuals. Contributing countries may either send a contingent of police, known as the FFPU, or they can send individual police officers—UN Police (UNPOL). Whether countries send contingents or individuals may affect the number of women that deploy because the recruitment process is different for groups versus individuals. In interviews with female peacekeepers in UNMIL, many of them pointed to the varying recruitment methods that affect women's participation.[7] If women are a part of a battalion or formed police unit at home and this unit gets selected for deployment, then more women deploy to the mission, but if there are no women in the battalions, as is normally the case, women do not get deployed. For this reason, there are fewer women deployed by the military. In contrast, for individual selection, there is usually an application system or a process of selection determined by authorities in the country, which could make it easier for women to participate. For example, Zimbabwean female police from the UNMIL mission said that the country commanders or province heads nominate individuals who apply for the job, whereas for women in the Nigerian military, they deployed because their unit was deployed to the mission. In this way, the type of recruitment has an effect on the numbers of women that deploy.

Karim and Beardsley have found that female peacekeepers tend to be deployed to countries that are safer for women, in particular countries with higher GDP, lower levels of conflict-related sexual violence, and lower levels of peacekeeper death (Karim and Beardsley 2013, 2015, 2017). Liberia could be considered on the dangerous side given that it experienced high levels of conflict-related sexual violence (Cohen and Hoover Green 2012), has low GDP, and peacekeeper deaths,[8] which could explain some contributing countries reluctance to send higher numbers of women.[9] Indeed, the condition of the mission country is important, because recruitment into peacekeeping missions is at the discretion of the contributing countries, and contributing countries take the safety of the mission into consideration when making decisions about the deployment of women (Karim and Beardsley 2015, 2017). Thus, women's participation in UNMIL is largely decided by the characteristics of the troops and police of the contributing countries that chose to deploy troops and/or police officers to Liberia, which means that even if there is a "need" for more women, as women may contribute in a unique way to the protection and prevention pillars, the UN has little discretion to increase their supply.

FEMALE PEACEKEEPERS' ROLE IN PROTECTION AND PREVENTION

As mentioned earlier, one of the main justifications for increases in female peacekeepers is that they are may be able to help protect women and girls from sexual and gender based violence (SGBV). UNMIL actively complied with the UN Security Council Resolution 1325 protection pillar by helping the Liberian government develop a National Action Plan for the implementation of the resolution. Since 2006, UNMIL participated in the National Task Force on Gender-Based Violence (GBV), chaired by the Ministry of Gender and Development. The Task Force developed a National Plan of Action on SGBV. UNMIL also introduced two major sensitization campaigns: The Campaign against Sexual Exploitation and Abuse (2006–2008); and the Anti-Rape Campaign (2007–2008). In 2005, to enhance law enforcement response, UNMIL was instrumental in the creation and training of officers for the Women and Children's Protection Unit (WCPU) in the Liberian National Police (LNP). UNMIL was also involved in the Ministry of Justice's SGBV Crimes Unit, which was established in 2007 to consolidate and speed up the process of prosecuting SGBV cases, as well as to ensure their appropriate response. The unit is responsible for coordinating the judicial response to SGBV cases from around the country. Additionally, UNMIL was involved in operationalizing Criminal Court "E," which was set up to prosecute sexual offences and respond to the backlog of SGBV cases.

In 2004, the transitional leaders of the Liberian National Police, along with UNMIL and other international partners, created a national gender policy that laid the groundwork for correcting imbalances of gender representation by setting up a Gender Unit and responding to the needs of SGBV survivors through the Women and Children's Protection Unit. The Gender Unit, which was established with help from female peacekeepers, was charged with promoting gender equality within the LNP. In 2008, the LNP introduced a 20 percent gender quota (and in 2012, a 30 percent quota) in an attempt to increase the number of women in the historically male-dominated institution, and to improve the LNP's capacity to respond to gender-based violence—as the LNP believed that Liberian women were more likely to report rape to female officers. Female peacekeepers were instrumental in the creation of the Women and Children's Protection Unit and the Gender Unit in the LNP by finding funding for the office. They have also helped write a sexual harassment policy for the LNP and provided input for the National Rape Law, among other activities (Karim and Beardsley 2017). By 2017, the LNP had 18 percent female officers (compared with the 2 percent in 2005), hundreds of officers trained in SGBV, and the security sector on the whole has seen more women in leadership positions than ever before (Huber and Karim 2017). The LNP has also launched a female police association to mentor women within the police force.

These activities toward gender mainstreaming and ensuring gender equality by and through UNMIL in coordination with the LNP were successful as they were supported and prioritized by the strong presence of women's groups in the country who fought to help achieve peace (Gizelis 2011), and also due to Liberian's electing the first female president in Africa (Scully 2016). These practices represent accomplishments that make UNMIL unique in how it helped implement the WPS agenda in Liberia. Reports by the UNMIL mission imply that the presence of female police and peacekeepers in UNMIL has led to enhanced protection for women and girls (UNMIL 2010). Thus, the combined efforts of local women and women in the peacekeeping missions contributed to enhanced protection.

Personal interviews with female peacekeepers in UNMIL highlight a belief among the women that they made a unique contribution to this previously-mentioned success of peacekeeping operations (Karim 2016). One anecdote from a Ugandan female UNPOL officer illustrates how the presence of women enhanced law enforcement responsiveness to rape in Monrovia. When participating in a joint patrol with UNPOL and the LNP, the patrol stopped at one of the police stations, where a Liberian female wanted to make a statement about the fact that she had been raped. The male LNP officer refused to take the complaint, because he said the rape case was outdated. The Ugandan UNPOL officer was able to calm her down and compel the LNP officer to take her case. Later, when interviewing her about the experience, she explained that she followed up on the case a few days later because "women are suffering this way, the sexual harassment, maybe I could help" (Karim 2016: 10). This means that she considered one of her roles, as a female, to directly help females in the community suffering from gender-based violence. UNMIL female peacekeepers may also advocate for awareness about rape and provide practical assistance, as described by some male peacekeepers. They also believe that they lead by example, because if locals see them, it may help legitimize roles for women locally, thereby promoting gender equality in the host country. In this way, both male and female peacekeepers appear to believe that female peacekeepers have a unique and positive impact on local women in the community.

Yet, even though policymakers and female peacekeepers view female UNMIL peacekeepers as effective in providing protection, most female peacekeepers in UNMIL have very little interaction with local girls and women. Rigid gender norms about the roles women play inhibited their participation in the wide range of mission roles, especially when it came to being able to leave the base and interact with locals (Karim and Beardsley 2017). These restrictions eroded leeway to engage local civilians, particularly women.

Most interactions with locals occurred while training the Liberian National Police, which means that female UNPOL officers have more interactions with locals than women in military contingents. The restrictions for military women included not being able to leave the base, not having a vehicle, and being required to travel with men. Some women reported that they left the base once or twice during their six-month or one-year deployment, and this was when the contingent participated in whole group community-outreach programs. Many women wanted to interact more with the local population but did not have the chance to do so because of the restrictions. A female from the Nigerian contingent, when asked about extending her stay in the mission, said, "We want to go home now, [we have] no freedom, we are in the cage. We don't make friends."[10]

Yet, even for female UNPOL, engagement with locals is infrequent. In one study using surveys in Monrovia conducted by the author, respondents indicated that even when female peacekeepers were active, most often local men had contact with them instead of local women. Furthermore, the survey responses suggested that there was no effect between contact with female peacekeepers and local men perceiving that rape is less of a problem, nor between contact with female peacekeepers and inspiration among local women to join the security forces (Karim 2016). The restrictions on interactions are particularly disconcerting and paradoxical given that in order for peacekeepers to provide protection, they have to spend time in the field. As such, it may be too much to expect that locals perceive female peacekeepers as bringing an added contribution to peacekeeping missions, because female peacekeepers are unable to fully engage in the type of community outreach that is needed for protection.

PARTICIPATION, PROTECTION, AND PREVENTION: THE INNOVATION OF ALL-FEMALE FORMED POLICE UNITS

One of the ways the UN sought to advance the WPS agenda and its three pillars—participation, protection, and prevention—was through the innovation of the FFPU. On January 31, 2007, India deployed one hundred and five Indian policewomen to UNMIL, becoming the first country in the world to deploy an all-female unit to a peacekeeping mission (Pruitt 2016). Even before the unit arrived on the ground, they were a global media sensation, and were heralded as a major success for peacekeeping operations. In 2010, then Secretary of State Hillary Clinton, called the unit "an example that must be repeated in UN peacekeeping missions all over the world" (Basu 2010). All-female formed police units deployed to UNMIL from 2007 to 2016, totaled nine rotations. President Ellen Johnson Sirleaf was impressed by the FFPU's performance in their capacity as protectors and asked them to become a part of her own security detail.

The FFPU was a joint initiative between the UN's Department of Peacekeeping Operations (DPKO) and India as a member state to the UN (Pruitt 2016). The UN saw it as a way to both increase peacekeeping personnel in Liberia, which was sorely needed at the time, and to dramatically increase the number of women in the peacekeeping mission, a key goal of Resolution 1325. India's rising prominence in peacekeeping—it is one of the top contributors of peacekeepers globally—paved the way for its leadership on the FFPU concept (Pruitt 2016). India saw the FFPU as a way to be at the forefront of peacekeeping innovation (Pruitt 2016). It also provided a way to demonstrate India's growing strength in the world and geopolitical power in the peacekeeping realm (Pruitt 2016: 39). Moreover, it had the resources and capacity to provide battalions of women to the mission. India has a strong tradition of female policing, particularly focusing on women's needs. India's Central Reserve Police Service, a paramilitary branch of the police force in India, has included all-female battalions since 1986. There are currently six-thousand in the reserve force (Pruitt 2016: 30). India also has a tradition of all-women police stations, which first emerged in the state of Kerala in the 1970s. Thus, there was a readily available supply of women police to send to the peacekeeping mission.

The FFPU model also provides an important benefit to women who may not otherwise be able to participate in peacekeeping. The FFPU offer an alternative or additional option for women seeking roles in peacekeeping without the discrimination and harassment frequently reported in male-majority units (Pruitt, 2016: 85). For many women, and perhaps due to conservative gender norms in some countries, mixed-sex units are barriers to increasing the participation of women in peacekeeping. By contrast, the all-female unit could provide a culturally appropriate and more comfortable environment for more women to participate. In this way, all-female units provide unique spaces for increased women's participation.

The UN has reported on the many successes by the FFPU in Liberia (UNMIL 2010). It has stated that the units were effective in reducing the instances of SGBV in the community by being a deterrent in the community and by establishing strong communication networks with community members. According to the reports, the unit also provided sensitization mechanisms for educating community members through frequent discussions about preventing rape, and the FFPU was a resource for women in the community to report their experiences of assault. The units also engaged in a number of community-related activities, including teaching classes at a local school on topics such as dancing and cooking, and they opened their medical clinic to Liberians. Carole Doucet, UNMIL`s Senior Gender Adviser, stated that "the new and important best practice in the case of the all-female Indian FFPU is the capacity of a women-only force to effectively implement formal security provision tasks while providing positive role modeling to citizens" (UNMIL 2010: 40).

What is noticeable from these comments, particularly by policymakers and the media, is the emphasis on human security. The objective of FFPUs in missions is to provide backup, riot control, and to provide security. Members of FFPUs are usually drawn from home state's paramilitary police organizations. FFPUs act as a bridge between military components of operations and the lightly armed (though not armed in missions), often institutionally "weak" local police (Anderholt 2012). In this sense, tackling SGBV is not one of the main tasks of the FFPU, nor is community policing or training (unlike UNPOL). Yet, according to UN reports, the women in Indian FFPU viewed their participation in the mission as part of a broader security mandate, compared to mostly male units, who view the mission mandate in terms of crime reduction (Pruitt 2016: 58).

While the emphasis on human security by the FFPU is an important contribution, women in the Indian FFPU were often lauded *only* for their accomplishments in preventing SGBV and inspiring local women to join the security forces instead of their overall roles in enhancing security. Despite their mandate, the media and UN have played up the all-female FFPU's community work rather than their security provision (Henry 2012; Pruitt 2016). The implication is that women are naturally inclined to lead community-oriented projects.

Women, therefore, are celebrated for doing "women's work" in the mission. However, as a result, the FFPU, which is mandated to help prevent violence, is not actually evaluated or commended for the job of providing protection.

It is very possible that all-female police units are more likely to provide security, conceptualized in terms of human security or more broadly. However, if they are *only* acknowledged as able to provide "softer" forms of security, this undermines progress for women more broadly, because it confines women's role in the security sector to basic gender stereotypes. Moreover, by assuming that women have a particular way of providing security (human security, community policing, or SGBV), men who do the same kind of work may not be recognized. Female peacekeepers in UNMIL were not unique in their community involvement, but they were unique in the extent to which they got credit for conducting such initiatives. All contingents (including the military and the FFPUs) in UNMIL have engaged with the community, usually through civil-military relations activities (CIMIC). If such important activities are considered gender-specific, then they will not receive the full weight of attention and recognition from all peacekeepers, and instead they will be relegated to all-female units. In this way, gender sensitivity is not "mainstreamed," but rather it is sidelined as "women's work."

Regardless of the challenges in recognizing women's provision of security, the FFPU is an important peacekeeping innovation developed in the Liberian mission that could serve as a future model for other peacekeeping missions seeking to expand women's participation. Indeed, the concept has already begun to spread, with FFPUs from Bangladesh and Rwanda deployed to the Democratic Republic of the Congo (DRC) and Haiti missions (United Nations 2017).

Conclusion

Since 2003, no major conflict or violent episode has occurred and Liberia has seen two peaceful election cycles, which makes the mission successful in the eyes of the UN (Druckman and Diehl 2013). The mission's record for female peacekeeper's participation, and female peacekeepers role in protection and prevention is more mixed. On one hand, it included a mandate that specified the importance of WPS from the beginning. Yet, with respect to female peacekeeper proportions overall, the mission did not boast high levels of women. With respect to protection and prevention, the mission, and women in the mission were involved in many institutional changes that advanced SGBV protection, and female peacekeepers felt that they uniquely contributed to the protection of girls and women. However, restrictions on mobility and interactions with locals may have prevented female peacekeepers from reaching their full potential when it came to providing protection and preventing violence.

With the deployment of the FFPU, all three goals became more attainable in the mission. The FFPU increased the ratio of female peacekeepers, actively sought to be involved in human security (protection), and their mandate required them to prevent relapses of violence. Yet, despite their contribution, international attention focused largely on their achievements related to feminized work. This means that despite innovations to peacekeeping that move the WPS agenda forward, female peacekeepers still face many barriers to advance the agenda. The deployment of the FFPU to Liberia is a step in the right direction, and other peacekeeping missions can learn from UNMIL's example, but more can be done to change the overall culture of missions to promote gender equality.

NOTES

1. The other pillars include the prevention of violence, and relief and recovery from violence.
2. See UN Security Council Resolution 1509 (2003), http://repository.un.org/handle/11176/26824.
3. See UN Security Council Resolution 1509 (2003), http://repository.un.org/handle/11176/26824.
4. Drawdown means lowering the numbers of all peacekeepers in preparation for the mission to formally exit.
5. LNP records from author's visit to Liberia in January of 2016.
6. See United Nations (2017).
7. The author conducted the interviews and focus groups with permission from the United Nations Department of Peacekeeping Operations and UNMIL in May–June 2012. The interviews were conducted in Monrovia, Buchanan, and Gbarnga, and included women in the military and policewomen. Contributing countries represented include Jordan, Nigeria, Philippines, Bangladesh, India, Ghana, Kenya, Pakistan, Switzerland, the United States, Sweden, Turkey, Zimbabwe, Denmark, Nepal, Bosnia, Uganda, Gambia, and Peru. The details of methodology can be found in Karim and Beardsley (2017: 204–210) or Karim (2016: 10–11).
8. The total number of peacekeeping deaths to date is 197. See UN Peacekeeping Fatalities data, http://www.un.org/en/peacekeeping/fatalities/documents/stats_4.pdf.
9. See Karim and Beardsley (2017: 76–77) for interviews conducted with Bangladeshi military leaders on selection criteria for female deployments.
10. Restrictions on leaving the base do apply to both men and women. However, none of the male peacekeepers interviewed voiced concern about the restrictions as a key impediment to their ability to serve as peacekeepers. See Karim (2016: 15) for the quote.

REFERENCES

Anderholt, Charlotte. "Female Participation in Formed Police Units: A Report on the Integration of Women in Formed Police Units of Peacekeeping Operations," US Army War College. Carlisle Barracks, PA: Peacekeeping and Stability Operations Institute, 2012, http://pksoi.armywarcollege.edu/default/assets/File/Formed_Police_Units.pdf.

Basu, Moni. "Indian Women Peacekeepers Hailed in Liberia," CNN, March 2, 2010, http://www.cnn.com/2010/WORLD/africa/03/02/liberia.women/index.html.

Ciment, James. *Another America: The Story of Liberia and the Former Slaves Who Ruled It.* New York: Hill and Wang, 2013.

Cohen, Dara Kay, and Amelia Hoover Green. "Dueling Incentives: Sexual Violence in Liberia and the Politics of Human Rights Advocacy." *Journal of Peace Research* 49, no. 3 (2012):445–458.

Cordell, Kristin. "Security or Tokenism: Evaluating Role of Women as Peacekeepers within the United Nations Department of Peacekeeping," PRIO, Oslo, 2011.

de Jonge Oudraat, Chantal, Kathleen Kuehnast, and Helga Hernes. *Women and War: Power and Protection in the 21st Century*. Washington, DC: US Institute of Peace Press, 2011.

Druckman, Daniel, and Paul F. Diehl, eds. *Peace Operation Success: A Comparative Analysis*. Boston: Martinus Nijhoff, 2013.

Gizelis, Theodora-Ismene. "A Country of Their Own: Women and Peacebuilding." *Conflict Management and Peace Science* 28, no. 5 (2011): 522–542.

Henry, Marsha. "Peacexploitation? Interrogating Labor Hierarchies and Global Sisterhood among Indian and Uruguyuan Female Peacekeepers." *Globalizations* 9, no.1 (2012): 15–33.

Huber, Laura, and Sabrina Karim. "The Internationalization of Security Sector Gender Reform in Post-Conflict Countries," *Conflict Management and Peace Science* 35, no. 3 (2017): 263–279.

Karim, Sabrina. "Re-Evaluating Peacekeeping Effectiveness: Does Gender Neutrality Inhibit Progress?" *International Interactions* 43, no. 5 (2016): 822–847. https://doi.org/10.1080/03050629.2017.1231113.

Karim, Sabrina, and Kyle Beardsley. "Female Peacekeepers and Gender Balancing: Token Gestures or Informed Policymaking?" *International Interactions* 39, no. 4 (2013): 461–488.

Karim, Sabrina, and Kyle Beardsley. "Ladies Last: Peacekeeping and Gendered Protection," In *A Systematic Understanding of Gender, Peace, and Security: Implementing UNSC 1325*, edited by Theodora-Ismene Gizelis and Louise Olsson, 62–95. London: Routledge, 2015.

Karim, Sabrina, and Kyle Beardsley. *Equal Opportunity Peacekeeping: Women, Peace, and Security in Post-Conflict States*. New York: Oxford University Press, 2017.

PeaceWomen. "Women, Peace, and Security: National Action Plan Development Toolkit." PeaceWomen, WILPF, 2013, http://www.peacewomen.org/assets/file/national_action_plan_development_toolkit.pdf.

Pruitt, Lesley J. *The Women in Blue Helmets: Gender, Policing, and the UN's First All-Female Peacekeeping Unit*. Oakland: University of California Press, 2016.

Scully, Pamela. *Ellen Johnson Sirleaf*. Athens: Ohio University Press, 2016.

United Nations. "Women in Peacekeeping," 2017, https://peacekeeping.un.org/en/women-peacekeeping .

UNMIL. "Gender Mainstreaming In Peacekeeping Operations Liberia 2003–2009. Best Practices Report." United Nations Mission in Liberia (UNMIL) and Office of the Gender Adviser (OGA). Accra, Ghana, September 2010, http://www.resdal.org/facebook/UNMIL_Gender_Mainstreaming_in_PKO_in_Liberia-Best.pdf.

CHAPTER 36

....

SECURING PARTICIPATION AND PROTECTION IN PEACE AGREEMENTS
The Case of Colombia

....

ISABELA MARÍN CARVAJAL AND EDUARDO
ÁLVAREZ-VANEGAS

THE participation of women in peace processes occurs mainly in informal ways and at the local and grassroots levels (Bell 2004; Porter 2007). Despite widespread mobilization and their contributions to peace processes as activists, community leaders, and survivors, their efforts have hardly ever been formally supported, recognized (Cockburn 1998; Rehn and Johnson-Sirleaf 2002), or translated at the negotiation table and into peace agreements (Anderlini 2007; Bouta et al. 2005). Within the Women, Peace, and Security (WPS) Resolutions, the United Nations Security Council (UNSC) included a series of provisions to transform this situation as well as to guarantee protection for women in contexts of armed conflict among other things.

Alongside the implementation of the WPS agenda, it is possible to identify some strategies and paths that have shown to be quite successful in terms of increasing women's participation and influence in peace processes. Nonetheless, the participation of women in peace processes is still very limited at least in formal or official spaces.

Some scholars have pointed out the limitations in how the WPS agenda conceives women in both the participation and protection pillars. According to these critiques, the Security Council overlooks the real practical and normative constraints of local contexts, and does not tackle the power structures nor the "political" reasons that women are excluded from decision-making in the first place (Heathcote 2014; Gizelis and Olsson 2015) and that produce gender-based violence.

In this chapter, we critically explore the development in scholarship and policy making, of the pillars of participation and protection in peace agreements. To do so, we draw upon the case of the Havana peace process, led by the Colombian government and the Revolutionary Armed Forces of Colombia (FARC), a non-state armed group, between 2012 and 2016. This analysis stems from our research experience during this period at the *Fundación Ideas para la Paz* (Bogotá, Colombia) working on women's participation in peace negotiations in Colombia.[1] Here we propose some answers to the following questions: How is the latest peace process in Colombia situated with respect to the evolution of the participation and protection of women in peace agreements? What insight does a critical approach to WPS issues offer with respect to the Colombian case?

The chapter has four parts.[2] First, we present a review of the academic and policy developments regarding women's participation in peace processes. Second, we summarize the critical approach to the conceptualization of the participation and protection pillars of the WPS framework. Third, we reconstruct the trajectory of women's participation in the Havana process.[3] Finally, we pose some key questions about the Havana process that emerge through a critical lens on WPS.

SECURING WOMEN'S PARTICIPATION IN PEACE AGREEMENTS

Literature on women's participation in peace processes and their influence on the outcomes of peace agreements demonstrates that their inclusion has been achieved through a series of strategies and actions adopted by women's organizations, by their relationship and interaction with other actors (for example, through the forging of strategic alliances and coalitions between social organizations, structural platforms of common interests, and lobbying at multiple levels), through the establishment of certain mechanisms of participation, and the creation of conditions that guarantee that women's voices are listened (Page et al. 2009; GIZ 2014; Simic 2014; Georgetown Institute for WPS 2015). O'Reilly, Súilleabháin, and Paffenholz (2015) have also drawn attention to the importance of establishing a transparent and well-grounded selection process, and of having politics—and the public—in mind. All in all, when analyzing women's participation in peace agreements, the interaction between collective actions and other social actors and institutions, and its gendered character, cannot be understood as independent spheres, since it is crucial for the outcome of mobilization. In other words, the encounter between subjects and institutions, and the power structures in which they operate can shape collective action. (Factors that affect women's participation and protection in peace agreements are examined in detail in chapters 13 and 14 of this volume.)

WOMEN'S PARTICIPATION AND PROTECTION IN PEACE AGREEMENTS: CRITICAL APPROACH TO THE WPS FRAMEWORK

The conceptualization of women's participation and protection in UN Security Council Resolution 1325 has receive critiques from feminist scholars due to perceived limitations with respect to the issues covered in the previous section. Although subsequent resolutions on WPS adopted by the Security Council have addressed some of these remarks regarding these two pillars, most remain unaddressed.

One of the main critiques of the Resolution 1325 is that women's participation is addressed through a singular focus on formal representation. The problem with this type of approach is that it neither addresses substantive issues, nor challenges gender essentialism, which is conceived as the assumption that all women are excluded from decision-making structures, while all men have access to such structures (Heathcote 2014; Gizelis and Olsson 2015). In line with this, some authors call for an understanding of women's participation where gender is seen as involved in power relations and that recognizes women's preexisting and diverse roles at the local level, and their capacity to contribute to policies and practices (Heathcote 2014). Through this path, it is more probable that when seeking to increase women's participation, the real practical and normative limitations of the specific context will be addressed (Gizelis and Olsson 2015).

In the follow-up resolutions to 1325, especially Resolution 2122, the approach to participation moves toward a more substantive understanding of the concept and thus away from the gender essentialism of previous documents (Global Study on Preventing Conflict 2015). However, for Heathcote (2014), the latest resolutions still have some problems. First, the use of "women and girls" language simplifies the diversity of the category; second, it is noticeable that the continuity of the still-limited models of participation, are similar to those in the earlier resolutions; third, the follow-up resolutions remain silent on the issue of male privilege and masculinity as a gendered practice (see chapter 8 in this volume). Hendricks (2015) points out a similar problem with regards to gender mainstreaming in general. She states that while the approach concentrates on inclusion and capacity building, it overlooks the fact that there could be resistance on women's equal participation, or even an explicit opposition to anything associated with feminism, or with the concept of gender as in the Colombian case.

In terms of the protection approach of Resolution 1325, two main issues have been identified. On the one hand, a common critique is that the issue of protection was articulated specifically to address the issue of sexual violence, which is reflected in the fact that peace agreements that have included provisions for an (en)gendered security have mainly focused on protection from sexual violence (Gizelis and Olsson 2015; Ellerby 2015). This has implications for how women are perceived in these context, as it considers them to be mainly victims (Gizelis and Olsson 2015). On the other hand, the diverse roles that women play in their communities has been largely overlooked, reinforcing assumptions of women only as peace activists and victims. Another problem has been the inability of these frameworks to reflect the complexities of women's identities, which also includes considerations of race, ethnicity, or socioeconomic status (Hudson 2010).

Women's Participation in the Havana Peace Process

The peace process held between the Colombian government and the FARC non-state armed group, which lasted four years (2012–2016), represents an unprecedented step toward the de-escalation of the armed conflict in the country. Nevertheless, this did not mean the end of all conflict, but rather it transformed into a more localized and fragmented scenario. This reality is evident, due to the continuation of fighting between other guerrilla groups (National Liberation Army and the Popular Liberation Army) and the adaptation of organized crime and criminal economies (Garzón et al. 2016) in the local and regional spheres (Álvarez-Vanegas 2017; Álvarez-Vanegas and Pardo 2017). Women, have been victims as well as key agents in some of these structures and activities. For example, they have taken on a range of roles within the different segments of criminal economies, including coca production, illegal mining, and contraband.[4]

In terms of securing women's participation, the Havana process is touted as an exemplar model. Alongside the negotiations, the collective and persistent efforts of women's organizations, their strategic networks, their lobbying exercises and the support of local allies and the international community, managed to increase their participation (Marin-Carvajal 2016). Together with a series of mechanisms disposed to facilitate consultations between certain social groups and the negotiators, and the inclusion of their concerns in the Peace Agreement, Colombia has been able to counter, in part, the gender inequity that usually prevails in peace decision-making.

In mid-2013, almost one year after the beginning of the peace process, there was only one woman among the main negotiators, Judith Simanca alias "Victoria Sandino," as a representative of the FARC. However, the creation of a platform by women's organizations changed this situation. This platform comprised several women's organizations with a long history and experience of mobilization in support of the peace initiative called the Summit of Women and Peace (*Cumbre de Mujeres y Paz* in Spanish).[5] Some of these organizations were created more than thirty years ago and have participated in at least three peace negotiations undertaken in the country during that period. Their principal goal has been to pressure the negotiators to include women, and their concerns in the negotiations, as well as in the Peace Agreement. The platform, which gathered more than five hundred women, representing multiple sectors and identities,[6] took place in October 2013. It led to a document that included key recommendations for the incorporation of a gender perspective in all six chapters of the Agreement (ONU Mujeres 2013a).

One month after the event, the government named two women representatives as part of its negotiating team.[7] Moreover, the continuous pressure by women's organizations and the support of the international community led to the establishment of a Gender subcommission in Havana. This subcommission was structured as a technical body responsible for the revision of the Peace Agreement under the recommendations of the six delegations of representatives from eighteen organizations concerned with the rights of women and sexual minorities. The representatives traveled to Havana between late 2014 and mid-2015 to present a speech and a document before the members of the Gender subcommission, as well as some of the negotiators.[8]

At the same time, women from different sectors and regions of the country were able to express their recommendations through the participation mechanism, which the negotiators arranged to increase the inclusion of civil society. Forums and Working Tables (*Consultas ciudadanas para la terminación del conflicto armado y la construcción de una paz estable y duradera* in Spanish) are, perhaps, visibile examples of these inclusive efforts. These mechanisms were organized by the UN and the National University of Colombia between November 2012 and February 2016, so that its participants could present or send their recommendations about each of the chapters, included in the Peace Agreement (ONU Mujeres 2013b). According to official information, women's organizations submitted 18 percent of the proposals. The information gathered was systematized and delivered to the negotiators.[9]

Furthermore, women were highly represented in the cycles of visits to victims, making up 60 percent of the sixty people who were included in the delegations that spoke directly to the negotiators. Under this frame, sexual violence was brought up as one of the main concerns among the organizations active during the peace process. In fact, some of the most visible women's organizations in the country created various platforms and led multiple campaigns to explain and promote the importance of the differential treatment of victims of sexual violence in conflict.[10]

Also, during the last months of negotiations two events are worth mentioning. The first is the Interethnic Commission of Peace (ICP), which was comprised of representatives from indigenous and afro-Colombian organizations. The ICP went to Havana in June 2016 and handed a document to the negotiators calling for the inclusion of a women's and gender perspective in the Peace Agreement, and for the effective participation of women from ethnic communities during the implementation phase (CONPI 2016).[11] Second, in September 2016, the Summit of Women and Peace organized an event, which enabled approximately five hundred women to discuss and design strategies to increase the presence of women during the verification and implementation of the Peace Agreement.

Finally, alongside the peace process, there were women who had important roles in the final decisions concerning the path of the negotiations, but not necessarily very visible ones. On the government side, there was a group of senior officers, mostly women, working for the Office of the High Commissioner for Peace; the main delegate, in charge of the peace negotiations, played a key role in the promotion of women's demands and the inclusion of a gender focus in the Peace Agreement.[12] On the guerrilla's side, the growing perception of the importance of a gender focus in the Peace Agreement among some of its female commanders also contributed to support the gender subcommission and the increased power of women's voices.[13]

All of these factors established the context for the inclusion of women's concerns and a gender perspective in the Final Peace Agreement.[14] Throughout the Peace Agreement of 2016, women are recognized as major actors in the peasant economy, and mechanisms for women's participation in decision-making, concerning land use and rural development programs, are established. The agreement includes measures to promote peasant women's human development in terms of health, housing, and education in nontraditional areas. In this respect, peace is understood as an integral process related to social well-being. It recognizes the disproportionate impact of armed conflict on women's lives; guarantees equal participation in the Truth Commission, as well as in the collective reparation programs; and includes a gender focus in the processes of return and resettlement. The agreement mentions the need to adopt affirmative measures to promote women's participation in politics, including political parties, public administration, and the various forms of citizenship participation. Furthermore, it highlights the importance of women's participation in the mechanism established for the implementation phase of the agreement, including those addressing security for leaders and communities. It also considers the application of measures to overcome the barriers to women's participation due to their caring responsibilities.

Finally, it includes the promotion of women's empowerment through the strengthening of women's leadership and women's social organizations.

However, the power structures and the gendered politics in which the negotiations took place, affected the outcomes of women's participation in terms of the substantive agreement. For example, the tone and content of the final Peace Agreement was influenced by patriarchal and heteronormative norms. This was the case not just in relation to the peace negotiations, but in terms of the multiple related discussions that were taking place at that time among the Congress, citizens, and the church.

We witnessed this in the period following the signing of the first agreement. After the victory of "No" in the plebiscite (Álvarez-Vanegas, Garzón et al. 2016) one of the most persistent claims of the opposition to renegotiate the Peace Agreement was the clarification (or even the exclusion) of its gender perspective. Other arguments of the opposition had to do with the way the transitional justice process was conceived in terms of punishments and benefits to the FARC.

The opposition groups, mainly on the right of the political spectrum, including religious leaders and other conservative sectors, were opposed to the idea that gender identity is a social construction, arguing that its inclusion in the first Peace Agreement was part of a global trend under the name of "gender ideology" (Mazzoldi et al. 2016). Their reason for rejecting a gender-inclusive approach to the agreement was to protect a particular conception of family, namely, one formed by a woman and a man. Discussions escalated to a broader dispute by some of the same people who objected to key provisions that strengthened the rights of women and sexual minorities, such as the approval of same-sex marriage, adopted in November 2015 by the Constitutional Courts. The dispute also involved the draft of an educational booklet published by the Ministry of Education and the UN concerning the importance of transforming discriminatory practices toward sexually diverse populations in schools.

INSIGHTS FROM THE COLOMBIAN CASE FROM A CRITICAL GENDER PERSPECTIVE

The Colombian case raises some key questions about the conception of participation and protection in the Women, Peace, and Security agenda. We now focus on three of them.

First, how far and in what ways does the final agreement move beyond the gender essentialist approach to women's roles in peace processes? Does it capture the multilayered experiences of women and recognize women's diverse roles? Does the gender focus included in the final agreement challenge the existing gender structure that hinders women participation in decision-making?

To address these questions, we must stress the importance of taking into account the gendered political context. The first version of the Peace Agreement included an understanding of women that went beyond their roles as victims and housewives, situating them as active participants of the peace-building project. And its gender focus included some steps toward the transformation of structural gender imbalances, mentioning expressions such as "non-sexist values," "sexual diversity and gender identity," "gender-based stereotypes," "systemic gender-violence," and a "gender-based approach." In this way, it considered that a gender perspective has to do with sexually diverse groups, as well as diverse groups of women (Cuesta and Mazzoldi 2017), a key dimension that goes beyond the limited understanding of gender relations in Resolution 1325 and its follow-up resolutions.

After this version of the agreement was negotiated with the opposition, however, there were multiple changes to the gendered focus. Although these changes seemed to be language-related, they actually have several implications on public policy. For instance, the opposition groups demanded more clarity in relation to the *gender* focus, asking that the provisions should specify that they referred only to the need to guarantee equality between men and women, women's active participation in peace-building, and the recognition of their victimization in the armed conflict. They clearly stated that all expressions that implied entitlements for sexually diverse groups be taken out of the agreement, arguing that they were unconstitutional. As such, the terms mentioned earlier were replaced by "equal opportunities," "vulnerable populations," "equality between men and women," "violence against women," and "affirmative action," shifting the broader, *gender* focus back to a rights-based approach. Furthermore, the importance of the family was reinforced, although it is explicit that women's rights do not depend on any association with the family (Cuesta and Mazzoldi 2017).

There is no doubt that even if such postures confirm the basis for women's inclusion in peace and security discussions, they intentionally do not challenge gendered power structures, including male privilege that largely excludes women from decision-making at the local level. However, the new version of the agreement had a more positive side for women's groups and lesbian, gay, bisexual, transgender, and intersex (LGBTI) organizations. The inclusion of the principle of the "right to equality" was complemented with a non-discrimination principle, which includes the search for equality of historically discriminated and excluded populations, mentioning explicitly LGBTI people and ethnic minorities. This can be read as a powerful opportunity for an intersectional approach to tackling inequalities in a comprehensive way (Cuesta and Mazzoldi 2017).

A second key question with respect to the Colombian Peace Agreement is how engendered the concept of *security* is in the final agreement and to what extent *protection* is focused on sexual violence? Following the WPS Resolutions, women's organizations in Colombia have insisted on the importance of taking into account conflict-related sexual violence. These organizations suggest that it is crucial to ensure that armed groups recognize their responsibility in cases of sexual violence as part of the both the politics of reparation and the justice and empowerment processes for the victims. The importance of these two variables is that they will allow women to transit beyond their identity as victims (Cumbre de Mujeres and Paz 2015). As a result of their mobilization, the government arranged a meeting in February 2015 between the president, experts, both national and international, and women victims of sexual violence during the Colombian conflict.[15] The agreement, in its transitional justice mechanisms (Special Jurisdiction for Peace), finally included a Special Unit to investigate cases of sexual violence, Moreover, it was established that in accordance with Colombia's responsibility under the Rome Statue, amnesty would never be considered in cases of sexual violence (Acuerdo Final 2016).

Further, with respect to conflict-related sexual violence, we should not overlook its relationship with security and truth-seeking in the Colombian case. Women's organizations at the local level during the transitional justice phase in 2005 (known as the Justice and

Peace process) uncovered the responsibility of state agents and paramilitary squads in relation to sexual violence. This process had important results in reconstructing some of the cases of sexual violence that occurred during the armed conflict and led to a series of legal achievements.

In 2008, the Constitutional Court published the sentence (*auto* in Spanish) "092." This case established that sexual violence had been a systematic, recurrent, extended and invisible practice committed by all parties to the conflict. It also determined that forcibly displaced women were particularly vulnerable to sexual violence by armed and non-armed actors. Furthermore, it ordered the adoption of measures to prevent sexual violence, abuse, and exploitation against this population and provide attention to its victims. Afterwards, the Constitutional Court, in sentence (*auto* in Spanish) 009 of 2015, sided with victims, concluding that the government had failed to adopt an integral strategy for guaranteeing basic rights, such as truth, justice, and reparation to victims of sexual violence. Specifically, it demonstrated that 97 percent of the 183 cases included in the first sentence have not been prosecuted, to which the court added 456 new cases to be investigated. The court also denounced the government for failing to implement any of the thirteen programs that were supposed to prevent the differential impact of forced displacement on women and to protect displaced women rights. This experience demonstrates that while the efforts of women's organizations are at an advanced stage, there remain concerns over the recent process: Can women civilians and ex-combatants count on proper security guarantees to enable them to tell their stories and those of others, about the sexual violence perpetrated by state forces and FARC members against civilians and their own comrades.

But what are the implications of focusing on sexual violence in order to understand the relevance of protection measures for women at a local level. On this point, it is important to bring up the conception of "security" and "non-repetition guarantees" included in the Final Peace Agreement, which sets up the basis for a comprehensive understanding of protection. The text establishes a relatively specific guide to build up new principles of coexistence (not necessarily reconciliation) during the implementation phase. The security guarantees are not limited to the demobilized ex-combatants; they include all communities from the prioritized regions for the implementation phase and the country as a whole (Acuerdo Final 2016).

In terms of women's protection, the implementation phase of the Final Agreement will face three preexisting conditions that go beyond sexual violence. First, in recent years, data have shown that in terms of gender-based violence the "private sphere" remains a highly dangerous domain for women.[16] So, how should this reality of the "continuum of violence" be articulated in relation to the protection pillar of the WPS framework? How is the transition from war to peace going to affect gender-based violence at home as well as in public realms and conflict-settings?

Second, both female ex-combatants and militias will face many challenges. Women that lay down their weapons will need special protection protocols so that their transitions do not reinforce, preexistent vulnerabilities concerning gender-based violence and gender injustice. Specifically, in order to fully transition from an armed group to a society that guarantees them security and all their rights, these transitions must ensure that women are able to move beyond these injustices. Therefore, it is fundamental to examine the specific variations of the contexts for reintegration processes and to consider the vulnerabilities of the peace agreement from a WPS perspective.

Third, the strategies are still not clear that the State intends to put forward to fill the authority, legitimacy, access to justice and security gaps, and to guarantee and protect women's participation, both ex-combatants and women's organizations. This must be a major concern for the Colombian government and international partners, considering that violence against community leaders (including women) has dramatically increased since 2014 during the peace negotiation phase, and persisted since the peace agreement signing and renegotiation.[17]

CONCLUSIONS

Recent approaches to women's participation in peace agreements demonstrate that there are some factors and strategies that actors, such as governments, international organizations, and women's collectives can follow to improve women's participation and influence in this context. However, the gendered dynamics of politics within formal and informal spheres continue to constrain the advancement of a gender perspective on peace processes. Women's mobilization is intertwined with the activities of other social actors and institutions and is therefore crucial to peace outcomes. In addition, power structures and political struggles are operating to reproduce patriarchal gender relations inside and outside the context of the peace negotiations and can severely restrain their achievements. The Colombian case shows that where there are sectors that believe that the transformation of gender roles and identities threatens the values of the family they may undermine a gender-inclusive peace process.

The chapter also emphasizes the importance of accounting for women's preexisting forms of participation and knowledge, and their multidimensional experiences in attending to the concrete and normative limitations of a specific context. Affirmative measures will be insufficient to move toward gender equity, for instance, if they do not address the structures that exclude women from decision-making. In this sense, the Final Agreement, by considering women as agents in the construction of their region, situates them as more than victims and articulates a non-discriminative, rights-based approach that offers an important foundation for recognizing intersectional experiences.

Regrettably the Final Peace Agreement itself does not challenge the gendered structures that exclude women from decision-making and that reproduce gender-based violence. Hence, the efforts of women's organizations, which have achieved so much during the negotiation process, must not stop now if a real transformation of gender relations in the peace agreement implementation phase is to be achieved. These historical, national-level organizations must work together with the grass-roots collective initiatives to pool their experience and gains in the agreement to ensure that what is written materializes in practice. Furthermore, they need to ensure that the implementation of the agreement takes into account the local needs of women in terms of protection. As the Colombian case highlights, it is important not to tie women's protection exclusively to sexual violence. It is essential, therefore, that the state closes the (in)security gaps that come with the demobilization of the FARC, so that women, former combatants included, can actively participate in the peace-building process, to ensure that certain invisible forms of violence do not continue or worsen.

Notes

1. The last version of the chapter was submitted on February 2017. Needless to say, since then the political context in the country and the dynamic of the implementation of the Peace Agreement has been very volatile.
2. We would like to thank Lisa Gormley and Bela Kapur from the Centre for Women, Peace, and Security from the London School of Economics and Political Science (LSE) for their valuable comments and recommendations on the draft of this chapter.
3. The main information included in this section was gathered by the authors during the development of a non-published research that explored women's participation in peace negotiations in Colombia and in some other peace negotiations around the world. The research was conducted as part of a project of the Foundation Ideas for Peace (*Fundación Ideas para la Paz* in Spanish) during 2015, and included the review of secondary sources, press review, and other types of official and nonofficial documents, as well as a series of interviews with representatives of national and regional women's organizations.
4. Currently, Eduardo Álvarez-Vanegas, head of the Armed Conflict and Peace Negotiations area at Fundación Ideas para la Paz (FIP), and Irina Cuesta, and Génica Mazzoldi, both researchers at FIP, are researching the impact on women by criminal economies in the southwest region of Putumayo. This research is part of a project sponsored by UN-Women Colombia.
5. The *Summit* was convened among the following ten organizations: Casa de la Mujer, Ruta Pacífica de las Mujeres, Red Nacional de Mujeres, Mujeres por la paz, Colectivo de Pensamiento y Acción Mujeres, Paz y Seguridad, Grupo de Seguimiento de la Resolución 1325, Conferencia Nacional de Organizaciones Afrocolombianas (CNOA), Iniciativa de Mujeres Colombianas por la Paz (IMP), and la Asociación Nacional de Mujeres.
6. The *Summit* had the presence of women coming from thirty out of the thirty-two regions of the country, from sectors such as feminist organizations, human rights movements, peasants, victims, indigenous, afro Colombian, youth and student sectors, environmentalists, grass-roots and communal organizations, sexual diversity organizations, the catholic church, cultural movements, political parties, the academic sector, research centers, union organizations, and media sectors (ONU Mujeres 2013a).
7. Nigería Rentería, senior counselor for women, and María Paulina Riveros, former director of Human Rights at the Ministry of Interior.
8. The delegations included sixteen women and two men from national and regional organizations on conflict victims; empowerment; and women's rights defense; peace-building; artistic movements; former combatants; sexual diversity rights; peasants; indigenous; and afro-Colombian communities; among others. These organizations were Iniciativa de Mujeres por la Paz, Corporación Colombiana de Teatro, Red Nacional de Artistas, Ruta Pacífica de las Mujeres, Sisma Mujer, la Casa de la Mujer, Asociación de Mujeres por la paz y los derechos de las Mujer (Asodemuc), la Alianza tejedoras de vida, la Corporación Caribe Afirmativo, el Departamento de Mujeres de la Coordinación Nacional de Desplazados, la Asociación Nacional de Mujeres Campesinas, Indígenas y Negras de Colombia (ANMUSIC), Red Mariposas Alas Nuevas, Red Nacional de Mujeres Ex Combatientes de la Insurgencia, la Federación de Estudiantes Universitarios, la Asociación Campesina del Catatumbo (Ascamcat), and el colectivo Narrar para vivir.

9. Still held as confidential information, all these data were systematized in order to pro-
    duce different types of reports by FIP that were delivered to the representatives of the
    Colombian government in Havana.

10. Some of the organizations that have been leading this process are Humanas Colombia,
    Sisma Mujer, and Red Nacional de Mujeres, and some of the projects they carried out
    during the Peace Agreement were "Si, sucedió en Colombia" and "No es hora de callar"—
    among many others. Likewise, an initiative from the dramatic arts field called "Ni con el
    pétalo de una rosa," meant to address awareness on this issue, has gained relevance over
    the years.

11. And in fact when this Commission was created, it included among its principles the
    parity and complementarity of men and women, and it was launched the 8th of March
    on the frame of The International Women's Day (ONIC 2016).

12. Two of the most relevant actors in the Office of the High Commissioner for Peace in
    terms of intermediation between the negotiators and the women's demands were Elena
    Ambrosi, thematic director of the Office, and Mónica Cifuentes, in charge of legal man-
    agement of the Peace Agreement.

13. Two of the main visible supporters of the gender focus in the Peace Agreement were alias
    "Victoria Sandino" and Tanja Nijmeijer, part of the FARC's negotiation team, alongside
    most of the process. The former was also one of the leaders of the gender subcommission.

14. A first version of the Peace Agreement was signed on the Havana on September 26, 2016,
    and subsequently it was voted in on the 2nd of October. On this instance the public
    rejected the agreement by a small margin (49.79 percent approved the agreement, and
    50.21 percent disapproved). After the defeat, the government initiated a negotiation with
    representatives of some of the sectors that were against the agreement in order to in-
    clude some of their demands, and a new version of the document was signed in Bogota
    on the 14th of November, which this time obtained legal validity being approved by the
    Congress the 1st of December.

15. One of these events was a closed-door meeting between the president and Nobel Peace
    Prize winners Jody Williams and Shirin Ebadi. The other one was a public forum with
    the two Nobel's, as well as Paula Gaviria, director of the Unity of Service and Reparation
    for Victims; Belén Sanz, UN Women representative for Colombia; Claudia Mejía, di-
    rector of Sisma Mujer; Jineth Bedoya, Colombian journalist and activist on sexual vio-
    lence; and Hania Moheeb, Egyptian journalist and activist on sexual violence. For more
    on this, see Presidencia de la República. "Presidente Santos compartió recomendaciones
    con mujeres víctimas de la violencia." Cartagena, February 2, 2015, http://wp.presidencia.
    gov.co/Noticias/2015/Febrero/Paginas/20150202_05-Presidente-Santos-compartio-
    recomendaciones-con-mujeres-victimas-de-la-violencia.aspx.

16. Data on violence show that women accounted for 86.7 percent of the cases of partner vi-
    olence in 2015, and this type of violence has incremented in the last ten years, registering
    19.592 cases in 2006 and 22.155 in 2015. In the case of sexual violence, women constituted
    85.2 percent of the cases of this type of violence, and in 88 percent of the cases, the person
    responsible was someone close to the victim (relative, partner or ex-partner, friend,
    or the person charged with taking care of the victim), and most cases occurred in the
    victim's house (77.8 percent). The data also show that the medium age of victims of sexual
    violence for that year was 12.4 years, and that this type of crime incremented in children
    from 0 to 5 by 12.5 percent in relation with the previous year (Medicina Legal 2016).
    [AU: As meant? Correct]

17. According to data gathered by Foundation Ideas for Peace, aggression against social leaders (which include threats, forced disappearance, arbitrary detention, homicide, attempted homicide, data theft, torture, and sexual violence) increased between
2013 and 2015, and showed a slight decrease in 2016. The Foundation registered 382
cases in 2013, 553 in 2014, 678 in 2015, and 633 in 2016—a total of 2.246 cases. In 159
of those cases, the victims were women, in 765 men, and in the rest, the sex of the
victim was not registered. This means that in the cases where the sex of the victim is
known, women represent 17 percent of the cases and men 82 percent. Some preliminary interpretations of these phenomena can be found at Álvarez-Vanegas, Eduardo
"¿Quién está matando a los líderes sociales en Colombia?" *Razón Pública*, April 24,
2016,   http://www.razonpublica.com/index.php/conflicto-drogas-y-paz-temas-30/
9397-%C2%BFqui%C3%A9n-est%C3%A1-matando-a-los-l%C3%ADderes-sociales-de-
colombia.html; see also Álvarez-Vanegas, Eduardo "¿Quién sigue matando a los líderes
sociales en Colombia?" *Razón Pública*, November 27, 2016, http://www.razonpublica.
com/index.php/conflicto-drogas-y-paz-temas-30/9895-qui%C3%A9n-sigue-matando-
a-los-l%C3%ADderes-sociales-en-colombia.html.

REFERENCES

Acuerdo Final. *Acuerdo final para la terminación del conflicto y la construcción de una paz estable y duradera*. Bogotá: OACP, 2016.

Álvarez-Vanegas, E., Garzón, J.C., and Bernal, J.L.Voting for Peace: Understanding the Victory of "No". Bogotá: Wilson Center/FIP, 2016.

Álvarez-Vanegas, E., and D. Pardo. *Entornos y riesgos de las zonas veredales y los puntos transitorios de normalización*. Bogotá: Fundación Ideas para la Paz, 2017.

Álvarez-Vanegas, E. "Agendas de paz, crimen organizado y conflicto híbrido." *Revista Javeriana* (2017): 56–59, http://cdn.ideaspaz.org/media/website/document/58a35676d3adf.pdf.

Anderlini, S. N. *Women Building Peace: What They Do, Why It Matters*. Boulder, CO: Lynne Rienner, 2007.

Bell, C. "Women Address the Problems of Peace Agreements." In *Peace Work. Women, Armed Conflict, and Negotiation*, edited by R. Coomaraswamy and D. Fonseka. New Delhi: Women Unlimited, 2004.

Bouta, T., G. Frerks, and I. Bannon. *Gender, Conflict, and Development*. Washington, DC: World Bank Publication, 2005.

Cockburn, C. *The Space Between Us: Negotiating Gender and National Identities in Conflict*. London: Zed Books, 1998.

Coordinación Nacional de Pueblos Indígenas - CONPI. "Los indígenas se pronuncian en la Mesa de Conversaciones de La Habana". Las2Orillas, julio, 2016, https://www.las2orillas.co/los-indigenas-se-pronuncian-en-la-mesa-de-conversaciones-de-la-habana/

Cuesta I., and Mazzoldi, G. "Gender Focus. Debates, Transformations, and Potentialities in Colombia's New Peace Accord." *OpenDemocracy*, February 2, 2017, https://www.opendemocracy.net/democraciaabierta/g-nica-mazzoldi-irina-cuesta/gender-focus-debates-transformations-and-potentialiti.

Cumbre de Mujeres y Paz. "Propuestas de la Cumbre Nacional de Mujeres y Paz a la Mesa de Negociación." La Habana, February 2015.

Ellerby, K. "(En)gendered Security? Gender Mainstreaming and Women's Inclusion in Peace Processes." In *Gender, Peace, and Security: Implementing UN Security Council Resolution 1325*, edited by T. I. Gizelis and L. Olsson, 185–209. New York: Routledge, 2015.

Gizelis, T. I., and L. Olsson. "An Introduction to Resolution 1325: Measuring Progress and Impact." In *Gender, Peace, and Security: Implementing UN Security Council Resolution 1325*, 1–15. New York: Routledge, 2015.

Garzón, J.C., Llorente, M.V., Álvarez-Vanegas, E., and Preciado, A. "Economías criminales en clave de postconflicto". Tendencias actuales y propuesta para hacerles frente. *Serie Notas Estratégicas No. 1*. Bogotá: FIP, 2016.

"Global Study on Preventing Conflict, Transforming Justice, Securing Peace: A Global Study on the Implementation of United Nations Security Council resolution 1325." UN Women, 2015.

Georgetown Institute for Women, Peace and Security. "Women Leading Peace. A Close Examination of Women's Political Participation in Peace Processes in Northern Ireland, Guatemala, Kenya, and the Philippines." Washington, DC: GIWPS, 2015.

GIZ. *Promoting Women's Participation in Peace Negotiations and Peace Processes.* Bonn and Eschborn, Germany: Deutsche Gesellschaft für Internationale Zusammenarbeit (GIZ), March 2014,

Heathcote, G. "Participation, Gender, and Security." In *Rethinking Peacekeeping, Gender Equality, and Collective Security*, edited by G. Heathcote and D. Otto, 48–69. Basingstoke, UK: Palgrave Macmillan, 2014.

Hendricks, C. "Creating Women's Leadership for Peace and Security in the Greater Horn of Africa: The Limitations of Capacity-Building as Remedy for Gender Inequality." *Feminist Africa* 20 (2015): 43–56.

Hudson, N. *Gender, Human Security, and the United Nations: Security Language as a Political Framework for Women.* London: Routledge, 2010.

Marin Carvajal, I. "Post-Conflict in Colombia. Uninvited: Women in Havana." *OpenDemocracy*, February 4, 2016, https://www.opendemocracy.net/democraciaabierta/isabela-mar-n-carvajal/post-conflict-in-colombia-4-uninvited-women-in-havana.

Mazzoldi, G., I. Cuesta, and E. Álvarez-Vanegas. "Gender Ideology: A Spoiler for Peace?" *OpenDemocracy*, October 2016, https://www.opendemocracy.net/democraciaabierta/g-nica-mazzoldi-irina-cuesta-eduardo-lvarez-vanegas/gender-ideology-spoiler-for-pe.

Medicina Legal. *Forensis 2015. Datos para la vida.* Bogotá: Instituto Nacional de Medicina Legal y Ciencias Forenses Grupo Centro de Referencia Nacional sobre Violencia, 2016.

ONU Mujeres. *Sistematización Cumbre Nacional de Mujeres y Paz.* Bogotá: Entidad de las Naciones Unidas para la Igualdad de Género y el Empoderamiento de las Mujeres, 2013a.

ONU Mujeres. *Sistematización de propuestas de las mujeres en las consultas ciudadanas para la terminación del conflicto y la construcción de una paz estable y duradera.* Bogotá, Entidad de las Naciones Unidas para la Igualdad de Género y el Empoderamiento de las Mujeres, 2013b.

Organización Nacional de Pueblos Indígenas - ONIC. Presentación Oficial de la Comisión Interétnica de Paz. *ONIC*, Marzo, 2016, http://www.onic.org.co/noticias/971-presentacion-oficial-de-la-comision-interetnica-de-paz

O'Reilly, M., Ó, Súilleabháin, and T. Paffenholz. *Reimagining Peacemaking: Women's Roles in Peace Processes.* New York: International Peace Institute, 2015.

Page, M., T. Whitman, and C. Anderson. "Strategies for Policymakers: Bringing Women into Peace Negotiations." Institute for Inclusive Security, October 2009.

Porter, E. *Peacebuilding: Women in International Perspective.* New York: Routledge, 2007.

Rehn, E., and E. Johnson-Sirleaf. *Women, War, Peace: The Independent Experts' Assessment on the Impact of Armed Conflict on Women and Women's Role in Peace-Building.* New York: UNIFEM, 2002.

Simic, O. "Increasing Women's Presence in Peacekeeping Operations: The Rationales and Realities of 'Gender Balance.'" In *Rethinking Peacekeeping, Gender Equality, and Collective Security*, edited by G. Heathcote and D. Otto, 185–199. Basingstoke, UK: Palgrave Macmillan, 2014.

....

CHAPTER 37

WPS AND WOMEN'S ROLES IN CONFLICT-PREVENTION

The Case of Bougainville

....

NICOLE GEORGE

In the late 1980s, Bougainville, an island territory of Papua New Guinea (PNG), was plunged into a devastating secessionist war lasting almost ten years. The conflict cost the lives of between 5 to 10 percent of the population and saw many more subject to trauma, injury, and displacement. Bougainville's women played an important role in bringing this conflict to a resolution. Their contributions to peace-building, both in localized contexts and within formalized peace processes, are celebrated within the country and have been accorded respect across the Pacific Islands region. But in the longer term, women have faced considerable difficulty in progressing the gender-just terms of the peace they worked so hard to build.

This becomes evident if consideration is given to the discriminatory continuities and ruptures evident in the way women have experienced the transition from conflict to peace. This perspective exposes, on the one hand, the continuity of gendered insecurity that emerged so starkly in the conflict, and which remains all too prevalent in the post-conflict environment. On the other hand, this perspective also exposes how in peacetime, expanded opportunities for women's political participation, which seemed to be promised in the wake of their prolific peace advocacy, have been ruptured.

Since 2000, the UN's Women, Peace, and Security (WPS) agenda has been taken up in Bougainville against this backdrop to resist the continuities and ruptures of war and peace. This is not, however, a simple story of forward moving progress. In this chapter I explain why. As I will show, WPS-oriented advocacy has been layered over the existing sociocultural, economic, and political institutions that are present in this context and which generate an "architecture of entitlement" determining who has authority to speak on peace and security issues in Bougainville and how (George 2016a, 2016b). As this chapter shows, this architecture tends to influence how women reflect on their experiences of conflict and ultimately, how they translate the WPS pillar area provisions on participation, conflict prevention and protection.

In this chapter, I develop this argument by drawing upon a body of twenty-five interviews conducted with women peace leaders and advocates in 2014, a series of surveys conducted in the same year with ninety local women in the community on questions of everyday gendered security, and later follow-up in-country research conducted in 2018. I have also consulted other published sources, such as NGO and UN agency reports and a wide range of feminist studies on peace, conflict, gender, and security. I progress my resulting analysis in five stages. In the first section, I provide a brief outline of the conceptual approach which guides my discussion. Next, I examine the gendered experiences of conflict on Bougainville. In the third section, I discuss women's peace-building in detail, showing the ways in which this work was supported by local sociocultural institutions. Following this, I discuss other darker aspects of the gendered experience of conflict on Bougainville by focusing on women's experiences of wartime violence and insecurity. I examine how these experiences are navigated in the present and the difficulties women continue to face in overcoming them to achieve protection from violence. In the final section, I draw the strands of the previous discussion together to reflect on the ways in which the global WPS agenda and local influences come together to establish an architecture of entitlement, which tempers how the terms of a gender-just peace are defined in this context.

GENDER AND ARCHITECTURES OF ENTITLEMENT

Observers of the conflict in Bougainville tend to reflect on the complex nature of the territory's regulatory environment showing how the state-building orientation of the contemporary peace process is layered over, and supported, or potentially undercut, by other informal, bottom-up institutions of customary and religious authority. The argument generally concludes that post-conflict order will be consolidated in Bougainville, only when the popular legitimacy of informal sites of regulatory authority is taken into account in the broader peace process (Boege 2009; Dinnen and Peake 2013).

In line with broader critiques of the liberal peace, this has been an influential argument in the fields of peace and conflict studies more generally (Mac Ginty 2012; Richmond 2009. It is not my intention to survey the full dimensions of this debate here, but rather to consider how women's post-conflict, political. and social ambitions fare in these hybridized contexts. In this regard, I follow the openings created in recent scholarship by Annika Björkdahl (2012) with Kristine Höglund (Björkdahl and Höglund 2013), and Johanna Mannegren Semilövic (Björkdahl and Mannegren Semilövic 2015), who have all reflected on the difficulties that hybridized systems of regulatory authority pose for women in post-conflict contexts. This work has exposed the gendered "frictions" occurring when there is an interplay between national, international, and local institutions, showing how these can be restrictive to the ambitions of women (Björkdahl and Mannegren Semilövic 2015: 167).

In my own work on gender and conflict transitions in the Pacific Islands region, I have shown that similar sorts of frictions have been generated through the interplay of international, national, and localized institutions and that these tend often to result in restrictive definitions of gendered order (George 2016b). In these contexts, women's efforts to defend rights to political participation or to bodily integrity and freedom from gendered violence may adhere to global advocacy refrains assumed to be emancipatory. But locally these claims can be cast as imposed, even "heartless" forms of globalism, ill-matched to the values of Pacific Island communities (Douglas 2002: 21). In those Pacific Island sites that have recently experienced nationalist conflict, some parochial political actors have also been effective in their efforts to cast women's rights claims as a form of gendered dissidence that poses a risk to the integrity and security of the indigenous community. As I will show, this kind of framing has important consequences for the ways in which women in Bougainville translate international norms such as those encapsulated within the WPS policy framework.

To understand these processes of translation, it is analytically useful to reflect on the "architecture of entitlements" (Adger and Kelly 1999: 257) that governs debate on peace and security in Bougainville and women's ability to participate in this dialogue. As I have shown elsewhere (George 2016a), references to an "architecture of entitlement" have emerged from the field of political geography to examine how the distribution of scare resources among individuals, groups, or institutions is guided by socially constructed ideas about groups and individual's legitimate claims to "entitlement" (Adger and Kelly 1999: 257). The contention that "social hierarchies and resource entitlement inequalities are rarely overturned in the course of adaptation" to external challenges but usually reinforced by them is important here. This forecasts, how "external changes," such as the experience of conflict, may "reinforce" the social and institutional hierarchies that shape how resources, material, and political (power), are distributed in conditions of insecurity (Adger and Kelly 1999: 257).

As I will show, this perspective is particularly pertinent when examining women's experiences of conflict in Bougainville. Here a range of interplaying customary, faith-based, national, and international institutions give shape to the architecture of entitlement that has determined how women participated in the conflict, and how they have experienced the gendered continuities and the gendered ruptures of the transition between conflict and peace. In some regards, this architecture has been enabling for women and opened possibilities for influential peace advocacy. But my discussion in later sections of this chapter will also show the constraints that have followed for women operating within this gendered architecture too. These have had profound implications for how women's leaders progress their ambitions for political participation in the post-conflict environment, how they have managed experiences of gendered insecurity both during and in the wake of conflict, and how they have chosen, in the longer term, to invoke the global WPS agenda as part of their efforts to progress a gender-just peace.

Gender and Changing Patterns of Conflict on Bougainville

The war that erupted in Bougainville at the end of the 1980s was triggered by short and long-term grievances. Many Bougainvilleans have long held frustration over their territory's incorporation into the colonial states of Papua and New Guinea, administered by Australia, and after 1975, into the post-independence state of Papua New Guinea. The secessionist unrest that led to war in the late 1980s reflected this frustration but was also fired by resistance to the environmental and social costs of one of the world's largest open-cut copper mines that had been operated by Conzinc Rio Tinto Australia in Panguna (in the territory's southern region) since the 1960s. Disputes between mine-owners and local land-owning groups over adequate compensation for land use and environmental damage had been on-going since the mine's opening but became more violent in the 1980s and saw some rebel groups engage in campaigns of sabotage against mine infrastructure.

The PNG national government, eager to protect the mine's lucrative export revenue, deployed mainland police and military to quell unrest in 1989. A blunt and indiscriminately violent incursion, this served only to increase the resolve and organization of the local re-sistance and culminated in the formation of the Bougainville Revolutionary Army or BRA. But not all Bougainvillean's felt opposition to the mine or sided with the independence cause. The PNG Defence Forces (PNGDF) were joined by a local faction which became known as the Bougainville Resistance Force.

Despite the fact that women's contributions to peace-building are commonly viewed as the most significant aspect of women's involvement in the conflict in Bougainville, women were also an important presence in the resistance movement, particularly in the early years. In large parts of the island, women's authority is upheld through matrilineal cus-tomary structures. Land is considered to be "owned by women," but men are understood to have a "sacred duty" to protect land on women's behalf (Titus, quoted in Savoana Spriggs 2010: 210).[1] Women therefore, have the power to instruct men about when and how to pro-tect their land and also to veto protective actions if they do not approve. Extending from these connections to land, women are understood to have the authority to "make war" and to "make peace," as it is put in the local idiom.[2] Women may not be involved in violence directly, but in many parts of the country they are understood to have customary authority to direct men to fight and when to give that fight up.

This authority was certainly evident in the early years of the conflict around Panguna. Women such as Perpetua Serero, cousin to rebel leader Frances Ono, played significant roles in the leadership of land-owner rebel groups in areas close to the Panguna mine (Laslett 2012: 708). At the height of the conflict, there is evidence that women also worked with rebel forces to lure PNG defense force troops into surprise attacks, such as the one that occurred in Kangu Beach and accounted for the deaths of twelve PNGDF troop members (Charlesworth 2008: 353). In other capacities, women were also involved in the supply and preparation of food for BRA forces and care for the wounded (UNIFEM 2004).

In a bid to weaken local support of this sort, the PNG government imposed a blockade on the islands in 1990, which lasted in some parts of the country for up to seven years and prevented imported food, medicines, and fuel from entering the island. This contributed to hardship and deprivation for everyday Bougainvilleans and increased the conflict's human cost dramatically. Women were particularly affected by restrictions placed on civilian movement and the crumbling health infrastructure which prevented them from accessing reproductive healthcare. Dramatic increases in maternal morbidity and infant mortality rates were recorded by local communities in the war years (Mirinka 1996)

As the conflict wore on, the lines separating separatist and loyalist groupings on the is-land became fractured. In these conditions, the use of force became more sporadic, un-controlled, and opportunistic. Customary authority and the matrilineal structures that had ensured women a respected place within local communities gave way to the "law of the gun," and violence was perpetrated among Bougainvilleans "brother against brother" as it is locally explained (anonymized source, June 2014). Many women were displaced during this period as they sought to escape the fighting with children and other dependents. A great number fled to the bush where they worked to establish food gardens and employed other "bush craft" technologies to cope with scarcity of fuel and medicines. There was enormous resilience displayed in these settings, but the bush camp existence was highly precarious. Women were frequently exposed to the predatory violence of both rebel and loyalist troops, who were themselves living in increasingly desperate conditions. One local peace activist, Sister Lorraine Garasu, described this situation for women as "life between two guns" (Garasu 2002: 29).

Other women chose, and were sometimes forced, to take their families to the "care camps" established by PNG authorities for those seeking refuge from the chaos of the war. But these were also places of precarity and violence. Camp authorities, both PNGDF personnel and sometimes BRF members, often displayed extreme suspicion of camp inmates and those suspected of enemy collaboration were subject to extrajudicial violence and torture. Women were also subjected to this violence when they refused to participate in PNGDF activities such as radio broadcasts designed to encourage rebel surrender, but also when they engaged in conflict resolution efforts too. This violence, including rape, was never brought to the attention of higher PNGDF authorities and generally committed with impunity (Amnesty 1997: 27).

Peace talks were underway from the earliest days of the conflict (Braithwaite et al. 2010), but it was not until 2001 that a formal peace agreement was ultimately brokered. This granted Bougainville political autonomy and ushered in a period of "fragile" peace. A disarmament and demobilization program was also undertaken in Bougainville in the wake of that agreement, with international support. Although the process was contested, subjected to various forms of funds misappropriation, and not fully open to the participation of women (elaborated upon in more detail in what follows), it did result in the destruction of 80 percent of the arms on Bougainville (UNIFEM 2004). These outcomes are important, but the achievement of Bougainville's peace has not necessarily increased protection or participation for those who were most integral to its initial foundation, Bougainville's women.

WOMEN'S LEADERSHIP IN CONFLICT PREVENTION: A FRAGILE LEGACY?

Women leaders in Bougainville are rightfully proud of their conflict prevention activities and commonly repeat the refrain that it was they who "brought peace to Bougainville" (George 2016b). Recognition of this work has extended across the Pacific Islands region, internationally, and even as far as deliberations within the United Nations Security Council (UNSC 2003).

This work began modestly. As a first step toward bridging lines of political division, some women began to send baskets of scarce goods to women in other parts of the territory. These "peace baskets" were designed to build a bottom-up sense of solidarity among women and to show those in isolated areas that they were not forgotten.[3] Church networks were also significant in this regard and allowed women to connect with each other and organize events such as prayer vigils and protest marches against violence in their communities (UNIFEM 2004; Hermkens 2011). As the impetus for peace increased, women's initiatives became more brazen and involved direct interventions with combatants. Here they would insert themselves physically between warring groups, or wrap their arms around combatants in a bid to halt gunfights. This work did not only occur within women's local communities; it became increasingly focused on building a momentum for peace across the country. To this end, women began to organize national meetings, in defiance of the PNGDF efforts to restrict movement. One of the most noteworthy of these events occurred in July 1996, when over seven hundred women gathered in Arawa. Reflecting on the utility of this event, one woman peace leader later explained; "when women met, they realised that they may have had different political views" but they were "not enemies."[4] Indeed, with concerns for their children, their families, and the future of their country mutually held across the lines of the conflict, women were easily united in agreement that continued perpetration of violence was in no one's interests. From these beginnings, women then began to approach the leaders of the warring camps and to plead with them to end the violence. In all of these efforts, from those occurring in grass-roots contexts, to those occurring on the national stage, women drew on highly feminized tropes to legitimize their peace-building. To do this they reminded their audience of their matrilineal status and the respect they deserved as maternal guardians of Bougainville's future generations, as well as its "sacred" land (see also Titus, quoted Savoana Spriggs).

References to Christian faith, particularly Marian traditions of Catholic belief, were particularly important for this activity. Mary is the patron saint of the territory, and was invoked by women to provide a sacred dimension to their peace-building efforts. As Anna Karina Hermkens has shown, Mary's attributes of virtue and peacefulness are entangled with customary representations of Bougainvillean motherhood. Women peace-builders, therefore, claimed that Mary, or "Mama Maria" in the local idiom, gave them the strength to promote peace, would protect them as they stood between lines of fighting, and lent persuasive weight to appeals that combatants lay down their arms (Hermkens 2011).

These strategies proved influential with Bougainville's broader political leadership. Indeed, in the final years of the conflict, women activists asserted that male political leaders had "rediscovered the value of women sharing in the decision-making process" and that this attitude would be "liberating" for all women in Bougainville (Titus, quoted Savoana Spriggs 2010, 211). The appointment of three women to the constitutional commission, established in September 2002 augured well for "a political future where women must take their rightful place beside men" (Titus, quoted in Savoana Spriggs 2010, 211).

But this constitutional process ultimately taught women the limits of their political influence. There was hope that women would be granted twelve reserved seats in the newly formed thirty-nine seat parliament to ensure there was female representation in each of Bougainville's twelve districts. When the final constitutional design was agreed, women were asked to accept only three reserved seats, a development that, as my interviews repeatedly demonstrated, remains a deep source of grievance for women across the country.[5]

Of course, in the ensuring elections women have been able to contest open seats. But their success in these contests has been negligible. In the three elections that have been held in the territory since the end of the conflict (on five-year electoral cycles), women candidates have succeeded in winning an open seat only once. Moreover, no woman candidate elected to a reserved seat has held onto it for a subsequent term. The general hesitancy toward women candidates in Pacific politics is well documented (Baker 2015; George 2014). In Bougainville, as elsewhere in the region, politics is understood to be the natural and rightful domain of men. But this general hesitancy is, in Bougainville, also compounded by the experience of the conflict and the resulting ways in which ideas about political participation have become gendered in the post-conflict setting in Bougainville.

Women took care to frame their conflict prevention activity so that it demonstrated their obedience to sociocultural norms of maternal virtue, religious faith, and gendered service to the community and the nation. Their peacebuilding can therefore be viewed as occurring in harmony with the prevailing architecture establishing where and how women can legitimately contribute to security debate. But activity framed in this way has not necessarily opened doors for women's participation in broader processes of conflict transition. Indeed, the overwhelming local focus on women's conflict prevention roles, in contradiction to their roles as "war-makers," has been invoked by some male political leaders to cast doubt on women's "entitlement" to participate in some fora. This was made particularly clear during the territory's Demobilisation, Disarmament, and Reintegration (DDR) process where combatant leaders expressed strong opposition to women's participation at meetings on weapons disposal, questioning their judgement on this issue because they "didn't fight" (UNIFEM 2004: 20).

In the sphere of electoral and parliamentary politics, similar ideas, although not as baldly stated, seem to be at play. Certainly, the emphasis placed on women's peacemaking roles and the consequent downplaying of women's involvement in the leadership or support of combat groups (particularly in the early years of the conflict) seems ultimately to have contributed to strongly feminized understandings of women's political capacity and a dismissal of this as valuable to the country in the longer term. Nonetheless, some recent reforms to Bougainville's system of local government have opened the way for increased participation by women with a new ward-based electoral system created with stipulations that each ward elects a male and female representative (ABG 2016a). In 2017, the first elections under this new system were held. There have been anecdotal reports that the system is being resisted in some areas[6] but there is also enthusiasm for the system from many women around the country. The challenge will be to see if inroads into the political system forged at this local level can open up the gendered architecture that shapes political representation at higher levels.

CONFRONTING THE LEGACIES OF GENDERED VIOLENCE AND INSECURITY

These maternalized and highly feminized framings of women's peace-building and conflict prevention have also had profound implications for the ways in which women have managed experiences of gendered violence and insecurity in the past and in the present. As previously noted, experiences of gender and sexual violence were widespread during the conflict. Some studies have suggested that many thousands of rapes were committed against women by warring groups from all sides (Braithwaite 2006; Braithwaite et al. 2010). Yet, in my interactions with women peace leaders in the present, this violence was often referred to in shadowy and veiled sorts of narratives.

References to this violence sometimes began by interview participants referring to experiences of "torture." Frequently my interlocutors displayed discomfort if this subject came up, and I usually avoided asking any question that might lead them to recall traumatic experiences. Nonetheless my interlocutors' references to experiences of violence during the conflict were recounted with enough frequency for me to understand that this was perpetrated indiscriminately (George 2016b).[7]

In most instances, the subject of violence was quickly followed by more positive stories that my interlocutors seemed much more inclined to recall and that demonstrated their agency and wartime resilience. As discussed earlier, women were often at the head of displaced family groups at this time, and frequently shouldered the burden of care for dependents in bush camps or in the care centers. The struggle for collective survival was therefore an overriding concern. But for some, the focus on survival seemed also to function as a distraction or a strategy for managing feelings of "trauma" or as an escape from "their tears."[8] Some of my interlocutors explained this idea stating that, to escape feelings of trauma, they clung to the ideas that gave them hope, such as their conclusion that they were doing something that "God wanted," and that they were building a future that would be positive for their country.[9]

For other women, silence on experiences of gender violence during the conflict years has been motivated by a personal decision to "make peace" with a negative experience (Terieken, quoted in Howley 2002: 13). This is reflected in the testimony of Gloria Terieken, recorded in a collection of writings on post-conflict reconciliation in Bougainville published just after the war (Howley 2002). Terieken discusses her response to a former assailant who tried to make amends some years later for the violence he had perpetrated; I said to him, "I have put it all behind me. I am settled down again and I do not want to think about this anymore. I do not want to talk about it . . . All I want to say is 'I forgive you' and put it behind me" (quoted in Howley, 2002: 13). Terieken went on to argue that this response was personally important because it allowed her to become "useful" again (cited Howley 2002: 13).

These reflections provide important insights into how the sensitivities of exposure to sexual violence are managed by women in an individual sense. But in Bougainville, they also show how notions of feminized obligation and virtue shape the prevailing architecture of the post-conflict environment and the ways women are "entitled" to manage these experiences of personal insecurity. The refusal to dwell on experiences of conflict-related gender violence, and to focus instead on survival or the achievement of a personal peace, is of course an agentic "coping" strategy that should not be diminished (Kent 2016). But in the Bougainvillean context, it might also be viewed as reflective of feminized peace-building discourse. As I have shown, women were often motivated to think beyond themselves and their own physical security, even as they put themselves in the line of fire, and saw their peace-building activity as a selfless defense of Bougainville's future. A similar sort of view is expressed by Terieken, who speaks of a desire to "make peace" and to be useful by putting experiences "behind" her. This suggests that women may also fear the broader costs of looking back and giving voice to events that have the potential to trigger friction in their communities. In this sense, the silence that women adopt on questions of conflict-related violence may reflect the expectation that in the post-conflict context, women are only "entitled" to be visible and active in the public domain as sources of peace and conflict prevention, rather than as catalysts for ongoing division.

There may be a personal cost incurred by women in all of this, but there are longer term and more generalized social costs that accrue for women in Bougainville from these "useful" silences too. The fact that gendered violence became so prevalent during the war, and that perpetrators were rarely made to account for their actions (either before customary or state-based regulatory authority), has resulted, in the longer term, in a diminishment of the seriousness of gender violence as a crime and the sites of regulatory order (particularly customary forms) that, before the war, protected women from abuses of this type (Department of Veterans Affairs and AusAID 2010; Braithwaite 2006; Eves 2016). My own research with women at the everyday community level on questions of gender and safety suggests that in the current context, feelings of vulnerability to violent assault have become almost a banal feature of everyday life. Indeed, in response to survey questions examining women's perceptions of safety within familial and communal settings, women study-participants in Bougainville referred to the risk of encounters with assailants that might result in violence, rape, and murder with a frequency that was both startling and disturbing. This suggests that women's efforts to manage past experiences of violence by making peace with them personally has preserved order at one level, but also preserved the environment of impunity that surrounds high levels of gender violence in the present. As the next section will show, this has implications for women's efforts to progress a gender-just form of peace in the longer term.

WOMEN PEACE AND SECURITY IN BOUGAINVILLE: GENDERING THE ARCHITECTURE OF ENTITLEMENT.

There is an increasing interest in the local applicability of the WPS framework in Bougainville, and women leaders invoke the ideas of UN Security Council Resolution 1325 as part of efforts to ensure that their rights to contribute to Bougainville's conflict transition is recognized. But the WPS agenda is not locally invoked as a "cut and paste" version of the resolutions that have been adopted in the distant chambers of the Security Council in New York. As I have established in the preceding sections, gendered patterns of conflict, gendered sociocultural institutions, and local trajectories of gendered agency and victimhood establish the architecture guiding debate on security in this context and the terms upon which women are understood to be "entitled" to participate in Bougainville's post-conflict transition. In Bougainville, this has therefore inclined women to "translate" the provisions of the WPS agenda in ways that fit within the prevailing local architecture of entitlements and to avoid any further gender-restrictive backlash.

This does not mean the WPS agenda is emptied of utility. Local women activists describe the WPS agenda, at least in abstract terms, as useful, and "very precious" in their campaigns to challenge the gendered terms of Bougainville's transition to peace (Hakena, quoted in FemLINKPACIFIC 2008). They have also joined with regional coalitions who describe Resolution 1325 as a "loud hailer" (FemLINKPACIFIC 2008) that provides influential international endorsement for their local and regional work.

Indeed, in recognition of this value, Bougainville's Minister for Women, Rose Pihei, worked with civil society partners between 2010 and 2015 to develop a draft National Action Plan (NAP) on Women, Peace, and Security. This was an impressive development, but as the minister moved to different executive portfolios in later years and then failed to hold her reserved seat at the 2015 election, forward movement on the NAP was halting.

In 2016 the Autonomous Bougainville Government's (ABG) Department for Community Development and Women's Affairs finally released its policy on Gender Equality, Peace and Security (ABG 2016), a document which provides detailed analysis of where and how gendered disadvantage impacts on women's access to decision-making spheres, economic participation, education and health and welfare services. It is followed by a matrix of action points designed to meet these challenges with a key focus on gender mainstreaming within government institutions. The Office of Gender Equality (newly formed since 2016) is nominated as providing oversight and technical assistance for specific aspects of the plan. These are all promising developments, but there is little evidence that the plan has attracted adequate resourcing for its implementation either from the AGB or external development partners. This will inevitably obstruct progress on goals outlined in the policy such as improved access to higher-level secondary education for girls, and efforts to arrest the high prevalence of gendered violence across the territory.

Ultimately, this means that women activists and women peace leaders will remain critical to the promotion of WPS principles in Bougainville. Yet without resourcing there are important limits to how far these groups can undertake this promotion so that it unsettles the gendered architecture of entitlement that shapes their participation in debate on Bougainville's post-conflict future. Presently, the agenda seems to be invoked predominantly by women activists to remind political leaders, local constituents, and interested foreign researchers about the importance of women's contributions to conflict prevention and peace-building. But reflective of the local socio-cultural terrain, this advocacy also tends to strongly reinforce the links between peace-building and conflict prevention in ways that are highly feminized. By this, I mean that local invocations of women's peacebuilding capacities tend to emphasize women's agency in conflict, but simultaneously reinforce cultural institutions reflecting women's maternal authority, sacred virtue, and obligations as "protectors" of land and the community.

While this is enabling on the one hand, it has also discouraged recognition of where and how women were centrally involved in the resistance movement, and the political acumen they acquired in these roles (George 2016b). Without this, as the example of the DDR process shows, it has become far too easy to marginalize women politically, to devalue their political views because they "didn't fight," and to therefore ensure their influence is ghettoized by the limits of their three reserved parliamentary seats.

This focus on women's peace-building agency also obscures the experiences of violence and intimidation that were highly prevalent for women across the country during the conflict period. The silence many women appear to have built around these experiences may be a decision to make peace with oneself, or to keep peace in the community. But it does little to challenge the impunity that allows gender violence to persist at extreme levels and in troubling continuity with the past, in a great many of Bougainville's communities today. The ongoing presence of this violence suggests the terms of the peace women worked so hard to achieve is still a long way from gender just.

Contemporary accounts of women's peace leadership in Bougainville have captured the imagination of local and international peace-builders and those in the region who work to promote awareness of the WPS framework. More attention focused on women's particular capacities to resolve disputes will, it is true, provide strong anchors for a sustainable peace in Bougainville. But it is important to also recognize the extent to which this agency in conflict has been tempered by the gender-restrictive architecture of entitlement that generally shapes debate on peace and security in Bougainville. While this architecture endures, the gender discriminatory continuities and ruptures I have discussed in these pages will remain a formidable challenge.

CONCLUSION

Women, Peace, and Security activists across the Pacific region regularly draw on the Bougainvillean example to illustrate the productive roles that women can play in Pacific societies as brokers of peace and to reinforce the idea that where recognition is given to the WPS pillar areas of prevention and participation, broader forms of stability and security can follow. But none of this negates the challenges pertinent to the other WPS pillar areas that also confront Bougainvillean women. Questions around women's inability to contribute to DDR processes because they "did not fight" are significant and have long-term implications both for gendered forms of security on the Island, and for the extent of women's influence in formal politics. Issues pertinent to the protection pillar, and particularly women's exposure to conflict-related sexual or gender-based violence, seem never to have been dealt with in any formalized way. These are sensitive questions and, for some, silence on these matters may be preferred. But these contentions are not universally shared and others have also called for more attention to these injustices (Miriori, 2004: 63).[10] As I have shown, these silences seem also to have sanctioned an environment of impunity around gendered violence which flourishes in the post-conflict context. Women active within the realm of institutionalized politics have made some steps to formalize the provisions of the WPS agenda in local policy, but financial resourcing of this policy has not been forthcoming, starkly illustrating the limits of women's influence to compete for material resources within the arena of formal politics.

This prompts questions about the kinds of supporting roles that the international WPS activist and policy community, and perhaps the UN Security Council itself, can provide in this context. Bougainvilleans are justly proud of the "home grown" quality of the "liberal-local" peace they have forged (Wallis 2012: 615). International actors who imagine they can advise on any aspect of conflict-transition practice without recognizing this strong commitment to the indigenous quality of Bougainville's hybrid peace do so at their peril. Nonetheless, international support, to assist the implementation of Bougainville's own, homegrown and locally formulated WPS policy is now critical. This kind of support could provide the territory's women with a much needed opening to build upon their achievements but also prise apart the architecture of entitlement that currently constrains their ability to advance a gender-just peace in this still fragile, transitional context. Key in all of this will be the development of partnerships that support, but do not suffocate, local women's considerable initiative and capacity.

NOTES

1. Bougainville Women's Press Statement, 1998, read by Mrs. Agnes Titus, Lincoln. Christchurch, New Zealand, quoted in Savoana-Spriggs (2010: 210).
2. Personal communication with "Therese," Arawa, June 2014.

3. Personal communication with "Angela," peace leader, Buka, June, 2014.
4. Personal communication with "Angela," Buka, June 2014.
5. This was a theme returned to many times in interviews with women leaders in Bougainville. Many of my interlocutors stated they have been part of the debate on the proposition for reserved seats for women and had nominated the need for twelve seats. Disappointment over the fact that only three seats were secured for women in the constitutions was universally expressed.
6. Personal communication with Volker Boege, Brisbane, April, 2018.
7. This testimony is corroborated by evidence gathered in an Amnesty International report on human rights abuses occurring during the Bougainville war which was published in 1997 (Amnesty International 1997).
8. Personal communication with "Therese," Arawa, June 24 2014.
9. Personal communication with "Therese," Arawa, June 24, 2014.
10. Personal communication with anonymized informant, Buka, June 2014.

References

ABG (Autonomous Government of Bougainville), 2016a. Community Government Act. Located at ARoB, 2004. *Constitution of the Autonomous Region of Bougainville*, located at http://www.abg.gov.pg/uploads/acts/16-01_Bougainville_Community_Government_Act_2016.pdf [accessed 2 March 2018]

ABG (Autonomous Government of Bougainville), 2016b. Policy for Women's Empowerment, Gender Equality, Peace and Security. Department of Community Development and Women's Affairs. Buka, August.

Adger, W. N., and M. P. Kelly. "Social Vulnerability to Climate Change and the Architecture of Entitlements." *Mitigation and Adaptation Strategies for Global Change* 4, nos. 3–4 (1999): 253–266.

Amnesty International. "Papua New Guinea: Bougainville: The Forgotten Human Rights Tragedy." February 26, 1997, https://www.amnesty.org/en/documents/asa34/001/1997/en/.

Baker, K. "Pawa Blong Meri: Women Candidates in the 2015 Bougainville Election." Discussion Paper, 2015/14. Australian National University, 2015, http://ssgm.bellschool.anu.edu.au/sites/default/files/publications/attachments/2016-07/dp-2015-14-baker-online.pdf

Björkdahl, A. "A Gender-Just Peace? Exploring the Post-Dayton Peace Process in Bosnia. *Peace and Change* 37, no. 2 (2012): 286–317.

Björkdahl, A., and K. Höglund. Precarious Peacebuilding: Friction in Global–Local Encounters. *Peacebuilding* 1, no. 3 (2013): 289–299.

Björkdahl, A., and J. Mannegren Selimovic. Gendering Agency in Transitional Justice. *Security Dialogue* 46, no. 2 (2015): 165–182.

Boege, V. "Peacebuilding and State Formation in Post-Conflict Bougainville." *Peace Review* 21, no. 1 (2009): 29–37.

Braithwaite, J. "Rape, Shame, and Pride." *Journal of Scandinavian Studies in Criminology and Crime Prevention* 7 (2006): 2–16

Braithwaite, J., H. Charlesworth, P. Reddy, and L. Dunn. *Reconciliation and Architectures of Commitment: Sequencing Peace in Bougainville* Canberra: ANU Press, 2010.

Charlesworth, H. "Are Women Peaceful? Reflections on the Role of Women in Peace-Building." *Feminist Legal Studies* 16, no. 3 (2008): 347–361.

Department of Veterans Affairs (Autonomous Region of Bougainville) and AusAID Democratic Governance Project. *Bougainville Peacebuilding Project Report*. Buka: DVA and AusAID, October 3, 2010.

Dinnen, S., and G. Peake. "More than Just Policing: Police Reform in Post Conflict Bougainville." *International Peacekeeping* 20, no. 5 (2013): 572.

Douglas, B. "Christian Citizens: Woman and Negotiations of Modernity in Vanuatu." *Contemporary Pacific* 14, no. 1 (2002): 1–38.

Eves, R. "Alcohol, Gender, and Violence in Bougainville." In Brief, 2016/15. State, Society, and Governance in Melanesia, 2016, http://ssgm.bellschool.anu.edu.au/sites/default/files/publications/attachments/2016-05/ib-2016-15-eves.pdf.

FemLINKPACIFIC. "Policy Brief on United Nations Security Council Resolution 1325." Suva: FemLINKPACIFIC, 2008, http://www.femlinkpacific.org.fj/_resources/main/files/FemLINKPACIFIC_WPS1325_Policy%20brief%201.pdf.

Garasu, L. "The Role of Women in Promoting Peace and Reconciliation." In *Weaving Consensus: The Papua New Guinea—Bougainville Peace Process,* edited by Andy Carl and Lorraine Garasu, 27–29. London: Conciliation Resources in Collaboration with Bougainville Inter-Church Women's Forum, 2002.

George, N. "Institutionalizing the Women, Peace, and Security Agenda in the Pacific Islands: Gendering the Architecture of Entitlements." *International Political Science Review* 37, no. 3 (2016a): 375–389.

George, N. "Light, Heat, and Shadows: Women's Reflections on Peacebuilding in Bougainville. *Peacebuilding* 4, no. 2 (2016b): 166–179.

George, N. "Women, Peace, and Security in the Pacific Islands: Hot Conflict/Slow Violence. *Australian Journal of International Affairs* 67, no. 3 (2014): 314–332.

Hermkens, A-K. "Mary, Motherhood and Nation: Religion and Gender Ideology in Bougainville's Secessionist Warfare." *Intersections: Gender and Sexuality in Asia and the Pacific*, February 25, 2011, http://intersections.anu.edu.au/issue25/hermkens.htm.

Howley, P. *Breaking Spears and Mending Hearts: Peacemakers and Restorative Justice in Bougainville*. Annandale, Australia: Federation Press, 2002.

Kent, L. "Sounds of Silence: Everyday Strategies of Social Repair in Timor-Leste." *Australian Feminist Law Journal* 42, no. 1 (2016): 31–50.

Laslett, K. "State Crime by Proxy." *British Journal of Criminology* 52, no. 3 (2012), 705–723.

Mac Ginty, R. *International Peacebuilding and Local Resistance: Hybrid Forms of Peace*. Basingstoke, UK: Palgrave MacMillan, 2012.

Mirinka, R. "Our Mothers and Children Are Dying: Military Offensives against the Island of Bougainville." In *Sustainable Development or Malignant Growth*, edited by A. Emberson-Bain, 229–235. Suva: Marama Publications, 1996.

Miriori, S. Rape, A Weapon of War, in As Mothers of the Land: the Birth of the Bougainville Women for Peace and Freedom, edited by J. T. Sirivi and M T Havini, 63–65. Canberra: Pandanus Books, 2004.

Richmond, O. "Beyond Liberal Peace? Responses to 'Backsliding.'" In *New Perspectives on Liberal Peacebuilding*, edited by E. Newman, R. Paris, and O. Richmond, 54–77. Tokyo: United Nations University Press, 2009.

Savoana Spriggs, R. "Bougainville Women's Role in Conflict Resolution in the Bougainville Peace Process." In *A Kind of Mending: Restorative Justice in the Pacific Islands*, edited by Sinclair Dinnen with Anita Jowitt, and Tess Newton-Cain, 195–253. Canberra: ANU Press, 2010.

UNIFEM (United Nations Development Fund for Women). *Getting it Right, Doing it Right: Gender and Disarmament, Demobilization, and Reintegration*. UNIFEM, 2004, http://www.poa-iss.org/CASAUpload/Members/Documents/15@Getting_it_Right_Doing_it_Right.pdf.

United Nations Security Council (UNSC). "Security Council Told Peace Agreement between Papua New Guinea, Bougainville Can Be Fully Implemented by Years End, Despite Serious Obstacles." Press Release sc/7700, March 28 2003, http://www.un.org/press/en/2003/sc7709.doc.htm.

Wallis, J., Building a Liberal-Local Peace and State in Bougainville. *Pacific Review* 25, no. 5 (2012): 613–635.

CHAPTER 38

WOMEN IN REBELLION
The Case of Sierra Leone

ZOE MARKS

THE Sierra Leone civil war was one of the conflicts at the forefront of policymakers' minds when the UN Security Council passed Resolution 1325. The war raged erratically and destructively across the small West African country of 5 million people from 1991 to 2002, and has become a paradigmatic case for understanding atrocity and the so-called "new wars" driven by inequality, weak states, and global profiteering (Straus 2012; Kaldor 2003). The primary rebel group, the Revolutionary United Front of Sierra Leone (RUF), was notorious for deploying child soldiers, amputating civilians' limbs, and using rape and sexual violence against women and girls of all ages (Guberek et al. 2006). After the war finally ended, Sierra Leone also became a paradigmatic case in liberal peace-building. Its post-conflict interventions—peacekeeping; disarmament, demobilization, and reintegration; security sector reform; and transitional justice—were on the whole, seen as a great success at the time and shaped the formula for other post-conflict reconstruction processes. The country thus served as an incubator for and an experiment in many of the issues that today define the Women, Peace, and Security (WPS) agenda.

Since the war's end, we have learned much more about what actually happened in Sierra Leone and the role of women and girls, and gender relations more broadly, in shaping the conflict (Coulter 2008; 2009). We also understand more clearly the limitations of post-war reconstruction efforts. This chapter focuses our attention on the varied experiences of women and girls in rebellion in order to highlight the practical realities of implementing WPS policies on the ground in conflict settings. Throughout, I primarily refer to "women" for efficiency and as a term inclusive of adolescent girls in Sierra Leone's cultural context; I specify age where salient, and acknowledge the importance of legal definitions from an advocacy perspective. The overarching research question framing this essay is how does positionality affect women's conflict experiences in armed groups and their post-conflict needs? Following Alcoff (1988), hooks (1981), Crenshaw (1991), and Yuval-Davis (2006), I use *positionality* to refer to the ways gender identity is both inherently relational, socially constructed, and understood in relation to other women, men, girls, boys, and is intersectional with other social categories including class, religion, ethnicity, age, and so on. This relational and intersectional approach enables us to analyze how gender constrains or shapes individual experiences, institutional and organizational power structures, and patterns of violence, victimization, and survival. It sharpens our understanding of the implications of armed group dynamics for WPS issues.

I first examine pathways of mobilization for female participants in the RUF, explaining how being a target of violence and mobilizing for violence were closely interrelated. I then turn to the gender-segregated power structures of the RUF and highlight the importance of the political organizational context for understanding women's widely varying experiences and access to power. I highlight the strategic importance of women in supporting the war machine and establishing a society in the bush. The final section pays special attention to the practical issues this raises for WPS policies and priorities in light of the fact that revolutionary movements often fail to deliver on their promise to transform gender roles and inequality.

MOBILIZATION AND VICTIMIZATION

Like all wars, the Sierra Leone civil war began before the first shots were fired, and the RUF's origins strongly shape how pathways to mobilization unfolded. Foday Sankoh, the founder and leader of the RUF, first recruited "Vanguard" members in neighboring Liberia in 1990 shortly after helping his friend and entrepreneurial counterpart, Charles Taylor, launch his own rebellion. Taylor's insurgency was rebuffed by the state Armed Forces of Liberia, as well as by the Sierra Leone Armed Forces and other members of the Economic Community of West African States Monitoring Group (ECOMOG), a regional peacekeeping force. To punish the Sierra Leone government for their intervention in his rebellion, Taylor ordered his troops to kill or capture all Sierra Leoneans residing in Liberia (Truth and Reconciliation Commission [TRC] 2004: 99–100). As a result, Sankoh had fertile ground on which to cajole Sierra Leoneans into joining the RUF Vanguard in Liberia, with many members "rescued" by Sankoh from the hands of Liberian rebels and motivated to join the RUF by their need for protection.

These violent origins of the RUF are crucial to understanding the prominent role played by physical insecurity and overt coercion in mobilizing people to fight in the RUF once the war moved into Sierra Leone. The "Vanguard," recruited in Liberia, numbered less than four hundred troops and had just seventeen women. As one of the female Vanguard members describes, in both Liberia and Sierra Leone, trust-based social networks, a coercive wartime context, and political grievances combined in powerful ways to lead people to join Sankoh's revolutionary project:

> [My best friend] is the one that made me to join in this war when we were [studying] in Liberia. We were Sierra Leonean, and she went to me and she said, "Mariatu, if you stay here, people are going to kill you. So, let us go and fight for our country." I said, "Which fight is that?" She said, "you don't know that the leader from the Sierra Leone rebel leadership is here?" (Interview: Mariatu Thomas, Vanguard/Women's Auxiliary Corps, Makeni, 2009; interviewee names are pseudonyms)

After nine months of training, the newly minted RUF Vanguard launched a pincer assault to liberate their home country from what they saw as corrupt and plundering one-party rule. They broke through the border and led invasion and recruitment campaigns in rural Southern and Eastern Sierra Leone. It was a fumbling, violent start: communication was soon cut off between the battalions; the military strategy of storming to the capital failed; and Liberian forces ransacked the same towns and villages from which the Sierra Leonean fighters sought to recruit adherents to their nascent revolution. However, decades of misrule, underdevelopment, and political marginalization also made the population sympathetic to their cause, if terrified of the means. The RUF operated an invade-rally-recruit strategy in nearly every village they entered, firing warning shots, corralling people into the local court *barrie* (where the chief presides), and announcing the arrival of the revolution. Further, although less than 1 percent of Vanguard members were women, they took up a gender equitable recruitment strategy after invading Sierra Leone in 1991, seeking to recruit both men and women as fighters and in support roles as medics, radio operators, secretaries, and more.

During its first few years, the RUF recruited teenaged and young adult men and women to their training camps through a combination of persuasion and coercion. One male Vanguard member described recruiting "gallant men [who] joined because they were tired of the rotting system" (Interview: Kai Fekkah, Vanguard/S4 Commander, Makeni 2009). But, a schoolboy who joined in the South provides a typical narrative from the perspective of those on the receiving end of recruitment:

> I was going to school. The rebels captured the town and called everyone in front of their houses, then started picking out the young men and women, and told them to join the movement. There was no resistance because we had heard they were at Zimmi a nearby border town. (Interview: Sylvester Kabbia, Junior commando, Makeni 2009)

His description reveals a mix of ambivalent local-level compliance with armed fighters, and resignation to the arrival of a war many saw as inevitable and necessary in Sierra Leone at the time.

The enthusiasm with which some communities welcomed the RUF, however, was largely short-lived. It quickly became clear that armed revolution was a violent and resource intensive endeavor, with taxes levied on local communities that were already struggling to survive. There were harsh penalties for noncompliance, and those trying to leave rebel territory risked being victimized by state forces unable to distinguish combatants from civilians. This narrowed the options available to people who found themselves behind RUF lines. At the individual level, women, children, and young people who became involved in the RUF had often been separated from their families. Trapped in a war zone, the group provided them the best chance for accessing food and physical security, albeit at great personal risk.

Future fighters were separated from civilians with other transferrable skills, such as teachers, medics, mechanics, and drivers. The military training in the RUF was particularly brutal, and female recruits were subject to the same strenuous and violent practices as male recruits. Recruits endured a litany of abusive drills designed to prepare them for a violent guerrilla existence in the bush. As one Women's Auxiliary Corps commander describes:

> [One] training was called "Escape for Survival," where they took us to the middle of the bush. We couldn't eat or drink for three days, so that at the frontline we can take hunger. They divided the group into two mock groups, the RUF and the "SLA" (Sierra Leone Army). There were two commanders and they gave us sticks as mock arms. We had to lay ambush while the other group makes like they're passing the road. The commander fired up with a real gun

to show the ambush. We would call the password, "commando!" and they had to say "brave, strong, intelligent" (Interview: Naberay Morrison, Women's Auxiliary Corps Commander, Makeni 2009).

From 1994 onward, mobilization patterns shifted as the RUF retreated from towns to guerrilla camps hidden in Sierra Leone's deepest forests and hills. This so-called jungle phase led to widespread forced recruitment as civilians were forced to carry supplies rebels looted from their villages into the RUF bush camps. The shift to guerrilla warfare also had a particularly pernicious gendered element, bringing intimate relationships and women's (re)productive labor more closely into the military sphere. From 1994 to 1995, Sankoh and other commanders encouraged male fighters to choose "wives" (also called "bush wives"), who they would keep in the camps to provide some of the logistical support previously provided by civilians living in villages in rebel-controlled territory. The result was twofold: a major increase in the rate of forced marriage, rape, and abduction (see Guberek et al. 2006; Smith et al. 2004; TRC 2004), and a marked shift in gender roles within the group, described in the next section. Within two years, however, the wife recruitment policy inaugurated under "Operation Fine Girl" was withdrawn, because supporting and protecting, as well as guarding, high numbers of untrained civilians drained security and material resources. Later mobilization patterns were characterized by continuity and change. In the second half of the war, from 1997 onward, participant numbers spiked as the RUF was joined by the mutinous SLA and together both fought against the community-mobilized Civil Defense Forces (CDF). Throughout this period, women and girls continued to be forced to join the RUF during raids on farms and villages. Such encounters were often characterized by rape and other forms of violence against family and community members (Marks 2014).

Coercion and violence persisted in contested territory and anti-civilian retaliation campaigns increased in response to CDF mobilization. But, recruitment and training declined across the organization. Gradually, as negotiated peace became an increasingly likely prospect, forced recruitment declined and members settled into more ordinary domestic units, often in towns and villages. In controlled territory, the RUF sought to attract followers and curry favor with local businessmen and women eager to tap into their social and economic networks. Mobilization patterns thus became even more stratified according to one's social station. Young girls and poor rural women had very little with which to bargain and were often at the mercy of diffuse groups of armed combatants they encountered. Yet, large stretches of urban areas and controlled zones saw life unfold day-to-day much as it did in peacetime.

These recruitment patterns are important for a few reasons. First, they reveal the close connection between coercion, violence, and mobilization. As decades of feminist security studies research has shown, there is often no bright line between victim and perpetrator (see, for example, Elshtain 1987; Moser and Clark 2001; Utas 2005), and the same was true in Sierra Leone (Cohen 2016). Most women who became RUF combatants had also themselves suffered extreme human rights violations in their initial encounter with the group, and as members they were subject to its harsh laws (Marks 2014). Many women and men were also complicit in perpetrating crimes on others that had been perpetrated on them, from forced recruitment and rape, to violent training and punishment within the organization. Second, I have highlighted change over time to underscore the importance of adapting policy solutions to a dynamic and shifting context. Preventing recruitment, whether voluntary or forced, requires understanding the patterns of insurgent mobilization on the ground and decriminalizing the highly constrained choices people are forced to make to survive. Finally, as the next section will explore, women's varied pathways into the group also shaped their roles and opportunities, and ultimately their experiences, within the RUF. More abject experiences of forced mobilization often translate into prolonged vulnerability.

MILITARY, SOCIAL, AND POLITICAL POWER

The fundamental distinction in armed conflict between combatants and civilians is often blurry and contested in civil war. Civilian neutrality is particularly difficult to protect when insurgents rely on the local population for support or cover, whether enthusiastic or elicited by force. Adding to the confusion, in Sierra Leone the RUF distinguished between "enemy civilians" and "RUF civilians." Under international humanitarian law, it is illegal to target any civilians with violence. However, in practice, the RUF governed civilian activities and relations within its own territory and camps with tight control, but largely failed to extend protection policies and organizational policing to people residing in government territory, who were seen as potential government collaborators. Falling within the rebels' sphere of influence was, therefore, a double-edged sword. While it meant protection from certain forms of frontline violence, it also exposed members to abuses that included restrictions on movement, controlled social relations, steep taxes on goods, and military judicial structures with harsh, often lethal, punishment. People's experiences of vulnerability within the organization, as such, followed internal logics of power. These can be best understood through the organization's military, social, and political hierarchies.

Everyone within the ambit of the RUF was distinguished according to whether or not they had been trained militarily. Most participants who joined in the first phase of the war received military training. In line with the shifting mobilization trajectories, women who joined in the early years were much more likely to be trained to handle weapons and conduct tactical missions than those who joined in the second and third phases of the conflict (1994–2001). Then, civilian numbers ballooned, partly as a result of people joining the RUF in the bush out of fear of being accused of collaborating with the insurgents and, therefore, targeted by pro-government forces. Women and girls who were forcibly recruited as wives or civilians had a more restricted set of options than female fighters. Civilian women primarily served in the private or domestic sphere of the organization, which itself was integral to the logistical capacity of the movement. Lastly, some of the more powerful women who opted into the group's project in the later stages did so as a form of social navigation, seeking to maximize their life chances in a militarily and politically shifting landscape.

According to early recruits into the RUF, female fighters suffered more than their male counterparts in battle in the early years of the war. As a result, unlike men, their participation in military operations was made optional, not compulsory, for much of the war. Some female fighters gained a reputation for being particularly fearsome in frontline operations, like "Adama Cut-Hands," and enjoyed going to fight because it gave them an opportunity to bring back loot and build their reputation. Mid-level female fighters had command over the child soldiers who made up the "small boys" (SBU) and "small girls" (SGU) units, respectively. They would take them on "food finding missions" in territory surrounding the rural bases and manage their labor in the camps. Trained women had their own command chain, the Women's Army Corps, or Women's Auxiliary Corps (referred to throughout the war as "WACs", there is some confusion among members as to what the acronym stood for), the name of which draws on similar structures in British and US military history. The WACs were intended to be a parallel structure with a female counterpart to each male military officer overseeing male troop operations. In practice, however, many WACs command positions went unfilled. After the overall WACs commander died in 1994, for example, the position was not filled again until 1997. Instead, throughout the "jungle" phase of the war, guerrilla military bases each had local WACs commanders who oversaw operations and assignments for trained women.

Toward the end of the war, the top-ranked overall training commander was a WACs member, and several of the female Vanguard members had risen in the ranks of the group. Senior WACs commanders presided over the Women's Task Force, which served as a pseudo-judicial liaison office between civilian women and male combatants. As a civilian wife described:

> If you have any problems with your man, you go to [the Task Force commander] and she will settle the matter. I went once because my husband was beating me. She talked to him, and he stopped for some time. If she told him, he had to stop. Sometimes she would call meetings for the women to show us how to fight. She would encourage the women and explain about the war. (Interview: Lettitia Ballah, April 2008, Mile 91)

The WACs commander and Women's Task Force thus had status within the male-dominated military apparatus of the organization and power over the civilian women's wing.

Civilian women's affairs were organized around wives' committees and a political Women's Wing. Women did most of the cooking, cleaning, fetching water, and laundering in camps. Those who were married, forcibly or voluntarily, to male fighters usually stayed in the camp and cared for their partner and children. Wives' commanders organized this female labor in a militarized fashion and delegated tasks on a daily basis. Women often delegated their tasks, in turn, to children or junior wives. Slivers of social hierarchy were thus sharpened in the labor intensive environment of low-budget insurgency.

Competition, harassment, and abuse were common between senior and junior wives where commanders had multiple female partners, and between trained and untrained women in the RUF. There were thus multiple gendered hierarchies at play. For trained women, their military skills garnered a level of legitimacy and cachet within the organization. They could access typically masculine militarized power by distinguishing themselves from the feminized "wife" role. There was value in being seen as brave and strong "as a man" at the frontlines, and good military performance underpinned promotion in the group. Moreover, within the camps, the ability to use violence curried respect and served as a source of protection in a highly insecure environment.

The incorporation of untrained women and girls into rebel camps threatened to destabilize the precarious security of female fighters and led to divisions between women. To avoid losing their status as equal to men, trained women fiercely differentiated themselves from untrained women. Within the wives' sphere, many women and girls described facing physical and verbal threats and intimidation from female fighters. Early female recruits saw themselves as original members and viewed later joiners with suspicion as less authentic or freeriding rather than fighting for the revolution. This internal cleavage was exacerbated by the fact that early joiners were overwhelmingly Mende-speaking, and subsequent recruitment waves incorporated more participants from other ethno-linguistic groups in the North of the country as the group expanded its territorial reach.

Because late joiners were less likely to be trained and more likely to be partnered or "married" to male combatants, they drew on different sources of social capital to secure their position in the organization. Many young women and girls were in an abject position of almost total insecurity and vulnerability (Marks 2014). Separated from their home communities and families and forced to join a violent organization with polyglot membership, the girls' primary source of security was often their "husband," the man who claimed responsibility for them at the G-5, the civilian governance branch of the RUF. Women's status thus varied in relation to that of their husbands or boyfriends. Unmarried and untrained women and girls were most susceptible to abuse by men and by commanders' wives. Those partnered with commanders, on the other hand, had privileged access to food and other supplies. They had bodyguards who controlled their movements but also protected them from others' advances or hostility. And they frequently looked after orphaned children who they fostered, and who they could also use (or abuse) as servants. As one of the top commanders' wives describes it:

> Because I was Superman's wife, I did not have to go on raids . . . Other girls who were not commanders' wives were not treated as well. They were flogged, abused, and had to go on ambushes and raids for food (Margaret Kanneh, quoted in Marks 2008: 35).

There was thus a social hierarchy within the RUF according to whether female members were married and if that marriage came with protections (see Marks 2014).

In interviews, women often referred to their political and military credentials to assert greater power and legitimacy than other women. Nowhere was the contentious relationship between trained and untrained women more apparent in the RUF than at the top, where WACs commanders resented the sudden political power wielded by senior male commanders' wives. Toward the end of the war, a group of civilian women within the RUF formed the Revolutionary United Sisters' Organization. Founded by a few senior civilian women and commanders' wives to unify RUF and SLA women, the group sought to provide medical care, food, and other services to wounded soldiers, and to create a social and political space for women in the male dominated organization. However, Vanguard women refused to join, saying they had not been properly consulted:

> They came to Freetown to ask me to join under [Alice] but I said I would never join because they did not consult the founder women. [A top commander] just fell in love with her; she didn't even join the revolution. She was just with a commander and had two *pikin* (children). If you are willing and you accept the ideology of the revolution you can be part of the revolution. (Interview: Fatu Tucker, Freetown, April 2008; also quoted in Marks 2014)

The formation of wives' committees and political groups by women who had not been part of the revolution from the beginning was seen as undermining the power and influence female fighters had fought hard to achieve. When it came time for peace talks at Lomé in 1999, both WACs and civilian women were tapped to attend. In the end, however, they were left behind due to military instability at the airfield where they were to be collected.

IMPLICATIONS FOR WOMEN, PEACE, AND SECURITY

The overarching lesson for the WPS agenda is that, even across diverse mobilization pathways, women's participation in armed groups cannot be conflated with empowerment. As we know from decades of research and dashed optimism, women's inclusion in revolutionary movements, insurgencies, state militaries, or local militias does not equate inherently with gender equality or emancipation. Women in armed groups often reinforce masculine militarism; they are not given equal leadership opportunities and decision-making power; they experience disproportionately high levels of harassment and oppression; and upon demobilization their contributions are often erased from the historical record or remembered for their exceptionalism. This disconnect between participation and empowerment is underscored in other chapters in this collection, particularly those on conflict prevention, feminist anti-militarism, and disarmament. Moreover, in patriarchal societies, the premise of equal opportunity often serves to occlude formal and informal power structures that continue to limit women's options, agency, and influence. The RUF was no exception. Women's vulnerability, and conversely their power and influence, was moderated by many of the same social factors that stratified society in peacetime Sierra Leone. Age, education, and social ties were important attributes for gaining even small amounts of respect in the RUF's society in the bush. Yet, the key factors influencing women's power and security were their military status—training, rank, and facility with violence—and their marital status, whether they were partnered with a powerful man. These gendered dimensions of rebellion dramatically shaped women's experiences of violence, protection, and participation.

Participation

A clear lesson from Sierra Leone is that rebel groups and other military organizations may have large numbers of female participants and often have dedicated leadership positions for women. Organizations like the RUF, which have a political wing and military wing, should have both wings represented at peace talks and other negotiations. Moreover, participation quotas should require women's inclusion from both branches. Women should not be included only as victims and civil society representatives in WPS. For the agenda to truly achieve its transformative potential, it must demand inclusion and representation from belligerents themselves. Including at peace talks representatives of the Women's Wing, the Women's Task Force, and the RUF's Ministry of Gender, for example, would have brought better representation of the range of women's issues within the RUF. It would also help transform gender equitable participation at the highest levels of rebel governance. Many of the female leaders within the RUF were involved in expanding education and medical care within the group's territory; their inclusion would have highlighted these issues. Conversely, some women were complicit in war crimes and abuse; their inclusion would also help strengthen accountability and help us better understand the gender dynamics of within-group impunity. Finally, low-ranked women must also be explicitly included in the structures and processes that broker peace. Often the political settlement agreed to by elites does little to redistribute power and resources to those who have been victimized and oppressed in civil war. This suggests we may need to identify space between track one and track two diplomacy, wherein stakeholder groups are given protected space to lobby for their needs as part of formal peace processes.

Protection and Prevention

From a prevention perspective, the RUF record for within-group policing was a ghastly failure. Women and girls (and men and boys) were victimized and abused at every stage of the conflict. Civilians were targeted for food and other material supplies, and were retaliated against when local communities mobilized in self-defense. Forced recruitment campaigns dragged women and girls into the rebellion against their will and often after suffering rape and other violent encounters with armed fighters. It is all the more worrying that many of these practices were not the official policy or strategy of the RUF, nor of many state and non-state armed groups elsewhere (Marks 2013). This widespread abuse, and the fact abuses were also carried out in large numbers by other parties to the conflict, raises serious questions for the WPS agenda about impunity and prevention.

Rape was outlawed in the code of conduct and was punishable by execution in the organization. Young girls, in particular, were supposed to be protected because they were considered too young for sexual relations. Yet, 25 percent of rape victims documented by the TRC were under the age of 13 (Conibere et al. 2004: 16) and many female combatants interviewed for this research described being raped upon capture. There is ample interview and archival evidence that the RUF did indeed also execute perpetrators of rape. However, it is undisputed that the organization continued to perpetrate rape throughout the war. How can we effectively disrupt cultures of violence and impunity within non-state armed groups?

One possibility is to lean more heavily on armed groups' own codes of conduct and internal laws. Where there are internal oversight and enforcement mechanisms, the international community and peace mediators can push for organizations to respect international humanitarian law by aligning and enforcing their own legal framework. A further lesson learned is that many of the worst abuses may happen within groups rather than between them, as women and girls are exposed to sustained violence and exploitation with only internal organizational rules and institutions for protection. Understanding the interwoven nature of victimization and perpetration of violence requires not criminalizing all members of insurgent organizations, but rather, recognizing the complex interplay between choice and coercion. A related lesson is the ambiguous commitment many participants had to the "revolution." Both men and women mobilized for violence in situations of extreme uncertainty and precarity, wherein generalized insecurity made joining the rebels one of the "least worst" options. More attention needs to be given to how conflict structures limit individual choices and actions. Treating combatants as people who may prefer to find themselves in different circumstances, rather than as militant ideologues, or lacking moral purpose, opens more avenues for demobilization.

Relief and Recovery

In the aforementioned context of widespread insecurity and coercive recruitment, women and girls may be the most vulnerable participants in disarmament, demobilization, and reintegration (DDR) campaigns. The Sierra Leone DDR process was at the time seen as a great success, with over seventy thousand fighters disarming. However, shortcomings were soon revealed. Only 6.5 percent of participants were women, despite an estimated 30 percent of RUF being female (Solomon and Ginifer 2008). There are a number of reasons DDR systematically excluded women and girls. First, and most simply, the process underestimated the number of female participants in the war, and as a result did not prepare adequate facilities to support their inclusion. For example, DDR camps rarely had gender segregated sleeping and bathing facilities. Second, the entry requirement of turning in a weapon excluded women and girls whose male partners or commanders largely controlled their access to weapons. Male commanders frequently distributed weapons as a form of "patronage" to ensure their male fighters' inclusion in DDR programs that were seen as a benefit, not a right. Third, many women and girls feared being labeled a rebel and potentially prosecuted if they participated in DDR. Much of the DDR process occurred amidst high levels of uncertainty and insecurity, and women who had already been harassed within the RUF may not have felt they would have adequate protection either from group members or other ex-combatants in the camps.

Women who participated either in DDR or in other post-conflict rehabilitative programs were largely shunted back into the restrictive gender roles of peacetime Sierra Leonean society. Megan MacKenzie (2009) describes the peace-building process as one of gendered reordering, where women and girls who were seen as violating social norms by participating in violence and rebellion were taught to be hairdressers, seamstresses, and other typically feminine vocations. A premium was put on reintegrating women into their families and home communities, though material resources focused on individual responsibility and independence recreating a post-conflict gender gap. Future programming needs to address lost social capital and social ties if reconstruction is going to successfully support reintegration. The United Nations Development Program (UNDP) began tracking temporary employment and livelihoods disbursements to women in 2013; however, the figures hover around one-third of economic benefits going to women (UN Women 2015: 9–10). Further limiting women's ability to secure sustainable livelihoods and personal wellbeing is a lack of mental and physical healthcare in the aftermath of war. Sierra Leone had a paucity of mental health professionals trained or qualified to work with victims of trauma. As a result, mental and emotional recovery often became lumped in with inappropriate community activities like reconciliation and transitional justice. There has been little to no sustained effort to help ex-combatants and other victims of the war intellectually and emotionally process the violence they have witnessed and experienced, which has knock-on effects on core personal and social functions. Stress and post-trauma leads to disrupted sleep, anxiety and stress management problems, damaged trust and communication, and problems with long-term planning that are compounded by Sierra Leone's extreme poverty. Moreover, women's health and the broader care economy are not prioritized after war, despite the increased importance of social cohesion in facilitating peace-building and post-conflict recovery. Many women I have interviewed complain of physical manifestations of this neglect, including pain associated with sexual violence, infections, or unattended births. It was not until 2010, eight years after the war ended, that pregnant and lactating women could access free medical care, and there is still no public provision for victims of violence and abuse during the war to receive treatment. As a result, people say in the local Krio language that they are "managing," but it is difficult, with poverty and lack of social protection the great equalizer between former combatants and civilians.

References

Alcoff, Linda. "Cultural Feminism versus Post-Structuralism: The Identity Crisis in Feminist Theory." *Signs: Journal of Women in Culture and Society* 13, no. 3 (1988): 405–436.

Cohen, Dara. *Rape during Civil War*. Ithaca, NY: Cornell University Press, 2016.

Conibere, Richard, Jana Asher, Kristen Cibelli, Jana Dudukovich, Rafe Kaplan, and Patrick Ball. *Statistical Appendix to the Report of the Truth and Reconciliation Commission of Sierra Leone*. Palo Alto, CA: Human Rights Data Analysis Group, 2004. https://hrdag.org/content/sierraleone/SL-TRC-statistics-chapter-final.pdf.

Coulter, Chris. *Bush Wives and Girl Soldiers: Women's Lives through War and Peace in Sierra Leone*. Ithaca, NY: Cornell University Press, 2009.

Coulter, Chris. "Female Fighters in the Sierra Leone War: Challenging the Assumptions?" *Feminist Review* 88, no. 1 (2008): 54–73.

Crenshaw, Kimberlé. "Mapping the Margins: Intersectionality, Identity Politics, and Violence against Women of Color." *Stanford Law Review* (1991): 1241–1299.

Guberek, Tamy, D. Guzmán, R. Silva, K. Cibelli, J. Asher, S. Weikart, P. Ball, and W. M. Grossman. "Truth and Myth in Sierra Leone: An Empirical Analysis of the Conflict, 1991–2000." A Report by the Benetech Human Rights Data Analysis Group and the American Bar Association. Palo Alto, CA: Benetech, 2006.

Elshtain, Jean Beth. *Women and War*. Chicago, IL: University of Chicago Press, 1987.

hooks, bell. *Ain't I a Woman: Black Women and Feminism*. Boston: South End, 1981, 665.

Kaldor, Mary. *New and Old Wars: Organised Violence in a Global Era*. New York: John Wiley & Sons, 2003.

MacKenzie, Megan. "Empowerment Boom or Bust? Assessing Women's Post-Conflict Empowerment Initiatives." *Cambridge Review of International Affairs* 22, no. 2 (2009): 199–215.

Marks, Zoe. Interview, Margaret Kanneh, Mile 91, April 11, 2008.

Marks, Zoe. "Sexual Violence Inside Rebellion: Policies and Perspectives of the Revolutionary United Front of Sierra Leone." *Civil Wars* 15, no. 3 (2013): 359–379.

Marks, Zoe. "Sexual Violence in Sierra Leone's Civil War: 'Virgination,' rape, and marriage." *African Affairs* 113, no. 450 (2014): 67–87.

Moser, Caroline O. N., and Fiona C. Clark, eds. *Victims, Perpetrators, or Actors? Gender, Armed Conflict, and Political Violence*. London: Zed Books, 2001.

Smith, L. Alison, Catherine Gambette, and Thomas Longley, "Conflict Mapping in Sierra Leone: Violations of International Humanitarian Law from 1991 to 2002," No Peace without Justice. Sierra Leone Conflict Mapping Programme. Freetown, Sierra Leone, March 2004): 561.

Solomon, Christiana, and Jeremy Ginifer. "Disarmament, Demobilisation, and Reintegration in Sierra Leone." Centre for International Cooperation and Security, July 2008.

Straus, Scott. "Wars Do End! Changing Patterns of Political Violence in Sub-Saharan Africa." *African Affairs* 111, no. 443 (2012): 179–201.

Truth and Reconciliation Commission (TRC), Sierra Leone. *Witness to Truth: Vol. 3A* Freetown, Sierra Leone, 2004.

UN Women. "Preventing Conflict, Transforming Justice, Securing the Peace: A Global Study on the Implementation of United Nations Security Council resolution 1325." PeaceWomen, 2015, http://www.peacewomen.org/sites/default/files/UNW-GLOBAL-STUDY-1325-2015%20(1).pdf.

Utas, Mats. "Agency of Victims: Young Women in the Liberian Civil War." In *Makers and Breakers: Children and Youth in Postcolonial Africa*, edited by Alcinda Honwana and Filip De Boeck, 53–80. Oxford: James Currey, 2005.

Yuval-Davis, Nira. "Intersectionality and Feminist Politics." *European Journal of Women's Studies* 13, no. 3 (2006): 193–209.

CHAPTER 39

PROTECTING DISPLACED WOMEN AND GIRLS
The Case of Syria

ELIZABETH FERRIS

OVER the past fifteen years, the issue of protecting displaced women and girls has been a major focus for the humanitarian community. Policies, guidelines, toolkits, and training manuals have all been produced in great abundance. Yet, despite these efforts, displaced women and girls continue to experience discrimination, gender-based violence, and restricted participation in decision-making. This chapter considers the impact of UN Security Council Resolution 1325 on displaced women and girls over the past fifteen years. It then examines the resolution's impact on the specific case of Syrian refugee and internally displaced women.

The adoption of Resolution 1325 in 2000 marked a major step forward in the international community's recognition of the importance of women to peace and security. In particular, the resolution highlighted women's contributions to a wide range of issues including participation, conflict-resolution, protection, and relief and recovery. Although Articles 7 and 12 of the resolution specifically mention refugee and displaced women, and advocates for refugee women participated actively in the drafting process, the focus of the resolution was primarily on the incorporation of women's concerns into peacekeeping, peacemaking, and peace-building, rather than on the particular needs and resources of refugee and displaced women. Indeed, the responsibility for responding to refugees and internally displaced persons (IDPs) has generally fallen to the governments concerned and to a constellation of humanitarian agencies. While humanitarian agencies, such as the Office for the Coordination of Humanitarian Affairs (OCHA) and the UN High Commissioner for Refugees (UNHCR) regularly brief the Security Council on their operations, the nuts and bolts of providing relief and solutions is largely left to the humanitarian agencies.

It is important to underscore at the outset that while both refugees and IDPs are displaced by conflict and often experience common threats, such as sexual and gender-based violence, family separation, and inadequate assistance and protection, there are important differences between refugees and IDPs which also affect their needs and possibilities. According to the 1951 Refugee Convention, refugees are individuals who have left their countries, can no longer avail themselves of the protection of their government and have a well-founded fear of persecution because of their race, religion, nationality, or membership in a particular social group or political opinion. There are presently 148 signatories to the 1951 Convention which imposes obligations on state parties, most fundamentally the obligation not to return refugees to situations where their lives are at risk. A large UN agency, UNHCR, has been entrusted by the international community with protecting and assisting refugees and currently has over ten thousand employees working in more than one hundred countries.[1] Although the international refugee regime has been stressed in recent years, the system is based on an international commitment to share responsibility for refugees.

On the other hand, the situation of those displaced within the borders of their countries, even when they flee for exactly the same reasons as refugees, is different. Rather than a binding international convention, there is a non-binding set of *Guiding Principles* (UN 1998) that call for respecting the rights of IDPs in specific areas. However, fundamental to the *Guiding Principles* is the affirmation that it is the responsibility of the national authorities of the concerned state to protect and assist IDPs, rather than the international community, even when state authorities themselves have been responsible or complicit in the displacement of IDPs. Rather than a single large international agency mandated to assist and protect them, different international agencies collaborate in responding to IDPs, with different agencies taking the lead in different sectors. Finally, the definition of IDPs as spelled out in the *Guiding Principles* is broader than that of refugees and includes those displaced by the effects of disasters and development projects, such as dams (Ferris 2015).[2] As of early 2017, estimates are that, of the world's 65 million conflict-displaced people, two-thirds of them (40 million) are IDPs. Because IDPs frequently live in areas of conflict, providing assistance to them and even collecting basic information about their numbers and needs is difficult to obtain. International assistance to IDPs is generally less than to refugees and, as Buscher (2010: 8) argues, these lower levels of international assistance are associated with a range of harms with respect to women IDPs, including comparatively poorer reproductive health outcomes. On the other hand, as residents or citizens of their country, internally displaced women generally do not face the same kinds of legal or administrative problems in accessing the labor market as women refugees do. In terms of normative frameworks, the 1951 Refugee Convention does not refer to gender, or mention women or girls. However, the provision that persecution because of "membership in a social group" has been interpreted in some countries to include those who have been persecuted because of their gender. UNHCR, as discussed more extensively in what follows, has worked hard to ensure that gender (as well as age and other characteristics of the refugee population) are mainstreamed into all of its policies and programs for refugees. Likely reflecting the fact that there was greater awareness of gender issues in the 1990s than in the 1950s, the *Guiding Principles* do refer to the importance of gender and specifically highlight the rights of IDP women to participate in decisions affecting their lives and their right to appropriate assistance.

As the main causes of displacement are conflicts and violence, this chapter begins with an assessment of refugee and displaced women's participation in peace processes, finding serious shortcomings in their engagement. However, humanitarian agencies have made impressive progress in recent decades toward ensuring that the particular needs and resources of displaced women are included in both assistance and protection programs, even though these initiatives do not seem to have been primarily influenced by Resolution 1325, but rather by other processes. The chapter goes on to address the seeming contradiction between significant progress in mainstreaming gender into field operations with the fact that conditions for refugee and displaced women have not significantly improved. The chapter then explores measures to increase the accountability of humanitarian actors to beneficiaries, before turning to a discussion of the situation facing Syrian refugee and displaced women. The chapter concludes with brief recommendations for improving conditions for refugee and displaced women in light of Resolution 1325.

REFUGEE AND DISPLACED WOMEN'S PARTICIPATION IN THE PEACE PROCESS: MINIMAL PROGRESS

It is important to underscore that preventing, resolving, and recovering from conflicts are of paramount importance to refugee and displaced women. It is conflict, after all, that forces people to leave their communities, and any progress in strengthening peace processes is of immediate benefit to refugee and displaced women. Women's participation in peace negotiations, peacekeeping forces, and the implementation of peace agreements is likely to strengthen prospects for peace and hence to benefit refugee and displaced women. However, it is also important to point out, as Bandarage (2010) does in the case of Sri Lanka, that women are not only victims, but they are also perpetrators and peacemakers.

While women are rarely present in peace processes, refugees and IDPs (both men and women) have also largely been excluded from such processes (Brookings-Bern Project 2007, 2010). Refugee and displaced women thus face dual barriers to participation: as women and as refugees or IDPs. Tinde (2009) finds that while women are more likely than men to advocate for a role for displaced women in peace, very few women are senior enough to change the status quo. There have been a few cases where refugee and displaced women have been involved—for example, the Guatemalan and Liberian cases are often cited, but by and large peace negotiations remain focused on dialogues between the leaders of the armed parties and do not include civilian representatives of those who have suffered the effects of the conflict. Even when mediators are sympathetic to the inclusion of refugees and IDPs, the armed parties tend to fear that their participation will create an imbalance in the negotiations (Brookings-Bern Project 2007). The three years of negotiations between FARC and the Colombian government are an exception where the participation of "victims," defined to include internally displaced persons, was intentional, gender-sensitive, broad-based and effective (Alsema 2015). Restrepo (2016) argues that women can overcome their victimhood by becoming agents of change in their communities and increase the likelihood of sustainable peace in their societies by facilitating empowerment and societal reconciliation. It is too early to evaluate the results of the historic peace agreement in Colombia on either women victims writ large or on IDP women in particular, but the signs are encouraging. It seems likely that the participation of both IDPs and women as "victims" in the peace process will be seen to have had a positive effect on long-term reconciliation efforts. As Snyder (2011) observes, in the cases of Burma (Myanmar), Sudan, and Tibet, the relative success of displaced women's participation in the Colombian peace processes stands in contrast to other situations where refugee women have had limited capacity to participate in peace-building processes.

While it seems that Resolution 1325 has produced few results in terms of the increased participation of refugee and displaced women in peace processes, the resolution also called for more attention to the particular needs of refugee and displaced women and called on humanitarian actors to incorporate gender into their programs and policies.

HUMANITARIAN AGENCIES: IMPRESSIVE RESPONSE IN ADDRESSING GENDER ISSUES

While a great deal of progress has been made by the international humanitarian community (at least on the policy level), in responding to the particular needs of refugee and displaced women and girls, it is difficult to attribute these changes to Resolution 1325. Other factors were likely more important in leading humanitarian actors to do more on gender issues than the Security Council resolution. For example, Buscher (2010) reports that the 2001 UNHCR-organized Dialogue with Refugee Women that enabled them to express their concerns directly to the High Commissioner for Refugees and led UNHCR to make five concrete commitments to refugee women (UNHCR 2001.)[3] The 2002 scandal in West Africa where a joint Save the Children/UNHCR Assessment report found that humanitarian workers had sexually exploited refugee women and children led the UN, donor governments, and NGOs to adopt a wide range of measures intended to prevent sexual exploitation and abuse (Ferris 2007). These changes may have been influenced by the 1325 resolution, but they were primarily influenced by other underlying drivers and triggers. For example, the UN Secretary-General's Bulletin (2003) made no mention of Resolution 1325 when it mandated a zero tolerance policy toward sexual exploitation and abuse, and it is rare to find more than a passing mention (if any) of Resolution 1325 in the many tools and policies adopted by humanitarian actors over the past twenty years.

Since the late 1990s, greater attention has been paid by the international humanitarian community to the needs of women and girls in conflict situations and to promoting gender-sensitive approaches to humanitarian and development assistance. Most of these efforts focused on refugees, although with the dissemination of the *Guiding Principles on Internal Displacement* (UN 1998), some efforts have also been made to address the particular needs of IDP women or to include them in them in the applicable general gender policies. The 2013 report of the Special Rapporteur on the Rights of Internally Displaced Persons spells out the many ways in which humanitarian and human rights actors have incorporated gender in their approaches to internally displaced women and girls (UN Human Rights Council 2013a).

Presenting an exhaustive list of all the tools, policies, and guidance developed over the past twenty years to address gender in humanitarian operations would take many more pages than is possible in this short chapter. Some of the important efforts in this process include the Inter-Agency Standing Committee's *Gender Handbook* (IASC 2006); UNHCR's *Handbook for the Protection of Women and Girls* (UNHCR 2008); UNHCR's 2011 Age, Gender, and Diversity policy; the International Organisation for Migration's Gender

Equality Policy: 2015–2019 (IOM 2015); and OCHA's Gender Equality resources (UN OCHA 2017) website which features a long list of tools for ensuring gender mainstreaming in coordination mechanisms, in preparedness, in emergency response funds, and so on. The IASC Gender Marker was rolled out in 2012 as a mechanism for determining the extent to which a given project responds to the needs of women and girls. It was intended to ensure that gender mainstreaming did not remain just at the policy level, but was also reflected in how budgets were allocated and spent. As with many of these resources, the Gender Marker includes not only the specific tool, but also guidance and training materials on using it, and a 2014 evaluation of its utility (IASC 2012–2014). Most recently, the Global Protection Cluster (2015) produced exhaustive (366 pages) guidelines for addressing gender-based violence in the context of humanitarian action. In addition to initiatives by international organizations, the International Federation of Red Cross and Red Crescent movement (IFRC 2013) and virtually all NGOs have developed their own resources (Groverman and Kloosterman 2010; Catholic Relief Services 2013).

Overall, significant progress has been made in addressing both protection and assistance issues, particularly in the area of improving reproductive health services. For example, the Inter-Agency Working Group on Refugee Productive Health (IAWG) developed a field manual with a Minimum Initial Service Package (MISP) addressing reproductive health in emergency settings (IAWG 2010). However, as is the case with all of the tools and policies, serious gaps remain in implementation (Martin 2003, 2011). There has also been progress in integrating women into assistance distribution systems, and implementing fuel strategies to reduce refugee and displaced women's exposure to violence when they collect firewood (see chapter 14 in this volume). In some cases, refugee and IDP women have received legal assistance to uphold their rights to land and property. For example, Colombia stands out for its development of strong associations between IDP and refugee women, which has increased their ability to participate in decision-making.

All of these initiatives (and many more) represent a significant commitment of staff time, both to develop the policies, to ensure institutional buy-in, to train staff, to monitor implementation, to report to governing bodies, to disseminate to partners, and so on. It is fair to stay that at the level of international agencies, the UN, NGO, and other international organizations all have made significant efforts to mainstream gender into their programs. At this level, the progress has been enormous. Yet, the situation for refugee and IDP women today is undoubtedly the worst in the modern history of international refugee protection regime.

IF GENDER IS SO MAINSTREAMED, WHY ARE CONDITIONS FOR WOMEN GETTING WORSE?

Since the adoption of Resolution 1325, the number of IDPs in the world has increased from 21.2 million in 2000 to 33.3 million in 2013 and to 41 million in 2016. In other words, the number of IDPs has doubled since the passing of Resolution 1325. On a more positive note, within the growing number of IDPs, the number assisted by UNHCR has increased even more—from assisting 6 million in 2000 to 23.9 million in 2013. In comparison, the number of refugees under UNHCR's mandate in 2000 was 15.87 million, a figure only slightly less than the 16.7 million refugees registered in 2013 (in comparison, the 2016 number of refugees is around 21.3 million) (IDMC 2017; UNHCR 2017a). This indicates that despite Resolution 1325, conflicts have displaced more people, and far more IDPs than refugees, although it should be noted that at least some of this increase is due to better collection of statistics on IDPs over the past twenty years.

Despite some promising initiatives, the 2015 review of 1325 found that the situation for refugees and displaced persons has become dire, with difficulties in a number of areas, from sexual and gender-based violence, to the lack of equity in post-conflict reparations, as well as a lack of participation in forums related to the particular needs of women displaced by disasters and the effects of climate change (UN Women 2015).

Refugee and internally displaced women have many specific needs related to their displacement, including lack of documentation or individual status. Male heads of household are still often the holders of the documentation or registration for the family, although strides have been made in refugee registration systems to register all adults. Refugees and IDPs almost always experience a decline in their previous standard of living. Both men and women often lose their traditional livelihoods. Women who have been responsible for livestock, agriculture, or trade often find that they are no longer able to pursue these activities, at least not in the same way. Women may have less mobility due to security situations that confine them to their homes, or in some cases, such as Syria, they are forced to travel or seek work outside the home because of the risk faced by men in venturing out (Davis et al. 2014; Dwyer and Cagoco-Guiam, 2011: 9). Without funds, they may resort to survival sex, petty crime, or early marriages. As the UN report summarizes,

> [refugee and displaced] women are at risk of human trafficking by organized crime; harassment, exploitation and discrimination by landlords and employers; and arbitrary arrest, detention and refoulement by the authorities (UN Women 2015: 69).

Family structures often change in displacement with women often assuming non-traditional roles. Sometimes it is easier for women to find employment in the informal sector than for men. These changing gender roles seem to be a factor in increasing domestic violence in families displaced by conflict, but may also have more positive long-term implications. Olivius (2014) engages with the topic of women's participation in refugee camps and uses case studies from two refugee camps in Bangladesh and Thailand. She finds within these camps that women's participation is used as a means to improve the efficiency of humanitarian aid in these contexts. In this process, women's participation can both reinforce existing gender inequalities but also open new opportunities to women. While the issue of sexual and gender-based violence (SGBV) is discussed more extensively in chapter 24 it is important to underscore here that displacement increases vulnerability to SGBV. Domestic violence seems to increase when men are frustrated by their inability to provide for their families. The breakdown of traditional norms and conflict-resolution mechanisms as a result of displacement may create a context of impunity where inhibitions and punishment for sexual assault no longer apply. The fact that refugees and IDPs are often dependent on aid providers for survival creates a situation where those in positions of power are able to sexually exploit those they are supposed to be aiding. Refugees and IDPs are also vulnerable to violence, including SGBV, because their social networks have been damaged. Refugee and displaced women are not a homogeneous group and often experience multiple forms of discrimination as gender intersects with race, age, civil status, socioeconomic status, disabilities and so on. Displacement seems to heighten the effects of such discrimination. Before turning to the specific case of Syrian refugees and IDPs, the following section discusses two of the major issues affecting refugee and IDP women, which are two areas where the international community has devoted significant resources.

Accountability and Participation

If refugee and displaced women are not active participants in the larger peace processes, how do they fare in participating in decisions about humanitarian assistance and programs?

NGOs in particular have taken up the issue of improving accountability of humanitarian organizations to beneficiaries, and not only to donors. This issue, which was also highlighted at the May 2016 World Humanitarian Summit, is reflected in the Sphere Standards, the work of the Humanitarian Partnership Initiative and now the Core Humanitarian Standard which sets out principles and practical ways of ensuring the participation of affected communities in humanitarian decision-making with accountability of NGOs to those they seek to serve (Core Humanitarian Standard 2017).

Despite these mechanisms, the participation of refugees and IDPs generally, and women in particular, in humanitarian decision-making has been lacking. In 2008, for example, UNHCR received a report that noted the agency's tendency to treat the displaced as "passive beneficiaries of aid" rather than as "equal partners with rights." The report found that this tendency hindered UNHCR's efforts to mainstream gender and highlighted the need to follow up on participatory assessment processes integral to the agency's policy on age, gender, and diversity mainstreaming (UNHCR EXCOM 2008). In 2011, UNHCR convened its second global dialogue with women, and took the important step of engaging internally displaced women in this process for the first time (UNHCR 2011b). Participatory assessments and "bottom-up" participatory planning processes are used by some agencies but few would say that they have been satisfactory. Internally displaced women have rarely played an active role in developing, implementing, and monitoring National Action Plans (NAPs) on Resolution 1325 (UN Human Rights Council, 2013a).

The participation of refugee and displaced persons generally, including women in transitional justice mechanisms, is an area where much greater work is needed. Too often, displacement is not included as one of the crimes considered by these mechanisms (Rimmer 2010; Duthie 2012) and gender-specific concerns may also be excluded. But particularly in looking at issues of post-conflict recovery, when refugees and IDPs may be able to return to their communities of origin, the need for inclusive transitional justice mechanisms is a prerequisite for sustaining peace agreements.

Syria Case Study

Since the Syrian conflict began in March 2011, displacement of Syrians has been rapid, massive, and dynamic. Presently over half of Syria's prewar population has been displaced with around 5 million living in other countries as refugees (though most without legal refugee status) and another 7 million as internally displaced persons. Most of the refugees are concentrated in the neighboring countries of Turkey (3 million), Lebanon (1.25 million), and Jordan (650,000 registered refugees, although the Jordanian government estimates their number as over a million) (UNHCR 2017a). Despite the media attention directed toward Syrian refugees making their way toward Europe or resettled in other countries, the vast majority of the refugees remain in the region where their host governments are increasingly concerned about their economic, political, and security impacts. Of these three countries, only Turkey has signed the 1951 Refugee Convention, but it maintains the original geographic restriction which stipulates that only Europeans can be considered as refugees. Turkey has given the Syrian refugees temporary protection status while both Jordan and Lebanon consider the refugees to be "guests" (a "friendlier" term than refugee but it carries with it no assumption of rights). Many of the refugees in Jordan and around 10 percent of those in Turkey live in refugee camps (UNHCR 2017b). But the rest of the refugees in these countries, and all of the refugees in Lebanon, live in rented or shared accommodation, or in what are euphemistically known as informal settlements. The fact that most of the refugees are not living in camps means that they are often "invisible" to both national authorities and international agencies. It is more difficult to monitor health conditions of refugees and their access to schools, much less incidences of SGBV when refugees are dispersed in large cities.

Inside Syria

As is the case with refugees and IDPs generally, much more is known about Syrian refugee women than about those displaced internally. The Independent International Commission of Inquiry on the Syrian Arab Republic has regularly reported on the human violations occurring inside Syria, including the impact on women. "Where men are the primary breadwinners," the most recent report states, "the enforced disappearance of adult male relatives has an acute impact" (Independent International Commission 2016: 14), as women are forced to rely on men in their extended families and are left in a legal limbo when their husbands are missing but not declared legally dead. Women have been particularly vulnerable to being taken hostage by various armed groups, and have experienced torture and detention. Rape and other forms of sexual violence have been used by Syrian officials during interrogations while in detention. In areas under ISIS control, women suffer lashings for not being adequately covered or being in the company of members of the opposite sex from outside their families. ISIS fighters have forcibly married Sunni women living in ISIS-controlled areas. Thousands of young Yazidi girls are sold in slave markets, and "passed from fighter to fighter as chattel" (Independent International Commission 2016: 15–17.) Additional reports of sexual violence committed by ISIS against women, men, boys, and girls are detailed in the Letter of the Secretary-General to the President of the Security Council (UNSG 2016).

The Special Rapporteur on the Human Rights of Internally Displaced Persons visited Syria in 2013 and reported that while sexual violence is a cause of displacement, women also experience sexual violence in flight and once they are displaced. Domestic violence appears to have increased and young women are increasingly adopting negative coping behaviors, including early marriage. Additionally, the report found that IDPs face the consequences of a lack of government capacity and the lack of a government policy on IDPs. Most IDPs in

Syria are living in areas that are difficult for humanitarian agencies to access (UN Human Rights Council 2013b: 20–21).

Alarmingly as governments of neighboring countries have all mostly closed their borders to Syrian refugees, it is likely that the number of Syrian IDPs will increase as presently evidenced on the Syria-Jordan border (Arraf 2017).

Syrian Refugee Women

The experiences of Syrian refugee women are in line with those of refugee women everywhere. Syrian refugee women have encountered violence during flight, family separation, changing household composition and responsibilities, a decreased standard of living, and protection threats. As their displacement drags on, their situation is likely to worsen. As such, even if the conflict were to end soon, it remains unlikely that they will be able to return to their communities. One aspect of Syrian refugees that differs from those of other nationalities is that there have been a number of reports and studies about the conditions they face, while other refugee women, in countries such as Chad, Cameroon, and the Democratic Republic of the Congo have received much less international attention.

Amnesty International (2016: 1) interviewed Syrian and Iraqi refugee women traveling in Northern Europe and found that refugee women and girls faced "violence, assault, exploitation and sexual harassment at every stage of their journey, including on European soil." A recent Oxfam (2016: 3) study on Syrian refugees in Greece began by asserting that "refugees and migrants were anything but helpless. They had overcome huge risks to escape danger and deprivation," but both men and women were frustrated by the slow nature of legal processes and eligibility. Women, because they could not access some public space, were particularly disadvantaged in their access to information and had reduced clarity about their options. On a daily level, Syrian refugee women in Greece, "felt that poor facilities, including accommodation and washing facilities, placed a heavy burden on them to care for the family, especially when traveling alone with their children. They mentioned the hardship of washing clothes by hand, and cleaning with limited implements and materials, and the burden of caring for children who have become unruly because of the absence of schooling and other boundaries" (Oxfam 2016: 4). While relief materials were available, there continued to be inequality in access to sexual and reproductive healthcare, to contraceptives, and to female doctors.

Household composition of Syrian refugee families is changing with consequences for the protection of refugee women and girls. By 2016, the number of female-headed Syrian households in Jordan had risen to nearly 40 percent from one-quarter a few years ago, while in Greece half of refugee households are estimated to be female-headed (Batha 2016). Batha found that rates of early marriage had doubled since the start of the war due to the increasing destitution of families. Similarly, Woldetsadik (2016) observed that in Lebanon the "absence of adult males in households has increased the vulnerability of women and children, who are at heightened risk for sexual and gender-based violence as well as child labor and other illicit activities." The 2014 study found that 30 percent of Syrian women respondents had experienced some form of violence, but 65 percent of them did not seek medical care. Woldetsadik also discovered that child marriage increased sharply among Syrian refugees living in Jordan due to the insecure environment, lack of work, and inability of heads of households to provide for their families. As elsewhere, the high prevalence of Syrian refugee women living outside of camps means that this population is unaware of or unable to access protection services.

Myers (2016) reports that domestic violence against Syrian refugee women has increased as a result of heightened male frustration due to their inability to find work and provide for their families. Even before the war, about 10 percent of Syrian marriages involved a girl under the age of 18, but that number has increased sharply. As UNICEF reports demonstrate, in some refugee camps 32 percent of registered marriages involved a child under the age of 18. Furthermore these reports also demonstrate that women are engaging in survival sex to support their families and that suicide among young girls is increasing (UNICEF, cited in Myer 2016).

Threats to the protection of refugee women almost always have repercussions for assistance. Charles and Denman (2013) report that the lack of access to basic services, such as education, is also related to the increase in gender-based violence. In looking at Syrian refugee women in Jordan, Lebanon, and Turkey, Williamson (2016) finds that women face legal restrictions that bar them from being full, legal participants in host country economies. Given the increase of female single-headed households, this restriction will have implications for the whole refugee family.

The Women's Refugee Commission in 2014 found real improvements in the way UN agencies and NGOs were responding to refugee women, including the deployment of a gender advisers to appreciate the gender dynamics among the Syrian refugee population. But at the same time, serious problems remained unresolved. Specifically, the distribution of relief items was often coordinated through male heads of household and most health facilities were staffed by male professionals, limiting access for refugee women.

CONCLUSION

Resolution 1325 was an important landmark in affirming the role of women in peace and security. With respect to refugee women, if the resolution has encouraged the participation of women in peacekeeping, peacemaking, and peace-building, and if this greater participation of women in these processes has led to peace, then refugee and displaced women are clear beneficiaries. Unfortunately, the evidence suggests that the number of refugees and especially IDPs, including women, has skyrocketed since the adoption of this resolution. The humanitarian community has taken important steps to address the needs of refugee women more effectively and certainly there is much greater awareness of the importance of gender in humanitarian responses. As the Syrian refugee and IDP cases demonstrate, where the humanitarian community falls short is in encouraging the full participation of refugee and IDP women in decision-making, as well as in their relief and recovery. The perennial problem for humanitarian actors is the conflict situation in which they operate and the gender dynamics among the refugee and IDP population under economic and protection stress. Until and unless conflicts are prevented and resolved, women who are displaced by their effects will continue to suffer the consequences.

In looking at the particular case of Syrian refugee and displaced women, the four pillars of WPS—participation, conflict-resolution, protection, and relief and recovery—are all in need of urgent attention. The resolution of the six-year old conflict seems distant as more international actors and armed opposition groups have entered the war. The ability of all Syrian refugees and IDPs to bring an end to their displacement largely depends on an end to the conflict. Bringing peace to Syria, and maintaining it, is a women's issue. As this chapter has demonstrated, Syrian refugee women face major protection and assistance challenges and, although data are lacking, it seems likely that internally displaced women face even greater challenges as they are closer to the violence and access by humanitarian actors is more difficult. Humanitarian actors are well aware of the threats facing refugee and displaced women and yet funding for Syrian refugees and for Syrians who remain within Syria is woefully inadequate. Yet, the situation is not completely bleak. Although often under the radar, Syrian refugee women are assuming new roles and participating in the decisions that affect their lives and those of their families. They are maintaining social networks, keeping their culture alive, and often providing financial support for their families. Syrian refugee and displaced women will have much to contribute to their country and their communities when the conflict ends. Until then, it is important that they receive the support they need, not only to survive, but also so their roles as leaders are recognized and affirmed.

NOTES

1. A separate UN agency, the UN Relief and Works Administration for Palestine Refugees in the Near East (UNRWA) has responsibility for Palestinian refugees.
2. For the purposes of this chapter, reference to IDPs focuses only on those displaced by conflict and serious human rights violations.
3. The five commitments were participation, individual registration and documentation, food and non-food items management and distribution, economic empowerment, and prevention and response to sexual and gender-based violence (UNHCR 2001).

REFERENCES

Alsema, Adriaan. "Colombia's Peace Deals in Depth: Victims." *Colombia Reports*, December 16, 2015, http://colombiareports.com/colombia-peace-deals-in-depth-victims/.

Amnesty International. "Female Refugees Face Physical Assault, Exploitation, and Sexual Harassment on Their Journey through Europe." January 16, 2016, https://www.amnesty.org/en/latest/news/2016/01/female-refugees-face-physical-assault-exploitation-and-sexual-harassment-on-their-journey-through-europe/.

Arraf, Jane. "Along Syria-Jordan Border, Refugees Struggle at a Camp Aid Workers Can't Visit." National Public Radio, March 20, 2017, http://www.npr.org/sections/parallels/2017/03/20/520857305/along-syria-jordan-border-refugees-struggle-at-a-camp-aid-workers-cant-visit.

Bandarage, Asoka. "Women, Armed Conflict, and Peacemaking in Sri Lanka: Toward a Political Economy Perspective." *Asian Politics & Policy* 2, no. 4 (October 1, 2010): 653–667.

Batha, Emma. "Syrian Refugee Crisis Is Changing Women's Traditional Roles in the Family." *Huffington Post*, September 12, 2016, http://www.huffingtonpost.com/entry/syrian-refugee-women-increasingly-serving-as-main-breadwinners_us_57d6b033e4b03d2d459b40e0.

Brookings-Bern Project on Internal Displacement. "Addressing Displacement in Peace Processes, Peace Agreements, and Peacebuilding." Brookings Institution, September 30, 2007, https://www.brookings.edu/research/addressing-internal-displacement-in-peace-processes-peace-agreements-and-peace-building/.

Brookings-Bern Project on Internal Displacement. "Integrating Internal Displacement in Peace Processes and Agreements." United States Institute of Peace/Brookings Institution, 2010, https://docs.unocha.org/sites/dms/Documents/Integrating%20IDPs%20in%20Peace%20Processes.pdf.

Buscher, Dale. "Refugee Women: Twenty Years On." *Refugee Survey Quarterly* 29, no. 2 (March 1, 2010): 4–20.

Catholic Relief Services. *CRS' Global Gender Strategy.* December 1, 2013, http://www.crs.org/our-work-overseas/research-publications/crs-global-gender-strategy.

Charles, Lorraine, and Kate Denman. "Syrian and Palestinian Syrian Refugees in Lebanon: The Plight of Women and Children." *Journal of International Women's Studies* 14, no. 5 (December 2013): 96–111. http://vc.bridgew.edu/cgi/viewcontent.cgi?article=1729&context=jiws.

Core Humanitarian Standard. "Core Humanitarian Standard." History, 2017, https://corehumanitarianstandard.org/the-standard/history.

Davis, Rochelle, Abbie Taylor, and Emma Murphy. "Gender, Conscription, and Protection, and the War in Syria." *Forced Migration Review*, September 2014, http://www.fmreview.org/syria/davis-taylor-murphy.

Duthie, Roger, ed. *Transitional Justice and Displacement.* New York: International Center for Transitional Justice, 2012, http://www.ssrc.org/publications/view/CF869AA8-B9D1-E111-BB1A-001CC477EC84/.

Dwyer, Leslie, and Rufa Cagoco-Guiam. *Gender and Conflict in Mindanao.* Asia Foundation, 2011, http://asiafoundation.org/publication/gender-and-conflict-in-mindanao-2/.

Ferris, Elizabeth. "Abuse of Power: Sexual Exploitation of Refugee Women and Girls," *Signs: A Journal of Women in Culture and Society* 32, no. 3 (Spring 2007): 584–590.

Ferris, Elizabeth. "Unseen Unheard: Gender-Based Violence in Disasters." IFRC, 2015, http://www.ifrc.org/Global/Documents/Secretariat/201511/1297700_GBV_in_Disasters_EN_LR2.pdf.

Global Protection Cluster. *Guidelines for Integrating Gender-Based Violence Interventions in Humanitarian Settings.* 2015, https://gbvguidelines.org/wp/wp-content/uploads/2015/09/2015-IASC-Gender-based-Violence-Guidelines_lo-res.pdf.

Groverman, Verona, and Jeanette Kloosterman. *Mainstreaming a Gender Justice Approach: A Manual to Support NGOs in Self-Assessing Their Gender Mainstreaming Competence.* Oxfam UK, September 27, 2010, http://policy-practice.oxfam.org.uk/publications/mainstreaming-a-gender-justice-approach-a-manual-to-support-ngos-in-self-assess-188709.

"Independent International Commission of Inquiry on the Syrian Arab Republic." UNHRC, 2016, http://www.ohchr.org/EN/HRBodies/HRC/IICISyria/Pages/IndependentInternationalCommission.aspx.

Internal Displacement Monitoring Centre (IDMC) "About the Global Internal Displacement Database (GIDD)." Internal Displacement, 2017, http://www.internal-displacement.org/global-figures.

Inter-Agency Working Group on Refugee Reproductive Health (IAWG). *The Inter-Agency Field Manual on Reproductive Health in Humanitarian Settings.* World Health Organization, 2010, http://www.who.int/reproductivehealth/publications/emergencies/field_manual/en/.

IASC. *Women, Girls, Boys & Men: Different Needs—Equal Opportunities. IASC Gender Handbook for Humanitarian Action.* December 21, 2006, https://interagencystanding-committee.org/gender-and-humanitarian-action-0/documents-public/women-girls-boys-men-different-needs-equal-5.

IASC. "The IASC Gender Marker Assessment." June 2014, https://www.humanitarianresponse.info/sites/www.humanitarianresponse.info/files/documents/files/IASC%20Gender%20Marker%20Assessment%20Report.pdf.

International Federation of Red Cross Red Crescent Societies (IFRC). "Strategic Framework on Gender and Diversity Issues 2013–2020." IFRC, 2013, http://www.ifrc.org/Global/Documents/Secretariat/201412/IFRC%20Strategic%20Framework%20on%20Gender%20and%20Diversity%20Issues-English.pdf.

International Organization for Migration (IOM). "Gender Equality Policy: 2015–2019." November 19, 2015, https://www.iom.int/sites/default/files/about-iom/gender/C-106-INF-8-Rev.1-IOM-Gender-Equality-Policy-2015-2019.pdf.

Martin, Susan. *Refugee Women*, 2nd ed., Lanham, MD: Lexington Books, 2003.

Martin, Susan. "Refugee and Displaced Women: Sixty Years of Progress and Setbacks." *Amsterdam Law Forum* 3, no. 2 (2011), https://papers.ssrn.com/sol3/papers.cfm?abstract_id=1919721.

Myers, Kristin. "Five Unique Challenges Facing Syrian Refugee Women." Concern USA, November 9, 2016, http://www.concernusa.org/story/five-unique-challenges-facing-syrian-refugee-women/.

Olivius, Elisabeth. "Displacing Equality? Women's Participation and Humanitarian Aid Effectiveness in Refugee Camps." *Refugee Survey Quarterly* 33, no. 3 (September 1, 2014): 93–117.

Oxfam. "Gender Analysis: The Situation of Refugees and Migrants in Greece." August, 2016, http://reliefweb.int/sites/reliefweb.int/files/resources/oxfam_gender_analysis_september2016.pdf.

Restrepo, Elvira Maria. "Leaders against All Odds: Women Victims of Conflict in Colombia." *Palgrave Communications* 2, no. 16014 (May 10, 2016), http://www.palgrave-journals.com/articles/palcomms201614.

Rimmer, Susan Harris. "Reconceiving Refugees and Internally Displaced Persons as Transitional Justice Actors." *Contemporary Readings in Law and Social Justice* 2, no. 2 (2010): 163–80. http://www.unhcr.org/4bbb2a589.pdf.

Snyder, A. C. "A Gendered Analysis of Refugee Transnational Bridgebuilding Capacity." In *Critical Aspects of Gender in Conflict Resolution, Peacebuilding, and Social Movements* (Research in Social Movements, Conflicts, and Change, Vol. 32), edited by A. C. Snyder and S. P. Stobbe, 13–44. Bingley, UK: Emerald Group Publishing Limited, 2011, https://www.emeraldinsight.com/doi/full/10.1108/S0163-786X%282011%290000032005.

Tinde, Gry Tina. "Top United Nations Peacebuilders and Advocacy for Women, Peace, and Security." *Refugee Survey Quarterly* 28, no. 1 (January 1, 2009): 140–50. https://academic.oup.com/rsq/article-abstract/28/1/140/1572067?redirectedFrom=fulltext.

United Nations (UN). "Guiding Principles on Internal Displacement." Report of the Representative of the Secretary-General, February 11, 1998, http://www.ohchr.org/EN/Issues/IDPersons/Pages/Standards.aspx.

UN Human Rights Council. "Report to the General Assembly of the Special Rapporteur on the Human Rights of Internally Displaced Persons." March 18, 2013a, https://documents-dds-ny.un.org/doc/UNDOC/GEN/G13/121/12/PDF/G1312112.pdf?OpenElement.

UN Human Rights Council. "Protection of and Assistance of Internally Displaced Persons in the Syrian Arab Republic." Report to the UN General Assembly of the Special Rapporteur on the Human Rights of Internally Displaced Persons. July 15, 2013b, http://www.ohchr.org/Documents/Issues/IDPersons/A_67_931Syria_report.pdf.

United Nations Secretary-General's Bulletin. "Special Measures for Protection from Sexual Abuse and Exploitation." UN Secretariat, October 9, 2003, http://www.securitycouncilreport.org/atf/cf/%7B65BFCF9B-6D27-4E9C-8CD3-CF6E4FF96FF9%7D/SE%20ST%20SGB%202003%2013.pdf.

UNHCR. "UNHCR's Commitments to Refugee Women." December, 12, 2001, http://www.refworld.org/docid/479f3b2a2.html.

UNHCR. *Handbook for the Protection of Women and Girls.* January 2008, http://www.unhcr.org/en-us/protection/women/47cfa9fe2/unhcr-handbook-protection-women-girls-first-edition-complete-publication.html.

UNHCR EXCOM. "Report on Age, Gender, and Diversity Mainstreaming." EC/59/SC/CRP.14: 3. June 2, 2008, http://www.unhcr.org/excom/EXCOM/484514c12.pdf.

UNHCR. "Age, Gender, and Diversity Policy: Working with People and Communities for Equality and Protection." June 1, 2011a, http://www.unhcr.org/en-us/protection/women/4e7757449/unhcr-age-gender-diversity-policy-working-people-communities-equality-protection.html.

UNHCR. "Survivors, Protectors, Providers: Refugee Women Speak Out." November 2011b, http://www.unhcr.org/en-us/protection/women/4ec5337d9/protectors-providers-survivors-refugee-women-speak-summary-report.html.

UNHCR. Figures at a Glance. "Global Internal Displacement Data," 2017a, ? http://www.internal-displacement.org/database/displacement-data.

UNHCR. "Syria Emergency." UNHCR Emergencies, 2017b, http://www.unhcr.org/syria-emergency.html.

UN OCHA. "Gender Equality Resources." OCHA, 2017, http://www.unocha.org/legacy/about-us/gender-equality-programming/gender-equality-resources.

UN Secretary-General (UNSG). "Special Report of the Special Representative of the Secretary-General on Sexual Violence in Conflict." Letter from the Secretary-General addressed to the President of the Security Council, December 20, 2016, http://reliefweb.int/report/iraq/special-report-office-special-representative-secretary-general-sexual-violence-conflict.

UN Women. "Transforming Justice, Securing the Peace. A Global Study on the Implementation of United Nations Security Council Resolution 1325 (2000)." Lead author: Radhika Coomaraswamy. UN Women, 2015, http://wps.unwomen.org/pdf.

UN Women. "The Effects of Gender Equality Programming on Humanitarian Outcomes." April 2015, http://www2.unwomen.org/-/media/headquarters/attachments/sections/library/publications/2015/unw%20effects%20of%20gender%20equlaity%20on%20humanitarian%20outcomessinglepgsweb.pdf?vs=5705.

Williamson, Sarah. "Syrian Women in Crisis: Obstacles and Opportunities." March 2016, http://www.protectthepeople.org/uploads/6/3/5/5/63555193/syrian.women.ptp.april2016.pdf.

Woldetsadik, Mahlet Atakilt. *The Precarious State of Syrian Refugee Women, Children in Lebanon*. Rand Corporation. September, 2016, http://www.rand.org/blog/2016/09/the-precarious-state-of-syrian-refugee-women-children.html.

Women's Refugee Commission. "Unpacking Gender: The Humanitarian Response to the Syrian Refugee Crisis in Jordan." March 12, 2014, https://www.womensrefugeecommission.org/resources/gender-issues/985-unpacking-gender-the-humanitarian-response-to-the-syrian-refugee-crisis-in-jordan.

CHAPTER 40

DONOR STATES DELIVERING ON WPS
The Case of Norway

INGER SKJELSBÆK AND TORUNN L. TRYGGESTAD

THE promotion of gender equality and women's empowerment has been a key component of Norwegian foreign policy since the early 1990s, irrespective of shifting governments. Before the 1990s, the main focus was on gender mainstreaming in Norwegian development cooperation, and considerable investments were made in programs and projects for women's empowerment in developing countries. Gradually, throughout the 1990s, other parts of the foreign policy service also started to address gender equality issues, most notably the sections within the Norwegian Ministry of Foreign Affairs (MFA) focusing on UN security politics and peacekeeping operations. As a direct follow-up to the 1995 Beijing Women's Conference, the MFA UN Section provided funding for a UN Expert Group Meeting in Santo Domingo in 1996 to explore the impact of gender differences on political decision-making and conflict resolution.[1] In the second half of the 1990s Norwegian diplomats were among the first at the UN to address the need for more women peacekeepers (Hernes 1998).[2] Together with Sweden, from 1999 to 2000, Norway also funded a study within the UN Department of Peacekeeping Operations (DPKO) on "Mainstreaming a Gender Perspective in Multidimensional Peacekeeping Operations" (Stiehm 2000). This study laid the foundation for the Windhoek Declaration and the Namibia Plan of Action (UN 2000), a document that outlines how to move from intentions to actions for more gender mainstreamed and balanced peace support operations. The Windhoek Declaration and the Namibia Plan of Action became a key reference document in the campaign to have a UN Security Council resolution adopted on the topic of women, peace, and security (WPS) (Tryggestad 2009). When UN Security Council Resolution 1325 was adopted in October 2000, Norway was among its sponsors; it was seen as a natural extension and continuation of Norwegian foreign policy priorities from the decades before.

Norway has gained international recognition as a key player in advancing the WPS agenda, normatively as well as financially (Norad 2016). Norway's engagement at the global level has intensified and it has also impacted the status of the agenda domestically. While WPS in the beginning was treated as a soft security issue relegated to the margins of Norwegian foreign policy, women's rights and gender equality are increasingly recognized as core norms and interests to be promoted by the foreign policy apparatus. A formal expression of this recognition came in 2016 when the government adopted the first-ever action plan for women's rights and gender equality in Norwegian foreign policy and development cooperation for the period 2016–2020 (Ministry of Foreign Affairs 2016a).

In this chapter, we aim to outline what Norway, as a small state, has achieved and gained by supporting the WPS agenda. More specifically, we will discuss what the Norwegian engagement has meant for the global implementation of Resolution 1325 and what the domestic ramification of this engagement has been.

Small States as Norm Entrepreneurs

What role can a small state like Norway play in promoting and reinforcing new ideas and norms within international society? In lack of power relative to size and military capabilities, small states often exercise issue-specific power (Egeland 1988, Ingebritsen 2002; Ingebritsen et al. 2006; Taulbee et al. 2014; de Carvalho and Neumann 2015). The Nordic countries exemplify how small states can influence international agendas and world politics by adopting the role of norm entrepreneurs (Björkdahl 2007a, 2007b), and have made their mark, individually and as a group, on issues such as conflict prevention, peace mediation, peacebuilding, human rights, and gender equality.

Engagement in peace-building, writ large, has been an important pillar of Norwegian foreign policy since the 1960s. It was former foreign minister Knut Frydenlund who defined that Norwegian foreign policy should be characterized by three core aspects: securing Norway's freedom and sovereignty; securing Norway's interests; and, last but not least, contributing to securing global peace and promoting cooperation between peoples (Frydenlund 1966: 143). These goals were formulated before Norway discovered oil in the North Sea in the early 1970s, which turned the small state of Norway into a wealthier and more influential actor on the geopolitical scene. Still, the insistence that Norwegian interests are served by engaging in *idealpolitik* has prevailed in policy and rhetoric. While recognizing that there are tensions, the argument that it is in Norway's interest to contribute to international peace-building has still been made by every foreign minister since Frydenlund's time.

At the same time as Norwegian peace engagement took form and became increasingly professionalized within the foreign policy domain, Norway also rose on the global scene as a gender equality nation. When Gro Harlem Brundtland had her second term as Prime Minister in 1986, eight ministers out of eighteen were women. This made headlines all over the world. In comparison, the global average of women parliamentarians in 1987 was 10 percent while the global average of women cabinet ministers in 1991 was 3.5 percent (UN 1991). Further, during the same time, legislative changes were made in Norway which prohibited discrimination based on gender; and secured equal pay for equal work, and abortion rights. The development and adoption of such "woman friendly" policies were, according to Helga Hernes (1987), a result of the interplay between agitation from below and state-driven integration policy from above, a dynamic coined "state feminism."

The close collaboration between state institutions and civil society organizations CSOs) in domestic politics is a model for collaboration which has also been adopted in Norwegian foreign policy, particularly in what is often referred to as the "Norwegian model for peace engagement."[3] This is a model that was introduced and operationalized at the MFA in the early 1990s (Neumann 2011), and it rests on the following principles (Ministry of Foreign Affairs 2016b):

- A long-term willingness to provide assistance; both for economic development and peace-building;
- Provision of resources; both human and financial;
- Close cooperation with Norwegian NGOs, which have served as door openers;
- Experience, built over many years, including working with non-state actors;
- Good relations with key international actors, both individual states and multilateral organizations (the UN in particular);
- No colonial past; Norwegian engagement is perceived to be sincere and not motivated by political or economic self-interest;
- Focus on peace facilitation rather than "mediation with muscle."

The Norwegian model for peace engagement has also positioned Norway as a credible and engaged norm entrepreneur on WPS (Tryggestad 2014); it combines a legacy of gender equality in social and political life with a long-standing peace-building commitment. Without a colonial history, Norway is regarded by many countries of the Global South as a neutral actor with no immediate material or geopolitical agendas. This has enabled Norway to enter into dialogue with governments and non-government actors that from the outset may have been skeptical of, or indifferent to, liberal normative agendas such as WPS. Nevertheless, to claim that no self-interests are involved in Norway's norm entrepreneurship would be to overlook the importance to small states of predictable and stable relations in the global system. Norway might not have an immediate material interest in advancing the WPS agenda, but it has a strong self-interest in promoting ideas and norms that contribute to the maintenance and strengthening of international law and order (Neuman 2011). The advancement of the WPS agenda is seen to contribute to such system maintenance.

Still, money talks. Norway's normative power and political leverage on WPS cannot be understood without also appreciating Norway's major donor role, multilaterally as well as bilaterally (see what follows). The provision of funding has been combined with an extensive collaboration with civil society actors such as national and international non-governmental organizations (NGOs), think tanks, advocacy groups and individual experts. In effect, the Norwegian MFA has taken advantage of the expertise of civil society actors and transnational advocacy networks and made *them* implementing partners on issues of high priority to Norwegian foreign policy. This approach has made Norwegian initiatives to advance the WPS agenda particularly effective, and has been applied in both multilateral and bilateral tracks of foreign policy. The relationship between the MFA and Norwegian NGOs in particular has been referred to as "symbiotic" (Taulbee 2014). Still, the Norwegian way of running its foreign policy in the area of WPS has been met with little criticism, possibly because of Norway's reputation as a benign political actor.

Norway's Normative Support of the WPS Agenda

Multilateral level

The Norwegian engagement with the WPS agenda comes partly from an ideal based foreign policy, but it is also seen as a reflection of particular Norwegian domestic experiences. For the younger generations of employees at the Norwegian Ministry of Foreign Affairs, the WPS agenda is not an alien agenda, but rather a logical extension of values, norms, and ideals from the everyday gender balanced life in Norwegian families and work life. In the words of a young diplomat, "gender equality is logical because it is an integral part of how we live."[4] This sociopolitical legacy is part of the backdrop of why the Norwegian WPS advocacy has been "broad and covers a range of different engagements at any given time, using a variety of channels, tactics and targets," according to a recent independent evaluation report (NORAD 2016: 13).

The UN has been the most prominent platform from which Norway could provide normative and political support of the WPS agenda. This has been done in different ways. First, in the form of supporting statements: Since Resolution 1325 was adopted, Norway has always given statements at the annual Security Council Open Debates on WPS (as the only Nordic country to do so), either individually or together with groups of other countries (like the Nordics). Second, by forming alliances: Norway was among the founding members of the New York based "Group of Friends of UNSCR 1325" in 2000, and has since been an active member of this group.[5] More recently Norway has been centrally involved in revitalizing Nordic cooperation within the context of the UN, including on gender equality issues (Nordic Council of Ministers 2017). Third, through seeking membership in various UN entities: As a nonpermanent member of the UN Security Council (2001–2002), Norway actively promoted the WPS agenda, but played an even more central WPS norm entrepreneur role as a member of the UN Peacebuilding Commission (PBC) during its formative years in 2006 to 2008. As co-chair of the PBC and chair of the so-called "Burundi configuration," Norway, among others, played an instrumental role in integrating provisions for women's empowerment and gender equality in strategy documents and facilitated women's participation in the negotiations of a peace-building strategy for Burundi (Tryggestad 2014). As a major donor and member of the boards of UNDP and UN Woman, Norway has also had a strong voice in support of the WPS agenda within these two organizations. In the years to come, WPS will form an integral part of Norway's campaign to be elected nonpermanent member of the UN Security Council for the period 2021–2022.

Beyond the UN, Norway has actively lobbied for the WPS agenda at NATO headquarters in Brussels and was instrumental in having the first NATO Special Representative for Women, Peace, and Security appointed in 2012. Not only did Norway come up with the idea, and rallied US support for it, Norway also funded the position for the first two years before it was included in the regular NATO budget. The first person to hold the position was Mari Skåre, a senior Norwegian diplomat, with in-depth knowledge of NATO.

More recently, the African Union (AU) has also emerged as an important partner organization. In 2015, Norway signed an agreement on a strategic partnership with the AU, in which WPS is one of the core issue areas to be supported, mainly through the provision of funding for the office of the AU Special Envoy on WPS. Clearly Norway has taken a leading normative role in promoting the WPS agenda on the global scene, but what are the domestic factors which have contributed to this prioritization?

Domestic Level

Norway's position as influential WPS advocate internationally has been made possible by bipartisan support at the domestic level, combined with implementing government structures that have collaborated closely with CSOs (including academic institutions). When the first National Action Plan (NAP) on WPS was launched in March 2006, it was signed by no less than five ministers.[6] While all five ministries were assigned with important implementing roles in their respective areas of concern, the Ministry of Foreign Affairs was left with the overall coordinating responsibility for the implementation of the NAP. Since then, two more NAPs have been launched, the last one 2015 (Ministry of Foreign Affairs 2015). At the launch event, Prime Minister Erna Solberg (Norway's second woman PM) gave the keynote address, underscoring the high priority given to the WPS agenda by the Norwegian government (Office of the Prime Minister 2015).

In terms of Norwegian domestic implementation efforts, the appointment of a Resolution 1325 Coordinator position within the MFA has been crucial. Established in 2008, the role of the coordinator was first and foremost to strengthen coordination and collaboration between the various entities involved in implementing the NAP, including Norwegian embassies in WPS priority countries.[7] The coordinator has served as liaison with CSOs and other relevant environments. However, the role of the coordinator has gone way beyond coordination. The various individuals filling the position have been active in promoting the WPS agenda both nationally and internationally, developing policies and providing substantive advice to colleagues and to the political leadership of the MFA. Serving as the point of contact, the coordinator has also been the person to turn to for CSOs when seeking advice on how to develop project proposals and how/where/when to apply for funding. In recent years, the coordinator has played a particularly important role internally at the MFA in support of mainstreaming WPS policies and concerns throughout the Norwegian foreign service.[8] However, Norwegian implementation efforts both nationally and internationally would not have come into force without a willingness to also fund the agenda.

FINANCIAL SUPPORT OF WPS AGENDA

A recurring criticism raised by international CSOs is the notorious underfunding of the WPS agenda. The Global Study (UN Women 2015) called for a substantial increase in funding, combined with the development of instruments for gender budgeting and resource tracking. Indicators and benchmarks are needed to properly measure progress with implementation of the WPS agenda, it is argued (UN Women 2015: 379). In Norway, civil society organizations have also criticized the government for lack of transparency and accountability toward commitments made in the NAPs, not least when it comes to how much money is actually spent on the WPS agenda (Forum Norway 1325 2015). They call for predictable and sustainable funding mechanisms, preferably in the form of increased earmarked funding.

Norwegian support for the WPS agenda is funded in various ways and from many different budget lines, primarily within the MFA. Since the second half of the 2000s, there has been a funding mechanism earmarked for WPS projects under the Section for Peace and Reconciliation. In recent years, this grant has amounted to NOK 30 million (approximately $3.6 million), of which NOK 20 million in 2016 was earmarked for civil society initiatives and projects in support of the WPS agenda. These NOK 20 million are administered by the Norwegian Agency for Development Cooperation (NORAD), and are subject to annual calls to which both Norwegian and international NGOs can apply. Throughout the years this grant has been a key source of funding of WPS activities for Norwegian and international CSOs operating in conflict settings. The remaining NOK 10 million of the grant is spent subject to decisions made by the Section for Peace and Reconciliation. The projects and activities that receive funding are often closely associated with thematic issues or countries of high priority to the Norwegian government, typically countries where Norway plays a role as peace facilitator (for example Colombia).

While the WPS grant for many years was the core source of funding for WPS activities, in recent years the funding portfolio has been broadened to include budget lines in an increasing number of departments and sections within the MFA, including embassies and Norwegian missions to organizations such as the AU, NATO, and the UN. According to the MFA Resolution 1325 Coordinator,[9] this is in line with the current NAP, which states that the WPS agenda shall be integrated into every peace and security effort of Norwegian foreign policy.

> It sends an important signal to earmark funding to WPS. But at the same time, it is important to emphasise that we have to work together to include WPS where it is natural in all our various peace and security efforts. When grants are provided for various WPS initiatives from the budget lines for humanitarian affairs, security policy, regional affairs, prevention of violent extremism, or promotion of human rights, it is because WPS is given a high priority and has become a dimension to be taken seriously throughout our foreign policy. Currently funding is generated from a wide range of sources within the MFA, generating an equally wide ownership to the various WPS initiatives. The collaboration on WPS is increasingly seen in the context of other activities the various sections and departments are involved in (MFA 1325 Coordinator, 2017).[10]

The broad funding portfolio makes it difficult, if not impossible, to know exactly how much funding the Norwegian government spends on WPS-related activities and initiatives. The following list of budget lines from which WPS work is funded, provides an indication of the scope of WPS integration in Norwegian foreign policy.

- *Section for Humanitarian Affairs*: In 2015 NOK 29 million was spent on projects and initiatives aimed at fighting gender-based and sexual violence. Funding was provided to partners at three different levels; the UN system, the International Red Cross, and NGOs (both Norwegian and international).
- *Section for Peace and Reconciliation*: The WPS grant (NOK 30 million) funds projects with an explicit women's rights and gender equality agenda. The emphasis is funding projects on women's political participation, including in peace processes, and the

prevention and management of conflict-related sexual violence. In addition to the WPS grant, this section also provides funding to WPS research activities.[11] Also, whenever embassies receive "Peace and Reconciliation Grants" they are encouraged to spend at least 10 percent of the funding on WPS-related activities.

- *Section for Human Rights and Democracy*: Support research on the role of women in conflict prevention and transitional justice in countries such as Tunisia and Colombia.
- *Section for Global Security and Disarmament*: From this budget line research projects on the gendered dimensions of violent extremism are funded, as well as the activities of CSOs, such as the Women's Alliance for Security Leadership (WASL).[12]
- *Department for Security Politics*: Funds the collaboration with the Ministry of Justice and Public Security on police contributions to international missions. This includes funds for the training of women police, and capacity building in gender awareness and how to fight sexual violence in a number of African countries and in Haiti; through the African Union's Training for Peace Programme; and through the funding of a gender advisor position within the UN Department of Peacekeeping Operations in New York.
- *Department for Regional Collaboration*: The collaboration with the AU Special Envoy on WPS is funded from this budget line. Activities following from Norway's recent identification of Nigeria as a WPS priority country is also funded from this budget line, along with a number of targeted women, peace and security efforts in all regions of the world.
- *Embassies*: Norwegian embassies in conflict-affected countries or regions do also provide funding for WPS activities, often in close collaboration with UN Women. At the time of writing (February 2017), the countries benefiting from such arrangements are East Timor, Jordan, Myanmar, South-Africa, South Sudan, and Zimbabwe. Norwegian embassies have also been involved in a long-term and comprehensive effort at fighting sexual violence in DRC. Funding has been channeled both through NGOs and the UN.

IMPACT OF NORWAY'S IMPLEMENTATION EFFORTS

For a small state like Norway the investments—both normatively, politically, and financially—in the WPS agenda have been, and continue to be, substantial, particularly in the context of the UN. Still, it has been argued that Norway's impact as a WPS influencer is limited, as long as it is not a member of the UN Security Council (NORAD 2016: 27). We would argue, however, that this is too narrow an understanding of influence. As a long-standing supporter of the UN, Norway has gained respect throughout the UN system and among UN member states. In terms of overall financial contributions to the UN, Norway has for many years been on the Top 10 list.[13] The exact level of financial contributions to the WPS agenda is more difficult to document (Norad 2016). However, both financial contributions and political and normative support have been long, consistent, and in line with overarching Norwegian UN policies. In UN circles, Norway is regarded as a country to trust and turn to when political and/or financial support are needed for normative agendas such as WPS. Further, Norwegian governments across different political constellations tend to respond positively when approached. In this way, Norway has played an important supportive role in the various WPS implementation efforts of the UN.

In terms of normative support, Norway has been at the forefront of supporting and advancing the broad normative framework of WPS, pointing to the importance of seeing the four pillars of the agenda as mutually dependent (Ministry of Foreign Affairs 2006). These are perspectives that have been advanced through the Friends of Resolution 1325 Group and by forming coalitions with the other Nordic countries. With the current NAP, however, Norway has adopted a policy of more focused and strategic engagements, identifying women's participation in peace mediation and peace-building processes as a particularly important, and neglected, dimension of the WPS agenda. This is an area where Norway might have a comparative advantage (Taulbee et al. 2014). Another topic that has emerged as a Norwegian priority issue under the WPS umbrella is the role of women in fighting violent extremism.

The impact of Norway's engagement with the WPS agenda has perhaps been particularly important in relation to CSOs (see chapter 33 in this volume). Because of Norway's long tradition of working closely with CSOs domestically—including those critical to the government—Norway has been one of few UN member states that has provided funding to organizations that serve important WPS watchdog or monitoring functions globally.[14] More importantly, Norway has also provided substantial funding to CSOs implementing WPS projects in conflict-affected areas, either individually or often in collaboration with UN agencies, such as UN Women. As funding became scarcer, in the wake of the global financial crisis in 2008, Norway remained a relatively stable donor. This applies both to direct funding of CSOs but also funding to UN Women.

Finally, the impact of Norway's WPS engagement is also visible in many of those peace processes where Norway has played a central role as facilitator, most notably in Colombia and the Philippines, but also in South Sudan and Sri Lanka. The format in several of these peace processes has been to invite input and viewpoints from women's groups across dividing political lines into the main political negotiations. While the goal is to have women be part of the main political processes, the early Norwegian experiences in peace mediation did value women's voices and inclusion, albeit to a limited extent, and with suboptimal peace settlements. The latest peace engagement in Colombia, however, opted for a much more comprehensive mediation design (Salvesen and Nylander 2017).

In the Colombian peace process, WPS was highlighted as one of three priority areas for the Norwegian facilitation team. Although all members of the Norwegian team shared responsibility for following up on Norwegian priorities, one diplomat was at all times charged with a particular responsibility for the WPS agenda. The Norwegian facilitation team pursued the WPS agenda along multiple tracks, by providing substantive input and advice on various gender issues to the parties and by providing funding for women's participation and the inclusion of gender experts in the negotiations. Norway also funded a number of conferences, seminars, and workshops for women's organizations to meet and discuss women's concerns and priorities for the peace process.

Conclusion

When Sweden announced its feminist foreign policy in 2015 (see chapter 61 in this volume), the relevance of gender equality and women's empowerment was elevated to a foreign policy level that we had not seen before, and it attracted a lot global media attention (Aggestam and Bergman-Rosamond 2016). Countries such as Australia and Canada, like-minded with the Nordics, have recently also elevated WPS and feminist analysis in their respective foreign policies (Rivas and Bardall 2016; True 2016; Government of Canada 2017).

While there has been no official reaction or response from Norwegian authorities to other countries' initiatives to frame gender equality as a central or integral part of their foreign policy, Norway cannot idly stand by as other states position themselves to take center stage on this normative agenda. The competitive space on this political agenda is thickening, and Norway may risk losing the moral high-ground when other countries seek to take a lead. The Norwegian framing so far has been that WPS as an agenda is not new, nor foreign, but a mainstream element of Norwegian politics, including foreign policy. There are three different arguments that can be detected in the ways in which the gender equality mainstreaming has taken form. First, it is linked to a *rhetoric of experiences* from domestic politics on successful economic development, welfare, and social well-being. Advancing WPS in Norwegian foreign policy is the smart thing to do in its own right. Second, it is linked to a *rhetoric of pragmatism*. Being an active and visible norm entrepreneur on WPS is a way of gaining access, while also strengthening Norway's small state status in other issue areas. Increased attention to the WPS agenda within the MFA, especially from around 2007 to 2008, is closely associated with policies being pursued at the time by Norway's close allies, the United States and the UK. During Hillary Clinton's tenure as Secretary of State, the United States sought out Norway as an ally on the issue of sexual violence in armed conflicts. In this period, Norway increased funding to various programs for survivors of conflict-related sexual violence, including co-funding with the United States of the Panzi Hospital in the Democratic Republic of the Congo. When Hillary Clinton visited Oslo in 2012 to open a conference on global health, focusing particularly on women and girls, it was highlighted in Norwegian media that it was even more important to the government that Clinton combined the opening of the conference with a visit to the High-North. The main goal for the MFA was to attract US attention to the climate/ecological/geopolitical challenges of the High-North, which is of particular national importance to Norway. On a number of occasions Norwegian diplomats have been open about how the WPS agenda has served as a door opener for discussing other issues of (greater) national interest with important allies (Danielsen et al. 2013).

The third argument for why WPS should be mainstreamed in Norwegian foreign policy is linked to a *rhetoric of values*. Whereas Norway's neighboring country Sweden has adopted an explicit feminist foreign policy, launched by a woman foreign minister (Sweden has had a number of women foreign ministers), Norway has not labeled its foreign policy in such terms. In practice, however, the policies of the two neighboring countries are quite similar. Norway's "soft" foreign policy, emphasizing peace mediation, peace-building, and, in recent years, humanitarian responses (Norway is a major donor) are in many ways associated with feminist values.

How Norway will respond to the increased competition on WPS from other small states and like-minded countries remains to be seen. What is clear is that by actively supporting the WPS agenda, Norway has not only contributed to the reinforcement of the agenda, but has also successfully reinforced its own small-state status in international politics.

Notes

1. The Expert Group Meeting was organized by the UN Division for the Advancement of Women (DAW, now part of UN Women) and the Peace Research Institute in Oslo (PRIO). The meeting sparked discussions and a number of follow-up activities within the UN system. The Norwegian MFA also provided funding for a scholarly output, the anthology *Gender, Peace and Conflict* (Skjelsbæk and Smith 2001).

2. Helga Hernes was the first woman within the Norwegian Ministry of Foreign Affairs to be appointed Ambassador for Peacekeeping Operations. She was also one of very few women serving in such a position at the global level.

3. The first effort at conceptualizing this model was made by Jan Egeland in 1988. He later became State Secretary at the MFA (1990–1997), and was during this period centrally involved in a number of peace facilitation processes.

4. Quote from interview with MFA employee, interviewed by the authors.

5. Currently, the following fifty-three UN member states are members of the "Group of Friends": Argentina, Australia, Austria, Bangladesh, Belgium, Botswana, Cameroon, Canada, Chile, Colombia, Croatia, Denmark, Finland, El Salvador, Estonia, France, Germany, Ghana, Guinea, Iceland, Ireland, Israel, Italy, Jamaica, Japan, Jordan, Kenya, Republic of Korea, Liberia, Liechtenstein, Lithuania, Mali, Mexico, Morocco, Namibia, Netherlands, New Zealand, Norway, Philippines, Portugal, Rwanda, Senegal, Singapore, South Africa, Spain, Sweden, Switzerland, Tanzania, United Arab Emirates, United Kingdom, Uruguay, United States of America, and Zambia. Information obtained from Simon Collard-Wexler, coordinator of the Group of Friends at the Canadian Mission to the UN, February 13, 2017 (email exchange).

6. These were the Ministry of Defence, the Ministry of Development Cooperation, the Ministry of Foreign Affairs, the Ministry of Justice and Public Security, and the Ministry of Children and Equality.

7. In the most recent NAP adopted by the Norwegian government in 2015 (for the period 2015–2018), the following countries were identified as priority countries: Afghanistan, Colombia, Myanmar, Palestine, and South Sudan. In 2016 Nigeria was added as the sixth priority country.

8. In September-October 2017 the coordinator position was upgraded to Special Envoy for Women, Peace and Security.

9. Email exchange, January 17, 2017.

10. Translated from Norwegian to English by the authors.

11. Among the research institutions that benefit from this budget line are the PRIO Centre on Gender, Peace, and Security.

12. WASL is an alliance of women rights and peace practitioners, organizations, and networks engaged in deradicalization efforts, prevention of violent extremism and peacebuilding.

13. For more on Norwegian financial contributions to the UN system, see http://www.un.org/pga/71/wp-content/uploads/sites/40/2015/08/Top-ten-providers-of-assessed-contributions-to-United-Nations-budget-and-of-voluntary-contributions-to-the-United-Nations-funds-programmes-and-agencies_3-Nov.pdf.

14. One such organization is the New York–based NGO Working Group on Women, Peace, and Security.

References

Aggestam, K., and A. Bergman-Rosamond. "Swedish Feminist Foreign Policy in the Making: Ethics, Politics, and Gender." *Ethics & International Affairs* 30 (2016): 323–334.

Björkdahl, A. "Norm Advocacy: A Small State Strategy to Influence the EU." *Journal of European Public Policy* 15 (2007a): 135–154.

Björkdahl, A. "Swedish Norm Entrepreneurship in the UN." *International Peacekeeping* 14 (2007b): 538–552.

Danielsen, H., E. Larsen, and I. W. Owesen. *Norsk Likestillingshistorie 1814–2013* [Norwegian History of Gender Equality 1814–2013]. Oslo: Fagbokforlaget, 2013.

de Carvalho, B., and I. B. Neumann, eds. *Small State Status Seeking. Norway's Quest for International Standing.* London and New York: Routledge, 2015.

Egeland, J. *Impotent Superpower—Potent Small State. Potentials and Limitations of Human Rights Objectives in the Foreign Policies of the United States and Norway.* Oslo: Norwegian University Press, 1988.

Forum Norway 1325. "15 Years of UNSCR 1325 Women, Peace, and Security. The Norwegian Civil Society Experience." Report. Oslo: Forum Norway 1325, 2015, https://issuu.com/folkehjelp/docs/290_forum_1325_anniversary_2015_pub.

Frydenlund, Knut. *Norsk utenrikspolitikk—i etterkrigstidens internasjonale samarbeid.* [Norwegian Foreign Policy—in Post-War International Collaboration]. Oslo: Norsk Utenrikspolitisk Intsitutt (NUPI), 1966.

Government of Canada. "Canada's Feminist International Assistance Policy." Global Affairs Canada, 2017, http://www.international.gc.ca/gac-amc/campaign-campagne/iap-pai/index.aspx?lang=eng.

Hernes, H. *Welfare State and Woman Power. Essays in State Feminism.* Oslo: Norwegian University Press, 1987.

Hernes, H. "Women in Armed Conflict. Statement Given at Expert Panel III: Women and Armed Conflict." Commission on the Status of Women, New York, March 4, 1998.

Ingebritsen, C. "Norm Entrepreneurs: Scandinavia's Role in World Politics." *Cooperation and Conflict* 37 (2002):11–23.

Ingebritsen, C., I. B. Neumann, S. Gstöl, and J. Beyer, eds. *Small States in International Relations.* Seattle/Reykjavik: University of Washington Press/University of Iceland Press, 2006.

Ministry of Foreign Affairs. "The Norwegian Government's Action Plan for the Implementation of UN Security Council Resolution 1325 (2000) on Women, Peace, and Security." Oslo: Ministry of Foreign Affairs, 2006, https://www.regjeringen.no/globalassets/upload/kilde/ud/pla/2006/0002/ddd/pdfv/279831-actionplan_resolution1325.pdf.

Ministry of Foreign Affairs. "Women, Peace, and Security. 2015–18. National Action Plan." Oslo: Norwegian Ministry of Foreign Affairs, 2015, https://www.regjeringen.no/globalassets/departementene/ud/vedlegg/fn/ud_handlingsplan_kfs_eng_nett.pdf.

Ministry of Foreign Affairs. "Freedom, Empowerment, and Opportunities. Action Plan for Women's Rights and Gender Equality in Foreign and Development Policy 2016–2020." National Action Plan. Oslo: Norwegian Ministry of Foreign Affairs, 2016a, https://www.regjeringen.no/globalassets/departementene/ud/vedlegg/fn/womens_rights.pdf.

Ministry of Foreign Affairs. "Norway's Approach to Peace and Reconciliation Work." November 9, 2016b, https://www.regjeringen.no/en/topics/freign-affairs/peace-and-reconciliation-efforts/innsiktsmappe/norway-peace-work/id446704/.

Neumann, I. B. "Peace and Reconciliation Efforts as Systems-Maintaining Diplomacy: The Case of Norway." *International Journal* 66 (2011): 563–579.

Norad. "Annex 5: Case Study on Norway's Engagement in Women, Peace, and Security." *Evaluation of Norway's Support for Advocacy in the Development Policy Arena.* Evaluation report commissioned by Norad, carried out by FCG SIPU International AB (SIPU) and Overseas Development Institute (ODI). Report 5, Evaluation Department. Oslo: Norad, 2016.

Nordic Council of Ministers. "Nordic Solutions to Global Challenges." Nordic Co-operation, 2017, http://www.norden.org/en/theme/nordic-solutions-to-global-challenges.

Office of the Prime Minister. Norway Intensifies Efforts to Promote Women, Peace, and Security. February 16, 2015, https://www.regjeringen.no/en/aktuelt/styrker-innsatsen-for-kvinner-fred-og-sikkerhet/id2396199/.

Rivas, A. M., and G. Bardall. "Women in Politics, Part 2: Moving Forward—Supporting Gender-Inclusive Political Participation." *CIPS Blog*, December 15, 2016, http://www.cips-cepi.ca/2016/12/15/women-in-politics-part-2-moving-forward-supporting-gender-inclusive-political-participation/.

Salvesen, H., and D. Nylander. "Towards an Inclusive Peace: Women and the Gender Approach in the Colombian Peace Process." Report. Oslo: Norwegian Centre for Conflict Resolution (NOREF), 2017.

Skjelsbæk, I., and D. Smith, eds. *Gender, Peace and Conflict.* London: Sage, 2001.

Stiehm, J. H. "Mainstreaming a Gender Perspective in Multidimensional Peace Support Operations." Report Prepared for the UN DPKOs Lessons Learned Unit. New York: United Nations Department of Peacekeeping Operations, 2000.

Taulbee, J. L. "Lesser States and Niche Diplomacy." In *Norway's Peace Policy: Soft Power in a Turbulent World*, edited by J. L. Taulbee, A. Kelleher, and P. C. Grosvenor. New York: Palgrave Macmillan, 2014.

Taulbee, J. L., A. Kelleher, and P. C. Grosvenor. *Norway's Peace Policy: Soft Power in a Turbulent World.* New York: Palgrave Macmillan, 2014.

True, J. "Gender and Foreign Policy." In *Navigating the New International Disorder, Australia in World Affairs 2011–2015*, edited by M. Beeson and S. Hameiri. Australian Institute of International Affairs. South Melbourne, Australia: Oxford University Press, 2016.

Tryggestad, T. L. "Trick or Treat? The UN and Implementation of Security Council Resolution 1325 on Women, Peace and Security." *Global Governance* 15 (2009): 539–557.

Tryggestad, T. L. "State Feminism Going Global. Norway on the UN Peacebuilding Commission." *Cooperation and Conflict* 49 (2014): 464–482.

UN. "The Windhoek Declaration and the Namibia Plan of Action on 'Mainstreaming a Gender Perspective in Multidimensional Peace Support Operations.'" May 31, 2000, http://www.un.org/womenwatch/osagi/wps/windhoek_declaration.pdf.

UN. *The World's Women 1970–1990. Trends and Statistics.* Social Statistics and Indicators, Series K, No. 8. New York: United Nations, 1991.

UN Women. "Preventing Conflict. Transforming Justice. Securing the Peace. A Global Study on the Implementation of United Nations Security Council Resolution 1325." New York: UN Women, 2015.

CHAPTER 41

WPS AS DIPLOMATIC VOCATION
The Case of China

LIU TIEWA

POLICY AND LITERATURE REVIEWS ON THE IMPLEMENTATION OF RESOLUTION 1325

FOR more than fifteen years, the Women, Peace, and Security (WPS) agenda has gradually moved toward the implementation phase at the institutional level. The United Nations and its institutions have contributed a lot to the transformation of this agenda from theory to practice through various multilateral discussions, further resolutions, and conferences.[1] In recent years, there have also been a number of state-led proactive engagement initiatives to promote UN Security Council Resolution 1325. For example, the Canadian-led Friends of 1325 was established in 2001, and the number of members varies between fifteen and twenty. The group meets every two or three months with the Secretary-General's Special Advisor on Gender Issues and the DPKO Gender Advisor.[2] More importantly, to translate the guidelines of Resolution 1325 into practice, sixty-six countries, as of May 2017, have developed National Action Plans (NAPs) (see Table 41.1). The goal of these NAPs is to strengthen and facilitate the implementation of Resolution 1325 in each local context.[3] Alongside the state driven NAPs, many civil societies, such as the NGO Working Group on Women, Peace, and Security (NGOWG), endeavor to help with the implementation of Resolution 1325 and its related resolutions.

Since the adoption of Resolution 1325 in 2000, a large body of literature has emerged which examines, both its implementation and impact (Hill et al. 2003; Anderlini 2007; Cockburn 2007; Tryggestad 2009; Deshmukh; 2010). In particular, some researchers have paid special attention to the NAPs on WPS, evaluating their effects and roles in implementing Resolution 1325 and the role of diplomacy in promoting WPS. Dr. Amy Barrow analyzed the development of the NAPs, comparing those in "donor states" (Denmark and UK) with the fragile states (Philippines and Nepal) to figure out the limited role of NAPs in operationalizing Resolution 1325 (Barrow 2016). She concluded that the success of the

Table 41.1 National Action Plans for the Implementation of Resolution 1325 on Women, Peace, and Security.

Year	Number of States	Name of States
2005	1	Denmark
2006	3	Norway, Sweden, UK
2007	3	Austria, Spain, Switzerland
2008	5	Finland, Iceland, Uganda, Ivory Coast, Netherlands
2009	6	Chile, Guinea, Belgium, Portugal, Liberia, Rwanda
2010	11	Bosnia Herz, Canada, DRC, Estonia, France, Italy, Philippines, Sierra Leone, Slovenia, Serbia, Guinea-Bissau
2011	6	USA, Senegal, Croatia, Ireland, Lithuania, Nepal
2012	8	Australia, Ghana, Mali, Burundi, Georgia, Togo, Burkina Faso, Gambia
2013	4	Kyrgyzstan, Macedonia, Nigeria, Germany
2014	5	Iraq, Republic of Korea, Kosovo, Indonesia, CAR
2015	8	Afghanistan, Palestine, Japan, New Zealand, Paraguay, Argentina, Tajikstan, South Sudan
2016	3	Ukraine, Kenya, Timor Leste
2017	3	Brazil, Montenegro, Czech Republic

Compiled by the author from statistics located at PeaceWomen, http://www.peacewomen.org/member-states.

early European NAPs was impacted by a lack substantive engagement with all the pillars of Resolution 1325. Furthermore, Barrow observes that "NAP[s] primarily help to support the operationalization of [Resolution] 1325 at the normative level with some trickle-down effect to the micro level" (Barrow 2016: 28–29). The Institute for Global and International Studies at George Washington University conducted a very intensive research project on WPS, "Women in Peace and Security through United Nations Security Resolution 1325: Literature Review, Content Analysis of National Plans, and Implementation" (Miller et al. 2014), which produced a detailed content analysis on forty NAPs. It confirmed the importance of NAPs as a bureaucratic tool for the implementation of Resolution 1325 and proposed other implementation strategies, including mainstreaming wider national policies and funding strategies (Miller et al. 2014). Furthermore, as Jacqui True explains, "the WPS NAP could therefore serve to integrate rather than aggregate common goals between peace and security, other agendas, and the SDGs [Sustainable Development Goals], such as those addressing displacement, climate change, conflict prevention and violent extremism" (True 2016: 6). This approach provides an even more integrated framework to better implement WPS in a more organized and practical approach.

Absent from these studies, however, is an understanding of why comparatively few countries in the Asian region have adopted NAPs.[4] This lack of implementation in the region raises a number of questions including, are NAPs the only "measure'" we can use to gauge state-level support and engagement with WPS? Does this mean those Asian countries with no NAPs are taking no action toward supporting Resolution 1325? To answer this question, this chapter examines the responsiveness of Asian countries to Resolution 1325 and considers whether the resolution's call for creating a NAP is necessary for the implementation of the WPS agenda. To date, few scholars have conducted research on how these countries think about Resolution 1325, and whether they realize their commitments to WPS in not adopting a NAP. This type of study is particularly vital in one country, the People's Republic of China. As a permanent member of the UN Security Council (UNSC) that holds the right to veto, their support for a WPS thematic agenda is crucial. To date, however, very little research has been done which examines China's understanding and engagement with the WPS agenda at the state level. Thus, this chapter focuses on China as a WPS case study to see how and if China has tried to live up to its commitments to the WPS agenda.

China's Attitude toward WPS

Up to now, China has not developed a National Plan of Action toward WPS. However, that does not mean China is not supportive of the WPS agenda. As a permanent member of the Security Council, China has emphasized the importance of gender equality on many diplomatic occasions and clearly expressed its consistent support for the global WPS agenda from the very outset. China understands the equally important role of women in the society and the process of civilization, and it has actively upheld the UN principle on gender equality. Thus, when the UN Economic and Social Council proposed a World Conference on Women in 1995, Mr. Qian Qichen, China's Foreign Minister at the time, invited the UN to hold the Fourth World Conference on Women in Beijing. In President Jiang Zemin's speech at the welcoming ceremony of that Conference, he expressed China's firm stand to fight for the equal status and rights of women in every aspect of their lives and China's determination to improve the status of women (Jiang 1995). The Conference marked an important turning point for gender equality and laid the foundation for the WPS agenda.

China has voted in favor (no abstention) of all the Security Council resolutions on WPS, and in all the Security Council public debates on issues related to WPS, China's position has always been affirmative (UNSC 2000: 17). Furthermore, China has showed its willingness to promote the prevention of violence against women, and the protection of women in conflict situations, as well as the participation and empowerment of women.

Not only has China been consistently supportive of the normative concept of WPS, it has also paid great attention to the implementation of these norms, both domestically and abroad. A desk review of all the speeches that Chinese representatives have made in the past during public debates at the Security Council on the WPS agenda highlights several points that China has made on the implementation of WPS.

First, China strongly supports the "participation" pillar of WPS that suggests that the international community should not only fight for women's inclusion in peace and security deliberations, but also tackle the root causes of conflict itself to promote women's peace and security. Only by "curbing conflicts, promoting development, reducing poverty, eliminating the root causes of strife and through development" (UNSC 2002: 15) can the international society truly protect women's safety and rights, and promote their participation in the peace process and post-conflict situations. This is a fundamental and consistent point of China's attitudes toward WPS and its implementation. In statements, China has never regarded crimes against women and girls in conflict situations, and their lack of participation in economic, political, and social life, as independent WPS issues. Instead they promote the incorporation of these ideas into the broader mandate of the United Nations, specifically the peace and development frameworks. China maintains the "the issue of women is that of development" (UNSC 2012: 24) and that conflicts, poverty and lack of development in concerned regions are the root causes of the crimes and discrimination against women and girls. Thus, to "avoid and reduce the harm suffered by women in armed conflict" (UNSC 2011: 22), greater resources should be invested in the prevention of war and reduction of conflict.

Second, with respect to the different roles that the international community and national states should play in the implementation of WPS, China stresses that incorporating WPS into the local context is the primary responsibility of the affected nations. China's representatives have more than once emphasized the essential role of national states in the protection and empowerment of women. During the 2007 Open Debate on WPS, Mr. Liu Zhenmin called on the countries concerned to "formulate, on the basis of their specific circumstances, national plans of action or strategies to implement resolution 1325" (UNSC 2007: 19). In the 2012 Open Debate, Mr. Wang Min pointed out that "governments bear the main responsibility for protecting women and combating sexual violence, as well as for implementing resolutions 1820, 1888, 1960" (UNSC 2010: 18). China presents the role of the international community as primarily concerned with delivering the relief and recovery pillar, including providing assistance to the countries concerned. As their submission to the 2010 open debate indicates, China believes that it is the international communities responsibility to "seek their understanding and cooperation, help strengthen their capacity-building, make progress in security sector reform and improve mechanisms in the areas of the rule of law, judicial assistance and compensation" (UNSC 2010: 18). Furthermore, they suggest that the international community should merely assist with the creation of gender balanced, stable leadership in these countries, while respecting their sovereignty. Responding to the rise of terrorist insurgencies in civil conflicts, China has specifically pointed out that terrorism and extremism in some countries and regions are causing "enormous harm to civilians in general and women in particular" (UNSC 2014: 18). Here again, China's position is that in assisting with the development of developing countries, this will mitigate the activities of terrorism and extremism.

Third, China also values the role of the United Nations and its relevant agencies, especially the Security Council, General Assembly, and Economic and Social Council, in implementing the prevention, protection, participation, and relief and recovery functions of WPS. China holds that the Security Council bears the primary responsibility for maintaining international peace and security, and for the removal of the direct causes of conflicts via prevention response initiatives. It therefore, creates an "enabling environment for the survival and development of all vulnerable groups, including women, children and civilians" (UNSC 2006: 18). Although China has frequently mentioned the role of the Security Council in preserving peace and preventing conflicts as "critical," "unique," and "primary," it has never regarded the Security Council as the sole authoritative agency of the UN system with respect to the implementation of WPS. The roles of the General Assembly, the Economic and Social Council, the Human Rights Council, UN Women, and other UN agencies are also emphasized by the Chinese delegation in open debates on WPS. These institutions should work closely with each other while carrying out their own functions based on their respective mandates. As Mr. Wang Min stated in the 2013 open debate on WPS, China believes that "the various organs of the United Nations must follow their own mandates and respect the division of labour, making every attempt to avoid any overlap of efforts" (UNSC 2013: 20). For example, the Security Council should "focus on conflict prevention, dispute mediation and post-conflict reconstruction" instead of "establishing universal standards with regard to women's issues and human rights" (UNSC 2013: 20; UNSC 2012: 24); the Economic and Social Council can provide humanitarian assistance to the conflict-affected countries; and the Human Rights Council can focus on the situation of human rights, especially that of women, in those countries. More importantly, China attach great significance of the women issues in both the National Action Plan of Human Rights and National Plan for the Implementation of the 2030 Agenda for Sustainable Development. In addition, it is worth mentioning that China also realizes the importance of regional, subregional and nongovernmental organizations in implementing WPS.

Last but not least, China has attached great significance to the prevention pillar of WPS, which their statements have defined as preventive, diplomatic, and peaceful solutions to the insecurity of women in conflict situations. In both the 2011 and 2016 open debates on WPS, China iterated that the international community should endeavor to find political solutions to conflicts and overcome differences through dialogue. For the protection of women in conflicts and wars, China particularly emphasizes the importance of mechanisms that prevention conflict. It has recommended that the Security Council "conduct active preventive diplomacy and promote the use of means such as dialogue, consultations and negotiations for the peaceful settlement of disputes" (UNSC 2011: 22). Furthermore, China appeals to the conflict-affected countries to focus on "capacity-building and socioeconomic development" (UNSC 2015: 21), and to the international community to help with post-conflict reconstruction in these countries, so as to eliminate the root causes of conflict and ensure the safety, development, and empowerment of women. Meanwhile, China firmly supports the enhanced participation of women in peace processes and post-conflict reconstruction, and believes that it can be achieved through economic development and empowerment of women. It maintains that the international community should "step up economic empowerment efforts" for women in weak countries and that the states should provide women with "better occupational-skills training and greater funding support for entrepreneurship"(UNSC 2016: 17).

From the speeches made by China's representatives on many diplomatic occasions, it is evident that China considers WPS to be an important global agenda that concerns the future of development and civilization. It is determined, at least rhetorically, to make this agenda a reality through the cooperation and coordination of the international community and nation states. In addition, China values the role of UN agencies, but requires the international community to respect the leadership role and sovereignty of states when implementing WPS. Moreover, it regards the maintenance of peace and the development as the fundamental solution to the problems of women, and hopes that the international community can find peaceful and meaningful ways to resolve these issues.

China's Actions to Implement WPS Agenda

Alongside its rhetorical commitments to the WPS agenda, China has also taken some concrete actions to realize them. It's true that China has neither developed, nor adopted a NAP on WPS. However it has, in its own way, endeavored to protect women in conflicts, engage them in peace-building processes, and empower them in daily life.

Internationally, China tries to implement WPS through UN frameworks, peacekeeping operations, and humanitarian assistance to conflict-affected countries. For example, in September 2015, the Global Summit of Women was convened under a joint China–United Nations initiative. At the Summit, President Xi Jinping announced that China would donate $10 million to the United Nations Entity for Gender Equality and the Empowerment of Women, in support of the implementation of the WPS agenda. Furthermore it promised to take measures to help developing countries address the challenges facing women and girls in the areas of health and education (UNSC 2015: 21). Additionally, China has attached great importance to women's issues in African countries, trying to support women in the political, economic, cultural, educational, and health domains. It has provided women and girls in Ebola-afflicted West African countries, such as Sierra Leone and Liberia, with a large amount of assistance to support Africa's efforts to upgrade its public-health system and emergency-response capacity on all fronts. Moreover, it has committed to "implement[ing] 200 Happy Life projects across Africa, and 100 village-level agricultural development projects, build industrial parks and vocational training centres on a collaborative basis, and provide training for 200,000 technical specialists" (UNSC 2016: 18).

Meanwhile, to promote women's participation in economic, political, and social life, as well as to enhance the empowerment of women in developing countries, China has also provided training courses for women from countries that could easily be affected by conflicts. For example, in December 2004, the Chinese government organized the first "Capacity Building Workshop for Female Officials from African Countries" to promote gender equality and women's development. Undertaken by the UN Educational, Scientific, and Cultural Organization (UNESCO) at the International Research and Training Centre for Suburban Education located in Baoding, the workshop attracted thirty-nine senior officials from twenty-one African countries, and covered themes such as gender equality, education, and development (Zou and Zhang 2005). In 2014, the Seminar on Social Management Capacity Building for Female Officials from African English Speaking Countries was sponsored by the Ministry of Commerce of the PRC and organized by China Women's University. About twenty female officials from twelve African countries including Egypt, Ethiopia, Ghana, Liberia, and Uganda attended the seminar. The seminar lasted fifteen days and shared China's experience in promoting women's equal participation in social management, economic development, and political domains with the African female officials.[5] By sharing its own experience of women's development with the African countries and providing them with various seminars and training courses, China is particularly focused on diplomatic engagement to help African countries promote gender equality and the empowerment of women.

Concerning the protection of women and children in conflict situations, China has deployed women peacekeepers to peacekeeping operations that report high rates of conflict-related sexual violence. In 2014, China dispatched an infantry battalion with a squad of thirteen infantry women to the peacekeeping operation in South Sudan. This was the first time that China had sent out women peacekeepers. They were trained in the same facilities and tasks as male peacekeepers and demonstrated particularly excellent operational capabilities to protect civilians in conflict areas. In 2016, China held, for the first time, an international training course specifically for women peacekeepers (China News 2016). About forty female military officers from twenty-four countries came to attend the training. The course was co-organized by the Office of Peacekeeping Affairs of Ministry of National Defense of the People's Republic of China (PRC), the Peacekeeping Center of Ministry of National Defense of PRC, and UN Women, in order to encourage troop-contributing countries to actively send women peacekeeping officers and improve their operational capacities.

The most recent great leap for China was a regional workshop themed on "Enhancing the Women, Peace and Security Agenda in Northeast Asia" held in Beijing on May 24, 2018. Organized by the UN Department of Political Affairs (DPA), in partnership with UN Women, United Nations Development Programme (UNDP), United Nations Educational, Scientific and Cultural Organization (UNESCO), Peace Research Institute Oslo (PRIO), and Stockholm International Peace Research Institute (SIPRI), the workshop aimed to create a platform for government officials, civil society representatives, academics and practitioners on issues related to the Women, Peace and Security (WPS) agenda in Northeast Asia. (China Women's news) The workshop raised Chinese people's awareness of WPS and at the same time provide more policy consultation and relevance both in China and the Northeast Asia in this regard.

On the domestic level, China pays great attention to the equal participation of women in the social and political aspects of their daily life. First, gender equality was promoted through law regulations and policy supports. In 1995, at the World Conference of Women, the Chinese government declared to the international community that it would consider the promotion of gender equality as a basic national strategy, which was later incorporated into the Law on the Protection of Women's Rights and Interests, amended in 2005. In 2013, when discussing with the leaders of the All-China Women's Association, President Xi Jinping explicitly pointed out that the gender difference and special interests of women should be taken into consideration during the processes of introducing laws and policy development (Xinhua News 2015). The tenth, eleventh, and twelfth Five-Year Plans also contain policies for women's development. These plans provide a more abundant content, clearer aims, and more effective measures to promote the development of women. Meanwhile, in 2011, the State Council issued the "Framework of Chinese Women Development" (2011–2020), which aims to protect women's interests, improve their social status, and enhance their equal participation in economic and social development. According to the Framework, Chinas is committed to improving the health, education, and economic situations of women and promoting their participation in decision-making and management affairs.[6]

China was among the first group of states to ratify the Convention on the Elimination of All Forms of Discrimination against Women (CEDAW) in 1980, upon its adoption by the UN General Assembly. In the following years, China submitted a couple of periodic reports to the Secretary-General of the United Nations in accordance with Article 18 of the Convention, the most recent one reviewed by the United Nations was in 2014. The protection of women's rights has also been incorporated into China's National Action Plan for Human Rights (2012–2015). It maintains that China will enforce laws on the protection of women's rights, promote gender equality, and safeguard the legitimate rights and interests of women (State Council Information Office 2012). As outlined in the National Action Plan for Human Rights, China will further promote women's participation in the management of national and social affairs, gradually increasing the number of women officials in the pro-vincial and state levels; it will endeavor to eliminate gender discrimination in employment and safeguard women's equal rights in acquiring economic resources; meanwhile, it will prevent and prohibit domestic violence against women, and fight against the trafficking of women (State Council Information Office 2012). Thus, although China has not yet devel-oped a NAP specifically for the WPS agenda, it has already incorporated the protection of women from violence and discrimination, and the promotion of women's rights and par-ticipation into daily life through different laws and regulations. To date, China has adopted three NAPs for Human Rights, (in 2009–2010, 2012–2015, 2016–2020), and produced two assessment reports on the NAP's implementation (2009–2010 and 2012–2015), all of which included a section on the protection of women's rights.[7]

Second, women in China have gained higher social status now and participated more than ever in both economic and political areas. For example, gender equality in the employ-ment sector is emphasized through laws and regulations, including the Law of the People's Republic of China on the Promotion of Employment, Special Provisions on Female Labors, and Law of Labor Contract. Since 2009, the Chinese government has offered microfinance loans equal to more than 222 billion RMB to encourage and help women to start their own businesses. Moreover, over two hundred thousand "women's schools" have been es-tablished to provide skills training for women in rural areas (China News 2015). As a re-sult, by 2013, the number of female entrepreneurs in China had increased to 25 percent of the total number of entrepreneurs (China News 2015). Chinese women are receiving more education and training than in the past, and seeing improvements in universal access to healthcare. In 2014, the percentage of female middle-school students and high-school students were, respectively, 46.7 percent and 50 percent; the percentage of female college students was about 52 percent; and the percentage of female PhD candidates increased to 36.9 percent (China News 2015). Currently, many schools have offered courses on gender equality and "femaleology" to promote public awareness of gender equality and the study of women. In addition, progress has been made on the participation of women in social and political domains. For example, the number of female representatives in both the National People's Congress and the provincial People's Congress has increased. In 2013, the female public servants recruited by the central government and its relevant agencies accounted for 47.8 percent of the total recruitment (China News 2015). Increased participation of women is also evident in the judicial branch. For example, in 2013, the percentage of female judges and prosecutors was, respectively, 28.8 percent and 29.3 percent, which was 12.1 percent and 12.3 percent higher than in 1995 (China News 2015). In general, as a result of China's gender equality policy, women in China have engaged more in the management of social and polit-ical issues, which will further improve women's social status and enhance the development of women.

It is true that China has not adopted a NAP on WPS like many Western countries, such as Australia, Denmark, UK and United States;[8] nor is it demonstrating any signs of making WPS a foreign policy priority like other states. However, China's endeavors to realize its commitments to WPS are present in the domestic and international arena. The absence of a NAP does not mean that China is not engaging with the agenda.

Internationally, China's implementation of the WPS agenda was mainly through cooperating with the UN and its relevant agencies, dispatching soldiers to peacekeeping missions, and providing assistance to conflict-affected countries. Domestically, China has tried to realize its commitments to the priority areas of WPS—prevention, relief and recovery, participation, and protection—by incorporating gender equality and women's development into various laws, and by taking concrete measures to improve the health, education, medical care, economic development, and political engagement of women. It's worth noting that, the implementation of WPS in China is in accordance with the belief that the primary responsibility for the protection of women from conflict situations and the improvement of their social status lies with the national government. Thus, when helping to implement WPS on the international level, China mainly chooses diplomatic or political solutions, offering financial support to related agencies within the UN framework and training courses to female officials from conflict-affected countries.

CONCLUSION

WPS is an agenda that emphasizes the importance of protecting women from violence in conflicts, and their equal participation in peacekeeping and peace-building processes. Almost sixteen years have passed since it was first proposed and it has gradually entered into the phase of implementation.

China considers WPS to be an important global agenda that concerns the future of development and civilization. It is determined to make this agenda a reality through the cooperation and coordination of the international community and nation states. More importantly, China is determined to raise awareness of, and thus mainstream the concept of, WPS domestically. Realizing that obstacles such as the absence of a national holistic mechanism though which multilevel organs can interact—namely, the National Working Committee on Children and Women under the State Council (central government); Internal and Judicial Affairs Committee (National People's Congress); and All-China Women's Federation (NGO)—constrains the capacity and impact of gender on legislation and policymaking, China should take significant steps toward providing a platform for this engagement. Moreover, China should consider creating a NAP for the implementation of Resolution 1325 on WPS.

Internationally, China's implementation of the WPS agenda occurs mainly, through cooperation with the UN and its relevant agencies, in dispatching soldiers to peacekeeping missions and providing assistance to conflict-affected countries. Domestically and internationally, it is worth noticing that China regards WPS as fundamentally a peace and development issue, instead of a problem associated with the silencing of women. Therefore, China's priorities for the implementation of WPS are usually combined with its commitment to assisting fragile countries in achieving lasting peace and security. China maintains that the nation-state should take primary responsibility for the implementation of WPS, and the international community should respect the sovereignty of nation-states during the implementation of WPS. Thus, it is more inclined to regard implementation of WPS as a diplomatic cause and realize it through peace and development solutions. In the future, China should increase its contribution to the UN framework, as it has been doing over the past years. The focus of this contribution should be on the alleviation of poverty and economic development in the least-developed and fragile states. In addition, China should look to speed up its systemic and holistic goal of mainstreaming WPS domestically, and possibly incrementally propose a NAP for WPS, similar to those which have been developed in the human rights field.

NOTES

1. At the international level, the UN Security Council has adopted seven resolutions on Women Peace, and Security, starting with UN Security Council Resolution 1325, followed by Resolutions 1820,1888, 1889, 1960, 2106, 2122, and 2242. For more information, please refer to http://www.un.org/en/peacekeeping/issues/women/wps.shtml.
2. Security Council Report, "Women, Peace, and Security" (October 28, 2005), http://www.securitycouncilreport.org/monthly-forecast/2005-11/lookup_c_glKWLeMTIsG_b_1141141.php.
3. See "Member States," PeaceWomen, http://www.peacewomen.org/member-states.
4. There are ten countries that have developed NAPs: Philippines, Nepal, Georgia, Kyrgyzstan, Iraq, Republic of Korea, Indonesia, Afghanistan, Japan, and Timor Leste.
5. China Women's University (CWU) held the opening ceremony of the Seminar on Social Management Capacity Building for Female Officials from African English Speaking Countries in 2014. See http://www.cwu.edu.cn/zhxw/3361.htm, last retrieved on October 6th, 2016.
6. Full text of "The Framework of Chinese Women Development (2011–2020)," August 8, 2011, see, http://www.china.com.cn/policy/txt/2011-08/08/content_23160230_2.htm.
7. Human Rights, China, http://www.humanrights.cn/html/wxzl/3/
8. For instance, in December 2011, President Barack Obama released the first-ever US National Action Plan on Women, Peace, and Security, and signed an Executive Order directing the Plan to be implemented. Together, the Executive Order and NAP chart a roadmap for how the United States will accelerate and institutionalize efforts across the government to advance women's participation in preventing conflict and keeping peace. The US NAP covers "National Integration and Institutionalization, Participation in Peace Processes and Decision- making, Protection from Violence, Conflict Prevention, and Access to Relief and Recovery." For more information, refer to https://obamawhitehouse.archives.gov/the-press-office/2011/12/19/fact-sheet-united-states-national-action-plan-women-peace-and-security.

REFERENCES

Anderlini, S. N. *Women Building Peace: What They Do, Why It Matters*. Boulder, CO: Lynne Rienner, 2007.
Barrow, A. "Operationalizing Security Council Resolution 1325: The Role of National Action Plans." *Journal of Conflict and Security Law* 21, no. 2 (2016): 247–275.
China News. "China Held an International Training Course for Women Peacekeepers for the First Time." June 27, 2016, http://www.chinanews.com/m/mil/2016/06-27/7918577.shtml.

China News. "White Paper on Chinese Gender Equality and Women Development." September 22, 2015, http://finance.chinanews.com/gn/2015/09-22/7537577.shtml.

China Women's News. "Enhancing the Women, Peace and Security Agenda in Northeast Asia' Regional Workshop Held in Beijing." May 25, 2018, http://www.womenofchina.cn/womenofchina/html1/news/international/1805/9329-1.htm

Chunfeng, Zou, and Bin Zhang. "Summary on the Capacity Building Workshop for Female Officials from African Countries." *World Education Information*, March 2005.

Cockburn, C. *From Where We Stand: War, Women's Activism and Feminist Analysis.* London: Zed Books, 2007.

Deshmukh, P. K. "United Nations Security Council Resolutions 1888 and 1889: Women, Peace, and Security." Introductory Note by Preeti Kundra Deshmukh. *International Legal Materials* 49, no. 1 (2010): 71–82.

Hill, F., M. Aboitiz, and S. Poehlman-Doumbouya. "Nongovernmental Organizations' Role in the Build-Up and Implementation of Security Council Resolution 1325." *Signs: Journal of Women in Culture and Society* 28, no. 4 (2003): 1255–1269.

Miller, B., M. Pournik, and A. Swaine. "Women in Peace and Security through United Nations Security Resolution 1325: Literature Review, Content Analysis of National Action Plans, and Implementation." Institute for Global and International Studies. Washington, DC: George Washington University, 2014.

State Council Information Office of the People's Republic of China. "National Action Plan for Human Rights (2012–2020)." June 11, 2012, http://www.scio.gov.cn/zxbd/nd/2012/Document/1172889/1172889_4.htm.

True, J. "Women, Peace, and Security in Asia Pacific: Emerging Issues in National Action Plans for Women, Peace, and Security." Discussion Paper. Asia-Pacific Regional Symposium on National Action Plans on Women, Peace, and Security. UN Women and the Embassy of Japan, Bangkok, Thailand, July 11–13, 2016, http://www2.unwomen.org/-/media/field%20office%20eseasia/docs/publications/2016/12/1-nap-jt-for-online-r3.pdf?v=1&d=20161209T0655.

Tryggestad, T. L. "Trick or Treat? The UN and Implementation of Security Council Resolution 1325 on Women, Peace, and Security." *Global Governance: A Review of Multilateralism and International Organizations* 15, no. 4 (2009): 539–557.

United Nations Security Council. "Open Debate on Women, Peace, and Security." S/PV.7658, March 28, 2016, http://www.securitycouncilreport.org/atf/cf/%7B65BFCF9B-6D27-4E9C-8CD3-CF6E4FF96FF9%7D/s_pv_7658.pdf.

United Nations Security Council. "Open Debate on Women, Peace, and Security." S/PV.7533, October 13, 2015, http://www.securitycouncilreport.org/un-documents/document/spv7533.php.

United Nations Security Council. "Open Debate on Women, Peace and Security." S/PV.7289, October 28, 2014, http://www.securitycouncilreport.org/un-documents/document/spv7289.php.

United Nations Security Council. "Open Debate on Prevention of Sexual Violence." S/PV.6984, June 24, 2013, http://www.securitycouncilreport.org/un-documents/document/spv6984.php.

United Nations Security Council. "Open Debate on Conflict-Related Sexual Violence." S/PV.6722, February 23, 2012, http://www.securitycouncilreport.org/un-documents/document/wps-s-pv-6722.php.

United Nations Security Council. *Women, Peace, and Security.* S/PV.6642, October 28, 2011, http://www.un.org/en/ga/search/view_doc.asp?symbol=S/PV.6642(Resumption1).

United Nations Security Council. "Open Debate on Conflict-Related Sexual Violence." S/PV.6453, December 16, 2010, http://www.securitycouncilreport.org/un-documents/document/WPS%20SPV%206453.php.

United Nations Security Council. "Open Debate on Women, Peace, and Security." S/PV.5766, October 23, 2007, http://www.securitycouncilreport.org/un-documents/document/WPS%20SPV5766resumption1.php.

United Nations Security Council. "Open Debate on Women, Peace, and Security." S/PV.5556, October 26, 2006, http://www.un.org/en/ga/search/view_doc.asp?symbol=S/PV.5556.

United Nations Security Council. "Open Debate on Women, Peace, and Security." S/PV.4635, October 28, 2002, http://www.securitycouncilreport.org/un-documents/document/WPS%20SPV%204635.php.

United Nations Security Council. "Women, Peace, and Security." S/PV.4208, October 24, 2000, http://www.un.org/en/ga/search/view_doc.asp?symbol=S/PV.4208.

Xinhua News. "Top 10 Issues on Gender Equality since Beijing World Conference on Women." October 14, 2015, http://news.xinhuanet.com/zgjx/2015-10/14/c_134712004.htm.

2005.

Zemin, Jiang. "Speech by the President of the People's Republic of China at the Welcoming Ceremony for the Fourth World Conference on Women." Beijing, September 4, 1995.

Chunfeng Zou, and Bin Zhang. "Summary on the Capacity Building Workshop for Female Officials from African Countries." World Education Information, March

CHAPTER 42

WOMEN CONTROLLING ARMS, BUILDING PEACE

The Case of the Philippines

JASMIN NARIO-GALACE

THIS chapter examines the effects of integrating the language of small arms and light weapons control into the Philippine National Action Plan (NAP) on Women, Peace, and Security (WPS).[1] It analyzes the context in which language on small arms control was infused, the structure of the integration, and the gains and challenges associated with implementing such language. As a lead player in the formulation and implementation of the first cycle of NAP on WPS in the Philippines, I consider how the convergence of small arms control and the WPS agenda in the Philippines has worked to change the attitudes and beliefs of those reached, and how it has helped inspire action from women to reduce small arms proliferation and violence. While men are primarily the wielders of weapons in the battlefield, women count largely among those caught in the crossfire and make up the majority of the displaced. To protect women from violence and prevent the violation of their rights, the NAP included the goal of adopting laws and mechanisms to regulate the transfer and use of small arms.

This chapter will discuss the role small arms and light weapons play in armed conflict and other situations of armed violence in general, and in the Philippines specifically. It will describe the effects of small arms proliferation on women, as well as the resolutions in the United Nations that establish the links between small arms proliferation, and Women, Peace, and Security. It will describe how the issue of small arms control got into the Philippine NAP on WPS, and will assess gains as well as lessons learned from its inclusion. It will end with a set of recommendations on how including the issue of small arms proliferation in NAPs on WPS could be better implemented.

SMALL ARMS VIOLENCE

Threats to peace and security abound. Armed violence, in both conflict and non-conflict settings, is one key threat. Every year throughout the world, armed violence kills around

526,000 people and more than 75 percent die in non-conflict settings (IISS 2015). That's approximately 1,441 killed on a daily basis. The International Institute for Strategic Studies reported that in 2014, 42 armed conflicts were waged in the world, resulting in 180,000 deaths which, roughly, translate to 493 fatalities per day.

A lot of theorizing has been done to explore the roots of armed violence. Krahe (1996) described some of these theories in her article "Aggression and Violence in Society." One theory looks at biological and psychological explanations, arguing that aggression is innate or inherent in human nature. Another looks at psychological explanations, such as frustration and aversive stimulation. A further theory posits that aggressive behavior is acquired through the process of socialization. Hence, if one is exposed to gangs, abusive neighborhoods, or harsh, domineering parenting styles, one is likely to be more aggressive

Political and economic analysts have also proposed various possible causes, such as territorial disputes, competition for resources, the search for independence or sovereignty, extreme nationalism, ideological or power struggles, or a history of colonialism (Navarro-Castro and Nario Galace 2010). Other researchers look at the root causes of violence from the perspectives of victims, suggesting that global inequalities in the distribution of wealth, extreme poverty, and unfair trading are significant influencers (Barnaby 1988). Furthermore, some scholars see deprivation and injustice, human rights abuses, and sympathy for aggrieved kin as powerful motivators for violence.

Other than death, armed violence brings other devastating effects to peace and security. War and criminality account for 14 percent of the 5.8 million people who die each year as a result of injuries (WHO 2010). Armed violence slows up access to even the most basic social services and diverts resources away from efforts at bettering lives. Countries plagued by armed violence in situations of crime or conflict, according to the United Nation Secretary-General Report to the Security Council on the subject of small arms, often perform poorly in terms of the Millennium Development Goals (United Nations 2008). Armed violence forms a serious impediment to economic growth and development, destroying livelihoods, property, and the environment.

Conflicts and violence have led to high records of human rights violations. Massacres, extrajudicial and political killings, torture, enforced disappearances, executions, assassinations, bombing, burning, and kidnapping are examples of atrocious acts. Armed violence also triggers displacement. According to the United Nations High Commissioner for Refugees (UNHCR) (2016), 65.3 million people were forced to flee their homes in 2015, or an average of twenty-four people fleeing from home each minute. With a global population of 7.4 billion, one in every 113 people, according to the UN agency, is an asylum seeker, internally displaced or a refugee.

Wars see children walk the battle zones instead of the playground. An estimated three hundred thousand children around the world are involved in armed conflict (Chatterjee 2012). Armed violence has other repercussions for children, including the disruption to education and creation of fear and trauma. It is interesting to note, that not many see the role proliferation and the availability of weapons play in enabling armed violence, sustaining armed conflicts, and destroying lives. In 14 of the 29 armed conflicts in 2015, Syria, Nigeria, Iraq, and Afghanistan were the bloodiest, with more than ten thousand deaths in each case (Project Ploughshares 2016). In these killings, both in conflict and non-conflict settings, small arms and light weapons are normally the weapons of choice.

The Small Arms Survey (2007) reported that there are approximately 875 million small arms in circulation worldwide, with 8 million new guns manufactured every year. Annual trade in small arms exceeds approximately, $8.5 billion. The International Action Network on Small Arms (IANSA) Women's Network posits that while the primary weapon holders, users, and traders, as well as the majority of victims, may be men, women also suffer the consequences of weapons proliferation. Weapons, guns in particular, have been used to facilitate rape, sexual abuse, and domestic or intimate-partner violence (Lyddon 2011). While men, mostly, are the wielders of weapons in armed violence situations, women count largely among those who are caught in the crossfire and make up the majority of the displaced. Women are particularly susceptible to sexual harassment, abduction, rape, and other threats of armed violence, with sexual violence being used deliberately as a tactic of war (Dehesa and Masters 2010). The UN reported, for example, that approximately two hundred thousand women and girls are survivors of rape in the Democratic Republic of the Congo; that between one hundred thousand and two hundred thousand girls and women were victims of rape in the Rwanda 1994 genocide; that more than forty thousand women in Liberia suffered some form of sexual violence during the 1989–2003 war; and that more than sixty thousand internally displaced women were sexually abused by armed combatants during the war in Sierra Leone (United Nations, n.d.). The Inter-Parliamentary Union (IPU), in a hearing at the UN in 2008, reported that armed conflict creates a climate of widespread sexual abuse, and counted the proliferation of weapons in communities, as one of the factors that enable rape with impunity.

Indeed, the proliferation of weapons is often overlooked as an enabling and sustaining factor in armed violence and conflict. Weapons play a central role in putting women's security at risk, in particular, and in tearing down peace and promoting insecurity in general.

Recognizing that the changing nature of warfare increasingly harms non-combatants and realizing that women are not included in decision-making on matters and mechanisms that relate to peace and security, including in peace processes, the United Nations Security Council adopted Resolution 1325 in 2000. The resolution, in essence, established the links between peace and security and the role women play, and can play, in promoting peace and security, particularly in the areas of peacekeeping, conflict prevention, conflict resolution, and peace-building. In 2010, the links between arms control and WPS were clearly established with the adoption of General Assembly (GA) Resolution 65/69 (UNGA 2011) which, recognizing women's participation in peace and security, urged member states to promote the equitable representation of women in decision-making processes related to disarmament, nonproliferation, and arms control. Subsequent GA resolutions were adopted to strengthen this. GA 67/48 (UNGA 2012, for instance, called upon all states to empower women, including through capacity-building efforts to participate in arms control efforts. GA 69/61 (UNGA 2014) encourages member states to better understand the impact of armed violence, particularly the impact of the illicit trafficking in small arms and light weapons (SALW) on women and girls.

With the clear links established by the resolutions previously mentioned between arms control, peace, and security, and the role women can play in disarmament, nonproliferation, and arms control, I consider whether the inclusion of the goal of small arms control in a NAP on women can help bring positive results in relation to peace and security. Specifically, I consider whether a NAP will be able to help protect women from armed violence and encourage their participation in arms control? And will it be able to help bring more peace and security?

GUNS AND VIOLENCE IN THE PHILIPPINES

This study will determine the effects of integrating the goal of small arms and light weapons control in a NAP on WPS. It will discuss if the peace and security context in the Philippines merits inclusion of language on small arms control in their NAP. It will describe the gains, including language, on small arms control, as well as the gaps and challenges in implementing language on small arms control in the NAP on WPS. It will discuss if the inclusion of the goal on small arms control in the first cycle of the Philippine NAP has brought positive results using Stufflebeam's (n.d.) Context, Input, Process, and Product (CIPP) evaluation model. CIPP is a program evaluation model developed by Daniel Stufflebeam and colleagues in the 1960s, and used in judging a program's value. CIPP is designed to systematically guide both evaluators and stakeholders conducting assessments at the beginning of a project, while the project is in progress, and at its end. The intention of the model is not to prove a project's worthiness, but rather to improve the program or project itself.

Thirteen women involved in WPS work were interviewed to help answer the questions of this study. The questionnaire formulated by this researcher was reviewed by experts on gender and disarmament prior to administration.

Guns and Women

The Philippines is awash in small arms. GunPolicy.org (n.d.) reported that there are approximately 3,900,000 guns, licit and illicit, held by civilians. The *Manila Times* (2014) reported that there are 1.7 million registered firearms in the country, 60 percent of which have been found using fictitious or questionable data (Lingao 2010). The Philippine National Police shared that there are nearly six hundred thousand loose or unregistered firearms. It also reported that there are roughly 150 new applications for gun licensing processed everyday (Gutierrez 2013). The Philippine Action Network on Small Arms (PhilANSA 2009) observed that there is a wide range of weapons in circulation: AK-47s, M-16s, M-14s, .38- and .45-caliber pistols and revolvers, rocket-propelled grenades, M-79s, PV-49s, landmines, machine guns (30/50/60) and 81 mm mortars. The current law does not help in regulating the proliferation of small arms. Republic Act No. 10951 (GOVPH 2013) allows a citizen to own and possess a maximum of fifteen registered firearms, and more than fifteen if the citizen is a certified gun collector. The law also exempts a long list of professionals from applying for a permit to carry their guns outside of their homes. Small arms proliferation enables and sustains the two major armed conflicts in the country, both of which have claimed thousands of lives. Since 1969, more than forty thousand have died in the armed conflict between the government and the Communist Party of the Philippines (Jamal 2017). From 1970 to 2015, between 100,000 and 150,000 died in the conflict in Mindanao (Rappler 2015). SALWs play a role in the ability of armed groups to commit gross human rights abuses, such as torture, arbitrary arrests, denial of fair trials, and extrajudicial and political killings. Hontiveros (2017) reported that there have been more than seven thousand drug-related killings since July 2016, with the police directly killing at least twenty-five hundred alleged drug offenders. In most of these cases, guns were used in snuffing out lives. Guns and private armed groups (PAGs), meanwhile, enable political dynasties to perpetuate themselves in power. A classic example of this is the Ampatuan political dynasty in Mindanao. The Ampatuan family, whose members are charged before the courts for the Maguindanao Massacre that killed 57 people, have at most 274 registered and licensed firearms, barely a fourth of the more than 1,200 total seized from in and around their properties, which included a 60-mm mortar, a 57-mm recoilless rifle, M-16 rifles, and a Barrett .50-caliber sniper rifle (Lingao 2010). The family employed two thousand militias while in office. The PNP reported that there are as many as 250 PAGs in the country working for politicians (Mendoza 2012). Guns enable politicians to destroy political opponents during elections. Elections in the country are always marred by killings. Some candidates use the bullet if they cannot win through the ballot. The elections of 2012, for example, killed 156 people (PhilANSA 2009). Most of these killings were done with the aid of a gun.

Small arms are also the weapons of choice in tribal wars. 183 people die each year from *rido* or family feuds in the Autonomous Region of Muslim Mindanao, according to the Philippine National Police (PNP) (IRIN 2009).

Women may not be the primary weapon users in the country, but they suffer from violence in the home or on the streets with the aid of guns. Of the fifty-seven killed in the Maguindanao Massacre, for instance, twenty-one were women. Results of police laboratory tests found traces of semen in five of the twenty-one slain women, evidence that they were raped (5 Women Killed 2009). The bodies of all five women had bruises or injuries to their genitals (Nario-Galace 2014). In 2009, 3,159 rape cases were tallied by the Philippine National Police. That's an average of nine rape cases daily or one incident every two-and-a-half hours (Flores and Diaz 2010). One study posited that "half of rape victims would not file a complaint because of the stigma and the embarrassment of recalling their ordeal to the authorities" (Flores and Diaz 2010). Additionally, 68 percent of gun violence against women reported in 2007, in the *Philippine Star*, were cases of rape (Center for Peace Education 2008).

Converging Agendas: Guns, Women, Peace and Security

That small arms and light weapons were a peace and security threat was validated in the consultations made in the process of formulating the first cycle of the Philippine National Action Plan on Resolution 1325. Consultation participants from conflict-affected communities, from North to South of the Philippines, identified guns as enablers of armed conflict and as tools that empower and sustain armed groups. As Miriam Coronel-Ferrer (2016), former chair of the Government Peace Panel observed, "gun proliferation is a real problem and has a real bearing on women, peace and security." Proliferation of small arms greatly adds to the armed violence in the country, both horizontal and vertical. Moreover, women are intensely affected by such armed violence, due to the responsibilities placed on them to care for internally displaced families and communities, and as victims/survivors of Sexual and Gender Based Violence (SGBV) or domestic violence (Tanada 2016.

As the NAP was formulated based on the communities' experiences of conflict, as well as their vision of peace, the control of their proliferation was included as an action point in the NAP with the following indicators: research on women's victims of gun violence is undertaken and publicized, training on women's human rights is added as a requirement before a license or renewal is issued, guns surrendered by rebel returnees are destroyed and not recirculated, and the firearms registration system is improved (WEAct1325 2010).

Philippines NAP

The Philippines NAP was adopted at the tail end of the Gloria Macapagal administration. When the administration of Benigno Aquino Jr. assumed power, the Office of the Presidential Adviser on the Peace Process (OPAPP) and chair of the National Steering Committee on WPS embarked on a NAP enhancement, arguing that the list of action points and indicators of the original NAP were too lengthy. They proposed the deletion of the language on SALW, but members of civil society in a consultation insisted that the language be retained. Fatmawati Salapuddin (2012) of Lupah Sug Bangsamoro, for instance, insisted on its retention, citing that the problem of small arms proliferation was very real in conflict-affected communities. OPAPP retained the SALW language but moved its location from an action point to an indicator. Namely, the "adoption of mechanisms to regulate the transfer and use of the tools of violence in armed conflict, particularly small arms and light weapons" was relocated under the action point that requires departments to "develop, enact and implement policies that ensure protection and security for women affected by armed conflict..." (OPAPP 2014).

The language inclusion may have been weakened but the link between WPS and arms control agendas was clearly established in this NAP. In various capacity-sharing and action research projects conducted in the next five years after the adoption of the NAP by the Women Engaged in Action on 1325 (WE Act 1325 2010)—a national network of women helping implement the NAP on WPS—training participants consistently mentioned the problem of small arms proliferation in their communities. One of these was at a recent action research on Women's Security Issues in the Bangsamoro (WE Act 1325 2016) where proliferation of firearms came out as one of the primary factors that made women feel unsafe and insecure in this region.

Including SALW in the NAP on WPS: Some Gains

The inclusion of the language of SALW in the Philippines NAP established the links between small arms proliferation and the WPS agenda. "You cannot take away guns from the peace and security issue," Coronel-Ferrer (2016), former chair of the Government Peace Panel said. Loreta Castro (2016), program director of the Center for Peace Education reinforced this belief suggesting that, "including such language enables all to recognize that this is a serious problem and should be addressed. It ceases to be invisible." Ana Natividad (2016), former program officer of WE Act 1325 expressed that

> the inclusion of such language establishes the intersection of a gender-sensitive outlook on peacebuilding and small arms proliferation in a landmark policy, mandating that it is an important aspect that needs to be given adequate consideration, ideally leading to corresponding action.

The inclusion of language on SALW helped raise awareness of the issue of SALW and its link to the WPS agenda. WE Act 1325, via its Women Working for Normalization Project, supported by DFAT Australia, gave space to the discussion of these links. Normalization was part of the Framework Agreement on the Bangsamoro (FAB) between the government and the Moro Islamic Liberation Front, signed in 2012. that pertained to the return of conflict-affected communities to conditions where people are free from fear of violence and crime, among others. Pathways to normalization included control of firearms and disbandment of private armies and armed groups. Frances Piscano (2016), former WE Act 1325 project officer, said that WE Act 1325's efforts have allowed for a better understanding that gun violence impedes human security. Carmen Lauzon-Gatmaytan (2017), former WE Act 1325 steering committee member, explained, "We were able to call attention to the importance of addressing the issue of small arms proliferation." Furthermore, Jogenna Jover (2016), executive director of the Kutawato Council for Justice and Peace, observed that the "women we engage now have a better understanding of the effects of gun proliferation, including intimidation of women in evacuation centers, workplace and in the family." Likewise, Mirma Tica (2016), of the Philippine Action Network on Small Arms, said that "the language helped people become aware of the connection between guns and women's protection, as well as their work on armed violence prevention," a view shared by Marylin Pintor of Mothers for Peace. Indeed, as Marylin Pintor (2016) suggests, "the inclusion of the language in NAP created and raised consciousness that arms control is necessary to protect women's rights and prevent violence."

The gain in including such language would be to make the stakeholders and duty bearers aware of this important issue and identify indicators for action (Tanada 2016). Including language of SALW in the NAP on WPS helped women recognize that they can use their agency to address the problem. There is now a gradual recognition of the agency of women and the need to include them in discussions on the issue (Hernandez 2016). The inclusion of such language opened a space for considerations of the role that women can play in addressing the impact of arms proliferation at the community level, given its disproportionate impact on them, and connecting to the larger framework of women's meaningful participation in various aspects of peace-building (Natividad 2016).

The inclusion of the language on NAP also gave some form of legitimacy to WPS activists to lobby for engendered policies. WE Act 1325 members, for example, made use of this provision in campaigning for support for an engendered Arms Trade Treaty within the country, region, and, during the negotiations, in the UN. In lobbying for a gender-sensitive firearms legislation, the Center for Peace Education referenced this provision in its statements made during public consultations and in its lobby work at the Senate calling for amendments to the law. Policymakers did not include the lobbied provision in the final text of the law, but the reference in the NAP was helpful in calling attention of policymakers to the issue (Viar 2016).

At the very least, indirect links between small arms and peace and security issues are in the normalization annex of the peace agreement between the government and the Moro Islamic Liberation Front (MILF). Many weapons are in the hands of private armed lords. The normalization annex addresses the issue of PAGs to pave the way for total demobilization (Coronel-Ferrer 2016).

Efforts at raising awareness on the ground have also produced some beliefs and attitudinal change. A study conducted by WE Act 1325 (2014) sought to find out if beliefs and attitudes toward arms control of community women affected by armed conflict will change after a peace training. Post-test scores using ANOVA indicated significant differences before and after the training. Training helped change participants' views that guns were necessary in providing personal and community security. A study conducted by the CPE among the youth prior to and after a peace camp also found significant differences in the youth's beliefs and attitudes toward arms control. After the training, the youth's belief that peace and normalcy will be more possible if arms were reduced, their proliferation controlled, and armed groups disbanded improved significantly (Nario-Galace 2017). A small arms control training also inspired a group of community women to invite politicians, the religious sector, and civil society to a meeting to discuss their concern about election violence. Where they lived was notorious for political killings especially during the election period. The dialogue resulted in politicians committing to tape the nozzles of their guns during the election period. The death rate during the said election period became significantly lower compared to previous election years (Bumogas 2013).

Gaps and Challenges in Implementing the Language on SALW in the NAP

There may have been some gains in the inclusion of the language, but there are also many gaps, in relation to the implementation of the provision. The NAP aimed at developing policies and mechanisms to control the proliferation of SALW to protect women's rights and the violation of these rights. The provision, however, was not widely disseminated to important stakeholders, such as the legislature, local government officials, and security sector groups, which had the power and mandate to create such laws and mechanisms. Civil society efforts at raising the awareness of women and youth in communities where arms proliferated was not complemented by awareness-raising efforts within and by government agencies. This, according to research participants, may be attributed to government's lack of awareness, interest, and/or capacity on the issue.

Some participants to this research went as far as saying that many government officials refused to recognize the link between gun proliferation and WPS, as many of them are gun collectors and gun enthusiasts who relied on these tools for their protection or perpetuation in power. One research participant posited, "the security sector being dominated by patriarchal values are often in support of arms ownership." Refusal to recognize the problem that SALWs bring to peace and security may also be due to the contention that some political families stock up on weapons for the use of their private armies.

Non-implementation of the provision may also be due to the nonrecognition that the proliferation and use of small arms is a real threat to peace and security. Hence, there is a lack of political will to control or do something about the problem (Castro 2016). This lack of recognition of the link is evidenced by the lack of knowledge the general public has on government commitments to international agreements such as the UN Program of Action on Small Arms and Light Weapons. Arms control discourse in the international arena does not seem to cascade to pertinent government agencies who have the power to implement them. Or if they have started to cascade, terms of office of those in charge have already ended. Disbandment of private armed groups in Regions 9, 12, and the ARMM would have started, for instance, but the Bangsamoro peace process got delayed with the assumption of a new government. The lack of push on the issue, however, was not relegated to duty bearers. In addition, women civil society organizations did not push the issue as much as they did with other goals in the NAP (Tanada 2016).

Research participants also pointed to masculinities, which shape notions of security as contributing factors to the lack of concern about arms proliferation. As Dayang Bahidjan (2016) of Nisa ul haqq fi Bangsamoro shared, "we have heard women complain that their husbands love their guns more than them." Others pointed to strong arguments espoused by many that guns are necessary for protection, especially in a country where there is a high crime rate and armed conflicts and other forms of armed violence exist.

Evaluating SALW Language Inclusion in NAP on WPS using the CIPP Model

An evaluation of context indicated that the Philippines is besieged by various forms of armed violence—two armed conflicts that have been there for nearly five decades each, extrajudicial killings, criminal violence, and *rido* or clan wars, among others. SALWs are normally the weapons of choice in enabling these. Guns are sourced from countries like the United States and China. Others are smuggled through the country's porous borders, while some are manufactured domestically and sold inexpensively. To acquire guns can be effortless, as gun sellers manage to get round government requirements and procedures (Gutierrez 2013). Guns also change hands from security sector to perpetrators either through *agaw-armas* (thievery) or illegal sale. PhilANSA (2009) approximated that twenty-eight people a day die from gun violence. Men are normally the users and victims of armed violence, but women are disproportionately affected by it. Clearly, something had to be done in relation to this context to save lives. Participants to the consultations on NAP on WPS constantly referenced this context in the conflict analysis and visioning of peace sessions held during the consultations. Participants cited the role women could play in controlling arms to reduce security threats and get to peace. Inclusion or input of language on arms control in the NAP on WPS required little thought. It became an imperative.

The NAP language on SALW was, however, implemented on a limited scale. Duty bearers either lacked awareness or refused to recognize the threat of SALW proliferation to peace and security. Important stakeholders, such as the legislature and security sector, who had the mandate to shape policies were not fully engaged in the process of NAP formulation and implementation. Implementation was left with a few civil society members who cared about the issue. And as this was a handful, initiatives were also a handful and limited to mainly awareness-raising and advocacy activities. The NAP on WPS went through some form of evaluation but not the particular indicator on SALW. Gender and disarmament advocates within WE Act 1325 did some form of reflection on why implementation did not go as planned but reflection results were not cascaded to those who could make a difference. NAP evaluation efforts were focused on the plan's main action points. SALW language was moved from its original location as an indicator to an action point. That the first cycle of the NAP on WPS had a long list of indicators did not help either.

The objective then in the NAP of controlling SALW to protect women from violence and prevent the violation of their rights via mechanisms and policies was not fully achieved. At best, the language was indirectly referenced in the peace agreement via the normalization annex that required disbandment of private armed groups as well as combatants' decommissioning. But language inclusion did help raise awareness of women on the ground on the impact of SALW proliferation to peace and security. In addition, training on the issue of small arms has led to changes in beliefs and attitudes about gun ownership. The inclusion of the small arms issue in the NAP also inspired women to advocate for engendered policies at the international, national, and community levels, as well as in organizing activities that reduced the risk of losing lives from guns during the 2013 national elections. Thus, effort to promote peace and security via SALW control language in the NAP on WPS was relatively useful.

CONCLUSION

Based on the gains and lessons learned, it is recommended, that the legislature, the security sector, and local government units be engaged in the process of formulating and implementing the NAP. Engaging them is crucial if WPS advocates want to see engendered firearms legislations, as well as mechanisms to control small arms proliferation and violence. These buy-ins of these government branches and units is critical to ensuring implementation of the SALW language in a NAP on WPS. Finding champions within these institutions will also help carry the agenda forward. Awareness-raising initiatives must also continue to promote norm change.

Second, since education had a positive impact on the beliefs, attitudes, and action of those who were engaged, capacity-sharing on women and arms control should be done systematically and on a broad scale to create impact.

Third, there is also a need to support peace processes and other political solutions to armed conflict as they have the potential of ending the conflicts, and paving the way to normalization, demobilization, and decommissioning.

Fourth, there is a need to work with Peace and Order Councils at various levels of governance as they are directly responsible for the peace and order situation in their communities. It is important to secure their commitment to include women in the work of promoting peace and security in their localities.

Fifth, we must continue with the advocacy of amending the firearms law, ratifying the arms trade treaty, and securing commitment to implement the UN Programme of Action (UN PoA) on Small Arms and Light Weapons. Adoption and/or implementation of these will help protect women from violence and promote their participation in small arms control processes.

Sixth, we must raise awareness of the Arms Trade Treaty, the UN PoA, and national firearms legislations and their implications to women, peace, and security, and make sure that international commitments cascade to agencies and groups that can help implement these commitments.

Seventh, to have solid data and evidence that may be used for education and lobbying, we must continue our research work on gun violence and women.

Eighth, we must continue to establish the links between the arms control and WPS agendas to highlight the role women can play in controlling arms and in promoting peace and security overall. Finally, we must continue to lobby for women's participation and leadership in peace processes to ensure that their lived realities on the ground are considered when crafting peace agreements and policies.

NOTES

1. This researcher expresses gratitude to the following for their support and assistance: Cynthia Alcantara, Dayang Bahidjan, Lourdes Quisumbing-Baybay, Loreta Castro, Anna Dinglasan, Miriam Coronel-Ferrer, Carmen Lauzon-Gatmaytan, Belle Hernandez, Jogenna Jover, Sarah Masters, Ana Natividad, Marylin Pintor, Frances Piscano, Karen Tanada, Mirma Tica, Jurma Tikmasan, and Iverly Viar.

REFERENCES

Bahidjan, Dayang. Nisa ul haqq fi Bansamoro member. Email correspondence with author, March 20, 2016.

Barnaby, F., ed. *GAIA Peace Atlas*. New York: Doubleday, 1988.

Bumogas, Paz. CCAGG Officer. Personal communication, 2013.

Center for Peace Education. "Women and Gun Violence: Philippines." Unpublished raw data, 2008.

Chatterjee, S. "For Child Soldiers, Every Day Is a Living Nightmare." *Forbes*, December 9, 2012, https://www.forbes.com/sites/realspin/2012/12/09/for-child-soldiers-every-day-is-a-living-nightmare/#1c2651d127bd.

Coronel-Ferrer, Miriam. Former chair of GPH Peace Panel. Email correspondence with author, March 20, 2016.

"5 Women Killed in Philippines Political Massacre May Have Been Raped, Tests Suggest." *New York Daily News*, December 3, 2009, http://www.nydailynews.com/news/world/5-women-killed-philippines-political-massacre-raped-tests-suggest-article-1.431967.

Dehesa, Cynthia, and Sarah Masters. "Joined-up Thinking: International Measures for Women's Security" *International Action Network on Small Arms (IANSA)*, 2010. http://www.iansa-women.org/sites/default/files/newsviews/en_iansa_1325_anniversary_paper_2010_final.pdf

Flores, H., and J. Diaz. "9 Women Raped Daily in RP in 2009." *PhilStar Global*, February 23, 2010, http://www.philstar.com/metro/551776/9-women-raped-daily-rp-2009.

GOVPH Official Gazette. "Republic Act No. 10591." May 29, 2013, http://www.officialgazette.gov.ph/2013/05/29/republic-act-no-10591/.

GunPolicy.org. "Philippines—Gun facts, Figures, and the Law." International Firearm Injury Prevention and Policy, n.d., http://www.gunpolicy.org/firearms/region/philippines.

Gutierrez, N. "Want to Own a Gun? Here's How Easy It Is." *Rappler*, January 10, 2013, http://www.rappler.com/nation/19462-want-to-own-a-gun-here-s-how-easy-it-is.

Hernandez, Belle. Balay Mindanaw Officer. Email correspondence with author, March 20, 2016.

Hontiveros, R. "Philippines: The Police's Murderous War on the Poor." Pagadian Diocese, February 1, 2017, http://www.pagadiandiocese.org/2017/02/01/philippines-the-polices-murderous-war-on-the-poor-amnesty-international-report/.

IANSA. *Joined-up Thinking: International Measures for Women, Security, and SALW.* London: IANSA Women's Network, September 29, 2010.

IISS. "Armed Conflict Survey 2015 Press Statement." May 2015, https://www.iiss.org/en/about%20us/press%20room/press%20releases/press%20releases/archive/2015-4fe9/may-6219/armed-conflict-survey-2015-press-statement-aobe.

IPU. "Sexual Violence against Women and Children in Armed Conflict." Parliamentary Hearing at the United Nations, November 20–21, 2008, http://www.ipu.org/splz-e/ungao8/s2.pdf.

IRIN. "Philippines: Vendettas and Violence Mindanao Analysis." ReliefWeb, June 24, 2009, http://www.irinnews.org/report/84979/philippines-vendettas-and-violence-mindanao-analysis.

Jamal, T. "Philippines-CPP/NPA (1969–2017)." Updated April 2017, http://ploughshares.ca/pl_armedconflict/philippines-cppnpa-1969-first-combat-deaths/.

Jover, Jo Genna. KCJP executive director. Email correspondence with author, March 20, 2016.

Krahe, B. "Aggression and Violence in Society." In *Applied Social Psychology*, edited by G. Semin and K. Fiedler, 343–373. London, SAGE, 1996.

Lauzon-Gatmaytan, Carmen. WE Act 1325 member. Email correspondence with author, March 20, 2016.

Lingao, E. "Ampatuans Used Public Office to Amass Illegal Arsenal." GMA News Online," February 4, 2010, http://www.gmanetwork.com/news/news/nation/183123/ampatuans-used-public-office-to-amass-illegal-arsenal/story/.

Lyddon, L. *Women, Gender, and Guns.* London, IANSA Women's Network, 2011.

Manila Times. "A Nation of Loose Guns." March 9, 2014, http://www.manilatimes.net/a-nation-of-loose-guns/81127/.

Mendoza, G. "85 Armed Groups Maintained by Politicians—PNP." *Rappler*, November 24, 2012, http://www.rappler.com/nation/politics/elections-2013/features/16706-85-armed-groups-politicians-pnp.

Nario-Galace, J. "Women Teaching Peace." Unpublished manuscript, 2017.

Nario-Galace, J. *Women's Agency against Guns.* ISIS International, July 27, 2014, http://www.isiswomen.org/index.php?option=com_content&view=article&id=1707:wo men-s-agency-against-guns&catid=22&Itemid=229.

Navarro-Castro, Loreta. CPE program director. Email Correspondence with author, March 20, 2016.

Navarro-Castro, L., and J. Nario-Galace. *Peace Education: A Pathway to a Culture of Peace*, 2nd ed. Quezon City, Philippines: Center for Peace Education, 2010.

Natividad, Ana. Former WE Act 1325 program officer. Email correspondence with author, March 22, 2016.

Office of the Presidential Advisor on the Peace Process (OPAPP). Bangsamoro Basic Law. 2014. https://www.hdcentre.org/wp-content/uploads/2016/07/Primer-on-the-proposed-Bangsamoro-Basic-Law-December-2014.pdf

PhilANSA. *Voices from the Ground: Peoples' Consultations on the Arms Trade Treaty.* Quezon City, Philippines: GZOPI, 2009.

Pintor, Marylin. Mothers for Peace executive director. Email correspondence with author, March 20 2016.

Piscano, Frances. Former WE Act 1325 project officer. Email correspondence with author, March 21, 2016.

Project Ploughshares. "Armed Conflict Report." Ploughshares, 2016, http://ploughshares.ca/wp-content/uploads/2016/10/PloughsharesAnnualReportReport2016.pdf.

Rappler. "Infographic: From Marcos to Aquino the Cost of War in Mindanao." *Rappler*, October 8, 2015, http://www.rappler.com/move-ph/issues/mindanao/107585-marcos-aquino-cost-war-mindanao.

Salapuddin, Fatmawatti. Lupah Sug Bangsamoro executive director. Personal Intervention: CSO Consultations on the National Action Plan Organized by OPAPP, 2012.

Small Arms Survey. *Guns and the City*. Geneva: Cambridge University Press, 2007.

Small Arms Survey. "Converging Agendas: Women, Peace, Security, and Small Arms." 2014, http://www.smallarmssurvey.org/fileadmin/docs/A-Yearbook/2014/en/Small-Arms-Survey-2014-Chapter-2-summary-EN.pdf.

Small Arms Survey. "Weapons and Markets." n.d., http://www.smallarmssurvey.org/weapons-and-markets.html.

Stufflebeam, D. L. "C.I.P.P. Evaluation Model." July 23, 2012, https://www.slideshare.net/0a1994/orly-cipp-model.

Tanada, Karen. GZOPI executive director. Email correspondence with author, March 20, 2016.

Tica, Mirma. PhilANCA member. Email correspondence with author, March 20, 2016.

UNGA. "Women, Disarmament, Non-Proliferation, and Arms Control." A/Res/65/69, January 13, 2011, http://www.un.org/en/ga/search/view_doc.asp?symbol=A/RES/65/69.

UNGA. Women, Disarmament, Non-Proliferation, and Arms Control. A/Res/67/48, 2012, http://www.un.org/en/ga/search/view_doc.asp?symbol=A/RES/67/48.

UNGA. "Women, Disarmament, Non-Proliferation, and Arms Control. A/Res/69/61, December 2014, http://www.un.org/en/ga/search/view_doc.asp?symbol=A/RES/69/61.

United Nations. "Outreach Programme on the Rwanda Genocide and the United Nations: Background Information on Sexual Violence Used as a Tool of War." UN.org, n.d., http://www.un.org/en/preventgenocide/rwanda/about/bgsexualviolence.shtml.

United Nations. "Universal Action Needed to Halt Illegal Proliferation of Small Arms and Light Weapons, says Secretary-General as He Opens Meetings of State Parties." Meetings Coverage and Press Releases, 2008, http://www.un.org/press/en/2008/dc3119.doc.htm.

UNHCR. "*With 1 Human in Every 113 Affected, Forced Displacement Hits Record High.*" June 20, 2016, http://www.unhcr.org/afr/news/press/2016/6/5763ace54/1-human-113-affected-forced-displacement-hits-record-high.html.

Viar, Iverly. Former WE Act 1325 project officer. Email correspondence with author, March 22, 2016.

WE Act 1325. *The Philippine National Action Plan*. Quezon City, Philippines: Women Engaged in Action on 1325, 2010.

WE Act 1325. *Women Speak: Perspectives on Normalization*. Quezon City, Philippines: Women Engaged in Action on 1325, 2014.

WE Act 1325. "Policy Paper on Women's Security Issues in the Bangsamoro." April 2016.

World Health Organization. *World Health Statitistics 2010*. Geneva: World Health Organization, 2010, http://www.who.int/gho/publications/world_health_statistics/EN_WHS10_Full.pdf

CHAPTER 43

TESTING THE WPS AGENDA
The Case of Afghanistan

CLAIRE DUNCANSON AND VANESSA FARR

THE US-led intervention in Afghanistan, framed initially as a "war on terror" and justified as self-defense, evolved to encompass both counterterrorist concerns and more complex questions of long-term stabilization, state-building, and peace-building (Ayub and Kuovo 2008; Suhrke 2012).[1] Launched only weeks after the adoption of United Nations Security Council Resolution 1325 on Women, Peace, and Security, the intervention presented "an important litmus test of UN and member states' resolve to integrate women into peace-building efforts" (Neuwirth 2002: 253). Yet, there was no mention of Resolution 1325 in any of the resolutions passed by the United Nations Security Council (UNSC) on Afghanistan in 2001, even in UNSCR 1401 in 2002, which created the United Nations Assistance Mission to Afghanistan (UNAMA) to support donor coordination and peace-building, and gender-just peace remains elusive in Afghanistan.[2] This chapter explores the reasons why the WPS agenda had such little traction in its first testing ground. First, we examine efforts to implement the WPS agenda in each of its four pillars; then we suggest three key interconnected reasons for the limited progress. We conclude with suggestions for enhancing women's security and participation in Afghanistan and the WPS agenda more broadly.

ASSESSMENT OF PROGRESS UNDER THE FOUR WPS PILLARS

At the time of the military intervention into Afghanistan, Resolution 1325 merely existed: no mechanisms had been set in place for its implementation. Its adoption created obligations applicable to all United Nations member states, including the governments of the United States, the UK, and Afghanistan; but these key players were still several years away from developing National Action Plans (NAPs) on how to meet these obligations on the ground.[3] Given the patriarchal extremism of the Taliban regime, local and international women's organizations pushed to protect Afghan women from the gendered harms of conflict and encourage their participation in efforts to build peace. Implementing Resolution 1325, however, was a challenge in the face of ongoing militarism and the persistence of Taliban-era decrees restricting women's freedoms (Tadjbakhsh 2009). In this section, we briefly assess this history.

Protection

Violence and injury, forced displacement, and war's long-term consequences are experienced differently by women and men (Rehn and Johnson Sirleaf 2002). Endless war in Afghanistan challenges women's access to the economic, health, education, and legal services necessary to survive and recover from war's gendered harms, including sexualized violence, rape, domestic violence, trafficking, abduction, and forced marriage (Ertük 2005). Eighty-seven percent of women in Afghanistan experience physical, sexual, or psychological violence during their lifetime, with 62 percent experiencing multiple forms (UN Women 2017). In her 2005 mission, United Nations Special Rapporteur (UNSR) on Violence against Women, Yakin Ertük (2005), concluded that levels of interpersonal violence were "dramatic and severe," and evidence suggests the situation has worsened as the political and security situation continues to decline. The Afghan Human Rights Commission (AIHRC), which releases yearly reports on violence against women, reported 2017 as another deadly year for women, with an 8 percent increase in violent crimes from the previous year's record, including not only lashing, stoning, and rape, but a perturbing rise in kangaroo courts, with corresponding impunity for crimes committed against women (AIHRC 2018). Perpetrators are most often family members (AIHRC 2018), but, from a feminist perspective, separating "private" from "public" violence that may be clearly ascribed to "war" is neither possible nor useful, as the rise in interpersonal violence in contexts of conflict is enabled by situations of lawlessness and militarization (True 2012: 124–33), and it is often the weaponry provided to men to pursue the aims of armed groups that is used to perpetrate domestic violence (Rehn and Johnson Sirleaf 2002; Farr et al. 2009).

On March 5, 2003, Afghanistan acceded to the Convention on the Elimination of Discrimination against Women (CEDAW) without reservation. Other protective legal frameworks have been adopted since then, including those that seek to address the problem of gendered violence. In the 2004 constitution, Article 22 declares women and men to be equal before the law. The National Action Plan for the Women of Afghanistan (NAPWA), developed under the leadership of the Ministry of Women's Affairs (MoWA) and ratified by President Karzai in 2007, is included as a benchmark in the Afghan National Development Strategy (ANDS), finalized in 2008. These advances arguably happened because of women's on-the-ground activism, with UNAMA's support; they are difficult to ascribe to the WPS agenda. Indeed, it was not until 2007 that UNAMA made preambular references to Resolution 1325, with more concrete references to discrimination appearing from 2008 (Tadjbakhsh 2009). Moreover, efforts to put the right to equality enshrined in these frameworks into practice are limited (Ayub, Kouvo, and Sooka 2009). No comprehensive review identified whether laws prior to it conform to the equal rights clause in the 2004 Constitution. As such, these preexisting laws, which fail to adequately protect women and girls from gender-based crimes, often prevail (Ayub, Kouvo, and Sooka 2009).[4] The hard-fought Elimination of Violence against Women (EVAW) law, passed by presidential decree in 2009, was accompanied by dedicated prosecution units, training programs for police, prosecutors, judges, and lawyers, and legal aid for women (Wimpelmann 2015). Yet, the consensus is that while it criminalizes violence, few mechanisms to identify and prosecute perpetrators exist (UNAMA 2013; AREU 2013; Afghan Women's Network 2016; Larson 2016). Meanwhile, women's shelters are under attack and the law is undermined by widespread use of mediation rather than adjudication.

Resolution 1325 calls for prosecutions and accountability for violence during wartime, yet there has been no "transitional justice" in Afghanistan. Indeed, the "National Stability and Reconciliation" amnesty law passed by parliament in 2007 disburdened the state from legal persecution of war criminals (Ayub et al. 2009). Key international powerbrokers, including the UN, have turned a blind eye to this law for the sake of stability, notwithstanding evidence of widespread war crimes including sexualized violence against women (Grau 2016: 412).

If efforts to develop a justice system that works for women have been slow, those to protect women and their rights in a more direct way, through the deployment of security personnel, have been differently flawed. In 2003, the UNSC voted to expand the NATO-led International Security Assistance Force (ISAF) beyond Kabul with a mandate to protect civilians; but observers argue that NATO intensified the conflict through air strikes, ground battles, night searches, and the like, while escalating the militarization of the country through distributing arms and money to militias to battle against Al Qaeda and the Taliban (Kandiyoti 2007b; Suhrke 2012). Ultimately, it is civilians who pay for these calculations about potential military gains, especially when there is an overall lack of expertise on how to take practical steps to dismantle decades-old systems of oppression. For example, while Provincial Reconstruction Teams (operating between 2006 and 2014), were told to promote gender equality, very few of those deployed understood what that meant or knew how to implement anything useful and practical (Jones 2009; Azarbaijani-Moghaddam 2014).

While global attention may have been diverted from the ongoing conflict in Afghanistan, insecurity has continued to worsen since 2011, with ever increasing numbers of civilian casualties and massive internal displacement as the Taliban has regained ground and the economy collapsed (Amnesty International 2016). Unsurprisingly, the Asia Foundation's 2017 survey found the national mood to be at a record low amid rising insecurity, civilian deaths, and economic challenges (Asia Foundation 2017). Later that year, the UN re-designated Afghanistan as a country in active conflict, a move brutally confirmed in the first half of 2018, which saw civilian casualties at the highest levels ever recorded (OCHA 2018; UNAMA 2018). More than 1 million remain internally displaced, and OCHA reported a further 360,000 displaced between January and December 2017 (OCHA 2018). Education, healthcare, and other basic rights have been severely compromised by this ongoing insecurity, reducing life expectancy over the last decade (Samar 2011), with a 21 percent increase in civilian trauma cases between 2016 and 2017 alone (UNAMA 2018). Afghanistan remains among the lowest ranking countries in the UNDP's Human Development Index and Gender Development Index (169th in both in 2016).

Participation

In its second pillar, Resolution 1325 emphasizes women's participation in all aspects of peace-building. In the various international summits and conferences devoted to discussing Afghanistan's future, however, women were often forgotten, or invited as an afterthought or deliberately excluded so as not to anger the Taliban (Cameron and Kamminga 2014). At the first Bonn Conference in 2002, only two out of twenty-three Afghans were women (Grenfell 2004; Heath and Zahedi 2011). Unsurprisingly, women's security needs were not reflected in the resulting power-sharing agreement between the Northern Alliance and the international community (Kandiyoti 2007b: 182). By the second Bonn conference in 2011, which aimed to plan Afghanistan's future following international withdrawal in 2014, Resolution 1325 was a full decade old, had been followed by more resolutions aimed at strengthening its goals, attracted donor support, and was factored into UN agency emergency and governance responses. Even so, it was only after a united outcry that Afghan women were included as participants (Haynes et al. 2012). More recent summits, such as Brussels in October 2016, the Quadrilateral Coordination Group's 2016 meetings to develop a "roadmap to peace," and 2017's "Kabul Process" have hardly challenged this pattern of exclusion.[5]

Turning to women's participation *within* Afghanistan, the situation was looking more promising until the decline in security of the last two years. Although with significant variations from region to region, women were moving around more freely, and and steady gains continued to be made in enrolling girls in formal education—which began to decline again as security worsened from 2016.[6] International pressure led to the inclusion of women in the Emergency Loya Jirga of 2002, which in turn recommended quotas for women in parliament (Grenfell 2004; Larson 2011). There are now more women holding positions of power than at any other time in history. Twenty-seven percent of the seats in parliament are held by women, four ministries and the AIHRC are led by women, and three women have been appointed as ambassadors (UN Women 2017). It is still difficult, however, to detect anything of a national women's movement. Female parliamentarians tend to retain allegiance to political parties or influential individuals, and tend not to promote women's gender interests; there are ongoing tensions between individual women parliamentarians, sometimes exacerbated by the donor community; and—crucially—there is a women face real physical danger as a result of upsetting conservative sensibilities in parliament and other public offices, in a context of chronic and highly gendered insecurity (Kandiyoti 2007b; Larson 2011, 2016).

There are quotas for women's inclusion in the High Peace Council (HPC), charged with overseeing the Afghan Peace and Reintegration Programme (APRP), which aims to persuade armed opposition members to disarm and reintegrate into society (UNDP 2011).[7] Perhaps unsurprisingly, some women on the HPC speak for their ethnicity or have ties to the Mujahadeen (Henry 2011) while others, who might want to present oppositional views, are ignored and sidelined (Lackenbauer and Harriman 2013; Larson 2015).[8] President Ghani appointed a new female deputy chair and two female advisors to the APRP in February 2016, but as the war also intensified that year, the impacts of their presence cannot easily be assessed.[9] Although it remains a challenge to impact upon the APRP (Quie 2012; Larson 2015), Afghan women, with the support of local and International NGOs, continue to build peace at the community-level and attempt to influence members of the HPC and parliament (Chilvers et al. 2016).

Considerable international effort to increase women's participation in the security sector—so that Afghan women are better able to report crimes and access desperately needed justice—has resulted in tiny advances; but communities continue to oppose women working in the security services, seeing policing as a disreputable job for an Afghan woman; commanders can be reluctant to recruit women; and relatively few women are qualified or drawn to working in a dangerous sector in which working conditions are difficult, with discrimination, assault, and sexual violence commonly aimed at women recruits (Hancock 2013).[10] The ANSF have developed a recruitment strategy and are conducting training inside and outside the country (Afghan Women's Network 2016), but recruitment of women is likely to remain challenging, especially given community opposition.

Not all suspicion emanates from conservative voices: many feminists question whether an increase of women in the security forces should be seen as a measure of success for the WPS agenda (see, for example, Hudson 2012). Cockburn, for one, has consistently asked whether feminists should in fact be "contesting the way the feminist agenda has been recuperated by armies justifying the recruitment of more women to the military in reference to Resolution 1325" (Cockburn 2011). Although Afghanistan represents a compromised space for advancing a liberal feminist agenda of inclusion in the security sector, it is perhaps easier to agree on the advantages of more women in the justice system. There is potential for optimism here, as in in 2014, 10 percent of judges and 22 percent of lawyers were female (Karlidag 2014: 16).

An overarching constraint, however, remains the deep insecurity that faces Afghans at every turn. Women in public life, whatever their role, are at risk of violence, even murder (Human Rights Watch 2009; Amnesty International 2015). Since NATO's withdrawal in 2014, human rights organizations have documented a steady conservative backlash against women's rights and an increase in public threats, intimidation, and attacks. In some parts of the country, it remains considerably more difficult for girls to access and remain in school than boys. Again, with great variations across Afghanistan, the social practice of early marriage is a contributing element to the problem, in that both fertility and maternal mortality rates remain extremely high (UNICEF 2017). Gains made in increasing female literacy may offer some hope of a future improvement in this cycle of female suffering, and may in time contribute to more women wanting to enter public life—whether at village level or nationally—than at present.

Prevention

Afghanistan's NAP on Resolution 1325, the existence of which itself demonstrates some progress in recent years in terms of the participation of women in building peace, interprets prevention work narrowly as the deterrence of violence against women. As such, the resolution's affirmation of "the important role of women in the prevention and resolution of conflicts and in peace-building" (UNSC 2000) is overlooked. This problem is exacerbated because there are few efforts to recognize and tackle the root causes of conflict. In Afghanistan, as we discuss in what follows, this would involve recognizing the legacies both of Cold War interventions, which include a surplus of armaments and a warlord-shaped narco-state, and contemporary economic policies that exacerbate rather than alleviate poverty, inequality, and precarity. The government of Afghanistan may claim to be tackling social grievances to create inclusive and egalitarian communities and prevent violent extremism, yet its approach to poverty reduction and development—the Afghan National Development Strategy (ANDS)—risks exacerbating these problems.[11]

Relief and Recovery

Although it is heartening that the Afghan government recognizes the need for a gender-inclusive program of sustainable development, the ANDS is based on classic neoliberal assumptions. At the behest of the International Financial Institutions (IFIs), Afghanistan aims to "ensure sustainable development through a private-sector-led market economy" (Islamic Republic of Afghanistan 2008) and focuses on the extraction and exploitation of natural resources, agricultural modernization, and infrastructural improvement, with an emphasis on attracting foreign investment. Observers note that development strategy is "premised on the principle that institutions must be put in place to ensure 'good governance' in a manner that delivers just enough 'state' to allow basic security for the functioning of markets and private-sector-led growth" (Kandiyoti 2007a: 504). This approach has gendered consequences. To take natural resource exploitation as an example, few women anywhere benefit from the extractive industries; they are unlikely to do so in Afghanistan (Lakhani et al. 2014; Global Witness 2016). Furthermore, a minimalist state in a context of a critical shortage of services exacerbates demands made on women as primary carers (Kandiyoti 2007b: 192), but it is exceedingly difficult for women to make this point in the absence of a national, inclusive, and effective women's movement.[12]

ANDS does have gender as a cross-cutting theme, but while the MoWA is mandated to take the lead role on monitoring and coordinating the outcome of government interventions for gender equality, it is limited by its under-resourced and marginalized position and is powerless to conduct regular and meaningful gender-impact assessments of IFI and government plans. This is a critical failure: feminists have argued for decades that women's organizations and ministries should be able to subject government development plans to scrutiny through gender-impact assessments (Ni Aoláin et al. 2011) or gender budgeting initiatives (Budlender 2010). NGOs do important work supporting women through small-scale economic empowerment projects,[13] but there is little space for civil society or international NGOs to challenge the overall economic strategy or object to its skewed impact on women's well-being (AREU 2013; see chapter 33 in this volume).

CHALLENGES TO PROGRESS

In this section, we elaborate on what we see as three interconnected and overlapping reasons for the limited progress of the WPS agenda in Afghanistan. The first is the fact that the initial military intervention was not primarily aimed at peace-building, but about US security in the wake of the 9/11 attacks—followed up by a large measure of greed from an international community that benefits from Afghanistan's war economy. The second is the scale of the challenge of implementing WPS in Afghanistan given the context of a legacy of decades of intervention, counter-intervention, and escalating conflict. The third is the way that implementation of the WPS agenda has focused more on civil and political rights, than on the inclusive social and economic transformation that women sorely need.

Self-Interested Intervention

Unlike other contemporary military adventures which ignore women altogether, the "need" to save suffering women was a major trope in the buildup to intervention and a loudly-expressed "interest" in their human rights was used as an emotive justification. Both George Bush and Tony Blair cynically represented Afghan women as somehow being eager to be drawn further into armed violence, making clichéd and hyperbolic claims about how their joint military attack on the Taliban would have the ultimate effect of freeing women. This message was pummeled home in a special radio broadcast as the buildup to the invasion began in earnest, when Laura Bush was put on the air to declare that the "fight against terrorism [in Afghanistan] is also a fight for the rights and dignity of women" (Bush 2001).[14] In reality, then as now, compromises with the Taliban and other conservative armed groups would always receive priority (Ayub and Kouvo 2008; Jones 2009; Kandiyoti 2009: 8; Heath and Zahedi 2011; Haynes et al. 2012; AREU 2013).

Meanwhile, observers have seen an increasing state of plunder in Afghanistan since the 2001 invasion. Afghanistan has been the world's greatest recipient of aid—$20 billion in the first decade post-intervention—but very little reaches the local economy or enables sustainable development. The allocation of vast reconstruction funds, totaling billions of dollars, to private (international and national) security and construction companies, which are wasteful, ineffective, or fraudulent, has entrenched a system of corruption (Curtis 2011; Gall 2012: 256–257; Rohde 2012).[15]

The WPS agenda took around a decade to take hold in Afghanistan because the intervening powers were, beyond rhetoric, unconcerned with its goals, acting primarily to secure their national security and wealth. Donors were not held to account for their promises to Afghan women (AREU 2013). Afghanistan offers woeful evidence of all the ways in which the WPS agenda remains vulnerable "to co-optation by militarist states and military institutions for military purposes" (Cockburn 2011). For many women, an overall decline in their standard of living has been the only lasting outcome of "Operation Enduring Freedom."

Legacies of Endless War

Secondly, the country now runs on an entrenched war economy whose structural drivers remain unaddressed, and is largely based in opium production and illegal drug trafficking, among other black market activities, from which a few warlords are the sole beneficiaries (Kandiyoti 2007b; Loewenstein 2012; Felbab-Brown 2017). Such war economies are profoundly gendered with most of the beneficiaries being male. In contrast, women, who are trying to survive, suffer increasing levels of hardship the further they are from commercial centers (Peterson 2008; see chapter 19 in this volume). Bluntly put, Afghanistan shows how challenging it is to make the ideals of the WPS agenda operational in face of an economically, physically, and socially devastated landscape.

The gendered effects of Afghanistan's narco-economy are of particular concern. Afghanistan now produces 90 percent of the world's heroin, twice as much as in 2000. The cultivation of opium benefits the few, and is now especially profitable for the Taliban and criminal gangs; but it causes massive health problems for ordinary people, and the misuse of land and water displaces other cultivation: poppy can be cheaper than food, but it cannot be eradicated because no other viable economy exists (Felbab-Brown 2017). These factors are both causes of, and exacerbate, violence against women and their children. In a country with virtually no treatment facilities, the number of female addicts continues to rise. Children, fed the drug to stave off hunger and fear, are now the largest group of addicts (Whitton 2016). Improving treatment facilities should become a key policy focus for both the government of Afghanistan and the international community (Felbab-Brown 2017).

Among the other gendered effects of the breakdown of Afghan society is a rise in forced and early marriages: men unable to meet their obligations in the drug trade resort to *Baad*, the practice of exchanging girls or women in marriage to pay a debt or settle a dispute. Women in such marriages are often underfed, overworked, depressed, and give birth too young, continuing the agonizing cycle (Samar 2011). Nonetheless, the international community attributes their plight to culture or religion, ignoring "the possibility that what to Western eyes looks like 'tradition' is, in many instances, the manifestation of new and more brutal forms of subjugation of the weak made possible by a commodified criminal economy, total lack of security and the erosion of bonds of trust and solidarity that were tested to the limit by war, social upheaval and poverty" (Kandiyoti 2009: 2; see also Abu-Lughod 2002; Hirschkind and Mahmood 2002).

Meanwhile, through the ANDS, Afghanistan promotes the policies that further entrench the inequalities produced by the war and narco-economies. Thus, it is hardly surprising that gains made in formal rights—which we argue to have been largely the focus of the WPS agenda to date—are "condemned to remain dead letters" in Afghanistan (Kandiyoti 2007b: 185).

WPS's Focus on Civil and Political Rights

The third reason that the WPS agenda has made such little progress in Afghanistan is related to its focus on civil and political rights, such as quotas for the participation of women in parliament, peace talks, and security sector and the development of legal frameworks to uphold women's rights, especially their right to be free from gender-based violence. Afghan women often see themselves as enmeshed in family relationships to the extent that individual rights can be less salient (Fluri 2011; Heath and Zahedi 2011). The focus on marriage and children, from which women draw material, as well as social and emotional, resources and security (Abirafeh 2009; Grace and Pain 2011), can act to constrain the pursuit of individual advantage and desires upon which the international community's model of peacebuilding, including the WPS agenda, are largely premised. Moreover, the WPS agenda, by appearing to be concerned with women at the expense of men, has not come across as relevant to all Afghan communities (Zahedi 2011).

Formal rights for women are arguably only ever translated into progress on the ground when there is a strong, coordinated, and active women's movement to hold institutions to account, to steer implementation, and to continue to advocate for women. Although many scholars testify to the resilience of Afghan women (see in particular the contributors to Heath and Zahedi 2011), few claim that there was in 2001 an Afghan women's movement strong enough to support effective implementation of the WPS agenda (see for example Billaud 2015). This is, in part, another legacy of the combination of decades of war and patriarchal attitudes which deprived many women of education and the ability to move freely outside the home (Kandiyoti 2009). Yet it may also be related to the WPS agenda's focus on individual civil and political rights, which can sometimes seem less relevant than the economic and social issues undermining women's security (Ahmed-Ghosh 2006; Kandiyoti 2007b; Kouvo 2008; Burki 2011). Our key point here is that the WPS agenda, with its emphasis on civil and political rights, has struggled to make inroads into challenging the entrenched war and narco-economies and their ongoing legacies that are the root cause of women's insecurity.

Conclusion

In this chapter, we have argued that the impact of the WPS agenda in Afghanistan has been limited, due to three main (overlapping) reasons: the self-interested nature of the intervening powers, the legacies of decades of conflict in Afghanistan, and the agenda's emphasis on civil and political rights. A key question, still, is whether the small achievements under the WPS agenda are steps upon which more progress for women can be built; or whether they are too marginal to be meaningful, or worse, counterproductive? While there is much to be optimistic about in terms of the WPS agenda in general—as evidenced throughout this handbook—growing inequality and insecurity in Afghanistan suggests to us that *in this particular context*, efforts to implement Resolution 1325 have come very close to doing more harm than good (also see Azarbaijani-Moghaddam 2007). The attempts to produce new laws to protect women from gender-based violence, and to facilitate their participation in public life, have led to a persistent and extremely violent backlash against women (Wimpelmann 2014). Violent men remain prominent in public life; the return to Kabul of the notorious warlord Gulbuddin Hekmatyar in early May 2017 struck terror in women activists and raises difficult questions about ongoing immunity for war crimes.[16] Meanwhile, efforts to mainstream gender into the prevention and relief and recovery pillars have been inadequate, leaving entrenched war economies intact and exacerbating inequalities.

That said, there are ways in which WPS advocates can move forward, which can build on the limited gains we identified in the first section. First, the international community— WPS advocates and the UN more generally—has to rethink how it can best support Afghan women. Researchers suggest donors must be less prescriptive, think beyond technocratic and project-based interventions, and be prepared to play a long-term supportive role as *facilitators of broader mobilization* (AREU 2013; Wimpelmann 2014; Larson 2016). Thinking about how to support women's rights in the context of their family relationships, and how to work to transform masculinities, will also be important ways forward (Zahedi 2011; AREU 2013). Second, the WPS agenda has to pay more attention to economic rights and empowerment.[17] WPS advocates need to argue for alternative economic models for post-conflict states. As well as community-level economic empowerment, NGOs need to put pressure on

IFIs and the donor community to direct the Afghan economy toward job creation, distribution of wealth, and sustainable inclusive prosperity. Above all, the most urgent task for WPS advocates remains oppositional—especially to commitments made by the government of Afghanistan, with international diplomatic support, to pursue "national security" with hard-line warlords whose words and deeds remain as misogynist and brutal as ever.

NOTES

1. We would like to acknowledge those who provided support and advice, pointed us in the direction of research and informants, and, in some cases, were kind enough to read and comment on earlier drafts. Attempting to do justice to the complexity of the situation of WPS in Afghanistan was a challenge, but we think we have come closer due to the solidarity and generosity of feminist colleagues who shared their insights: Sippi Azarbaijani-Moghaddam, Wazhma Frogh, Deniz Kandiyoti, Sari Kouvo, Anna Larson, Henry Myrttinen, and Torunn Wimpelmann. Thanks also to the editors of this handbook who provided very useful comments on an earlier draft and were generous with support throughout.

2. These are SCR1363, July 30, 2001; SCR1378, November 14, 2001; SCR1383, December 6, 2001; SCR1386, December 20, 2001. Women receive a single mention in the last of them.

3. The UK adopted its first NAP in 2006; the United States in 2011; Afghanistan in 2015. PeaceWomen, http://www.peacewomen.org/member-states.

4. Indeed, Article 3 of the 2004 Constitution states: "No law can be contrary to the beliefs and provisions of the sacred religion of Islam," providing the opportunity to invalidate Article 22 (Grenfell 2004; Kandiyoti 2007a).

5. See Human Rights Watch commentary by Heather Barr in "Afghanistan's Mysterious Vanishing Plan on Women and Peace Talks" (October 27, 2016), https://www.hrw.org/news/2016/10/27/afghanistans-mysterious-vanishing-plan-women-and-peace-talks; and "Afghanistan Donors Splash Cash, Bury Rights" (October 6, 2016), https://www.hrw.org/news/2016/10/06/afghanistan-donors-splash-cash-bury-rights; and "Women Excluded Again from Peace Talks" (June 6, 2017), https://www.hrw.org/news/2017/06/06/women-excluded-again-afghanistans-peace-talks.

6. By-and-large, women and girls had begun to enjoy greater freedom in Kabul and more freedom in the largest provincial cities than in rural areas in recent years. For example, women were able to move around fairly freely and often did not wear the Burka in Kabul, which was a significant change from 2002; and more girls were beginning to attend school, who were more likely to complete more years of schooling, in cities than the rural areas. These gains have sharply reversed in the catastrophic urban violence of 2017-18, reflecting family anxieties that it is, once more, not safe for women to leave home. Ethnographic observation by Vanessa Farr in Kabul, Jalalabad, Herat, Kandahar, and Bamian from 2015–2018.

7. The HPC is an eighty-member body providing political support to the peace process and overseeing the implementation of the Afghan Peace and Reintegration Program signed in May 2010. Nine (13 percent) of seventy members are women, while thirty-one Provincial Peace Councils (PPCs) have three to five women in each (17 percent).

8. This appears to be the fate of the similar project of Community Development Committees (CDCs) part of the National Solidarity Programme (NSP) (Kandiyoti 2007b: 189).

Perceived and real resistance from the Taliban is often cited as the reason for this exclusion, but that may be a convenient excuse to continue to do "men's business" as usual.

9. The year 2016 was the most violent on record and the prospects for peace declined even further in 2017 and 2018. Daesh/ISIS, under the name ISIS-Khorasan Province (ISIS-KP), is a rising armed opposition group with an apparent focus on disrupting any progress towards democracy.

10. By 2013, 1 percent of the Afghanistan National Police (ANP) and 0.4 percent of the Afghanistan National Army (ANA) were female (Karlidag 2014). The ANA Officer Academy, founded in October 2013, has recruited women since 2014 and graduated several dozen. The nine hundred women currently serving in the ANA falls short of a goal of five thousand set by donors, a problem ascribed to the overall difficulty of women serving in the public sector. In one effort to address the recruitment lag, in 2018, construction work began on a "Women's Police Town" in Kabul, whose aim is to enable women to support both the "Resolute Support mission and the Afghan National Defense and Security Forces Roadmap through increased recruitment and retention of talented leadership within the Afghan National Police." See "Women in Afghan Army Overcome Opposition, Threats," Reuters (November 3, 2016), http://www.reuters.com/article/us-afghanistan-women-army-idUSKBN12Z05W and "Ceremony Marks Start Of Work On Women's Police Town," Tolo News (9 April 2018). https://www.tolonews.com/afghanistan/ceremony-marks-start-work-women%E2%80%99s-police-town.

11. See Ambassador to the UN, H. E. Mahmoud Saikal's statement at the "Security Council Debate on Conflict Prevention and Peace" (January 10, 2017), http://afghanistan-un.org/2017/01/security-council-debate-on-conflict-prevention-and-sustaining-peace/.

12. A prime example of the on-the-ground impacts of neoliberal national policy can be seen in the basic health services pillar of the Ministry of Public Health, which at the very humblest level relies on a cadre of unpaid Community Health Workers (CHWs) of whom around half are women. As such, this sector can be seen as the most important public service space for women—but it is also one of the least remunerated and relies on highly gendered ideologies premised on women's voluntary and unpaid caring work being made available to their community (see Farr 2018).

13. See, for example, the UN's internship program for Afghan women (August 18, 2016), http://asiapacific.unwomen.org/en/news-and-events/stories/2016/08/unlocking-the-potential-of-afghan-women.

14. Laura Bush was then First Lady of the United States, and, as a woman with absolutely no feminist credentials, her intervention can only be read as a cynical effort to manipulate public opinion in favor of an illegitimate military project.

15. Examples abound: a $125 million contract to build a new road was initially granted to an American company, which then subcontracted to a firm from a regional country for $80 million, making a profit of $45 million (see Gall 2012: 141).

16. See Patricia Gossman, May 5, 2017, "Afghanistan Warlord's Grandiose, and Damaging, Return: Hekmatyar Criticizes Media, Rejects Accountability," Human Rights Watch (May 5, 2017), (https://www.hrw.org/news/2017/05/05/afghanistan-warlords-grandiose-and-damaging-return).

17. The Asia Foundation's survey found that a record number (74 percent) of Afghans feel women should be able to work outside the home. While this is due more to economic necessity than a commitment to women's rights, it provides some opportunity for optimism (Asia Foundation 2016).

REFERENCES

Abirafeh, Lina. *Gender and International Aid in Afghanistan: The Politics and Effects of Intervention*. Jefferson, NC: McFarland, 2009.

Abu-Lughod, Lila. "Do Muslim Women Really Need Saving? Anthropological Reflections on Cultural Relativism and Its Others." *American Anthropologist* 104, no. 3 (2002): 783–790.

Afghan Women's Network. "From Documents to Implementation: Afghan Women's Network First Monitoring Report on Implementation of Afghanistan National Action Plan (NAP) UNSCR 1325 on Women, Peace and Security." AWN, 2016.

Ahmed-Ghosh, Huma. "Voices of Afghan Women: Human Rights and Economic Development." *International Feminist Journal of Politics* 8, no. 1 (2006): 110–128.

AIHRC. "AIHRC Records 4,000 Cases Of Violence Against Women."Afghan Independent Human Rights Commission, 2018, https://www.tolonews.com/afghanistan/aihrc-records-4000-cases-violence-against-women.

Amnesty International. "Afghanistan: Their Lives on the Line: Women Human Rights Defenders under Attack in Afghanistan." ASA 11/1279/2015. April 7, 2015, https://www.amnesty.org/en/documents/document/?indexNumber=asa11%2f1279%2f2015&language=en.

Amnesty International. "My Children Will Die This Winter: Afghanistan's Broken Promise to the Displaced." ASA 11/4017/2016. May 31, 2016, https://www.amnesty.org/en/documents/asa11/4017/2016/en/.

AREU. "Women's Rights, Gender Equality, and Transition: Securing Gains, Moving Forward." Afghan Research and Evaluation Unit. September 2013, https://areu.org.af/archives/publication/1308.

Asia Foundation. "A Survey of the Afghan People." Asia Foundation, 2017, http://asiafoundation.org/where-we-work/afghanistan/survey/.

Ayub, Fatima, and Sari Kouvo. "Righting the Course? Humanitarian Intervention, the War on Terror, and the Future of Afghanistan." *International Affairs* 84, no. 4 (2008): 641.

Ayub, Fatima, Sari Kouvo, and Yasmin Sooka. "Addressing Gender-Specific Violations in Afghanistan." New York: International Centre for Transitional Justice, February 2009, https://www.ictj.org/sites/default/files/ICTJ-Afghanistan-Gender-Violations-2009-English.pdf.

Azarbaijani-Moghaddam, Sippi. "On Living with Negative Peace and a Half-Built State: Gender and Human Rights." *International Peacekeeping* 14, no. 1 (2007): 127–142.

Azarbaijani-Moghaddam, Sippi. "Seeking Out Their Afghan Sisters: Female Engagement Teams in Afghanistan." CMI Working Paper, 2014, https://www.cmi.no/publications/5096-seeking-out-their-afghan-sisters.

Billaud, Julie. *Kabul Carnival: Gender Politics in Postwar Afghanistan*. Philadelphia: University of Pennsylvania Press, 2015.

Budlender, D. "Price of Peace: Financing for Gender Equality in Post-Conflict Reconstruction." United Nations Development Programme, New York. October 2010, http://www.undp.org/content/undp/en/home/librarypage/womens-empowerment/price-of-peace-financing-for-gender-equality-in-post-conflict-reconstruction.html.

Burki, Shireen Khan. "The Politics of Zan from Amanullah to Karzai: Lessons for Improving Afghan Women's Status." In *Land of the Unconquerable: The Lives of Contemporary Afghan Women*, edited by Jennifer Heath and Ashraf Zahedi. Berkeley: University of California Press, 2011.

Bush, Laura. "Radio Address by Mrs. Bush." White House Press Release, November 17, 2001, http://georgewbush-whitehouse.archives.gov/news/releases/2001/11/20011117.html.

Cameron, Elizabeth, and Jorrit Kamminga. "Behind Closed Doors: The Risk of Denying Women a Voice in Determining Afghanistan's Future." Oxfam International, November 24, 2014, http://oxfamilibrary.openrepository.com/oxfam/bitstream/10546/335875/1/bp200-behind-doors-afghan-women-rights-241114-en.pdf.

Chilvers, Richard, Sodaba Khairkhowa, and Annabel Morrissey. "Women and Peace Building in Afghanistan: Building Local and National-Level Peace with the Meaningful Participation of Women." Oxfam International, September 2016, http://policy-practice.oxfam.org.uk/publications/women-and-peace-building-in-afghanistan-building-local-and-national-level-peace-619867.

Cockburn, Cynthia. "Snagged on the Contradiction." Presented at the Annual Meeting of No to War—Not to NATO. Dublin, Ireland, April 15–17, 2011, http://www.cynthiacockburn.org/BlogNATO1325.pdf.

Curtis, Mark. "The Great Game: The Reality of Britain's War in Afghanistan." War on Want, February 2011, https://waronwant.org/resources/great-game.

Ertük, Yakin. "Integration of the Human Rights of Women and the Gender Perspective: Violence against Women." Report of the Special Rapporteur on Violence against Women: Its Causes and Consequences. Addendum: Mission to Guatemala. E/CN.4/2006/61/Add.5. New York: United Nations Commission on Human Rights, March 2005.

Farr, Vanessa. "Securing Health in Afghanistan: Gender, Militarized Humanitarianism, and the Legacies of Occupation." In Global Health and Security: Critical Feminist Perspectives, edited by Colleen O'Manique and Pieter Fourie. Abingdon, UK: Routledge, 2018.

Farr, Vanessa, Henri Myrttinen, and Albrecht Schnabel. Sexed Pistols: The Gendered Impacts of Small Arms and Light Weapons. Tokyo: United Nations University Press, 2009, http://unu.edu/publications/books/sexed-pistols-the-gendered-impacts-of-small-arms-and-light-weapons.html.

Felbab-Brown, Vanda. "Afghanistan's opium production is through the roof—why Washington shouldn't overreact." November 21, 2017. https://www.brookings.edu/blog/order-from-chaos/2017/11/21/afghanistans-opium-production-is-through-the-roof-why-washington-shouldnt-overreact/.

Fluri, Jennifer. "Armored Peacocks and Proxy Bodies: Gender Geopolitics in Aid/Development Spaces of Afghanistan." Gender, Place & Culture 18, no. 4 (2011): 519–536.

Gall, Sandy. War Against the Taliban: Why It All Went Wrong in Afghanistan. London: Bloomsbury, 2012.

Global Witness. "Why Extractive Sector Abuses Matter for Women's Rights in Afghanistan." October 2016, https://www.globalwitness.org/fr/campaigns/afghanistan/why-extractive-sector-abuses-matter-womens-rights-afghanistan/.

Grace, Jo, and Adam Pain. "Rural Women's Livelihood Their Position in the Agrarian Economy." In Land of the Unconquerable, edited by Jennifer Heath and Ashraf Zahedi. Berkeley: University of California Press, 2011.

Grau, Bele. "Supporting Women's Movements in Afghanistan: Challenges of Activism in a Fragile Context." Gender & Development 24, no. 3 (2016): 409–426.

Grenfell, Laura. " The Participation of Afghan Women in the Reconstruction Process." Human Rights Brief 12, no. 1 (2004): 22–25.

Hancock, Louise. "Women and the Afghan Police: Why a Law Enforcement Agency That Respects and Protects Females Is Crucial for Progress." Oxfam International, 2013, http://

policy-practice.oxfam.org.uk/publications/women-and-the-afghan-police-why-a-law-enforcement-agency-that-respects-and-prot-300653.

Haynes, Dina Francesca, Naomi Cahn, and Fionnuala D. Ni Aolain. "Women in the Post-Conflict Process: Reviewing the Impact of Recent UN Actions in Achieving Gender Centrality." SSRN, 2012, http://papers.ssrn.com/sol3/papers.cfm?abstract_id=2250703.

Heath, Jennifer, and Ashraf Zahedi. "Introduction." In *Land of the Unconquerable: The Lives of Contemporary Afghan Women*. Berkeley: University of California Press, 2011.

Heath, Jennifer, and Ashraf Zahedi. *Land of the Unconquerable: The Lives of Contemporary Afghan Women*. Berkeley: University of California Press, 2011 http://www.ucpress.edu/book.php?isbn=9780520261860.

Henry, Sheilagh. "The Missing Piece in Afghanistan's Peace Talks." Asia Foundation, January 12, 2011, http://asiafoundation.org/2011/01/12/the-missing-piece-in-afghanistans-peace-talks/.

Hirschkind, Charles, and Saba Mahmood. "Feminism, the Taliban, and Politics of Counter-Insurgency." *Anthropological Quarterly* 75, no. 2 (2002): 339–354.

Hudson, Heidi. "A Bridge Too Far? The Gender Consequences of Linking Security and Development in SSR Discourse and Practice." In *Back to the Roots: Security Sector Reform and Development*, edited by Albrecht Schnabel and Vanessa Farr. Geneva: DCAF, 2012, http://www.isn.ethz.ch/Digital-Library/Publications/Detail/?lng=en&id=153074. https://www.files.ethz.ch/isn/153074/Back%20to%20the%20Root_Security%20Sector%20Reform%20and%20Development_YB2011.pdf

Human Rights Watch. "'We Have the Promises of the World': Women's Rights in Afghanistan." December 6, 2009, https://www.hrw.org/report/2009/12/06/we-have-promises-world/womens-rights-afghanistan#70daa9.

Islamic Republic of Afghanistan. "Afghanistan National Development Strategy (ANDS)." Ministry of Foreign Affairs, Islamic Republic of Afghanistan, 2008, http://mfa.gov.af/en/page/6547/afghanistan-national-development-strategy/afghanistan-national-development-strategy-ands.

Jones, Ann. "Remember the Women?" *The Nation*, October 21, 2009, https://www.thenation.com/article/remember-women/.

Kandiyoti, Deniz. "Between the Hammer and the Anvil: Post-Conflict Reconstruction, Islam, and Women's Rights." *Third World Quarterly* 28, no. 3 (2007a): 503–517. doi:10.1080/01436590701192603.

Kandiyoti, Deniz. "Old Dilemmas or New Challenges? The Politics of Gender and Reconstruction in Afghanistan." *Development and Change* 38 (2007b): 169–199. doi:10.1111/j.1467-7660.2007.00408.x.

Kandiyoti, Deniz. "The Anthony Hyman Memorial Lecture." SOAS, the University of London, March 16, 2009.

Karlidag, Melike. "UN Security Council Resolution 1325 in Afghanistan Civil Society Monitoring Report 2014." Afghan Women's Network, 2014.

Kouvo, Sari. "A 'Quick and Dirty' Approach to Women's Emancipation and Human Rights?" *Feminist Legal Studies* 16 (2008): 37–46. doi:10.1007/s10691-007-9077-7.

Lackenbauer, Helené, and David Harriman. "Women at the Peace Table: Rhetoric or Reality? Women's Participation and Influence in the Peace and Reintegration Process in Afghanistan." Swedish Ministry of Foreign Affairs, April 2013.

Lakhani, Sadaf, Marine Durand, and Javed Noorani. "Women and Afghanistan's Extractive Industries." United States Institute of Peace, Policy Brief #3, June 2014, https://iwaweb.org/wp-content/uploads/2014/12/women_and_afghanistans_extractive_industries1.pdf.

Larson, Anna. "Women's Political Presence A Path to Promoting Gender Interests?" In *Land of the Unconquerable: The Lives of Contemporary Afghan Women*, edited by Jennifer Heath and Ashraf Zahedi. Berkeley: University of California Press 2011.

Larson, Anna. "Afghanistan." In *Women in Conflict and Peace*, edited by Jenny Hedström and Thiyumi Senarathna. International IDEA, 2015, http://www.idea.int/sites/default/files/publications/women-in-conflict-and-peace.pdf.

Larson, Anna. "Women and Power: Mobilising around Afghanistan's Elimination of Violence against Women Law." London: Overseas Development Institute, February 2016, https://www.odi.org/publications/10299-women-power-afghanistan-violence-against-women-law.

Loewenstein, Antony. "Natural Resources Were Supposed to Make Afghanistan Rich. Here's What's Happening to Them." *The Nation,* January 11–18, 2012, https://www.thenation.com/article/resources-were-supposed-to-make-afghanistan-rich/.

Neuwirth, J. "Women and Peace and Security: The Implementation of UN Security Council Resolution 1325." *Duke Journal of Gender Law & Policy* 9 (2002.): 253.

Ni Aoláin, Fionnuala, Dina Francesca Haynes, and Naomi Cahn. *On the Frontlines: Gender, War, and the Post-Conflict Process.* New York: Oxford University Press, 2011.

OCHA. "Afghanistan." 2017. http://www.unocha.org/afghanistan.

OCHA. "2018 Humanitarian Needs Overview." https://reliefweb.int/sites/reliefweb.int/files/resources/afg_2018_humanitarian_needs_overview_1.pdf

Peterson, V. Spike. "'New Wars' and Gendered Economies." *Feminist Review* 88, no. 1 (2008): 7–20.

Quie, Marissa. "Peace-Building and Democracy Promotion in Afghanistan: The Afghanistan Peace and Reintegration Programme and Reconciliation with the Taliban." *Democratization* 19, no. 3 (2012): 553–574.

Rehn, Elizabeth, and Ellen Johnson Sirleaf. "Women, War, Peace: The Independent Experts' Assessment of the Impact of Armed Conflict on Women and Women's Role in Peacebuilding." UN Women, 2002, http://www.unwomen.org/en/digital-library/publications/2002/1/women-war-peace-the-independent-experts-assessment-on-the-impact-of-armed-conflict-on-women-and-women-s-role-in-peace-building-progress-of-the-world-s-women-2002-vol-1.

Rohde, David. "Visit Afghanistan's 'Little America,' and See the Folly of For-Profit War." *The Atlantic,* June 1, 2012, https://www.theatlantic.com/international/archive/2012/06/visit-afghanistans-little-america-and-see-the-folly-of-for-profit-war/257962/.

Samar, Sima. "The Hidden War against Women: Health Care in Afghanistan." In *Land of the Unconquerable: The Lives of Contemporary Afghan Women*, edited by Jennifer Heath and Ashraf Zahedi. Berkeley: University of California Press, 2011.

Suhrke, Astri. "Waging War and Building Peace in Afghanistan." *International Peacekeeping* 19, no. 4 (2012): 478–491. doi:10.1080/13533312.2012.709759.

Tadjbakhsh, Shahrbanou. "Afghanistan." In *Council Resolutions under Chapter VII*, edited by Maud Edgren-Schori, Débora García-Orrico, Pierre Schori, Shahrbanou Tadjbakhsh, and Gilles Yabi. Madrid: FRIDE, 2009, http://fride.org/publication/655/security-council-resolutions-under-chapter-vii.

True, Jacqui. *The Political Economy of Violence against Women.* New York: Oxford University Press, 2012.

UNAMA. "A Way to Go: An Update on Implementation of the Law on Elimination of Violence against Women in Afghanistan." United Nations Assistance Mission in Afghanistan, December 2013, https://unama.unmissions.org/sites/default/files/unama_evaw_law_report_2013_revised_on_16_dec_2013.pdf.

UNAMA 2016: "Afghanistan: Protection of Civilians in Armed Conflict Annual Report 2016. Kabul, Afghanistan, February 2017. https://unama.unmissions.org/sites/default/files/protection_of_civilians_in_armed_conflict_annual_report_8feb_2016.pdf.

UNAMA. 2017. "Afghanistan Quarterly Report on the Protection of Civilians in Armed Conflict Quarterly Report." Kabul: United Nations Assistance Mission in Afghanistan, January 1 to September 30, 2017, https://unama.unmissions.org/sites/default/files/unama_protection_of_civilians_in_armed_conflict_quarterly_report_1_january_to_30_september_2017_-_english.pdf.

UNAMA. "Latest UN Update Records Continuing Record High Levels of Civilian Casualties in 2018," April 12, 2018, https://unama.unmissions.org/latest-un-update-records-continuing-record-high-levels-civilian-casualties-2018.

UNDP. "Afghanistan Peace and Re-Integration Program (APRP) UNDP Support." First Quarter Progress Report, 2011, http://www.undp.org/content/dam/afghanistan/docs/crisisprev/APRP_00076674_QPR_Q1_2011.pdf.

UNICEF. "Annual Report 2017." February 2018. https://www.unicef.org/afghanistan/reports/annual-report-2017.

UNSC. "United Nations Security Council Resolution 1325." United Nations Security Council, October 31, 2000, http://www.un.org/ga/search/view_doc.asp?symbol=S/RES/1325(2000).

UN Women. "UN Women: Afghanistan Country Office." UN Women, Asia and the Pacific, 2017, http://asiapacific.unwomen.org/en/countries/afghanistan.

Whitton, Michaela. "The War in Afghanistan Has Turned a Generation of Children into Heroin Addicts." Anti-Media, May 9, 2016, http://theantimedia.org/afghanistan-child-heroin-addicts/.

Wimpelmann, Torunn. "Leaving Them to It? Women's Rights in Transitioning Afghanistan." The Royal Institute of International Affairs, Chatham House (Asia Programme, Afghanistan), 2014.

Wimpelmann, Torunn. "One Step Forward and Many to the Side: Combating Gender Violence in Afghanistan, 2001–2014." Women's Studies International Forum 51 (2015): 101–109. doi:10.1016/j.wsif.2014.11.007.

Zahedi, Ashraf. "When the Picture Does Not Fit the Frame: Engaging Afghan Men in Women's Empowerment." In Land of the Unconquerable: The Contemporary Lives of Afghan Women, edited by Jennifer Heath and Ashraf Zahedi. Berkeley: University of California Press, 2011.

CHAPTER 44

MAINSTREAMING WPS IN THE ARMED FORCES
The Case of Australia

JENNIFER WITTWER

THE adoption of UN Security Council Resolution 1325 on Women, Peace, and Security (WPS) in 2000 offered a solid foundation for mainstreaming WPS principles into armed forces around the world, as it was the first time that the disproportionate impact of conflict on women and girls was institutionally recognized. Resolution 1325 called on UN member states to ensure women's equal participation and full involvement in all efforts for the maintenance and promotion of peace and security, and urged all actors to increase the participation of women and incorporate gender perspective into peacekeeping. In addition, it spelled out a role for the armed forces in the implementation of Resolution 1325 in national institutions and in peacekeeping.

The implementation of Resolution 1325, and its subsequent resolutions, has generally been translated globally to armed forces through the development of National Action Plans (NAP) by UN member states. The release of the *National Action Plan on Women Peace and Security 2012–2016* by the Australian Government in 2012, marked recognition by the Australian Defence Force (ADF)[1] and the Department of Defence[2] (collectively known as "Defense")[3] that implementation of the WPS agenda was an imperative to improving military capability and increasing operational effectiveness. Indeed, in 2013, the then Vice Chief of the Defence Force, Air Marshal Mark Binskin, acknowledged that "stability and peace can only be achieved through a gender-inclusive approach to conflict resolution and peace building" (Vice Chief Directive).

Defense has, since then, made considerable inroads toward ensuring that the practical implementation of the NAP achieves the WPS outcomes being sought by the Australian Government through political, social, aid, and diplomatic actions, that it aligns closely with those of allied armed forces, and that it builds on its already significant global contribution to Resolution 1325. This includes recognizing UN and North Atlantic Treaty Organization (NATO)[4] frameworks on WPS, working closely with civil society to identify current and emerging WPS issues, supporting and assisting the development of implementation strategies for other armed forces, and contributing to national and international initiatives on integrating gender perspective into military operations.

The Australian NAP enabled Defense to focus its attention on, and fully embed, the principles of Resolution 1325, particularly on the inclusion of gender considerations as an important factor in promoting gender equality for women and girls in countries threatened by war, violence, and insecurity, and in the planning and conduct of military peace and security efforts for national and global security.

Defense recognized that ensuring the safety and security of women and girls in conflict contributes significantly to a reduction in conflict levels and the maintenance of sustainable peace. Using the NAP, Defense formulated key WPS thematic areas for implementation, guided by the principles of Resolution 1325, global commitments to WPS, international best practice in security sector reform, and building on pre-Resolution 1325 initiatives that supported the WPS agenda. Defense's key strategy was to integrate a gender perspective into operations. This chapter provides a case study of the actions taken by Australian Defense to mainstream WPS into its military business and operations through the Australian NAP.

RESOLUTION 1325 AND THE ROLE OF THE ARMED FORCES

Resolution 1325 reaffirms the important role of women in the prevention and resolution of conflicts, peace negotiations, peace-building, peacekeeping, and humanitarian responses. Furthermore, it stresses the importance of their equal participation and full involvement in all efforts for the maintenance and promotion of peace and security. Resolution 1325 urges all actors to increase the participation of women and incorporate gender perspectives in all UN peace and security efforts. It also calls on all parties to conflict to take special measures to protect women and girls from gender-based violence, particularly rape and other forms of sexual abuse, in situations of armed conflict.

A critical point to draw from Resolution 1325 is that it does not seek to address issues solely related to women and girls. While there are numerous linkages to issues of diversity and gender equality, the scope of the initiative is broader, calling on nations to consider the impact of armed conflict on populations at risk and to acknowledge that those impacts may affect men, women, girls, and boys differently. Recognizing these differences and adapting actions to account for them is known as applying "gender perspectives" to operations, policies, and programs. The resolution notes that gender perspectives must be incorporated into the planning and execution of military operations, and that nations have a responsibility to protect populations at risk during armed conflicts (Vance 2016).

Giving women an active role to play in the security sector is essential, not only to ensure equal rights of both women and men, but to make these institutions more efficient and effective in responding to the different security needs of women and men. Their inclusion is an operational imperative due to their diverse range of skill sets. In the context of peace and stability operations, notably in Iraq and Afghanistan, women contributed substantially to widening the net of intelligence gathering, performing the cordon and search of women, and assisting in the aftermath of sexual violence (Valasek 2008).

Including women enables the military to better deal with the complexities of current conflicts especially where gender-based violence has become a weapon of war and where human rights violations and humanitarian crisis have become a mainstay of conflict issues (Hendricks and Hutton 2008: 4). Current evidence suggests that mixed gender peacekeeping units have significant effect: the contingent is more trusted by the community; more equipped to undertake key tasks, such as house and body searches, working in prisons, providing escorts for victims/witnesses, and screening combatants at disengagement, demobilization, and reintegration sites; more able to make meaningful contact with vulnerable groups and civil societies in local communities; easier to support conflict-affected women who would have difficulty speaking to male personnel; less likely to have problems with sexual exploitation and abuse; and they find it promotes and encourages the participation of local women and their organizations in post-conflict political processes (UN-INSTRAW, n.d.).

Understanding the needs and concerns of women and girls in conflict environments enables more comprehensive and effective planning of, and approach to, operational responses. The acknowledged benefits of applying a gender perspective into military operations include: more extensive information gathering capacities to improve access and communication with the local population in order to make better and more balanced decisions; overall situational awareness of all parties involved in the conflict to increase credibility and acceptance of the operation and the troops in theatre; and enhanced mutual understanding and respect to assure a better force protection (NATO 2009: 18).

Pre-NAP Platform for The ADF's Implementation of WPS

Australia has been integrally involved in global efforts to build and restore peace for more than sixty-five years, and has provided personnel to more than fifty UN and other multilateral peace and security operations since 1947. Prior to 1994, however, women were unable to undertake combat-related roles, and were further excluded from combat until 2011, which limited their capacity to be involved in peacekeeping. They were heavily concentrated in nontechnical and support roles, such as clerical, administrative, logistical, and health services, and under-represented in technical and war-fighting / combat roles. An expansion of their roles in military operations, ensuring gender equality through their participation, and identifying supporting protection mechanisms—inherently meeting the obligations of Resolution 1325—were the outcomes of three major initiatives that occurred prior to NAP implementation.

The first was the 2011 decision by the Australian Government to remove the gender restrictions on the remaining ADF combat roles.[5] From January 2016, females have been recruited directly into combat employment categories.

The second initiative was the conduct of two independent reviews in 2011 and 2012 by the Federal Sex Discrimination Commissioner, Elizabeth Broderick, into the treatment of women at the Australian Defence Force Academy (Broderick 2011) and in the ADF (Broderick 2012). These reviews examined the adequacy and appropriateness of measures to promote gender equality, women's safety, and to prevent sexual harassment and abuse, and sex discrimination, as well as efforts to increase women's participation in the ADF and in key leadership positions.[6]

Thirdly, in an effort to meet operational imperatives,[7] the Australian provincial reconstruction teams in Uruzgan Province, Afghanistan, deployed female engagement teams. This enabled them to tap into the local community and identify pressing security and domestic needs and concerns. They established a female development assistance program with a number of projects relating to education programs and economic development, and the provision of health services, school supplies and medicine to the local population. They also worked with the women's ministries in the provincial Afghanistan government to improve the living conditions and access to basic services for rural Afghan women and their families. These activities contributed to the overall effectiveness of the operation by winning the "hearts and minds" of the local population.

These activities serendipitously aligned with the NAPs objectives on the role of armed forces; increasing the number of women in the armed forces and in international missions, integrating a gender perspective in pre-deployment training, and promoting protection of women's rights in conflict and post-conflict areas (UN-INSTRAW, n.d.). These factors were critical for sustaining efforts to enhance capability building, improve operational effectiveness, and meet ADF's commitments under Resolution 1325.

The Australian NAP

Australia's work to implement Resolution 1325 is guided by its NAP, providing a coordinated approach across a number of government departments to integrating gender into Australia's peace and security efforts.[8] It identifies the strategies and actions that Australia is undertaking, nationally and internationally, to advance this important work and highlights the specific responsibilities.

The NAP sets out Australia's plans to integrate a gender perspective into its peace and security efforts, protect the human rights of women and girls, and promote their participation in conflict prevention, management, and resolution. It seeks to structure its activities equally around the Resolution 1325 pillars—prevention of armed conflict; participation of women in all aspects of peace and security work; protection of women and girls in conflict situations; ensuring a gender perspective in all relief and recovery efforts; and integrating a gender perspective across all peace and security work (NAP 2012: 15). Australia recognized that determined and coordinated efforts were required to promote the protection and participation of women and girls, and to respond to their needs in fragile, conflict and post conflict situations (Australian NAP 2012: 19).

The NAP contains five high-level strategies aligned with the five thematic areas identified by the UN for conceptualizing and organizing activities in the implementation of the WPS agenda.[9] There are twenty-four actions, which outline how each strategy will be practically delivered. Collectively, Defense and the Australian Civil Military Centre[10] are responsible for seventeen actions; the majority are heavily focused on its contribution to peace and security efforts, implementation of WPS internationally, training for deployed forces, relationships with civil society in operations, and enhanced participation of women in peace and security operations.

The NAP is premised on the nexus between gender equality and peace; for Defense, this has played out in two ways. First, as described in the preceding paragraphs, with a greater focus on operations. The NAP reaffirms that implementation of the WPS agenda is long-term and transformative, and importantly, that it is about changing the approach to peace and security efforts. (Australian NAP 2012: 15)

The second approach involves ensuring that Defense is held accountable for its role in implementing the WPS agenda. Since 2013, Australian civil society has come together with government to hold an annual dialogue on WPS, which brings together the key agencies engaged in the implementation of the NAP to outline their actions and reflect on progress to ensure that implementation of the NAP remains both accountable to civil society and informed by its input and deliberations (Annual Civil Society Report Card 2013: 2).

Defense Strategy for the Implementation of Resolution 1325 and the Australian NAP

In 2013, Defense formally acknowledged its obligations to the NAP, and recognized it as the mechanism to drive integration of gender perspectives into its operations, to enhance understanding of complex operational environments, improve capability and performance of the workforce through increased diversity, and enhance its reputation within the Australian and international community. The implementation strategy for Defense was specifically aligned with the intent of Resolution 1325, ensuring delivery of outcomes that built on the positive achievements of current cultural reform programs, and making certain that the process of planning, execution, and conduct of Defense-related NAP actions comprehensively and effectively demonstrated implementation of those actions. (CDF 2014: 1)

To facilitate this, Defense appointed a senior officer [11] in August 2013, initially reporting to the Vice Chief of the Defence Force, until July 1, 2014, when the Chief of the Defence Force assumed responsibility. This demonstrated senior leadership commitment to, and leadership on, WPS. It highlighted the importance of the WPS agenda to Defense's strategic policy, gave prominence to Defense's implementation strategy, and was pivotal to a coordinated, holistic approach in responding to its NAP responsibilities. Primary responsibilities included the development of a NAP implementation plan,[12] liaising with the other government agency partners responsible for NAP implementation,[13] and facilitating whole-of-government progress.

A working group was also established, with representatives from the three armed services, Joint Operations Command, and relevant Defense agencies, which met quarterly to report progress and to facilitate NAP actions within their respective areas. The inclusion of a civil society representative on the working group[14] enabled transparency, collaboration, and the strengthening of Defense's relationship with civil society, an important factor in accountability and ownership by Defense.

Defense NAP Implementation Plan

The development of an implementation plan from late 2013 was seen as the primary means for mainstreaming WPS within Defense. The plan was informed by the outcomes of the

2013 Jumonji University Seminar and the 2013 Global Technical Review meeting,[15] and the then NATO–revised policy and action plan for the implementation of Resolution 1325 (NATO 2014).[16] This included regional, national, and international engagement with NATO allies and partners, international organizations, and civil society, and academia; operational responses, such as the inclusion of a gender perspective in the planning and conduct of operations and major exercises; addressing conflict-related sexual and gender-based violence; appointing gender advisers and developing female engagement capability; national initiatives to improve women's participation in armed forces and military responses to conflict; and training and education in gender and the WPS agenda.

These core outcomes influenced the design of initiatives and tasks that Defense could implement that supported NAP actions, grouped under the NAP strategies but aligned with one of six thematic areas shown in Box 44.1. The Defense implementation plan was endorsed by key senior Defense officials, and has progressed over the past four years as a fluid and live matrix of activities.

IMPORTANCE OF LEADERSHIP
IN IMPLEMENTING WPS

Defense's progress against the NAP has been quite significant in a short period of time and this has been influenced by ministerial and senior ADF leader commitment and action, and Defense's active engagement and transparency in collaboration with civil society. Air Chief Marshal, and currently Chief of Defence Force, Mark Binskin confirmed this approach during the 2014 Defence Women in Peace and Security conference when he said the following:

> By 2019, one year after the NAP is completed, the WPS agenda will be fully embedded in our approach to personnel management, the planning and conduct of operations, throughout our policy frameworks and in our corporate guidance. It will enhance our ability to effectively contribute to peace and security operations within our region and internationally. We will have an increased relationship of collaboration and engagement with civil society and other Government organisations to ensure a coordinated and whole of government approach to the implementation of women, peace and security objectives. So—how can we be sure we will keep up with our early momentum? My intention is to continue my personal commitment to the women, peace and security agenda—and I expect everyone in Defence to do the same.

Box 44.1 Six Key Thematic Areas of the Defense Implementation Plan

1. Key strategic guidance and operational planning documents and processes training;
2. WPS training and education;
3. Development of products by ACMC;
4. Increasing deployment and leadership opportunities for women;
5. Developing the gender advisor and female engagement capability;
6. National and international engagement on WPS.

The Chief of the Defence Force has personally driven the strategy to implement the NAP within the Australian armed forces. The participation by Lieutenant General David Morrison, the then Chief of the Army, at the United Kingdom Summit on the Prevention of Sexual Violence in Conflict in June 2014, and his closing ceremony speech—which included the now famous "the standard you walk past is the standard you set" quote—cemented Defense's role in, and commitment to, addressing sexual and gender-based violence in conflict-affected communities. This and other events helped reinforce Australia's position on WPS and its implementation of the NAP as a best practice example of effective implementation of Resolution 1325.

INTEGRATING GENDER PERSPECTIVE INTO PEACE AND SECURITY POLICIES

Primary to the success of mainstreaming WPS has been the development of a gender advisor capacity. In April 2014, the Chief of the Defence Force appointed the then executive director of the Australian National Committee for UN Women[17] as his gender advisor. This not only enabled him to better address gender diversity within the ADF, it also increased the collaboration and engagement with civil society. Defense created additional positions to fully embed WPS into operational business, including a gender advisor to directly support Joint Operations Command; strategic gender / women's advisors to the military chiefs of service; and a gender focal point supporting operations in the Middle East.

This gender advisor capacity has been instrumental to the introduction and streamlining of WPS initiatives and activities across the whole of Defense. Foremost among these accomplishments is the successful integration of WPS into key strategic Defense policy and guidance, and into operational planning documents and processes, thereby cementing its importance and priority for and within the operational context. This impacted Australian military planning considerations for major exercises, including the 2015 Australian / United States bilateral Exercise Talisman Sabre,[18] with eight military gender advisers attached for the duration. Since 2014, Defense has included WPS goals in its corporate and annual business plans. [19] In 2016, the Defence White Paper[20] provided specific reference to Defense's obligations and initiatives under the NAP, and progress of the Defense implementation plan is reported to government as part of the White Paper implementation and as required under the accountability framework in the NAP.

The redevelopment of joint doctrine has further enabled the integration of WPS into operational considerations, with the inclusion of WPS into the lead doctrine development guide, as well as peacekeeping-specific doctrine relating to mission planning, humanitarian responses, and supporting international operations.[21] Additionally, in December 2015, Defense published strategic guidelines for the protection of civilians, which provide a whole-of-government perspective on protection of civilians in international situations of armed conflict and other situations of violence. As a measure of the high regard in which these guidelines are held, Japan is translating them for their use in training Japanese military personnel for peacekeeping operations.

Building on the WPS training already conducted through the ADF peace operations training center for personnel deploying to UN missions,[22] Defense also embedded WPS into force preparation training for the Middle East and other international operations. To compliment this, work has commenced to include WPS into the professional military and training continuum for all ADF personnel, and currently training is conducted for officers attending junior and senior command and staff colleges.[23] To support all aspects of training, Defense published a WPS training manual and facilitator guide, and two key research documents to enhance understanding of, and training in, WPS.[24]

Defense is also examining ways to provide increased deployment and leadership opportunities for women. In the main, this effort is being captured by the implementation of the Broderick Review and the removal of the gender restrictions, which over time will increase the participation of women across all employment categories of the ADF.[25]

Over the last fifteen years, Australia's operational experience has coincided with a growing awareness and understanding of women's unique experiences in conflict-affected environments and their valuable contribution to peace and security efforts (Shteir 2015: 1). An increasing number of senior ADF women are deploying to and commanding on operations—as the 2016 Force Commander for Afghanistan, the Deputy Commander for Australian forces in the Middle East, and, in 2015, a senior female officer commanded the ADF's contingent to the UN Truce Supervision Organization. Operations in Afghanistan over the last decade have given Defense an appreciation of the role that women can play in security sector reform. This awareness enhances the mainstreaming of WPS into Defense operations to continue to develop and deploy women across a range of increasingly nontraditional operational roles.

SUPPORTING CIVIL SOCIETY TO INCREASE WOMEN'S PARTICIPATION

The implementation of WPS has brought about a more collaborative and trusted relationship between Defense and civil society, which has contributed to the development of international best practice and increased Defense's understanding and capability for WPS through a better understanding of how conflict impacts women and girls, and more holistic approaches and responses to address this issue. Defense's primary focus has been on cooperating with other agencies and civil society in developing policy, educating the Defense workforce, and in the development of subject matter experts, such as gender advisers for key military international exercises and international operations.

Defense has also sponsored and funded numerous activities with civil society organizations to broaden its knowledge and understanding of conflict-related WPS issues. These include training with UN agencies in the Asia and Pacific, supporting and participating in the annual civil society dialogues to assess NAP implementation, and dialogues with international civil society organizations on gender justice, security, and women's rights.

Promoting WPS Implementation Internationally

Defence's progress with the NAP has enhanced its reputation globally, and enabled increased opportunities for international engagement on WPS. The ADF has committed to permanent representation at the annual NATO Committee on Gender Perspective since 2011. In 2014, the committee considered the topic of "Recruitment and Retention in the [NATO] Armed Forces—National Human Resource Polices and Exchange of Best Practices." The participation by the ADF, and by Elizabeth Broderick, in this conference, largely influenced two of the three major recommendations to the NATO Military Committee arising from the Committee's syndicate efforts: that nations be encouraged to conduct assessments to identify and address potential gaps in policies and programs that may negatively impact the retention of women in the armed forces, and that nations be encouraged to establish an Advisory Committee to inform and shape military gender equality priorities (NATO 2014).

From 2014–2017, the Australian Human Rights Commission and the ADF participated in a NATO project to assess the impact of Resolution 1325 on the recruitment and retention of women in NATO armed forces.[26] The project identified six principles, largely influenced by the Broderick Review, as best practice recommendations for security sector reform within other armed forces (UNSCR 1325 Reload 2015: 33).

Also in 2014, the annual ADF Gender Conference included presentations on the operationalization of Resolution 1325 in military operations from senior international military delegates.[27] This contributed to lessons learned, information sharing, and raising the level of understanding and awareness of the importance of WPS and gender perspective in operations. This conference, which was attended by ADF members, civil society, academics, other government department representatives, senior Defense officials, and both the Minister for Defence and the Minister Assisting the Prime Minister for Women, left the audience in no doubt as to their commitment to the WPS agenda and the ongoing progress of the NAP within Defense and the broader Australian community.[28]

The ADF has continued to support international implementation of WPS: working with the Japanese Self Defense Force to develop a NAP implementation plan; creating a gender adviser capacity and exploring employment of gender advisers and female engagement teams in Japanese peacekeeping operations; supporting WPS seminars, workshops, and operations in the Asia and Pacific region; presenting at international and academic WPS conferences; participating in and conducting female military observer courses at international peacekeeping centers; contributing to public consultations on the development of the New Zealand NAP and New Zealand Defence Force implementation; assisting Canadian Armed Forces with the development of an implementation plan and gender positions; and participating in, and presenting at, key seminars and training sessions conducted at international military institutions.

To leverage global efforts to mainstream WPS, Defense is enhancing opportunities for senior ADF women to deploy in key peace and security positions overseas. In addition to the gender focal point in the Middle East, supporting the mainstreaming of WPS in multilateral operations, and as testament to the credibility and expertise of our gender advisers, the ADF has also maintained liability for gender adviser positions in NATO operations in

Afghanistan since 2013; and in 2016, a female officer deployed as the first Military Gender Adviser to the UN Mission in South Sudan. Defense also established a five-year funded, non-ongoing position to UN Women in New York which commenced in 2017.

Overall, Defense has made a considerable contribution to the global implementation of the WPS agenda in military organizations and operations. This has reinforced Defense's internal efforts to implement the NAP, and ensured that Resolution 1325 and the WPS principles were embedded into Defense business, which would not have occurred in the absence of a NAP, and without the leadership and direction of senior leaders within Defense.

CONCLUSION

Since the adoption of Resolution 1325 by the UNSC in 2000, Australia has been actively involved in and supported a large number of high-level commitments to addressing the role of women in peace and security. In the main, this has been focused on political, social, diplomatic, and aid responses to crisis and conflict management, human rights, gender equality, and peacekeeping. The ADF's initial comprehension of WPS principles was demonstrated only through the recognition that military women could play a role in engaging with the local population in peacekeeping missions, and this occurred informally in regional missions in the early 2000s, and more formally through the use of female engagement teams in Afghanistan after 2011.

However, a more thorough integration of Resolution 1325 and related resolutions into the ADF's approach to military operations through the Australian NAP has recognized the unique role that both men and women bring to peace and security efforts, and the need to capitalize on this capability to improve operational effectiveness. Using the NAP actions as a strategic framework, Defense identified six core areas that supported the Resolution 1325 principle of gender perspective in operations and were likely to increase operational effectiveness and enhance mission outcomes. The current suite of initiatives in the Defense implementation plan are not exhaustive and are designed to lay the groundwork for ongoing implementation as understanding and knowledge of Resolution 1325 and the WPS agenda increases within the Defense community.

NOTES

1. Royal Australian Navy, the Australian Army, and the Royal Australian Air Force.
2. A Department of State, headed by the Secretary of the Department of Defence.
3. The "Defence" portfolio consists of a number of component organizations that together are responsible for supporting the defense of Australia and its national interests. This includes the Department of Defence and the ADF.
4. NATO is an intergovernmental military alliance based on the North Atlantic Treaty, which was signed on April 4, 1949. The organization constitutes a system of collective defense whereby its member states agree to mutual defense in response to an attack by any external party.

5. In 2011, the remaining combat roles previously excluding women were (Navy) Clearance Divers and Mine Warfare and Clearance Diving Officers; (Air Force) Airfield Defence Guards and Ground Defence Officers; and (Army) Infantry and Armoured Corps, some Artillery roles, Explosive Ordnance Disposal Squadrons, and Combat Engineer Squadrons—this represents 7 percent of total employment trades in the ADF.

6. Details about, and content of, these reviews can be found at "Collaboration for Cultural Reform in Defence," http://defencereview.humanrights.gov.au.

7. In 2011, in response to NATO policy to integrate Resolution 1325 into military operations, and building on the US military's experience and success in Iraq, the International Security Assistance Force in Afghanistan required all military units to create female engagement teams to build relations with Afghan women. These teams had dual and linked military and civilian purposes, one as a force multiplier and important part of evolving counter-insurgency strategy, and the second to promote the participation of women in conflict and post-conflict settings to help build more peaceful, equitable, and democratic societies. In taking this approach, the coalition was implementing a 1325 strategy that translated into practical measures and leadership opportunities for women on the ground.

8. The departments are, namely, the Department of Prime Minister and Cabinet (Office for Women); Department of Defence; Australian Federal Police; the Attorney-General's Department; the Australian Civil-Military Centre; and the Department of Foreign Affairs and Trade.

9. These themes are prevention, participation, protection, relief and recovery, and normative.

10. The Australian Civil Military Centre is an Australian Government initiative to improve Australia's effectiveness in civil-military collaboration for conflict and disaster management overseas.

11. This officer was a colonel equivalent.

12. The Defence Implementation Plan remains as the guiding program to support the ADF's implementation of the NAP and provides direction on mainstreaming WPS.

13. These included the Australian Federal Police, the Department of Foreign Affairs and Trade, the Attorney General's Department, the Australian Civil Military Centre, and the Department of the Prime Minister and the Cabinet.

14. Currently, Julie McKay, of the Australian National Committee for UN Women (2014).

15. The meeting was held November 5–7, 2013, organized by UN Women in collaboration with civil society and with financial support from Austria, Finland, and the Netherlands, to examine building accountability for the implementation of Resolution 1325.

16. The ADF has been working closely with NATO since 2012 on the development of its action plans on Resolution 1325, specific projects relating to women's participation in armed forces, input into national reports, and development of products arising from the annual Committee on Gender Perspective.

17. National Committees for UN Women are independent nongovernmental organizations that support the mission of UN Women through their public awareness initiatives about UN Women and global women's issues, and fundraising efforts to support UN Women programs worldwide.

18. Exercise Talisman Saber (also spelled Talisman Sabre, the spelling alternating between US and Australia) is a biannual joint Australia–United States military exercise conducted every two years.

19. The Defence Corporate Plan (DCP) sets out the purpose, activities, and results for four financial years, and builds on the longer-term strategic guidance contained in the Defence White Paper. The Defence Business Plan articulates how the activities in the DCP will be implemented.

20. The Defence White Paper sets out the government's direction to Defense to guide strategy, capability, and organizational and budget planning.

21. The policy guidance on all joint doctrine development and review. The JDDG is provided to all joint doctrine developers and provides specific guidance on developing the detailed analysis of requirements that establish the context, scope and content of ADF joint doctrine.

22. This training uses UN accredited core training material.

23. Australian Defence Force Academy, the Australian Command and Staff College, and the Australian Defence College.

24. Sarah Shteir, "Conflict-related Sexual and Gender-based Violence: An Introductory Overview to Support Prevention and Response Efforts." Civil-Military Occasional Papers, Australian Civil Military Centre, 2014; and Sarah Shteir, "Gender Crisis, Gendered Response; The Necessity and Utility of a Gender Perspective in Armed Conflict and Natural Disasters." Civil-Military Occasional Papers, Australian Civil Military Centre, 2014.

25. Defense and the AHRC have an ongoing collaborative relationship which looks at, among other areas, gender diversity and the treatment of women in the ADF.

26. The preliminary outcomes of this review were presented to the UN as part of the global review conducted for the fifteenth anniversary of Resolution 1325 in 2015, and the final report was released in October 2016.

27. Major General Jody Osterman, US Marine Corps, (ex-Deputy Chief of Staff Operations, Afghanistan); Captain Herve Auffret (Head of Policy and Doctrine in the Office of Military Affairs, Department of Peacekeeping Operations, UN Headquarters); and Lieutenant Colonel Jesus Gil Ruiz (NATO Office of the Gender Advisor).

28. Defense's progress regarding the NAP from March 2012 to December 2013, and an update of 2014 initiatives, has been recorded in the first Progress Report to Government, which was tabled in parliament in July 2014.

REFERENCES

Annual Civil Society Report Card. "Australia's National Action Plan—Women, Peace, and Security." August 2013, https://acfid.asn.au/sites/site.acfid/files/resource_document/Civil-Society-Report-Card-2013.pdf.

"Australian National Action Plan on Women, Peace, and Security 2012–2018." Australian Government, 2012, https://www.pmc.gov.au/office-women/international-forums/australian-national-action-plan-women-peace-and-security-2012-2018.

Australian National Committee for UN Women. "Women, Peace, and Security: An Introductory Manual." Australian Government, 2014, https://www.acmc.gov.au/publications/women-peace-and-security-an-introductory-manual/.

Broderick, E. "Review into the Treatment of Women at the Australian Defence Force Academy." Phase 1 Report. Australian Human Rights Commission, 2011.

Broderick, E. "Review into the Treatment of Women in the Australian Defence Force." Phase 2 Report. Australian Human Rights Commission, 2012.

Chief of Defence Force (CDF). Directive 17/24, EAPC(C)D(2014)0001, 2014.

Hendricks, C., and L. Hutton. "Defence Reform and Gender." In *Gender and Security Sector Reform ToolKit*, edited by M. Bastick and K. Valasek. Geneva: Democratic Control of Armed Forces/UN-INSTRAW, 2008.

NATO. "Gender Training and Education: Recommendations on Implementation of UNSCR 1325." 2009: 18, https://www.nato.int/issues/women_nato/pdf/2010/BrochureGender.pdf.

NATO. NATO Committee on Gender Perspective—2014 Annual Conference—Recommendations, 5 Jun 14. B. MC 0458/3 (Final), NATO, IMSM-0286-2014, June 5, 2014.

Shteir, S. "Women, Peace, and Security: Reflections from Australian Male Leaders." Civil-Military Occasional Papers, edited by Helena Studdert and Sarah Shteir. Australian Civil Military Centre, November 2015.

UN-INSTRAW. "Virtual Discussion on the Role of the Armed Forces in the Implementation of UNSCR 1325." Discussion Summary. United Nations INSTRAW, UN Women, n.d.

UNSCR 1325 Reload. "An Analysis of Annual National reports to the NATO Committee on Gender Perspectives from 1999–2013: Polices, Recruitment, Retention, and Operations." Findings and Recommendations. NATO Science for Peace and Security Program, 2015: 33.

Valasek, K. "*Security Sector Reform and Gender.*" In *Gender and Security Sector Reform Toolkit*, edited by Megan Bastick and Kristin Valasek. Geneva: Centre for the Democratic Control of Armed Forces/UN-INSTRAW, 2008.

Vance, J. H. "CDS Directive for Integrating UNSCR 1325 and Related Resolutions into CAF Planning and Operations." January 2016, http://www.forces.gc.ca/en/operations-how/cds-directive.page.

Vice Chief of Defence Force Directive. Recommendation 5, 2013. No 5/2013, 2013.

PART V

CROSS-CUTTING AGENDA? CONNECTIONS AND MAINSTREAMING

CHAPTER 45

WPS AND RESPONSIBILITY TO PROTECT

ALEX J. BELLAMY AND SARA E. DAVIES

THIS chapter explores the evolving relationship between Women, Peace, and Security (WPS) and the Responsibility to Protect (R2P). It begins by outlining the emergence of R2P in the wake of failures to respond adequately to mass atrocities in Rwanda, Bosnia, and elsewhere, and evaluating the charge that, as originally conceived, R2P was "gender blind." The chapter moves on to show how the UN Secretary-General and others have attempted to build bridges between the two agendas and how the Security Council has looked to simultaneously implement both—in general terms and within specific conflict settings. This section also considers some of the feminist critiques of R2P in light of these efforts. The final part of the chapter sets out the similarities and differences between the two agendas and calls for greater cross-fertilization between them, including through the incorporation of a gender lens into atrocity prevention and an atrocity-prevention lens into WPS. Overall, we argue that the two agendas should be understood as mutually reinforcing, such that the attainment of one requires the attainment of the other, but that they are complementary rather than synonymous agendas inasmuch as they contain important differences.

EMERGENCE OF R2P

Stemming from the horrors of Srebrenica, a UN "safe area" from which over seven thousand men and boys were taken and slaughtered by Bosnian Serb forces in 1995, and Rwanda, which a year earlier, had experienced full blown genocide, the Responsibility to Protect (R2P) is a disarmingly simple idea. It holds that sovereign states have a responsibility to protect their own populations from four crimes that indisputably "shock the conscience of humankind" (Walzer 1977): genocide, war crimes, ethnic cleansing, and crimes against humanity. It requires that the international community assist individual states to fulfill their responsibility, because some states lack the physical capacity and resources of legitimacy needed to protect their populations from these crimes. R2P calls specifically for the prevention of the four crimes and their incitement. Finally, R2P says that when states "manifestly fail" to protect their populations from these four crimes, whether through lack of capacity or will or as a result of deliberate intent, the international community should respond in a "timely and decisive" fashion with diplomatic, humanitarian, and other peaceful means and, failing that, with all the tools that are available to the United Nations Security Council. This can include the use of military force.

These are the three pillars of the Responsibility to Protect: (1) the primary responsibility of the state to protect its own population from genocide, war crimes, ethnic cleansing, and crimes against humanity; (2) the international community's duty to assist; (3) the international responsibility to take timely and decisive action to protect populations from these crimes when the state fails to do so (UNGA 2009). The principle is not ambiguous; it is the politics that surround it and the challenge of realizing its ambition in practice that is so difficult.

The phrase "responsibility to protect"—R2P—was first coined in 2001 by the International Commission on Intervention and State Sovereignty (ICISS), a group of retired politicians, diplomats, and humanitarians chaired by former Australian Foreign Minister Gareth Evans and highly respected former Algerian diplomat Mohammed Sahnoun. The Commission was tasked by the Canadian government with the job of reconciling the tensions between state sovereignty and humanitarian necessity made abundantly obvious by the Northern Atlantic Treaty Organization's (NATO) intervention in Kosovo in 1999. Specifically, the Canadian government asked the Commission to find a way of avoiding repetitions of, on the one hand, cases like the 1994 Rwandan genocide, where the world stood aside and did nothing as eight hundred thousand people were butchered in just one hundred days and, on the other hand, cases like Kosovo where a group of states took it upon themselves to use force to protect people without a mandate from the UN Security Council (Bellamy 2009; Evans 2008).

The Commission's answer came in the form of R2P—a call for a shift away from sterile debates about the prerogatives of interveners and inalienable rights of sovereigns toward a focus on protection for vulnerable populations and the responsibilities of individual governments and the international community as a whole (ICISS 2001). The Commission argued that there was a duty to prevent as well as respond to these crimes and maintained that armed intervention should be reserved for the most severe cases and guided by a set of prudential criteria (Thakur 2016: 417). This would ensure that force would only be used for the right reasons and only when likely to do more good than harm.

The journey of translating R2P from idea to political principle and diplomatic practice began with former UN Secretary-General Kofi Annan. Annan (2012: 118) welcomed the advent of R2P, describing it in his memoir as "a brilliant innovation." He judged that by reframing debates about how the world should respond to mass atrocities and focusing on the responsibilities of sovereignty, R2P held the promise of reconciling two fundamental principles of the UN Charter that had all too often worked to opposite ends: state sovereignty and the protection of fundamental human rights.

In September 2005, more than 150 heads of state and government arrived in New York to conclude negotiations on a blueprint for UN reform. In paragraphs 138 and 139 of the World Summit's Outcome Document, subsequently adopted as a General Assembly resolution, the UN's Member States committed themselves to R2P and its three pillars. Their commitment was subsequently reaffirmed by the Security Council in Resolutions 1674 (adopted in 2006), 1894 (adopted in 2009), 2171 (adopted in 2014), and 2220 (adopted in 2015), among others.

In 2009, the General Assembly passed a unanimous resolution in which it pledged to continue its consideration of the implementation of R2P. Since then, the Secretary-General has issued a report on R2P each year and the General Assembly has debated it in an informal and interactive dialogue.

Since 2005, R2P has become part of the diplomatic language used, albeit unevenly and with patchy results, to prevent and respond to atrocity crimes. The practical use of R2P got off to a slow and discouraging start, largely because states were uncertain about what they had agreed to, unsure about how to conceptualize and operationalize R2P, and concerned about its potential implications. In the almost five years between Security Council Resolution 1674 (adopted in 2006) and Resolution 1970 on Libya (adopted in 2009), the Council referred to the concept only once (though it did refer to R2P prior to Resolution 1674, in Resolution 1653 [adopted in 2006] on the Great Lakes Region of Africa). This came in a highly contentious preambular paragraph in Resolution 1706 (2006) on the situation in Darfur, where Sudanese government forces and their notorious allies, the "Janjaweed" militia, had conducted a reign of terror resulting in the death of some two hundred thousand people and forced displacement of over 2 million more.

Given the UN and its member states hesitance to implement their 2005 commitment to R2P, few—if any—anticipated the role that the principle would play in the dramatic events of 2011. In February 2011, the "Arab Spring" reached Libya. Protests there quickly turned into a major uprising. The following month, in March 2011, the Security Council responded to the unfolding crisis by throwing almost its entire portfolio of preventive measures at the situation in Libya in Resolution 1970. When the Gadhafi regime failed to comply with the Council's demands and looked likely to topple the rebel stronghold of Benghazi and commit a massacre there, the Council took the unprecedented step of authorizing the use of force against a state to protect civilians from imminent danger, enforce a no-fly zone, and enforce an arms embargo (Resolution 1973). NATO and its allies hastily arranged a coalition of the willing that prevented the fall of Benghazi and the widely anticipated massacre there. The conflict dragged on into a stalemate but eventually the regime collapsed.

A few days after the adoption of its landmark resolution on Libya, the Security Council unanimously adopted Resolution 1975 on Côte d'Ivoire. Having lost an election, the country's now former president, Laurent Gbagbo, refused to stand down. Following the advice of international election monitors, the Security Council declared Alassane Ouattarra to be the country's president and authorized the use of force to protect the civilian population. UN forces, already stationed in Côte d'Ivoire as part of the UNOCI operation deployed to oversee an end to the country's civil war and transition to a new, democratic government, acted alongside French forces to stop the escalating violence, remove Gbagbo, and allow the elected president to take his place at the head of the new government.

The Council's responses to the crises in Libya and Cote d'Ivoire demonstrated a newfound determination (on which, see Bellamy and Williams 2011) to act on the responsibility to protect populations from atrocity crimes, including through the use of force when necessary. But the responses proved highly controversial. Critics complained that NATO and the UN had overstepped their mandates by contributing to regime change, that they had used disproportionate force which increased civilian casualties, and that they had ignored or outright rejected opportunities for further political dialogue. Russia in particular argued that the Libyan experience colored its thinking on the subsequent crisis in Syria, pushing it to resist Western pressure on the al-Assad regime (Averre and Davies 2015).

Although the Security Council has indeed been deadlocked on Syria, the Council has employed R2P in other contexts. Resolution 1996, adopted in July 2011, established a UN peace operation for South Sudan and called upon the international community to provide assistance to help the new government there to fulfill its responsibility to protect. Resolution 2014, adopted in October 2011, reminded the government of Yemen of its primary responsibility to protect its population. In its September 2011 Presidential Statement on preventive diplomacy, the Council again recalled its commitment to R2P. Resolution 2085 (adopted in 2012) on Mali authorized an international mission to assist the government there in fulfilling its responsibility to protect. Resolution 2117 (adopted in 2013) on small arms and light weapons recognized their capacity to result in the commission of R2P crimes; and Resolution 2121 (adopted in 2013) on the Central African Republic underscored the government's responsibility to protect its own population.

Thus, in a remarkably short space of time R2P has been transformed from a concept proposed by an international commission into an international norm endorsed by the world's governments and usefully employed in more than a dozen situations. It is a principle that increasingly frames how world governments and international organizations think about the prevention of genocide and mass atrocities and responses to them.

Gender Blindness

From the start, gender has been identified as a major weakness in R2P (Bond and Sherret 2006; Charlesworth 2010). Critics pointed to the fact that ICISS commission, which first coined the phrase R2P in 2001, had a distinct lack of expertise on gender issues and was unbalanced with only one of the twelve commissioners being female. This imbalance was echoed on the Commission's advisory board (the small number of women represented did not make presentations to the panel), and of two thousand publications listed as sources by the commission's database, only seven reportedly explored gender and atrocities, and four examined women and security (Davies 2016). The ICISS report contained only three references to women and gender (all in relation to rape) and made no mention of the unique role of women in conflict, peacemaking, and peace-building. Charlesworth (2010: 242) provides one explanation for this: the gender stereotypes held by key "architects" of R2P, such as Gareth Evans, who in his book on R2P presents women in two narrow frames—as victims of mass rape or the motherly, inclusive peace-builders.

When the ICISS report referred to women the frame was even narrower, essentially viewing women as victims, specifically victims of rape (ICISS 2001: 33). Gender—the relations between women and men, the social roles attributed to each sex, and its role in conflict—was not addressed (Caprioli and Boyer 2001), although rape as a political act was, which may be interpreted as acceptance that gender norms are significant in situations where mass atrocities are committed (see Piza-Lopez and Schmeidl 2002). However, the report left unanswered questions concerning how interventions inspired by R2P could address gender equity concerns and it ignored gender inequalities as root causes of atrocities from which gender inequity becomes a concern. Furthermore, as mentioned already, there was no reference at all to the WPS agenda adopted only a year earlier (in 2000) by the UN Security Council in Resolution 1325. Specifically, the ICISS report was silent on Resolution

1325's reference to the responsibility of all states to "put an end to impunity and to prosecute those responsible for genocide, crimes against humanity, and war crimes including those relating to sexual and other violence against women and girls" (para. 11). It was also silent on the 1998 Rome Statute's recognition that sexual and gender-based violence (not only rape and not only women as survivors of rape) constituted crimes against humanity and war crimes.

The 2004 report of the UN Secretary-General's High Level Panel on Threats, Challenges and Change, "A More Secure World," reaffirmed the centrality of both Security Council Resolution 1325 and R2P, but kept them separate and distinct (Rehn and Sirleaf 2002). Likewise, the 2005 World Summit Outcome Document included references to both R2P and WPS but treated them as separate and distinct agendas, shaping how the two would continue to be viewed. The question is how do we explain this early conceptual segregation of R2P and WPS?

Writing after the 2005 agreement on R2P, Jennifer Bond and Laurel Sherret (2006) argued that if the population most in need of R2P in number—women and girls—were persistently excluded from the debate about the implementation of R2P, the principle would falter in its aim of protecting civilians from atrocity crimes (Bond and Sherret 2006: 74). The problem they argued, lay in the failure of R2P to engage with the WPS agenda. Other critics noted that R2P advocates tended not to acknowledge the complementarity of R2P's three pillars with the four pillars of the WPS agenda—though the reverse was also true: advocates of WPS have tended to be wary of positively engaging with the R2P agenda (see Hall and Shepherd 2013; Harris-Rimmer 2014).

Interestingly, however, Bond and Sherret (2006) stopped short of arguing that gender equality advocates should abandon R2P. Instead, they identified areas of mutual agreement and compatibility across the two agendas, where advocacy for gender equality across the broader areas of economic and social development, civil and political rights, as well as peace and security, could be effective for both (Bond and Sherret 2006: 74). They suggested that the two agendas shared some common goals and occupied a similar institutional space given their association with the two principal organs of the UN (General Assembly and Security Council). This view came to be supported by others who saw opportunities for deeper alignment between the two agendas on the Security Council in strengthening action to combat sexual and gender-based violence, promoting the inclusion of women in the security sector, the involvement of women combatants and non-combatants in peace-building agreements, greater gender equity within UN institutions, and, in particular, the organization's field missions (Hunt 2009; International Coalition for the Responsibility to Protect 2012).

Despite these efforts, R2P has developed largely in isolation of other efforts to protect and empower women as agents of peace and security, including conflict prevention. The principle now stands accused of offering a much less radical and progressive set of policies than those developed by other agendas, notably efforts to implement the Security Council's resolutions on WPS. According to the critics, not only does this make R2P less transformative than it ought to be, it carries the danger that the principle's conservatism might "crowd-out" other initiatives, create a degree of backsliding, especially with respect to WPS, or lead to humanitarian interventions that further compromise women's security (Charlesworth 2010; Hall and Shepherd 2013; Harris-Rimmer 2014).

This critique is correct to the extent that until recently, there has been little explicit engagement between R2P and the wide range of institutions and initiatives relating to the much broader WPS agenda. This is starting to change, however. Hilary Charlesworth (2010), Eli Stamnes (2012), and Sara Davies and Sarah Teitt (2012) explored the potential for deepening the alignment of the two agendas as first suggested by Bond and Sherret. Davies and Teitt (2012) concurred that while the ICISS report was indeed "gender blind," this did not apply to the R2P principle itself or efforts after 2005 to implement it. They proposed a need to update the gendered analysis of R2P to take account of developments since the 2005 World Summit adopted R2P and suggested potential areas of engagement and research (specifically) for R2P advocates, namely early warning frameworks, the pursuit of common goals on the Security Council (between R2P and WPS), prioritization of gender equality rights in national human rights institutions, and a focus on specific prevention of crimes of sexual violence and gender-based violence (2012: 215-221).

Research in an edited volume (see Davies et al. 2013) catalyzed thinking about the relationship between R2P and WPS, provoking both scholarly debate and policy engagement on the relationship between R2P, WPS, and the prevention of mass atrocities (Bond and Sherret 2012; Hudson et al. 2012; Skjelsbæk 2012; Caroni and Seiberth 2015). The majority of this research has approached the conceptual relationship between R2P and WPS as requiring a responsible state—one best placed to realize the security of individuals through adherence to rules and norms concerning human rights and gender equality. It is a normative position: states fulfilling their responsibility to protect is the most durable solution of internally displaced populations and civilians trapped in situations where they are being targeted for mass atrocities, or deprived of human rights (Mooney 2010). This literature points to growing international engagement with both the WPS agenda and the R2P principle—reflected in the increasing number of commitments to and invocations of both R2P and WPS agenda, in various international forums such as the Security Council (Bellamy 2014: 99–101; Davies 2016; Tryggestad 2009). It has also spurred fresh thinking on practical issues such as the place of gender in atrocity early warning (Davies and True 2015; Davies et al. 2015; Hewitt 2016; Spitka 2016).

Turning to a more policy-oriented aspect of the critique, there is no evidence to suggest that in diplomatic or operational practice, R2P "crowds-out" other initiatives, including those relating to gender. Nor is it true that R2P principle itself (as opposed to some of its advocates) is "gender blind." On the one hand, each of the crimes to which R2P relates has an explicit gender component. For instance, crimes listed under the rubric of widespread or systematic sexual- and gender-based violence, the prevention of which was fought for as a central tenet of the WPS agenda, are expressly prohibited by international law as crimes of genocide, war crimes, or crimes against humanity (depending on their context). On the other, there is nothing in the R2P principle to suggest that it ought to replace or transcend the implementation of the Security Council's Resolution 1325 and subsequent resolutions on Women, Peace, and Security, or do the same to any other thematic agenda for that matter. No UN officials, diplomats, or serious analysts have suggested that it should. From the Security Council's vantage point, the two agendas are distinct but complementary. What is more, regional debates beyond the West among governments and civil society has traversed the boundaries between R2P and WPS, recognizing the tangible connections between them (Davies 2014b).

From this, it seems fair to suggest that the best remedy for the lack of gender sensitivity detected by some feminist scholars lies not, therefore, in abandoning R2P but in identifying and closing the gap that lies between it and the effort to end gender discrimination and inequality (Hewitt 2016). Indeed, significant progress has been made since 2005 to identify and build a cross-cutting agenda between WPS and R2P. It is to this that we now turn.

DISTINCT BUT COMPLEMENTARY AGENDAS

One advocate of the shared agenda between R2P and WPS was the UN Secretary-General Ban Ki-moon. The UN Secretary-General recognized the connection between the four R2P crimes and widespread or systematic sexual-and gender-based violence. In addition to enumerating the connections between the protection of women and the four crimes associated with the R2P, in 2009 the Secretary-General specifically referred to Security Council Resolutions 1612 (adopted in 2005) and 1820 (adopted in 2008) as underscoring that rape and other forms of sexual violence constituted "war crimes, crimes against humanity or constitutive acts with respect to genocide" that states have a responsibility to end and the international community has a concomitant responsibility to respond to (UNGA 2009: para. 34). He observed that in Resolution 1820 on WPS, for instance, the Security Council had agreed that "rape and other forms of sexual violence can constitute a war crime, a crime against humanity, or a constitutive act with respect to genocide . . . and calls upon Member States to comply with their obligations for prosecuting persons responsibility for such acts" (para. 34). The Secretary-General also noted that the resolution called upon the Security Council to monitor sexual violence as a "security problem," due to its propensity to be as destructive to communities as conventional weapons, and to bring these situations to the attention of the Security Council.

Since then, the Secretary-General has gradually amplified the connections between the two agendas. In 2013, the Secretary-General report argued that gender discrimination was significant for R2P in and of itself: "gender discrimination and inequality increase underlying risks associated with sexual and gender-based violence, which can constitute genocide, war crimes and crimes against humanity in some circumstances." The report went on to note, "specific gender discrimination practices include the denial or inadequate protection of basic rights relating to physical security and the status of women, compulsory birth control and unequal access to services and property" (UNGA 2013: para. 19). This was an important step not only because it recognized gender inequality as a matter of concern for R2P, but because it promoted the need to close the institutional gaps between the UN's R2P and its gender-focused work. Most notably, it implicitly directed the UN's Office on Genocide Prevention and R2P to engage with the UN's Special Adviser on Gender Issues and the Advancement of Women, the Special Representative for Children and Armed Conflict, the Special Representative on Sexual Violence in Conflict, and key organization, UN Women.

The Secretary-General went on to note the need to direct more attention and research to record best practices in the alleviation of gender inequality and promotion of gender empowerment to prevent mass atrocities. This was well received by a number of member states in the United Nations General Assembly's Informal Interactive Dialogue on R2P. Several countries, including Brazil, Cote d'Ivoire, United Kingdom, Norway, Switzerland, and New Zealand specifically referred to the importance of preventive action that is gender sensitive and emphasized the relationship between R2P and WPS in noting that sexual and gender-based violence in armed conflict can constitute R2P crimes (Davies 2014b).

This line of thinking has led to the articulation of a series of specific reflections and recommendations on actionable policy. In the area of prevention, specifically the role of local early warning to prevent mass atrocities, the Secretary-General argued in 2009 that "less well known is the role of individuals, advocacy groups, women's groups and the private sector in shaping the international response to crimes and violations relating to the responsibility to protect" (UNGA January 2009: para.3). On the responsibility to protect populations subjected to one or more of the four crimes, the Secretary-General's 2009 report repeatedly referred to the need for R2P advocates to ensure that gender responsiveness and engagement be addressed in efforts to implement each of the three pillars. Here, the Secretary-General made a number of recommendations for establishing the protection of women and promotion of gender equality as part of a framework for implementing R2P. In relation to pillar one, he called for further study into why some societies plunge into mass violence while their neighbors remain stable and on "why it has been so difficult to stem widespread and systematic sexual violence" (para.15). The report called for an investigation into how some states protect the rights of women despite internal diversity and adversity. In keeping with the call in Resolution 1325 for an end to amnesty and immunity for those who commit crimes against humanity and genocide that entail crimes against women— the Secretary-General also argued that states needed to do more to end impunity for four crimes, that states should become parties to the Rome Statute of the International Criminal Court (ICC), and that post-conflict regimes should locate and apprehend individuals "at whatever level, who are accused of committing or inciting crimes and violations relating to the responsibility to protect" (paras. 19, 59). Finally, the Secretary-General identified the incorporation of the protection of women into the training for police, soldiers, the judiciary and legislators as a core component of the prevention of genocide and mass atrocities, and called upon states to assist their peers in this area of capacity building (paras. 25–26, 39).

The 2009 Secretary-General's report therefore provided the most significant and direct attempt to date to link R2P to the protection of women (Davies 2014b). Subsequently, the Secretary-General has repeatedly included references to both WPS and gender equality in his annual reports on R2P. This has included a focus on the relationship between documenting reports of sexual and gender-based violence and identifying patterns of mass atrocities (UNGA 2010), the need to ensure gender equity across rule of law institutions (UNGA 2011), the prevention of sexual violence in conflict (UNGA 2012), gender equality and its relationship to preventing mass atrocities (UNGA 2013), support for national strategies to prevent gender-based violence (UNGA 2014), the importance of transnational justice mechanisms directed at sexual and gender-based violence (UNGA 2014), and enduring patterns of gender discrimination (UNGA 2015). In the 2015 report, the Secretary-General also emphasized a continued need to direct more attention and research to record best practices in the alleviation of gender inequality and promotion of gender empowerment to prevent mass atrocities, including sexual and gender-based crimes.

These sentiments have been translated into practice, albeit still only in modest ways. Despite acute political and budgetary pressure, the Security Council has given increased focus to women's security and women's role in peace and security in the face of mass atrocities—such as in the creation of women's human rights advisors in UN Missions, such as in South Sudan, Mali, and Cote D'Ivoire; the UN Informal Experts Group (IEG) on Women, Peace, and Security, with oversight for specific country situations; the adoption of resolutions that address the particular needs of civilians and their right to humanitarian access in Syria; statements on the need to protect displaced populations, the majority of which are women; and the adoption of a new thematic agenda on Arms Trade Treaty (ATT). In particular, the General Assembly's adoption of ATT and its entry into force in 2014 could be interpreted as a notable achievement for both R2P and WPS advocates with the ATT having specific provisions on states not being supplied with arms if they have engaged in or permitted one of the four R2P crimes on their territory, with specific mention of sexual and gender-based crimes (Hiniker 2014). Sweden's 2017 decision to withhold the sale of arms to Saudi Arabia on these grounds is a good case in point. There was also further provision in the ATT to ensure that disarmament and demobilization programs are gender equitable for both former combatants and victims of crimes committed by combatants. Each of these developments contributes, in its own way, to R2P's goal of preventing atrocity crimes and WPS's protection components.

Conclusion: Forward Thinking

Neither R2P nor WPS are emerging agendas seeking to find a voice at the international table. They are different in their focus and scope but both have been successful in securing the support of UN member states and finding a regular place in the agendas and working practices of the Security Council. There is little evidence to suggest that either WPS or R2P is weakened, or diluted by mutual conceptual and policy engagement; but there are areas where working across conceptual, political, and institutional silos might be reasonably thought to deliver better outcomes for both. It is fair to argue, in looking at other international agendas, that the goals of each will be harder to achieve without the full use of all available instruments and networks (Carpenter 2013). Moreover, where pushback has occurred against R2P and WPS, it has done so independently of any linkage between them. As noted earlier, WPS advocates have long been critical of the Security Council's focus on sexual and gender-based violence at the expense of other parts of the WPS agenda (often raised is the eight-year gap between the four pillar focus of Resolution 1325 and the sexual violence in conflict focus of Resolution 1820; see chapter 24 in this volume). This pushback against the wider elements of the agenda occurred despite the *absence* of linkage with R2P at the time. We conclude, therefore, by offering five practical suggestions of steps that might support both R2P and WPS and their actual implementation on the ground where human rights violations and atrocities are still occurring.

First, there are important operational synergies. Where progress has been made in improving international responses to the most serious humanitarian crises, this has often come in the context of Security Council engagements that included both WPS *and* R2P. In these settings, such as in the UN's responses to crises in South Sudan, Mali, the Central African Republic, Cote d'Ivoire, and the Democratic Republic of Congo, the Security Council has referred to preventing and addressing gender discrimination that gives rise to atrocity crimes in the first place. The creation of the IEG on Women, Peace, and Security, to hear briefings and reports on country situations where there is the risk of atrocities or a history of atrocities, lifts both WPS and R2P out of their silos to be understood holistically with reference to countries that require the attention of the Security Council (Security Council Report 2017).

Second, as we noted earlier, it is increasingly recognized that widespread sexual and gender-based violence constitutes an atrocity crime and should therefore be core business for R2P. In 2014, the Secretary-General referred to sexual and gender-based violence in the context of the role of regional organizations in supporting the documentation and prevention of these crimes. Several non-Western states, such as Thailand and Malaysia, continue to engage with and support mutual agendas shared by WPS and R2P in the area of preventing sexual and gender-based violence and specific action to protect populations from this violence. The ICC has made clear determinations to this effect. Resolution 2106 (adopted in 2013) on sexual and gender-based violence was explicit in calling on states to take responsibility to prevent these crimes by adopting military and police protocols concerning the investigation and prosecution of sexual crimes; by introducing legislation and judicial processes to document, investigate, and prosecute sexual violence in conflict and post-conflict; and by cooperating with UN Commissions of Inquiry.

Third, R2P advocates are championing the role of women as agents of protection and change. Champions should be sought at the Security Council in New York and the Human Rights Council in Geneva, and we need to broaden the networks further. It is particularly important to look for avenues in different regional and institutional contexts. The 2013 Secretary-General report specifically referred to the need for the inclusion of gender indicators to support early warning and the recognition of women's groups as agents of protection. The incorporation of gender equality into the security and justice sectors, for instance, is recognized as a core component of the prevention of atrocity crimes. This recognition is sparking practical work. In 2017, one of the principal sites of R2P advocacy, the Asia Pacific Centre for R2P, teamed up with the ASEAN Commission on the Protection and Promotion of the Rights of Women and Children to explore the linkages between atrocity prevention, gender empowerment, and the elimination of discrimination (ASEAN Secretariat 2017). This agenda has also been identified as a core priority of the Asia Pacific Partnership for Atrocity Prevention, a group of thirteen organizations—including the ASEAN Parliamentarians for Human Rights group—from across that region (APCR2P 2017).

Fourth, there is greater recognition of the need for R2P advocates to ensure that gender responsiveness and engagement be addressed in efforts to implement each of the three pillars. Here, as we noted earlier, the UN Secretary-General made a number of recommendations for establishing the protection of women and promotion of gender equality as part of a framework for implementing R2P. Incorporating gender discrimination and gender-rights–abuse indicators into the operationalization of the Office of the Special Representative for the Prevention of Genocide and the Responsibility to Protect, particularly when making country specific recommendations and statements on high-risk situations, would be a valuable contribution to IEG on WPS, IASC (see chapters 24 and 49 in this volume), and Human Rights Council processes (see chapter 25 in this volume).

Fifth, there is synergy on the question of accountability and the imperative of ending impunity. In keeping with the call in Resolution 1325 for an end to amnesty and immunity for those who commit crimes against humanity and genocide that entail crimes against women—the Secretary-General also argued that states needed to do more to end impunity for the four atrocity crimes, that states should become parties to the Rome Statute of the International Criminal Court, and that post-conflict regimes should locate and apprehend individuals "at whatever level, who are accused of committing or inciting crimes and violations relating to the responsibility to protect." Advocacy on the importance of international human rights law and international humanitarian law is of vital interest to both R2P and WPS advocates, yet, again, there has been little collective advocacy from either agenda in this area to date.

Going forward, R2P advocates and office holders need to embrace the struggle against gender discrimination and inequality on its own terms and recognize the multiple roles that women and girls play in contexts of genocide and mass atrocities as victims, bystanders, perpetrators, protectors, and peacemakers. The Secretary-General has essentially recognized that R2P can achieve its objectives only when the UN's goals in WPS, and in relation to ending gender discrimination more broadly, are achieved. At the same time, however, advocates of WPS must also recognize that they will not achieve the goals set by their own agenda while that of eliminating atrocity crimes remains unfulfilled.

REFERENCES

Annan, Kofi. *Interventions: A Life in War and Peace*. New York: Allen Lane, 2012.

ASEAN Secretariat. "The ASEAN Commission on the Promotion and Protection of the Rights of Women and Children (ACWC) to Advance Gender, Peace, and Security Agenda in the Region." Association of South East Asian Nations, March 31, 2017, http://asean.org/asean-to-advance-gender-peace-and-security-agenda-in-the-region/.

Asia Pacific Centre for Responsibility to Protect (APCR2P). "Asia Pacific Partnership for Atrocity Prevention (APPAP)." Brisbane: University of Queensland, (2017, https://r2pasiapacific.org/asia-pacific-partnership-atrocity-prevention-appap.

Averre, Derek, and Lance Davies. "Russia, Humanitarian Intervention and the Responsibility to Protect: The Case of Syria." *International Affairs* 91, no. 2 (2015): 813–834.

Bellamy, Alex J. *The Responsibility to Protect: The Global Effort to End Mass Atrocities*. Cambridge: Polity, 2009.

Bellamy, Alex J., and Paul D. Williams. "The New Politics of Protection? Cote d'Ivoire, Libya, and the Responsibility to Protect." *International Affairs* 87, no. 4 (2011): 825–850.

Bellamy, Alex J. *Responsibility to Protect: A Defense*. Oxford, UK: Oxford University Press, 2014.

Bond, Jennifer, and Laurel Sherret. *A Sight for Sore Eyes: Bringing Gender Vision to the Responsibility to Protect Framework*. United Nations International Research and Training Institute for the Advancement of Women. March 2006, http://iwrp.org/new/wp-content/uploads/2010/07/nv-bond.pdf.

Bond, Jennifer, and Laurel Sherret. "Mapping Gender and the Responsibility to Protect: Seeking Intersections, Finding Parallels." *Global Responsibility to Protect* 4, no. 2 (2012): 133–153.

Caroni, Martina, and Corinna Seiberth. "From Gender-Blind to Gender-Sensitive: The Relevance of the UN Women, Peace, and Security Agenda for Operationalizing Responsibility to Protect." In *Responsibility to Protect: A New Paradigm of International Law?*, edited by Peter Hilpold, 253–273. Boston: Brill Nijhoff, 2015.

Carpenter Charli. " 'Lost' Causes: Agenda Vetting in Global Issue Networks and the Shaping of Human Security." New York: Cornell University Press, 2013.

Caprioli, Mary, and Mark A. Boyer. "Gender, Violence, and International Crisis." *Journal of Conflict Resolution* 45, no. 2 (2001): 503–518.

Charlesworth, Hilary. "Feminist Reflections on the Responsibility to Protect." *Global Responsibility to Protect* 2, no. 3 (2010): 232–249.

Davies, Sara E., Kimberly Nackers, and Sarah Teitt. "Women, Peace, and Security as an ASEAN Priority." *Australian Journal of International Affairs* 68, no. 3, (2014a): 333–355.

Davies, Sara E. "R2P and Gender: The Marginalisation of Responsibilities." *E-IR*, March 13, 2014b, http://www.e-ir.info/2014/03/13/r2p-and-gender-the-marginalization-of-responsibilities/.

Davies, Sara E. "Gender." In *Oxford Handbook of the Responsibility to Protect,* edited by Alex J. Bellamy and Tim Dunne. Oxford: Oxford University Press, 2016.

Davies, Sara E., and Sarah Teitt. "Engendering the Responsibility to Protect." *Global Responsibility to Protect* 4, no. 2 (2012): 198–222.

Davies, Sara E., and Jacqui True. "Reframing Conflict-Related Sexual and Gender-Based Violence: Bringing Gender Analysis Back in" *Security Dialogue* 46, no. 6 (2015): 495–512.

Davies, Sara E., Sarah Teitt, and Zim Nwokora. "Bridging the Gap: Early Warning, Gender, and the Responsibility to Protect." *Cooperation and Conflict* 50, no. 2 (2015): 228–249.

Davies, Sara E., Zim Nwokora, Eli Stamnes, and Sarah Teitt, eds. *Responsibility to Protect and Women Peace and Security Agenda.* Boston: Brill, 2013.

Evans, Gareth. *The Responsibility to Protect: Ending Mass Atrocity Crimes Once and for All.* Washington, DC: Brookings Institution, 2008.

Hall, Lucy, and Laura J. Shepherd. "WPS and R2P: Theorising Responsibility and Protection." In *Responsibility to Protect and Women, Peace, and Security,* edited by Sara E. Davies, Zim Nwokora, Eli Stamnes, and Sarah Teitt, 53–80. Leiden, Belgium: Martinus Nijhoff, 2013.

Harris-Rimmer, Sue. "Feminist Ripostes to the Responsibility to Protect." Gender Institute 2014 Public Lecture Series Feminist Theory Now. Australian National University. Podcast, July 22, 2014, http://genderinstitute.anu.edu.au/feminist-ripostes-responsibility-protect-doctrine-o.

Hewitt, Sarah. "Overcoming the Gender Gap: The Possibilities of Alignment between the Responsibility to Protect and the Women, Peace, and Security Agenda." *Global Responsibility to Protect* 8, no. 1 (2016): 3–28.

Hiniker, Alexandra. "The Unexplored Links between Humanitarian Disarmament and the Responsibility to Protect." International Coalition for the Responsibility to Protect [Blog], September 5, 2014, http://icrtopblog.org/tag/arms-trade-treaty/.

Hudson, Valerie M., Bonnie Ballif-Spanvill, Mary Caprioli, and Chad F. Emmett. *Sex and World Peace.* New York: Colombia University Press, 2012.

Hunt, Swanee. "The UN's R2P Report Is Missing Out by Half." *Huffington Post,* April 2, 2009, http://www.huffingtonpost.com/swanee-hunt/the-uns-r2p-report-is-mis_b_171198.html.

International Coalition for the Responsibility to Protect. "Women and the Responsibility to Protect." March 9, 2012, http://icrtopblog.org/2012/03/09/women-and-the-responsibility-to-protect/.

International Commission on Intervention and State Sovereignty. *The Responsibility to Protect.* Ottawa: IDRC, 2001.

Mooney, Erin D. "Something Old, Something New, Something Borrowed . . . Something Blue? The Protection Potential of a Marriage of Concepts between R2P and IDP Protection." *Global Responsibility to Protect* 2, no. 1 (2010): 60–85.

Piza-Lopez, Eugenia, and Susanne Schmeidl. *Gender and Conflict Early Warning: A Preliminary Framework*. Geneva: Swisspeace with International Alert, 2002.

Rehn, Elizabeth, and Ellen J Sirleaf. "Women, War, and Peace: The Independent Experts." Assessment of the Impact of Armed Conflict on Women and Women's Role in Peace-building. New York: United Nations Development Fund for Women, 2002.

Security Council Report. "In Hindsight: Women, Peace, and Security–Closing the Security Council's Implementation Gap." March 31, 2017, http://www.securitycouncilreport.org/monthly-forecast/2017-04/in_hindsight_women_peace_and_securityclosing_the_security_councils_implementation_gap.php.

Skjelsbæk, Inger. "Responsibility to Protect or Prevent? Victims and Perpetrators of Sexual Violence Crimes in Armed Conflicts." *Global Responsibility to Protect* 4, no. 2 (2012): 154–171.

Spitka, Timea. "Drawing the Red Lines: Gender and Responsibility to Protect in BiH and Israel/Palestine." The Responsibility to Protect at 10 Conference. Boston: Brandeis University, 2016, http://www.brandeis.edu/ethics/pdfs/internationaljustice/r2p/march%202015%20papers/r2p-spitka.pdf.

Stamnes, Eli. "The Responsibility to Protect: Integrating Gender Perspectives into Policies and Practices." *Global Responsibility to Protect* 4, no. 2 (2016): 172–197.

Thakur, Ramesh. "Review Article: The Responsibility to Protect at 15." *International Affairs* 92, no. 2 (2016): 415–434.

Tryggestad, Torunn L. "Trick or Treat? The UN and Implementation of Security Council Resolution 1325 on Women, Peace, and Security." *Global Governance: A Review of Multilateralism and International Organizations* 15, no. 4 (2009): 539–557.

United Nations General Assembly. "Implementing the Responsibility to Protect." Report of the Secretary-General, A/63/677, 2009, http://www.responsibilitytoprotect.org/index.php/about-rtop/the-un-and-rtop.

United Nations General Assembly. "Early Warning, Assessment, and the Responsibility to Protect." Report of the Secretary-General, A/64/864, 2010, http://www.responsibilitytoprotect.org/index.php/about-rtop/the-un-and-rtop.

United Nations General Assembly. "Role of Regional and Sub-Regional Arrangements on Implementing the RtoP." Report of the Secretary-General, A/65/877, 2011, http://www.responsibilitytoprotect.org/index.php/about-rtop/the-un-and-rtop.

United Nations General Assembly. "Responsibility to Protect—Timely and Decisive Response." Report of the Secretary-General, A/66/874, 2012, http://www.responsibilitytoprotect.org/index.php/about-rtop/the-un-and-rtop.

United Nations General Assembly. "Responsibility to Protect: State Responsibility and Prevention." Report of the Secretary-General, A/67/929, 2013, http://www.responsibilitytoprotect.org/index.php/about-rtop/the-un-and-rtop.

United Nations General Assembly. "Responsibility to Protect: International Assistance." Report of the Secretary-General, A/68/947, 2014, http://www.responsibilitytoprotect.org/index.php/about-rtop/the-un-and-rtop.

United Nations General Assembly. "A Vital and Enduring Commitment: Implementing the Responsibility to Protect." Report of the Secretary-General, A/69/981, 2015, http://www.responsibilitytoprotect.org/index.php/about-rtop/the-un-and-rtop.

Walzer, Michael. *Just and Unjust Wars: A Moral Argument with Historical Illustrations*. New York: Basic Books, 1977.

CHAPTER 46

....

WPS AND PROTECTION OF CIVILIANS

....

LISA HULTMAN AND
ANGELA MUVUMBA SELLSTRÖM

PROTECTION of civilians (POC) has become a core feature of United Nations peace-keeping. A normative shift in the 1990s led to new mandates and priorities in peace-keeping operations. This has occurred in parallel to the policy shift toward emphasizing the security of women. This chapter compares these two agendas and asks whether these two goals—protection of civilians and security of women—go hand in hand or if there are any tensions in the way these are pursued. We focus both on the expectations formulated by the UN Security Council and on the operational activities and priorities on the ground. The provision for the protection of civilians initially differed from the Women, Peace, and Security (WPS) agenda, since it was mainly formulated in gender-neutral language (although the understanding of "civilians" was partly gendered). Still, over time the two frameworks have begun to overlap, albeit through focusing on deterring and preventing sexual and gender-based violence (SGBV). The apparent focus on SGBV arises from an underlying normative assumption by UN actors that the WPS claim for sensitivity to gender translates into addressing wartime rape and other forms of sexual abuse. Preventing such harms is the main intersecting link between the POC and WPS frameworks. Initially, efforts to shield civilians from this violence were possible because of the dominant narrative of sexual violence as a "weapon of war," but additional logics for this violence are increasingly acknowledged and may thus influence the way protection is carried out in the future.

We begin by providing a brief overview of the policy development of POC, and its consequences. The chapter then turns to how gender is addressed in the POC agenda, and highlights relatively new efforts such as patrolling and escorts within peace support operations. The next section reflects on the focus on protection in the WPS agenda, including a brief summation of its gender-sensitive orientation and types of actions by the UN. Finally, we compare the two agendas and consider how the different frameworks and explanations for SGBV influence protection.

The POC Policy Shift and Its Consequences

The year 1999 marked a significant shift in the focus and character of UN peacekeeping operations. The ongoing violence against the civilian population in Sierra Leone led the Security Council to authorize the United Nations Mission in Sierra Leone (UNAMSIL) with the explicit mandate to take the necessary action "to afford protection to civilians under imminent threat of physical violence" (UNSC 1999a: sec.14). This was the result of years of failure, frustration, and self-reflection for UN peacekeeping. After a few years in the early 90s of successful facilitation of transitions from war to peace in a number of cases, such as Mozambique and El Salvador (Howard 2008), the mid-1990s instead offered a dark period for UN peacekeeping. In 1994, the Security Council failed to take decisive action to stop the genocide in Rwanda. The small UN presence in the country was not sufficiently equipped or mandated to interfere with the escalating violence. The critique of UN peacekeeping was strengthened further the year after when the mission in Bosnia was unable to prevent the genocidal violence perpetrated in Srebrenica and armed actors forced the withdrawal of UN peacekeepers from Somalia, leaving the country in a state of anarchy (Howard 2008; Adebajo 2011). While these failures scarred the whole international community, leading eventually to the development of the Responsibility to Protect (see chapter 45 in this volume), it also scarred UN peacekeeping more specifically. According to Holt and Taylor (2009: 4), "the inability of peacekeeping missions to address violence against civilians in the past has damaged the standing of the United Nations and threatened to discredit the practice of peacekeeping in general." Nevertheless, after a few years of critical discussion, the Security Council thus decided in 1999 that UN peacekeeping should play an important role in protecting civilians during armed conflict.

The provision for protection of civilians has now become normative practice in UN peacekeeping missions (Wills 2009: 66). Research has recently begun to examine the consequences of this policy shift for the way peacekeeping is conducted and its impact on the ground. One pertinent question is of course whether the normative shift toward protection also serves as a motivation for the Security Council to intervene in cases of civilian atrocities. Some studies indicate that the Security Council is indeed more likely to deploy a peacekeeping mission when there are high levels of violence against civilians and that this effect has become stronger after 1999 (Hultman 2013). This would indicate an increasing willingness of the Security Council to intervene in the conflicts where civilians are most at risk, such as Mali and South Sudan (see chapter 14 in this volume). The extent to which peacekeepers—once a mission is established—then deploy to the areas where civilians are most at risk is debated. Costalli (2014) finds that in Bosnia, the UN did in fact deploy to the most violent areas, whereas Powers et al. (2015) argue that the UN does not do so. Fjelde et al. (2019) find that the UN deploys to areas where rebels target civilians, but not where governments do. Given that missions are mandated to protect civilians within their area of deployment, this is a critical question for the credibility of POC within UN peacekeeping.

Even if the protection norm seems to have an impact on how the UN Security Council addresses violence against civilians, there are enormous challenges when it comes to implementing those mandates and offering civilians protection from physical violence. In a systematic assessment of the first ten years of POC mandates, Holt and Taylor (2009) identify a number of challenges and obstacles to their successful implementation. For example, mission commanders interpret and prioritize POC in different ways. Another problem is when the mission is tasked to collaborate with the government forces when those same forces are also perpetrating violence against civilians, like the case of the United Nations Organization Stabilization Mission in the Democratic Republic of the Congo (MONUSCO) (also see chapter 14 in this volume). This particular problem of how peacekeeping forces interact with the host state has been highlighted by other studies that emphasize how the need for consent *de facto* means that the peacekeepers are unable to forcefully interfere when violence is perpetrated by government forces (see e.g., Wills 2009 on United Nations Stabilization Mission in Haiti [MINUSTAH]). The increased focus on protection from sexual violence is also a great challenge for the UN, and peacekeepers have been criticized for failing to enforce protection—for example, with the mass rapes in eastern Democratic Republic of the Congo (DRC) (UNJHRO 2011).

Despite these challenges on the ground, quantitative studies have shown that UN peacekeeping reduces the overall level of violence against civilians under certain conditions. The capacity of the mission is crucial for the ability to protect civilians. The more troops and police that the UN is able to provide, the better the protection (Hultman et al. 2013). High capacity is not a guarantee for success; however, it provides the necessary means for carrying out such a challenging task as protecting civilians. Diversity of the troops on the ground is an additional important factor for the effectiveness of reducing violence against civilians (Bove and Ruggeri 2016).

GENDER IN THE POC AGENDA

Looking at many of the mandates for peacekeeping missions with POC provisions, POC has primarily meant the authorization to use force at the tactical level to protect civilians under imminent threat of physical violence within the mission's area of deployment. As such, it is a gender-neutral concept. Nevertheless, the way that protection is discussed in the Security Council meetings suggest that it is a gendered concept in the sense that "innocent civilians" is often taken to mean "women and children" (Carpenter 2006). For example, the motivations brought up in the meeting establishing UNAMSIL in 1999 included the need to protect innocent women and children (UNSC 1999b). For several missions, and particularly for more recent missions, the protection language in UN Security Council resolutions also includes a clause about protection from sexual violence. For example, the mandate for MONUSCO specifies that the mission needs to work with the government of the DRC "to ensure the protection of civilians from abuses and violations of human rights and violations of international humanitarian law, including all forms of sexual and gender-based violence" (UNSC 2014: sec. 4a [iii]). The United Nations Multidimensional Integrated Stabilization Mission in Mali (MINUSMA) has a mandate: "To provide specific protection for women and children affected by armed conflict, including through Child Protection Advisors and Women Protection Advisors, and address the needs of victims of sexual and gender-based violence in armed conflict" (UNSC 2015, sec.14d[iv]).

These formulations are clearly influenced by the WPS agenda, and the general move toward acknowledging SGBV as a particular problem. However, they also reveal different ways of seeing the relation between POC and WPS. If the initial focus on protection of civilians in UNAMSIL was driven by an understanding of civilians as being primarily women and children, the MINUSMA mandate makes a distinction between protection of civilians in general and protection of women. The MONUSCO mandate also specifies protection from SGBV as a specific category, although without limiting this to a question of protecting women. However, the MONUSCO mandate does call for a deployment of Women Protection Advisers, that are tasked with setting up and supporting systems for monitoring and reporting SGBV incidents and patterns. This particular type of protection component is related to the WPS agenda and emblematic of the increasing overlap between the two frameworks.

In practice, the POC formulations in the mandate mean that peacekeepers have some operational guidance and scope to use force for protection, particularly through patrolling and escorts. For the most part, peace support operations appear to concentrate on non-coercive engagement. The 2015 Global Study on the Implementation of UN Security Council Resolution 1325 (see also chapter 11 in this volume) identifies a number of measures that have been used to protect women and girls from sexual violence. These include joint protections teams involving civil-military cooperation. UN peacekeeping patrols in and around refugee and IDP camps in the DRC, Haiti, and Darfur have been recognized as important measures for protection. Peacekeeping operations have also distributed fuel-efficient stoves and rolling water containers (to save women and girls from having to gather firewood or carry water, two activities that contribute to their vulnerability to armed actors and to sexual violence) (UNSC Women 2015: 144). Other activities include quick impact projects such as construction of latrines or more suitable shelters. The Global Study, however, notes that "these innovations still remain piecemeal and limited, more often pilot projects and special initiatives rather than the core business" (UN Women 2015: 144).

Relatedly, mission operations now include gender advisors and women protection advisors, who carry out gender sensitivity training toward the implementation of human rights law and norms; devise trainings, also for UN Police; support local prosecution and mobile courts; as well as contribute to monitoring, analysis and reporting arrangements (MARA) (UN Women 2015: 144). In addition, the deployment of all-female police units in missions has been attributed to enhancing the likelihood of reporting sexual violence, and to protection, leading to the establishment of female police networks in conflict-affected settings. Efforts to improve judicial and police capacity have been introduced in the DRC, Guinea, Sierra Leone, and Somalia (UN Women 2015: 144).

One of the main challenges to both the success and the credibility of POC is the recurrent problem of sexual exploitation and abuse (SEA) by peacekeepers themselves (see chapter 18 in this volume). Reports of SEA by peacekeepers in as many as fourteen missions over a four-year period (2009–2013) (Karim and Beardsley 2016) have undermined confidence in DPKO's protection role. This is beginning to receive more attention within the UN organization. On January 6, 2017, the UN Secretary-General appointed a new task force that will develop a strategy to prevent and respond to sexual exploitation and abuse (UN 2017). Even though this is not a strategy unique to peacekeeping, it is clearly a response to the widespread problem of SEA by peacekeepers. Some missions, such as the United Nations Operation in Côte d'Ivoire (UNOCI) and the United Nations Mission in Liberia (UNMIL), also have specific training to reduce SEA.

PROTECTION IN THE WPS AGENDA

The WPS progenitors have placed protection, along with prevention, participation, peace-building, and recovery, as the main pillars (UN Women 2015; and chapter 16 in this volume). Since its beginning, the primary feature of protection in the WPS framework (as opposed to the POC's original scope) has been its orientation toward SGBV (also at times referred to as conflict-related sexual violence within the WPS) for all intents and purposes through Security Council Resolutions 1325 (UNSC 2000), 1820 (UNSC 2008), 1888 (UNSC 2009), 1960 (UNSC 2010), and 2106 (UNSC 2013). Resolution 1325 specifically "calls upon all parties to armed conflict to respect . . . the rights and protection of women and girls, especially as civilians" (UNSC 2000: oper. para. 9). It frames protection as based on international legal instruments such as the Geneva Conventions, the Convention on the Elimination of All Forms of Discrimination against Women, and the Rome Statute of the International Criminal Court, and not "merely" operational mandates of peacekeepers and their humanitarian obligations under the UN Charter. Moreover, parties to armed conflict should "take *special measures to protect women and girls from gender-based violence* . . . and all other forms of violence in situations of armed conflict" (emphasis ours, UNSC 2000: oper. para 10). In contrast, POC operational clauses in resolutions mandate peacekeeping missions to address physical violence *as well as* SGBV; WPS language and rhetoric placed the latter at the forefront of protection. Although these distinct interpretations have overlapped over time, these differences in emphasis have had some implications for when and how to prevent, deter, and respond to different types of violence.

How has protection evolved within the WPS then? The UN's protection work under WPS has been coercive and non-coercive, short-term and long-term, and ranged from instituting targeted sanctions against actors that are credibly suspected of committing sexual violence, to training military, police, and peacekeepers on the prevention of these abuses. For instance, Resolution 1820 requests the UN Secretary-General and UN agencies to develop mechanisms for protection against sexual violence in refugee and IDP camps. Resolution 1888 demands that armed conflict parties take military disciplinary measures, invoking the importance of command and control responsibilities. In addition, Resolution 1960 goes further by requesting the prohibition of sexual violence in Codes of Conduct and military field manuals.

The tasks carried out by the Security Council to stop armed actors from committing sexual violence through sanctions in particular, have a coercive, short-term quality to them. It has included SGBV in its sanctions regimes for the DRC, Somalia, and the Central African Republic (CAR) (Nabti 2015). In contrast, conflict resolution and peace-building activities through other UN actors are better suited to changing attitudes, values, and discriminatory practices in conflict contexts and are non-coercive and long-term strategies. In either set of engagements, protection is framed by a gendered lens, which rhetorically positions women and girls as the main victims and, therefore, objects of protection. Sanctions in particular, have retained a security and masculinist hue, focusing on the behavior of armed actors, with males viewed as the primary culprits of sexual violence (see Nabti 2015).

The Security Council's work has included stimulating protection through binding language that would constrain against the commission of sexual violence. Yet, a steady increase in language on gender has not necessarily enhanced protection. In 2016, 48 percent of Council resolutions included references to the WPS agenda, but the depth of these references with regard to coercive enforcement of protection is uneven (Security Council Report 2013; and see chapter 14 in this volume). The complex nature of wedding the WPS framework with international refugee, humanitarian, and human rights law, remains operationally muddy (see chapter 39 in this volume).

The WPS frame implies that a broad range of actions, and therefore actors, is important as well. Civil society and the media, for instance, have a role to play in programs that can shape gender hierarchies and values and attitudes that are associated with sexual violence. Entities such the Office of the United Nations High Commissioner for Human Rights (OHCHR), the Peacebuilding Commission, or the Human Rights Council, for instance, are important in terms of their relative influence in rule of law, governance, or peace-building processes. They may have an impact by contributing to a protective, gender-sensitive environment. Troop- and police-contributing countries to peace support operations are obliged to act appropriately to prevent SEA.

Finally, in the context of the WPS, protection intersects with other pillars of prevention, participation, and peace-building. The WPS frame calls for cross-pollination to transform the conditions that give rise to SGBV, and violence against women more broadly. The causes of violence are assumed as associated with gender discrimination, and its attendant asymmetries and hierarchies. Consequently, the tools for protection, at least indirectly, also pivot around notions of transforming deeply rooted values and attitudes. Striving to change them entails gender mainstreaming as well as increasing women's participation in political processes, economic activities, and the security sector (see UN Women 2015).

COMPARING THE TWO AGENDAS

The WPS agenda frames protection as gendered, and has influenced greater attention on SGBV against women and girls within the POC. It embraces a broader range of sexual violence acts (such as rape, sexual slavery, enforced prostitution, forced pregnancy, enforced sterilization) as the concerns of protection. These acts are not always visible, and are notoriously difficult to monitor and report. Moreover, to a certain extent, the UN is accountable for these harms both when civilians and combatants are victims. POC, as the name implies, is limited to civilians at risk of physical harm. This is a subtle yet important difference in terms of defining vulnerability and needs for protection.

While POC has been justified with reference to women and children, the protection language in peacekeeping mandates is generally gender-neutral, highlighting protection of civilians at risk of physical harm. Recent mandates more often see specific reference to protection from SGBV. This is then listed as a separate task and hence an addendum to the gender-neutral protection task. Protection measures in the WPS, on the other hand, have been fixated on female victimhood. For the majority of the last decades, the idea of protection has operated with an implicit assumption that women and girls are victims, and men and boys are perpetrators. The UN has placed conceptual emphasis on physical security of civilians in their gendered construction, making "her" or "him" implicit, direct beneficiaries of protection. This is thus fundamentally different from the overall

POC framework, which focuses on preventing harm to civilians at an aggregate level of the "conflict-affected population." This is likely a consequence of having arisen out of different normative and political roots.

The narrative of sexual violence as a weapon of war (see Eriksson Baaz and Stern 2013) facilitates the link between POC and WPS. This portrayal of wartime SGBV has dominated policy, at times reducing the reasons for its use by armed actors and groups to one particular motivation and discounting other explanations. Nevertheless, in policy terms, saying that sexual violence is a weapon of war helps to elevate the problem within the hierarchy of threats to peace and security (Carter 2010). This fits with the POC framework, and as such provides a reasonable basis for peace operations to act. If SGBV is always strategic, then similar measures taken to protect civilians in general, such as deterrence through patrols, should also be effective measures to protect women from sexual violence. The problem, however, is that sexual violence is a multifaceted phenomenon. Research suggests a number of other explanations for why sexual violence occurs within armed conflicts, focusing among other things on group-level functions (see e.g., Wood 2006, 2009, 2010, 2014; Lieby 2009; Cohen 2013; Cohen and Nordås 2014; Muvumba Sellström 2015a, 2015b; Hoover Green 2016). Case studies also highlight the more complex nature of sexual violence. For example, in a study of the UN mission in Chad and protection from SGBV, Solhjell, Karlsrud, and Lie (2010: 16) explicitly conclude that "SGBV is not a tactic of war in Chad." Hence, protection from SGBV may require particular responses from a peace operation that have not yet been sufficiently developed within the POC framework.

By moving away from the dominating "weapon of war" narrative, SGBV and gender-informed protection could be viewed in a more comprehensive way. This is not to say that these views are necessarily competitive. Nevertheless, with the current practice, POC strengthens only part of the WPS agenda, potentially at the cost of other WPS goals. The militarized approach to protection within the WPS agenda has also been critiqued for its "short-term, often physical" appeal to "a dominant masculinist logic," while participation and prevention are considered to focus more on "long-term social transformation" (Lee-Koo 2013: 40). Moreover, if POC pushes peacekeeping toward more robust mandates, involving the use of force to a greater extent, we cannot expect this to automatically translate into improved protection for women. Protection of women and protection from SGBV may require specific strategies and approaches on the ground (see, for example, chapter 35 in this volume, on delivering protection by all female peacekeeping forces). Furthermore, as pointed out by Nagelhus Schia and de Carvalho (2013), the problem of SGBV needs to be addressed in all rule-of-law institutions. The strong emphasis by the UN Special Representative on Sexual Violence on ending impunity may be a way forward in developing a wider array of tools for offering civilian protection equally for the whole civilian population.

Conclusions

This chapter has summarized the main trajectory of the POC framework, and related its content and evolution to the WPS agenda. The protection of civilians is specific to conflict and related humanitarian crises and is likely to remain limited to preventing physical harm. This is an important distinction from the WPS lens, which has erected the prevention, participation, and peace-building pillars, together with protection. All these are ideally meant to be mutually reinforcing. In contrast, the POC frame is positioned within the mandates of peace support operations and toward the shielding of civilians in gender neutral terms. The POC only focused on women in relation to their categorization as "innocents" and, to a certain degree, lumped them together with children. This formulation of "innocents" as "women and children" has not shifted dramatically over time, but the integration of the WPS agenda with the POC has led to other developments. A preeminent example of these developments is the turn toward protection against SGBV. Underscored by the "weapon of war" narrative for the logic of this violence, the POC now grasps physical vulnerability differently, expanding its conceptualization beyond killing or conflict-related physical violence and introducing new forms of protection at the level of peacekeeping operations. This expansion has its limitations, particularly since the WPS framework mainly conceived of sexual violence as a strategy used by armed actors (the weapon of war narrative) and originally limited its lens of victimhood to women and girls. With time and new research, these limitations are diminishing to conceive of other logics of sexual violence, to see its multifaceted forms in terms of motivation and type and to develop a wider, more holistic toolset for protection.

As UN actors move away from a singular focus on the weapon of war narrative, protection will thus evolve further. Efforts to insist on the establishment and enforcement of codes of conduct by the UN will take on greater importance. Peace support operations that tackle values and attitudes through training may address gender hierarchies and relations, while also securing the safety of women through patrols and escorts. When these measures cross-pollinate, either through engaging other WPS pillars or different POC tiers and strategies, protection will be better suited to disrupting the many logics of violence. To a certain extent, it is difficult to distinguish between the POC and WPS in relation to this particular form of protection, since the former is influenced by the latter and as the general tendency within policy development is to mainstream gender across a wide array of frameworks. In the realm of protection of civilians, this is a positive sign of advancement.

REFERENCES

Adebajo, A. *UN Peacekeeping in Africa: From the Suez Crisis to the Sudan Conflicts*. Boulder, CO: Lynne Rienner, 2011.

Bove, V., and A. Ruggeri. "Kinds of Blue. Diversity in UN Peacekeeping Missions and Civilian Protection." *British Journal of Political Science* 46, no. 3 (2016): 681–700.

Carpenter, C. R. *'Innocent Women and Children': Gender, Norms, and the Protection of Civilians*. Aldershot, UK: Ashgate, 2006.

Cohen, D. K. "Explaining Rape during Civil War: Cross-National Evidence (1980–2009)." *American Political Science Review* 107, no. 3 (2013): 461–477.

Cohen, D. K., and R. Nordås. "Sexual Violence in Armed Conflict: Introducing the SVAC Dataset, 1989–2009." *Journal of Peace Research* 51, no. 3 (2014): 418–428.

Costalli, S. "Does Peacekeeping Work? A Disaggregated Analysis of Deployment and Violence Reduction in the Bosnian War." *British Journal of Political Science* 44, no. 2 (2014): 357–380.

Eriksson Baaz, M., and M. Stern. *Sexual Violence as a Weapon of War? Perceptions, Prescriptions, Problems in the Congo, and Beyond*. London and New York: Zed Books, 2013.

Fjelde, H., L. Hultman, and D. Nilsson. "Protection through Presence: UN Peacekeeping and the Costs of Targeting Civilians." *International Organization* 73, no 1 (2019).

Holt, V. K., G. Taylor, and M. Kelly. "Protecting Civilians in the Context of UN Peacekeeping Operations: Successes, Setbacks, and Remaining Challenges." United Nations, Office for the Coordination of Humanitarian Affairs, 2009.

Hoover Green, A. "The Commander's Dilemma: Creating and Controlling Armed Group Violence." *Journal of Peace Research* 53, no. 5 (2016): 619–632.

Howard, L. M. *UN Peacekeeping in Civil Wars*. Cambridge: Cambridge University Press, 2008.

Hultman, L. "UN Peace Operations and Protection of Civilians: Cheap Talk or Norm Implementation?" *Journal of Peace Research* 50, no. 1 (2013): 59–73.

Hultman, L., J. Kathman, and M. Shannon. "United Nations Peacekeeping and Civilian Protection in Civil War." *American Journal of Political Science* 57, no. 4 (2013): 875–891.

Karim, S., and K. Beardsley. "Explaining Sexual Exploitation and Abuse in Peacekeeping Missions: The Role of Female Peacekeepers and Gender Equality in Contributing Countries." *Journal of Peace Research* 53, no. 1 (2016): 100–115.

Lee-Koo, K. "Translating UNSCR 1325 into Practice: Lessons Learned and Obstacles Ahead." In Davies, S. E., Nwokora, Z., and Stamnes, E., eds. *Responsibility to Protect and Women, Peace and Security: Aligning the Protection Agendas*. Leiden, NL: Brill, 2013.

Lieby, M. 2009. "Wartime Ssexual Vviolence in Guatemala and Peru." *International Studies Quarterlyy*, 53 (2009): 445–468.

Muvumba Sellström, A. "Stronger than Justice: Armed Group Impunity for Sexual Violence." Doctoral Dissertation, University of Uppsala's Department of Peace and Conflict Research, 2015a.

Muvumba Sellström, A. "Impunity for Conflict-Related Sexual Violence: Insights from Burundi's Former Fighters." In *Deconstructing Women, Peace, and Security: A Critical Review of Approaches to Gender and Empowerment*, edited by S. I. Cheldelin and M. Mutisi, 228–254. Cape Town: Human Sciences Research Council, 2015b.

Nabti, N. M. "Increasing the Cost of Rape: Using Targeted Sanctions to Deter Sexual Violence in Armed Conflict." In *Economic Sanctions under International Law: Unilateralism, Multilateralism, Legitimacy, and Consequences*, edited by A. Marossi and M. Bassett, 43–67. The Hague: T. M. C. Asser Press, 2015.

Nagelhus Schia, N., and B. de Carvalho. "Sexual and Gender-Based Violence and the Rule of Law in Liberia." In *The Protection of Civilians in UN Peacekeeping: Concept, Implementation, and Practice*, edited by B. de Carvalho and O. J. Sending, 181–196. Baden-Baden: Nomos, 2013.

Powers, M., B. W. Reeder, and A. A. Townsen. "Hot Spot Peacekeeping." *International Studies Review* 17, no. 1 (2015): 46–66.

Security Council Report. "Women, Peace, and Security: Sexual Violence in Conflict and Sanctions." Cross-cutting Report, no. 2, April 10, 2013, http://www.securitycouncilreport.org/atf/cf/%7B65BFCF9B-6D27-4E9C-8CD3-CF6E4FF96FF9%7D/cross_cutting_report_2_women_peace_security_2013.pdf.

Solhjell, R., J. Karlsrud, and J. H. S. Lie. "Protecting Civilians against Sexual and Gender-Based Violence in Eastern Chad." Security in Practice 7, Norwegian Institute of International Affairs, 2010.

United Nations Joint Human Rights Office (UNJHRO). Report on the Investigatin Missions of the United Nations Joint Human Rights Office into the Mass Rapes and other Human Rights Violations Committed in the Villages of Bushani and Kalamahiro, in Masisi

Territory, North Kivu, 31 December 2010 and 1 January 2011. July 2011, https://reliefweb.int/sites/reliefweb.int/files/resources/Full_report_174.pdf.

United Nations News. "New Task Force to Develop Strategy to Strengthen UN Response to Sexual Exploitation and Abuse." January 6, 2017. http://www.un.org/apps/news/story.asp?NewsID=55922&&Cr=sexual%20violence&&Cr1=#.WHY-x4W4USS

UN Secretary-General. "Report of the Secretary-General on Conflict-Related Sexual Violence." S/2016/361, 2016.

UN Security Council (UNSC). "Resolution 1270." [4054th Meeting]. S/RES/1270, 1999a.

UNSC. "Meeting Record." [4054th Meeting]. S/PV.4054, 1999b.

UNSC. "Resolution 1325." [On Women, Peace, and Security]. S/Res/1325, 2000.

UNSC. "Resolution 1674." [On Protection of Civilians]. S/Res/1674, 2006.

UNSC. "Resolution 1820." [On Acts of Sexual Violence against Civilians in Armed Conflicts]. S/Res/1820, 2008.

UNSC. "Resolution 1888." [On Acts of Sexual Violence against Civilians in Armed Conflicts]." S/Res/1888, 2009.

UNSC. "Resolution 1960." [On Women, Peace, and Security]. S/Res/1960, 2010.

UNSC. "Resolution 2106." [On Sexual Violence in Armed Conflict]. S/Res/2106, 2013.

UNSC. "Resolution 2147." [7150th Meeting]. S/Res/2147, 2014.

UNSC. "Resolution 2227." [7474th Meeting]. S/Res/2227, 2015.

UN Women. "Preventing Conflict, Transforming Justice, Securing the Peace—A Global Study on the Implementation of United Nations Security Council Resolution 1325." UN Entity for Gender Equality and the Empowerment of Women. October 12, 2015, http://www.peacewomen.org/sites/default/files/UNW-GLOBAL-STUDY-1325-2015%20(1).pdf.

Wills, S. Protecting Civilians: The Obligation of Peacekeepers. Oxford: Oxford University Press, 2009.

Wood, E. J. "Variation in Sexual Violence during War." Politics and Society 34, no. 3 (2006): 307–342.

Wood, E. J. "Armed Groups and Sexual Violence: When Is Wartime Rape Rare?" Politics and Society 37, no. 1 (2009): 131–161.

Wood, E. J. "Sexual Violence during War: Variation and Accountability." In Collective Crimes and International Criminal Justice: An Interdisciplinary Approach, edited by A. Smeulers, 295–322. Antwerp: Intersentia, 2010.

Wood, E. J. "Sexual Violence in Armed Conflict." International Review of the Red Cross 96, no. 894 (2014):457–478.

CHAPTER 47

....

WPS, CHILDREN, AND ARMED CONFLICT

....

KATRINA LEE-KOO

SINCE the publication of UNICEF's *Machel Report into the Impact of Armed Conflict on Children* in 1996, the United Nations has established significant global architecture around the protection of children living in conflict-affected zones. Children and Armed Conflict (CaAC), like Women, Peace, and Security (WPS), has become an important cross-cutting theme for the UN Security Council. The two agendas have had, in many ways, parallel trajectories. This has allowed the agendas to align in their common purpose to highlight the experiences of civilian groups in armed conflict. It also provides opportunities to strengthen the institutionalization of the agendas, build mechanisms for compliance, share data in overlapping areas of concern, and generate momentum in advocacy. Thus, there are areas where alignment is to the mutual benefit of each agenda. Despite these similarities, however, "women" and "children" are discrete constituencies, with unique experiences of armed conflict, and different needs and roles in post-conflict societies. As a consequence, they must be considered as independent categories of analysis. The tendency to collapse "womenandchildren" into a single conceptualization of victimized civilians can stifle and misrepresent both agendas.

The purpose of this chapter therefore is to map the opportunities for alignment, and areas of divergence of these two thematic Security Council agendas. It does so by comparing three areas of the agendas: their institutionalization and structural frameworks; their content, particularly as outlined in the thematic UN Security Council resolutions; and conceptualization of the central concepts of women, girls, and children within the agendas. Ultimately, this chapter recognizes that further alignment can reap rewards for both agendas, but that this must be pursued cautiously and reflectively so as to avoid endangering the potential each has to advance a better understanding of the relationship between each group, and peace and security. Thus, this chapter argues that while there are structural and technical benefits to alignment of the two agendas, they are conceptually unique and must be recognized as such.

THE CHILDREN AND ARMED CONFLICT AGENDA

The UN's Children and Armed Conflict agenda is animated by a single pillar: the protection of children in conflict zones. Tabled at the General Assembly in 1996, the report prepared by Graca Machel, entitled "Impact of Armed Conflict on Children," provided a grim overview of the task that lay ahead of the UN in establishing a protection framework:

> More and more of the world is being sucked into a desolate moral vacuum. This is a space devoid of the most basic human values; a space in which children are slaughtered, raped, and maimed; a space in which children are exploited as soldiers; a space in which children are starved and exposed to extreme brutality. Such unregulated terror and violence speak of *deliberate victimisation*. There are few further depths to which humanity can sink (UNGA 1996; emphasis added).

This report provided an urgent call for the UN to acknowledge the hidden devastation that armed conflict visits upon children. In 1999, the Security Council responded with the first of what are currently eleven thematic resolutions addressing Children and Armed Conflict (see Table 47.1). The foundational resolution, Resolution 1261 (UNSC 1999: [1]), brings to the Security Council's attention the harmful impact of armed conflict upon children, and highlights the "long-term consequences this has for durable peace, security and development." As the agenda has developed, a focus upon "six grave violations" has been identified. These are: (1) the recruitment and use of children; (2) the killing and maiming of children; (3) sexual violence against children; (4) attacks on schools and hospitals; (5) abduction of children; and (6) denial of humanitarian access (Office of the Special Representative, n.d.). While this is not a comprehensive list of issues affecting children in conflict zones, these six grave violations establish the priority areas for the Security Council, and the broader UN and NGO system.

While the Security Council has been largely responsible for setting this agenda, the bulk of dedicated advocacy and policy development within the UN system now sits with the UN Special Representative to the Secretary-General for Children and Armed Conflict, appointed in 1997, and her office. Established as a result of the recommendations of the *Machel Report*, the role of the Special Representative "is to strengthen the protection of children affected by armed conflict, raise awareness, promote the collection of information about the plight of children affected by war and foster international cooperation to improve their protection" (Office of the Special Representative, n.d.; see also UNGA 1997). The Office reports to the General Assembly and the Human Rights Council and provides advocacy and advice to the Security Council and individual member states on the implementation of the Security Council resolutions. While it coordinates and drives implementation practices, it relies upon partner UN agencies such as UNICEF and the UN Department of Peacekeeping Operations' Child Protection Unit, and NGOs to support on-the-ground activities including data collection and implementation of protection measures.

Table 47.1 A Shorthand Guide to the CaAC Resolutions

Resolution	Overview
1261 (1999)	Brings to the attention of the UN Security Council the harmful and widespread impact of conflict on children and its consequences for durable peace;
1314 (2000)	Stresses the importance of the protection of children in situations of conflict, and emphasizes the responsibility of all states to put an end to impunity and prosecute those responsible for abuses and violations of children;
	Reaffirms the importance of including child protection advisers in peace operations;
1379 (2001)	Calls upon parties to armed conflict to ensure the protection of children;
	Expresses readiness to include specific provisions in the mandates of peacekeeping operations;
	Requests the compilation of a list of parties who recruit and use children in violation of international law;
1460 (2003)	Calls for application of international norms and standards on the protection of children in armed conflict;
	Notes the cases of sexual exploitation and abuse of women and children, especially girls, in humanitarian crisis;
1539 (2004)	Requests the Secretary-General to urgently devise an action plan for a systematic and comprehensive monitoring and reporting mechanism, and calls on parties involved in the recruitment and use of children to prepare concrete time-bound action plans to halt this harmful process;
1612 (2005)	Establishes the monitoring and reporting mechanisms (MRM);
	Decides to establish a Security Council Working Group on Children and Armed Conflict to review implementation of the monitoring and reporting mechanism and action plans;
	Highlights the link between the use of child soldiers and the illicit trafficking of small arms and light weapons;
1882 (2009)	Expresses deep concern about the incidents of rape and other forms of sexual violence committed against children, including the use of sexual violence in some situations as a tactic of war;
	Calls upon member states to take decisive and immediate action against persistent perpetrators of violations and abuses committed against children;
	Calls to integrate the protection, rights, well-being, and empowerment of children into all peace processes and post-conflict recovery and reconstruction planning;
1998 (2011)	Urges parties to conflict to refrain from actions that impede children's access to education and health services including in particular attacks on schools and hospitals;
	Pays considerable attention to sexual violence committed against children in the situations of conflict; directs the Working Group on Children and Armed Conflict to support the Special Representative in increasing pressure on persistent perpetrators of violations and abuses committed against children;
	Invites the Special Representative to brief the Security Council;

Table 47.1 (*Contd.*)

Resolution	Overview
2068 (2012)	Expresses deep concern about persisting perpetrators of violations against children in armed conflict, and calls to bring them to justice through national justice systems and, where applicable, international justice mechanisms and mixed criminal courts and tribunals in order to end impunity; reiterates the readiness to adopt targeted and graduated measures against persistent perpetrators in line with earlier resolutions;
2143 (2014)	Urges member states to mainstream child protection when undertaking security sector reform; recommends the inclusion of child protection in military trainings and standard operating procedures; Recalls the importance of ensuring children's access to basic services;
2225 (2015)	Expresses grave concern about the abduction of children in situations of armed conflict, perpetrated in particular by non-state armed groups and violent extremist groups, and following abuses of their human rights, including sexual violence and slavery, particularly targeting girls; Urges for immediate release of abducted children; Stresses the importance of addressing the root cause of conflict to enhance the protection of children on a long-term basis.

INSTITUTIONAL ALIGNMENT BETWEEN WPS AND CaAC

From its inception, the CaAC agenda has developed a strong institutional framework that has subsequently facilitated its implementation. In this sense, it has had a different trajectory to WPS, which has struggled to establish a robust framework that ensures compliance. Swaine (2009: 409–410) notes that in terms of components that compel states to act, WPS can be compared unfavorably to—or seen to be lagging behind—the CaAC agenda. The strength of the CaAC agenda when compared to WPS is evident in the language used in the resolutions, mechanisms for implementation, reporting and monitoring, and the institutional infrastructure that has been developed to support advocacy and implementation. Established earlier than WPS, the CaAC framework has therefore provided a pathway, momentum, and lessons learned that the WPS agenda has benefited from.

Unlike WPS, the institutional infrastructure for CaAC was established early. The Office of the Special Representative was created in 1997 out of the recommendations of the *Machel Report* and was in operation to support the first thematic Security Council resolution adopted in 1999 (Resolution 1261). Alternatively, no equivalent office was established around the adoption of Resolution 1325. Reflecting one of the four WPS pillars, the Special Representative for Sexual Violence in Conflict and its associated office was established in 2010 under Resolution 1888 (UNSC 2009b: [4]), over a decade after the Children and Armed Conflict Office. Similarly, the Council's Children and Armed Conflict Working Group was created in 2005 pursuant to Resolution 1612 while no counterpart exists for WPS. However, in 2016 the Informal Experts Group on WPS was created in Resolution

2242 (UNSC 2015b: [5a]) as a result of recommendations of the 2015 *Global Study on the Implementation of UNSCR1325* (see UN Women 2015). This hybrid model—in which UN Women plays a Secretariat role—seeks to improve upon areas of perceived ineffectiveness and inflexibility of the Working Group model.

Monitoring and reporting mechanisms were created early in the Children and Armed Conflict agenda. Resolution 1379 (UNSC 2001: [16]) requests that the Secretary-General list in his annual report all state and non-state parties to conflicts listed on the Council's agenda who recruit or use children. Subsequent resolutions expanded this to include not just recognized conflicts but all situations of concern to the Secretary-General, and all six of the grave violations against children (beyond child recruitment). Parties which appear in this "naming and shaming" process are encouraged to develop and implement action plans to end the abuse of children, or remain on the list until the Secretary-General is convinced that the action plan has been implemented and the abuse has substantially ended. The formal establishment of the MRM—which reports on the six grave violations—occurred in Resolution 1612 (UNSC 2005). The MRM is designed to "to collect and provide timely, objective, accurate and reliable information on the recruitment and use of child soldiers in violation of applicable international law and other violations and abuses committed against children affected by armed conflict" (UNSC 2005: [2]). As demonstrative of the operation of the MRM, the Secretary-General's 2016 Report (UNGA 2016), lists fifty-nine parties in fourteen states as being responsible for such crimes.

A half a decade after Resolution 1612, Resolution 1960 (UNSC 2010: [8]) created a similar "naming and shaming" mechanism on sexual and gender-based violence within the Secretary-General's annual report. Here, offenders are similarly asked to make a commitment to prohibit and punish sexual violence. However, the language established in MARA (monitoring, analysis, and reporting arrangements) is arguably weaker than the MRM. Resolution 1612 (UNSC 2005: [2],[3])

> *requests the Secretary-General to implement without delay*, the abovementioned monitoring and reporting mechanism, beginning with its application, within existing resources, *in close consultation with countries concerned*, to parties in situations of armed conflict listed in the annexes to the Secretary-General's report . . .

In far less assertive language Resolution 1960 (UNSC 2010; emphasis added) "*expresses its intention* to use this list [of parties perpetrating sexual and gender-based violence] as a basis for *more focused United Nations engagement* with those parties including, as appropriate . . . with the procedures of the relevant sanctions committees." While there are procedures for action here, they are inhibited by weaker language.

However, even though the 2015 *Global Study on the Implementation of UNSCR1325* lamented the slow implementation of the WPS agenda, it is important to note that the agenda is supported by substantial civil society activism. This activism has been influential in encouraging UN member states particularly to develop implementation measures. At the time of writing, sixty-three UN member states have established National Action Plans (or NAPs) to guide their state's implementation of the agenda (PeaceWomen, n.d.). This is further supported by civil society monitoring of NAP implementation in many states, and robust, research-based debate on the agenda as evidenced in this handbook. This level of research and activism is not matched in the Children and Armed Conflict agenda. Outside of the activism of dedicated NGOs, there does not exist an extensive research base engaging with the agenda or advocating for its development.

CONTENT AND CONCEPTUALIZATION

The Children and Armed Conflict agenda embraced, from the beginning, a strong focus upon gender. Two months prior to the adoption of Resolution 1325 in October 2000, Resolution 1314 (UNSC 2000a: [16e]) urged regional organizations to "[i]ntegrate a gender perspective into all policies, programmes and projects." Elsewhere, the resolutions seek to highlight the particular vulnerabilities of the girl child. Again, Resolution 1314 (UNSC 2000a:[13]) acknowledges the special needs of girls "heading households, orphaned, sexually exploited and used as combatants." Passed in 2004, Resolution 1539 (UNSC 2004: [8]) emphasizes "the specific needs and capacities of girls" with reference to disarmament, demobilization, and reintegration processes. However, the remainder of gender-specific references to girls in the resolutions relate to sexual and gender-based violence. Indicative of this, Resolution 1379 (UNSC 2001: [8]) calls upon parties to conflict to "meet the special needs of girls affected by armed conflict and put to an end to all forms of violence and exploitation, including sexual violence, particularly rape." Similarly, Resolution 1539 (UNSC 2004: [10]) highlights sexual violence against girls when it "[n]otes with concern all the cases of sexual exploitation and abuse of women and children, especially girls, in humanitarian crisis, including those cases involving humanitarian workers and peacekeepers."

Importantly however, this initially strong focus upon gender is not maintained throughout the resolutions. This is evident in two ways. First, after 2004 there are no specific references to girls as uniquely or particularly vulnerable groups of children in conflict. Indicative of this, subsequent resolutions which "condemn rape and other forms of sexual violence" do so not against women and/or girls but "*against children*" (UNSC 2009a: [3]; emphasis added). Second, again after 2004, CaAC resolutions no longer reference Resolution 1325 or the WPS agenda in the Preamble, and no longer reference either "women and girls" or "women and children" in the text of the resolutions. The adoption of gender-neutral language is an important shift in the Council's conceptualization of the agenda. In part, this may have been prompted by data showing the extent to which sexual and gender-based violence targets both boys and girls. This was highlighted in 2005 when the UN launched an investigation into peacekeeper abuse of children and it was recognized that a number of the victims were boys. The change in language was therefore a corrective to a gendered assumption that it was solely or overwhelmingly girls who were targeted for sexual violence. This, in turn highlights the problems associated with overlaying the experiences of adult civilians onto children. Consequently, the extraction of "women" from the familiar terms "women and children" or "women and girls" is a move that recognizes the problems of associating the two groups without critical engagement or evidence-based translation of the issues from one group to another.

The WPS resolutions, on the other hand, have made consistent references to children. Interestingly, in all resolutions this is done within the "women and children" and "women and girls" terminology. Resolution 1325 (UNSC 2000b: preamble; emphasis added), for instance, expresses "concern that civilians, particularly *women and children*, account for the vast majority of those adversely affected by armed conflict" while the recent Resolution 2242 (UNSC 2015b: [15]) speaks of the need to consider "the specific impact of conflict and post-conflict environments on *women's and girls'* security, mobility, education, economic activity and opportunities . . ." References to girls and children are primarily made within the protection pillar or to a much lesser extent in the relief and recovery pillar. Boys—in the context of "men and boys"—have also been explicitly referenced in the more recent WPS resolutions in three capacities: as having a role to play in combatting violence against women, as being "secondarily traumatized as forced witnesses of sexual violence," both in Resolution 2106 (UNSC 2013a: preamble), and as needing to be engaged "as partners in promoting women's participation" in Resolution 2242 (UNSC 2015b: preamble). However, the primary reference to children as a subcategory of adulthood—predominantly womanhood—provides important insights into how the WPS agenda conceptualizes children as gendered beings and as people who experience conflict.

The collapsing of "womenandchildren" into a single conceptual framing has received substantial critique from feminist international relations scholars (see Enloe 1990; Brocklehurst 2006; Burman 2008). Feminists argue that joining these two categories presents women *as if they were children*, which in turn has a deleterious impact upon their capacity for agency and voice in sites of public or political decision-making. In this sense women, like children, are infantilized, domesticated, in need of protection, lack political consciousness, and have no agency, skill or, potentially, moral right to engage in public sphere activities such as peace-building or combat. The frustrating insistence upon continued linkage, feminists argued, has reinforced exclusionary practices that have culminated in women's absence from global peace and security activities and supported the overwhelming emphasis shown in the WPS agenda upon protection over participation.

However, there has been substantially less analysis on the impact that the "womenandchildren" conceptualization has upon children and the operation of children's rights in conflict-affected zones. Scholars and advocates should similarly engage with the representation of children's agency. In this vein, it is important to note that girls are virtually excluded from the participation pillar of the WPS agenda. Within the operative paragraphs of the resolutions, all references to girls are made within the framework of the Council's need to protect them. While there are four references to the participation and empowerment of girls in the WPS resolutions, these are strictly limited to the perambulatory paragraphs. Like the Children and Armed Conflict agenda, this serves to deny children agency, particularly within the realm of peace and security activities. In this sense, children are conceptualized as wholly victims of armed conflict with no recognized capacity to meaningfully contribute to transitions out of conflict or sustainable peace-building. The feminization of children similarly reinforces the denial of agency that is generated when women become infantilized in the "womenandchildren" framing. In both agendas, this approach denies the complex lived experiences of children who may demonstrate agency and impact in conflict zones (see Huynh 2015; Lee-Koo 2015; Berents 2014). Moreover, it also fails to substantially challenge masculinist imaginings of peace and security participation as activities that only occurs in formal spaces.

Where the Children and Armed Conflict agenda does acknowledge an active role for children is in the issue of child soldiering. While the agenda encompasses the aforementioned "six grave violations," the resolutions have developed a particular focus upon the first of these violations: ending the recruitment of children into armed groups. This is further emphasized in the 2002 Optional Protocol on the Convention of the Rights of the Child, and more recently the "Paris Principles" in 2007, which establishes a much stronger protection framework for child soldiers, a more inclusive definition of child soldiering (particularly to include noncombatant recruited children), and a stronger gender focus. Collectively, these documents underpin a number of the campaigns supported by the Office of the Special Representative around this issue. For instance, the 2010–2012 "Zero under 18" campaign generated twenty-one new ratifications of the Optional Protocol, while the 2014 "Children Not Soldiers" project (with UNICEF) similarly seeks to lobby conflict parties to end child recruitment.

While strong arguments can be made that child soldering represents a grave violation of children's rights, particularly where children's recruitment is forced, the Security Council's focus upon this issue nonetheless requires critical engagement. This is particularly the case when considered alongside the Security Council's focus within the WPS agenda on sexual and gender-based violence. In essence, both foci preference protection over empowerment and participation. In the case of child soldiering it should be noted that the participation being denied is likely to be both negative and super-empowered (see Lee-Koo 2011). However, the failure to recognize the complexities around children's recruitment and evidence of the capacity of some children to negotiate, manipulate, or be voluntarily recruited (see Huynh 2015) illuminates the Security Council's blanket denial of children's agency. This protection ethic is similarly evident in the Security Council's focus on sexual violence in the WPS resolutions. While this issue undeniably constitutes a major security concern for women in conflict-affected regions, it has been argued that the Security Council's primary focus upon this is problematic for at least two reasons. First, it similarly fails to acknowledge the complexities around some women's identities as *both* survivors of violence and agents of peace (see Shepherd 2011). Second, it reinforces a masculinist and paternal ethic of militarized protection that the Security Council finds both familiar and comfortable (Cook 2009).

This may also explain the divergent commitments to implementation by the Security Council. The stronger consensus and commitment to implementing CaAC—as opposed to WPS—is telling. Part of this might be explained by the fact that the CaAC agenda does not challenge the hierarchies that have been established in normative and mainstream visions of peace and security in sites such as the UN Security Council. The protection of children from violence in conflict—a single protection pillar of the agenda—might be seen as peripheral, but does not fundamentally disrupt hegemonic and masculinist regime of protection that the Security Council imagines for itself. As noted earlier, the same may be said about the preponderant focus and willingness to develop stronger implementation structures around sexual and gender-based violence in the WPS agenda, while the participation, prevention, and relief and recovery pillars have encountered significant implementation roadblocks. This may be because these agendas require structural reform and challenge the gendered hierarchies and relationships of power in peace and security economies.

CONCLUSION

Both the WPS and CaAC agendas have been animated by advocacy that identifies a direct link between the conflict-related experiences of women and children, and the UN Security Council's mandate to safeguard peace and security. These links have enabled attention to be shone on the relationship between conflict and the breadth of violence experienced by civilian groups. What the Security Council has been slower to engage with is the role that these groups can play—through both formal and informal participation—in the prevention and resolution of conflict, and the sustainability of peace. In the case of the WPS agenda, the framework for women's participation is there in the resolutions, but the implementation has been belabored. In the case of children, the resolutions offer virtually no capacity for children's agency to be identified or harnessed. As argued in this chapter, neither case is assisted by the conflating of children and girls with women.

However, while the rights of conflict-affected women, and conflict-affected children, need to be conceptualized and operationalized discretely, they are nonetheless allied agendas. There is visible institutional alignment between the two thematic causes. This creates opportunities for shared momentum, advocacy on implementation and compliance, data sharing, and learning from each other's experiences. In efforts to better ensure the protection of civilians and build an inclusive and sustainable approach to peacebuilding, the closer—albeit at times cautious—alignment of the two agendas will be an asset.

REFERENCES

Berents, H., "'It's about Finding a Way': Children, Sites of Opportunity, and Building Everyday Peace in Colombia." *The International Journal of Children's Rights* 22, no. 2 (2014), 361–384.
Brocklehurst, H. *Who's Afraid of Children? Children, Conflict, and International Relations.* London: Ashgate, 2006.
Burman, E. "Beyond 'Women vs. Children' or 'Womenandchildren': Engendering Childhood and Reformulating Motherhood." *International Journal of Children's Rights* 16, no. 2 (2008), 177–194.
Cook, S. "Security Council Resolution 1820: On Militarism, Flashlights, Raincoats, and Rooms with Doors—A Political Perspective on Where it Came From and What it Adds." *Emory International Law Review* 23 (2009): 125–139.
Enloe, C. "Womenandchildren: Making Feminist Sense of the Persian Gulf Crisis." *Village Voice*, September 25, 1990, 29–32.
Huynh, K. "Children and Agency: Caretakers, Free-Rangers, and Everyday Life.: In *Children and Global Conflict*, edited by K. Huynh, B. D'Costa, and K. Lee-Koo. Cambridge: Cambridge University Press, 2015.
Lee-Koo, K. "Children and Peace Building: Propagating Peace." In *Children and Global Conflict*, edited by K. Huynh, B. D'Costa, and K. Lee-Koo. Cambridge: Cambridge University Press, 2015.
Lee-Koo, K. "Horror and Hope: (Re)presenting Militarised Children in Global North—South Relations." *Third World Quarterly* 32, no. 4 (2011): 725–742.

Office of the Special Representative of Secretary-General. "Children and Armed Conflict, Children and Armed Conflict." Mandate, n.d.,

PeaceWomen. National Action Plans." Member states, n.d., http://www.peacewomen.org/member-states.

Shepherd, L. J. "Sex, Security, and Superhero(in)es: From 1325 to 1820 and Beyond." *International Feminist Journal of Politics* 13, no. 4 (2011): 504–521.

Swaine, A. "Assessing the Potential of National Action Plans to Advance Implementation of United Nations Security Council Resolution 1325." *Yearbook of International Humanitarian Law* 12 (2009): 403–433.

United Nations General Assembly (UNGA). "Children and Armed Conflict: Report of the Secretary-General." A/70/836, 2016.

United Nations General Assembly (UNGA). "Impact of Armed Conflict on Children. Report of the Expert of the Secretary-General, Ms. Graca Machel." A/51/306, 1996.

United Nations General Assembly (UNGA). "Resolution 51/77." A/RES/51/77, 1997.

United Nations Security Council (UNSC). "Resolution 1261." S/RES/1261, 1999.

United Nations Security Council (UNSC). "Resolution 1314." S/RES/1314, 2000a.

United Nations Security Council (UNSC). "Resolution 1325." S/RES/1325, 2000b.

United Nations Security Council (UNSC). "Resolution 1379." S/RES/1379, 2001.

United Nations Security Council (UNSC). "Resolution 1539." S/RES/1539, 2004.

United Nations Security Council (UNSC). "Resolution 1612." S/RES/1612, 2005.

United Nations Security Council (UNSC). "Resolution 1882." S/RES/1882, 2009a.

United Nations Security Council (UNSC). "Resolution 1888." S/RES/1888, 2009b.

United Nations Security Council (UNSC). "Resolution 1960." S/RES/1960, 2010.

United Nations Security Council (UNSC). "Resolution 2106." S/RES/2106, 2013a.

United Nations Security Council (UNSC). "Resolution 2242." S/RES/2242, 2015b.

UN Women. "Transforming Justice, Securing the Peace. A Global Study on the Implementation of United Nations Security Council Resolution 1325 (2000)." Lead author: Radhika Coomaraswamy. UN Women, 2015, http://wps.unwomen.org/pdf/en/GlobalStudy_EN_Web.pdf.

CHAPTER 48

WPS, GENDER, AND DISABILITIES

DEBORAH STIENSTRA

ONE of the key gaps, and thus an important opportunity, in implementing UN Security Council Resolution 1325 on Women, Peace, and Security (WPS) is found at the intersections of women and disability. While normative frameworks exist in relation to both women and disability, the Convention on the Elimination of All Forms of Discrimination against Women (CEDAW, adopted in 1979 and ratified by 189 countries) and the Convention on the Rights of Persons with Disabilities (CRPD, adopted in 2008 and ratified by 177 countries), women and girls with disabilities are disproportionately vulnerable to violence in conflicts and remain invisible and excluded from most post-conflict processes, including peace-building. While an increasing number of policy frameworks and scholarly publications call for an intersectional response that includes disabilities, there is little substantive analysis that addresses the unique situations of women with disabilities and by women with disabilities in conflict-affected situations.

WOMEN WITH DISABILITIES AND CONFLICT

Disability is a social construct that reflects the values and meanings given to diverse bodies and ways of walking, talking, perceiving, learning, thinking, and knowing. In many cultures, those whose bodies are outside what is considered "normal" or whose ways of being in or going through the world is different from the "norm" are considered disabled. The CRPD links those diverse bodies and ways of being with barriers in the environment that prevent full participation. "Persons with disabilities include those who have long-term physical, mental, intellectual or sensory impairments which in interaction with various barriers may hinder their full and effective participation in society on an equal basis with others" (CRPD 2008: Article 1). The 2011 World Disability Report (WHO and World Bank 2011) illustrates that approximately 1 billion people experience disabilities around the world, with the vast majority in countries of the Global South. In addition, more than half of people with disabilities are women and girls.

The CRPD goes beyond simply advocating access and participation for women with disabilities. It calls upon states parties to cultivate the capacity of women with disabilities to participate by promoting positive images of people with disabilities, and initiating measures to enable individual and independent participation by women with disabilities. This has particular implications for post-conflict settings.

> The CRPD obligates that persons with disabilities are able to act on their own behalf, creating an implicit guarantee regarding the provision and development of skills and resources that would permit this. When conflict ends, states and other organizations can draw on this obligation to ensure that programs move beyond aiding women with disabilities in accessing justice and developmental aid. Instead, these programs should also provide skills training, education, and similar capacity-oriented activities (Cornelsen 2012: 125).

In discussions related to conflict, peace, and security, having a disability is often equated with something wrong or lacking in one's body, and being vulnerable and in need of protection. Drawing on research from Smith-Khan et al. (2014) into refugee camps in Uganda, Malaysia, Pakistan. and Indonesia, Berghs (2015) suggests that the human rights and socially constructed approach to disability found in the CRPD is not widely used in these refugee and post-conflict settings. "In most of the refugee camps, despite the CRPD, disability was still seen as linked to a medical issue or health and identified mainly through physical impairment—easily identifiable and measurable" (749). In addition, most of the discourse related to disability found in relation to conflict is about the vulnerability of or protection for women with disabilities, rather than about their capacity and leadership in their own communities (Ortoleva 2011-2012: 400). As one woman with disabilities from the Democratic Republic of the Congo articulates, "Get to know us, not just as victims, but as women working to improve our own futures" (Sherwood et al. 2016: 30).

In many conflict-affected societies, there can be a hierarchy of impairments, with those who were soldiers in a war and acquired physical impairments, such as loss of limbs, receiving the greatest support, and often valorized for their roles in the conflict, while those who have congenital or non-conflict–related impairments are left with few supports and little access to education (Trani et al. 2012: 360). These cultural differences in response to disability, together with gender discrimination, mean that girls and women with disabilities have significantly less access to services, including education, and are usually invisible and excluded from the post-conflict transition processes (Trani et al. 2012; Bakhshi and Trani 2011).

In response to the predominantly medical view of disability, and the charity response often taken by donors and nongovernmental organizations, much of what is considered "disability-related" post-conflict funding may be for the prevention of impairments (landmine removal), equipment (wheelchairs and prosthetic devices), or rehabilitation services, rather than for capacity building or education (Stienstra and Estey 2016; Cornelsen 2012). For example, Canadian development assistance directed approximately 58 percent of its disability-identified funding to prevention and rehabilitation projects including preventing diseases, removing landmines, and rehabilitation. This is compared with roughly 46 percent of funding directed to all projects in the areas of inclusion, capacity building, and human rights (Stienstra 2017: 126–127). Lord and Stein (2015) argue that a medical approach to disability in conflict "misses the complex array of factors that contribute to the stigma and discrimination inhibiting the social inclusion of persons with disabilities generally in society, and ex-combatants in particular" and results in portraying those with disabilities as a burden to recovery rather than highlighting factors and barriers to their integration in post-conflict societies and the value of their participation. Berghs (2014) argues that the humanitarianism being promoted, in this case by the United Kingdom, is not focused "on inclusion but rather on impairment as a particular and at times preventable problem that costs money and affects state resources....That policy has as its goal a tactical approach that seeks to intervene to stop conflict, prevent causes of violence, and ensure neoliberalism" (Berghs 2014: 30).

Situations of conflict can be a cause of disability, as well as have significant impacts on those with disabilities. The World Bank (2007) argues, that conflict can directly and indirectly create disability:

> They cause significant numbers of physical and psycho-social disability directly through injuries, sexual abuse, mental and emotional distress, or indirectly though disruption of health and education services, lack of fuel, water, energy and jobs. Conflict and disasters are major causes of disability, but they also have a greater impact on those who are disabled, as such events with lack of access to information and services (13).

They argue further, that conflict can have significant long-term disability-related implications for societies.

> [C]onflicts and disasters are often associated with high prevalence of mental and psycho-social health problems, including post-traumatic stress disorder (PTSD). These "hidden disabilities" often affect a large proportion of the general population over a long period of time, and the economic and social impact can be quite devastating unless addressed at an early point. Recent research reveals that in post-conflict societies, mental health disorders represent a major obstacle to economic development through lost productivity, loss of learning capacity, and cost of treatment and care (World Bank 2007: 13).

Women and girls disproportionately experience the disabling effects of conflict, even though they are often not seen as affected by conflict. Cultural norms and stereotypes around women and disability combine to make women with disabilities uniquely invisible after conflict (Cornelsen 2012: 120). Women and girls with disabilities experience greater gender-based violence than women without disabilities or men with disabilities (Ortoleva 2010), which in turn can lead to increased risk for HIV and significantly effects their mental health. As a Women's Refugee Commission study (Pearce et al. 2014: 11) illustrates, adolescent girls with intellectual disabilities and women with mental health disabilities are particularly vulnerable to sexual violence. The same study reported that in conflict-affected Mindanao, girls with intellectual disabilities who did not live with their mothers and had traveled to urban areas to get income experienced sexual violence (Pearce et al. 2014: 12) in part because the community-related protective structures were absent. In addition, their credibility in reporting the violence to authorities was questioned, and made them reluctant to access services or report violence.

Women are also disabled by war and conflict, including through bombs, land-mines, and similar devices, and through the use of sexual violence as a weapon of war (Cornelsen 2012: 106). In northern Uganda, a Human Rights Watch study reported that "during the fighting, many women lost the use of limbs due to landmines or gunshot wounds, were mutilated by rebels, sustained injuries in fires, or were never vaccinated for disabling illnesses such as polio" (Barriga 2010: 6).

Some women experience disability-specific situations in conflict. For example, deaf and hearing-impaired women may not be able to hear conflict and flee (Jerry et al. 2015: 15). Some women with disabilities are abandoned or locked in a room when conflict occurs, or may be separated from their care providers (Jerry et al. 2015). For some women with disabilities escaping violence may mean leaving mobility or other disability-related aids behind (Jerry et al. 2015: 16; Ortoleva 2010).

In addition, women with disabilities may experience gender-specific situations in conflict, especially related to their caregiving responsibilities. Women with disabilities are often responsible for caring for their children, and women may also be responsible for the care of children with disabilities, and in conflict settings, this work is often unrecognized or undervalued (Berghs 2015: 750–751). In many situations, it is assumed that women will take on the caregiving of their spouses with impairments during and after conflicts (Samararatne and Soldatic 2015: 767). Those women with caregiving responsibilities may be isolated and not able to participate in their communities or activities because of these responsibilities. (Pearce et al. 2014: 13). This is a key post-conflict issue under the WPS "relief and recovery" pillar which tends to emphasize economic rather than social reconstruction.

Supports and services necessary for women with disabilities are often disrupted or inaccessible in situations of conflict (Ortoleva 2010). For those in refugee camps, services may be inappropriate or they may not be able to get to those services (Pearce 2015; Mizra 2011; Reilly 2010). Women with disabilities experienced the loss of community structures and protective mechanisms, especially in the context of new displacements (Pearce et al. 2014: 12) and have lost their own caregivers. As one researcher from Nigeria reported, "In crisis situations, women with disabilities suffer the most. I can run from danger but them, they cannot see. Their caregivers tend to leave them. Their caregivers violate them" (Jerry et al. 2015: 16).

All of this suggests, that while women and girls with disabilities are created and significantly affected by crisis situations, they are often invisible to those addressing the conflicts or providing supports for refugees. In addition, as countries move away from conflicts, their invisibility leads to their absence in peace-building discussions and decisions. The process of returning to peacetime society regularly excludes women with disabilities, and one of the most common approaches is to ignore them (Cornelsen 2012; Lord and Stein 2015), as research in Sri Lanka identifies:

> The interviews conducted among women who had acquired physical disabilities due to the internal armed conflict suggested that they had been marginalized both as victims of war and in any measures towards transitional justice and reconciliation (Samararatne and Soldatic 2015: 767).

Similarly, Nigerian women with disabilities spoke of their exclusion or absence from community peace forums. "When they did take part, they were not given a role and so were unable to contribute their perspectives, skills and talents" (Jerry et al. 2015: 17), and some were unable to participate because materials were not provided in a format that was accessible to them. In general, women with disabilities still do not largely take place in peace-building and continue to be marginalized after war. There is little access for women with disabilities to transitional justice post-conflict despite the disproportionate harm they experience (Cornelsen 2012).

NORMATIVE FRAMEWORKS RELATED TO WOMEN AND DISABILITIES

International normative frameworks address both the rights of women (CEDAW) and the rights of persons with disabilities (CRPD), among other norms related to indigenousness, culture, economic, and political rights. In this discussion CEDAW and the CRPD are the primary focus, even though CEDAW only addresses women with disabilities directly in several comments (Cornelsen 2012: 118), while the CRPD includes women with disabilities in Article 6. The CRPD Article 11 also requires that state parties implement positive measures of protection and safety for people with disabilities affected by humanitarian emergency and risk (Lord and Stein 2015: 286). As Cornelsen argues:

> Reading the CEDAW and the CRPD together constructs a stronger right to access, capacity, and agency, meaning a guarantee that the disabled woman will be empowered to act on her own. This can help her to escape common paradigm of "victim in need of help" after the conflict ends (2012: 118; see also chapter 52 in this volume).

In addition to Article 6 of the CRPD on women with disabilities, the Committee on the Rights of Persons with Disabilities (2016) recognized the importance of focusing on the intersections of women and disability by releasing a special interpretive comment. In it, they argue that states parties need to ensure that women with disabilities are full participants in decision-making.

> In line with a human rights-based approach, ensuring the empowerment of women with disabilities means promoting their participation in public decision-making. Women and girls with disabilities have historically encountered many barriers to participation in public decision-making. Due to power imbalances and multiple forms of discrimination, they have had fewer opportunities to establish or join organizations that can represent their needs as women and persons with disabilities. States parties should reach out directly to women and girls with disabilities and establish adequate measures to guarantee that the perspectives of women and girls with disabilities are fully taken into account. (Committee on the Rights of Persons with Disabilities 2016: 7)

In situations of armed conflict and humanitarian emergencies, the Committee notes that women with disabilities are at greater risk of sexual violence and less likely to have access to recovery and rehabilitation services or access to justice. They suggest that there are unique disability-related barriers that affect access to services, including having information in an accessible format. "When women with disabilities do receive information, they may not be able to physically access distribution points. Even when they do, they may not be able to communicate with staff" (2016: 12-13).

In her analysis of both CEDAW and CRPD, Cornelsen argues that because of CEDAW, women with disabilities can assert that they should be part of the post-conflict process (2012: 124). As a normative framework, the CRPD works to increase individual capacity, not simply to open up the space within which an individual can act (Cornelsen 2012: 125). Both CEDAW and CRPD, and international norms more generally, provide rallying points for social movement advocacy (Sabatello and Schultze 2014). Thus, it requires attention to both conventions to ensure the participation of women with disabilities in a post-conflict peace-building effort.

But creating systems that are open and accessible to women with disabilities is not sufficient, because of the historical invisibility of women and girls with disabilities and the stigma and prejudice they experience. As a result of their marginalized place in society, women and girls with disabilities may have little understanding of their rights or legal protections (Samararatne and Soldatic 2015). In situations of crisis or post-conflict, they may ask aid agencies for what they believe an agency can provide anyone, like household items or a latrine, rather than the disability specific needs they may have (Barriga 2010).

As a result, a prior step to the involvement of women with disabilities in post-conflict transitional processes is the development of the women's knowledge about rights. Lord and Stein (2015) suggest that legal empowerment of those who are marginalized in society not only helps their economic, social, and political participation, but rebuilds more inclusive legal and institutional frameworks for transition. This could be part of DDR (disarmament, demobilization, and reintegration) programs (Cornelsen 2012: 129). For rural women with disabilities, the challenges of gaining knowledge of and claiming their rights becomes even more profound:

> The combination of having a disability, being a woman and living in a rural area created a legal vacuum for these women, in that they were unable to access the law and legal systems—whether that was access to legal information to interpret the law and the necessary regulations, and understanding how to interpret and interact with the law and its regulatory framework via the administration process to advocate on one's behalf (Samararatne and Soldatic 2015: 769).

As women with disabilities learn about and claim their rights, it is also essential to ensure access to justice. This may be as simple as allowing a woman to tell her own story, which when someone has been invisible or told they were not an important part of society, can be very empowering.

> Building on this paradigm, a disabled woman's access to justice in the form of judicial institutions or ad hoc tribunals will require more than just a development of her legal capacity. Ensuring her capability to act as her own agent and realize her rights are two important elements to add to the standard (Cornelsen 2012: 133).

Women with Disabilities and Resolution 1325

A significant measure to support the inclusion of women in peace and security is Resolution 1325. (UN Women 2015) recognizes the diverse identities and situations of women, including disability, around the world and the impacts these can have on their abilities to participate and contribute to post-conflict rebuilding.

> It is well understood that these identities can intersect to amplify vulnerability; the Global Study also seeks to explore how intersectional identities can be tapped as a resource, to provide unique perspectives for the establishment and maintenance of peace and security in a world that is full of diversity (UN Women 2015: 34).

Despite this promise, there is little in the Global Study that addresses the situations of women with disabilities in peace, conflict, and security. When disability is addressed, it is primarily in the context of women providing care for those who have been disabled in conflict and concerns about reliance on their unpaid labor (UN Women 2015: 177–179). A particularly troubling part of the Study is its negative use of "blindness" as way to describe the absence of attention to gender by governments. This reinforces the view that disability, in this case blindness, is a lack in a human, rather than just another way of experiencing the world. Indeed, some have argued that only in the context of blindness does sight get its meaning (Michalko 2010). One noteworthy strength in the Global Study is its call for the involvement of grass-roots organizations in peace-building, especially those who experience "intersectional discrimination" (UN Women 2015: 303), which includes disability.

Resolution 1325 is made real through national action plans (NAPs), thus, it is important to examine how women with disabilities are addressed in these NAPs, especially in countries that have ratified both CEDAW and CRPD. Ortoleva (2011-2012) reviewed thirty-four NAPs noting that few countries included any reference to women with disabilities or issues of concern to them. Only nine countries, Austria, Finland, Italy, Liberia, Nepal, Rwanda, the United States, Uganda, and Georgia, included any mention of women with disabilities. Her findings confirm the themes identified earlier that there is a tendency "to focus merely on protection, rehabilitation, and victimization, rather than on the participation of women with disabilities in peace building and post conflict national institution and societal development" (399). She notes that there is little recognition of the impacts that war and conflict have on women with disabilities; organizations of women with disabilities appear not to have been consulted in the development of the reports; there is a lack of baseline indicators related to the situations of women with disabilities; and there is a significant gap between the normative human rights frameworks, especially the CRPD, and the approach to disability taken in NAPs.

These are significant gaps, and research to monitor and address them are critical to the successful implementation of Resolution 1325 generally. Ortoleva and her colleagues (2017) provide essential analysis and recommendations for the inclusion of women with disabilities in the NAP on Resolution 1325 of the United States, including the development of infrastructure, such as an internal disability liaison and support for the participation of women with disabilities and their organizations in developing peace-building and humanitarian relief programs. Australia's National Action Plan (Australian Government 2012) has also included some attention to the situations of women with disabilities. In addition, Canada's 2017 commitment to a feminist foreign policy, as well as its second NAP (Canada 2017), in conjunction with the government's commitment to new accessibility legislation in 2018, also offers some strategic opportunities.

CONCLUSIONS

Resolution 1325 provides a significant opportunity to ensure the full participation of women in peace-building and post-conflict transitions. The normative framework adopted in the 2015 Global Study on the implementation of 1325 is an intersectional approach. Yet, the type of intersectionality adopted is a "gender-first" approach. As I argue in relation to Canadian foreign and development policies (Stienstra 2017), a gender-first approach assumes that gender is the predominant factor and deals with other intersecting power relations in the context of gender. But the gender-first approach brings with it a set of often unexamined assumptions:

> This approach may be less useful for illustrating experiences in which other social locations, including disability, are the dominant factor. A gender-first approach may inadvertently make invisible other power relations at the expense of identifying gender inequalities. A gender-first intersectional approach may not be effective in explaining situations in which other power relations, such as disability, colonialism, or racism, shape the experiences of women, nor in supplying measures to provide redress for these inequalities (Stienstra 2017: 121).

As the scholarship discussed in this chapter suggests, women with disabilities remain invisible in post-conflict societies as well as in the measures taken to ensure the participation of women in peace and security. Women with disabilities are rarely viewed as leaders or actors in their own right or for the rights of all women. They are rarely viewed as peacebuilders, nor as those involved in revitalizing their countries post-conflict (Sherwood et al. 2016; Ortoleva 2011-2012). The exclusion of women with disabilities comes because no one thinks that they have anything to contribute and there are underlying negative attitudes and stigma related to both women and disabilities.

> Due to their perceived low intellect, it is often thought women with disabilities cannot play roles in decision-making in the household and community. As a result, women with disabilities are viewed as irrelevant, as being without contributions to make and so are marginalised from society (Jerry et al. 2015: 17).

Implementing an intersectional approach to Women, Peace, and Security in practice requires the support and participation of women with disabilities and their representative organizations; the shift to a human rights approach to disability in conflict, post conflict, and humanitarian crises, in line with the CRPD rather than a medical or health oriented approach; recognition and redress of the unique aspects of sexual and gender-based violence for women and girls with disabilities; critical reflection on social protection mechanisms to respond to women and girls with disabilities; donor initiatives that support capacity building including legal and human rights capacity, political participation, and education; and development and leadership of humanitarian actions and programs by women with disabilities. In addition, an intersectional approach to WPS will require women without disabilities to recognize and value the contributions of women with disabilities, and ensure they can contribute and provide leadership in rebuilding communities.

References

Australian Government. *Australian National Action Plan on Women, Peace, and Security 2012–2018*. March 2012, https://www.dss.gov.au/sites/default/files/documents/05_2012/aus_nap_on_women_2012_2018.pdf.

Bakhshi, P., and J. F. Trani. "A Gender Analysis of Disability, Vulnerability, and Empowerment in Afghanistan. In *Development Efforts in Afghanistan: Is There a Will and a Way? The Case of Disability and Vulnerability*, edited by J. F. Trani, 123–160. Paris: L'Harmattan, 2011.

Barriga, Shantha Rau. *"'As If We Weren't Human': Discrimination and Violence against Women with Disabilities in Northern Uganda."* New York: Human Rights Watch, 2010.

Berghs, Maria. "Radicalising 'Disability' in Conflict and Post-Conflict Situations." *Disability & Society* 30, no. 5 (2015): 743–758. doi:10.1080/09687599.2015.1052044.

Berghs, Maria. "The New Humanitarianism: Neoliberalism, Poverty, and the Creation of Disability." In *Disability, Human Rights, and the Limits of Humanitarianism*, edited by Michael Gill and Cathy J. Schlund-Vials, 27–43. Farnham, UK: Ashgate, 2014.

Committee on the Rights of Persons with Disabilities (CRPD). *General Comment: No. 3 (2016) Article 6: Women and Girls with Disabilities*. United Nations, CRPD/C/GC/3, September 2, 2016, http://www.ohchr.org/Documents/HRBodies/CRPD/GC/Women/CRPD-C-GC-3.doc.

Cornelsen, Kathleen. "Doubly Protected and Doubly Discriminated: The Paradox of Women with Disabilities after Conflict." *William & Mary Journal of Women and the Law* 19 (2012): 105.

Government of Canada. *Gender Equality: A Foundation for Peace: Canada's National Action Plan 2017–2022*. Ottawa: Global Affairs Canada, 2017.

Jerry, Grace, Patricia Pam, Chukwuma Nnanna, and Chitra Nagarajan. "What Violence Means to Us: Women with Disabilities Speak." Nigeria Stability and Reconciliation Programme and Inclusive Friends, 2015, .

Lord, Janet E., and Michael Ashley Stein. "Peacebuilding and Reintegrating Ex-Combatants with Disabilities." *The International Journal of Human Rights* 19, no. 3 (2015): 277–292. doi:10.1080/13642987.2015.1031515.

Michalko, R. "What's Cool about Blindness?" *Disability Studies Quarterly* 30, no. 3/4 (2010), http://dx.doi.org/10.18061/dsq.v30i3/4.1296.

Mirza, Mansha. "Disability and Humanitarianism in Refugee Camps: The Case for a Travelling Supranational Disability Praxis." *Third World Quarterly* 32, no. 8 (2011): 1527–1536. doi:10.1080/01436597.2011.604524.

Ortoleva, Stephanie. "Women with Disabilities: The Forgotten Peace Builders." *Loyola of Los Angeles International and Comparative Law Review* 33 (2010): 83–142.

Ortoleva, Stephanie, and Alec Knight. "Who's Missing—Women with Disabilities in UN Security Council Resolution 1325 National Action Plans." *ILSA Journal of International & Comparative Law* 18 (2011-2012): 395.

Ortoleva, Stephanie, Amanda McRae, and Rhianna Hoover. "When War Forgets Women and Girls with Disabilities: Recommendations for the US National Action Plan on Women, Peace, and Security." US Civil Society Working Group Policy Brief, March 22, 2017, https://www.usip.org/sites/default/files/7th-US-CSWG-Policy-Brief-March-31-2017-v3.pdf.

Pearce, Emma. "'Ask Us What We Need': Operationalizing Guidance on Disability Inclusion in Refugee and Displaced Persons Programs." *Disability and the Global South* 2, no. 1 (2015): 460–478.

Pearce, Emma, Dale Buscher, and Women's Refugee Commission. *Disability Inclusion: Translating Policy into Practice in Humanitarian Action*. New York: Women's Refugee Commission, 2014.

Reilly, Rachael. "Disabilities among Refugees and Conflict-Affected Populations." *Forced Migration Review* 35 (2010): 8–10.

Sabatello, Maya, and Marianne Schultze, eds. *Human Rights and Disability Advocacy*. Philadelphia: University of Pennsylvania Press, 2014.

Samararatne, Dinesha W. V. A., and Karen Soldatic. "Inclusions and Exclusions in Law: Experiences of Women with Disability in Rural and War-Affected Areas in Sri Lanka." *Disability & Society* 30, no. 5 (2015): 759–772. doi:10.1080/09687599.2015.1021760.

Sherwood, Elizabeth, Emma Pearce, and Women's Refugee Commission. "'Working to Improve Our Own Futures': Inclusion of Women and Girls with Disabilities in Humanitarian Action." Women's Refugee Commission, May 2016, https://www.womensrefugeecommission.org/populations/disabilities/research-and-resources/1342-networks-women-disabilities.

Smith-Khan, L., M. Crock, B. Saul, and R. McCallum. "To 'Promote, Protect and Ensure': Overcoming Obstacles to Identifying Disability in Forced Migration." *Refugee Studies* (2014). doi:10.1093/jrs/feu020.

Stienstra, D. "Lost without Way-Finders? Disability, Gender, and Canadian Foreign and Development Policy." In Obligations and Omissions: Canada's Ambiguous Actions on Gender Equality, edited by Rebecca Tiessen and Stephen Baranyi, 115–138. Montreal: McGill-Queen's University Press, 2017.

Stienstra, Deborah, and Steve Estey. "Canada's Responses to Disability and Global Development." *Third World Thematics: A TWQ Journal* 1, no. 3 (2016): 382–395.

Trani, J. F., Parul Bakhshi, and Anand Nandipati. "'Delivering' education; Maintaining Inequality: The Case of Children with Disabilities in Afghanistan." *Cambridge Journal of Education* 42, no. 3 (2012): 345–365.

UN Women. "Transforming Justice, Securing the Peace. A Global Study on the Implementation of United Nations Security Council Resolution 1325 (2000)." Lead author: Radhika Coomaraswamy. UN Women, 2015, http://wps.unwomen.org/pdf/en/GlobalStudy_EN_Web.pdf.

United Nation. Convention on the Rights of Persons with Disabilities. 2008. http://www.un.org/disabilities/documents/convention/convoptprot-e.pdf

World Bank. *Incorporating Disability-Inclusive Development into Bank-Supported Projects*. Washington DC: Social Development Department, World Bank, 2007.

World Health Organization and the World Bank. *World Report on Disability*. Geneva: World Health Organization, 2011.

CHAPTER 49

WPS AND HUMANITARIAN ACTION

SARAH MARTIN AND DEVANNA DE LA PUENTE

ROSALBA[1] a woman in her fifties, sits by a dirt road in a rural Colombian community in a country emerging from fifty-two years of armed conflict. Years ago, she was displaced by the fighting and currently lives in an informal settlement. She could only find work in an illegal mine where she worked until she lost her right leg in an accident at a mine that is the main source of work for the community. Armed groups (that are not involved in the peace process) control the mine. The government does not provide this informal settlement with any services—no healthcare or secondary education and she supports her 5-year-old grand-daughter who was abandoned by her parents.

Fatima[2] is a 35-year-old Rohingya woman living in the Rakhine region of Myanmar. She fled to this remote settlement with her four children after militant Buddhist groups burned their village. In the remote camp where she lives, there is no school for her children and very few services. The government has blocked many international NGOs from working there. Her husband would like to marry her 12-year old daughter off to an older man to alleviate household costs. Their closest neighbors, Buddhist Rakhine villagers, often attack the camp and women have stopped using the latrines near the settlement at night for fear of sexual assault.

Both of these women are living in "humanitarian settings," supported by a system designed to deliver short-term relief for disaster- and war-affected people who were expected to return home relatively quickly. Yet in many humanitarian settings around the world, return is uncertain and generations remain displaced (Bennett et al. 2016). In the ideal humanitarian system, there is a smooth cycle as humanitarians deliver essential life-saving support and then the people rebuild their houses and move home as soon as the "good guys" win and a peace agreement is signed. The humanitarian aspect of this scenario is focused on essential services—food, water, shelter, emergency healthcare, and basic sanitation delivered to gender-neutral "people" living in camps.

In theory, there is a continuum from humanitarian relief to recovery: a clear end to the humanitarian relief phase where the peace-building and development actors (like the government) step in. In this theory, humanitarians and peace-building actors work together with men and women to build the peace and improve gender equality. Unfortunately, this does not occur in practice. The "tyranny of the urgent" excuses humanitarians from having to think about gender-specific humanitarian response or promoting gender equality, pushing it off to "later" and reflecting the too-common reality that "later is a patriarchal time zone" (Enloe 2006) which leaves the voices of displaced women ignored.

Rosalba and Fatima are representative of the many women around the world affected by armed conflict whose needs fall somewhere in the grey area between "humanitarian," "peacebuilding," and "development." They live in a typical protracted post-conflict humanitarian settings—places that still experience violence despite the presence of peace dialogues and agreements. During the "relief to recovery" pillar of the UN Security Council Resolution 1325, Rosalba and Fatima are voiceless. As displaced women, they still struggle to survive and keep their families together in absence of either humanitarian or development support.

This chapter uses examples drawn from the authors' experiences as gender specialists in humanitarian settings[3] to illustrate the gap that threatens the implementation of the "relief and recovery" pillar of 1325. It argues that by ignoring gender issues and failing to incorporate women's specific needs and interests into humanitarian response, the sector deepens the divide between humanitarian, post-conflict, and development, making it more difficult for displaced and affected women to be properly and effectively engaged in the relief peace-to-development continuum. Peacebuilding and humanitarian actors must more work closely together and align their interventions to promote gender equality and a women, peace, and security agenda. Women affected by the crises, and the local women's organizations who might give these women a voice, must be allowed to lead. Most importantly, all actors should ensure that they provide support to overcome the blockages to allow for their meaningful participation, particularly for women who might experience greater barriers, such as refugees, stateless, ethnic, and rural women.

UNDERSTANDING GENDER
IN HUMANITARIAN ACTION

Gender in Humanitarian Action (GiHA) is the term for the integration of gender equality in the humanitarian sector and ensuring that the needs of women, girls, men, and boys are reflected in humanitarian needs assessments, program design, and implementation. Often, practitioners focus on women and girls, due to the assumption that they are more vulnerable and therefore require emergency attention. Humanitarians strive to meet the practical needs of their program beneficiaries by delivering life-saving services, which are always prioritized but usually in a gender-blind way. Even if humanitarians acknowledge women and girls' particular biological needs, they are rarely prioritized in humanitarian programs. For example, humanitarian needs assessments have highlighted the importance of menstrual hygiene management for women and adolescent girls (Sommer 2012; Krishnan and Twigg 2016). In a multisectoral assessment conducted after the 2015 Nepal earthquake, women and adolescent girls prioritized sanitary materials and safe access to bathing facilities. About 48 percent of women said that they had not been able to access services or information specific to proper sanitation practice and disposal of menstrual pads (OCHA and UN Women 2016). Menstrual hygiene was of particular protection concern in Nepal given the issue of *chhaupadi*, a harmful traditional practice where girls are forced to live outside of the house while menstruating. *Chhaupadi* places Nepali girls at increased risk of sexual violence and abuse—in fact, girls who slept elsewhere during their periods were more than twice as likely to report they had been raped since the earthquake (4 percent) than other girls (1.7 percent) (Her Safety Assessment Report 2015). Yet, the issue was still not adequately addressed by humanitarians in Nepal (or many other contexts) (Robinson and Obrecht, 2016; Sommer et al. 2016). Helping the humanitarian sector see, understand, and then address women and girl's basic needs is challenging. Ensuring that women and girls meaningfully participate in decision-making within the humanitarian response is even more so.

The Challenges of Incorporating Gender into Humanitarian Action

The global governing body for humanitarians, the Inter-Agency Standing Committee (IASC)'s gender policy outlines the humanitarian sector's commitment to promote gender equality in humanitarian response (Inter-Agency Standing Committee 2008). It states that the human rights of women, girls, boys, and men are to be equally promoted and protected in humanitarian action and that gender equality should be taken into consideration at all program levels, from contingency planning prior to the onset of an emergency to all stages of humanitarian response (i.e., immediate response to early recovery and to reconstruction and transition). The key humanitarian guidance tools to support this include the IASC Gender Handbook (Inter-Agency Standing Committee, 2005), the IASC Gender Marker,[4] the deployment of Gender Capacity (GenCap) Advisors[5] to Humanitarian Country Teams (HCT), and an increased focus on incorporating gender into the humanitarian architecture, also known as the cluster system.[6]

The dedicated work of gender advocates, feminists, and engaged policymakers who are committed to ensure that local women have their voices heard and taken into account has resulted in progress in several policy frameworks and processes to promote gender equality. The 2016 World Humanitarian Summit (WHS) has as one of its seven High Level Roundtable commitments, the promise to "catalyze action to achieve gender equality" to make humanitarian programming gender responsive and to empower women and girls as change agents and leaders (UN 2016). Some international organizations have begun to promote these commitments. In 2017, after Hurricane Matthew, ActionAid Haiti's women-led community committees (comprised of community representatives that required 60 percent women) were established very early in the response (Mitaru et al. 2017). In Colombia, the HCT has also promoted the inclusion of local women's organizations in coordination teams to promote women's role as decision-makers and not just as victims (de la Puente and Morales 2016).

Despite the copious global commitments, tools, and progressive discourse, there are still major gaps. Working on gender equality by prioritizing women's leadership, particularly the leadership of local women, is still not meaningfully incorporated into humanitarian action. The WHS one-year self-report on gender stated that several respondents spoke of the difficulty of cultural norms and beliefs hindering efforts to advance gender equality and the empowerment of women and girls. Local women's organizations continue to have difficulties accessing humanitarian funding and engaging in humanitarian processes. At the WHS, a national NGO based in India vocalized the opinions of many women's groups—that most global processes remain dominated by powerful actors who still do not adequately engage frontline organizations, but continue to make decisions on their behalf.

So despite progress in global strategies and policies, actual humanitarian response continues as normal. The issue of water and sanitation is a good example of the failure to incorporate women into leadership. In every humanitarian setting, it is a fact that women become more vulnerable to violence when they have to go to urinate in dark unlit places in order to preserve their modesty. Some men take advantage of this vulnerability and attack women and girls. Because of this, women are afraid of going alone to the bathroom in the dark of night—even armed female combatants (Benedict 2007). Despite this knowledge, in over thirty years of humanitarian response, water and sanitation colleagues have been unable to prioritize consulting women about their safety while taking care of this most basic of needs. In the words of Julie Lafrenière at a 2015 conference on Women, Peace, and Security, "*We cannot achieve long-term change that transforms the lives of those living in poverty or those affected by conflict and natural disasters if half of the world's population isn't included in the consultations, design, or implementation, whether of latrines, or camps, or peace processes*" (Alowis et al. 2015).

Humanitarian actors often create community WASH committees but fail to insure women are meaningfully involved, which means that women are rarely consulted about where latrines should be placed. Water points are placed far from areas where women cook which leads to girls being taken out of school to fetch water all day. Shelters are constructed without adequate privacy considerations that place women and girls in dangerous proximity to men and boys and leading to increased risks of sexual exploitation, rape, and sexual harassment. Even in humanitarian responses in countries in the Global North, like Germany and Greece, which have access to a stable and secure operating space, ample financial resources, and access to trained international organizations and global tools, these same problems arise (Müller et al. 2017). Despite many years of efforts by gender equality activists like the authors, the humanitarian sector has not meaningfully incorporated the perspectives of women and girls into their needs assessments or program design. The net result is that ignoring the views and experiences of women and girls in humanitarian programming has resulted in violence against women and girls. Solving the problem of how to effectively insure women (and their local women's organizations) are listened to in humanitarian action will also solve some of the wider problems of including women's involvement in the full continuum of peace, security, and development.

Neglecting Gender Equality in Disaster Preparedness and Risk Reduction

In humanitarian emergencies, the "business as normal" reigns due to pressure to respond. The "humanitarian cowboy" often arrives in emergencies to lead the international response and immediately begins to organize actions based on their experience from the past. They neglect to seek out information on local capacity—particularly the capacity of women's organizations, and instead jump to conclusions based on their own experiences and assumptions

The 2015 Nepal earthquake response is an example. In 2011, the European Commission for Humanitarian Aid Operations (ECHO) funded a GBV in emergency capacity-building intervention in Nepal (Martin 2011). There were four Nepali women's organizations that worked on peacebuilding and development that were taught the basics of responding to GBV in humanitarian emergencies. One recommendation was that UN agencies in Nepal should link the local women's organizations with disaster risk reduction (DRR) actors to prepare for natural disasters. After the earthquake, before international actors were deployed, the project investment paid off as these organizations responded immediately to the needs of disaster-affected women. During a post-disaster discussion, it came out that the UN's initial needs assessments used no female data collectors. The male-dominated international first responders made excuses—women were "too frightened to go out"—that were quickly disproven as local women's organizations had mobilized humanitarian response within hours of the earthquake. Another excuse was that trekking companies were used for recruitment and since "no women are able to carry heavy things up and down mountains," no women were recruited (ignoring the fact that women who live in the mountain communities carry heavy things regularly and that there are many women sherpas who work commercially to lead treks). Valuable information was lost due to these assumptions.

Targeted outreach to local women's organizations in DRR programs is an effective way to mainstream gender equality into humanitarian response. In 2014, the authors were involved in organizing a conference in the Philippines on "*Disaster prevention, preparedness, and response in South and Southeast Asia: Maximizing a Gender Inclusive Approach.*" At first, some DRR specialists felt that the workshop should help DRR specialists develop tools to improve understanding gender issues. However, with the assistance of the gender experts, the agenda was eventually changed to engage local women's organizations in Pakistan, Nepal, Philippines, Vietnam, and Bangladesh to show the DDR community the vibrant work that local women's organizations were already doing on gender and disasters. The blockage was not that no one was paying attention to gender—it was that the mostly male DDR specialists and national disaster management officers were either unaware or uninterested in looking at the work that women's groups were already doing on the issue. The combination of a lack of awareness of women's organizations, poor prioritization of women's issues, and that there were very few women in the room in the first place to point out the issue led to it being overlooked.

Integrating Gender in Humanitarian Response Leads to Greater Participation of Women in Post-Conflict

A conflict doesn't necessarily end just because a ceasefire is signed and the signing of a peace agreement doesn't necessarily end violence—particularly against women and girls. During conflict, the use of violence and power over women, particularly sexual violence, is often normalized. Even when the conflict is over, armed groups and criminal gangs continue to use violence. Illegal trade, smuggling, and drug trafficking flourish in many post-conflict areas and women are still subjected to GBV.[7] Governments that have signed peace agreements are often keen to end the humanitarian phase and move rapidly to the "post-conflict" or development stage in order to end sanctions and encourage economic investment, ignoring the violence that is targeting women.

In 2003–2005, the demobilization and disarmament settings in Liberia and Sierra Leone found that the needs of female combatants were ignored in favor of pushing them quickly through a demobilization, disarmament, and reintegration process to move the country into the development/post-conflict agenda. Many female combatants were rape survivors and ostracized from their communities, leaving them unable to return home. Female former combatants expressed the desire to start small businesses in Monrovia because of ostracization from their communities. To support themselves and their children, some had returned to the areas where they had been demobilized to sell sex to UN peacekeepers in order to feed and support their children. Vulnerable female combatants found that their livelihood needs were not prioritized in the push to move from humanitarian response to economic development (Martin, 2005).

In 2009, in Sri Lanka, three years after the end of the conflict between the *Liberation Tigers of Tamil Elam* and the Sri Lankan government, the humanitarian community was alarmed by the government's haste in phasing out humanitarian support in the North and Eastern part of the country. The government was eager to promote foreign investment and economic development in the North, something that might be hampered by the presence of humanitarian actors. Humanitarian actors were still raising concerns regarding the safety of single women, conflict widows, and those left by their partners who had migrated for work (Niland et al. 2014). This shift from humanitarian programming to government-led development programming meant that the international humanitarian community that supported GBV programming lost funding, ending support to security and safety mechanisms for women and girls in highly militarized areas of return, placing them at high risk of violence and affecting women's access to land, income, and political participation (de la Puente 2012).

In Myanmar, after the country's move toward constitutional reform in 2010, the military junta proactively sought peace agreements with many armed groups throughout the country to avoid the appearance of ongoing instability and to encourage the lifting of economic sanctions. It also limited humanitarian organizations from working in the southern Rakhine State where the ethnic Muslim minority, the Rohingya, were being forcibly displaced, persecuted, and attacked by Rakhine Buddhists. Development agencies that did not work too closely with the displaced Rohingyas were allowed more freedom. Médecins Sans Frontières (MSF), a humanitarian organization that provides medical care, was harassed by the government as it treated victims of violence, as well as sexual violence, in their medical and mental health programs (Hodal 2014) and was eventually expelled (Perlez 2014). Rohingya women alleged sexual abuse by the military, and MSF's policy of bearing witness (*témoignage*) to the abuse was leading to international scrutiny of the newly elected government, which claimed to be moving toward peace agreements and democracy (Bradford 2017). The government succeeded in getting the sanctions lifted, but the violence, particularly sexual violence, has continued unabated (Human Rights Watch 2017, Refugees International 2017).

Often, the local women's organizations and women human rights defenders who speak out about this violence become the target of the violence, as documented in Colombia, Honduras, Myanmar, and Sri Lanka (Barcia 2011). In an unpublished report, women human rights defenders in Myanmar spoke of being subjected to harassment, arbitrary detention, and violence, including sexual assault by the government. They are branded as "rebel wives," putting them at risk of interrogation, extrajudicial punishment, torture, or sexual assault under the pretext of national security. As a result, many women activists have found it difficult to continue visiting sexual violence survivors for fear of attack and have fled Myanmar. Those in exile fear having their name added to the Ministry of Home Affair's "blacklist" and denied the right to return (Article 19 n.d.).

In 2016, the government of Colombia and the main rebel group, *Las Fuerzas Armadas Revolucionarias de Colombia—Ejército del Pueblo* (FARC-EP) signed a peace deal to end fifty years of conflict. Enthusiastic media coverage about the historic peace deal allowed the Colombian government to promote their economic development agenda as the "war was over." During the conflict, sexual violence was prevalent and is still being perpetrated by armed groups who are not party to the peace deal and who have taken control of former FARC-controlled areas. The Ombudsman's office reported an increase in conflict-related sexual violence for eighty-five municipalities where conflict continues with other armed groups who are not part of the peace deal (Defensoria del Pueblo, Colombia 2017). The government would like to refocus donor attention toward their economic development agenda but the ongoing violence threatens the safety of the population, particularly women and girls. The number of threats to women human rights defenders has increased by 31 percent, which is limiting active engagement of women in peace-building (United Nations Security Council 2017). The international community has followed the government's lead and begun reducing humanitarian operations in the country, ignoring the threats and risks to peace that the ongoing violence poses, particularly for women and girls, including FARC's female ex-combatants who comprise about 35 percent of the armed forces.

Women from Post-Conflict Areas Are Excluded

Despite progress in trying to bring gender awareness into DDR, humanitarian, peace-building, and development efforts, the cohort of women who are allowed to participate in any of these peace agreement discussions is small. It is considered a huge success getting any women to the table at all—let alone having diversity within the women and attempting meaningful representation of women living in humanitarian settings. If certain women do succeed in being heard in these fora, it is often because these women are often considered "exceptional," and that is how they are able to sit in with the men—for example, they tend to be a member of the elite with access to education.

Women's rights activists at the national level often do not represent the needs and voices of women in rural and remote areas—let alone the displaced women. Peacebuilding efforts that do focus on incorporating women often ignore first responders during humanitarian efforts, like the local Nepali rural women's groups, and tend to be dominated at the national and international levels, rather than meaningfully involving and consulting with women who have experienced the conflict themselves. The process of involving women in peacebuilding and humanitarian response often suffers from "elite capture"—the process whereby resources designated for the benefit of the larger population are usurped by a few individuals of the superior status—be it economic, political, educational, ethnic, or otherwise. Most of the women's groups who are the most represented in peace talks, international conferences, and in literature are the ones who are from the urban areas and have accessed formal education and speak English better than those displaced from the mostly rural areas where conflicts take place. Representatives from women's organizations who do not speak English and may not be perceived as very Western-friendly are often excluded from the table and decision-making completely.

For example in Pakistan, the women of the local NGOs in urban strongholds of Karachi and Islamabad are fearless advocates of women´s rights. However, they don't necessarily represent the perspective of women in the rural areas of Sindh or Federally Administered Tribal Areas—where women have little to no rights and no space to exercise them.[8] The national agenda around women´s rights is led by highly educated women who have achieved great results on women´s participation and engagement in politics and labor, yet they don´t represent women in remote rural areas, most of whom are not permitted to be seen in public, who are illiterate, or must work in dangerous settings to provide basic necessities for their families.

In Nepal, the Maoist insurgency impacted rural areas the most. Despite efforts of the international community to create fora and events to promote women's involvement in the peace processes, the actual negotiations that took place were mostly male dominated. Even in these international efforts to get women involved, small women's NGOs from rural areas felt that they were marginalized and pushed aside in favor of well-known women's organizations from Kathmandu whose leaders have traveled internationally and were educated outside the country.[9]

In some cases, the women at the table might be the women of the diaspora who are returning to help rebuild their countries (as it has been in post-conflict times in Libya, Afghanistan, Liberia, and Northern Uganda). In 2013, the Preventing Sexual Violence Initiative (PSVI) launched a mission to Libya to document conflict-related sexual violence and provide guidance to incorporating women into the peace and security agenda (Foreign and Commonwealth Office 2014). A consultative meeting with women's rights activists found that the loudest and most engaged voices came from the Libyan diaspora in the United States, the UK, and Tunisia, women who had returned to work on women's issues. Women who had lived in Libya during the Qadaffi regime were present, but were more reluctant to speak out on issues. Internally displaced women were not present at all.

This raises the question, how can women from conflict-affected areas be involved meaningfully? Specifically, how can alignment of humanitarian efforts and Resolution 1325 address this imbalance in women's participation? Can Rosalba, a single women living with disabilities in poverty, caring for her granddaughter, and with no safe access to livelihoods, services, or protection contribute to meetings around women's participation in the peace process? How can Fatima, who is forbidden to get a travel permit to even leave Rakhine State, let alone travel freely to Yangon, afford transport to get to meetings in urban areas? How will they find the time to participate in consultations of women when they struggle daily for a minimum income for survival? How can displaced women be vocal to speak out for women´s rights when there is no one around to ensure their safety and the safety of their families?

Even humanitarian providers who try to incorporate women into their programming fail to see the additional burdens that their programming can place on women's lives—scheduling sessions during their meal preparation time, failing to provide childcare, or putting meetings in places where it is difficult for women to attend. And during the transition to peacebuilding and development, as political structures start back up, women's contributions continue to be ignored. The burdens of caring for their families and others in society combined with a lack of access to resources, limit women's opportunities to participate in civil society. There is rarely a budget or any real tangible support to directly help women go to these areas to consult with displaced women or to find ways to get information from the humanitarians or local women's groups who are working on the front line. Displaced women cannot be expected to drop everything they are doing to support their communities and keep their families together to attend meetings in faraway places, but there must be a way to bring their voices to the processes.

How Can the Gaps Be Bridged?

The failure to focus on gender in DRR, disaster preparedness, and humanitarian action continues through the cycle leading to more and more women being ignored in peace-building and development. Better integration of women and their organizations who are directly impacted by natural disasters and conflict into disaster preparedness and humanitarian response can stop this cycle. Women understand and live with peace and security concerns every day in all phases of this cycle. But when women are struggling to get their humanitarian needs met, and their family's, they are unable to even begin to conceive of how to get more involved in peace-building and fulfill their full potential. Where there are no safe toilets, no healthcare, no clean water, no shelter, women find it difficult to get involved in abstract issues like peace processes that take place far away in foreign cities or in the capital. Without these basic humanitarian needs met, the Resolution 1325 agenda is a luxury that few can afford.

Building the Bridge between Humanitarian and Peacebuilding

Local women's rights organizations are the overlooked actors that can bridge the divide between development and humanitarian action and implement the women, peace, and security agenda so that it accurately includes women and girl´s concerns in disaster risk reduction, humanitarian settings, recovery, and post-conflict. As UN Women's Global Study on 1325 report makes clear, "the original champions of women's rights in conflict— women's civil society organizations— continue to mobilize around women's peace and security issues, driving the agenda forward in local, national, and international settings" (UN Women 2015).

This was recognized at the WHS where the UN Secretary-General reinforced the issue when he said, "Full and equal participation by women and girls in civil, political, economic and social spheres and in decision-making at all levels must become the standard to which all actors, including the United Nations, are held accountable in their development and humanitarian programming and funding" (United Nations General Assembly 2016). The common component of the humanitarian, peace-building, and developing agenda is that without women, there is no peace, there is no effective humanitarian response, and there would be no sustainable development.

Despite the WHS commitments and UN Security Council Resolution 2242, there is still very little action on the ground. We continue to fail to ensure that either global women's organizations or local women's organizations have long-term continued access to the resources and funding that they need for sustainable work or for space at the decision-making tables to promote this agenda in humanitarian action and peace-building. In a recent Oxfam report, the humanitarian community and donors in Iraq, the Occupied Palestine Territories, and Yemen have been accused of inadvertently causing a near disappearance of gender equality work in these countries because local women's organizations have had to prioritize responding to humanitarian needs. Donors and INGOs have exerted a disproportionate influence on the local women's organization's priorities, type of work, and opportunities, and most found it difficult to pursue their own agendas and strategies if they did not line up with donor priorities (Anderson 2017).

Development actors also fail to capitalize on opportunities to align with humanitarians where they could coordinate and bring the voices of women from hard to reach communities into the dialogue, such as in the Myanmar and Sri Lanka cases. The development agenda with its framework in the Sustainable Development Goals (SDGs) promotes gender equality through goal 5: *Gender Equality and Women and Girls' Empowerment*. However there is no target under this goal that specifically references women and girls living in conflict situations—meaning that the humanitarian agenda is not adequately included in the development architecture (Alowis et al. 2015). As one woman activist said in Colombia "(Women´s organizations) have survived war but we don´t know if we will survive peace. Whichever organization survives peace, those are the one who will remain for the future." Without dedicated resources, it is difficult for women´s organizations to meaningfully participate in the peace implementation. Despite global commitments, their work increases significantly yet their resources remain the same or decrease.

Many women's rights activists expected that the formation of UN Women would elevate their power as its predecessor, UNIFEM, had an extensive network of grass-roots women's organizations that they had worked with in the development sector. The inclusion of UN Women in humanitarian response could have served to ensure that local women's groups are meaningfully involved in humanitarian response. However, UN Women has very little capacity to respond in humanitarian emergencies, relies heavily on GenCap advisors instead of recruiting staff,[10] and is often sidelined in humanitarian response by others (Sandler et al. 2012). UN inter-agency competition over resources and mandates doesn't help. The struggle for limited funds to work on gender equality combined with an unclear mandate for humanitarian response means that UN Women has not yet succeeded in its attempt to join the major humanitarian actors to better integrate gender equality work into humanitarian action.

Building the capacity of humanitarians to work closely with local women's organizations is a key way of ensuring that women can participate. Often successful humanitarian programming around gender equality looks to humanitarians like development programming. This limits how much humanitarians interact with women at the grass-roots level through local women's organizations, because it is seen as "development work." However, humanitarian services that are set up in times of crises can end up becoming a part of long-term development work if coordinated with local women's activists. In Myanmar, ten years post-cyclone Nargis, the women's safe spaces set up during the cyclone response have morphed into women's community centers and are now used as women's safe spaces for displaced women returning to Myanmar following peace agreements. Humanitarian coordination mechanisms established in the cyclone response also became a network of local women's organizations that have now engaged the government in responding to women's rights in the transition to democracy.[11]

In the 2016 humanitarian response to Syrian and Afghan refugees moving from Turkey to Greece through the Balkans to Germany and Sweden, local anti-trafficking women's organizations were engaged to screen refugees for GBV and offer services. Many of these organizations were formed from women's organizations that came together before and during the Balkans conflict in the 1990s. The author[12] facilitated a nine-country, twenty-two–agency regional training to introduce the international basics on setting up safe houses, understanding the gendered needs of refugees, and training local organizations to advocate on behalf of refugees (Martin 2016). By linking domestic violence initiatives, anti-trafficking groups, and refugee/humanitarian actors in future humanitarian emergencies, there can be more capacity to respond to the needs of women and girls and the structures to support women and girls, living in these countries can been strengthened.

In Colombia, there is an effort to include women´s organizations into the local humanitarian coordination teams. To do this, there first had to be a dialogue with the local coordination teams to sensitize them to the value of the women's participation, and with the women´s organization to understand humanitarian architecture and the value of participating in it. The leader of one women´s group expressed confusion about the "humanitarianism" saying, "For me, humanitarian meant the response to floods or earthquakes. I didn´t understand it meant response to conflict as well."

It is critical to improve coordination. Humanitarians and peace-builders must come together and join efforts to support the humanitarian efforts to peacebuilding and recovery continuum while promoting gender equality as a priority. Problematically, neither peace building actors nor humanitarian actors and service providers see the need for connection in their struggles to improve women's participation, yet they interact with the same women on the ground. The gender experts working on WPS often sit in the development sector, while gender and GBV experts working in humanitarian action sit in different offices and interact in humanitarian coordination mechanisms. While the same agency may work on the same issues in the same countries, they do not always communicate within or with others.

Conclusions

The international community cannot wait until the peace process starts to try to bring women to the table. Humanitarian action and its precursors, disaster risk reduction and disaster preparedness, are the first steps in addressing the needs of the displaced and if that fails to meet the needs of women and girls, it can further entrench inequality and impede sustainable development for years to come. Engaging and letting local women's organizations lead in every step of the way is key to success, and local women's participation must remain central to all humanitarian action. Displaced women and girls are already acting as leaders in their families and communities to keep the family together, and they must be more formally engaged as leaders and agents of change, not just as victims or passive recipients of aid to be protected. The humanitarian community must start listening to women and girls, and the local women's organizations that represent them and women and girls must be given the tools and resources to facilitate their meaningful participation in relief, recovery, and peace-building. Only then, will UNSCR 1325 be able to reach its full potential.

NOTES

1. Woman interviewed in Colombia by the author, 2016 (name changed to protect privacy).
2. Composite portrait of different women living in Rakhine State in Myanmar.
3. Through the article, the word "women" refers to women of all ages, race, and religion. Lesbian, gay, bisexual, transgender, and intersex (LGBTI) men and boys also have been affected by conflict and disasters, but this article focuses on women as the main victims of gender inequality and gender-based violence in most humanitarian crises.
4. IASC Gender Marker is a tool that codes, on a 0–2 scale, whether or not a humanitarian project is designed well enough to ensure that women/girls and men/boys will benefit equally from it or if it will advance gender equality in another way. https://www.humanitarianresponse.info/sites/www.humanitarianresponse.info/files/documents/files/Introduction%20to%20IASC%20Gender%20Marker.pdf.
5. IASC maintains a roster of Senior Gender Advisors (aka "GenCaps") who are deployed to humanitarian crises to support the inclusion of gender equality into the humanitarian response. This roster is co-managed by OCHA and Norwegian Refugee Council. Humanitarian Response, "GenCap," https://www.humanitarianresponse.info/en/coordination/gencap.
6. The Humanitarian Cluster System are groups of humanitarian organizations, both UN and non-UN, in each of the main humanitarian response sectors (e.g., water and sanitation, food security, health, and the like). They are designated by the IASC and have clear responsibilities for coordination.
7. As is seen in the Democratic Republic of the Congo, Guatemala, Papua New Guinea-Bougainville, currently in Colombia, and in many other post-conflict places.
8. This was Devanna de la Puente's experience in Pakistan.
9. This was Sarah Martin's experience in Nepal.
10. A June 2017 call for GenCap deployments saw 40 percent being hosted by UN Women.
11. The Gender Equality Network in Myanmar arose from coordination in the humanitarian response to Cyclone Nargis in 2008, and it was created to specifically focus on multisectoral and cross-cutting issues faced by women in cyclone-affected areas. The Women's Protection Technical Working Group evolved to become the Gender Equality Network, which is now a major actor in incorporating women into the peace and security discussions in Myanmar.
12. This was Sarah Martin's experience in Nepal.

REFERENCES

Alowis, H., M. Alam, A. AlHefeiti, A. Binetti, H. Beswick, M. D'Amico, and R. Turkington. "Gender-Responsive Humanitarian Intervention in the Aftermath of Conflict: The Humanitarian-Development Continuum." United Arab Emirates Panel Series on Women, Peace, and Security: Panel 5. New York: Permanent Mission of the United Arab Emirates to the United Nations, May 5, 2015, https://www.un.int/uae/sites/www.un.int/files/United%20Arab%20Emirates/uae_giwps_publication_2015.pdf.

Anderson, K. "Now is the Time: Research on Gender Justice, Conflict, and Fragility in the Middle East and North Africa." Oxfam International, June 2017, https://www.oxfam.org/en/research/now-time-research-gender-justice-conflict-and-fragility-middle-east-and-north-africa.

Article 19. *Silencing Sensitivities: Women Human Rights Defenders and the Risk of Challenging Gender Inequality in Myanmar.* Article 19, n.d.

Barcia, I. *Urgent Responses for Women Human Rights Defenders at Risk: Mapping and Preliminary Assessment.* Women Human Rights Defenders. Toronto, Mexico City, Cape Town: Association of Women's Rights in Development, 2011.

Benedict, H. *The Private War of Women Soldiers. Salon*, March 7, 2007, http://www.salon.com/2007/03/07/women_in_military/.

Bennett, C., M. Foley, and S. Pantuliano. *Time to Let Go: Remaking Humanitarian Action for the Modern Era.* London: Overseas Development Institute and Humanitarian Policy Group, April 2016, https://www.odi.org.uk/sites/odi.org.uk/files/resource-documents/10421.pdf.

Bradford, A. "Mass Sexual Violence Leaves Rohingya Women Traumatized and Stateless." *News Deeply*: Women & Girls, June 8, 2017, https://www.newsdeeply.com/womenandgirls/articles/2017/06/08/mass-sexual-violence-leaves-rohingya-women-traumatized-and-stateless?utm_content=buffer9e219&utm_medium=social&utm_source=facebook.com&utm_campaign=buffer.

de la Puente, D. "Report of the Rapid Needs Assessment of Women's Protection Needs in Kachin, Myanmar." IASC Gender-Based Violence Area of Responsibility (GBV AOR), 2012.

de la Puente, D., and C. Morales. *Compendio de prácticas prometedoras en la inclusión del enfoque de género en la acción humanitaria en Colombia.* IASC GenCap Project and OCHA, 2016, https://reliefweb.int/sites/reliefweb.int/files/resources/buenas_practicas.pdf.

Defensoria del Pueblo, Colombia. "Defensoría del Pueblo advierte que en 85 municipios hay riesgo vigente de violencia sexual contra mujeres y niñas." May 25, 2017, http://www.defensoria.gov.co/es/nube/noticias/6380/Defensor%C3%ADa-del-Pueblo-advierte-que-en-85-municipios-hay-riesgo-vigente-de-violencia-sexual-contra-mujeres-y-ni%C3%B1as-Mujeres-ayuda-ni%C3%B1os-riesgo-posacuerdo-Farc-dominio-comunicado-violencia-sexual-Mujeres.htm.

Enloe, C. *The Curious Feminist.* Berkeley: University of California Press, 2004.

Foreign and Commonwealth Office, Government of the United Kingdom. *Human Rights and Democracy Report 2013.* London, June 2014.

Her Safety Assessment Report. "People in Need." Humanitarian Response Info, 2015, https://www.humanitarianresponse.info/sites/www.humanitarianresponse.info/files/assessments/her_safety_assessment_final.pdf.

Hodal, K. "Burma Tells Medécins Sans Frontières to Leave State Hit by Sectarian Violence." *The Guardian*, February 28, 2014, https://www.theguardian.com/world/2014/feb/28/burma-medecins-sans-frontieres-rakhine-state.

Human Rights Watch. *Burma: Security Forces Raped Rohingya Women, Girls.* February 6, 2017, https://www.hrw.org/news/2017/02/06/burma-security-forces-raped-rohingya-women-girls.

Inter-Agency Standing Committee. *Gender Handbook in Humanitarian Action. Women, Girls, Boys and Men: Different Needs, Equal Opportunities.* IASC, 2006.

Inter-Agency Standing Committee. "Policy Statement: Gender Equality in Humanitarian Action." IASC, June 20, 2008, https://interagencystandingcommittee.org/system/files/legacy_files/IASC Gender Policy 20 June 2008.pdf.

Kastner, E. "Addressing Gender-Based Violence in Emergencies: Analytical Paper on WHS Self-Reporting on Agenda for Humanity Transformations 2D and 3D." UNFPA, 2017.

Krishnan, S., and J. Twigg. "Menstrual Hygiene: A 'Silent' Need during Disaster Recovery. *Waterlines* 35, no. 3 (2016): 265–276.

Martin, S. "*Must Boys Be Boys? Ending Sexual Exploitation and Abuse in UN Peacekeeping Missions.*" Refugees International, October 2005, http://www.pseataskforce.org/uploads/tools/mustboysbeboysendingseainunpeacekeepingmissions_refugeesinternational_english.pdf.

Martin, S. *Lessons Learned Workshop for Asia Region: Nepal, Pakistan, and Afghanistan.* 2011.

Martin, S. *Europe Refugee Crisis: Balkans Regional Workshop on Gender-Based Violence.* Belgrade, Serbia: International Rescue Committee, 2016.

Mitaru, A., J. Timoney, A. Varghese, and J. Lund. "Empower Women and Girls (Transformation 3D) and Gender as a Cross-Cutting Issue: Analytical Paper on WHS Self-Reporting." ActionAid, Women's Refugee Commission, and UN Women. Agenda for Humanity, 2017, http://www.agendaforhumanity.org/sites/default/files/AP_3D%26Gender_0.pdf.

Müller, P., D. Sukharchuck, and Y. Polat. "Women Refugees at Risk of Sexual Assault in Berlin Shelters." IRIN News, May 10, 2017, https://www.irinnews.org/investigations/2017/05/10/women-refugees-risk-sexual-assault-berlin-shelters.

Niland, N., J. Holmes, and M. Bradley. "Policy Debate—Humanitarian Protection in the Midst of Civil War: Lessons from Sri Lanka." International Development Policy, May 2014, https://poldev.revues.org/1629.

OCHA and UN Women. "Gender Profile (March 2016)." OCHA / UN Women, 2015, http://reliefweb.int/sites/reliefweb.int/files/resources/nepal_gender_profile_-_updated_8th_march_2016.pdf.

Perlez, J. "Death Stalks Muslims as Myanmar Cuts Off Aid." *New York Times,* May 2, 2014, https://www.nytimes.com/2014/05/03/world/asia/death-stalks-muslims-as-myanmar-cuts-off-aid.html?_r=0.

Refugees International. "Myanmar," 2017, https://www.refugeesinternational.org/search?q=myanmar.

Robinson, A.. with A. Obrecht. "Improving Menstrual Hygiene Management in Emergencies: IFRC's MHM Kit." HIF/ALNAP Case Study. London: ODI/ ALNAP, 2016.

Sandler, J., A. Rao, with R. Eyben. "Strategies of Feminist Bureaucrats: United Nations Experiences." *IDS Working Papers* 2012, no. 397 (July 2012): 1–35.

Sommer, M. "Menstrual Hygiene Management in Humanitarian Emergencies: Gaps and Recommendations." *Waterlines* 31, no. 1 (2012): 83–104.

Sommer, M., M. Schmitt, D. Clatworthy, G. Bramucci, E. Wheeler, and R. Ratnayake. "What is the Scope for Addressing Menstrual Hygiene Management in Complex Humanitarian Emergencies? A Global Review." *Waterlines* 35, no. 3 (2016): 245–264.

United Nations General Assembly. "One Humanity: Shared Responsibility. Report of the Secretary-General for the World Humanitarian Summit." United Nations, A/70/709, 2016.

United Nations Security Council. "Report of the Secretary-General on the United Nations Mission in Colombia." United Nations, S/2017/252, 2017.

United Nations (UN). "*High-Level Leaders' Roundtable—World Humanitarian Summit.*" Agenda for Humanity, 2016, https://www.worldhumanitariansummit.org/summit/roundtables.

UN Women. "Transforming Justice, Securing the Peace. A Global Study on the Implementation of United Nations Security Council Resolution 1325 (2000)." Lead author: Radhika Coomaraswamy. UN Women, 2015, http://wps.unwomen.org/pdf/en/GlobalStudy_EN_Web.pdf.

CHAPTER 50

....

WPS, MIGRATION, AND DISPLACEMENT

....

LUCY HALL

UN Security Council Resolution 1325, the "mother resolution" (True 2012: 115) of the Women, Peace, and Security agenda (hereafter WPS) acknowledges that women (and children) are over-represented in populations of refugees and internally displaced persons (United Nations Security Council [UNSC] 2000: 1). This chapter explores the normative, institutional, and historical relationships between WPS and refugee protection, and WPS and the protection of internally displaced persons (here after IDPs). Although the normative, institutional, and historical relationship between refugee and IDP protection overlaps significantly, as this chapter will illustrate, attempts at aligning refugee protection and IDP protection with WPS have followed significantly different paths. Following this distinction the chapter is organized into four sections. First, it outlines gender in relation to refugee protection and attempts to align refugee protection to WPS. Second, the chapter traces how IDP protection and gender branched out from feminist critiques of the gender blindness of refugee protection. The third section discusses the alignment of WPS with both IDP and refugee protection agendas with reference to recent attempts to draw WPS closer to the IDP and refugee protection agendas. Fourth, the chapter argues that there is considerable potential for closer alignment between these three normative frameworks. This argument is premised, however, on three narratives referred to as (1) the continuum of violence; (2) the political economy approach; and (3) recognizing agency and capturing (feminist) gains. These three narratives, the chapter suggests, provide points of departure for displaced women, advocates, and scholars to reinvigorate feminist visions of peace and security that could more strongly unite these three normative agendas.

GENDER AND REFUGEE PROTECTION

....

This section outlines the efforts to correct the gender blindness of refugee law and highlights the potential of more closely aligning refugee protection with the WPS agenda. The legal foundations of refugee protection laid out in the 1951 Convention Relating to the Status of

Refugees (hereafter 1951 Convention) were completely blind to women, gender, and issues of sexual inequality (Edwards 2010: 22). The implications of this are clearly illustrated, albeit horrifically so, by the following example cited by international human rights lawyers in their ultimately successful attempt to challenge the legal recognition of women as refugees:

> A man was tied to a chair and forced at gunpoint to watch his common-law wife being raped by soldiers. In determining the case for refugee status, he was deemed to have been tortured. His partner was not (Pittaway and Bartolomei 1991: 26).

Such criticism of international refugee law's inability to protect women benefited from the momentum generated by the UN Decade on Women (1976–1985) and the efforts of scholars and activists who galvanized around the idea that "women's rights are human rights" during the World Conference on Human rights in 1993 (Bunch 1990). Gender asylum law, as Anker frames it, was constructed on the edifice of international women's human rights law (Anker 2002: 138–139). The feminist critique of the androcentric basis of refugee law resulted in two key developments in refugee law and policy: (1) recognizing women as refugees; and (2) recognizing women refugees as beneficiaries of protection (Edwards 2010: 23–24).

Before delving further into these developments in refugee law and policy, it is first important to note that to be granted refugee protection, an applicant must first be outside the country of their nationality and second "owing to well-founded fear of being persecuted" on the grounds of race, religion, nationality, membership of a particular social group or political opinion and be "unwilling or unable to avail himself (*sic*) of the protection of that country" (United Nations High Commissioner for Refugees [UNHCR] 2011:10). Gender is therefore absent as an over ground for determining refugee status and protection (McPherson et al. 2001: 324). Advocacy efforts to correct the masculine bias of refugee law coalesced in a political climate that was unfavorable to refugees. In the post–Cold War context, refugees no longer served the West as symbols of the oppressive Soviet regimes. In the early 1990s, it was simply too risky to open up the 1951 Refugee Convention and add sex and gender to the existing five grounds for persecution (Macklin 2009: 32). The omission of gender from the 1951 Convention did not dissuade UNHCR and several states from developing guidelines to inform the gender sensitive interpretation of refugee law (Macklin 2009: 33).

UNHCR's guidelines on gender-related persecution state the following:

> Even though gender is not specifically referenced in the refugee definition, it is widely accepted that it can influence, or dictate, the type of persecution or harm suffered and the reasons for this treatment. The refugee definition, properly interpreted, therefore covers gender-related claims. As such, there is no need to add an additional ground to the 1951 Convention definition (UNHCR 2002: 3).

The "proper interpretation," however, requires clear guidance which, following Macklin (2009: 33), needs to address three elements: the agent of persecution, the form of persecution, and the reason for persecution. Macklin writes that broadening the definition of the agent of persecution to include both state and non-state actors draws on feminist critique of the public/private distinction that values and recognizes public violations and devalues and silences private violations. Gender guidelines therefore emphasize that the agent of persecution may be the state, or a non-state actor (spouse, relative, employer, insurgent group) in circumstances where the state is unable or unwilling to provide protection. (Macklin 2009: 33)

In addition, Macklin notes that "a pattern of state denial of protection to women abused by non-state actors could also contribute to a finding of persecution" (UNHCR 2002, para. 14, as quoted in Macklin 2009: 33). Overcoming, or acknowledging refugee law's bias toward public forms of harm and persecution are also central to ensuring a gender sensitive interpretation of refugee law. For example, gender guidelines outline that for women, persecution may include female genital mutilation, domestic violence, rape, dowry-related violence, and trafficking (Macklin 2009: 33). Building on the feminist critique of the public/private divide, this recognizes the political nature of so-called "private" forms of persecution.

Gender guidelines also highlight how gender may overlap with other forms of persecution—for example, race, religion, or political opinion. Women of a racial or ethnic minority may be subjected to sexual violence and reproductive controls (Macklin 2009: 33). Macklin illustrates that while persecution may be gendered in form, it is on account of race, ethnicity or nationality that refugee status may be granted (2009: 33). Women may also be targeted through their association with certain political parties or trade unions and be subjected to different forms of violence than male colleagues. In these situations, while the persecution is gendered in form, the grounds for refugee status may be based on real or imputed political opinion (Macklin 2009: 33). While progress has been made in terms of recognizing and correcting the masculine bias of refugee law and should be celebrated, there are elements of gender asylum law, to use Anker's (2002) term, that remain problematic. This chapter now turns to the limitations of gender asylum law and what the implications of this mean for closer alignment of refugee protection with the WPS.

Gender asylum law tends to depoliticize women's roles in times of conflict and persecution. For example, Edwards illustrates that despite progress toward recognizing "refugee rights are women's rights," international refugee law and policy at times reinforces the perception that women are principally social and cultural in nature (Edwards 2010: 27). For example, questions of real or imputed political opinion are raised in relation to refugee status; gender guidelines tend to construct women as political only through their "family or male relatives" (UNHCR 2002: 9). In addition, UNHCR's 2002 Guidelines on International Protection regarding gender-related persecution state that

> women are less likely than their male counterparts to engage in high profile political activity and are more often involved in 'low level' political activities that reflect dominant gender roles. For example, a woman may work in nursing sick rebel soldiers, in the recruitment of sympathisers, or in the preparation and dissemination of leaflets. Women are also frequently attributed with political opinions of their family or male relatives, and subjected to persecution because of the activities of their male relatives (UNHCR 2002: 9).

This, as Edwards notes, underpins "essentialist" or "gendered" depictions of "women claimants as less than political in nature, and certainly less political than their male counterparts" (Edwards 2010: 27). Interestingly, Edwards acknowledges that her own role in drafting these guidelines during her employment at UNHCR is "rather confronting" (2010: 27). Edwards writes that the process of developing the guidelines strengthens MacKinnon's complaint that: "When what happens to women also happens to men, like being beaten and disappearing and being tortured to death, the fact that those it happened to are *women* is not registered in the record of human atrocity" (Edwards 2010: 27). This pattern of not recognizing or registering atrocities against women is also evident in the ways in which "particular social group" (hereafter PSG) is interpreted as grounds for refugee status determination (Edwards 2010: 27). Edwards explains that despite gender guidelines acknowledging that women may have claims to refugee status on any of the five grounds (listed earlier) codified in the 1951 Convention, there is a tendency in many jurisdictions to use PSG as the default grounds (2010: 27–28). For example, in Australia and Canada decision-makers concede that domestic violence is linked in some way to gender, but neither gender nor sex are listed as grounds for persecution (Macklin 1999: 298). This forced the consideration of "women," or "women subject to domestic violence" as constituting a particular social group (Macklin 1999: 298). Crawley has critiqued the overemphasis of PSG in determining the refugee status of women claimants, and she notes that while PSG

> may provide a "safety net" for some refugee women, it also reflects a particular static conceptualization of gender that rests on, and ultimately replicates, the existing and paradigmatically masculine normative structures of international refugee law. (Crawley 1999: 326)

It is clear that while there have been significant advances in developing a gender sensitive interpretation and application of refugee law, progress to correct the masculine bias of the law remains precarious and is at times problematic. A similar diagnosis could be applied to the second of two key developments in refugee law and policy: recognizing women refugees as beneficiaries of protection.

Parallel to the interpretation of refugee law through a feminist-informed perspective as discussed earlier is the recognition of "refugee women as beneficiaries of protection" (Edwards 2010: 31). The main objective of policies that seek to address the particular rights and needs of refugee women emphasize that men and women are affected differently by forced displacement and that "protection responses and strategies must take this into account" (Edwards 2010: 31). This is encapsulated in UNHCR's 1990 Policy on Refugee Women, which was later updated in 2008. Whilst this policy framework does attempt to illustrate the "multifaceted nature of women's lives," it is haunted by earlier protective constructions of women that emphasize vulnerability and women's maternal, familial, and domestic roles (Edwards 2010: 32). Attempts to reshape these essentialist constructions—for example, by describing refugee women as also "resilient, resourceful and courageous"—have been described as awkward and patronizing (Edwards 2010: 32; Kneebone 2005: 13). Despite this, it is recognized that the meaningful participation of refugee women in camps and urban contexts is critical in order to reduce women's exposure to violence and enhance their access to justice, healthcare, education, shelter, food, and non-food items. When women are not consulted or involved in the distribution of food or fuel and firewood, their exposure to sexual violence and sexual exploitation and abuse increases. A well-documented and frequently cited example is the threat posed for women refugees who risked being raped due to their responsibility for collecting firewood (Edwards 2010: 34). Furthermore, the sexual exploitation and abuse of refugee and IDP women and children continues to be documented (HRW 2016). This indicates that while progress has been made in gendering refugee law and policy, and progress in recognizing "refugee rights as women's rights," its application remains limited.

ALIGNING REFUGEE PROTECTION WITH WPS

There are several ways in which more closely aligning refugee law and policy with the WPS agenda could overcome the limitations inherent to refugee law, particularly in terms of its limited application and its tendency to depoliticize women. Using WPS Agenda as an advocacy tool could strengthen the claims of refugee or exiled women to be included in peace negotiations. The closer alignment of the WPS and refugee protection agendas could cultivate important avenues to build on these important gains. The inclusion of refugees, exiles, and diaspora groups in the development and monitoring of National Action Plans (NAPs) also suggests that the intersections between the WPS and refugee protection agendas are, at least in policy, evident. For example The Netherlands third NAP on 1325 (2016 – 2019) is developed by the state and civil society, and migrant, refugee, and diaspora groups are well represented. The NAP states:

> Many migrant and refugee women's organisations in the Netherlands are involved in peacebuilding activities. These activities take place both within their communities in the Netherlands and in their countries of origin, with which they have strong ties. (Dutch NAP 2011–2015: 21)

Women from Burundi, Ethiopia, Eritrea, Indonesia, Iraq, Liberia, the Philippines, Rwanda, Somalia, South Sudan, and Sudan are represented in civil society through the Multicultural Women Peacemakers Network (MWPN) which is an umbrella organization of migrant and refugee women's organizations in the Netherlands (Dutch NAP 2011–2015: 21). E-Quality, a Dutch research institution focusing on gender and diversity, is further evidence of the awareness of the intersections between diaspora and refugee communities and the WPS agenda; they are developing a Diaspora Toolkit for Conflict-Sensitive Strategies to support diaspora organizations' efforts to implement Resolution 1325 in their countries of origin (Dutch NAP 2011-2015: 37).

While the Dutch NAP suggests the inclusion of refugee and exiled women is based on recognizing their role in peace-building activities, the Australian NAP on 1325 interprets the inclusion of refugee women in the realm of WPS by following a different logic. The Australian NAP on WPS refers to the Women at Risk category established in 1989, which was intended to provide a pathway to resettlement for "vulnerable women refugees and their dependents" (Australian NAP 2012–2018: 37). The introduction of the "women at risk" category in Australia's Humanitarian Program is linked to the increased attention toward refugee women in the late 1980s, as discussed earlier (see *inter alia* Edwards 2010: 24–25). Manderson et al. (1998) write that the:

> Women at Risk Program was introduced by the Australian (federal) Government in 1989 in response "to the priority given the UNHCR to the protection of refugee women in particularly vulnerable situations" (DIMA 1996 in Manderson et al. 1998: 271).

Manderson et al. (1998: 275) continue to highlight that the "women at risk" category contains "certain immediate advantages to women in recognizing their subordinate status to men, the Women at Risk visa category is limited." Indeed, the intention of the program is to identify women who do not have this family or social support, have been or are "at risk" by virtue of the absence of "traditional support" (i.e., male partner), and who therefore have an "obvious" need for resettlement, in addition to a history of gender-related abuse and violence (Manderson et al. 1998: 272).

While this is absolutely an "important step in recognizing the heightened vulnerability of women refugees," Manderson et al. highlight that upon resettlement to Australia, women are frustrated by "their inability to advocate for themselves and their dependency on the state" (1998: 282). This again indicates the tendency for gender asylum law and policy to de-politicize women refugees by emphasizing their vulnerability. The "women at risk" category assumes that women's vulnerability stems from the absence of "traditional," therefore patri-archal, protection. This contradicts the granting of refugee protection to women escaping situations of domestic violence, which acknowledge that the family can be a deep source of insecurity for many women. The limitations and criticisms of the "women at risk" category are not reflected in Australia's NAP on WPS (2012–2018). Therefore while the reference to the "Women at Risk" refugee policy denotes an awareness of connections between refugee protection and the WPS agenda, it also reinforces ideas about women, vulnerability, and being "at risk" due to the absence of a husband, father, or "male partner," which run counter to the WPS agenda's interest in recognizing women's agency in times of conflict.

GENDER AND IDP PROTECTION

The evolution of norms concerning the protection of persons displaced within the borders of a state emerged in the late 1980s and early 1990s as debates surrounding the relevance and application of refugee protection norms escalated (Mertus 1998). The provision of *international* protection in the context of rising *internal* conflicts arose in parallel to the tightening of asylum procedures following the end of the Cold War. In addition, increased interest in preventing refugee flows directed attention toward "protecting and assisting persons dis-placed within their own countries" (Cohen and Deng 1998: 3). These developments in the normative realm of forced displacement also merged with increased attention to the plight of women refugees as previously discussed (see *inter alia* Edwards 2010: 24–25). As this section demonstrates, this milieu influenced the evolution of the main normative mech-anism for IDPs, the Guiding Principles on Internal Displacement (hereafter the Guiding Principles). Notwithstanding the numerous significant and persistent protection gaps for internally displaced women (hereafter IDW), the Guiding Principles articulate a sensitivity to the gendered repercussions of forced displacement, which could provide a favorable con-text for closer alignment between the WPS and IDP protection agendas.

Indeed these agendas share a conceptual history. As mentioned, debates surrounding refugee protection corresponded with a rise in activism and norm building which pivoted around the (re)conception of women's rights as human rights and prevention of violence against women (Bunch 1990). Activism and the work of norm entrepreneurs in conjunc-tion with the post-Cold War context "unleashed a series of events that were beneficial to women's organizations because it opened new space for thinking about the world" (Joachim 2003: 260).

The result of NGO activism in the early 1990s concerning the inclusion of women's rights as human rights had concrete implications, including the UN General Assembly adopting the Declaration on the Elimination of All Forms of Violence Against Women (United Nations 1993), and the appointment of a Special Rapporteur (Joachim 2003: 260). In the activist and NGO realm, the campaign against gender violence created and strengthened networks (Joachim 2003: 260). There are interesting parallels between the "women's rights as human rights" and IDP protection agendas. These include the increase of internal armed conflict and concomitant easing of Cold War alignments; the engagement and entrepreneurial work directed at the UN; and the institutionalization of human rights issues in the form of Special Rapporteurs. It is not only the contextual similarities that the "women's rights as human rights" and IDP protection agendas share. Indeed, as this chapter will continue to explore, there is a robust foundation that the WPS and IDP protection agendas have inherited in common that is being, and could be further, strengthened.

The Guiding Principles draw from, and arguably benefit from, two normative frameworks that were the outcome of feminist theorizing and activism. First, the Declaration on the Elimination of Violence Against Women (DEVAW) (United Nations 1993), which was preceded by the UN Decade for Women (1975–1985), and a series of world conferences on women (Joachim 1999: 143). Second, the outcome document of the 1995 UN Conference on Women: the Beijing Platform for Action (BPfA). Both DEVAW and the BPfA are referenced by the Guiding Principles. For example, Guiding Principles' definition of "gender specific violence" (Annotated Guidelines 2000: 28–29) follows the one contained in Article 1 of DEVAW. The BPfA underscores Guiding Principle 18, which states that "special efforts should be made to ensure the full participation of women in the planning and distribution of these basic supplies [food, water, shelter, housing, medical and sanitation services]" (annotated Guidelines 2000: 45–48). The Guiding Principles and the WPS Agenda are both informed and shaped by the outcomes documented in the BPfA. As Shepherd notes, the objectives of the BPfA are closely related to the actions mandated in Resolution 1325 (Shepherd 2008: 110).

What is evident, and present in the references that both the BPfA and the Guiding Principles make, is the shared conceptual foundations that both agendas inherited. This connection is further iterated in the preamble of Resolution 1325 as well as in the BPfA recommendation that the UN High Commissioner for Human Rights and the UN High Commissioner for Refugees (UNHCR) take into account the

> close link between massive violations of human rights, especially in the form of genocide, ethnic cleansing, systematic rape of women in war situations and refugee flows and displacements, and the fact that refugee, displaced and returnee women may be subject to particular rights abuses (Report of the Fourth World Conference on Women thanks United Nations Fourth World Conference on Women [UNFWCW] 1995: 95–96).

To draw attention to the important place the BPfA has in the normative ancestry of both the WPS and IDP protection agendas demonstrates that their initial iterations were inflicted with an acute awareness of the complex connections between gendered violence and forced displacement.

In addition to the BPfA and DEVAW the Guiding Principles also draws from the Convention on the Elimination of Discrimination Against Women (CEDAW) to underscore the responsibility of states to, *inter alia*, take appropriate measures to suppress all forms of traffic in women and exploitation, as well as in eliminating discrimination against women in the field of healthcare (United Nations 1979: Articles 6 and 12, respectively). By drawing from existing human rights instruments that specifically address discrimination and violence against women, the Guiding Principles created a strong foundation for the mandate to develop a sensitivity to gendered inequality and violence. Furthermore, it demonstrates that, rather than being an afterthought, the architects of the Guiding Principles wrote gendered violence into the foundations of IDP protection. This provided a strong basis for IDP protection to continue to evolve as a normative framework with an acute awareness and understanding of the gendered nature of violence that precedes, precipitates, and follows forced displacement.

References to CEDAW, DEVAW, and the BPfA in the Guiding Principles demonstrate that, unlike refugee protection, IDP protection from its inception displayed an awareness of how forcibly displaced persons face a continuity of gendered violence (Ferris 1990). This can be traced to the experiences and criticisms of two key figures in the evolving IDP mandate: Elisabeth Ferris and Roberta Cohen. Ideas about continuity and gendered violence can be traced back to Elizabeth Ferris's work in the early 1990s, in particular her article "Refugee Women and Violence" (Ferris 1990). In this paper, Ferris highlights five patterns of gendered violence in relation to—as the title suggests—refugee women. Ferris delineates between violence, as a cause of flight, violence during flight, violence in camps, family violence and violence and prostitution (1990: 4–6). Krause draws on both Ferris (1990) and Cockburn's (2004) work on the continuum of violence to challenge the "prevailing notion that violence during conflict and displacement are separate cases" (Krause 2015: 2). Instead, to paraphrase Cockburn (2004: 43), conflict and displacement are linked by violence at different points on a scale reaching from the personal to the international, from the home to the tank column. Roberta Cohen wrote of her experience consulting on a review of UNHCR's Refugee Women Policy in the early 1990s in an article titled, " 'What's So Terrible about Rape?' and Other Attitudes at the United Nations" (Cohen 2000). Such comments were encountered by Roberta Cohen during in her consulting work with UNHCR in the early 1990s (Cohen: 2000). The attention and sensitivity to the gendered and violent implications of forced displacement can be traced to the work of Ferris and Cohen, who were among a team of "norm entrepreneurs" determined not to replicate the gender blindness of refugee protection. The Guiding Principles attentiveness to the continuity of violence and its (re)articulation of CEDAW, DEVAW, and the BPfA, demonstrates a deep and preexisting affinity with the WPS agenda. This shared heritage provides a strong normative basis for strengthening the already existing interaction between the IDP and WPS agendas.

Aligning IDP Protection with WPS

The common ground between the WPS and IDP protection agendas is evident not only in their shared normative roots, but also in the annual report(s) of the Special Rapporteur on the Human Rights of IDPs and his statement to the 2014 Security Council Debates on the WPS Agenda. The recent creation of this institutional space for the IDP and WPS agendas to, quite literally, speak to each other at the Security Council contrasts significantly with the lack of institutional space for refugee and WPS agendas to converse. In this section, the chapter turns to look at these two examples (the 2013 Report of the Special Rapporteur on IDPs and his 2014 Statement to the Security Council) as sites of existing interaction and what it might mean for the closer alignment of the WPS and IDP agendas in the future.

The Report to the Human Rights Council from the Special Rapporteur on the Human Rights of IDPs "provides a thematic analysis of the particular situation of internally displaced women, taking stock of progress to date with regard to the protection and assistance for them, examining some of the outstanding challenges . . ." (United Nations General Assembly [UNGA] 2013: 1). The report explicitly refers to WPS, noting

> the [Security] Council's resolutions on women, peace and security, including its landmark resolution 1325 (2000), are particularly important tools for strengthening and systematizing responses to the rights and needs of IDW (UNGA 2013: 9).

Furthermore the report notes that National Action Plans for the implementation of 1325 presents a "valuable opportunity" to include and engage IDW (UNGA 2013: 9). Although both IDP and WPS agendas emphasize the violence, displacement, and deprivation characteristic of armed conflict, they can also bring about opportunities for women, as recent reporting on IDW by the Special Rapporteur notes that IDW are rarely involved in "developing, implementing and monitoring national action plans on Security Council resolution 1325" (UNGA 2013: 15). This represents a significant, yet overlooked, opportunity for closer and constructive alignment of the WPS and IDP Protection agendas. While the connection between IDW and WPS are clearly expressed in national and international policy documents, indicating that the importance of dialogue between these two normative agendas exists, it remains to be seen if this translates into meaningful participation for IDW.

In addition to these policy intersections, the former Special Rapporteur on the Human Rights of IDPs Chaloka Beyani was invited to address the 2014 Security Council Debates on the WPS Agenda. He stated in his address that

> the intersection of peace between security, human rights and development is critical to dealing with the issue of internal displacement. We must not lose sight of the important role that internally displaced women can play in negotiating peace, ensuring their human rights and bringing about development in post-conflict situations (Beyani 2014: 6)

In his address, Beyani also referred to the normative developments in the 1990s concerning women's rights in "emergency and post-conflict situations" as well as the Guiding Principles "which detail specific rights of internally displaced women and girls" (2014, 6). Beyani invoked the previously mentioned report, noting that this thematic report was dedicated to the situation of IDW (Beyani 2014: 7). Notwithstanding these important normative advances, Beyani highlights that "responses to internal displacement still do not adequately address the specific concerns and roles of women and girls" (2014: 7). As discussed earlier, while on paper the connections between the WPS and IDP agendas are expressed, and those expressions appear to be increasing in momentum; however much remains to be done to ensure the "participation and leadership of IDP women in finding durable solutions that address their very specific concerns" (Beyani 2014: 8). The final section of this chapter considers the points at which narratives of refugee and IDP protection intersect with WPS, which very much speak to ensuring the participation and leadership of displaced women in conflict situations.

INTERSECTING NARRATIVES OF GENDER/DISPLACEMENT AND WOMEN, PEACE, AND SECURITY

The conceptual history that the WPS and forced displacement agendas share provides substantial evidence that the normative goals of each agenda do not significantly diverge and that there is considerable potential for a closer alignment. As this chapter draws to a close, we discuss three intersecting narratives that could form the basis for which to consider the costs and benefits of such an alignment. These three narratives are referred to as (1) the continuum of violence; (2) the political economy approach; and (3) recognizing agency and capturing (feminist) gains. What links these three narratives is their potential to address several feminist criticisms that the WPS agenda has significantly narrowed since Resolution 1325 (True 2012; Kirby and Shepherd 2016a).

As previously discussed, ideas about continuity and gendered violence were developed in response to weak and inadequate refugee law and incorporated into the development of IDP Protection. Further aligning the IDP Protection and WPS agendas could provide some measure against the narrowing of the WPS agenda that currently precludes recognition of the continuum of violence (Kirby and Shepherd 2016b: 380). Increasing the conversations among the forced displacement and WPS realms, inclusive of displaced women, advocates and scholars could contribute to further understanding the implications of the narrowing of the WPS agenda and investigate how this might be countered.

Understanding gendered violence as existing across a continuum, which questions the bracketing of time into pre-, during-, and post-conflict phases, links well with a feminist political economy approach—also absent from the WPS Agenda (True 2012). True writes the political economy approach "avoids the compartmentalization and selective treatment of violence against women that disconnects the problem from its underlying causes" (2012: 7). For example, within norms that address the rights of returning IDPs and refugees, questions around systemic discrimination against women in national laws concerning property rights, inheritance rights and land ownership rights are explicitly addressed (Internal Displacement Monitoring Centre [IDMC] 2014). In his address to the Security Council Debate on the WPS Agenda, Chaloka Beyani, the Special Rapporteur on the Human Rights of IDPs, noted that, "pre-existing patterns of discrimination in many of those contexts are exacerbated during conflict and contribute to violations of women's rights to housing, land and property" (Beyani 2014: 7). The 2013 report from the Special Rapporteurs (UNGA 2013), which focused specifically on IDW also draws out the gendered links between protection from physical violence and the loss of livelihoods, lack of adequate housing, and denial of property rights (UNGA 2013: 7, 9, 16). While in the IDP and refugee protection frameworks, attention is given to how discrimination against women, linked to economic inequality, typified by gendered patterns of land and property ownership, correlates with increased exposure to physical violence. This resonates with the feminist political economy approach, which, to paraphrase True, would suggest that for WPS to achieve its feminist vision of peace, something that its current and near exclusive focus on redressing sexual violence through legal prosecution and juridical structures ignores—and, therefore, does not seek to alter the unequal economic and social structures (True 2012: 133)—it would need to renew efforts to lay the foundations of sustainable peace by addressing chronic gender inequality (Kirby and Shepherd 2016b: 249). Again, dialogue with displaced women, advocates, and scholars from the forced displacement and WPS agendas could facilitate understanding of the repercussions of the current narrow WPS agenda and explore how this might be countered.

The final intersecting narrative this chapter explores draws on the emphasis that both the forced displacement and WPS agendas place on recognizing women as "makers and beneficiaries of peace" (Kirby and Shepherd 2016a: 376). The narrowing of the WPS agenda diluted of one of its initial goals to increase the representation and participation of women in peace and security governance (United Nations Security Council 2000; Kirby and Shepherd 2016b: 251). Recognizing women's agency in times of extreme violence is central to the feminist revision of peace and security discourses, that seem to be unable to conceive of women beyond their roles as mothers, wives/widows, dependents, and as always and already vulnerable, weak, and sick (Puechguirbal 2010). At its core the WPS agenda seeks to acknowledge, encourage, and support women at all levels of decision-making in conflict and peace processes (United Nations Security Council 2000: 2). This resonates strongly with the IDP Protection policy architecture, which highlights the following:

> While uprooted, many women take on new roles as leaders and breadwinners, which they sustain after displacement by, for example, developing new businesses and promoting peaceful coexistence at the grassroots level (UNGA 2013: 17).

Furthermore attention is paid to maintaining the gains that IDW and refugee women may have made while displaced (UNGA 2013: 22). Again this resonates with feminist critiques which point to the masculine logics embedded in post-conflict discourses that position returning to "normal" as desirable or even possible (Pankhurst 2008: 3). Not only does the "return to normal" approach sideline and ignore the gains women make during times of conflict it ushers in a violent backlash against women (Pankhurst 2008: 3). Closer alignment of the IDP and WPS protection agendas could create a strong normative basis to recognize women's agency in both conflict and post-conflict situations.

Conclusions

The integration of the refugee, IDP, and WPS agendas could provide the foundation for furthering the feminist vision of peace and security. The shared conceptual history of these normative frameworks provides a certain gravitas for further building on and honoring this his(her)tory, while the intersecting narratives previously discussed—(1) the continuum of violence; (2) the political economy approach; and (3) recognizing agency and capturing (feminist) gains—provide points of departure for displaced women, advocates, and scholars to explore the ways in which this creates the foundation for a feminist (re)definition/(re)visioning of peace. Importantly, and as this chapter has argued, this (re)definition/(re)visioning of peace should resist the idealized notion of peace associated with women, but move toward "broad, multidimensional terms that include the elimination of all social hierarchies leading to political and economic injustice" (; True 2012: 19). Further exploration of the intersecting narratives of gender, violence, and displacement within the refugee, IDP, and WPS agendas would provide a meaningful contribution to realizing this feminist (re)definition/(re)visioning of peace and security.

References

Anker, D. E., 2002. Refugee law, gender, and the human rights paradigm. *Harv. Hum. Rts. J.*, 15, p.133.

Beyani, C. (Special Rapporteur), 7289th meeting on Women and peace and security—Security Council, 2014, http://webtv.un.org/meetings-events/treaty-bodies/watch/chaloka-beyani-special-rapporteur-on-women-and-peace-and-security-security-council-7289th-meeting/3862727973001/?term=&lan=french?lanchinese

Bunch, C. "Women's Rights as Human Rights: Toward a Re-Vision of Human Rights." *Human Rights Quarterly* 12, no. 4 (1990): 486–498. doi:10.2307/762496.

Cockburn, C. "The Continuum of Violence: A Gender Perspective on War and Peace." In *Sites of Violence: Gender and Conflict Zones*, edited by W. Giles and J. Hyndman. Berkeley: University of California Press, 2004.

Cohen, R. "What's So Terrible about Rape? and Other Attitudes at the United Nations." *SAIS Review* 20, no. 2 (Fall–Summer 2000), 73–77.

Cohen, R., and F. M. Deng. "Masses in Flight: The Global Crisis of Internal Displacement." Washington, DC: Brookings Institution Press, 1998.

Crawley, H. 1999. "Women and Refugee Status: Beyond the Public/Private Dichotomy in UK Asylum Policy". In *Engendering Forced Migration: Theory and Practice*, edited by Doreen Marie Indra. New York: Bergham Books.

Department of Families, Housing, Community Services and Indigenous Affairs Australian National Action Plan on Women, Peace and Security 2012–2018, http://www.peacewomen.org/sites/default/files/aust_nap2012_2018.pdf

DIMA (Department Of Immigration And Multicultural Affairs) (1996) Refugee and Humanitarian Visa Applicants. Guidelines on Gender Issues for Decision Makers. Canberra: DIMA. Women at Risk. Information Sheet 965i. Canberra: DIMA, 1996.

Edwards, A. "Transitioning Gender: Feminist Engagement with International Refugee Law and Policy 1950–2010." *Refugee Survey Quarterly* 29, no. 2 (2010), 21–45. doi:10.1093/rsq/hdq021.

Ferris, E. G. "Refugee Women and Violence." Paper presented at the World Council of Churches, Geneva, 1990.

Human Rights Watch. "Central African Republic: Rape by Peacekeepers." February 4, 2016, http://www.refworld.org/docid/56b459b64.html.

Internal Displacement Monitoring Centre (IDMC). "The Kampala Convention: Make It Work for Women." Norwegian Refugee Council and IDMC, 2014, https://www.nrc.no/globalassets/pdf/reports/the-kampala-convention---make-it-work-for-women.pdf.

Joachim, J. "Shaping the Human Rights Agenda." In *Gender Politics in Global Governance*, edited by M. K. Meyer and E. Prugl. Lanham, MD: Rowman & Littlefield Publishers, 1999.

Joachim, J. "Framing Issues and Seizing Opportunities: The UN, NGOs, and Women's Rights." *International Studies Quarterly* 47, no. 2 (2003): 247–274.

Kalin, W. *Guiding Principles on Internal Displacement: Annotations*. American Society of International Law, Issue 32 of Studies in transnational legal policy, 2000.

Kirby, P., and L. J. Shepherd. "The Futures Past of the Women, Peace, and Security Agenda." *International Affairs* 92, no. 2 (2016a): 373–392.

Kirby, P., and L. J. Shepherd. "Reintroducing Women, Peace, and Security." *International Affairs* 92, no. 2 (2016b): 249–254.

Kneebone, S. "Women Within the Refugee Construct:'Exclusionary Inclusion'in Policy and Practice—The Australian Experience". *International Journal Of Refugee Law* 17, no. 1 (2005): 7–42.

Krause, U. "A Continuum of Violence? Linking Sexual and Gender-based Violence during Conflict, Flight, and Encampment." *Refugee Survey Quarterly* 34, no. 4 (2015): 1–19.

Macklin, A. "Legal Aspects of Conflict-Induced Migration by Women." In *Women, Migration, and Conflict: Breaking a Deadly Cycle*, edited by Susan Forbes Martin and John Tirman. Dordrecht, Netherlands: Springer, 2009.

Macklin, A. "A Comparative Analysis of the Canadian, US and Australian Directives on Gender Persecution and Refugee Status." In *Engendering Forced Migration: Theory and Practice*, edited by Doreen Marie Indra. New York: Bergham Books, 1999.

Manderson, L., M. Kelaher, M. Markovic, and K. McManus. "A Woman without a Man Is a Woman at Risk: Women at Risk in Australian Humanitarian Programs." *Journal of Refugee Studies* 11, no. 3 (1998): 267–283. doi:10.1093/jrs/11.3.267.

McPherson, M., L. S. Horowitz, D. Lusher, S. Di Giglio, L. E. Greenacre, and Y. B. Saalman. "Marginal Women, Marginal Rights: Impediments to Gender-Based Persecution Claims by Asylum-seeking Women in Australia." *Journal of Refugee Studies* 24, no. 2 (2001): 323–347.

Mertus, J. "The State and the Post–Cold War Refugee Regime: New Models, New Questions." *International Journal of Refugee Law* 10, no. 3 (1998), 321–348. doi:10.1093/ijrl/10.3.321.

The Netherlands Ministry of Foreign Affairs (2012–2015). "Women: Powerful Agents for Peace and Security." http://www.peacewomen.org/sites/default/files/dutch_nap_2012-2015.pdfNAP

Pankhurst, D. "Introduction: Gendered War and Peace." In *Gendered Peace: Women's Struggles for Post-War Justice and Reconciliation*. New York: Routledge, 2008.

Pittaway, E., and L. Bartolomei. "Refugees, Race, and Gender: The Multiple Discrimination against Refugee Women." *Refuge* 19, no. 6 (1991): 21–32.

Puechguirbal, N. "Discourses on Gender, Patriarchy, and Resolution 1325: A Textual Analysis of UN Documents." *International Peacekeeping* 17, no. 2 (2010): 172–187. doi:10.1080/13533311003625068.

Puechguirbal, N. "The Cost of Ignoring Gender in Conflict and Post-Conflict Situations: A Feminist Perspective." *Amsterdam Law Forum* 4, no. 1 (2012), http://amsterdamlawforum.org/article/viewFile/245/437.

Shepherd, L. J. *Gender, Violence and Security*. New York: Zed Books, 2008.

True, J. *The Political Economy of Violence against Women*. New York: Oxford University Press, 2012.

United Nations. "Convention on the Elimination of Discrimination Against Women." UN Women, 1979, http://www.un.org/womenwatch/daw/cedaw/.

United Nations. "Declaration on the Elimination of Violence Against Women." UNGA, 1993, http://www.un.org/documents/ga/res/48/a48r104.htm.

United Nations Fourth World Conference on Women (UNFWCW). "Beijing Platform for Action." September 4–5, 1995, http://www.un.org/womenwatch/daw/beijing/pdf/BDPfA%20E.pdf.

United Nations General Assembly (UNGA). "Report of the Special Rapporteur on the Human Rights of Internally Displaced Persons." Chaloka Beyani, 2013, https://documents-dds-ny.un.org/doc/UNDOC/GEN/G13/121/12/PDF/G1312112.pdf?OpenElement.

United Nations High Commissioner for Refugees (UNHCR). "UNHCR Policy on Refugee Women," August 20, 1990, http://www.refworld.org/docid/3bf1338f4.html.

United Nations High Commissioner for Refugees (UNHCR). "Guidelines on International Protection No. 1: Gender-Related Persecution Within the Context of Article 1A(2) of the 1951 Convention and/or its 1967 Protocol Relating to the Status of Refugees." HCR/GIP/02/01, May 7, 2002, http://www.refworld.org/docid/3d36f1c64.html.

United Nations High Commissioner for Refugees (UNHCR). "Handbook and Guidelines on Procedures and Criteria for Determining Refugee Status under the 1951 Convention and the 1967 Protocol Relating to the Status of Refugees." HCR/1P/4/ENG/REV. 3, December 2011, http://www.refworld.org/docid/4f33c8d92.html.

United Nations High Commissioner for Refugees (UNHCR). "From 1975 to 2013: UNHCR's Gender Equality Chronology." July 3, 2013, http://www.refworld.org/docid/53a2a5f54.html.

United Nations High Commissioner for Refugees (UNHCR). "UNHCR Age, Gender, and Diversity: Accountability Report 2015." June 2016, http://www.refworld.org/docid/576a31804.html.

United Nations Security Council., Women Peace and Security Debate, S/PV.7289, (2014). http://www.peacewomen.org/sites/default/files/wpsdebateoctober2014.pdf

United Nations Security Council. "Resolution 1325." S/RES/1325, 2000.

United Nations Security Council. "Resolution 1820." S/RES/1820, 2008.

United Nations Security Council. "Resolution 1888." S/RES/1888, 2009.

United Nations Security Council. "Resolution 1889." S/RES/1889, 2009.

United Nations Security Council. "Resolution 1960." S/RES/1960, 2010.

United Nations Security Council. "Resolution 2106." S/RES/2106, 2013.

United Nations Security Council. "Resolution 2122." S/RES/2122, 2013.

CHAPTER 51

....

WPS AND LGBTI RIGHTS

....

LISA DAVIS AND JESSICA STERN

WHILE United Nations Security Council Resolution 1325 and its subsequent resolutions[1] have galvanized worldwide efforts to address the challenges women face in conflict and post-conflict settings, it has lacked a holistic approach to gender. The interpretation of gender under the Women, Peace, and Security (WPS) agenda is outdated, binary, and heteronormative. This narrow approach has overlooked the experiences of lesbians, bisexual women, transgender, and intersex (LBTI) people in conflict and disaster settings, failing to capture threats and/or create tailored responses to meet survivors' needs.[2] As Jamie Hagen points out, the result has been "[t]hose vulnerable to insecurity and violence because of their sexual orientation or gender identity remain largely neglected by the international peace and security community" (Hagen 2016: 313).

In response, lesbian, gay, bisexual, transgender, intersex (LGBTI), and women's rights activists have begun to collaborate, raising awareness about how gender and sexuality are intertwined. Broadening the WPS agenda's understanding of gender should be in everyone's interest. A broader interpretation of gender builds coalitions across the women's and LGBTI movements, which amount to a larger movement committed to ending violence against individuals for defying traditionally ascribed gender roles. This broader understanding within the WPS framework also helps strengthen the concept of gender equality and underscores the need to address long-standing gender-based violence and discrimination in transitional justice and peace-building processes.

How can women and LGBTI movements unite under the women peace and security agenda? This chapter[3] explores current activism and debates on the discourse of gender within the WPS agenda and studies Iraq as a case study where women's and LGBTI rights organizing have converged.

HISTORICAL CHALLENGES TO ADDRESSING GENDER-BASED VIOLENCE IN CONFLICT

Sexual violence in conflict has traditionally been trivialized. In the humanitarian context, it used to be argued that sexual violence was simply "a product of war" or the "private acts of renegade soldiers." The reluctance to recognize gender-based violence as a human rights violation is in part rooted in the traditional view that violence against women is a private matter. Designed to uphold male dominance and heteronormative values, protecting "family values" became a justification for the failure of states to intervene when violence was committed within the home (United Nations 2006: 36).

This is primarily because in all societies, women are less powerful than men, meaning that their ability to live free from gender-based violence, their right to make decisions about their sexuality, their reproductive choices, where they work, if they inherit, and who they marry are not prioritized in states' obligations to uphold human rights. As Charlotte Bunch[4] notes, "[F]emale subordination runs so deep that it is still viewed as inevitable or natural, rather than seen as a politically constructed reality maintained by patriarchal interests, ideology, and institutions" (Bunch 1990: 491).

For this reason, the WPS agenda is a tool of survival. Such gendered violence requires a remedy different from those meant to address more broadly defined conflict-related violence. This is because acute stigma coupled with multiple forms of discrimination compounds individuals' vulnerability to severe rights abuses, including loss of life. Disproportionate vulnerability in insecure times exacerbates the consequences of gender-based violence, such as disease, disability, depression, and exploitation.

QUEER VULNERABILITIES IN TIMES OF WAR

While the work of women's rights activists to dismantle institutional discrimination is far from complete, the added work of addressing gendered violence and discrimination at vulnerable intersections has come to a head. As Julie Goldscheid asserts, "[D]espite its history as a political and organizing tool, the 'violence against women' frame is problematic [. . .] and reinforces a binary view of gender that is inconsistent with queer, feminist and other critical theory" (Goldscheid 2014: 625).

Often left out of the discussion altogether have been LGBTI survivors of gender-based violence and others who fall outside normative gender expressions and identities. The effect of this discrimination compounded when added to the double or triple discrimination and violence experienced by lesbians and transgender persons of color, youth, elders, religious and ethnic minorities, and others with multiple forms of marginalized identities (Crenshaw 1989). The result has been the perpetuation of institutionalized discrimination as inadequate resources, insufficient laws, and weak enforcement mechanisms have allowed gender-based violence to persist.

Yet, LGBTI people are at heightened risk in conflict. First, the community networks that enable people to survive during times of conflict are often not available to LGBTI people who have been rejected by their family or community. Second, the empowerment of military actors nationally erodes the safety of LGBTI people because military power is generally premised on essentializing "two sexes" and de facto recognition (and acceptance) of only heterosexual intimacy (Sjoberg 2014). Third, in times of war, dissent is discouraged, which makes LGBTI human rights defenders and all who challenge the status quo outsiders to nationalist fervor.

The disproportionate effect that gender-based violence has on women and LGBTI persons requires taking a different approach to conflict through the WPS agenda to ensure its prevention and redress. If gender-based violence is not addressed from its root causes during post-conflict reconstruction, anti-woman and anti-LGBTI discrimination and violence will continue along with a proliferation of other forms of bigotry. Such failure commonly stems from pre-conflict discriminatory beliefs or norms on gender.

Broadening the Gender Lens in the WPS Agenda: ISIS as a Case Study

Women and LGBTI Iraqis and Syrians were persecuted long before the emergence of the Islamic State in Iraq and Syria (ISIS). The extremist militia's rise comes against a backdrop of a long-running armed conflict in Syria and Iraq in which gender-based violence has been continuous (MADRE and Women's International League for Peace and Freedom 2014). In this context, three organizations united in a multifaceted strategy for international advocacy to address the rights of women and LGBTI Iraqis: OutRight Action International,[5] MADRE,[6] and the Organization for Women's Freedom in Iraq (OWFI).[7] The three organizations hold a joint commitment to the empowerment of Iraqi women and are working together to find ways to support the bourgeoning LGBTI community.

Motivating this work is the shared recognition that the conservative gender norms which render Iraqi women vulnerable exist on a continuum of violence also targeting LGBTI Iraqis. Discrimination and violence against women in Iraq is well-documented (Efrati 2005; MADRE 2008; Al-Ali and Pratt 2009). While the occupation of parts of Iraq by ISIS has dramatically worsened the human rights situation there, human rights violations against women and girls should be understood as a continuation of the deterioration of women's human rights over the last couple of decades in Iraq, as well as of long-standing discriminatory policies and practices. Severe gender discrimination in Iraq's personal status laws further erodes women's rights in the current climate. Norms of "family honor" recognized in Iraq's penal code, which permit honor considerations to mitigate sentences, have been a long-standing threat to women and girls. Such policies exacerbate the vulnerabilities of those fleeing conflict-related gender-based violence, including those who have been detained or abused by ISIS fighters.

Lesser known is the plight of LGBTI Iraqis. The number of Iraqis perceived as LGBTI killed by state and non-actors was always difficult to confirm due to lack of state reporting and community fear. However, one poster in Sadr City, Baghdad, documented by OutRight in 2012, was indicative. It called on "every male and female in the strongest terms to stop their dirty deeds," singling out thirty-three people by name and decorated with two handguns. While media reports alleged that the number of "emos" killed during that campaign spanned anywhere from dozens to hundreds, rights groups were unable to confirm the number of people killed, LGBTI or otherwise.[8] Instead, the groups focused on the harsh realities reported by LGBTI community members. Today, the vast majority of LGBTI Iraqis almost exclusively keep their sexual orientation and gender identities secret. They live in constant fear of discrimination, rejection by family, violence, and death. Since LGBTI advocacy work is highly dangerous and puts advocates and their families' lives at risk, less than a handful of groups currently engage in protecting LGBTI persons in Iraq.

In the partnership's early days, the groups focused on human rights documentation and trainings by OutRight and MADRE in support of OWFI's expansion from women's rights into the new area of LGBTI rights. The trainings began simply and privately. OWFI would send small, brave and compassionate numbers of its staff. OutRight and MADRE would debunk stereotypes, introduce facts, and feature LGBTI community members to tell their own stories.

While these organizations had been working together in different capacities for some years, their formalized relationship took on more dramatic implications and a different strategic direction with the rise of ISIS. In the face of conflict-related violence by government members, ISIS and other militias, women and LGBTI Iraqis remain in urgent need of physical protection and emergency assistance. For these reasons in 2014, OutRight, MADRE, and OWFI documented their findings together by releasing two publications highlighting the long history of discrimination and abuse against LGBT[9] persons in Iraq and situating the issues alongside the more established discourse of gender-based violence (Organization of Women's Freedom in Iraq, OutRight Action International, and MADRE 2014a, 2014b).[10] Because of their sensitive nature, the reports were disseminated to Iraqi LGBTI community members and to a carefully created list of NGOs, press, UN officials, and governments. In 2015, a report was submitted to UN Human Rights Committee outlining the Government of Iraq's failures in its obligations under the International Covenant on Civil and Political Rights (Human Rights and Gender Justice, MADRE, and Organization of Women's Freedom in Iraq 2015). These publications provided insight on gendered discrimination and violence in Iraq where there is a dearth of information.

An Arria-Formula for LGBT Rights Violations

With the rise of ISIS, the groups decided to increase their strategic focus on the UN Security Council. It was clear that the safety of women and LGBTI Iraqis would be heavily influenced by the international community, nowhere more acutely than by the powerful Security Council itself.

With their two publications, the groups enjoyed their first success with the Security Council: following the release of these reports, in March 2015, then-UN Secretary-General Ban Ki-Moon's report to the Security Council on conflict-related sexual violence acknowledged for the first time the targeting of LGBT individuals in Iraq (United Nations Security Council 2015: 10). This may be the first official submission to the Security Council to refer to LGBT individuals and it was certainly the first such reference by a UN Secretary General. Yet, these first steps were not enough, so the groups' efforts to bring together the WPS agenda and LGBTI inclusion in the Security Council continued.

The groups' efforts took a big step forward when, on August 24, 2015, the UN Security Council held the first-ever Arria-Formula on LGBT violations (Stern 2016). The invitation described the Arria as an "Open Meeting on Vulnerable Groups in Conflict: ISIL's Targeting LGBT Individuals." Arria-Formula discussions are informal meetings called by UN Security Council members where states may engage in private discussions on issues of international importance.[11] Apart from the Secretary General's brief reference in his report on sexual violence in conflict, this was the first time in the Security Council's more than seventy-year history that it formally or informally addressed the experiences of LGBT people in conflict.

The Permanent Missions of Chile and the United States co-hosted the Arria. The Chilean Ambassador Cristian Barros-Melet opened with remarks reinforcing the notion that LGBT violations in conflict fall within the purview of the Council's work. He explained its purpose was to address human rights violations based on sexual orientation and gender identity in the context of the ISIS conflict, linking ISIS's extremist violence to the global context of homophobia and transphobia.

In her opening remarks, then-US Ambassador Samantha Power stated, "This is the first time in history that the Council has held a meeting on the victimization of LGBT persons. It is the first time we are saying, in a single voice, that it is wrong to target people because of their sexual orientation and gender identity. It is a historic step. And it is, as we all know, long overdue" (Power 2015). She went on to say, "while today's session is focused on the crimes against LGBT persons committed by ISIS, we know the scope of this problem is much broader," recognizing the continuum of LGBT rights violations beyond the scope of ISIS.

LGBTI community members shared personal accounts of violence perpetrated by ISIS. Subhi Nahas from Syria and "Adnan" from Iraq underscored that LGBT persons in Iraq and Syria had been subjected to discrimination and violence by state authorities and community members prior to and since the emergence of the conflict. Jessica Stern provided expert testimony about OutRight's research of ISIS's claims of killing LGBTI Iraqis and Syrians, including its documentation that ISIS officials took responsibility for killing at least thirty people on the basis of their perceived homosexual conduct (Stern 2016). She highlighted the efforts of local and international groups to document crimes pertaining to gender-based persecution and presented the Council members with concrete recommendations formulated by locally based LGBTI and women's rights activists known from OutRight's joint project with OWFI and MADRE.

From the groups' perspective, the Arria was vital. The Security Council had already held multiple hearings about the vulnerabilities of Iraqi women and other groups to violence from ISIS. This hearing was the first to connect LGBT killings to the larger conflict context and the WPS agenda. Stern recognized this in her remarks, "Our concerns are not only for LGBTI people. We condemn in the strongest terms the sexual enslavement of women, ISIS attacks on Christians, Turkmanis, Kurds, and its intent to destroy the Yazidi as a group. Only by working across the human rights spectrum will we get to the other side" (Stern 2016).

Thirteen out of the fifteen members of the Security Council, including all five permanent members, attended the meeting.[12] Council members as well as other UN member states delivered supportive statements, citing the inclusion of sexual orientation and gender identity (SOGI) as protected classes under the Universal Declaration of Human Rights (UDHR). These recommendations echoed previous calls to the international community for policy reforms that meet the immediate needs of LGBTI persons but also remedy the root causes of the crisis. The remarks from the states repeated certain themes, including condemnation of the killings and connecting this issue to a larger pattern of attacks on vulnerable groups. At least half a dozen states invoked the UDHR to name SOGI along with historically recognized protected classes such as sex, race, religion, and ethnicity—further normalizing the concept of LGBT rights as human rights. States discussed LGBT rights on a continuum, recognizing rights violations over history and not just through the silo of ISIS or conflict.

The Arab Group discussed the Arria for several hours in a private session later that day—specifically whether to issue a condemnation of the Arria for its focus on LGBT rights violations. In other UN venues, such as the Human Rights Council and General Assembly, the Arab Group would frequently issue hostile statements when these rights appeared in resolutions or statements, even questioning the definition of "sexual orientation" and "gender identity" (Rserven 2012). Significantly, the states did not issue a joint statement of condemnation. This understated conclusion from the Arab Group is notable because it seems the Arria was not viewed as one country's initiative alone or simply as an LGBT problem but as a part of the broader issue of the responsibility of the Security Council to address acts of violence by ISIS, including against vulnerable minorities.

Following the event, UN member states and representatives of UN agencies informed OutRight and MADRE that recommendations from the panel helped them build the case for more substantive programming, particularly in Iraq and Syria, that is responsive to the needs and concerns of LGBT persons in times of conflict.

Utilizing the UN Security Council's Informal Expert Group to Create Change

In October 2015, during the annual debate on WPS, the UN Security Council adopted Resolution 2242 creating the Council's Informal Expert Group on Women, Peace, and Security ("IEG" or "Expert Group") (UN Women 2015).

Each year, MADRE, OutRight, and other international organizations work in partnership with the local Iraqi and Kurdish women's organizations, OWFI and Asuda, to organize a convening with Iraqi and Kurdish women's rights activists. In March 2016, participants from different regions, religions, sects, and political affiliations met in Erbil to create a unified advocacy platform of demands for gender-sensitive reconstruction and stabilization processes in Iraq. Significantly, at least two organizations at the women's rights meeting addressed the violence against LGBT people by ISIS as among their concerns. Participants compiled recommendations for a submission to the UN Security Council's Expert Group (MADRE, Organization of Women's Freedom in Iraq, Asuda, and Women's International League for Peace and Freedom 2016) that would meet on April 29, 2016, to discuss Iraq.

Following the March convening, representatives from OWFI and IraQueer,[13] Iraq's first and only LGBTI rights organization, traveled to New York in preparation for the Expert Group's spring review on Iraq. OutRight and MADRE organized a briefing at the Dutch mission to the UN, and several government members of the Expert Group attended.

Following its official meeting on Iraq in April, the Expert Group produced a report compiling key recommendations for the Security Council to integrate into their decisions and work in Iraq. Notably, the Expert Group urged the UN Security Council, "in all relevant decisions about Iraq, including UNAMI's [the United Nations Assistance Mission for Iraq] mandate, and the Council's interactions with the government of Iraq and mission leaderships," to "call on the government of Iraq to issue a directive clarifying that Iraqi

NGOs may provide much-needed services to survivors of gender-based violence, including shelter" (Informal Experts Group on Women, Peace, and Security 2016: 3).

The inclusion of recommendations by local Iraqi organizations in the list of recommendations by the Expert Group is a clear advocacy win. It demonstrates that local Iraqi women and LGBTI groups working together have influenced the debate and policies within the WPS agenda and multilateral system, and they have done so based on perspectives and priorities of Iraqi activists on the ground. Furthermore, as a result of this advocacy, in the fall of 2016, OWFI was invited by UNAMI, the institution assisting the government in facilitating civil society input, to propose amendments to a draft law on domestic violence entitled the "Family Protection Law."

Gendering Formal Recommendations to the UN Security Council

Following the Arria-Formula, Yanar Mohammed, co-founder of OWFI, addressed the UN Security Council at the annual Open Debate on Women, Peace, and Security in October 2015. She drew Council Members' attention to ISIS's gender-based persecution of both women and LGBTI people in the larger Iraqi context where gender rights were already degraded, leaving members of these vulnerable groups far more vulnerable to abuse by ISIS and other combatants. She also emphasized the importance of the international community taking a sustainable approach to the ISIS conflict, highlighting the importance of prosecuting ISIS militia members but also reforming discriminatory laws and policies to build a more equitable and sustainable foundation for the long-term in Iraq (Mohammed 2015).

On June 2, 2016, Lisa Davis delivered the civil society statement for the UN Security Council's Open Debate on Sexual Violence in Conflict (Davis 2016). Davis cited the issues raised at the LGBT Arria-Formula the year before and urged Security Council members to support documentation efforts that ensure that crimes committed against all marginalized persons, including women and LGBTI persons, in conflict are accounted for in tribunals and other transitional justice processes. These comments provoked a lively debate between states. The United States and Uruguay cited the international community's responsibility to end sexual and gender-based violence—including violence against LGBTI individuals perpetrated by ISIS. The delegate from Russia retorted that LGBTI documentation "distracts" from the Security Council's mandate on the issue.

The positive reverberations of these advocacy efforts have slowly but surely manifested themselves, particularly in the language of key UN documents. For example, shortly after the Arria-Formula on LGBT issues, UNAMI for the first time devoted an independent section to attacks on individuals on the basis of real or perceived sexual orientation in its periodic report on the human rights situation in Iraq (United Nations Assistance Mission for Iraq and United Nations Human Rights Office of the High Commissioner for Human Rights 2015: 17). Notably, in the subsequent report, UNAMI also stated that together with the Office of the United Nations High Commissioner on Human Rights, the Mission has "started collecting information on LGBTI-related cases with a view to establishing a dedicated database" (United Nations Assistance Mission for Iraq and United Nations Office of the High Commissioner for Human Rights 2016: 35). Additionally, in his 2016 report on Women, Peace, and Security issues, the UN Secretary-General voiced concern over threats against and systematic persecution of "those who do not conform to gender norms" (United Nations Security Council 2016a: 10). While this annual report has, in previous years, addressed security threats against women human rights defenders, political leaders, and LBT women, this is the first time that these violations were recognized as part of the larger framework of persecution on the basis of presumed gender transgression.

Moving Forward

These illustrations are useful for academics and activists committed to the safety and security of women and LGBTI people in times of conflict, disaster, and post-conflict. As these examples show, community-based organizations are increasingly expanding the WPS agenda to be more inclusive of a broader interpretation of gender. Perhaps surprisingly, states are accepting this approach. States have both taken the initiative at the UN Security Council and applied dialogue in that space to increase access for local civil society organizations to policy creation and reform, as when the government of Iraq invited OWFI to comment on its Family Violence Protection draft law. The international system has also responded favorably to the expansion, both through the UN Secretary-General's report on conflict-related sexual violence to the Security Council and in surprising new developments. In what might be seen as the culmination of many of these efforts, the UN Security Council recognized "sexual orientation" for the first time ever in a historic statement condemning the biased motivation for the attack on the Pulse Nightclub in Orlando (United Nations Security Council 2016b).

Moving forward, we must draw inspiration from this progress and continue pushing the WPS Agenda to be broader and more inclusive. In a time where globally we are seeing increased attacks on women, increased attacks on LGBTI people, more conflict, and more war, women and LGBTI people need coalitions with one another more than ever. The fear that expanding the interpretation of gender in the WPS Agenda will weaken the cause has been shown to be both outdated and wrong. At a time when states are threatening to withdraw from the International Criminal Court, we need to invest more heavily in these institutions' reach to ensure the preservation of the international system itself.

While the inclusion of language regarding these violations is not an end in itself, it constitutes a critical step in prioritizing the situation of LGBTI persons among key international stakeholders, and galvanizing them into action. Importantly, this inclusion helps establish a normative framework for addressing the full spectrum of gender-based persecution in transitional justice mechanisms and post-conflict reconstruction processes in Iraq. It further signals that these issues have been incorporated into the work of the UN Security Council and other UN bodies, and thus increases the likelihood that input and recommendations from Iraqi civil society on these issues will guide their policies and programming in-country.

Similarly, as member states each communicate the Security Council's priority issues to their respective capitals, these governments are also more likely to provide political support and mobilize resources for implementing policy recommendations formulated by Iraqi civil society that address not only these violations, but also their root causes.

Lastly, while there is little we can do for women, religious or ethnic minorities, or LGBTI persons—or anyone living in ISIS-controlled areas—there is much we can do when they flee. We hope that this conversation with all of its benefits and risks helps lead to actions for all marginalized groups affected by the conflict. Only time will tell if it does.

NOTES

1. Security Council Resolution 1325 (2000); subsequent resolutions include 1820 (2008); 1888 (2009); 1889 (2009); 1960 (2010); 2106 (2013); 2122 (2013); and 2242 (2015).
2. Additionally, this approach overlooks the ways in which gay men are targeted for defying traditional gender and sexual assumptions about masculinity and manliness. This problem will not be the subject of this chapter but does deserve future investigation.
3. The authors would like to thank J. M. Kirby for her editorial assistance, and Stephanie Chaban and Afarin Dadkhah for their research assistance. The authors would also like to thank Yanar Mohammed, Amir Ashour, and all the activists at the Organization for Women's Freedom in Iraq (OWFI), IraQueer, and the many other men and women human rights activists in Iraq who cannot be named for safety reasons.
4. Charlotte Bunch is the founding director and senior scholar of the Center for Women's Global Leadership at Rutgers University and a Board of Governor's Distinguished Service Professor in Women's and Gender Studies. In 1996, Professor Bunch was inducted into the National Women's Hall of Fame.
5. OutRight is an international human rights organization dedicated to improving the lives of people who experience discrimination or abuse on the basis of their sexual orientation, gender identity, gender expression, or sex characteristics.
6. MADRE is an international women's human rights organization that partners with community-based women's groups worldwide facing war and disaster.
7. The work of the Organization for Women's Freedom in Iraq (OWFI) runs the gamut from service delivery to advocacy. OWFI traditionally focused on advocating for and providing services like shelter to the most vulnerable women but more recently, its staff have expanded to provide shelter to LGBTI Iraqis and also engage in life-threatening activities to document anti-LGBTI abuses.
8. As described in a press release from OutRight (then IGLHRC), Human Rights Watch, and Amnesty International, *emos* were "a cross-section of people seen locally as nonconformists. They include people suspected of homosexual conduct, but also people with distinctive hairstyles, clothes, or musical taste. In English, 'emo' is short for 'emotional,' referring to self-identified teens and young adults who listen to alternative rock music, often dress in black, close-fitting clothes, and cut their hair in unconventional ways. People perceived to be gay, lesbian, transgender or effeminate are particularly vulnerable" (OutRight 2012).
9. The "I" in the acronym "LGBTI" was not included because of a lack of documented cases of violence against intersex persons available.

10. All of the documentation had been carried out before Mosul fell to ISIS. With the new conflict ensuing, OWFI requested the Arabic versions of the reports not be released for safety reasons.
11. For more information, see United Nations Security Council (2002).
12. The only members of the Security Council to be absent were Angola and Chad.
13. Having a diverse team of young activists between the age of 18–32 residing mostly inside Iraq and the Kurdistan region, IraQueer represents the start of the first queer movement in Iraq's public history.

References

Al-Ali, N., and N. Pratt. *What Kind of Liberation? Women and the Occupation of Iraq*. Berkeley: University of California Press, 2009.

Bunch, C. "Women's Rights as Human Rights: Toward a Re-Vision of Human Rights." *Human Rights Quarterly* 12, no. 4 (1990): 486–498.

Crenshaw, K. "Demarginalizing the Intersection of Race and Sex: A Black Feminist Critique of Antidiscrimination Doctrine, Feminist Theory, and Antiracist Politics. *The University of Chicago Legal Forum* 1, no. 8 (1989): 139–167.

Davis, L. "Statement by Lisa Davis, UN Security Council Open Debate on Sexual Violence in Conflict." June 2, 2016, http://www.womenpeacesecurity.org/resource/statement-unsc-svic-open-debate-june-2016/.

Efrati, N. "Negotiating Rights in Iraq: Women and the Personal Status Law. *The Middle East Journal* 5, no. 4 (2005): 577–595.

Goldscheid, J. "Gender Neutrality, The 'Violence against Women' Frame, and Transformative Reform." *UMKC Law Review* 82, no. 3 (2014): 623–662.

Hagen, J. J. "Queering Women, Peace, and Security." *International Affairs* 92, no. 2 (2016): 313–332.

Human Rights and Gender Justice Clinic [formerly IWHR Clinic], MADRE, Organization of Women's Freedom in Iraq, et al. "Seeking Accountability and Demanding Change: A Report on Women's Human Rights Violations in Iraq." Response to the Fifth Periodic Report of the Republic of Iraq. October 2015, http://www.law.cuny.edu/academics/clinics/iwhr/publications/ICCPR-Iraq-Shadow-Report-GBV-ENG-PDF.pdf.

Informal Experts Group on Women, Peace, and Security. "Security Council Informal Experts Groups on Women, Peace, and Security, Republic of Iraq." [On file with the authors.] April 29, 2016.

MADRE. "Promising Democracy, Imposing Theocracy: Gender-Based Violence and the US War in Iraq." New York: MADRE, 2008, https://www.madre.org/press-publications/human-rights-report/promising-democracy-imposing-theocracy-gender-based-violence

MADRE and Women's International League for Peace and Freedom. "Joint Written Statement Submitted by the MADRE, Women's International League for Peace and Freedom (WILPF), Non-governmental Organizations in Special Consultative Status." UN Doc. A/HRC/S-22/NGO/13, September 1, 2014.

MADRE, Organization of Women's Freedom in Iraq, Asuda, and Women's International League for Peace and Freedom. "Letter to the UN Security Council Expert Group on

Women, Peace and Security." April 20, 2016, https://www.madre.org/press-publications/human-rights-report/letter-un-security-council.

Mohammed, Y. "Statement at the UN Security Council Open Debate on Women, Peace, and Security." NGO Working Group on Women, Peace, and Security. October 13, 2015, http://www.womenpeacesecurity.org/resource/statement-unsc-wps-open-debate-october-2015/.

Organization of Women's Freedom in Iraq, OutRight Action International [formerly IGLHRC], and MADRE. *We're Here: Iraqi LGBT People's Accounts of Violence and Rights Abuse.* Madre, 2014a, https://www.madre.org/sites/default/files/PDFs/We%27re%20Here%20AR-ENG%20Revised%20w%20Security%20Statement-%20050115.pdf.

Organization of Women's Freedom in Iraq, OutRight Action International [formerly IGLHRC], and MADRE. "When Coming Out Is a Death Sentence: Persecution of LGBTI Iraqis." OutRight, November 2014b, https://www.outrightinternational.org/sites/default/files/ComingOutDeathSentence_Iraq_0.pdf.

OutRight Action International [formerly IGLHRC], Human Rights Watch, and Amnesty International. "Iraq: Investigate Emo Attacks." OutRight, March 16, 2012, https://www.outrightinternational.org/content/iraq-investigate-'emo'-attacks.

Power, S. "Remarks at a UN Security Council Arria-Formula Meeting on ISIL's Targeting of LGBT Individuals." United States Mission to the United Nations, August 24, 2015, https://2009-2017-usun.state.gov/remarks/6799.

Rserven. "UN Votes to Protect People on Basis of Sexual Orientation, Gender Identity: US Abstains." *Daily Kos*, November 22, 2012, https://www.dailykos.com/stories/2012/11/22/1164003/-UN-votes-to-protect-people-on-basis-sexual-orientation-gender-identity.

Sjoberg, L. *Gender, War, and Conflict.* Cambridge: Polity Press, 2014.

Stern, J. "The U.N. Security Council's Arria-Formula Meeting on Vulnerable Groups in Conflict: ISIL's Targeting of LGBTI Individuals." *New York University Journal of International Law and Politics* 48 (2016), 1191–1198.

United Nations. "Ending Violence against Women: From Words to Action." Study of the Secretary-General, 2006, http://www.unwomen.org/-/media/headquarters/media/publications/un/en/englishstudy.pdf?vs=954.

United Nations Assistance Mission for Iraq and Office of the United Nations High Commissioner for Human Rights. "Report on the Protection of Civilians in Armed Conflict in Iraq, 1 May–31 October 2015." OHCHR, 2015, http://www.ohchr.org/Documents/Countries/IQ/UNAMIReport1May31October2015.pdf.

United Nations Assistance Mission for Iraq and Office of the United Nations High Commissioner for Human Rights. "Report on the Protection of Civilians in Armed Conflict in Iraq, January to June 2016." OHCHR, December 5, 2016, http://uniraq.com/index.php?option=com_k2&view=item&id=5974:report-on-human-rights-in-iraq-january-to-june-2016&Itemid=650&lang=en.

United Nations Security Council. "Working Methods Handbook: Background Note on the 'Arria-Formula' Meetings of the Security Council Members." October 25, 2002, https://www.un.org/en/sc/about/methods/bgarriaformula.shtml.

United Nations Security Council. "Conflict-Related Sexual Violence: Report of the Secretary-General." March 23, 2015, http://www.securitycouncilreport.org/atf/cf/%7B65BFCF9B-6D27-4E9C-8CD3-CF6E4FF96FF9%7D/s_2015_203.pdf.

United Nations Security Council. "Report of the Secretary-General on Women and Peace and Security." UN Doc. S/2016/822, September 29, 2016a, http://www.securitycouncilreport. org/atf/cf/%7B65BFCF9B-6D27-4E9C-8CD3-CF6E4FF96FF9%7D/s_2016_822.pdf.

United Nations Security Council. "Security Council Press Statement on Terrorist Attack in Orlando, Florida." June 13, 2016b, https://www.un.org/press/en/2016/sc12399.doc.htm.

UN Women. "Statement by UN Women on the Adoption of Security Council Resolution 2242 on Women, Peace, and Security." October 14, 2015, http://www.unwomen.org/en/news/ stories/2015/10/ed-statement-unsc-resolution-1325.

....

CHAPTER 52

WPS AND CEDAW, OPTIONAL PROTOCOL, AND GENERAL RECOMMENDATIONS

....

CATHERINE O'ROURKE WITH AISLING SWAINE

A key conclusion of the Global Study on UN Security Council Resolution 1325 was the need for improved synergies between the treaty-based human rights system and the Women, Peace, and Security (WPS) agenda:

> To fully realize the human rights obligations of the women, peace and security agenda, all intergovernmental bodies and human rights mechanisms must act in synergy to protect and promote women's and girls' rights at all times, including in conflict and post-conflict situations (United Nations 2015: 350).

This chapter considers the current and potential role of the Convention on the Elimination of All Forms of Discrimination Against Women (hereafter "CEDAW" or "the Convention") and the CEDAW Committee (hereafter "CEDAW Committee" or "the Committee") to enhance implementation of the WPS resolutions.

The chapter begins by providing an introduction and overview of CEDAW, the Optional Protocol, and the CEDAW Committee's activities. The chapter then turns to specific activities by the CEDAW Committee to address the WPS agenda and its implementation by state parties to CEDAW. Further, the chapter addresses tensions emerging from the concurrent implementation of both agendas, as well as efforts to resolve such tensions. The chapter argues that the CEDAW Convention and Committee offer unique opportunities for improved implementation of the resolutions by UN member states and further structured opportunities for civil society involvement in the interpretation, monitoring, and enforcement of WPS commitments. Nevertheless, the chapter concludes, there is also value in the tensions between the human rights focus of CEDAW and the peace and security priorities of WPS.

CEDAW, THE OPTIONAL PROTOCOL
AND GENERAL RECOMMENDATIONS

It was in response to the identified gendered shortcomings of the human rights canon that CEDAW was adopted in 1979 and the CEDAW Committee was established to monitor its implementation (Bunch 1990; Charlesworth and Chinkin 2000). The Convention's radical departure from the established canon at the time of its adoption was demonstrated in its broad definition of discrimination against women encompassing both public and private life (Article 1), its integration of civil and political (Articles 7–9), and social and economic rights (Articles 10–13), the permissive provision for temporary special measures to remedy gender inequality (Articles 4), and its requirement on state parties to modify discriminatory social and cultural patterns (Article 5).

Much more than its symbolic importance, however, the entry into force of the Convention in 1981 established a treaty-based system of state accountability for an enumerated list of women's human rights, involving periodic review of state compliance (Article 18) by an independent committee of experts (Article 17). Firstly, and most importantly, the Committee has led the periodic review of state compliance with obligations under the Convention. This takes place through connected procedures of state reporting, effectively engaging NGOs in shadow reporting, and pursuing a "constructive dialogue" with states' party representatives based on the Committee's compliance concerns. The Committee's written "Concluding Observations" detail specific recommendations to the state party, which are reviewed on subsequent reporting cycles. Secondly, the Committee has enhanced these periodic reporting procedures through the activation of what might be termed "monitoring-plus" activities, in the form of "statements" addressing particular women's human rights' situations of concern, and the request for "exceptional reports" from state parties, outside of the normal reporting cycle, where the circumstances merit such a request (Article 18). The Committee has established itself as the key institution advancing feminist informed normative and legal developments on women's rights under international law (Freeman et al. 2012: 13).

The CEDAW Committee plays a unique and critical role in advancing feminist-informed interpretations of the treaty's provisions and ultimately in shaping normative development of international human rights law. The Committee undertakes this work in particular by articulating authoritative interpretations of the Convention through General Recommendations. Because the Convention itself guarantees broad rights of non-discrimination against women, the Committee plays a key role in developing and interpreting the application of those broad rights to specific settings and challenges. Under the Convention's article 21, the General Recommendations are informed by the Committee's state monitoring activities, where it identifies systematic or structural issues that are best dealt with by a more general statement, rather than specific comments to state parties. The Committee's most significant General Recommendation to date has been General Recommendation 19 (1992) on violence against women. The significance of this recommendation lies in the fact that the Convention does not explicitly address gender-based violence as a human rights violation. General Recommendation 19 has been significant throughout the international human rights system in identifying gender-based violence as both a cause and consequence of historically unequal gender relations, and, further, in articulating how violence against women prevents victims from enjoying the full plethora of rights guaranteed under CEDAW. Another General Recommendation of significance to this chapter is General Recommendation 28 (2010) on the nature of state obligations under CEDAW. General Recommendation 28 is explicit in determining that obligations on state parties under CEDAW prevail even in contexts of armed conflict and also apply extra-territorially to the conduct of state parties outside of their borders. Finally, General Recommendation Number 30 (2013) on the rights of women in conflict-prevention, conflict, and conflict resolution, addresses the application of rights guaranteed under CEDAW to the specific context of conflict.

Scholarship on the limitations of CEDAW has focused on its structural weaknesses. Foremost among these is the challenge posed by far-reaching reservations to the Convention, whereby states seek to "hollow out the heart of their obligations" (Charlesworth and Chinkin 2000: 113). Compounding the challenge of reservations, the Convention's lack of an individual complaints procedure, and the Committee's mandate under Article 17(1) to "consider the progress made in the implementation" of the Convention—as distinct from monitoring compliance or determining violations—has historically posed a significant structural obstacle to the protection and promotion of women's rights. Weaker implementation and obligation procedures contribute to a picture of a fragile infrastructure for the protection and promotion of women's human rights under CEDAW.

There have been two important responses to the recognized structural weaknesses of CEDAW. The first, to emerge from some related scholarly work, has been to advocate a shift away from understanding the Convention as a legal instrument. Largely due to its endemic problems of under-enforcement, CEDAW is often conceptualized as principally a "cultural" rather than "legal" tool for the advancement of women's rights. Sally Engle Merry, for example, argues that the Convention is more important for the cultural work that it does than for its specific repressive function:

> Human rights law is itself primarily a cultural system. Its limited enforcement mechanisms mean that the impact of human rights law is a matter of persuasion rather than force, of cultural transformation rather than coercive change. Its documents create new cultural frameworks for conceptualizing social justice (Merry 2006: 16).

CEDAW's under-enforcement is usefully located within broader challenges of state commitment and compliance confronted across the spectrum of international human rights treaties (Simmons 2009). The Convention is not unique, therefore, in the enforcement challenges that it confronts. Looking comparatively across a range of rights protected by international treaties, Beth Simmons concludes that the treaties' impacts lie less in their direct relationship with state parties, but rather in the mobilizing framework that they offer to domestic reform constituencies. Moreover, the prerequisites for such impacts are supportive conditions for social mobilization and strategic litigation. Where such circumstances are absent, human rights treaty ratification cannot, of itself, compel progressive change (Simmons 2009: 253–254). Simmons's findings indicate broadly positive outcomes for women's rights if CEDAW is re-conceptualized not principally as a set of legally binding obligations on states, but rather to provide a supportive mobilizing framework for domestic reform constituencies. These findings support the chapter thesis that CEDAW offers unique opportunities for civil society involvement in the interpretation, monitoring, and enforce-ment of WPS commitments.

The second response to CEDAW's structural weaknesses, intended as a legal and insti-tutional remedy, has been successful advocacy for the adoption of an Optional Protocol to CEDAW. The Optional Protocol, which was adopted by the United Nations General Assembly in 1999, established two new enforcement procedures. Firstly, it established the right of individual petition for individuals from state parties to seek recourse for violations of their rights guaranteed under CEDAW (Article 1), subject to a number of procedural requirements, most notably the obligation to first exhaust domestic remedies (Article 4). Significantly, however, the Optional Protocol also empowers the Committee to conduct an inquiry "where it has received reliable information of grave or systematic violations by a State Party of rights established in the Convention" (Article 8). The enforcement procedures have afforded the Committee an opportunity not just to encourage states to move toward compliance, but to actually determine violations of the Convention in spe-cific incidences. The individual petition procedure has gathered significant momentum and the Committee regularly considers complaints from individuals alleging violations of their rights guaranteed under CEDAW. The inquiry procedure for the investigation of "grave or systematic violation" of the Convention has, by contrast, been characterized by "under-usage" (Freeman et al. 2012: 617). It has been activated only three times since the Optional Protocol entered into force in 2000. In the case of both the individual petition and in-quiry procedures, the Committee has not yet addressed violations emerging specifically from conflict. The adoption of General Recommendation 30 (2013) addressing the rights of women in conflict-prevention, conflict, and post-conflict reconstruction may yet prompt increased use of the Optional Protocol to vindicate the rights guaranteed by CEDAW to women and girls in conflict-affected settings.

OVERVIEW OF DEVELOPMENTS ON WPS AND CEDAW

CEDAW does not specify its application to armed conflict, in contrast, for example, to the Convention on the Rights of the Child. Further, its provisions do not specifically address the needs and rights of women that prevail in conflict-affected settings. Rather, they are general statements of women's rights to be interpreted and applied as necessary to end all forms of discrimination against women. Because none of the enumerated rights formally address conflict, there is potential for selective state reporting on the impact of conflict on women's rights. Nevertheless, the Convention does not provide for derogation during periods of conflict and public emergency, and the Committee has consistently affirmed the Convention's application to conflict, civil strife, and public emergency (Committee on the Elimination of All Forms of Discrimination 2013: para. 11).

The CEDAW Committee engaged in some monitoring of state party activity on UN Security Council Resolution 1325 (2000) prior to its adoption of General Recommendation 30. In particular, the Committee has scrutinized state party adoption of National Action Plans (NAPs) on WPS. The Committee has fostered the adoption of

NAPs by commending state parties that have done so (CEDAW 2006a: para. 6), and in encouraging other state parties to do likewise. Further, the Committee has scrutinized NAP content and implementation (CEDAW 2011: para. 35). In addition to its scrutiny of NAP adoption, content, and implementation, the Committee has also framed its recommendations to state parties on conflict-specific issues as constitutive of their implementation of resolution 1325 (CEDAW 2006b: para. 34). It is noteworthy that the Committee's scrutiny of state party activity on WPS extends to both conflict-affected countries and donor countries.

The adoption by the Committee of General Recommendation Number 30 (2013) on the rights of women in conflict prevention, conflict, and post-conflict reconstruction therefore arose from the recognized silences of the Convention in specifically addressing challenges to women's rights in such settings. Evidencing inter-institutional cooperation to advance the rights of women in conflict, the initial Concept Note that led to the ultimate General Recommendation was written by UN Women. Further, UN Women funded and supported the regional consultations that were held with women's organizations to inform the drafting of General Recommendation 30. Thematically, General Recommendation 30, in line with all of the Committee's General Recommendations, takes the Convention as its starting point. The bulk of the General Recommendation is dedicated to articulating the ways in which the rights guaranteed under CEDAW are impacted by conflict, specifically the prohibition of discrimination in law, policy, and custom; the obligation on states to challenge discriminatory social and cultural patterns; the prohibition on trafficking; the right to political participation in domestic and international affairs; access to education, employment, health; and the rights of rural women; right to nationality; right to equality in marriage and family relations; and the right to enter into contracts. General Recommendation 30 notes the consequent obligations on states to remedy violations caused by conflict and makes several recommendations to states parties to this end.

General Recommendation 30 specifically addresses the relationship of CEDAW to the WPS resolutions, substantively, in terms of the importance of implementing the resolutions in order to comply with state obligations under CEDAW and, procedurally, in terms of the obligations on states to report on their WPS activities in their periodic reporting to the CEDAW Committee. General Recommendation 30 further addresses the territorial application of the Convention, to state party activities within their borders, but also in bilateral relations with neighboring states, in donor activities and foreign affairs, and in multilateral memberships of UN and regional organizations. As such, General Recommendation 30 not only addresses states currently or recently in conflict, but rather addresses all state parties. It reflects a longer-term body of work by the Committee to bring domestic implementation of the resolutions under its purview and within the Convention's formal mechanisms of state accountability.

General Recommendation 30 responds both to concerns about the legal status and under-enforcement of Security Council Resolution 1325. The Recommendation interprets implementation of the resolutions as constitutive of state obligations under CEDAW "as all areas of concern addressed in those resolutions find expression in the substantive provisions of the Convention" (CEDAW 2013: para. 26). In addition, this intervention by the Committee formally brings the domestic implementation of the resolutions under the monitoring role of the Committee:

States parties are to provide information on the implementation of the Security Council agenda on women, peace and security, in particular resolutions 1325 (2000), 1820 (2008), 1888 (2009), 1960 (2010) and 2106 (2013), including by specifically reporting on compliance with any agreed United Nations benchmarks or indicators developed as part of that agenda (para. 83).

The adoption of General Recommendation 30 has prompted a number of efforts from both civil society and responsible UN actors to harness the potential synergies between CEDAW and the WPS agenda. Very quickly after its adoption, UN Women commissioned a Guidebook to inform states how to achieve synergies between the implementation of both their CEDAW and WPS obligations (O'Rourke and Swaine 2015). The civil society organization, Global Network for Women Peacebuilders, began holding trainings with their in-country partners on how to utilize Shadow Reporting in order to improve international scrutiny of state performance on implementing WPS commitments. The UN Secretary-General, in his 2016 annual report on Women, Peace, and Security, specifically addressed the CEDAW Committee's activities under General Recommendation 30 and requested further guidance to states from the Committee on the detail of WPS commitments that could be implemented as part of broader CEDAW compliance activities (UN Secretary-General 2016: para. 73). Finally, and perhaps most importantly, in December 2016 an *Arria Formula* meeting was held between the Security Council and members of the CEDAW Committee, to discuss how synergies could be advanced. (Proposals emerging from this meeting are discussed further in what follows.) The holding of such a meeting is, in international law terms, unprecedented. That the two bodies would pursue cooperation and collaboration in this manner is potentially very significant for the mutually reinforcing implementation of both agendas.

INTERSECTIONS BETWEEN WPS AND CEDAW

Some Implementation Tensions

CEDAW and the WPS resolutions of the Security Council emerge from distinct UN organs, with distinct mandates and compositions. In formal institutional terms, CEDAW's roots lie in the Economic and Social Council established by the UN Charter in 1948 with a mandate to *inter alia* make and initiate studies and recommendations on human rights, as well as set up commissions "for the promotion of human rights." One such commission was the Commission on the Status of Women, which took a lead role in drafting the treaty text. The text was ultimately adopted by resolution of the General Assembly, the single most democratic and inclusive organ of the six established by the UN Charter. UN member states then separately ratify the treaty, whereby they consent to being bound by its obligations and to the authority of the monitoring body established by the Convention, namely the Committee on the Elimination of All Forms of Discrimination against Women.

The open and democratic process underpinning CEDAW, which includes the specific consent of individual states to international obligations, contrasts in several meaningful ways from the WPS resolutions of the Security Council. The Security Council was also established under the UN Charter, though without any expressed role in the advancement of equality and human rights. Rather, the Security Council is an enforcement body that responds to threats to international peace and security. Its membership is highly selective; five states have permanent membership while the remainder of member states vie for ten rotating nonpermanent memberships of two years duration. Further, its resolutions cannot be appealed or judicially reviewed. The resolutions of the Security Council proceed, therefore, with little required democratic input, broader state consent, or formal connection to the human rights mandate of the UN.

The key practical consequence of these distinct mandates is that, while CEDAW offers a mechanism for maintaining state accountability of all state parties with a clear basis in treaty law, the Security Council has no comparable accountability mechanism under the UN Charter. Rather, the Security Council's resources and infrastructure are more closely tailored to monitor UN system and intergovernmental activity. Beyond these practical differences are theoretical and doctrinal issues, such as the definition of "conflict" underpinning the activities of the respective bodies. Whereas the CEDAW Committee has adopted a broad understanding of "conflict," which includes protracted and low-intensity civil strife, ethnic and communal violence, and states of emergency (CEDAW 2013: para. 4), the Security Council has largely resisted such a broad definition, with some permanent members arguing that the agenda applies only to the country situations on the agenda of the Council.

In comparing the thematic focus of activity between the CEDAW Committee and the Security Council, the significance of a structural understanding of gender and conflict becomes evident. While both institutions share some common thematic concerns, such as conflict prevention, gender-based violence, and women's participation in peace-building, CEDAW and General Recommendation 30 go beyond the WPS resolutions in several critical respects. The WPS agenda, for example, does not address trafficking, nationality and statelessness, or marriage and family relations, yet these are specifically addressed in CEDAW and General Recommendation 30. Differences are not just evident in the themes addressed; they are perhaps even more telling in the approach adopted. In General Recommendation 19, General Recommendation 30, and throughout CEDAW's activities, the Committee has advanced an understanding of gender-based violence as both a cause and consequence of historically unequal relations between men and women. When addressing the specifics of conflict-related violence, therefore, the Committee understands and articulates the relationship of conflict-related violence to gender-based violence that precedes and survives the end of conflict. Moreover, the Committee situates such violence within the broader exacerbating effects of conflict on gender inequality and women's vulnerabilities to all forms of violence.

The approach contrasts in meaningful ways with the WPS resolutions' focus on "sexual violence when used or commissioned as a tactic of war to deliberately target civilians or as part of a widespread or systematic attack against civilian populations" (for example, UN Security Council 2008: para. 1). Differences are further evident in approaches to perhaps the most fundamental gender issue in conflict: its prevention. Whereas the WPS resolutions advocate the increased participation of women in conflict prevention (for example, UN Security Council 2000: para. 1), the CEDAW Committee advocates conflict prevention per se in order to address the causes of conflict—for example by calling on state parties to robustly regulate the arms trade and to appropriately control the circulation of conventional and small arms (CEDAW 2013: para. 29–38).

It is also possible to discern some clear and important trends in the state-monitoring activities by the Committee in conflict-affected state parties since it adopted General Recommendation 30. First and foremost, it is clear that the Committee is prioritizing women's participation in peace processes and transitional justice processes, in its monitoring of state activities. Given that this issue of participation is one of the four priority pillars of the WPS resolutions, it is noteworthy that it is the Committee, rather than the Security Council, that is pursuing meaningful accountability in this regard. The priority given by the Committee to women's participation is best-illustrated by the selection of this issue for "follow-up" by the Committee, in Georgia, in the Central African Republic, Iraq, and Syria. Further, NAPs continue to be an area of scrutiny. The Concluding Observations also address issues around statelessness, and employment and economic opportunities affected by conflict, as specified in General Recommendation 30. Of particular interest are the Committee's Concluding Observations to Syria in 2014, which deal almost exclusively with conflict-related challenges to women's human rights (CEDAW 2014). The Committee draws heavily on General Recommendation 30 to that end, and importantly draws attention also to shortcomings beyond the state party, specifically in donor funding to the country, and the conduct of non-state armed actors. To quote the Global Study on the Implementation of Resolution 1325, the Concluding Observations to Syria are a "model for the engagement of civil society with human rights mechanisms on the WPS agenda" (United Nations 2015: 357).

From the perspective of the Security Council, by contrast, the potential for any synergy between its work and that of the human rights system has been tentative to this point. The WPS agenda and the wider thematic as well as routine work of the Security Council has continued to develop almost in isolation from obligations on women's and human rights in the wider UN system. Procedurally, this has meant little crossover in terms of account-ability in respect of the Security Council itself with procedural human rights mechanisms such as the CEDAW Committee. While the Security Council does reference broader nor-mative and human rights instruments of the UN system in its resolutions, actual sub-stantive engagement with CEDAW has been sparse. Noteworthy is that CEDAW is not referenced in all of the WPS resolutions, and less so in the resolutions addressing conflict-related sexual violence. CEDAW is cited in the operational paragraphs of resolution 1325 (2000) and resolution 2250 (2015), wherein states parties and parties to armed conflict are called upon to comply with applicable obligations under CEDAW; and in resolution 2145 (2014) and resolution 2210 (2015), where duplicate requests are made to the UN mission in Afghanistan to continue support to that states' compliance to CEDAW. Otherwise, where CEDAW is mentioned, it appears in the preambular paragraphs, which are considered by some as a "dumping ground" for proposals not acceptable in the operative paragraphs (Wood 1998: 86).

How Implementation Tensions Might be Addressed

Practically speaking, there are ways that the activity of each regime can be engaged with, shared, and used to influence progress on women's rights in conflict by both regimes. The evidence gathered by the CEDAW Committee through periodic and exceptional state party reports, civil society shadow reports, and Committee hearings provide data that is of use to the Security Council as it makes decisions on situations on its agenda. The Security Council can rely on that data and demonstrate its willingness to make use of and reference that work in its own working methods. The Informal Experts Group of the Security Council established under resolution 2242 (2015) has already made use of reports by the CEDAW Committee in its briefing on Mali, for example. This mechanism facilitates briefings to the Security Council about situations on its agenda that are delivered by experts and civil society members. This mechanism could also include the outputs of CEDAW state party monitoring or members of the Committee. This is a particular opportunity for civil society, a constituency with considerably fewer opportunities for formal engagement with the Security Council than the CEDAW Committee, to have their insights and outputs considered.

The Security Council can, in turn, maximize the potential of its own areas of authority, most notably its power under its sanctions regime. A High-Level Review of the Security Council's sanctions regime made specific recommendations for expanded sanctions criteria that would include inducing thematic areas of concern to be considered as "threats" under the Security Council's mandate in respect of sanctions. This included a recommendation that the Security Council "should use existing sanctions regimes more effectively to enforce thematic priorities, including . . . the Women, Peace and Security Agenda[s]" (UN Security Council and General Assembly 2015: 68). A further recommendation was made to adopt thematic sanctions regimes that would include not only sexual violence (which has been its only focus to date as noted earlier), but significantly "gross violations of women's rights" (UN Security Council and General Assembly 2015: 82). Whether and how women's rights become mapped onto and reach the threshold of "threat" to international peace and security remains to be seen. The sanctions committee can, for example, make use of the reports of states parties and the concluding observations of the CEDAW Committee, drawing in data from the CEDAW Committee to inform moves toward this development and in its overall decisions-making. Cross-regime dialogue could also be expanded, such as briefings by members of the CEDAW Committee to the sanctions committee on women's rights in the situation under purview, and civil society members responsible for shadow reports could also be invited to make submissions relevant to establishing violations of women's rights as evidence for sanctions. Likewise, the reports of peacekeeping missions and the UN Secretary-General's now annual report on this issue could be shared with CEDAW, reinforcing joined-up reporting, data sharing, and approaches to addressing sexual exploitation within the UN system by both regimes. The opportunities that exist for enhanced data-sharing and cross-regime dialogue, in the pursuit of improved overall accountability for women's rights in conflict, are considerable.

CONCLUSION

The adoption of concurrent provisions on women and conflict by both the CEDAW Committee and the Security Council has brought these two entities into direct conversation with each other, albeit from different legal, normative, and mandate-driven standpoints. The CEDAW Committee, through General Recommendation 30, has provided guidance to states on their obligations to women's rights in settings of conflict and peace-building. The WPS resolutions have ensured that the Security Council is engaged in institutional activity regarding women's rights within its mandate, such as using its specific powers to address issues like conflict-related sexual violence through its sanctions regime. For both regimes, it is evident that moving forward on modalities for the practical enforcement and implementation of the concerns and rights of women in conflict cannot be advanced in isolation from the other. Clearly, therefore, there is an important role for complementarity.

Such complementarity should be accompanied also, however, by "productive friction" (Young 2012: 88) between the regimes, in which each seeks to hold the other to account for its activities on women's rights in conflict. In the increasingly complex terrain of international law, proposals for regime interaction need to be contextual and institution-specific, and judged with respect to the democracy, transparency, and openness of the respective institutions. Proposals that maximize accountability (broadly understood) will enhance legitimacy also. This is something that should motivate both regimes. Rather than seeing the differences in mandate and focus as obstacles to the advancement of women's rights in conflict, it is important also to recognize the value in tensions between the security-focus of the Security Council and the feminist and rights-based approach of the CEDAW Committee.

REFERENCES

Bunch, C. "Women's Rights as Human Rights: Toward a Re-Vision of Human Rights." *Human Rights Quarterly* 12 (1990): 486–498.

Charlesworth, H., and C. Chinkin. *The Boundaries of International Law: A Feminist Analysis.* Manchester, UK: Manchester University Press, 2000.

Committee on the Elimination of All Forms of Discrimination against Women. "Concluding Observations to Cyprus." UN Doc. CEDAW/C/CYP/3-5, 2006a.

Committee on the Elimination of All Forms of Discrimination against Women. "Concluding Observations to Denmark." UN Doc. CEDAW/C/DEN/CO6, 2006b.

Committee on the Elimination of All Forms of Discrimination against Women. "Concluding Observation to Nepal." UN Doc. CEDAW/C/NPL/CO/4-5, 2011.

Committee on the Elimination of All Forms of Discrimination against Women. "Concluding Observations to Syria.: UN Doc CEDAW/C/SYR/CO/2, 2014.

Committee on the Elimination of All Forms of Discrimination against Women. "General Recommendation Number 30 on the Rights of Women in Conflict Prevention, Conflict, and Conflict Resolution." UN Doc CEDAW/C/GC/30, 2013.

Freeman, M. A., C. Chinkin, and B. Rudolf. *The UN Convention on the Elimination of All Forms of Discrimination against Women: A Commentary.* Oxford: Oxford University Press, 2012.

Merry, S. E. *Human Rights and Gender Violence: Translating International Law into Local Justice.* New York: Cambridge University Press, 2006.

O'Rourke, C., and A. Swaine. *Guidebook on CEDAW General Recommendation Number 30 and the UN Security Council Resolutions on Women, Peace, and Security.* New York: UN Women, 2015.

Simmons, B. A. *Mobilizing for Human Rights: International Law in Domestic Politics.* New York: Cambridge University Press, 2009.

United Nations. "Preventing Conflict, Transforming Justice, Securing the Peace: A Global Study on the Implementation of United Nations Security Council Resolution 1325." New York: United Nations, 2015.

United Nations General Assembly and Security Council. "Compendium of the High-Level Review of the United Nations Sanctions." UN Doc A/69/941-S/2015/432, 2015.

United Nations Secretary-General. "Annual Report to the Security Council on Women, Peace, and Security." UN Doc S/2016/822, 2016.

United Nations Security Council. "Resolution 1325." UN Doc S/RES2122/2013, 2000.

United Nations Security Council. "Resolution 1820." UN Doc S/RES1820/2008 2008.

Wood, M. "The Interpretation of UN Security Council Resolutions." *Max Planck Yearbook of United Nations Law* 2 (1998): 73–95.

Young, M. A. "Regime Interaction in Creating, Implementing, and Enforcing International Law. In *Regime Interaction in International Law: Facing Fragmentation*, edited by M. A. Young, 85–110. Cambridge: Cambridge University Press, 2012.

CHAPTER 53

WOMEN'S ROLES IN CVE

SRI WIYANTI EDDYONO WITH SARA E. DAVIES

IN 2000, the UN Security Council adopted UN Security Council Resolution (UNSCR) 1325 regarding Women, Peace, and Security (WPS). This Resolution sought to redress the absence of discussion and understanding on the deep impact of conflict on women. Several remarkable inclusions were attached to the successive WPS UN Security Council Resolutions (UNSCR) 1820 (2008), 1888 (2009), 1889 (2009), 1960 (2010) and 2106 (2013), and 2122 (2013). While UNSCRs 1820, 1888, 1960, and 2106 primarily focus on women's experience in conflict relating to sexual violence, the UNSCR 1889 and 2122 have expanded to discuss the significance of women's participation in peace agreements, post-conflict reconstruction, and governance. These developments reflect the shifting ideas and approaches from women as a passive subject into the active role as an agent in peace-building. The approach resonates the importance to discuss women's agenda in peace and security arena, not only because women are affected deeply and excessively from the conflict, but women can also play significant roles in maintaining peace.

One of the significant resolutions with regard to the conceptualization of women's role is the UNSCR 2122, which reaffirms UNSCR 1325 and states that the implementation of UNSCR 1325 can only effectively achieved "through dedicated commitment to women's empowerment, participation, and human rights, and through concerted leadership, consistent information and action, and support, to build women's engagement in all levels of decision-making." Women's empowerment, women's leadership, and women's participation and engagement in all levels of decision-making are powerful ideas which resonate clearly in the contemporary women, peace, and security agenda. This chapter examines recent attempts to integrate these ideas of empowerment, leadership, and participation associated with the WPS agenda to the issue of preventing and countering violence extremism (P/CVE). The chapter first presents the relevant frameworks concerning WPS that can be utilized in addressing P/CVE; and in the second part of the chapter, we explore whether and how women can play significant roles—empowerment, leadership, and participation roles in P/CVE.

DEFINING P/CVE

The United Nations Global Counter-Terrorism Strategy Resolution (Resolution 60/288 2006) states "that acts, methods and practices of terrorism in all its forms and manifestations are activities aimed at the destruction of human rights, fundamental freedoms and democracy, threatening territorial integrity, security of States and destabilizing legitimately constituted Governments." It emphasized that terrorism has a deep impact on development, peace and security, and human rights. The UN Security Council Resolution 2178 (UNSC 2014) states that terrorism and, in all its forms and manifestations, denotes one of the most serious threats to international peace and security where "any acts of terrorism are criminal and unjustifiable regardless of their motivations, whenever and by whomsoever committed."

The UN has not yet established a clear definition of violence extremism (VE), but it has been referred to as a phenomenon that is not specific to a certain region, nationality, or system of belief (UNSG 2015). What has been agreed upon is that addressing VE and countering its occurrence constitutes a significant impact on potential acts of terror (terrorism) (UNSC 2014; UNSG 2015). In Resolution 2718, a direct link was made between countering violent extremism and the mitigation of terrorism. Specifically, this resolution contends that countering violent extremism can be conducive to preventing terrorism, and countering violent extremism (P/CVE) can serve to prevent radicalism, recruitment, and mobilization of individuals joining with terrorist groups, and thus becoming foreign terrorist fighters.

Terrorism and violent extremism have undergone significant shifts in how foreign terrorist fighters are being recruited. The activities are being conducted in various regions from the Middle East and Africa to Europe and Asia; and the recruitment process itself depends upon spreading hatred, intolerance, and violence in the fighters' own communities (UN Women 2015). The activities also target and violate women. Young women in particular are targeted for gender based violence that incudes sexual violence (Iman and Yuval-Davis 2004; UNSG 2015; True and Eddyono 2017); and recruitment activity seeks to involve women to spread ideology and conduct terrorist acts (D'Estaing 2017; Bakker and Leede 2015). Bakker and Leede (2015) and D'Estaing (2017) have discussed the increased phenomena of women's involvement as foreign fighters, particularly young women.

Women have long participated and engaged in activities of terrorist groups and violent extremism. It is therefore important to be sensitive to the different roles of women in terrorism and violent extremism–this engagement reflects the diversity of women (Dufour-Genneson and Alam 2014). In radicalized communities, according to Dufour-Genneson and Alam (2014), women can be at once victims, violent actors, as well as agents in positive action. Women's roles in this area of peace and security are very dynamic. Women have the ability to influence situations involving extreme violence activities; the question is what agenda and strategy is best suited to establish and encourage empowered women's roles in P/CVE.

WPS FRAMEWORKS AND P/CVE

The relevant UN Security Council documents that have sought to establish a conceptual and policy cross-cutting approach between WPS and P/CVE are UNSCR 2178 (2014), UNSCR 2242 (2015), UN Secretary General's Plan of Action to Prevent Violent Extremism (UNGA 2015) and the Fifth Review on the Global Counter-Terrorism Strategy (UNGA 2016). These documents all refer to WPS agenda stated in UNSCR 1325 (2000) as well as UNSCR 2242 (2015). Briefly, we detail below how each resolution has paid attention to the embedding the WPS agenda in the P/CVE strategies.

The adoption of UNSCR 2178 in 2014 was a vital step toward preventing terrorism by promoting a focus on CVE. It was also significant for the WPS agenda as it was the first time the UN Security Council acknowledged the urgency to empower women as a strategy to mitigate factors contributing to the spread of violent extremist and radicalism (UN Women 2015). The adoption of UNSCR 2178 was also a sign of the significant development in approaches toward violent extremism, as the UN Security Council endorsed nonviolent and peaceful alternative strategies to decrease the risk radicalization to terrorism within this resolution. A nonviolent approach is particularly relevant to the WPS agenda and women's experiences, as many studies presented to date have revealed that the "hard" violent approach to combat terrorism and violent extremism often places women in (more) dangerous and difficult situations (UN Women 2015).

In 2015, UNSCR 2242 followed. This resolution was the first attempt to develop a framework on the WPS agenda in addressing terrorism and violent extremism. Although the previous resolution UNSC 2178 (2014) mentioned the WPS agenda and a commitment to empower women, it did not provide a framework or strategy to enhance women's role. In contrast, UNSCR 2242 (2015) elaborates a number of recommendations with regard to women's roles in addressing terrorism and violent extremism. The resolution also notes the need for a differentiated gender sensitive understanding of CVE, for women,

> terrorism and violent extremism, including in the context of their health, education, and participation in public life, and that they are often directly targeted by terrorist groups, and expressing deep concern that acts of sexual and gender-based violence are known to be part of the strategic objectives and ideology of certain terrorist groups, used as a tactic of terrorism, and an instrument to increase their power through supporting financing, recruitment, and the destruction of communities . . .

The UNSCR 2242 (2015) framework focuses on several keys points that acknowledge the need to incorporate the WPS agenda to P/CVE:

(a) The urgency to increase of funding on WPS, specifically to provide more aid in conflict and post-conflict situations for programs that further gender equality and women's empowerment and civil society organization capacity building.
(b) The greater integration of agendas on WPS, counterterrorism, and countering violent extremism by members states, and UN offices and agencies.
(c) The integration of gender as a cross-cutting issue throughout the activities within their respective mandates, including within country-specific assessments and reports, recommendations in the Counter-Terrorism Committee (CTC), and the Counter-Terrorism Committee Executive Directorate (CTED). This includes the task to facilitate technical assistance to member states by open consultation with women's groups.
(d) Collaboration among UN bodies relating to P/CVE, particularly UN Women, in conducting and gathering gender-sensitive research and data collection on the drivers of radicalization for women, and the impacts of counterterrorism strategies on women's human rights and women's organizations.
(e) Ensuring participation and leadership of women and women's organizations in establishing strategies to counter terrorism and violent extremism.

In addition to the guidance from the UN Security Council, the UN Secretariat itself introduced important suggestions on the linkage between WPS and P/CVE. First came the release of the UN Secretary-General's Plan of Action to Prevent Violent Extremism (UNGA 2015). One recommendation in the Plan of Action was to strengthen women's roles. Specifically, the Plan recommends a focus on seven priority areas in which two were devoted to gender—gender equality and empowering women.[1] The framework also defined prevention and countering violent extremism as two interrelated approaches: first, a gender-integrated approach, placing women and men inclusively as part of the broader society dealing with diverse and interrelates issues; and second, a specific approach through a gender and women's empowerment strategy. In some aspects, this action plan reemphasizes but also broadening the strategies and framework stated in UNSCR 2242 (UNGA 2015).

The key points of the gender integration approach of the Plan of Action can be seen from the platform to establish national action plans in member countries, develop law and human rights reform, and in the youth platform. It was recommended that national action plans be established through a consultation process or gathering input from a wide range of government actors (different departments and law enforcement), as well as nongovernmental actors who work for youth, families, women, religious, cultural, and education sectors (including civil society organizations, media, and private sector actors). The national plans to prevent violent extremism were advised to link the analysis of the drivers of violence extremism with development policies on the Sustainable Development Goals, especially the SGD goal one: ending poverty in all its forms; goal four: ensuring inclusive and equitable quality education and promoting lifelong learning opportunities for all; and goal five: achieving gender equality and empowering all women and girls.

The Platform of Action introduces approaches of disengagement, rehabilitation, and counseling programs for persons engaged in violent extremism—and stresses that these programs be gender-sensitive and children-sensitive to facilitate reintegration into society for these people.[2] The gender-equality and empowering-women approaches designed in the Plan of Action are included out of acknowledgement that

> women's empowerment is a critical force for sustainable peace. While women do sometimes play an active role in violent extremist organizations, it is also no coincidence that societies for which gender equality indicators are higher are less vulnerable to violent extremism. We must therefore ask ourselves how we can better promote women's participation, leadership, and empowerment across society, including in governmental, security sector, and civil society institutions.

The Action Plan reiterates UNSCR 2242 (2015) in that the strategies designed for addressing terrorism and violent extremism have to ensure the protection and empowerment of women as central considerations. The strategy has to consider—crucially—whether it can cause negative impact on women's rights. The Plan establishes five strategies on gender equality and women's empowerment, as follows:

1. Mainstream gender perspective across activities in preventing violent extremism;
2. Establish gender sensitive research and data collection on women's roles in C/PVE;

3. Involve women and other underrepresented groups in the implementation of law and security agency, which includes counterterrorism prevention and response frameworks;
4. Offer opportunities for women in capacity building and encourage their civil society groups to engage in prevention and response efforts related to violent extremism;
5. Provide adequate funds for projects that address women's specific needs or that empower women in preventing violent extremism.

Finally, the UN General Assembly's Fifth Review Resolution on the Global Counter-Terrorism Strategy was adopted in 2016 (UNGA 2015). The review acknowledges the significant contribution of women activists in advocacy for the implementation of the Global Counter-Terrorism Strategy to ensure women's participation and leadership to prevent and counter violent extremism. The review discusses how acts of sexual and gender-based violence, for example, are a financing and recruitment strategy of particular terrorist groups because trafficking women generates income (via trafficking networks) and attracts recruits from fundamentalist communities. Therefore, the review urges to all member states to do the following:

(a) emphasize the significant role of women in addressing terrorism and violent extremism;
(b) integrate a gender analysis to study the impact of radicalization of women to terrorism and the impacts of counterterrorism strategies on women's human rights and women's organizations;
(c) consult with women and women's organizations when establishing strategies to counterterrorism and violent extremism.

From the development of the Global Strategy on countering and preventing violent extremism, its review, and the Plan of Action, the last three years have achieved significant progress in conceptualizing an empowered and inclusive WPS agenda into countering and preventing P/CVE. In particular, the Global Strategy (UNGA 2016) acknowledged the significant contributions of national and international women's movement in ensuring the integration of gender perspective and the importance of women's role in addressing VE. The Global Strategy, however, has yet to be broken down into more detailed plans for implementation to ensure consistent impact at the regional and local levels (Ní Aoláin 2016). It is also important to make sure that the implementation of the P/CVE strategy avoids the instrumentalization of women and women's rights, where women are only seen as tools or are being utilized or perceived as assets to prevent and counter VE (UN Women 2015; d'Estaing 2017).

Developing Strategy on Enhancing Women's Roles from Best Practices

Given the complexity and dynamic forms of VE, multiple strategies are necessary to prevent and address the local risks. Iman and Yuval-Davis (2004) analyzed the link between the rise of fundamentalism and extreme violence, finding that fundamentalism and radicalism often place women as their center of struggle as submissive objects to achieve their violent acts and support their objectives. Through a pilot study in Indonesia, True and Eddyono (2017) also found the link between the rise of extreme violence and the presence of fundamentalism ideology in everyday life. Thus, it is essential to create differentiated local opportunities to support and encourage women's empowerment, women's leadership, and women's participation to address P/CVE. Establishing a range of programs may be necessary to access women within often diverse communities, rather than adopting a one issue–one community approach. Based on evidence from the field, there are three core aspects that need to be considered to develop an empowered women's agenda in P/CVE: the diversity of women's roles; the promotion of women's human rights; and the inclusion of women in interfaith dialogue.

First, it is necessary to recognize women's multiple roles and support women's agency in these different fora. Women's roles may need to remain diverse for some time. Therefore, it is crucial to support women in these different roles and their agency in various arenas, rather than focusing on training women or reforming women to take on different or more "progressive" roles. What does this look like in practice? In studying women's roles in Indonesia (and the wider South East Asian context), True and Eddyono (2017) looked at the importance of the role of women in the family: as daughters, sisters, wives, or mothers. Women have different positions in their families, and they may have single or multiple roles. True and Eddyono (2017) found evidence of women having significant influence within their families to maintain peace, but it depended on their role within the family. One example is the daughter who is also a sister. After his return from Saudi Arabia, a sister opposed her brother's request to only open an Islamic boarding school for boys. She did not openly oppose her brother, but she appealed to her father as his daughter to continue to open the Islamic boarding school for girls. In the same study, it was found that in certain Islamic cultures, those who wants to do jihad have to ask for a blessing from their mothers: the mother plays a significant role in blessing the children to act on jihad or to prevent them from conducting jihad (True and Eddyono 2017). Meanwhile, when released from jail, the wife can be the crucial figure who encourages her husband to not return to join the local terrorist group.

However, there are criticisms in emphasizing women's roles in the family for P/CVE programs, particularly for mothers and wives. In certain conflict contexts, D'Estaing (2017) finds that the narrative of the mother as the one who approves jihad can lead to these mothers becoming a target of violence conducted by extremists in their own community. In addition, this strategy may legitimate the state's intrusion into the "responsibility" of the mother by creating or reinforcing stereotypes attached to women as the "good mother" or "failed mother." A good mother prevents their son or daughter's involvement with extremism; failure to do so means she has failed to be a good mother. Attaching P/CVE to gendered familial roles risks fueling a narrow perspective on the leading factors of violent extremism and why people participate in it (D'Estaing 2017).

As such, supporting women's roles in P/CVE is not a simple matter. Women are in the middle of a battle between those who support or those who oppose violent extremism (Ní Aoláin 2015). In one situation paying attention to women's family roles may lead to success, but in another setting it may lead a women to being targeted for coercion and harm. In addition, even when such a strategy is deemed to be an effective approach,[3] it may risk re-emphasizing women's gender roles if it is not pursued in a broader framework of gender equality within the family and society.

Therefore, it is important to recognize women's roles in the family, but along with it to support their roles beyond traditional domestic functions. Investment in upscaling women's agency in the community, organizations, and public sectors is vital. In studying women's roles in Indonesia (and the wider South East Asian context), True and Eddyono (2017) found that women often serve in significant and dynamic roles as religious teachers/ assistants, in religious peer groups in *majelis ta'lim* (prayer or retaliation group), and as community organizers and leaders. These informal positions may be filled in addition to their formal roles as lecturer, teacher, and civil servant. Because of their informality, it may be difficult to locate women who are serving in these roles; yet these positions may be fundamental and significant in countering and preventing fundamentalist ideology. What these roles often lack, however, is the funding necessary to upscale the programs they are already delivering in an attempt to prevent the rise of fundamentalism in community levels.

Coomaraswamy (UN Women 2015) argues there is a correlation between women's rights and a decrease in violent extremism: countries with relative gender equality are less prone to violent extremism. However, the discourse of women's rights can also become a target to legitimize intervention by extremist or radical groups (True and Eddyono 2017). The fundamentalists have developed social media campaigns to promote their "counter-arguments" to women's rights campaigns: promoting child marriage, polygamy, and dress code to protect girls and women (True and Eddyono 2017). Therefore, countering the narratives of violent extremists by developing messages on gender equality is very important.

D'Estaing (2017) has argued that it is vital the P/CVE program focus is gender sensitive— programs must address extremism but also support local women's empowerment. The inclusion of women's human rights framework within P/CVE programs is vital, and success will be dependent on supporting the women's organizations and women activists who provide crucial opportunities for women's leadership and empowerment within the same community. Extremism will be addressed through supporting organizations who work on advocating basic rights and safer conditions for women, who organize to assist the community in addressing women's various problems, such as violence against women, the rights of LGBT, or child marriage, and polygamy. Women's empowerment activities enhance women's roles in preventing violent extremism and create a sustainable social environment for ensuring positive change continues.

Third, it is vital to recognize and enhance women's roles in interfaith dialogue. As violent extremism grows in religious fundamentalism, there is equal skepticism with regard to the religious approach in preventing violent extremism. Yet, the international conference of women's religious leaders (women's ulama) in Indonesia in 2017 is one of the promising cross-cutting ideas where women's religious leaders have prominent roles in their own community, and across communities, in both upholding women's rights as well as peace and security (Kongres Ulama Perempuan Indonesia 2017). These women ulamas have reinterpreted the Koran in line with gender equality principles, and organize to communicate and campaign for women's rights in Islam. Their work is evidence of the need to incorporate women's representation and agendas in education and religious organizations (True and Eddyono 2017).

Finally, related to the role of education on gender equality in religious teaching, interfaith dialog is also crucial to prevent tension and to break the block between religions and their interpretation. Women activists and ulamas have played significant roles to initiate the development of an interfaith forum, and it is evidentially effective in addressing violent extremism (True and Eddyono 2017).

Conclusion

The integration of the WPS agenda in the UNSCR on P/CVE and the 2016 Global Strategy for Countering and Preventing Terrorism and Violent Extremism has been a crucial and welcome development for CVE response The Global Strategy (2016) has established two approaches, the integration of a gender perspective across the framework and a more targeted, specific focus on gender equality and women's empowerment within high-risk situations. This progress needs to be maintained, however, through effective implementation strategies that rely on evidence of best practices while also contextualizing the strategy to very diverse local settings. Therefore, the chapter recommends three strategies to build upon and strengthen the inclusion of the women-empowerment agenda in the CVE Global Strategy: first, acknowledge the diversity of women's roles and their agency in different areas, particularly in the more private and less public spaces. Private spaces and relationships can be sources of power to secure peace and security. Second, enhance and upscale the women's human rights activities and organization; and finally, recognize, respect, and support women's roles through religious framework and interfaith dialogue.

Notes

1. The seven priorities of the Platform of Action for Preventing Violence Extremism: (1) dialogue and conflict prevention; (2) strengthening good governance, human rights, and the rule of law; (3) engaging communities; (4) Empowering youth; (5) gender equality and empowering women; (6) education, skill development, and employment facilitation; and (7) strategic communications, including through the Internet and social media (UNGA 2015).
2. The Action Plan recommended gender integration in youth programs by:

    (1) supporting and strengthening young women and men's participation in activities aimed at preventing violent extremism, including providing a physically, socially, and emotionally safe and supportive environment for their participation, reaching the youth from underrepresented groups, and establishing mentoring programs;
    (2) integrating young women and men into decision-making processes at local and national levels;
    (3) building intergenerational dialogue and youth–adult confidence-building activities and training that aims to grow trust between decision-makers and young women and men (UNGA 2015).
3. See also Women Without Borders (n.d.).

REFERENCES

Bakker, Edwin, and Seran de Leede. "European Female Jihadists in Syria: Exploring an Under-Researched Topic." International Centre for Counter Terrorism, April 2015, https://www.icct.nl/download/file/ICCT-Bakker-de-Leede-European-Female-Jihadists-In-Syria-Exploring-An-Under-Researched-Topic-April2015.pdf.

Couture, Krista London. "A Gendered Approach to Countering Violent Extremism." Policy Paper. Center for 21st Century Security and Intelligence. Washington DC: Brookings, July 30, 2014, https://www.brookings.edu/research/a-gendered-approach-to-countering-violent-extremism-lessons-learned-from-women-in-peacebuilding-and-conflict-prevention-applied-successfully-in-bangladesh-and-morocco/.

D'Estaing, Sophie Giscard. "Engaging Women in Countering Violent Extremism: Avoiding Instrumentalization, and Furthering Agency." Gender and Development 25, no. 1 (2017): 103–118.

Iman, A., and N. Yuval-Davis. "Warning Signs of Fundamentalisms." In Warning Signs of Fundamentalisms, edited by A. Iman, J. Morgan, and N. Yuval-Davis.. Nottingham, UK: Russell Press, 2004.

Kongres Ulama Perempuan Indonesia (KUPI). "Women's Ultimate Congress Indonesia." Cirebon, April 25–27, 2017, https://infokupi.com.

Langham, Keith, and Abdul Faqihuddin Kodir, eds. "Congress of Indonesian Women Ulama: Official Documents on Process and Outcome." Cirebon: Kongres Ulama Perempuan Indonesia, 2017.

Ní Aoláin, Fionnuala. "Jihad, Counter-Terrorism, and Mothers." Just Security, March 4, 2015, https://www.justsecurity.org/20407/jihad-counter-terrorism-mothers/.

Ní Aoláin, Fionnuala. "The 'War on Terror' and Extremism: Assessing the Relevance of the Women, Peace, and Security Agenda." International Affairs 92 (2016): 275–291.

Dufour-Genneson, Ségolène, and Mayesha Alam. "Women and Countering Violent Extremism," Georgetown Institute for Women, Peace, and Security, Information2Action, January 2014.

Shepherd, L. J. "Advancing the Women, Peace, and Security Agenda: 2015 and Beyond," Norwegian Peacebuilding Resource Centre Policy Brief, August 28, 2014, http://www.peacebuilding.no/Themes/Inclusivity-and-gender/Publications/Advancing-the-Women-Peace-and-Security-agenda-2015-and-beyond.

Shepherd Laura, J. "The Women, Peace, and Security Agenda at the United Nations." In Global Insecurity, edited by A. Burke and R. Parker. London: Palgrave Macmillan, 2017.

True, Jacque, and Sri Eddyono. "Preventing Violent Extremism: Gender Perspective and Women's Roles." Monash Centre for Gender Peace and Security, 2017, http://docs.wixstatic.com/ugd/b4aef1_5fb20e84855b45aabb5437fe96fc3616.pdf.

United Nation General Assembly (UNGA). "Resolution 60/288: United Nations Global Counter-Terrorism Strategy." September 8, 2006, https://documents-dds-ny.un.org/doc/UNDOC/GEN/N05/504/88/PDF/N0550488.pdf?OpenElement.

United Nation General Assembly (UNGA). "Plan of Action to Prevent Violent Extremism, The United Nations Global Counter-Terrorism Strategy. Report of the Secretary-General." A/70/674, United Nation General Assembly, 2015.

United Nations General Assembly (UNGA). "Resolution 70/291: United Nation Global Counter-Terrorism Strategy Review." A/RES/70/291, July 1 2016, http://www.un.org/en/ga/search/view_doc.asp?symbol=A/RES/70/291.

United Nations Security Council (UNSC). "Resolution 2178." September 24, 2014, https://www.un.org/sc/ctc/wp-content/uploads/2015/06/SCR-2178_2014_EN.pdf

United Nations Security Council (UNSC). "Resolution 2242." October 13, 2015. http://undocs.org/S/RES/2242(2015).

UN Women. "Preventing Conflict, Transforming Justice, Securing the Peace: A Global Study on the Implementation of United Nations Security Council Resolution 1325." Lead author Radhika Coomaraswamy. New York: United Nations, 2015.

Women Without Borders. "Mothers Schools: Sensitizing Mothers to Recognize Signs of Radicalisation." Women Without Borders, n.d., http://www.women-without-borders.org/projects/underway/42/.

CHAPTER 54

WPS AND ARMS TRADE TREATY

RAY ACHESON AND MARIA BUTLER

LIVING in a globalized world of violence and militarism requires WPS to focus on where conflict is and also from where it is being exported. Weapons sold and transferred internationally contribute to and facilitate armed conflict, and cause social and political upheaval. From small arms used in femicides or domestic violence (Nowak 2012), to explosive weapons used in populated areas with potentially unique impacts on women (Irsten 2014), women are either targeted by those wielding weapons or are specifically impacted by their use. Small arms, the most common weapon used against women in general, facilitate violence both during and outside armed conflict. Adopted in April 2013 by the United Nations General Assembly (UNGA), the ATT is an historic international agreement. It is the first treaty to regulate the sale and transfer of conventional weapons and to explicitly recognize the links between the international arms trade and gender-based violence (GBV).[1] Both are important for the WPS agenda.

This chapter addresses the relationship between the Women, Peace, and Security (WPS) agenda and the Arms Trade Treaty (ATT or Treaty) starting with the journey to a gendered ATT. Then, we explore implementing synergies and tensions of ATT and WPS. Finally, we look critically at two common impediments to advancing implementation: culture and economies.

THE JOURNEY TO A GENDERED ATT

When states, civil society, and international organizations came together in 2006 to initiate a negotiation process for what would become the ATT, the key motivation for many was to disrupt the relentless flows of weapons that perpetuate cycles of armed violence and armed conflict around the world (Acheson 2016). In part, this meant challenging states and other entities that facilitate war for economic gain, interrupting their seemingly unappeasable profiteering from the scourge of violent death and destruction. These motivations echoed those of women's groups who had worked for the adoption of United Nations Security

Council Resolution 1325 in 2000 (UNSC 2000), and pushed for the WPS agenda to prevent and end war (Hill et al. 2003). But ensuring inclusion of a gender perspective was not a priority for most of the seven years of ATT preparatory work or the six weeks of negotiations. It was a gender-blind process like most disarmament spaces.[2]

The Women's International League for Peace and Freedom (WILPF) and the International Action Network on Small Arms Women's Network (IANSA Women's Network) initiated a civil society campaign to support the transformative potential of the first international arms trade treaty and to address the lack of gender analysis in the text. The "Make it Binding" campaign advocated for a legally binding provision in the ATT prohibiting the sale and transfer of weapons where there is risk or evidence of GBV.[3] The campaign grew organically and the advocacy strategy evolved as politics and positions changed through the first negotiation conference in July 2012 to the final negotiations in March 2013. In 2012, WILPF and others released a joint policy paper calling for explicit inclusion of GBV in the ATT (WILPF et al. 2012). Members and partners of the four organizations used the paper in their advocacy with governments in capitals around the world. Over 100 organizations worldwide signed onto a declaration calling for the inclusion of GBV in the treaty. With the aim of making the gendered consequences and women's experiences of armed violence visible, WILPF and others organizations also published other pieces of analysis and advocacy (Chinkin 2012; Green et al. 2013).

Pushback on the inclusion of GBV, however, came from active lobbying by The Holy See (Acheson 2015c). The Holy See, using its Observer Status,[4] aligned with some governments to attempt to block any reference to "gender," proposing only reference to "women and children" (Enloe [1989] 2014). The delegations of Algeria, The Holy See, Egypt, the Islamic Republic of Iran, the United Arab Emirates, and the Solomon Islands asked that the wording "GBV" be changed to "violence against women" (VAW) (Acheson 2015c). This reflects ongoing struggles in multilateral fora against "gender" (News.va 2012), as discussed by Baden and Goetz (1997) in their reflections on the 1995 Beijing Platform for Action. Although the UN bodies use "GBV," its definition and use are debated. In the ATT discussions, civil society explained the difference between GBV and VAW, arguing that the broader concept of GBV is important for capturing violence perpetrated on the basis of sex, sexuality, gender identity, or transgression of gender norms, rather than only against a specific sex (Gerome and Butler 2012).

A reference to "women" in the ATT was included in the preamble, which bears in mind "that civilians, particularly women and children, account for the vast majority of those adversely affected by armed conflict and armed violence" (ATT). The final text reflects the negotiations' focus on the protection of women and women's vulnerability, rather than their agency, or how unequal gender relations cause that vulnerability. The language on women's participation was deleted from the final agreed text. This exclusive focus on "protection" and discourse is a well-known challenge in WPS: "There was much in the [UNSCR] 1325 text about women's sexual vulnerability, nothing about those who were the main source of danger to women" (Cockburn 2013). Women are treated exclusively as victims, grouped together with children and the vulnerable, stripped of their agency and diverse identities, experiences, and capacities. This language reinforces persistent constructions of women as the weaker and innocent sex in need of protection, and of men as the more "powerful sex," who are neither innocent nor vulnerable, but with a responsibility to "protect" women. Such

692 RAY ACHESON AND MARIA BUTLER

language entrenches militaristic social constructions that link masculinity with prepared-ness for military action (Carpenter 2005).[5] Moreover, the ATT's preamble inaccurately states that women account for the "*vast majority*" of those adversely affected by conflict.

The devaluation of certain perspectives, ideas, and, interests because they are marked as "feminine," coupled with the equation of masculinity with violence, gives war positive value as a show of masculine power. At the same time the perception that not going to war is weak makes it more difficult for political leaders to take decisions not to embark on mil-itary action.

Parallel to the challenges on the language in the criteria and preamble, there was the im-portant "numbers game" that needed to be won. Support from a high number of states was re-quired to ensure that the right language in the criteria would not be sacrificed at the eleventh hour. Campaigns need energizing moments to keep the momentum and one such moment came on July 20, 2012, during the first negotiation conference. Nicole Améline, French expert from the UN Committee on the Elimination of Discrimination against Women (CEDAW) and a former minister and parliamentarian, walked across the halls of the UN from where CEDAW was meeting to where the official ATT negotiation were underway. Améline had been a speaker at the WILPF organized side-event, "Women's Human Rights, the ATT, and CEDAW," held that day with partners IANSA, IAW, and UN Women, where she had learned that France was not supportive of including language on GBV in the ATT criteria. She approached the head of the French ATT delegation for a brief tête–à–tête. Minutes later, France indicated to the Chair that it wanted to take the floor, and proceeded to state that GBV is a "main preoccupation" for its government and it must be in the criteria of the ATT. The French delegate also noted that the "notion of gender is already very well established within the UN." It was a turning point. The European Union had not yet been on board, but it soon thereafter changed its position and became a staunch supporter of the provision. After that occurrence, the momentum turned in favor of the inclusion of GBV in the Treaty.

In the process of advocating for inclusion of GBV in the ATT, WILPF and its part-ners referenced WPS as a precedent for agreed language and the normative agenda. WPS data and information (national implementation, shadow reports, global indicators, UN Secretary-General's annual report on conflict-related sexual violence) were cited as pos-sible sources of information for future treaty-based assessments related to GBV (WILPF et al. 2012). The constituencies built up among states and civil society on WPS were useful for highlighting the importance of including GBV in the ATT. Concerted civil society ad-vocacy led to the inclusion of language on the relationship between "illicit use of, and illicit trade in, small arms and light weapons and aggravated violence against women and girls"[6] in the Commission on the Status of Women, "Agreed Conclusions," in March 2013. On July 24, 2012, the CEDAW Committee adopted a strong statement on the need for a gender perspective in the ATT. It recalled "that the arms trade has specific gender dimensions and direct links to discrimination and gender-based violence against women with far reaching implications for efforts to consolidate peace, security, gender equality, and to secure devel-opment" (CEDAW Committee 2012).

Thus support for the legally binding GBV provision went from a handful of states at the beginning of the preparatory process to over one hundred by the end of the second round of negotiations in March 2013 (Acheson 2013a). All of the advocacy, and collaborations, worked. The final text of the Treaty, adopted on April 2, 2013, included, in Article 7 on "Export and Export Assessment," a provision that the exporting state party, in making its export risk assessment mandated by the Treaty, "shall take into account the risk of the conventional arms covered under Article 2(1) or of the items covered under Article 3 or Article 4 being used to commit or facilitate serious acts of gender-based violence or serious acts of violence against women and children" (Arms Trade Treaty 2013: Article 7[4]). The inclusion of GBV in Article 7(4) captures the violence against any person who is being targeted because their behavior does not conform to socially defined norms of appropriate behavior for men and women or girls and boys (Acheson et al. 2013). This provision is groundbreaking in its recognition that acts of GBV can be facilitated by the international arms trade and its requirement of assessing the risk of GBV as a distinct violation of international human rights law (IHRL) or international humanitarian law (IHL).

An understanding of Article 7(4) noted that it does not permit states parties to authorize transfers of the conventional weapons, ammunition, munitions, parts, or components covered by the treaty where there is a risk of GBV, "when it constitutes one of the negative consequences of Article 7(1)—for example, when it is a violation of international humanitarian law (IHL) or international human rights law (IHRL), when it undermines peace and security, or when it forms part of transnational organized crime." Furthermore, "Where GBV is broader than IHL or IHRL, it must still be taken into account," WILPF argued. Article 7(4) requires states to act with due diligence to ensure that the arms transfer will not be diverted to non-state actors such as death squads, militias, or gangs that commit acts of GBV." Finally, WILPF noted, "All acts of GBV are serious in nature and therefore are covered by the reference in ATT."[7]

Implementing Synergies of ATT and WPS

As previously discussed, there are numerous synergies and commonalities between the WPS and the ATT's agendas. Realizing the WPS resolutions requires actions to prevent conflict and to protect women and girls from the harm of war, including GBV and conflict-related sexual violence. The ATT's Article 7(4), aimed at preventing arms transfers that risk facilitating acts of GBV, potentially helps make the WPS agenda operational (Gerome 2016).[8]

In parallel, there has been some advance in strengthening an integrated approach to WPS. The latest WPS resolution, Resolution 2242, demonstrates that there are ways to acknowledge the unique and grave impacts of the use or trade of weapons on women and girls, as distinct to men or boys or others, without categorizing them as innocent, vulnerable, or victims. It calls for actions to mitigate the risk of women becoming active players in the illicit transfer of small arms and light weapons, for example (UNSC 2015).

The ATT and WPS also have synergies with other instruments focusing on women's rights and gender equality. In November 2013, the CEDAW Committee noted that conflict prevention includes "robust and effective regulation of the arms trade, in addition to appropriate control over the circulation of existing and often illicit conventional arms, including small arms, to prevent their use to commit or facilitate serious acts of gender-based violence" (UN CEDAW 2013). Recommendation 30 also highlights first, the correlation between increased prevalence of GBV and the outbreak of conflict, suggesting that increasing rates of GBV can serve as an early warning of conflict, and second, that proliferation of conventional weapons affects women in situations of conflict-related GBV, domestic violence, and also as protestors or actors in resistance movements. It simultaneously highlights the potential targeting of women as victims as well as their agency in a variety of roles. Recommendation 30 encourages states to "address the gendered impact of international transfers of arms, especially small and illicit arms including through the ratification and implementation" of the ATT. The recommendation "could and should have gone further to promote women's participation in designing solutions to the challenges it identifies. However, it is a concrete example of a tool that has drawn together concerns about GBV and power structures in the use, trade, and proliferation of arms" (Acheson 2015c).

Using the tools together, we can see the synergies of the ATT, WPS, and CEDAW, which enable civil society and states to question and demand actions from exporting states using exterritorial obligations. WILPF has utilized these synergies to hold states accountable. In 2016, working with WILPF sections in these countries, we submitted CEDAW reports on Sweden (arms transfers; TNCs) and France (arms transfers; nuclear testing). The CEDAW Committee recommendation to Sweden was the first time that "CEDAW Committee has reminded States on their responsibility towards their impact on the rights of persons outside the borders of the State" and to "ensure that the new legislation to regulate export of arms includes a strong and robust gender-specific perspective" (CEDAW 2016a). The recommendation to France was to integrate "a gender dimension in its strategic dialogues with the countries purchasing French arms and continue conducting rigorous, transparent and gender sensitive risk assessments, in accordance with the Arms Trade Treaty" (CEDAW 2016b). Other examples of engagement can be found in a shadow report to the Committee on the impact of Germany's arms transfers on women (WILPF 2016a, WILPF and ECCHR 2017); a shadow reports to the Committee on Economic, Social, and Culture Rights regarding the arms transfers to Saudi Arabia by France, Sweden, and the United Kingdom (WILPF 2016b, WILPF 2016c, and, WILPF 2016d); a statement to the Human Rights Council on the use of weapons and arms transfers to parties in the conflict in Yemen (WILPF 2016e); and in a statement on the report of the Commission of Inquiry on Syria (WILPF 2016f).

THE COMMON IMPEDIMENTS OF CULTURE AND ECONOMIES

The implementation of the ATT and WPS face similar cultural and economic impediments, namely, patriarchal gendered power, including the marginalization of women, and militarism. Militarism, as both an ideology and as a political economy, undermines effective regulation of the international arms trade, prevention of violence or conflict, or the promotion of women's rights and equality.

Culture of Militarism

As has been examined and exposed through feminist analysis, militarism "as an ideology creates a culture of fear and supports the use of aggression, violence and military interventions for settling disputes and enforcing economic and political interests" (LaForgia 2011). Similarly, the Global Study on WPS argues, "Militarism and cultures of militarized masculinities create and sustain political decision-making where resorting to the use of force becomes a normalized mode for dispute resolution" (UN Women 2015). If the use of force is normalized as the measure of security and dispute resolution, the production and proliferation of weapons is necessary. This ideology of militarism is highly gendered (Enloe [1989] 2014; Cockburn 2013), privileging violent forms of masculinity, requiring the dehumanization of others, and imposing inferiority on women (Vine 2015). This results in many forms of gendered power and inequalities, including GBV, both during and after conflict. Indeed, weapons transferred through international arms deals continue to be used to kill, injure, or threaten people on the basis of sex, identity, and sexuality long after conflicts have ended. There is a normalization of the presence and use of arms.

There are other tensions between the effective implementation of the ATT within the nexus of the WPS agenda that are also underpinned by the culture of militarism. The way the UN Security Council resolutions on WPS have been interpreted and used "risks promoting women's participation foremost within the highly masculine militarized security structures that tend to generate rather than prevent or end armed conflict" (Acheson 2015c). Cockburn notes a lack of "any reference to the causes of war, let alone to ending war" in UNSCR 1325, and she goes on to pose a key question "Was it the fact that some of the worst offending states were actually members of the Council that made it seem so impossible to voice issues such as militarization, the arms trade, and disarmament?" (Cockburn 2013).

In the course of engaging governments and militaries to promote the implementation of Resolution 1325, the inherent contradictions of the text became clear to those wanting to use the resolution as a vehicle to recognize women as actors necessary in, and capable of, ending war, achieving peace, and redefining security, whereas the militaries have instead used it as a vehicle to promote and enlarge women's contributions to war (Acheson 2015c; Cockburn 2012.

Because it aims to protect women in war and insists they have an equal right to participate in the processes and negotiations that end wars, Resolution 1325 fails to lend itself to war prevention or to challenging the legitimacy of systems that generate war (Cohn 2008). Original supporters of the resolution, "particularly women on the ground, for whom armed violence and conflict is a daily reality," have found themselves further removed from its implementation (Butler 2012). This is problematic for an antimilitarist, anti-war agenda, in which the ATT could and should play a key role. Instead, like the WPS agenda, the ATT is often implemented to reinforce militarism instead of challenging it.

Political Economy of Militarism

Economic incentives of militarism remain a significant impediment to the effective implementation of WPS and ATT. War is embedded in the global economy, and in particular in the economies of the most economically powerful countries.

Global military spending reached $1.68 trillion in 2017—about a 50 percent increase from 2001 (Sipri.org 2017a). The international arms trade is currently valued at about $375 billion per year (Sipri.org 2017b). The top six arms exporters—the United States, Russia, France, Germany, China, and the United Kingdom—are responsible for nearly 75 percent of the arms trade. The volume of international arms transfers has risen by 10 percent since the adoption of the Arms Trade Treaty (Sipri.org 2018). The top ten arms companies sold $204.5 million worth of arms in 2016 (Sipri.org 2017b). This is where money goes, rather than on programs or tools to enhance inclusive peace and gender equality.

While austerity measures cut budgets for gender equality, education, housing, and health around the world, the arms production industry continues to grow; and as can be seen in mounting conflicts around the globe, commercial interests often influence arms export policy. According to SIPRI, "the USA has long seen arms exports as a major foreign policy and security tool, but in recent years exports are increasingly needed to help the US arms industry maintain production levels at a time of decreasing US military expenditure" (Sipri. org 2015b).

Meanwhile, the mass circulation of arms devastates: "developing countries are on the receiving end of most flows of arms, suffer the consequences of their proliferation and use, and then have to divert resources from development to deal with the aftermath of this destruction" (Acheson 2015a). They are also the largest purchasers of weapons from developed countries. "Military cooperation," including the purchase of equipment, is often a part of development aid funding.

A case study for the intersection of these failures is the Saudi-led military intervention in Yemen. As stated by the Secretary-General during a Security Council briefing in February 2015, "Yemen is collapsing before our eyes."[9] As Yemen faces war, economic collapse, and rising violence, women are increasingly vulnerable and destitute. As WILPF noted in a letter dated February 26, 2015, to the Security Council "Women in Yemen have limited access to healthcare, economic opportunities, education, and are often victims of child marriage" urging, together with our partners in Yemen "the Council to strengthen consideration of Women, Peace, and Security obligations in all aspects of the Council's work on Yemen" (WILPF 2015).[10]

At the same time, ATT states parties, including France, Germany, the Netherlands, South Africa, Spain, Sweden, Switzerland, and the United Kingdom, and signatories Turkey and the United States, all transferred weapons to Saudi Arabia in 2014 (ATT Monitor 2016). Several of these continued to issue export licenses to Saudi Arabia in 2015 to the current day, while Saudi Arabia relentlessly bombed Yemen. The arms industry is profiting wildly from these sales (Wearing 2016, Stone 2016).

The bombing in populated areas in Yemen is continuing to result in civilian casualties and the destruction of civilian assets, leading to death, injury, mass displacement, and extreme food insecurity. A UN panel investigating the Saudi-led bombing campaign in Yemen uncovered "widespread and systematic" attacks on civilian targets in violation of international humanitarian law (MacAskill 2016). When explosive weapons have been used in populated areas in Yemen, civilians make up 95 percent of reported deaths and injuries (Perkins 2015). Arms transfers to Saudi Arabia have been condemned by many human rights and disarmament or arms control groups, the Committee of the International Covenant on Economic, Social, and Cultural Rights,[11] and the UN Secretary-General (Wintour 2016) for resulting in IHRL and IHL violations in Yemen. Eminent legal scholars have found the UK government to be violating domestic, regional, and international law, including the ATT (Amnesty.org 2015). A UK NGO is challenging the UK government's decision to continue to license the export of military equipment to Saudi Arabia (CAAT.org.uk 2018).

The ATT should be just the instrument to prevent arms transfers in a situation like this. However, just as the WPS agenda can be (mis)used to legitimize structures of militarism and war, the ATT can be, and is being, used to legitimate the arms trade. The UK government, for example, has repeatedly claimed that its sales to Saudi Arabia meet its arms exports regulations. One member of the UK defense committee insisted that the Saudi-led coalition in Yemen is trying to avoid hitting civilians. "They are doing their level best to sort it out," he told BBC Radio 4's *Today* program. "I reckon they have made some mistakes and have breached in the past, but I can tell you this . . . things have been really tightened up" (Graham-Harrison 2016).

The final ATT text does contain a number of problematic elements that civil society, including WILPF, warned at the time could be manipulated in the future by states looking to exploit the treaty to justify arms sales instead of preventing them from taking place. In particular, there is no prohibition against transferring weapons to states that are clearly violating IHRL or IHL—states must only conduct a risk assessment to determine if the risk of such violations are "overriding"—an undefined concept that pits IHL and human rights violations against an assessment of the weapons' possible "contribution" to peace and security. This contains "no recognition that respect for IHL and human rights themselves *contribute to* peace and security," WILPF pointed out at the time. "The phrase "overriding risk" in Article 7 ultimately gives exporting states a blank check to authorize any export they wish, despite the provisions of this treaty," argued WILPF. "It arguably implies that even if the exporting state is 90 percent certain the weapons will be used to slaughter civilians, it could decide the weapons contribute to promoting some other, undefined interest, and thus approve the transfer" (Acheson 2013b). The ATT in effect treats the international arms trade as a legitimate business rather than as a key contributor to armed violence and armed conflict around the world.

Because the ATT is seen by many of its states parties as both a trade treaty as well as a human rights or arms control treaty, implementation efforts risk pitting the interests of industry against the interests of preventing humanitarian harm. The concept of "responsible" or "legitimate" arms transfers, contrasted with "irresponsible" or "illicit" trade, glosses over the fact that every transfer and use of weapons results in violence in some form, and that many so-described legitimate transfers result in destabilization and destruction. The relentless bombing and bombardment in populated areas in Yemen is but one example. It contributes nothing to peace, security, or stability; does not promote "responsible action" by states parties; and above all, exacerbates, rather than reduces, human suffering.

Conclusion

The WPS agenda and the ATT have overlapping aims and the potential to reinforce each other in promoting peace. But both become meaningless at best, or counterproductive at worst, when they are used to legitimize militarism and undermine peace and security. The culture and political economy of militarism work against effective implementation of the ATT and WPS agenda. Neither of them fundamentally challenges the culture or economies of war or violence; they were negotiated and are being implemented in ways consistent with the historic perpetuation of military intervention and violent masculinities.

To be effective, implementation of the ATT and WPS must oppose militarism. In order to do so, it must constantly and tirelessly challenge the dominant norm of associating maleness with militancy. ATT states parties must view the Treaty as a legal and moral counterweight to profiteers of death and destruction, and begin to use the Treaty as a tool to combat and prevent the actions that undermine it.

WPS must focus on conflict *prevention* above engagement in the systems that generate and sustain conflict. The reduction of arms export and import remains an integral part of the WPS. In their national budgets, states must prioritize peace over the arms industry. Excessive spending on military resources directly and indirectly diverts and reduces available resources for social and economic development, including resources for gender equality. It also reinforces weapons as the solution to problems, rather than nonviolent means of conflict resolution and prevention.

Arms transfers to recipients that violate human rights at home or abroad should be ended. Implementation of the ATT with a view to preventing armed conflict and armed violence is imperative. In this context, the UN Security Council in particular must be challenged: the permanent five UN Security Council members are also among the biggest arms exporters in the world and they are directly contradicting the WPS agenda. The same countries that discuss the implementation of the WPS in Yemen or protection against sexual violence in the Democratic People's Republic of Congo, for example, fail to address how they fuel the conflict through their export of weapons.

Furthermore, gender diversity in disarmament, nonproliferation, and arms control must promote the experiences and influence anyone not conforming to dominant gender or sexuality norms. Armed violence has differential impacts on LGBTQI people, which should be reflected in discussions about weapons, conflict, and violence. A range of perspectives must be presented in discussions and negotiations, including critiques of dominant structural inequalities and normative framings.

Following from this, "meaningful" participation of women and others would create space for alternative conceptions of security and focus on preventing armed conflict and armed violence rather than on responding to it with military force. All those promoting the implementation of WPS and the ATT should include a critique of militarism, violence, war, and patriarchy in order to help ensure that women are not integrated into the structures generating and sustaining conflict, and that international arms deals are subjected to appropriate scrutiny rather than accepted as legitimate business.

Notes

1. There is more than one interpretation of gender-based violence. WILPF and others categorize GBV as violence that is directed at a person based on her or his specific sex or gender role in society. For more information, see Acheson 2015a.
2. Recall the words of Eleanor Roosevelt "too often the great decisions are originated and given form in bodies made up wholly of men, or so completely dominated by them that whatever of special value women have to offer is shunted aside without expression" (quoted in Tickner 1992: 1).
3. "Make It Binding!" (WILPF 2013), http://wilpf.org/make-it-binding-join-our-petition-on-the-arms-trade-treaty/.

4. See statement such as "Holy See Statement Regarding 'All States' Formula Participation" (July 3, 2012), http://reachingcriticalwill.org/images/documents/Disarmament-fora/att/negotiating-conference/statements/3July_HolySee.pdf.

5. Though Charli Carpenter has noted that even where women constitute a high ratio of combatants, sex is used "as a shortcut to distinction" between civilians and combatants; see (Carpenter 2006: 89–90).

6. Commission on the Status of Women, "Agreed Conclusions," 57th Session (2013).

7. Acheson et al., "Preventing Armed Gender-Based Violence," 9.

8. The "Guide to Effective Implementation of This Provision of the ATT," goes deeper into how to do this with information on how to assess the risk of GBV in a recipient country and why arms transfers must be denied where such risk exists.

9. "'Yemen Is Collapsing before Our Eyes,' Secretary-General Tells Security Council, Calling for International Support to Help Re-Establish Legitimate Government" (February 12, 2015), http://www.un.org/press/en/2015/sgsm16526.doc.htm.

10. Women's International League for Peace and Freedom, "Re: Security Council Consideration of Yemen and Women, Peace, and Security" (February 26, 2015), http://peacewomen.org/sites/default/files/Letter%20to%20Security%20Council_Yemen_WILPF.pdf.

11. "UK Called to Control Its Arms Exports after Disastrous Consequences for Human Rights in Yemen," Women's International League for Peace and Freedom, July 6, 2016, http://wilpf.org/the-review-of-sweden-the-uk-and-france-under-the-committee-on-economic-social-and-cultural-rights.

References

Acheson, Ray, Maria Butler, and Sofia Tuvestad. "Preventing Armed Gender-Based Violence: A Binding Requirement in the New Draft ATT Text." *ATT Monitor* 6, no. 9 (2013): 9, http://reachingcriticalwill.org/images/documents/Disarmament-fora/att/monitor/ATTMonitor6.9.pdf.

Acheson, Ray. "100 States Support Strengthening the Criterion on Preventing Gender-Based Violence." *ATT Monitor* 6, no. 8 (2013a): 5. http://reachingcriticalwill.org/images/documents/Disarmament-for a/att/monitor/ATTMonitor6.8.pdf.

Acheson, Ray. "A Tale of Two Treaties." *ATT Monitor* 6, no. 9 (2013b): 3. http://reachingcriticalwill.org/images/documents/Disarmamfor afora/att/monitor/ATTMonitor6.9.pdf.

Acheson, Ray. "Profits of Pain: Stopping the War Economy to Stop Wars." Women Peacemakers Program, *"Women, Peace, and Security: Business as Usual?"* 2015a, https://www.womenpeacemakersprogram.org/assets/CMS/May-24-gender-/Article-6-Acheson-Profits-of-Pain-.pdf

Acheson, Ray. "Gender-Based Violence and the Arms Trade Treaty." Women's International League for Peace and Freedom, 2015b, http://www.reachingcriticalwill.org/images/documents/Publications/GBV_ATT-brief.pdf.

Acheson, Ray. *Women, Weapons, and War: A Gendered Critique of Multilateral Instruments.* Women's International League for Peace and Freedom, 2015c, http://www.reachingcriticalwill.org/images/documents/Publications/women-weapons-war.pdf.

Acheson, Ray. "Editorial: Struggling for the Soul of the ATT." *ATT Monitor* 9, no. 5 (2016): 1. http://www.reachingcriticalwill.org/images/documents/Disarmament-fora/att/monitor/ATTMonitor9.6.pdf.

Amnesty.org. "UK Government Breaking the Law Supplying Arms to Saudi Arabia, Say Leading Lawyers." Amnesty International, December 17, 2015, https://www.amnesty.org/en/latest/news/2015/12/uk-government-breaking-the-law-supplying-arms-to-saudi-arabia.

Arms Trade Treaty. Adopted as General Assembly Resolution 67/234B, April 2, 2013.

ATT Monitor. "Dealing in Double Standards: How Arms to Saudi Arabia Are Causing Human Suffering in Yemen." Control Arms, 2016, http://armstreatymonitor.org/en/wp-content/uploads/2016/02/ATT-Monitor-Case-Study-2-Saudi-Arabia-.pdf.

Baden, Sally, and Anne Marie Goetz. "Who Needs [Sex] When You Can Have [Gender]? Conflicting Discourses on Gender at Beijing." Feminist Review 56, no. 1 (1997): 3–25.

Butler, Maria. "The Women, Peace, and Security Agenda: The Two Silent 'Ps': Proliferation and Profit." Women's International League for Peace and Freedom, July 13, 2012, http://www.peacewomen.org/node/90649.

CAAT.org.uk, "Stop Arming Saudi: Judicial Review." Last updated 12 April 2018. https://www.caat.org.uk/campaigns/stop-arming-saudi/judicial-review.

Carpenter, Charli R. "'Women, Children, and Other Vulnerable Groups': Gender, Strategic Frames and the Protection of Civilians as a Transnational Issue." International Studies Quarterly 49, no. 2 (2005a): 295–334.

Carpenter, Charli R. "Recognizing Gender-Based Violence against Civilian Men and Boys in Conflict Situations." Security Dialogue 37, no. 1 (2006): 83–103.

CEDAW Committee 2012. "Statement of the Committee on the Elimination of Discrimination against Women on the Need for a Gender Perspective in the Text of the Arms Trade Treaty." Agreed Conclusions, Commission on the Status of Women, July 24, 2012, http://www.ohchr.org/Documents/HRBodies/CEDAW/Statements/StatementGenderPerspective.pdf.

CEDAW Committee. Concluding Observations on Sweden. CEDAW/C/SWE/CO/8-9, para. 35, 2016a.

CEDAW Committee. Concluding Observations on France. CEDAW/C/FRA/CO/7-8, para. 22, 2016b.

Chinkin, Christine. Gender and the Arms Trade Treaty—A Legal Overview. Women's International League for Peace and Freedom, 2012, http://wilpf.org/wp-content/uploads/2013/02/Gender-and-the-Arms-Trade-Treaty-a-legal-overview.pdf.

Cockburn, Cynthia. "Snagged on the Contradiction: NATO, Resolution 1325, and Feminist Responses." Women in Action on Women in Peacebuilding (2012): 48–57. http://www.isiswomen.org/phocadownload/print/isispub/wia/wia2012/WIA2012_07TalkingPointsCynthiaCockBurn.pdf.

Cockburn, Cynthia. "War and Security, Women and Gender: An Overview of the Issues." Gender & Development 21, no. 3 (2013): 433–452.

Cohn, Carol. "Mainstreaming Gender in UN Security Policy: A Path to Political Transformation?" In Global Governance: Feminist Perspectives, edited by Shirin M. Rai and Georgina Waylen, 185–206. Basingstoke, UK: Palgrave Macmillan, 2008.

Commission on the Status of Women, "Agreed Conclusions," 57th Session, 2013.

Enloe, Cynthia. Bananas, Beaches, and Bases: Making Feminist Sense of International Politics. Berkeley: University of California Press, (1989) 2014.

Gerome, Rebecca. Preventing Gender-Based Violence through Arms Control: Tools and Guidelines to Implement the Arms Trade Treaty and UN Programme of Action. Geneva: Women's International League for Peace and Freedom, 2016.

Gerome, Rebecca, and Maria Butler. "A Step back? 'Gender-Based Violence' vs 'Violence against Women and Children.'" *ATT Monitor* 5, no. 11 (2012): 2–3. http://www.reachingcriticalwill. org/images/documents/Disarmament-fora/att/monitor/ATTMonitor5.11.pdf.

Graham-Harrison, Emma. "UK in Denial over Saudi Arms Sales Being Used in Yemen, Claims Oxfam." *The Guardian*, August 23, 2016, https://www.theguardian.com/world/2016/aug/23/ uk-in-denial-over-saudi-arms-sales-being-used-in-yemen-claims-oxfam.

Green, Caroline, Deepayan Basu Ray, Claire Mortimer, and Kate Stone. "Gender-Based Violence and the Arms Trade Treaty: Reflections from a Campaigning and Legal Perspective." *Gender & Development* 21, no. 3 (2013): 551–562.

Hill, Felicity, Mikele Aboitiz, and Sara Poehlman-Doumbouya. "Nongovernmental Organizations' Role in the Buildup and Implementation of Security Council Resolution 1325." *Signs* 28, no. 4 (2003): 1255–1269.

Irsten, Gabriella. *Women and Explosive Weapons*. Women's International League for Peace and Freedom, 2014, http://www.reachingcriticalwill.org/images/documents/Publications/ WEW.pdf.

LaForgia, Rachel. "Intersections of Violence against Women and Militarism." Meeting Report, Center for Women's Global Leadership, June 9–11, 2011: 5. http://www.cwgl.rutgers.edu/ docman/violence-against-women-publications/387-intersectionsvaw-militarism-pdf-1/ file.

MacAskill, Ewen. "UN Report into Saudi-Led Strikes in Yemen Raises Questions over UK Role." *The Guardian*, January 27, 2016, https://www.theguardian.com/world/2016/jan/27/ un-report-into-saudi-led-strikes-in-yemen-raises-questions-over-uk-role.

News.va. "Holy See Addresses UN Human Rights Council on Gender." March 9, 2012, http:// www.news.va/en/news/holy-see-addresses-un-human-rights-council-on-gender.

Nowak, Matthias. "Femicide: A Global Problem." *Small Arms Survey* Nowak, Matthias. "Femicide: A Global Problem." *Small Arms Survey; Research Notes: Armed Violence* 14 (2012) 14 (February 2012), http://www.smallarmssurvey.org/fileadmin/docs/H-Research_ Notes/SAS-Research-Note-14.pdf.

Perkins, Robert. "State of Crisis: Explosive Weapons in Yemen." Action on Armed Violence and the UN Office for the Coordination of Humanitarian Affairs, 2015, http://www.inew. org/site/wp-content/uploads/2015/09/State-of-Crisis.pdf.

SIPRI.org. "The United States Leads Upward Trend in Arms Exports, Asian and Gulf States Arms Imports Up, Says SIPRI." March 16, 2015b. http://www.sipri.org/media/pressreleases/ 2015/at-march-2015.

SIPRI.org, "World military spending: Increases in the USA and Europe, decreases in oil-exporting countries." 2017a. https://www.sipri.org/media/press-release/2017/ world-military-spending-increases-usa-and-europe.

SIPRI.org, "The SIPRI Top 100 arms-producing and military services companies, 2016." December 2017. https://www.sipri.org/publications/2017/sipri-fact-sheets/ sipri-top-100-arms-producing-and-military-services-companies-2016.

SIPRI.org, "Trends in International Arms Transfers, 2017." March 2018. https://www.sipri.org/ sites/default/files/2018-03/fssipri_at2017_0.pdf.

Stone, Joe. "British Government Signed Off £3.3bn of Arms Exports to Saudi Arabia in First Year of Brutal Yemen Bombardment." *The Independent*, July 27, 2016, http://www.inde-pendent.co.uk/news/uk/politics/british-government-arms-sales-saudi-arabia-yemen-3-billion-bombs-missiles-war-crimes-houthi-a7157856.html.

Tickner, Ann J. *Gender in International Relations: Feminist Perspectives on Achieving Global Security*. New York: Columbia University Press, 1992.

UN Committee on the Elimination of Discrimination Against Women (CEDAW Committee). "General Recommendation No. 30 on Women in Conflict Prevention, Conflict, and Post-Conflict situations." CEDAW/C/GC/30, November 1, 2013.

UN Security Council Resolution 1325, UN Doc S/RES/1325 (October 31, 2000).

UN Security Council Resolution 2242, UN Doc S/RES/2242 (October 13, 2015).

UN Women. "Transforming Justice, Securing the Peace. A Global Study on the Implementation of United Nations Security Council Resolution 1325 (2000)." Lead author: Radhika Coomaraswamy. UN Women, 2015, http://wps.unwomen.org/pdf/en/GlobalStudy_EN_Web.pdf.

Vine, David. "Base Nation: How U.S. Military Bases Abroad Harm America and the World." New York: Metropolitan Books, 2015.

Wearing, David. "A Shameful Relationship: UK Complicity in Saudi State Violence." Campaign against Arms Trade, 2016, https://www.caat.org.uk/campaigns/stop-arming-saudi/a-shameful-relationship.pdf.

WILPF and the European Center for Constitutional and Human Rights (ECCHR). "The Impact of Germany's Arms Transfers on Women: Germany's Extraterritorial Obligations under CEDAW. Joint Shadow Report, February 2, 2017, http://www.reachingcriticalwill.org/images/documents/Publications/CEDAW-Germany.pdf.

WILPF. "Re: Security Council Consideration of Yemen and Women, Peace, and Security." February 26, 2015, http://peacewomen.org/sites/default/files/Letter%20to%20Security%20Council_Yemen_WILPF.pdf

WILPF. "The Extraterritorial Obligations of States towards Human's Rights." Statement before the CEDAW Committee's Pre-session Review of Germany. July 25, 2016a, http://wilpf.org/wilpf_statements/the-extraterritorial-obligations-of-states-towards-human-rights/.

WILPF. "Explosive Weapons and the Right to Health, Education, and Adequate Housing: Extraterritorial Obligations of France under CESCR." Shadow Report to the CESCR 58th Session, 2016b, http://www.reachingcriticalwill.org/images/documents/Publications/wilpf-cescr-france.pdf.

WILPF. "Explosive Weapons and the Right to Health, Education, and Adequate Housing: Extraterritorial Obligations of Sweden under CESCR." Shadow Report to the CESCR 58th Session, 2016c, http://www.reachingcriticalwill.org/images/documents/Publications/wilpf-cescr-sweden.pdf.

WILPF. "Explosive Weapons and the Right to Health, Education, and Adequate Housing: Extraterritorial Obligations of the United Kingdom under CESCR." Shadow Report to the CESCR 58th Session, 2016d, http://www.reachingcriticalwill.org/images/documents/Publications/wilpf-cescr-uk.pdf.

WILPF. "Statement on the Use of Weapons and Arms Transfers to Parties in the Conflict in Yemen." Reaching Critical Will, 2016e, http://www.reachingcriticalwill.org/news/latest-news/11177-wilpf-statement-on-the-use-of-weapons-and-arms-transfers-to-parties-in-the-conflict-in-yemen.

WILPF. "Statement on the Report of the Commission of Inquiry on Syria." Reaching Critical Will, 2016f, http://www.reachingcriticalwill.org/news/latest-news/11178-wilpf-statement-on-the-report-of-the-commission-of-inquiry-on-syria.

WILPF, IANSA Women's Network, Amnesty International, and Religions for Peace. "The Arms Trade Treaty: Securing Women's Rights and Gender Equality." Reachingcriticalwill.

org, June 2012, http://reachingcriticalwill.org/images/documents/Disarmament-fora/att/policypaper.pdf.

Wintour, Patrick. "Ban Ki-Moon Adds to Pressure on UK to Stop Arms Sales to Saudis." *The Guardian*, February 5, 2016, https://www.theguardian.com/world/2016/feb/05/ban-ki-moon-yemen-war-uk-arms-sales-saudi-arabia.

CHAPTER 55

WPS AND SUSTAINABLE DEVELOPMENT GOALS

RADHIKA BALAKRISHNAN AND KRISHANTI DHARMARAJ

THE economic policies that have been followed since the 1980s have accelerated inequality both within and between countries. This inequality, in conjunction with growing militarism and conflict within and between countries, has made sustainable peace and genuine security unattainable in the current context. Despite this, the inequality within and among nations continues to increase, now ensuring that eight men own the same amount of wealth as 3.6 billion people who make up the poorest half of humanity (Oxfam 2017). In 2014, the World Economic Forum identified inequality as, "a major risk of human progress, impacting social instability within countries and threatening security on a global scale" (Oxfam 2014: 2).

In order to examine the issues surrounding women, peace, and security it is critical to unpack the relationship between existing economic policy and violent conflicts, and how women are disproportionately affected at this intersection. This requires dismantling the current objectives of the economic system of profit over people and planet, and posits a new normative framework that centers on the fulfillment of human rights. This framework ensures the principles of equality and non-discrimination, resulting in gender equality, which is fundamental to achieving and sustaining peace, also one of the pillars of the 2030 Agenda for Sustainable Development (2030 Agenda).

The preamble of the 2030 Agenda states: "We are determined to foster peaceful, just and inclusive societies which are free from fear and violence. There can be no sustainable development without peace and no peace without sustainable development" (United Nations 2015: 3). In 2015, the UN General Assembly, in adopting the 2030 Agenda, set seventeen Sustainable Development Goals (SDGs) with a clear pledge that "no one will be left behind" (United Nations 2015: 3). This chapter posits that achieving sustainable development requires a change in the current economic system and advances the idea that an economic system based on the fulfillment of human rights and a peace and security agenda must consider what polices are needed to achieve sustainable peace, beyond the absence of war and violence. (See also chapter 26 on IFI and chapter 12 on Conflict Prevention in this volume.)

Though the Universal Declaration of Human Rights was adopted in 1948, International Covenant Civil and Political Rights and the International Covenant of Economic, Social, and Cultural Rights went into effect in 1966, the Convention on the Elimination of all forms of Discrimination against Women in 1979, and United Nations Security Council Resolution 1325 was adopted in 2000, we continue to live in a world of perpetual violent conflict and war. These circumstances accelerate civilian casualties and disproportionately impact women at an unprecedented level, including through the use of sexual violence as a weapon of war. The 2030 Agenda is guided by a full respect for international law including those just mentioned and the Declaration on Right to Development (United Nations 2015). Though there is an emphasis on the importance of the human rights framework in the 2030 Agenda, there is an absence of utilizing the normative framework of human rights to question the economic system that impacts development. The current economic system is governed by a narrow set of policy goals, such as increasing GDP and keeping inflation low. These policy measures are guided by mainstream economic thinking that believes in the virtues of the market and efficiency as the main goal rather than distribution or fulfillment of rights. These policy measures impact women and men differently, making women more vulnerable and excluded from benefiting from economic gain, whether during peacetime or violent conflict.

In addition to the economic system, another challenge to the development and implementation of the SDGs is violent conflict, war, and occupation. A connection exists between development and peace where, without one, the other is not possible and without human rights neither can exist. In a report by the Institute for Economics and Peace (2016: 4) the economic impact of violence in the world is estimated as 13.3 percent of world Gross Domestic Product (GDP). In addition, the level of violence reduces the amount of money invested in sectors such as those that allocate funds towards long-term social benefits. Countries experiencing violence and conflict also often face a decline in foreign direct investment as well as a serious capital flow. The relationship is both ways; low economic performance, inequality, and social fragmentation can lead to violence and conflict (Institute for Economics of Peace: 2016: 4–9). The economic policies that lead to growing levels of inequality resulting in exclusion and discrimination are inextricably linked to violence and militarism.

Human rights as the normative framework to construct economic policy will not only help in terms of securing development but will also result in promoting a peaceful world for all. The six main tenants of the human rights framework are universality, indivisibility, participation, accountability, transparency, and non-discrimination. Universality and non-discrimination ensures that women, as humans, are entitled to fundamental human rights and should not be discriminated against based on their multiple and intersecting identities, such as but not limited to gender, gender identity, race, ethnicity, caste, sexual orientation, class, ability, religion, and/or nationality (Center for Women's Global Leadership 2013). Indivisibility ensures that rights are interdependent, and therefore policies must prioritize respecting, protecting, and fulfilling all rights in order to fully realize any. Peace would be a natural outcome if transparency and accountability of governments along with participation of civil society were a deliberative process of developing economic policy.

One challenge to human rights implementation is that war and conflict are rarely contained within a country's borders. Though states are still the main actors held accountable for the implementation of human rights, not all conflict is within borders and many of the consequences of conflict bleed to other countries. For example, there are currently more than 65 million displaced persons worldwide. This constitutes over 21 million refugees. While half of the refugee population are children, over 50 percent of the adult population are women (UNHCR 2015). To ensure full inclusion, especially of women and other marginalized communities such as the disabled and ethnic minorities, the human rights framework is vital when implementing policies at local, national, regional, and international levels. Therefore, the aid agencies, development banks, and international entities committed to the sustainability of peace and development must work at the intersection of Resolution 1325 and the 2030 Agenda (see also chapter 26 in this volume).

To ensure that the 2030 Agenda is implemented in a manner where "no one is left behind," Resolution 1325 must be integrated using an intersectional approach that recognizes multiple and intersecting identities of all people, and the relevance of the document must be recognized when implementing the SDGs in conflict zones (United Nations 2015: 3). High levels of violations and suppression of human rights can give rise to conflict and may result in war, and during violent conflict and war, the level of human rights violations increases leading to vulnerability for women. While all women may face the threat of violence in such an environment, those who are marginalized due to their multiple and intersecting identities face significant threats that result in loss of livelihood, an inadequate standard of living, and violence, including torture and even death.

Resolution 1325, adopted in 2000, encompasses four pillars to address women, peace and security as this handbook outlines and summarizes as protection, participation, prevention, and peace-building and recovery. This implies that the participation of women in decision-making must exist at all levels including conflict resolution, protection of women and girls from sexual and all forms of violence, prevention of violence against women and girls through measures such as the development of intervention strategies, and peace-building and recovery through a gendered approach.

The Global Study on the implementation of Resolution 1325, conducted in 2015, (UN Women 2015) affirms that peace is only sustainable if women are fully included in peace processes, gender is integrated into all aspects of program, resource allocation and service delivery, and equality between men and women is realized. It is important to recognize that the equality sought is substantive equality, which is the equality of results rather than only the equality of access. SDG 5 on gender equality (based on CEDAW), which calls for an end to all forms of discrimination against all women and girls everywhere, reinforces the need for equality between women and men for the sustainability of development and peace. It is important to recognize that for gender equality to be realized within the SDGs, both the implementation of SDG 5 and the integration of gender into all SDGs, specifically SDG 16 on promoting inclusive and peaceful societies, are critical.

The SDG Agenda includes peace as one of its five key concepts along with people, planet, prosperity, and partnership. Peace is amplified through SDG 16: "Promote peaceful and inclusive societies for sustainable development, provide access to justice for all and build effective, accountable and inclusive institutions at all levels." This goal exhibits a clear shift in the development paradigm, which recognizes that inequality and insecurity do not happen in isolation. Yet, this goal misses a critical component—the reference to women, peace, and security. SDG 16 has twelve targets, yet none of these refer to women or consider gender. Therefore, the implementation of the SDGs, especially Goal 16, must integrate gender along with UNSCR 1325 to ensure that women are positioned not merely as beneficiaries, but as agents of change.

PREVENTION OF CONFLICT AND WAR

In order to attempt to prevent war and violent conflict, there is a need to understand its underlying causes. The World Bank report on the dimensions of violent conflict has highlighted several issues related to this from 2000–2015. They claim that 56 percent of conflicts were due to issues surrounding access to land, 58 percent were described as subnational, 25 percent political inclusion, 6 percent due to illicit drug trafficking, 17 percent mining, 21 percent migration related, and 62 percent were spill over and overlap of the other issues described.

These data illustrate very clearly the relationship between economic resources and the dimensions of violent conflict. The World Bank report states that, "identifying viable measures for addressing issues of inequity and lack of economic and political inclusion should be an important complement to efforts to build the institutional capacities of the state. The lack of recognition of the need to adapt development policies is at the origin of many of the relapses of violence" (United Nations World Bank 2016).

In order for states to adequately address issues of inequity and lack of economic and political inclusion within a country requires resources. Access to resources is often limited due to the growing levels of inequality among countries as a result of the ongoing and new imperialist agendas around the world. The data from the World Bank report clearly illustrate that access to land, mining, and extractive industries and migration, to name a few, are some of the important dimensions of violent conflict.

Though institutions, such as the World Bank, refer to these needs, the response is most often a singular focus of economic policy targeted toward increased growth. Little if any attention is paid to how resources are allocated and what the priorities are of economic policymaking. It is important to further the World Bank findings with a gendered approach. In developing countries, statutory and customary laws continue to restrict women's access to land and other assets, and women's control over household economic resources is limited. In nearly a third of developing countries, laws do not guarantee the same inheritance rights for women and men, and in an additional half of countries discriminatory customary practices against women are found. Moreover, about one in three married women from developing regions has no control over household spending on major purchases and about one in ten married women is not consulted on how their own cash earnings are spent (UN Women 2015). When inequality is exasperated due to gender-based discrimination, the solution sought to secure and protect land and other natural resources must recognize and integrate women's equality as fundamental to preventing violent conflict. The implementation of SDGs therefore adds value to addressing inequality and preventing violent conflict.

We argue that if the fulfillment of human rights was at the center of economic policymaking, the way in which the state gets and distributes resources would be very different. Most often what is done in terms of security issues is to react to existing conflict rather than to prevent it through a deliberate focus on the fulfillment of rights. One of the critical issues in terms of economic policy and the fulfillment of rights is access to resources. The International Covenant on Economic, Social, and Cultural Rights states that a government must take steps "to the maximum of its available resources" to support the progressive realization of human rights (Office of the High Commissioner on Human Rights 1966). For example using the maximum of available resources to fulfill rights, such as an adequate standard of living, will decrease the conflicts that often arise due to levels of inequality. Prevention must address the realization of human rights and the interdependence of civil and political rights with economic, social, and cultural rights. Human rights stress a much broader range of issues and objectives and increase the substantive freedoms and choices people enjoy in their lives (Balakrishnan et al. 2016: 3).

There are a range of policy options that are available to governments when looking at resources. The first of course is to look at how the government actually spends them. For example, if we were to look at the difference between expenditure on social spending versus military spending in most countries we would find that there is a much higher percentage of government revenue that goes to the military. Though there has been a decrease in military expenditure since the end of the Cold War, there has been a steady increase since 2001. Global military expenditure in 2015 was an estimated $1,676 billion, an increase of about 1.0 percent from 2014. In total, 2.3 percent of GDP was spent on the military (Perlo-Freeman et al. 2016). Though these numbers are the global total, the amount spent on military is much higher in countries that are ravaged by war. The United States, though not having conflict within its borders, is the highest military spender in the world, nearly three times the second, which is China (Perlo-Freeman et al. 2016). Who decides on how resources are spent and how priorities are set will be a critical factor in the fulfillment of human rights.

Another case of how resources are spent to the detriment of human rights and equitable development is that of Sri Lanka. In 2013, the government of Sri Lanka allocated 290 billion Rupees ($US 2.2 billion) to the combined defense and urban development ministry. This was a 26 percent increase from 2012, making it the highest ever, even after the government won the war against the separatist Liberation Tigers of Tamil Eelam (LTTE) in 2009. While the building of social infrastructure remains crucial after the civil war, the Sri Lankan government increased the education budget by only 7.5 billion rupees and health by 18 billion rupees, compared with the 60 billion rupee increase for defense (Gunadasa 2012).

Examining how resources are spent is crucial, but so is how resources are mobilized. Taxes are one of the most important ways that states mobilize resources. What tax policy regimes are followed is critical. A trend within neoliberal economic reform is the impetus to decrease taxes on wealthy individuals and corporations, which shrinks the pool of resources available to government to fulfill rights. Other than looking at the use of maximum available resources, the human rights framework also provides guidance in terms of global tax policies and the issues of extraterritorial obligations. The issue of tax revenue is both national and global, as it includes areas such as problems of tax shelters and global corporate tax evasion. Therefore, looking at revenues requires not only national mobilization of resources but global coordination (ETO 2013).

The decisions made on fiscal and monetary policy, such as those regarding deficit spending if there is a downturn in the economy and how much debt is sustainable, are also important. The focus on austerity in many parts of Europe after the crisis in 2008 has had some impact on the marginalization of people and the increase in violent extremism and conflict within Europe (Halikiopoulou 2016). The nationalist trend in many parts of the world, giving forth to policy decisions such as Brexit in the United Kingdom and the voting of Trump as President in the United States, is clear evidence that people are frustrated and the level of inequality is fostering a right wing nationalist trend. The particular use of neoliberal policy since the 1980s and financialization of the world economy has limited the role of the state in the provision of social welfare and has exasperated the level of inequality (Balakrishnan 2016: 4).

Another aspect of the ways in which neoliberal economic policy has had an impact on maximum available resources is how monetary and financial policy is conducted. For example, the United States has a dual mandate to conduct monetary policy to increase employment and decrease inflation. Many countries, due to the imposition of neoliberal economic policy by institutions such as the International Monetary Fund, are only allowed to have inflation targets. This limits the scope of monetary policy and allows the interests of creditors to override the interests of people. Financial policy and regulation also has an impact. With the huge increase in the financialization of the world economy, the volatility of economies has made sustainable development very precarious. South Africa, for example, has shown that to embrace some of the neoliberal polices toward capital mobility and not employment generation has made the economy vulnerable to crisis (McKenzie and Pons-Vignon 2012: 23). The ability to implement the SDGs with increasing volatility in capital markets is not possible. There is a need to regulate finance to limit capital mobility to decrease the boom and bust cycles the world is experiencing.

The last consideration is the important role of overseas development assistance (ODA). Though the 2030 Agenda set up important goals, one thing it did not do was increase the resources needed for its proposed development. The discussion on financing for development (FFD) did nothing to increase ODA and barely kept the prior commitments of 0.07 percent. ODA has also become very explicitly a part of the foreign policy considerations by donor governments and often in the interest of industry that is exploiting resources in other countries (Balakrishnan et al. 2016). The Trump Administration, in its budgetary rollout, not only cut development assistance globally, but has also asked to have it become a program that is tied closely to national security objectives (Harris et al. 2017).

As the 2030 Agenda posits that the overall approach to the implementation of the SDGs is through a human rights framework, a particularly useful set of human right guidelines is the framework set out in the Maastricht Guidelines on Violations of Economic, Social, and Cultural Rights, which differentiates three dimensions of obligations:

1. The obligation to respect requires states to refrain from interfering with the enjoyment of economic, social, and cultural rights. Thus the right to housing is violated if the state engages in arbitrary forced evictions.
2. The obligation to protect requires states to prevent violations of such rights by third parties. Thus the failure to ensure that private employers comply with basic labour standards may amount to a violation of the right to work or the right to just and favorable conditions of work.
3. The obligation to fulfill requires states to take appropriate legislative, administrative, budgetary, judicial and other measures towards the full realization of such rights. Thus, the failure of States to provide essential primary health care to those in need may amount to a violation (Committee on Economic, Social, and Cultural Rights 1999).

A problem in utilizing these principles has been the use of their obligation to protect as a reason for invasions and imperialist attacks in the name of defending, very often, women's rights, as was certainly the case in Afghanistan. The obligations in the Maastricht Guidelines are written to examine economic and social rights, not to be a justification for war.

Though the 2030 Agenda is rooted in human rights and Resolution 1325 is the responsibility of the member states, these do not have strong implementation and accountability mechanisms that would allow civil society to monitor progress including demanding resource allocation to the fulfillment of the goals. Given that both documents are influenced by human rights norms, it is imperative that the implementation has a rights-based approach that includes accountability through integration into human rights reporting. The resolution must be integrated into the implementation of the SDGs and reported within the Universal Periodic Review (UPR) process at the Human Rights Council where member states are engaged in peer review of human rights progress. The SDGs can also be integrated within the reporting mechanism of the International Covenant of Economic, Social, and Cultural Rights. SDG 5 could be specifically addressed within CEDAW reporting, and with respect to countries in conflict, SDG 16 targets should be integrated into the reporting process of CEDAW, making the protection of women in conflict and post-conflict a priority. CEDAW general recommendation 30, along with SDG 16 and UNSCR 1325, provides a comprehensive platform for addressing women, peace, and security.

While peace and security are inextricably linked to the realization of human rights, there remains a clear divide between the UN Human Rights Bodies and the functioning of the UN Security Council. The five permanent members of the Security Council (P5)— the United States, China, the United Kingdom, Russia, and France—have the largest defense budgets that comprise 61 percent of total military expenditure in the world. Of this, the United States is responsible for 43 percent and is the largest manufacturer of arms in the world (Stockholm International Peace Research Institute 2015). In 2013, the US Special Operations Command (SOCOM), one of the nine organizational units that make up the Unified Combatant Command, had special operations forces (SOFs) in 134 countries, where they were either involved in combat, special missions, or advising and training foreign forces (Turse 2014). During President Obama's first six years in office, agreements for $190 billion worth of weapons sales were made. His administration sold more weapons than any other since WWII (Hartung 2016). Given this investment of the P5 towards militarization and especially that of the United States, policy is often led by vested interests rather than the advancement of peace (see chapter 54 in this volume). War is marketable and therefore militarization contributes to the current system of economic growth.

Both the SDGs and Resolution 1325 are universal documents. Therefore the responsibility of implementation and monitoring belong to governments in both the Global North and South. The aim of a national plan of action is to implement policies that impact its country positively. Yet the governments of the Global North have developed plans to hold governments accountable of those they have invaded or occupy. For example, the United States National Action Plan (NAP) for Resolution 1325 in 2011 focuses on Afghan women's participation and empowerment rather than the accountability of the United States for the impact of its invasion on women of Afghanistan, Iraq, or the occupation of Puerto Rico and the Pacific Islands marked as Territories of the United States. Similarly, the United States has not acknowledged its role in the implementation of the SDGs, yet a city such as Flint, Michigan, for example, which faced a water crisis, could deeply benefit by the implementation of SDG 6, ensuring availability and sustainable management of water and sanitation for all.

One important aspect of using a human rights–based approach is that it provides venues for civil society to hold governments accountable. The treaty bodies previously mentioned as well as the UPR review are important places for governments to report on their fulfillment of human rights and for civil society to hold them to account. An example of a civil society win is the historic judgment from the African Court of Human and Peoples

Rights in Arusha in favor of the Ogiek community of Kenya. Following an eight-year legal battle, the Court found that the Kenyan government violated seven separate articles of the African Charter in a land rights case that dates back to colonial times. "Crucially the Court has recognized that the Ogiek—and therefore many other indigenous peoples in Africa—have a leading role to play as guardians of local ecosystems, and in conserving and protecting land and natural resources, including the Mau Forest" (Minority Rights Group 2017). This accountability becomes critical when assessing the progress of occupied and militarized zones such as Palestine or the North of Sri Lanka, after the end of the war eight years ago (2009), the north of Sri Lanka remains heavily militarized (Amnesty International 2017).

Sustainability of peace demands a structural shift that challenges the current status quo. Human rights must be the normative framework assessing economic policy and its efficacy has to be judged by the ability to fulfill rights, not just economic growth. Realization of rights, including non-discrimination and equality, must be included in shaping and measuring peace. The structural shift necessary for the sustainability of peace must include the full and equal participation of women at every level. Without women's equality an authentic practice of peace will not be possible. Shifting this status quo also requires a redefinition of peace beyond the absence of war, conflict, and militarization. Peace must encompass the realization of human rights, including the indivisibility and interdependency of economic, social, cultural, civil, and political rights; protection and sustainability of natural resources including the climate; and inclusion and equality of *all* within and among communities and nations.[1]

SDG GOAL 5—Women's Equality

5.1 End all forms of discrimination against all women and girls everywhere

5.2 Eliminate all forms of violence against all women and girls in the public and private spheres, including trafficking and sexual and other types of exploitation

5.3 Eliminate all harmful practices, such as child, early, and forced marriage, and female genital mutilation

5.4 Recognize and value unpaid care and domestic work through the provision of public services, infrastructure, and social protection policies, and the promotion of shared responsibility within the household and the family as nationally appropriate

5.5 Ensure women's full and effective participation and equal opportunities for leadership at all levels of decision-making in political, economic, and public life

5.6 Ensure universal access to sexual and reproductive health and reproductive rights as agreed in accordance with the Programme of Action of the International Conference on Population and Development and the Beijing Platform for Action and the outcome documents of their review conferences

5.a Undertake reforms to give women equal rights to economic resources, as well as access to ownership and control over land and other forms of property, financial services, inheritance, and natural resources, in accordance with national laws

5.b Enhance the use of enabling technology, in particular information and communications technology, to promote the empowerment of women

5.c Adopt and strengthen sound policies and enforceable legislation for the promotion of gender equality and the empowerment of all women and girls at all levels

SDGs

(1) End poverty in all its forms everywhere. (2) End hunger, achieve food security and improved nutrition, and promote sustainable agriculture. (3) Ensure healthy lives and promote well-being for all at all ages. (4) Ensure inclusive and equitable quality education and promote lifelong learning opportunities for all. (5) Achieve gender equality and empower all women and girls. (6) Ensure availability and sustainable management of water and sanitation for all. (7) Ensure access to affordable, reliable, sustainable, and modern energy for all. (8) Promote sustained, inclusive, and sustainable economic growth, full and productive employment, and decent work for all. (9) Build resilient infrastructure, promote inclusive and sustainable industrialization, and foster innovation. (10) Reduce inequality within and among countries. (11) Make cities and human settlements inclusive, safe, resilient, and sustainable. (12) Ensure sustainable consumption and production patterns. (13) Take urgent action to combat climate change and its impacts (taking note of agreements made by the UNFCCC forum). (14) Conserve and sustainably use the oceans, seas, and marine resources for sustainable development. (15) Protect, restore, and promote sustainable use of terrestrial ecosystems; sustainably manage forests; combat desertification; halt and reverse land degradation; and halt biodiversity loss. (16) Promote peaceful and inclusive societies for sustainable development, provide access to justice for all and build effective, accountable, and inclusive institutions at all levels. (17) Strengthen the means of implementation and revitalize the global partnership for sustainable development.

NOTES

1. Working definition from the Center for Women's Global Leadership's strategic plan.

REFERENCES

Amnesty International. "Only Justice Can Heal Our Wounds." May 8, 2017, https://www.amnesty.org/en/documents/asa37/5853/2017/en/.

Balakrishnan, Radhika, James Heintz, and Diane Elson. *Rethinking Economic Policy for Social Justice: Radical Potential of Human Rights*. New York: Routledge, 2016.

Center for Women's Global Leadership (CWGL). "Framing Questions on Intersectionality." US Human Rights Network, 2013, http://www.ushrnetwork.org/sites/ushrnetwork.org/files/framing_questions_on_intersectionality_1.pdf.

Committee on Economic, Social, and Cultural Rights (CESCR). "The Nature of States Parties' Obligations." General Comment 3, 1999.

ETO. *Maastricht Principles on Extraterritorial Obligations on States in the Area of Economic, Social, and Cultural Rights*. Heidelberg: Fian International, 2013, https://www.ilsa.org/jessup/jessup17/Batch%202/Maastricht%20Principles%20on%20Extraterritorial%20Obligations%20of%20States%20in%20the%20Area%20of%20Economic,%20Social%20and%20Cultural%20Rights.pdf.

Gunadasa, Saman. "Unprecedented Military Budget in Sri Lanka". World Socialist Website, 2012, https://www.wsws.org/en/articles/2012/10/slec-019.html.

Halikiopoulou, Daphne. "Austerity Brings Extremism: Why the Welfare State Is the Key to Understanding the Rise of Europe's Far Right." Huffington Post, September 23, 2016, http://www.huffingtonpost.co.uk/daphne-halikiopoulou/austerity-brings-extremis_b_8182866.html.

Harris, Bryant, Robbie Gramer, and Emily Tamkin. "The End of Foreign Aid as We Know It." *Foreign Policy*, April 24, 2017, http://foreignpolicy.com/2017/04/24/u-s-agency-for-international-development-foreign-aid-state-department-trump-slash-foreign-funding/.

Hartung, William D. "The Obama Administration Has Brokered More Weapons Sales Than Any Other Administration since World War II." *The Nation*, July 26, 2016, https://www.thenation.com/article/the-obama-administration-has-sold-more-weapons-than-any-other-administration-since-world-war-ii/.

Institute for Economics and Peace. "The Economic Value of Peace: Measuring the Global Economic Impact of Violence and Conflict." IEP, 2016. http://visionofhumanity.org/app/uploads/2017/02/The-Economic-Value-of-Peace-2016-WEB.pdf.

McKenzie, Rex A., and Nicolas Pons-Vignon. "Volatile Capital Flows and a Route to Financial Crisis in South Africa." AUGUR Working Paper, February 2012 (WP #2).

Minority Rights Group. "Huge Victory for Kenya's Ogiek as African Court Sets Major Precedent for Indigenous Peoples' Land Rights." May 26, 2017, http://minorityrights.org/2017/05/26/huge-victory-kenyas-ogiek-african-court-sets-major-precedent-indigenous-peoples-land-rights/.

Office of the High Commissioner for Human Rights. "International Covenant on Economic Social and Cultural Rights." ICESCR, December 16, 1966.

Oxfam. "An Economy for the 99%." Oxfam Briefing Paper, January 2017, https://www.oxfam.org/sites/www.oxfam.org/files/file_attachments/bp-economy-for-99-percent-160117-en.pdf.

Oxfam. "Working for the Few." Oxfam Briefing Paper, January 20, 2014, https://www.oxfam.org/sites/www.oxfam.org/files/file_attachments/bp-working-for-few-political-capture-economic-inequality-200114-en_3.pdf.

Perlo-Freemanf, Sam, Aude Fleurant, Pieter D. Wezeman, and Siemon T. Wezeman. "Trends in World Military Expenditure, 2015." Stockholm International Peace Research Institute, April 2016, https://www.sipri.org/publications/2016/sipri-fact-sheets/trends-world-military-expenditure-2015.

Stockholm International Peace Research Institute (SIPRI). "The United States Leads Upward Trend in Arms Exports, Asian and Gulf States Arms Imports up, Says SIPRI." March 16, 2015, https://www.sipri.org/media/press-release/2015/united-states-leads-upward-trend-arms-exports-asian-and-gulf-states-arms-imports-says-sipri.

Turse, Nick. "America's Secret War in 134 Countries." *The Nation*, January 16, 2014, https://www.thenation.com/article/americas-secret-war-134-countries/.

UN Security Council. "Security Council Resolution 1325 (2000)" [on women and peace and security]. S/RES/1325, 2000.

UN Women. "Preventing Conflict, Transforming Justice, Securing the Peace: A Global Study on the Implementation of United Nations Security Council Resolution 1325." UN Women, 2015, http://www.peacewomen.org/sites/default/files/UNW-GLOBAL-STUDY-1325-2015%20(1).pdf.

UNHCR. "Figures at a Glance." UNHCR, 2015, http://www.unhcr.org/en-us/figures-at-a-glance.html.

United Nations. "Transforming Our World: The 2030 Agenda for Sustainable Development." A/Res/70/1, 2015, https://sustainabledevelopment.un.org/content/documents/21252030%20Agenda%20for%20Sustainable%20Development%20web.pdf.

United Nations World Bank. "Sustaining Peace: Making Development Work for the Prevention of Violence Conflicts." Concept note, October 13, 2016, https://www.prio.org/utility/Download.ashx?x=545.

CHAPTER 56

....

WPS AND THE CONVENTION AGAINST TORTURE

....

ANDREA HUBER AND THERESE RYTTER

THE emergence of the women, peace, and security (WPS) agenda with the adoption of the landmark UN Security Council resolution 1325 in 2000 effectively marked the end of an era where the international peace and security paradigm had been "gender-blind" to the detriment of millions of women and girls worldwide. While being grounded in the UN Charter, the WPS agenda cuts across four branches of international law, notably human rights law. This chapter explores to what extent the UN Security Council resolutions on WPS take into account the international human rights framework against torture and ill-treatment, notably the UN Convention against Torture (GA Resolution 39/46) and how the UN human rights mechanisms with a mandate relating to torture have addressed situations specific to women and girls in conflict and post-conflict situations.

DO UN SECURITY COUNCIL RESOLUTIONS ON WPS REFLECT THE INTERNATIONAL HUMAN RIGHTS FRAMEWORK AGAINST TORTURE AND ILL-TREATMENT?

....

Resolution 1325 was essentially conceived as part of the international legal framework that upholds the rights of women and girls in the context of conflict and post-conflict, and it was lobbied for as a human rights resolution (UN Women 2015: 15). Accordingly, Resolution 1325 reaffirms the need to fully implement international human rights law that protects the rights of women and girls during and after conflicts. However, the WPS policy architecture does not refer to any core international human rights treaties other than CEDAW (GA Resolution 34/180) and the Convention on the Rights of the Child (GA Resolution 44/25), let alone the absolute and non-derogable prohibition of torture (Nowak and McArthur 2008: 89). Yet, of the WPS agenda's four-pillar mandate (George and Shepherd 2006: 298; and Rees and Chinkin 2016: 1211–1226)—protection, prevention, participation, and relief and recovery—the UN Convention against Torture (UNCAT) is particularly relevant to the pillars of protection and prevention.

The *"protection pillar"* addresses the protection of women against sexual and other forms of gender-based violence (GBV) (S/RES/1820 2008; S/RES/1888 2009; S/RES/1889 2009; and S/RES/1960 2010). Seen through a human rights and criminal justice lens, the concept of protection primarily revolves around the obligation to end impunity for such violence. This overall obligation is accompanied by several specific obligations, such as ensuring full accountability for acts of sexual exploitation and abuse, prosecuting those responsible, undertaking thorough and timely investigations, prohibiting sexual violence, ensuring that victims are protected and receive redress for their suffering, and undertaking legal and judicial reforms.

The WPS obligations related to the protection against violence are firmly rooted in international humanitarian, human rights, and/or criminal law. Importantly, the Convention against Torture requires States Parties to criminalize torture (UNCAT, Articles 1, 4), to establish jurisdiction (UNCAT, Article 5), to undertake prompt and impartial investigations (UNCAT, Article 12), to submit cases of alleged torture to competent authorities for prosecution (UNCAT, Article 7), to protect victims and witnesses (UNCAT, Article 13), and to ensure an enforceable right to redress for victims (UNCAT, Article 14). As such, there is a large degree of congruency between the WPS regime and UNCAT.

By comparison, the *"preventive pillar"* has historically been less developed, (Skjelsbæk 2012: 163; and Kirby and Shepherd 2016: 377–378) arguably because the effective prevention would require states to take measures addressing the underlying structural barriers to substantive and transformative equality. Currently, preventive measures—within the scope of UNCAT—are limited to training of police and military personnel, and heightening awareness and responsiveness to protect women and children.

By contrast, the Convention against Torture contains a broad spectrum of preventive obligations, with their point of departure being a general obligation to take effective legislative, judicial, or other measures to prevent such acts (UNCAT, Articles 2 and 16). Added to this are specific obligations to respect the principle of *non-refoulement* (UNCAT, Article 3), to review detention and interrogation practices (UNCAT, Article 11), and to ensure training of public officials involved in the custody or interrogation of individuals (UNCAT, Article 10). When comparing the WPS agenda with UNCAT, it becomes evident that the interface between the two is rather limited, and that the UN Security Council resolutions only mirror a fraction of UNCAT's preventive obligations.

In sum, several obligations embodied in UNCAT are reflected in the WPS regime, particularly with regard to protection and to some extent prevention. However, the obligations in the resolutions are clearly drawn from other international treaties, notably CEDAW, given the lack of any reference to UNCAT and the divergence in language between the WPS resolutions and UNCAT.

HAVE UN HUMAN RIGHTS MECHANISMS WITH A SPECIFIC MANDATE RELATING TO TORTURE ADDRESSED WOMEN AND GIRLS IN CONFLICT AND POST-CONFLICT SITUATIONS?

This section explores whether and how the UN human rights bodies with a mandate relating to torture—the Committee against Torture, the Sub-Committee on Prevention of Torture, and the Special Rapporteur on Torture—each within their mandate, have integrated the WPS agenda into their respective monitoring of state compliance with the Convention against Torture vis-à-vis women and girls during and after conflict.

Committee against Torture

Protection of women during armed conflict is the WPS dimension that is addressed most often by the Committee. In the context of conflict, the Committee routinely expresses concern about reports of sexual violence against women; the systematic use of rape as a "weapon of war" (Committee against Torture [CAT] 2007; 2010); the underreporting of rape and other sexual violence against women and girls (CAT 2013b), the limited number of investigations, the absence of sentences, and the lack of effective redress to victims of rape and other sexual violence (CAT 2011a; 2005; 2008; 2011b; and 2013b)

In continuation hereof, the Committee regularly recommends State Parties to criminalize violence against women in conflict areas (CAT 2015a); to promptly and impartially investigate all allegations of rape and other sexual violence; to prosecute and punish perpetrators with penalties appropriate; and to end impunity for both state officials and non-state actors (CAT 2005; 2008a; 2008b; 2013a; 2015b). In some cases, the Committee has also required States to ensure that women fleeing conflict-related sexual violence have access to shelter, medical and psychological care and rehabilitation, and that they are able to access such services without discrimination based on gender (CAT 2015b). Finally, in order to facilitate the monitoring of states' implementation of UNCAT, the Committee increasingly requires states to provide statistical data, disaggregated by sex (CAT 2012).

Prevention of violence against women in conflict and post-conflict settings has been given less, although increasing attention since the adoption of the General Comment no. 2 on the implementation of Article 2 of the Convention in 2008. The General Comment reinforces the obligation to prevent torture vis-à-vis women by emphasizing the principle of non-discrimination as integral to the definition of torture, the gendered nature of violations that women—and men—suffer, and the need to build a culture of respect for women.

In its examination of state parties, the Committee has required that a variety of gender-specific preventive measures be taken, notably to redouble efforts to prevent sexual violence and abuse against women and children (CAT 2008c); to ensure that procedures are in place to monitor law enforcement officials (CAT 2005); to provide mandatory training on human rights, and the prohibition of SGBV, in particular against women and children, for the military and other officials (CAT 2006; 2011b); and to conduct information campaigns to raise awareness that sexual violence are offences under criminal law, to break the taboo on sex crimes, and to eliminate the stigmatization and exclusion of victims (CAT 2007).

Women's *participation* in peace-building or peacekeeping is seldom addressed by the Committee. A rare exception is the recent consideration of Burundi, where the Committee recommended the State Party to ensure that women police officers take part in security operations as a measure to protect women against sexual violence during searches and protest control operations (CAT 2016).

Overall, it emerges from the Committee's concluding observations that it has expanded its sensitivity to and awareness of the issue of violence against women in the past decade (Gaer 2012: 303). It addresses a wide range of violations vis-à-vis women within the broader continuum of violence in conflict and post-conflict settings as well as beyond, and while its focus has predominantly been on state actors, growing attention is given to violence perpetrated by non-state actors. Despite the developments in understanding sexual and other GBV as torture and the explicit mention of women and girls in many cases, SGBV is nevertheless often not addressed in an engendered manner that takes into account underlying structural barriers to substantive and transformative equality.

Subcommittee on Prevention of Torture

The Subcommittee on Prevention of Torture[1] (SPT) (GA Resolution 57/199).[2] has not explored torture and ill-treatment in times of conflict or post-conflict, let alone gender-specific violations. In its eighth annual report it addresses women deprived of their liberty,[3] but without reference to conflict or post-conflict situations. A short section in the seventh annual report on "Conflict and Political Repression" also does not reflect on such settings or the WPS agenda.[4]

However, it should be recognized that the SPT's mandate only covers a limited part of the WPS agenda, and that its working methods are rather unsuitable for countries in conflict and post-conflict situations. Primarily acting through country visits, fragile security situations restrict the ability to engage meaningfully.[5]

UN Special Rapporteur on Torture

The challenges associated with country visits by the Special Rapporteur on Torture (SRT)[6] to states involved in armed conflict may also explain the limited coverage of torture in these contexts by the SRT.[7] A screening of the mandate's country reports shows that where violations specific to women have been addressed, they did not relate to conflict or post-conflict situations.[8] However, in recognition of the need to address gender-specific forms of torture and other ill-treatment, the SRT dedicated the 2016 thematic report to this topic.

The report provides a valuable source for identifying women-specific violations (SRT 2016),[9] which are "often amplified during conflict." (SRT 2016)[10]

The *"protection pillar"* of the WPS agenda is reflected in a chapter on rape and other forms of sexual violence as a gender-specific form of torture and ill-treatment when carried out by, at the instigation of, or with the consent or acquiescence of public officials, or through lack of due diligence. The SRT reiterates that such acts "unequivocally amount to torture under international criminal law jurisprudence," and that torture can be committed by both states and non-state armed groups (SRT 2016).[11] Importantly, the SRT's report provides insights into the relationship between the WPS terminology of *"violence"* and UNCAT language (*"torture and ill-treatment"*).

The SRT clarifies that gender-specific forms of torture are those "committed against any person because of their sex and socially constructed gender roles." (SRT 2016) Noting a tendency to consider violations against women as *ill-treatment* even where they would more appropriately be identified as torture,[12] the SRT recalls that "if an act [of violence] is gender-specific or perpetrated against persons on the basis of their sex, gender identity (. . .) or non-adherence to social norms around gender and sexuality," the "purpose and intent elements of the definition of torture are always fulfilled." (SRT 2016)[13]

With regard to investigations into abuse, the SRT stresses the need for gender-sensitive practices of inquiry and emphasizes that "States" due diligence obligations to ensure redress remain intact when non-State actors perpetrate conflict-related sexual violence.[14] At the same time, the Rapporteur states that "Reparations must be premised on a full understanding of the gendered nature and consequences of the harm suffered and take existing gender inequalities into account."[15] In fact, victims must be empowered to help determine what forms of reparation are best suited to their situation.[16] Moreover, the importance of gender equality in judicial procedures is singled out alongside the need for equal weight afforded to the testimony of women and the prohibition of "discriminatory evidence."[17] The SRT also recalls refugees as a population exposed to torture and other ill-treatment in the context of armed conflict, noting that women and girls are "particularly vulnerable to sexual violence, exploitation and slavery along migration routes."[18]

Reflecting the *"prevention pillar,"* although in less detail, the SRT notes the failure of states to comply with their obligations where "laws, policies or practices perpetuate harmful gender stereotypes in a manner that enables or authorizes, explicitly or implicitly, prohibited acts to be performed with impunity," where "failure to intervene encourages and enhances the danger of privately inflicted harm" and where states fail to "exercise due diligence to protect against such violence."[19]

Practices reflected in the report include female genital mutilation, child and forced marriage, and honor-based violence, representing acknowledged types of GBV that constitute ill-treatment and torture.[20] While these forms of violence do not specifically occur during conflict or in post-conflict situations, due to the non-derogable nature of the prohibition of torture,[21] states continue to be obliged to exercise due diligence to prevent and protect from such acts. Moreover, the SRT notes that child and other forms of forced marriages "increase during conflict."[22] The *"participation pillar"* is not reflected in the SRT's reports, *"relief and recovery"* is not part of the mandate.

How Have Resolutions Setting Up Peacekeeping Operations Reflected the Framework against Torture and Ill-Treatment Specific to Women and Girls?

The restricted focus of the WPS framework is also reflected in resolutions establishing UN peacekeeping operations (PKR), which determine their mandate and priorities to re-establish peace and security.[23]

The PKR reflect an imbalance in favor of protection to the detriment of prevention and participation. Although formulated in general terms and with little detail, women are regularly highlighted as particular beneficiaries, with the deployment of "Women Protection Advisers" constituting the most common commitment to addressing issues for women and girls within peacekeeping forces. The aspect of investigations and prosecution of SGBV *during* conflict is the most common task specified for peacekeeping missions, while most resolutions remain silent on victims' assistance needs and ongoing and future exposure to gender-specific violence (Huber and Rytter 2017). For example, UN Security Council Resolution 2100 (2013) requested "that MINUSMA take fully into account the need to protect civilians (. . .), including, in particular women."[24] In the case of MINUSCA,[25] the "specific protection for women and children affected by armed conflict" featured as one of the priority tasks of the mission.[26]

The *"preventive pillar"* in PKR is usually limited to the provision of training for security forces, and coaching needs tend to be formulated in general terms (human rights training) rather than explicitly requiring the incorporation of gender-specific training. For instance, UN Security Council Resolution 2313 (2016) encompasses a provision on capacity-building and training of police and corrections personnel, but lacks mention of training on gender issues or the protection of women.[27]

With regard to the *"participation pillar,"* PKO at times call for "robust vetting, enhanced recruitment procedures and training"[28] or for professional, ethnically representative, and regionally balanced recruitment,[29] but they do not mention the objective of a gender balance within security forces. Despite efforts by UN agencies to this end, in 2014 women still only represented 3 percent of the military personnel and 10 percent of police personnel.[30]

Conclusion

Overall, the WPS paradigm and the UN human rights bodies with a mandate relating to torture have led relatively separate lives with a few noticeable exceptions. While recognizing the importance of ensuring coherence and avoiding duplication among UN human rights bodies, UNCAT could be attributed a greater role by the Security Council within the WPS framework. As Barrow argues, Resolution 1325 often appears to be considered as an independent framework, and stronger links need to be established with legal provisions of international law (Barrow 2010: 229, 234). Drawing upon UNCAT as a normative basis for future WPS resolutions would strengthen the focus on post-conflict security and justice sector reform, which is currently overshadowed by the focus on "coming to terms" with past violations. This would also help bolster the WPS agenda, which does not recognize the "continuum of violence" (Cockburn 2004) that characterizes the experience of women whose lives are not only marked by the "extraordinary violence of 'rape as a weapon of war,'" but everyday forms of violence that occur in all contexts (Kirby and Shepherd 2016: 380).

NOTES

1. The SPT was established by the Optional Protocol to the Convention against Torture (OPCAT, Articles 5–17) and started its work in February 2007. Its mandate is the prevention of torture and ill-treatment in any place where persons may be deprived of their liberty. The Subcommittee's main functions are to undertake visits to states parties, which may include visits to any place of detention, and an advisory role with regard to National Preventive Mechanisms, which OPCAT requires state parties to establish at the national level.

2. For the purposes of this article, the author screened the Subcommittee's annual reports (First Annual Report of the Subcommittee on Prevention of Torture and Other Cruel, Inhuman, or Degrading Treatment or Punishment [CAT/C/40/2], May 14, 2008; Second Annual Report of the Subcommittee on Prevention of Torture and Other Cruel, Inhuman, or Degrading Treatment or Punishment [CAT/C/42/2], April 7, 2009; Third Annual Report of the Subcommittee on Prevention of Torture and Other Cruel, Inhuman, or Degrading Treatment or Punishment [CAT/C/44/2], March 25, 2010; Fourth Annual Report of the Subcommittee on Prevention of Torture and Other Cruel, Inhuman, or Degrading Treatment or Punishment [CAT/C/46/2], February 3, 2011; Fifth annual Report of the Subcommittee on Prevention of Torture and Other Cruel, Inhuman, or Degrading Treatment or Punishment [CAT/C/48/3], March 19, 2012; Sixth Annual Report of the Subcommittee on Prevention of Torture and Other Cruel, Inhuman, or Degrading Treatment or Punishment [CAT/C/50/2], April 23, 2013; Seventh Annual Report of the Subcommittee on Prevention of Torture and Other Cruel, Inhuman, or Degrading Treatment or Punishment [CAT/C/52/2], March 20, 2014; Eighth Annual Report of the Subcommittee on Prevention of Torture and Other Cruel, Inhuman, or Degrading Treatment or Punishment [CAT/C/54/2], March 26, 2015; Ninth Annual Report of the Subcommittee on Prevention of Torture and Other Cruel, Inhuman, or Degrading Treatment or Punishment [CAT/C/57/4, March 22, 2016).

3. Eighth Annual Report of the Subcommittee on Prevention of Torture and Other Cruel, Inhuman, or Degrading Treatment or Punishment [CAT/C/54/2], March 26 2015, paras. 63 et sqq.

4. It notes that state agents "use more violence, including torture and ill-treatment" in countries where there is or has been conflict; however, it only explores general links to democracy, referring to a "heightened risk of suppression or political dissent by means of torture" in non-democratic states (Seventh Annual Report of the Subcommittee on Prevention of Torture and Other Cruel, Inhuman, or Degrading Treatment or Punishment [CAT/C/52/2], March 20 2014, chap. F, paras. 87, 88).

5. In fact, reviewing visits undertaken by the SPT to countries associated with conflict or post-conflict, the mission was either conducted prior to escalation of conflict (e.g., Mali in 2011, Ukraine in 2011), and/or the respective report remains confidential (e.g., Lebanon,

Turkey). SPT country visits have taken place, for example, to Mali (visit December 2011); Lebanon (report confidential); Nigeria (July 2014, report confidential); Ukraine (planned visit suspended May 2016; previous report on visit May 2011); Tunisia (April 2016, no report yet); Turkey (October 2015, report confidential); Philippines (May/June 2015, report confidential).

6. The Special Rapporteur on Torture and Other Cruel, Inhuman, or Degrading Treatment or Punishment was established with a mandate to work on all countries, irrespective of whether they have ratified the Convention against Torture and Other Cruel, Inhuman, or Degrading Treatment or Punishment. The mandate comprises the following main activities: urgent appeals to states with regard to individuals at risk of torture; communications on alleged individual cases of torture; fact-finding country visits; and annual reports to the Human Rights Council and the General Assembly.

7. For example, visit requests have been pending to Afghanistan (first made in 2005), Côte D'Ivoire (requested since 2005), Egypt (request first made in 1996), Iraq (2005), Israel (2002), Libyan Arab Jamahiriya (2005), Pakistan (2011), Russian Federation, with respect to the Republic of Chechnya (2000), Syrian Arab Republic (2005), Thailand (2011), and Yemen (2005).

8. For the purposes of drafting this article, the authors have conducted a search using the Universal Human Rights Index (http://uhri.ohchr.org/). Reports reviewed included, for example, "Report of the Special Rapporteur on Torture and Other Cruel, Inhuman, or Degrading Treatment or Punishment, Juan E. Méndez— Addendum, Mission to Ghana" (A/HRC/25/60/Add.1), March 5 2014: para. 103; "Report of the Special Rapporteur on Torture and Other Cruel, Inhuman, or Degrading Treatment or Punishment, Manfred Nowak, to the General Assembly—Addendum, Mission to Jordan" (A/HRC/4/33/Add.3), January 5, 2007: para. 70(4); "Report of the Special Rapporteur on Torture and Other Cruel, Inhuman, or Degrading Treatment or Punishment to the Human Rights Council— Addendum, Mission to Papua New Guinea" (A/HRC/16/52/Add.5), February 7, 2011: paras. 69, 84; "Report of the Special Rapporteur on Torture and Other cruel, Inhuman, or Degrading Treatment or Punishment, Manfred Nowak, to the Human Rights Council— Addendum, Mission to Jamaica" (A/HRC/16/52/Add.3), October 11, 2010: summary; paras. 31–33; "Report of the Special Rapporteur on Torture and Other Cruel, Inhuman, or Degrading Treatment or Punishment, Juan E. Méndez—Addendum, Mission to Morocco" (A/HRC/22/53/Add.2), April 30, 2013: para. 92; "Report of the Special Rapporteur on Torture and Other Cruel, Inhuman, or Degrading Treatment or Punishment, Manfred Nowak, to the Human Rights Council, Mission to the Republic of Moldova" (A/HRC/10/44/Add.3), February 12, 2009: paras. 49–55; "Report of the Special Rapporteur on Torture and Other Cruel, Inhuman, or Degrading Treatment or Punishment, Manfred Nowak, to the Human Rights Council, Mission to Togo" (A/HRC/7/3/Add.5), January 6, 2008: paras. 2, 53, 54, 71, 97, 104; "Report of the Special Rapporteur on Torture and Other Cruel, Inhuman, or Degrading Treatment or Punishment, Manfred Nowak—Addendum, Mission to Uruguay" (A/HRC/13/39/Add.2), December 21, 2009: para. 68–76, 84, 103, 105(s) et al.<AU: Please check the usage of et al here is appropriate.>

9. "Report of the Special Rapporteur on Torture and Other Cruel, Inhuman, and Degrading Treatment or Punishment, Human Rights Council" (A/HRC/31/57), January 5, 2016.

10. A/HRC/31/57, para. 7.

11. A/HRC/31/57, para. 51.

12. A/HRC/31/57, para. 8.

13. A/HRC/31/57, paras. 8, 9.

14. A/HRC/31/57, para. 53.
15. A/HRC/31/57, para. 66.
16. A/HRC/31/57, para. 66, referring to the Nairobi Declaration on Women and Girls' Right to a Remedy and Reparation.
17. A/HRC/31/57, para. 67.
18. A/HRC/31/57, para. 31; for considerations regarding victims of trafficking see paras. 40–41.
19. A/HRC/31/57, paras. 10, 55.
20. A/HRC/31/57, paras. 59–64.
21. Convention against Torture, Article 2(2); International Convention on Civil and Political Rights, Article 4(2). According to the Committee against Torture, the absolute and non-derogable character of the prohibition of torture has become accepted as a matter of customary international law (CAT /C/GC/2/CRP.1/Rev.4, Committee against Torture, General Comment no. 2, para. 1). The prohibition of torture is also enshrined in international humanitarian law—for example, the Geneva Conventions of 1949 and their Additional Protocols of June 8, 1977.
22. A/HRC/31/57, para. 64. The SRT also notes that, like rape, forced marriage is used as a tactic of war and to fulfill strategic objectives such as domination, intimidation, and degradation. It has been recognized as a crime against humanity by the Special Court for Sierra Leone (para. 64, with reference to Inter-American Court of Human Rights, *González et al.* [*"Cotton Field"*] *v. Mexico*, judgment of November 16, 2009).
23. For the purpose of this article, the most recent Security Council Resolutions extending the existing UN peacekeeping operations as well as a selection of older resolutions have been screened: S/RES/2285 (2016), Security Council Resolution 2285 (2016), April 29, 2016; S/RES/2127 (2013), Security Council Resolution 2127 (2013), December 5, 2013; S/RES/2301 (2016), Security Council Resolution 2301 (2016), July 26, 2016; S/RES/2100 (2013), Security Council Resolution 2100 (2013), April 25, 2013; S/RES/2295 (2016), Security Council Resolution 2295 (2016), June 29, 2016; S/RES/2313 (2016), Security Council Resolution 2313 (2016), October 13, 2016; S/RES/2211 (2015) Security Council Resolution 2211 (2015), March 26, 2015; S/RES/2296 (2016), Security Council Resolution 2296 (2016), June 29, 2016; S/RES/2257 (2015), Security Council Resolution 2257 (2015), December 22, 2015; S/RES/2234 (2015), Security Council Resolution 2234 (2015), July 29, 2015.
24. MINUSMA (United Nations Multidimensional Integrated Stabilization Mission in Mali), S/RES/2100 (2013), April 25, 2013, OP26. By comparison, S/RES/2100 (2013), April 25, 2013 (OP26) "*Encourages* MINUSTAH to continue assisting the Government of Haiti in providing adequate protection to the civilian population, with particular attention to (. . .) vulnerable groups, especially women" (S/RES/2313 2016, Security Council Resolution 2313 [2016], October 13, 2016, OP30). See also S/RES/2211 (2015) Security Council Resolution 2211 (2015), March 26, 2015, MONUSCO, DRC, OP 7(c).
25. MINUSCA (Mission multidimensionnelle intégrée des Nations Unies pour la stabilisation de la République centrafricaine).
26. S/RES/2301 (2016), Security Council Resolution 2301 (2016), July 26, 2016, OP33(a)(ii).
27. S/RES/2313 (2016), October 13, 2016, OP17 and OP18. By comparison, SCR 2100 (2013) "*Urges* Member States, regional and international organizations to provide coordinated assistance, expertise and training, including on human rights and international humanitarian law, especially concerning the protection of women and children" (S/RES/2100 [2013], April 25, 2013, OP23).
28. S/RES/2313 (2016), Security Council Resolution 2313 (2016), October 13, 2016, OP18.

29. S/RES/2301 (2016), Security Council Resolution 2301 (2016), July 26, 2016, OP9. See also OP25, 26, 27.

30. United Nations Peacekeeping, http://www.un.org/en/peacekeeping/issues/women/womeninpk.shtml.

References

Barrow, A. "UN Security Council Resolutions 1325 and 1820: Constructing Gender in Armed Conflict and International Humanitarian Law." *International Review of the Red Cross* 92, no. 77 (2010): 211–234.

Cockburn, C. "The Continuum of Violence: A Gender Perspective on War and Peace." In *Sites of Violence: Gender and Conflict Zones*, edited by Winona Giles and Jennifer Hyndmann. Berkeley: University of California Press, 2004.

Committee against Torture (CAT). "Concluding Observations on Algeria." CAT/C/DZA/CO/3, 2008a.

Committee against Torture (CAT). "Concluding Observations on Burundi." CAT/C/BDI/CO/1, 2007.

Committee against Torture (CAT). "Concluding Observations on Burundi." CAT/C/BDI/CO/2/Add.1, 2016.

Committee against Torture (CAT). "Concluding Observations on Chad." CAT/C/TCD/CO/1, 2009.

Committee against Torture (CAT). "Concluding Observations on Colombia." CAT/C/COL/CO/4, 2010.

Committee against Torture (CAT). "Concluding Observations on Congo." CAT/C/COG/CO/1, 2015a.

Committee against Torture (CAT). "Concluding Observations on Ethiopia" CAT/C/ETH/CO/1, 2011a.

Committee against Torture (CAT). "Concluding Observations on Indonesia." CAT/C/IND/CO/2, 2008b.

Committee against Torture (CAT). "Concluding Observations on Iraq." CAT/C/IRQ/CO/1, 2015b.

Committee against Torture (CAT). "Concluding Observations on Kenya." CAT/C/KEN/CO/2, 2013a.

Committee against Torture (CAT). "Concluding Observations on Peru." CAT/C/PER/CO/5-6, 2013b.

Committee against Torture (CAT). "Concluding Observations on Sri Lanka." CAT/C/LKA/CO/2/Add.1, 2005.

Committee against Torture (CAT). "Concluding Observations on Sri Lanka." CAT/C/LKA/CO/3-4, 2011b, .

Committee against Torture (CAT). "Concluding Observations on Togo." CAT/C/TGO/CO/2, 2012.

Committee against Torture (CAT). "General Comment no. 2 on Implementation of Article 2 by State Parties." CAT/C/GC/2, January 24 2008c.

Convention against Torture and Other Cruel, Inhuman, or Degrading Treatment or Punishment. "General Assembly Resolution 39/46." December 10, 1984.

Convention on the Elimination of All Forms of Discrimination against Women. "General Assembly Resolution 34/180." December 18, 1979.

Convention on the Rights of the Child. "General Assembly Resolution 44/25," November 20, 1989.

Gaer, F. "Rape as a Form of Torture: The Experience of the Committee against Torture," *CUNY Law Review* 15 (2012): 295–308.

George, N., and L. J. Shepherd. "Women, Peace, and Security: Exploring the Implementation and Integration of UNSCR 1325." *International Political Science Review* 37, no. 3 (2006): 297–306.

Huber, Andrea, and Therese Rytter. "Women, Gender-Specific Abuse, and Peacekeeping Operations." Penal Reform International, April 18, 2017, https://www.penalreform.org/blog/women-gender-specific-abuse-and-peacekeeping-operations-2/.

Kirby, P., and L. Shepherd. "The Futures Past of the Women, Peace, and Security Agenda." *International Affairs* 92, no. 2 (2016): 373–392.

Nowak, M., and E. McArthur. *The United Nations Convention against Torture: A Commentary.* Oxford Commentaries on International Law. New York: Oxford University Press, 2008.

Optional Protocol to the Convention against Torture and other Cruel, Inhuman, or Degrading Treatment or Punishment. "General Assembly Resolution 57/199." December 18, 2002.

Rees, M., and C. Chinkin. "Exposing the Gendered Myth of Post Conflict Transitions: The Transformative Power of Economic, Social, and Cultural Rights." *Journal of International Law and Politics* 48 (2016): 1211–1226.

Report of the Special Rapporteur. "SR On Torture and Other Cruel, Inhuman, and Degrading Treatment or Punishment." Human Rights Council, A/HRC/31/57, January 5, 2016.

Skjelsbæk, I. "Responsibility to Protect or Prevent? Victims and Perpetrators of Sexual Violence Crimes in Armed Conflicts." *Global Responsibility to Protect* 4 (2012): 154–171.

UN Department of Peacekeeping Operations, Department of Field Support. "Gender Forward Looking Strategy 2014-2018" 2014

UN Security Council, "Resolution 2100 (2013) Adopted by the Security Council at its 6952nd meeting, on 25 April 2013", S/RES/2100 (2013), April 25, 2013

UN Security Council, "Resolution 2313 (2016) Adopted by the Security Council at its 7790th meeting, on 13 October 2016", S/RES/2313 (2016), October 13, 2016

CHAPTER 57

··

WPS AND CLIMATE CHANGE

··

ANNICA KRONSELL

THIS chapter explores the problem of climate change as a gendered problem and connects it to the UN Women, Peace, and Security (WPS) agenda. It shows that in both the policy and scholarly context, the debate on climate and gender has been dominated by framing the problem as about women's vulnerability to climate events and how women's livelihoods are adversely effected by climate change. The violence of climate change comes through immediate weather events, such as floods and storms, but also as slow violence in everyday life, often exacerbated by other pressures and conflicts. In the feminist literature, the vulnerability of women is explained in terms of structural violence and a combined violence to women and nature. Thus, in attempts to achieve climate peace, a complexity of security needs should be considered. It is argued that the human security focus, already an important element of the UN and the WPS agenda, is a fruitful way to connect the aspirations for peace with climate concerns.

THE INTERNATIONAL AGENDA AND GENDERED CLIMATE CHANGE

Climate change issues have only recently come to the feminist peace agenda. It is due to a number of factors. First, the climate change agenda has mainly been assigned to natural science expertise, such as meteorologists and climatologists. When climate issues came on the global agenda they were scientized and also depoliticized, lacking social perspectives (Kronsell 2017). Second, climate change has become an element of attention on the women's and feminist agenda only fairly recently. While the UN Women's Conference, convened in Beijing in 1995, adopted a section on women and the environment in its platform for action, the importance of climate change issues was not noted there and slow to emerge. Third, the involvement of women and women's groups in climate change negotiations and decision-making only began in the mid-2000s (Kronsell 2015). Finally, climate change is not yet prominent on the WPS agenda nor a salient feature in the scholarly literature on WPS. This chapter outlines the main arguments for making this connection and begins by presenting how the literature considers the connection between gender and climate change.

Women as Vulnerable Victims of Climate Change

The early scholarship on gender and climate change demonstrated sex differences in the impacts of climate change by highlighting the vulnerability of women particularly in the South, and emphasizing women's specific role in mitigating climate change. The renowned Intergovernmental Panel on Climate Change (IPCC) noted how rural women in developing countries are among the groups most vulnerable to climate change. A major emphasis of earlier studies on gender and climate change (Dankelman 2010; Terry 2009) was in this vein, focusing on women as vulnerable victims in the South, often studying this in the local context (cf. Resurrección 2013). In much of the literature, whether it is studies of climate mitigation or adaptation, women in the Global South are discussed as vulnerable victims (Aquilar 2013; Bendlin 2014: 684). Indeed, the risks of climate change vary for women and men; women are more likely to become victims of climate change because they do not have the same access to resources, have different living conditions, and have more restricted capabilities than men as a group do (Alston 2013a, 2013b; Singh et al. 2010). This is due to their different social, political, and economic conditions. While women in the rural South are likely to be more vulnerable to climate change, climate change is gendered also in other parts of the world. There are considerable differences within both the North and the South (Johnsson-Latham 2007) —for example, homeless people or poor retired women in the North hardly produce any climate gases at all, while rich male elites in the South may emit more carbon than the average citizen in the North (EIGE 2012: 21).

Vulnerability Framing Depoliticizes Gender Power

Djoudi et al., who analyzed research on climate change adaptation, found a strong tendency to "depict a feminization of vulnerability and reinforce a victimization discourse within climate change studies" (Djoudi et al. 2016: S248). The tendency to equate gender with women and thereby depoliticize gender power relations is found across this literature (Kronsell 2015, 2017). With this focus, the literature tends to ignore structural inequalities and power relations. Chris Cuomo (2011: 695) explains that if structural inequalities are framed as differential vulnerability or susceptibility to harm, the result is that attention is drawn to the "supposed weaknesses or limitations of those who are in harm's way, but says little about whether injustices or other harms have put them in such precarious positions." Concepts like vulnerability to socioecological crises are political phenomena that can and should not be thought of as outside relations of power (Hackfort and Burchardt 2016: 2).

Apart from being a concern for critical gender scholars, this can also have practical consequences for attempts to deal with climate problems. Efforts toward climate mitigation and adaptation may be misdirected if power relations remain invisible and "the associated structures of inequalities and vulnerabilities with respect to climate change" are not noted, argue Hackfort and Burchardt (2016: 9). They underscore that a gendered perspective on climate change recognizes that the possibility and capability to adapt to climate change is "shaped by power relations determining access to resources" and information in turn, this determines the availability of options and choices, factors that relate to societal positions of groups (Djoudi et al. 2016: S248).

This critique notwithstanding, vulnerability can be a relevant concept, the climate problem certainly accents human as well as species vulnerability, and the concept is thus, frequently used in climate change research, but we also see that various framings "are not simply about different interpretations of the word vulnerability. They are about fundamentally different" understandings of the climate change problem as well as representing different worldviews and scientific understandings that influence what knowledge is produced, which policies are adopted and what actors are considered relevant (O'Brien et al. 2007: 76–78). One such framing is the human-security understanding of vulnerability which also has resonance with the peace agenda. It has not yet been adopted in the climate change debate that involves national governments and international institutions. However, it is this framing that best lends itself to grasp the climate change problem in relation to the complexities of ecosystems and in broader communities, according to Karen O'Brien and her colleagues (2007: 85). We return to human security below.

CLIMATE CHANGE AS A SECURITY CONCERN

In mainstream security theories the depiction of an acute threat is constitutive of what can become a security issue, and while vulnerability is recognized as a situation that may lead to instability and conflict (Buzan et al. 1998), vulnerability lacks the acuteness of a proper security issue (Liotta 2005; Galliard 2010) and also because no simple, direct link between climate change, conflict, and war has been established (cf. Carleton et al. 2016; Gleditsch and Nordås 2014; Schleussner et al. 2016). Gleick (2014), however, argues that the war in Syria can be connected to climate change vulnerability, in the context of a set of complex interrelated factors, including the effects of climate change on available water resources that contributed to the escalation of conflict into war. Feminist security scholars (i.e., Wibben 2011) are particularly critical to a framing of security that only considers acute threats and that is limited to when a proper "threat" or "enemy" can be defined (Jansson and Eduards 2016). Climate change has relevance for security often in an indirect way, in the way that weather events related to climate change affect the conditions for agriculture and livelihoods in general. Often there are more drastic climate change implications when floods, storms, droughts and fires displace people, leading also to climate related migration. Migration too is gendered, in who stays behind and who can leave. Mainstream security studies are less able to consider vulnerabilities like this nor how complexities like those mentioned earlier are also security concerns, and, furthermore, they lack the tools to problematize gendered structures as a threat. Hence, a feminist security perspectives seems more appropriate in considering the relation between violence, peace, and climate change.

WOMEN AS CLIMATE CHANGE AGENTS

Somewhat paradoxically, at the same time as women are cast as vulnerable to climate change they are also frequently depicted as virtuous heroines (cf. Arora-Jonsson 2011: 745). This resonates with the WPS agenda. UN Security Council Resolution (UNSCR) 1325 both recognizes the vulnerability of women in conflict and war—for example, to sexual violence and abuse—and, at the same time, argues that they should be included in peacekeeping efforts and be expected to provide alternative views and solutions. According to Bernadette Resurrección (2013), the framing of women—as vulnerable and virtuous heroines—reflects a general discourse on gender found in global governance (e.g., Leach 2007), which appears to have been carried over to the contemporary climate change agenda (Resurrección 2013: 37; Holvoet and Inberg 2014).

However, the celebration of women's agency as "heroic" and "virtuous" is also an important yet, controversial element in feminist thought. Standpoint theory posits that women's positions in society shape ways of knowing and provide other experiences than those lived by dominant male elites (Hartsock 1985; Harding 1991). Ecofeminists have argued that based on caring experiences and skills, women can contribute with alternatives by "healing the wounds" of the earth (Plant 1989) through "earthcare" (Merchant 1996). In relation to climate change specifically, empirical studies that focus on women as a group also show that women collectively contribute less carbon emissions than men as a group do. In this sense, women's behavior as a group could be considered more climate-friendly than men's behavior as a group. The sex difference in terms of climate impact is most apparent in the South but also evident in the North (Bendlin 2014: 684–687; OECD 2008; Räty and Carlsson-Kanyama 2010; Schultz and Stiess 2009). In various surveys, women in the European Union and the United States are more concerned about climate issues and more inclined to take climate action (European Commission 2009; McCright 2010), and, hence, it has been shown that there are gender differences in terms of attitudes to climate change issues (Goldsmith et al. 2013; McCright and Dunlap 2011). While these sex differences in climate behavior and attitudes may be relevant as a basis for climate agency and for generating alternatives (MacGregor 2014), it does not address the gender and climate problem in terms of power. If virtuous women are the ones who are called on to solve the problem, it effectively diverts attention from power.

POWER AND GENDERED CLIMATE CHANGE

When both the problem and the solution for gender issues are confined to women, it leaves little room to conceptualize gender as being about power relations. A way to bring power into the analysis of the climate agenda and connect it with gendered peace is through a structural perspective. To look at the connection between climate change, gender, and peace I begin with the Swedish international peace activist Elin Wägner who in 1941 wrote Väckarklockan (The Alarm Clock; Wägner 1941). Elin Wägner is interesting because she was extremely foresighted (Forsås-Scott 1999: 15) when she anticipated that humans' relation to the earth, demonstrated through the political economic system, was putting humankind in much danger. In her earlier work she connected the violence of war to the violence of patriarchy in terms of a quest for domination, but in Väckarklockan, she worried particularly about the exploitation of the earth. She feared it would continue also in peacetime if patriarchy was not dismantled—with patriarchy intact there could be no peace. She spoke much about the land, the soil, but also the domination by men over all species. So, although mainly known as a suffragette and peace activist, Wägner early noted the importance of thinking about the relationship between patriarchy, war, conflicts, and the exploitation of nature to achieve peace. Her arguments were often articulated through the concept of earth mother, referring to the violence done to the land through humans striving for progress, modernization, and industrialization, as well as the damage that war, weapons, and armed struggles would inflict on the land (Isaksson and Linder 2003). Wägner was concerned with the land, and did not foresee the climate problems that science later revealed; climate change, however, can fruitfully be perceived in terms of her ideas—for example, as caused by violence done to the land, to the earth, through violent and devastating mining practices, and the extraction of coal and oil, which are also damaging processes to nature. Climate change is a much later symptom of this violence to nature, when coal and oil burned as energy, with carbon (CO_2) emissions that accumulate in the atmosphere and lead to temperature increase and climate change.

Elin Wägner poignantly points to the various violences of patriarchy and suggests that peace can only be reached by counteracting the violence conducted by patriarchy to humans, nations, as well as to nature together in one effort. In a book "Peace with Earth" [my translation of Swedish Fred med Jorden] which she authored together with Elisabeth Tamm in 1940, she wrote that the world's problems require nothing less than a re-evaluation of men and women's relation to the earth and to life. Her peace activism was thus not only devoted to ending wars and military struggle, but she propagated for a radically changed world order, the end of weapons production and sales, a changed political-economic system that did not focus on material production and ruthless exploitation, but, for example, with a caring type of biological agriculture (Forsås-Scott 1999: 24f). Thus, Wägner connects women, peace, and environmental issues with a critique of a destructive patriarchal politico-economic structure. Wägner and Tamm (1985: 15) wrote that there can be no separate solution to concerns for peace, land use, health, population, or education. All concerns have to be included in a solution that includes a re-assessment of humans' relation to the earth and to livelihoods.

As Forsås-Scott (1999: 55) argues, Wägner's perspective is an example of early ecofeminism in that it points to how the oppression of women is similar to the oppression of nature in western civilization. A connection between the two also developed for Carolyn Merchant (1980), Val Plumwood (1993), and numerous other ecofeminists; however, while peace to them is a given requirement for a sustainable society (Warren and Duane 1996), peace is not further theorized. Climate change is an issue which pushes this to the forefront as it is about survival and an existential concern. Scientists argue that we are living in the Anthropocene (Steffen et al. 2007), a new geological era where the effects of the lives of humans have geological consequences—that is, consequences for entire earth systems. It is climate change that is making it happen. Climate change is the result of the burning of fossil fuels, industrialization, globalization, excessive production, and extreme consumption, but also of greed and the belief in constant growth, the result of advanced capitalism.

Climate change is gendered, due to gendered economic structures and gendered livelihoods. It is well established that increased temperatures are already leading to droughts, forest fires, floods, rising sea levels, extreme heat, storms, and hurricanes that are affecting human livelihoods and lives, particularly women's lives. In the Global South, women are often responsible for subsistence farming, for collecting water for the household, which becomes more difficult when the climate becomes hotter. Due to cultural norms, women might not learn how to swim, not be allowed to leave the house, and more likely be injured or killed by hurricanes and floods. In cities and in more affluent societies there is evidence of such structural inequalities: older and poor women are often severely affected by heat; they cannot afford fans or air conditioning and get health problems, while at the same time they have made the lowest carbon footprint of everyone in that society. Storms, fires, and floods can drastically impact human security because they are immediate; climate change is also evident in slower acts of violence leading to insecurities that are felt in the individual's everyday life.

That the sea level rises is a serious problem; entire countries are threatened—low-island countries most immediately—but sea levels advance fairly slowly. In her article on women, peace, and security in the Pacific Islands, Nicole George connects the ideas on violence with the WPS agenda. George suggests that WPS's perspective on violence as it has been applied and translated in the regional context focuses "on the links between gendered insecurity and 'hot' conflict" and thereby tends to overlook "questions of attenuated and structural violence" (George 2014: 324). According to her, to achieve peace, it makes more sense in the context of women's security struggles in the Pacific Islands to think of violence not only as "hot" and immediate but also as "slow." Here George relies on Rob Nixon's (2011) idea of "slow violence" to identify what Pacific Island women consider as security threats that are slowly compounding impacts of environmental degradation—rising sea levels and climate change—with other security threats such as militarism and colonialism (George 2014: 320).

A similar argument, that too much attention is paid to immediate and violent security threats, was made by Kathleen De Onis (2012) who suggested that women's bodies are at the nexus of climate and reproductive justice but often the focus is on what happens during disasters and single events. It is often argued that "women are more vulnerable to rape and other sexual violence during natural crises, particularly disasters that cause mass displacement, such as those caused by climate change" (Rojas-Cheatham et al. 2009) but this may limit the understanding of how climate issues are gendered to that which happens during disasters and single events, thus, excluding the effects of climate change that lead to changes in biodiversity, food production, and impact the livelihood and health of people in their everyday life (de Onis 2012: 316).

The structural power perspective applied earlier suggests that there is a complexity in the power relations associated with climate change, in respect to how different power structures—patriarchy, capitalism, militarism, and (post)colonialism—are all implicated in climate change, and in relation to its effects, leading to injustices and inequalities regarding the possibilities to respond and adapt. In terms of the violence of climate change, we have noted forms of structural violence but also that climate changes can have violent immediate effects as well as the slower violence that impacts everyday lives over a longer period of time. There appears to be a need for a broader security perspective in the WPS agenda to be able to include climate security as well.

Positive Peace and Climate Peace

Climate change issues are related to questions around structural forms of power and violence. It regards who has power over the production and consumption patterns and over the climate agenda. The call to build resilience in society to deal with climate change resembles the need to build a peace in line with what peace researchers, like Johan Galtung (1969, 1990) have associated with positive peace. While negative peace is achieved when there is an absence of overt violence and conflict, in positive peace, there is an absence of structural violence. Climate change can be perceived as the result of structural violence. The responsibility as well as the consequences of climate change are deeply unjust and intersectional factors are relevant—north-south, class, ethnicity, as well as gender. The most privileged emit most greenhouse gases today and historically have a huge carbon footprint compared to the less privileged whether they live in the global south or in the north. A climate peace has to deal with structural violence, through the promotion of equality and social justice.

As Nobel Peace laureate Wangari Maathai writes "peace cannot exist without equitable development, just as development requires sustainable management of the environment in a democratic and peaceful space" (Maathai 2008). In current debates, the connection to peace is often articulated as the need to build resilience in society against the effects of climate change. Often, such resilience needs to be built closer to people's livelihoods where climate change puts increased pressure on "already fragile, undervalued and precarious gendered roles and responsibilities at community level" (UNEP 2016: 13). Wangari Maathai envisioned that women due to their livelihoods have a special place in the work with peace: "women are the primary caretakers, holding significant responsibility for tilling the land and feeding their families. As a result, they are often the first to become aware of environmental damage as resources become scarce and incapable of sustaining their families" (Maathai 2005). As Maathai suggests, women in the global south are on the average more vulnerable to environmental effects, also because they are not likely to have the resources to adjust to climate change, nor do they live in states or regions with such capacities, while the privileged do. The privileged are likely to be less effected by climate changes, as they have the means to adapt—for example, through adaptive flood management in city planning or climate regulation in buildings. Hence, when the WPS agenda calls for the inclusion of women in peace negotiation processes, this could be extended toward efforts at building climate peace, and women may have a particular expertise highly useful as inputs to build climate resilient communities.

Climate Peace through a Human Security Focus

This final section elaborates on how a human security focus can be the way forward in efforts to include climate concerns on the WPS agenda. Human security is already part of the WPS agenda and "entails the protection of people from critical and pervasive threats and situations and the empowerment of people to enhance their potential" (Nasu 2012: 97).

Human security is also a core concept in the UN Security Council and incorporated in key policy documents and debates (Nasu 2012: 98, 108), and the UNSCR 1325 is a resolution that takes a human security perspective when it recognizes the under-valued and under-utilized contributions women can make to peace (Atienza 2015). While the Security Council has discussed the climate issue on several occasions, and, for example, articulated it as "the threat of sea-level rise to small island States and food security" (Nasu 2012: 119), it has not been in relation to gender issues. However, it may be ripe for such discussion, and a human security perspective can take into account how structural and slow violence is perceived in a specific context.

This was illustrated in the literature reviewed for this chapter, and I turn to an example from Maria Atienza (2015) who studied how people in risky environments define human security. Human security allowed her to get to people's sense of security and their threats and risks because it takes its starting point in the individual; the threat itself—what it is or how it is named: war or climate, land degradation—is secondary. Atienza suggests that human security is something which can be understood by listening to people who are dealing with everyday risks. "Recognition and identification of threats is fundamental to human security" (Atienza 2015: 451). However, Atienza points to a weakness in current analysis of human security—in line with George's (2014) criticism referred to earlier—its tendency to differentiate between extraordinary risks and everyday or daily risks. In her empirical study of five municipalities in the Philippines, Atienza noted that from the human bottom-up perspective, risks are not necessarily differentiated as peoples' perceptions of security cover "the range of economic, food, health, environment, political, personal and community security" (Atienza 2015: 462). Different threats—environmental, climate hazards, poverty, and ethnic conflicts—are often entangled (Atienza 2015; see also Davies et al. 2016: 468). Taking a starting point in human security can cover a wider range of security threats, those that are relevant from the perspective of the individual, which in turn can lead to a more inclusive way to interpret security. The possibility for peace relates to security and the need to address security concerns in terms of interconnectedness and multidimensionality. To place climate peace on the WPS agenda suggests that a starting point in human security can help in taking seriously how individuals are possibly effected differently by climate events, risks, and threat, how those effects are gendered, and how they may be entangled and overlap with other threats and risks.

This chapter argued that the violence of climate change is felt through immediate weather events as well as through slow violence in everyday life. Livelihoods are gendered and so are the effects of climate change. This has generally been noted as the vulnerability of women to climate change, however, little interest has been devoted to try to understand climate change as slow violence. Slow violence is the result of the power relations associated with climate change. Ecofeminists have called attention to the interactions of power structures— patriarchy, capitalism, militarism, and the exploitation of nature—that in combination lead to climate change and to conflicts. The WPS agenda should consider climate change as a security issue in terms of both immediate and slow effects on women's lives. There is a need to recognize the importance of power relations in order to build resilience in societies to deal with climate change. To approach climate change this way can be a venue toward achieving a positive peace. The WPS agenda is grounded in human security and calls for the inclusion of women in peace negotiation processes, this should be extended toward efforts at dealing with the effects of climate change. The human security perspective is helpful in understanding the complexity of climate power relations because it takes the perspective of everyday life and gives value to human experience. Women's different experiences and knowledge are instrumental in building climate resilient communities and achieving climate peace.

REFERENCES

Alston, M. "Introducing Gender and Climate Change: Research, Policy, and Action." In *Research, Action, and Policy: Addressing the Gendered Impacts of Climate Change*, edited by M. Alston and K. Whittenbury, 3–14. Dordrecht, the Netherlands: Springer, 2013a.

Alston, M. "Gender Mainstreaming and Climate Change." *Women's Studies International Forum* 47, no. B (2013b): 287–294.

Aquilar, L. "A Path to Implementation: Gender-Responsive Climate Change Strategies. In *Research, Action, and Policy: Addressing the Gendered Impacts of Climate Change*, edited by M. Alston and K. Whittenbury, 149–157. Dordrecht, the Netherlands: Springer, 2013.

Arora-Jonsson, S. "Virtue and Vulnerability: Discourses on Women, Gender, and Climate Change." *Global Environmental Change* 21 (2011): 744–751.

Atienza, M. "People's Views about Human Security in Five Philippine Municipalities." *Disaster Prevention and Management* 24, no. 4 (2015): 448–467.

Bendlin, L. "Women' s Human Rights in a Changing Climate: Highlighting the Distributive Effects of Climate Policies. *Cambridge Review of International Affairs* 27, no. 4 (2014): 680–698.

Buzan, B., O. Wæver, and J. de Wilde. *Security. A New Framework for Analysis*. Boulder, CO: Lynne Rienner, 1998.

Carleton, T., S. M. Hsiang, and M. Burke. "Conflict in a Changing Climate." *The European Physical Journal Special Topics* 225, no. 3 (2016): 489–511.

Cuomo, C. "Climate Change, Vulnerability, and Responsibility." *Hypatia* 26, no. 4 (2011): 690–714.

Dankelman, I., ed. *Gender and Climate Change: An Introduction*. London and Washington DC: Earthscan, 2010.

Davies, S. E., J. True, and M. Tanyag. "How Women's Silence Secures the Peace: Analysing Sexual and Gender-Based Violence in a Low-Intensity Conflict." *Gender & Development* 24, no. 3 (2016): 459–473.

de Onís, K. M. "Looking Both Ways: Metaphor and the Rhetorical Alignment of Intersectional Climate Justice and Reproductive Justice Concerns." *Environmental Communication* 6, no. 3 (2012): 308–327.

Djoudi, H., B. Locatelli, C. Vaast, K. Asher, M. Brockhaus, and B. Basnett Sijapati. "Beyond Dichotomies: Gender and Intersecting Inequalities in Climate Change Studies." *Ambio* 45, Suppl. 3 (2016): S248–S262.

EIGE. *Review of the Implementation in the EU of Area K of the Beijing Platform for Action: Women and Environment—Gender Equality and Climate Change*. European Institute of Gender Equality. Luxembourg: Publications Office of the EU, 2012.

European Commission. *European Attitude towards Climate Change*. Brussels: EU Commission, 2009.

Forsås-Scott, H. *Elin Wägner Vad tänker du mänsklighet? Texter om feminism, fred och miljö i urval*. Stockholm: Nordsteds Förlag, 1999.

Gaillard, J-C. "Vulnerability, Capacity, and Resilience: Perspectives for Climate and Development Policy." *Journal of International Development* 22 (2010): 218–232.

Galtung, J. "Violence, Peace, and Peace Research." *Journal of Peace Research* 6 no. 3 (1969): 167–191.

Galtung, J. "Cultural Violence." *Journal of Peace Research* 27, no. 3 (1990): 291–305.

Gleditsch, P. N., and R. Nordås. "Conflicting Messages? The IPCC on Conflict and Human Security." *Political Geography* 43, Special Issue (2014): 82–90.

Gleick, P. H. "Water, Drought, Climate Change, and Conflict in Syria. *Weather, Climate, and Society* 6, no. 3 (2014): 331–340.

George, N. "Promoting Women, Peace, and Security in the Pacific Islands: Hot Conflict/Slow Violence." *Australian Journal of International Affairs* 68, no. 3 (2014): 314–332.

Goldsmith, R. E., I. Feygina, and J. Jost. "The Gender Gap in Environmental Attitudes: A System Justification Perspective." In *Research, Action, and Policy: Addressing the Gendered Impacts of Climate Change,* edited by M. Alston and K. Whittenbury, 159–171. Dordrecht, the Netherlands: Springer, 2013.

Hackfort, S., and H-J. Burchardt. "Analyzing Socio-Ecological Transformations—A Relational Approach to Gender and Climate Adaptation" *Critical Policy Studies,* November 22, 2016, http://dx.doi.org/10.1080/19460171.2016.1191363.

Harding, S. *Whose Science? Whose Knowledge? Thinking from Women's Lives.* Buckingham, UK: Open University Press, 1991.

Hartsock, N. *Money, Sex, and Power: Toward a Feminist Historical Materialism.* Boston: Northeastern University Press, 1985.

Holvoet, N., and L. Inberg. "Gender Sensitivity of Sub-Saharan Africa National Adaptation Programmes of Action: Findings from a Desk Review of 31 Countries." *Climate and Development* 6, no. 3 (2014): 266–276.

Isaksson, U., and E. H. Linder. *Elin Wägner- en biografi.* Stockholm: Albert Bonniers Förlag, 2003.

Jansson, M., and M. Eduards. "The Politics of Gender in the UN Security Council Resolutions on Women, Peace, and Security." *International Feminist Journal of Politics* 18, no. 4 (2016): 590–604.

Johnsson-Latham, G. "A Study on Gender Equality as a Prerequisite for Sustainable Development: What We Know About the Extent to Which Women Globally Live in a More Sustainable Way Than Men, Leave a Smaller Ecological Footprint, and Cause Less Climate Change." Stockholm: Ministry of the Environment, 2007.

Kronsell, A. "The Contribution of Feminist Perspectives to Climate Governance." In *Understanding Climate Change through Gender Relations,* edited by S. Buckingham and V. Le Masson. London: Routledge, 2017.

Kronsell, A. "Feminism." In *Research Handbook on Climate Governance,* edited by K. Bäckstrand and E. Lövbrand, 73–83. Cheltenham, UK, and Northampton, MA: Edward Elgar, 2015.

Leach, M. "Earth Mother Myths and Other Ecofeminist Fables: How a Strategic Notion Rose and Fell. *Development and Change* 38, no. 1 (2007): 67–85.

Liotta, P. H. "Through the Looking Glass: Creeping Vulnerabilities and the Reordering of Security." *Security Dialogue* 36, no. 1 (2005): 49–70.

Maathai, W. "An Unbreakable Link: Peace, Environment, and Democracy. *Harvard International Review* 29, no. 4 (2008): 24.

Maathai, W. "Nobel Peace Prize Speech: Nobel Lecture, Oslo, 10 December 2004." *Meridians: Feminism, Race, Transnationalism* 6, no. 1 (2005): 195–201.

MacGregor, S. "Only Resist: Feminist Ecological Citizenship and the Post-Politics of Climate Change." *Hypatia* 29, no. 3 (2014): 617–633.

McCright, A. "The Effects of Gender on Climate Change Knowledge and Concern in the American Public." *Population and Environment* 32 (2010): 66–87.

McCright, A., and R. Dunlap. "Cool Dudes: The Denial of Climate Change among Conservative White Males in the United States." *Global Environmental Change* 21 (2011): 1163–1172.

Merchant, C. *The Death of Nature. Women, Ecology, and the Scientific Revolution.* San Francisco: Harper, 1980.

Merchant, C. *Earthcare: Women and the Environment.* New York: Routledge, 1996.

Nasu, H. "The Place of Human Security in Collective Security." *Journal of Conflict & Security Law* 18, no. 1 (2012): 95–129.

Nixon, R. *Slow Violence and the Environmentalism of the Poor.* Cambridge, MA: Harvard University Press, 2011.

O'Brien, K., S. Eriksen, L. Nygaard, and A. Schjolden. "Why Different Interpretations of Vulnerability Matter in Climate Change Discourses." *Climate Policy* 7, no. 1 (2007): 73–88.

OECD. *Household Behavior and the Environment, Reviewing the Evidence.* Paris: Organisation for Economic Co-operation and Development, 2008.

Plant, J., ed. *Healing the Wounds: The Promise of Ecofeminism,* Santa Cruz, CA: New Society, 1989.

Plumwood, V. *Feminism and the Mastery of Nature.* London and New York: Routledge, 1993.

Resurrección, B. "Persistent Women and Environment Linkages in Climate Change and Sustainable Development Agendas." *Women's Studies International Forum* 40 (2013): 33–43.

Rojas-Cheatham, A., D. G. Paredes, S. Griffin, A. Shah, and E. Shen. *Looking Both Ways: Women's Lives at the Crossroads of Reproductive Justice and Climate Justice.* January 2009, https://vawnet.org/material/looking-both-ways-womens-lives-crossroads-reproductive-justice-and-climate-justice.

Räty, R., and A. Carlsson-Kanyama. "Energy Consumption by Gender in Some European Countries." *Energy Policy* 38, no. 1 (2010): 646–649.

Schleussner, C-F., J. Donges, R. V. Donner, and H. J. Schelinhuber. "Armed-Conflict Risks Enhanced by Climate-Related Disasters in Ethnically Fractionalized Countries." *PNAS* 113, no. 33 (2016): 9216–9221

Schultz, I., and I. Stiess. *Gender Aspects of Sustainable Consumption Strategies and Instruments.* Frankfurt: Institute for Social-Ecological Research, 2009.

Steffen, W., P. Crutzen, and J. R. McNeill. "The Anthropocene: Are Humans Now Overwhelming the Great Forces of Nature?" *AMBIO* 36, no. 8 (2007): 614–621.

Singh, A., J. Svensson, and A. Kalyanpur. "The State of Sex-Disaggregated Data for Assessing the Impact of Climate Change." *Procedia Environmental Sciences* 1 (2010): 395–404.

Terry, G., ed. *Climate Change and Gender Justice.* London: Oxfam, 2009.

UNEP. *Global Gender and Environment Outlook.* Nairobi, Kenya: United Nations Environment Programme, 2016.

Warren, K. J., and L. C. Duane., eds. *Bringing Peace Home: Feminism, Violence, and Nature.* Bloomington and Indianapolis: Indiana University Press, 1996.

Wibben, A. *Feminist Security Studies: A Narrative Approach.* London: Routledge, 2011.

Wägner, E. *Väckarklockan.* Stockholm: Bonnier, 1941/2007.

Wägner, E., and E. Tamm. Fred med jorden. Knivsta, Sweden: Arkturus, 1985.

PART VI

ONGOING
AND FUTURE
CHALLENGES

CHAPTER 58

GLOBAL STUDY
Looking Forward

RADHIKA COOMARASWAMY AND EMILY KENNEY

On the fifteenth anniversary of the passage of UN Security Council Resolution 1325 (UN 2000) in October 2015, the Security Council held a high-level review on the implementation of the resolution. In anticipation of the high-level review, in Resolution 2122 (UN 2013), the Council had requested the Secretary-General to commission a global study to highlight good practice examples, implementation gaps, and challenges, as well as emerging trends and priorities for action. The resulting report, "Preventing Conflict, Transforming Justice, and Securing the Peace: A Global Study on the Implementation of United Nations Security Council Resolution 1325" (UN Women 2015) (hereinafter, the *Global Study*) was presented to the Council during the high-level review, sharing key recommendations for the future of the Women, Peace, and Security (WPS) agenda.

The 400-page *Global Study* was shaped by broad consultations with states, regional organizations, and civil society, as well as by research commissioned to explore understudied aspects of the WPS agenda, and a survey of women's civil society organizations working on peace and security around the world. A high-level advisory group provided strategic guidance on the content of the report, and was comprised of seventeen well-known leaders on WPS, including former diplomats, civil society champions, and human rights experts. The report includes ten guiding principles for the future of the WPS agenda, alongside dozens of technical recommendations for a range of actors to accelerate implementation of the agenda.

Today, in global policymaking forums, interest in the WPS agenda has never been greater. Attendance at the 2015 high-level review on Resolution 1325 was unprecedented: with 111 registered speakers, it was the best-attended open debate in the history of the Security Council (Ní Aoláin 2016: 275). At the high-level review, the Security Council adopted its eighth resolution on WPS, Resolution 2242 (UN 2015d), which had seventy-two member state co-sponsors. The UN Secretary-General's annual report on Women and Peace and Security summarized the key findings of the *Global Study* and endorsed many of its recommendations, committing to action in five key areas: (1) bringing women's participation and leadership to the core of peace and security efforts; (2) protecting the human rights of women and girls during and after conflict; (3) ensuring gender-responsive planning and accountability for results; (4) strengthening gender architecture and technical expertise;

and (5) financing the women, peace, and security agenda (UN 2015c: paras. 151–173). The Secretary-General also committed to "personally task the senior leadership of the United Nations to make a priority of implementing recommendations related to women and peace and security across all three peace and security reviews relevant to the United Nations system" (UN 2015c: para. 152).

Since the 2015 high-level review, the WPS agenda has continued to gain traction within the UN and among its member states, and women's participation now plays a central role in the emerging discourse on "sustaining peace"—the new paradigm for conflict prevention, resolution, and resilience, which was developed in the UN's 2015 peace-building architecture review (UN 2015b), and further established in two substantively identical resolutions on the topic in 2016: Security Council Resolution 2282 (UN 2016a) and General Assembly Resolution 70/262 (UN 2016b. However, one must contrast the rosy picture of commitment to gender equality and women's rights in UN headquarters in New York, with the reality on the ground: the continued backlash against women's rights from political and religious extremists of all stripes alongside rising nationalism, populism, and anti-globalization. The WPS agenda is increasingly salient in this era of uncertainty; an important platform for peace activists to advocate and hold states to account, and a tool to advance a transformative vision of justice, security, and peace.

This chapter explores three key areas of focus that emerged from the *Global Study* and 2015 high-level review on Resolution 1325: (1) preventing conflict and sustaining peace, (2) countering terrorism and violent extremism, and (3) transforming gender inequality through justice. We argue that these areas are central to the WPS agenda and essential to ensuring that it remains a relevant framework into the future. In each of these areas, the chapter draws on related themes from the *Global Study*—participation, human rights, demilitarization, and localization—to provide additional guidance on the application of recommendations in light of current global discussions and trends.

PREVENTING CONFLICT AND SUSTAINING PEACE

The *Global Study* was one of three parallel independent reviews of the United Nations' peace and security architecture that took place in 2015. The other two reviews, the report of the High-Level Independent Panel on United Nations Peace Operations (UN 2015a), and the report of the Advisory Group of Experts for the 2015 Review of United Nations Peacebuilding Architecture (UN 2015b), shared a number of common themes with the *Global Study*. The three reviews emphasized that the UN needed to take a new approach, if it was to effectively and sustainably respond to the increasingly globalized and entrenched nature of conflict. Each report includes a section on the changing context for the work of the UN on peace and security (UN 2015a: vii; 2015b: 14–16; UN Women 2015: 20–21), highlighting factors including the growth in violent extremism, the availability of new technologies of war, illicit markets and organized crime, the proliferation of small arms and light weapons, and entrenched inequalities within and among states.

The reviews urged the UN system to move away from the unsustainable and often ineffective approach of responding to conflicts with lengthy and costly peacekeeping efforts. The *Global Study* and the peace operations review both emphasize the importance of seeking political and other nonmilitary avenues of conflict prevention and resolution, rather than resorting to peacekeeping (e.g., UN 2015a: vii; UN Women 2015: 153), and leveraging new technologies to enhance impact (UN 2015a: paras. 285–287; UN Women 2015: 201–202). Moreover, the UN should focus on building "sustaining peace"—a term coined in the peace-building architecture review that encompasses "not only efforts to prevent relapse into conflict, but also to prevent lapse into conflict in the first place" (UN 2015b: para. 7). The 2016 General Assembly and Security Council resolutions on "sustaining peace" articulate a comprehensive approach to conflict prevention, focused on addressing its root causes. The "sustaining peace" resolutions do not directly state the root causes of conflict, but reference those outlined in the peace-building architecture review, which include unresolved social and economic grievances, and impunity for human rights violations (UN 2015b: 19–20).

While the United Nations has always been concerned with preventing conflict, the "sustaining peace" paradigm that has emerged over the past two years includes a new emphasis on the benefits of inclusion—and of women's participation, in particular. The resolutions note the "substantial link between women's full and meaningful involvement in efforts to prevent, resolve, and rebuild from conflict and those efforts' effectiveness and long-term sustainability" (UN 2016a; 2016b). This echoes language in the peace-building architecture review: "[I]t is, at last, becoming widely recognized that women's participation is [. . .] crucial to the success of economic recovery, political legitimacy, and social cohesion" (UN 2015b: para. 56).

In what must be viewed as a success for the WPS agenda, women's participation is now being taken forward as a key element of mainstream discussions on peace and security—not only in parallel processes led by gender equality advocates. While discussions outside of male-dominated spaces have proved essential to the development of the WPS agenda, engagement within these spaces is critical, if the WPS agenda is to shift the broader discourse on peace and security. At the same time, the rhetoric of states in support of women's participation has not always been matched with increased political will to implement commitments, or with funding for organizations and programming which focus on gender equality and women's empowerment. With increasing attention to inclusion and gender equality in processes and programs aimed at preventing conflict and sustaining peace, the *Global Study* offers several guiding recommendations to policymakers and activists.

First, the "sustaining peace" resolutions note "the substantial link between women's full and meaningful involvement in efforts to prevent, resolve, and rebuild from conflict and those efforts' effectiveness and long-term sustainability" (UN 2016a; 2016b). While evidence of the effect of women's participation on outcomes, including that shared in the *Global Study*,[1] can be very useful in convincing policymakers of the value of inclusion—particularly those who are not typically swayed by human rights-based arguments—an overreliance on the instrumental value of participation risks drowning out the intrinsic argument that ensuring women's participation is a state obligation. Too often, human rights and rights-based approaches are considered as something to be added on if time and money allow, and which quickly fall out of focus in favor of political expediency, or addressing urgent security concerns.

The *Global Study* emphasized that women's human rights are the foundation of the WPS agenda (UN Women 2015: 15). Human rights principles[2] dictate women should participate in decision-making, regardless of the impact they might have on outcomes. Evidence of the positive effects of women's participation in peace and security efforts adds critical weight to arguments in favor of inclusion, and we should continue to gather data and examples to reinforce this message. However, by relying solely on these arguments, and not emphasizing the *obligation* to be inclusive, advocates risk inadvertently sending the message that women's participation is optional but encouraged. Those implementing the "sustaining peace" resolutions should not lose sight of the goals of gender equality and universal respect for women's human rights, which will make the ultimate contribution toward conflict prevention and resolution.

Second, while the rhetoric around the importance of women's participation gains traction, it bears reminding that the actual rate of women's participation and leadership in peace and security efforts remains paltry and will require a sustained and concerted effort to redress. For example, the *Global Study* cited a study of thirty-one major peace processes between 1992 and 2011, which revealed that only 9 percent of negotiators were women (Castillo Diaz and Tordjman 2012). One needs look no further than jarring recent photographs of overwhelmingly male negotiators present in Geneva for both the Syrian and Cyprus peace talks for evidence that little progress has been made in the five years since that study was completed—and women's participation in peace negotiations is but one element of peace and security decision-making.

The *Global Study* offers a number of recommendations aimed at increasing levels of women's participation in peace and security processes, including heightened accountability for UN leaders vis-a-vis gender parity obligations (UN Women 2015: 58), developing and implementing strategies to ensure that women's organizations participate in peace processes, and funding to support women's networks to engage in peace efforts (UN Women 2015: 386). Financial support for women peacemakers remains particularly dismal. In 2012–2013, only 6 percent of all aid to fragile states targeted gender equality as the main objective (OECD DAC Network on Gender Equality 2015). With increasing calls for inclusion, one must not lose sight of the real challenge of increasing the number, and diversity, of women included in processes, including at the decision-making level; and ensuring that women can contribute meaningfully to these processes, when they do have a seat at the table.

One of the *Global Study* recommendations to enhance women's participation that has been taken forward by the United Nations, states, and civil society groups is the establishment of the Women's Peace and Humanitarian Fund (WPHF) (formerly known as the Global Acceleration Instrument on Women, Peace and Security and Humanitarian Action) (UN Women 2015: 386). The WPHF is a rapid, pooled funding mechanism to support women's participation, leadership, and empowerment in humanitarian response and peace and security settings. For example, in Burundi in 2016, the WPHF began funding a nation-wide network of 516 women mediators, who dealt with more than 6,000 local conflicts from January to July 2016 (GAI 2016: 19, 22). If diplomats and policymakers are serious about inclusive conflict prevention, they must continue to shift their resources to support women and gender equality-focused interventions like those funded through the WPHF.

Third, in the "sustaining peace" resolutions, the Security Council and General Assembly identify a long list of ways to address the root causes of conflict: strengthen the rule of law, promote sustainable economic growth, eradicate poverty, encourage national unity and reconciliation, enhance access to justice, and promote gender equality and respect for human rights. Noticeably absent from the "sustaining peace" resolutions: language addressing a major root cause of conflict identified in the *Global Study*, militarism. Militarism is a sociopolitical process which normalizes violence and promotes the use of force as an acceptable, primary mode of dispute resolution. In 2015, global military expenditure reached an estimated $1.6 billion, and the ongoing conflicts in many parts of the world often had direct links to arms acquisitions from abroad (Stockholm International Peace Research Institute [SIPRI] 2015: 20). The volume of international transfers of major weapons grew by 14 percent between 2006 and 2010, and from 2011 to 2015; yet, only just over a quarter of all UN member states used the UN's mechanism to report basic data on imports and exports (SIPRI 2015: 21). The UN spent approximately $8.47 billion on peacekeeping efforts during the 2014–2015 fiscal year (UN Women 2015: 382).

In light of current trends, the absence of a response to militarism or arms trafficking in the recent "sustaining peace" resolutions, is jarring—but not entirely surprising. Global weapons sales implicate all member states, but particularly the most powerful: the five permanent members of the Security Council were among the top six global weapons exporters and importers of weapons between 2010 and 2014 (SIPRI 2015: 17). Perhaps for this same reason, the eight WPS resolutions have also been very limited in their focus on demilitarization, rarely looking beyond enhancing women's participation in demobilization, disarmament, and reintegration processes.[3] To counteract the forces of militarism and encourage all states to address their role in perpetuating cycles of conflict, the *Global Study* recommended robust implementation of the Arms Trade Treaty, and gender-responsive national budgeting (UN Women 2015: 214). Article 7(4) of the Arms Trade Treaty (2014) asks state parties to assess the risk of arms "being used to commit or facilitate serious acts of gender-based violence or acts of violence against women and girls" and makes it illegal to transfer weapons if there is an overriding risk of gender-based violence occurring as a consequence of such a transfer. Through the process of developing a gender-responsive national budget, the destabilizing impact of military spending on international peace and security and women's rights can be exposed and mitigated (UN Women 2015: 214).

For the concept of "sustaining peace" to work, the solution is simple: wealthy and powerful states must prioritize peace over profit, and address their complicity in conflict through global arms dealing and militarization—the proverbial elephant in the Security Council chamber. This dramatic shift will be possible only when the voices of constituents demanding demilitarization rise above those of the complacent. *Global Study* concluded with a "Call to Action," inviting the creation of national, regional, and international networks of women working for peace, "so that their voices reach and activities can reach a climax and stem the current tide of recurrent militarization and mindless violence" (UN Women 2015: 397).

COUNTERING TERRORISM AND VIOLENT EXTREMISM

The General Assembly and Security Council shied away from identifying any specific drivers of conflict and insecurity in the "sustaining peace" resolutions; not only avoiding militarism, but also inequality, climate change, migration, criminal organizations, and violent extremist and terrorist groups. However, while not mentioned in the resolutions, the Security Council and General Assembly are increasingly consumed with responding to terrorist and extremist violence, including in relation to the WPS agenda. In UNSCR 2242 (2015), the Security Council called for greater integration of the agendas on WPS and countering terrorism and violent extremism (CT/CVE). The *Global Study* foreshadowed this move, with a chapter focused on countering violent extremism as an issue of increasing relevance to WPS. This chapter, alongside other recommendations in the *Global Study*, provides guidance to those working on gender mainstreaming in the context of preventing and responding to violent extremism and terrorism.

First, the *Global Study* provides a useful context for the interpretation of the Security Council's request, in UNSCR 2242, that the UN's two main counterterrorism bodies, the Counter-Terrorism Committee (CTC) and Counter-Terrorism Committee Executive Directorate (CTED), "integrate gender as a cross-cutting issue throughout the activities within their respective mandates, including within country-specific assessments and reports, recommendations made to Member States, facilitating technical assistance to Member States, and briefings to the Council" (UN 2015d: para. 11). While a gender analysis is central to understanding the drivers of any form of violent conflict, including conflict driven by terrorism and extremist groups, the *Global Study* insists that this analysis move beyond simplistic depictions of women as victims, or as mothers or daughters who might serve as informants or deterrents to their male relatives involved in violent extremist groups. These tropes exclude the large numbers of women, including those who participate in extremist groups (UN Women 2015: 226). Furthermore, a gender analysis requires moving beyond simply examining *women*, to explore the ways in which social constructions of *gender*—and gender inequality—are a driver of individual and group acts of terrorist and extremist violence.

Second, UNSCR 2242 calls for the CTC and CTED to consult with women and women's organizations, to inform their work (UN 2015d: para. 11). WPS advocates have long sought to increase the interaction between women's civil society and decision-making bodies—particularly with the Security Council. In UNSCR 2242, the Council "expressed its intention to invite civil society, including women's organizations, brief the Council in country-specific considerations and relevant thematic areas" (UN 2015d: para. 5c), which had been recommended in the *Global Study* (UN Women 2015: 342). Civil society briefings and consultations could play an important role in strengthening the work of decision-making bodies, such as the Security Council, CTC, and CTED. However, member states must make a concerted effort to act on their promises for greater interaction—from the intentions expressed in UNSCR 2242, to the "sustaining peace" resolutions, which stress "the need to increase women's role in decision-making with regard to conflict prevention and resolution and peacebuilding" (UN 2016b, 2016a). In 2016, the Security Council invited only one briefing from a civil society representative on a country-specific deliberation.[4] Furthermore, it must be noted that "consultation" with women and women's civil society organizations is a far cry from women's participation in decision-making, and must only be viewed as a first step toward increasing women's representation on these bodies. Of the fifteen states comprising the members of the Security Council and CTC in 2017, only one had a woman as permanent representative.[5]

As envisaged in UNSCR 2242, consultations with women's civil society organizations on the topic of CVE or CT must be undertaken with great care, and within a clear framework—with the intention to enhance the quality of gender analysis, and not use women's voices and women's rights as a tool in militarized efforts to fight extremist violence and terrorism. [6]

The *Global Study* shared the emphatic call of women around the world to respect the independence of local women's activism (UN Women 2015: 222). Consultations with women and women's organizations should avoid creating an obvious association between women's rights and CVE/CT efforts—or risk feeding into the narrative that women's rights are a foreign, Western agenda, and put women human rights defenders at heightened risk for reprisal by extremist groups (Saferworld 2017).

Third, the *Global Study* called for a greater emphasis on prevention rather than militarized responses to conflict—a call that was repeated in the peace operations and peace-building architecture reviews, and ultimately in the "sustaining peace" resolutions. This call applies equally to traditional inter-state conflict, as it does to interventions relating to non-state actors, including terrorist and violent extremist groups. Rather than focusing on militarized responses to extremist violence, CVE and CT efforts must follow the progression of the broader framework of peace and security. The UN's new "sustaining peace" paradigm calls for greater attention to the root causes and drivers of radicalization and violence: inequality and exclusion, among others. As such, the entire *Global Study*, with its focus on building resilience to conflict through inclusion and equality, is relevant for those working on preventing violent extremism and terrorism as well.

Transformative Justice

The "sustaining peace" resolutions emphasize the need for a comprehensive approach to transitional justice to build societies that are resilient to conflict. Transitional justice refers to the range of judicial and nonjudicial mechanisms employed to achieve redress for past human rights violations, including truth commissions, criminal trials, reparations programs and institutional reforms. The *Global Study* gives added nuance to the concept of comprehensive transitional justice, exploring how these mechanisms might do more than redress individual rights violations—how they might be used to *transform* gender inequality as a root cause of conflict and insecurity. Transitional justice mechanisms, from reparations processes, to the vetting of the security sector, must work in synergy to enable women's full enjoyment of their human rights. In post-conflict states, where rule-of-law institutions are weak or non-existent, there are clear practical challenges to acting on the *Global Study*'s recommendation to "support legal orders to challenge socio-cultural norms and contexts of inequality" (UN Women 2015: 401). In light of the growing attention to transitional justice as a key aspect of "sustaining peace," this recommendation bears further interrogation.

First, a core recommendation of the *Global Study* was that peace-building efforts must be participatory and tailored to the local context, avoiding a one-size-fits-all approach (UN Women 2015: 15–16). The 2015 peace operations review also bemoaned UN missions and mandates that are "produced on the basis of templates instead of tailored to support situation-specific political strategies" (UN 2015a: vii). This concern over imported peace-building models is not new, and extends to transitional justice; in a 2004 report on the rule of law and transitional justice, the Secretary-General decried "one-size-fits-all formulas and the importation of foreign models," encouraging support based on national assessments, national participation, and national needs and aspirations (UN 2004: 1).

Community-based and victim-centered transitional justice processes adhere to human rights principles, and provide the strongest foundation for transitional justice to become transformative, and contribute to sustaining peace. Locally driven processes can move the discourse of justice and repair beyond the strictly legal approaches prescribed by national and international elites, to a wider range of social, economic, and political policy responses that advance equality and sustainable peace in the longer-term (Gready and Robins 2014). Processes that originate at the community level can also bypass weakened or non-existent national rule of law institutions, while strengthening critical local infrastructure, including the capacity of civil society organizations. However, it is important to bear in mind that women do not benefit universally from locally driven justice processes, particularly when these processes are informed by discriminatory custom and practice. Locally driven processes can also be as political—and averse to real change, or accountability for crimes—as those driven by national or international actors. Financial and political support for women's civil society groups working on local-level justice is essential to ensure that women's voices drive these processes so that they transform—rather than entrench—existing inequalities. As with all peace-building efforts, transitional justice processes must work from the bottom up, and prioritize local experiences and voices, even when this requires additional resources.

Second, a key finding of the *Global Study* was that when women participate in decision-making relating to peace and security efforts, including transitional justice, outcomes improve. For example, the *Global Study* referenced research showing that, from 1993 to 2004, in every case before the International Criminal Tribunal for the Former Yugoslavia resulting in significant redress of sexual violence crimes perpetrated against both women and men, women judges were on the bench (Mertus et al. 2004: 11). Whether a process operate at the local, national, or international level, a human rights-based approach to transitional justice requires that women participate in its design, implementation, and monitoring—with a particular eye to the diversity of women's participation and leadership (e.g., ensuring representation of rural women, indigenous women, young women, and so on).

Transitional justice mechanisms often focus on women's participation as victims rather than as agents of change or as leaders in peace-building. By emphasizing women's meaningful participation and leadership, transitional justice mechanisms can shift the focus so that the process itself becomes a site of empowerment for women and of transformation for communities. Furthermore, by creating alternative avenues for women's participation beyond their victimhood, transitional justice mechanisms can move away from solely examining the crimes of individual perpetrators, and begin to also focus on the structural inequality that underpins sexual and gender-based violence, for example (Gready and Robins 2014). Enhancing women's meaningful participation in transitional justice processes creates an opportunity for narratives of women's rights and gender equality to emerge or gain strength. For example, 100 of the 198 statement-takers employed by the Liberian Truth and Reconciliation Commission (TRC) were women. Gender parity was the result of a conscious effort, and was achieved through public service announcements that specifically encouraged applications from women, and by posting fliers about employment opportunities at places frequented by women, such as beauty salons and university campuses (Republic of Liberia 2009: vol. 3, app. 14).

Third, the *Global Study* reaffirmed that women's human rights are central to the maintenance of international peace and security. Women's civil, political, economic, social, and cultural rights are universal, indivisible, and non-hierarchical. Nonetheless, transitional justice mechanisms have historically focused on civil and political rights violations over economic, social, and cultural rights violations (Valji 2012: 2), and have failed at "taking into account the interdependence and interrelatedness of all human rights violations which have occurred during conflict" (CEDAW 2013: para. 76). To bring about social transformation, transitional justice mechanisms must move away from this narrow focus on the types of civil and political violations often experienced by men, such as forced disappearances, or violence in detention facilities. Justice processes must equally investigate the economic and social rights violations that women often prioritize for redress, and which underpin gender-based violence and discrimination that women experience before, during, and after conflict. By focusing on the full range of human rights, transitional justice processes reaffirm the interdependence of human rights that underpin gender equality, and which are central to the WPS agenda.

The Global Study sought to advance a notion of justice that is as much about redress for conflict-related gender-based violence as it is about addressing structural gender inequality. By situating post-conflict justice alongside other key concepts of localization, participation, and respect for human rights, the tall task of contributing to social transformation and sustaining peace comes closer into reach.

Conclusion

The WPS agenda sets out a framework for enhancing women's right to participate in sustainable conflict prevention and to address the entrenched root causes of conflict. This chapter has sought to further contextualize key concepts and recommendations from the *Global Study*, to make them more tangible and applicable to the current context. In light of the global shift in attention toward "sustaining peace," with inclusion as a central tenant, the WPS agenda is more relevant than ever. The themes of conflict prevention, countering violent extremism and terrorism while respecting women's autonomy, and transformative justice must continue to move to the center of global and local peace and security efforts—with key concepts of participation, human rights, demilitarization, and localization informing their content. The Women, Peace, and Security agenda, with its calls for a permanent peace, human security, gender equality, remains as salient as ever in this era of uncertainty.

Notes

1. For example, in the *Global Study* chapter on women's participation in peace processes, the report draws on research undertaken by the Graduate Institute in Geneva. The in-depth analysis of forty peace processes since the end of the Cold War, shows that in cases where women's groups exercised a strong influence on the negotiation process, there was

a much higher chance that an agreement would be reached than when women's groups exercised weak or no influence (Paffenholz et al. 2015).

2. There are several basic principles which are always a part of human rights implementation. These principles include: universality, indivisibility, interdependence, participation, accountability, transparency, and non-discrimination. People have the right to participate in decision-making processes that affect their lives and well-being (National Economic and Social Rights Initiative, n.d.; UNFPA 2005).

3. Perhaps the broadest reference comes in UNSCR 2242, which "*Encourages* empowering women, including through capacity-building efforts, as appropriate, to participate in the design and implementation of efforts related to the prevention, combating and eradication of the illicit transfer, and the destabilizing accumulation and misuse of small arms and light weapons" (UN 2015d: para. 15).

4. Under the presidency of Sweden, Victoria Wollie, National Coordinator for the West Africa Network for Peacebuilding—Women in Peacebuilding Network in Liberia, was invited to brief the Security Council during a debate on Liberia on December 2, 2016 (UN 2016c).

5. As of July 1, 2017, the lone woman ambassador on the Security Council was Nikki Haley of the United States.

6. For a detailed discussion of the securitization of women's rights in CT and CVE, see posts by Fionnuala Ní Aoláin (2015) and Jayne Huckerby (2015) on the "Just Security" blog.

REFERENCES

Arms Trade Treaty. United Nations Office for Disarmament Affairs, December 24, 2014, https://www.un.org/disarmament/att/.

Castillo Diaz, Pablo, and Simon Tordjman. "Women's Participation in Peace Negotiations: Connections between Presence and Influence." In *UN Women Sourcebook on Women, Peace and Security*. New York: UN Women, 2012.

CEDAW. "General Recommendation No. 30 on Women in Conflict Prevention, Conflict, and Post-Conflict Situations." CEDAW/C/GC/30 . Committee on the Elimination of Discrimination against Women, 2013.

Global Acceleration Instrument (GAI) for Women, Peace, and Security, and Humanitarian Action. "Annual Report: January–December 2016." PeaceWomen, 2016, http://peacewomen. org/sites/default/files/UNW%20GAI%20Annual%20Report%202016%20FINAL.pdf.

Gready, P., and S. Robins. "From Transitional to Transformative Justice: A New Agenda for Practice." *International Journal of Transitional Justice* 8, no. 3 (2014): 339–361. doi: 10.1093/ijtj/iju013.

Huckerby, Jayne. "The Complexities of Women, Peace, Security, and Countering Violent Extremism." *Just Security*, September 24, 2015, https://www.justsecurity.org/26337/womens-rights-simple-tool-counterterrorism/#https://www.justsecurity.org/25983/counter-terrorism-committee-addressing-role-women-countering-terrorism-violent-extremism/%20.

Mertus, Julie, Olja Hocevar van Wely, Women Waging Peace, and the Policy Commission. *Women's Participation in the International Criminal Tribunal for the Former Yugoslavia (ICTY): Transitional Justice for Bosnia and Herzegovina*. Washington, DC: Hunt Alternatives Fund, July 2004.

National Economic and Social Rights Initiative. "What Are the Basic Principles of the Human Rights Framework?" NESRI, n.d., https://www.nesri.org/programs/what-are-the-basic-principles-of-the-human-rights-framework.

Ni Aolain, Fionnuala. "Counter-Terrorism Committee: Addressing the Role of Women in Countering Terrorism and Violent Extremism." *Just Security*, September 17, 2015, https://www.justsecurity.org/25983/counter-terrorism-committee-addressing-role-women-countering-terrorism-violent-extremism/.

Ní Aoláin, Fionnuala. "The 'War on Terror' and Extremism: Assessing the Relevance of the Women, Peace, and Security Agenda." *International Affairs* 92, no. 2 (2016): 275–291.

OECD DAC Network on Gender Equality. "Financing UN Security Council Resolution 1325: Aid in Support of Gender Equality and Women's Rights in Fragile Contexts." March 2015.

Paffenholz, Thania, Nick Ross, Anna-Lena Schluchter, Jacqui True, and Steven Dixon. "Making Women Count: Assessing Women's Inclusion and Influence on the Quality and Sustainability of Peace Negotiations and Implementation." Graduate Institute Geneva, Centre on Conflict, Development and Peacebuilding, 2015.

Republic of Liberia. "Truth and Reconciliation Commission Report," Vol. 3. 2009.

Saferworld. "The Countering Violent Extremism Agenda Risks Undermining Women Who Need Greater Support." April 26, 2017, https://www.saferworld.org.uk/resources/news-and-analysis/post/221-the-countering-violent-extremism-agenda-risks-undermining-women-who-need-greater-support.

Stockholm International Peace Research Institute (SIPRI). "SIPRI Yearbook 2015: Armaments, Disarmament, and International Security: Summary." Solna, Sweden: SIPRI, 2015.

United National Population Fund (UNFPA). "Human Rights Principles." UNFPA, 2005, http://www.unfpa.org/resources/human-rights-principles.

United Nations (UN). "Security Council Resolution 1325 (2000)." UN Doc. S/RES/1325 S/RES/1325. United Nations Security Council, 2000.

United Nations (UN). "Report of the Secretary General: The Rule of Law and Transitional Justice in Conflict and Post-Conflict Societies." S/2004/616, 2004.

United Nations (UN). "Security Council Resolution 2122 (2013)." S/RES/2122, 2013.

United Nations (UN). "Report of the High-Level Independent Panel on United Nations Peace Operations: Uniting Our Strengths for Peace—Politics, Partnership, and People." A/70/95–S/2015/446, 2015a.

United Nations (UN). "Report of the Advisory Group of Experts for the 2015 Review of the United Nations Peacebuilding Architecture: The Challenge of Sustaining Peace." A/69/968–S/2015/490, 2015b.

United Nations (UN). "Report of the Secretary-General: Women and Peace and Security." S/2015/716, 2015c.

United Nations (UN). "Security Council Resolution 2242 (2015)." S/RES/2242. United Nations Security Council, 2015d.

United Nations (UN). "Security Council Resolution 2282 (2016)." 2016a.

United Nations (UN). "General Assembly Resolution 70/262 (2016)." 2016b.

United Nations (UN). "Meetings Coverage: Greater Investment in Security, Justice, Correction Sectors Key to Liberia's Stability, Peacekeeping Chief Tells Security Council." Text. *Meetings Coverage and Press Releases*. December 2, 2016c, https://www.un.org/press/en/2016/sc12608.doc.htm.

UN Women. "Preventing Conflict, Transforming Justice, Securing the Peace: A Global Study on the Implementation of United Nations Security Council Resolution 1325." New York: UN Women, 2015.

Valji, Nahla. "A Window of Opportunity: Making Transitional Justice Work for Women." Guidance Paper. UN Women, 2012.

CHAPTER 59

···

MEASURING WPS
A New Global Index

···

JENI KLUGMAN

WOMEN are at the heart of efforts to achieve sustainable peace worldwide. This has been explicitly recognized by the international community, from the agenda established by United Nations Security Council Resolution 1325 on Women, Peace, and Security, to the 2030 Agenda for Sustainable Development (discussed in chapter 55), which recognizes the need to build inclusive, just, and peaceful societies for all.

Global indices are an increasingly popular way to assess progress against such goals by distilling an array of complex information into a single number or ranking. A notable early example is the Human Development Index, inspired by the work of Nobel Laureate Amartya Sen and published annually by the United Nations Development Programme since 1990. This has been followed by an enormous proliferation of indices used to assess various aspects of well-being, development, peace, and security. Recent research has shown how "scorecard diplomacy" can be a powerful agent for change (Kelley 2017). The boom in indices has been at least partly due to their growing use by governments, NGOs, and campaigners to lobby for and shape new laws and policies. Highly comparative and easy to understand numbers can call out low performers and help to reinforce good performance.

The new global Women, Peace, and Security (WPS) Index bridges insights from gender and development indices with those from peace and security indices in a way that is simple and transparent and that reflects women's autonomy and empowerment as agents at home, in the community, and in society. The index is structured around three basic dimensions of women's well-being: inclusion (economic, social, political); justice (formal laws and informal discrimination); and security (at the individual, community, and societal levels). This is depicted in Figure 59.1. The WPS Index captures and quantifies these three dimensions through carefully selected indicators. It ranks 153 countries along these three dimensions in a way that highlights key achievements and deficits, and provides a tool to monitor progress over time.

This chapter[1] examines the need and rationale for a new global index and how it has been constructed, before presenting key results and insights that emerge from the rankings and associated analysis. It concludes by underlining the need for better data to inform future knowledge and updates of the index.

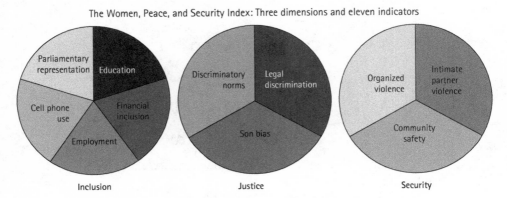

The Women, Peace, and Security Index: Three dimensions and eleven indicators

Inclusion   Justice   Security

FIGURE 59.1 The WPS Index, dimensions, and indicators.

WHY IS A WOMEN, PEACE, AND SECURITY INDEX NEEDED?

A primary goal of this index is to accelerate progress on the international Women, Peace, and Security agenda and the Sustainable Development Goals, bringing partners together around an agenda for women's inclusion, justice, and security, by contributing to the evidence base and understanding about key patterns of achievements and gaps. This reiterates a recurring theme in this volume, well-argued by Chantal de Jonge Oudraat; Louise Olsson and Theodora-Ismene Gizelis; and Krishanti Dharmaraj and Radhika Balakrishnan, among others, that good evidence and better data are needed to advance the WPS agenda. The analysis is designed to stimulate interest and give a broad group of stakeholders and the international community a comprehensive picture of achievements and gaps across a critical range of fronts. As underlined by Sanam Naraghi Anderlini in this volume, *if not for civil society*, empirical evidence and data is key to deepening the institutionalization of the WPS agenda.

While there has been a proliferation of global indices, none have sought to address the WPS agenda (Cooley and Snyder 2015). The new index brings together three broad dimensions of this agenda: inclusion, justice, and security. Several innovative features set the WPS Index apart from existing gender indices and security indices. It incorporates several indicators that have never been used in other prominent gender indices: specifically, women's perceptions of safety in the community and organized violence, as well as whether women's paid work is deemed acceptable by men in the society. The index also incorporates several other indicators that have seldom been included elsewhere: including financial inclusion, cell phone use, a bias for sons, and intimate partner violence.[2]

Existing gender indices—such as the World Economic Forum's Gender Gap Index—are typically limited to such aspects as whether women have completed secondary school or are in paid work. These aspects of inclusion are undoubtedly important, but they are incomplete in the absence of aspects of justice and security. For instance, it is surely misleading to focus on girls' schooling where girls are not safe in their home or community and as a result may only intermittently be able to attend the school they are enrolled in. And girls' non-attendance at school has been found to be an early warning sign for domestic violence (Holt et al. 2008). The WPS Index shares some commonalities with the Social Institutions and Gender Inequality (SIGI) Index, published by the Organisation for Economic Co-operation and Development (OECD), and the Economist Intelligence Unit's Women's Economic Opportunity Index. But those two indices rely extensively on expert judgment to measure various concepts or to address missing data, and they are far more complex in construction. And the SIGI Index does not include any economic dimensions (such as employment and cell phone use) or any indicators of organized violence.[3]

The set of indices around peace and security tend to focus either on state fragility or on forecasting the probability of armed conflict or political instability in the future. The Index of State Weakness in the Developing World (from the Brookings Institution), the Fragile States Index (Fund for Peace and *Foreign Policy*), and the Global Peace Index published by the Institute for Economics and Peace include an array of conflict indicators and assessments, but invariably ignore systematic bias and discrimination against women and girls (Rice and Patrick 2008; Messner et al. 2017; Global Peace Index 2017). The exclusion of sexual and gender-based violence from measures of human security remains a pressing problem. The Global Peace Index, Joint Proposal to Create a Human Security Report, and Human Rights Dialogue all reflect this absence (Bunch 2002). The Country Indicators for Foreign Policy Fragility Index does include a handful of indicators related to women in parliament and in the labor force, among the large number (70) and range of indicators tracked (Carment et al. 2016).

The WPS Index is also the first gender index to be developed in the framework of the 2030 Agenda for Sustainable Development, and it is firmly grounded in the goals, targets, and indicators that 193 governments agreed to in September 2015.[4] As far as possible, we drew on the global indicator framework developed by the Inter-Agency and Expert Group on SDG Indicators that was agreed to, as a practical starting point at the 47th session of the UN Statistical Commission held in March 2016, and was then taken note of by ECOSOC at its 70th session in June 2016.[5]

At the same time, the Index confronted major gaps and deficits on the data front—which means that we need to rely on the best available, rather than the best possible, indicators. The importance of better data is now well recognized. SDG 17.18 commits to "by 2020, enhance capacity-building support to developing countries to increase significantly the availability of high-quality, timely and reliable data disaggregated by income, gender, age, race, ethnicity, migratory status, disability, geographic location and other characteristics relevant in national contexts." Likewise, the Women, Peace. and Security agenda calls for international actors and national governments to improve data on gender and conflict (UN Women 2015).[6] But for the time being, the Index had to work with what is currently available.

How Is the Index Constructed?

The index comprises three dimensions—inclusion, justice and security—each of which is measured using a carefully selected set of comparable indicators. For example, inclusion is measured by women's achievements in education, employment, and parliamentary representation, as well as access to cell phones and financial services. Justice is captured in both formal and informal aspects—lack of discrimination in the legal system, alongside discriminatory norms. Security is measured at three levels—the family, community, and societal level. The indicator definitions, data sources, and rationale for inclusion are given in.[7]

One obvious question to address is: why these three dimensions? As exemplified in the seven targets and twenty or so indicators under the gender equality goal of the Sustainable Development Agenda,[8] and many more targets and indicators relevant to women under an array of other goals, from education and health to productive work and the environment, there are a large number of components that could be included in a gender index. The three chosen for the WPS Index were carefully selected, echoing the emphasis of the 2030 Agenda on the need to build peaceful, just, and inclusive societies.[9] Exclusion and injustice are drivers of violence and insecurity.

The WPS Index was also designed to support the emerging agenda around SDG16+, which highlights the links among the SDGs and emphasizes the integrated and cross-cutting nature of the peace and security agenda.[10] It has been well argued that SDG16 should not be seen in isolation, given the strong links with other goals, in line with the integrated and indivisible nature of the agenda.

Inclusion is at the core of both to the Women, Peace, and Security agenda and to the 2030 Agenda for Sustainable Development. This has multiple dimensions in both outcomes and processes. It has been persuasively argued that political, social, and economic inclusion holds the key to fostering more peaceful societies (Steven 2018). We selected several key indicators of inclusion that are relevant to diverse groups of women, and seek to capture how well women are included in economic, social and political life. Likewise, *justice* and *security* are not only core to women's well-being, but they also underpin SDG 16 on promoting peaceful and inclusive societies for sustainable development, making access to justice available for all, and building effective, accountable institutions at all levels. These aspects have special resonance and relevance to women and girls, who too often face injustice due to formal and informal discrimination and the lack of security at home, in the community, and in society at large. In Burundi, for example, the resumption of conflict poses major threats to women's well-being. Sexual violence and loss of life are widespread, reportedly often perpetrated by security agents, police, military, and members of *Imbonerakure*—the youth wing of the ruling party (Vigaud-Walsh 2015; Human Rights Watch 2016).

Choosing indicators to capture the aspects of interest requires dealing with data constraints, which can be severe when trying to identify global measures that are widely accepted and comparable across a large set of diverse countries. To keep the index as simple and transparent as possible, the following criteria were applied in their selection:

- **Global relevance**. Applicable to a broad range of country settings and linked to the SDGs.
- **Actionability**. Not only deeply relevant to women's well-being, but actionable by policymakers and partners.
- **Data adequacy**. Data are collected and processed in a statistically reliable way without large or frequent revisions and are available for at least 120 countries for a recent year. Most of the data related to 2014–2016, with some earlier data points as needed, depending on country level availability.

- **Data quality**. Represent widely agreed-on measures for the topic and are derived from official national or international sources (for example, national statistical offices, UN organizations) or other reputable international sources (for example, Gallup, Peace Research Institute Oslo, peer-reviewed journals). Louise Olsson and Theodora-Ismene Gizelis in this volume have shown how bad data can undermine progress on the WPS agenda.
- **Transparent. Based on population or representative-survey data.** Capture data from a population- or a survey-based measure and do not rely solely on expert judgment to score performance, since such measures can be criticized as subjective.

The legal discrimination indicator is drawn from the widely cited *Women, Business, and the Law,* a World Bank Group product that collects data on laws and regulations that constrain women's economic opportunities, available here.[11] We aggregate seventy-eight different laws and regulations that differentiate between men and women across the following categories—accessing institutions, using property, going to court, providing incentives to work, building credit and getting a job—with six laws (specifically those that require married women to obey their husband, mandates for paternity leave, equal remuneration for work of equal value, non-discrimination based on gender in hiring, and prohibitions of dismissal of pregnant workers and of child or early marriage) given a larger weight. The "accessing institutions" category includes several types of constitutional provisions for gender equality. This score thereby captures the host of laws that can support or impede full equality in accessing basic rights, services, and economic opportunities in all countries, including conflict-affected states.

The inclusion of indicators of women's security is a major innovation of the WPS Index. Security is captured at three levels that matter for women's well-being: home and family, community, and society, as defined in Figure 59.1. Among the insights from the security dimension are that violence perpetrated by an intimate partner during a woman's lifetime is high around the world, and not only in countries affected by organized violence. In the European Union, one in five women have experienced physical or sexual violence by a partner since the age of 15, and worldwide about 30 percent of women who have been in an intimate relationship have experienced violence from their partner (European Union Agency for Fundamental Rights 2014; García-Moreno et al. 2013). Even higher rates of intimate partner violence have been documented in a range of conflict settings. A multi-country study found that living in a fragile or conflict-affected state was associated with a 35 percent higher risk of intimate partner violence relative to living in other developing countries in the sample (Hanmer and Klugman 2016). It is also important to recognize the data limitations that plague studies of domestic violence: most formal studies likely underestimate the extent of intimate partner violence (Palermo et al. 2013).[12]

The feeling that one can walk alone near one's home at night without fear (perception of community safety indicator) is one of the basic measures of how safe and secure people feel. The index incorporates the measured level of safety recorded by women according to the 2015 Gallup World Poll, which reveals a global gender gap of about 7 percentage points, and the share of women feeling safe falling as low as 10 percent in Venezuela (the lowest score Gallup has recorded in the decade since the measure was launched). Fewer than one in three women feel safe in several Latin American countries, including Argentina, Brazil, Dominican Republic, and El Salvador, and in some Sub-Saharan African countries, including Botswana, Gabon, and South Africa. Only 31 percent of Malaysian women reported feeling safe in their neighborhood. At the other end of the spectrum, women in Singapore and in several Scandinavian countries report a high sense of safety—exceeding 85 percent. These patterns in community safety are correlated to patterns of intimate partner violence. We find that women who feel unsafe in their community are also generally more likely to feel unsafe at home.

The WPS Index uses the UCDP/PRIO (Uppsala Conflict Data Program [UCDP]/Peace Research Institute Oslo) measure of organized violence: state-based, non-state-based, and one-sided violence leading to more than twenty-five battle deaths annually per 100,000, for the period 2010–2015. UCDP/PRIO defines battle deaths as "deaths caused by warring parties that can be directly related to combat over the contested incompatibility." These include military and civilian deaths caused during battlefield fighting, guerrilla activities, bombardments, assassinations, and urban warfare, but not indirect deaths due to disease, starvation, criminality, or one-sided violence against civilians when there is no opposing party (UCDP 2006).[13]

This is now the most used dataset on war, and is based on rigorous and independent coding criteria (Nygard et al. 2016), but has been criticized for its narrow focus. Restrepo, Spagat, and Vargas (2006) find in the cases of Colombia and Northern Ireland that the UCDP has a tendency to underestimate killings due to its restrictive criteria, and that more detailed micro-datasets are better representative of the two conflicts. Kaldor (2013) argues that the UCDP concept of conflict misses the nuances of contemporary war characterized by transnational violence, or persistent low-intensity fighting that may fall below the UCDP threshold. Most importantly for the WPS Index, the battle death measure fails to account for sexual and gender-based violence, or any form of interpersonal violence, which often disproportionately affect women (True 2015).

Despite these limitations, the UCDP/PRIO measure provides the best country coverage and comparability needed for our index. There are no micro-level datasets that have generated comparable data for a large number of countries. Homicide data were not used in the index because they are generally incomplete and at times not comparable (Regoeczi and Riedel 2003). Recognizing the partiality of the battle -death measure, the security dimension includes two additional indicators that are most important to women—intimate partner violence and safety in the community—which better reflect the personal security of women than battle deaths alone.

WHAT ARE THE HEADLINE RESULTS?

The index highlights key achievements and major deficits in women's inclusion, justice, and peace, by country group and for individual countries. We rank 153 countries based on their index score, which ranges from zero (worst performance) to one (best performance). The global rankings reveal that even though good performers often do well across the board, performance is uneven across dimensions in several regions and many countries. And alongside commonalities, there are large differences within regions, illustrating the feasibility of improvements in countries that are below their neighbors' standards.

Who Are the Top Performers?

The top performing countries on the WPS Index (ranking 1–12, with ties for some positions) in descending order are Iceland, Norway, Switzerland, Slovenia, Spain, Finland, Canada, Netherlands, Sweden, Belgium, Singapore,[14] Denmark, Germany, and the United Kingdom. They share some important characteristics. Each of these societies is generally peaceful and stable. Each has high scores on multiple aspects of inclusion, especially women's education, financial inclusion, and cell phone use, and very low shares of men believing that it is unacceptable for women to work. None of the societies has recorded levels of organized violence.

It is notable that all these top-performing countries also rank much higher on the WPS Index than on per capita GDP. Slovenia (with the largest difference) is thirty positions higher on the WPS Index than on per capita income, and Spain twenty-four higher. Iceland is distinguished by very high rates of parliamentary representation and the highest reported rate of women's employment.

No country has excellent scores on all aspects, however. Both Norway and Sweden record high rates of intimate partner violence, for example, and fewer than half of women in Belgium and Spain are in paid work. And all eleven of these top-performing countries maintain legal differences between how men and women are treated. For example, although Singapore has a non-discrimination clause in its constitution, it does not explicitly mention gender as a category protected against discrimination. Iceland's constitution does not contain a clause on non-discrimination by gender.

Who Performs Worst: The Bottom Dozen Rankings

The worst performing countries on the WPS Index (ranking 141–152, with a tie for last position) are, starting from the bottom, Afghanistan and Syria (tied for worst place), Yemen, Pakistan, Central African Republic, Iraq, Mali, Sudan, Niger, Lebanon, Cameroon, and Chad. These countries all perform poorly on aspects of each dimension and especially poorly on organized violence. Almost every one of these countries has significant levels of organized violence, with Syria having the highest score of nearly 173 battle deaths per 100,000 people. Besides, all except for the Central African Republic and Niger experience rates of organized violence above the global average. The total number of deaths from organized violence in Syria has escalated rapidly over the past decade, from around one recorded death in 2008 to more than 49,000 deaths in 2016. In 2015 and 2016, three countries in the bottom dozen—Afghanistan, Central African Republic, and Syria—accounted for more than two-thirds of total global deaths from organized violence.

On the inclusion and justice dimensions, the bottom dozen group includes the countries with the worst global scores on female employment (notably Syria, where only one in eight women are in paid work) and discriminatory norms (most markedly Pakistan), while the bottom dozen all score worse than the global average on legal discrimination. Women's employment in Syria was low prior to the conflict—at least since 2008, for all the years for which International Labour Organization data are available. Several of the countries in the bottom dozen do badly on the WPS Index even relative to a low regional average: Afghanistan is 35 percent lower than its regional average, Syria 27 percent, and Pakistan 25 percent.

Behind the Headlines

Looking behind the overall ranking and top and bottom performers, several key headlines emerge:

First, the index demonstrates that good things often go together. Around thirty countries score in the top third for all three dimensions, with achievements in each dimension reinforcing progress more broadly. Among country groups, such mutual reinforcement is seen notably for the Developed Country group, Central and Eastern Europe and Central Asia, and East Asia and the Pacific.[15]

For most indicators and most regions, there are countries that are close to or above the global average. For example, the global average for women's schooling is about seven years, and in all regions except South Asia some countries are above that level. Likewise it is striking that there are countries in all regions that have surpassed the global mean rate of women's cell phone use of about 78 percent, including Iraq, Mongolia, and Chile. The same is true of women's employment rates around the world, including Rwanda, Lao PDR, and Madagascar. That there are countries in all regions that have met if not exceeded global averages in women's inclusion and justice has the important and encouraging implications.

Second, however, such positive synergies are not a given, as patterns of unbalanced achievement across dimensions are also common. For example, Sub-Saharan Africa does relatively well on justice but performs unimpressively on inclusion—a dimension on which the Middle East and North Africa and South Asia also perform poorly. Relatively weak achievements on specific fronts reveal areas where investments or policy reforms are needed, and windows into potential opportunities for improvement.

Analysis of the worst performers in each country group reveals extensive legal discrimination in the worst-scoring countries in all regions. All regions have countries scoring worse (a higher score indicates worse performance) than 23, the global average; Saudi Arabia has a score of 54, the highest in the world. More progress is needed in much of the world: currently thirty-two countries score worse than 30 on our measure of legal discrimination.[16]

Third, while there are clear regional patterns in performance, there are also major differences *within* regions, illustrating the scope for improvement in order to reach the standards of neighbors. This is shown in Figure 59.2.[17]

Thus, although the Middle East and North Africa is the bottom-ranked region on the WPS Index, which can be traced largely to high levels of organized violence and discriminatory laws, its within-region differences are also striking. For example, the United Arab Emirates (UAE) ranks among the top third of countries on the WPS Index overall, while several neighbors are in the bottom tercile globally, including Saudi Arabia and Egypt, with Lebanon, Iraq, Yemen, and Syria all in the bottom dozen. At the same time, UAE's achievements are constrained by its retention of many discriminatory laws, resulting in a rank of 124 out of 153 countries on the justice dimension of the WPS Index. The Sharia-based Law of Personal Affairs, which covers marriage, divorce, and succession, is restrictive and discriminatory, with clauses requiring a male guardian to approve a woman's marriage and gives men a unilateral right to divorce, for example (Begum 2015). Moreover, protection measures for victims of sexual assault are weak, and there is no comprehensive law against domestic violence (Salem 2015).

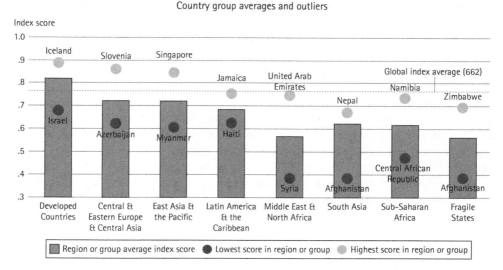

FIGURE 59.2 WPS Index Group, averages, and outliers.

Fourth, attainments in too many countries are well below global averages. In the inclusion dimension, for example, parliamentary representation of women ranges from a global high of 56 percent in Rwanda to zero in Qatar, and in nearly two dozen countries, this representation is in single digits. On women's employment, behind a global average of about 50 percent, Syria is the lowest at 12 percent, and in five of eight country groups the regional low is less than half the global average. In the justice dimension, as noted earlier, legal discrimination is extensive. The share of men who do not think it is acceptable for women to work outside the home is likewise high in several country groups, averaging one-fourth of men in the fragile states group, one-third in South Asia, and ranging as high as 37 percent in the Middle East and North Africa. This indicator is a valuable measure of societal norms toward women's agency. Cross-country analysis shows how adverse norms toward women's work are systematically associated with lower rates of female labor force participation (Klugman and Tyson 2016).

But even among the countries that do poorly overall, each country performs at least as well as the regional average on at least one indicator. For example, Yemen's measure of organized violence during the period was far below the regional average: below 7 per 100,000, compared to the MENA regional average of almost 21 deaths per 100,000. In Afghanistan, for example, it is women's parliamentary representation (due to quotas[18]), and in Niger it is indicators in the security dimension. For three indicators there are no countries scoring much worse than the regional average—mean years of schooling, legal discrimination, and lifetime intimate partner violence—reflecting a convergence of performance on these indicators at the regional level.

Finally, money matters, but many countries do far better on the WPS Index—or far worse—than their per capita income rank. Fifty-seven countries rank at least ten places better on the WPS Index than on their global income ranking—notably Zimbabwe,[19] Lao People's Democratic Republic (Lao PDR), and Nicaragua—while more than fifty countries do much worse: Saudi Arabia, for example, drops a massive eighty-nine places on the WPS Index relative to its per capita income. This underlines the important insight that improvements in women's inclusion, justice, and security are not an inevitable result of greater national wealth, not least because economic growth is often unequally distributed, including by gender, and the importance of specific policy and investment choices made by governments.

Advancing the WPS agenda requires a constellation of factors and actors—the importance of which has been well articulated elsewhere in this volume. For example, Yifat Susskind and Diana Duarte explore the concept of women's networked advocacy as a means to reframe the discussion around peace and conflict resolution by incorporating the perspectives of many and varied stakeholders. Chantal de Jonge Oudraat similarly identifies the need to broaden the WPS agenda by overcoming the divides that separate the security, academic, policy, and gender communities—among others. This index has a related, and more specific motivation: informing and strengthening the evidence needed to argue for change and greater efforts, and to hold governments and others to account.

The WPS Index and the findings it reveals should be useful to a range of groups:

- *Policymakers* can draw on the results to set priorities for actions to improve women's inclusion, justice, or security (or all three dimensions) in countries that are performing poorly and where achievements are unbalanced across the three dimensions and the underlying indicators. Such patterns reveal the potential for improvements, as well as more generalized deficits that require attention.
- *Civil society* can utilize the results to spotlight achievements as well as injustice and to hold decision-makers to account, especially given the links to the Sustainable Development Goals to which all national governments have committed.
- *Business and investors* can better analyze risks and assess the policy environment in countries based on rankings on inclusion, justice, and security.
- *Academics from a range of disciplines*—peace and security studies, development economics, gender specialties—can exploit a wealth of possibilities for research from the WPS Index, which provides a major database for analysis as well as online tools to investigate the data.[20]
- *The international development community* can see a comprehensive picture of achievements and gaps along a range of fronts, including areas needing greater focus and investment.

The Index both exposes key data gaps, and demonstrates the importance of better data. Holding governments and decision-makers to account for their international commitments relies on timely and high-quality data that are disaggregated by sex, as well as other relevant characteristics. Progress on the data agenda is critical to inform effective decision-making. The data revolution called for by the 2030 Agenda for Sustainable Development must have women and girls at its heart.

The global rankings on women's inclusion, justice, and security offer multiple insights. They highlight priority areas in which policy reforms and investments are needed to accelerate progress, especially in countries that are performing poorly or where achievements are unbalanced across dimensions. The results show that that few countries perform uniformly well or badly across key indicators of inclusion, justice, and security. By building an integrated picture, we have exposed some key data and evidence gaps and promote consensus around actions to address those gaps.

The analysis and results are designed to both inform and contribute to an evidence-based narrative that inspires political action and social movements. Indeed, a primary objective of the index is to inspire further thought and analysis to better understand the constrainers and enablers of progress for women and girls to meet the international community's goals and commitments.

Notes

1. This chapter draws on work presented in a joint report by Georgetown Institute of Women, Peace, and Security and PRIO, led by Jeni Klugman. The author is grateful to the following people for background statistical and empirical analysis: Amie Gaye, Arjun Krishnan, Patty Chang, Marianne Dahl, and Roudabeh Kishi.
2. For full information on the Index, see GIWPS, https://giwps.georgetown.edu/the-index/.
3. The WomanStats Project offers a database on the status of women, covering over 350 variables. It also includes country rankings for specific topics, such as Women's Physical Security and Laws Concerning Property Rights for Women, estimated at particular points in time: see http://www.womanstats.org/newmapspage.html.
4. "Sustainable Development Goals," https://sustainabledevelopment.un.org/?menu=1300.
5. "Sustainable Development Goal 5," https://sustainabledevelopment.un.org/sdg5.
6. See Coomaraswamy (2015), which calls for using the gender, conflict, and crisis database to inform programming and to facilitate knowledge sharing, following good practice, and disseminating data through an online repository, http://wps.unwomen.org/pdf/en/CH14.pdf.
7. Two steps are basic in estimating any index: normalization and aggregation. Details are available in Klugman (2017). Here we simply note that the Index is constructed as a geometric mean of the arithmetic mean of the normalized scores of the indicators included in each of the three dimensions. A geometric mean was used in order to reflect that, consistent with the SDG agenda, all three dimensions are equally important and that countries are expected to perform well on each dimension.
8. See https://unstats.un.org/sdgs/files/metadata-compilation/Metadata-Goal-5.pdf for an assessment of proposed indicators and challenges.
9. "Goal 5: Achieve Gender Equality and Empower All Women and Girls," March 31, 2016, https://sustainabledevelopment.un.org/post2015/transformingourworld.
10. See in particular the recent work of the Center for International Cooperation at New York University: Steven (2018), http://cic.nyu.edu/programs/sdg16plus.
11. Please see http://wbl.worldbank.org/data/exploretopics/all-indicators.
12. Gender-based violence is vastly underreported phenomenon, especially in formal settings. Palermo et al. (2013) analyze DHS data from 284,281 women in twenty-four countries between 2004 and 2011 and find that, in sum, only 7 percent of the women who experienced gender-based violence reported to a formal source. Estimates of gender-based violence prevalence based on health systems data or on police reports may underestimate the total prevalence of gender-based violence.
13. Database available for download here: UCDP Downloads, http://ucdp.uu.se/downloads/.

14. At the same time Singapore has been dominated by the same political party and family since 1969. The country is ranked as only partly free by Freedom House (aggregate score of 51/100 where 100 is most free) with ratings of 4/7 for both political rights and civil liberties, where 1 is most free. See https://freedomhouse.org/report/freedom-world/2017/singapore.

15. We adopt the Regional Groupings in the UN Women report, "Progress of the World's Women," http://progress.unwomen.org; and for fragile states, the World Bank, http://www.worldbank.org/en/topic/fragilityconflictviolence/brief/harmonized-list-of-fragile-situations.

16. They are, in ascending order: Pakistan, Sierra Leone, Madagascar, Botswana, Tunisia, Haiti, Democratic Republic of the Congo, Liberia, Gabon, Algeria, Myanmar, Nepal, Egypt, Guinea, Malaysia, Cameroon, Republic of the Congo, Lebanon, Kuwait, Mauritania, Qatar, Iraq, Swaziland, Bahrain, Afghanistan, Yemen, Iran, United Arab Emirates, Syria, Sudan, Jordan, and finally Saudi Arabia, with a score of 54.

17. The index ranges from a possible low score of 0 to a high score of 1. The Regional groupings and Developed Country group are from UN Women's *Progress of the World Women 2015–2016* [http://progress.unwomen.org]. The Fragile States group follows the harmonized World Bank definition (http://www.worldbank.org/en/topic/fragilityconflictviolence/brief/harmonized-list-of-fragile-situations). The thirty-five countries in the fragile states group are also included in their respective regions.)

18. Globally there is a correlation between the enactment of quotas and levels of female parliamentary representation, although much more needs to be done to ensure substantive representation: see Krook and Zetterberg (2015). Afghanistan has reserved seat provisions for directly elected positions, decided province-wise by all voters. This is to ensure women's substantive political representation. See Fleschenberg and Bari (2015) for more details on their gender equality implications.

19. It should be noted that Zimbabwe's relatively good performance here appears to reflect the contrast between economic collapse—income per capita fell by more than one-third between 2000 and 2015—against earlier investments in human development which helped to assure women's inclusion, at least for the time being, on such fronts as women's education and employment. A notable exception is the low rate of financial inclusion, not surprising given the recent hyper-inflation.

20. The "Women, Peace, and Security" icon is available here: https://giwps.georgetown.edu/the-index.

References

Begum, R. "Time to Take Action for Women in the United Arab Emirates." Human Rights Watch (Blog), March 8, 2015, https://www.hrw.org/news/2015/03/08/time-take-action-women-united-arab-emirates.

Bunch, C. "Feminism, Peace, Human Rights, and Human Security." *Canadian Women Studies* 22, no. 2 (2002): 6.

Carment, D., S. Langlois-Bertrand, and Y. Samy. "Assessing State Fragility, With a Focus on Climate Change and Refugees: A 2016 Country Indicators for Foreign Policy Report." Country Indicators for Foreign Policy, Norman Paterson School of International Affairs,

Carleton University, Ottawa. March 15, 2016, https://carleton.ca/cifp/wp-content/uploads/CIFP-2016-Fragility-Report-March-16-2016.pdf.

Cooley, A., and J. Snyder, eds. *Ranking the World*. Cambridge: Cambridge University Press, 2015.

European Union Agency for Fundamental Rights. "Violence against Women: An EU-Wide Survey." Main Results Report, 2014.

Fleschenberg, A., and F. Bari. "Unmaking Political Patriarchy through Gender Quotas?" Policy Brief, Publication Series: Reviewing Gender Quotas in Afghanistan and Pakistan, 2015, https://www.boell.de/sites/default/files/unmaking_political_patriarchy_through_gender_quotas1.pdf?dimension1=division_afghanistan.

García-Moreno, C., C. Pallitto, K. Devries, H. Stöckl, C. Watts, and N. Abrahams. "Global and Regional Estimates of Violence against Women: Prevalence and Health Effects of Intimate Partner Violence and Non-Partner Sexual Violence." World Health Organization, 2013, http://www.who.int/reproductivehealth/publications/violence/9789241564625/en.

Global Peace Index, *Global Peace Index 2017*. Institute for Economics & Peace, 2017, http://visionofhumanity.org/app/uploads/2017/06/GPI-2017-Report-1.pdf.

Hanmer, L., and J. Klugman. "Exploring Women's Agency and Empowerment in Developing Countries: Where Do We Stand?" *Feminist Economics* 22, no. 1 (2016): 237–263.

Holt, S., H. Buckley, and S. Whelan. "The Impact of Exposure to Domestic Violence on Children and Young People: A Review of the Literature." *Child Abuse & Neglect* 32, no. 8 (2008): 797–810.

Human Rights Watch. "Burundi: Gang Rapes by Ruling Party Youth." HRW, July 27, 2016, https://www.hrw.org/news/2016/07/27/burundi-gang-rapes-ruling-party-youth.

Kaldor, M. "In Defence of New Wars." *Stability: International Journal of Security and Development* 2, no. 1 (2013).

Kelley, J. G. *Scorecard Diplomacy: Grading States to Influence Their Reputation and Behavior*. Cambridge: Cambridge University Press, 2017.

Klugman, Jeni G. "World Development Report 2017: Gender Based Violence and the Law." *World Development Report*. Washington, D.C. : World Bank Group, 2017, http://documents.worldbank.org/curated/en/611461487586627507/World-development-report-2017-gender-based-violence-and-the-law

Klugman, J., and Tyson, L. "Leave No One Behind: A Call to Action for Gender Equality and Women's Economic Empowerment." UN Secretary-General's High-Level Panel on Women's Economic Empowerment, 2016, http://hlp-wee.unwomen.org/-/media/hlp%20wee/attachments/reports-toolkits/hlp-wee-report-2016-09-call-to-action-en.pdf?la=en.

Krook, M. L., and P. Zetterberg. *Gender Quotas and Women's Representation: New Directions in Research*. New York: Routledge, 2015.

Messner, J. J., N. Haken, H. Blyth, C. Murphy, A. Quinn, G. Lehner, and D. Ganz. "Fragile States Index Annual Report 2017." Fund for Peace, 2017, http://reliefweb.int/sites/reliefweb.int/files/resources/951171705-Fragile-States-Index-Annual-Report-2017.pdf.

Nygard, H. M., T. Wheeler, and H. Urdal. "Options for Measuring Conflict Deaths in Goal 16." Saferworld/PRIO. PRIO Paper, 2016, https://www.prio.org/Publications/Publication/?x=9008.

Palermo, T., J. Bleck, and A. Peterman. "Tip of the Iceberg: Reporting and Gender-Based Violence in Developing Countries." *American Journal of Epidemiology* 179, no. 5 (2013): 602–612.

Regoeczi, W. C., and M. Riedel. The Application of Missing Data Estimation Models to the Problem of Unknown Victim/Offender Relationships in Homicide Cases. *Journal of Quantitative Criminology* 19, no. 2 (2003): 155–183.

Restrepo, J. A., M. Spagat, and J. F. Vargas. Special Data Feature; the Severity of the Colombian Conflict: Cross-Country Datasets versus New Micro-Data. *Journal of Peace Research* 43, no. 1 (2006): 99–115.

Rice, S. E., and S. Patrick. "Index of State Weakness in the Developing World." *Global Economy and Development*. Brookings Institution, 2008, https://www.brookings.edu/wp-content/uploads/2016/06/02_weak_states_index.pdf.

Salem, O. "FNC Investigates Domestic Violence Problem in UAE." *The National*, January 27, 2015, http://www.thenational.ae/uae/courts/fnc-investigates-domestic-violence-problem-in-uae.

Steven, David. "Justice for All: Challenge Paper for the First Meeting of the Task Force on Justice", Center on International Cooperation, New York: New York University, 2018, https://cic.nyu.edu/challenge-paper-task-force-on-justice.

True, J. "Winning the Battle but Losing the War on Violence: A Feminist Perspective on the Declining Global Violence Thesis." *International Feminist Journal of Politics* 17, no. 4 (2015): 554–572.

UN Women. "Transforming Justice, Securing the Peace. A Global Study on the Implementation of United Nations Security Council Resolution 1325 (2000)." Lead author: Radhika Coomaraswamy. UN Women, 2015, http://wps.unwomen.org/pdf/en/GlobalStudy_EN_Web.pdf.

Uppsala Conflict Data Program (UCDP). "Definitions, Sources, and Methods for Uppsala Conflict Data Program Battle-Death Estimates." Department of Peace and Conflict Research, Uppsala University, 41 (2006): 3–4. http://ucdp.uu.se/downloads/old/brd/ucdp-brd-conf-41-2006.pdf.

Vigaud-Walsh, F. "Women and Girls Failed: The Burundian Refugee Response in Tanzania." Washington, DC: Refugees International, 2015, https://www.refugeesinternational.org/s/20151222-Tanzania.pdf.

CHAPTER 60

....

PURSUING GENDER
SECURITY

....

AISLING SWAINE

THE concept of security has long been subject to debate, variably attached to the security of the state, while, increasingly, if tentatively, linked to the security of people. Even where centered around "people," approaches taken to advance security within global policy spaces have not comprehensively or equally included all. Nor has the development of policy approaches to security been grounded in the ways that social norms will influence what security is and means for differing people in different social contexts. Feminist scholars and activists have advocated for a gendered understanding of security, making it relevant to the lives of women and girls and the ways that gender norms and inequalities underpin connections in insecurities across public and private spaces. That is an understanding of security that gives as much legitimacy and attention to security in personal and interpersonal realms, to the ways that insecurities are empirically experienced within intimate lives and relationships, as that situated within political and public spaces and systems.

As discussed in earlier chapters in this handbook, the Women, Peace, and Security (WPS) agenda was, in many ways, a step toward that idea. UN Security Council (UNSC) Resolution 1325 represented an effort to draw gender as a framework into the wider realm of international peace and security. It was an attempt to reform the perception that concepts and experiences of peace and security, and responses to them, are gender neutral. Rather, by introducing women's specific and gendered experiences of conflict, and making visible women's exclusion from policy processes, the agenda pointed to how the current state of global affairs operates from an exclusionary gender dynamic that inherently disfavors women. As argued by Terrell Carver, social, political and economic systems globally rely on the "stealth devalue[ing] of the feminine" to operate and exercise power and influence (Carver 2014: 115–116). Power evolves covertly and overtly on the basis of the resulting gendered ranking, presenting a perceived "natural" advantage for masculinity. Where masculinity is understood to operate in both a gendered mode, men claiming identities as male, as well as a de-gendered mode, as representing the "generic human," those claiming masculine identity, men, may also claim representation of all human beings (Carver 2014: 117). In turn, the systems of international relations are attributed the same assumed generic and neutral status that, when viewed through the prism of gender, are evidently covertly coded masculine. Gender neutrality, and the idea that systems of peace and security are gender neutral, thereby becomes impossible. Rather, as long argued by feminists, systems of international affairs and security are endemically gendered in nature (Tickner 1992). The WPS agenda was an essential step toward unveiling the privileging of these generic overt and covert masculinized norms of security and the need to tackle the ways that these generate exclusion and harm for women.

Where the endeavor to advance understanding of security through a gendered prism has got to is the subject of this chapter. Focusing on gender with respect to insecurities in women's lives, this chapter looks back as well as forwards. To do so, it considers what may be meant by the idea of gendered security and how may it be pursued going forward? The chapter begins at the beginning, first setting out a frame for understanding gender and security and then discussing where and how concepts of gendered security came about in global policy spaces. It maps the trajectory of the emergence of gendered understandings of security and how these have fared in respect of the evolution of relevant global policy. It sets out three critical elements of gender security as a concept as it has emerged and continues to find positioning going forward. This is followed by exploring suggestions for key policy areas and issues that require engagement for pursuing gender security going forward.

Gendering Security

In considering the pursuit of gender security, we must first ask, what is ultimately being pursued? I borrow from Gunhild Hoogensen and Svein Vigeland Rottem to further ask "are we on a mission to securitize all and sundry?" (2004: 156). What might securitizing some or all of the inequalities, issues, and interests in women's lives imply and result in? Pursuing an understanding of gender security has been driven by an ultimate necessity: to redefine the ways that security has been nominally conceived and understood (Cockburn 2013: 441). This has meant transforming the idea that it is the state that holds the capacity and thereby the monopoly on defining what security is and means (Hoogensen and Stuvøy 2006: 211). Importantly, it also means upending assumptions that the predominant understanding of security (as employed in dominant academic disciplines and international institutions) is impartial and generically relevant, whether to individual people or variant social contexts. Ultimately, advancing feminist understandings of security attempts to redraw the assumptions that underpin reductive militarized approaches to security, toward one redefined by an understanding of the subtle and not-so-subtle systems of power that disadvantage some over others.

Historically, a belief in two distinctive categories of male and female with oppositional qualities that empower masculine over feminine, has conditioned society to accept a taken-for-granted idea of the dominance of the generic or neutral masculine, systematically disadvantaging women (Cohn 2013). Gender and its workings thereby should be understood less as a binary and more as a hierarchy (Carver 2014: 116), with significant if omnipotent influence over the construction of roles, norms, and power within political as well as private spheres. Gendering security is a means to refocus the concept's normative basis toward this dynamic and ground it in the ways that gender norms structure people's lives (and in respect to the scope of this chapter, a focus on women's lives). From this viewpoint, gender as a lens brings about an understanding of security that "reflects the empirical world and becomes open to the voices of those who in fact experience insecurity in all its variations and manifestations" (Hoogensen and Stuvøy 2006: 211). It is an understanding of security that is infused with the relevance of politicized understandings of gender that point to the dynamic of power relations, ultimately transforming inequalities across women's lives.

In furthering the pursuit of this complex understanding of security going forward, we must first consider its "beginnings" within global policy and how far that has come in respect of the gendered complexity of security. What were the origins of pursuing an idea of security that was rooted in an understanding of the gendered social order and women's place in it? A starting point for consideration of this question is the early organized activism of women's movements aimed at furthering peace and security. The first Women's Peace Congress in The Hague in 1915 attempted to influence multilateral negotiations and bring an end to World War I. The congress adopted a resolution that made the critical link between the rights of women and the prevention of warfare, and the insecurities it brought with it. It stated opposition to "the assumption that women can be protected under the conditions of modern warfare" and protested "the horrible violation of women which attends all war" (International Congress of Women 1915: Articles 2, 9). While the links between women's liberation and the achievement of peace were debated within this movement (Confortini 2012: 10), from these beginnings, security, the prevention of conflict, and the political rights of women were tentatively intertwined.

As feminists increasingly raised critical questions and observations of the social world, gender evolved as the frame through which continuums of inequalities, misogyny, and violence were identified and mapped across all facets of women's lives. An understanding of the impacts of militarism on women's everyday lives was also advanced, exposing the multifaceted nature of everyday insecurities and their relationship with the military industrial complex (Enloe 2000; 1988). Feminist activists identified the ways that insecurities for women presented across multiple spheres, from intimate violence in the home, to economic security and political freedoms and authority (Cockburn 2004; Moser 2001; Kelly 1998). While much of feminist thinking and activism evolved outside of multilateral systems, the establishment of the UN provided a focal point to again, and on a sustained basis, attempt to influence global multilateral peace and security processes. The UN presented the opportunity and entry point through which to advance feminist understandings of women's lives into the emerging global policies and norms that would impact them. The evolving UN system also presented challenges, however, namely in whether and how the complex concept of gender would be captured and become employed, particularly in the arena of peace and security, with its very definite militarist basis.

Through the UN women's world conferences from the 1970s, insecurities impacting women within and outside of armed conflict were progressively captured within UN debate and outcome documents (Cockburn 2013: 442). The growing legitimacy of concepts of human rights were drawn upon and new normative frameworks evolved. The concept of human security which evolved within the UN system during the 1990s made it possible for different kinds of insecurity to be understood in respect of human need and experience (United Nations Development Programme (UNDP) 1994). However, "[w]ithout gender analysis, a fundamental power relation is erased from reality" (UNDP 1994: 212) and even with human-centered approaches, more is required in respect of parsing out the gendered norms that underpin the human experience, particularly in the empirical world.

A human-centric security focused on the individual remains an assumed universal or generic (and also thereby masculine) reading of the human experience of security, unless the gendered underpinnings of that experience are acknowledged. People's lives are not generic, but rather gendered. They are in turn made to map into an assumed generic order. The gendered nature of that order requires attention so that the human-centric focus on security goes beyond the individual to cognizance of the gender norms that give meaning to that individual's life and experiences of insecurities, in context. Human security approaches that have evolved have still required a gender analysis so that what is normalized and covert in respect of gender hierarchies is illuminated as the political basis of the range of inequalities that generate and sustain multifaceted human insecurities in the first place.

The Beijing Platform for Action (BPFA) adopted in 1995 (United Nations 1995) was the first, and possibly the most progressive normative outcome document, to outline a comprehensive critical framework that fully draws complex linkages between gender, national security, development, economic growth, militarism, and empowerment for women. The BPFA frequently references power, power relations, and power structures as the basis for the critical discriminations and obstacles in women's lives. It pushed for a much-needed reduction in militarization and increased spending on social and economic initiatives that would advance the status of women. It set out "an active and visible policy of mainstreaming a gender perspective into all policies and programmes" taken by the UN system and its members "so that before decisions are taken an analysis is made of the effects on women and men, respectively" (United Nations 1995: Strategic Action E). This gendered framing, and linkages to wider economic, security, and social imperatives, offered a comprehensive and progressive approach to security within global policy, drawing links between macro and micro level policy processes, from the public to the private spheres.

These developments of the 1990s offered the critical entry point for the advent of a clear tie in policy between concepts of gender and security. The call for and adoption of UN Security Council Resolution 1325 (UNSC 2000) was motivated by acknowledgment of gendered norms and hierarchies that infuse prevailing understandings of security. The resolution stems from the need to bring changes to discriminatory gender norms and to fulfill women's rights (UN Women 2015: 15), a normative basis for which had been absent specifically from the peace and security realm. The basis of the adoption of Resolution 1325 is to build on the provision for gender mainstreaming made by the BPFA and later officially adopted as the UN strategy toward the achievement of gender equality (United Nations 1997), and bring that into the security realm. The adoption of the seven subsequent WPS resolutions have established further institutional modalities that work to mainstream gender within the substantive focus and ways of working of all facets of the global peace and security realm.

Gains have clearly been made since the link between women's political rights and security were tentatively begun in the 1915 women's congress. Recognition of the inter-relationship between concepts of gender and security has been advanced; the voices of women and gendered insecurities within women's lives have been made visible; the global multilateral system has adopted gender and gender equality as a frame for its work through normative developments such as the BPFA; the foremost multilateral security institution in the world has adopted a series of resolutions that are drawn from and aim toward ideas of gendered security. However, while an instrument such as the BPFA offers a more comprehensive articulation of gender security, its normative status leaves it with little legal might; and while the WPS resolutions have gained much more traction than the BPFA, becoming "the most significant normative framework" relating to gender and security (True 2016), they are also estimated to fall short of achieving a comprehensive approach to gender security. On the one hand, it was aptly strategic that the UN's security body, the Security Council, which has the mandate to make the UN's decisions on peace and security (United Nations 1945), has been to the forefront of evolving gender security through global policy. This brought gender and gender mainstreaming right into the heart of the international security realm. On the other hand, while the WPS agenda is groundbreaking in this regard, because of the framing offered through the Security Council's mandate, it may be questioned whether the WPS resolutions fulfill and drive a comprehensive understanding of gender security. The transformative elements of the pursuit of gender security earlier described—changing gender power relations, redefining the meaning and understanding of security, militarism, and norms that determine discriminatory practices of security—are somewhat missing from the language of the resolutions. The concept of "gender" does not appear within the resolutions in an explicitly political feminist way—for example, in ways that specifically articulate the structural basis of the gender norms that inhibit the rights of women, and that have determined generic concepts and understandings of security that are exclusionary of women. Rather, the implicit focus given to women appears in the resolutions "in the form of a binary opposition between men and women in which women-in-general were subordinate to men-in-general" missing the opportunity to "foster [the] critical consciousness" (Cornwall 2014: 128, 137) that is required for engagement with a comprehensive understanding of the gendered hierarchies that are institutionalized through current approaches to security.

As a result, what has tended to occur in practice is a focus on security as determined by and instrumental to the Security Council and its membership. Under this approach, gender and women's positioning is integrated and becomes "securitised" in line with existing definitions, rather than the systems reflecting a gendered understanding of multifaceted securities offered through the more fulsome idea of "gender security." Women's rights are addressed only as far as they are instrumental to pursuing existing definitions of security, and modes of conflict prevention, response and resolution (Hudson 2009). In this integrationist mode of application, traditional concepts of security remain intact and are paramount in how the agenda becomes applied in practice, with women's rights per se taking a secondary role (Hudson 2009). Making gender security palatable to security actors in this instrumentalist way more often than not comes into tension with the transformative end of the approach more akin to the idea of gender security earlier outlined. A transformative approach is rooted in human rights norms and is about reforming the very ways and means of understanding and doing security, overturning militarization and structural inequalities as the root of the current gendered order. In this mode of understanding and application, the traditional notions of peace and security are challenged, and key equality concerns that drive a focus on peace rather than militarism inform implementation.

In some estimations, the more reductive instrumental and integrationist approach has taken precedence since the inception of the WPS agenda, diminishing its gender and equality basis and shrinking the wider gains made on women's rights (Otto 2010). Nonetheless, it must be acknowledged that while this approach does not fulfill women and girl's rights *because they are entitled to human rights*, it does make gendered concerns palatable to adoption by security actors who may not otherwise accept its relevance (Hudson

2009). In this mode, instrumentalist approaches have garnered substantive engagement on women's rights and needs globally within peace and security policy and programming. It is the case that steps forward that are essentially instrumental in approach can lead to longer-term and strategic gains. For example, security actors, such as peacekeeping battalions, may increase the number of female officers as a means to enhance operational effectiveness, such as gathering better and varied intelligence from host country civilian women. The growing presence of female officers may however lead to longer-term changes in cultural acceptance of women's right to hold senior roles in security operations, the appointment of women to senior positions, an enhanced understanding of the need for gendered analysis of security situations, and better responses to the empirical and longer-term needs of women in the host population (Puechguirbal 2003; Dharmapuri 2013).

While the approaches taken to date offer much and lend themselves toward longer-term strategic changes, much like the critique of broader women's rights instruments, the WPS resolutions, which are to the forefront of advancing gender security through policy and practice, are characterized by depoliticized ideas of gender that rely on integrating women rather than the political project of upending inequalities (Taylor 2007). From the Women's Peace Congress in 1915 to the Beijing conference in 1995, and the advent of the WPS agenda in the new millennium, challenges remain in evolving a political understanding of gender hierarchies of power in ways that make practical changes in how international security is approached. It may be argued that a *selective* gendered security prevails, whereby a reductive version of a gendered analysis of security neutered of radical political and transformational potential in and of itself, has become employed. Gains toward a political and comprehensive understanding of gender security that tends to the transformational remains evolving and this is where the potential lies for the pursuit of gender security going forward. Critical consideration is still required of whether advancing gender security is dependent on a zero-sum approach of securitizing some or all of the inequalities, issues, and interests in women's lives in order to garner a response to them. Or instead, more effort is made to connect the transformative potential and tenets set out in the WPS resolutions with the broader peace and security realm it is meant to influence. Moving from a narrow and selective to a comprehensive gendered security requires building upon and going beyond 1915—to the foundation offered by human rights in the contemporary era and an understanding of gender beyond bifurcated relations between men and women.

Going Forward: Pursuing Gender Security

Global policy approaches to peace and security will continue to evolve on the basis of an assumed gender neutrality unless a comprehensive and transformational gendered lens of security is applied. "UNSCR 1325 is a human rights mandate" (UN Women 2015: 15), and its success requires the entire system thinking and acting in ways conscious of gendered inequalities and the transformational end of what is meant by gender security. The critical basis for the advancement of a comprehensive gender security is the practical implementation of the foundations that are laid in instruments such as the WPS agenda. The "depoliticising tendency of a bureaucratic gender mainstreaming" approach (Taylor 2007: 74) that begins as instrumentalism can be built on so that the political context to the steps taken is given more attention and engagement. Often, it is the practical or integrationist engagement on women's interests that allows an entry point for broader understanding of gender and women's rights to be made visible. It is critical that practical engagement on women's needs and interests is then used as a basis to further more strategic, longer-term and equality focused approaches (Moser 1993; Swaine 2016). Pursuing gender security thereby requires ensuring that gender mainstreaming approaches simultaneously address women's interests, or in instrumentalist ways engage with or integrate women, while at the same time, concurrently building on the steps taken and gains made to promote and advance equality-focused agendas that work toward gender transformation (Moser 2014). Rather than resting at the point of securitizing women's rights, steps toward security and peace are developed on the basis of illuminating the bias inherent in the normative ways of doing. Links between women's rights and participation are recognized as not just tentative, but central to what is an acceptable standard of peace and security. And that realization is mapped into all facets of global approaches to the achievement of a security inclusive of all.

Moving the instrumental or practical toward the strategic requires a depth of understanding of the concept of gender and the potential that gender security offers. Going forward, I highlight some elements of security that, when made visible and engaged with, may support further attention toward a more transformational approach. These are elements that build on the requirements of making women's rights instrumental or simply integrating them to the existing system, to getting at the underpinning inequalities that make the need for a comprehensive concept of gender security within global policy so important.

Pursuing gender security requires critical understanding and engagement with the strategic and practical elements of achieving security:

- security as *economic or material:* recognition is required of the basic facets of everyday survival for individuals and that these are as significant as broad macroeconomic imperatives that states prioritize as part of their specific frameworks of national security. Understanding that meeting women's interests and rights begins with ensuring they can practically sustain themselves and their families remains a gap. The links between women's basic needs (e.g., food, water), often neglected, for example, in humanitarian operations, and how those needs determine broader economic security, as well as contribute to, for example, protection from insecurities (e.g., sexual exploitation, sexual attacks when collecting water), requires further action through implementation of the WPS agenda (Swaine 2016);
- security as inherently *political:* mapping security from private to public, and identifying underlying connections between insecurities in the home across differing spaces. For example, there remains need for recognition within the WPS agenda of the links between women's experience of violence in the home and the ways that women will be targeted for sexual violence in conflict; and the underpinning basis of this violence in gender inequalities;
- security as *sociocultural and contextually specific:* deeper recognition is required of the ways that security and insecurities are structurally influenced and will vary across culturally diverse gendered social orders. Approaches are required that do not treat security as a monolith concept centered on the state, but rather variant, fluid, and changing depending on the context. This includes recognition of insecurities that

women and men will identify that may differ greatly from the universal idea of security that the state or security actors prioritize during and after conflict. Implementation of the WPS agenda, whether by security actors or policy makers, requires recognition of who is defining what security is and means, and who does not get their voices heard. For example, peace-building measures require more engagement with the ways that women of differing identities will determine what security for them is and means after a conflict—whether that's securing a sustainable income, not being forced to live in the vicinity of perpetrators of mass violence, or ownership rights over land and property. Making the link from the practical (securing a basic income) to the strategic (women's property rights) is imperative for implementation of the WPS agenda to achieve a comprehensive security.

Ultimately, gendered understanding of the political, economic, societal, and contextual facets of security ensures that the fundamental power relations that determine the meaning of security per individual and collective identities, are recognized. If gendered security is about countering state monopoly on defining security, and advancing security for humans beyond assumed gender neutrality to the gendered nature of insecurities, engagement with these critical elements is required, so that over time, current selective or reductive approaches may be advanced toward a comprehensive security.

With that in mind, going forward, the isolation of the WPS agenda within the confines of the UN Security Council and its mandate requires unshackling and comprehensive approaches to gendered security need to be advanced across all initiatives relating to peace and security. I argue that two conceptual frames, human rights and inclusivity, are critical underpinning concepts for comprehensive gender security to be achieved. I then analyze how global processes related to development and peace could be informed by a comprehensive notion of gendered security.

Human Rights

Reorienting the securitization of the concept of gender toward the normative and practical effect offered through human rights frameworks will provide a route toward a more comprehensive and potentially transformative effect. As Catherine O'Rourke discusses elsewhere in this handbook, the Convention on the Elimination of Discrimination against Women (United Nations 1979), and particularly its General Recommendation No. 30 (GR 30) (United Nations 2013), provide a means to link the WPS agenda directly with human rights frameworks. The focus on conflict and security through CEDAW is grounded in human rights principles, portending to the transformational potential of drawing gender into those security realms. In the CEDAW Committee's constructive dialogues, the aims and tasks set out by the WPS agenda are examined on the basis that "their implementation must be premised on a model of substantive equality and cover all rights enshrined in the Convention" (United Nations 2013: para. 26). Going forward, an approach that draws CEDAW and the WPS resolutions together will advance a more fulsome conceptual and practical approach to achieving gendered security (O'Rourke and Swaine 2015).

Inclusivity

To pursue a fulsome gendered security, more attention is required to unique empirical experiences of insecurities for individuals. This is a cognizance of the "individual" and "human" security that, as discussed before, goes beyond the assumed universal or covert masculinized generic human, to the gendered nature of social and political location. Further, it is cognizance and response to the ways that individual identity characteristics and their gender normative ordering will create specific insecurities, inequalities, and marginalization. Implementation of the WPS agenda, for example, is not currently resulting in attention to differing women and the conditions of differing social contexts. An inclusivity analysis of nine WPS National Action Plans in the Asia-Pacific region for example, found that the degree to which action plans address multiple and intersecting identity factors of women and girls varies considerably. This is in a context where women of multiple racial, ethnic, religious, political, and other identities are involved in, caught up in, and experiencing conflict and its aftermath, and an approach responsive to those realities should be standard. These plans, that in effect strive toward achieving gendered security, are not necessarily translating into actions that are accountable to women of differing identities, or tackling differing and intersecting sources of discriminations (Swaine 2016).

While engaging with the uniqueness of experience requires balance with the blanket approach required by policy, engaging with multiplicities of inequalities is not a new endeavor for women themselves. Women caught up in conflict are navigating those contexts with acute awareness of how their ethnicity, age, bodily abilities, and other factors inform risk as well as mobility, and ultimately their security, within conflict and political spaces. The actors, entities, and technocratic solutions to the gaps in women's rights in conflict and to gendered security simply have to catch up. The complexity of the multiplier effect of the convergence of identity factors within specific social and political systems of discrimination requires attention in programming and policy. This would mean for example that women with disabilities receive services, while at the same time ensuring that their voices inform peace-building measures in the longer-term, and specific actions are taken to advance their rights. Further, attention is needed to the ways that in contemporary conflicts addressing intersectional identities is not just about how characteristics such as gender, age, ethnicity, and ability come together to generate sustained social, political, and economic exclusions, but also how some identity characteristics will take on hyper political significance due to the exigencies and drivers of a conflict. More and more contemporary conflicts and conflict violence are driven by identity politics (UN Women 2015: 21). Policy approaches must respond to identity dynamics in context in order to further inclusivity and moves toward comprehensive gendered security.

Going forward and addressing this critical gap in the WPS agenda, "the aim is not to show that one group is more victimized or privileged than another, but to reveal meaningful distinctions and similarities in order to overcome discriminations and put the conditions in place for all people to fully enjoy their human rights" (Symington 2004: 2). Approaches should be framed by critical analysis that uncovers *who are the women and what are the specifics of gendered insecurity for them that processes of development, peace, and security should be tailored to in this social context?*

The relationship with CEDAW again offers most potential here. CEDAW recognizes the need for states to address all forms of "gender-based discrimination" which are "inextricably linked with other factors that affect women, such as race, ethnicity, religion or belief, health, status, age, class, caste, and sexual orientation and gender identity" (United Nations 2010: paras 5, 18). The CEDAW Committee has outlined that "an identical or neutral treatment of women and men might constitute discrimination" where "such treatment resulted in or had the effect of women being denied the exercise of a right because there was no recognition of the pre-existing gender-based disadvantage and inequality that women face" (United Nations 2010: para. 5). In GR 30, the Committee requests that states address the needs of women "subjected to multiple and intersecting forms of discrimination, including women with disabilities, older women, girls, widows, women who head households, pregnant women, women living with HIV/AIDS, rural women, indigenous women, women belonging to ethnic, national, sexual or religious minorities, and women human rights defenders" (Committee on the Elimination of Discrimination against Women 2013: para. 57 [b]). The human rights and inclusivity lens furthers normative and practical implementation that inch closer to diversified and more comprehensive understandings of security.

Sustainable Development and Sustainable Peace

Three major reviews of the peace and security architecture of the United Nations system that were conducted in 2015 all broadly pointed to the changing nature of conflict, the rising numbers of deaths from conflict globally, the increasing range of actors within contemporary armed conflicts, and the differing roles women and girls might play. These reviews identified similar findings and critical steps required going forward. They all found that across the UN system, investment in the prevention of conflict is fundamentally lacking (Advisory Group of Experts 2015; High-Level Independent Panel on Peace Operations 2015; UN Women 2015). Conflict prevention through sustaining development and positive peace is a critical aspect of achieving gendered security, and, of course, achieving gender equality contributes to stable and secure societies. Sustainable development as a prerequisite to the prevention of armed conflict not only requires more engagement with human rights, inclusivity, and comprehensive ideas of gendered security, but also with that of sustainable, positive peace. The challenge of the UN architecture's current framework—development done here (UN General Assembly) and security done there (UN Security Council) is ultimately a major barrier to a comprehensive approach to development and security. In turn, the rivalry between human rights based versus securitized approaches, in what are sometimes exclusive, and more often shared, spaces of development and security, prevents understanding of gendered security as a prerequisite to global peace and security.

A UN Security Council resolution adopted in 2016 offers hope. Resolution 2282 (United Nations Security Council 2016) commits in its operational paragraphs: "[T]o promote an integrated, strategic and coherent approach to peacebuilding, noting that security, development and human rights are closely interlinked and mutually reinforcing;" (op. 4 ([b]) *[B]y emphasizing that* sustaining peace requires coherence between the General Assembly, the Security Council, and the Economic and Social Council (op. 2), it ultimately sets out ways forward:

> Stress[ing] the importance of closer cooperation between the Economic and Social Council and Peacebuilding Commission, in accordance with their respective mandates, including

through enhanced dialogue in support of promoting coherence and complementarity between the United Nations' peace and security efforts and its development, human rights and humanitarian work, and encourages the Peacebuilding Commission to draw on the expertise of relevant Economic and Social Council subsidiary bodies, as appropriate (op. 10).

To draw together the foundational tenets of the normative frameworks and practical work of the Security Council, CEDAW and broader human rights agendas, the BPFA, and the 2030 agenda for sustainable development, would be a radical change in approach. Where the 2030 agenda places an emphasis on "inclusive societies," and the interconnectedness of sustainable development with peace and security (United Nations 2015: para. 20, 35), an entry point for comprehensive gendered security emerges. The importance of women's non-militaristic approaches to operational as well as structural forms of conflict prevention would also become relevant here. As emphasized in the Global Study, women's peace dialogues in locations such as South Sudan, women-run situation rooms in multiple countries monitoring for and preventing political violence at times of elections, all contribute to non-forceful yet sustainable approaches to the prevention of conflict (UN Women 2015: 195). Peace and, thereby, comprehensive security, inextricably linked with and reliant on the achievement of gender equality, is reliant on the system operating in more congruent ways. Implementation of the WPS agenda in ways that secure gendered peace and a gendered security means working across all bodies of the architecture on peace, development, and human rights, so that much like building peace, pursuing gendered security as part of that, is an inherently political endeavor.

CONCLUSION

The enterprise of pursuing gender security has brought with it a series of successes and setbacks. It has required reappraising existing ways of considering security and injecting those with keen and critical questions about women's lives and gendered power dynamics, often employing academic frames of discourse in spaces that do not welcome such questioning. It has meant critiquing institutions for militarist and statist approaches to security, while at the same time engaging with those same institutions as the modalities through which practical change can be achieved. It has become an enduring strategy of attempting to tackle and prevent the causes of war, while striking a delicate balance in maintaining a pacifist centric approach that requires working through and compromising with the very institutions that instigate and exist to manage war and its impacts. Pursuing gender security has meant arguing for acknowledgment of "war and gender relations as mutually shaping" each other (Cockburn 2013: 445). It is thereby a complex endeavor that requires understanding security, war, and gender as concepts in and of themselves in disaggregated ways; and at the same time illuminating the impossibility of disaggregating one from the other: war and insecurity cannot be understood without understanding their gendered nature, while the dynamics of contemporary gender relations are inseparable from the insidious influence of norms of militarism and militarized masculinities that overtly and covertly infuse our societies.

The value of the concept of gender security is the frame that gender brings an understanding of relations of power within how security is conceived and furthered.

"Since 1325's passage, feminists inside and outside the UN have put tremendously creative thought and energy into making it a living document—an ongoing commitment for the Security Council, rather than a one-time rhetorical gesture" (Cohn 2004: 8). Going forward, it is not that human rights, development, and peace-building must be securitized in order for gender security to be achieved. Rather, global policy and programming processes must be infused with and operate through interconnectedness. That interconnectedness is enabled by working from and through the underlying thread that is common across them all: gender inequalities, multiple and intersecting gendered identities that operate within multifarious gendered orders globally. These are the orders in which insecurity is experienced and through which development, peace, and security must be pursued. It is thereby imperative that the normative ideas of rights and equality have a practical affect within and across development, human rights, and peace-building, all of which is available through, and will achieve, a global comprehensive gendered security.

References

Advisory Group of Experts. "The Challenge of Sustaining Peace: Report of the Advisory Group of Experts for the 2015 Review of the United Nations Peacebuilding Architecture." June 29, 2015, https://reliefweb.int/report/world/challenge-sustaining-peace-report-advisory-group-experts-2015-review-united-nations.

Carver, T. "Men and Masculinities in International Relations Research." *Brown Journal of World Affairs* 21, no. 1 (2014): 113–126.

Cockburn, C. "The Continuum of Violence: A Gender Perspective on War and Peace." In *Sites of Violence: Gender and Conflict Zones*, edited by W. Giles and J. Hyndman, 24–44. Berkeley: University of California Press, 2004.

Cockburn, C. "War and Security, Women and Gender: An Overview of the Issues. *Gender & Development* 21, no. 3 (2013): 433–452.

Cohn, C. "Feminist Peacemaking." *The Women's Review of Books* 21, no. 5 (2004): 8–9.

Cohn, C. "Women and Wars: Towards a Conceptual Framework." In *Women and Wars*, 1–35. Cambridge, UK: Polity Press, 2013.

Confortini, C. C. *Intelligent Compassion: Feminist Critical Methodology in the Women's International League for Peace and Freedom.* New York: Oxford University Press, 2012.

Cornwall, A. "Taking Off International Development's Straightjacket of Gender." *Brown Journal of World Affairs* 21, no. 1 (2014): 127–139.

Dharmapuri, S. *Not Just a Numbers Game: Increasing Women's Participation in UN Peacekeeping.* New York: International Peace Institute, 2013.

Enloe, C. *Does Khaki Become You?* London: Pluto Press, 1988.

Enloe, C. *Maneuvers: The International Politics of Militarizing Women's Live.* Berkeley: University of California Press, 2000.

High-Level Independent Panel on Peace Operations. "Report of the High-level Independent Panel on Peace Operations on Uniting Our Strengths for Peace: Politics, Partnership, and People." New York: United Nations General Assembly, Security Council, A/70/95, S/2015/446, 2015.

Hoogensen, G., and S. V. Rottem. "Gender Identity and the Subject of Security." *Security Dialogue* 35 (2004): 155–171.

Hoogensen, G., and K. Stuvøy. "Gender, Resistance, and Human Security." *Security Dialogue* 37, no. 2 (2006): 207–228.

Hudson, N. F. "Securitizing Women's Rights and Gender Equality." *Journal of Human Rights* 8, no. 1 (2009): 53–70.

International Congress of Women. *Resolutions Adopted.* The Hague, April 28–May 1, 1915.

Kelly, L. *Surviving Sexual Violence.* Cambridge, UK: Polity Press, 1998.

Moser, Caroline. *Gender Planning and Development: Theory, Practice, and Training.* New York and London: Routledge, 1993.

Moser, Caroline O. N. "The Gendered Continuum of Violence and Conflict: An Operational Framework." In *Victims, Perpetrators, or Actors? Gender, Armed Conflict, and Political Violence,* 30–52. New York: Zed Books, 2001.

Moser, Caroline O. N. "Gender Planning and Development: Revisiting, Deconstructing, and Reflecting." DPU60 Working Paper Series: Reflections No. 165/60, 2014.

O'Rourke, C., and A. Swaine. *Guidebook on CEDAW General Recommendation No. 30 and the Security Council Resolutions on Women, Peace, and Security.* New York: UN Women, 2015.

Otto, Dianne. "Power and Danger: Feminist Engagement with International Law through the UN Security Council." *Australian Feminist Law Journal* 32 (2010): 97–121.

Puechguirbal, N. *Gender Training for Peacekeepers: Lessons from the DRC. International Peacekeeping* 10, no. 4 (2003): 113–128.

Swaine, A. "Making Women's and Girl's Needs, Wellbeing, and Rights Central to National Action Plans in the Asia-Pacific Region." UN Women, 2016.

Symington, A. *Intersectionality: A Tool for Gender and Economic Justice.* Women's Rights and Economic Change, No. 9. Toronto: Association for Women in Development, August 2004.

Taylor, M. "Gender and the White Paper on Irish Aid." *Trocaire Development Review* (2007): 65–77.

Tickner, J. A. *Gender in International Relations.* New York: Columbia University Press, 1992.

True, J. "Explaining the Global Diffusion of the Women, Peace, and Security Agenda." *International Political Science Review* 37, no. 3 (2016): 307–323.

United Nations. "Beijing Declaration and Platform for Action." A/conf.177/20 and A/conf.177/20/add. Fourth World Conference on Women, Beijing, September 15, 1995.

United Nations. "Charter of the United Nations." San Francisco: United Nations, 1945.

United Nations. "Convention on the Elimination of Discrimination against Women." CEDAW, December 18, 1979.

United Nations. "Transforming Our World: The 2030 Agenda for Sustainable Development." A/RES/70/1, United Nations General Assembly, 2015.

United Nations. "UN Economic and Social Council Resolution 1997/2: Agreed Conclusions." UN Economic and Social Council. ECOSOC, July 18 1997.

United Nations Committee on the Elimination of Discrimination against Women. "General Recommendation No. 28 on the Core Obligations of States Parties under Article 2 of the Convention on the Elimination of All Forms of Discrimination against Women." CEDAW/C/2010/47/GC.2, Geneva: United Nations, 2010.

United Nations Committee on the Elimination of Discrimination against Women. "General Recommendation No. 30 on Women in Conflict Prevention, Conflict, and Post-Conflict Situations." CEDAW/C/2010/47/GC.2, Geneva: United Nations, 2013.

United Nations Development Programme (UNDP). "Human Development Report." New York: United Nations, 1994.

United Nations Security Council. "Resolution 1325." S/RES/1325(2000), New York: United Nations, 2000.

United Nations Security Council. "Resolution 2282." S/RES/2282 (2016), New York: United Nations, 2016.

UN Women. "Transforming Justice, Securing the Peace. A Global Study on the Implementation of United Nations Security Council Resolution 1325 (2000)." Lead author: Radhika Coomaraswamy. UN Women, 2015, http://wps.unwomen.org/pdf/en/GlobalStudy_EN_Web.pdf.

CHAPTER 61

....

THE CHALLENGE OF FOREIGN POLICY IN THE WPS AGENDA

....

VALERIE M. HUDSON AND LAUREN A. EASON

MARGOT Wallström, appointed Swedish foreign minister in the fall of 2014, has famously articulated that her nation will follow a "feminist foreign policy." Sweden is one of the largest foreign aid donors in the world on a per capita basis. Sweden is also one of the largest arms exporters in the world, again on a per capita basis. Are these foreign policy choices consistent? Are they feminist?

Hillary Clinton, while US Secretary of State, similarly articulated a foreign policy in which the subjugation of women was deemed a security threat to the United States (Hudson and Leidl 2015). The Quadrennial Diplomacy and Development Review (QDDR) of 2010, written first under her watch and designed to put Diplomacy/Development planning on a par with defense planning, asserted, "The protection and empowerment of women and girls is key to the foreign policy and security of the United States . . . To that end, women are at the center of our diplomacy and development efforts—not simply as beneficiaries, but also as agents of peace, reconciliation, development, growth, and stability" (US Department of State 2010: 23). The QDDR was, among other things, an exercise in gender-mainstreaming, with 133 references to women and girls within its 220 pages. And yet Clinton advocated a Responsibility to Protect (R2P) operation in Libya that set the situation of Libyan women back decades, and never raised, at least in public, any issues concerning women with US ally Saudi Arabia.

It seems, then, that there are both conceptual issues as well as practical barriers to the implementation of a feminist foreign policy. The experiences of these two nations, one a very powerful nation and one an international norm leader on gender equality, will be instructive as we probe the potential of a feminist foreign and security policy (FFSP). Because of the different gender norms in the United States, and because the United States is a great power which is often drawn into conflict, the two cases are quite different, yet in tandem they highlight important dimensions of the task. In one sense, as we shall see, Clinton faced a far more difficult time—and enjoyed arguably far less success—than Wallström.

Lamentably, at this juncture it is also worth asking if the day of feminist foreign policy is already over in the United States after the 2016 election of President Donald Trump. During the Trump Administration's transition period, which is when this essay was written, transition leaders asked the State Department for a list of all personnel working on gender issues within the organization (including at the Agency for International Development [USAID]), and a tally of funds used to promote gender equality by the United States. The Trump Administration's initial budget zeroed out all funding for the State Department's Office of Global Women's Issues; the latest budget restores funding but indicates the office may disappear in a promised restructuring of the State Department.

Given this stunning *volte face*, we feel the time may be right for some reflection. In this essay, we will probe the various types of conceptual issues and implementation barriers that Sweden and the United States have encountered when attempting to implement a "feminist foreign policy." On the United States side, we delimit our analysis to the Obama Administration, particularly the years in which Hillary Clinton was Secretary of State.

Conceptual Issues

An examination of the Swedish stance might be advantageous in discerning the conceptual issues that must be tackled in pursuing a feminist foreign policy. For example, is an FFSP pacifist? We raised at the outset the example of Sweden, one of the largest per capita aid donors in the world. However, in addition to being the third largest arms exporter (per capita in the world), in 2015 the Swedish government announced a billion dollar increase in defense spending, largely to address concerns about Russia provocation. Swedish academics assert that this is not hypocrisy, but rather practicality. In a world where some national and subnational actors have malign motives, "hard" power will continue to be a necessity, as Karin Aggestam and Annika Bergman-Rosamund (2016) suggest:

> [A] feminist foreign policy is not as closely associated with pacifism as is often assumed, but encourages pragmatism in the alternation between the use of soft and hard power as the most appropriate diplomatic and military strategy to manage security threats . . . Feminist foreign policy . . . does not rule out the use of force in very exceptional circumstances so as to ensure the rights and entitlements of women and men in war zones.

This means, therefore, that war and military intervention short of war are not necessarily incompatible with the goals of a FFSP, at least in the Swedish view.

Second, the issue of arms sales is equally nuanced in the Swedish case. SIPRI data show that Sweden sells mostly to Western alliance countries or West-leaning nations, such as Japan, South Korea, Finland, and Australia. However, despite canceling a major arms deal with Saudi Arabia in 2015 over human rights concerns, sales continued to Pakistan, the UAE, and Thailand (SIPRI, n.d.).

Once more, notice that this means the production of weapons and their sale to other countries is not necessarily incompatible with the goals of an FFSP in the Swedish perspective, though apparently there are some red lines surrounding who can be a recipient of such arms. Pakistan made the cut, but the Saudis saw a cancellation and then a resumption; a full understanding of the criteria used and how these were implemented would be enlightening.

Furthermore, having a feminist foreign policy in the Swedish view also does not exclude military, or quasi-military, alliances. After announcing its new feminist foreign policy in 2015, Sweden announced in 2016 that it was signing a host-nation support agreement with NATO, again probably in response to Russian provocations (Duxbury 2016).

Up to this point, then, an FFSP simply looks very much like a foreign policy crafted along traditional just war principles (in this case, *jus ad bellum*). Given right intent, legitimate authority, and reasonable hope of success, military acquisitions, agreements, and operations can be undertaken after ethical deliberation in light of national interests. Of course, the idea that ethical deliberation must accompany more traditional interest-based argument in foreign policy is an important one. Nevertheless, the Swedes have clearly ducked the following critique: "A[n] objection raised against a feminist foreign policy is its association with soft normative power and its inability to confront aggression, hardcore security issues, and threats emanating from actors such as hostile states" (Aggestam and Rosamund 2016: 5). With the Swedish combination of hard and soft power, this critique appears to be a nonissue.

So what is the difference, then, between feminist foreign policy and foreign policy based on just war principles?

We suggest that there are several areas of discernible difference, specifically: (a) a gendered revision of *jus in bello* principles; (b) a revision of the *jus ad bellum* principle of legitimate authority; (c) the creation of gender-sensitive *jus ex bello* principles; and (d) a broader agenda of gender equality as a security issue.

Since we have begun our analysis with the Swedish case, let us continue with its analysis to see these two points more clearly, though it must be recognized that other nations have also moved in the same direction, such as Canada (Government of Canada 2017). In her numerous speeches on the topic, Margot Wallström consistently reiterates what she calls the four R's of a feminist foreign policy: reality check, women's rights, women's representation, and fairer resource distribution. We begin our discussion with a reality check on traditional just war theory as created primarily by male thinkers.

A Reality Check for Just War Theory: Jus In Bello. What "reality check" means to Wallström is that an analysis of any foreign or security policy situation must include an analysis of what is going on with women on the ground. She best expressed this perspective in a question-and-answer session after her March 2016 speech to the Marshall Fund in Brussels. Noting that military planners dealing with the situation in Syria might typically look at a map and note areas controlled by Daesh, areas controlled by the regime, areas controlled by al-Nusra, and so on, Wallström suggests such a map would not offer a full "reality check": "Women have to ensure the continuity . . . somebody has to take care of the kids, somebody has to make food, somebody has to do all those practical things . . . If this sounds naive, it is not. It is just a very, very practical measure that has to be included" (Lesser and Horst 2016). Though this off-the-cuff response is not fully fleshed out, Wallström appears to be suggesting that military commanders need to take into consideration not only an operation's effect on the enemy, but also on the women who must keep families provisioned and safe in the midst of such operations. The totality of the reality of war—including women's reality—must be considered at the highest levels of strategic planning. In a sense, the *jus in bello* principle of proportionality can never be met without a full understanding of what harm will be caused women by the proposed action—and that understanding cannot be had without a sex-differentiated analysis.

Furthermore, another principle of *jus in bello*—target discrimination—is also in need of revision to include a gender perspective. For example, the targeting by the Bush and Obama administrations in the United States of all "military age men" in certain areas, to include those individuals assumed by fuzzy drone video to be aged 16 and above, whether or not these "men" can be confirmed as militants, or as being at least 16, or even identified after having been killed, is called euphemistically a "signature strike" (De Luce and McLeary 2016). We submit that signature strikes are not ethically justified, particularly if, for example, we were to imagine asking mothers of teenaged sons—of any nationality—for their opinion of this indiscriminate targeting strategy.

Jus Ad Bellum. This raises another important issue concerning the *jus ad bellum* principle of legitimate authority. Can a government really be the legitimate authority that just war theory demands if women—half of the nation's citizenry—are not fully represented at the highest levels of decision-making, especially with reference to foreign/security policy? This is one of the reasons that Wallström says bluntly, "I believe in quotas" (Lesser and Horst 2016). In that same speech, Wallström asserted the importance of full female representation as heads of delegations and their deputies, peacekeepers, negotiators, and mission staff. The Swedish government has certainly made strides in this area, as Wallström noted in another forum:

> Representation, which includes influence over agenda-setting, starts by asking a simple question: Who takes part in conducting foreign policy—at all levels? It starts at the highest level over at the Swedish Ministry for Foreign Affairs—where all the four top positions, two ministers and two state secretaries, are held by women. It must continue in every other part of the Ministry: when ambassadors are appointed, when mediators and their teams are sent to conflicts, and when a position as mid-level executive is filled. But it is also about the knowledge and awareness about gender equality among all our staff in the Ministry, both at home and abroad (Wallström 2014).

In addition, Wallström's feminist foreign policy declares women's representation to not only be obligatory in their home country, but that Sweden should play a role in overcoming obstacles to female representation abroad, as well. This conviction about the need for women's representation is not based on some purported inherent peacefulness of women, but rather because gender equality is a mechanism to break norms of coercive domination at all levels of decision-making. In addition, it adds to the decision-making discussion those viewpoints, priorities, and experiences of half the citizenry that would otherwise be invisibilized. In line with these beliefs, Sweden supported the unsuccessful movement to select a female UN Secretary-General in 2016, it has weighed in on the importance of full female representation in the Syrian peace talks by supporting the Women's Advisory Board (Wallström 2016), and Sweden has been active in training a multinational network of trained female mediators available to be tapped by the United Nations or regional intergovernmental organizations to serve peace negotiations (Government Offices of Sweden 2015b, 2015c). Concerning the last, Wallström has called mediation "the weapon of inclusion" for women; that is, a trained cadre of female mediators can create room for other women at the table during peace negotiations.

Jus Ex Bello. We would also suggest that a feminist foreign policy requires a revision not only of *jus ad bellum* and *jus in bello*, but also the development of *jus ex bello* principles. Women are often left to pick up the pieces after the soldiers have decided that the conflict, at least as far as they are concerned, is over. A feminist foreign policy would assert that how conflict is ended and how troops are withdrawn is just as ethically fraught an enterprise as going to war in the first place. To take a US example, to wit, the US drawdown of troops in Afghanistan, ethicist Darrel Moellendorf (2011) expresses this well:

> [T]here is a peculiar, and possibly more important, moral issue that arises when a war that satisfies just cause should be ended on grounds of the unlikelihood of success or disproportionality. For to end such a war is to admit failure for the cause of justice . . . But the considerations that make the cause just also serve to make it appropriate to mitigate the resulting injustices of failure, to whatever extent this can be done within the constraints of the likelihood of success and proportionality. On the assumption, then, that national protection against terrorist attacks and rescuing the Afghan people from Taliban domination are just causes for continued prosecution of the war, an argument on behalf of ending the war should pay attention to the manner in which the resultant injustices—such as greater room for terrorist organizations to operate freely and poorer prospects for women, girls, minorities, and dissidents—might be mitigated.

Moellendorf is absolutely right. Someone must be tasked with thinking about the physical safety of Afghan women during and even after the Coalition pull-out. We know from decades of research that women are often marginalized with respect to rights and participation, and violence frequently continues and may even be exacerbated in some situations (Jones 2011). However, there is no sign that this discussion ever took place in the US Department of Defense (DoD) under the Obama Administration. If not DoD, then surely State and USAID under Obama took seriously the peril in which the US anticipated leaving Afghan women? USAID's Promote Program, which was the flagship program of the Obama Administration for Afghan women post–pull-out, included no programming to protect the physical security of its beneficiaries (USAID 2013).[1] Wallström's idea of a reality check based on women's perspectives is sorely needed to address this ethical failure, but we submit that discussion will not take place at all under the Trump Administration.

In sum, a core part of a truly FFSP must be a reevaluation of *jus ad bellum* and *jus in bello* principles using a gender perspective, as well as a realization that war does not stop for women when the shooting is over; in other words, what is needed is the development of principles and logistics for a *jus ex bello* that considers women's reality.

Gender Equality as a National Security Issue. Broadening one's vision to see women's reality as important to just war theory is critical, but so are the other "R's" mentioned by Wallström: women's rights, women's representation, and a fairer resource distribution. Because we have spoken of women's representation in the previous section, we will examine the first and last of these in more detail here.

As Wallström has noted, a feminist foreign policy "is really defining gender equality as a peace and security issue" (Tung 2015). As the Foreign Ministry elaborates,

> Equality between women and men is a fundamental aim of Swedish foreign policy. Ensuring that women and girls can enjoy their fundamental human rights is both an obligation within the framework of our international commitments, and a prerequisite for reaching Sweden's broader foreign policy goals on peace, and security and sustainable development (Government Offices of Sweden 2016c).

This is really quite an extraordinary statement. While academics have made the case that the security of women affects the security of nation-states, it is rare that a Foreign Ministry has done so (Hudson et al. 2012). The view that gender equality is requisite for peace and security, and the idea that a nation-state would therefore make it a fundamental aim not only of domestic policy, but also of foreign policy, puts Sweden in a very small club of nations, a club which is now at least one nation smaller due to the recent US election. As articulated by Wallström (2014), efforts to bring about gender equality must strive to eradicate harmful practices, while shoring up progress already won:

> If you aim at pursuing a feminist foreign policy, the work must follow two paths when dealing with women's human rights. There are areas where we must aim for prohibition, such as in relation to gender-based discrimination, forced marriages and female genital mutilation. Secondly, there are areas where the aim is progress, such as in regard to equal rights to inheritance, access to education and health, including sexual and reproductive health and rights. These areas are key to women's empowerment.

To that end, Sweden put forth its first National Action Plan on Women, Peace, and Security in 2006 and is now on its third iteration of that plan (Government Offices of Sweden 2016d). In addition, there is also a complementary Swedish Foreign Service Action Plan (Government Offices of Sweden 2015c), as well as a ten-year National Strategy to prevent and combat men's violence against women (Government Offices of Sweden 2016a). Sweden also has a formal position of Minister for Gender Equality[2] within the government, and in 2016 Sweden announced "the Government states its intention to establish a gender equality agency, to be operational from the beginning of 2018" (Government Offices of Sweden 2016b).

Sweden also makes gender equality part of the conversation in bilateral talks. For example, when the Indian president visited Sweden in 2015, Wallström published an opinion piece in *The Hindu* newspaper, averring,

> Women's full enjoyment of human rights is a top priority for Sweden, domestically as well as globally. Rather than perceiving gender equality merely as a goal in itself, we regard equality to be a prerequisite for achieving our wider foreign and security policy objectives. Sweden's feminist foreign policy aims to respond to one of the greatest unresolved problems of our time, namely that the human rights of women and girls are still being violated in so many ways around the world. Human rights are women's rights. Progress in empowering women and women's representation and rights benefits society as a whole. It is my firm belief that India and Sweden can work together as partners to find ways of addressing this critical challenge, both bilaterally and multilaterally (Wallström 2015).

While this type of statement is a prelude to further dialogue with a partner nation, there of course have been instances where a feminist foreign policy stance seems to preclude close relations. Much has been made of Saudi Arabia's reaction to remarks made by Wallström to the Swedish parliament concerning the subordination of Saudi women, which caused a cancellation in 2015 of her invitation to address the Arab League, a cancellation of an arms sale agreement with Saudi Arabia, and a subsequent recall of the Saudi ambassador to his home country (Tung 2015). Eventually, Wallström made plain her remarks were not an attack on Islam, though she did not apologize for them, and the Saudis returned their ambassador, and arms sales eventually resumed.

In another work, we have alluded to a possible FFSP principle that we called the "Steinem Rule" (Hudson and Leidl 2015). Named after famed feminist activist Gloria Steinem, it refers to an insight that came to Steinem while attending a State Department briefing the very day the Soviets invaded Afghanistan:

> Newspapers were full of articles about the *mujahideen* and their declaration of war against their own Soviet-supported government. Their leaders gave three reasons for why they wanted to drive the Soviets out: girls were permitted to go to school; girls and women could no longer be married off without their consent; and women were being invited to political meetings.

During the discussion that followed the meeting, Steinem stood up and posed an obvious question to her State Department hosts: Given what the *mujahideen* themselves had said that day, wasn't the United States supporting the wrong side? Steinem remembers the question falling into that particular hush reserved for the ridiculous. She doesn't remember the exact answer, but the State Department made it clear that the United States opposed anything that the Soviets supported . . . Steinem says she has never stopped regretting that she didn't chain herself to the seats of that State Department auditorium in public protest (Hudson and Leidl 2015: 8–9).

An inventory of where foreign aid and military assistance is going—for example, is it going to deeply misogynist regimes?—might well be an important pillar of a feminist foreign policy. Why would a nation committed to gender equality aid and arm the forces of egregious misogyny in the world? A focus on women's rights remains rhetorical unless accompanied by commitment of—or refusal to commit—resources. The Swedish decision to temporarily cut arms sales to Saudi Arabia is an example of the power of such refusal, though resumption of such sales calls that power into question.

Knowing that resource commitment is the bottom line, Wallström advocates her final "R": a more equitable distribution of resources. In response, Sweden has promoted the concept of "gender-responsive budgeting," which is explained by the Finance Ministry in the following terms:

> Sweden has a feminist government that works to achieve gender equality between women and men at all levels of society. . . . Gender-responsive budgeting means that the gender equality effects of budget policy are to be evaluated and that a gender equality perspective is to be integrated at all levels of the budgetary process. It also means a redistribution of revenue and expenditure to promote gender equality. This includes, for example, the use of sex disaggregated statistics, thorough analyses from a gender equality perspective, and reforms and other measures that lead to increased gender equality—and which make a tangible difference in people's daily lives in the short or long term (Government Offices of Sweden 2015a).

In sum, then, in this discussion of the conceptual issues surrounding an FFSP, we see a fuller conception of feminist foreign policy come into view from examination of the Swedish case. A revision of just war theory—informed by a gender perspective—complements a more holistic effort to improve rights, increase women's representation, and address resource gaps. While an FFSP stance can justifiably countenance the use of military instruments, it also aims higher: it aims for gender equality for all as a sturdy underpinning of domestic and international peace.

Implementation Barriers

Having a clear conception of feminist foreign policy in the abstract, as already outlined, does not necessarily free a government from various barriers related to the implementation thereof.[3] Given that we are more familiar with the US case, we now leave Sweden to discuss what was learned about the implementation of an FFSP under Secretary of State Hillary Clinton from 2009 to 2013.

Moral Quandaries Faced by Clinton. While in the Swedish case, feminist foreign policy had sincere support from the highest levels of government and gender equality norms were prevalent within the society, Clinton did not have that luxury. Whereas the Swedes were able to temporarily suspend arms sales to Saudi Arabia, for example, in part because of its extreme subordination of women, there was no support within the Obama Administration for any similar action. As a result, Clinton faced profound moral quandaries in attempting to be true to her belief in FFSP and yet function within the foreign policy mindset of the administration.

For example, Clinton was castigated for not openly confronting the Saudis on their treatment of women. However, it is also true that those waiting in the wings to overthrow the Saudi royal family would arguably be a hundred times worse for women. Why, then, Clinton might ask, undermine a regime that has steadily worked to improve women's situation, though perhaps not at the pace desired? And yet it is equally true that the Saudis finance the spread of Wahhabism throughout the Islamic world, which has a very atavistic stance on women. Islamic cultures that have a more tolerant view of women's rights, such as in Indonesia, have seen that tolerance profoundly undermined by Saudi-financed preachers. This was a real moral quandary for Clinton, in a way that it was not for Wallström.

Another quandary is that US state support for women in other countries can leave those women much more vulnerable. Once again this issue is much more difficult for the United States than it is for Sweden—indeed, the United States, in trying not to harm women's groups, has on occasion even channeled the money through Nordic countries. While all human rights defenders, men and women, can be vulnerable in this way, it can be argued that women are doubly vulnerable, given that they do not possess the structural economic power of men in many countries and also given the great cultural controversy provoked by the issue of women's rights in many lands. For example, when one of the authors (Hudson) visited UN Women in spring 2013, she was taken aback to hear that some at that organization felt Hillary Clinton would have "blood on her hands," meaning that Clinton had encouraged Afghan women to stand up, and as they did, they would surely be killed. Two years later, when the Taliban briefly seized Kunduz in October 2015, they reportedly had lists of women activists and working women who were targeted for summary execution (Hackel 2015). The Kunduz episode demonstrates the concerns expressed at UN Women are not fantastical.

Perhaps the most profound quandary facing Clinton was her support for the principle of Responsibility to Protect. What she discovered, surely to her sorrow, is that R2P does not logically entail R2PW (Responsibility to Protect Women). That is, "humanitarian military intervention" by states, if that is not an oxymoron, always produces grave consequences for women. The Libyan R2P action which Clinton championed has hurt women, with many women activists assassinated and women sidelined in the current political chaos. The Syrian civil war, which gained assent from the West as an R2P-like process designed to oust a brutal dictator, has destroyed women's prospects in that country. The Arab "Spring" itself, meant to overthrow sclerotic autocrats in favor of nascent democracy, was surely an Arab Winter for women. Even before the time of the Obama Administration, the pattern was visible: Iraqi women were set back a century in terms of security by the American invasion to neutralize Saddam Hussein. The use of military force—whether by the state or by revolutionary groups—typically results in a real regress for women. The R2P versus R2PW contradiction is thus also a persistent quandary for an FFSP—at least by a great power such as the United States.

Bureaucratic Shenanigans. We'd like to highlight three ways in which bureaucratic forces can also undermine a state's attempt to pursue a feminist foreign policy, as illustrated in the US case when Hillary Clinton was Secretary of State. The first is what we call "the pet rock problem." The "pet rock" problem alludes to the infamous 2011 statement by an anonymous US senior official quoted in the *Washington Post* about the situation in Afghanistan: "Gender issues are going to have to take a back seat to other priorities. There's no way we can be successful if we maintain every special interest and pet project. All those pet rocks in our rucksack were taking us down" (Chandrasekaran 2011). Women—fully half the population of Afghanistan—were a *pet rock* to senior US officials in the Obama Administration. Genuflection to the idea that women were important in US foreign policy was commonplace, no doubt in part due to Clinton's stature; however, "when push came to shove," commitments to women's empowerment and security evaporated.

Sanam Anderlini (2013) concurs: "[Clinton's] president [wa]sn't behind her. You're raising expectations of the women, you're making it part of the American agenda, and then your own guys don't follow through. They're the first ones to sell you down the river. One US official told me, 'The issue of Afghan women is not our issue.' They didn't take it seriously, they were late to it . . . Don't just talk about it and then behind the scenes let it all go."

Part of the problem was that even during Clinton's tenure women remained underrepresented in the US foreign policy establishment, which normalized the lack of women in foreign policy discussions overall. For example, in the Afghan and Syrian cases, the US did not insist on hard targets for women's participation in delegations from other countries—and as Micah Zenko (2011) indicated while Clinton was Secretary of State, this may have been because of the United States' own lack of women at the table:

> [A]t 10 prominent think tanks with a substantial foreign-policy focus . . . I found that women constituted only 21 percent of the policy-related positions (154 of 723) and only 29 percent of the total leadership staff (250 of 874) . . . Given this disparity, it should come as no surprise that women are also underrepresented in the halls of power. The Pentagon's "Senior Defense Officials" website lists 129 positions, of which 21 (16 percent) are filled by women . . . Of the 171 chiefs of mission at U.S. embassies, 50 are women (29 percent). Data for top staffers at the U.S. Agency for International Development (USAID) is less readily available, but a Women in International Security (WIIS) study found that, in 2007 "women only held 29 percent of the Senior Foreign Service positions [at USAID]."

Besides senior positions, those who are actually there on the ground in lower-ranking positions are also key. And to understand who is there, we have to understand that much of the programming carried out under US government auspices is performed by for-profit contractors, which, while their headquarters may be based in the United States, use a series of sub- and sub-subcontractors to actually carry out the work. Heads of projects (COPs) may be Americans, but generally the staff may be subcontractors from countries such as India or Pakistan where the culture of gender equality is underdeveloped—and virtually all of these subcontractors are male. And if the COP isn't thinking about gender, you can be sure the subcontractors are not either.

An interviewee put it this way: "It seems like a lot of COPs are selected because they have grey hair and a penis. It doesn't seem like they are vetted for quality, development skills or a sound development philosophy. I don't think they even think about women enough to have some kind of hard line position against women. They are dealing with their political world, because there are no women, women are kind of a non-entity. It just doesn't even enter their universe" (Hudson and Leidl 2015). Or, alternatively, women enter their universe in unhappy ways at the ground level: the problem of contractor and subcontractor purchase of commercial sex has dogged US programming in the field. Even though all federal employees, contractors, and even subcontractors are prohibited from purchasing sex acts 24/7, incidents when Clinton was Secretary of State were all too common, and remain so to this day. All this added up to a deep disconnect between the rhetoric of Clinton's feminist foreign policy and what actually transpired on the ground where the programming actually does—or does not—make a difference.

In sum, the US case is a nice complement to that of Sweden. While the experiences of Sweden highlight some of the more vexing conceptual issues attending the development of an FFSP, the US case places into sharp relief some of the stiff implementation obstacles faced.

Conclusion

Women are not inherently more peaceful than men, though men have had millennia to perfect the art of coercive control due to humankind's sexual dimorphism. Despite this long history, male domination is not an inevitable social structure. The surest mechanism by which to break the template of male dominance is the promulgation of norms of gender equality. If a male dominance system produces highly dysfunctional sequelae of instability, insecurity, and belligerence, then to the degree a nation-state can instantiate gender equality in its government and its policy—including its foreign policy—the greater the prospects for stability, security, and peace.

In a stunning new piece of empirical research, Elin Bjarnegard and Erik Melander (2017) find that attitudes toward other nationalities and religious groups are not predictable by biological sex—but are significantly predicted by attitudes toward gender equality. Those with the ability to treat the other half of their own population with respect were those who were capable of treating outgroups similarly. This is strong evidence that norms of gender equality within a society shape attitudes that underlie a nation's foreign policy. The authors comment, "both men and women who reject gender equality are much more hostile both to other nations and to minorities in their own country" (2017: 1). If the very First Other encountered—the other sex—can be lived with in peace and equality, then other "Others" can be lived with as well. World peace may well depend on the ability of the two halves of humanity to live in peace first, which is why the Swedes have been adamant that "gender equality is a peace and security issue."

Several principles and recommendations follow from our analysis of the Swedish and US cases, and are instructive for those building an FFSP pursuant to the Women, Peace, and Security agenda originally set forth in Resolution 1325:

- Feminist foreign policy admits no contradiction in the simultaneous use of soft power and hard power instruments. Feminist foreign policy is not inherently pacifist, though it does seek peace. That means that the use of military instruments, and the pursuit of military alliances and military acquisitions are not anathema—but they must be carefully evaluated along feminist just war theory principles, perhaps including the Steinem Rule. Ethical deliberation must inform discussions of national interest.
- Feminist foreign policy does not argue that women are inherently peaceful; rather, it argues that the promulgation of gender equality norms will make possible deep attitudinal change about the possibility and the desirability of living in peace, respect, and equality with others who are different. These norms concerning the treatment of the "First Difference" deeply color foreign and security policy.
- The promulgation of gender equality norms is thus a *mechanism* by which the old templates of violent coercion through male dominance are shed, permitting greater stability, security, and peace for the nation.
- Such promulgation requires, at a minimum:

  o A revamping of just war theory to include women's reality. This involves revision not only of *jus ad bellum* and *jus in bello* principles, but also the development of new *jus ex bello* principles.
  o Hard target quotas for women's participation in all aspects of foreign and security decision-making and implementation so that gender equality is lived by those who govern and who act for the government.
  o Constant vigilance to improve women's rights within one's own country, and dedicated observation of the situation of women's rights in the countries with which one interacts. It may be necessary to forego close relations with nations that grievously subordinate women, and foreign aid programming to improve women's rights abroad should be a priority issue.
  o Constant vigilance also to foresee implementation issues which will undermine a feminist foreign policy. For example, contractors and subcontractors must be scrutinized for their propensity to undermine feminist foreign policy. While there must be will at the highest levels of government for gender equality norms to really take root, attention to gender must be a skill cultivated not only among generals, but among sergeants, as well.
  o Adequate resource commitment to achieve gender equality goals must be a priority for the government, and this means sex-disaggregated data will be key for gender-sensitive budgeting purposes.

It may seem to some that this agenda is impossible, but to that, Wallström in March of 2016, quoting Nelson Mandela, retorts, "It always seems impossible until it is done" (Lesser and Horst 2016).

Notes

1. For an extended discussion of this point, please see Hudson and Leidel (2015).
2. Technically, the Minister for Children, the Elderly, and Gender Equality; however, with the new agency there will be a Minister of Gender Equality.
3. This section adapted from Hudson and Leidl (2015).

References

Aggestram, K., and A. Bergman-Rosamond. "Swedish Feminist Foreign Policy in the Making: Ethics, Politics, and Gender." *Ethics & International Affairs* [Blog]. September 15, 2016, https://www.ethicsandinternationalaffairs.org/2016/swedish-feminist-foreign-policy-in-the-making-ethics-politics-and-gender/.

Anderlini, S. Telephone Interview by Valerie M. Hudson, November 21 2013.

Bjarnegård, E., and E. Melander. "Pacific Men: How the Feminist Gap Explains Hostility." *The Pacific Review* (2017): 1–16.

Chandrasekaran, Rajiv. "In Afghanistan, U.S. shifts strategy on women's rights as it eyes wider priorities." *The Washington Post*, March 14, 2011, http://www.washingtonpost.com/wp-dyn/content/article/2011/03/05/AR2011030503668.html.

De Luce, D., and P. McLeary. "Obama's Most Dangerous Drone Tactic Is Here to Stay." *Foreign Policy*, April 5, 2016, http://foreignpolicy.com/2016/04/05/obamas-most-dangerous-drone-tactic-is-here-to-stay/.

Duxbury, C. "Sweden Ratifies NATO Cooperation Agreement." *The Wall Street Journal*, May 25, 2016, https://www.wsj.com/articles/sweden-ratifies-nato-cooperation-agreement-1464195502.

Government of Canada. "Canada's Feminist International Assistance Policy." Government of Canada, 2017, http://international.gc.ca/world-monde/issues_development-enjeux_developpement/priorities-priorites/policy-politique.aspx?lang=eng.

Government Offices of Sweden. "Gender-Responsive Budgeting." Government Offices of Sweden, 2015a, http://www.government.se/articles/2015/11/gender-responsive-budgeting/.

Government Offices of Sweden. "Minister for Foreign Affairs Margot Wallström Hosts High-Level Meeting on Women's Roles in Peace Processes." Government Offices of Sweden, December 15, 2015b, http://www.government.se/articles/2015/12/minister-for-foreign-affairs-margot-wallstrom-hosts-high-level-meeting-on-womens-role-in-peace-processes/.

Government Offices of Sweden. "Swedish Foreign Service Action Plan for Feminist Foreign Policy 2015–2015 Including Focus Areas for 2016." Government Offices of Sweden, 2015c, http://www.government.se/4ad6e7/contentassets/b799e89a0e06493f86c63a561e869e91/action-plan-feminist-foreign-policy-2015-2018.

Government Offices of Sweden. "Swedish Government Presents Feminist Policy for a Gender-Equal Future." Government Offices of Sweden, November 18, 2016a, http://www.government.se/press-releases/2016/11/swedish-government-presents-feminist-policy-for-a-gender-equal-future/.

Government Offices of Sweden. "Swedish Government to Establish Gender Equality Agency." Government Offices of Sweden, September 16, 2016b, http://www.government.se/press-releases/2016/09/swedish-government-to-establish-gender-equality-agency/.

Government Offices of Sweden. "Today Is International Women's Day." Government Offices of Sweden, March 8, 2016c, http://www.government.se/articles/2016/03/today-is-international-womens-day/.

Government Offices of Sweden. "Women, Peace & Security: Sweden's National Action Plan for the implementation of the UN Security Council Resolutions on Women, Peace, and Security 2016–2020." Government Offices of Sweden, 2016d, http://www.government.se/49ef7e/contentassets/8ae23198463f49269e25a14d4d14b9bc/swedens-national-action-plan-for-the-implementation-of-the-united-nations-security-council-resolutions-on-women-peace-and-security-2016-2020-.pdf.

Hackel, J. "The Taliban Had a Hit List of Working Women When They Took Over Kunduz." *Public Radio International*, October 15, 2015, http://www.pri.org/stories/2015-10-15/taliban-had-hit-list-working-women-when-they-took-over-kunduz.

Hudson, V., B. Ballif-Spanvill, M. Caprioli, and C. Emmett. *Sex and World Peace*, New York: Columbia University Press, 2012.

Hudson, V., and P. Leidl. *The Hillary Doctrine: Sex and American Foreign Policy.* New York: Columbia University Press, 2015.

Jones, A. *War Isn't Over When It's Over.* New York: Picador, 2011.

Lesser, I., and C. Horst. "A Conversation with Margot Wallström, Swedish Foreign Minister: On Women, Peace, and Security." GMF, March 14, 2016, http://www.gmfus.org/events/conversation-margot-wallström-swedish-foreign-minister-women-peace-and-security.

Moellendorf, D. "Jus ex Bello in Afghanistan." *Ethics & International Affairs 25*, no. 2 (June 30, 2011): 155–164.

SIPRI. "Importer/Exporter TIV Tables." Stockholm International Peace Research Institute, n.d., https://www.sipri.org/databases/armstransfers.

Tung, Liam. "Swedish Foreign Minister Margot Wallström Explains Why the World Needs Feminist Foreign Policy." *Sydney Morning Herald*, July 3, 2015, http://www.smh.com.au/world/swedish-foreign-minister-margot-wallstrom-explains-why-the-world-needs-feminist-foreign-policy-20150702-gi3y6y.html.

USAID. "Promoting Gender Equality in National Priority Programs (PROMOTE)." FedBizOpps.Gov., 2013, https://www.fbo.gov/?s=opportunity&mode=form&id=17a9531dfa7d35ca6a30d6b303c7433b&tab=core&_cview=0.

US Department of State. "Leading through Civilian Power: The First Quadrennial Diplomacy and Development Review." QDDR, 2010, https://www.state.gov/documents/organization/153108.pdf.

Wallström, M. "Speech by the Minister for Foreign Affairs Margot Wallström at the Seminar about #Femdefenders, Arranged by Kvinna till Kvinna [Speech Transcript]." Government Offices of Sweden, November 28, 2014, http://www.government.se/speeches/2014/11/speech-by-the-minister-for-foreign-affairs-margot-wallstrom-at-the-seminar-about-femdefenders-arranged-by-kvinna-till-kvinna/.

Wallström, M. "A New Landmark in India-Sweden Relations." *The Hindu*, May 30, 2015, http://www.thehindu.com/todays-paper/tp-opinion/a-new-landmark-in-indiasweden-relations/article7262205.ece.

Wallström, M. "Syria's Peace Talks Need More Women at the Table." Government Offices of Sweden, March 8, 2016, http://www.government.se/opinion-pieces/2016/03/syrias-peace-talks-need-more-women-at-the-table/.

Zenko, M. "City of Men." *Foreign Policy*, July 14, 2011, http://foreignpolicy.com/2011/07/14/city-of-men/.

CHAPTER 62

NETWORKED ADVOCACY

YIFAT SUSSKIND AND DIANA DUARTE

RIGHTS advocates today find themselves strangers in a strange landscape of global governance. The institutions and political conditions that allowed for human rights gains as recently as the 1990s (see chapter 25 in this volume) have mutated: The space for civil society participation has been forced shut and opportunities for policy influence closed off. This steady constriction of civil society space demands that advocates for human rights and peace re-evaluate and retool existing strategies to achieve policy aims, namely in the realm of peace and conflict resolution. Reframing conventional understandings of what constitutes advocacy and peace processes is a critical point of entry for this inquiry, one that allows us to center the experiences of the women most threatened by human rights violations associated with armed conflict, including sexual violence.

In this chapter, we will posit women's networked advocacy as a vital strategy to overcome civil society's exclusion from policymaking and to imagine new spaces of peacemaking power beyond the negotiating table. We define networked advocacy as an approach that unites activists and organizations operating at multiple levels from the grass-roots to the global to share knowledge and information, including documentation of local rights violations and community conditions. From this basis, they can devise common strategies that maximize each participant's expertise and access to spaces of power, whether policymaking bodies or community organizing spaces; create, monitor, and ensure peace implementation at the local and national levels; foster community familiarity and constituencies of support for rights standards and peace processes; build coherence between peace policy and practice at the global, national, and local levels; and create openings for gains in-country. Networked advocacy also reinforces the feedback loop between grass-roots and official policymaking arenas, creating the conduits necessary for local conditions to influence policy and for policy gains to translate to the local level.

In the sections to follow, we will first concentrate on peace and national reconciliation processes, with two aims: (1) to analyze women's strategies advocating for effective participation and leadership roles in these official processes, and (2) to assess frankly the limitations of such processes. We will then shift focus to grass-roots sites where women lead community reconciliation efforts and combat stigma against sexual violence survivors, and we will present methodologies that create a feedback loop between spaces of grass-roots mobilizing and official processes, strengthening policy recommendations and fostering lasting peace. In particular, we argue that grass-roots initiatives can better mobilize peace agents and constituencies at the local level, generating alternative and vital peace processes, beyond official negotiating mechanisms, and better answering the basic question of all peacemaking efforts: how will we live together when the war ends?

WOMEN'S STRATEGIES FOR INCLUSION WITHIN PEACE AND NATIONAL RECONCILIATION PROCESSES

Women's groups have often been the targets of backlash that narrows civil society space, particularly those groups who address the root causes of violations women face and call for systemic change. On the one hand, such activist groups have been accused of "immoral" behaviors that pose a threat to the family or society, whether they are speaking out in favor of women's political leadership or setting up protections for women's rights, like anti-violence shelters or ensuring access to reproductive rights (Sakr 2013; Msimang 2015). Right-wing actors mobilize popular opposition to such women's groups by emphasizing the perceived threats to social norms that these groups are said to pose.

Alternatively, when not vilified as threats to culture and community, women's groups are waved away as inessential to substantial policymaking processes (Leimbach 2015). Relegating women to the private sphere, these so-called traditional norms and discriminatory attitudes are used by political gatekeepers to prevent women from weighing in on policymaking questions, from economics to military policy and even to women's health and reproductive rights.

The overall efforts to constrain civil society space coupled with the specific backlash against women's political participation is particularly palpable in the realm of peacebuilding and national reconciliation. The project of ending an armed conflict is also the project of determining how postwar society will be run—with all the allocation of power and privilege that entails. The incentives are arrayed for those currently in power to stave off interlopers who might try to create more just or equitable outcomes responsive to the needs of the most conflict-affected or marginalized. Women's civil society groups have a proven tendency to act as those interlopers, and a growing body of evidence demonstrates that their effective participation in peace processes greatly increases the chances that the resulting peace will last: by 20 percent over two years and by 35 percent over fifteen years (Stone 2015: 34). Yet, they have often been insufficiently prepared to counter the opposition they face from more powerful actors seeking to guard their own interests in the outcome of negotiations. As Thania Paffenholz (2015: 3) explains, resistance by such elites has been an enduring obstacle to women's successful inclusion in peace processes.

Women have nevertheless made headway in this arena. In 2000, successful advocacy led to the adoption by the United Nations Security Council of Resolution 1325, mandating a role for women civil society representation in peace and national reconciliation processes, and now serving as a cornerstone of the Women, Peace, and Security (WPS) Agenda.

Since winning this recognition on paper, gatekeepers of official peace negotiations have failed to fully implement Resolution 1325's provisions (see chapter 64 in this volume), often ignoring its requirements altogether. As a result, women peace advocates have been compelled to employ a wide range of strategies to secure a role at the negotiating table and otherwise influence peacemaking agendas. Such strategies, to be examined shortly, include lobbying in official policymaking spaces, mobilizing nonviolent civic resistance, setting up parallel and consultative processes, or creating third-way political parties. Taken together, these approaches offer a blueprint that women today can follow to seize potential opportunities and avoid obstacles. Below is a brief explanation of some of those strategies and their pitfalls, as well as the potential of networked advocacy to accelerate or deepen the approach.

In the Suites

Women peacemakers have taken advantage of sympathetic allies within policymaking spaces to assist with maneuvering their way into otherwise inaccessible spaces. When advocates are knocking and pushing on one side of a door, it helps to have a friend on the other side to turn the knob. Such policymaking allies can supply valuable information, make other introductions, and offer their expertise to create shared insider-outsider strategies. However, allies in positions of power may be few, may serve governments with shifting or competing priorities, may be replaced, or may prove unreliable in other ways. The success of such a strategy also may depend on esoteric knowledge of how to navigate those spaces once the door is opened.

A networked advocacy approach that leverages the combined strengths of insider policymaking knowledge with the expertise and moral authority of grass-roots activists can make for a powerful intervention. Success relies on an egalitarian alliance between professional advocates and grass-roots activists equipped with the skills to advocate effectively. This approach is augmented by other support, like training, financial backing, translation, assistance with childcare, dialogue with families to overcome strictures against women traveling or speaking publicly, and other means to navigate obstacles that may prevent grass-roots women's participation in negotiations.

Networked advocacy further allows for a consolidation of contacts and leveraging of relationships. Women's organizations map out potential entry points into policymaking spaces. The net they cast can be more broad and effective than in a purely bilateral relationship between a civil society group and its policymaking allies, deriving the benefit of multiple viewpoints and broader representation.

In the Streets

When official channels for participation in peace processes have been denied or eliminated by governments or other gatekeepers, women have led grass-roots mobilizations to generate external pressure on decision-makers. A notable and successful example of this transpired in the case of the Liberian civil war, where women dressed in white as a visible symbol of peace, networked across religious and community lines, staged months-long sit-ins, and eventually wore down policymakers to accede to women's demands with their relentless peaceful protest (Disney 2008; Gbowee 2009).

The limitations of this strategy lie in the inherent difficulty of sustaining that level of grass-roots mobilization. Resource constraints, physical and emotional dangers, the pressures of wage-earning and family-care responsibilities, challenges of strategic communications and messaging to build and maintain public support, and activist fatigue combine as obstacles mitigating against long-term public mobilizations.

However, through networked advocacy, local activists seeking to maintain popular street mobilizations can benefit from both moral and material support, and borrow from a wider library of protest strategies. Accelerating communications technologies have furthered this networked approach, enabling rapid coordination. For example, in 2016, women-led Indigenous activists in Standing Rock, North Dakota, organized against an oil pipeline that both threatened their water supply and represented a violation of the 1868 Treaty of Fort Laramie that resolved a land conflict between the Sioux Nation and the United States. Their peaceful protests were bolstered over months by worldwide donations and delegations of activist allies. A networked advocacy approach was evident in the broad range of allies, with diverse agendas and identities that supported the mobilization, from women's organizations to Indigenous Peoples around the world to former adversaries like US military veterans and local ranchers (Monet 2016; Medina and Davis 2016). Networked advocacy also supported the legal challenges to the pipeline, locally, nationally, and internationally (Earthjustice 2017; Payne 2016). These in turn, were boosted by coordinated lobbying efforts, mobilizing people across a range of sectors to call their congressional representatives, divest from banks supporting the pipeline, and more.

In Parallel

To reveal and overcome the deficiencies of an official peace or national reconciliation process, women's groups have also opted to set up parallel mechanisms, such as side forums and consultations. Whether or not these spheres are concretely connected to official decision-making, they can still serve as a normative counterweight offering an alternative vision and new models of work.

A case study of networked advocacy in parallel spaces can be found in the initiative called Women Lead to Peace. In January 2014, nearly three years into the Syrian conflict, negotiators reconvened for a second round at the Geneva Conference peace process. Like prior gatherings of the Geneva Conference, this round excluded women's civil society groups and their pro-democracy and human rights expertise. Advocates came together to launch an alternative forum, called Women Lead to Peace, held simultaneously and in an adjacent location to the Geneva II Conference. Women Lead to Peace brought together women peace-builders from Guatemala, Sri Lanka, Northern Ireland, and Bosnia, who could share their strategies to influence official processes as well as their grass-roots conflict prevention experiences with Syrian women civil society. International allies who convened the space also offered their expertise on legal tactics, strategic communications, and advocacy skills.[1] The interplay at this convening helped to position Syrian women peace-builders as leaders and to generate pressure for the creation of an official Syrian women's consultative body for future peace negotiating rounds (Gambale 2016).

In setting up a parallel space to an official peace process, women may benefit from comparative perspectives and resources from other nodes in an activist network. For instance, in different times and spaces, women civil society leaders have devised differing models, such as popular tribunals, consultative bodies, and advisory groups to generate recommendations.

REFRAMING ADVOCACY AND PEACE PROCESSES TO REVEAL NEW SPACES OF POWER

These previously noted strategies, which seek to influence official policymaking, involve no small amount of time, resources, and expertise. Grass-roots women's peace-building groups with limited resources and competing priorities may ask themselves whether action within official spaces is worthwhile, or whether their investment of energy would be squandered if they lose the fight to entry. In times when intractable political negotiations are slow, ineffective, or stalled, such as attempts over years to end Syria's war or over decades to end Colombia's war, women may find their most effective avenues for action exist at the levels of community building and culture change. Operating at these levels offers opportunities to constitute and strengthen alternative arenas for civil society power at the grassroots, and shift the battleground upon which attacks on civil society space are confronted.

Turning our analytical gaze to the grass-roots, we discover new dimensions to terms such as advocacy and peace process. If we define advocacy too narrowly as legal strategies to apply pressure for policy change, we might miss grass-roots forms of advocacy—often led by women—that generate policy directly: consider the peace communities established by women activists in Colombia or the local ceasefires and prisoner exchanges negotiated by women activists in Syria (Rojas 2004: 26; Williams and Barsa 2014). If we define a peace process solely as that which occurs around an officially designated negotiating table, we might miss cases like women's community-based conflict reconciliation efforts. If we overly focus on how women's civil society space is constrained in official arenas, we might miss how it is flourishing in informal spaces. By looking at these two specific conflicts—the wars in Syria and Colombia—we can trace the impacts of women's leadership in the two focal areas of (1) community-based national reconciliation, and (2) social norm change to combat stigma against wartime sexual violence survivors.

It is important to note that a focus on women's leadership at the grass-roots level does not cede their claim to a role in official policymaking spaces. Rather, as evidenced in the research of Mala Htun and S. Laurel Weldon (2012: 551–552), autonomous feminist movements, through their connections to specific communities and social groups outside of dominant power structures, are able to generate, capture, and spread knowledge that influences both public perceptions and institutional practices. Leveraging this dynamic through networked advocacy enables grass-roots women and their transnational allies to create a positive feedback loop between grass-roots and policymaking spaces. In doing so, women bridge persistent gaps between communities and official peace processes, a key to ensuring effective implementation of any peace accord.

This framing—a positive feedback loop—allows us to further emphasize the mutually reinforcing and amplifying nature of the interaction between the local and transnational, as well as the substantive roles that local activists can play at the transnational level and that transnational allies can play at the local level. Using networked advocacy to sustain this feedback loop guards against work at the grass-roots that risks only addressing symptoms of crisis, as well as official policymaking that risks operating in a vacuum devoid of the realities of local communities.

Grass-roots Community Reconciliation Interventions

In Colombia, decades of armed conflict between government forces, FARC rebels, and paramilitary groups ensnared communities in violence. Widespread recruitment and exploitation of children as soldiers, massive displacement, and the use of sexual violence as a mode of terror and control tore apart the community structures that people depend upon for their resilience in the face of trauma.

The war in Syria has meant the siege and bombardment of entire communities and triggered a surge of refugees living precariously and struggling to accommodate their urgent needs for food, housing, healthcare, and other basics. As in many other conflicts, gender-based violence has featured prominently in the war, with, for example, Syrian women and girls often citing the threat of sexual violence as a primary motivator for their displacement (Human Rights and Gender Justice Clinic et al. 2016).

Whereas Colombia's decades-long conflict reached a historic milestone in 2016 with the signing of a peace agreement between the government and the FARC, as of this writing Syria's peace process is effectively at a standstill (Casey 2016). Despite these differences, both Colombian and Syrian women's local civil society groups have been essential to protect individual and community resilience through periods of violence and to lay the groundwork for future peace and reconciliation.

In Colombia, in communities that were surrounded on all sides by warfare, organizing by grass-roots women created pockets of peace, such as areas specifically delineated as free of armed actors or community gatherings where people could talk about the trauma they had endured and their visions for peace (Rojas 2009). While each instance was small in scope, they offered a basis to reconstitute the community bonds that are frayed by violence. Furthermore, women continued to work over decades to preserve these pockets of peace, even as official peace processes repeatedly sprung up, faltered, failed, and started again. Women's groups played a leading role in documenting and highlighting the gendered impacts of the war, including sexual violence and the impact of displacement on women (ABColombia et al. 2013). When a viable peace process was finally underway, beginning in 2012, women peace activists had already seeded its chances for success, by priming communities to accept its outcomes and by demanding accountability for the violations they had documented.

With the peace agreement between the Colombian government and FARC rebels now in its implementation phase, the question of popular acceptance is preeminent. A key

mechanism for planned demobilization and disarmament is the establishment of "concentration zones," where combatants will congregate to hand over weaponry and register for
reintegration and transitional justice processes. These zones are crucial for the monitoring
and maintenance of ceasefire. However, the exclusion of civil society from policymaking
was reproduced in these zones, with communities poorly informed about the initiative. The
lack of information is a direct consequence of the government's failure to invest in public
education and community consultation, and its disregard for partnering with civil society
groups to serve that outreach role (Vigaud-Walsh 2016: 13–14). As a result, communities are
apprehensive about the policy and fearful about their proximity to armed encampments,
rendering the concentration zones sites of potential volatility and violence.

Meanwhile, in areas where women's civil society groups have been able to mobilize the
resources and capacity to sustain community outreach, people are better prepared for the
realities of demobilization. For instance, in the community of Chocó slated to serve as a
"concentration zone," groups like the human rights organization Taller de Vida (Spanish
for "Workshop of Life") have implemented community-based programming to build resilience through expressive art programs, answer questions, allay fears, minimize volatility,
and create more stable conditions to reintegrate former combatants.

Concurrent with the adoption of the peace agreement has been a wave of killings largely
perpetrated by right-wing militias and targeted against human rights activists, labor and
land reform organizers, and prominent voices on the left. A report by Corporacion Arco
Iris indicated that these assassinations of human rights defenders are part of an organized
right-wing effort to destabilize the peace process. This grimly recalls a failed attempt at
peace in the 1980s, in which an earlier iteration of a demobilized political alternative to the
FARC was targeted with an extermination campaign (Murphy 2016). These attacks serve
not only as a powerful disincentive for rebel combatants to lay down arms today but are
killing off the civil society leadership needed to foster community trust and implement
lasting peace.

Syrian women's groups have similarly engaged in community level work to create
conditions for future peace, a process that deepened even amidst high levels of violence.
A 2015 study of women's peace-building groups tracked a spike in new groups established,
beginning in 2012 and flourishing despite extremely difficult conditions in 2013 and 2014
(Ghazzawi et al. 2015: 11). This research also illuminated the myriad modes of peace-
building employed by women's groups: a campaign to prevent the spread of small arms,
craft workshops and social activities to foster coexistence, human rights documentation to
lay the groundwork for redress in future justice processes, efforts to combat child soldier
recruitment, and leadership training to promote women's participation in local government and broader political processes (Ghazzawi et al. 2015: 22–23). All the while, the official
Geneva Conference peace process lurched through multiple failed rounds, unable to establish a basis for negotiation among the warring parties.

In Syria and Colombia, the efforts of women's groups to mend community rifts simultaneously enables people to forge new postwar identities critical to long-term prospects for
peace. Activities organized by women's civil society groups allow both victims and former
combatants to gain new agency as citizens as they voice their experiences and demands.
For instance, as ex-FARC rebels take the leap to give up their weapons or as Syrian child
soldiers recruited by the Islamic State group are demobilized, many have little or no experience with civilian life: their sense of self is equated with their status as a combatant.

Community dialogues and training opportunities offered by civil society organizations allow newly demobilized combatants to reimagine identities that became warped and entrenched through violence and warfare. Ultimately, they are able to answer the question of "who am I, if not a soldier?" with "I am a contributing member of this community." The ability to transition to this new identity, thanks in large part to programs of women's civil society groups, reduces the likelihood that former combatants will take up arms again. In a personal communication, Colombian human rights activist Stella Duque explained, "[Y]ou cannot ask a person to give up their identity without offering them an alternative and a new path forward." As such, these programs are essential to ensuring that peace accords can move from paper to practice.

Networked advocacy enables these community-based efforts that reshape identities and communities to loop back to the policy space and exert influence. For example, beginning in 2015, international allies mobilized to bring together Syrian grass-roots women peace activists in a series of gatherings, termed "Strategies for Change." These gatherings allowed these women to consolidate their expertise and strengthen relationships to fuel their grass-roots organizing. Crucially, these international allies also orchestrated the space for government representatives and policymakers to participate in these meetings, allowing the women leaders to present their demands directly and creating conduits between civil society and government spaces.

Additionally, despite the repeated failures of the Geneva peace process to end the war in Syria, networked advocacy has enabled grass-roots and international level advocacy to continue to nourish each other. In particular, advocates have used the international treaty body system to highlight gender-based violence in conflict at the international level and collate documentation for later use. Though the gains are not visible via a peace agreement, history has shown that this type of work by grass-roots groups and their international allies plants the seeds to hold armed actors accountable and to ensure that women are part of future peace negotiations.

COMBATING STIGMA AGAINST SEXUAL VIOLENCE SURVIVORS

The deliberate use of rape and other forms of sexual violence to terrorize and impose control over both individuals and entire communities has been documented in armed conflicts worldwide. Armed actors target their sexualized attacks based upon the logic of gendered power dynamics that predate the outbreak of the conflict, targeting both women and gender nonconforming people. Gender-based violence becomes a vehicle to enforce political ideology.

Unless official peace and national reconciliation processes grapple directly with this form of violence and its consequences, the resulting agreement will fail to include relevant solutions that can meet the needs of survivors, offer accountability, and check the recurrence and normalization of violence (see Davies et al. 2016). Neglecting to distinguish gender-based violence as a particular form of violation, with specific manifestations and consequences, has resulted in that violence coming to define life for women and gender nonconforming people in so-called peace time. In Nicaragua, the normalization of gender-based and sexual violence as a weapon during the Contra war of the 1980s still reverberates, as perpetrators continue to mimic those tactics (Prieto-Carron et al. 2007). In Guatemala, where rape was used as a weapon during its three-decade civil war, women continue to endure a femicide crisis more than twenty years after a peace agreement was signed (Carey Jr. and Torres 2010).

Research by Htun and Weldon (2012: 553) has shown that when women civil society groups organize together, they "generate social knowledge about women's position as a group in society," and establish those issues as priorities on the policymaking agenda. Conversely, when these groups are absent or marginalized, gender-based violence is perceived as tangential or "only" important to women. Women civil society actors, in both the Syrian and Colombian case studies, have thus worked to include sexual violence in peace negotiations. After an initial draft of the Colombian peace agreement left room for impunity for perpetrators of sexual violence, women both inside and outside the official process mobilized pressure for changes. As a result, the final agreement as signed does not include crimes such as massacres, kidnapping, and sexual violence under amnesty provisions.

Even outside of those official policymaking spaces, women's civil society groups work at the grass-roots level to de-normalize rape as a mode of community control and terror, just as many such groups confront sexual violence during peace time. They accomplish this by offering medical aid, counseling, and other care, in ways that are sensitive to survivors' needs and that demonstrate to community members what acceptance of survivors looks like. By fostering this acceptance, women civil society actors disarm the power of sexual violence as a weapon of war by denying its ability to destroy the social fabric of communities through stigmatization of survivors.

These efforts serve to shift community and cultural norms, yet they also create new spaces for political action separate from official processes. Htun and Weldon's research has revealed how autonomous women's groups engage in a form of "everyday politics," talking directly to community members about clearly relevant realities of their lives, shaping new models of social organization, and preparing communities to accept new ideas (2012: 554). For instance, the work of the Colombian organization Taller de Vida invites survivors of sexual violence and forced recruitment to share their personal stories with the community, through art installations, dramatic performances and public conversations. This "everyday politics" may happen far from the negotiating table yet remains indispensable to the cultural change that undergirds effective peace-building. Furthermore, when the doors of the negotiating room remain locked to women civil society actors, these grass-roots spaces can cooperate as laboratories for the creation of new peacemaking strategies.

Once again, networked advocacy provides the conduit for a feedback loop from the grass-roots realm back into the policy space. In 2017, the first full year of implementation of Colombia's peace agreement, grass-roots organizations prepared to turn their years of community organizing and documentation of wartime rights violations into concrete policy actions to propose at the national level, including to offer reparation for survivors of sexual violence and to better reintegrate former combatants into civilian society.

CONCLUSION

Grass-roots organizing, particularly through women's leadership, is fundamental to the success of peace processes, as has been argued by many proponents of the global Women, Peace, and Security Agenda. In fact, in contrast to what occurs in an official negotiating room, women's grass-roots peace-building is a truer, more fundamental, and long-lasting peace process. It is the foundation upon which peace agreements must be built, and it is the vehicle for implementation at the community level.

Networked advocacy, combining local and international women's rights actors in the service of a common goal, aids this noteworthy shift in emphasis by arraying a network of support around grass-roots in women's civil society. As actors in the network move through spaces of advocacy, official and community-based, they measure their success not through achievement in official spaces, but by impacts at the local level. Influential stakeholders—including governments, funders, and international organizations that operate as gatekeepers to peace processes—must recognize the power of these networks and mobilize resources and support to sustain them.

NOTE

1. The Women Lead to Peace Convening was spearheaded by the women's organizations MADRE, WILPF, CODEPINK, the Nobel Women's Initiative, and Kvinna till Kvinna.

REFERENCES

ABColombia, Corporación Sisma Mujer, and The U.S. Office on Colombia (USOC). "Colombia: Women, Conflict-Related Sexual Violence, and the Peace Process." November 2013, http://reliefweb.int/sites/reliefweb.int/files/resources/ABColombia_Conflict_related_sexual_violence_report.pdf.

Carey Jr., D., and M. G. Torres. "Precursors to Femicide: Guatemalan Women in a Vortex of Violence." *Latin American Research Review* 45, no. 3 (2010): 142–164.

Casey, N. "Colombia's Congress Approves Peace Accord with FARC." *New York Times,* 2016, https://www.nytimes.com/2016/11/30/world/americas/colombia-farc-accord-juan-manuel-santos.html.

Davies, S., True, J., and Tanyag, M. "How women's silence secures the peace: analysis of sexual and gender-based violence in a low-intensity conflict." Gender & Development 24, no. 3 (2016): 459–473.

Disney, A. *Pray the+ Devil Back to Hell (Film).* Fork Films, April 2008.

Earthjustice. "Standing Rock Sioux Tribe Asks federal Court to Set Aside Trump's Pipeline Reversal." December 4, 2017, http://earthjustice.org/features/faq-standing-rock-litigation.

Gambale, M. L. "How Syrian Women Landed at the UN Peace Talks and What It All Means." *PassBlue,* 2016, http://www.passblue.com/2016/05/10/how-syrian-women-landed-at-the-un-peace-talks-and-what-it-all-means/.

Gbowee, L. "Effecting Change through Women's Activism in Liberia." Institute for Development Studies Bulletin, Vol. 40, no. 2. Malden, MA: Blackwell, 2009.

Ghazzawi, R., A. Mohammed, and O. Ramandan. "Peacebuilding Defines Our Future Now: A Study of Women's Peace Activism in Syria." Istanbul: Badael Foundation, 2015.

Htun, M., and S. L. Weldon. "The Civic Origins of Progressive Policy Change: Combating Violence against Women in Global Perspective, 1975–2005." *American Political Science Review* 106 (2012): 548–569.

Human Rights and Gender Justice Clinic, City University of New York School of Law, MADRE, and The Women's International League for Peace and Freedom (WILPF). "Human Rights Violations against Women and Girls in Syria." Submission to the United Nations Universal Periodic Review, July 25, 2016, https://www.madre.org/sites/default/files/PDFs/Syria%20UPR%20submission%20Final.pdf.

Leimbach, D. "As Syrian Peace Talks Take Shape, How Will Women Take Part?" *PassBlue*, December 26, 2015, http://www.passblue.com/2015/12/26/as-syrian-peace-talks-take-shape-how-will-women-take-part/.

Medina, D. A., and R. Davis. "Veteran Finds Forgiveness, Peace in Standing Rock Fight." *NBC News*, December 9, 2016, http://www.nbcnews.com/storyline/dakota-pipeline-protests/veteran-finds-forgiveness-peace-standing-rock-fight-n694226.

Monet, J. "Standing Rock Joins the World's Indigenous Fighting for Land and Life." *Yes! Magazine*, September 30, 2016, http://www.yesmagazine.org/people-power/standing-rock-joins-the-worlds-indigenous-fighting-for-land-and-life-20160930.

Murphy, H. "Colombia Accepts Role in 1980s Killings of Leftist Politicians." *Reuters*, September 15, 2016, http://www.reuters.com/article/us-colombia-rebels-idUSKCN11M052.

Msimang, S. "The Backlash against African Women." *New York Times*, January 10, 2015, https://www.nytimes.com/2015/01/11/opinion/sunday/the-backlash-against-african-women.html.

Paffenholz, T. "Beyond the Normative: Can Women's Inclusion Really Make for Better Peace Processes?" Policy Brief. Graduate Institute of International and Development Studies' Centre on Conflict, Development, and Peacebuilding, 2015.

Payne, C. "Standing Rock Goes to the Inter-American Commission on Human Rights." *IntLawGrrls*, December 3, 2016, https://ilg2.org/2016/12/03/standing-rock-goes-to-the-inter-american-commission-on-human-rights/.

Prieto-Carron, M., M. Thomson, and M. Macdonald. "No more killings! Women Respond to Femicides in Central America." *Gender & Development* 15, no. 1 (2007): 25–40.

Reuters. "Colombia Approves Amnesty Deal for Thousands of Farc Rebels." *The Guardian*, December 28, 2016, https://www.theguardian.com/world/2016/dec/29/colombia-approves-amnesty-deal-for-thousands-of-farc-rebels.

Rojas, C. "In the Midst of War: Women's Contributions to Peace in Colombia." Women Waging Peace Policy Commission, Hunt Alternatives Fund, April 2004.

Rojas, C. "Women and Peacebuilding in Colombia: Resistance to War, Creativity for Peace." In *Colombia: Building Peace in a Time of War*, edited by V. M. Bouvier, 207–224. Washington, DC: United States Institute of Peace Press, 2009.

Sakr, A. "Iraqi Government Rejects Plans for Women's Shelters." *Al-Monitor*, December 9, 2013, http://www.aina.org/news/2013129170017.htm.

Stone, L. "Annex II: Quantitative Analysis of Women's Participation in Peace Processes." In *Reimagining Peacemaking: Through Women's Roles in Peace Processes*, edited by Marie O'Reilly, Andrea Süilleabháin, and Thania Paffenholz, 34. New York: International Peace Institute, 2015.

Vigaud-Walsh, F. "A Battle Not Yet Over: Displacement and Women's Needs in Post-Peace Agreement Colombia." Refugees International Field Report, 2016.

Williams, K., and M. Barsa. "Syrian Women Know How to Defeat ISIS." *Time*, 2014, http://time.com/3513830/syrian-women-defeat-isis/.

CHAPTER 63

....

WOMEN'S PEACEMAKING
IN SOUTH ASIA

....

MEENAKSHI GOPINATH AND RITA MANCHANDA

IN South Asia with conflicted borders, multiple sociocultural communities, divided and deeply unequal groups jostling for power and resources, the Women, Peace, and Security (WPS) discourse has had to grapple with global assumptions that tended to homogenize the category of women in conflict situations. In South Asia's conflict-peace continuum, gender identities get subsumed along the pervasive fault lines of caste, class, region, and religion. Women confront multiple barriers as they negotiate the complicities between the patriarchies of family, community, and state that thwart cross-community peace politics. Transcending these internal fault lines is the vibrant counter narrative of South Asian women's peace networks. Solidarities across borders and boundaries in the face of extremely entrenched state centric and military centric discourses (Khattak 1997: 38–52) are the distinct marker of the region's WPS activism. Especially where states are in official denial of the existence of internal conflicts, local women's engagement around the substantive global norms enunciated in the WPS (1325 +) policy framework has substantially expanded its contours to include issues of justice, marginalization, and militarism. The development discourse and issues of human security have remained an integral part of the region's WPS engagement. Women's "peace-work" has been impacted by their mobilization around civil society movements for political economic and social justice (Coomaraswamy and Fonseca 2004).

We argue that South Asia's rich and textured experience of peace-work at the micro level has recognized and positioned the everyday resistance and resilience of women within the framework of the complex dialectic of "victimhood" and "agency." It is a nonlinear and nuanced understanding of the structural constraints and "enabling spaces" that women negotiate through the continuum of conflict (Gopinath and DasGupta 2006: 192). South Asia's varied and innovative styles of peace-work are negotiated through culturally rooted strategies. These include performing, mourning, and politicizing motherhood to demand justice from a protector state often experienced as predator; inverting the politics of shame through naked protests; harnessing the moral force of protracted "fasting" to speak truth to power; and consciously building regional solidarities to foreground the imperative of peace in a conflicted region. Building theory from praxis it unpacks women's marginalization as rooted in governance structures, the political economy of violence, impunity, and cultural practices.

These innovative strategies and conceptual insights, many often preceding Resolution 1325, have remained comparatively invisibilized in national and global discussions and frameworks. This chapter maps the trajectory of South Asian women scripting their WPS agenda even as they negotiate the fault lines of identity and sociocultural constraints of inequality to build openings for peace in heavily masculinized and militarized spaces. We argue that the narrative of structural constraints and enabling spaces needs to more effectively enter the global discourse to make it less normatively prescriptive and more sensitive to contextual specificities so as to recognize the politics of peacemaking in diverse conflicts. The first part of the chapter addresses the complexities and specificities of women's peacework in some heightened spaces of conflict in the region, the strategies employed, and the organizations and platforms that have facilitated this work. The second part of the chapter engages with the reasons for this comparative invisibility and the consequent implications for the dilution of the global WPS agenda.

FROM INVISIBILITY TO PROTAGONISM

Across South Asia in the hills and valley of India's Northeast and Jammu and Kashmir; Bangladesh's Chittagong Hill Tracts (CHT); Pakistan's Balouchistan; in Nepal, Afghanistan, and Sri Lanka—women mobilizing for peace finds reflection in myriad Mothers Fronts, Association of Parents of Disappeared, Conflict Victims Platform, Association of War Affected Women, and the like. Performing in public space the act of grieving, Mothers Fronts in Sri Lanka's North and South, as in Kashmir and Balouchistan, demanded that the state return their "disappeared" children so as to enable them as mothers to fulfill their duty. Strategies were innovated using weapons of the weak, like ritualistic wailing and cursing, as public protest by Sri Lankan mothers of "missing" youth cadres of *Janatha Vimukthi Perumana* (de Mel 2001: 233–281). Widows of the 1984 anti-Sikh carnage in Delhi shamed an accused state by refusing to end their public enactment of mourning rituals (Das 1990: 345–398). Naga Mothers Association (NMA) initiated a peace campaign centered around the motto: "Shed No Blood," which turned on ritually restoring through the shawl ceremony human value to every unclaimed "body" so as to end violence among splintered Naga armed groups (Manchanda 2004: 39). Everyday activities were politicized. NMA's *kitchen politics* evolved around the comforting symbols of hearth and food so as to appeal to factional leaders to end violence. Not only did they facilitate indirect talks among top leaders, but asserted themselves as trusted ceasefire monitors. In Sri Lanka mothers of missing soldiers brokered a temporary ceasefire between the government and LTTE (Visaka Dharmadasa, quoted in Manchanda 2017a: xvii). Batticaloa saw the remarkable effort of mothers and wives of the "disappeared" using Sri Lanka's Right to Information (RTI) Act to push for answers at government offices (Bastian 2017).

Women's collectives emerged as the front line against militarization, war hysteria, and human rights violations (including sexual violence), entering the public sphere as a group for the first time. In Pakistan, defying extreme patriarchies, two dozen Baloch women marched for a month over seven hundred kilometres (435 miles) to Karachi to seek justice for their brothers, sons and husbands who had "disappeared." Decades earlier, in the 1980s, the rallies of Pakistan's Women Action Forum (WAF) stood as the bulwark against state sponsored Islamization and the undermining of women's rights (Jilani 1986). In Manipur province of Northeast India, neighborhood collectives of Mothers, the *Meira Paibis* (torch bearers) patrolled the night streets to sound the alarm against counter insurgency raids by soldiers, performing resistance in mass "sit-ins," silent vigils, and rallies against state militarization. Characteristic of the panoply of organizations involved in peacemaking in the region is the tradition of alliance building with other social movements for asserting human security. This is evident in the involvement of the Meira Paibis and women's groups across the Northeast asserting livelihood and environmental security and resisting mega hydroelectric and tourism projects, which are often militarily enforced (Hans 2016: 160–184).

As elsewhere, the dominant idiom of women's peace politics is motherhood politics. By its side is another significant trope of activism—the inversion of the politics of the body and the politics of shame. From using their bodies as human shields to prevent clashes and lying prostrate for hours to stop army vehicles loaded with "our boys" from being taken away, women innovated an inversion of *body politics*. Women, whose bodies were sexually assaulted and mutilated in their homes and fields during the conflict, used their bodies in the public space to confront a more powerful opponent, the Indian security forces, by shaming the "protector" authority, the state,[1] in naked protests in Odhisha province in India against a mega development project, and in Manipur against the impunity afforded by the Armed Forces Special Powers Act (AFSPA).[2]

In 2004, twelve Meira Paibis stripped and enacted a naked protest at the gate of the historic Kangla Fort, the headquarters of Assam Rifles in Imphal, province of Manipur. Through their legacy of anti-colonial protests, the Mothers, holding aloft a banner "Indian Army, Come Rape Us," howled their outrage at the abduction, rape, torture, killing, and mutilation of the body of their "daughter" Manorma Devi on suspicion of being a member of an armed group. In custody, she was shot and her genitalia mutilated. Their *body politics* shamed the state into setting up a review committee. It recommended repeal, but AFSPA has stayed.

Amidst the Meira Paibis was South Asia's peace icon, Irom Chanu Sharmila, on hunger strike (force-fed nasally in custody) from 2000 to 2016. Irom's punitive denial of her body in sixteen long years of hunger strike, abjuring food and water, is also an inversion of body politics (Mehrotra 2009). It is a strategy of bodily renunciation to assert the moral force of truth to power. The state's conscious policy of invisibilizing the moral protest of this latter day Gandhian with a section of the nationalist media colluding in this strategy of erasure, led her to finally abandon her fast for a sad debut into electoral politics.

Solidarity networks across conflicted borders are a hallmark of the region's peacemaking initiatives. Women across the region share a struggle with decades of internal conflicts which have their causes in, and consequences for, interstate and regional conflicts. The opportunities for strategic intervention have predicated working regionally, sharing lessons learned and exchanging good practices. For instance, women have boldly acknowledged the excesses of their own state against women during conflicts with neighboring states. Pakistan's influential WAF, in an important symbolic act of solidarity, publicly apologized for war crimes perpetrated by Pakistan soldiers on East Pakistan's women in the 1971 Liberation War for Bangladesh (Sarwar 2015). More recently, cross-border gender accountability initiatives received a new impetus with women's groups using the CEDAW reporting mechanism in 2014 to demand that India's extraterritorial development assistance projects in neighboring countries, such as Sri Lanka, incorporate gender sensitivities.

Across the militarized and masculinized Pakistan-India border, women engaging in *bus diplomacy* have transgressed the dominant national security discourse and visited the other, humanizing "the enemy." Dialogues across fault lines within and across borders have explored the possibility of building a transversal politics (Samuel 2017: 80–96). Multiple regional and subregional networks of women have shared and forged common strategies— for example, Naga women interacting with Sri Lankan peace activists (Banerjee 2003); and women from the Chittagong Hill Tracts (Bangladesh) and the Naga hills have discussed their conflict resolution accords (Perera 1999). Women have worked regionally to contribute to the global WPS agenda (Goswami et al. 2017: 50–79).

The failure of states across the region to provide institutional mechanisms for the peaceful resolution of conflicts has produced a plethora of cross-border civil society initiatives for peace. Among the most vibrant are women's peace networks such as WISCOMP (Women in Security Conflict Management and Peace), WIPSA (Women's Initiatives for Peace in South Asia), ASR (Institute of Women's Studies, Lahore), SANGAT (South Asia Network of Gender Advocacy and Training), and WRN (Women's Regional Network). Women have played a prominent role in other forums, such as SAFHR (South Asia Forum for Human Rights); SAHR (South Asian for Human Rights); and ICES (International Centre for Ethnic Studies) and PIFPD (Pak-India Forum for Peace and Democracy), which facilitated regional thinking and strategizing on peace and security and nurtured a Pak-India peace constituency.

Organizations like WISCOMP were among the first to recognize the importance of cross-border learning of women organizing for peace and enabled Naga—Sri Lanka exchanges, India- Pakistan joint training exposures, and provided an inclusive platform for multistakeholder regional dialogues. The activities of WISCOMP, SAFHR, SIMORGH, and ICES (especially under the directorship of Radhika Coomaraswamy) seeded a South Asian feminist peace discourse rooted in the everyday peace-work of women addressing issues of quotidian transgressions on human security. Their research and advocacy work claimed space for women's experiences to redefine "hard security issues" deemed a masculine bastion (Rajagopalan and Faizal 2005).

It was at the confluence of the expanding global conceptualization of human security and feminist knowledge that local women's peace-work became not only visible but recognized as "political" agency. It encouraged national, regional, and international women's peace networks to engage for the first time with local women living in conflict. In India, women's mobilization around Beijing 1995 fostered the emergence of organizations such as North East Network, whose advocacy work drew national attention to the impact of AFSPA on women's rights and lives in this conflict zone (Goswami et al. 2005), even entering the policy text of the government's XI (2005–2011) and XII (2012–2017) Five Year Plans. Independent research bodies across the region such as WISCOMP (Delhi), Calcutta Research Group (Kolkata), SAFHR (Kathmandu), ICES (Colombo), and ASR (Lahore), and *Ain o Salish Kendra* (Dhaka) facilitated pioneering studies that located women's collective activism as a part of wider social movements asserting human security and inclusive citizenship rights. Importantly, the creative outpouring of advocacy and research on what later came to inform the global WPS agenda was already out there in the 1980s and 1990s. It was galvanized further by the expanding global WPS architecture of policy norms.

NEGOTIATING GENDERED POWER SYSTEMS

Despite evidence of the richness and value of women's peace-work, women are missing at and around the region's peace tables where discussions are animated by the self-interested language of power brokerage. They are instrumentalized as victims of the war atrocity narrative and mobilized for mass protest rallies but are denied voice and autonomy by state and non-state authorities. For instance, in Sri Lanka, the vibrant and independent Mothers Front in Jaffna subsequently was reined in by the LTTE as it consolidated its authoritarian control over the struggle (de Mel 2001: 238). Similarly, WISCOMP's intervention in peace-building in Kashmir revealed that although women were part of the community's struggle for self-determination, "the majority saw themselves as largely acted upon rather than conscious actors" (DasGupta and Sinha 2008: 11, 19). Even in the case of the *Meira Paibis*, although their moral authority peaked following the naked protest in 2004, and their resistance status was further sanctified by several months in prison, when it came to asserting leadership in the civil society sphere, they were excluded. Moreover, changes in the political economy have undermined further the socioeconomic base of their solidarity in the all women *Ima* Market (Laimayum 2012). Part of the difficulty of leveraging women's activism is that women themselves do not see their activity as political, but often as an extension of their domestic roles.

While the contingent situations may be different in Bangladesh, India, Nepal, and Sri Lanka, the gendered politics of instrumentalizing women in power narratives and marginalizing them in power structures are the same across cultures and histories. An important exception was Sri Lanka's Gender Sub Committee during the 2002–2003 peace talks. Supported by the Norwegian facilitator, women mobilized to influence the peace talks and established a women's committee of five nominated by the government and five by the LTTE (Samuel 2010). The abrupt collapse of the peace talks aborted this pioneering initiative. Even in the region's internationally backed peace processes: Nepal and Afghanistan, women voices were absent from the peace table. Sima Samar, head of Afghanistan's Human Rights Commission, bitterly observed that vulnerable groups whose lived experiences of oppression made them have the greatest stake in working for peace and justice are not listened to. Instead, armed groups who know nothing but war determine decisions on peace and justice (cited in Manchanda 2017a: xxix). Even in the Indo-Naga peace process, where civil society bodies are playing an iconic role in sustaining a difficult peace process over eighteen years of an uneasy ceasefire, the interim Indo-Naga Framework Agreement of 2015 involved no civil society, a space where women are largely present (Manchanda and Bose 2015: 78–97).

However, it is in the long Naga conflict–peace continuum that we witness the scope and limits of the empowering potential of women's practice of peace work. Naga women's collectives have moved their work beyond the apolitical archetype of *Mother Sorrow* to political assertion aimed at transforming gendered power systems. Five decades of Naga statehood and market penetration, galvanized further by the long cold peace, has produced a new order of elite stratification in Naga hills which is not only reworking relations within traditional tribal hierarchies, but also class, youth, and gender relations. A generation of educated and professional tribal women have emerged, many of whom are linked with national, regional (Sri Lanka), and international indigenous women's networks. The ceasefire has provided the context for women to translate their moral authority as "peacekeepers" and push for inclusion in the all-male public sphere, traditional and modern (Manchanda and Kakran 2017). Women's claim to representation in the public sphere is stymied by the influential males of the community as a transgression of Naga community identity and in violation of Article 371A of the Indian Constitution which guarantees upholding customary laws and practices. The gender question has polarized Naga society bringing to a head tensions inherent in the relationship of gender, ethnicity, and nation.

The context of South Asia illustrates the complexity of addressing women, peace, and security issues given multiple social layers, and women negotiating contradictory and complicit patriarchies of state, community, and family. The region's multi-ethnic societies and cross-border co-ethnicities posit belonging to collectivities other than the nation state. Women who are embedded in their communities thus experience the state as oscillating between "protector" of status quo interests and as "predator" when their community contends for power and resources (de Mel 2001). Their articulation of autonomy gets enmeshed in the overall identity struggles of the community (Manchanda and Bose 2015:138–166). Yet, after the guns fall silent, "normalcy" restores gendered norms. Tamil women's postwar experience in Sri Lanka is one of deepening victimization as they negotiate a climate of fear and vulnerability at the hands of the security forces and from within their own communities (Gowrinathan and Cronin-Furman 2015). The state is nowhere near gender neutral as narratives of state building expose. Gendered narratives of the Great Partition (1947) of the Indian subcontinent tell the sordid story of the Indian and Pakistan states stripping away rights from women abducted during the communal violence, and uprooting and "restoring" them forcibly to their territorial belonging, following the demarcation of the two nation states (Menon and Bhasin 2002). In Bangladesh, it is the story of a patriarchal state giving away for foreign adoption babies born to women raped in the war as "spoilt" and thus unfit to become Bangladeshi citizens (D'Costa 2011: 110–143).

Gender identities get subsumed particularly as women organize in Northeast India, Bangladesh, and Sri Lanka around ethnic belonging. Solidarities, in particular, crumble when mainstream women's groups (outside conflict zones) internalize national security discourses and cartographic anxieties. "When nationalism is part of the equation with militarization," scholar activist Meghna Guhathakurta (2010: 74–76) observed, there was little room for dialogue between CHT women and Bangladesh's mainstream women's movement. Solidarities cracked when Bangladeshi women at the Women's Conference in Beijing in 1995 excluded from the country presentation their own military's sexual abuse of the hill women.

The challenge has been to create a space where identities matter less, and where militarization, cultures of impunity, and exclusionary politics are seen as common areas of women's engagement. In South Asia, within the evolving WPS agenda, environment, antiwar, and antinuclear protests are areas of common struggle, as too is the economy and the decline in women's labor force participation. Sarla Emmanuel's (2008) strategic mapping of Sri Lankan women's peace activism demonstrates the integral interconnectedness of peacework with the broader work of addressing issues of socioeconomic marginalization, cultural oppression, patriarchal practices, labor rights, political rights, and justice. Building on that tradition, Sri Lankan feminists are forging difficult alliances on the basis of "transversal solidarities" among the three ethnicities in Sri Lanka exploring common spaces of socioeconomic rights entitlements (Samuel 2017: 50).

The ascendancy of hyper-nationalism in India and elsewhere, however, has seen mainstream women's groups retreat from engaging, even on humanitarian issues in conflict areas, especially with the media's obsessive focus on the casualties of the security forces defending national sovereignty. Arguably, the invisibilization of South Asian women's peace-work in the global template has something to do with its invisibilization in national gender and security discourses.

PARADOX OF INVISIBILITY: WOMEN'S PEACE-WORK

It is at the grass-roots where women's fecund activism in the many conflicts and peace processes of South Asia is found and confined. The Naga women, the CHT hill women, and Pashto women of Swat (Pakistan) are not to be found at the formal peace tables. In Pakistan's Swat district, women lobbied to be included in the peace talks between the ruling Awami National Party (ANP) in Khyber Pakhtunkhwa and the Taliban (2009), insisting on "no peace talks about us, without us," determined to defend women's rights being traded away for ending the "war." The gender-apartheid Taliban made women's exclusion a deal breaker. Refusing to be marginalized, ANP women organized a separate peace table, a women's *Jirga* (Manchanda 2017: xvii). In Bangladesh, Amin Mohsin, the chronicler of the country's hegemonic nationalism and of the CHT hill tribes struggle for their identity and rights, describes the exclusive peace negotiations of 1997 in distant Dhaka, isolating the CHT "elite" representatives from their support base including the Hill Women's Federation, which had been mobilized during twenty years of struggle (Mohsin 2003).

South Asian feminist intellectuals are critical of this focalization of women's agency to one indicator—the number of women at peace tables. Nighat Khan, who has been an influential voice in shaping the Global South WPS discourse asserted that the "issue (in engendering peace processes) was not about getting more women and expertise at the table but more about, what is it that women are negotiating or mediating for? What is on the table during peace talks and who determines what should be on the peace table? What do or should women bring to the peace table? What can be compromised and how can women's rights not be traded away?" (Gowami et al 2017: 61). It is a perspective that finds echo in WISCOMP's monographs, which popularized the notion of "more women *around* the peace table" (Gopinath and DasGupta 2006).

Is there an "ill fit" in South Asian praxis of peace-building and the global WPS discourse? South Asian experiences and feminist expertise remains comparatively invisible in the 2012 global compendium UN Women Sourcebook. The Global Study's analysis in 2015 does resonate with the region's experiences, but only Nepal and Afghanistan find some attention, and Sri Lanka's Gender Subcommittee, a brief mention. Only where the "internationals" are involved do these processes and women's experiences within them get reflected in global policy discussions and frameworks. Do they "fit" better the global WPS paradigm of peacemaking, structured around adoption of National Action Plans and getting women to the peace table? Drawing upon her experience as a participant in Sri Lanka's Gender Subcommittee process, Kumudini Samuel (2010) concluded that while women's presence in official peace negotiations could place women's needs and concerns on the peace agenda, their presence in and of itself would not guarantee an engendered discussion, especially if participants at high-level negotiations are distanced from their communities' grass-roots peace movement.

That skepticism has been reinforced by the mixed experiences of the "gains" of conflict and peace-building in internationalized processes in Nepal and Afghanistan, which have promoted women's inclusion. Women's quotas did ensure impressive representation in the post-accord peace architecture. Admittedly, in Nepal, women's mobilization during the Maoist conflict and women's resistance in the subsequent political transformation, created the context for the internationals to support women occupying a third of the seats in the Constituent Assembly (Yadav 2016: 60–71). In Afghanistan, an overtly top–down process vaulted women into public office. The peace momentum enabled gender rights to be incorporated in the constitutions. Progressive policies were formulated despite intransigent patriarchies (Oxfam 2011). National Action Plans on 1325 and 1820 were adopted in both countries though with questionable commitments on implementation (Buchanan et al. 2012; Afghan Women's Network 2014). However, in Nepal, power struggles and ascendant caste, ethnic, and regional affiliations vitiated the national peace-building consensus, divided the women, and gender equality was disappointingly set back, especially with international commitments weakening. In Afghanistan, the alliances that political women had made with warlords and power brokers for leveraging influence and security distanced them from the solidarities of women's networks and reduced them to proxies. Also, women who, emboldened by the assurances of the internationals, had joined government service and become development workers and human rights defenders found themselves vulnerable targets and isolated from their communities as the international community withdrew and extremist forces regained control. "Peace" with the Taliban, it was feared, would trade away women's rights (Manchanda 2017a: xxviii).

In non-internationalized negotiated settlements such as Bangladesh's CHT accord in 1997, the Hill Women's Federation, which had been mobilized during twenty years of struggle, was marginalized in the peace processes that delivered a "violent peace," with women feeling even more insecure and from multiple sources (D'Costa 2014). However, the indigenous roots of their resistance, and their expanding alliances with broader social movements in Bangladesh and abroad, has made it possible to sustain their continuing struggle for rights. This is more robustly demonstrated within the Naga peace process, where women are effectively leveraging their moral authority as peacemakers and through alliance building with other social solidarities to claim entry into the public sphere, challenging their customary exclusion from decision-making. The patriarchal backlash, in which the women's question became a pawn in the chessboard of power politics, has set back the movement, but not without instilling a bitter lesson in political strategy (Changkija 2017). The Naga women's story exemplifies the dialectic of structural constraints and enabling spaces, a nonlinear narrative of an organically rooted movement to transform the nature of gender exclusion and inequality.

This narrative needs to more effectively enter the policy discussions and normative framework of the 1325+ discourse, if it is to expand beyond an elite women-driven project of peripheral value, especially in non-internationalized conflict zones. This "ill fit" has contributed to the ambivalence of government officials and the region's gender experts toward Resolution 1325 as an enabling frame. Political sensitivities have made Indian officials, with Pakistan and Sri Lanka closely following, assert, "*[T]here are no situations of 'armed* conflict' within the territory of India, and hence the Security Council Resolution 1325 relating to Women in Armed Conflict is not applicable to India."[3]

Official disfavor regarding mechanisms that bring in international accountability have discouraged mainstream and, especially, "funded" women's groups to avoid such international instruments as 1325+. Consequently Resolution 1325 has had relatively limited impact in protecting or promoting women as key drivers in peace-building in the region. Instead, gender equality activists have focused on using country commitments under CEDAW (including General Recommendation 30: 2013) and the normative framework of the Beijing Platform for Action (BPFA) to oppose militarization and support local women building "human security." Importantly, CEDAW GR30's more expanded conceptualization of conflict and attention to structural constraints provides a better "fit" to the South Asian reality. This is not to deny that in Nepal and Afghanistan, but also elsewhere in South Asia, the political international endorsement for Resolution 1325 has encouraged women's groups to use it as a tool for mobilization and an important normative compass for building accountability and solidarities around the spirit of a shared framework (Hans 2016). However, its greater effectiveness requires a realignment of the WPS discourse to resonate with the contextual specificities of the Global South reality.

RE-SCRIPTING WPS DISCOURSE

The international discourse on Women, Peace, and Security, especially from the beginning of the twenty-first century, has tended to focus overwhelmingly on sexual violence against girls and women in conflict and the notion of a "post-conflict" situation. Women's peacemaking in South Asia has, on the other hand, focused on a plethora of issues germane to human security. In the "freedom from want" and "freedom from fear" continuum, sexual violence figures as an important but not "exclusive" concern.

Even in Nepal, where a NAP process was successfully initiated, largely facilitated by the international donor community, it provided a context to conjoin "peace work" with issues of representation in the aftermath of the democratic mobilization against the monarchy. While the concept of "resistance" is not integral to Resolution 1325, it was very much in evidence in the internationalized WPS initiatives in this Himalayan state. The normative compass provided by 1325+ has been pushed further in the South Asian context to include issues of disarmament, displacement, militarism, patriarchy, environment, and development. The politics has been transversal, building solidarities across several sectors of the women's movements and progressive civil society initiatives.

Broadly Center and Left in orientation, these mobilizations have not traditionally been in sync with state ideologies on nationalism or neoliberal paradigms of economic growth. Typically, South Asian women's peace-work has straddled the *divides* between human rights initiatives and nonviolent peace activism that are reflected largely as two discrete, often contradictory streams in national and international narratives. South Asian women's peacemaking has tweaked the 1325 narrative's linearity, recognizing that on the ground, even when the guns are silent, the neat conceptual divisions of "pre-conflict," "conflict," and "post-conflict" stages fly in the face of the continuum of violence women confront on a daily basis.

An ethics of care is deeply inscribed when *doing* peace, as the *Shed No Blood* slogan or *kitchen politics* in India's Northeast has demonstrated. The deft play of transgression and bricolage in their approach to building peace, underscores that while the battle lines may not be always formally drawn, conflict and violence colors the quotidian experience encompassing not just combatants but entire families and kin communities. The personal has in this sense always remained the palpably political. South Asian women's groups have striven consistently to break the barriers between the "private" and the "public" in their peace work, even as different forms and manifestations of overt and structural violence come down heavily on their everyday resistances. Here the resistances of women in what is apolitically designated as the "private" sphere assume the magnitude of major transgressions on entrenched structures of patriarchy. These are structures that embed and legitimize cultures of militarism and impunity—the ultimate Bastille for women's peace-work. While these local initiatives may appear miniscule from the hallowed precincts of international policymaking, persistence and courage in the face of the magnitude of violent reaction they evoke from deeply entrenched structures of power need to be more visibilized.

Violent extremism, while sustained by large international networks of arms, drugs, and funds, depends also on homegrown, alienated youth, nurtured by intransigent cultures of militarism. This has been the pervasive battlefield for women making peace in South Asia. Alongside, there is the use of extrajudicial methods by states to contain secessionist tendencies and armed insurgencies in regions of conflict. Here, the state of exception becomes the norm of governance. How women negotiate spaces for dialogue, caught as they are between two armed patriarchies of the state and the militants, is also a narrative of tactics that the global script would do well to foreground. Using a Lederacian lens, this would constitute the *matrix of multilogues* that women's peace-work can bring to the high table—a simultaneity of conversations both vertical and horizontal with multiple stakeholders.[4] The aphorism, from the "village council to the negotiation table" (coined by International Alert), with the importance of each stage as supportive and contributing to the next in a cycle of interlinkages to build expanding circles of engagement, could be the *mantra* that reflects the work of women peacemakers in South Asia.

South Asian women's rich and fecund peace-work holds the possibility of enriching the vocabulary of the international discourse on WPS, of emphasizing the continuum of violence that women confront even during "cessation of hostilities," and the dialectic between victimhood and agency which is rooted in the specificity of women's complex negotiation of "structural constraints" and the creation of "enabling spaces" for women's peace-building efforts. That narrative needs to impact the global WPS discourse. What the visibilization of women's peace-work in South Asia has the potential of doing, is to redefine the scope and language of political action, and thereby the practice of engaged citizenship across the continuum of peace and conflict.

NOTES

1. Body politics to shame and disempower brutal state authorities has been dramatically captured in Mahasweta Devi's short story "Draupadi," *Multitudes* 2, no. 2 (2007): 37–49.

2. The Armed Forces (Special Powers) Act (AFSPA) of 1958 grants special powers to army and paramilitary forces in what are deemed "disturbed areas." It provides for impunity from criminal prosecution.

3. CEDAW: 37th session, January 15–February 2, 2007; (India) responses to queries on its 2nd and 3rd periodic report.

4. John Paul Lederach's model of conflict transformation involves a non linear approach and a process of "multilogues" that is, by fostering multilevel horizontal relationships across social cleavages as well as vertical links within a conflict party from elite to grassroots to bridge the "interdependence gap".

REFERENCES

Afghan Women's Network. "UN Security Council Resolution 1325 in Afghanistan." Kabul: AWN, 2014.

Banerjee, P. *Across the Experiences: Naga Women in Sri Lanka*. New Delhi: WISCOMP, 2003.

Bastians, D. "Families of the Missing Seek Answers through Right to Information Act." *Daily FT*, February 6, 2017, http://www.ft.lk/article/596166/ft.

Buchanan, C., A. Cooper, C. Griggers, L. Low, R. Manchanda, R. Peters, and A. P. Prentice. *From Clause to Effect. Including Women's Rights and Gender in Peace Agreements*. Geneva: Centre for Humanitarian Dialogue, 2012, https://peacemaker.un.org/sites/peacemaker.un.org/files/IncludingWomensRightsInPeaceAgreements_HDC2012.pdf.

Changkija, M. "Pride as Well as Prejudice." *The Hindu*, February 8, 2017, http://www.thehindu.com/opinion/op-ed/Pride-as-well-as-prejudice/article17242990.ece.

Coomaraswamy, R., and D. Fonseca. *Peace-Work*. Colombo, Sri Lanka: ICES/Kali for Women, 2004.

D'Costa, B. *Nationbuilding, Gender, and War Crimes in South Asia*. New York: Routledge, 2011.

D'Costa, B. "Marginalisation and Impunity: Violence among Women and Girls in the Chittagong Hill Tracts." Dhaka, Bangladesh: Chittagong Hill Tracts Commission, May 26, 2014.

Das, V. "Our Work to Cry. Your Work to Listen." In *Mirrors of Violence: Communities, Riots, and Survivors in South Asia*, edited by V. Das, 345–398. Delhi: Oxford University, 1990.

DasGupta, S., and N. Sinha. *Gender, Violence, and Rights*. New Delhi: WISCOMP, 2008.

De Mel, N. *Women and the Nation's Narrative*. New Delhi: Women Unlimited, 2001.

Emmanuel, S. *Strategic Mapping of Women's Peace Activism in Sri Lanka*. Colombo, Sri Lanka: Women and Media Collective, April 28, 2008, http://womenandmedia.org/strategic-mapping-of-womens-peace-activism-in-sri-lanka/.

Gopinath, M., and S. DasGupta. "Structural Challenges, Enabling Spaces: Gender and Non-Traditional Formulations of Security in South Asia." In *Studying Non-Traditional Security in Asia*, edited by R. Emmers, M. Caballero-Anthony, and A. Acharya, 192–209. Singapore: Cavendish Academic, 2006.

Goswami, R., K. Samuel, and N. S. Khan. "Herstory: Peace Movements in South Asia." In *Women and Politics of Peace*, edited by R. Manchanda, 59–79. New Delhi: Sage, 2017.

Goswami, R., M. G. Sreekala, and M. Goswami. "Women in Armed Conflict Situations." Guwahati, India: North East Network, 2005.

Gowrinathan, N., and K. Cronin-Furman. *The Forever Victims? Tamil Women in Post-War Sri Lanka*. New York: Colin Powell School, 2015.

Guhathakurta, M. "Resistance Politics in the Hills." In *Ashes and Hopes,* edited by Mohaiemen Naeem, 74–76. Dhaka, Bangladesh: Drishtipath Writers Collective, 2010.

Hans, A. "Women of Manipur: A Space for UNSC R 1325." In *Openings for Peace: UNSCR 1325 Women and Security in India,* edited by A. Hans and S. Rajagopalan, 160–184. New Delhi: Sage, 2016.

Jilani, H. "The Pakistan Women's Action Forum." *Canadian Woman Studies* 7, nos. 1–2 (1986): 107–110.

Khattak, S. "Gendered and Violent: Inscribing the Military on the Nation State." In *Engendering the Nation State,* Vol. 2, edited by N. Hussain, S. Mumtaz, and R. Saigol, 38–52. Lahore: Simorgh, 1997.

Laimayum, B. "Women's Protest Movement and Ideology of Motherhood in Manipur." PhD dissertation, Jawaharlal Nehru University, 2012.

Lederach, J. P. *Preparing for Peace: Conflict Transformation.* Syracuse: Syracuse University Press, 1995.

Manchanda, R. "Endgame in the Naga Peace Process." In *Bridging State and Nation,* Vol. 2, edited by R. Manchanda, T. Bose, and S. Nag, 35–121. New Delhi: Sage, 2015.

Manchanda, R. "Gender, Power, and Peace Politics: A Comparative Analysis." In *Women and Politics of Peace,* 21–57. New Delhi: Sage, 2017b.

Manchanda, R. "Introduction." In *Women and Politics of Peace,* xvii–xlii. New Delhi: Sage, 2017a.

Manchanda, R. *We Do More Because We Can: Women in the Naga Peace Process.* Kathmandu: SAFHR, 2004.

Manchanda, R., and S. Kakran. "Gendered Power Transformations in India's Northeast." *Cultural Dynamics* 29, nos. 1–2 (2017): 63–82.

Manchanda, R., and T. Bose. *Making War, Making Peace,* Vol 1. New Delhi: Sage, 2015.

Mehrotra, D. *Burning Bright: Irom Sharmila and the Struggle for Peace in Manipur.* New Delhi: Penguin, 2009.

Menon, R., and K. Bhasin. *Borders and Boundaries.* New Delhi: Kali for Women, 2000.

Oxfam. *A Place at the Table: Safeguarding Women's Rights in Afghanistan.* Oxfam International, 2011, https://www.oxfam.org/en/research/place-table-safeguarding-womens-rights-afghanistan.

Mohsin, Amina. *The Chittagong Hill Tracts: The Difficult Road to Peace.* Boulder, CO: Lynne Rienner, 2003.

Perera, J., ed. *Peace Process in Nagaland and the Chittagong Hill Tracts.* Kathmandu: SAFHR, 1999.

Rajagopalan, S., and F. Faizal, eds. *A Clearing in the Thicket.* New Delhi: Sage, 2005.

Rajagopalan, S. "The 1325 Resolution." In *Openings for Peace: UNSCR 1325 Women and Security in India,* edited by A. Hans and S. Rajagopalan, 8–32. New Delhi: Sage, 2016.

Samuel, K. *The Centrality of Gender in Securing Peace.* New Delhi: WISCOMP, 2010.

Samuel, K. "Women's Activism and the Search for Peace in Sri Lanka." In *Women and Politics of Peace,* edited by R. Manchanda, 80–96. New Delhi: Sage, 2017.

Sarwar, Beena. "Should Pakistanis Apologise to Bangladeshis? An Online Appeal Reopens Old Wounds." *Scroll.in,* December 7, 2015, https://scroll.in/article/773523/should-pakistanis-apologise-to-bangladeshis-an-online-appeal-reopens-old-wounds.

Yadav, P. *Social Transformation in Post-Conflict Nepal.* New Delhi: Routledge, 2016.

CHAPTER 64

WPS, PEACE NEGOTIATIONS, AND PEACE AGREEMENTS

KARIN AGGESTAM

PEACE negotiations and their outcomes have long-term repercussions for post-conflict politics and societies. Peace negotiations can therefore be viewed as "windows of opportunities" to renegotiate power relations and relationships in order to build a more durable and just peace (Anderson 2016). Yet, one of the most striking patterns of contemporary peace diplomacy is the gross underrepresentation of women at the negotiation table, which reflects the gendered nature of diplomacy as an institution (Aggestam and Towns 2018). To give some empirical illustrations, 85 percent of the ambassadors in the world are men (Towns and Niklasson 2016); the United Nations appointed its first-ever female mediator Mary Robinson in 2013; the External Action Service of the European Union is headed by a woman, Federica Mogherini, but all nine Special Envoys are men (as of 2017); and only 2.5 percent of all chief mediators and 9 percent of all negotiators are women in peace processes (UN Women 2012). What these figures reflect is the presence of some major gendered barriers that inhibit women's broader participation in peace diplomacy and negotiation. The gendered dynamics of inclusion and exclusion are particularly prevalent in peace negotiations due to their securitized and militarized framing. They are also distinct by their informal, secretive, and homosocial contexts. Hence, to analyze gender and peace negotiations does not only relate to the extent women are present in the process and what outcomes they produce, but regards also the forms and structures of the overarching process itself and to what extent such process is gendered. In other words, it means looking inside the "black box" of negotiations. By analyzing gendered norms, rules, and practices that shape the negotiators' strategies and preferences, we are able to gain greater insights to the formal and informal institutional setting and design of the negotiation process (Waylen 2014: 495–496).

At the same time, we need to recognize that formal and informal institutions are dynamic and transformative. Women are today seeking out diplomatic careers in increasing numbers, and they are rising in rank within diplomacy (Aggestam and Towns 2018). The landmark resolution of the United Nations Security Council 1325, which was endorsed in 2000, is a significant milestone in the quest for inclusive representation and participation in peace negotiations. The resolution put the Women, Peace and Security (WPS) on to the global agenda of the international community. The resolution underlines the important role women do and should play in the prevention and resolution of conflicts, peace negotiations, and wider peace support operations. Consequently, as part of the WPS agenda, the UN and other regional organizations have made serious attempts to gender-mainstream their organizations and institutions (Krook and True 2012). There is today a coalition of "Friends of WPS," consisting of around thirty member states, which is coordinated by Canada. Some of these countries, such as Australia, Sweden, and Canada have even included the WPS agenda as part of their foreign policies (True 2016). Recently, the Swedish government has taken one step further by declaring that the country is pursuing a feminist foreign policy. As part of that effort, foreign minister Margot Wallström has taken on a normative entrepreneurial leadership in peace diplomacy where one of the top priorities is the inclusion of women in peace negotiations (Aggestam and Bergman Rosamond 2016). As such, the WPS agenda serves as a powerful and salient normative framework. At the same time, we are far from inclusive peace negotiations since such a shift entails reassessing gender hierarchies, power relations, and inequalities.

The research question raised in this chapter is how gender impacts peace negotiations, and how women's participation is conceptualized in theory and framed in policy? The overarching aim is threefold: (a) to examine the descriptive representation of women as peacemakers in the formal negotiation process; (b) to analyze the gendered nature of the informal process; and (c) to identify some restraining and enabling conditions for enhanced participation of women in peace negotiation. Peace negotiations, which aim to resolve, build, and sustain peace, relate to all four pillars of participation, prevention, protection, and peace-building and recovery. This chapter, however, focuses mainly on participation whereas contributions to this handbook (see Part II: Pillars of WPS) discuss the others in greater details.

The chapter proceeds as follow. The first part takes stock of contemporary policy discourses on women's participation and the state-of-the art of scholarly work on gender and peace negotiations. The second part discusses where women are descriptively positioned in peace negotiation and analyzes the gendered dynamics of peace negotiations. Based on a recent empirical study we conducted of fifty-plus peacemakers, some important gender dynamics that enable and constrain women's participation in peace negotiation are identified. The chapter ends with a discussion how the research agenda can be advanced on gender and peace negotiation.

Taking Stock of International Policy Discourses on Women's Participation

There exist today impressive transnational advocacy networks that promote the WPS agenda. They have spurred a number of international initiatives and practices—for example, the UN Institute for Training and Research (UNITAR), which supports women in leadership and diplomacy at the UN headquarter in New York and pushes for gender expertise and the appointments of more women to peace negotiations. Moreover, the UN Security Council restated and passed a new resolution (Resolution 2122) in 2013, requesting the UN Secretary General to mobilize support for an increase in appointments of women as chief mediators. A network of Nordic women mediators (NWM), comprised of a contact group (the Nordic MFAs) together with an advisory group of senior women mediators, was launched in 2015. The overarching ambition of the NWM is to make visible senior women mediators and how they can be utilized as a resource pool for international assignments, as well as to assist more broadly in peace negotiations by interacting with similar women's networks.[1]

Yet, despite nearly two decades of advocacy work, women continue to play marginal roles in formal peace negotiations. In contemporary international advocacy discourses, two major lines of arguments can be delineated on women's participation. The first one is based on women rights and a justice approach, which has sprung from the global women's movement (Garner 2010). The underpinning rationale is that women have the same right to participate in peace negotiations as men. Women constitute 50 percent of the population, and this, it is argued, should be reflected more fairly on the international scene and for sure in matters of peace and security that affect women's everyday life. As mentioned, peace processes open up "windows of opportunities" to negotiate an emancipatory peace (Anderson 2016). In their capacity, mediators and negotiators are centrally positioned to redesign negotiation processes toward greater inclusion. It is argued that actions taken in that direction should be based on principles of justice and fairness, which therefore do not need any further justification (Charlesworth 2008; El-Bushra 2007).

The second line of argument has become more prevalent in recent years and relies more on instrumental reasoning. Here, the presence of women is believed to bring something valuable and different to diplomacy. Women are frequently portrayed as peaceful and with a different set of qualities than men. To include women becomes a "smart" policy since it enhances the prospect for efficient negotiations and peaceful outcomes (Clinton 2011). By way of illustration, after the successful conclusion of the negotiations between Iran and the P5+1 (the UN's five permanent members—China, France, Russia, United Kingdom, and United States—plus Germany) in 2015, the High Representative of the European Union for Foreign Affairs and Security Policy, Federicia Mogherini, stated that "[h]aving many women at the table in key positions . . . helped us to be concrete and pragmatic the whole way" (Kianpour 2015). Indeed, there is a widespread assumption about a positive correlation between women participation, successful negotiations, and sustainable outcomes. Some of these arguments reflect the prevalence of the "women-peace hypothesis," which represents an idealized version of "femininity" where the inclusion of women assumes to generate compromises and sustainable peace (Anderlini 2003 Maoz 2009).

However, there are some conundrums in these contemporary policy discourses. First, the two dominant discourses seem to work and at times even contradict each other, since the first one emphasizes sameness of rights whereas the second builds on arguments of difference and essentialism (Palmiano 2014). Furthermore, an instrumental approach risks prioritizing women's agency within a particular framework that restricts participation to a certain type of women and securitizes women's representation in the sense that it is framed basically as a question about security (Hudson 2012; Shepherd 2011). Second, there is a strong focus in the policy discourses on counting women and on entry points at the negotiation table, whereas much less attention is put on the gendered dynamics of the process itself. Third, there is an overarching inclination to conflate gender and women (Palmiano 2014). For instance, UN officials seem to be aware of the dangers of making women's participation contingent upon essentialist assumptions and positive outcomes, but argue that such instrumental reasoning is still required because it is seen as the most effective and persuasive way to push forward toward broader representation of women on the global diplomatic scene (Hudson 2012: 46). Thus, one central task for academia is to critically probe these underlying assumptions and assess how gendered practices and power relations affect outcomes.

GENDER AND PEACE AGREEMENTS

Contemporary policy discourses also build on an underlying assumption that women's participation in peace negotiations increases the likelihood that gender-specific provisions will be adopted in peace agreements (UN Women 2012). Since the launching of UN resolution 1325 there is a growing number of peace agreements that contain gender provisions, up from 11 percent to 27 percent (Bell 2015, 2010). Moreover, in UN-sponsored peace processes, the WPS-agenda plays an integral part in 67 percent of all these peace agreements (Bell 2015). This pattern probably reflects the growing practice of including gender expertise as part of the negotiation teams. Again, peace mediators are critically positioned and have unique opportunities to enforce the norms entailed in Resolution 1325. They also have the leverage to bring in the required expertise, coordinate, and include women's groups at the civil society level (track 2 and 3) with formal peace negotiations (track 1), thus reinforcing women's agency, empowerment, and interests. The UN mediation in the Great Lakes by the Special Envoy Mary Robinson in 2013 provides a case in point. Robinson made clear from the start that she sought as a mediator to put the principles of 1325 into action by reinforcing women's agency by inclusion at all levels of the peace-building process (O'Reilly and Súilleabháin 2013).

In a recent study, Paffenholz et al. (2016) found a positive correlation in cases where women have been able to exercise strong influence in the peace negotiations and the drafting of agreements. At the same time, the authors caution to give too much weight to numerical presence in formal negotiations. For example, the case of Liberia showed how women's groups *outside* the formal negotiations were able to exert powerful pressure on the negotiating delegations. The Women in the Peacebuilding Network (WIPNET) successfully mobilized a series of effective mass actions in parallel to the peace negotiations, demanding that the parties should reach an agreement (O'Reilly et al. 2015). Hence, Paffenholz et al.'s study does not confirm a correlation between greater representation of women and influence over the negotiation process. For example, female "observers" to peace negotiations have recently been increasing in numbers, but they are rarely influencing the process itself in any substantive ways. This is why the Paffenholz study also concludes that rather than counting women, the focus should be on assessing women's activities and the degree of influence over the decision-making bodies at the negotiation table. As such, these activities relate to what extent women are able to influence the start of peace negotiations; to set the negotiation agenda; to add gender provisions to an agreement and to push for it to be signed. Most important is to assess the extent an agreement is gender-sensitive and if it addresses women rights. There is also a need to explore further the link between the existence of women's rights in peace agreements and their political representation in post-conflict governance. When it comes to durable peace agreements, it seems that women's participation, as witnesses, signatories, mediators, and negotiators, has a positive impact. According to Laurel Stone, (2015) women's participation increases the chances that peace agreements will hold over time by 20 to 35 percent. Yet, Christine Bell (2015: 1) underlines that the major challenge for gender-sensitive peace agreements lies in their quest to be fully implemented. References to women and gender issues tend to be infused with "constructive ambiguity" and "holistic interpretations" that often reflect the absence of shared understandings among the parties. Thus, these clauses become notoriously difficult to implement without further negotiations.

State-of-the-Art on Gender and Peace Negotiation

Three strands of research are relevant to the study of gender in peace negotiations. First, peace and conflict research (PCR) has a longstanding interest in studying and promoting inclusive peace processes because they are intimately linked to the legitimacy and quality of durable peace (see, for example, Stedman et al. 2002; Wallensteen 2015). Civil society engagement in peace processes is also central to the paradigm of conflict transformation, which is dominant in the field. As such, the importance of local ownership, bottom–up/local approaches and the combination of various tracks of negotiations are stressed (Lederach 1998, 2010). At the same time, specific gender analyses are less common in the peace-building field (Shepherd 2016; Duncanson 2016; Björkdahl and Selimovic 2016), and in those cases where gender is taken seriously, it is assessed as part of the wider peace process, civil society engagement, and outcomes, rather than specifically analyzing gender and women's participation in formal negotiations (Kellerby 2013; Waylen 2014).

Second, large parts of feminist scholarship in International Relations (IR) build on a longstanding peace activism around the globe. Thus, there is today a broad range of studies on women and peacemaking as alternatives to militarism (Garner 2010; Porter 2007; Enloe 2016). At the same time, there are surprisingly few studies, which address women and gender in peace diplomacy and international negotiations (Aggestam and Towns 2018; Anderson 2016; Cassidy 2017). One reason for this gap may be related to the general ambivalence that exists among feminist IR scholars to study token women in top leading diplomatic positions as they are linked to state power. More surprising is the near absence of critical feminist analysis on the specific gendered structures and dynamics of formal peace negotiation, which can be contrasted to the growing number of critical feminist studies on military institutions (Kronsell 2012; Sjoberg 2010). One unfortunate consequence of that is that feminist scholarship on peacemaking ends up analyzing women mostly as peaceful agents. As such, it may generate notions of women that feminist scholars seek to deconstruct (Palmiano 2014).

The third research stream is international negotiation theory, which rarely has any research on gender and peace negotiations. This is somewhat of a paradox in a field that otherwise underlines the importance of process dynamics, communication, relation, and context. There are several studies that problematize inclusion/exclusion (see, for example, Wanis St John 2008; Pfaffenholz 2014) in terms of conflicting parties and they underline the importance of culture, cognitive factors, and relational skills such as empathy (Broome 2009). Furthermore, the field of international mediation has taken a quantitative turn in recent years (Bercovitch and Fretter 2007; Greig and Diehl 2012). Due to the low number of empirical cases of women negotiators, over time such longitudinal datasets are restricted. Yet, single and comparative case methodology can serve as a useful alternative approach to the study of gender and peace negotiations. Such studies have great potential to advance new hypotheses as well as theoretical and empirical knowledge in an otherwise underdeveloped field (Ackerly and True 2010: 129).

There are also some studies on gender and international negotiations that are using simulation and experiments (Boyer et al. 2009; Florea et al. 2003). However, their results tend to confirm essentialist assumptions, which underline how men and women approach negotiations differently. Women are often portrayed as having a more relational view of others in negotiations. Women also tend to prefer problem-solving dialogue more often than men. Florea et al. (2003: 230) add that women bring a personalized component of empathy, which is a skill undervalued in male-dominated settings of negotiation. Furthermore, masculine traits are frequently associated with competitive transactional negotiation behavior, whereas feminine characteristics are linked to cooperative and transformational problem-solving. Masculine characteristics typically include self-affirmation, competition, and dominance, while feminine characteristics entail cooperation and inclusion (Florea et al. 2003). These propositions resemble the classical distinction in negotiation theory between distributive and integrative negotiations and in mediation theory between power and pure mediation.

In sum, few studies have critically assessed and analyzed in-depth the gendered structures of peace negotiations and the impact of their hyper-masculine and securitized framing. Sarai Aharoni (2018) depicts peace negotiations as structureless, and highly infused by secrecy and exceptionalism. It is often not clear at what time peace negotiations start, where they take place, and who is participating, which restricts women's opportunity to partake in the process.

WOMEN'S DESCRIPTIVE REPRESENTATION IN PEACE NEGOTIATIONS AND MEDIATION

The most commonly referred study to probe women's descriptive representation in peace negotiation is the UN study from 2012, which was mentioned at the beginning of this chapter. In another unique study on women as formal peace mediators, Aggestam and Svensson (2018) identify thirty-six cases of women as peacemakers from 1991 to 2014. This counts for about 8 percent of the total number of mediation interventions, which is remarkably low; yet, the figure differs somewhat from the UN Women study probably because the latter focuses strictly on chief mediators. However, despite the low number of cases, a clear trend is identified in the last two decades since the launching of Resolution 1325 with an increasing number of women acting as peace mediators, from eleven to twenty-five (Aggestam and Svensson 2018). Furthermore, what stands out in this study is that Nordic, African, and North American mediators constitute approximately two-thirds of all the cases. This result is corroborated by the findings of Towns and Niklasson (2016) on women ambassadors, who also identified a higher number of Nordic, North American, and African ambassadors.[2] It, therefore, seems more likely that women act as mediators when they advance in greater numbers to senior positions in diplomacy more generally.

These figures generate a number of potentially interesting propositions, which should be further explored in empirical studies. First, are women advancing in greater numbers as negotiators and mediators due to the Nordic countries' degree of gender equal society and strong historical commitment to international peacemaking (see also chapter 40 in this volume)? Second, is there a correlation between the number of women acting as foreign ministers and mediators? For example, in the case of US mediators, the pattern is striking. Finally, can traditional cultural authority, as seen in some African cases (cf. Paffenholz 2016), be an important additional source of power for women to advance as peace negotiators? By way of illustration, during the formal negotiations in Bougainville in the 1990s, women were able to draw upon their matrilineal cultural roles as "mothers of the land" to legitimize their calls for peace and participation in the peace process (George 2017: 172).

GENDERED DYNAMICS AT THE NEGOTIATION TABLE

Peace negotiations are particularly ingrained with masculinized norms of power and leadership as they are strongly associated with security interests and military affairs. Yet, there are surprisingly few studies that analyze these gendered processes. In most cases, peace negotiations take place in the midst of crises and are set against emergency settings that trigger "exceptional politics" (Aharoni 2018). Exceptional politics is thus intimately related to securitization, where democratic politics, transparency, and communication flows are put on hold (Agamben 2005). Hence, what is observed and visible in peace negotiations is often only the "top of the iceberg" of the overall process. Feminist institutionalist scholarship provides a useful analytical lens to explain these informal and gendered processes by showing how gender norms, roles, and practices are producing and reproducing constructions of femininity and masculinity (see, for example, Kenny 2014; Waylen 2014). Such analysis highlights how informal male networks often are at play between selected groups of negotiators and military leaders as a way to build and nurture homosocial relationships. The combination of secrecy and the lack of formal structures thereby disguise power and make peace negotiations per definition exclusionary and notoriously difficult for women to enter and navigate (Aharoni 2011: 402; Potter 2005:10). As a consequence of this informal environment, women's participation is often contested or met with indifference. In a recently conducted study of fifty-plus peacemakers,[3] we explored some of these broad questions. The interviews focused on the different ways gender interacts with institutional contexts and process dynamics in an effort to identify the enabling and restraining conditions of women's inclusion in formal peace negotiations. Drawing upon these findings, the brief discussion that follows illustrates some of the gender dynamics women and men experience during the negotiation process.

Involving Men on Gender Issues

In the study, we found an overall expressed desire among the peacemakers to see more men engaged and committed to the work on gender and women issues. The WPS-agenda may otherwise become "ghettoized" and turned into a silo of concern only for women. As one peace mediator noted: "People think that 'gender' = 'women issues,' full stop. No discussion about masculinity. If you mention that, they say 'what are you talking about?'" Many of the peacemakers also pointed to the general lack of shared definitions on "women issues," which gives an indication that a more explicit normative and feminist platform is required in negotiations.

Sending Mixed Messages with Training

In the international policy discourses, there is a strong emphasis that women need more training in order to prepare them to negotiate at the table. However, several peacemakers underlined that the emphasis on training sends mixed messages and signals to women that they lack skills men already acquire. As one chief mediator reflects: "The women said to me: 'we need no training in mediation; we need training on golf and whiskey drinking.'" Again, this quote highlights the gendered dynamics of informal homosocial negotiations.

Western Framing

There is an overall concern among the interviewed peacemakers that the framing of women's rights and gender issues is "Western." In some instances, women's rights have from the outset been perceived as highly contested and controversial. As a consequence, it has been difficult to push for the WPS agenda during the negotiations. The resistance against women rights was also expressed as being part of a "gender ideology," which contradicts family values. This has at times triggered counterproductive results and even caused deadlocks. At the same time, such outcomes have also been countered and mitigated by women's groups putting pressure on the delegations to continue the negotiations as seen in Burundi and Guatemala.

Gendered Styles of Negotiation

The difference between men and women regarding styles of negotiation were partly confirmed in the interviews. Male negotiators were frequently described as driven by a quest for power and with strong egos. Women negotiators were portrayed as being less concerned with loss of face and more inclined toward a societal orientation of negotiation, which emphasizes responsibility to the family and society at large as well as to education, justice, protection, livelihood, development, and so on. Consequently, the presence of women assumes to change the dynamics of negotiation and communication, making the overall setting less aggressive by steering away from zero-sum power games. At the same time, several peacemakers pointed to the dilemma of pushing for broader participation of women at the formal negotiation table as some women feel "uncomfortable to sit with men . . . many women, really most, are not accustomed to seeing themselves sitting at the table (figuratively speaking), or being in the process in general; they don't think they belong here." On the other hand, a gender metaphor that reappeared among the interviewees was the one of "mother," which was utilized as a resource to generate legitimacy, access, and leverage during the process. As mentioned earlier, matrilineal cultural power has effectively been used in the Bougainville and Uganda peace talks.

Intersectionality

Several peacemakers noted that the inclusion of women tends to favor a special "type" of woman as a negotiator who is well educated and from middle/upper class. This points to the importance of integrating an intersectional approach to the analysis—that is, an awareness how race, class, and ethnicity interact with gender. It also reflects how women negotiators are assumed to fit gendered scripts and roles, which again may have "western bias." Furthermore, some of the women negotiators were recruited and expected first and foremost to deliver on political mandates, but not to promote women's issues specifically. This reflects the tension between descriptive representation of women and substantive representation of women's issues.

Peace vs. Gender Justice Dilemma

One overarching concern that many of the peacemakers raised was the intricate incentive structures of peace negotiation to reach an agreement. There seems to be a reoccurring tension between ending violence with a ceasefire and promoting gender justice long-term in order to consolidate a sustainable peace. Often times, women rights are perceived as secondary. This resonates with the wider debates on peace versus justice where the priority, it is argued, is first to stop the bloodshed and then to seek reconciliation, restoration, and retribution. This dilemma raises questions about what the criteria for inclusion and agenda setting are, and of timing and design—that is, how the negotiations are sequenced and structured.

Gendered Division of Labor

Many peacemakers share a concern that women tend to end up in supportive functions during the negotiations. Madame Anstee (2003), with long experience of UN mediation, has warned that "women should never learn to type" as a way of avoiding administrative positions in diplomacy. Yet, what is interesting to note is that women are increasingly gaining access and presence in peace negotiations as part of the "technical staff." Hence, women gain entry in their capacity as experts, advisors, and advocates although they are rarely expected to exercise any political roles. As a consequence, women negotiators end up in the "second row" and rank in the process. As one of the female mediators underlined: "I've experienced negotiation teams in which the leader doesn't even know the name of the women in the team; they are only there because they have to comply with 1325. You have to check [make sure] that they [the women] have positions in society; that they are empowered to partici- pate on an equal basis." This underscores again the importance of making women count at the table, not only counting the number of women participating.

Process Design

Most of the peacemakers stress that the negotiation process need to be reframed and redesigned in such a way as to enable other tracks of diplomacy to be included: "the further away from the process, the more women there are." This again relates to the importance of timing—that is, at what time women are included in the process. It was pointed out that women need to be on board early on in the pre-negotiation phase in order to influence the agenda and the parameters of the formal negotiation.

Homosociality and Insecurity

Peace negotiations are distinguished from other types of negotiations by the strong dom- inance of men at the table. Hence, to include more women challenges such a homoso- cial negotiation environment, which partly explains why women negotiators are still so contested. As one negotiator observed: "There are certain social spaces, where the political decision-making happens, where women are not allowed . . . With men—they understand each other immediately." This points to the fact that women are perceived differently than men. Moreover, in some contexts they face specific vulnerabilities, insecurity, and social pressures where women negotiators have to "watch their language" and "behave respectful at all times."

CONCLUSION: WHERE DO WE GO FROM HERE?

This chapter has sought to provide an overview and analysis of gender and peace negotiations in theory, policy, and practice by highlighting the interplay between actors and the gen- dered forms and structures of peace negotiations. As such, some restraining and enabling conditions for enhanced participation of women in peace negotiation have been discussed. Still, there is a large gap in research on gender and peace negotiations that needs to be addressed by conducting more theoretical and empirical studies. By way of conclusion, three remarks are made that can further the research agenda on gender and peace negotiations. First, in order to understand the structural gendered barriers, we need to move beyond the focus on women's presence in peace negotiation and instead unpack the deeper gendered dynamics of the process itself so that theoretical and empirical knowledge can be gained and advanced. Such scholarly work also has the potential of generating relevant insights for policymakers who strive to understand the conditions for inclusion and formulate more effective strategies for gender equality. Second, the peace versus gender-justice dilemma is surprisingly underresearched in regards to the barriers it generates and how it relates to the broader ethical and normative debates on peace and justice. From a practitioner's perspective, it may be less of a surprise as the dominant international policy frames of women's participation in peace negotiations are mostly instrumental, depoliticized, and technocratic. They tend to avoid the more contested and gendered political power struggles, which are related to the quest for substantive representation and gender equality. Following on from that, as our final conclusion, we need to rethink and visualize a new peace diplomacy and design based on a more explicit normative and feminist platform that can empower actors and groups seeking conflict transformation and sustainable peace.

NOTES

1. See further information at the Folke Bernadotte Academy [FBA], http://www.fba.se.
2. The overarching patterns on representation of ambassadors (Towns and Niklasson 2016) and peace mediators (Aggestam and Svensson 2017) are strikingly similar in the way that Nordic 35 percent / 25 percent, American 25 percent / 23 percent and African 20 percent / 17 percent have the larger number of women diplomats.
3. Fifty-three structured interviews (forty-six women, seven men) were conducted via Skype or telephone between December 2016 and February 2017. Most of the peacemakers are or have been working for IGOs, NGOs, and MFAs. They are mostly senior negotiators with extensive experience in formal peace negotiations in various regions. They also have different national backgrounds ranging from Africa, Europe, United States, South America, and Middle East. The interviews lasted between thirty and forty-five minutes and the interviewees were informed that all answers will be anonymized as soon as they were coded for analysis. I want to express my sincerest appreciation to my research assistant Jakob Frizell for his dedicated and professional contribution to the work with the interview survey.

REFERENCES

Ackerley, B., and J. True. *Doing Feminist Research in Political and Social Science.* New York: Palgrave Macmillan, 2010.

Agamben, G. *State of Exception.* Chicago: University of Chicago Press, 2005.

Aggestam, K., and A. Bergman Rosamond. "Feminist Foreign Policy in the Making: Ethics, Politics, and Gender." *Ethics and International Affairs* 30, no. 3 (2016): 323–334.

Aggestam, K., and A. Towns. *Gendering Diplomacy and International Negotiation.* Basingstoke, UK: Palgrave Macmillan, 2018.

Aggestam, K., and I. Svensson. "Where Are the Women in Peace Mediation?" In *Gendering Diplomacy and International Negotiation*, edited by K. Aggestam and A. Towns. Basingstoke, UK: Palgrave Macmillan, 2018.

Aharoni, S. "Diplomacy as Crisis: An Institutional Analysis of Gender and the Failure to Negotiate Peace in Israel." In *Gendering Diplomacy and International Negotiation*, edited by K. Aggestam and A. Towns. Basingstoke, UK: Palgrave, 2018.

Aharoni, S. "Gender and 'Peace Work': An Unofficial History of Israeli-Palestinian Peace Negotiations." *Politics & Gender* 7 (2011): 391–416.

Anderlini, S. "The Untapped Resource: Women in Peace Negotiations." *Conflict Trends* 3 (2003): 18–22.

Anderson, M. *Windows of Opportunity: How Women Seize Peace Negotiations for Political Change.* Oxford: Oxford University Press, 2016.

Anstee, M. J. *Never Learn to Type: A Woman at the UN.* Chichester, UK: Wiley, 2003.

Bell, C. "Text and Context. Evaluating Peace Agreements for Their 'Gender Perspective.'" UN Women, October 2015, http://www.unwomen.org/-/media/headquarters/attachments/sections/library/publications/2017/text-and-context_en.pdf?vs=4743.

Bell, C. "Peace Agreements or Pieces of Paper? The Impact of UNSC Resolution 1325 on Peace Processes and Their Agreements." *International and Comparative Law Quarterly* 59, no. 4 (2010): 941.

Bercovitch, J., and J. Fretter. "Studying International Mediation: Developing Data Sets on Mediation, Looking for Patterns, and Searching for Answers." *International Negotiation* 12 (2007): 145–173.

Björkdahl, A., and J. Manngren Selimovic. "Gender: The Missing Piece in the Peace Puzzle." In *The Palgrave Handbook of Disciplinary and Regional Approaches to Peace*, edited by O. Richmond, S. Pogodda, and J. Ramovic. London: Palgrave Macmillan, 2016.

Boyer, M., N. Hudson, A. Niv-Solomon, L. Janik, M. Butler, and S. Brown. "Gender and Negotiation: Some Experimental Findings from an International Negotiation Simulation." *International Studies Quarterly* 53 (2009): 23–47.

Broome, B. "Building Relational Empathy Through an Interactive Design Process." In *Handbook of Conflict Analysis and Resolution*, edited by D. J. D. Sandole, S. Byrne, I. Sandole-Staroste, and J. Senehi. Oxon, UK, and New York: Routledge, 2009.

Cassidy, J., ed. *Gender and Diplomacy.* London: Routledge, 2017.

Charlesworth, H. "Are Women Peaceful? Reflections on the Role of Women in Peace-Building." *Feminist Legal Studies* 16, no. 3 (2008): 347–361.

Clinton, H. "Keynote Address at the International Crisis Group." New York, December 16, 2011, https://still4hill.com/2011/12/17/secretary-clintons-keynote-address-at-the-international-crisis-groups-in-pursuit-of-peace-award-dinner/.

Duncanson, C. *Gender and Peacebuilding.* Cambridge, UK: Polity Press, 2016.

El-Bushra, J. "Feminism, Gender, and Women's Peace Activism." *Development and Change* 38, no. 1 (2007): 131–147.

Enloe, C. *Globalization and Militarism.* Boulder, CO: Rowman and Littlefield, 2016.

Florea, N., S. Brown, M. Butler, and M. Hernandez. "Negotiating from Mars to Venus: Gender in Simulated International Negotiations." *Simulation Gaming* 24 (2003): 226–248.

Garner, K. *Shaping a Global Women's Agenda: Women's NGOs, and Global Governance, 1925–85.* Manchester, UK: Manchester University Press, 2010.

George, N. "Light, Heat, and Shadows. Women's Reflections on Peacebuilding in Post-Conflict Bougainville." *Peacebuilding* 4, 2 (2017): 166–179.

Greig, M., and P. Diehl. *International Mediation.* Cambridge, UK: Polity Press, 2012.

Hudson, N. *Gender, Human Security, and the United Nations.* London: Routledge, 2012.

Kellerby, K. "(En)Gendering Security? The Complexities of Women's Inclusion in Peace Processes." *International Interactions* 39, no. 4 (2013): 435–460.

Kenny, M. "A Feminist Institutionalist Approach." *Politics & Gender* 10, no 4 (2014): 679–684.

Kianpour, S. "Iran Negotiations: The Women Who Made the Iran Nuclear Deal Happen." BBC, August 6, 2015.

Kronsell, A. *Gender, Sex, and Post-National Defence*. Oxford: Oxford University Press, 2012.

Krook, M., and J. True. "Rethinking the Life Cycles of International Norms: The United Nations and the Global Promotion of Gender Equality." *European Journal of International Relations* 18, no. 1 (2012): 103–127.

Lederach, J. *The Moral Imagination*. Oxford: Oxford University Press, 2010.

Lederach, J. *Building Peace*. Washington, DC: United States Institute for Peace, 1998.

Maoz, I. "The Women and Peace Hypothesis? The Effect of Opponent Negotiators' Gender on the Evaluation of Compromise Solutions in the Israeli-Palestinian Conflict." *International Negotiation* 14, no. 3 (2009): 519–536.

O'Reilly, M., A. Ó Súilleabháin, and T. Paffenholz. "Reimagining Peacemaking: Women's Roles in Peace Processes." New York: International Peace Institute, June 2015.

O'Reilly, M., and A. Ó Súilleabháin. "Issue Brief. Women in Conflict Mediation. Why it Matters." New York: International Peace Institute, September 2013.

Paffenholz, T. "Participation of Civil Society in Peace Negotiations." *Negotiation Journal* 30, no.1 (2014): 69–91.

Paffenholz, T., N. Ross, S. Dixon, A-L. Schluchter, and J. True. "Making Women Count—Not Just Counting Women: Assessing Women's Inclusion and Influence on Peace Negotiations." Report ITI and UN Women, January 4, 2016, http://www.inclusivepeace.org/content/making-women-count-not-just-counting-women-assessing-womens-inclusion-and-influence-peace.

Palmiano, J. "Fighting 'Feminist Fatigue'? Women and Peace Negotiations." Working Paper, No. 2. Swiss Peace, 2014.

Porter, E. *Peacebuilding. Women in International Perspective*. New York: Routledge, 2007.

Potter, A. "Opinion. We the Women. Why Conflict Mediation Is Not Just a Job for Men." Geneva: Centre for Humanitarian Dialogue, 2005.

Shepherd, L. "Gender and Global Social Justice: Peacebuilding and the Politics of Participation." In *Global Social Justice*, edited by Heather Widdows and Nicola Smith. London and New York: Routledge, 2011.

Shepherd, L. "Victims of Violence or Agents of Change? Representations of Women in UN Peacebuilding Discourse", *Peacebuilding*, 4 no.2. (2016): 121-135.

Sjoberg, L. "Women Fighters and the 'Beautiful Soul' Narrative", *International Review of the Red Cross* 92 no.877 (2010): 53–68.

Stedman, S., D. Rothchild, and E. Cousens. *Ending Civil Wars: The Implementation of Peace Agreements*. Boulder, CO: Lynne Rienner 2002.

Stone L. "Quantitative Analysis of Women's Participation in Peace Processes." In *Reimagining Peacemaking: Women's Roles in Peace Processes*, edited by M O'Reilly, A. Ó Súilleabháin, and T. Paffenholz, Annex II. A Study of 156 Peace Agreements, Controlling for Other Variables, 2015, http://www.unwomen.org/en/news/stories/2016/10/experts-take-womens-meaningful-participation-in-peacebuilding#notes.

True, J. "Gender and Foreign Policy." In *Australia in World Affairs: Navigating New International Disorders*, edited by Mark Beeson and Shahar Hamieri. Oxford: Oxford University Press, 2016.

Towns, A., and B. Niklasson. "Gender, International Status, and Ambassador Appointments." *Foreign Policy Analysis* 13, no. 3 (2016): 1–20.

UN Woman. "Women's Participation in Peace Negotiations: Connections between Presence and Influence." October 2012, http://www.unwomen.org/~/media/headquarters/attachments/sections/library/publications/2012/10/wpssourcebook-03a-womenpeacenegotiations-en.pdf.

Wallensteen, P. *Quality Peace*. Oxford: Oxford University Press, 2015.

Wanis-St. J. "Civil Society and Peace Negotiations: Confronting Exclusion." *International Negotiation* 13, no. 1 (2008): 11–36.

Waylen, G. "A Seat at the Table—Is it Enough? Gender, Multiparty Negotiations, and Institutional Design in South Africa and Northern Ireland." *Politics & Gender* 10, no. 4 (2014): 495–523.

CHAPTER 65

THE WPS AGENDA
A Postcolonial Critique

SWATI PARASHAR

WOMEN Peace and Security (WPS) is now considered a global "norm," deriving legitimacy from the Beijing declaration, the Convention on the Elimination of All Forms of Discrimination Against Women (CEDAW), UN Security Council Resolution 1325, and seven subsequent resolutions. Taken together, these instruments and the norms that underpin them are referred to as the WPS "agenda." Feminist scholars and practitioners have argued that the WPS agenda with its transformatory potential enables stakeholders to mainstream gender in policymaking and implementation (True 2016). The primary aim of this agenda is to address women's concerns in conflict affected regions to leverage more equitable and gender-just peace, while international resources in the form of foreign aid and research/study grants continue to be directed toward these efforts. As a derivative of this agenda the Swedish Feminist Foreign Policy launched in 2014 (Government of Sweden 2017), prioritizing gender equality and human rights both among the domestic constituents and audiences abroad, has become a benchmark by which to measure the success of democratic, liberal, and progressive governments. Similarly, Canada's Feminist International Assistance Policy, targets "gender equality and the empowerment of women and girls" (Government of Canada 2018). These new developments have generated debates globally about whether the WPS "agenda" and the concepts and practices it inspires have any purchase in the Global South, and how might we extend our scrutiny and critique, especially from a postcolonial feminist perspective.

At the outset, one could argue that the WPS "agenda" is inattentive to gender relations, masculinities, and gender hierarchies in the Global South (see UN Women 2015). It assumes that peace is the natural outcome of women's involvement in post-conflict processes, essentializing women's roles and experiences. However, the Western centric nature of WPS calls for greater scrutiny of this "agenda" and its relationship to the Global North and South, where the latter is often assumed to be a mere recipient of norms (Basu 2016). For this "agenda" to acquire a discursive meaning and universal character, the Global South must perform the site of innumerable "case studies," where people and societies are framed in a perpetual state of conflict and violence. As an illustrative example, the chapter draws from WPS interventions in countering violent extremism (CVE) policies which fail to account for the complex histories of political violence and extremist ideologies rooted in colonial encounters. The chapter, thus, adopts a postcolonial feminist approach and methodology to caution against the hierarchy of knowledge production in the WPS agenda; the uncritical instrumentalization of women's rights, "empowerment," and "gender equality" in policies; and the problematic framing by feminists who contribute to statist narratives of conflicts "out there," which can be fixed by holding Global South states and non-state actors account-able to Western concepts and practices.

In the next section, I discuss the colonial origins, intent, and language of the WPS "agenda" by engaging with the problematic nature of agenda setting, the concept of "best practices," and ideas regarding "case studies," "gender equality," and "empowerment," which endorse the neoliberal projects of Western governments. I also consider the epistemic violence and marginalization that present the Global South as contexts and sites without agency and lacking in any "progressive" gender discourse, as well as the complicity of feminists in promoting statist agendas without querying their own positionality, ethical commitments, and privilege. This is illustrated by the example of the uneasy encounters be-tween WPS and CVE policies. Finally, I conclude with a call to scholars and practitioners to revisit the debates and commitments of third wave feminism and to rescue feminism from its increasing co-optation into neocolonial and neoliberal agendas that are focused on the "protection" of women in the Global South.

WPS "Agenda": Old Wine in a New Bottle?

Although Western discourses of the "other" and the concept of "global sisterhood" have been critiqued by postcolonial feminists, the knowledge about the "other" continues to be (re)produced in Western discourses, and feminists, both in the Global North and South, are complicit in it (Mohanty 1988; hooks 1989; Trinh 1989; Suleri 1992). Postcolonial theorists have paid attention to the dual oppression of women in postcolonial states, and the fluidity of gender norms that were challenged under colonial masculinity. Edward Said (1993) pointed out that "anti-colonial resistance" was not "anti-colonial critique," and that the chauvinism and authoritarianism of colonial states had to be challenged, while also recognizing the struggles within the larger anti-colonial movements, such as women's movements against patriarchal traditions and violence. Postcolonial feminists have unpacked the image of the universal "third world woman" and the overruling of gender hierarchies in racialized spaces. They have highlighted the lack of acknowledgment of "differences" in feminist understandings of women's global oppressions, where the difference is not just between the West and non-West but within these geographies and temporalities as well (Mohanty 1998; Trinh 1989).

The debate around the "third world" woman has addressed the issue of the dual coloni-zation of women, oppressed by both native and foreign patriarchies. Mohanty's (2003) dis-cursive colonialism critiques both "global sisterhood" and the othering of the "third world" woman, highlighting the problematic history of feminism as imperialism, where feminists have been complicit in both the production and the marginalization of the gendered sub-altern. Feminist criteria to bolster the civilizing mission of Western states was not only ap-plied during the colonial rule but continues to inform postcolonial politics enacted through the WPS "agenda." There is a scramble to establish the efficacy of WPS in bringing gender equality and justice to women in conflict areas in the Global South (True 2016; Otto 2016; Pratt 2013; Pratt and Richter-Devroe 2011). Specifically, there is considerable pressure to improve the lot of the women "out there," from state agencies, neoliberal global institutions and even corporate interests, who fund both WPS research and practical initiatives (Pratt 2013). In this context, I make four interrelated arguments about the WPS norm/agenda setting, the politics of "best practices" and "case studies," how "gender equality" and "empowerment" serve neocolonial statist agendas and neoliberal Western modernity, and the overall epistemic violence and marginalizations practiced by WPS advocates.

WHOSE NORMS, WHOSE AGENDA?

The WPS agenda is associated ". . . with successful advocacy efforts of non-governmental organizations (NGOs)—and other gender advocates—with offices in New York, London and Geneva" (Basu 2016). In addition, efforts to push the agenda forward are also identified with "governments, NGOs, and international organizations that are based primarily in the Global North" (Basu 2016). In these contexts, the Global South is represented as "conflict affected" sites of intervention, notwithstanding their limited power in the UN and their lack of resources (Pratt 2013). Feminists from the Global South, however, have debunked the widely shared assumptions about the Global North as the "conceptual, material and institutional home" of UN Security Council Resolutions (Basu 2016). The Global South is not a mere recipient of policies formulated elsewhere, but can claim "ownership" of the WPS resolutions, which had a number of Global South inputs prior to its adoption in 2000. However, my critique goes beyond the mere acceptance of the "role" of the Global South in the formulation of the WPS agenda to engaging with its problematic politics and its discursive marginalizations.

The Global North has access to funds and resources and, barring China and Russia, constitutes the three main actors within the UN Security Council, entrusted with passing critical resolutions that form the core of WPS. Large scale military interventions to restore peace are sanctioned by the UN Security Council, reviving colonial "rescue narratives" in sites of conflict in the Global South (Pratt 2013; Pratt and Richter-Devroe 2011). For example, Gibbings mentions:

> The references to 1325 in the preamble of Security Council Resolution 1483 (22 May 2003) on Iraq can be seen as positive, in that it gives legitimacy to advocates' demand for women's rightful inclusion in the reconstruction and nation-building process in Iraq. But you could also see it in another way—that 1325 is being used as a tool to justify military occupation on behalf of "liberating" women (cited in Cohn et al. 2004: 138).

The Global War on Terror is another appropriate example of Western efforts aimed to rescue Afghan women from the Taliban, and feminists were complicit in supporting that effort (Elshtain 2003). States, societies, and scholars in the Global North are invested in the WPS "agenda," providing a moral compass to governments and people. For feminists in the North, engaging with WPS as a global "agenda" means easy access and influence within policy circles, to enter into conversations with the "mainstream" and to pitch themselves as "experts."

The Politics of "Best Practices" and "Case Studies"

Feminists have deployed the concept of "best practices" in the implementation of the WPS agenda, however, there is a need to exercise caution about adapting "best practices" from one conflict region to another without taking account of the specific context (D'Costa 2016; Basu 2016). The resilience and flexibility of local gender hierarchies during and after conflicts have played a crucial role in post-conflict transformations (Parpart 2016). This resilience cannot be explained simply as a longing for social order and stability engendered by the chaos of war, which can be effectively generalized. In fact, even two situations of conflict in the same temporal and spatial geographies can demonstrate completely different gender norms, before, during, and after the conflict (Parashar 2014). Gender in these conflicts is part of a complex intersectional identity formation, which could include the privileging of caste, class, religion, ethnicity, language, and nationalism—or a combination of these identities. "Best practices" thus, may be a useful policy term, but it does not capture the complexity of the situation on the ground.

For the WPS "agenda" to acquire a discursive meaning and universal character, the Global South must perform the site of innumerable "case studies" where people and societies are framed in a perpetual state of conflict and violence. This framing denies agency to the Global South and mediates the understanding of the "case studies" through armed conflicts within nation-states. It fails to highlight the complexities of these conflicts in which states are parties waging wars against their own citizens, but it also ensures that theories and approaches from the Global North provide the normative knowledge and framing for understanding these case studies. Bina D'Costa (2016) has highlighted the problem of "hypervisibility," with respect to certain kinds of "case studies" that suit the narratives and theoretical frames of the Global North. For example, the recognition of rape and sexual violence as a crime in wars. The uncritical focus on and framing of wartime rape in locations "out there" (Africa and Asia) contribute to a certain kind of "hypervisibility" of case studies that makes it difficult to distinguish between silence as a "speech act," useful for individual women as a negotiated survival strategy, and silence that needs to be deconstructed for purposes of transitional justice (D'Costa 2016).

Feminist movements in the Global South have been nomadic, drawing from various social reform movements and anti-colonial nationalisms. Transnationalism has been articulated by postcolonial feminists (Grewal and Kaplan 2000) who do not restrict themselves to speaking about countries or borders and have highlighted the asymmetries of power not just between the West and the non-West but also within postcolonial societies.[1] Therefore, locating "case studies" within specific nation-states/ regional geographies is unhelpful as it is important to recognize women's lives outside normative institutions.

"Gender Equality" and "Empowerment" serving Western Neoliberal Nation-States

The "situatedness" of WPS within an international/global discourse needs to be further unsettled in meaningful ways. The notion of "international" is delimiting and relies predominantly on the "nation state," which fails to provide a people-centric approach. Prior to the creation of nation-states and access to citizenship rights, the modes of belonging were located within broader national cultures. Postcolonial subjectivities are now shaped exclusively within neoliberal Western modernity, recognizing only the nation-state and overriding other means of being and belonging (Parashar et al. 2018). Citizenship rights in many states elude women and other minorities, but when state-led National Action Plans (NAP) are emphasized as part of the WPS agenda, they end up endorsing the state's narrative of the conflict and its marginalizations and discrimination. Conflicts in which the (postcolonial) state is targeted by its citizens are hardly recognized, as such, in order to protect the sovereignty and international prestige of the state and retain monopoly over violence. In such situations, "gender equality" and "empowerment," as defined and appropriated by/mediated through statist agendas, are unproductive and even potentially damaging concepts.

Through its focus on women's access to decision-making and support for gender equality, the WPS discourse endorses a particular liberal vision of equality and peace that does not appear to be inclusive of all interests and experiences. It does not accommodate women's agency that does not seek individual emancipation/empowerment, or work within secular-liberal frameworks (Basu 2016). It should come as no surprise that gender equality is both contested and contentious in how it is understood as a norm pushed by the Global North on the South; in fact, in specific contexts, women may value gender complementarity rather than gender equality. Similarly, the concept of empowerment has been critiqued by scholars who have argued that the non-Western woman is hardly recognized as a full subject and that "empowerment programming is explicitly depoliticizing, obscuring women's relationships to power and the state" (Cronin-Furman et al. 2017: 7). Empowerment, thus, continues to be co-opted and invoked by Western women to "save" women in the developing world, as part of the colonial/imperial project (Ibid: 2).

WPS, Epistemic Violence, and Marginalizations

Epistemic violence and marginalizations are an outcome of feminist research and practice, and scholars and practitioners who advocate the implementation of the WPS agenda are complicit in (re)producing these marginalizations by being inattentive to their own "privilege," "location," and "politics" (D'Costa 2016). As discussed previously, in order to accommodate statist agendas backed by neoliberal financing and funding of WPS projects,[2] feminists in the Global North have stopped paying attention to how research questions are framed and what constitutes a legitimate area of study. Furthermore, they have failed to consider what methodologies can be ethically grounded and collaborative research networks can bring insightful knowledge. Case studies are carefully selected to suit the Western governments strategic priorities, intervention goals, and funding rationale; some areas are over-researched (like sexual violence in wars), while others are marginalized (such as state violence against indigenous people and gender minorities). Merely making "women" visible is an insufficient step toward intellectually and politically satisfying explanations of the subordination of women's interests to the nation-state.

The intersectional analyses pioneered by postcolonial feminists highlight the multiple marginalizations, inequalities, and injustices at the local, national, and international levels that shape women's experiences of insecurity[3] and transnational feminism (Basu 1995). In addition, they also highlight the various insecurities imposed on women and other minorities in the Global South by the actions of Western states in their neoliberal interventionist avatars, controlling weak states and civil society agendas of the Global South through donor grants, research funding, and support for outreach activities.[4] In such situations, it is essential to underscore that the WPS agenda runs the risk of Western neoliberal state appropriating feminist ethical commitments to perpetuate epistemic violence and marginalizations on the Global South. In the next section, I discuss the problems with the WPS agenda in the context of countering violent extremism.

WPS and CVE: Uneasy Encounters

The field of Countering Violent Extremism has become the most visible and contested area of research and policy intervention by governments and international organizations. Post 9/11, states have created and strengthened new legal apparatus within the ambit of the UN to meet their needs in addressing violent, transnational, and non-state actors along with the protection of vulnerable populations.[5] In Western contexts, CVE expanded as an area of research and praxis as a response to the US agencies' focus on the threat of violent extremism and the conditions that support it. It has now become a catch-all category embraced by all the agencies and bureaus across the US policy system. In line with this trend, other governments and international institutions, including the UK, the UN, the Gulf Cooperation Council (GCC), and the European Union, have all developed their own CVE programs.[6] Several countries in the Global South have also adopted national CVE policies that address both right and left-wing extremisms, acknowledging that they have a long history of violent extremism and terrorism in their societies which predate 9/11 and the Global War on Terror.

Extremist and terrorist violence in many Global South contexts have origins in colonial policies and legacies, while postcolonial states have adopted similar methods and strategies as their colonial predecessors to deal with them (Parashar 2018). As countries struggle to counter the effects of violent extremism, the response mechanisms have primarily centered on militarism and security-related methods, like increased border monitoring and control, intelligence gathering, law enforcement, and military defense mechanisms that can be implemented and made visible in the public discourse. In many cases of extremism, particularly emanating from the spread of left-wing revolutionary ideologies among marginalized sections within states, the security-development nexus has been introduced in CVE policies to address the inequalities and development deficit that fuel violence (Parashar 2013).

Policymakers and grass-roots practitioners, in analyzing the drivers of violence and extremism in prolonged conflicts, have identified "push factors" emanating from weak governance, underdevelopment, and human rights violations. Naureen Chowdhury Fink (2014), in her study on CVE, observes how these "push factors" often get generalized globally, but create a particular set of environmental enablers in different contexts. This allows extremist groups and recruiters to exploit local grievances and offer alternative narratives and mechanisms for addressing them. There are also certain other factors, identified as "pull factors," such as charismatic recruiters, appealing communications, and material benefits that may prompt recruitment and support for extremist groups (Fink 2014; Fink et al. 2016). Conflicts in South Asia, the Sahel, and the Horn of Africa, for example, have demonstrated that violent extremism is not only related to terrorism but can play a large role in fueling sectarian tensions, intra and interstate violence, transnational insecurity and criminality, and hindering socioeconomic development.

The UN Global Counter-Terrorism Strategy in 2006 first marked the recognition of women's roles in countering terrorism and violent extremism. Women's prevention roles in conflict were recognized in Resolution 1325, and specifically in relation to CVE in Resolutions 2122 and 2242. Resolution 2242 in particular, directly addresses the impact of the rise of violent extremism on the lives of women. Through Resolution 2242, the international security regime aims to derive legitimizing benefits from the co-option of Women, Peace, and Security to its operational framework with a focus on the "inclusion" of women in CVE. Other multilateral actors such as the Organization for Security and Co-operation in Europe (OSCE), the Global Counterterrorism Forum, and the EU have also advanced women's inclusion within the field of CVE. They emphasize strategic coherence and coordination within a statist masculine paradigm and are less attentive to gender perspectives. Their approach is to simply include women who are potentially impactful social actors owing to their inherent peacefulness and problem-solving skills, and more so as the cultural bearers of society. Fionnuala Ní Aoláin (2013) finds a pattern of selective entreaty in multiple resolutions and in the language of Resolution 2242 in particular, which essentializes women as either wicked perpetrators of extremist violence or virtuous saviors of sons, husbands, and communities.

The various elements of the WPS agenda seem to be discordant in the multiple understandings of conflict and terrorism. For example, the CEDAW Committee's understanding of "conflict" is broad, including "protracted and low-intensity civil strife, ethnic and communal violence and states of emergency" (O'Rourke and Swaine 2018). The Security Council, on the other hand, has a narrow and securitized view of conflicts and terrorism in country specific situations. WPS locates women's agency, but tends to default to a binary view of gender (men as combatants and perpetrators of violence versus women as peacemakers and victims of violence). Practitioners and policymakers ascribe specific roles for women in CVE, usually as maternal figures who can assist in focused deradicalization programs that serve militarized agendas. Research based evidence arising from contemporary conflicts, however, points to the varied roles essayed by women—as agents of change, violent, suicidal, survivors, negotiators, and peacemakers. Extremist organizations appeal to women based on the glorification of stereotypical notions of "power," invoking traditional gender roles of mothers juxtaposed against hyper-masculine ideals. Motherhood is also used by local women's groups to counter the appeal of radical ideologies[7] (see Parashar 2014). These complex understandings of gender roles at the local level, make it difficult for state authorities and communities to come to an agreement about developing counter narratives to extremism from a gender lens.

In support of the concerns often raised by women from the Global South, the UN Global Study on Women, Peace, and Security (see UN Women 2015) cautioned against the securitization of women's rights even though it argued that women's role is pivotal in CVE, and women's empowerment can decrease the likelihood of extremism. In consultations with women leaders and local women's rights organizations for the Study, there was deep skepticism of and opposition to including women's empowerment programs within counter-terrorism operations. Although feminist scholarship advocates empowerment of women as vital to combating terrorism and extremism, making gender a national security issue and advancing "gender equality" raises questions about appropriation of local conflicts in driving liberal feminist agendas. This does not recognize and support women's roles at the local level, particularly where both the notion of gender norms and "gender equality" can be vastly different from Western norms and expectations. Equal participation of women in peace and security efforts should be a goal in its own right, while taking local contexts into consideration; the interface between WPS and CVE agendas only engender further militarization and insecurities for women and other vulnerable sections of the population.

Conclusion: From Saving "Women" to Rescuing "Feminism"

WPS remains a contested site of feminist political struggles in both discourse and practice. It highlights that the anxieties of third wave feminism about diversity and difference and postcolonial critiques of "global sisterhood" remain relevant (Parashar 2016). The WPS "agenda" is currently deployed through a limited understanding of gender norms and relations in the Global South, paying little attention to masculinities, intersectionality, and gender hierarchies. The contested terms of peace and conflict in the WPS discourse and the type of conflicts and sites also require greater exploration, especially as they stand at variance with many Global South states' understanding of conflicts within and beyond their borders. Moreover, gender based violence is experienced on a continuum that does not recognize the rupture between peace and conflict, and nation-state borders which became part of a postcolonial quest for modernity.

The postcolonial feminist framing of this chapter cautioned against the hierarchy of knowledge production, the erasures of colonial histories of violence and gender marginalizations, the uncritical instrumentalization of women's rights and gender equality, and the state-led securitization of conflict situations that result in human rights violations and racial stereotyping of vulnerable minorities. The chapter highlighted how feminists are complicit in the (re)production of racial hierarchies and work closely with neoliberal Western states in their grand missions to promote good liberal values, such as gender equality and empowerment to the rest of the world. The inclusion of the WPS agenda, particularly in CVE policies, makes "gender equality" a militarized tool that securitizes women's lives and discounts the opinions and experiences of women on the ground in affected countries and local contexts.

Feminist research has demonstrated how women negotiate everyday life and resistance within conflict spaces regulated by multiple patriarchies, and how the fragmentary resistance and negotiations occur within the context of disparate social and cultural locations in the Global South. Women's transnational movements are the strongest in the Global South, looking beyond states and borders to create networks for women/gender activism; they have also altered their vocabularies of resistance from "protection" and "security" to "freedom" and "access." However, the current global feminist discourse seems to have adopted colonial overtones looking down on the Global South as sites of unmanageable conflicts that can provide the empirical testing ground for Western approaches to peacebuilding and rescuing women from their oppressive patriarchies. The WPS "agenda" serves as a cog in the wheel of the larger protection/savior narrative that seems to have become part of the contemporary feminist vocabulary.

NOTES

1. South Asian feminism, for example, has always been about challenging and contesting borders and geographies, building solidarities based on the standpoint approach. See, for example, the works of Kamla Bhasin and *Sangat,* http://www.sangatnetwork.org/vision-history.html; and WISCOMP, http://wiscomp.org/.
2. These projects have included examining violence against women in conflicts to make recommendations to governments; examining women's roles in CVE policies; and explicitly engaging with Western governments' agendas to bring about "gender equality" as part of a "global" campaign.
3. For example, intersectional feminists in India have highlighted the insecurities faced by lower caste *(Dalit)* and tribal *(Adivasi)* women and how they are marginalized in mainstream discourses. In "case studies" about India, nuanced analyses of different experiences of mainstream, *dalit*, and *adivasi* women can be completely missing.
4. Pakistan, Afghanistan, and Rwanda are good examples of post-conflict states that have thrived on Western donors driving their agendas for "gender equality." In most cases, these grants are part of bilateral power arrangements between post-conflict states and their Western donors. These state-sponsored and state-led interventions leave little space for conflict narratives and dynamics that challenge the statist version of events.
5. See, for example, Resolutions 2178, 2242, 2250, and a host of UNGA resolutions such as 60/288, 49/60, and the 2005 World Summit Outcome, https://www.un.org/sc/ctc/focus-areas/countering-violent-extremism/.
6. In December 2012, an international coalition of governments established the *Hedayah International Centre of Excellence for Countering Violent Extremism* in the United Arab Emirates.
7. Mossarat Qadeem in Pakistan, for example, has built on her experience of dissuading youth from joining violent extremist groups and created a network of women and mother activists to provide alternative solutions to the youth subject to joining or leaving violent extremist groups. See "The Women Waging Peace Network," https://www.inclusivesecurity.org/experts/mossarat-qadeem/.

References

Aoláin, F. N. "Situating Women in Counterterrorism Discourses: Undulating Masculinities and Luminal Femininities." *Boston University Law Review* 93, no. 3 (2013): 1085–1122.

Basu, S., ed. *The Challenge of Local Feminisms: Women's Movements in Global Perspective*, Boulder, CO: Westview Press, 1995.

Basu, S. "The Global South Writes 1325 (Too)." *International Political Science Review* 37, no. 3 (2016): 362–374.

Cohn, C., H. Kinsella, and S. Gibbings. "Interviewing Felicity Hill, Maha Muna, and Isha Dyfan. Women, Peace, and Security: Resolution 1325." *International Feminist Journal of Politics* 6, no. 1 (2004): 130–140.

Cronin-Furman, K., N. Gowrinathan, and R. Zakaria. *Emissaries of Empowerment*. Colin Powell School for Civic and Public Leadership. New York: City College of New York, 2017.

D'Costa, B. "Learning to Be a Compassionate Academic." *Australian Journal of International Affairs* 71, no. 1 (2016): 3–7.

Elshtain, J. *Just War against Terror: The Burden of American Power in a Violent World*, New York: Basic Books, 2003.

Fink, N. C. "Something Old, Something New: The Emergence and Evolution of CVE Effort." *United States Institute of Peace Insights Newsletter* 1 (Spring 2014), Washington DC, https://www.usip.org/sites/default/files/Insights-Spring-2014.pdf.

Fink, N. C., S. Zeiger, and R. Bhulai. *A Man's World: Exploring the Roles of Women in Countering Terrorism and Violent Extremism*. Washington DC, New York, London: Hedayah and The Global Center on Cooperative Security, 2016.

Government of Canada. "Canada's Feminist International Assistance Policy." April 5, 2018, http://international.gc.ca/world-monde/issues_development-enjeux_developpement/priorities-priorites/policy-politique.aspx?lang=eng.

Government of Sweden. "Sweden's Feminist Foreign Policy: Examples from Three Years of Implementation," 2017, http://www.government.se/4ab455/contentassets/654bcc72d8f44da087386b4906043521/swedens-feminist-foreign-policy--examples-from-three-years-of-implementation.pdf.

Grewal, I., and C. Kaplan. "Postcolonial Studies and Transnational Feminist Practices." *Jouvert: A Journal of Postcolonial Studies* 5, no. 1 (2000), http://english.chass.ncsu.edu/jouvert/v5i1/grewal.htm.

hooks, b. *Talking Back: Thinking Feminist, Thinking Black*. Boston: South End Press, 1989.

Mohanty, C. T. "Under Western Eyes: Feminist Scholarship and Colonial Discourses." *Feminist Review* 30 (Autumn1988): 61–88.

Mohanty, C. T. *Feminism without Borders: Decolonizing Theory, Practicing Solidarity*. Durham, NC: Duke University Press, 2003.

O'Rourke, C., and A. Swaine. "CEDAW and the Security Council: Enhancing Women's Rights in Conflict." *International & Comparative Law Quarterly* 67, no. 1 (2018), .

Otto, D. "Women, Peace, and Security: A Critical Analysis of the Security Council's Vision." London: LSE Women, Peace and Security Working Paper Series, 2016.

Parashar, S. "Armed Resistance, Economic (In)security, and the Household: A Case Study of the Maoist Insurgency in India." In The *Global Political Economy of the Household*, edited by J. Elias and S. Gunawardana. London: Palgrave, 2013.

Parashar, S., J. A. Tickner, and J. True., eds. *Revisiting Gendered States: Feminist Imaginings of the State in International Relations*. London and New York: Oxford University Press, 2018.

Parashar, S. "Is Transnational Feminist Solidarity Possible?" In *Handbook of Gender in World Politics*, edited by J. Steans and D. Tepe-Belfrage. Oxford: Edward Elgar, 2016.

Parashar, S. *Women and Militant Wars: The Politics of Injury*. London: Routledge, 2014.

Parashar, S. "Terrorism and the Postcolonial 'State.'" In *Routledge Handbook of Postcolonial Politics*, edited by O. U. Rutazibwa and R. Shilliam. London and New York: Routledge, 2018.

Parpart, J. L. "Imagined Peace, Gender Relations, and Post-Conflict Transformation: Anti-Colonial and Post-Cold War Conflicts." In *Women, Gender Equality, and Post-Conflict Transformation: Lessons Learned, Implications for the Future*, edited by J. P. Kaufman and K. P. Williams, 51–71. New York: Routledge, 2016.

Peters, A. "Creating Inclusive National Strategies to Counter Violent Extremism." Policy Recommendations. Institute for Inclusive Security, August 10 2015, https://www.inclusivesecurity.org/wp-content/uploads/2015/08/CVE_Policy_Recommendations_Brief.pdf.

Pratt, N. "Reconceptualizing Gender, Reinscribing Racial–Sexual Boundaries in International Security: The Case of UN Security Council Resolution 1325 on 'Women, Peace, and Security.'" *International Studies Quarterly* 57, no. 4 (2013): 772–783.

Pratt, N., and S. Richter-Devroe. "Critically Examining UNSCR 1325 on Women, Peace, and Security." *International Feminist Journal of Politics* 13, no. 4 (2011): 489–503.

Said, E. *Culture and Imperialism*. New York: Vintage, 1993.

Sinha, M. *Specters of Mother India: The Global Restructuring of an Empire*. Durham, NC: Duke University Press, 2006.

Suleri, S. "Woman Skin Deep: Feminism and the Postcolonial Condition." *Critical Inquiry* 18, no. 4 (1992): 756–769.

Trinh, T. Minh-ha. *Woman, Native, Other: Writing Postcoloniality and Feminism*. Bloomington: Indiana University Press, 1989.

True, J. "Explaining the Global Diffusion of the Women, Peace, and Security Agenda." *International Political Science Review* 37, no. 3 (2016): 307–323.

UN Women. "Transforming Justice, Securing the Peace. A Global Study on the Implementation of United Nations Security Council Resolution 1325 (2000)." Lead author: Radhika Coomaraswamy. UN Women, 2015, http://wps.unwomen.org/pdf/en/GlobalStudy_EN_Web.pdf.

White, C. "15 Years On, A New Opportunity: UNSCR 2242." Georgetown Institute for Women, Peace, and Security. *GIPWS Blog*, October 28, 2015, http://giwps.georgetown.edu/15-years-on-a-new-opportunity-unscr-2242/.

Wright, H. "The High-Level Review on Women, Peace, and Security: A Tale of Two Viewpoints." *Saferworld*, October 21, 2015, https://www.saferworld.org.uk/resources/news-and-analysis/post/172-the-high-level-review-on-women-peace-and-security-a-tale-of-two-viewpoints.

CHAPTER 66

THE WPS AGENDA AND STRATEGY FOR THE TWENTY-FIRST CENTURY

CHANTAL DE JONGE OUDRAAT

UN Security Council Resolution 1325, adopted in 2000, recognized the critical roles women can and must play in advancing international peace and security. Subsequent UN Security Council resolutions on Women, Peace, and Security (WPS) strengthened the protection of women, particularly with regard to conflict-related sexual and gender-based violence, and they reaffirmed the important roles of women in restoring and maintaining peace.

The United Nations and regional security organizations (such as the African Union, NATO, and the OSCE) have developed organization-wide policies and action plans to integrate gender perspectives into their deliberations and operations. The international community has also adopted legal and normative frameworks, which recognize the pernicious effects of sexual and gender-based violence in conflict and provide a basis for prosecuting sexual crimes, including rape, as crimes against humanity and as war crimes.[1] At the national level, more than sixty states, including the United States, have developed National Action Plans, which acknowledge the importance of the participation of women in advancing peace and security and seek to translate the principles of Resolution 1325 in national policies and programs.

Despite these international and national commitments, gender perspectives in the analyses of international security challenges remain underdeveloped, and the roles and numbers of women in the national and international security field continue to be marginal. Indeed, the participation of women in decision-making and operational positions in peace processes and in national and international security institutions remains limited. As of 2015, at the United Nations only 16 percent of appointments to top posts were women. In 2016, the UN Security Council did not appoint a woman for the Secretary-General post, despite seven highly qualified women candidates. Women still make up less than 10 percent of peace negotiators, and are sorely underrepresented in most national law enforcement and security forces. On the protection side, while the legal and normative framework at the global level is robust, implementation is lagging and there have been very few prosecutions for sexual violence (see Chapters 14 and 24). Similarly, while many governments claim to support the principles of Resolution 1325, funding for programs aimed at women's empowerment and participation in peace and security is appallingly low (see Chapter 62). Lastly, gender perspectives are insufficiently integrated into analyses of global dynamics that underpin international security challenges. Gender perspectives are often afterthoughts, if they are thought about at all.

In sum, while Resolution 1325 has helped civil society organizations "as a framing tool and a source of legitimacy to demand action from their governments and the international community" (UN Women 2015: 304), many civil society actors recognize that UNSCR 1325 has not lived up to its "transformative potential."[2]

In this chapter I do two things. First, I identify three main challenges that hold the WPS agenda back. Second, I discuss how to overcome these challenges.

The Challenges

The lack of progress on the WPS agenda is due to structural challenges, including legal barriers, social norms, as well as more immediate political challenges. Three major challenges stand out.

The first challenge is political and conceptual. The WPS agenda is fundamentally an agenda about gender equality. Strategies and policies to promote gender equality in the economic and political fields have been difficult to implement. Indeed, gender equality policies challenge basic social, economic, and political patriarchal power relations within societies.[3] Demands for gender equality and women's rights are opposed by male-dominated cultures—in almost every corner of the globe (Guterres 2017). Gender gaps in the economic and political spheres remain large worldwide (World Economic Forum 2016; United Nations 2016, 2017; Oxfam 2017). Women are grossly underrepresented in the formal economy and frequently work in vulnerable, low paying, and undervalued jobs. Their average earnings are well below those of men—$11,000 versus $20,000. In addition, many women, even those who have entered the formal economy, are most often also engaged in unpaid household and care work (World Economic Forum 2016; World Bank 2017). The World Bank has estimated that a majority of countries have at least one legal restriction with regard to women's economic opportunities and many have laws that restrict the types of jobs they can do (UN Women 2017a; World Bank 2017). Similarly, at the political level, women remain hugely underrepresented. As of January 2017, of the 193 UN member states, only ten had a woman serving as head of state and nine serving as head of government. In 2016, only 23 percent of all national parliamentarians were women, and in 2015 only 17 percent of government ministers were women (UN Women 2017b).

The international political environment has changed considerably since the adoption of Resolution 1325 in 2000—unfortunately not in the right direction.[4] The rise of extremisms, including the rise of populist authoritarianism, has led to a backlash against feminist agendas, including the WPS agenda. In March 2017, UN Secretary-General António Guterres recognized that "around the world, tradition, cultural values and religion are being misused to curtail women's rights, to entrench sexism and defend misogynistic practices," and he urged UN member states to reaffirm their commitment to gender equality (Guterres 2017).

For the WPS agenda to advance, I argue that the WPS community needs to reframe how it talks about this agenda in the peace and security field. The Women, Peace, and Security agenda is not just about women and women rights, but also about gender—that is, about the distribution of power within societies among men and women.

The second challenge is that the communities that deal with security challenges, most notably the WPS community and the security community, live in silos. They are not connected to each other. Divides and silos ("fiefdoms") also exist within each of these communities (Sylvester 2009; see Chapter 67). Unless these silos are broken down, little headway will be made on the WPS agenda and the resolution of twenty-first century security challenges.

The third challenge is a lack of awareness and expertise on gender. Despite a growing body of research that emphasizes the roles of women and gender in examining security challenges, these perspectives remain "off the radar screen" in mainstream academic discussions of security challenges. (Sjoberg 2015, 2009; Maliniak et al. 2008, 2012, 2013) Similarly, despite the passage of Resolution 1325 and the recognition in many national and international policy documents of the importance of gender mainstreaming, gender perspectives remain largely absent when it comes to implementation. In addition, for many policymakers gender mainstreaming remains synonymous with gender balancing—that is, adding women.

To advance the WPS agenda, three things need to happen. First, the WPS community needs to broaden the WPS agenda to include a Gender, Peace, and Security (GPS) agenda. The WPS community needs to reframe the WPS agenda as a WPS + GPS agenda. Second, the WPS and the security communities need to overcome the divides that keep them apart. Third, the academic and policy communities need to increase expertise on WPS and GPS issues and better train the next generation of security experts in WPS + GPS. In the remainder of the chapter, I discuss these proposals in greater depth.

Reframing the Issues: From WPS to WPS + GPS

Since the adoption of Resolution 1325 in 2000, the WPS agenda has focused largely on the protection of women in conflict, particularly protection from sexual and gender-based violence. Unfortunately, an important component of the WPS agenda—the participation of women in peace and security—has not been sufficiently advanced. A focus on participation would have required that policymakers examine and redress economic and political inequalities between men and women and question traditional gender norms and roles.

The focus on protection has had a tendency to skew the analysis of policymakers toward women as victims. This reinforces traditional gender roles. Similarly, the focus on "women and children," which is prevalent in WPS resolutions, tends to infantilize women and diminish their agency. Lastly, the focus on protection has had a tendency to ignore the structural reasons for violence against women, such as gender inequalities (True and Tanyag 2017; Cockburn 2010).

In addition, because the WPS agenda has been framed in terms of women, it has been easy for the traditional security community to pigeonhole the WPS agenda as a "women's" issue and treat it as secondary or tertiary in national and international security policy. To overcome these problems and advance the WPS agenda, the WPS community needs to broaden the lens from "women" to "women and gender." It needs to develop a parallel track of work that has a more expansive and more inclusive GPS framework.

There are two main reasons for reframing these issues. First, from an analytical perspective, policymakers, activists, analysts, and scholars need to focus clearly and explicitly on the central issue—gender. It is not enough to advance women's representation in the international peace and security arena. The issue is gender equality. A gender perspective is needed to uncover the relationships and power structures that define genders, their relationships, and their access to resources and opportunities.

Gender is one of the main attributes that define the identity of people (Ridgeway 2011, 2009, 2006). Most societies are based on assumptions of gender differences and politics of gender inequality at both individual and structural/institutional levels. These inequalities "affect politics and security at both the national and international levels" (Hudson et al. 2012: 5).

Existing power imbalances, gender inequalities, and the lack of participation by women in peace and security efforts justify a focus on women. However, to address the root causes of these inequalities and imbalances it is necessary to adopt a whole-of-society approach that addresses the structural power imbalances created by gender inequality. To create a more effective way of thinking about, and advancing, this agenda, policymakers, activists, analysts, and scholars need a WPS + GPS framework.

Second, from a political perspective, a WPS + GPS agenda will help to overcome the idea that the WPS agenda is a "women's" issue. The WPS + GPS framework is broader and more inclusive. This will make it easier to connect the WPS agenda to issues that the traditional security community cares about, such as violent conflict and terrorism. It will also help to connect the WPS agenda to other international priorities, such as the Sustainable Development Goals, particularly Goal 5 on Gender Equality and Women's Empowerment.

BREAKING DOWN SILOS

In 2015, the United Nations launched three major reviews on UN peace operations; the UN peacebuilding architecture; and the implementation of UNSCR 1325 (United Nations 2015a, 2015b; UN Women 2015). All three reviews recognized the changing security environment. They recognized that contemporary security challenges are interconnected and will require whole-of-society approaches in which the security of people is central.

The peace operations and peace-building reviews also acknowledged the importance of the WPS agenda for the work of the United Nations. They admitted that existing divides between the traditional security community and the WPS community hinder the search for solutions. They recognized that these divides needed to be bridged, as well as the divides within those communities.

Indeed, the traditional security community, which is comprised mainly of men and is anchored in the policy establishment, has largely failed to focus on the role of women and gender in security (Maliniak et al. 2008, 2012, 2013; K 2017; Yao & Delatolla 2017; Brechenmacher 2017). For members of this community, matters of war and peace are about power—mainly military and economic power. The traditional security community has treated women and gender as peripheral issues.

Similarly, within the academic world, feminist international relations (IR) and feminist security studies continue to be marginalized.[5] Feminist scholars point to the dominance of a realist, state-centric, and positivist approach to the study of international relations to explain the lack of gender perspectives in traditional IR or security studies. Traditional security specialists also tend to separate the international from the national and the private from the public. These different approaches have translated into different research priorities for mainstream IR and feminist IR scholars (Tickner 2011, 1992; True 2015; True and Tanyag 2017). As a result, these different strands of study within the IR and international security fields have been talking past each other and living in their own academic bubbles.

At the same time, the WPS community, comprised mainly of women, is anchored in civil society and mistrusts the traditional security community and its focus on military action (see Chapters 4, 12, and 58). Numerous members in this community argue that many of the security problems that plague the world today are brought about by an emphasis on the military aspects of security. Most of the WPS community focuses on human security, gender inequality, and the subjugation of women as a source of conflict, including violent conflict. Within this community there are also deep divides between those who focus on inequalities at the individual and local level and those who focus on the structural level, as well as those who focus on security issues and those focusing more broadly on gender equality issues.[6]

All of these communities care deeply about international peace and security and have much to contribute to policy analysis and policy action, but they do not mix and often ignore each other. They are stovepiped.[7] To advance the WPS + GPS agenda, those who care about peace and security and gender equality need to knock down stovepipes, build bridges, and create spaces where diverse groups of scholars, analysts, activists, and policymakers can come together.

Those who care about peace and security and gender equality need to promote a better understanding between these communities and bridge the divides that keep them apart— including divides that set up artificial tensions between structural and individual approaches to gender inequalities. This will lead to a broader, more diverse, and smarter global security community. This, in turn, will lead to smarter and more effective policies.

For example, policies and programs that seek to prevent and counter violent extremism need to understand how structural gender inequalities may be a root cause for radicalization. At the same time policies and programs need to reflect on how structural inequalities manifest themselves differently in different parts of the world. To be able to respond in an appropriate and effective manner, it is absolutely critical that the policymaker, the academic, the analyst work hand in hand with those active in their communities.

BOLSTER AWARENESS AND EXPERTISE ON WPS + GPS

In the *Global Trends 2025* report, published in 2008, the US National Intelligence Council (USNIC) highlighted women as agents of geopolitical change and predicted that the "economic and political empowerment of women could transform the global landscape" (USNIC 2008: 16). [8] This acknowledgment was a significant step toward the recognition of gender as an important element when examining global security challenges. Unfortunately, the NIC's Global Trends Report, published in 2017, largely ignores how gender dynamics impact security in the future.

The 2017 report paints a future where both US dominance and the rules-based international order may come to an end. The intensifying crisis in global governance is mirrored by profound national differences of opinion around the roles of government. According to the NIC "debates over moral boundaries—to whom is owed what—will become more pronounced, while divergence in values and interest between states will threaten international security" (USNIC 2017: ix) The 2017 Global Trends report underscores how domestic political debates about power and the distribution of resources influence international security. However, it does not examine how gender roles and norms define power relations within states and how unequal access to economic and political resources and opportunities may affect peace and prosperity. The Global Trends report does not recognize that gender is a key explanatory variable of societal dynamics—including the dynamics that determine peace and security.

The NIC is not alone in ignoring gender when discussing security challenges. Most academic and policy discussions about international security challenges ignore gender perspectives. For example, a 2016 survey by the New America Foundation found that the majority of US national security policymakers had little knowledge or understanding of gender. Most policymakers equated gender with women and were not familiar with the WPS agenda. The majority of policymakers believed that an "add women and stir" approach would be sufficient. Lastly and more importantly, most policymakers in the survey believed that gender is relevant for only a handful of subjects, such as sex trafficking, sexual violence, and sex slavery in ISIS. They did not believe that gender was relevant to subjects like economics, trade, or issues related to defense (Hurlburt et al. 2017). [9]

This lack of understanding of the role of gender in international affairs and security policies is widespread and not restricted to US policymakers. The 2015 UN reviews on peacekeeping operations and the peace-building architecture acknowledged that UN member states and the UN Secretariat insufficiently integrated gender perspectives in their peace and security analyses and processes (United Nations 2015a, 2015b). These reviews also recognized that for many UN member states, as well as many in the UN secretariat, gender continues to be seen as an "add-on" (United Nations 2015a, 2015b; Stammes and Osland 2016; Security Council Report 2017).

There is a tremendous need for WPS + GPS expertise in the policy world. Gender perspectives are desperately needed in policy development and policy implementation, but they are usually left out—in part because of neglect, but also because gender experts are not always available. There is a small and growing community of WPS and gender experts, but given the breadth and depth of security challenges in the twenty-first century, this community needs to be supported and expanded. Gender needs to become a regular item in the curricula of international relations and international security studies. Students need to be introduced to the concepts of gender and gender analyses early on. Gender and gender analyses also need to be part of the curricula of military training and education. [10]

Conclusion

The WPS agenda is based on the proposition that lasting peace cannot be achieved without gender equality. The WPS agenda posits that gender balancing and the integration of gender perspectives into the analysis of policy challenges, including security challenges—are critical tools for advancing peace and security (Krook and True 2012).

Unfortunately, most policymakers and experts in the traditional security community remain oblivious to the gender dimensions of international peace and security challenges. For many policymakers and experts, the WPS agenda remains a "women's" agenda and is therefore easily sidelined. Even within the UN Security Council, references to the WPS agenda are consistently overlooked when Council members make decisions about "hard" security issues or when it is in "crisis" mode and responds to new and emerging crisis (Security Council Report 2017)

For the WPS agenda to advance, the WPS community needs to emphasize that this is not only a women's agenda but also, and importantly, a peace and security agenda. Gender inequalities and gender-based violence are indicative of dysfunctional and disruptive patterns of state domination that make interstate and intra-state aggression more likely (Hudson et al. 2012).

To underscore this point, the WPS community needs to reframe the WPS agenda into a WPS + GPS agenda—that is, an agenda that recognizes that a focus on women is necessary, but not sufficient. To fully address security challenges in the twenty-first century, the focus also needs to be on gender—that is, on the power structures that define and defy international peace and security.

In addition, the WPS and the security communities need to bridge the divides between and among them. Finally, analysts and academics need to advance our understanding and knowledge about the gender dimensions of international security challenges so that policymakers can truly incorporate a gender perspective in the analyses of these challenges and in the policies to deal with these challenges. To do this, policymakers need to invest in a next generation of scholars and policymakers. Only then can the regressive forces that want women to remain subordinate to men be stopped. Only then will the truly transformative nature of Resolution 1325 become a reality.

Notes

1. For example, the Statute of the International Criminal Court allows for the prosecution of sexual crimes, including rape, as crimes against humanity and war crimes. The Statute also provides for reparation and the protection of victims. In addition, the UN Security Council has adopted many resolutions dealing with sexual violence in conflict. UNSCR 1820 (2008) recognized sexual violence as a weapon and tactic of war and requested the UN Secretary General to appoint a Special Representative on Sexual Violence in Conflict. In 2012, the United Kingdom launched the Preventing Sexual Violence in Conflict Initiative (PSVI). It developed an international protocol on the documentation and investigation of sexual violence in conflict, which was published in 2016.
2. Many chapters in this Handbook also emphasize this point.

3. While gender norms and gender relations vary greatly over time and across societies, most societies are founded upon assumptions of gender differences and gender inequalities. Patriarchal structures and the norms and gender stereotypes that accompany them are hard to change.

4. In this Handbook Christine Chinkin points to the hollowing out of international human rights law in the 1990s. See Chapter 3.

5. Brooke Ackerly and Jacqui True argue that the marginalization of feminist scholars is less prominent in Australia, Canada, and the UK, where the IR field is more pluralist. See Ackerly and True 2008.

6. These divides often break down as among academics, NGO analysts, and activists, as well as along disciplinary lines. The divide between those focusing on security and those focusing on gender equality narrowed somewhat in October 2013 when the Monitoring Committee of the Convention for the Elimination of Discrimination Against Women (CEDAW) adopted General Recommendation 30 (GR 30) on the rights of women in conflict prevention, conflict, and post-conflict situations. GR 30 explicitly links to the WPS agenda and calls on states to report on the implementation of their WPS commitments in their reports to CEDAW (see O'Rourke and Swaine 2015 and Chapter 52).

7. Despite much talk about the importance of interdisciplinarity, academic disciplines remain very walled off from each other. The security expert rarely mingles with the anthropologist or the region specialist, and their careers proceed in different lanes and according to different criteria. Similarly, the activist often speaks a different language and frequently has different priorities from the academic, think tanker, or even the international activist. Finally, policymakers have their own vocabulary and priorities that may not overlap.

8. The report posited: "Although data on political involvement are less conclusive than those regarding economic participation, political empowerment of women appears to change governmental priorities. Examples as disparate as Sweden and Rwanda indicate that countries with relatively large numbers of politically active women place greater importance on societal issues such as healthcare, the environment, and economic development. If this trend continues over the next 15-20 years, as is likely, an increasing number of countries could favor social programs over military ones. Better governance also could be a spin-off benefit, as a high number of women in parliament or senior positions correlates with lower corruption."

9. I have found in my own research and travel in Asia, Africa, and Europe that the United States is not unique in this regard.

10. The Scandinavian countries, Australia, Canada, and the UK have been better at integrating gender into curricula.

REFERENCES

Ackerly, Brooke, and Jacqui True. "An Intersectional Analysis of International Relations: Recasting the Discipline." *Politics and Gender* 4, no. 1 (2008): 156–173.

Brechenmacher, Saskia. "Here's Why Closing the Foreign Policy Gender Gap Matters." *New America Weekly*, March 16, 2017, http://carnegieendowment.org/2017/03/16/here-s-why-closing-foreign-policy-gender-gap-matters-pub-68325.

Cockburn, Cynthia. "Gender Relations as Causal in Militarization and War." *International Feminist Journal of Politics* 12, no. 2 (2010): 139–157.

Guterres, António. "UN Secretary-General, Remarks." *UN Press Service*, March 8, 2017.

Hudson, Valerie M., Bonnie Balif-Spanvill, Mary Caprioli, and Chad F. Emmet. *Sex and World Peace*. New York: Columbia University Press, 2012.

Hurlburt, Heather, Elizabeth Weingarten, and Carolina Marques de Mesquita. *A Guide to Talking Women, Peace, and Security Inside the U.S. Security Establishment*. Washington, DC: New America Foundation, 2017.

K., Pablo. "What We Talked About at ISA: The Climate for Women in International Relations and Politics." March 6, 2017, https://thedisorderofthings.com/2017/03/06/what-we-talked-about-at-isa-the-climate-for-women-in-p-international-relations/.

Krook, Mona Lena, and Jacqui True. "Rethinking the Life Cycles of International Norms: The United Nations and the Global Promotion of Gender Equality." *European Journal of International Relations* 18, no. 1 (2012): 103–127.

Maliniak, Daniel, Amy Oakes, Susan Peterson, and Michael J. Tierney. "Women In International Relations." *Politics and Gender* 4, no. 1 (2008): 122–144.

Maliniak, Daniel, Susan Peterson, and Michael J. Tierney. "TRIP around the World: Teaching, Research, and Policy Views of International Relations Faculty in 20 Countries." Williamsburg, VA: Institute for the Theory and Practice of International Relations at the College of William and Mary, May 2012. See also the other Reports at https://trip.wm.edu/home/.

Maliniak, Daniel, Ryan Powers, and Barbara F. Walter. "The Gender Citation Gap in International Relations." *International Organization* 67, no. 4 (2013): 889–922.

O'Rourke, Catherine, and Aisling Swaine. *Guidebook on CEDAW General Recommendation No.30 and the Security Council Resolutions on Women, Peace, and Security*. New York: UN Women, 2015.

Oxfam. "An Economy That Works for Women: Achieving Women's Economic Empowerment in an Increasingly Unequal World." Oxford: Oxfam, March 2017.

Ridgeway, Cecilia. *Framed by Gender: How Gender Inequality Persists in the Modern World*. New York: Oxford University Press, 2011.

Ridgeway, Cecilia. "Framed Before We Know It: How Gender Shapes Social Relations." *Gender and Society* 23, no. 2 (2009): 145–160.

Ridgeway, Cecilia. "Gender as an Organizing Force in Social Relations: Implications for the Future of Inequality." In *The Declining Significance of Gender*, edited by F. D. Blau, M. C. Brinton, and D. B. Grusky, chap. 9. New York: Russell Sage Foundation, 2006.

Security Council Report. "Women, Peace, and Security: Closing the Security Council's Implementation Gap." Research Report, No. 2, February 24, 2017, http://www.securitycouncilreport.org/research-reports/women-peace-and-security-closing-the-security-councils-implementation-gap.php.

Sjoberg, Laura. "From Unity to Divergence and Back Again: Security and Economy in Feminist International Relations." *Politics and Gender* 11, no. 2 (2015): 408–413.

Sjoberg. Laura. "Introduction to Security Studies: Feminist Contributions." *Security Studies* 18, no. 2 (2009): 183–213.

Stamnes, Eli, and Kari M. Osland. "Synthesis Report: Reviewing UN Peace Operations, the UN Peacebuilding Architecture, and the Implementation of UNSCR 1325." Oslo: NUPI, NUPI Report (2), 2016.

Sylvester Christine. "Roundtable Discussion: Reflections on the Past, Prospects for the Future in Gender and International Relations." *Millennium: Journal of International Studies* 37, no. 1 (2009).

Tickner, Ann J. "Feminist Security Studies: Celebrating an Emerging Field." *Politics and Gender* 7, no. 4 (2011): 576–581.

Tickner, Ann J. *Gender in International Relations: Feminist Perspectives on Achieving Global Security.* New York: Columbia University Press, 1992.

True, Jacqui. "A Tale of Two Feminisms in International Relations? Feminist Political Economy and the Women, Peace, and Security Agenda." *Politics and Gender* 11, no. 2 (2015): 419–424.

True, Jacqui, and Maria Tanyag. "Global Violence and Security from a Gendered Perspective. In *Global Insecurity: Futures of Global Chaos and Governance,* edited by A. Burke and R. Parker, 43–63. London: Palgrave MacMillan, 2017.

United Nations. "Report of the High-Level Independent Panel on Peace Operations: On Uniting Our Strengths for Peace: Politics, Partnerships, and People." UN Document A/70/95—S/2015/446, June 17, 2015a.

United Nations. "The Challenges of Sustaining Peace: A Report of the Advisory Group of Experts for the 2015 Review of the United Nations Peacebuilding Architecture." UN Document S/2015/419, June 29, 2015b.

United Nations. "Leave No One Behind: A Call to Action for Gender Equality and Women's Economic Empowerment." Report of the UN Secretary-General's High Level Panel on Women's Empowerment, 2016, http://www2.unwomen.org/-/media/hlp%20wee/attachments/reports-toolkits/hlp-wee-report-2016-09-call-to-action-en.pdf?la=en&vs=1028.

United Nations. "Leave No One Behind: Taking Action for Transformational Change on Women's Economic Empowerment." UN Secretary-General's High Level Panel on Women's Empowerment, 2017, http://www2.unwomen.org/-/media/hlp%20wee/attachments/reports-toolkits/hlp-wee-report-2017-03-taking-action-en.pdf?la=en&vs=5226.

UN Women. "Transforming Justice, Securing the Peace. A Global Study on the Implementation of United Nations Security Council Resolution 1325 (2000)." Lead author: Radhika Coomaraswamy. UN Women, 2015, http://wps.unwomen.org/pdf/en/GlobalStudy_EN_Web.pdf.

UN Women. "Fact and Figures: Economic Empowerment." July 2017a, http://www.unwomen.org/en/what-we-do/economic-empowerment/facts-and-figures.

UN Women. " Fact and Figures: Women's Leadership and Political Participation." July 2017b, http://www.unwomen.org/en/what-we-do/leadership-and-political-participation/facts-and-figures.

USNIC (US National Intelligence Council). *Global Trends 2025: A Transformed World.* Washington, DC: National Intelligence Council. November 2008.

USNIC (US National Intelligence Council). *Global Trends: Paradox of Progress.* Washington, DC: National Intelligence Council. January 2017.

World Bank. "Gender Data Portal." World Bank, 2017, http://datatopics.worldbank.org/gender/.

World Economic Forum. "Global Gender Gap Report." 2016, http://reports.weforum.org/global-gender-gap-report-2016/.

Yao, Joanne, and Andrew Delatolla. "Gender and Diversity in the IR Curriculum: Why Should We Care?" The Disorder of Things [Blog], April 20, 2017, https://thedisorderofthings.com/2017/04/20/gender-and-diversity-in-the-ir-curriculum-why-should-we-care/.

CHAPTER 67

....

THE CHALLENGES OF MONITORING AND ANALYZING WPS FOR SCHOLARS

....

NATALIE FLOREA HUDSON

INTRODUCTION

....

FIFTEEN years after the unanimous adoption of UN Security Council Resolution 1325 and the subsequent development of the Women, Peace, and Security (WPS) agenda, the field of scholarship on WPS has been described as "extensive, detailed and crowded" (Kirby and Shepherd 2016: 252). As this analysis demonstrates, the field is better understood as uneven, unfinished, and undervalued. This Oxford Handbook is evidence of the incredible amount of time and energy that individuals have dedicated to researching and advocating for women's security and gender equality in times of conflict and in peace. We can now say a body of literature on WPS exists in a way that simply did not in 2000, and a group of scholars, practitioners, and policymakers live in and constitute this WPS space at local, national, and global levels.

As some begin to think about whether or not WPS as an area of research and advocacy is entering into a second phase or next generation,[1] it is important to take this moment to assess past scholarship and reflect upon future challenges for WPS scholars. While generational categorization may not be the most useful terminology to describe development of the field, the chapters in this section certainly call for taking stock of achievements and reflection for how best to move the WPS forward in inclusive and transformative ways. Part of this moment involves taking a closer look at who actually constitutes this burgeoning area of research. Understanding who counts themselves as a WPS scholar, how they came to do this work, what parts of the world their experiences reflect, and how they think about research connecting to policy, advocacy, and civil society is critical for understanding the literature and the challenges that exist for this field in years to come. These questions are particularly relevant for feminist scholars grappling with methodology that makes it imperative to reflexively situate ourselves in our research fields (Ackerly et al. 2006; Wibben 2016).

This chapter takes a closer look at the growing group of scholars who work in the WPS space. Some in this space identify as feminists, others as human rights defenders, some as activists, others as lawyers, and some even step into the policy world for brief moments. The goals of their research vary from a focus on the development of WPS architecture to the implementation of global and national policy to address the impact of conflict and conflict resolution on women's lives. As the positions of the scholars and the focus of the scholarship vary, so too does the motivation behind the research and the ways in which the research intersects with advocacy, policy, and practice. Using information from a survey of those who claim to work in the WPS space, this chapter examines the positionality of this group of scholars. This means taking into account the external environment that surrounds the subject, giving the subject complex and multiple identities, and making individual voices critical to the analysis (Alcoff 1988). This chapter also considers the practical and ethical challenges that this group faces in conducting research on (and at times engaging in advocacy for) WPS, and the ways in which these scholars and their research intersect with WPS policy and politics.

Data in this chapter rely upon a voluntary survey questionnaire conducted in January and February 2017 using a confidential online survey platform. At the time of writing, forty questionnaires have been completed. While the data generated do not reflect a representative sample of WPS scholars, they do provide a rich source of information and experiences worth analyzing. Specific survey questions and the institutional approval for this human subject research can be found in Appendix A.

POSITION AND PRIVILEGE OF WPS SCHOLARS

When asking WPS scholars how they came to do this area of research, there is an important distinction between those who came to study Resolution 1325 and the WPS agenda in direct and intentional ways and those who came to this space unintentionally and sometimes with great hesitation. Examining our own positionality in this research is a fundamental starting point as feminist scholars. For me, "positionality" describes where I "stand," literally and figuratively, in relation to that which I seek to investigate (Merriam et al. 2001: 411). Reflecting on the spaces we occupy as scholars is critical to feminist research. As Sandra Harding maintains, "only in this way can we hope to produce understandings and explanations which are free of distortion from the unexamined beliefs of social scientists themselves" (Harding 1987: 9). At one level the goal is more objective social science, but at another level the purpose is to show how and to appreciate the ways in which human interests affect knowledge production as a starting point.

As a white, Western woman pursuing a PhD, I come to this area of research from a particular place of privilege. I was in graduate school working on my doctoral prospectus shortly after Resolution 1325 was adopted. At that time, my research focused on advocacy for women's human rights in the context of global governance, and I began investigating the link between advocacy for women's rights and gender equality with those focused on human security in the UN. I wanted to understand what the human security approach did (and did not do) for women, for human rights advocacy, and for the security agenda of the

UN Security Council. Resolution 1325 was an ideal case study for exploring the intersection of women rights, human security, and global governance (Hudson 2009).

Survey respondents shared some similar identity markers and positionality to mine. The majority were women (88 percent), age 25–44 (75 percent), self-identifying as white or Caucasian (71 percent), and from the United States (49 percent). Other countries of origin included 40 percent from Europe, 8 percent from Australia, and 11 percent from the "Global South,"[2] including Afghanistan, India, and Uganda.[3] Certainly, more work needs to be done to reach and collect survey responses from the many scholars doing WPS research in Latin America, Africa, Asia, and the Middle East, and this will be part of future survey research. Time and access are key challenges here to this sort of data collection. Nonetheless, it is striking to consider how WPS scholarship is dominated by white women from Australia, the United States, and Western Europe, many of whom have not experienced the armed conflict that is so often the subject of their research. The contributions from authors to this OUP handbook do reflect greater diversity in perspectives and experiences, with chapters from scholars and practitioners from South Africa, Nigeria, the Philippines, Fiji, Sri Lanka, New Zealand, Thailand, India, China, Kenya, and Colombia. Still, the majority of the content in the handbook comes from individuals living and working in Australia, the United States, and Western Europe. Certainly, many contributors have transnational backgrounds, multiple identities, and even dual citizenship; for example, some may be born outside of these three regions or have substantial family or personal experiences with armed conflict. But the point of many coming from places of privilege still holds. WPS scholarship is not immune to moral hierarchies and power dynamics in the production and consumption of knowledge, where "the politics of knowledge/information include whose questions are pursued, whose concerns are silenced, whose health needs are prioritized, whose methods are authorized, whose paradigm is presumed, whose project is funded, whose findings are publicized, whose intellectual property is protected [which] are all deeply structured by gender, as well as racial, economic and national hierarchies" (Peterson 2005: 515).

WHAT DRIVES WPS SCHOLARSHIP

Beyond these identity markers connected to positionality, the survey did reflect an important divergence in how individuals came to WPS research. Many discussed becoming WPS scholars "through the back door" or "by necessity" or even "reluctantly"—indicating that they never really set out to be WPS scholars. Numerous respondents reflected on how they started with focus on or a passion for a particular women's issue, such as women's roles in the peace process; or gendered effects of Disarmament, Demobilization and Reintegration (DDR) programs; or women's participation in peacekeeping; or sexual and gender-based violence in war zones; and in order to connect this research to policy and/or advocacy, they had to situate themselves in the WPS space. In this way, WPS was (and continues to be) the necessary language and conceptual framework to engage with policymakers, practitioners, and advocacy organizations.

Engagement with the WPS agenda has become essential for many feminist scholars, despite the fact feminists have critiqued WPS for being narrow, reductionist, and even counterproductive. One of the earliest critiques from Sandra Whitworth (2004) examined how

1325, and gender more broadly, was used as a problem-solving tool for the UN, losing all capacity for radical critique of the institution, much less transformative change. Building on this, Gibbings (2011) points to the way in which the narrow focus on women as peacemakers leads to exclusive narratives about security and whose voices count in WPS advocacy. Dharmapuri (2011) argued that WPS understands the problem, but doesn't know how to solve it—adding women and stirring does not work. Postcolonial feminist critiques argue that the technical tasks of WPS have done little to enhance women's participation and protection needs in everyday lives (Hudson 2012). Others explain the lack of progress because of inadequate resources and political will (Olsson and Gizeljis 2013). Even scholars who are WPS advocates have found the impact to be slow, inconsistent, and uneven (Tryggestad 2009). That is not to say that feminist scholars who came to WPS in more direct ways do not feel the same limitations and frustrations; certainly, these categories of scholars (and the challenges) are fluid. Still, it matters what brings WPS scholars to this research in the first place and what keeps them there. At the core of feminist scholarship must be the motivation to take women's lives seriously and to conduct research that benefits women and not just the researcher. This motivation is important to remember in light of the fact that the WPS agenda and the creation of new policy space has led to the opening of academic space and provided opportunities—both in terms of resources and points of access in the policymaking process, which scholars may not have had otherwise.

Carol Cohn and Claire Duncanson (2016) talk about academics who work in the WPS space in similar terms. They see a distinction between those who start with WPS as an agenda and an architecture with new units, positions, and programs, and those who are focused on ending war and what armed conflict does to women. The former being focused more on the bureaucracy and the implementation of the resolutions in formal institutional spaces, and the latter focused more on women's lived experiences. This latter group are often those most skeptical of WPS as a product of neoliberal peace-building, and all the cost that comes along with it (Hudson 2016). While there is a significant amount of research that challenges this dichotomous view, and many feminists would argue for building alliances across these different starting points, the distinction is important for understanding some of the challenges that WPS scholars face. This is especially relevant in analyzing architecture and institutional design as different from but related to implementation, which is different from but related to impact.

This thinking also challenges WPS scholars to consider whether or not engagement is a softening of feminist opposition to war. WPS squarely situates women's rights and gender equality concerns in international security arenas, and, certainly, this particular placement of these long-standing issues might actually be limiting for women's emancipation and a more radical transformative shift (Cohn 2008; Shepherd 2008; Shepherd 2011). For example, WPS scholarship and advocacy put a great deal of emphasis on the UN Security Council and how it is or could be better implementing the WPS agenda. This emphasis not only reinforces the power and the authority of the Security Council and the major state powers that comprise the organization, it also relies upon a very flawed institution historically guided by militaristic approaches to security in order to implement a radical human security-based agenda. Where, how, and by whom these issues are addressed matter, and it is important to understand how the WPS framework and language can simultaneously create opportunities for equality while reinforcing existing patriarchal, militaristic, and imperialist power structures (Hudson 2013; Pratt 2013). This tension is apparent when we consider a major component of WPS scholarship and advocacy focuses on increasing women's participation in peace operations as military or police personnel. What does it mean that implementing WPS means more people (women), uniformed and armed are being deployed across the globe? In this way, we must head Cora Weiss's warning that WPS should not be a means of "making war safe for women" (Weiss 2011).

MARGINALIZED REALITIES OF ACADEMIA AND GLOBAL POLICYMAKING

One of the consistent themes in the survey was the challenge of "being taken seriously" that many academics still face in academic disciplines, departments and among their colleagues. Research on women and gender continue to be marginalized in international relations studies just as in global policy circles; there is a particular lack of mainstreaming of WPS issues and principles with other core elements of UN Security Council business, such as Security Council country mandates (UN Women 2015).

That is not to say that WPS has not found a home in the field of feminist international relations; it certainly has. For example, there were seven full panels dedicated to WPS (based on the panel title) at the 2017 International Studies Association (ISA) Annual Convention in Baltimore.[4] One could also point to the emergence of Women or Gender, Peace, and Security research centers, including LSE Centre for Women, Peace, and Security; Oslo's Gender, Peace, and Security Centre at the Peace Research Institute; Monash University's Centre for Gender, Peace, and Security; and Georgetown University's Institute for Women, Peace, and Security. But when WPS is contextualized in field of International Relations, which is still highly steeped in (neo)realist and masculinized research questions, WPS is largely marginalized from scholarship in security studies, development, global governance, and even human rights. The policy world is no different. On the tenth anniversary of Resolution 1325, Willett points out that WPS continues to face obstacles due to "limitations of mainstreaming gender in existing institutional and discursive frameworks that are still dominated by state-centric, patriarchal and militaristic practices" (Willet 2010: 149). The politics of seriousness still affects what counts and what does not in terms of research and funding priorities in the academy and in politics.

Many (but not all) WPS scholars, as evident in the survey data, also struggle because so many endeavor to conduct research that is politically palatable for policymakers, practitioners, and advocacy organizations. Over 90 percent of respondents articulated a desire to "influence policy outcomes" or "galvanize activists" or "engage with policy-makers" or "inform women's advocacy groups." Here we see an interesting conflation of doing research that is applied and research that is politically palatable, and the extent to which research can be both independent and yet useful and accessible to policymakers. WPS scholars seem uniquely committed to inspire and inform those working for women's rights and gender equality in conflict-affected areas around the world, as well as those who know nothing of women's experiences in conflict but who work in international peace and security.

Conducting policy-relevant research does not come easy and very little WPS "research and commentary has made it into journals with a policy audience" (Kirby and Shepherd

2016: 253). Many survey respondents referred to the challenges of living "the slash": scholar/
activist/advocate/consultant. Navigating the slashes means writing for different audiences
with very different demands and timelines. This requires using different language and different processes for disseminating the work. It means navigating very different WPS spaces
and, at times, feeling like we don't operate in any one of these spaces particularly well.
Further, many grapple with finding the balance between being critical, feminist, and intellectually honest, while also being politically relevant and accessible. As one respondent
stated:

> I see my research as a way of pushing the agenda to be more feminist and radical. In contrast
> to my earlier work as an NGO practitioner, I feel like academia offers the space to think more
> creatively about WPS and its radical potential as compared to policy and practitioner spaces.
> It seems like the role of academia is to counter-balance the traditionalizing and moderating
> tendencies of policy processes.

While the challenges of connecting theory to practice is certainly not unique to WPS
scholars, there are some common methodological approaches that guide feminist research and embrace these challenges in distinctive way. These include "a deep concern with
which research questions gets asked and why; the goal of designing research that is useful
to women . . . and the centrality of questions of reflexivity and the subjectivity of the researcher" (Tickner 2006: 22). WPS scholars are well-positioned to embrace these important methodological standards. Undoubtedly the survey data reflected a group of scholars
driven by deep passion (and compassion) for empowering women and ending armed conflict, as well as individuals committed to connecting with the lived experiences of women
and girls (and men and boys for that matter), and to understanding the role of the researcher in larger process.

GLOBAL NORTH AND GLOBAL SOUTH DISCONNECT

By asking questions about who WPS scholars are and the challenges they encounter, certain tensions emerge around the engagement with and representation of the Global South
in WPS research, policy, and advocacy. To date, the writing of WPS and what counts as
expertise has been more closely associated to the Global North, both in terms of research
generated by practitioners and research published in academic journals (Pratt and Richter-
Devroe 2011). More specifically, there are "some widely shared assumptions about the
Global North being the conceptual, material and (not least) institutional home" of the WPS
agenda (Basu 2016: 362). These shared assumptions manifest themselves, for example, in
who gets published, where, and what "counts" as scholarship.[5] Survey respondents reflected
this concern as one of the challenges in connecting research to policy and/or advocacy. The
responses revealed a desire to better connect and build relationships with women or civil
society organizations in conflict-affected countries and the challenges faced in doing that in
an ethical and sustainable way. The Women's International League for Peace and Freedom
(WILPF) Academic Network in an excellent example of WPS scholars attempting to build
bridges and forge alliances across countries and regions.[6]

There are at least two issues at stake here. One is the disconnect between researchers and practitioners in conflict-affected countries with those who are not living in or have ever experienced a war zone. The second is a disconnect in how Global South scholars and their scholarship is represented in WPS. Both lead to the silencing, the marginalizing, and the making invisible the multifaceted ways that the Global South, both state and nonstate actors, have contributed to WPS. The fact that governments and civil society organizations from the Global South have contributed to the creation of, the implementation of, and contestation around the WPS agenda deserves greater attention. For example, Bangladesh, Namibia, and Jamaica played a pivotal role as nonpermanent members on the Security Council when 1325 was adopted in 2000, but there has been very little published research looking more closely at the implementation of WPS in these three states since 2000 and what their leadership (or lack thereof) means today.

In highlighting the silencing of the Global South's experience with implementing, and not implementing the WPS agenda, Basu maintains that WPS would be well-served to pay "attention to the non-implementation of WPS resolutions that is evident in the Global South" (2016: 370–371). The meaningful work of Women in Security, Conflict Management, and Peace (WISCOMP) focused on peace-building in South Asia since 1999, is particularly instructive here. In this way, Basu pushes WPS scholars to dig deeper into experiences of "non-implementation" at the "local" level as these instances can provide a much fuller understanding of various reasons why civil society groups choose not to engage. She argues that there might be any number of reasons why civil society doesn't implement WPS, including lack of interest, limited utility, differences in CSOs, as well as more fundamental opposition to the ideological underpinnings of the resolutions. She warns that "not taking these narratives seriously comes at a political cost" (2016: 370). That is not to suggest a romanticization of the local, but rather taking seriously various local realities that simply get lost, as they do in many global policy processes.

HIERARCHY AND HEGEMONY OF WPS RESEARCH AND ADVOCACY

Research, analysis, and monitoring of WPS is very much affected by which issues, actors, and locations are elevated by governments, international organizations, donors, and advocacy groups as being the most urgent and most in need of global attention and intervention. Undoubtedly, a hierarchy of issues exist within the WPS agenda. It is no accident that the second, third, fourth, and fifth WPS resolution narrow in on sexualized violence in armed conflict, giving more attention to the protection pillar than the participation or conflict-prevention pillar of SCR 1325. Here, the tendency is for WPS institutions to essentialize and simplify women's experiences in conflict (Hudson 2009; Gibbings 2011), situating them as vulnerable actors who require little more than protection (Puechguirbal 2010). Given these institutional biases, the research has also narrowed in many ways on sexual violence and increasing prosecutions with far less attention on demilitarization and prevention of conflict (Basu and Confortini 2016).

Acknowledging victims while also being able to move beyond the frame of victimhood is a real challenge for WPS scholars, especially if they are trying to influence policy and practice. Of course, WPS scholarship and advocacy can also be affected by and contribute to a hierarchy of victimhood, where certain victims like those who survive rape in war are constructed as the most vulnerable and the issue that needs most urgently attended to in terms of humanitarian intervention or peacekeeping. There is also a hierarchy here (and beyond WPS circles), as Ticktin outlines, between the protector and the victim where protection ensure power asymmetry and not equality, where "regimes of care ultimately work to displace possibilities for larger forms of collective change, particularly for those most disenfranchised" (2011: 3). For example, many WPS scholars point to a disturbing gap between the matters that are considered relevant and important to formal institutional deliberation on WPS issues and the matters that are prioritized by local actors and civil society group (Basini and Ryan 2016). This is particularly true when we look at institutional pressures to better measure women's security and insecurity and to subsequently provide quantitative data for policymakers to use (Simić 2013). "Hard data" are still in demand and often necessary for explaining and justifying the importance of gender issues to international peace and security policymakers. The challenges are normative and political, ranging from the those who want to frame WPS as a luxury or a secondary issue to be handled once the peace agreement has been signed, to those who frame WPS as a political threat to populist (conservative) authoritarianism sweeping the globe (as seen in chapter 66 in this volume).

What Do We Know and Where Do We Go From Here?

There was a general consensus in the surveys that this field of scholarship is expanding, and while such growth is often seen as valuable, there is also reason to be cautious. WPS scholars are paying attention to different intersectional forms of analysis as well as new subjects, including men and masculinity, LGBTQ concerns, refugees, and countering violent extremism.[7] Further, there is a desire among many to create and deepen connections between WPS and human rights, or development and global health, or sustainability and climate justice. In looking at these new areas, however, WPS scholars are also more apt to consider how WPS has been co-opted in troubling ways by neoliberal initiatives that privilege the state and its military as well as capitalist economic ideals. Consider, for example, the anti-feminist politics so deeply embedded with the "war on terrorism" and all that goes into countering violent extremism. What does it mean to make the prevention of terrorism and violent extremism central to the WPS agenda? In what ways does such a focus reinforce problematic and violent ideas about who counts as a terrorist and the central role of the military in "combatting" extremism. How can WPS scholarship best engage with this global policy priority? At one level, there must be a balance struck between creating meaningful connections without creating new forms of co-optation. At another level, some disorder and incoherence may be okay, perhaps even desirable for feminist IR that embraces diverse theories, knowledge, and methodologies. Baaz and Stern embrace the notion of "unease" in the seduction that so often goes along with stories about women's insecurity and gender-based violence (Baaz and Stern 2013: 15). As feminist researchers, the aim is not to resolve unease, but to hold on to it, be honest about it, and work with it.

While more is certainly being written, we must wonder if we are saying anything new, and whether or not we should be. From Afghanistan to Syria to South Sudan to Burma to Colombia, violence against women is rampant and women continue to be excluded from decision-making bodies. In this way, protection and participation remain core issues for women's civil society organizations across the globe, and WPS scholarship has a responsibility to maintain focus on these foundational issues and to co-produce knowledge on these issues with women most directly affected by armed conflict. As Wibben reminds us, these narratives are "sites of the exercise of power" that enable us to "not only investigate but also invent an order for the world" (2011: 2). WPS scholars constitute that which they study, and the research is performative and powerful in this way. We must remain focused on who we are, what we claim to represent, the motivations that drive our research, and the way in which our scholarship informs (and doesn't inform) policy, practice, and advocacy.

NOTES

1. See, for example, the recent workshop entitled, "The Futures of Women, Peace, and Security: New Directions in Research on the Women, Peace, and Security Agenda" (International Studies Association Annual Convention, Baltimore, MD, February 21, 2017) and the upcoming WIIS Next Generation WPS + GPA Symposium (Women in International Security, Washington, DC, November 12–19, 2017).

2. I recognize that the Global North/Global South distinction is problematic, often obscuring more than clarifying. Such distinctions also tend to overemphasize differences rather than identify similarities. Still I use these two categories to concisely talk about those that live in the "wealthy" or "economically developed" parts of the world which largely tend to be in the geographic north from those in the geographic south, particularly Asia, Africa, and Latin America. Australia, New Zealand, Japan, among others, don't fit the geographic distinction.

3. The lack of respondents from scholars in Latin America, Africa, the Middle East, and Asia is particularly problematic and is part of my focus for a second round of data collection later this year.

4. They were many more that did not have WPS in the title but focused on core elements of WPS, including sexual- and gender-based violence in conflict, women as combatants, women in the peace process, gendered security sector reform, and gendered peace-building, just to name a few.

5. There are attempts by WPS scholars to address questions of representation, power, and positionality in the performances of WPS research. See, for example, a special forum in *International Studies Perspective* 14, no. 4 (2013) entitled "The State of Feminist Security Studies: Continuing the Conversation."

6. At the time of writing, the WILPF Academic Network consisted of thirty-seven members of professors, doctoral students, and independent researchers from all regions of the world. For updates, see http://wilpf.org/academic-network.

7. See the special issue of *International Affairs* 92, no. 2 (March 2016) on "The Futures of Women, Peace, and Security."

References

Ackerly, B. A., M. Stern, and J. True. *Feminist Methodologies for International Relations.* Cambridge: Cambridge University Press, 2006.

Alcoff, L. "Cultural Feminism versus Post-Structuralism: The Identity Crisis in Feminist Theory." *Signs* 13, no. 3 (1988): 405–436.

Baaz, M. E., and M. Stern. *Sexual Violence as a Weapon of War? Perceptions, Prescriptions, and Problems in the Congo and Beyond.* London: Zed Books, 2013.

Basini, H., and C. Ryan. "National Action Plans as an Obstacle to Meaningful Local Ownership of UNSCR 1325 in Liberia and Sierra Leone." *International Political Science Review* 37, no. 3 (2016): 390–403.

Basu, S. "The Global South Writes 1325 (Too)." *International Political Science Review* 37, no. 3 (2016): 362–374.

Basu, S., and C. Confortini. "Weakest "P" in the 1325 Pod? Realizing Conflict Prevention through Security Council Resolution 1325." *International Studies Perspectives* 18, no. 1 (2016): 43–63.

Cohn, C. "Mainstreaming Gender in UN Security Policy: A Path to Political Transformation. In *Global Governance: Feminist Perspectives,* edited by S. M. Rai and G. Waylen, 185–206. New York: Palgrave Macmillan, 2008.

Cohn, C., and C. Duncanson. "Tackling Neoliberal Post-War Reconstruction Models: The Post-2015 Agenda for Women, Peace, and Security Advocates." Paper presented at the International Feminist Journal of Politics Conference, Cincinnati, Ohio, May 20–22, 2016.

Dharmapuri, S. "Just Add Women and Stir?" *Parameters* (Spring 2011): 56–66.

Gibbings, S. "No Angry Women at the United Nations: Political Dreams and Cultural Politics of United Nations Security Council Resolution 1325." *International Feminist Journal of Politics* 13, no. 4 (2011): 522–538.

Harding, S., ed. *Feminism and Methodology: Social Science Issues.* Bloomington: Indiana University Press, 1987.

Hudson, H. "A Double-edged Sword of Peace? Reflections on the Tension between Representation and Protection in Gendering Liberal Peacebuilding." *International Peacekeeping* 19, no. 4 (2012): 443–460.

Hudson, H. "Decolonising Gender and Peacebuilding: Feminist Frontiers and Border Thinking in Africa." *Peacebuilding* 4, no. 2 (2016): 194–209.

Hudson, N. F. "UNSCR 1325: The Challenges of Framing Women's Rights as a Security Matter." NOREF Norwegian Peacebuilding Resource Centre Policy Brief, 2013, http://reliefweb.int/sites/reliefweb.int/files/resources/4814ab8970493cca48dbbafdbb4e92bc.pdf.

Hudson, N. F. *Gender, Human Security, and the UN: Security Language as a Political Framework for Women.* London: Routledge, 2009.

Kirby, P., and L. Shepherd. "Reintroducing Women, Peace, and Security." *International Affairs* 92, no. 2 (2016): 249–254.

Merriam, S. B., J. Johnson-Bailey, M. Lee, Y. Kee, G. Ntsean, and M. Muhamad. "Power and Positionality: Negotiating Insider/Outsider Status within and across Cultures." *Journal of Lifelong Education* 20, no. 5 (2001): 405–416.

Olsson, L., and T. Gizeljis. "An Introduction to UNSCR 1325." *International Interactions* 39, no. 4 (2013): 425–434.

Peterson, V. S. "How (the Meaning of) Gender Matters in Political Economy." *New Political Economy* 10, no. 4 (2005): 499–521.

860   NATALIE FLOREA HUDSON

Puechguirbal, N. "Discourses on Gender, Patriarch, and Resolution 1325: A Textual Analysis of UN Documents." *International Peacekeeping* 17, no. 2 (2010): 172–187.

Pratt, N. "Reconceptualizing Gender, Reinscribing Racial-Sexual Boundaries in International Security: The Case of UN Security Council Resolution 1325 on Women, Peace, and Security." *International Studies Quarterly* 57, no. 4 (2013): 616–622.

Pratt, N., and S. Richter-Devroe, ed. *Gender, Global Governance, and International Security.* London: Routledge, 2011.

Shepherd, L. J. "Power and Authority in the Production of United Nations Security Council Resolution 1325." *International Studies Quarterly* 52, no. 2 (2008): 383–404.

Shepherd, L. J. "Sex, Security, and Superhero(in)es: From 1325 to 1820 and Beyond." *International Feminist Journal of Politics* 13, no. 4 (2011): 504–521.

Simić, O. "Moving beyond the Numbers: Integrating Women into Peacekeeping Operations. NOREF Norwegian Peacebuilding Resource Centre Policy Brief, March 13, 2013, http://www.ceipaz.org/images/contenido/movingbeyondnumbers.pdf.

Tickner, J. A. "Feminism Meets International Relations: Some Methodological Issues." In *Feminist Methodologies for International Relations*, edited by B. A. Ackerly, M. Stern, and J. True. Cambridge: Cambridge University Press, 2006.

Ticktin, M. *Casualties of Care: Immigration and the Politics of Humanitarianism in France*, 3. Berkeley: University of California Press, 2011.

Tryggestad, Torunn L. "Trick or Treat? The UN and Implementation of Security Council Resolution 1325 on Women, Peace, and Security." *Global Governance* 15 (2009): 539–557.

UN Women. "Transforming Justice, Securing the Peace. A Global Study on the Implementation of United Nations Security Council Resolution 1325 (2000)." Lead author: Radhika Coomaraswamy. UN Women, 2015, http://wps.unwomen.org/pdf/en/GlobalStudy_EN_Web.pdf.

Weiss, C. "We Must Not Make War Safe for Women." 50.50 Inclusive Democracy, May 24, 2011, https://www.opendemocracy.net/5050/cora-weiss/we-must-not-make-war-safe-for-women.

Whitworth, S. *Men, Militarism, and UN Peacekeeping: A Gendered Analysis.* Boulder, CO: Lynne Rienner, 2004.

Wibben, A. T. R. *Feminist Security Studies: A Narrative Approach.* London: Routledge, 2011.

Wibben, A. T. R., ed. *Researching War: Feminist Methods, Ethics, and Politics.* London: Routledge, 2016.

Willet, S. "Introduction: Security Council Resolution 1325: Assessing the Impact on Women, Peace, and Security." *International Peacekeeping* 17, no. 2 (2010): 142–158.

APPENDIX A

SURVEY: WHAT MAKES A WPS SCHOLAR?

You have been asked to participate in a research project conducted by Natalie Florea Hudson from the University of Dayton, in the Department of Political Science. This survey will contribute to a research project aimed at understanding the identity, motivation and aims of scholars conducting research in the WPS space. This survey is only ten questions long and should take you less than twenty minutes to complete. Thank you for taking the time. [EXEMPT B-2; Approved 1/6/17 by IRB, University of Dayton]

Your Participation: Read the information below, and ask questions about anything you do not understand before deciding whether or not to participate.

- Your participation in this research is voluntary. You have the right not to answer any question and to stop participating at any time for any reason. Answering the survey questions will take about twenty minutes.
- You will not be compensated for your participation.
- All of the information you tell us will be confidential.
- Only the researcher and faculty advisor will have access to your responses. If you are participating in an online survey: We will not collect identifying information, but we cannot guarantee the security of the computer you use or the security of data transfer between that computer and our data collection point.
- I understand that I am ONLY eligible to participate if I am over the age of 18. If you have any questions or concerns, please contact Dr. Natalie Florea Hudson, University of Dayton, Department of Political Science, 937-229-3617, nhudson1@udayton.edu. If you have questions regarding your rights as a research participant, you may contact Candise Powell, J.D., Chair of the Institutional Review Board at the University of Dayton, IRB@udayton. edu; Phone: (937) 229-3515.

Survey Questions

1. What led you to conduct research on WPS?
2. How do you define the purpose of your research on WPS?
3. What are some of the challenges you face in conducting research on WPS?
4. How does your research inform policy and/or advocacy?
5. What are the challenges in making connections between your research and policy and/ or advocacy?
6. How has this field of scholarship and/or body literature changed since your engagement with it?
7. I identify my gender as
   a. Woman
   b. Man
   c. Trans*
   d. Prefer not to disclose
   e. Don't identify with any of the choices
8. What is your age?
   a. 18 to 24
   b. 25 to 34
   c. 35 to 44
   d. 45 to 54
   e. 55 to 64
   f. 65 to 74
   g. 75 or older
9. What is your country of origin?
10. How do you identify in terms of race or ethnicity?

Index

Boxes, figures, notes, and tables are indicated by b, f, n, and t following the page numbers.

al-Abadi, Haider, 284
abuse. *See* sexual exploitation and
    abuse (SEA)
Accra Peace Agreement (2003), 112
Acheson, Ray, 690
action plans. *See* national action plans
    (NAPs)
activism. *See* advocacy; civil society activism;
    women's activism
ADB (Asian Development Bank), 347–348n8
Addams, Jane, 20–23
adolescents. *See* children and adolescents
advocacy
    civil society in, 430–431
    conceptual and analytical framework
        for, 41, 42
    consensus-driven approach to, 69
    for disarmament, 143
    for ICC, 360, 432
    networked (*see* networked advocacy)
    for Resolution 1325, 26, 28, 29, 43–45, 47
    for women in peacemaking processes, 16
    WPS advocacy assessment in UNSC, 69–74
Afghanistan, 553–568
    forced marriage in, 560
    internally displaced persons in, 555
    mandate for UN mission in, 70
    military deployment of women to, 257n1,
        570, 572, 578, 579n7
    national action plan for, 276, 279, 554, 557
    NATO operations in, 371, 372
    participation of women in peace processes
        in, 156–157, 556–557
    police women in, 265, 563n10
    prevention of violence in, 557–558
    protection of women in, 554–555

relief and recovery efforts in, 187, 558,
    561–562
sanctions imposed upon, 32
US drawdown of troops in, 783
World Bank projects in, 344
WPS implementation in, 83, 553–561
Africa Gender Scorecard, 381, 385n5
African Charter on Human and People's
    Rights. *See* Maputo Protocol
African Peace and Security Architecture
    (APSA), 376–378
African Union (AU), 375–387. *See also specific
    countries*
    adoption of Women's Situation Room as
        best practice, 442
    establishment of, 376–377
    gender sensitive peace and security
        architecture in, 378–381
    human rights investigations by, 324–325
    ICC opposition from, 359
    national action plan development and, 274,
        384, 385n4
    in peacekeeping operations, 209
    as practice site for Africanization of WPS,
        375–376, 378, 381, 384–385
    special representatives on WPS agenda
        from, 68
    strategic partnerships with, 519–520
    WPS implementation efforts in, 376–385
agency of women. *See also* women's activism
    in conflict prevention, 5, 6
    maternalism in denial of, 20
    political, 60
    prevention of violence and, 106
    protection and, 104
    in victimization discourse, 55, 91

Aggestam, Karin, 5, 780, 815, 820

Aharoni, Sarai, 430, 820

AIDS. *See* HIV/AIDS

Alam, Mayesha, 681

Alison, M., 128

Al-Qaeda, 555

Álvarez-Vanegas, Eduardo, 461

Améline, Nicole, 692

Amnesty International, 44,
   486n7, 509

Ampatuan dynasty, 544

Anderson, Hilary, 419–421

Anderson, M., 151

Aning, Kwesi, 240

Annan, Kofi, 40–41, 41*b*, 161,
   287, 586

Anstee, M. J., 823

Aoláin, Fionnuala Ní, 835

Arab Spring (2011), 587, 787

Arat, Z., 124, 126, 130n2

architectures of entitlement, 475–477,
   482–485

armed forces. *See* military forces

arms control. *See* disarmament,
   demobilization, and reintegration
   (DDR) process

Arms Trade Treaty of 2013 (ATT), 690–703
   CEDAW and, 694
   criticisms of, 697
   cultural and economic impediments to
      implementation, 694–697
   gender perspectives in, 201, 690–693
   Global Study recommendations for, 743
   overview, 690
   principles of, 142
   Responsibility to Protect and, 593
   WPS agenda and, 693–694, 697–698

Aroussi, S., 149, 151

Arria Formula meetings, 48, 71, 116, 117,
   660–662, 674

ASEAN. *See* Association of South East Asian
   Nations

Ashrawi, Hanan, 45

Asian Development Bank (ADB), 347–348n8

Association of South East Asian Nations
   (ASEAN), 388–401. *See also specific
   countries*

conflict resolution in, 389

human rights commitment by, 389–391,
   393–394, 399n6

members of, 389

national action plan development and, 275,
   391–393

WPS advancement in, 393–398

ATT. *See* Arms Trade Treaty of 2013

AU. *See* African Union

Australia, 569–581
   civil society organizations in, 576
   defense strategy for WPS implementation
      in, 572–575, 574*b*, 578
   foreign policy of, 524
   gender integrated into peace and security
      policies in, 575–576
   international engagement on WPS,
      577–578
   national action plan for, 569–570, 572–574,
      578, 624, 647–648

participation of women in military,
   571–572, 578

Baaz, M. E., 857–858

Bachelet, Michele, 422

Baden, Sally, 691

Bahidjan, Dayang, 548

Bakker, Edwin, 681

Balakrishnan, Radhika, 704

Bandarage, Asoka, 503

Bangsamoro peace process, 398n3, 546, 548

Bangura, Zainab Hawa, 303

Ban Ki-Moon, 122, 208, 212, 660

Barnett, M., 61

Barros-Melet, Cristian, 661

Barrow, Amy, 528–529, 720

Bartky, Sandra, 21

Basu, Soumita, 100, 856

Batliwala, Srilatha, 201

Beardsley, K., 212, 255, 454

Beijing Platform for Action (BPFA)
   gendered framing of issues in, 215, 768
   implementation review of, 43, 44,
      46–47, 80
   influences on formulation of, 379, 649
   on women in conflict resolution, 31, 41, 67

Belém do Pará Convention (1994), 416–417, 419, 421, 422, 423n4

Bell, Christine, 111, 150, 819

Bellamy, Alex J., 585

Bemba, Jean-Pierre, 357–359

Bensouda, Fatou, 351, 356, 358, 359

Berghs, Maria, 619, 620

Bergman-Rosamond, Annika, 5, 780

Better Peace Tool (ICAN), 51, 115

Beyani, Chaloka, 651, 652

Bhagwan-Rolls, Sharon, 402

bias. *See* discrimination; stereotypes

Binskin, Mark, 569, 574

bisexuals. *See* lesbian, gay, bisexual, transgender, and intersex (LGBTI) persons

Bjarnegard, Elin, 788

Björkdahl, Annika, 428, 476

Blair, Tony, 559

body politics, 805

Boko Haram, 382

Bond, Jennifer, 589, 590

Bosnia-Herzegovina
economic transition following, 143–144
national action plan for, 276, 278–279, 286–287, 432, 434
sexual exploitation and abuse in, 223

Bosnian War (1992–1995)
human trafficking and, 183–184
peacekeeping operations during, 599
sexual violence during, 17, 26–27, 78–79, 207
UNSC response to human rights violations in, 29
warning signs prior to, 139

Bougainville (Papua New Guinea), 475–488
architectures of entitlement in, 475–477, 482–485
bush camps in, 478–479, 482
gender and changing patterns of conflict in, 477–479
legacies of gendered violence and insecurity in, 481–483
national action plan for, 404, 483
participation of women in peace processes in, 157, 475, 478–481, 485
secessionist war in, 475, 477–478
sexual violence in, 479, 481–483, 485
WPS applicability in, 483–485

box-ticking exercises, 197, 218, 276

BPFA. *See* Beijing Platform for Action

Brahimi report (Panel on UN Peace Operations), 32, 81, 213

Brexit, 708

Broderick, Elizabeth, 571, 577

Brundtland, Gro Harlem, 517

Bunch, Charlotte, 421, 658, 665n4

Burchardt, H-J., 728

Burma. *See* Myanmar

Burundi
human rights violations in, 324
participation of women in peace processes in, 198, 718
relief and recovery efforts in, 187
women's peace coalitions in, 39
WPHF in, 742

Buscher, Dale, 502, 504

bus diplomacy, 806

Bush, George W., 559, 782

Bush, Laura, 559, 563n14

bush camps, 478–479, 482, 490, 492, 496

Butler, Maria, 690

Buttenheim, Lisa, 212

CaAC. *See* Children and Armed Conflict agenda

Cambodia
Khmer Rouge regime in, 388, 392, 396–397
national action plan for, 391, 392
prostitution in, 223
sexual violence in, 396–397

Canada, foreign policy of, 524, 624, 625

CAR. *See* Central African Republic

Carayon, G., 358

care ethics, 21–23, 812

care work, 21, 138, 241, 621

Carpenter, Charli, 366, 699n5

Carreiras, Helena, 248, 250

Cartesian dualisms, 19

Carvajal, Isabela Marín, 461

Carver, Terrell, 765

Castro, Loreta, 545

CEDAW. *See* Convention on the Elimination of All Forms of Discrimination against Women

Central African Republic (CAR)
  peacekeeping operations in, 214, 382
  relief and recovery efforts in, 187
  Responsibility to Protect utilized in, 588
  sanctions regime for, 602
  sexual violence and exploitation in, 222, 227–228, 357, 383

Chandhoke, Neera, 429

Chappell, L., 61, 352

Charles, Lorraine, 510

Charlesworth, Hilary, 88–89, 588, 590

children and adolescents
  as casualties in new wars, 16
  in conflict zones (*see* Children and Armed Conflict (CaAC) agenda)
  feminization of, 614
  marriage of, 184, 189n9, 421, 510
  recruitment as soldiers, 354, 489, 493–494, 615
  in refugee camps, 17, 184
  sexual exploitation and abuse of, 29–30, 222–224, 226, 230
  small arms availability and impact on, 541
  UNSC resolutions for protection of, 29–30

Children and Armed Conflict (CaAC) agenda, 608–617
  content and conceptualization of, 613–615
  emergence of, 609
  institutional alignment with WPS, 608, 611–613, 616
  monitoring and reporting mechanisms in, 612
  overview, 608
  principles of, 609
  UNSC resolutions related to, 609, 610–611t, 611, 613

China, WPS agenda in, 530–537

Chinkin, Christine, 26, 186

Chowdhury, Anwarul, 45, 46, 83, 116, 125

CIM (Inter-American Commission of Women), 414–422

CIPP (Context, Input, Process, and Product) evaluation model, 543, 548–549

civilians. *See* protection of civilians (POC)

civil rights, 77, 337, 560–561

civil society, defined, 429

civil society activism
  for Arms Trade Treaty, 691, 692
  for human rights of women, 28–29
  for International Criminal Court, 360
  for Resolution 1325, 29, 43, 48–50, 80–81, 431
  for victim reparations, 352
  in WPS implementation, 71, 74, 612

civil society organizations (CSOs), 428–438.
    See also networked advocacy
  in agenda-setting and advocacy, 430–431, 435
  autonomy of, 49, 429
  challenges for, 434–436
  disarmament advocacy by, 143
  in domestic politics, 518, 520, 523
  Global Study input from, 90, 125, 129
  growth of, 430–431
  in humanitarian action and development, 636–638
  in institutionalization and practice of norms, 431–434
  mobilization of, 102
  in national action plan formulation, 278, 279, 432, 434, 612
  in peace negotiations, 150, 152, 819
  in protection against sexual violence, 105
  regional, 405, 408
  on superficial forms of conflict resolution, 59
  transformative feminist leadership in, 201
  World Bank consultations with, 345
  WPS agenda and, 98, 107, 428–436, 576

civil wars, 49, 58, 135, 207, 388, 489–493

Clark, Helen, 19, 23n10

climate change, 726–736
  causes of, 730
  human security and, 732–734
  international agenda on, 726
  mitigation efforts by women, 19, 729
  in national action plans, 286
  natural disasters associated with, 19, 406
  positive peace and, 732
  power and gender related to, 729–731
  as security concern, 728
  women as vulnerable victims of, 727–728

Clinton, Hillary, 79, 85, 456, 524, 779, 786–788
Cockburn, Cynthia, 557, 650
Cohen, Carol, 128, 853
Cohen, Roberta, 650
Colombia
    gender equality plan for, 274, 433
    grass-roots mobilization in, 797–798
    in Havana peace process, 461,
        463–469, 471n14
    humanitarian action in, 630, 634, 638
    measure of violence in, 756
    participation of displaced persons in peace
        negotiations, 503–504
    refugee and IDP women in, 505
    sexual and domestic violence in, 471n16
    UPR outcome report on, 326
    WPS implementation in, 12, 50, 83, 523
comfort women, 27
Commission on the Status of Women
        (CSW), 41–45
community-based protection, 169–170
complementarity principle, 325, 353
conflict prevention and resolution, 135–147.
        See also peace; prevention of violence
    architectures of entitlement in, 475–477,
        482–485
    in ASEAN, 389
    categorization of measures for, 137
    current state of policies for, 136–137
    gender mainstreaming in, 53
    Global Study and, 137, 740–743
    international financial institutions in,
        338–339
    intersection with participation pillar,
        198–199
    overview, 135–136
    participation of women in, 31, 475, 479–481
    patriarchy and militarization impacting,
        138–143
    pragmatic approach to, 5
    resistance to superficial forms of, 58–60
    restorative agency in promotion of, 145
    social and economic development in, 143–144
    socioeconomic rights and, 343
    in Sustainable Development Goals, 707–711
    transformational shifts required for, 141–145
    UNSC resolutions on, 48, 105–106

Confortini, Catia C., 100, 440
Congolese Armed Forces (FARDC), 165, 166
Context, Input, Process, and Product (CIPP)
        evaluation model, 543, 548–549
Convention on the Elimination of All Forms
        of Discrimination against Women
        (CEDAW), 669–679. See also General
        Recommendation 30
    Arms Trade Treaty and, 694
    on disabilities, 618, 622–623
    on equality in political participation, 31
    General Recommendation 19, 670–671, 675
    General Recommendation 28, 671
    national action plan alignment with, 284,
        285, 404
    Optional Protocol proposal, 672
    overview, 669, 773–774
    protection of women and, 602, 649–650
    ratification of, 117, 534, 554
    Resolution 1325 and, 390–391, 676
    on sexual and gender-based violence, 27
    structural weaknesses of, 671–672
    under-enforcement of, 671–672
    WPS, intersection with, 674–678
Convention on the Rights of Persons
        with Disabilities (CRPD), 618–619,
        622–623, 625
Convention on the Rights of the Child
        (1989), 102
Convention Relating to the Status of Refugees
        (1951), 501–502, 508, 643–644
Coomaraswamy, Radhika, 124, 403, 405,
        686, 739
Cornelsen, Kathleen, 622, 623
Coronel-Ferrer, Miriam, 544, 545
Costalli, S., 599
Côte d'Ivoire
    relief and recovery efforts in, 187
    Responsibility to Protect utilized in, 587
    sexual violence in, 307
countering violent extremism (CVE), 680–
        689. See also violent extremism
    community project financing and, 314n4
    Global Study recommendations for, 743–745
    in militarization of peacekeeping, 217
    in national actions plans, 285–287, 683
    overview, 680–681

countering violent extremism (CVE) (*Cont.*)
  participation of women in, 84, 152, 683–687
  UNSC resolutions on, 285, 308
  WPS frameworks and, 107, 285, 681–684,
    687, 834–836
Cravero, Kathleen, 304
Crawley, H., 646
crimes against humanity
  human rights violations as, 322, 323, 325
  jurisdiction for prosecution of, 28
  Responsibility to Protect against, 585,
    586, 589
  sexual violence as, 28, 70, 194, 322–323, 352,
    357, 432
CRPD (Convention on the Rights of Persons
    with Disabilities), 618–619, 622–623, 625
CSOs. *See* civil society organizations
CSW (Commission on the Status of
    Women), 41–45
Cuomo, Chris, 727
CVE. *See* countering violent extremism
Cyprus
  external resistance to peace agenda in,
    59, 154
  peacekeeping operations in, 212

Dahrendorf, Nicola, 226
Dallaire, Roméo, 82–83
Davies, Sara E., 3, 585, 590, 680
Davis, Lisa, 657, 663
D'Costa, Bina, 832
DDR process. *See* disarmament,
    demobilization, and reintegration process
de Carvalho, Benjamin, 604
Declaration on the Elimination of Violence
    against Women (DEVAW), 27, 389–390,
    394, 649
de Jonge Oudraat, Chantal, 760, 840
demobilization. *See* disarmament,
    demobilization, and reintegration
    (DDR) process
Democratic Republic of Congo (DRC)
  community-based protection mechanisms
    in, 169–170
  human right violations in, 165, 167,
    174n13

international policing in, 260, 458, 601
MARA implementation in, 171–172
national action plan for, 277
participation of women in peace processes
    in, 153, 154, 156–157
peacekeeping operations in, 209, 212,
    214, 217
protection mandates in, 163–167
relief and recovery efforts in, 187
sanctions regime for, 602
sexual violence and exploitation in, 226,
    230, 304, 306, 542, 600
Women Protection Advisors in, 168–169
Democratic Republic of Korea, human rights
    violations in, 322–323
Denman, Kate, 510
de Onis, Kathleen, 731
Dersnah, Megan, 293
D'Estaing, Sophie Giscard, 681, 685, 686
DEVAW (UN Declaration on the Elimination
    of Violence against Women), 27, 389–
    390, 394, 649
De Vos, Dieneke, 359
Dharmaraj, Krishanti, 704
Diop, Bineta, 378, 382
disabled women. *See* women with disabilities
disarmament, demobilization, and
    reintegration (DDR) process
  conflict prevention and, 142–143, 197
  gender-sensitive approaches to, 59, 183, 196
  marginalization of women in, 481, 484,
    485, 633
  in peace agreements, 479
  protection mandates and, 164
  relief and recovery in, 179
  women's participation in, 20, 24n13,
    497–498
disaster risk reduction (DRR), 392–394,
    631–632, 634
discrimination. *See also* Convention
    on the Elimination of All Forms
    of Discrimination against Women
    (CEDAW); stereotypes
  in access to resources, 337
  in cycle of violence, 138
  economic, 182
  internally displaced persons and, 506–507

in international military missions, 255
intersectional, 624
of LGBTI persons, 466, 467, 658
norms in perpetuation of, 94
sanctions as form of, 32
sexual and gender-based violence as, 27, 591
structural, 59, 144, 186
of women with disabilities, 620
division of labor, 18, 238, 240–241, 823–824
Djoudi, H., 727
Dlamini-Zuma, Nkosasana, 378
Doe, Samuel, 452
Dolan, C., 91, 358
domestic violence
armed groups and, 62n5
coping behaviors for, 508
economic influences on, 510
gender and, 646
Pacific Islands Forum and, 407
police response to, 266
relationship with large scale conflict and violence, 55, 320, 506
weapons in facilitation of, 142, 542
Domingo, P., 150, 151
Dönges, Hannah, 161
Doucet, Carole, 457
DPA. See United Nations Department of Political Affairs
DPKO. See United Nations Department of Peacekeeping Operations
DRC. See Democratic Republic of Congo
DRR (disaster risk reduction), 392–394, 631–632, 634
Duarte, Diana, 760, 792
Dufour-Genneson, Ségolène, 681
Duncanson, Claire, 553, 853
Duque, Stella, 799
Dyfan, Isha, 44

Eason, Lauren A., 779
East Timor, UNSC response to humanitarian crisis in, 31
Ebola epidemic, 112, 277, 533
ecofeminism, 729, 730, 733
economic rights. See socioeconomic rights

economic security, 18, 771
Eddyono, Sri Wiyanti, 680, 685, 686
Edu-Afful, Fiifi, 240
Edwards, A., 645
Egeland, Jan, 525n3
Eghobamien-Mshelia, Esther, 284
Egnell, Robert, 367
elite capture, 634–635
elite resistance in peace negotiations, 156
Ellerby, K., 149–151
Elshtain, J. B., 215
empowerment of women
crisis response mechanisms for, 7
CSOs in, 430
with disabilities, 623
economic, 344
financing for, 184
in foreign policy, 523–524
initiatives for, 516
peace and, 22, 60
as precondition for prevention of violence, 106
in relief and recovery, 181, 186, 187
in social conflicts, 399n9
UNSC resolutions on, 103, 150, 683–684
in Western neoliberal nation-states, 833
Enloe, Cynthia, 93, 94, 145, 225
environmental security, 18–19, 406. See also climate change
Eritrea, human rights violations in, 323
Ertük, Yakin, 554
essentialism
association of women and peace in, 16, 101
avoidance in theory of maternalism, 21
in male-female binaries, 215, 463
victimization and protection discourses in, 54–55, 89
ethical policing, 261
ethics of care, 21–23, 812
ethnic cleansing, 585, 586, 649. See also genocide
ethnic wars, 17
European Union
adoption of Resolution 1325, 81
analysis of WPS use in, 375
Arms Trade Treaty and, 692
national action plan development and, 274, 287

Evans, Gareth, 33, 586, 588
exploitation. *See* sexual exploitation and
    abuse (SEA)
extremism. *See* violent extremism

FARC. *See* Revolutionary Armed Forces of
    Colombia
FARDC (Congolese Armed Forces), 165, 166
Farr, Vanessa, 553
female formed police units (FFPUs), 214, 265,
    451–452, 456–459, 601
female genital mutilation, 77, 323, 645,
    719, 784
females. *See* women
femicide, 414, 417, 420, 421, 690, 800
femininity
    critical analysis of, 94
    devaluation of ideas associated with, 692
    hyper-visibilization of, 88–89
    peace and, 16, 101
    strategic use of, 242
feminist foreign and security policy (FFSP),
    779–791
    arms sales under, 57
    barriers to implementation, 779, 786–788
    conceptual issues related to, 780–785
    disabilities and, 624
    four R's of, 781–785
    gender perspectives in, 201, 523–524
    pragmatism and, 5
    recommendations for, 789
    Steinem Rule in, 785
    traditional just war principles vs.,
        781–783
feminist theory
    on androcentric bias of refugee law, 644
    constructivist approach to, 4, 6
    critiques of WPS in, 56, 366, 462–463,
        852–853
    ecofeminism, 729, 730, 733
    on gender equality, 101
    in International Relations, 16, 19, 857
    on militarism, 694–695
    on peace associated with women, 20–22
    political economy approach in, 652
    political institution analysis based on, 61

postcolonial, 440, 441, 447, 830–834,
    836–837
pragmatic approach to, 4–6, 8
research perspectives in, 123, 126, 127,
    129, 130
on security, 16, 18, 22–23, 766–767
third-world feminism, 379
transformative leadership in, 200–202
on war, 17
women's activism in development of, 16
femLINKpacific, 403, 405, 406, 408–410
Ferris, Elizabeth, 501, 650
FFPUs. *See* female formed police units
FFSP. *See* feminist foreign and security policy
Fiji
    domestic violence in, 407
    media networks in, 410
    natural disasters in, 406
    political participation by women in, 402
financial institutions. *See* international
    financial institutions (IFIs)
Fink, Naureen Chowdhury, 835
Finland, national action plan for, 84, 282,
    286, 624
Finnemore, M., 61
Fjelde, Hanne, 599
forced marriage
    in bush camps, 492
    as citizen security issue, 421
    as human rights issue, 323, 324
    in Khmer Rouge regime, 392
    in post-conflict societies, 340, 560
    Rome Statute on, 359
Ford Foundation, 43
foreign policy. *See* feminist foreign and
    security policy (FFSP)
formed police units (FPUs)
    female, 214, 265, 451–452, 456–459, 601
    militarization of, 262
    UN characterization of, 268n3
Forsås-Scott, H., 730
Forster, A., 250
Foundation Ideas for Peace, 470, 472n17
four pillars of WPS, 193–199
    hierarchy among, 7
    international policing in relation to, 259,
        261–267

intersection of, 9, 197–199, 202
locations for assessing progress of, 10
origins of, 99–100, 193, 218n1
participation (*see* participation of women in peace processes)
prevention (*see* prevention of violence)
protection (*see* protection of women)
relief and recovery. *See* relief and recovery (R&R)
uneven implementation of, 194–197
FPUs. *See* formed police units
Fragoso, Teresa, 248
Fraser, Arvonne, 78
Frydenlund, Knut, 517

GAI (Global Acceleration Instrument or women's peace and humanitarian fund), 185
Galtung, Johan, 18, 732
Garasu, Lorraine, 479
gays. *See* lesbian, gay, bisexual, transgender, and intersex (LGBTI) persons
Gbagbo, Laurent, 587
Gbowee, Leymah, 125, 137
GBVIMS (Gender-Based Violence Information Management System), 309, 314n5
gender. *See also* men; women
    as analytical tool, 93, 94
    architectures of entitlement and, 475–477, 482–485
    climate change and, 729–731
    definition in international law, 352
    domestic violence and, 646
    in dynamics of violence, 91, 93–94, 139, 140, 744
    in humanitarian action, 504–505, 629–636
    institutional dynamics shaped by, 61, 440
    integrated into peace and security policies, 575–576
    internally displaced person protection and, 643–646
    intersection with displacement and WPS, 652–653
    military policies on, 249–251
    peace and, 16, 20–22, 101, 818–819
    positionality and, 489–490
    protection of civilians and, 600–601
    reframing WPS to include gender, 842–843, 846
    refugee protection and, 643–646
    in Responsibility to Protect, 588–591
    use of term in WPS resolutions, 88
gender advisors
    gender mainstreaming through deployment of, 216, 575
    in humanitarian action, 630, 639n5
    for NATO, 365, 367, 369–372, 370f
    in peacekeeping operations, 5, 115–116, 118, 601
    technical reporting on number of, 62
    UNSC resolutions on, 104, 150
Gender asylum law, 644, 645
gender balancing, 206–208, 212–215, 369, 842, 846
gender-based violence. *See* sexual and gender-based violence (SGBV)
Gender-Based Violence Information Management System (GBVIMS), 309, 314n5
gender budgeting, 184–185, 187, 342, 743, 785
gender capture, 61
gendered protection norm, 212, 255
gender inequality
    conflict and, 138, 440
    hierarchies of, 91, 138
    neoliberalism and, 143
    in political office, 84
    post-conflict exacerbation of, 17, 183
    poverty and, 18, 182
    in refugee camps, 17, 23n5
    sexual exploitation and abuse caused by, 229
    structural, 22, 126, 337
    UNDP index of, 382–383, 385n6
Gender Is My Agenda Campaign (GIMAC), 380, 441
gender mainstreaming
    bureaucratic approach to, 770
    in conflict prevention and resolution, 53
    criticisms of, 463
    CSO promotion of, 431, 432

gender mainstreaming (*Cont.*)
   in DDR programs, 196
   defense strategies for, 573–576
   in inter-American system, 418–421
   in international policing, 259, 260, 262–263
   in military forces, 7–8
   national action plans for, 422
   organizational structures supportive of,
      115–116
   in peacekeeping operations, 7–8, 110–118,
      206–208, 215–216, 218
   in policymaking, 8, 369
   in relief and recovery, 187, 561
   research and evaluation of, 115
   in security sector reform, 260
   by UNMIL, 455
   UNSC devotion to, 116–117
   UN system-wide efforts for, 294–296,
      298–300
Gender Marker (IASC), 185, 189n11, 296, 505,
      630, 639n4
gender roles
   in bush camps, 492
   cultural variation in, 364
   in patriarchy, 91, 138, 469
   in peacekeeping operations and economies,
      156–157, 240
   war in transformation of, 85n6, 139, 183, 184
gender security, 765–778
   advancement through policy and
      practice, 770
   comprehensive approach to, 768–769, 771,
      775–776
   human rights and, 772
   inclusivity and, 773
   for sustainable development and peace,
      774–775
   theoretical understandings of, 16–19, 766–767
   transformative elements in, 769
General Assembly. *See generally United
      Nations headings*
General Recommendation 19 (CEDAW),
      670–671, 675
General Recommendation 28 (CEDAW), 671
General Recommendation 30 (CEDAW)
   on arms transfers, 142
   development of, 672–674

   on human rights obligations, 339, 772
   mandate for, 391
   on national action plans, 287
   on sexual and gender-based violence,
      396–398, 675
   transformative capacity of, 201
   on women in conflict, 671, 672, 677
   WPS agenda in relation to, 8, 9, 284–285
Geneva Conventions (1949), 58, 63n7, 602
genocide
   jurisdiction for prosecution of, 28
   in Khmer Rouge regime, 388
   Responsibility to Protect against, 585,
      586, 589
   Rwandan, 26, 39, 40, 542, 586, 599
   sexual violence and, 194
George, Nicole, 475, 731
Germany, national action plan for, 283,
      284, 348n13
Ghali, Boutros-Boutros, 431
Gibbings, S., 831, 853
GIMAC (Gender Is My Agenda Campaign),
      380, 441
Gizelis, Theodora-Ismene, 122
Gleick, P. H., 728
Global Acceleration Instrument (GAI or
      women's peace and humanitarian
      fund), 185
global financial crisis (2008), 12, 340, 523
Global Network of Women Peacebuilders
      (GNWP), 125, 280, 674
Global North
   climate change and, 727, 729, 732
   consumption habits of, 239
   humanitarian action in, 631
   national action plans in, 275
   WPS agenda in, 129, 829–834, 855–856
Global Partnership for the Prevention of
      Armed Conflict (GPPAC), 403, 405–407
Global South
   climate change and, 727, 729, 731, 732
   environmental security in, 18–19
   military missions in, 422
   Norway as viewed by, 518
   security as defined by women of, 15
   stereotypes of, 440
   troop-contributing countries from, 212

women's movements in, 441
WPS agenda in, 129, 829–834, 836, 837, 855–856
Global Study on the Implementation of UNSC Resolution 1325 (2015), 122–132, 739–750
conflict prevention and sustaining peace in, 137, 740–743
on countering violent extremism, 743–745
disabilities and, 624
on funding, 63n9, 185, 282, 347–348n8, 520
on gender advisors, 116
on ICC gender justice project, 352–353, 356–357, 360
LGBTI persons in, 91
mandate for, 122, 739
measurement, data, and voice in, 128–129
men and masculinity in, 90–92, 95n4
on militarized approach to security, 140, 435
on objectives of Resolution 1325, 136
obstacles and challenges identified in, 3, 4, 7, 309
overview, 739–740
on participation of women in peace processes, 157, 706, 742, 747–748n1
on peacekeeping operations, 213, 216, 229, 263–264
politics of measurement and production in, 123–126, 130
on protection from sexual violence, 601
on relief and recovery, 179, 196
theoretical standpoints and concepts in, 126–128
on transitional justice, 397, 745–747
GNWP (Global Network of Women Peacebuilders), 125, 280, 674
Goetz, Anne Marie, 61, 150, 200, 691
Goldscheid, Julie, 658
Goldsmith, A., 261, 266
Goldstone, J. A., 261
Gopinath, Meenakshi, 803
Gottemoeller, Rose, 368
GPPAC (Global Partnership for the Prevention of Armed Conflict), 403, 405–407
grass-roots mobilization, 794–799, 801, 809
Greener, Bethan, 259
Greenham Common Women's Peace Camp, 20

Guatemala
national action plan for, 422
participation of women in peace processes in, 198, 503
sexual violence in, 800
Guiding Principles on Internal Displacement (UN), 502, 504, 648, 649
Guinea
international policing in, 601
political violence in, 70
sexual exploitation and abuse in, 223
guns. *See* small arms and light weapons (SALWs)
Guterres, António, 117, 137, 195, 229, 841

Haass, Richard, 81–82
Haastrup, Toni, 375
Hackfort, S., 728
Hagen, Jamie, 657
Hague Appeal for Peace (HAP), 40, 43, 44
Hall, Lucy, 643
Hamidi, Samira, 279
Hammarskjöld, Dag, 112
harassment. *See* sexual harassment
Harris, V., 261, 266
Havana peace process, 461, 463–469, 471n14
Hayes, Niamh, 354, 355, 358
Heathcote, G., 463
Heinecken, L., 215
Hekmatyar, Gulbuddin, 561
Hendricks, C., 463
Henry, Marsha, 225, 238
Hermkens, Anna Karina, 480
Hernes, Helga, 517, 525n2
Hewitt, Sarah, 178
Heyzer, Noeleen, 39, 45
Higate, Paul, 238
high-impact national action plans, 277–284, 278f, 281f, 288
High Level Independent Panel on Peace Operations (HIPPO)
on conflict prevention policy, 136
on peacekeeping operations, 213, 217
protests regarding appointment of, 130n6
WPS implementation review by, 117–118, 125, 126, 312

High-Level Panel final report on Women's
    Economic Empowerment, 343
high-level problem-solving workshops,
    154–155
Hill, Felicity, 44, 49
Hillary Doctrine, 85
Hills, A., 261
HIV/AIDS, 49, 117, 182, 223, 394, 434, 620
Höglund, Kristine, 476
Holt, V. K., 599, 600
homosexuality. *See* lesbian, gay, bisexual,
    transgender, and intersex (LGBTI)
    persons
Hontiveros, R., 543
Hoogensen, Gunhild, 766
HRW (Human Rights Watch), 70, 383,
    620–621
Htun, Mala, 796, 800
Huber, Andrea, 715
Hudson, Natalie Florea, 385n3, 850
Hudson, Valerie M., 779
Hull House settlement, 20. *See also*
    Addams, Jane
Hultman, Lisa, 598
Human Development Index (UNDO),
    555, 751
Human Development Report (UNDP),
    22, 32–33
humanitarian action, 628–642
    allocation of resources for, 295, 296
    development and, 636–638
    disaster risk reduction and, 631–632
    funding for, 185
    gender in, 504–505, 629–636
    institutional mechanisms for, 297
    overview, 628–629
    participation of women in, 632–634,
        636–639
    for refugees and internally displaced
        persons, 504–505, 638
    for sexual violence and exploitation,
        504, 505
human rights. *See also* United Nations
    Human Rights Council
    ASEAN commitment to, 389–391,
        393–394, 399n6
    basic principles of, 748n2
    civil society activism for, 28–29
    conditionality policies and, 165
    gender security and, 772
    in inter-American system, 415–417
    in international policing, 261–262, 267
    monitoring, 410
    in national action plans, 534–535
    political nature of, 144
    protection of, 102–103, 171
    relationship with human security, 32–33, 77
    sexual and gender-based violence as
        violation of, 27–28
    Sustainable Development Goals and,
        704–711
    Universal Declaration of Human Rights,
        661, 704–705
    violence and, 541
    World Conference on Human Rights, 27
    WPS and, 319–321, 328–329, 741–742
Human Rights Watch (HRW), 70, 383,
    620–621
human security
    as basis for WPS and POC agendas, 162
    climate change and, 732–734
    defined, 22
    feminist theory on, 22, 23
    FFPUs and, 457–458
    gendered nature of, 377, 767–768
    global movement on, 431, 806
    gun violence as impediment to, 546
    promotion of, 137, 405, 407, 409
    relationship with human rights, 32–33, 77
human trafficking
    declarations against, 394
    in peacekeeping economies, 223, 241
    by police officers, 266
    in post-conflict environments, 27, 183–184,
        222, 320, 340
Hunt, Swanee, 76, 81
Al-Hussein, Zeid Ra'ad, 226

IA (International Alert), 39, 41, 43, 44, 48, 90
IANSA (International Action Network on
    Small Arms), 39, 542, 691
IAP (Inter-American Program), 417–419
IASC. *See* Inter-Agency Standing Committee

IBRD (International Bank for Reconstruction and Development), 338, 347n5
ICAN (International Civil Society Action Network), 51, 125
ICBL (International Campaign Ban Landmines), 20, 28–29
ICC. See International Criminal Court
ICISS (International Commission on Intervention and State Sovereignty), 33, 586, 588–590
ICSID (International Center for Settlement of Investment Disputes), 338
IDA (International Development Association), 337–339, 345, 347n5
idealpolitik, 517
IDPs. See internally displaced persons
IFC (International Finance Corporation), 338
IFIs. See international financial institutions
Iman, A., 684–685
IMF. See International Monetary Fund
Inclusive Security, 81, 276, 277, 283, 287
Inder, Brigid, 353, 357
India
    failure to invoke WPS in, 57
    police women in, 214, 268–269n5, 456–457
indigenous populations
    cosmologies of, 19
    exclusion from WPS, 68
    networked activism of, 795
Individual Partnership Action Plans (IPAPs), 287
Indonesia
    ethnic and religious conflict in, 388
    national action plan for, 280, 391–393
    peace processes in, 388
    roles of women in, 685, 686
    sexual violence in, 396
inequality. See gender inequality
Informal Experts Group on Women, Peace, and Security, 5, 73, 107, 117, 611–612, 662–663, 677
Inter-Agency Standing Committee (IASC)
    Gender Marker tool, 185, 189n11, 296, 505, 630, 639n4
    review of gender policy, 298
    roster of gender advisors kept by, 639n5
    on sexual violence and exploitation, 91, 227

Inter-American Commission of Human Rights, 416–417
Inter-American Commission of Women (CIM), 414–422
Inter-American Convention on the Prevention, Punishment, and Eradication of Violence against Women. See Belém do Pará Convention
Inter-American Court of Human Rights, 416–417
Inter-American Program (IAP), 417–419
Intergovernmental Panel on Climate Change (IPCC), 727
internally displaced persons (IDPs), 501–515. See also refugees
    comparison with refugees, 501–502
    discrimination and, 506–507
    gender and protection of, 648–650
    humanitarian response to, 504–505
    Maputo Protocol on, 382
    participation in peace processes, 503–504, 507
    prevalence of, 502, 505–506, 541
    sexual violence and exploitation of, 226, 506, 542
    Syrian case study on, 507–511
    UNSC resolutions on, 643
    WPS framework and, 510–511, 650–654
International Action Network on Small Arms (IANSA), 39, 542, 691
International Alert (IA), 39, 41, 43, 44, 48, 90
International Bank for Reconstruction and Development (IBRD), 338, 347n5
International Campaign Ban Landmines (ICBL), 20, 28–29
International Center for Settlement of Investment Disputes (ICSID), 338
International Civil Society Action Network (ICAN), 51, 125
International Commission on Intervention and State Sovereignty (ICISS), 33, 586, 588–590
International Criminal Court (ICC), 351–363
    advocacy for, 360, 432
    contributions to WPS agenda, 351–353, 360
    gender justice developments in, 356–359
    global accountability in, 353

International Criminal Court (ICC) (*Cont.*)
  human rights cases referred to, 325
  opposition to, 359
  Rome Statute and, 351–356, 358–360, 432,
    592, 595, 602
  on sexual violence, 91, 194, 352, 432, 594
  statute for, 28, 55
  victims' mandate for, 352, 355–356, 432
International Development Association
    (IDA), 337–339, 345, 347n5
International Finance Corporation (IFC), 338
international financial institutions (IFIs),
    336–350. *See also specific institutions*
  in conflict prevention, 338–339
  economic influence of, 143–144
  entry points and opportunities for WPS in,
    340–343
  institutional operations of, 342–343
  political leadership and state commitment
    by, 341–342
  relevance of WPS agenda to, 336–340, 346
  in relief and recovery, 183, 337–340, 558
  UNSC resolutions on, 338
International Monetary Fund (IMF)
  austerity policies of, 340, 347n7
  economic influence of, 183
  institutional operations of, 342
  leadership of, 341
  neoliberalism and, 709
  in post-conflict relief and recovery, 337–340
  relevance of WPS agenda to, 346
international policing, 259–272. *See also*
    female-formed police units (FPUs)
  categorization of roles in, 260
  defined, 259
  ethical concerns in, 261
  gender mainstreaming in, 259, 260,
    262–263
  human rights–centered, 261–262, 267
  participation of women in, 141, 198, 259,
    264–265, 268–269n5
  for prevention and protection, 259, 261–264
  in relief and recovery, 259, 266–267
  sexual exploitation and abuse in, 261,
    263, 268n4
  of sex workers, 17
  WPS agenda and, 259, 261–268

International Red Cross, 91, 505
International Relations (IR), 16, 19, 22, 819,
    844, 857
International Security Assistance Force
    (ISAF), 371, 372
intersectional discrimination, 624
intersex people. *See* lesbian, gay, bisexual,
    transgender, and intersex (LGBTI)
    persons
intimate partner violence. *See* domestic
    violence
IPAPs (Individual Partnership Action
    Plans), 287
IPCC (Intergovernmental Panel on Climate
    Change), 727
IR. *See* International Relations
Iran nuclear accord (2015), 24n13
Iraq
  child marriage in, 184
  failure to invoke WPS in, 58
  LGBTI persons in, 659–663
  military deployment of women to, 257n1,
    570, 579n7
  national action plan for, 284
  refugees in, 509
  sanctions imposed upon, 17, 48
ISAF (International Security Assistance
    Force), 371, 372
Isfahani, Mahnaz, 43
ISIS. *See* Islamic State in Iraq and Syria
Islamic State in Iraq and Syria (ISIS), 284,
    308, 324, 508, 659–663
Israeli-Palestinian conflict
  external resistance to peace agenda
    in, 59–60
  failure to invoke WPS in, 63n8
participation of women in peace processes
    in, 151

Jacevic, Mirsad Miki, 273
Jaffer, Mobina, 82
Japan, national action plan for, 280, 286
Jenkins, Rob, 125, 126, 150, 200
Jennings, Kathleen M., 237
jihad, 685
Joachim, J., 648

Johal, Ramina, 44
Johnson Sirleaf, Ellen, 112, 238, 274, 456
Jordan
    child marriage in, 184, 189n9
    national action plan for, 84, 282, 286
    Syrian refugees in, 508–510
    World Bank projects in, 344
Jover, Jogenna, 546
justice. *See* social justice; transitional justice
just war theory, 781–783
juveniles. *See* children and adolescents

Kabila, Joseph, 166
Kaldor, Mary, 26
Kapur, Bela, 135
Karim, Sabrina, 212, 255, 451, 454
Karlsrud, John, 206, 604
Katanga, Germain, 355, 356
Kenney, Emily, 739
Kenya
    national action plan for, 84, 189n14, 285–286
    participation of women in peace processes
        in, 154, 156
    violation of African Charter, 711
    Women's Situation Room in, 442
Khan, Nighat, 809
Khmer Rouge regime, 388, 392, 396–397
Kim, Jim Yong, 344
Klugman, Jeni, 751
Koomen, Jonneke, 351
Kosovo
    exclusion of women from economic
        reconstruction planning in, 185
    international policing in, 260
    military intervention in, 33
    NATO operations in, 33, 371, 586
    UNSC response to humanitarian
        crisis in, 31
Kottok, Sharon, 43
Krahe, B., 541
Krause, U., 650
Kreft, A. K., 216
Kronsell, Annica, 726
Kuehnast, Kathleen, 17
Kullenberg, Janosch, 161
Kunnie, Julius, 19

Lafrenière, Julie, 631
La Garde, Christine, 341
Landgren, Karin, 110
landmines, 20, 28–29, 620–621
LAPs (local action plans), 286–287
Latin America, political movements in, 77–78
Lauzon-Gatmaytan, Carmen, 546
Lavulavu, Akosita, 403
Lebanon
    child marriage in, 184
    peacekeeping operations in, 209
    Syrian refugees in, 508–510
    World Bank projects in, 344
Leede, Seran de, 681
Lee-Koo, Katrina, 608
Le Hoai Trung, 395
lesbian, gay, bisexual, transgender, and
        intersex (LGBTI) persons, 657–668
    discrimination against, 466, 467, 658
    exclusion from WPS, 68, 657
    formal recommendations to UNSC
        regarding, 663–664
    in *Global Study*, 91
    ISIS and, 659–663
    marriage rights for, 466
    sexual and gender-based violence against,
        658–659
    vulnerabilities in conflict, 658–659, 665
Li, Q., 189n7
Liberia. *See also* United Nations Mission in
        Liberia (UNMIL)
    background on conflict in, 452
    CSO influence in, 433
    DDR process in, 633
    Ebola epidemic in, 112, 533
    national action plan for, 84, 276, 279,
        454, 624
    participation of women in peace processes
        in, 153, 155, 156, 503
    peacekeeping operations in, 112–114,
        214, 217
    police women in, 265
    sexual violence and exploitation in, 207,
        223, 224, 306
Libya
    Arab Spring in, 587, 787
    human rights violations in, 323–324

Libya (*Cont.*)
   participation of women in peace processes
      in, 154
   Responsibility to Protect utilized in, 587,
      779, 786–787
   women's activism in, 635
Lie, Jon Harald Sande, 604
light weapons. *See* small arms and light
      weapons (SALWs)
Liyambo, Aina, 47, 48
local action plans (LAPs), 286–287
Lopez, Eugenia Piza, 39, 41, 48
Lord, Janet E., 619–620, 623
Lubanga, Thomas, 354–356, 358
Lund, Kristin, 212
Lute, Jane Holl, 228

Maathai, Wangari, 78, 732
Macapagal, Gloria, 545
Machel, Graça, 29, 609
*Machel Report into the Impact of Armed
      Conflict on Children* (UNICEF), 608,
      609, 611
MacKenzie, Megan, 498
MacKinnon, Catharine, 353
Macklin, A., 644–645
MADRE, 659–662, 665n6
Maguindanao Massacre (2009), 544
Mahmoud, Youssef, 125
*Mainstreaming Gender in Peacebuilding: A
      Framework for Action* (Naraghi-
      Anderlini & Pankhurst), 42
males. *See* men
Mali
   national action plan for, 382
   peacekeeping operations in, 212, 217
   protection of civilians in, 600
   Responsibility to Protect utilized in, 588
Manchanda, Rita, 803
Mandela, Nelson, 789
Manderson, L., 647–648
Manjoo, Rashida, 317
Mannergren Selimovic, Johanna, 428, 476
Maori feminine principle, 19
Maputo Protocol (2003), 378–380, 382,
      384–385

Marks, Zoe, 489
marriage
   of children, 184, 189n9, 421, 510
   forced (*see* forced marriage)
   same-sex, 466
Martin, Florence, 44, 46
Martin, Sarah, 628
masculinity. *See also* men
   critical analysis of, 93, 94
   defined, 88, 239
   in *Global Study*, 90, 95n4
   in international policing, 267
   invisibilization of, 88, 89, 91–93
   militarized, 141, 238, 494, 496
   power dynamics and, 225, 765
   refugee law and, 644
   security and, 16, 766
   violence and, 343, 692
mass action, 155, 433, 818
mass rape, 70, 324, 588, 600
maternalism, as instrument for peace, 20–21, 23
matrilineal structures, 478, 480, 821, 823
Mayanja, Rachel, 451
Mbarushimana, Callixte, 355
Médecins Sans Frontières (MSF), 633
media
   in civil rights movement, 77
   FFPUs in, 457
   gender hierarchies and, 603
   in regional networks, 405–406, 408
   representation of women in, 403
   sexual exploitation and abuse reports in,
      223, 226
   social media, 263
   in WPS advancement, 117, 377, 409–410
Melander, Erik, 788
men. *See also* gender inequality; masculinity
   as agents for provision of national
      security, 20
   in division of labor, 18, 823–824
   in *Global Study*, 90–92
   involvement with gender issues, 822
   in protector/protected myth, 18, 56, 139
   as sexual and gender-based violence
      victims, 55, 90–92, 358
   in victimization discourses, 55
   in WPS architecture, 89–94, 107

Méndez, Luz, 80, 125
Merchant, Carolyn, 730
Merkel, Angela, 284
Merry, Sally Engle, 671
Meyer McAleese, Mary K., 413
MIGA (Multilateral Investment Guarantee
    Agency), 338
MILF (Moro Islamic Liberation Front), 83,
    388, 389, 546
militarism and militarization
    conflict prevention impacted by, 138–143
    culture of, 694–695
    defined, 742–743
    of formed police units, 262
    of masculinity, 141, 238, 494, 496
    of national action plans, 139
    of peacekeeping operations, 217
    political economy of, 695–697
    of Resolution 1325, 139–140
    of WPS, 6, 139–140, 423
military forces, 248–258
    defense strategy for WPS implementation
        in, 572–575, 574b, 578
    deployment of women to combat areas,
        254, 257n1, 570
    expenditure growth for, 139–140, 743
    factors affecting national policies on
        gender in, 139, 249–251, 256–257
    gender mainstreaming in, 7–8
    military college applicants by gender, 84, 85n5
    NATO gender-related policies, 251–252
    overview, 248–249
    representation of women in, 59, 253–256,
        254–255f
    Resolution 1325 and role of, 570–571
    sexual harassment among, 248, 252
Miller, Barbara, 422
Mills, S., 440
Min, Wang, 531, 532
Mine Ban Treaty of 1997, 20, 28–29
Mintrom, M., 431
MINUSMA (United Nations
    Multidimensional Integrated
    Stabilization Mission), 212, 217,
    600–601, 720
Mission in Liberia. See United Nations
    Mission in Liberia (UNMIL)

Mission in the Congo. See United Nations
    Stabilization Mission in the Congo
    (MONUSCO)
MNLF (Moro National Liberation Front),
    388, 389, 398n2
Moellendorf, Darrel, 783
Moghadam, V. M., 440
Mogherini, Federica, 24n13, 815, 817
Mohammed, Yanar, 663
Mohanty, C. T., 830
Mohsin, Amin, 809
Möller-Loswick, Anna, 314
Monitoring, Analysis, and Reporting
    Arrangements (MARA), 170–172, 307–
    308, 601, 612
MONUSCO. See United Nations Stabilization
    Mission in the Congo
Moon, Katherine, 17
Moosa, Z., 150
Moreno, Carmen, 419
Moreno Ocampo, Luis, 353, 354, 357
Moro Islamic Liberation Front (MILF), 83,
    388, 389, 546
Moro National Liberation Front (MNLF),
    388, 389, 398n2
Morrison, David, 575
Mothers of the Plaza de Mayo, 20
MPTF (Multi-Partner Trust Fund),
    304–306, 311
MSF (Médecins Sans Frontières), 633
Multilateral Investment Guarantee Agency
    (MIGA), 338
Multi-Partner Trust Fund (MPTF),
    304–306, 311
Muna, Maha, 44
Myanmar
    ethnic conflict in, 388, 389
    humanitarian action in, 633, 638, 639n11
    national action plan for, 295, 391, 393
    peace processes in, 347n8, 388–389, 503–504
    sexual violence in, 396, 633, 634
Myers, Kristin, 510
Myrttinen, Henri, 88

Nagelhus Schia, Niels, 604
Nahas, Subhi, 661

Naraghi-Anderlini, Sanam, 38, 80, 752, 787
Nario-Galace, Jasmin, 540
national action plans (NAPs), 273–290
    African Union and, 274, 384, 385n4
    ASEAN and, 275, 391–393
    CIPP evaluation model for, 543, 548–549
    countering violent extremism in,
        285–287, 683
    CSOs in formulation of, 278, 279, 432,
        434, 612
    design and implementation of, 278–280
    disabilities in, 624
    emerging trends in, 285–287
    environmental and climate change issues
        in, 286
    externalized application of WPS
        through, 57–58
    for gender mainstreaming, 422
    growth of, 68, 84–85, 179, 200, 273
    high-impact NAP methodology, 277–284,
        278f, 281f, 288
    history of, 273–274
    human rights in, 534–535
    ICC support in, 360
    in inter-American system, 413, 422
    international organizations in promotion
        of, 287
    localization of, 286–287
    militarization of, 139
    motivations for development of, 274–277
    political will and, 283–284
    refugees and internally displaced persons
        in, 507, 647, 651
    regional (see regional action plans
        (RAPs))
    relief and recovery in, 187, 189n14
    resource identification and allocation for
        implementation of, 282–283
    results-based monitoring and evaluation
        of, 280–282, 281f
    small arms and light weapons control in,
        544–549
    tools and frameworks to link to, 284–285
    on women in conflict resolution, 53, 275
    for WPS implementation, 528–529,
        529t, 537n8
Natividad, Ana, 545

NATO. See North Atlantic Treaty
    Organization
Nderitu, Alice Wairimu, 76, 78, 84, 85n6
neoliberalism
    economics of, 143, 336, 341, 709
    in national policy, 563n12
    on post-conflict recovery, 183
    social benefits scaled back in, 18
    structural violence and, 420
Nepal
    earthquake in (2015), 629–630, 632
    humanitarian action in, 629–630, 632, 635
    mobilization of women in, 810
    national action plan for, 432, 624
    participation of women in peace processes
        in, 153, 347n8
Netherlands, national action plan for, 279–280,
    282, 283, 647
networked advocacy, 792–802
    defined, 792
    grass-roots mobilization, 794–799, 801
    for inclusion in peace and national
        reconciliation processes, 793–796
    overview, 792–793
    parallel mechanisms in, 795–796
    policymaking allies, 794
    reframing peace processes through, 796–797
    sexual violence survivor stigma and, 799–800
Newer Ideals of Peace (Addams), 20–21
new wars, 26, 29, 30, 33, 268n1, 489
NGO Working Group on Women, Peace, and
    Security (NGOWG), 69, 72–74, 74–75n2,
    125, 431, 528
Ngudjolo Chui, Mathieu, 355
Nguyen Phuong Nga, 395–396
Ní Aoláin, Fionnuala, 53
    APSA (African Peace and Security
        Architecture), 376–378
Nigeria
    abduction of school-aged girls in, 382
    national action plan for, 284, 442–444
    Women's Situation Room in, 442–445
    women with disabilities in, 621
Niklasson, B., 821
Nixon, Rob, 731
norms
    feminist constructivist approach to, 6

of gender-balance in economic governance, 12

gendered protection, 212, 255

implementation and practice of, 433–434

institutionalization of, 431–432

international contestation of, 6, 8

in perpetuation of discrimination, 94

small states as norm entrepreneurs, 517–518

of violence, 94, 138

North Atlantic Treaty Organization (NATO), 364–374

civilian staff by gender, 368, 368*f*

creation of, 578n4

female military college applicants in member countries, 84, 85n5

gender advisors for, 365, 367, 369–372, 370*f*

gender-related policies of, 251–252, 372–373

Kosovo military intervention by, 33, 371, 586

literature review on WPS and, 365–367

national action plan development and, 287, 574

operational gender perspective, 369–372

reporting mechanisms, 367–369

representation of women in NATO forces, 250–251, 253–255, 254–255*f*

Science for Peace and Security Programme, 287, 366, 372

WPS promotion by, 9, 364–365, 569, 577

Northern Ireland

failure to invoke WPS in, 57, 63n7

measure of violence in, 756

participation of women in peace processes in, 153–156, 198

North Korea, human rights violations in, 322–323

Norway, 516–527

conscription for women in, 139

financial support for WPS agenda in, 520–522, 524

foreign policy of, 516, 517, 524

gender equality and women's empowerment initiatives in, 516, 517

impact of WPS implementation efforts in, 522–523

military participation by women in, 251

national action plan for, 283, 337, 348n13, 520–523, 525n7

normative support for WPS agenda in, 519–520

peace engagement model in, 518

as small state norm entrepreneur, 517–518

strategic partnerships with, 519–520

World Bank programming in, 342

Ntaganda, Bosco, 358

nuclear weapons. *See* disarmament, demobilization, and reintegration (DDR) process

Nyanjiru, Mary Muthoni, 78

OAS. *See* Organization of American States

Obama, Barack

arms sales and, 710

foreign policy of, 782, 783

gender issues under, 787

NAP on WPS released by, 537n8

Obradovic, Lana, 367

O'Brien, Karen, 728

ODA (overseas development assistance), 709

Office for Global Women's Affairs, 52n3

Office of the High Commissioner for Human Rights (OHCHR), 116, 223, 295, 307, 322, 603

O'Gorman, Eleanor, 302

Oldenburg, Silke, 242

Olivius, Elisabeth, 506

Olsson, Louise, 122

Ongwen, Dominic, 358–359

Onyesoh, Joy, 439

Operation Enduring Freedom (2001), 559

O'Reilly, Marie, 193, 462

Organization for African Unity. *See* African Union (AU)

Organization for Security and Cooperation in Europe (OSCE), 40–42, 81, 274, 283, 287, 835

Organization for Women's Freedom in Iraq (OWFI), 659–663, 665n7

Organization of American States (OAS), 413–427

history of, 414–415

human rights and gender equality regime of, 416–419

pillars and mandates of, 419

WPS agenda in, 413–414, 417, 419–423

O'Rourke, Catherine, 62n5, 150, 669, 772
Ortoleva, Stephanie, 624
OSCE. *See* Organization for Security and
    Cooperation in Europe
Ottawa Convention (Mine Ban Treaty of
    1997), 20, 28–29
Otto, Dianne, 60
Ouattara, Alassane, 587
OutRight Action International,
    659–662, 665n5
overseas development assistance (ODA), 709
OWFI (Organization for Women's Freedom
    in Iraq), 659–663, 665n7

Pacific Islands Forum (PIF), 402–412. *See also*
    specific countries
    climate change and, 731
    GPPAC Pacific Regional Secretariat, 4–05
    international policing and, 268
    media networks utilized by, 409–410
    national action plan development and, 274
    participation of women in, 402–403
    progression of Resolution 1325 in,
        406–407, 411
    regional networks and activities within,
        405–406, 408–409
    WPS advancement in, 404, 408–409
Paffenholz, Thania, 148, 150–152, 195, 462,
    793, 818
Pakistan, women's activism in, 635
Palestine. *See also* Israeli-Palestinian conflict
    gender mainstreaming in, 295
    human rights violations in, 323
Palme, Olaf, 23n2
pan-Africanism, 379, 384
Pankhurst, Donna, 42
Parashar, Swati, 829
participation of women in peace processes,
    148–160. *See also* conflict prevention
    and resolution; peacekeeping
    operations (PKOs)
    from armed groups, 496–497
    civil society organizations and, 576
    consultation, 153–154
    counting women and gender provisions
        for, 149–150

critical approach to WPS framework on,
    462–463
descriptive representation, 820–821
direct representation, 153
division of labor and, 823–824
enabling and constraining process factors,
    155–157
female peacekeepers, 208–216, 209–211*f*,
    451–459
gendered styles of negotiation and, 822–823
Global Study recommendations for, 157,
    706, 742, 747–748n1
Havana peace process, 464–469
high-level problem-solving workshops,
    154–155
inclusive commissions, 154
international policy discourses on, 816–818
intersectionality and, 823
intersection with protection, prevention,
    and recovery, 102–105, 197–199
literature review, 462, 819–820
observer status, 153
obstacles to, 150–151, 557
peace vs. gender justice dilemma and, 823
policing, 141, 198, 259, 264–265, 268–269n5
refugees and IDP women, 503–504, 507
research on benefits of, 148–149,
    151–152, 195
rights-based approach to, 148, 149, 469
in South Asia (*see* South Asia women's
    peace networks)
training for, 822
transformative feminist leadership and,
    200–202
UNSC resolutions on, 99–105, 149, 152, 195,
    413, 434, 463
women with disabilities, 619, 625
patriarchy
    care work in, 138
    characteristics of, 138–139
    conflict prevention impacted by, 138–141
    gender roles in, 91, 138, 469
    maintenance of, 93, 94, 138, 266, 496
    in peace negotiations, 469
    protector/protected myth and, 56, 139
    in Taliban regime, 553
    violence in, 730

war and peace as defined in, 56
WPS as challenge to, 4
Paul, Ancil Adrian, 41
peace. *See also* conflict prevention and
    resolution; participation of women
    in peace processes; peacekeeping
    operations (PKOs)
definitions of, 15
empowerment as element of, 22, 60
engendering, 16, 20–22, 101, 818–819
Global Study on sustainment of, 740–743
maternalism as instrument for, 20–21, 23
obstacles to achievement of, 16
positive peace, 15, 22, 50, 193, 732
in Sustainable Development Goals, 706
peacekeeping economies, 237–247
    actors involved in, 239
    defined, 237
    gendered nature of, 238, 240–241, 244
    human trafficking in, 223, 241
    interventions to combat inequities in,
        243, 244
    investment and infrastructure development
        in, 239–240
    sex industry in, 183, 223–225, 230–231,
        241–243
    use of term, 238
    WPS agenda and, 238, 241–243
peacekeeping operations (PKOs), 206–221.
        See also High Level Independent
        Panel on Peace Operations (HIPPO);
        peacekeeping economies; United
        Nations Department of Peacekeeping
        Operations (DPKO)
    community engagement and active
        listening in, 112–114, 118
    complexity of UN mandates for, 111
    consolidation process within, 169
    gender balancing in, 206–208, 212–215
    gender mainstreaming in, 7–8, 110–118,
        206–208, 215–216, 218
    innovations in, 5
    leadership of, 212
    militarization of, 217
    multidimensional nature of, 207, 218n3
    recruitment process for, 453
    research and evaluation of, 114–115, 118

sexual exploitation and abuse in, 124, 214,
    222–229, 382–384, 601
troop-contributing countries, 173, 212–213,
    217–218, 227–228
UNSC gendered perspective on, 32, 34,
    110–112, 208
women's participation in, 208–216, 209–
    211f, 451–459
working conditions in, 216–217
Peet, J., 55, 62–63n6, 62n4
Pena, M., 358
Philippines
    guns and violence in, 543–549
    national action plan for, 277, 391–392, 397,
        540, 544–549
    peace processes in, 388, 398n2, 523
    sexual violence in, 544
    violent conflict in, 388, 389
    WPS implementation in, 83–84
physical security, 17, 138, 161, 491
PIF. *See* Pacific Islands Forum
Pihei, Rose, 483
Pillay, Anu, 243
Pintor, Marylin, 546
Piscano, Frances, 546
Pitanguy, Jacqueline, 77–78
PKOs. *See* peacekeeping operations
Plan of Action to Prevent Violent Extremism
    (United Nation General Assembly), 107,
    683, 684, 687nn1–2
Plumwood, Val, 730
POC. *See* protection of civilians
policing. *See* international policing
political violence, 70, 137, 421
Porter, Elisabeth, 21–22
positionality, 489–490, 851–852
positive complementarity, 353
positive peace, 15, 22, 50, 193, 732
postcolonial feminist theory, 440, 441, 447,
    830–834, 836–837
poverty
    eradication of, 21, 340
    gender inequality and, 18, 182
    in post-conflict societies, 498
    vulnerability to violence and, 138
Power, Samantha, 661
Powers, M., 599

Pratt, N., 440
prejudice. *See* discrimination; stereotypes
prevention of violence. *See also* conflict
    prevention and resolution
  in armed groups, 497
  extremism, 107
  female peacekeepers in, 454–458
  international policing for, 259, 261–264
  intersection with participation pillar,
    198–199
  lack of progress on, 196–197
  sexual, 104–105, 417
  terrorism, 107
  UNSC resolutions on, 99, 105–107, 197,
    241, 413
prostitution
  peacekeeper use of, 223
  in post-conflict environments, 27, 222
  security politics and, 17
protection advisors. *See* Women Protection
    Advisors (WPAs)
Protection of Civilians in Armed Conflict
    (UNSC), 30, 32
protection of civilians (POC), 598–
    607. *See also* Responsibility to
    Protect (R2P)
  ambiguity in, 162–163
  delinking sexual exploitation and abuse
    from, 229
  gender and, 600–601
  implementation challenges, 161, 163, 601
  integration with WPS, 10, 172, 601–605
  international policing for, 261, 262
  operationalization of, 167
  overview, 598
  policy shifts and consequences for,
    599–600
  prioritization of, 166
  reporting mechanisms for, 73
  rights-based approach to, 162
  UNSC resolutions on, 29–33, 104, 165
protection of women, 161–177. *See also*
    Responsibility to Protect (R2P); Women
    Protection Advisors (WPAs)
  ambiguity in, 162–163
  in armed groups, 497
  community-based, 169–170

critical approach to WPS framework on,
    462–463
  female peacekeepers in, 454–458
  gender-specific methods for, 162
  human rights and, 102–103, 171
  implementation challenges, 161, 172–173,
    554–555
  international policing for, 259, 261–264
  intersection with participation pillar, 102–
    105, 197–198
  Monitoring, Analysis, and Reporting
    Arrangements for, 170–172 (*see
    also* MARA)
  prioritization of, 6–7, 12n4, 194–195, 310
  rights-based approach to, 162
  from sexual violence, 102–104, 163–166,
    194–195
  in social conflicts, 399n9
  UNSC resolutions on, 99, 102–105, 111, 194,
    225, 413, 463, 602
protector/protected myth, 18, 56, 108n1, 139
public buy-in of peace negotiations, 156
public decision-making processes,
    154–155, 622
Puechguirbal, Nadine, 93
Puente, Devanna de la, 628

Qadeem, Mossarat, 837n7
Qichen, Qian, 530
Quadrennial Diplomacy and Development
    Review (QDDR), 779

R&R. *See* relief and recovery
rape. *See also* sexual and gender-based
    violence (SGBV)
  in bush camps, 492
  ICC convictions for, 357–358
  of internally displaced persons, 508
  mass rape, 70, 324, 588, 600
  in refugee camps, 223
  in war, 17, 26–27, 30, 479, 489
  weaponization of, 78–79, 207, 308, 717
RBM&E (results-based monitoring and
    evaluation), 280–282, 281f
Reach Critical Will project, 20

realpolitik, 60, 388
Reardon, Betty, 40, 44
recovery. *See* relief and recovery (R&R)
Reed, Melinda, 357
Reeder, B. W., 599
Rees, Madeleine, 135, 186
refugees, 643–648. *See also* internally
    displaced persons (IDPs)
    comparison with internally displaced
        persons, 501–502
    exploitation of, 184
    gender and protection of, 643–646
    gender inequality among, 17, 23n5
    humanitarian response to, 504–505, 638
    Maputo Protocol on, 382
    participation in peace processes, 503, 507
    sexual violence and exploitation among, 17,
        223–224, 509, 646
    Syrian case study, 509–511
    UNSC resolutions on, 30, 501, 643
    women with disabilities as, 619, 621
    WPS framework and, 510–511, 647–648,
        653–654
regional action plans (RAPs)
    in African Union, 376
    in ASEAN, 392, 394
    in Pacific Islands Forum, 404, 408
    UNSC resolutions on, 284
Rehn, Elisabeth, 125, 238, 274
reintegration process. *See* disarmament,
    demobilization, and reintegration
    (DDR) process
relief and recovery (R&R), 178–192. *See also*
    humanitarian action
    armed groups and, 497–498
    challenges to, 188
    defined, 179
    empowerment in, 181, 186, 187
    frameworks for implementation of, 179, 181
    gender mainstreaming in, 187, 561
    gender perspective and women's
        participation in, 182–184
    international financial institutions in, 183,
        337–340, 558
    international policing in, 259, 266–267
    intersection with participation pillar,
        197–198

from natural disasters, 406
overview, 178–179
post-conflict financing and gender
    budgeting, 184–185, 187, 337–340
securing economic and social rights in,
    181–182
for sexual violence victims, 182, 186, 352,
    355–356
transitional justice in, 186–187
UNSC resolutions on, 100, 179, 180t,
    196, 413
reproductive rights, 47, 182
Resolution 794 (UNSC), 29
Resolution 1261 (UNSC), 29–30, 609, 610t
Resolution 1265 (UNSC), 30, 32
Resolution 1296 (UNSC), 30–31
Resolution 1314 (UNSC), 610t, 613
Resolution 1325 (UNSC), 26–52. See also
    *Global Study on the Implementation of
    UNSC Resolution 1325;* Women, Peace,
    and Security (WPS)
    action plans for (*see* national action plans
        (NAPs))
    agenda-setting text of, 100
    armed forces and, 570–571
    CEDAW and, 390–391, 676
    civil society activism for, 29, 43, 48–50,
        80–81, 431
    on conflict prevention, 48
    declarative nature of, 430
    depersonalization of, 38–39, 50
    events leading up to adoption of, 27–31
    gendered perspective on peacekeeping in,
        32, 34, 110–112, 208
    gender mainstreaming in, 111, 112
    implications of, 34, 50
    limitations of, 55, 68, 462–463
    literature and policy reviews on
        implementation of, 528–530
    militarization of, 139–140
    objectives of, 8, 26, 99, 99t, 136, 145–146n1
    origins and evolution of, 39–40, 375
    Pacific Islands Forum implementation of,
        406–407, 411
    parallel developments with, 33
    on participation of women in peace
        processes, 100–101, 149, 195, 413, 463

Resolution 1325 (UNSC) (*Cont.*)
    partnerships and politics in campaign
        for, 43–48
    policy framing for, 41–42
    on prevention of violence, 105, 241, 413
    on protection of women, 102, 163, 194, 225,
        413, 463, 602
    on refugees and internally displaced
        persons, 501, 643
    on relief and recovery, 179, 180*t*, 196, 413
    transformative capacity of, 51, 178, 197
    women with disabilities and, 623–624
Resolution 1379 (UNSC), 610*t*, 612, 613
Resolution 1539 (UNSC), 610*t*, 613
Resolution 1612 (UNSC), 591, 610*t*, 611, 612
Resolution 1820 (UNSC)
    application of, 48
    key issues and provisions of, 98, 99*t*, 180*t*
    on participation of women in peace
        processes, 101
    on prevention of violence, 105, 146n1
    on protection of women, 102–103, 602
    on sexual violence, 91, 164, 214, 591, 602
    on SRSG–SVC, 302, 308
Resolution 1888 (UNSC)
    key issues and provisions of, 99*t*, 180*t*
    on prevention of violence, 105
    on protection of women, 103, 602
    on relief and recovery, 179
    on sexual violence, 611
    on SRSG–SVC, 302–304, 308
Resolution 1889 (UNSC)
    on gender advisors, 150
    key issues and provisions of, 72, 99*t*
    on national action plans, 432
    on participation of women in peace
        processes, 101, 195
    on prevention of violence, 105
    on protection of women, 103, 104
    on relief and recovery, 179, 180*t*, 196
    on sexual violence, 164
    on socioeconomic rights, 182
    on SRSG–SVC, 302
Resolution 1960 (UNSC)
    key issues and provisions of, 99*t*, 180*t*
    on peacekeeping operations, 114
    on prevention of violence, 105

    on protection of women, 104, 602
    on sexual violence, 164, 602, 612
    on SRSG–SVC, 302, 308
Resolution 2106 (UNSC)
    key issues and provisions of, 99*t*, 180*t*
    on participation of women in peace
        processes, 102
    on protection of women, 104–105, 602
    on sexual violence, 89–92, 95n3, 358, 594,
        602, 614
    on SRSG–SVC, 308
Resolution 2117 (UNSC), 68, 71
Resolution 2122 (UNSC)
    key issues and provisions of, 71, 99*t*,
        119n8, 180*t*
    on mandate for *Global Study*, 124, 739
    on participation of women in peace
        processes, 102, 116, 150, 195, 434, 463, 680
    on prevention of violence, 105–106, 146n1
    on relief and recovery, 196
    on small arms and light weapons, 68
Resolution 2178 (UNSC), 681, 682
Resolution 2185 (UNSC), 264
Resolution 2242 (UNSC)
    on arms transfers, 693
    on civil society actors, 435
    on empowerment of women, 683–684
    on engagement by men and boys, 90, 91
    on female peacekeepers, 84
    funding initiatives in, 185
    on gender advisers, 115
    group meetings on, 119n9
    on international policing, 264
    key issues and provisions of, 71, 73, 99*t*,
        180*t*, 406, 612
    on national action plans, 284, 287
    on participation of women in peace
        processes, 102, 152, 195
    on peacekeeping operations, 209
    on prevention of violence, 106–107, 197
    on protection of women, 105, 614
    on violent extremism and terrorism, 285,
        308, 682–683, 744
Resolution 2243 (UNSC), 58
Resolution 2272 (UNSC), 228, 229
Resolution 2282 (UNSC), 338, 347n1,
        774–775

Responsibility to Protect (R2P), 585–597.
    See also protection of civilians (POC);
    protection of women
  applications of, 587–588, 779
  Clinton's support for, 786–787
  complementary relationship with, 591–595
  criticisms of, 587, 589–590
  emergence of, 585–588, 599
  gender in, 588–591
  implementation challenges, 593–595
  principles and pillars of, 33, 585–586
  sexual violence and, 594
  UNSC resolutions on, 586, 587
Restrepo, Elvira Maria, 503
Restrepo, J. A., 756
results-based monitoring and evaluation
    (RBM&E), 280–282, 281*f*
Resurrección, Bernadette, 729
Revolutionary Armed Forces of Colombia
    (FARC), 83, 461, 463–466, 468–469, 503,
    634, 797
Revolutionary United Front of Sierra Leone
    (RUF), 489–498
Richter-Devroe, S., 440
Robinson, Fiona, 21, 22
Robinson, Mary, 815, 818
Rohingyas, 389, 628, 633
Rolls, Sian, 402
Romaniuk, Oksana, 82
Rome Statute of 1998, 351–356, 358–360, 432,
    592, 595, 602
Roosevelt, Eleanor, 698n2
Rottem, Svein Vigeland, 766
R2P. *See* Responsibility to Protect
Ruane, Abigail, 403
Ruddick, Sara, 21, 22
RUF (Revolutionary United Front of Sierra
    Leone), 489–498
rule of law, 26, 61, 119n11, 193, 300n2, 397, 531,
    603, 742, 745
  Rule of Law Team of Experts, 303, 307
Rupesinghe, Natasja, 206
Rwanda
  CSO influence in, 434
  democratic transition in, 84
  female legislators in, 84
  gender roles in, 85n6

  genocide in, 26, 39, 40, 542, 586, 599
  International Criminal Tribunal for, 27–28
  national action plan for, 283, 434, 624
  police women in, 265, 458
  poverty in, 182
  relief and recovery efforts in, 187
  sexual violence in, 79, 207, 542
  UNSC response to human rights
      violations in, 29
Rytter, Therese, 715

Safi, Hasina, 279
Sahnoun, Mohammed, 586
Said, Edward, 830
Salapuddin, Fatmawati, 545
SALWs. *See* small arms and light weapons
Samar, Sima, 807
same-sex marriage, 466
Samuel, Kumudini, 809–810
sanctions
  CEDAW and, 677
  for human rights violations, 325
  negative effects on vulnerable populations,
      17, 32, 48
  sexual violence and, 602
Sankoh, Foday, 490, 492
Santiago, Irene, 79
Save the Children, 189n9, 223, 504
Sayo, Bernadette, 357
Schjølset, A., 253
Schulze, Kirsten, 389
Schuurman, Marriët, 369
SDGEA (Solemn Declaration on Gender
    Equality in Africa), 380
SDGs. *See* Sustainable Development Goals
SEA. *See* sexual exploitation and abuse
Secretary-General. *See* United Nations
    Secretary-General
Secretary-General Special Representative. *See*
    Special Representative of the Secretary-
    General on Sexual Violence in Conflict
    (SRSG–SVC)
security. *See also* human security;
    international policing
  definitions of, 15–16, 18, 23n2, 140
  economic, 18, 771

security (*Cont.*)
   environmental, 18–19, 406
   feminist theory on, 16, 18, 22–23, 766–767
   gendering (*see* gender security)
   Hillary Doctrine on, 85
   in inter-American system, 420–422
   physical, 17, 138, 161, 491
Security Council. *See* United Nations Security
   Council (UNSC)
security sector reform (SSR), 119n11, 179, 260,
   570, 576–577, 858
Sellström, Angela Muvumba, 598
Sen, Amartya, 751
September 11 terrorist attacks (2001), 34, 49
Serero, Perpetua, 478
Seven-Point Action Plan on Gender-
   Responsive Peacebuilding, 179, 181–183,
   196, 282, 296
sexual and gender-based violence (SGBV).
   See also Special Representative of the
   Secretary-General on Sexual Violence in
   Conflict (SRSG–SVC)
   ASEAN action against, 393–398
   children as victims of, 29–30
   criminalization of, 27–28, 352, 432
   CSO advocacy against, 434, 435
   Havana peace process and, 467–468
   historical challenges to addressing, 657–658
   humanitarian operations, 505
   institutionalization of mandates for,
      309–312
   in inter-American system, 416–417,
      420–421
   international recognition of, 17, 27, 29–30,
      32, 207
   LGBTI persons and, 658–659
   men as victims of, 55, 90–92, 358
   Monitoring, Analysis, and Reporting
      Arrangements on, 170–172, 307–308,
      601, 612
   networked advocacy and, 799–800
   policy and institutional developments at
      UN, 303–304
   prevention of, 104–105, 417
   protection from, 102–104, 163–166,
      194–195
   rape (*see* rape)

refugees and internally displaced persons
      and, 17, 506, 508, 509, 542
   relief and recovery for victims of, 182, 186,
      352, 355–356
   resolutions and presidential statements on,
      6–7, 12n3
   Responsibility to Protect and, 594
   small arms and light weapons in, 119n11
   terminology considerations, 310
   UNSC resolutions on, 91, 164–165, 214, 601,
      611, 614
   in victimization discourse, 55, 89, 463
   in violent extremism and terrorism, 57, 308
   in war, 17, 26–27, 30, 479, 489, 604
   women as perpetrators of, 95n5
   women with disabilities as victims of, 620
   World Bank approach to, 343–344
sexual exploitation and abuse (SEA), 222–236
   defined, 222
   delinking from WPS and POC, 222, 224–
      226, 229–232
   humanitarian operations, 504
   by international police personnel, 261,
      263, 268n4
   obstacles to reporting of, 227
   in peacekeeping operations, 124, 214, 222–
      229, 382–384, 601
   of refugees, 646
   technocratic responses to, 232
   UN policy on, 184, 224, 226–229
sexual harassment
   discipline of soldiers for, 225
   of female mediators and peacekeepers,
      156–157, 217
   in military, 248, 252
   national policies on, 455
   in post-conflict societies, 340
sexuality. *See* lesbian, gay, bisexual,
      transgender, and intersex (LGBTI)
      persons
sex work. *See* prostitution; transactional sex
SGBV. *See* sexual and gender-based violence
Sharmila, Irom Chanu, 805
Shepherd, Laura J., 98
Sherret, Laurel, 589, 590
Sierra Leone, 489–500
   bush camps in, 490, 492, 496

civil war in, 489–493
DDR process in, 497–498, 633
Ebola epidemic in, 277, 533
exclusion of women from economic reconstruction planning in, 185
international policing in, 601
military, social, and political hierarchies in, 493–495
mobilization and victimization in, 490–493
national action plan for, 84, 277, 280, 283
participation of women in peace processes in, 156
positionality and gender in, 489–490
sexual violence and exploitation in, 207, 223, 489, 492, 542
Women's Situation Room in, 442
WPS agenda in, 496–498
siloed implementation phenomenon, 194, 229, 843–844
Simanca, Judith, 464
Simat, Mary, 84
Simić, O., 215
Simmons, Beth, 671
Sion, L., 215
Sjoberg, Laura, 17, 55, 62–63n6, 62n4, 95n5, 366
Skåre, Mari, 519
Skjelsbæk, Inger, 516
small arms and light weapons (SALWs), 540–552
deaths resulting from, 541
flow of, 73
minimizing buildup of, 197
national action plans on control of, 544–549
prevalence of, 542, 543
sexual violence and, 119n11
UNSC resolutions on, 68, 71
violence involving, 540–542
WPS agenda and, 545–547, 549–550
SMART indicators and outcomes, 281, 282
Smith-Khan, L., 619
Snyder, A. C., 503
Sochua, Mu, 45
social justice
human rights in realization of, 144
obstacles to achievement of, 16
peace in relation to, 21
promotion of, 15, 323
social media, 263
socioeconomic rights
conflict prevention and, 343
focus of Global North on, 129
IFI conditionalities and, 144
in peacekeeping economies, 242–244
in relief and recovery, 181–182
UNSC resolutions on, 182
WPS agenda and, 561–562
socioeconomic status. See poverty
Solemn Declaration on Gender Equality in Africa (SDGEA), 380
Solhjell, Randi, 604
Solomon Islands
domestic violence in, 407
international policing in, 260
national action plan for, 404
natural disasters in, 406
political participation by women in, 402
Somalia
gender inequality in, 382–383, 385n6
human rights violations in, 29
international policing in, 601
peacekeeping operations during, 599
sanctions regime for, 602
sexual exploitation and abuse in, 382–384
transition processes for women in, 50
South Africa
military participation by women, 139
neoliberalism and, 709
participation of women in peace processes in, 154, 156
peacekeeping operations in, 207
South Asia women's peace networks, 803–814
emergence of, 804–805
grass-roots mobilization of, 809
innovations in, 804–806
negotiation of gendered power systems by, 807–809
overview, 803–804
paradox of invisibility in, 809–811
reframing WPS discourse for, 811–812
South Sudan
community-based protection mechanisms in, 170

South Sudan (*Cont.*)
exclusion of women from economic reconstruction planning in, 185
human rights violations in, 325
international policing in, 263
MARA implementation in, 171
peacekeeping operations in, 209
protection mandates in, 163–167
Responsibility to Protect utilized in, 588
Women Protection Advisors in, 168, 169
Sow, Ndeye, 39
Spagat, M., 756
Special Rapporteurs
on certain human rights issues and groups as part of Special Procedures, 327–328, 649
on Eritrea human rights violations, 323
on Human Rights of Internally Displaced Persons, 504, 508, 650–652
on promotion of truth, justice, reparations, and guarantees of non-recurrence, 328
on rights of Freedom of Peaceful Assembly, 328
on Situation of Human Rights Defenders, Torture, and Violence against Women, 328
on Terrorism, 328–329
on Torture, 717, 718–719, 722n6
on Violence against Women, 554, 649
Special Representative of the Secretary-General on Sexual Violence in Conflict (SRSG–SVC), 302–316
accountability mechanisms for, 307
advisors to, 168
annual reports from, 72, 166, 172
appointment of women as, 212, 303
creation of, 302–304
integration into UN system, 304–311
lessons and insights from, 311–312
Sri Lanka
exploitation of women in, 184
humanitarian action in, 633
human rights violations in, 323
participation of women in peace processes in, 503
resource allocation in, 708
women with disabilities in, 621
World Bank projects in, 344

SRSG–SVC. *See* Special Representative of the Secretary-General on Sexual Violence in Conflict
SSR. *See* security sector reform
Stamnes, Eli, 206, 590
standpoint theory, 729
state feminism, 517
Stein, Michael Ashley, 619–620, 623
Steinberg, Donald, 82
Steinem, Gloria, 785
stereotypes. *See also* discrimination
in division of labor, 18
encapsulation derived from, 254
gendered, 151, 199
of Global South, 440
in Responsibility to Protect, 588
in security, 82
of victimhood, 55
Stern, Jessica, 657, 661
Stern, M., 857–858
Stewart-Harawira, Makere, 19
Stiehm, Judith, 18
Stienstra, Deborah, 618
Stoltenberg, Jens, 365
Stone, Laurel, 151, 819
Strategic Results Framework, 179, 181, 296
structural discrimination, 59
structural violence, 18, 21, 56
Stufflebeam, Daniel, 543
Sudan. *See also* South Sudan
conflict and violence in, 70, 587
peacekeeping operations in, 209, 217
peace processes in, 503–504
Súilleabháin, Ó, 462
Summit of Women and Peace (2013), 464, 465, 470nn5–6
Summits of the Americas, 415, 418, 423n3
Susskind, Yifat, 760, 792
Sustainable Development Goals (SDGs), 704–714
assessment of progress using WPS Index, 752–754
conflict prevention in, 707–711
development and implementation of, 141, 185, 704–706
on gender equality, 637
human rights framework for, 704–711

peace in, 706
relief and recovery in, 179, 196
transformative capacity of, 201, 409
for women's equality, 711–712
WPS agenda in relation to, 284–285, 341,
    529, 843
Svedberg, Barbro, 336
Svensson, I., 820
Swaine, Aisling, 382, 669, 765
Sweden
    arm sales by, 57, 593, 780
    conscription for women in, 139
    feminist foreign policy of, 57, 201, 311,
        523–524, 780–782, 784–785, 816 (*see
        also* FFSP)
    gender relation education in, 141
    national action plan for, 57, 286, 784
    NATO responsibilities for, 367
    World Bank programming in, 342
Swiss, L., 151
Syria
    CSO influence in, 433
    exploitation of women in, 184
    external resistance to peace agenda in, 59
    failure to invoke WPS in, 58
    grass-roots mobilization in, 797, 798
    human rights violations in, 324
    LGBTI persons in, 659–663
    participation of women in peace processes
        in, 150, 154
    refugees and internally displaced persons
        in, 506–510
    World Bank projects in, 344
WPS implementation in, 83

Taliban, 553–556, 559–560, 786, 809–810, 831
Talisman Sabre military exercises, 575, 579n18
Tamm, Elisabeth, 730
Tarr-Whelan, Linda, 43, 45
Taylor, Charles, 112, 452, 490
Taylor, G., 599, 600
Taylor, Sarah, 67
TCCs. *See* troop-contributing countries
Teakeni, Josephine, 404
Teitt, Sarah, 590
Terieken, Gloria, 482

terrorism. *See* violent extremism and
    terrorism
TFNs (transnational feminist networks),
    439–442. *See also* Women's Situation
    Room (WSR)
TFV (Trust Fund for Victims), 352, 355,
    359, 360
Thailand
    gender equality plan for, 274
    refugee camps in, 506
    terrorism in, 389
third-world feminism, 379
Tica, Mirma, 546
Tickner, J. Ann, 5, 8, 15, 60
Ticktin, M., 857
Tiewa, Lu, 528
Timor-Leste
    exclusion of women from economic
        reconstruction planning in, 185
    international policing in, 260, 266
    relief and recovery efforts in, 186
Tinde, Gry Tina, 503
Titus, Agnes, 404
tokenism, 94, 195, 206, 218, 253, 254
Tolbert, William R., Jr., 452
Tonga
    domestic violence in, 407
    natural disasters in, 406
    political participation by women in, 402–403
torture. *See* United Nations Convention
    against Torture (UNCAT)
Towns, A., 821
Townsen, A. A., 606
trafficking. *See* human trafficking
transactional sex, 183, 184, 223–225, 230–231,
    241–243. *See also* prostitution
transfer strategies, 155
transformative feminist leadership, 200–202
transgender people. *See* lesbian, gay, bisexual,
    transgender, and intersex (LGBTI)
    persons
transitional justice
    advancement of, 113, 398
    ASEAN recognition of, 395
    gender-sensitive mechanisms of, 56, 397
    Global Study recommendations for,
        745–747

transitional justice (*Cont.*)
Havana peace process and, 467
mandate for, 62, 555
for refugees and internally displaced
persons, 507
in relief and recovery, 179, 186–187
women with disabilities and, 622
transnational feminist networks (TFNs),
439–442. *See also* Women's Situation
Room (WSR)
treaties. *See specific names of treaties*
Tripp, A. M., 441
troop-contributing countries (TCCs), 173,
212–213, 217–218, 227–228
True, Jacqui, 3, 5, 150, 178, 275, 276, 336, 431,
529, 652, 685–686
Trump, Donald
funding for women's issues under, 780
International Criminal Court and, 359
nationalism and, 193, 708
Trust Fund for Victims (TFV), 352, 355, 359, 360
Tryggestad, Torunn L., 124, 516
Turshen, Meredeth, 243

UCDP (Uppsala Conflict Data Program),
23n3, 756
UDHR (Universal Declaration of Human
Rights), 661, 704–705
Uganda
landmines in, 620–621
national action plan for, 624
participation of women in peace processes
in, 150
sexual violence in, 344, 348n18
Women's Situation Room in, 442
Ukraine, military participation by women
in, 139
Ünaldi, Zeliha, 80
UNCAT. *See* United Nations Convention
against Torture
UNDP. *See* United Nations Development
Programme
UNFPA (United Nations Population Fund),
187, 305
UNHCR. *See* United Nations High
Commissioner for Refugees

UNICEF (United Nations Children's Fund),
296, 305, 510, 608, 609
UNIFEM. *See* United Nations Development
Fund for Women
United Kingdom
Brexit and, 708
failure to invoke WPS in, 57
Foreign and Commonwealth Office, 91
military participation by women, 251
national action plan for, 283, 360
Preventing Sexual Violence Initiative in, 92
United Nations (UN). *See also headings
following that start with United Nations*
in advancement of women's rights, 124
Advisory Group of Experts on
Peacebuilding, 135–136, 142
CEDAW (*see* Convention on the
Elimination of All Forms of
Discrimination against Women)
Commission on the Status of
Women, 41–45
Convention on the Rights of Persons with
Disabilities, 618–619, 622–623, 625
Convention on the Rights of the Child, 102
DEVAW (*see* Declaration on the
Elimination of Violence against Women)
fundamental restructuring of, 300n1
gender-focused budget allocations from,
296, 300n2
High-Level Panel final report on Women's
Economic Empowerment, 343
Peacebuilding Fund, 185, 296
power positions within, 61
sexual exploitation and abuse as defined
by, 222
sexual violence policy and institutional
developments at, 303–304
system-wide efforts for gender
mainstreaming, 294–296, 298–300
Universal Declaration of Human Rights,
661, 704–705
World Bank partnership with, 347n1, 347n6
WPS advancement within, 295–299
United Nations Action Against Sexual
Violence in Conflict, 61, 296, 302–311
United Nations Children's Fund (UNICEF),
296, 305, 510, 608, 609

United Nations Convention against Torture
(UNCAT), 716–721
on criminalization of torture, 716
on gender-sensitive inquiries into
abuse, 719
participation of women in peace processes
and, 718, 720
peacekeeping operations and, 720
for post-conflict situations, 717–719
preventive obligations in, 716–720
protection of women in, 716, 717, 719, 720
Special Rapporteur on Torture, 717,
718–719, 722n6
WPS agenda in relation to, 716, 720–721
United Nations Department of Peacekeeping
Operations (DPKO)
coordination with other UN agencies, 295,
305, 307, 311
on female formed police units, 456
on gender balancing, 206, 208, 214, 215
gender mainstreaming efforts of, 124, 207,
216, 296
mandate for, 62
operational concept of POC developed
by, 163
shortcomings in WPS implementation, 70
United Nations Department of Political
Affairs (DPA), 62, 70, 295, 296, 305, 311
United Nations Development Fund for
Women (UNIFEM)
activism for Resolution 1325 by, 29, 40–42,
41b, 44, 48, 49
merger with UN Women, 294
on nexus of CEDAW and Resolution
1325, 390
United Nations Development Programme
(UNDP), 22
coordination with other UN agencies, 307
gender budgeting analysis by, 184–185
Gender Inequality Index of, 382–383,
385n6
gender mainstreaming efforts of, 296
Human Development Index of, 555, 751
Human Development Report, 22, 32–33
relief and recovery efforts of, 196, 498
training initiatives for women, 23n10
workshops held by, 408

United Nations Entity for Gender Equality
and the Empowerment of Women (UN
Women), 293–301
challenges for, 297–300
creation of, 294, 306
funding for, 523, 533
gender mainstreaming efforts of,
294–296, 300
gender-specific briefings by, 117
Global Study coordinated by, 90, 295
in humanitarian response, 637
international policing partnerships
with, 264
national action plan support from, 282
overview, 293
on participation of women in peace
processes, 150, 274
predecessors to, 40, 294
WPS advancement by, 62, 295–300
United Nations High Commissioner for
Refugees (UNHCR)
community engagement and, 112–113
gender mainstreaming by, 502, 507
on gender-related persecution, 644, 645
on internally displaced persons, 541
mandate for, 505–506
refugees and, 649
on sexual exploitation and abuse, 223, 504
UNSC and, 47, 501
United Nations Human Rights Council,
317–335
Advisory Committee to, 319–320
commissions of inquiry and fact-finding
missions, 321–325
establishment of, 318
institution-building process adopted by,
318–319
legal and governmental influence of, 603
overview, 317–318
resolutions adopted by, 320–321
Special Procedures mechanism of,
327–329
Universal Periodic Review process for,
325–327, 710
United Nations Mission in Liberia (UNMIL),
451–460
civilian perceptions of, 114

United Nations Mission in Liberia
(UNMIL) (*Cont.*)
community links between field offices,
112–113
female participation in, 214, 451–459
mainstreaming Resolution 1325 by, 112
mandate for, 452–453
sensitization campaigns of, 454
site of headquarters for, 243
transactional sex and, 224
WPS implementation by, 451, 455, 458–459
United Nations Mission in South Sudan
(UNMISS), 163–172, 209
United Nations Multidimensional Integrated
Stabilization Mission (MINUSMA), 212,
217, 600–601, 720
United Nations Population Fund (UNFPA),
187, 305
United Nations Secretariat
gender inadequacy in peace and security
analyses and processes of, 845
gender mainstreaming efforts by, 110,
115–117, 119n11
linkage between WPS and P/CVE, 683
Resolution 1325 and, 124
women peacekeepers and, 213
United Nations Secretary-General
annual report on Responsibility to Protect
(R2P), 587
annual report on WPS, 10, 62, 106,
674, 739
annual report to cover Children and
Armed Conflict agenda, 612
annual report to Security Council on
conflict related sexual violence, 72, 172,
660, 664, 692
annual report to Security Council on small
arms, 541
collaboration with World Bank and,
338, 347n1
on conflict prevention, 135, 137, 142
country-specific reports paying attention
to WPS issues, 116, 117, 119n9
on field missions to have increased
participation of women, 207–208,
212, 451
on gender in the work of UNMIL, 112

gender parity in senior appointments by,
117, 205, 309
"Global Study on the implementation
of resolution 1325," 3, 122, 125 (*see also*
Resolution 1325)
on insecurity in Africa, 30
need to understand gender perspectives on
peace process issues, 114, 118
*Plan of Action to Prevent Violent
Extremism,* 107, 683
on post-conflict peace-building, 196
Protection of Civilians in Armed Conflict, 32
on relief and recovery work, 179, 196
"Report on Mainstreaming a Gender
Perspective into All Policies and
Programmes in the UN System," 115
Responsibility to Protect (R2P) role, 585–
587, 591–592 (*see also* Responsibility to
Protect (R2P))
on rule of law and transitional justice, 745
Security Council convened for hearings on
sexual violence against women, 7
Seven-Point Action Plan on Gender-
Responsive Peacebuilding, 179, 181–183,
196, 282, 296
on sexual exploitation and abuse (SEA)
policy (*see* sexual exploitation and
abuse (SEA))
*Special Measures for Protection from Sexual
Exploitation and Abuse,* 224
Special Representative (*see* Special
Representative of the Secretary-
General on Sexual Violence in Conflict
(SRSG–SVC))
task force appointed to develop strategy
to prevent and respond to sexual
exploitation and abuse, 601
urging defense of women's rights in face of
sexism and misogynistic practices, 841
Yemen briefing by (2015), 696
United Nations Security Council (UNSC). *See
also specific resolutions*
accountability in, 71–73
Arria Formula meetings of, 48, 71, 116, 117,
660–662, 674
assessment of WPS advocacy in, 69–74
on child protection, 29–30

gender mainstreaming efforts by, 110, 116–117
LGBTI recommendations for, 663–664
organizational structure of, 71
product outcomes in, 71, 75n3
Protection of Civilians in Armed Conflict, 30, 32
on refugee protection, 30
women in political and peace deliberations of, 5
United Nations Stabilization Mission in the Congo (MONUSCO), 163–172, 174n7, 209, 212, 306, 600–601
United States
civil rights movement in, 77
combat restrictions for women lifted in, 257n1
drawdown of troops in Afghanistan, 783
foreign policy of, 786–788
integration of women into policing in, 198
national action plan for, 57–58, 537n8, 624, 710, 840
women's national protest activities in, 20, 60
Universal Declaration of Human Rights (UDHR), 661, 704–705
Universal Periodic Review (UPR), 325–327, 710
UNMIL. *See* United Nations Mission in Liberia
UNMISS (United Nations Mission in South Sudan), 163–172, 209
UNSC. *See* United Nations Security Council
UN Women. *See* United Nations Entity for Gender Equality and the Empowerment of Women
Uppsala Conflict Data Program (UCDP), 23n3, 756

Valji, Nahla, 53
Vargas, J. F., 756
Veneracion-Rallonza, Ma. Lourdes, 388, 394
victimization discourse, 54–55, 89, 91, 463, 503, 727
Vienna Declaration (1993), 77, 79
violence. *See also* conflict prevention and resolution; domestic violence; sexual

and gender-based violence (SGBV); violent extremism; war
continuum of, 55–57, 310, 468, 652, 721
cycle of, 138
empowerment as precondition for prevention of, 106
femicide, 414, 417, 420, 421, 690, 800
gendered dynamics of, 91, 93–94, 139, 140, 744
genocide (*see* genocide)
human rights and, 541
masculinity and, 343, 692
measures of, 756
norms of, 94, 138
political, 70, 137, 421
prevention of (*see* prevention of violence)
SALWs and, 540–542
structural, 18, 21, 56, 413–414, 420
torture (*see* United Nations Convention against Torture (UNCAT))
violent extremism and terrorism. *See also* countering violent extremism (CVE)
definitions of, 680–681
gendered perspectives prevention of, 7
misogyny in relation to, 55
in national action plans, 285–286
prevention of, 107
recruitment for, 681
sexual violence as used in, 57, 308
UNSC resolutions on, 285, 308, 682–683
war on, 49, 553, 831, 834, 857
WPS application to, 58
von Hlatky, Stéfanie, 364

Wägner, Elin, 729–730
Walleyn, Luc, 356
Wallström, Margot, 303, 306, 779, 781–785, 789, 816
war. *See also* war crimes
casualties of, 16–17, 23n3, 32
civilian neutrality in, 493
civil wars, 49, 58, 135, 207, 388, 489–493
ethnic wars, 17
gendered history of, 60
as impediment to WPS implementation, 559–560

war (*Cont.*)
    mobilization and victimization patterns in,
        490–493
    new wars, 26, 29, 30, 33, 268n1, 489
    rationale for, 18, 62–63n6
    sexual and gender-based violence in, 17,
        26–27, 30, 479, 489, 604
    women, impact on, 17, 183, 189n7
war crimes
    human rights violations as, 323
    jurisdiction for prosecution of, 28
    relief and recovery for victims of, 179
    Responsibility to Protect against, 585,
        586, 589
    in Rwandan genocide, 79
    sexual violence as, 194, 310, 322, 352, 357
    by women in armed groups, 496
war on terror, 49, 553, 831, 834, 857
Waylen, G., 61
Weiss, Cora, 44, 48, 80, 106, 854
Weldon, S. Laurel, 796, 800
Wen, M., 189n7
Westendorf, Jasmine-Kim, 222
Whitworth, Sandra, 129, 852–853
WHO (World Health Organization), 305, 309–310
Wiatrowski, M. D., 261
Wibben, A. T. R., 858
Wiener, Antje, 6, 8
WIGJ (Women's Initiatives for Gender
    Justice), 353, 354, 357
Willett, Susan, 129, 854
Williams, Jody, 20
Williamson, Sarah, 510
WILPF. *See* Women's International League for
    Peace and Freedom
Windhoek Declaration and Namibia Plan of
    Action (2000), 67, 207, 379, 516
Wittwer, Jennifer, 367, 569
Woldetsadik, Mahlet Atakilt, 509–510
women. *See also* femininity; gender
    inequality; marriage
    activism by (*see* women's activism)
    agency of (*see* agency of women)
    in armed groups, 490–498
    in climate change mitigation, 19
    in countering violent extremism, 84, 152,
        683–687

    in DDR process, 20, 24n13, 497–498
    with disabilities (*see* women with
        disabilities)
    in division of labor, 18, 823–824
    dual colonization of, 830
    empowerment of (*see* empowerment
        of women)
    heterogeneity of identities of, 156
    in humanitarian action, 632–634, 636–639
    infantilization of, 46, 100, 231, 614, 842
    in military (*see* military forces)
    in peace processes (*see* participation of
        women in peace processes)
    protection of (*see* protection of women)
    in protector/protected myth, 18, 56,
        108n1, 139
    reproductive rights for, 47, 182
    in victimization discourse, 55, 89, 91, 463,
        503, 727
    war, impact on, 17, 183, 189n7
Women, Peace, and Security (WPS). *See also*
    Resolution 1325
    action plans for (*see* national action plans
        (NAPs))
    in African Union (*see* African Union (AU))
    armed groups and, 496–498
    in ASEAN (*see* Association of South East
        Asian Nations)
    assessment of advocacy in UNSC, 69–74
    CaAC, institutional alignment with, 608,
        611–613, 616
    CEDAW, intersection with, 674–678
    civil society and (*see* civil society
        organizations (CSOs))
    community of practice in, 5, 8, 9, 376, 385
    conflict prevention and (*see* conflict
        prevention and resolution)
    countering violent extremism and, 107, 285,
        681–684, 687, 834–836
    criticisms of, 54–60, 366, 461–463,
        852–853
    delinking sexual exploitation and abuse
        from, 222, 224–226, 229–232
    feminist pragmatist approach to, 4–6, 8
    four pillars of (*see* four pillars of WPS)
    funding for, 61, 63n9, 93, 95n7
    future outlook for, 107–108, 857–858

in Global North vs. Global South, 129, 829–834, 836, 837, 855–856
hierarchy and hegemony of research and advocacy related to, 856–857
human rights and (*see* human rights)
ICC contributions to, 351–353, 360
institutionalization of, 61–62, 276, 311–313, 440, 444–447
integration with POC, 10, 172, 601–605
international awareness of, 844–845
international financial institutions in advancement of, 336–346
marginalization of, 854–855
measurement of. (*see* Women, Peace, and Security Index)
men and boys in, 89–94, 107
militarization of, 6, 139–140, 423 (*see also* military forces)
motivations for engagement with, 852–854
NATO in promotion of, 9, 364–365, 569, 577
in OAS (*see* Organization of American States)
objectives and scope of, 3–5, 53, 67, 98
obstacles to implementation of, 3, 4, 70–71, 84, 420
patterns of application, 57–58
in peacekeeping economies, 238, 241–243
in PIF (*see* Pacific Islands Forum)
in policing, 259, 261–268
as political movement, 76–85
position and privilege of WPS scholars, 851–852
postcolonial feminist theory on, 830–834, 836–837
reframing to include gender, 842–843, 846
for refugees and internally displaced persons, 510–511, 647–648, 650–654
reporting mechanisms for, 72–73
research-policy dialogue on, 126–129
resolutions in agenda formation, 99–108, 99*t*
Responsibility to Protect and, 591–595
siloed implementation phenomenon and, 843–844
small arms proliferation and, 545–547, 549–550

structural challenges for, 841–842
UN advancement of, 295–299
Women, Peace, and Security (WPS) Index, 751–764
applicability of, 760
comparison with existing indices, 752–753
dimensions and indicators, 751, 752*f*, 753–756
global rankings based on, 756–761, 759*f*
objectives of, 752
Sustainable Development Goals and, 752–754
Women, War, and Peace (Rehn & Johnson Sirleaf), 238
Women at the Peace Table: Making a Difference (Narghi-Anderlini), 42, 45
Women Building Peace Campaign, 39, 43, 44
Women Lead to Peace initiative, 795
Women Protection Advisors (WPAs)
functions of, 167–169, 171, 194
in peacekeeping operations, 5, 72, 601
UNSC resolutions on, 104
women's activism. See *also* agency of women
in conflict zones, 21
exclusion of women from post-conflict areas, 634–636
in feminist theory development, 16
history of, 428
for International Criminal Court, 360
longitudinal assessment of, 53
in multitrack peace processes, 128
in Pacific Island region, 404, 410
on sexual and gender-based violence, 27
for UN accountability, 408
Women's Caucus for Gender Justice, 28
Women's Initiatives for Gender Justice (WIGJ), 353, 354, 357
Women's International League for Peace and Freedom (WILPF)
disarmament initiatives of, 20, 140, 142, 691–693, 697
establishment of, 430
four pillars of WPS and, 193
international alliances facilitated by, 855, 858
in Resolution 1325 working group, 44
on strategies for counteracting war, 126–127
translation of Resolution 1325 by, 49

Women's International Peace Conference (1985), 15
Women's Peace and Humanitarian Fund (WPHF), 742. *See also* GAI (Global Acceleration Instrument)
Women's Peace Congress (1915), 15, 20, 92, 767
Women's Situation Room (WSR), 439–447
  establishment of, 441
  implementation of, 441–442, 447
  objectives of, 439, 441, 442
  replication of, 442–445, 447
  WPS institutionalization through, 444–447
Women's Strike for Peace (1961), 20
Women Waging Peace. *See* Inclusive Security
women with disabilities, 618–627
  conflict and, 618–622
  discrimination of, 620
  hierarchy of impairments, 619
  medical approach to, 619–620
  normative frameworks related to, 618, 622–623
  participation in peace processes, 619, 625
  prevalence of, 618
  Resolution 1325 and, 623–624
  sexual and gender-based violence among, 620
  WPS inclusiveness of, 446
World Bank
  collaboration with United Nations, 338, 347n1
  on conflict and disability, 620
  in conflict prevention, 338–339
  on dimensions of violent conflict, 707
  economic influence of, 143, 144, 183
  gender strategy of, 343–346
  institutional operations of, 342–343
  leadership of, 341
  in post-conflict relief and recovery, 337–340

  promotion of political agendas through, 342
  relevance of WPS agenda to, 346
  Systematic Country Diagnostics, 342, 344–345
  UN partnership with, 347n1, 347n6
World Health Organization (WHO), 305, 309–310
World Humanitarian Summit (2016), 410, 507, 630–631, 637
WPAs. *See* Women Protection Advisors
WPHF (Women's Peace and Humanitarian Fund), 742. *See also* Global Acceleration Instrument (GAI)
WPS. *See* Women, Peace, and Security
WPS Index. *See* Women, Peace, and Security Index
WSR. *See* Women's Situation Room

Xi Jinping, 533, 534

Yemen
  failure to invoke WPS in, 58
  measure of violence in, 759
  military interventions in, 696–697
  participation of women in peace processes in, 153, 154, 156–157
Young, Angelic, 282
youth. *See* children and adolescents
Yuval-Davis, N., 684–685

Zeid Report (2005), 226, 227
Zemin, Jiang, 530
Zenko, Micah, 787
Zhenmin, Liu, 531